THE ECONOMICS OF LABOR MARKETS

4, 5, 13, 14, 15, 16, 17, 21, 29, 34, 7, 23, 9

18 The Markets for the Factors of Production

19 Earnings and Discrimination

20 Income Inequality and Poverty

These chapters examine the special features of labor markets, in which most people earn most of their income.

TOPICS FOR FURTHER STUDY

21 The Theory of Consumer Choice

22 Frontiers of Microeconomics

Additional topics in microeconomics include household decision making, asymmetric information, political economy, and behavioral economics.

THE DATA OF MACROECONOMICS

23 Measuring a Nation's Income

24 Measuring the Cost of Living

The overall quantity of production and the overall price level are used to monitor developments in the economy as a whole.

THE REAL ECONOMY IN THE LONG RUN

25 Production and Growth

26 Saving, Investment, and the Financial System

27 The Basic Tools of Finance

28 Unemployment

These chapters describe the forces that in the long run determine key real variables, including growth in GDP, saving, investment, real interest rates, and unemployment.

MONEY AND PRICES IN THE LONG RUN

4,5   29,34

29 The Monetary System

30 Money Growth and Inflation

The monetary system is crucial in determining the long-run behavior of the price level, the inflation rate, and other nominal variables.

THE MACROECONOMICS OF OPEN ECONOMIES

31 Open-Economy Macroeconomics: Basic Concepts

A nation's economic interactions with other nations are described by its trade balance, net foreign investment, and exchange rate.

32 A Macroeconomic Theory of the Open Economy

A long-run model of the open economy explains the determinants of the trade balance, the real exchange rate, and other real variables.

SHORT-RUN ECONOMIC FLUCTUATIONS

33 Aggregate Demand and Aggregate Supply

34 The Influence of Monetary and Fiscal Policy on Aggregate Demand

35 The Short-Run Trade-off between Inflation and Unemployment

The model of aggregate demand and aggregate supply explains short-run economic fluctuations, the short-run effects of monetary and fiscal policy, and the short-run linkage between real and nominal variables.

FINAL THOUGHTS

36 Six Debates over Macroeconomic Policy

A capstone chapter presents both sides of six major debates over economic policy.

Seventh Edition

Principles of
Economics

Seventh Edition

Principles of
Economics

N. Gregory Mankiw

CENGAGE
Learning®

Australia • Brazil • Japan • Korea • Mexico • Singapore • Spain • United Kingdom • United States

Principles of Economics, 7e
N. Gregory Mankiw

Senior Vice President, Global
  Product Manager, Higher Education:
  Jack W. Calhoun

Vice President, General Manager,
  Social Science & Qualitative Business:
  Erin Joyner

Product Director: Mike Worls

Developmental Editor: Jane Tufts

Product Development Manager:
  Jennifer E. Thomas

Content Developers: Clara Goosman and
  Elizabeth A. Beiting-Lipps

Product Assistant: Anne Merrill

Sr. Content Project Manager:
  Colleen A. Farmer

Sr. Market Development Manager:
  John Carey

Sr. Marketing Manager: Robin LeFevre

Marketing Coordinator: Christopher Walz

Media Developer: Anita Verma

Digital Content Designer: Kasie Jean

Sr. Content Digitization Project Manager:
  Jaclyn Hermesmeyer

Manufacturing Planner: Kevin Kluck

Sr. Marketing Communications Manager:
  Sarah Greber

Production Service: PreMediaGlobal

Sr. Art Director: Michelle Kunkler

Cover and Internal Designer:
  Beckmeyer Design

Internal Illustrations by: Greg LaFever

Cover Painting by: Wojciech Gerson
  (1831–1901)

Rights Acquisitions Specialist
  (Text and Photo): John Hill

For product information and technology assistance, contact us at
Cengage Learning Customer & Sales Support, 1-800-354-9706

For permission to use material from this text or product, submit all requests online at **www.cengage.com/permissions**
Further permissions questions can be emailed to
permissionrequest@cengage.com

Unless otherwise noted, all items © Cengage Learning.

Library of Congress Control Number: 2013944588

ISBN-13: 978-1-285-16587-5

ISBN-10: 1-285-16587-X

Cengage Learning
200 First Stamford Place, 4th Floor
Stamford, CT 06902
USA

Cengage Learning is a leading provider of customized learning solutions with office locations around the globe, including Singapore, the United Kingdom, Australia, Mexico, Brazil, and Japan. Locate your local office at:
www.cengage.com/global

Cengage Learning products are represented in Canada by Nelson Education, Ltd.

To learn more about Cengage Learning Solutions, visit
www.cengage.com

Purchase any of our products at your local college store or at our preferred online store **www.cengagebrain.com**

Printed in the United States of America
2 3 4 5 17 16 15 14

About the Author

N. Gregory Mankiw is the Robert M. Beren Professor of Economics at Harvard University. As a student, he studied economics at Princeton University and MIT. As a teacher, he has taught macroeconomics, microeconomics, statistics, and principles of economics. He even spent one summer long ago as a sailing instructor on Long Beach Island.

Professor Mankiw is a prolific writer and a regular participant in academic and policy debates. His work has been published in scholarly journals, such as the *American Economic Review, Journal of Political Economy,* and *Quarterly Journal of Economics,* and in more popular forums, such as the *New York Times* and *The Wall Street Journal.* He is also author of the best-selling intermediate-level textbook *Macroeconomics* (Worth Publishers). In addition to his teaching, research, and writing, Professor Mankiw has been a research associate of the National Bureau of Economic Research, an adviser to the Congressional Budget Office and the Federal Reserve Banks of Boston and New York, and a member of the ETS test development committee for the Advanced Placement exam in economics. From 2003 to 2005, he served as chairman of the President's Council of Economic Advisers.

Professor Mankiw lives in Wellesley, Massachusetts, with his wife Deborah, three children, Catherine, Nicholas, and Peter, and their border terrier, Tobin.

Jordi Cabre

Brief Contents

Part **I** Introduction   1

  1 Ten Principles of Economics   3
  2 Thinking Like an Economist   19
  3 Interdependence and the Gains from Trade   47

Part **II** How Markets Work   63

  4 The Market Forces of Supply and Demand   65
  5 Elasticity and Its Application   89
  6 Supply, Demand, and Government Policies   111

Part **III** Markets and Welfare   133

  7 Consumers, Producers, and the Efficiency of Markets   135
  8 Application: The Costs of Taxation   155
  9 Application: International Trade   171

Part **IV** The Economics of the Public Sector   193

  10 Externalities   195
  11 Public Goods and Common Resources   215
  12 The Design of the Tax System   233

Part **V** Firm Behavior and the Organization of Industry   257

  13 The Costs of Production   259
  14 Firms in Competitive Markets   279
  15 Monopoly   299
  16 Monopolistic Competition   329
  17 Oligopoly   347

Part **VI** The Economics of Labor Markets   371

  18 The Markets for the Factors of Production   373
  19 Earnings and Discrimination   395
  20 Income Inequality and Poverty   413

Part **VII** Topics for Further Study   433

  21 The Theory of Consumer Choice   435
  22 Frontiers of Microeconomics   461

Part **VIII** The Data of Macroeconomics   481

  23 Measuring a Nation's Income   483
  24 Measuring the Cost of Living   505

Part **IX** The Real Economy in the Long Run   521

  25 Production and Growth   523
  26 Saving, Investment, and the Financial System   547
  27 The Basic Tools of Finance   569
  28 Unemployment   585

Part **X** Money and Prices in the Long Run   607

  29 The Monetary System   609
  30 Money Growth and Inflation   633

Part **XI** The Macroeconomics of Open Economies   657

  31 Open-Economy Macroeconomics: Basic Concepts   659
  32 A Macroeconomic Theory of the Open Economy   683

Part **XII** Short-Run Economic Fluctuations   705

  33 Aggregate Demand and Aggregate Supply   707
  34 The Influence of Monetary and Fiscal Policy on Aggregate Demand   745
  35 The Short-Run Trade-off between Inflation and Unemployment   769

Part **XIII** Final Thoughts   793

  36 Six Debates over Macroeconomic Policy   795

Preface to the Student

"Economics is a study of mankind in the ordinary business of life." So wrote Alfred Marshall, the great 19th-century economist, in his textbook, *Principles of Economics*. Although we have learned much about the economy since Marshall's time, this definition of economics is as true today as it was in 1890, when the first edition of his text was published.

Why should you, as a student at the beginning of the 21st century, embark on the study of economics? There are three reasons.

The first reason to study economics is that it will help you understand the world in which you live. There are many questions about the economy that might spark your curiosity. Why are apartments so hard to find in New York City? Why do airlines charge less for a round-trip ticket if the traveler stays over a Saturday night? Why is Leonardo DiCaprio paid so much to star in movies? Why are living standards so meager in many African countries? Why do some countries have high rates of inflation while others have stable prices? Why are jobs easy to find in some years and hard to find in others? These are just a few of the questions that a course in economics will help you answer.

The second reason to study economics is that it will make you a more astute participant in the economy. As you go about your life, you make many economic decisions. While you are a student, you decide how many years to stay in school. Once you take a job, you decide how much of your income to spend, how much to save, and how to invest your savings. Someday you may find yourself running a small business or a large corporation, and you will decide what prices to charge for your products. The insights developed in the coming chapters will give you a new perspective on how best to make these decisions. Studying economics will not by itself make you rich, but it will give you some tools that may help in that endeavor.

The third reason to study economics is that it will give you a better understanding of both the potential and the limits of economic policy. Economic questions are always on the minds of policymakers in mayors' offices, governors' mansions, and the White House. What are the burdens associated with alternative forms of taxation? What are the effects of free trade with other countries? What is the best way to protect the environment? How does a government budget deficit affect the economy? As a voter, you help choose the policies that guide the allocation of society's resources. An understanding of economics will help you carry out that responsibility. And who knows: Perhaps someday you will end up as one of those policymakers yourself.

Thus, the principles of economics can be applied in many of life's situations. Whether the future finds you reading the newspaper, running a business, or sitting in the Oval Office, you will be glad that you studied economics.

N. Gregory Mankiw
December 2013

Acknowledgments

In writing this book, I benefited from the input of many talented people. Indeed, the list of people who have contributed to this project is so long, and their contributions so valuable, that it seems an injustice that only a single name appears on the cover.

Let me begin with my colleagues in the economics profession. The seven editions of this text and its supplemental materials have benefited enormously from their input. In reviews and surveys, they have offered suggestions, identified challenges, and shared ideas from their own classroom experience. I am indebted to them for the perspectives they have brought to the text. Unfortunately, the list has become too long to thank those who contributed to previous editions, even though students reading the current edition are still benefiting from their insights.

Most important in this process have been Ron Cronovich (Carthage College) and David Hakes (University of Northern Iowa). Ron and David, both dedicated teachers, have served as reliable sounding boards for ideas and hardworking partners with me in putting together the superb package of supplements.

The following reviewers of the sixth edition provided suggestions for refining the content, organization, and approach in the seventh.

Mark Abajian, *San Diego Mesa College*

Rahi Abouk, *University of Wisconsin Milwaukee*

Nathanael Adams, *Cardinal Stritch University*

Seemi Ahmad, *Dutchess Community College*

May Akabogu-Collins, *Mira Costa College–Oceanside*

Ercument Aksoy, *Los Angeles Valley College*

William Aldridge, *University of Alabama–Tuscaloosa*

Donald L. Alexander, *Western Michigan University*

Basil Al-Hashimi, *Mesa Community College*

Rashid Al-Hmoud, *Texas Tech University*

Hassan Aly, *Ohio State University*

Michelle Amaral, *University of the Pacific*

Shahina Amin, *University of Northern Iowa*

Catalina Amuedo, *San Diego State University*

Vivette Ancona, *Hunter College–CUNY*

Diane Anstine, *North Central College*

Carolyn Arcand, *University of Massachusetts Boston*

Ali Ataiifar, *Delaware County Community College*

Shannon Aucoin, *University of Louisiana Lafayette*

Lisa Augustyniak, *Lake Michigan College*

Wesley Austin, *University of Louisiana Lafayette*

Sang Hoo Bae, *Clark University*

Karen Baehler, *Hutchinson Community College*

Mohsen Bahmani-Oskooee, *University of Wisconsin Milwaukee*

Stephen Baker, *Capital University*

Tannista Banerjee, *Auburn University*

Bob Barnes, *DePaul University*

Hamid Bastin, *Shippensburg University*

Leon Battista, *Albertus Magnus College*

Gerald Baumgardner, *Susquehanna University*

Christoph Bauner, *University of Massachusetts–Amherst*

Elizabeth Bayley, *University of Delaware*

Mike Belleman, *St Clair County Community College*

Cynthia Benelli, *University of California Santa Barbara*

Charles Bennett, *Gannon University*

Bettina Berch, *Borough of Manhattan Community College*

Stacey Bertke, *Owensboro Community & Technical College*

Tibor Besedes, *Georgia Institute of Technology*

Abhijeet Bhattacharya, *Illinois Valley Community College*

Ronald Bishop, *Lake Michigan College*

Janet Blackburn, *San Jacinto South College*

Natalia Boliari, *Manhattan College*

Antonio Bos, *Tusculum College*

Jennifer Bossard, *Doane College*

James Boudreau, *University of Texas–Pan American*

Mike Bowyer, *Montgomery Community College*

William Brennan, *Minnesota State University–Mankato*

Scott Broadbent, *Western Kentucky University*

Greg Brock, *Georgia Southern University*

Stacey Brook, *University of Iowa*

Keith Brouhle, *Grinnell College*

Byron Brown, *Michigan State University*

Christopher Brunt, *Lake Superior State University*

Laura Bucila, *Texas Christian University*

Donna Bueckman, *University of Tennessee–Knoxville*

Joe Bunting, *St. Andrews University*

Rob Burrus, *University of North Carolina–Wilmington*

James Butkiewicz, *University of Delaware*

Anna Cai, *University of Alabama–Tuscaloosa*

Michael Carew, *Baruch College*

William Carner, *Westminster College*

Onur Celik, *Quinnipiac University*

Kalyan Chakraborty, *Emporia State University*

Suparna Chakraborty, *Baruch College–CUNY*

Dustin Chambers, *Salisbury University*

Silvana Chambers, *Salisbury University*

Krishnamurti Chandrasekar, *New York Institute of Technology*

Yong Chao, *University of Louisville*

David Chaplin, *Northwest Nazarene University*

Xudong Chen, *Baldwin-Wallace College*

Yi-An Chen, *University of Washington, Seattle*

Ron Cheung, *Oberlin College*

Dmitriy Chulkov, *Indiana University Kokomo*

Lawrence Cima, *John Carroll University*

Cindy Clement, *University of Maryland*

Matthew Clements, *Saint Edward's University*

Tina Collins, *San Joaquin Valley College*

Scott Comparato, *Southern Illinois University*

Stephen Cotten, *University of Houston Clear Lake*

Jim Cox, *Georgia Perimeter College*

Michael Craig, *University of Tennessee–Knoxville*

Matt Critcher, *University of Arkansas Community College at Batesville*

George Crowley, *Troy University, Troy*

David Cullipher, *Arkansas State University-Mountain Home*

Dusan Curcic, *University of Virginia*

Maria DaCosta, *University of Wisconsin–EauClaire*

Bruce Dalgaard, *St. Olaf College*

Anusua Datta, *Philadelphia University*

Amanda Dawsey, *University of Montana*

William DeFrance, *University of Michigan-Flint*

Paramita Dhar, *Central Connecticut State University*

Ahrash Dianat, *George Mason University*

Stephanie Dieringer, *University of South Florida St. Petersburg*

Parks Dodd, *Georgia Institute of Technology*
Veronika Dolar, *Long Island University*
Kirk Doran, *University of Notre Dame*
Caf Dowlah, *Queensborough Community College–CUNY*
Tanya Downing, *Cuesta College*
Michael J. Driscoll, *Adelphi University*
Ding Du, *Northern Arizona University*
Kevin Dunagan, *Oakton Community College*
Nazif Durmaz, *University of Houston–Victoria*
Tomas Dvorak, *Union College*
Eva Dziadula, *Lake Forest College*
Dirk Early, *Southwestern University*
Ann Eike, *University of Kentucky*
Harold Elder, *University of Alabama–Tuscaloosa*
Lynne Elkes, *Loyola University Maryland*
Diantha Ellis, *Abraham Baldwin College*
Noha Emara, *Columbia University*
Michael Enz, *Framingham State University*
Lee Erickson, *Taylor University*
Pat Euzent, *University of Central Florida–Orlando*
Timothy Ewest, *Wartburg College*
Amir Farmanesh, *University of Maryland*
Donna Fisher, *Georgia Southern University*
Nikki Follis, *Chadron State College*
Joseph Franklin, *Newberry College*
Ted Fu, *Shenandoah University*
Winnie Fung, *Wheaton College*
Marc Fusaro, *Arkansas Tech University*
Todd Gabe, *University of Maine*
Mary Gade, *Oklahoma State University*
Jonathan Gafford, *Columbia State Community College*
Iris Geisler, *Austin Community College*
Jacob Gelber, *University of Alabama at Birmingham*
Robert Gentenaar, *Pima Downtown Community College*
Soma Ghosh, *Albright College*
Edgar Ghossoub, *University of Texas at San Antonio*

Alex Gialanella, *Manhattanville College*
Bill Gibson, *University of Vermont*
Kenneth Gillingham, *Yale University*
Gregory Gilpin, *Montana State University*
Jayendra Gokhale, *Oregon State University*
Joel Goldhar, *IIT/Stuart School of Business*
Michael Goode, *Central Piedmont Community College*
Michael J Gootzeit, *University of Memphis*
Jackson Grant, *US Air Force Academy*
Jeremy Groves, *Northern Illinois University*
Ilhami Gunduz, *Brooklyn College–CUNY*
Michele Hampton, *Cuyahoga Community College Eastern*
James Hartley, *Mount Holyoke College*
Mike Haupert, *University of Wisconsin LaCrosse*
David Hedrick, *Central Washington University*
Sara Helms, *Samford University*
Jessica Hennessey, *Furman University*
Thomas Henry, *Mississippi State University*
Bob Holland, *Purdue University*
Glenn Hsu, *University of Central Oklahoma*
Jim Hubert, *Seattle Central Community College*
Christopher Hyer, *University of New Mexico*
Kent Hymel, *California State University–Northridge*
Miren Ivankovic, *Anderson University*
Eric Jacobson, *University of Delaware*
Ricot Jean, *Valencia College*
Michal Jerzmanowski, *Clemson University*
Bonnie Johnson, *California Lutheran University*
Bruce Johnson, *Centre College*
Paul Johnson, *University of Alaska Anchorage*
Philipp Jonas, *KV Community College*
Adam Jones, *University of North Carolina–Wilmington*

Jason Jones, *Furman University*
Roger Jordan, *Baker College*
James Jozefowicz, *Indiana University of Pennsylvania*
Simran Kahai, *John Carroll University*
David Kalist, *Shippensburg University*
David Karemera, *St. Cloud State University*
Wahhab Khandker, *University of Wisconsin–LaCrosse*
Jongsung Kim, *Bryant University*
Kihwan Kim, *Rutgers*
Todd Knoop, *Cornell College*
Fred Kolb, *University of Wisconsin–EauClaire*
Oleg Korenok, *Virginia Commonwealth University*
Mikhail Kouliavtsev, *Stephen F. Austin State University*
Ben Kyer, *Francis Marion University*
Daniel Lawson, *Oakland Community College*
Elena Lazzari, *Marygrove College*
Chun Lee, *Loyola Marymount University*
Daniel Lee, *Shippensburg University*
Jihoon Lee, *Northeastern University*
Jim Lee, *Texas A&M–Corpus Christi*
Sang Lee, *Southeastern Louisiana University*
Qing Li, *College of the Mainland*
Carlos Liard-Muriente, *Central Connecticut State University*
Larry Lichtenstein, *Canisius College*
Jenny Liu, *Portland State University*
Jialu Liu, *Allegheny College*
Michael Machiorlatti, *Oklahoma City Community College*
Bruce Madariaga, *Montgomery College and Northwestern University*
C. Lucy Malakar, *Lorain County Community College*
Gabriel Manrique, *Winona State University*
Katherine McClain, *University of Georgia*
Michael McIlhon, *Century College*
Jennifer McNiece, *Howard Payne University*
Charles Meyrick, *Housatonic Community College*

Heather Micelli, *Mira Costa College*
Laura Middlesworth, *University of Wisconsin–Eau Claire*
Phillip Mixon, *Troy University–Troy*
Evan Moore, *Auburn University–Montgomery*
Francis Mummery, *California State University–Fullerton*
John Mundy, *St. Johns River State University*
James Murray, *University of Wisconsin–LaCrosse*
Christopher Mushrush, *Illinois State University*
John Nader, *Davenport University*
Max Grunbaum Nagiel, *Daytona State College*
Scott Niederjohn, *Lakeland College*
George Norman, *Tufts University*
Yanira Ogrodnik, *Post University*
David O'Hara, *Metropolitan State University*
Wafa Orman, *University of Alabama in Huntsville*
Brian O'Roark, *Robert Morris University*
Glenda Orosco, *Oklahoma State University Institute of Technology*
Orgul Ozturk, *University of South Carolina*
Maria Papapavlou, *San Jacinto Central College*
Nitin Paranjpe, *Wayne State University*
Irene Parietti, *Felician College*
Jooyoun Park, *Kent State University*
Michael Patton, *St. Louis Community College–Wildwood*
Wesley Pech, *Wofford College*
Germain Pichop, *Oklahoma City Community College*
Florenz Plassmann, *Binghamton University*
Lana Podolak, *Community College of Beaver County*
Gyan Pradhan, *Eastern Kentucky University*
Silvia Prina, *Case Western Reserve University*
Thomas Prusa, *Rutgers University*

Robert Rebelein, *Vassar College*
Matt Rendleman, *Southern Illinois University*
Kristen Roche, *Mount Mary College*
Antonio Rodriguez, *Texas A&M International University*
Debasis Rooj, *Kishwaukee College*
Larry Ross, *University of Alaska*
Jeff Rubin, *Rutgers University–New Brunswick*
Jason C. Rudbeck, *University of Georgia*
Jeff Ruggiero, *University of Dayton*
Robert Rycroft, *University of Mary Washington*
Allen Sanderson, *University of Chicago*
Nese Sara, *University of Cincinnati*
Naveen Sarna, *Northern Virginia Community College–Alexandria*
Eric Sartell, *Whitworth University*
Martin Schonger, *Princeton University*
Michael Schultz, *Menlo College*
Gerald Scott, *Florida Atlantic University*
Reshmi Sengupta, *Northern Illinois University*
David Shankle, *Blue Mountain College*
Robert Shoffner, *Central Piedmont Community College*
Johnny Shull, *Wake Tech Community College*
Suann Shumaker, *Las Positas College*
Nicholas Shunda, *University of Redlands*
Milan Sigetich, *Southern Oregon University*
Jonathan Silberman, *Oakland University*
Joe Silverman, *Mira Costa College–Oceanside*
Catherine Skura, *Sandhills Community College*
Gary Smith, *Canisius College*
Richard Smith, *University of South Florida–St. Petersburg*
Joe Sobieralski, *Southwestern Illinois College–Belleville*
Soren Soumbatiants, *Franklin University*
Dean Stansel, *Florida Gulf Coast University*

Sylwia Starnawska, *D'Youville College*
Keva Steadman, *Augustana College*
Rebecca Stein, *University of Pennsylvania*
Michael Stroup, *Stephen F. Austin State University*
Edward Stuart, *Northeastern Illinois University*
Yu-hsuan Su, *University of Washington*
Abdul Sukar, *Cameron University*
John Susenburger, *Utica College*
James Swofford, *University of South Alabama*
Vera Tabakova, *East Carolina University*
Eric Taylor, *Central Piedmont Community College*
Erdal Tekin, *Georgia State University*
Noreen Templin, *Butler Community College*
Thomas Tenerelli, *Central Washington University*
Charles Thompson, *Brunswick Community College*
Flint Thompson, *Chippewa Valley Technical College*
Deborah Thorsen, *Palm Beach State College–Central*
James Tierney, *University of California Irvine*
Julie Trivitt, *Arkansas Tech University*
Ross vanWassenhove, *University of Houston*
Ben Vaughan, *Trinity University*
Rubina Vohra, *St. Peter's College*
Will Walsh, *Samford University*
Chih-Wei Wang, *Pacific Lutheran University*
Chad Wassell, *Central Washington University*
Christine Wathen, *Middlesex Community College*
Oxana Wieland, *University of Minnesota, Crookston*
Christopher Wimer, *Bowling Green State University–Firelands College*
Ken Woodward, *Saddleback College*
Eric Zemljic, *Kent State University*
Zhen Zhu, *University of Central Oklahoma*
Kent Zirlott, *University of Alabama–Tuscaloosa*

The team of editors who worked on this book improved it tremendously. Jane Tufts, developmental editor, provided truly spectacular editing—as she always does. Mike Worls, economics product director, did a splendid job of overseeing the many people involved in such a large project. Jennifer Thomas, product development manager; Clara Goosman, content developer; and Elizabeth Beiting-Lipps, associate content developer, were crucial in assembling an extensive and thoughtful group of reviewers to give me feedback on the previous edition while putting together an excellent team to revise the supplements. Colleen Farmer, senior content project manager, and Katy Gabel, project manager, had the patience and dedication necessary to turn my manuscript into this book. Michelle Kunkler, senior art director, gave this book its clean, friendly look. Greg LaFever, the illustrator, helped make the book more visually appealing and the economics in it less abstract. Pamela Rockwell, copyeditor, refined my prose, and PreMediaGlobal prepared a careful and thorough index. John Carey, senior market development manager, and Robin LeFevre, senior brand manager, worked long hours getting the word out to potential users of this book. The rest of the Cengage team was also consistently professional, enthusiastic, and dedicated.

I am grateful also to Lisa Mogilanski and Alex Sareyan, two star Harvard undergraduates, who helped me refine the manuscript and check the page proofs for this edition.

As always, I must thank my "in-house" editor, Deborah Mankiw. As the first reader of most things I write, she continued to offer just the right mix of criticism and encouragement.

Finally, I would like to mention my three children, Catherine, Nicholas, and Peter. Their contribution to this book was putting up with a father spending too many hours in his study. The four of us have much in common—not least of which is our love of ice cream (which becomes apparent in Chapter 4). I am grateful to Nicholas in particular for helping me check the page proofs for this edition. In case you didn't notice, Nick, it was just my way of tricking you into learning a bit of economics.

N. Gregory Mankiw
December 2013

Contents

Preface: To the Student   xi

Acknowledgments   xiii

Part I Introduction   1

CHAPTER 1

Ten Principles of Economics   3

1-1 How People Make Decisions   4
   1-1a Principle 1: People Face Trade-offs   4
   1-1b Principle 2: The Cost of Something Is What You Give Up to Get It   5
   1-1c Principle 3: Rational People Think at the Margin   6
   1-1d Principle 4: People Respond to Incentives   7
   Case Study: The Incentive Effects of Gasoline Prices   8

1-2 How People Interact   9
   1-2a Principle 5: Trade Can Make Everyone Better Off   9
   1-2b Principle 6: Markets Are Usually a Good Way to Organize Economic Activity   10
   1-2c Principle 7: Governments Can Sometimes Improve Market Outcomes   11
   FYI: Adam Smith and the Invisible Hand   11

1-3 How the Economy as a Whole Works   13
   1-3a Principle 8: A Country's Standard of Living Depends on Its Ability to Produce Goods and Services   13

   1-3b Principle 9: Prices Rise When the Government Prints Too Much Money   13
   In The News: Why You Should Study Economics   14
   1-3c Principle 10: Society Faces a Short-Run Trade-off between Inflation and Unemployment   15

1-4 Conclusion   16
Summary   16
Key Concepts   17
Questions for Review   17
Quick Check Multiple Choice   17
Problems and Applications   18

CHAPTER 2

Thinking Like an Economist   19

2-1 The Economist as Scientist   20
   2-1a The Scientific Method: Observation, Theory, and More Observation   20
   2-1b The Role of Assumptions   21
   2-1c Economic Models   22
   2-1d Our First Model: The Circular-Flow Diagram   22
   2-1e Our Second Model: The Production Possibilities Frontier   24
   2-1f Microeconomics and Macroeconomics   27

2-2 The Economist as Policy Adviser   27
   2-2a Positive versus Normative Analysis   28
   2-2b Economists in Washington   28
   2-2c Why Economists' Advice Is Not Always Followed   29

2-3 Why Economists Disagree   30
   2-3a Differences in Scientific Judgments   30
   2-3b Differences in Values   31
   2-3c Perception versus Reality   31
   In The News: Actual Economists and Virtual Realities   33

2-4 Let's Get Going   34
Summary   34
Key Concepts   34
Questions for Review   35
Quick Check Multiple Choice   35
Problems and Applications   35

APPENDIX   Graphing: A Brief Review   37
   Graphs of a Single Variable   37
   Graphs of Two Variables: The Coordinate System   38
   Curves in the Coordinate System   39
   Slope   41
   Cause and Effect   43

CHAPTER 3

Interdependence and the Gains from Trade   47

3-1 A Parable for the Modern Economy   48
3-1a Production Possibilities   48
3-1b Specialization and Trade   50

3-2 Comparative Advantage: The Driving Force of Specialization   52
3-2a Absolute Advantage   52
3-2b Opportunity Cost and Comparative Advantage   52
3-2c Comparative Advantage and Trade   53
3-2d The Price of the Trade   54
FYI: The Legacy of Adam Smith and David Ricardo   55

3-3 Applications of Comparative Advantage   55
3-3a Should Tom Brady Mow His Own Lawn?   55
In The News: Economics within a Marriage   56
3-3b Should the United States Trade with Other Countries?   57

3-4 Conclusion   58
Summary   59
Key Concepts   59
Questions for Review   59
Quick Check Multiple Choice   59
Problems and Applications   60

Part II How Markets Work   63

CHAPTER 4

The Market Forces of Supply and Demand   65

4-1 Markets and Competition   66
4-1a What Is a Market?   66
4-1b What Is Competition?   66

4-2 Demand   67
4-2a The Demand Curve: The Relationship between Price and Quantity Demanded   67
4-2b Market Demand versus Individual Demand   68
4-2c Shifts in the Demand Curve   69
Case Study: Two Ways to Reduce the Quantity of Smoking Demanded   71

4-3 Supply   73
4-3a The Supply Curve: The Relationship between Price and Quantity Supplied   73
4-3b Market Supply versus Individual Supply   74
4-3c Shifts in the Supply Curve   75

4-4 Supply and Demand Together   77
4-4a Equilibrium   77
4-4b Three Steps to Analyzing Changes in Equilibrium   79

4-5 Conclusion: How Prices Allocate Resources   83
In The News: Price Increases after Disasters   84

Summary   84
Key Concepts   86
Questions for Review   86
Quick Check Multiple Choice   86
Problems and Applications   87

CHAPTER 5

Elasticity and Its Application   89

5-1 The Elasticity of Demand   90
5-1a The Price Elasticity of Demand and Its Determinants   90
5-1b Computing the Price Elasticity of Demand   91
5-1c The Midpoint Method: A Better Way to Calculate Percentage Changes and Elasticities   91
5-1d The Variety of Demand Curves   92
5-1e Total Revenue and the Price Elasticity of Demand   94
FYI: A Few Elasticities from the Real World   94
5-1f Elasticity and Total Revenue along a Linear Demand Curve   96
5-1g Other Demand Elasticities   97

5-2 The Elasticity of Supply   98
5-2a The Price Elasticity of Supply and Its Determinants   98
5-2b Computing the Price Elasticity of Supply   99
5-2c The Variety of Supply Curves   99

5-3 Three Applications of Supply, Demand, and Elasticity   101
5-3a Can Good News for Farming Be Bad News for Farmers?   102
5-3b Why Did OPEC Fail to Keep the Price of Oil High?   104
5-3c Does Drug Interdiction Increase or Decrease Drug-Related Crime?   105

5-4 Conclusion   107
Summary   107
Key Concepts   108
Questions for Review   108
Quick Check Multiple Choice   108
Problems and Applications   109

CHAPTER 6

Supply, Demand, and Government Policies   111

6-1 Controls on Prices   112
6-1a How Price Ceilings Affect Market Outcomes   112
Case Study: Lines at the Gas Pump   114
Case Study: Rent Control in the Short Run and the Long Run   115
6-1b How Price Floors Affect Market Outcomes   116
Case Study: The Minimum Wage   117
6-1c Evaluating Price Controls   119
In The News: Venezuela versus the Market   120

6-2 Taxes   121
6-2a How Taxes on Sellers Affect Market Outcomes   122
6-2b How Taxes on Buyers Affect Market Outcomes   123
Case Study: Can Congress Distribute the Burden of a Payroll Tax?   125
6-2c Elasticity and Tax Incidence   126
Case Study: Who Pays the Luxury Tax?   128

6-3 Conclusion   128
Summary   129
Key Concepts   129
Questions for Review   129
Quick Check Multiple Choice   129
Problems and Applications   130

Part III Markets and Welfare   133

CHAPTER 7

Consumers, Producers, and the Efficiency of Markets   135

7-1 Consumer Surplus   136
7-1a Willingness to Pay   136
7-1b Using the Demand Curve to Measure Consumer Surplus   137
7-1c How a Lower Price Raises Consumer Surplus   138
7-1d What Does Consumer Surplus Measure?   139

7-2 Producer Surplus   141
7-2a Cost and the Willingness to Sell   141
7-2b Using the Supply Curve to Measure Producer Surplus   142
7-2c How a Higher Price Raises Producer Surplus   143

7-3 Market Efficiency   144
7-3a The Benevolent Social Planner   145
7-3b Evaluating the Market Equilibrium   146
In The News: The Invisible Hand Can Park Your Car   148
Case Study: Should There Be a Market in Organs?   148

7-4 Conclusion: Market Efficiency and Market Failure   150
Summary   151
Key Concepts   151
Questions for Review   151
Quick Check Multiple Choice   151
Problems and Applications   152

CHAPTER 8

Application: The Costs of Taxation   155

8-1 The Deadweight Loss of Taxation   156
8-1a How a Tax Affects Market Participants   157
8-1b Deadweight Losses and the Gains from Trade   159

8-2 The Determinants of the Deadweight Loss   160
Case Study: The Deadweight Loss Debate   162

8-3 Deadweight Loss and Tax Revenue as Taxes Vary   163
Case Study: The Laffer Curve and Supply-Side Economics   164
In The News: The Tax Debate   166

8-4 Conclusion   168
Summary   168
Key Concept   168
Questions for Review   168
Quick Check Multiple Choice   169
Problems and Applications   169

CHAPTER 9

Application: International Trade   171

9-1 The Determinants of Trade   172
9-1a The Equilibrium without Trade   172
9-1b The World Price and Comparative Advantage   173

9-2 The Winners and Losers from Trade   174
9-2a The Gains and Losses of an Exporting Country   174
9-2b The Gains and Losses of an Importing Country   175
9-2c The Effects of a Tariff   177
FYI: Import Quotas: Another Way to Restrict Trade   179
9-2d The Lessons for Trade Policy   179
9-2e Other Benefits of International Trade   180
In The News: Threats to Free Trade   181

9-3 The Arguments for Restricting Trade   182
In The News: Should the Winners from Free Trade Compensate the Losers?   183

9-3a The Jobs Argument   183
9-3b The National-Security Argument   184
In The News: Second Thoughts about Free Trade   184
9-3c The Infant-Industry Argument   185
9-3d The Unfair-Competition Argument   186
9-3e The Protection-as-a-Bargaining-Chip Argument   186
Case Study: Trade Agreements and the World Trade
   Organization   187

9-4 Conclusion   188
Summary   189
Key Concepts   189
Questions for Review   189
Quick Check Multiple Choice   189
Problems and Applications   190

Part IV The Economics of the Public Sector   193

CHAPTER 10

Externalities   195

10-1 Externalities and Market Inefficiency   197
10-1a Welfare Economics: A Recap   197
10-1b Negative Externalities   198
10-1c Positive Externalities   199
In The News: The Externalities of Country Living   200
Case Study: Technology Spillovers, Industrial Policy, and
   Patent Protection   201

10-2 Public Policies toward Externalities   202
10-2a Command-and-Control Policies: Regulation   202
10-2b Market-Based Policy 1: Corrective Taxes and Subsidies   203
Case Study: Why Is Gasoline Taxed So Heavily?   204
10-2c Market-Based Policy 2: Tradable Pollution Permits   205
10-2d Objections to the Economic Analysis of Pollution   207
In The News: What Should We Do about Climate Change?   208

10-3 Private Solutions to Externalities   208
10-3a The Types of Private Solutions   208

10-3b The Coase Theorem   209
10-3c Why Private Solutions Do Not Always Work   211

10-4 Conclusion   211
Summary   212
Key Concepts   212
Questions for Review   212
Quick Check Multiple Choice   213
Problems and Applications   213

CHAPTER 11

Public Goods and Common Resources   215

11-1 The Different Kinds of Goods   216

11-2 Public Goods   218
11-2a The Free-Rider Problem   218
11-2b Some Important Public Goods   218
Case Study: Are Lighthouses Public Goods?   221
11-2c The Difficult Job of Cost–Benefit Analysis   221
Case Study: How Much Is a Life Worth?   222

11-3 Common Resources   223
11-3a The Tragedy of the Commons   223
In The News: The Case for Toll Roads   224
11-3b Some Important Common Resources   225
Case Study: Why the Cow Is Not Extinct   227

11-4 Conclusion: The Importance of Property Rights   228
Summary   228
Key Concepts   229
Questions for Review   229
Quick Check Multiple Choice   229
Problems and Applications   229

CHAPTER 12

The Design of the Tax System   233

12-1 A Financial Overview of the U.S. Government   234
12-1a The Federal Government   235
Case Study: The Fiscal Challenge Ahead   238
12-1b State and Local Governments   240

12-2 Taxes and Efficiency   242
12-2a Deadweight Losses   243
Case Study: Should Income or Consumption Be Taxed?   243
12-2b Administrative Burden   244
12-2c Marginal Tax Rates versus Average Tax Rates   245
12-2d Lump-Sum Taxes   245

12-3 Taxes and Equity   246
12-3a The Benefits Principle   246
12-3b The Ability-to-Pay Principle   247
Case Study: How the Tax Burden Is Distributed   248
12-3c Tax Incidence and Tax Equity   249
In The News: Tax Expenditures   250
Case Study: Who Pays the Corporate Income Tax?   250

**11-4 Conclusion: The Trade-off between Equity and
Efficiency   252**

Summary 253
Key Concepts 253
Questions for Review 253
Quick Check Multiple Choice 254
Problems and Applications 254

Part V Firm Behavior and the Organization of Industry 257

CHAPTER 13

The Costs of Production 259

13-1 What Are Costs? 260
13-1a Total Revenue, Total Cost, and Profit 260
13-1b Costs as Opportunity Costs 260
13-1c The Cost of Capital as an Opportunity Cost 261
13-1d Economic Profit versus Accounting Profit 262

13-2 Production and Costs 263
13-2a The Production Function 263
13-2b From the Production Function to the Total-Cost Curve 265

13-3 The Various Measures of Cost 265
13-3a Fixed and Variable Costs 266
13-3b Average and Marginal Cost 267
13-3c Cost Curves and Their Shapes 268
13-3d Typical Cost Curves 270

13-4 Costs in the Short Run and in the Long Run 271
13-4a The Relationship between Short-Run and Long-Run Average Total Cost 271
13-4b Economies and Diseconomies of Scale 272
FYI: Lessons from a Pin Factory 273

13-5 Conclusion 274
Summary 274
Key Concepts 275
Questions for Review 275

Quick Check Multiple Choice 275
Problems and Applications 276

CHAPTER 14

Firms in Competitive Markets 279

14-1 What Is a Competitive Market? 280
14-1a The Meaning of Competition 280
14-1b The Revenue of a Competitive Firm 280

14-2 Profit Maximization and the Competitive Firm's Supply Curve 282
14-2a A Simple Example of Profit Maximization 282
14-2b The Marginal-Cost Curve and the Firm's Supply Decision 283
14-2c The Firm's Short-Run Decision to Shut Down 285
14-2d Spilt Milk and Other Sunk Costs 286
Case Study: Near-Empty Restaurants and Off-Season Miniature Golf 287
14-2e The Firm's Long-Run Decision to Exit or Enter a Market 288
14-2f Measuring Profit in Our Graph for the Competitive Firm 288

14-3 The Supply Curve in a Competitive Market 289
14-3a The Short Run: Market Supply with a Fixed Number of Firms 290
14-3b The Long Run: Market Supply with Entry and Exit 290
14-3c Why Do Competitive Firms Stay in Business If They Make Zero Profit? 292
14-3d A Shift in Demand in the Short Run and Long Run 293
14-3e Why the Long-Run Supply Curve Might Slope Upward 293

14-4 Conclusion: Behind the Supply Curve 295
Summary 296
Key Concepts 296
Questions for Review 296
Quick Check Multiple Choice 296
Problems and Applications 297

CHAPTER 15

Monopoly 299

15-1 Why Monopolies Arise 300
15-1a Monopoly Resources 301
15-1b Government-Created Monopolies 301
15-1c Natural Monopolies 302

15-2 How Monopolies Make Production and Pricing Decisions 303
15-2a Monopoly versus Competition 303
15-2b A Monopoly's Revenue 304
15-2c Profit Maximization 306
15-2d A Monopoly's Profit 308
FYI: Why a Monopoly Does Not Have a Supply Curve 308
Case Study: Monopoly Drugs versus Generic Drugs 309

15-3 The Welfare Cost of Monopolies 310
15-3a The Deadweight Loss 311
15-3b The Monopoly's Profit: A Social Cost? 313

15-4 Price Discrimination   314
15-4a A Parable about Pricing   314
15-4b The Moral of the Story   315
15-4c The Analytics of Price Discrimination   315
15-4d Examples of Price Discrimination   317
In The News: Price Discrimination in Higher Education   318

15-5 Public Policy toward Monopolies   319
15-5a Increasing Competition with Antitrust Laws   319
15-5b Regulation   319
15-5c Public Ownership   321
15-5d Doing Nothing   321

15-6 Conclusion: The Prevalence of Monopolies   322

Summary   323
Key Concepts   323
Questions for Review   323
Quick Check Multiple Choice   324
Problems and Applications   324

CHAPTER 16

Monopolistic Competition   329

16-1 Between Monopoly and Perfect Competition   330

16-2 Competition with Differentiated Products   332
16-2a The Monopolistically Competitive Firm in the Short Run   332
16-2b The Long-Run Equilibrium   332
16-2c Monopolistic versus Perfect Competition   335
16-2d Monopolistic Competition and the Welfare of Society   336
In The News: Insufficient Variety as a Market Failure   338

16-3 Advertising   338
16-3a The Debate over Advertising   339
Case Study: Advertising and the Price of Eyeglasses   340
16-3b Advertising as a Signal of Quality   341
16-3c Brand Names   342

16-4 Conclusion   343
Summary   344
Key Concepts   344
Questions for Review   345
Quick Check Multiple Choice   345
Problems and Applications   345

CHAPTER 17

Oligopoly   347

17-1 Markets with Only a Few Sellers   348
17-1a A Duopoly Example   348
17-1b Competition, Monopolies, and Cartels   349
In The News: Public Price Fixing   350
17-1c The Equilibrium for an Oligopoly   351
17-1d How the Size of an Oligopoly Affects the Market Outcome   352

17-2 The Economics of Cooperation   353
17-2a The Prisoners' Dilemma   353
17-2b Oligopolies as a Prisoners' Dilemma   355

Case Study: OPEC and the World Oil Market   356
17-2c Other Examples of the Prisoners' Dilemma   356
17-2d The Prisoners' Dilemma and the Welfare of Society   358
17-2e Why People Sometimes Cooperate   358
Case Study: The Prisoners' Dilemma Tournament   359

17-3 Public Policy toward Oligopolies   360
17-3a Restraint of Trade and the Antitrust Laws   360
Case Study: An Illegal Phone Call   361
17-3b Controversies over Antitrust Policy   361
Case Study: The Microsoft Case   363

17-4 Conclusion   364
In The News: Should the N.C.A.A. Be Taken to Court?   365

Summary   366
Key Concepts   366
Questions for Review   366
Quick Check Multiple Choice   366
Problems and Applications   367

Part VI The Economics of Labor Markets   371

CHAPTER 18

The Markets for the Factors of Production   373

18-1 The Demand for Labor   374
18-1a The Competitive Profit-Maximizing Firm   375
18-1b The Production Function and the Marginal Product of Labor   375
18-1c The Value of the Marginal Product and the Demand for Labor   377
18-1d What Causes the Labor-Demand Curve to Shift?   378
FYI: Input Demand and Output Supply: Two Sides of the Same Coin   379

18-2 The Supply of Labor   380
18-2a The Trade-off between Work and Leisure   380
18-2b What Causes the Labor-Supply Curve to Shift?   380

18-3 Equilibrium in the Labor Market   381
18-3a Shifts in Labor Supply   381
18-3b Shifts in Labor Demand   383
In The News: The Economics of Immigration   384
Case Study: Productivity and Wages   384
FYI: Monopsony   386

18-4 The Other Factors of Production: Land and Capital   386
18-4a Equilibrium in the Markets for Land and Capital   387
FYI: What Is Capital Income?   388
18-4b Linkages among the Factors of Production   388
Case Study: The Economics of the Black Death   389

18-5 Conclusion   390
Summary   390
Key Concepts   390
Questions for Review   391
Quick Check Multiple Choice   391
Problems and Applications   391

CHAPTER 19

Earnings and Discrimination   395

19-1 Some Determinants of Equilibrium Wages   396
19-1a Compensating Differentials   396
19-1b Human Capital   396
Case Study: The Increasing Value of Skills   397
In The News: Higher Education as an Investment   398
19-1c Ability, Effort, and Chance   399
Case Study: The Benefits of Beauty   400
19-1d An Alternative View of Education: Signaling   401
19-1e The Superstar Phenomenon   402
19-1f Above-Equilibrium Wages: Minimum-Wage Laws, Unions, and Efficiency Wages   402

19-2 The Economics of Discrimination   403
19-2a Measuring Labor-Market Discrimination   403
Case Study: Is Emily More Employable than Lakisha?   405
19-2b Discrimination by Employers   405
Case Study: Segregated Streetcars and the Profit Motive   406
19-2c Discrimination by Customers and Governments   406
Case Study: Discrimination in Sports   407
In The News: Gender Differences   408

19-3 Conclusion   408
Summary   409
Key Concepts   410
Questions for Review   410
Quick Check Multiple Choice   410
Problems and Applications   411

CHAPTER 20

Income Inequality and Poverty   413

20-1 The Measurement of Inequality   414
20-1a U.S. Income Inequality   414
20-1b Inequality around the World   416
20-1c The Poverty Rate   417

20-1d Problems in Measuring Inequality   418
Case Study: Alternative Measures of Inequality   420
20-1e Economic Mobility   420

20-2 The Political Philosophy of Redistributing Income   421
20-2a Utilitarianism   421
20-2b Liberalism   422
20-2c Libertarianism   423

20-3 Policies to Reduce Poverty   424
20-3a Minimum-Wage Laws   424
20-3b Welfare   425
20-3c Negative Income Tax   425
20-3d In-Kind Transfers   426
20-3e Antipoverty Programs and Work Incentives   427
In The News: International Differences in Income Redistribution   428

20-4 Conclusion   428
Summary   430
Key Concepts   430
Questions for Review   430
Quick Check Multiple Choice   430
Problems and Applications   431

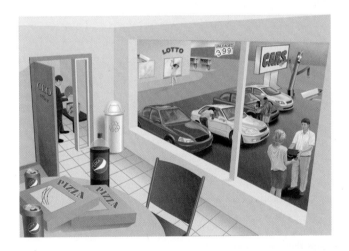

Part VII Topics for Further Study   433

CHAPTER 21

The Theory of Consumer Choice   435

21-1 The Budget Constraint: What the Consumer Can Afford   436

21-2 Preferences: What the Consumer Wants   437
21-2a Representing Preferences with Indifference Curves   438
21-2b Four Properties of Indifference Curves   439
21-2c Two Extreme Examples of Indifference Curves   440

21-3 Optimization: What the Consumer Chooses 442
21-3a The Consumer's Optimal Choices 442
FYI: Utility: An Alternative Way to Describe Preferences and Optimization 443
21-3b How Changes in Income Affect the Consumer's Choices 444
21-3c How Changes in Prices Affect the Consumer's Choices 445
21-3d Income and Substitution Effects 446
21-3e Deriving the Demand Curve 448

21-4 Three Applications 449
21-4a Do All Demand Curves Slope Downward? 449
Case Study: The Search for Giffen Goods 450
21-4b How Do Wages Affect Labor Supply? 450
Case Study: Income Effects on Labor Supply: Historical Trends, Lottery Winners, and the Carnegie Conjecture 453
21-4c How Do Interest Rates Affect Household Saving? 454

21-5 Conclusion: Do People Really Think This Way? 456
Summary 457
Key Concepts 457
Questions for Review 457
Quick Check Multiple Choice 458
Problems and Applications 458

CHAPTER 22

Frontiers of Microeconomics 461

22-1 Asymmetric Information 462
22-1a Hidden Actions: Principals, Agents, and Moral Hazard 462
FYI: Corporate Management 463
22-1b Hidden Characteristics: Adverse Selection and the Lemons Problem 464
22-1c Signaling to Convey Private Information 465
Case Study: Gifts as Signals 465
22-1d Screening to Uncover Private Information 466
22-1e Asymmetric Information and Public Policy 466

22-2 Political Economy 467
22-2a The Condorcet Voting Paradox 467
22-2b Arrow's Impossibility Theorem 468
22-2c The Median Voter Is King 469
22-2d Politicians Are People Too 471

22-3 Behavioral Economics 471
22-3a People Aren't Always Rational 471
Case Study: Left-Digit Bias 473
22-3b People Care about Fairness 474
22-3c People Are Inconsistent over Time 475
In The News: Can Brain Science Improve Economics? 476

22-4 Conclusion 476
Summary 478
Key Concepts 478
Questions for Review 478
Quick Check Multiple Choice 478
Problems and Applications 479

Part VIII The Data of Macroeconomics 481

CHAPTER 23

Measuring a Nation's Income 483

23-1 The Economy's Income and Expenditure 484

23-2 The Measurement of GDP 486
23-2a "GDP Is the Market Value . . ." 486
23-2b ". . . of All . . ." 486
23-2c ". . . Final . . ." 487
23-2d ". . . Goods and Services . . ." 487
23-2e ". . . Produced . . ." 487
23-2f ". . . Within a Country . . ." 487
23-2g ". . . In a Given Period of Time." 487

23-3 The Components of GDP 488
FYI: Other Measures of Income 489
23-3a Consumption 489
23-3b Investment 489
23-3c Government Purchases 490
23-3d Net Exports 490
Case Study: The Components of U.S. GDP 491

23-4 Real versus Nominal GDP 491
In The News: The BEA Changes the Definitions of Investment and GDP 492
23-4a A Numerical Example 492
23-4b The GDP Deflator 494
Case Study: Real GDP over Recent History 495

23-5 Is GDP a Good Measure of Economic Well-Being? 496
Case Study: International Differences in GDP and the Quality of Life 497
In The News: The Underground Economy 498
In The News: Measuring Macroeconomic Well-Being 500

23-6 Conclusion 500
Summary 502
Key Concepts 502

Questions for Review 502
Quick Check Multiple Choice 502
Problems and Applications 503

CHAPTER 24

Measuring the Cost of Living 505

24-1 The Consumer Price Index 506
  24-1a How the CPI Is Calculated 506
  FYI: What Is in the CPI's Basket? 508
  24-1b Problems in Measuring the Cost of Living 509
  In The News: Monitoring Inflation in the Internet Age 510
  24-1c The GDP Deflator versus the Consumer Price Index 512

24-2 Correcting Economic Variables for the Effects of Inflation 513
  24-2a Dollar Figures from Different Times 514
  24-2b Indexation 514
  FYI: Mr. Index Goes to Hollywood 515
  24-2c Real and Nominal Interest Rates 515
  Case Study: Interest Rates in the U.S. Economy 517

24-3 Conclusion 518
Summary 518
Key Concepts 519
Questions for Review 519
Quick Check Multiple Choice 519
Problems and Applications 519

Part IX The Real Economy in the Long Run 521

CHAPTER 25

Production and Growth 523

25-1 Economic Growth around the World 524

25-2 Productivity: Its Role and Determinants 526
  FYI: Are You Richer Than the Richest American? 526
  25-2a Why Productivity Is So Important 527
  25-2b How Productivity Is Determined 527
  FYI: A Picture Is Worth a Thousand Statistics 528
  FYI: The Production Function 531
  Case Study: Are Natural Resources a Limit to Growth? 532

25-3 Economic Growth and Public Policy 532
  25-3a Saving and Investment 533
  25-3b Diminishing Returns and the Catch-Up Effect 533
  25-3c Investment from Abroad 535
  25-3d Education 536
  25-3e Health and Nutrition 536
  25-3f Property Rights and Political Stability 537
  In The News: Does Food Aid Help or Hurt? 538
  25-3g Free Trade 539
  25-3h Research and Development 540
  25-3i Population Growth 540
  In The News: One Economist's Answer 542

25-4 Conclusion: The Importance of Long-Run Growth 544
Summary 545
Key Concepts 545
Questions for Review 545
Quick Check Multiple Choice 545
Problems and Applications 546

CHAPTER 26

Saving, Investment, and the Financial System 547

26-1 Financial Institutions in the U.S. Economy 548
  26-1a Financial Markets 548
  26-1b Financial Intermediaries 550
  FYI: Key Numbers for Stock Watchers 551
  26-1c Summing Up 552
  In The News: Should Students Sell Equity in Themselves? 553

26-2 Saving and Investment in the National Income Accounts 554
  26-2a Some Important Identities 554
  26-2b The Meaning of Saving and Investment 556

26-3 The Market for Loanable Funds 556
  26-3a Supply and Demand for Loanable Funds 557
  26-3b Policy 1: Saving Incentives 558
  26-3c Policy 2: Investment Incentives 560
  26-3d Policy 3: Government Budget Deficits and Surpluses 561
  Case Study: The History of U.S. Government Debt 563
  FYI: Financial Crises 565

26-4 Conclusion 565
Summary 566
Key Concepts 566
Questions for Review 566
Quick Check Multiple Choice 567
Problems and Applications 567

CHAPTER 27

The Basic Tools of Finance 569

27-1 Present Value: Measuring the Time Value of Money 570
 FYI: The Magic of Compounding and the Rule of 70 572

27-2 Managing Risk 572
 27-2a Risk Aversion 572
 27-2b The Markets for Insurance 573
 27-2c Diversification of Firm-Specific Risk 574
 27-2d The Trade-off between Risk and Return 575

27-3 Asset Valuation 576
 27-3a Fundamental Analysis 577
 27-3b The Efficient Markets Hypothesis 577
 Case Study: Random Walks and Index Funds 578
 27-3c Market Irrationality 579
 In The News: Is the Efficient Markets Hypothesis Kaput? 580

27-4 Conclusion 581
Summary 581
Key Concepts 581
Questions for Review 581
Quick Check Multiple Choice 582
Problems and Applications 582

CHAPTER 28

Unemployment 585

28-1 Identifying Unemployment 586
 28-1a How Is Unemployment Measured? 586
 Case Study: Labor-Force Participation of Men and Women in the U.S. Economy 589
 28-1b Does the Unemployment Rate Measure What We Want It To? 590
 28-1c How Long Are the Unemployed without Work? 592
 28-1d Why Are There Always Some People Unemployed? 592
 FYI: The Jobs Number 593

28-2 Job Search 593
 28-2a Why Some Frictional Unemployment Is Inevitable 594
 28-2b Public Policy and Job Search 594
 28-2c Unemployment Insurance 595
 In The News: Why Has Employment Declined? 596

28-3 Minimum-Wage Laws 596

28-4 Unions and Collective Bargaining 598
 FYI: Who Earns the Minimum Wage? 599
 28-4a The Economics of Unions 599
 28-4b Are Unions Good or Bad for the Economy? 600

28-5 The Theory of Efficiency Wages 601
 28-5a Worker Health 601
 28-5b Worker Turnover 602
 28-5c Worker Quality 602

 28-5d Worker Effort 603
 Case Study: Henry Ford and the Very Generous $5-a-Day Wage 603

28-6 Conclusion 604
Summary 604
Key Concepts 604
Questions for Review 605
Quick Check Multiple Choice 605
Problems and Applications 605

Part X Money and Prices in the Long Run 607

CHAPTER 29

The Monetary System 609

29-1 The Meaning of Money 610
 29-1a The Functions of Money 611
 29-1b The Kinds of Money 611
 In The News: Why Gold? 612
 29-1c Money in the U.S. Economy 613
 FYI: Why Credit Cards Aren't Money 614
 Case Study: Where Is All the Currency? 615

29-2 The Federal Reserve System 615
 29-2a The Fed's Organization 615
 29-2b The Federal Open Market Committee 616

29-3 Banks and the Money Supply 617
 29-3a The Simple Case of 100-Percent-Reserve Banking 617
 29-3b Money Creation with Fractional-Reserve Banking 618
 29-3c The Money Multiplier 619

29-3d Bank Capital, Leverage, and the Financial Crisis of 2008–2009   620

29-4 The Fed's Tools of Monetary Control   622
29-4a How the Fed Influences the Quantity of Reserves   622
29-4b How the Fed Influences the Reserve Ratio   623
29-4c Problems in Controlling the Money Supply   624
Case Study: Bank Runs and the Money Supply   625
In The News: Bernanke on the Fed's Toolbox   626
29-4d The Federal Funds Rate   628

29-5 Conclusion   629
Summary   629
Key Concepts   629
Questions for Review   630
Quick Check Multiple Choice   630
Problems and Applications   630

CHAPTER 30

Money Growth and Inflation   633

30-1 The Classical Theory of Inflation   634
30-1a The Level of Prices and the Value of Money   635
30-1b Money Supply, Money Demand, and Monetary Equilibrium   635
30-1c The Effects of a Monetary Injection   637
30-1d A Brief Look at the Adjustment Process   638
30-1e The Classical Dichotomy and Monetary Neutrality   639
30-1f Velocity and the Quantity Equation   640
Case Study: Money and Prices during Four Hyperinflations   642
30-1g The Inflation Tax   642
30-1h The Fisher Effect   644
FYI: Hyperinflation in Zimbabwe   644

30-2 The Costs of Inflation   646
30-2a A Fall in Purchasing Power? The Inflation Fallacy   647
30-2b Shoeleather Costs   647
30-2c Menu Costs   648
30-2d Relative-Price Variability and the Misallocation of Resources   648
30-2e Inflation-Induced Tax Distortions   649
30-2f Confusion and Inconvenience   650
30-2g A Special Cost of Unexpected Inflation: Arbitrary Redistributions of Wealth   651
30-2h Inflation Is Bad, But Deflation May Be Worse   652
Case Study: *The Wizard of Oz* and the Free-Silver Debate   652

30-3 Conclusion   654
Summary   654
Key Concepts   654
Questions for Review   655
Quick Check Multiple Choice   655
Problems and Applications   655

Part XI The Macroeconomics of Open Economies   657

CHAPTER 31

Open-Economy Macroeconomics: Basic Concepts   659

31-1 The International Flows of Goods and Capital   660
31-1a The Flow of Goods: Exports, Imports, and Net Exports   660
Case Study: The Increasing Openness of the U.S. Economy   661
In The News: The Changing Nature of U.S. Exports   662
31-1b The Flow of Financial Resources: Net Capital Outflow   664
31-1c The Equality of Net Exports and Net Capital Outflow   665
31-1d Saving, Investment, and Their Relationship to the International Flows   666
31-1e Summing Up   667
Case Study: Is the U.S. Trade Deficit a National Problem?   668

31-2 The Prices for International Transactions: Real and Nominal Exchange Rates   670
31-2a Nominal Exchange Rates   670
FYI: The Euro   671
31-2b Real Exchange Rates   672

31-3 A First Theory of Exchange-Rate Determination: Purchasing-Power Parity   673
31-3a The Basic Logic of Purchasing-Power Parity   674
31-3b Implications of Purchasing-Power Parity   674
Case Study: The Nominal Exchange Rate during a Hyperinflation   676
31-3c Limitations of Purchasing-Power Parity   677
Case Study: The Hamburger Standard   677

31-4 Conclusion   678
Summary   679
Key Concepts   679
Questions for Review   679
Quick Check Multiple Choice   679
Problems and Applications   680

CHAPTER 32

A Macroeconomic Theory of the Open Economy   683

32-1 Supply and Demand for Loanable Funds and for Foreign-Currency Exchange   684
32-1a The Market for Loanable Funds   684
32-1b The Market for Foreign-Currency Exchange   686
FYI: Purchasing-Power Parity as a Special Case   688

32-2 Equilibrium in the Open Economy   689
32-2a Net Capital Outflow: The Link between the Two Markets   689
32-2b Simultaneous Equilibrium in Two Markets   690
FYI: Disentangling Supply and Demand   692

32-3 How Policies and Events Affect an Open Economy   692
32-3a Government Budget Deficits   692
32-3b Trade Policy   694
32-3c Political Instability and Capital Flight   697
Case Study: Capital Flows from China   699
In The News: Is a Strong Currency Always in a Nation's Interest?   700

32-4 Conclusion   700
Summary   702
Key Concepts   702
Questions for Review   702
Quick Check Multiple Choice   702
Problems and Applications   703

Part XII Short-Run Economic Fluctuations   705

CHAPTER 33

Aggregate Demand and Aggregate Supply   707

33-1 Three Key Facts about Economic Fluctuations   708
33-1a Fact 1: Economic Fluctuations Are Irregular and Unpredictable   708
33-1b Fact 2: Most Macroeconomic Quantities Fluctuate Together   710
33-1c Fact 3: As Output Falls, Unemployment Rises   710

33-2 Explaining Short-Run Economic Fluctuations   710
33-2a The Assumptions of Classical Economics   710
33-2b The Reality of Short-Run Fluctuations   711
In The News: The Social Influences of Economic Downturns   712
33-2c The Model of Aggregate Demand and Aggregate Supply   712

33-3 The Aggregate-Demand Curve   714
33-3a Why the Aggregate-Demand Curve Slopes Downward   714
33-3b Why the Aggregate-Demand Curve Might Shift   717

33-4 The Aggregate-Supply Curve   719
33-4a Why the Aggregate-Supply Curve Is Vertical in the Long Run   720
33-4b Why the Long-Run Aggregate-Supply Curve Might Shift   721
33-4c Using Aggregate Demand and Aggregate Supply to Depict Long-Run Growth and Inflation   722
33-4d Why the Aggregate-Supply Curve Slopes Upward in the Short Run   723
33-4e Why the Short-Run Aggregate-Supply Curve Might Shift   727

33-5 Two Causes of Economic Fluctuations   728
33-5a The Effects of a Shift in Aggregate Demand   729
FYI: Monetary Neutrality Revisited   731
Case Study: Two Big Shifts in Aggregate Demand: The Great Depression and World War II   732
Case Study: The Recession of 2008–2009   733
In The News: What Have We Learned?   734
33-5b The Effects of a Shift in Aggregate Supply   736
Case Study: Oil and the Economy   738
FYI: The Origins of the Model of Aggregate Demand and Aggregate Supply   739

33-6 Conclusion   740
Summary   740
Key Concepts   741
Questions for Review   741
Quick Check Multiple Choice   742
Problems and Applications   742

CHAPTER 34

The Influence of Monetary and Fiscal Policy on Aggregate Demand 745

34-1 How Monetary Policy Influences Aggregate Demand 746
34-1a The Theory of Liquidity Preference 747
34-1b The Downward Slope of the Aggregate-Demand
Curve 749
FYI: Interest Rates in the Long Run and the Short Run 750
34-1c Changes in the Money Supply 751
34-1d The Role of Interest-Rate Targets in Fed Policy 753
FYI: The Zero Lower Bound 753
Case Study: Why the Fed Watches the Stock Market
(and Vice Versa) 754

34-2 How Fiscal Policy Influences Aggregate Demand 755
34-2a Changes in Government Purchases 755
34-2b The Multiplier Effect 756
34-2c A Formula for the Spending Multiplier 757
34-2d Other Applications of the Multiplier Effect 758
34-2e The Crowding-Out Effect 758
34-2f Changes in Taxes 759
FYI: How Fiscal Policy Might Affect Aggregate Supply 760

34-3 Using Policy to Stabilize the Economy 760
34-3a The Case for Active Stabilization Policy 761
Case Study: Keynesians in the White House 762
In The News: How Large Is the Fiscal Policy
Multiplier? 762
34-3b The Case against Active Stabilization Policy 764
34-3c Automatic Stabilizers 764

34-4 Conclusion 765
Summary 766
Key Concepts 766
Questions for Review 766
Quick Check Multiple Choice 767
Problems and Applications 767

CHAPTER 35

The Short-Run Trade-off between Inflation and Unemployment 769

35-1 The Phillips Curve 770
35-1a Origins of the Phillips Curve 770
35-1b Aggregate Demand, Aggregate Supply, and the Phillips
Curve 771

35-2 Shifts in the Phillips Curve: The Role of Expectations 773
35-2a The Long-Run Phillips Curve 773
35-2b The Meaning of "Natural" 775
35-2c Reconciling Theory and Evidence 776
35-2d The Short-Run Phillips Curve 777
35-2e The Natural Experiment for the Natural-Rate
Hypothesis 778

**35-3 Shifts in the Phillips Curve: The Role of Supply
Shocks 780**

35-4 The Cost of Reducing Inflation 782
35-4a The Sacrifice Ratio 783
35-4b Rational Expectations and the Possibility of Costless
Disinflation 784
35-4c The Volcker Disinflation 785
35-4d The Greenspan Era 787
35-4e A Financial Crisis Takes Us for a Ride along the Phillips
Curve 788

35-5 Conclusion 789
Summary 790
Key Concepts 790
Questions for Review 790
Quick Check Multiple Choice 790
Problems and Applications 791

Part XIII Final Thoughts 793

CHAPTER 36

Six Debates over Macroeconomic Policy 795

**36-1 Should Monetary and Fiscal Policymakers Try to Stabilize
the Economy? 796**
36-1a Pro: Policymakers Should Try
to Stabilize the Economy 796
36-1b Con: Policymakers Should Not Try to Stabilize the
Economy 796
In The News: How Long Will the Fed Keep Interest Rates at
Zero? 798

**36-2 Should the Government Fight Recessions with
Spending Hikes Rather Than Tax Cuts? 798**
36-2a Pro: The Government Should Fight Recessions with
Spending Hikes 798

36-2b Con: The Government Should Fight Recessions
with Tax Cuts   800

36-3 Should Monetary Policy Be Made by Rule Rather Than by Discretion?   802
36-3a Pro: Monetary Policy Should Be Made by Rule   802
36-3b Con: Monetary Policy Should Not Be Made by Rule   803
FYI: Inflation Targeting   804

36-4 Should the Central Bank Aim for Zero Inflation?   804
36-4a Pro: The Central Bank Should Aim for Zero
Inflation   805
36-4b Con: The Central Bank Should Not Aim for Zero
Inflation   806
In The News: What Is the Optimal Inflation Rate?   807

36-5 Should the Government Balance Its Budget?   808
36-5a Pro: The Government Should Balance Its Budget   808
36-5b Con: The Government Should Not Balance Its
Budget   809

In The News: What Would an American Fiscal Crisis Look
Like?   810

**36-6 Should the Tax Laws Be Reformed to Encourage
Saving?   812**
36-6a Pro: The Tax Laws Should Be Reformed to Encourage
Saving   812
36-6b Con: The Tax Laws Should Not Be Reformed to
Encourage Saving   813

36-7 Conclusion   814
Summary   815
Questions for Review   815
Quick Check Multiple Choice   815
Problems and Applications   816

Glossary   817
Index   825

PART

I

Introduction

Ten Principles of Economics

The word *economy* comes from the Greek word *oikonomos*, which means "one who manages a household." At first, this origin might seem peculiar. But in fact, households and economies have much in common.

A household faces many decisions. It must decide which household members do which tasks and what each member receives in return: Who cooks dinner? Who does the laundry? Who gets the extra dessert at dinner? Who gets to drive the car? In short, a household must allocate its scarce resources (time, dessert, car mileage) among its various members, taking into account each member's abilities, efforts, and desires.

Like a household, a society faces many decisions. It must find some way to decide what jobs will be done and who will do them. It needs some people to grow food, other people to make clothing, and still others to design computer software. Once society has allocated people (as well as land, buildings, and machines) to various jobs, it must also allocate the goods and services

3

they produce. It must decide who will eat caviar and who will eat potatoes. It must decide who will drive a Ferrari and who will take the bus.

The management of society's resources is important because resources are scarce. **Scarcity** means that society has limited resources and therefore cannot produce all the goods and services people wish to have. Just as each member of a household cannot get everything she wants, each individual in a society cannot attain the highest standard of living to which she might aspire.

Economics is the study of how society manages its scarce resources. In most societies, resources are allocated not by an all-powerful dictator but through the combined choices of millions of households and firms. Economists, therefore, study how people make decisions: how much they work, what they buy, how much they save, and how they invest their savings. Economists also study how people interact with one another. For instance, they examine how the multitude of buyers and sellers of a good together determine the price at which the good is sold and the quantity that is sold. Finally, economists analyze forces and trends that affect the economy as a whole, including the growth in average income, the fraction of the population that cannot find work, and the rate at which prices are rising.

The study of economics has many facets, but it is unified by several central ideas. In this chapter, we look at *Ten Principles of Economics*. Don't worry if you don't understand them all at first or if you aren't completely convinced. We explore these ideas more fully in later chapters. The ten principles are introduced here to give you an overview of what economics is all about. Consider this chapter a "preview of coming attractions."

scarcity
the limited nature of society's resources

economics
the study of how society manages its scarce resources

1-1 How People Make Decisions

There is no mystery to what an economy is. Whether we are talking about the economy of Los Angeles, the United States, or the whole world, an economy is just a group of people dealing with one another as they go about their lives. Because the behavior of an economy reflects the behavior of the individuals who make up the economy, we begin our study of economics with four principles about individual decision making.

1-1a Principle 1: People Face Trade-offs

You may have heard the old saying, "There ain't no such thing as a free lunch." Grammar aside, there is much truth to this adage. To get something that we like, we usually have to give up something else that we also like. Making decisions requires trading off one goal against another.

Consider a student who must decide how to allocate her most valuable resource—her time. She can spend all of her time studying economics, spend all of it studying psychology, or divide it between the two fields. For every hour she studies one subject, she gives up an hour she could have used studying the other. And for every hour she spends studying, she gives up an hour that she could have spent napping, bike riding, watching TV, or working at her part-time job for some extra spending money.

Or consider parents deciding how to spend their family income. They can buy food, clothing, or a family vacation. Or they can save some of the family income for retirement or for children's college education. When they choose to spend an extra dollar on one of these goods, they have one less dollar to spend on some other good.

When people are grouped into societies, they face different kinds of trade-offs. One classic trade-off is between "guns and butter." The more a society spends on national defense (guns) to protect its shores from foreign aggressors, the less it can spend on consumer goods (butter) to raise the standard of living at home. Also important in modern society is the trade-off between a clean environment and a high level of income. Laws that require firms to reduce pollution raise the cost of producing goods and services. Because of these higher costs, the firms end up earning smaller profits, paying lower wages, charging higher prices, or some combination of these three. Thus, while pollution regulations yield the benefit of a cleaner environment and the improved health that comes with it, the regulations come at the cost of reducing the incomes of the regulated firms' owners, workers, and customers.

Another trade-off society faces is between efficiency and equality. **Efficiency** means that society is getting the maximum benefits from its scarce resources. **Equality** means that those benefits are distributed uniformly among society's members. In other words, efficiency refers to the size of the economic pie, and equality refers to how the pie is divided into individual slices.

When government policies are designed, these two goals often conflict. Consider, for instance, policies aimed at equalizing the distribution of economic well-being. Some of these policies, such as the welfare system or unemployment insurance, try to help the members of society who are most in need. Others, such as the individual income tax, ask the financially successful to contribute more than others to support the government. Though they achieve greater equality, these policies reduce efficiency. When the government redistributes income from the rich to the poor, it reduces the reward for working hard; as a result, people work less and produce fewer goods and services. In other words, when the government tries to cut the economic pie into more equal slices, the pie gets smaller.

Recognizing that people face trade-offs does not by itself tell us what decisions they will or should make. A student should not abandon the study of psychology just because doing so would increase the time available for the study of economics. Society should not stop protecting the environment just because environmental regulations reduce our material standard of living. The poor should not be ignored just because helping them distorts work incentives. Nonetheless, people are likely to make good decisions only if they understand the options that are available to them. Our study of economics, therefore, starts by acknowledging life's trade-offs.

efficiency
the property of society getting the most it can from its scarce resources

equality
the property of distributing economic prosperity uniformly among the members of society

1-1b Principle 2: The Cost of Something Is What You Give Up to Get It

Because people face trade-offs, making decisions requires comparing the costs and benefits of alternative courses of action. In many cases, however, the cost of an action is not as obvious as it might first appear.

Consider the decision to go to college. The main benefits are intellectual enrichment and a lifetime of better job opportunities. But what are the costs? To answer this question, you might be tempted to add up the money you spend on tuition, books, room, and board. Yet this total does not truly represent what you give up to spend a year in college.

There are two problems with this calculation. First, it includes some things that are not really costs of going to college. Even if you quit school, you need a place to sleep and food to eat. Room and board are costs of going to college only to the extent that they are more expensive at college than elsewhere. Second, this calculation ignores the largest cost of going to college—your time. When you spend a year listening to lectures, reading textbooks, and writing papers, you cannot spend that time working at a job. For most students, the earnings they give up to attend school are the single largest cost of their education.

opportunity cost
whatever must be given up to obtain some item

The **opportunity cost** of an item is what you give up to get that item. When making any decision, decision makers should be aware of the opportunity costs that accompany each possible action. In fact, they usually are. College athletes who can earn millions if they drop out of school and play professional sports are well aware that the opportunity cost of their attending college is very high. It is not surprising that they often decide that the benefit of a college education is not worth the cost.

1-1c Principle 3: Rational People Think at the Margin

rational people
people who systematically and purposefully do the best they can to achieve their objectives

Economists normally assume that people are rational. **Rational people** systematically and purposefully do the best they can to achieve their objectives, given the available opportunities. As you study economics, you will encounter firms that decide how many workers to hire and how much of their product to manufacture and sell to maximize profits. You will also encounter individuals who decide how much time to spend working and what goods and services to buy with the resulting income to achieve the highest possible level of satisfaction.

marginal change
a small incremental adjustment to a plan of action

Rational people know that decisions in life are rarely black and white but usually involve shades of gray. At dinnertime, the question you face is not "Should I fast or eat like a pig?" More likely, you will be asking yourself "Should I take that extra spoonful of mashed potatoes?" When exams roll around, your decision is not between blowing them off and studying twenty-four hours a day but whether to spend an extra hour reviewing your notes instead of watching TV. Economists use the term **marginal change** to describe a small incremental adjustment to an existing plan of action. Keep in mind that *margin* means "edge," so marginal changes are adjustments around the edges of what you are doing. Rational people often make decisions by comparing *marginal benefits* and *marginal costs*.

For example, suppose you are considering calling a friend on your cell phone. You decide that talking with her for 10 minutes would give you a benefit that you value at about $7. Your cell phone service costs you $40 per month plus $0.50 per minute for whatever calls you make. You usually talk for 100 minutes a month, so your total monthly bill is $90 ($0.50 per minute times 100 minutes, plus the $40 fixed fee). Under these circumstances, should you make the call? You might be tempted to reason as follows: "Because I pay $90 for 100 minutes of calling each month, the average minute on the phone costs me $0.90. So a 10-minute call costs $9. Because that $9 cost is greater than the $7 benefit, I am going to skip the call." That conclusion is wrong, however. Although the *average* cost of a 10-minute call is $9, the *marginal* cost—the amount your bill increases if you make the extra call—is only $5. You will make the right decision only by comparing the marginal benefit and the marginal cost. Because the marginal benefit of $7 is greater than the marginal cost of $5, you should make the call. This is a principle that people innately understand: Cell phone users with unlimited minutes (that is, minutes that are free at the margin) are often prone to make long and frivolous calls.

Thinking at the margin works for business decisions as well. Consider an airline deciding how much to charge passengers who fly standby. Suppose that flying a 200-seat plane across the United States costs the airline $100,000. In this case, the average cost of each seat is $100,000/200, which is $500. One might be tempted to conclude that the airline should never sell a ticket for less than $500. But a rational airline can increase its profits by thinking at the margin. Imagine that a plane is about to take off with 10 empty seats and a standby passenger waiting at the gate is willing to pay $300 for a seat. Should the airline sell the ticket? Of course, it should. If the plane has empty seats, the cost of adding one more passenger is tiny. The *average* cost of flying a passenger is $500, but the *marginal* cost is merely the cost of the bag of peanuts and can of soda that the extra passenger will consume. As long as the standby passenger pays more than the marginal cost, selling the ticket is profitable.

Marginal decision making can help explain some otherwise puzzling economic phenomena. Here is a classic question: Why is water so cheap, while diamonds are so expensive? Humans need water to survive, while diamonds are unnecessary; but for some reason, people are willing to pay much more for a diamond than for a cup of water. The reason is that a person's willingness to pay for a good is based on the marginal benefit that an extra unit of the good would yield. The marginal benefit, in turn, depends on how many units a person already has. Water is essential, but the marginal benefit of an extra cup is small because water is plentiful. By contrast, no one needs diamonds to survive, but because diamonds are so rare, people consider the marginal benefit of an extra diamond to be large.

A rational decision maker takes an action if and only if the marginal benefit of the action exceeds the marginal cost. This principle explains why people use their cell phones as much as they do, why airlines are willing to sell tickets below average cost, and why people are willing to pay more for diamonds than for water. It can take some time to get used to the logic of marginal thinking, but the study of economics will give you ample opportunity to practice.

"Is the marginal benefit of this call greater than the marginal cost?"

incentive
something that induces a person to act

1-1d Principle 4: People Respond to Incentives

An **incentive** is something (such as a prospect of a punishment or reward) that induces a person to act. Because rational people make decisions by comparing costs and benefits, they respond to incentives. You will see that incentives play a central role in the study of economics. One economist went so far as to suggest that the entire field could be summarized as simply "People respond to incentives. The rest is commentary."

Incentives are crucial to analyzing how markets work. For example, when the price of an apple rises, people decide to eat fewer apples. At the same time, apple orchards decide to hire more workers and harvest more apples. In other words, a higher price in a market provides an incentive for buyers to consume less and an incentive for sellers to produce more. As we will see, the influence of prices on the behavior of consumers and producers is crucial for how a market economy allocates scarce resources.

Public policymakers should never forget about incentives: Many policies change the costs or benefits that people face and, as a result, alter their behavior. A tax on gasoline, for instance, encourages people to drive smaller, more fuel-efficient cars. That is one reason people drive smaller cars in Europe, where gasoline taxes are high, than in the United States, where gasoline taxes are low. A higher gasoline tax also encourages people to carpool, take public transportation, and live closer to where they work. If the tax were larger, more people would be driving hybrid cars, and if it were large enough, they would switch to electric cars.

When policymakers fail to consider how their policies affect incentives, they often end up with unintended consequences. For example, consider public policy regarding auto safety. Today, all cars have seat belts, but this was not true fifty years ago. In the 1960s, Ralph Nader's book *Unsafe at Any Speed* generated much public concern over auto safety. Congress responded with laws requiring seat belts as standard equipment on new cars.

How does a seat belt law affect auto safety? The direct effect is obvious: When a person wears a seat belt, the probability of surviving an auto accident rises. But that's not the end of the story because the law also affects behavior by altering incentives. The relevant behavior here is the speed and care with which drivers operate their cars. Driving slowly and carefully is costly because it uses the driver's time and energy. When deciding how safely to drive, rational people compare, perhaps unconsciously, the marginal benefit from safer driving to the marginal cost. As a result, they drive more slowly and carefully when the benefit of increased safety is high. For example, when road conditions are icy, people drive more attentively and at lower speeds than they do when road conditions are clear.

Consider how a seat belt law alters a driver's cost–benefit calculation. Seat belts make accidents less costly because they reduce the likelihood of injury or death. In other words, seat belts reduce the benefits of slow and careful driving. People respond to seat belts as they would to an improvement in road conditions—by driving faster and less carefully. The result of a seat belt law, therefore, is a larger number of accidents. The decline in safe driving has a clear, adverse impact on pedestrians, who are more likely to find themselves in an accident but (unlike the drivers) don't have the benefit of added protection.

At first, this discussion of incentives and seat belts might seem like idle speculation. Yet in a classic 1975 study, economist Sam Peltzman argued that auto-safety laws have had many of these effects. According to Peltzman's evidence, these laws produce both fewer deaths per accident and more accidents. He concluded that the net result is little change in the number of driver deaths and an increase in the number of pedestrian deaths.

Peltzman's analysis of auto safety is an offbeat and controversial example of the general principle that people respond to incentives. When analyzing any policy, we must consider not only the direct effects but also the less obvious indirect effects that work through incentives. If the policy changes incentives, it will cause people to alter their behavior.

case study **The Incentive Effects of Gasoline Prices**

From 2005 to 2008 the price of oil in world oil markets skyrocketed, the result of limited supplies together with surging demand from robust world growth, especially in China. The price of gasoline in the United States rose from about $2 to about $4 a gallon. At the time, the news was filled with stories about how people responded to the increased incentive to conserve—sometimes in obvious ways, sometimes in less obvious ways.

Here is a sampling of various stories:

- "As Gas Prices Soar, Buyers Are Flocking to Small Cars"
- "As Gas Prices Climb, So Do Scooter Sales"
- "Gas Prices Knock Bicycles Sales, Repairs into Higher Gear"
- "Gas Prices Send Surge of Riders to Mass Transit"
- "Camel Demand Up as Oil Price Soars": Farmers in the Indian state of Rajasthan are rediscovering the humble camel. As the cost of running gas-guzzling tractors soars, even-toed ungulates are making a comeback.
- "The Airlines Are Suffering, but the Order Books of Boeing and Airbus Are Bulging": Demand for new, more fuel-efficient aircraft has never been greater.

The latest versions of the Airbus A320 and Boeing 737, the single-aisle work-horses for which demand is strongest, are up to 40 percent cheaper to run than the vintage planes some American airlines still use.

- "Home Buying Practices Adjust to High Gas Prices": In his hunt for a new home, Demetrius Stroud crunched the numbers to find out that, with gas prices climbing, moving near an Amtrak station is the best thing for his wallet.
- "Gas Prices Drive Students to Online Courses": For Christy LaBadie, a sophomore at Northampton Community College, the 30-minute drive from her home to the Bethlehem, Pa., campus has become a financial hardship now that gasoline prices have soared to more than $4 a gallon. So this semester she decided to take an online course to save herself the trip—and the money.
- "Diddy Halts Private Jet Flights Over Fuel Prices": Fuel prices have grounded an unexpected frequent-flyer: Sean "Diddy" Combs. . . . The hip-hop mogul said he is now flying on commercial airlines instead of in private jets, which Combs said had previously cost him $200,000 and up for a roundtrip between New York and Los Angeles. "I'm actually flying commercial," Diddy said before walking onto an airplane, sitting in a first-class seat and flashing his boarding pass to the camera. "That's how high gas prices are."

Many of these developments proved transitory. The economic downturn that began in 2008 and continued into 2009 reduced the world demand for oil, and the price of gasoline declined substantially. No word yet on whether Mr. Combs has returned to his private jet. ◢

Quick Quiz *Describe an important trade-off you recently faced.* • *Give an example of some action that has both a monetary and nonmonetary opportunity cost.* • *Describe an incentive your parents offered to you in an effort to influence your behavior.*

1-2 How People Interact

The first four principles discussed how individuals make decisions. As we go about our lives, many of our decisions affect not only ourselves but other people as well. The next three principles concern how people interact with one another.

1-2a Principle 5: Trade Can Make Everyone Better Off

You may have heard on the news that the Chinese are our competitors in the world economy. In some ways, this is true because American and Chinese firms produce many of the same goods. Companies in the United States and China compete for the same customers in the markets for clothing, toys, solar panels, automobile tires, and many other items.

Yet it is easy to be misled when thinking about competition among countries. Trade between the United States and China is not like a sports contest in which one side wins and the other side loses. In fact, the opposite is true: Trade between two countries can make each country better off.

To see why, consider how trade affects your family. When a member of your family looks for a job, she competes against members of other families who are looking for jobs. Families also compete against one another when they go shopping because each family wants to buy the best goods at the lowest prices. In a sense, each family in an economy competes with all other families.

"For $5 a week you can watch baseball without being nagged to cut the grass!"

Despite this competition, your family would not be better off isolating itself from all other families. If it did, your family would need to grow its own food, make its own clothes, and build its own home. Clearly, your family gains much from its ability to trade with others. Trade allows each person to specialize in the activities she does best, whether it is farming, sewing, or home building. By trading with others, people can buy a greater variety of goods and services at lower cost.

Countries as well as families benefit from the ability to trade with one another. Trade allows countries to specialize in what they do best and to enjoy a greater variety of goods and services. The Chinese, as well as the French and the Egyptians and the Brazilians, are as much our partners in the world economy as they are our competitors.

1-2b Principle 6: Markets Are Usually a Good Way to Organize Economic Activity

The collapse of communism in the Soviet Union and Eastern Europe in the 1980s was one of the last century's most important changes. Communist countries operated on the premise that government officials were in the best position to allocate the economy's scarce resources. These central planners decided what goods and services were produced, how much was produced, and who produced and consumed these goods and services. The theory behind central planning was that only the government could organize economic activity in a way that promoted economic well-being for the country as a whole.

market economy
an economy that allocates resources through the decentralized decisions of many firms and households as they interact in markets for goods and services

Most countries that once had centrally planned economies have abandoned the system and are instead developing market economies. In a **market economy**, the decisions of a central planner are replaced by the decisions of millions of firms and households. Firms decide whom to hire and what to make. Households decide which firms to work for and what to buy with their incomes. These firms and households interact in the marketplace, where prices and self-interest guide their decisions.

At first glance, the success of market economies is puzzling. In a market economy, no one is looking out for the economic well-being of society as a whole. Free markets contain many buyers and sellers of numerous goods and services, and all of them are interested primarily in their own well-being. Yet despite decentralized decision making and self-interested decision makers, market economies have proven remarkably successful in organizing economic activity to promote overall economic well-being.

In his 1776 book *An Inquiry into the Nature and Causes of the Wealth of Nations*, economist Adam Smith made the most famous observation in all of economics: Households and firms interacting in markets act as if they are guided by an "invisible hand" that leads them to desirable market outcomes. One of our goals in this book is to understand how this invisible hand works its magic.

As you study economics, you will learn that prices are the instrument with which the invisible hand directs economic activity. In any market, buyers look at the price when determining how much to demand, and sellers look at the price when deciding how much to supply. As a result of the decisions that buyers and sellers make, market prices reflect both the value of a good to society and the cost to society of making the good. Smith's great insight was that prices adjust to guide these individual buyers and sellers to reach outcomes that, in many cases, maximize the well-being of society as a whole.

Smith's insight has an important corollary: When a government prevents prices from adjusting naturally to supply and demand, it impedes the invisible hand's ability to coordinate the decisions of the households and firms that make up an economy. This corollary explains why taxes adversely affect the allocation of resources: They distort prices and thus the decisions of households and firms. It also explains the great harm caused by policies that directly control prices, such as rent control. And it explains the failure of communism. In communist countries, prices were not determined in the marketplace but were dictated by central planners. These planners lacked the necessary information about consumers' tastes and producers' costs, which in a market economy is reflected in prices. Central planners failed because they tried to run the economy with one hand tied behind their backs—the invisible hand of the marketplace.

1-2c Principle 7: Governments Can Sometimes Improve Market Outcomes

If the invisible hand of the market is so great, why do we need government? One purpose of studying economics is to refine your view about the proper role and scope of government policy.

One reason we need government is that the invisible hand can work its magic only if the government enforces the rules and maintains the institutions that are

---

FYI

Adam Smith and the Invisible Hand

It may be only a coincidence that Adam Smith's great book *The Wealth of Nations* was published in 1776, the exact year in which American revolutionaries signed the Declaration of Independence. But the two documents share a point of view that was prevalent at the time: Individuals are usually best left to their own devices, without the heavy hand of government guiding their actions. This political philosophy provides the intellectual basis for the market economy and for free society more generally.

Why do decentralized market economies work so well? Is it because people can be counted on to treat one another with love and kindness? Not at all. Here is Adam Smith's description of how people interact in a market economy:

Bettmann/Corbis

Adam Smith

> Man has almost constant occasion for the help of his brethren, and it is in vain for him to expect it from their benevolence only. He will be more likely to prevail if he can interest their self-love in his favour, and show them that it is for their own advantage to do for him what he requires of them. . . . Give me that which I want, and you shall have this which you want, is the meaning of every such offer; and it is in this manner that we obtain from one another the far greater part of those good offices which we stand in need of.

> It is not from the benevolence of the butcher, the brewer, or the baker that we expect our dinner, but from their regard to their own interest. We address ourselves, not to their humanity but to their self-love, and never talk to them of our own necessities but of their advantages. Nobody but a beggar chooses to depend chiefly upon the benevolence of his fellow-citizens. . . .

> Every individual . . . neither intends to promote the public interest, nor knows how much he is promoting it. . . . He intends only his own gain, and he is in this, as in many other cases, led by an invisible hand to promote an end which was no part of his intention. Nor is it always the worse for the society that it was no part of it. By pursuing his own interest he frequently promotes that of the society more effectually than when he really intends to promote it.

Smith is saying that participants in the economy are motivated by self-interest and that the "invisible hand" of the marketplace guides this self-interest into promoting general economic well-being.

Many of Smith's insights remain at the center of modern economics. Our analysis in the coming chapters will allow us to express Smith's conclusions more precisely and to analyze more fully the strengths and weaknesses of the market's invisible hand. ◢

property rights
the ability of an individual to own and exercise control over scarce resources

key to a market economy. Most important, market economies need institutions to enforce **property rights** so individuals can own and control scarce resources. A farmer won't grow food if she expects her crop to be stolen; a restaurant won't serve meals unless it is assured that customers will pay before they leave; and an entertainment company won't produce DVDs if too many potential customers avoid paying by making illegal copies. We all rely on government-provided police and courts to enforce our rights over the things we produce—and the invisible hand counts on our ability to enforce our rights.

Yet there is another reason we need government: The invisible hand is powerful, but it is not omnipotent. There are two broad reasons for a government to intervene in the economy and change the allocation of resources that people would choose on their own: to promote efficiency or to promote equality. That is, most policies aim either to enlarge the economic pie or to change how the pie is divided.

Consider first the goal of efficiency. Although the invisible hand usually leads markets to allocate resources to maximize the size of the economic pie, this is not always the case. Economists use the term **market failure** to refer to a situation in which the market on its own fails to produce an efficient allocation of resources. As we will see, one possible cause of market failure is an **externality,** which is the impact of one person's actions on the well-being of a bystander. The classic example of an externality is pollution. When the production of a good pollutes the air and creates health problems for those who live near the factories, the market left to its own devices may fail to take this cost into account. Another possible cause of market failure is **market power,** which refers to the ability of a single person or firm (or a small group) to unduly influence market prices. For example, if everyone in town needs water but there is only one well, the owner of the well is not subject to the rigorous competition with which the invisible hand normally keeps self-interest in check; she may take advantage of this opportunity by restricting the output of water so she can charge a higher price. In the presence of externalities or market power, well-designed public policy can enhance economic efficiency.

market failure
a situation in which a market left on its own fails to allocate resources efficiently

externality
the impact of one person's actions on the well-being of a bystander

market power
the ability of a single economic actor (or small group of actors) to have a substantial influence on market prices

Now consider the goal of equality. Even when the invisible hand yields efficient outcomes, it can nonetheless leave sizable disparities in economic well-being. A market economy rewards people according to their ability to produce things that other people are willing to pay for. The world's best basketball player earns more than the world's best chess player simply because people are willing to pay more to watch basketball than chess. The invisible hand does not ensure that everyone has sufficient food, decent clothing, and adequate healthcare. This inequality may, depending on one's political philosophy, call for government intervention. In practice, many public policies, such as the income tax and the welfare system, aim to achieve a more equal distribution of economic well-being.

To say that the government *can* improve on market outcomes at times does not mean that it always *will*. Public policy is made not by angels but by a political process that is far from perfect. Sometimes policies are designed simply to reward the politically powerful. Sometimes they are made by well-intentioned leaders who are not fully informed. As you study economics, you will become a better judge of when a government policy is justifiable because it promotes efficiency or equality and when it is not.

Quick Quiz *Why is a country better off not isolating itself from all other countries?* • *Why do we have markets, and according to economists, what roles should government play in them?*

1-3 How the Economy as a Whole Works

We started by discussing how individuals make decisions and then looked at how people interact with one another. All these decisions and interactions together make up "the economy." The last three principles concern the workings of the economy as a whole.

1-3a Principle 8: A Country's Standard of Living Depends on Its Ability to Produce Goods and Services

The differences in living standards around the world are staggering. In 2011, the average American had an income of about $48,000. In the same year, the average Mexican earned about $9,000, the average Chinese about $5,000, and the average Nigerian only $1,200. Not surprisingly, this large variation in average income is reflected in various measures of quality of life. Citizens of high-income countries have more TV sets, more cars, better nutrition, better healthcare, and a longer life expectancy than citizens of low-income countries.

Changes in living standards over time are also large. In the United States, incomes have historically grown about 2 percent per year (after adjusting for changes in the cost of living). At this rate, average income doubles every 35 years. Over the past century, average U.S. income has risen about eightfold.

What explains these large differences in living standards among countries and over time? The answer is surprisingly simple. Almost all variation in living standards is attributable to differences in countries' **productivity**—that is, the amount of goods and services produced by each unit of labor input. In nations where workers can produce a large quantity of goods and services per hour, most people enjoy a high standard of living; in nations where workers are less productive, most people endure a more meager existence. Similarly, the growth rate of a nation's productivity determines the growth rate of its average income.

productivity
the quantity of goods and services produced from each unit of labor input

The fundamental relationship between productivity and living standards is simple, but its implications are far-reaching. If productivity is the primary determinant of living standards, other explanations must be of secondary importance. For example, it might be tempting to credit labor unions or minimum-wage laws for the rise in living standards of American workers over the past century. Yet the real hero of American workers is their rising productivity. As another example, some commentators have claimed that increased competition from Japan and other countries explained the slow growth in U.S. incomes during the 1970s and 1980s. Yet the real villain was not competition from abroad but flagging productivity growth in the United States.

The relationship between productivity and living standards also has profound implications for public policy. When thinking about how any policy will affect living standards, the key question is how it will affect our ability to produce goods and services. To boost living standards, policymakers need to raise productivity by ensuring that workers are well educated, have the tools they need to produce goods and services, and have access to the best available technology.

1-3b Principle 9: Prices Rise When the Government Prints Too Much Money

In January 1921, a daily newspaper in Germany cost 0.30 marks. Less than two years later, in November 1922, the same newspaper cost 70,000,000 marks. All other prices in the economy rose by similar amounts. This episode is one of

IN THE NEWS
·············

Why You Should Study Economics

In this excerpt from a commencement address, the former president of the Federal Reserve Bank of Dallas makes the case for studying economics.

The Dismal Science? Hardly!

By Robert D. McTeer, Jr.

My take on training in economics is that it becomes increasingly valuable as you move up the career ladder. I can't imagine a better major for corporate CEOs, congressmen, or American presidents. You've learned a systematic, disciplined way of thinking that will serve you well. By contrast, the economically challenged must be perplexed about how it is that economies work better the fewer people they have in charge. Who does the planning? Who makes decisions? Who decides what to produce?

For my money, Adam Smith's invisible hand is the most important thing you've learned by studying economics. You understand how we can each work for our own self-interest and still produce a desirable social outcome. You know how uncoordinated activity gets coordinated by the market to enhance the wealth of nations. You understand the magic of markets and the dangers of tampering with them too much. You know better what you first learned in kindergarten: that you shouldn't kill or cripple the goose that lays the golden eggs. . . .

Economics training will help you understand fallacies and unintended consequences. In fact, I am inclined to define economics as the study of how to anticipate unintended consequences. . . .

Little in the literature seems more relevant to contemporary economic debates than what usually is called the broken window fallacy. Whenever a government program is justified not on its merits but by the jobs it will create, remember the broken window: Some teenagers, being the little beasts that they are, toss a brick through a bakery window. A crowd gathers and laments, "What a shame." But before you know it, someone suggests a silver lining to the situation: Now the baker will have to spend money to have the window repaired. This will add to the income of the repairman, who will spend his additional income, which will add to another seller's income, and so on. You know the drill. The chain of spending will multiply and generate higher income and employment. If the broken window is large enough, it might produce an economic boom! . . .

Most voters fall for the broken window fallacy, but not economics majors. They will say, "Hey, wait a minute!" If the baker hadn't spent his money on window repair, he would have spent it on the new suit he was saving to buy. Then the tailor would have the new income to spend, and so on. The broken window didn't create net new spending; it just diverted spending from somewhere else. The broken window does not create new activity, just different activity. People see the activity that takes place. They don't see the activity that *would* have taken place.

The broken window fallacy is perpetuated in many forms. Whenever job creation or retention is the primary objective I call it the job-counting fallacy. Economics majors understand the non-intuitive reality that real progress comes from job destruction. It once took 90 percent of our population to grow our food. Now it takes 3 percent. Pardon me, Willie, but are we worse off because of the job losses in agriculture? The would-have-been farmers are now college professors and computer gurus. . . .

So instead of counting jobs, we should make every job count. We will occasionally hit a soft spot when we have a mismatch of supply and demand in the labor market. But that is temporary. Don't become a Luddite and destroy the machinery, or become a protectionist and try to grow bananas in New York City. ◢

inflation
an increase in the overall level of prices in the economy

history's most spectacular examples of **inflation,** an increase in the overall level of prices in the economy.

Although the United States has never experienced inflation even close to that of Germany in the 1920s, inflation has at times been an economic problem. During the 1970s, for instance, when the overall level of prices more than doubled, President Gerald Ford called inflation "public enemy number one." By contrast, inflation in the first decade of the 21st century ran about 2½ percent per year; at this rate, it would take almost 30 years for prices to double. Because high inflation imposes various costs on society, keeping inflation at a low level is a goal of economic policymakers around the world.

What causes inflation? In almost all cases of large or persistent inflation, the culprit is growth in the quantity of money. When a government creates large quantities of the nation's money, the value of the money falls. In Germany in the early 1920s, when prices were on average tripling every month, the quantity of money was also tripling every month. Although less dramatic, the economic history of the United States points to a similar conclusion: The high inflation of the 1970s was associated with rapid growth in the quantity of money, and the low inflation of more recent experience was associated with slow growth in the quantity of money.

1-3c Principle 10: Society Faces a Short-Run Trade-off between Inflation and Unemployment

Although a higher level of prices is, in the long run, the primary effect of increasing the quantity of money, the short-run story is more complex and controversial. Most economists describe the short-run effects of monetary injections as follows:

"Well it may have been 68 cents when you got in line, but it's 74 cents now!"

- Increasing the amount of money in the economy stimulates the overall level of spending and thus the demand for goods and services.
- Higher demand may over time cause firms to raise their prices, but in the meantime, it also encourages them to hire more workers and produce a larger quantity of goods and services.
- More hiring means lower unemployment.

This line of reasoning leads to one final economy-wide trade-off: a short-run trade-off between inflation and unemployment.

Although some economists still question these ideas, most accept that society faces a short-run trade-off between inflation and unemployment. This simply means that, over a period of a year or two, many economic policies push inflation and unemployment in opposite directions. Policymakers face this trade-off regardless of whether inflation and unemployment both start out at high levels (as they did in the early 1980s), at low levels (as they did in the late 1990s), or someplace in between. This short-run trade-off plays a key role in the analysis of the **business cycle**—the irregular and largely unpredictable fluctuations in economic activity, as measured by the production of goods and services or the number of people employed.

business cycle
fluctuations in economic activity, such as employment and production

Policymakers can exploit the short-run trade-off between inflation and unemployment using various policy instruments. By changing the amount that the government spends, the amount it taxes, and the amount of money it prints, policymakers can influence the overall demand for goods and services. Changes in demand in turn influence the combination of inflation and unemployment that the economy experiences in the short run. Because these instruments of economic policy are potentially so powerful, how policymakers should use these instruments to control the economy, if at all, is a subject of continuing debate.

This debate heated up in the early years of Barack Obama's presidency. In 2008 and 2009, the U.S. economy, as well as many other economies around the world, experienced a deep economic downturn. Problems in the financial system, caused by bad bets on the housing market, spilled over into the rest of the economy, causing incomes to fall and unemployment to soar. Policymakers responded in various ways to increase the overall demand for goods and services. President Obama's first major initiative was a stimulus package of reduced taxes and increased government spending. At the same time, the nation's central bank, the Federal Reserve, increased the supply of money. The goal of these policies was to reduce unemployment. Some feared, however, that these policies might over time lead to an excessive level of inflation.

Quick Quiz   *List and briefly explain the three principles that describe how the economy as a whole works.*

1-4 Conclusion

You now have a taste of what economics is all about. In the coming chapters, we develop many specific insights about people, markets, and economies. Mastering these insights will take some effort, but it is not an overwhelming task. The field of economics is based on a few big ideas that can be applied in many different situations.

Throughout this book, we will refer back to the *Ten Principles of Economics* highlighted in this chapter and summarized in Table 1. Keep these building blocks in mind: Even the most sophisticated economic analysis is founded on the ten principles introduced here.

TABLE 1

Ten Principles of Economics

How People Make Decisions
1: People Face Trade-offs
2: The Cost of Something Is What You Give Up to Get It
3: Rational People Think at the Margin
4: People Respond to Incentives

How People Interact
5: Trade Can Make Everyone Better Off
6: Markets Are Usually a Good Way to Organize Economic Activity
7: Governments Can Sometimes Improve Market Outcomes

How the Economy as a Whole Works
8: A Country's Standard of Living Depends on Its Ability to Produce Goods and Services
9: Prices Rise When the Government Prints Too Much Money
10: Society Faces a Short-Run Trade-off between Inflation and Unemployment

Summary

- The fundamental lessons about individual decision making are that people face trade-offs among alternative goals, that the cost of any action is measured in terms of forgone opportunities, that rational people make decisions by comparing marginal costs and marginal benefits, and that people change their behavior in response to the incentives they face.

- The fundamental lessons about interactions among people are that trade and interdependence can be mutually beneficial, that markets are usually a good way of coordinating economic activity among people, and that the government can potentially improve market outcomes by remedying a market failure or by promoting greater economic equality.

- The fundamental lessons about the economy as a whole are that productivity is the ultimate source of living standards, that growth in the quantity of money is the ultimate source of inflation, and that society faces a short-run trade-off between inflation and unemployment.

Key Concepts

scarcity, *p. 4*
economics, *p. 4*
efficiency, *p. 5*
equality, *p. 5*
opportunity cost, *p. 6*
rational people, *p. 6*

marginal change, *p. 6*
incentive, *p. 7*
market economy, *p. 10*
property rights, *p. 12*
market failure, *p. 12*
externality, *p. 12*

market power, *p. 12*
productivity, *p. 13*
inflation, *p. 14*
business cycle, *p. 15*

Questions for Review

1. Give three examples of important trade-offs that you face in your life.

2. What items would you include to figure out the opportunity cost of a vacation to Disneyworld?

3. Water is necessary for life. Is the marginal benefit of a glass of water large or small?

4. Why should policymakers think about incentives?

5. Why isn't trade among countries like a game with some winners and some losers?

6. What does the "invisible hand" of the marketplace do?

7. Explain the two main causes of market failure and give an example of each.

8. Why is productivity important?

9. What is inflation and what causes it?

10. How are inflation and unemployment related in the short run?

Quick Check Multiple Choice

1. Economics is best defined as the study of
   a. how society manages its scarce resources.
   b. how to run a business most profitably.
   c. how to predict inflation, unemployment, and stock prices.
   d. how the government can stop the harm from unchecked self-interest.

2. Your opportunity cost of going to a movie is
   a. the price of the ticket.
   b. the price of the ticket plus the cost of any soda and popcorn you buy at the theater.
   c. the total cash expenditure needed to go to the movie plus the value of your time.
   d. zero, as long as you enjoy the movie and consider it a worthwhile use of time and money.

3. A marginal change is one that
   a. is not important for public policy.
   b. incrementally alters an existing plan.
   c. makes an outcome inefficient.
   d. does not influence incentives.

4. Adam Smith's "invisible hand" refers to
   a. the subtle and often hidden methods that businesses use to profit at consumers' expense.
   b. the ability of free markets to reach desirable outcomes, despite the self-interest of market participants.
   c. the ability of government regulation to benefit consumers, even if the consumers are unaware of the regulations.
   d. the way in which producers or consumers in unregulated markets impose costs on innocent bystanders.

5. Governments may intervene in a market economy in order to
   a. protect property rights.
   b. correct a market failure due to externalities.
   c. achieve a more equal distribution of income.
   d. All of the above.

6. If a nation has high and persistent inflation, the most likely explanation is
   a. the central bank creating excessive amounts of money.
   b. unions bargaining for excessively high wages.
   c. the government imposing excessive levels of taxation.
   d. firms using their monopoly power to enforce excessive price hikes.

Problems and Applications

1. Describe some of the trade-offs faced by each of the following:
   a. a family deciding whether to buy a new car
   b. a member of Congress deciding how much to spend on national parks
   c. a company president deciding whether to open a new factory
   d. a professor deciding how much to prepare for class
   e. a recent college graduate deciding whether to go to graduate school

2. You are trying to decide whether to take a vacation. Most of the costs of the vacation (airfare, hotel, and forgone wages) are measured in dollars, but the benefits of the vacation are psychological. How can you compare the benefits to the costs?

3. You were planning to spend Saturday working at your part-time job, but a friend asks you to go skiing. What is the true cost of going skiing? Now suppose you had been planning to spend the day studying at the library. What is the cost of going skiing in this case? Explain.

4. You win $100 in a basketball pool. You have a choice between spending the money now and putting it away for a year in a bank account that pays 5 percent interest. What is the opportunity cost of spending the $100 now?

5. The company that you manage has invested $5 million in developing a new product, but the development is not quite finished. At a recent meeting, your salespeople report that the introduction of competing products has reduced the expected sales of your new product to $3 million. If it would cost $1 million to finish development and make the product, should you go ahead and do so? What is the most that you should pay to complete development?

6. The Social Security system provides income for people over age 65. If a recipient of Social Security decides to work and earn some income, the amount received in Social Security benefits is typically reduced.
   a. How does the provision of Social Security affect people's incentive to save while working?
   b. How does the reduction in benefits associated with higher earnings affect people's incentive to work past age 65?

7. A 1996 bill reforming the federal government's anti-poverty programs limited many welfare recipients to only two years of benefits.
   a. How does this change affect the incentives for working?
   b. How might this change represent a trade-off between equality and efficiency?

8. Explain whether each of the following government activities is motivated by a concern about equality or a concern about efficiency. In the case of efficiency, discuss the type of market failure involved.
   a. regulating cable TV prices
   b. providing some poor people with vouchers that can be used to buy food
   c. prohibiting smoking in public places
   d. breaking up Standard Oil (which once owned 90 percent of all oil refineries) into several smaller companies
   e. imposing higher personal income tax rates on people with higher incomes
   f. instituting laws against driving while intoxicated

9. Discuss each of the following statements from the standpoints of equality and efficiency.
   a. "Everyone in society should be guaranteed the best healthcare possible."
   b. "When workers are laid off, they should be able to collect unemployment benefits until they find a new job."

10. In what ways is your standard of living different from that of your parents or grandparents when they were your age? Why have these changes occurred?

11. Suppose Americans decide to save more of their incomes. If banks lend this extra saving to businesses, which use the funds to build new factories, how might this lead to faster growth in productivity? Who do you suppose benefits from the higher productivity? Is society getting a free lunch?

12. During the Revolutionary War, the American colonies could not raise enough tax revenue to fully fund the war effort; to make up the difference, the colonies decided to print more money. Printing money to cover expenditures is sometimes referred to as an "inflation tax." Who do you think is being "taxed" when more money is printed? Why?

Go to CengageBrain.com to purchase access to the proven, critical Study Guide to accompany this text, which features additional notes and context, practice tests, and much more.

Thinking Like an Economist

Every field of study has its own language and its own way of thinking. Mathematicians talk about axioms, integrals, and vector spaces. Psychologists talk about ego, id, and cognitive dissonance. Lawyers talk about venue, torts, and promissory estoppel.

Economics is no different. Supply, demand, elasticity, comparative advantage, consumer surplus, deadweight loss—these terms are part of the economist's language. In the coming chapters, you will encounter many new terms and some familiar words that economists use in specialized ways. At first, this new language may seem needlessly arcane. But as you will see, its value lies in its ability to provide you with a new and useful way of thinking about the world in which you live.

The purpose of this book is to help you learn the economist's way of thinking. Just as you cannot become a mathematician, psychologist, or lawyer overnight, learning to think like an economist will take some time. Yet with a combination of theory, case studies, and examples of economics in the news, this book will give you ample opportunity to develop and practice this skill.

Before delving into the substance and details of economics, it is helpful to have an overview of how economists approach the world. This chapter discusses the field's methodology. What is distinctive about how economists confront a question? What does it mean to think like an economist?

2-1 The Economist as Scientist

Economists try to address their subject with a scientist's objectivity. They approach the study of the economy in much the same way a physicist approaches the study of matter and a biologist approaches the study of life: They devise theories, collect data, and then analyze these data in an attempt to verify or refute their theories.

To beginners, the claim that economics is a science can seem odd. After all, economists do not work with test tubes or telescopes. The essence of science, however, is the *scientific method*—the dispassionate development and testing of theories about how the world works. This method of inquiry is as applicable to studying a nation's economy as it is to studying the earth's gravity or a species' evolution. As Albert Einstein once put it, "The whole of science is nothing more than the refinement of everyday thinking."

Although Einstein's comment is as true for social sciences such as economics as it is for natural sciences such as physics, most people are not accustomed to looking at society through a scientific lens. Let's discuss some of the ways in which economists apply the logic of science to examine how an economy works.

"I'm a social scientist, Michael. That means I can't explain electricity or anything like that, but if you ever want to know about people, I'm your man."

2-1a The Scientific Method: Observation, Theory, and More Observation

Isaac Newton, the famous 17th-century scientist and mathematician, allegedly became intrigued one day when he saw an apple fall from a tree. This observation motivated Newton to develop a theory of gravity that applies not only to an apple falling to the earth but to any two objects in the universe. Subsequent testing of Newton's theory has shown that it works well in many circumstances (although, as Einstein would later emphasize, not in all circumstances). Because Newton's theory has been so successful at explaining observation, it is still taught in undergraduate physics courses around the world.

This interplay between theory and observation also occurs in economics. An economist might live in a country experiencing rapidly increasing prices and be moved by this observation to develop a theory of inflation. The theory might assert that high inflation arises when the government prints too much money. To test this theory, the economist could collect and analyze data on prices and money from many different countries. If growth in the quantity of money were completely unrelated to the rate of price increase, the economist would start to doubt the validity of this theory of inflation. If money growth and inflation were strongly correlated in international data, as in fact they are, the economist would become more confident in the theory.

Although economists use theory and observation like other scientists, they face an obstacle that makes their task especially challenging: In economics, conducting experiments is often impractical. Physicists studying gravity can drop many objects in their laboratories to generate data to test their theories. By contrast, economists studying inflation are not allowed to manipulate a nation's monetary policy simply to generate useful data. Economists, like astronomers and evolutionary biologists, usually have to make do with whatever data the world happens to give them.

To find a substitute for laboratory experiments, economists pay close attention to the natural experiments offered by history. When a war in the Middle East interrupts the flow of crude oil, for instance, oil prices skyrocket around the world. For consumers of oil and oil products, such an event depresses living standards. For economic policymakers, it poses a difficult choice about how best to respond. But for economic scientists, the event provides an opportunity to study the effects of a key natural resource on the world's economies. Throughout this book, therefore, we consider many historical episodes. These episodes are valuable to study because they give us insight into the economy of the past and, more important, because they allow us to illustrate and evaluate economic theories of the present.

2-1b The Role of Assumptions

If you ask a physicist how long it would take a marble to fall from the top of a ten-story building, he will likely answer the question by assuming that the marble falls in a vacuum. Of course, this assumption is false. In fact, the building is surrounded by air, which exerts friction on the falling marble and slows it down. Yet the physicist will point out that the friction on the marble is so small that its effect is negligible. Assuming the marble falls in a vacuum simplifies the problem without substantially affecting the answer.

Economists make assumptions for the same reason: Assumptions can simplify the complex world and make it easier to understand. To study the effects of international trade, for example, we might assume that the world consists of only two countries and that each country produces only two goods. In reality, there are numerous countries, each of which produces thousands of different types of goods. But by considering a world with only two countries and two goods, we can focus our thinking on the essence of the problem. Once we understand international trade in this simplified imaginary world, we are in a better position to understand international trade in the more complex world in which we live.

The art in scientific thinking—whether in physics, biology, or economics—is deciding which assumptions to make. Suppose, for instance, that instead of dropping a marble from the top of the building, we were dropping a beach ball of the same weight. Our physicist would realize that the assumption of no friction is less accurate in this case: Friction exerts a greater force on a beach ball than on a marble because a beach ball is much larger. The assumption that gravity works in a vacuum is reasonable for studying a falling marble but not for studying a falling beach ball.

Similarly, economists use different assumptions to answer different questions. Suppose that we want to study what happens to the economy when the government changes the number of dollars in circulation. An important piece of this analysis, it turns out, is how prices respond. Many prices in the economy change infrequently; the newsstand prices of magazines, for instance, change only once every few years. Knowing this fact may lead us to make different assumptions when studying the effects of the policy change over different time horizons. For studying the short-run effects of the policy, we may assume that prices do not change much. We may even make the extreme and artificial assumption that all prices are completely fixed. For studying the long-run effects of the policy, however, we may assume that all prices are completely flexible. Just as a physicist uses different assumptions when studying falling marbles and falling beach balls, economists use different assumptions when studying the short-run and long-run effects of a change in the quantity of money.

2-1c Economic Models

High school biology teachers teach basic anatomy with plastic replicas of the human body. These models have all the major organs—the heart, the liver, the kidneys, and so on—which allow teachers to show their students very simply how the important parts of the body fit together. Because these plastic models are stylized and omit many details, no one would mistake one of them for a real person. Despite this lack of realism—indeed, because of this lack of realism—studying these models is useful for learning how the human body works.

Economists also use models to learn about the world, but unlike plastic manikins, their models mostly consist of diagrams and equations. Like a biology teacher's plastic model, economic models omit many details to allow us to see what is truly important. Just as the biology teacher's model does not include all the body's muscles and capillaries, an economist's model does not include every feature of the economy.

As we use models to examine various economic issues throughout this book, you will see that all the models are built with assumptions. Just as a physicist begins the analysis of a falling marble by assuming away the existence of friction, economists assume away many of the details of the economy that are irrelevant for studying the question at hand. All models—in physics, biology, and economics—simplify reality to improve our understanding of it.

2-1d Our First Model: The Circular-Flow Diagram

The economy consists of millions of people engaged in many activities—buying, selling, working, hiring, manufacturing, and so on. To understand how the economy works, we must find some way to simplify our thinking about all these activities. In other words, we need a model that explains, in general terms, how the economy is organized and how participants in the economy interact with one another.

circular-flow diagram
a visual model of the economy that shows how dollars flow through markets among households and firms

Figure 1 presents a visual model of the economy called a **circular-flow diagram**. In this model, the economy is simplified to include only two types of decision makers—firms and households. Firms produce goods and services using inputs, such as labor, land, and capital (buildings and machines). These inputs are called the *factors of production*. Households own the factors of production and consume all the goods and services that the firms produce.

Households and firms interact in two types of markets. In the *markets for goods and services*, households are buyers, and firms are sellers. In particular, households buy the output of goods and services that firms produce. In the *markets for the factors of production*, households are sellers, and firms are buyers. In these markets, households provide the inputs that firms use to produce goods and services. The circular-flow diagram offers a simple way of organizing the economic transactions that occur between households and firms in the economy.

The two loops of the circular-flow diagram are distinct but related. The inner loop represents the flows of inputs and outputs. The households sell the use of their labor, land, and capital to the firms in the markets for the factors of

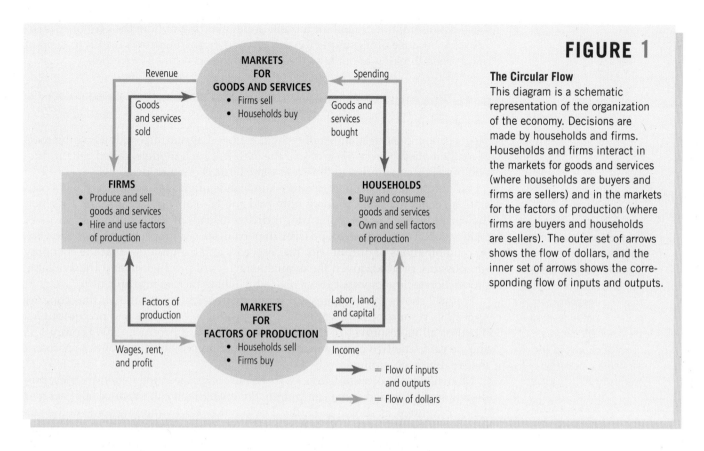

FIGURE 1

The Circular Flow
This diagram is a schematic representation of the organization of the economy. Decisions are made by households and firms. Households and firms interact in the markets for goods and services (where households are buyers and firms are sellers) and in the markets for the factors of production (where firms are buyers and households are sellers). The outer set of arrows shows the flow of dollars, and the inner set of arrows shows the corresponding flow of inputs and outputs.

production. The firms then use these factors to produce goods and services, which in turn are sold to households in the markets for goods and services. The outer loop of the diagram represents the corresponding flow of dollars. The households spend money to buy goods and services from the firms. The firms use some of the revenue from these sales to pay for the factors of production, such as the wages of their workers. What's left is the profit of the firm owners, who themselves are members of households.

Let's take a tour of the circular flow by following a dollar bill as it makes its way from person to person through the economy. Imagine that the dollar begins at a household, say, in your wallet. If you want to buy a cup of coffee, you take the dollar to one of the economy's markets for goods and services, such as your local Starbucks coffee shop. There, you spend it on your favorite drink. When the dollar moves into the Starbucks cash register, it becomes revenue for the firm. The dollar doesn't stay at Starbucks for long, however, because the firm uses it to buy inputs in the markets for the factors of production. Starbucks might use the dollar to pay rent to its landlord for the space it occupies or to pay the wages of its workers. In either case, the dollar enters the income of some household and, once again, is back in someone's wallet. At that point, the story of the economy's circular flow starts once again.

The circular-flow diagram in Figure 1 is a very simple model of the economy. It dispenses with details that, for some purposes, are significant. A more complex and realistic circular-flow model would include, for instance, the roles of government and international trade. (A portion of that dollar you gave to Starbucks might be used to pay taxes or to buy coffee beans from a farmer in Brazil.) Yet these details are not crucial for a basic understanding of how the economy is organized. Because of its simplicity, this circular-flow diagram is useful to keep in mind when thinking about how the pieces of the economy fit together.

2-1e Our Second Model: The Production Possibilities Frontier

Most economic models, unlike the circular-flow diagram, are built using the tools of mathematics. Here we use one of the simplest such models, called the production possibilities frontier, to illustrate some basic economic ideas.

Although real economies produce thousands of goods and services, let's consider an economy that produces only two goods—cars and computers. Together, the car industry and the computer industry use all of the economy's factors of production. The **production possibilities frontier** is a graph that shows the various combinations of output—in this case, cars and computers—that the economy can possibly produce given the available factors of production and the available production technology that firms use to turn these factors into output.

Figure 2 shows this economy's production possibilities frontier. If the economy uses all its resources in the car industry, it produces 1,000 cars and no computers. If it uses all its resources in the computer industry, it produces 3,000 computers and no cars. The two endpoints of the production possibilities frontier represent these extreme possibilities.

More likely, the economy divides its resources between the two industries, producing some cars and some computers. For example, it can produce 600 cars and 2,200 computers, as shown in Figure 2 by point A. Or, by moving some of the factors of production to the car industry from the computer industry, the economy can produce 700 cars and 2,000 computers, represented by point B.

production possibilities frontier
a graph that shows the combinations of output that the economy can possibly produce given the available factors of production and the available production technology

FIGURE 2

The Production Possibilities Frontier
The production possibilities frontier shows the combinations of output—in this case, cars and computers—that the economy can possibly produce. The economy can produce any combination on or inside the frontier. Points outside the frontier are not feasible given the economy's resources. The slope of the production possibilities frontier measures the opportunity cost of a car in terms of computers. This opportunity cost varies, depending on how much of the two goods the economy is producing.

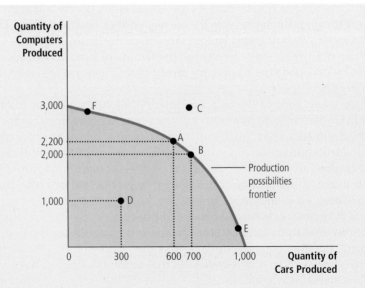

Because resources are scarce, not every conceivable outcome is feasible. For example, no matter how resources are allocated between the two industries, the economy cannot produce the amount of cars and computers represented by point C. Given the technology available for manufacturing cars and computers, the economy does not have enough of the factors of production to support that level of output. With the resources it has, the economy can produce at any point on or inside the production possibilities frontier, but it cannot produce at points outside the frontier.

An outcome is said to be *efficient* if the economy is getting all it can from the scarce resources it has available. Points on (rather than inside) the production possibilities frontier represent efficient levels of production. When the economy is producing at such a point, say point A, there is no way to produce more of one good without producing less of the other. Point D represents an *inefficient* outcome. For some reason, perhaps widespread unemployment, the economy is producing less than it could from the resources it has available: It is producing only 300 cars and 1,000 computers. If the source of the inefficiency is eliminated, the economy can increase its production of both goods. For example, if the economy moves from point D to point A, its production of cars increases from 300 to 600, and its production of computers increases from 1,000 to 2,200.

One of the *Ten Principles of Economics* discussed in Chapter 1 is that people face trade-offs. The production possibilities frontier shows one trade-off that society faces. Once we have reached an efficient point on the frontier, the only way of producing more of one good is to produce less of the other. When the economy moves from point A to point B, for instance, society produces 100 more cars but at the expense of producing 200 fewer computers.

This trade-off helps us understand another of the *Ten Principles of Economics:* The cost of something is what you give up to get it. This is called the *opportunity cost*. The production possibilities frontier shows the opportunity cost of one good as measured in terms of the other good. When society moves from point A to point B, it gives up 200 computers to get 100 additional cars. That is, at point A, the opportunity cost of 100 cars is 200 computers. Put another way, the opportunity cost of each car is two computers. Notice that the opportunity cost of a car equals the slope of the production possibilities frontier. (If you don't recall what slope is, you can refresh your memory with the graphing appendix to this chapter.)

The opportunity cost of a car in terms of the number of computers is not constant in this economy but depends on how many cars and computers the economy is producing. This is reflected in the shape of the production possibilities frontier. Because the production possibilities frontier in Figure 2 is bowed outward, the opportunity cost of a car is highest when the economy is producing many cars and few computers, such as at point E, where the frontier is steep. When the economy is producing few cars and many computers, such as at point F, the frontier is flatter, and the opportunity cost of a car is lower.

Economists believe that production possibilities frontiers often have this bowed shape. When the economy is using most of its resources to make computers, such as at point F, the resources best suited to car production, such as skilled autoworkers, are being used in the computer industry. Because these workers probably aren't very good at making computers, increasing car production by one unit will cause only a slight reduction in the number of computers produced.

At point F, the opportunity cost of a car in terms of computers is small, and the frontier is relatively flat. By contrast, when the economy is using most of its resources to make cars, such as at point E, the resources best suited to making cars are already at work in the car industry. Producing an additional car means moving some of the best computer technicians out of the computer industry and turning them into autoworkers. As a result, producing an additional car will mean a substantial loss of computer output. The opportunity cost of a car is high, and the frontier is steep.

The production possibilities frontier shows the trade-off between the outputs of different goods at a given time, but the trade-off can change over time. For example, suppose a technological advance in the computer industry raises the number of computers that a worker can produce per week. This advance expands society's set of opportunities. For any given number of cars, the economy can now make more computers. If the economy does not produce any computers, it can still produce 1,000 cars, so one endpoint of the frontier stays the same. But if the economy devotes some of its resources to the computer industry, it will produce more computers from those resources. As a result, the production possibilities frontier shifts outward, as in Figure 3.

This figure illustrates what happens when an economy grows. Society can move production from a point on the old frontier to a point on the new frontier. Which point it chooses depends on its preferences for the two goods. In this example, society moves from point A to point G, enjoying more computers (2,300 instead of 2,200) and more cars (650 instead of 600).

The production possibilities frontier simplifies a complex economy to highlight some basic but powerful ideas: scarcity, efficiency, trade-offs, opportunity cost, and economic growth. As you study economics, these ideas will recur in various forms. The production possibilities frontier offers one simple way of thinking about them.

FIGURE 3

A Shift in the Production Possibilities Frontier
A technological advance in the computer industry enables the economy to produce more computers for any given number of cars. As a result, the production possibilities frontier shifts outward. If the economy moves from point A to point G, then the production of both cars and computers increases.

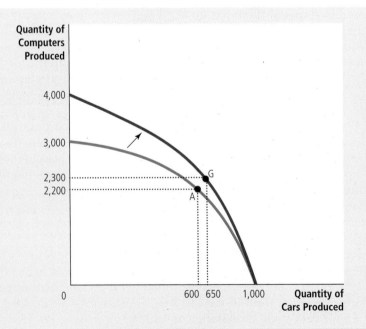

2-1f Microeconomics and Macroeconomics

Many subjects are studied on various levels. Consider biology, for example. Molecular biologists study the chemical compounds that make up living things. Cellular biologists study cells, which are made up of many chemical compounds and, at the same time, are themselves the building blocks of living organisms. Evolutionary biologists study the many varieties of animals and plants and how species change gradually over the centuries.

Economics is also studied on various levels. We can study the decisions of individual households and firms. Or we can study the interaction of households and firms in markets for specific goods and services. Or we can study the operation of the economy as a whole, which is the sum of the activities of all these decision makers in all these markets.

The field of economics is traditionally divided into two broad subfields. **Microeconomics** is the study of how households and firms make decisions and how they interact in specific markets. **Macroeconomics** is the study of economy-wide phenomena. A microeconomist might study the effects of rent control on housing in New York City, the impact of foreign competition on the U.S. auto industry, or the effects of compulsory school attendance on workers' earnings. A macroeconomist might study the effects of borrowing by the federal government, the changes over time in the economy's rate of unemployment, or alternative policies to promote growth in national living standards.

Microeconomics and macroeconomics are closely intertwined. Because changes in the overall economy arise from the decisions of millions of individuals, it is impossible to understand macroeconomic developments without considering the associated microeconomic decisions. For example, a macroeconomist might study the effect of a federal income tax cut on the overall production of goods and services. But to analyze this issue, he must consider how the tax cut affects households' decisions about how much to spend on goods and services.

Despite the inherent link between microeconomics and macroeconomics, the two fields are distinct. Because they address different questions, each field has its own set of models, which are often taught in separate courses.

microeconomics
the study of how households and firms make decisions and how they interact in markets

macroeconomics
the study of economy-wide phenomena, including inflation, unemployment, and economic growth

Quick Quiz *In what sense is economics like a science? • Draw a production possibilities frontier for a society that produces food and clothing. Show an efficient point, an inefficient point, and an infeasible point. Show the effects of a drought. • Define* microeconomics *and* macroeconomics.

2-2 The Economist as Policy Adviser

Often, economists are asked to explain the causes of economic events. Why, for example, is unemployment higher for teenagers than for older workers? Sometimes, economists are asked to recommend policies to improve economic outcomes. What, for instance, should the government do to improve the economic well-being of teenagers? When economists are trying to explain the world, they are scientists. When they are trying to help improve it, they are policy advisers.

2-2a Positive versus Normative Analysis

To help clarify the two roles that economists play, let's examine the use of language. Because scientists and policy advisers have different goals, they use language in different ways.

For example, suppose that two people are discussing minimum-wage laws. Here are two statements you might hear:

> Polly: Minimum-wage laws cause unemployment.
> Norm: The government should raise the minimum wage.

Ignoring for now whether you agree with these statements, notice that Polly and Norm differ in what they are trying to do. Polly is speaking like a scientist: She is making a claim about how the world works. Norm is speaking like a policy adviser: He is making a claim about how he would like to change the world.

In general, statements about the world come in two types. One type, such as Polly's, is positive. **Positive statements** are descriptive. They make a claim about how the world *is*. A second type of statement, such as Norm's, is normative. **Normative statements** are prescriptive. They make a claim about how the world *ought to be*.

positive statements
claims that attempt to describe the world as it is

normative statements
claims that attempt to prescribe how the world should be

A key difference between positive and normative statements is how we judge their validity. We can, in principle, confirm or refute positive statements by examining evidence. An economist might evaluate Polly's statement by analyzing data on changes in minimum wages and changes in unemployment over time. By contrast, evaluating normative statements involves values as well as facts. Norm's statement cannot be judged using data alone. Deciding what is good or bad policy is not just a matter of science. It also involves our views on ethics, religion, and political philosophy.

Positive and normative statements are fundamentally different, but they are often intertwined in a person's set of beliefs. In particular, positive views about how the world works affect normative views about what policies are desirable. Polly's claim that the minimum wage causes unemployment, if true, might lead her to reject Norm's conclusion that the government should raise the minimum wage. Yet normative conclusions cannot come from positive analysis alone; they involve value judgments as well.

As you study economics, keep in mind the distinction between positive and normative statements because it will help you stay focused on the task at hand. Much of economics is positive: It just tries to explain how the economy works. Yet those who use economics often have normative goals: They want to learn how to improve the economy. When you hear economists making normative statements, you know they are speaking not as scientists but as policy advisers.

2-2b Economists in Washington

President Harry Truman once said that he wanted to find a one-armed economist. When he asked his economists for advice, they always answered, "On the one hand, ... On the other hand, ..."

Truman was right in realizing that economists' advice is not always straightforward. This tendency is rooted in one of the *Ten Principles of Economics*: People face trade-offs. Economists are aware that trade-offs are involved in most policy decisions. A policy might increase efficiency at the cost of equality. It might help future generations but hurt current generations. An economist who says that all policy decisions are easy or clear-cut is an economist not to be trusted.

Truman was not the only president who relied on the advice of economists. Since 1946, the president of the United States has received guidance from the Council of Economic Advisers, which consists of three members and a staff of a few dozen economists. The council, whose offices are just a few steps from the White House, has no duty other than to advise the president and to write the annual *Economic Report of the President*, which discusses recent developments in the economy and presents the council's analysis of current policy issues.

The president also receives input from economists in many administrative departments. Economists at the Office of Management and Budget help formulate spending plans and regulatory policies. Economists at the Department of the Treasury help design tax policy. Economists at the Department of Labor analyze data on workers and those looking for work to help formulate labor-market policies. Economists at the Department of Justice help enforce the nation's antitrust laws.

Economists are also found outside the administrative branch of government. To obtain independent evaluations of policy proposals, Congress relies on the advice of the Congressional Budget Office, which is staffed by economists. The Federal Reserve, the institution that sets the nation's monetary policy, employs hundreds of economists to analyze economic developments in the United States and throughout the world.

The influence of economists on policy goes beyond their role as advisers: Their research and writings often affect policy indirectly. Economist John Maynard Keynes offered this observation:

> The ideas of economists and political philosophers, both when they are right and when they are wrong, are more powerful than is commonly understood. Indeed, the world is ruled by little else. Practical men, who believe themselves to be quite exempt from intellectual influences, are usually the slaves of some defunct economist. Madmen in authority, who hear voices in the air, are distilling their frenzy from some academic scribbler of a few years back.

These words were written in 1935, but they remain true today. Indeed, the "academic scribbler" now influencing public policy is often Keynes himself.

2-2c Why Economists' Advice Is Not Always Followed

Any economist who advises presidents or other elected leaders knows that his recommendations are not always heeded. Frustrating as this can be, it is easy to understand. The process by which economic policy is actually made differs in many ways from the idealized policy process assumed in economics textbooks.

Throughout this text, whenever we discuss economic policy, we often focus on one question: What is the best policy for the government to pursue? We act as if policy were set by a benevolent king. Once the king figures out the right policy, he has no trouble putting his ideas into action.

In the real world, figuring out the right policy is only part of a leader's job, sometimes the easiest part. After a president hears from his economic advisers about what policy is best from their perspective, he turns to other advisers for related input. His communications advisers will tell him how best to explain the proposed policy to the public, and they will try to anticipate any misunderstandings that might make the challenge more difficult. His press advisers will tell him how the news media will report on his proposal and what opinions will likely be expressed on the nation's editorial pages. His legislative affairs advisers will

"Let's switch. I'll make the policy, you implement it, and he'll explain it."

tell him how Congress will view the proposal, what amendments members of Congress will suggest, and the likelihood that Congress will pass some version of the president's proposal into law. His political advisers will tell him which groups will organize to support or oppose the proposed policy, how this proposal will affect his standing among different groups in the electorate, and whether it will affect support for any of the president's other policy initiatives. After hearing and weighing all this advice, the president then decides how to proceed.

Making economic policy in a representative democracy is a messy affair—and there are often good reasons why presidents (and other politicians) do not advance the policies that economists advocate. Economists offer crucial input into the policy process, but their advice is only one ingredient of a complex recipe.

Quick Quiz *Give an example of a positive statement and an example of a normative statement that somehow relates to your daily life.* • *Name three parts of government that regularly rely on advice from economists.*

2-3 Why Economists Disagree

"If all economists were laid end to end, they would not reach a conclusion." This quip from George Bernard Shaw is revealing. Economists as a group are often criticized for giving conflicting advice to policymakers. President Ronald Reagan once joked that if the game Trivial Pursuit were designed for economists, it would have 100 questions and 3,000 answers.

Why do economists so often appear to give conflicting advice to policymakers? There are two basic reasons:

- Economists may disagree about the validity of alternative positive theories about how the world works.
- Economists may have different values and therefore different normative views about what government policy should aim to accomplish.

Let's discuss each of these reasons.

2-3a Differences in Scientific Judgments

Several centuries ago, astronomers debated whether the earth or the sun was at the center of the solar system. More recently, meteorologists have debated whether the earth is experiencing global warming and, if so, why. Science is an ongoing search to understand the world around us. It is not surprising that as the search continues, scientists sometimes disagree about the direction in which truth lies.

Economists often disagree for the same reason. Economics is a young science, and there is still much to be learned. Economists sometimes disagree because they have different hunches about the validity of alternative theories or about the size of important parameters that measure how economic variables are related.

For example, economists disagree about whether the government should tax a household's income or its consumption (spending). Advocates of a switch from the current income tax to a consumption tax believe that the change would encourage households to save more because income that is saved would not be taxed. Higher saving, in turn, would free resources for capital accumulation, leading to more rapid growth in productivity and living standards. Advocates of the current income tax system believe that household saving would not respond much to a change in the tax laws. These two groups of economists hold different normative views about the tax system because they have different positive views about saving's responsiveness to tax incentives.

2-3b Differences in Values

Suppose that Peter and Paula both take the same amount of water from the town well. To pay for maintaining the well, the town taxes its residents. Peter has income of $100,000 and is taxed $10,000, or 10 percent of his income. Paula has income of $20,000 and is taxed $4,000, or 20 percent of her income.

Is this policy fair? If not, who pays too much and who pays too little? Does it matter whether Paula's low income is due to a medical disability or to her decision to pursue an acting career? Does it matter whether Peter's high income is due to a large inheritance or to his willingness to work long hours at a dreary job?

These are difficult questions on which people are likely to disagree. If the town hired two experts to study how the town should tax its residents to pay for the well, we would not be surprised if they offered conflicting advice.

This simple example shows why economists sometimes disagree about public policy. As we know from our discussion of normative and positive analysis, policies cannot be judged on scientific grounds alone. Sometimes, economists give conflicting advice because they have different values. Perfecting the science of economics will not tell us whether Peter or Paula pays too much.

2-3c Perception versus Reality

Because of differences in scientific judgments and differences in values, some disagreement among economists is inevitable. Yet one should not overstate the amount of disagreement. Economists agree with one another to a much greater extent than is sometimes understood.

Table 1 contains twenty propositions about economic policy. In surveys of professional economists, these propositions were endorsed by an overwhelming majority of respondents. Most of these propositions would fail to command a similar consensus among the public.

The first proposition in the table is about rent control, a policy that sets a legal maximum on the amount landlords can charge for their apartments. Almost all economists believe that rent control adversely affects the availability and quality of housing and is a costly way of helping the neediest members of society. Nonetheless, many city governments ignore the advice of economists and place ceilings on the rents that landlords may charge their tenants.

The second proposition in the table concerns tariffs and import quotas, two policies that restrict trade among nations. For reasons we discuss more fully later in this text, almost all economists oppose such barriers to free trade. Nonetheless, over the years, presidents and Congress have chosen to restrict the import of certain goods.

Why do policies such as rent control and trade barriers persist if the experts are united in their opposition? It may be that the realities of the political process stand as immovable obstacles. But it also may be that economists have not yet convinced enough of the public that these policies are undesirable. One purpose of this book is to help you understand the economist's view of these and other subjects and, perhaps, to persuade you that it is the right one.

Quick Quiz *Why might economic advisers to the president disagree about a question of policy?*

TABLE 1

Propositions about Which Most Economists Agree

Proposition (and percentage of economists who agree)

1. A ceiling on rents reduces the quantity and quality of housing available. (93%)
2. Tariffs and import quotas usually reduce general economic welfare. (93%)
3. Flexible and floating exchange rates offer an effective international monetary arrangement. (90%)
4. Fiscal policy (e.g., tax cut and/or government expenditure increase) has a significant stimulative impact on a less than fully employed economy. (90%)
5. The United States should not restrict employers from outsourcing work to foreign countries. (90%)
6. Economic growth in developed countries like the United States leads to greater levels of well-being. (88%)
7. The United States should eliminate agricultural subsidies. (85%)
8. An appropriately designed fiscal policy can increase the long-run rate of capital formation. (85%)
9. Local and state governments should eliminate subsidies to professional sports franchises. (85%)
10. If the federal budget is to be balanced, it should be done over the business cycle rather than yearly. (85%)
11. The gap between Social Security funds and expenditures will become unsustainably large within the next 50 years if current policies remain unchanged. (85%)
12. Cash payments increase the welfare of recipients to a greater degree than do transfers-in-kind of equal cash value. (84%)
13. A large federal budget deficit has an adverse effect on the economy. (83%)
14. The redistribution of income in the United States is a legitimate role for the government. (83%)
15. Inflation is caused primarily by too much growth in the money supply. (83%)
16. The United States should not ban genetically modified crops. (82%)
17. A minimum wage increases unemployment among young and unskilled workers. (79%)
18. The government should restructure the welfare system along the lines of a "negative income tax." (79%)
19. Effluent taxes and marketable pollution permits represent a better approach to pollution control than the imposition of pollution ceilings. (78%)
20. Government subsidies on ethanol in the United States should be reduced or eliminated. (78%)

Source: Richard M. Alston, J. R. Kearl, and Michael B. Vaughn, "Is There Consensus among Economists in the 1990s?" *American Economic Review* (May 1992): 203–209; Dan Fuller and Doris Geide-Stevenson, "Consensus among Economists Revisited," *Journal of Economics Education* (Fall 2003): 369–387; Robert Whaples, "Do Economists Agree on Anything? Yes!" *Economists' Voice* (November 2006): 1–6; Robert Whaples, "The Policy Views of American Economic Association Members: The Results of a New Survey," *Econ Journal Watch* (September 2009): 337–348.

Actual Economists and Virtual Realities

For professional economists, video games may be the next frontier.

The Economics of Video Games

By Brad Plumer

Inflation can be a headache for any central banker. But it takes a certain type of economist to know what to do when a belligerent spaceship fleet attacks an interstellar trading post, causing mineral prices to surge across the galaxy.

Eyjólfur Guðmundsson is just that economist. Working for the Icelandic company CCP Games, he oversees the virtual economy of the massively multiplayer video game Eve Online. Within this world, players build their own spaceships and traverse a galaxy of 7,500 star systems. They buy and sell raw materials, creating their own fluctuating markets. They speculate on commodities. They form trade coalitions and banks.

It's a sprawling economy, with more than 400,000 players participating in its virtual market—more people, in fact, than live in Iceland. Inflation, deflation and even recessions can occur. Which is why, from his office in Reykjavik, Guðmundsson leads a team of eight analysts poring over reams of data to make sure everything in Eve Online is running smoothly. His job bears more than a passing resemblance to that of Ben Bernanke, who oversees the U.S. economy from the Federal Reserve.

"For all intents and purposes, this is an economy that has activity equal to a small country in real life," Guðmundsson says. "There's nothing 'virtual' about this world."

Nowadays, many massively multiplayer online video games have become so complex that game companies are turning to economists for help. Without oversight, the games' economies can go badly awry—as when a gambling ban triggered a virtual bank run in the online world of Second Life in 2007, with one bank alone costing players $750,000 in real-life money.

But there's a flip side, too. Just as video game designers are in dire need of economic advice, many academic economists are keen on studying video games. A virtual world, after all, allows economists to study concepts that rarely occur in real life, such as full-reserve banking, a popular libertarian alternative to the current banking system that cropped up in Eve Online. The data is richer. And it's easier to run economy-wide experiments in a video game—experiments that, for obvious reasons, can't be run on countries.

That ability to experiment on a massive scale, academics say, could revolutionize economics.

"Economic theory has come to a dead end—the last real breakthroughs were in the 1960s," says Yanis Varoufakis, a Greek economist recently hired by the video-game company Valve. "But that's not because we stopped being clever. We came up against a hard barrier. The future is going to be in experimentation and simulation—and video game communities give us a chance to do all that."

At least, that's the dream. The reality, as always, is more complicated. Game companies are often wary of meddling economists trying to conduct experiments that suck the fun out of their virtual worlds. And some academics scoff at the notion that there's anything to learn from universes filled with warlocks and starfleets. Game companies and economists may need each other. Now if only they could learn to share the controller.

In June, Varoufakis announced on his blog that he had been hired as an in-house economist by Valve, the maker of the popular Half-Life games. Varoufakis wasn't an obscure number-cruncher. From his perch at the University of Athens, he had become famous for his trenchant analyses of Greece's debt woes and the euro crisis.

It was clear why Valve was interested. The company oversees a network of games such as Team Fortress 2 that run on its online gaming platform, called Steam.

Valve wanted to link different Steam games together so players could trade virtual items. As Gabe Newell, the chief executive of Valve, explained in an e-mail to Varoufakis: "We are discussing an issue of linking economies in two virtual environments (creating a shared currency), and wrestling with some of the thornier problems of balance of payments."

Whom better to ask, Newell figured, than an expert on the difficulties that Germany and Greece faced after joining the euro?

To date, only two companies—CCP and Valve—have gone so far as to hire in-house economists. But several academics who study virtual worlds say they have consulted with game designers.

"If you're creating a game with 100,000 users, with things that they can buy and sell, you need an economist just to help you tweak that system so that it doesn't spin out of control," says Robert Bloomfield, an economist who studies virtual worlds at Cornell's Johnson School of Management. ◢

Source: *The Washington Post*, September 28, 2012.

2-4 Let's Get Going

The first two chapters of this book have introduced you to the ideas and methods of economics. We are now ready to get to work. In the next chapter, we start learning in more detail the principles of economic behavior and economic policy.

As you proceed through this book, you will be asked to draw on many of your intellectual skills. You might find it helpful to keep in mind some advice from the great economist John Maynard Keynes:

> The study of economics does not seem to require any specialized gifts of an unusually high order. Is it not … a very easy subject compared with the higher branches of philosophy or pure science? An easy subject, at which very few excel! The paradox finds its explanation, perhaps, in that the master-economist must possess a rare *combination* of gifts. He must be mathematician, historian, statesman, philosopher—in some degree. He must understand symbols and speak in words. He must contemplate the particular in terms of the general, and touch abstract and concrete in the same flight of thought. He must study the present in the light of the past for the purposes of the future. No part of man's nature or his institutions must lie entirely outside his regard. He must be purposeful and disinterested in a simultaneous mood; as aloof and incorruptible as an artist, yet sometimes as near the earth as a politician.

This is a tall order. But with practice, you will become more and more accustomed to thinking like an economist.

Summary

- Economists try to address their subject with a scientist's objectivity. Like all scientists, they make appropriate assumptions and build simplified models to understand the world around them. Two simple economic models are the circular-flow diagram and the production possibilities frontier.

- The field of economics is divided into two subfields: microeconomics and macroeconomics. Microeconomists study decision making by households and firms and the interaction among households and firms in the marketplace. Macroeconomists study the forces and trends that affect the economy as a whole.

- A positive statement is an assertion about how the world *is*. A normative statement is an assertion about how the world *ought to be*. When economists make normative statements, they are acting more as policy advisers than as scientists.

- Economists who advise policymakers sometimes offer conflicting advice either because of differences in scientific judgments or because of differences in values. At other times, economists are united in the advice they offer, but policymakers may choose to ignore the advice because of the many forces and constraints imposed by the political process.

Key Concepts

circular-flow diagram, *p. 22*
production possibilities frontier, *p. 24*

microeconomics, *p. 27*
macroeconomics, *p. 27*

positive statements, *p. 28*
normative statements, *p. 28*

Questions for Review

1. How is economics a science?

2. Why do economists make assumptions?

3. Should an economic model describe reality exactly?

4. Name a way that your family interacts in the factor market and a way that it interacts in the product market.

5. Name one economic interaction that isn't covered by the simplified circular-flow diagram.

6. Draw and explain a production possibilities frontier for an economy that produces milk and cookies. What happens to this frontier if disease kills half of the economy's cows?

7. Use a production possibilities frontier to describe the idea of "efficiency."

8. What are the two subfields into which economics is divided? Explain what each subfield studies.

9. What is the difference between a positive and a normative statement? Give an example of each.

10. Why do economists sometimes offer conflicting advice to policymakers?

Quick Check Multiple Choice

1. An economic model is
   a. a mechanical machine that replicates the functioning of the economy.
   b. a fully detailed, realistic description of the economy.
   c. a simplified representation of some aspect of the economy.
   d. a computer program that predicts the future of the economy.

2. The circular-flow diagram illustrates that, in markets for the factors of production,
   a. households are sellers, and firms are buyers.
   b. households are buyers, and firms are sellers.
   c. households and firms are both buyers.
   d. households and firms are both sellers.

3. A point inside the production possibilities frontier is
   a. efficient, but not feasible.
   b. feasible, but not efficient.
   c. both efficient and feasible.
   d. neither efficient nor feasible.

4. An economy produces hot dogs and hamburgers. If a discovery of the remarkable health benefits of hot dogs were to change consumers' preferences, it would

   a. expand the production possibilities frontier.
   b. contract the production possibilities frontier.
   c. move the economy along the production possibilities frontier.
   d. move the economy inside the production possibilities frontier.

5. All of the following topics fall within the study of microeconomics EXCEPT
   a. the impact of cigarette taxes on the smoking behavior of teenagers.
   b. the role of Microsoft's market power in the pricing of software.
   c. the effectiveness of antipoverty programs in reducing homelessness.
   d. the influence of the government budget deficit on economic growth.

6. Which of the following is a positive, rather than a normative, statement?
   a. Law X will reduce national income.
   b. Law X is a good piece of legislation.
   c. Congress ought to pass law X.
   d. The president should veto law X.

Problems and Applications

1. Draw a circular-flow diagram. Identify the parts of the model that correspond to the flow of goods and services and the flow of dollars for each of the following activities.
   a. Selena pays a storekeeper $1 for a quart of milk.
   b. Stuart earns $4.50 per hour working at a fast-food restaurant.
   c. Shanna spends $30 to get a haircut.

   d. Salma earns $10,000 from her 10 percent ownership of Acme Industrial.

2. Imagine a society that produces military goods and consumer goods, which we'll call "guns" and "butter."
   a. Draw a production possibilities frontier for guns and butter. Using the concept of opportunity cost, explain why it most likely has a bowed-out shape.

b. Show a point that is impossible for the economy to achieve. Show a point that is feasible but inefficient.

c. Imagine that the society has two political parties, called the Hawks (who want a strong military) and the Doves (who want a smaller military). Show a point on your production possibilities frontier that the Hawks might choose and a point that the Doves might choose.

d. Imagine that an aggressive neighboring country reduces the size of its military. As a result, both the Hawks and the Doves reduce their desired production of guns by the same amount. Which party would get the bigger "peace dividend," measured by the increase in butter production? Explain.

3. The first principle of economics discussed in Chapter 1 is that people face trade-offs. Use a production possibilities frontier to illustrate society's trade-off between two "goods"—a clean environment and the quantity of industrial output. What do you suppose determines the shape and position of the frontier? Show what happens to the frontier if engineers develop a new way of producing electricity that emits fewer pollutants.

4. An economy consists of three workers: Larry, Moe, and Curly. Each works 10 hours a day and can produce two services: mowing lawns and washing cars. In an hour, Larry can either mow one lawn or wash one car; Moe can either mow one lawn or wash two cars; and Curly can either mow two lawns or wash one car.

a. Calculate how much of each service is produced under the following circumstances, which we label A, B, C, and D:
- All three spend all their time mowing lawns. (A)
- All three spend all their time washing cars. (B)
- All three spend half their time on each activity. (C)
- Larry spends half his time on each activity, while Moe only washes cars and Curly only mows lawns. (D)

b. Graph the production possibilities frontier for this economy. Using your answers to part (a), identify points A, B, C, and D on your graph.

c. Explain why the production possibilities frontier has the shape it does.

d. Are any of the allocations calculated in part (a) inefficient? Explain.

5. Classify the following topics as relating to microeconomics or macroeconomics.
a. a family's decision about how much income to save
b. the effect of government regulations on auto emissions
c. the impact of higher national saving on economic growth
d. a firm's decision about how many workers to hire
e. the relationship between the inflation rate and changes in the quantity of money

6. Classify each of the following statements as positive or normative. Explain.
a. Society faces a short-run trade-off between inflation and unemployment.
b. A reduction in the rate of money growth will reduce the rate of inflation.
c. The Federal Reserve should reduce the rate of money growth.
d. Society ought to require welfare recipients to look for jobs.
e. Lower tax rates encourage more work and more saving.

Go to CengageBrain.com to purchase access to the proven, critical Study Guide to accompany this text, which features additional notes and context, practice tests, and much more.

Appendix

Graphing: A Brief Review

Many of the concepts that economists study can be expressed with numbers—the price of bananas, the quantity of bananas sold, the cost of growing bananas, and so on. Often, these economic variables are related to one another: When the price of bananas rises, people buy fewer bananas. One way of expressing the relationships among variables is with graphs.

Graphs serve two purposes. First, when developing economic theories, graphs offer a way to visually express ideas that might be less clear if described with equations or words. Second, when analyzing economic data, graphs provide a powerful way of finding and interpreting patterns. Whether we are working with theory or with data, graphs provide a lens through which a recognizable forest emerges from a multitude of trees.

Numerical information can be expressed graphically in many ways, just as there are many ways to express a thought in words. A good writer chooses words that will make an argument clear, a description pleasing, or a scene dramatic. An effective economist chooses the type of graph that best suits the purpose at hand.

In this appendix, we discuss how economists use graphs to study the mathematical relationships among variables. We also discuss some of the pitfalls that can arise in the use of graphical methods.

Graphs of a Single Variable

Three common graphs are shown in Figure A-1. The *pie chart* in panel (a) shows how total income in the United States is divided among the sources of income, including compensation of employees, corporate profits, and so on. A slice of the pie represents each source's share of the total. The *bar graph* in panel (b) compares income for four countries. The height of each bar represents the average

The pie chart in panel (a) shows how the U.S. national income in 2011 was derived from various sources. The bar graph in panel (b) compares the 2011 average income in four countries. The time-series graph in panel (c) shows the productivity of labor in U.S. businesses from 1950 to 2010.

FIGURE A-1

Types of Graphs

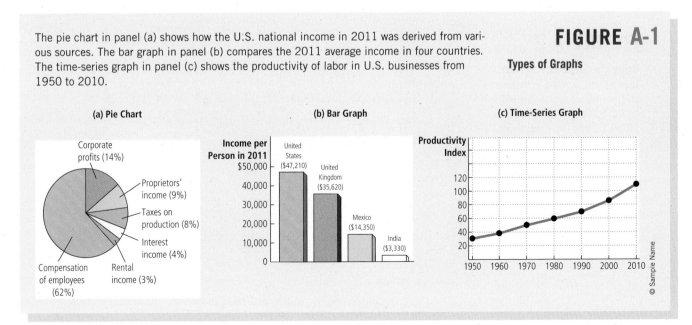

(a) Pie Chart

Corporate profits (14%)
Proprietors' income (9%)
Taxes on production (8%)
Interest income (4%)
Rental income (3%)
Compensation of employees (62%)

(b) Bar Graph

Income per Person in 2011
$50,000
40,000
30,000
20,000
10,000
0
United States ($47,210)
United Kingdom ($35,620)
Mexico ($14,350)
India ($3,330)

(c) Time-Series Graph

Productivity Index
120
100
80
60
40
20
1950 1960 1970 1980 1990 2000 2010

© Sample Name

income in each country. The *time-series graph* in panel (c) traces the rising productivity in the U.S. business sector over time. The height of the line shows output per hour in each year. You have probably seen similar graphs in newspapers and magazines.

Graphs of Two Variables: The Coordinate System

The three graphs in Figure A-1 are useful in showing how a variable changes over time or across individuals, but they are limited in how much they can tell us. These graphs display information only about a single variable. Economists are often concerned with the relationships between variables. Thus, they need to display two variables on a single graph. The *coordinate system* makes this possible.

Suppose you want to examine the relationship between study time and grade point average. For each student in your class, you could record a pair of numbers: hours per week spent studying and grade point average. These numbers could then be placed in parentheses as an *ordered pair* and appear as a single point on the graph. Albert E., for instance, is represented by the ordered pair (25 hours/week, 3.5 GPA), while his "what-me-worry?" classmate Alfred E. is represented by the ordered pair (5 hours/week, 2.0 GPA).

We can graph these ordered pairs on a two-dimensional grid. The first number in each ordered pair, called the *x-coordinate*, tells us the horizontal location of the point. The second number, called the *y-coordinate*, tells us the vertical location of the point. The point with both an *x*-coordinate and a *y*-coordinate of zero is known as the *origin*. The two coordinates in the ordered pair tell us where the point is located in relation to the origin: *x* units to the right of the origin and *y* units above it.

Figure A-2 graphs grade point average against study time for Albert E., Alfred E., and their classmates. This type of graph is called a *scatterplot* because it plots scattered points. Looking at this graph, we immediately notice that points farther to the right (indicating more study time) also tend to be higher (indicating a better grade point average). Because study time and grade point average typically move in the same direction, we say that these two variables have a *positive correlation*.

FIGURE A-2

Using the Coordinate System
Grade point average is measured on the vertical axis and study time on the horizontal axis. Albert E., Alfred E., and their classmates are represented by various points. We can see from the graph that students who study more tend to get higher grades.

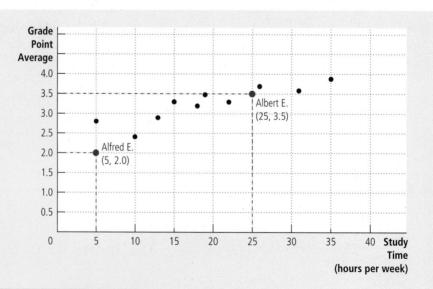

By contrast, if we were to graph party time and grades, we would likely find that higher party time is associated with lower grades; because these variables typically move in opposite directions, we say that they have a *negative correlation*. In either case, the coordinate system makes the correlation between the two variables easy to see.

Curves in the Coordinate System

Students who study more do tend to get higher grades, but other factors also influence a student's grades. Previous preparation is an important factor, for instance, as are talent, attention from teachers, even eating a good breakfast. A scatterplot like Figure A-2 does not attempt to isolate the effect that studying has on grades from the effects of other variables. Often, however, economists prefer looking at how one variable affects another, holding everything else constant.

To see how this is done, let's consider one of the most important graphs in economics: the *demand curve*. The demand curve traces out the effect of a good's price on the quantity of the good consumers want to buy. Before showing a demand curve, however, consider Table A-1, which shows how the number of novels that Emma buys depends on her income and on the price of novels. When novels are cheap, Emma buys them in large quantities. As they become more expensive, she instead borrows books from the library or chooses to go to the movies rather than read. Similarly, at any given price, Emma buys more novels when she has a higher income. That is, when her income increases, she spends part of the additional income on novels and part on other goods.

We now have three variables—the price of novels, income, and the number of novels purchased—which are more than we can represent in two dimensions. To put the information from Table A-1 in graphical form, we need to hold one of the three variables constant and trace out the relationship between the other two. Because the demand curve represents the relationship between price and quantity demanded, we hold Emma's income constant and show how the number of novels she buys varies with the price of novels.

Suppose that Emma's income is $30,000 per year. If we place the number of novels Emma purchases on the *x*-axis and the price of novels on the *y*-axis, we can graphically represent the middle column of Table A-1. When the points that represent these entries from the table—(5 novels, $10), (9 novels, $9), and so on—are

TABLE A-1

Price	For $20,000 Income:	For $30,000 Income:	For $40,000 Income:
$10	2 novels	5 novels	8 novels
9	6	9	12
8	10	13	16
7	14	17	20
6	18	21	24
5	22	25	28
	Demand curve, D_3	Demand curve, D_1	Demand curve, D_2

Novels Purchased by Emma
This table shows the number of novels Emma buys at various incomes and prices. For any given level of income, the data on price and quantity demanded can be graphed to produce Emma's demand curve for novels, as shown in Figures A-3 and A-4.

FIGURE A-3

Demand Curve
The line D_1 shows how Emma's purchases of novels depend on the price of novels when her income is held constant. Because the price and the quantity demanded are negatively related, the demand curve slopes downward.

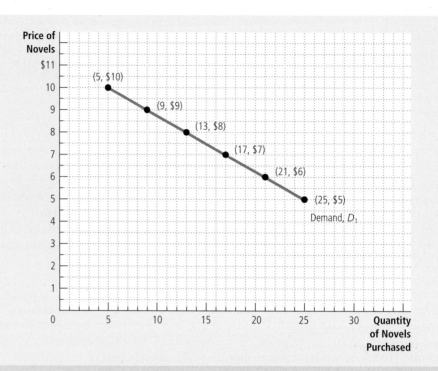

connected, they form a line. This line, pictured in Figure A-3, is known as Emma's demand curve for novels; it tells us how many novels Emma purchases at any given price. The demand curve is downward sloping, indicating that a higher price reduces the quantity of novels demanded. Because the quantity of novels demanded and the price move in opposite directions, we say that the two variables are *negatively related*. (Conversely, when two variables move in the same direction, the curve relating them is upward sloping, and we say that the variables are *positively related*.)

Now suppose that Emma's income rises to $40,000 per year. At any given price, Emma will purchase more novels than she did at her previous level of income. Just as earlier we drew Emma's demand curve for novels using the entries from the middle column of Table A-1, we now draw a new demand curve using the entries from the right column of the table. This new demand curve (curve D_2) is pictured alongside the old one (curve D_1) in Figure A-4; the new curve is a similar line drawn farther to the right. We therefore say that Emma's demand curve for novels *shifts* to the right when her income increases. Likewise, if Emma's income were to fall to $20,000 per year, she would buy fewer novels at any given price and her demand curve would shift to the left (to curve D_3).

In economics, it is important to distinguish between *movements along a curve* and *shifts of a curve*. As we can see from Figure A-3, if Emma earns $30,000 per year and novels cost $8 apiece, she will purchase 13 novels per year. If the price of novels falls to $7, Emma will increase her purchases of novels to 17 per year. The demand curve, however, stays fixed in the same place. Emma still buys the same number of novels *at each price*, but as the price falls, she moves along her demand curve from left to right. By contrast, if the price of novels remains fixed at $8 but her income rises to $40,000, Emma increases her purchases of novels from 13 to 16 per year. Because Emma buys more novels *at each price*, her demand curve shifts out, as shown in Figure A-4.

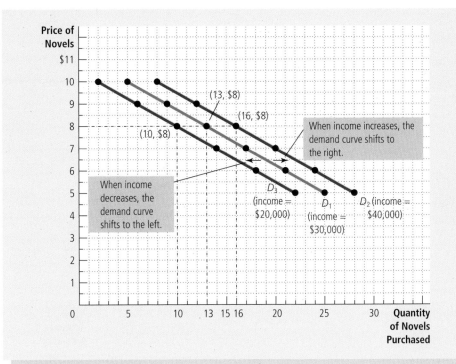

FIGURE A-4

Shifting Demand Curves
The location of Emma's demand curve for novels depends on how much income she earns. The more she earns, the more novels she will purchase at any given price, and the farther to the right her demand curve will lie. Curve D_1 represents Emma's original demand curve when her income is $30,000 per year. If her income rises to $40,000 per year, her demand curve shifts to D_2. If her income falls to $20,000 per year, her demand curve shifts to D_3.

There is a simple way to tell when it is necessary to shift a curve: *When a relevant variable that is not named on either axis changes, the curve shifts.* Income is on neither the *x*-axis nor the *y*-axis of the graph, so when Emma's income changes, her demand curve must shift. The same is true for any change that affects Emma's purchasing habits, with the sole exception of a change in the price of novels. If, for instance, the public library closes and Emma must buy all the books she wants to read, she will demand more novels at each price, and her demand curve will shift to the right. Or if the price of movies falls and Emma spends more time at the movies and less time reading, she will demand fewer novels at each price, and her demand curve will shift to the left. By contrast, when a variable on an axis of the graph changes, the curve does not shift. We read the change as a movement along the curve.

Slope

One question we might want to ask about Emma is how much her purchasing habits respond to price. Look at the demand curve pictured in Figure A-5. If this curve is very steep, Emma purchases nearly the same number of novels regardless of whether they are cheap or expensive. If this curve is much flatter, the number of novels Emma purchases is more sensitive to changes in the price. To answer questions about how much one variable responds to changes in another variable, we can use the concept of *slope*.

The slope of a line is the ratio of the vertical distance covered to the horizontal distance covered as we move along the line. This definition is usually written out in mathematical symbols as follows:

$$\text{slope} = \frac{\Delta y}{\Delta x},$$

FIGURE A-5

Calculating the Slope of a Line
To calculate the slope of the demand curve, we can look at the changes in the x- and y-coordinates as we move from the point (21 novels, $6) to the point (13 novels, $8). The slope of the line is the ratio of the change in the y-coordinate (−2) to the change in the x-coordinate (+8), which equals −¼.

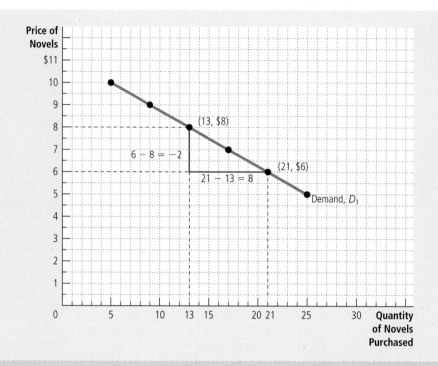

where the Greek letter Δ (delta) stands for the change in a variable. In other words, the slope of a line is equal to the "rise" (change in y) divided by the "run" (change in x). The slope will be a small positive number for a fairly flat upward-sloping line, a large positive number for a steep upward-sloping line, and a negative number for a downward-sloping line. A horizontal line has a slope of zero because in this case the y-variable never changes; a vertical line is said to have an infinite slope because the y-variable can take any value without the x-variable changing at all.

What is the slope of Emma's demand curve for novels? First of all, because the curve slopes down, we know the slope will be negative. To calculate a numerical value for the slope, we must choose two points on the line. With Emma's income at $30,000, she will purchase 21 novels at a price of $6 or 13 novels at a price of $8. When we apply the slope formula, we are concerned with the change between these two points; in other words, we are concerned with the difference between them, which lets us know that we will have to subtract one set of values from the other, as follows:

$$\text{slope} = \frac{\Delta y}{\Delta x} = \frac{\text{first } y\text{-coordinate} - \text{second } y\text{-coordinate}}{\text{first } x\text{-coordinate} - \text{second } x\text{-coordinate}} = \frac{6 - 8}{21 - 13} = \frac{-2}{8} = \frac{-1}{4}$$

Figure A-5 shows graphically how this calculation works. Try computing the slope of Emma's demand curve using two different points. You should get exactly the same result, −1/4. One of the properties of a straight line is that it has the same slope everywhere. This is not true of other types of curves, which are steeper in some places than in others.

The slope of Emma's demand curve tells us something about how responsive her purchases are to changes in the price. A small slope (a number close to zero) means that Emma's demand curve is relatively flat; in this case, she adjusts the number of novels she buys substantially in response to a price change. A larger slope (a number farther from zero) means that Emma's demand curve is relatively steep; in this case, she adjusts the number of novels she buys only slightly in response to a price change.

Cause and Effect

Economists often use graphs to advance an argument about how the economy works. In other words, they use graphs to argue about how one set of events *causes* another set of events. With a graph like the demand curve, there is no doubt about cause and effect. Because we are varying price and holding all other variables constant, we know that changes in the price of novels cause changes in the quantity Emma demands. Remember, however, that our demand curve came from a hypothetical example. When graphing data from the real world, it is often more difficult to establish how one variable affects another.

The first problem is that it is difficult to hold everything else constant when studying the relationship between two variables. If we are not able to hold other variables constant, we might decide that one variable on our graph is causing changes in the other variable when those changes are actually being caused by a third *omitted variable* not pictured on the graph. Even if we have identified the correct two variables to look at, we might run into a second problem—*reverse causality*. In other words, we might decide that A causes B when in fact B causes A. The omitted-variable and reverse-causality traps require us to proceed with caution when using graphs to draw conclusions about causes and effects.

Omitted Variables   To see how omitting a variable can lead to a deceptive graph, let's consider an example. Imagine that the government, spurred by public concern about the large number of deaths from cancer, commissions an exhaustive study from Big Brother Statistical Services, Inc. Big Brother examines many of the items found in people's homes to see which of them are associated with the risk of cancer. Big Brother reports a strong relationship between two variables: the number of cigarette lighters that a household owns and the probability that someone in the household will develop cancer. Figure A-6 shows this relationship.

What should we make of this result? Big Brother advises a quick policy response. It recommends that the government discourage the ownership of cigarette lighters by taxing their sale. It also recommends that the government require warning labels: "Big Brother has determined that this lighter is dangerous to your health."

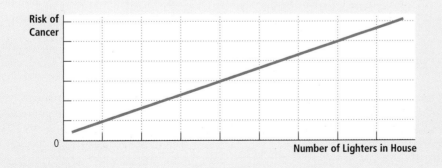

FIGURE A-6

Graph with an Omitted Variable
The upward-sloping curve shows that members of households with more cigarette lighters are more likely to develop cancer. Yet we should not conclude that ownership of lighters causes cancer because the graph does not take into account the number of cigarettes smoked.

Courtesy of Randall Munroe/XKCD.com

In judging the validity of Big Brother's analysis, one question is key: Has Big Brother held constant every relevant variable except the one under consideration? If the answer is no, the results are suspect. An easy explanation for Figure A-6 is that people who own more cigarette lighters are more likely to smoke cigarettes and that cigarettes, not lighters, cause cancer. If Figure A-6 does not hold constant the amount of smoking, it does not tell us the true effect of owning a cigarette lighter.

This story illustrates an important principle: When you see a graph used to support an argument about cause and effect, it is important to ask whether the movements of an omitted variable could explain the results you see.

Reverse Causality   Economists can also make mistakes about causality by misreading its direction. To see how this is possible, suppose the Association of American Anarchists commissions a study of crime in America and arrives at Figure A-7, which plots the number of violent crimes per thousand people in major cities against the number of police officers per thousand people. The anarchists note the curve's upward slope and argue that because police increase rather than decrease the amount of urban violence, law enforcement should be abolished.

If we could run a controlled experiment, we would avoid the danger of reverse causality. To run an experiment, we would randomly assign different numbers of police to different cities and then examine the correlation between police and crime. Figure A-7, however, is not based on such an experiment. We simply observe that more dangerous cities have more police officers. The explanation for

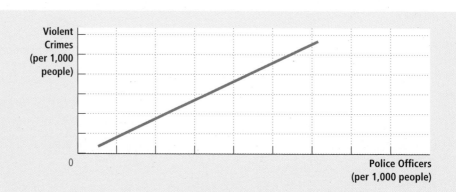

FIGURE A-7

Graph Suggesting Reverse Causality

The upward-sloping curve shows that cities with a higher concentration of police are more dangerous. Yet the graph does not tell us whether police cause crime or crime-plagued cities hire more police.

this may be that more dangerous cities hire more police. In other words, rather than police causing crime, crime may cause police. Nothing in the graph itself allows us to establish the direction of causality.

It might seem that an easy way to determine the direction of causality is to examine which variable moves first. If we see crime increase and then the police force expand, we reach one conclusion. If we see the police force expand and then crime increase, we reach the other. Yet there is also a flaw with this approach: Often, people change their behavior not in response to a change in their present conditions but in response to a change in their *expectations* of future conditions. A city that expects a major crime wave in the future, for instance, might hire more police now. This problem is even easier to see in the case of babies and minivans. Couples often buy a minivan in anticipation of the birth of a child. The minivan comes before the baby, but we wouldn't want to conclude that the sale of minivans causes the population to grow!

There is no complete set of rules that says when it is appropriate to draw causal conclusions from graphs. Yet just keeping in mind that cigarette lighters don't cause cancer (omitted variable) and minivans don't cause larger families (reverse causality) will keep you from falling for many faulty economic arguments.

Interdependence and the Gains from Trade

Consider your typical day. You wake up in the morning and pour yourself juice from oranges grown in Florida and coffee from beans grown in Brazil. Over breakfast, you watch a news program broadcast from New York on your television made in China. You get dressed in clothes made of cotton grown in Georgia and sewn in factories in Thailand. You drive to class in a car made of parts manufactured in more than a dozen countries around the world. Then you open up your economics textbook written by an author living in Massachusetts, published by a company located in Ohio, and printed on paper made from trees grown in Oregon.

Every day, you rely on many people, most of whom you have never met, to provide you with the goods and services that you enjoy. Such interdependence is possible because people trade with one another. Those people providing you with goods and services are not acting out of generosity. Nor is some government agency directing them to satisfy your desires. Instead, people provide you and other consumers with the goods and services they produce because they get something in return.

In subsequent chapters, we examine how an economy coordinates the activities of millions of people with varying tastes and abilities. As a starting point for this analysis, in this chapter we consider the reasons for economic interdependence. One of the *Ten Principles of Economics* highlighted in Chapter 1 is that trade can make everyone better off. We now examine this principle more closely. What exactly do people gain when they trade with one another? Why do people choose to become interdependent?

The answers to these questions are key to understanding the modern global economy. Most countries today import from abroad many of the goods and services they consume, and they export to foreign customers many of the goods and services they produce. The analysis in this chapter explains interdependence not only among individuals but also among nations. As we will see, the gains from trade are much the same whether you are buying a haircut from your local barber or a T-shirt made by a worker on the other side of the globe.

3-1 A Parable for the Modern Economy

To understand why people choose to depend on others for goods and services and how this choice improves their lives, let's look at a simple economy. Imagine that there are two goods in the world: meat and potatoes. And there are two people in the world—a cattle rancher named Rose and a potato farmer named Frank—each of whom would like to eat both meat and potatoes.

The gains from trade are most obvious if Rose can produce only meat and Frank can produce only potatoes. In one scenario, Frank and Rose could choose to have nothing to do with each other. But after several months of eating beef roasted, boiled, broiled, and grilled, Rose might decide that self-sufficiency is not all it's cracked up to be. Frank, who has been eating potatoes mashed, fried, baked, and scalloped, would likely agree. It is easy to see that trade would allow them to enjoy greater variety: Each could then have a steak with a baked potato or a burger with fries.

Although this scene illustrates most simply how everyone can benefit from trade, the gains would be similar if Frank and Rose were each capable of producing the other good, but only at great cost. Suppose, for example, that Rose is able to grow potatoes but her land is not very well suited for it. Similarly, suppose that Frank is able to raise cattle and produce meat but he is not very good at it. In this case, Frank and Rose can each benefit by specializing in what he or she does best and then trading with the other person.

The gains from trade are less obvious, however, when one person is better at producing *every* good. For example, suppose that Rose is better at raising cattle *and* better at growing potatoes than Frank. In this case, should Rose choose to remain self-sufficient? Or is there still reason for her to trade with Frank? To answer this question, we need to look more closely at the factors that affect such a decision.

3-1a Production Possibilities

Suppose that Frank and Rose each work 8 hours per day and can devote this time to growing potatoes, raising cattle, or a combination of the two. The table in Figure 1 shows the amount of time each person requires to produce 1 ounce of

Panel (a) shows the production opportunities available to Frank the farmer and Rose the rancher. Panel (b) shows the combinations of meat and potatoes that Frank can produce. Panel (c) shows the combinations of meat and potatoes that Rose can produce. Both production possibilities frontiers are derived assuming that Frank and Rose each work 8 hours per day. If there is no trade, each person's production possibilities frontier is also his or her consumption possibilities frontier.

FIGURE 1

The Production Possibilities Frontier

(a) Production Opportunities

	Minutes Needed to Make 1 Ounce of:		Amount Produced in 8 Hours	
	Meat	**Potatoes**	**Meat**	**Potatoes**
Frank the farmer	60 min/oz	15 min/oz	8 oz	32 oz
Rose the rancher	20 min/oz	10 min/oz	24 oz	48 oz

(b) Frank's Production Possibilities Frontier

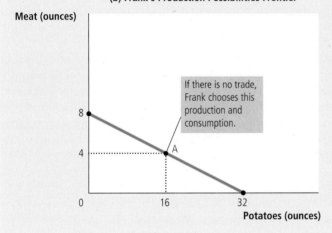

(c) Rose's Production Possibilities Frontier

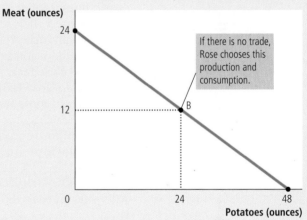

each good. Frank can produce an ounce of potatoes in 15 minutes and an ounce of meat in 60 minutes. Rose, who is more productive in both activities, can produce an ounce of potatoes in 10 minutes and an ounce of meat in 20 minutes. The last two columns in the table show the amounts of meat or potatoes Frank and Rose can produce if they devote all 8 hours to producing only that good.

Panel (b) of Figure 1 illustrates the amounts of meat and potatoes that Frank can produce. If Frank devotes all 8 hours of his time to potatoes, he produces 32 ounces of potatoes (measured on the horizontal axis) and no meat. If he devotes all his time to meat, he produces 8 ounces of meat (measured on the vertical axis) and no potatoes. If Frank divides his time equally between the two activities, spending 4 hours on each, he produces 16 ounces of potatoes and 4 ounces of meat. The figure shows these three possible outcomes and all others in between.

This graph is Frank's production possibilities frontier. As we discussed in Chapter 2, a production possibilities frontier shows the various mixes of output that an economy can produce. It illustrates one of the *Ten Principles of Economics* in Chapter 1: People face trade-offs. Here Frank faces a trade-off between producing meat and producing potatoes.

You may recall that the production possibilities frontier in Chapter 2 was drawn bowed out. In that case, the rate at which society could trade one good for the other depended on the amounts that were being produced. Here, however, Frank's technology for producing meat and potatoes (as summarized in Figure 1) allows him to switch between the two goods at a constant rate. Whenever Frank spends 1 hour less producing meat and 1 hour more producing potatoes, he reduces his output of meat by 1 ounce and raises his output of potatoes by 4 ounces—and this is true regardless of how much he is already producing. As a result, the production possibilities frontier is a straight line.

Panel (c) of Figure 1 shows the production possibilities frontier for Rose. If Rose devotes all 8 hours of her time to potatoes, she produces 48 ounces of potatoes and no meat. If she devotes all her time to meat, she produces 24 ounces of meat and no potatoes. If Rose divides her time equally, spending 4 hours on each activity, she produces 24 ounces of potatoes and 12 ounces of meat. Once again, the production possibilities frontier shows all the possible outcomes.

If Frank and Rose choose to be self-sufficient rather than trade with each other, then each consumes exactly what he or she produces. In this case, the production possibilities frontier is also the consumption possibilities frontier. That is, without trade, Figure 1 shows the possible combinations of meat and potatoes that Frank and Rose can each produce and then consume.

These production possibilities frontiers are useful in showing the trade-offs that Frank and Rose face, but they do not tell us what Frank and Rose will actually choose to do. To determine their choices, we need to know the tastes of Frank and Rose. Let's suppose they choose the combinations identified by points A and B in Figure 1. Based on his production opportunities and food preferences, Frank decides to produce and consume 16 ounces of potatoes and 4 ounces of meat, while Rose decides to produce and consume 24 ounces of potatoes and 12 ounces of meat.

3-1b Specialization and Trade

After several years of eating combination B, Rose gets an idea and goes to talk to Frank:

ROSE: Frank, my friend, have I got a deal for you! I know how to improve life for both of us. I think you should stop producing meat altogether and devote all your time to growing potatoes. According to my calculations, if you work 8 hours a day growing potatoes, you'll produce 32 ounces of potatoes. If you give me 15 of those 32 ounces, I'll give you 5 ounces of meat in return. In the end, you'll get to eat 17 ounces of potatoes and 5 ounces of meat every day, instead of the 16 ounces of potatoes and 4 ounces of meat you now get. If you go along with my plan, you'll have more of *both* foods. [To illustrate her point, Rose shows Frank panel (a) of Figure 2.]

FRANK: (sounding skeptical) That seems like a good deal for me. But I don't understand why you are offering it. If the deal is so good for me, it can't be good for you too.

ROSE: Oh, but it is! Suppose I spend 6 hours a day raising cattle and 2 hours growing potatoes. Then I can produce 18 ounces of meat and 12 ounces of potatoes. After I give you 5 ounces of my meat in exchange for 15 ounces of your potatoes, I'll end up with 13 ounces of meat and 27 ounces of potatoes, instead of the 12 ounces of meat and 24 ounces of potatoes that I now get. So I will also consume more of both foods than I do now. [She points out panel (b) of Figure 2.]

The proposed trade between Frank the farmer and Rose the rancher offers each of them a combination of meat and potatoes that would be impossible in the absence of trade. In panel (a), Frank gets to consume at point A* rather than point A. In panel (b), Rose gets to consume at point B* rather than point B. Trade allows each to consume more meat and more potatoes.

FIGURE 2

How Trade Expands the Set of Consumption Opportunities

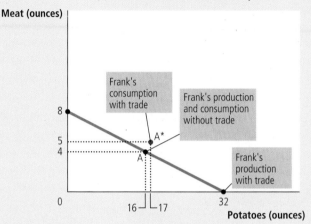

(a) Frank's Production and Consumption

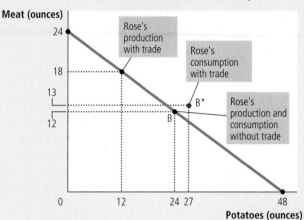

(b) Rose's Production and Consumption

(c) The Gains from Trade: A Summary

	Frank		Rose	
	Meat	**Potatoes**	**Meat**	**Potatoes**
Without Trade:				
Production and Consumption	4 oz	16 oz	12 oz	24 oz
With Trade:				
Production	0 oz	32 oz	18 oz	12 oz
Trade	Gets 5 oz	Gives 15 oz	Gives 5 oz	Gets 15 oz
Consumption	5 oz	17 oz	13 oz	27 oz
GAINS FROM TRADE:				
Increase in Consumption	+1 oz	+1 oz	+1 oz	+3 oz

FRANK: I don't know. . . . This sounds too good to be true.

ROSE: It's really not as complicated as it first seems. Here—I've summarized my proposal for you in a simple table. [Rose shows Frank a copy of the table at the bottom of Figure 2.]

FRANK: (after pausing to study the table) These calculations seem correct, but I am puzzled. How can this deal make us both better off?

ROSE: We can both benefit because trade allows each of us to specialize in doing what we do best. You will spend more time growing potatoes and less time raising cattle. I will spend more time raising cattle and less time growing potatoes. As a result of specialization and trade, each of us can consume more meat and more potatoes without working any more hours.

3-2 Comparative Advantage: The Driving Force of Specialization

Rose's explanation of the gains from trade, though correct, poses a puzzle: If Rose is better at both raising cattle and growing potatoes, how can Frank ever specialize in doing what he does best? Frank doesn't seem to do anything best. To solve this puzzle, we need to look at the principle of *comparative advantage*.

As a first step in developing this principle, consider the following question: In our example, who can produce potatoes at a lower cost—Frank or Rose? There are two possible answers, and in these two answers lie the solution to our puzzle and the key to understanding the gains from trade.

3-2a Absolute Advantage

absolute advantage
the ability to produce a good using fewer inputs than another producer

One way to answer the question about the cost of producing potatoes is to compare the inputs required by the two producers. Economists use the term **absolute advantage** when comparing the productivity of one person, firm, or nation to that of another. The producer that requires a smaller quantity of inputs to produce a good is said to have an absolute advantage in producing that good.

In our example, time is the only input, so we can determine absolute advantage by looking at how much time each type of production takes. Rose has an absolute advantage both in producing meat and in producing potatoes because she requires less time than Frank to produce a unit of either good. Rose needs to input only 20 minutes to produce an ounce of meat, whereas Frank needs 60 minutes. Similarly, Rose needs only 10 minutes to produce an ounce of potatoes, whereas Frank needs 15 minutes. Based on this information, we can conclude that Rose has the lower cost of producing potatoes, if we measure cost in terms of the quantity of inputs.

3-2b Opportunity Cost and Comparative Advantage

opportunity cost
whatever must be given up to obtain some item

There is another way to look at the cost of producing potatoes. Rather than comparing inputs required, we can compare opportunity costs. Recall from Chapter 1 that the **opportunity cost** of some item is what we give up to get that item. In our example, we assumed that Frank and Rose each spend 8 hours a day working. Time spent producing potatoes, therefore, takes away from time available for producing meat. When reallocating time between the two goods, Rose and Frank give up units of one good to produce units of the other, thereby moving along the production possibilities frontier. The opportunity cost measures the trade-off between the two goods that each producer faces.

Let's first consider Rose's opportunity cost. According to the table in panel (a) of Figure 1, producing 1 ounce of potatoes takes 10 minutes of work. When Rose spends those 10 minutes producing potatoes, she spends 10 minutes less

TABLE 1

The Opportunity Cost of Meat and Potatoes

	Opportunity Cost of:	
	1 oz of Meat	1 oz of Potatoes
Frank the farmer	4 oz potatoes	¼ oz meat
Rose the rancher	2 oz potatoes	½ oz meat

producing meat. Because Rose needs 20 minutes to produce 1 ounce of meat, 10 minutes of work would yield ½ ounce of meat. Hence, Rose's opportunity cost of producing 1 ounce of potatoes is ½ ounce of meat.

Now consider Frank's opportunity cost. Producing 1 ounce of potatoes takes him 15 minutes. Because he needs 60 minutes to produce 1 ounce of meat, 15 minutes of work would yield ¼ ounce of meat. Hence, Frank's opportunity cost of 1 ounce of potatoes is ¼ ounce of meat.

Table 1 shows the opportunity costs of meat and potatoes for the two producers. Notice that the opportunity cost of meat is the inverse of the opportunity cost of potatoes. Because 1 ounce of potatoes costs Rose ½ ounce of meat, 1 ounce of meat costs Rose 2 ounces of potatoes. Similarly, because 1 ounce of potatoes costs Frank ¼ ounce of meat, 1 ounce of meat costs Frank 4 ounces of potatoes.

Economists use the term **comparative advantage** when describing the opportunity costs faced by two producers. The producer who gives up less of other goods to produce Good X has the smaller opportunity cost of producing Good X and is said to have a comparative advantage in producing it. In our example, Frank has a lower opportunity cost of producing potatoes than Rose: An ounce of potatoes costs Frank only ¼ ounce of meat, but it costs Rose ½ ounce of meat. Conversely, Rose has a lower opportunity cost of producing meat than Frank: An ounce of meat costs Rose 2 ounces of potatoes, but it costs Frank 4 ounces of potatoes. Thus, Frank has a comparative advantage in growing potatoes, and Rose has a comparative advantage in producing meat.

Although it is possible for one person to have an absolute advantage in both goods (as Rose does in our example), it is impossible for one person to have a comparative advantage in both goods. Because the opportunity cost of one good is the inverse of the opportunity cost of the other, if a person's opportunity cost of one good is relatively high, the opportunity cost of the other good must be relatively low. Comparative advantage reflects the relative opportunity cost. Unless two people have the same opportunity cost, one person will have a comparative advantage in one good, and the other person will have a comparative advantage in the other good.

comparative advantage
the ability to produce a good at a lower opportunity cost than another producer

3-2c Comparative Advantage and Trade

The gains from specialization and trade are based not on absolute advantage but on comparative advantage. When each person specializes in producing the good for which he or she has a comparative advantage, total production in the economy rises. This increase in the size of the economic pie can be used to make everyone better off.

In our example, Frank spends more time growing potatoes, and Rose spends more time producing meat. As a result, the total production of potatoes rises from 40 to 44 ounces, and the total production of meat rises from 16 to 18 ounces. Frank and Rose share the benefits of this increased production.

We can also look at the gains from trade in terms of the price that each party pays the other. Because Frank and Rose have different opportunity costs, they can both get a bargain. That is, each of them benefits from trade by obtaining a good at a price that is lower than his or her opportunity cost of that good.

Consider the proposed deal from Frank's viewpoint. Frank receives 5 ounces of meat in exchange for 15 ounces of potatoes. In other words, Frank buys each ounce of meat for a price of 3 ounces of potatoes. This price of meat is lower than his opportunity cost for an ounce of meat, which is 4 ounces of potatoes. Thus, Frank benefits from the deal because he gets to buy meat at a good price.

Now consider the deal from Rose's viewpoint. Rose buys 15 ounces of potatoes for a price of 5 ounces of meat. That is, the price of potatoes is $\frac{1}{3}$ ounce of meat. This price of potatoes is lower than her opportunity cost of an ounce of potatoes, which is $\frac{1}{2}$ ounce of meat. Rose benefits because she gets to buy potatoes at a good price.

The story of Rose the rancher and Frank the farmer has a simple moral, which should now be clear: *Trade can benefit everyone in society because it allows people to specialize in activities in which they have a comparative advantage.*

3-2d The Price of the Trade

The principle of comparative advantage establishes that there are gains from specialization and trade, but it raises a couple of related questions: What determines the price at which trade takes place? How are the gains from trade shared between the trading parties? The precise answer to these questions is beyond the scope of this chapter, but we can state one general rule: *For both parties to gain from trade, the price at which they trade must lie between the two opportunity costs.*

In our example, Frank and Rose agreed to trade at a rate of 3 ounces of potatoes for each ounce of meat. This price is between Rose's opportunity cost (2 ounces of potatoes per ounce of meat) and Frank's opportunity cost (4 ounces of potatoes per ounce of meat). The price need not be exactly in the middle for both parties to gain, but it must be somewhere between 2 and 4.

To see why the price has to be in this range, consider what would happen if it were not. If the price of meat were below 2 ounces of potatoes, both Frank and Rose would want to buy meat, because the price would be below each of their opportunity costs. Similarly, if the price of meat were above 4 ounces of potatoes, both would want to sell meat, because the price would be above their opportunity costs. But there are only two members of this economy. They cannot both be buyers of meat, nor can they both be sellers. Someone has to take the other side of the deal.

A mutually advantageous trade can be struck at a price between 2 and 4. In this price range, Rose wants to sell meat to buy potatoes, and Frank wants to sell potatoes to buy meat. Each party can buy a good at a price that is lower than his or her opportunity cost. In the end, each person specializes in the good for which he or she has a comparative advantage and is, as a result, better off.

Quick Quiz   *Robinson Crusoe can gather 10 coconuts or catch 1 fish per hour. His friend Friday can gather 30 coconuts or catch 2 fish per hour. What is Crusoe's opportunity cost of catching 1 fish? What is Friday's? Who has an absolute advantage in catching fish? Who has a comparative advantage in catching fish?*

Bettmann/CORBIS

FYI

The Legacy of Adam Smith and David Ricardo

Economists have long understood the gains from trade. Here is how the great economist Adam Smith put the argument:

It is a maxim of every prudent master of a family, never to attempt to make at home what it will cost him more to make than to buy. The tailor does not attempt to make his own shoes, but buys them of the shoemaker. The shoemaker does not attempt to make his own clothes but employs a tailor. The farmer attempts to make neither the one nor the other, but employs those different artificers. All of them find it for their interest to employ their whole industry in a way in which they have some advantage over their neighbors, and to purchase with a part of its produce, or what is the same thing, with the price of part of it, whatever else they have occasion for.

This quotation is from Smith's 1776 book *An Inquiry into the Nature and Causes of the Wealth of Nations*, which was a landmark in the analysis of trade and economic interdependence.

David Ricardo

Smith's book inspired David Ricardo, a millionaire stockbroker, to become an economist. In his 1817 book *Principles of Political Economy and Taxation*, Ricardo developed the principle of comparative advantage as we know it today. He considered an example with two goods (wine and cloth) and two countries (England and Portugal). He showed that both countries can gain by opening up trade and specializing based on comparative advantage.

Ricardo's theory is the starting point of modern international economics, but his defense of free trade was not a mere academic exercise. Ricardo put his beliefs to work as a member of the British Parliament, where he opposed the Corn Laws, which restricted the import of grain.

The conclusions of Adam Smith and David Ricardo on the gains from trade have held up well over time. Although economists often disagree on questions of policy, they are united in their support of free trade. Moreover, the central argument for free trade has not changed much in the past two centuries. Even though the field of economics has broadened its scope and refined its theories since the time of Smith and Ricardo, economists' opposition to trade restrictions is still based largely on the principle of comparative advantage.

3-3 Applications of Comparative Advantage

The principle of comparative advantage explains interdependence and the gains from trade. Because interdependence is so prevalent in the modern world, the principle of comparative advantage has many applications. Here are two examples, one fanciful and one of great practical importance.

3-3a Should Tom Brady Mow His Own Lawn?

Tom Brady spends a lot of time running around on grass. One of the most talented football players of all time, he can throw a pass with a speed and accuracy that most casual athletes can only dream of. Most likely, he is talented at other physical activities as well. For example, let's imagine that Brady can mow his lawn faster than anyone else. But just because he *can* mow his lawn fast, does this mean he *should*?

To answer this question, we can use the concepts of opportunity cost and comparative advantage. Let's say that Brady can mow his lawn in 2 hours. In that same 2 hours, he could film a television commercial and earn $20,000. By contrast,

© Cliff Welch/Icon SMI/Corbis

"They did a nice job mowing this grass."

IN THE NEWS

Economics within a Marriage

An economist argues that you shouldn't always unload the dishwasher just because you're better than your partner at it.

You're Dividing the Chores Wrong

By Emily Oster

No one likes doing chores. In happiness surveys, housework is ranked down there with commuting as activities that people enjoy the least. Maybe that's why figuring out who does which chores usually prompts, at best, tense discussion in a household and, at worst, outright fighting.

If everyone is good at something different, assigning chores is easy. If your partner is great at grocery shopping and you are great at the laundry, you're set. But this isn't always—or even usually—the case. Often one person is better at everything. (And let's be honest, often that person is the woman.) Better at the laundry, the grocery shopping, the cleaning, the cooking. But does that mean she should have to do everything?

Before my daughter was born, I both cooked and did the dishes. It wasn't a big deal, it didn't take too much time, and honestly I was a lot better at both than my husband. His cooking repertoire extended only to eggs and chili, and when I left him in charge of the dishwasher, I'd often find he had run it "full" with one pot and eight forks.

After we had a kid, we had more to do and less time to do it in. It seemed like it was time for some reassignments. But, of course, I was still better at doing both things. Did that mean I should do them both?

I could have appealed to the principle of fairness: We should each do half. I could have appealed to feminism—surveys show that women more often than not get the short end of the chore stick. In time-use data, women do about 44 minutes more housework than men (2 hours and 11 minutes versus 1 hour and 27 minutes). Men outwork women only in the areas of "lawn" and "exterior maintenance." I could have suggested he do more chores to rectify this imbalance, to show our daughter, in the *Free To Be You and Me* style, that Mom and Dad are equal and that housework is fun if we do it together! I could have simply smashed around the pans in the dishwasher while sighing loudly in the hopes he would notice and offer to do it himself.

But luckily for me and my husband, I'm an economist, so I have more effective tools than passive aggression. And some basic economic principles provided the answer. We needed to divide the chores because it is simply not *efficient* for the best cook and dishwasher to do all the cooking and dishwashing. The economic principle at play here is increasing marginal cost. Basically, people get worse when they are tired. When I teach my students at the University of Chicago this principle, I explain it in the context of managing their employees. Imagine you have a good employee and a not-so-good one. Should you make the good employee do literally everything?

Usually, the answer is no. Why not? It's likely that the not-so-good employee is better at 9 a.m. after a full night of sleep than the good employee is at 2 a.m. after a 17-hour workday. So you want to give at least a few tasks to your worse guy. The same principle applies in your household. Yes, you (or your spouse) might be better at everything. But anyone doing the laundry at 4 a.m. is likely to put the red towels in with the white T-shirts. Some task splitting is a good idea. How much depends on how fast people's skills decay.

To "optimize" your family efficiency (every economist's ultimate goal—and yours, too), you want to equalize effectiveness on the final

Forrest Gump, the boy next door, can mow Brady's lawn in 4 hours. In that same 4 hours, Gump could work at McDonald's and earn $40.

In this example, Brady has an absolute advantage in mowing lawns because he can do the work with a lower input of time. Yet because Brady's opportunity cost of mowing the lawn is $20,000 and Gump's opportunity cost is only $40, Gump has a comparative advantage in mowing lawns.

The gains from trade in this example are tremendous. Rather than mowing his own lawn, Brady should make the commercial and hire Gump to mow the lawn. As long as Brady pays Gump more than $40 and less than $20,000, both of them are better off.

task each person is doing. Your partner does the dishes, mows the lawn, and makes the grocery list. You do the cooking, laundry, shopping, cleaning, and paying the bills. This may seem imbalanced, but when you look at it, you see that by the time your partner gets to the grocery-list task, he is wearing thin and starting to nod off. It's all he can do to figure out how much milk you need. In fact, he is just about as good at that as you are when you get around to paying the bills, even though that's your fifth task.

If you then made your partner also do the cleaning—so it was an even four and four—the house would be a disaster, since he is already exhausted by his third chore while you are still doing fine. This system may well end up meaning one person does more, but it is unlikely to result in one person doing everything.

Once you've decided you need to divide up the chores in this way, how should you decide who does what? One option would be randomly assigning tasks; another would be having each person do some of everything. One spousal-advice website I read suggested you should divide tasks based on which ones you like the best. None of these are quite right. (In the last case, how would anyone ever end up with the job of cleaning the bathroom?)

To decide who does what, we need more economics. Specifically, the principle of

comparative advantage. Economists usually talk about this in the context of trade. Imagine Finland is better than Sweden at making both reindeer hats and snowshoes. But they are much, much better at the hats and only a little better at the snowshoes. The overall world production is maximized when Finland makes hats and Sweden makes snowshoes.

We say that Finland has an *absolute advantage* in both things but a *comparative advantage* only in hats. This principle is part of the reason economists value free trade, but that's for another column (and probably another author). But it's also a

Illustration by Robert Neubecker

guideline for how to trade tasks in your house. You want to assign each person the tasks on which he or she has a comparative advantage. It doesn't matter that you have an absolute advantage in everything. If you are much, much better at the laundry and only a little better at cleaning the toilet, you should do the laundry and have your spouse get out the scrub brush. Just explain that it's efficient!

In our case, it was easy. Other than using the grill—which I freely admit is the husband domain—I'm much, much better at cooking. And I was only moderately better at the dishes. So he got the job of cleaning up after meals, even though his dishwasher loading habits had already come under scrutiny. The good news is another economic principle I hadn't even counted on was soon in play: *learning by doing.* As people do a task, they improve at it. Eighteen months into this new arrangement the dishwasher is almost a work of art: neat rows of dishes and everything carefully screened for "top-rack only" status. I, meanwhile, am forbidden from getting near the dishwasher. Apparently, there is a risk that I'll "ruin it."

Ms. Oster is a professor of economics at the University of Chicago. ◢

Source: *Slate*, November 21, 2012. The article is found in the link: http://www.slate.com/articles/double_x/doublex/2012/11/dividing_the_chores_who_should_cook_and_who_should_clean.2.html

3-3b Should the United States Trade with Other Countries?

Just as individuals can benefit from specialization and trade with one another, as Frank and Rose did, so can populations of people in different countries. Many of the goods that Americans enjoy are produced abroad, and many of the goods produced in the United States are sold abroad. Goods produced abroad and sold domestically are called **imports**. Goods produced domestically and sold abroad are called **exports**.

imports
goods produced abroad and sold domestically

exports
goods produced domestically and sold abroad

To see how countries can benefit from trade, suppose there are two countries, the United States and Japan, and two goods, food and cars. Imagine that the two countries produce cars equally well: An American worker and a Japanese worker can each produce one car per month. By contrast, because the United States has more and better land, it is better at producing food: A U.S. worker can produce 2 tons of food per month, whereas a Japanese worker can produce only 1 ton of food per month.

The principle of comparative advantage states that each good should be produced by the country that has the smaller opportunity cost of producing that good. Because the opportunity cost of a car is 2 tons of food in the United States but only 1 ton of food in Japan, Japan has a comparative advantage in producing cars. Japan should produce more cars than it wants for its own use and export some of them to the United States. Similarly, because the opportunity cost of a ton of food is 1 car in Japan but only ½ car in the United States, the United States has a comparative advantage in producing food. The United States should produce more food than it wants to consume and export some to Japan. Through specialization and trade, both countries can have more food and more cars.

In reality, of course, the issues involved in trade among nations are more complex than this example suggests. Most important among these issues is that each country has many citizens with different interests. International trade can make some individuals worse off, even as it makes the country as a whole better off. When the United States exports food and imports cars, the impact on an American farmer is not the same as the impact on an American autoworker. Yet, contrary to the opinions sometimes voiced by politicians and pundits, international trade is not like war, in which some countries win and others lose. Trade allows all countries to achieve greater prosperity.

Quick Quiz   *Suppose that a skilled brain surgeon also happens to be the world's fastest typist. Should she do her own typing or hire a secretary? Explain.*

3-4 Conclusion

You should now understand more fully the benefits of living in an interdependent economy. When Americans buy tube socks from China, when residents of Maine drink orange juice from Florida, and when a homeowner hires the kid next door to mow the lawn, the same economic forces are at work. The principle of comparative advantage shows that trade can make everyone better off.

Having seen why interdependence is desirable, you might naturally ask how it is possible. How do free societies coordinate the diverse activities of all the people involved in their economies? What ensures that goods and services will get from those who should be producing them to those who should be consuming them? In a world with only two people, such as Rose the rancher and Frank the farmer, the answer is simple: These two people can bargain and allocate resources between themselves. In the real world with billions of people, the answer is less obvious. We take up this issue in Chapter 4, where we see that free societies allocate resources through the market forces of supply and demand.

Summary

- Each person consumes goods and services produced by many other people both in the United States and around the world. Interdependence and trade are desirable because they allow everyone to enjoy a greater quantity and variety of goods and services.

- There are two ways to compare the ability of two people to produce a good. The person who can produce the good with the smaller quantity of inputs is said to have an *absolute advantage* in producing the good. The person who has the smaller opportunity cost of producing the good is said to have a *comparative*

  advantage. The gains from trade are based on comparative advantage, not absolute advantage.

- Trade makes everyone better off because it allows people to specialize in those activities in which they have a comparative advantage.

- The principle of comparative advantage applies to countries as well as to people. Economists use the principle of comparative advantage to advocate free trade among countries.

Key Concepts

absolute advantage, *p. 52*

opportunity cost, *p. 52*

comparative advantage, *p. 53*

imports, *p. 57*

exports, *p. 57*

Questions for Review

1. Under what conditions is the production possibilities frontier linear rather than bowed out?

2. Explain how absolute advantage and comparative advantage differ.

3. Give an example in which one person has an absolute advantage in doing something but another person has a comparative advantage.

4. Is absolute advantage or comparative advantage more important for trade? Explain your reasoning using the example in your answer to Question 3.

5. If two parties trade based on comparative advantage and both gain, in what range must the price of the trade lie?

6. Why do economists oppose policies that restrict trade among nations?

Quick Check Multiple Choice

1. In an hour, David can wash 2 cars or mow 1 lawn, and Ron can wash 3 cars or mow 1 lawn. Who has the absolute advantage in car washing, and who has the absolute advantage in lawn mowing?
   a. David in washing, Ron in mowing.
   b. Ron in washing, David in mowing.
   c. David in washing, neither in mowing.
   d. Ron in washing, neither in mowing.

2. Once again, in an hour, David can wash 2 cars or mow 1 lawn, and Ron can wash 3 cars or mow 1 lawn. Who has the comparative advantage in car washing, and who has the comparative advantage in lawn mowing?
   a. David in washing, Ron in mowing.
   b. Ron in washing, David in mowing.
   c. David in washing, neither in mowing.
   d. Ron in washing, neither in mowing.

3. When two individuals produce efficiently and then make a mutually beneficial trade based on comparative advantage,
   a. they both obtain consumption outside their production possibilities frontier.
   b. they both obtain consumption inside their production possibilities frontier.
   c. one individual consumes inside her production possibilities frontier, while the other consumes outside hers.
   d. each individual consumes a point on her own production possibilities frontier.

4. Which goods will a nation typically import?
   a. those goods in which the nation has an absolute advantage

b. those goods in which the nation has a comparative advantage

c. those goods in which other nations have an absolute advantage

d. those goods in which other nations have a comparative advantage

5. Suppose that in the United States, producing an aircraft takes 10,000 hours of labor and producing a shirt takes 2 hours of labor. In China, producing an aircraft takes 40,000 hours of labor and producing a shirt takes 4 hours of labor. What will these nations trade?

a. China will export aircraft, and the United States will export shirts.

b. China will export shirts, and the United States will export aircraft.

c. Both nations will export shirts.

d. There are no gains from trade in this situation.

6. Mark can cook dinner in 30 minutes and wash the laundry in 20 minutes. His roommate takes half as long to do each task. How should the roommates allocate the work?

a. Mark should do more of the cooking based on his comparative advantage.

b. Mark should do more of the washing based on his comparative advantage.

c. Mark should do more of the washing based on his absolute advantage.

d. There are no gains from trade in this situation.

Problems and Applications

1. Maria can read 20 pages of economics in an hour. She can also read 50 pages of sociology in an hour. She spends 5 hours per day studying.
   a. Draw Maria's production possibilities frontier for reading economics and sociology.
   b. What is Maria's opportunity cost of reading 100 pages of sociology?

2. American and Japanese workers can each produce 4 cars a year. An American worker can produce 10 tons of grain a year, whereas a Japanese worker can produce 5 tons of grain a year. To keep things simple, assume that each country has 100 million workers.
   a. For this situation, construct a table analogous to the table in Figure 1.
   b. Graph the production possibilities frontiers for the American and Japanese economies.
   c. For the United States, what is the opportunity cost of a car? Of grain? For Japan, what is the opportunity cost of a car? Of grain? Put this information in a table analogous to Table 1.
   d. Which country has an absolute advantage in producing cars? In producing grain?
   e. Which country has a comparative advantage in producing cars? In producing grain?
   f. Without trade, half of each country's workers produce cars and half produce grain. What quantities of cars and grain does each country produce?
   g. Starting from a position without trade, give an example in which trade makes each country better off.

3. Pat and Kris are roommates. They spend most of their time studying (of course), but they leave some time for their favorite activities: making pizza and brewing root beer. Pat takes 4 hours to brew a gallon of root beer and 2 hours to make a pizza. Kris takes 6 hours to brew a gallon of root beer and 4 hours to make a pizza.
   a. What is each roommate's opportunity cost of making a pizza? Who has the absolute advantage in making pizza? Who has the comparative advantage in making pizza?
   b. If Pat and Kris trade foods with each other, who will trade away pizza in exchange for root beer?
   c. The price of pizza can be expressed in terms of gallons of root beer. What is the highest price at which pizza can be traded that would make both roommates better off? What is the lowest price? Explain.

4. Suppose that there are 10 million workers in Canada and that each of these workers can produce either 2 cars or 30 bushels of wheat in a year.
   a. What is the opportunity cost of producing a car in Canada? What is the opportunity cost of producing a bushel of wheat in Canada? Explain the relationship between the opportunity costs of the two goods.
   b. Draw Canada's production possibilities frontier. If Canada chooses to consume 10 million cars, how much wheat can it consume without trade? Label this point on the production possibilities frontier.
   c. Now suppose that the United States offers to buy 10 million cars from Canada in exchange for 20 bushels of wheat per car. If Canada continues to consume 10 million cars, how much wheat does this deal allow Canada to consume? Label this point on your diagram. Should Canada accept the deal?

5. England and Scotland both produce scones and sweaters. Suppose that an English worker can produce 50 scones per hour or 1 sweater per hour. Suppose that a Scottish worker can produce 40 scones per hour or 2 sweaters per hour.
   a. Which country has the absolute advantage in the production of each good? Which country has the comparative advantage?
   b. If England and Scotland decide to trade, which commodity will Scotland trade to England? Explain.
   c. If a Scottish worker could produce only 1 sweater per hour, would Scotland still gain from trade? Would England still gain from trade? Explain.

6. The following table describes the production possibilities of two cities in the country of Baseballia:

	Pairs of Red Socks per Worker per Hour	Pairs of White Socks per Worker per Hour
Boston	3	3
Chicago	2	1

   a. Without trade, what is the price of white socks (in terms of red socks) in Boston? What is the price in Chicago?
   b. Which city has an absolute advantage in the production of each color sock? Which city has a comparative advantage in the production of each color sock?
   c. If the cities trade with each other, which color sock will each export?
   d. What is the range of prices at which trade can occur?

7. A German worker takes 400 hours to produce a car and 2 hours to produce a case of wine. A French worker takes 600 hours to produce a car and X hours to produce a case of wine.
   a. For what values of X will gains from trade be possible? Explain.

   b. For what values of X will Germany export cars and import wine? Explain.

8. Suppose that in a year an American worker can produce 100 shirts or 20 computers and a Chinese worker can produce 100 shirts or 10 computers.
   a. For each country, graph the production possibilities frontier. Suppose that without trade the workers in each country spend half their time producing each good. Identify this point in your graphs.
   b. If these countries were open to trade, which country would export shirts? Give a specific numerical example and show it on your graphs. Which country would benefit from trade? Explain.
   c. Explain at what price of computers (in terms of shirts) the two countries might trade.
   d. Suppose that China catches up with American productivity so that a Chinese worker can produce 100 shirts or 20 computers. What pattern of trade would you predict now? How does this advance in Chinese productivity affect the economic well-being of the citizens of the two countries?

9. Are the following statements true or false? Explain in each case.
   a. "Two countries can achieve gains from trade even if one of the countries has an absolute advantage in the production of all goods."
   b. "Certain very talented people have a comparative advantage in everything they do."
   c. "If a certain trade is good for one person, it can't be good for the other one."
   d. "If a certain trade is good for one person, it is always good for the other one."
   e. "If trade is good for a country, it must be good for everyone in the country."

Go to CengageBrain.com to purchase access to the proven, critical Study Guide to accompany this text, which features additional notes and context, practice tests, and much more.

How Markets Work

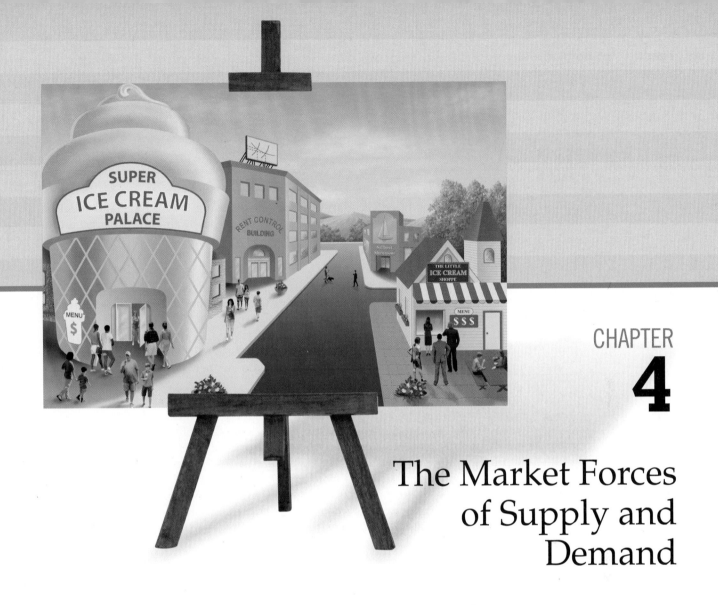

The Market Forces of Supply and Demand

W hen a cold snap hits Florida, the price of orange juice rises in supermarkets throughout the country. When the weather turns warm in New England every summer, the price of hotel rooms in the Caribbean plummets. When a war breaks out in the Middle East, the price of gasoline in the United States rises and the price of a used Cadillac falls. What do these events have in common? They all show the workings of supply and demand.

Supply and *demand* are the two words economists use most often—and for good reason. Supply and demand are the forces that make market economies work. They determine the quantity of each good produced and the price at which it is sold. If you want to know how any event or policy will affect the economy, you must think first about how it will affect supply and demand.

This chapter introduces the theory of supply and demand. It considers how buyers and sellers behave and how they interact with one another.

It shows how supply and demand determine prices in a market economy and how prices, in turn, allocate the economy's scarce resources.

4-1 Markets and Competition

The terms *supply* and *demand* refer to the behavior of people as they interact with one another in competitive markets. Before discussing how buyers and sellers behave, let's first consider more fully what we mean by the terms *market* and *competition.*

4-1a What Is a Market?

market
a group of buyers and sellers of a particular good or service

A **market** is a group of buyers and sellers of a particular good or service. The buyers as a group determine the demand for the product, and the sellers as a group determine the supply of the product.

Markets take many forms. Some markets are highly organized, such as the markets for many agricultural commodities. In these markets, buyers and sellers meet at a specific time and place where an auctioneer helps set prices and arrange sales.

More often, markets are less organized. For example, consider the market for ice cream in a particular town. Buyers of ice cream do not meet together at any one time. The sellers of ice cream are in different locations and offer somewhat different products. There is no auctioneer calling out the price of ice cream. Each seller posts a price for an ice-cream cone, and each buyer decides how much ice cream to buy at each store. Nonetheless, these consumers and producers of ice cream are closely connected. The ice-cream buyers are choosing from the various ice-cream sellers to satisfy their cravings, and the ice-cream sellers are all trying to appeal to the same ice-cream buyers to make their businesses successful. Even though it is not as organized, the group of ice-cream buyers and ice-cream sellers forms a market.

4-1b What Is Competition?

The market for ice cream, like most markets in the economy, is highly competitive. Each buyer knows that there are several sellers from which to choose, and each seller is aware that his product is similar to that offered by other sellers. As a result, the price and quantity of ice cream sold are not determined by any single buyer or seller. Rather, price and quantity are determined by all buyers and sellers as they interact in the marketplace.

competitive market
a market in which there are many buyers and many sellers so that each has a negligible impact on the market price

Economists use the term **competitive market** to describe a market in which there are so many buyers and so many sellers that each has a negligible impact on the market price. Each seller of ice cream has limited control over the price because other sellers are offering similar products. A seller has little reason to charge less than the going price, and if he charges more, buyers will make their purchases elsewhere. Similarly, no single buyer of ice cream can influence the price of ice cream because each buyer purchases only a small amount.

In this chapter, we assume that markets are *perfectly competitive.* To reach this highest form of competition, a market must have two characteristics: (1) The goods offered for sale are all exactly the same, and (2) the buyers and sellers are so numerous that no single buyer or seller has any influence over the market price. Because buyers and sellers in perfectly competitive markets must accept the price the market determines, they are said to be *price takers.* At the market price, buyers can buy all they want, and sellers can sell all they want.

[Handwritten annotations at top of page:]
Perfect Competition
Goods are the same
Many buyers + sellers

Monopoly
only one seller

There are some markets in which the assumption of perfect competition applies perfectly. In the wheat market, for example, there are thousands of farmers who sell wheat and millions of consumers who use wheat and wheat products. Because no single buyer or seller can influence the price of wheat, each takes the market price as given.

Not all goods and services, however, are sold in perfectly competitive markets. Some markets have only one seller, and this seller sets the price. Such a seller is called a *monopoly*. Your local cable television company, for instance, may be a monopoly. Residents of your town probably have only one company from which to buy cable service. Still other markets fall between the extremes of perfect competition and monopoly.

Despite the diversity of market types we find in the world, assuming perfect competition is a useful simplification and, therefore, a natural place to start. Perfectly competitive markets are the easiest to analyze because everyone participating in the market takes the price as given by market conditions. Moreover, because some degree of competition is present in most markets, many of the lessons that we learn by studying supply and demand under perfect competition apply in more complicated markets as well.

Quick Quiz   *What is a market? • What are the characteristics of a perfectly competitive market?*

4-2 Demand

We begin our study of markets by examining the behavior of buyers. To focus our thinking, let's keep in mind a particular good—ice cream.

4-2a The Demand Curve: The Relationship between Price and Quantity Demanded

The **quantity demanded** of any good is the amount of the good that buyers are willing and able to purchase. As we will see, many things determine the quantity demanded of any good, but in our analysis of how markets work, one determinant plays a central role—the price of the good. If the price of ice cream rose to $20 per scoop, you would buy less ice cream. You might buy frozen yogurt instead. If the price of ice cream fell to $0.20 per scoop, you would buy more. This relationship between price and quantity demanded is true for most goods in the economy and, in fact, is so pervasive that economists call it the **law of demand**: Other things being equal, when the price of a good rises, the quantity demanded of the good falls, and when the price falls, the quantity demanded rises.

The table in Figure 1 shows how many ice-cream cones Catherine buys each month at different prices of ice cream. If ice cream is free, Catherine eats 12 cones per month. At $0.50 per cone, Catherine buys 10 cones each month. As the price rises further, she buys fewer and fewer cones. When the price reaches $3.00, Catherine doesn't buy any cones at all. This table is a **demand schedule**, a table that shows the relationship between the price of a good and the quantity demanded, holding constant everything else that influences how much of the good consumers want to buy.

The graph in Figure 1 uses the numbers from the table to illustrate the law of demand. By convention, the price of ice cream is on the vertical axis, and the

quantity demanded
the amount of a good that buyers are willing and able to purchase

[Handwritten:] Price↓ Demand↑ vice versa

law of demand
the claim that, other things being equal, the quantity demanded of a good falls when the price of the good rises

demand schedule
a table that shows the relationship between the price of a good and the quantity demanded

FIGURE 1

Catherine's Demand Schedule and Demand Curve

The demand schedule is a table that shows the quantity demanded at each price. The demand curve, which graphs the demand schedule, illustrates how the quantity demanded of the good changes as its price varies. Because a lower price increases the quantity demanded, the demand curve slopes downward.

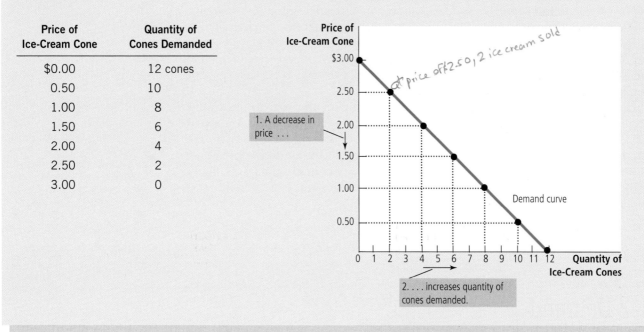

Price of Ice-Cream Cone	Quantity of Cones Demanded
$0.00	12 cones
0.50	10
1.00	8
1.50	6
2.00	4
2.50	2
3.00	0

quantity of ice cream demanded is on the horizontal axis. The line relating price and quantity demanded is called the **demand curve**. The demand curve slopes downward because, other things being equal, a lower price means a greater quantity demanded.

demand curve
a graph of the relationship between the price of a good and the quantity demanded

4-2b Market Demand versus Individual Demand

The demand curve in Figure 1 shows an individual's demand for a product. To analyze how markets work, we need to determine the *market demand*, the sum of all the individual demands for a particular good or service.

The table in Figure 2 shows the demand schedules for ice cream of the two individuals in this market—Catherine and Nicholas. At any price, Catherine's demand schedule tells us how much ice cream she buys, and Nicholas's demand schedule tells us how much ice cream he buys. The market demand at each price is the sum of the two individual demands.

The graph in Figure 2 shows the demand curves that correspond to these demand schedules. Notice that we sum the individual demand curves horizontally to obtain the market demand curve. That is, to find the total quantity demanded at any price, we add the individual quantities, which are found on the horizontal axis of the individual demand curves. Because we are interested in analyzing how markets function, we work most often with the market demand curve. The market demand curve shows how the total quantity demanded of a good varies as the price of the good varies, while all the other factors that affect how much consumers want to buy are held constant.

The quantity demanded in a market is the sum of the quantities demanded by all the buyers at each price. Thus, the market demand curve is found by adding horizontally the individual demand curves. At a price of $2.00, Catherine demands 4 ice-cream cones and Nicholas demands 3 ice-cream cones. The quantity demanded in the market at this price is 7 cones.

FIGURE 2

Market Demand as the Sum of Individual Demands

Price of Ice-Cream Cone	Catherine		Nicholas		Market
$0.00	12	+	7	=	19 cones
0.50	10		6		16
1.00	8		5		13
1.50	6		4		10
2.00	4		3		7
2.50	2		2		4
3.00	0		1		1

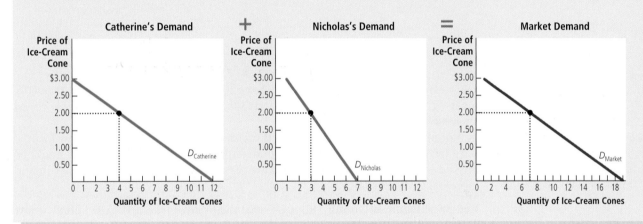

4-2c Shifts in the Demand Curve

Because the market demand curve holds other things constant, it need not be stable over time. If something happens to alter the quantity demanded at any given price, the demand curve shifts. For example, suppose the American Medical Association discovered that people who regularly eat ice cream live longer, healthier lives. The discovery would raise the demand for ice cream. At any given price, buyers would now want to purchase a larger quantity of ice cream, and the demand curve for ice cream would shift.

Figure 3 illustrates shifts in demand. Any change that increases the quantity demanded at every price, such as our imaginary discovery by the American Medical Association, shifts the demand curve to the right and is called an *increase in demand*. Any change that reduces the quantity demanded at every price shifts the demand curve to the left and is called a *decrease in demand*.

There are many variables that can shift the demand curve. Here are the most important.

Income What would happen to your demand for ice cream if you lost your job one summer? Most likely, it would fall. A lower income means that you have

Reduce→ left→ decrease demand

FIGURE 3

Shifts in the Demand Curve
Any change that raises the quantity that buyers wish to purchase at any given price shifts the demand curve to the right. Any change that lowers the quantity that buyers wish to purchase at any given price shifts the demand curve to the left.

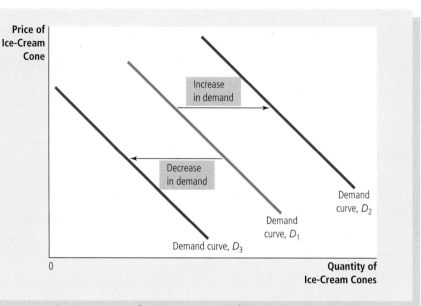

[handwritten] Normal good = income falls, demand falls
Inferior good = income falls, demand goes up

normal good
a good for which, other things being equal, an increase in income leads to an increase in demand

inferior good
a good for which, other things being equal, an increase in income leads to a decrease in demand

substitutes
two goods for which an increase in the price of one leads to an increase in the demand for the other

complements
two goods for which an increase in the price of one leads to a decrease in the demand for the other

less to spend in total, so you would have to spend less on some—and probably most—goods. If the demand for a good falls when income falls, the good is called a **normal good**.

Not all goods are normal goods. If the demand for a good rises when income falls, the good is called an **inferior good**. An example of an inferior good might be bus rides. As your income falls, you are less likely to buy a car or take a cab and more likely to ride a bus.

Prices of Related Goods   Suppose that the price of frozen yogurt falls. The law of demand says that you will buy more frozen yogurt. At the same time, you will probably buy less ice cream. Because ice cream and frozen yogurt are both cold, sweet, creamy desserts, they satisfy similar desires. When a fall in the price of one good reduces the demand for another good, the two goods are called **substitutes**. Substitutes are often pairs of goods that are used in place of each other, such as hot dogs and hamburgers, sweaters and sweatshirts, and movie tickets and DVD rentals. *[handwritten]* Substitute = Ice cream and frozen yogurt

Now suppose that the price of hot fudge falls. According to the law of demand, you will buy more hot fudge. Yet in this case, you will likely buy more ice cream as well because ice cream and hot fudge are often used together. When a fall in the price of one good raises the demand for another good, the two goods are called **complements**. Complements are often pairs of goods that are used together, such as gasoline and automobiles, computers and software, and peanut butter and jelly. *[handwritten]* complements;

Tastes   The most obvious determinant of your demand is your tastes. If you like ice cream, you buy more of it. Economists normally do not try to explain people's tastes because tastes are based on historical and psychological forces that are beyond the realm of economics. Economists do, however, examine what happens when tastes change.

Expectations   Your expectations about the future may affect your demand for a good or service today. If you expect to earn a higher income next month, you may choose to save less now and spend more of your current income buying ice cream. If you expect the price of ice cream to fall tomorrow, you may be less willing to buy an ice-cream cone at today's price.

Number of Buyers   In addition to the preceding factors, which influence the behavior of individual buyers, market demand depends on the number of these buyers. If Peter were to join Catherine and Nicholas as another consumer of ice cream, the quantity demanded in the market would be higher at every price, and market demand would increase.

Summary   The demand curve shows what happens to the quantity demanded of a good when its price varies, holding constant all the other variables that influence buyers. When one of these other variables changes, the demand curve shifts. Table 1 lists the variables that influence how much of a good consumers choose to buy.

If you have trouble remembering whether you need to shift or move along the demand curve, it helps to recall a lesson from the appendix to Chapter 2. A curve shifts when there is a change in a relevant variable that is not measured on either axis. Because the price is on the vertical axis, a change in price represents a movement along the demand curve. By contrast, income, the prices of related goods, tastes, expectations, and the number of buyers are not measured on either axis, so a change in one of these variables shifts the demand curve.

TABLE 1

Variable	A Change in This Variable . . .
Price of the good itself	Represents a movement along the demand curve
Income	Shifts the demand curve
Prices of related goods	Shifts the demand curve
Tastes	Shifts the demand curve
Expectations	Shifts the demand curve
Number of buyers	Shifts the demand curve

Variables That Influence Buyers
This table lists the variables that affect how much consumers choose to buy of any good. Notice the special role that the price of the good plays: A change in the good's price represents a movement along the demand curve, whereas a change in one of the other variables shifts the demand curve.

case study

Two Ways to Reduce the Quantity of Smoking Demanded

Public policymakers often want to reduce the amount that people smoke because of smoking's adverse health effects. There are two ways that policy can attempt to achieve this goal.

One way to reduce smoking is to shift the demand curve for cigarettes and other tobacco products. Public service announcements, mandatory health warnings on cigarette packages, and the prohibition of cigarette advertising on television are all policies aimed at reducing the quantity of cigarettes demanded at any given price. If successful, these policies shift the demand curve for cigarettes to the left, as in panel (a) of Figure 4.

FIGURE 4

Shifts in the Demand Curve versus Movements along the Demand Curve

If warnings on cigarette packages convince smokers to smoke less, the demand curve for cigarettes shifts to the left. In panel (a), the demand curve shifts from D_1 to D_2. At a price of $2.00 per pack, the quantity demanded falls from 20 to 10 cigarettes per day, as reflected by the shift from point A to point B. By contrast, if a tax raises the price of cigarettes, the demand curve does not shift. Instead, we observe a movement to a different point on the demand curve. In panel (b), when the price rises from $2.00 to $4.00, the quantity demanded falls from 20 to 12 cigarettes per day, as reflected by the movement from point A to point C.

(a) A Shift in the Demand Curve

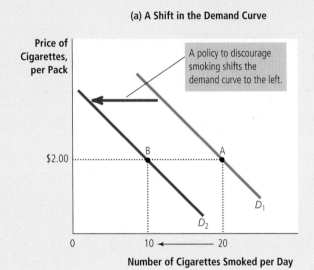

(b) A Movement along the Demand Curve

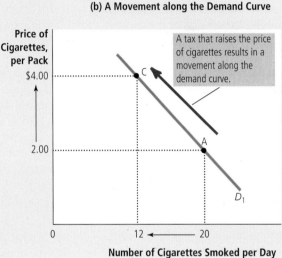

"What is the best way to stop this?"

Edyta Pawlowska/Shutterstock.com

Alternatively, policymakers can try to raise the price of cigarettes. If the government taxes the manufacture of cigarettes, for example, cigarette companies pass much of this tax on to consumers in the form of higher prices. A higher price encourages smokers to reduce the numbers of cigarettes they smoke. In this case, the reduced amount of smoking does not represent a shift in the demand curve. Instead, it represents a movement along the same demand curve to a point with a higher price and lower quantity, as in panel (b) of Figure 4.

How much does the amount of smoking respond to changes in the price of cigarettes? Economists have attempted to answer this question by studying what happens when the tax on cigarettes changes. They have found that a 10 percent increase in the price causes a 4 percent reduction in the quantity demanded. Teenagers are especially sensitive to the price of cigarettes: A 10 percent increase in the price causes a 12 percent drop in teenage smoking.

A related question is how the price of cigarettes affects the demand for illicit drugs, such as marijuana. Opponents of cigarette taxes often argue that tobacco and marijuana are substitutes so that high cigarette prices encourage marijuana use. By contrast, many experts on substance abuse view tobacco as a "gateway drug" leading the young to experiment with other harmful substances. Most studies of the data are consistent with this latter view: They find that lower cigarette prices are associated with greater use of marijuana. In other words, tobacco and marijuana appear to be complements rather than substitutes. ◢

Quick Quiz   *Make up an example of a monthly demand schedule for pizza and graph the implied demand curve. Give an example of something that would shift this demand curve, and briefly explain your reasoning. Would a change in the price of pizza shift this demand curve?*

4-3 Supply

We now turn to the other side of the market and examine the behavior of sellers. Once again, to focus our thinking, let's consider the market for ice cream.

4-3a The Supply Curve: The Relationship between Price and Quantity Supplied

The **quantity supplied** of any good or service is the amount that sellers are willing and able to sell. There are many determinants of quantity supplied, but once again, price plays a special role in our analysis. When the price of ice cream is high, selling ice cream is profitable, and so the quantity supplied is large. Sellers of ice cream work long hours, buy many ice-cream machines, and hire many workers. By contrast, when the price of ice cream is low, the business is less profitable, so sellers produce less ice cream. At a low price, some sellers may even choose to shut down, and their quantity supplied falls to zero. This relationship between price and quantity supplied is called the **law of supply**: Other things being equal, when the price of a good rises, the quantity supplied of the good also rises, and when the price falls, the quantity supplied falls as well.

The table in Figure 5 shows the quantity of ice-cream cones supplied each month by Ben, an ice-cream seller, at various prices of ice cream. At a price below

quantity supplied
the amount of a good that sellers are willing and able to sell

Price high = supply high
Price low = supply low

law of supply
the claim that, other things being equal, the quantity supplied of a good rises when the price of the good rises

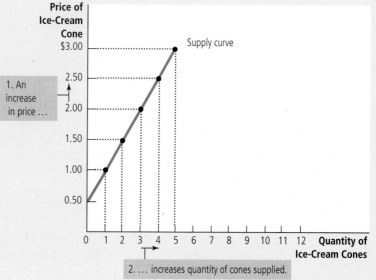

The supply schedule is a table that shows the quantity supplied at each price. This supply curve, which graphs the supply schedule, illustrates how the quantity supplied of the good changes as its price varies. Because a higher price increases the quantity supplied, the supply curve slopes upward.

FIGURE 5

Ben's Supply Schedule and Supply Curve

Price of Ice-Cream Cone	Quantity of Cones Supplied
$0.00	0 cones
0.50	0
1.00	1
1.50	2
2.00	3
2.50	4
3.00	5

$1.00, Ben does not supply any ice cream at all. As the price rises, he supplies a greater and greater quantity. This is the **supply schedule**, a table that shows the relationship between the price of a good and the quantity supplied, holding constant everything else that influences how much producers of the good want to sell.

The graph in Figure 5 uses the numbers from the table to illustrate the law of supply. The curve relating price and quantity supplied is called the **supply curve**. The supply curve slopes upward because, other things being equal, a higher price means a greater quantity supplied.

4-3b Market Supply versus Individual Supply

Just as market demand is the sum of the demands of all buyers, market supply is the sum of the supplies of all sellers. The table in Figure 6 shows the supply schedules for the two ice-cream producers in the market—Ben and Jerry. At any price, Ben's supply schedule tells us the quantity of ice cream that Ben supplies,

FIGURE 6

Market Supply as the Sum of Individual Supplies

The quantity supplied in a market is the sum of the quantities supplied by all the sellers at each price. Thus, the market supply curve is found by adding horizontally the individual supply curves. At a price of $2.00, Ben supplies 3 ice-cream cones and Jerry supplies 4 ice-cream cones. The quantity supplied in the market at this price is 7 cones.

Price of Ice-Cream Cone	Ben		Jerry		Market
$0.00	0	+	0	=	0 cones
0.50	0		0		0
1.00	1		0		1
1.50	2		2		4
2.00	3		4		7
2.50	4		6		10
3.00	5		8		13

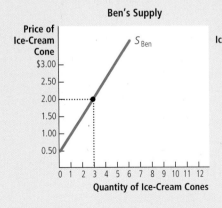

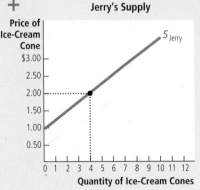

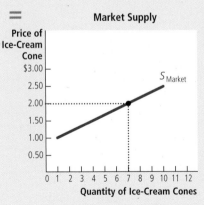

and Jerry's supply schedule tells us the quantity of ice cream that Jerry supplies. The market supply is the sum of the two individual supplies.

The graph in Figure 6 shows the supply curves that correspond to the supply schedules. As with demand curves, we sum the individual supply curves *horizontally* to obtain the market supply curve. That is, to find the total quantity supplied at any price, we add the individual quantities, which are found on the horizontal axis of the individual supply curves. The market supply curve shows how the total quantity supplied varies as the price of the good varies, holding constant all the other factors beyond price that influence producers' decisions about how much to sell.

4-3c Shifts in the Supply Curve

Because the market supply curve is drawn holding other things constant, when one of these factors changes, the supply curve shifts. For example, suppose the price of sugar falls. Sugar is an input into the production of ice cream, so the fall in the price of sugar makes selling ice cream more profitable. This raises the supply of ice cream: At any given price, sellers are now willing to produce a larger quantity. The supply curve for ice cream shifts to the right.

Figure 7 illustrates shifts in supply. Any change that raises quantity supplied at every price, such as a fall in the price of sugar, shifts the supply curve to the right and is called an *increase in supply*. Similarly, any change that reduces the quantity supplied at every price shifts the supply curve to the left and is called a *decrease in supply*.

There are many variables that can shift the supply curve. Here are some of the most important.

Input Prices To produce their output of ice cream, sellers use various inputs: cream, sugar, flavoring, ice-cream machines, the buildings in which the ice cream is made, and the labor of workers to mix the ingredients and operate the machines. When the price of one or more of these inputs rises, producing ice cream is less profitable, and firms supply less ice cream. If input prices rise substantially, a firm

[handwritten margin notes]
what causes
shift in supply curve:
Ingredient prices↑ supply↓
Technology ↑ supply ↑
expectations ↑ supply ↓
number of sellers ↓ supply↓

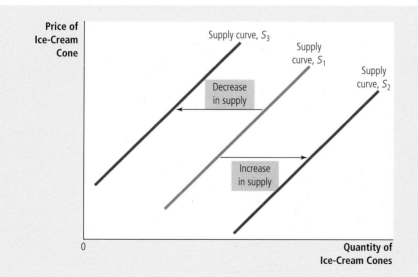

Price of Ice-Cream Cone

Supply curve, S_3
Supply curve, S_1
Supply curve, S_2

Decrease in supply

Increase in supply

0

Quantity of Ice-Cream Cones

FIGURE 7

Shifts in the Supply Curve
Any change that raises the quantity that sellers wish to produce at any given price shifts the supply curve to the right. Any change that lowers the quantity that sellers wish to produce at any given price shifts the supply curve to the left.

might shut down and supply no ice cream at all. Thus, the supply of a good is negatively related to the price of the inputs used to make the good.

Technology   The technology for turning inputs into ice cream is another determinant of supply. The invention of the mechanized ice-cream machine, for example, reduced the amount of labor necessary to make ice cream. By reducing firms' costs, the advance in technology raised the supply of ice cream.

Expectations   The amount of ice cream a firm supplies today may depend on its expectations about the future. For example, if a firm expects the price of ice cream to rise in the future, it will put some of its current production into storage and supply less to the market today.

Number of Sellers   In addition to the preceding factors, which influence the behavior of individual sellers, market supply depends on the number of these sellers. If Ben or Jerry were to retire from the ice-cream business, the supply in the market would fall.

Summary   The supply curve shows what happens to the quantity supplied of a good when its price varies, holding constant all the other variables that influence sellers. When one of these other variables changes, the supply curve shifts. Table 2 lists the variables that influence how much producers choose to sell of a good.

Once again, to remember whether you need to shift or move along the supply curve, keep in mind that a curve shifts only when there is a change in a relevant variable that is not named on either axis. The price is on the vertical axis, so a change in price represents a movement along the supply curve. By contrast, because input prices, technology, expectations, and the number of sellers are not measured on either axis, a change in one of these variables shifts the supply curve.

Quick Quiz   *Make up an example of a monthly supply schedule for pizza, and graph the implied supply curve. Give an example of something that would shift this supply curve, and briefly explain your reasoning. Would a change in the price of pizza shift this supply curve?*

TABLE 2

Variables That Influence Sellers
This table lists the variables that affect how much producers choose to sell of any good. Notice the special role that the price of the good plays: A change in the good's price represents a movement along the supply curve, whereas a change in one of the other variables shifts the supply curve.

Variable	A Change in This Variable . . .
Price of the good itself	Represents a movement along the supply curve
Input prices	Shifts the supply curve
Technology	Shifts the supply curve
Expectations	Shifts the supply curve
Number of sellers	Shifts the supply curve

4-4 Supply and Demand Together

Having analyzed supply and demand separately, we now combine them to see how they determine the price and quantity of a good sold in a market.

4-4a Equilibrium

Figure 8 shows the market supply curve and market demand curve together. Notice that there is one point at which the supply and demand curves intersect. This point is called the market's **equilibrium**. The price at this intersection is called the **equilibrium price**, and the quantity is called the **equilibrium quantity**. Here the equilibrium price is $2.00 per cone, and the equilibrium quantity is 7 ice-cream cones.

The dictionary defines the word *equilibrium* as a situation in which various forces are in balance—and this also describes a market's equilibrium. *At the equilibrium price, the quantity of the good that buyers are willing and able to buy exactly balances the quantity that sellers are willing and able to sell.* The equilibrium price is sometimes called the market-clearing price because, at this price, everyone in the market has been satisfied: Buyers have bought all they want to buy, and sellers have sold all they want to sell.

The actions of buyers and sellers naturally move markets toward the equilibrium of supply and demand. To see why, consider what happens when the market price is not equal to the equilibrium price.

Suppose first that the market price is above the equilibrium price, as in panel (a) of Figure 9. At a price of $2.50 per cone, the quantity of the good supplied (10 cones) exceeds the quantity demanded (4 cones). There is a **surplus** of the good: Suppliers are unable to sell all they want at the going price. A surplus is sometimes called a situation of *excess supply*. When there is a surplus in the ice-cream market, sellers of ice cream find their freezers increasingly full of ice cream they would like to sell but cannot. They respond to the surplus by cutting their

equilibrium
a situation in which the market price has reached the level at which quantity supplied equals quantity demanded

equilibrium price
the price that balances quantity supplied and quantity demanded

equilibrium quantity
the quantity supplied and the quantity demanded at the equilibrium price

surplus =excess supply
a situation in which quantity supplied is greater than quantity demanded

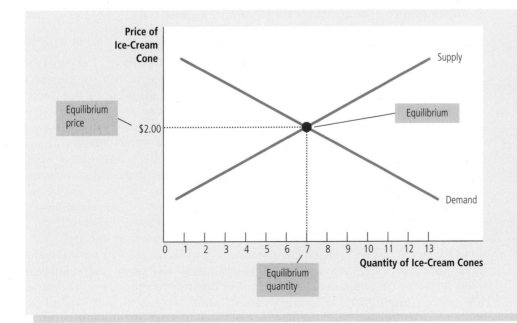

FIGURE 8

The Equilibrium of Supply and Demand
The equilibrium is found where the supply and demand curves intersect. At the equilibrium price, the quantity supplied equals the quantity demanded. Here the equilibrium price is $2.00: At this price, 7 ice-cream cones are supplied and 7 ice-cream cones are demanded.

FIGURE 9

Markets Not in Equilibrium

In panel (a), there is a surplus. Because the market price of $2.50 is above the equilibrium price, the quantity supplied (10 cones) exceeds the quantity demanded (4 cones). Suppliers try to increase sales by cutting the price of a cone, and this moves the price toward its equilibrium level. In panel (b), there is a shortage. Because the market price of $1.50 is below the equilibrium price, the quantity demanded (10 cones) exceeds the quantity supplied (4 cones). With too many buyers chasing too few goods, suppliers can take advantage of the shortage by raising the price. Hence, in both cases, the price adjustment moves the market toward the equilibrium of supply and demand.

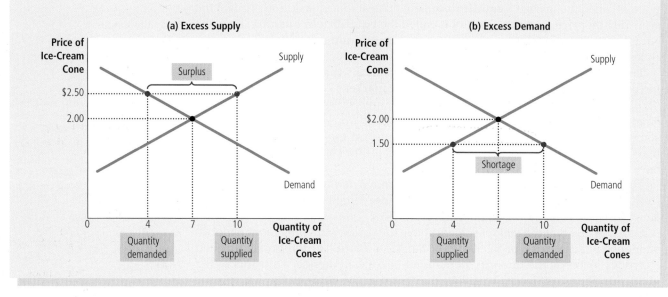

prices. Falling prices, in turn, increase the quantity demanded and decrease the quantity supplied. These changes represent movements *along* the supply and demand curves, not shifts in the curves. Prices continue to fall until the market reaches the equilibrium.

Suppose now that the market price is below the equilibrium price, as in panel (b) of Figure 9. In this case, the price is $1.50 per cone, and the quantity of the good demanded exceeds the quantity supplied. There is a **shortage** of the good: Demanders are unable to buy all they want at the going price. A shortage is sometimes called a situation of *excess demand*. When a shortage occurs in the ice-cream market, buyers have to wait in long lines for a chance to buy one of the few cones available. With too many buyers chasing too few goods, sellers can respond to the shortage by raising their prices without losing sales. These price increases cause the quantity demanded to fall and the quantity supplied to rise. Once again, these changes represent movements *along* the supply and demand curves, and they move the market toward the equilibrium.

Thus, regardless of whether the price starts off too high or too low, the activities of the many buyers and sellers automatically push the market price toward the equilibrium price. Once the market reaches its equilibrium, all buyers and sellers are satisfied, and there is no upward or downward pressure on the price. How quickly equilibrium is reached varies from market to market depending on how quickly prices adjust. In most free markets, surpluses and shortages are

shortage *Excess demand*
a situation in which quantity demanded is greater than quantity supplied

only temporary because prices eventually move toward their equilibrium levels. Indeed, this phenomenon is so pervasive that it is called the **law of supply and demand**: The price of any good adjusts to bring the quantity supplied and quantity demanded for that good into balance.

law of supply and demand
the claim that the price of any good adjusts to bring the quantity supplied and the quantity demanded for that good into balance

4-4b Three Steps to Analyzing Changes in Equilibrium

So far, we have seen how supply and demand together determine a market's equilibrium, which in turn determines the price and quantity of the good that buyers purchase and sellers produce. The equilibrium price and quantity depend on the position of the supply and demand curves. When some event shifts one of these curves, the equilibrium in the market changes, resulting in a new price and a new quantity exchanged between buyers and sellers.

When analyzing how some event affects the equilibrium in a market, we proceed in three steps. First, we decide whether the event shifts the supply curve, the demand curve, or, in some cases, both curves. Second, we decide whether the curve shifts to the right or to the left. Third, we use the supply-and-demand diagram to compare the initial and the new equilibrium, which shows how the shift affects the equilibrium price and quantity. Table 3 summarizes these three steps. To see how this recipe is used, let's consider various events that might affect the market for ice cream.

Example: A Change in Market Equilibrium Due to a Shift in Demand
Suppose that one summer the weather is very hot. How does this event affect the market for ice cream? To answer this question, let's follow our three steps.

1. The hot weather affects the demand curve by changing people's taste for ice cream. That is, the weather changes the amount of ice cream that people want to buy at any given price. The supply curve is unchanged because the weather does not directly affect the firms that sell ice cream.
2. Because hot weather makes people want to eat more ice cream, the demand curve shifts to the right. Figure 10 shows this increase in demand as a shift in the demand curve from D_1 to D_2. This shift indicates that the quantity of ice cream demanded is higher at every price.
3. At the old price of $2, there is now an excess demand for ice cream, and this shortage induces firms to raise the price. As Figure 10 shows, the increase in demand raises the equilibrium price from $2.00 to $2.50 and the equilibrium quantity from 7 to 10 cones. In other words, the hot weather increases the price of ice cream and the quantity of ice cream sold.

TABLE 3

Three Steps for Analyzing Changes in Equilibrium

1. Decide whether the event shifts the supply or demand curve (or perhaps both).
2. Decide in which direction the curve shifts.
3. Use the supply-and-demand diagram to see how the shift changes the equilibrium price and quantity.

FIGURE 10

How an Increase in Demand Affects the Equilibrium
An event that raises quantity demanded at any given price shifts the demand curve to the right. The equilibrium price and the equilibrium quantity both rise. Here an abnormally hot summer causes buyers to demand more ice cream. The demand curve shifts from D_1 to D_2, which causes the equilibrium price to rise from $2.00 to $2.50 and the equilibrium quantity to rise from 7 to 10 cones.

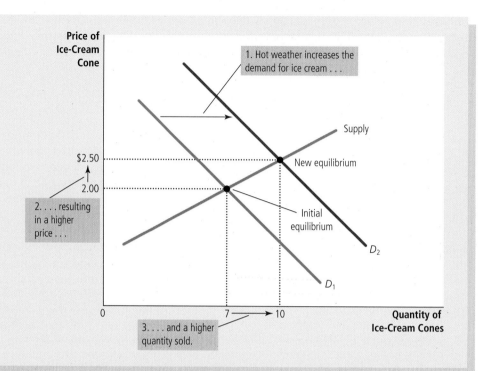

Shifts in Curves versus Movements along Curves   Notice that when hot weather increases the demand for ice cream and drives up the price, the quantity of ice cream that firms supply rises, even though the supply curve remains the same. In this case, economists say there has been an increase in "quantity supplied" but no change in "supply."

Supply refers to the position of the supply curve, whereas the *quantity supplied* refers to the amount suppliers wish to sell. In this example, supply does not change because the weather does not alter firms' desire to sell at any given price. Instead, the hot weather alters consumers' desire to buy at any given price and thereby shifts the demand curve to the right. The increase in demand causes the equilibrium price to rise. When the price rises, the quantity supplied rises. This increase in quantity supplied is represented by the movement along the supply curve.

To summarize, a shift *in* the supply curve is called a "change in supply," and a shift *in* the demand curve is called a "change in demand." A movement *along* a fixed supply curve is called a "change in the quantity supplied," and a movement *along* a fixed demand curve is called a "change in the quantity demanded."

Example: A Change in Market Equilibrium Due to a Shift in Supply
Suppose that during another summer, a hurricane destroys part of the sugarcane crop and drives up the price of sugar. How does this event affect the market for ice cream? Once again, to answer this question, we follow our three steps.

1. The change in the price of sugar, an input for making ice cream, affects the supply curve. By raising the costs of production, it reduces the amount of ice cream that firms produce and sell at any given price. The demand curve does not change because the higher cost of inputs does not directly affect the amount of ice cream households wish to buy.

2. The supply curve shifts to the left because, at every price, the total amount that firms are willing and able to sell is reduced. Figure 11 illustrates this decrease in supply as a shift in the supply curve from S1 to S2.

3. At the old price of $2, there is now an excess demand for ice cream, and this shortage causes firms to raise the price. As Figure 11 shows, the shift in the supply curve raises the equilibrium price from $2.00 to $2.50 and lowers the equilibrium quantity from 7 to 4 cones. As a result of the sugar price increase, the price of ice cream rises, and the quantity of ice cream sold falls.

Example: Shifts in Both Supply and Demand   Now suppose that a heat wave and a hurricane occur during the same summer. To analyze this combination of events, we again follow our three steps.

1. We determine that both curves must shift. The hot weather affects the demand curve because it alters the amount of ice cream that households want to buy at any given price. At the same time, when the hurricane drives up sugar prices, it alters the supply curve for ice cream because it changes the amount of ice cream that firms want to sell at any given price.

2. The curves shift in the same directions as they did in our previous analysis: The demand curve shifts to the right, and the supply curve shifts to the left. Figure 12 illustrates these shifts.

3. As Figure 12 shows, two possible outcomes might result depending on the relative size of the demand and supply shifts. In both cases, the equilibrium price rises. In panel (a), where demand increases substantially while supply falls just a little, the equilibrium quantity also rises. By contrast, in panel (b), where supply falls substantially while demand rises just a little, the equilibrium quantity falls. Thus, these events certainly raise the price of ice cream, but their impact on the amount of ice cream sold is ambiguous (that is, it could go either way).

on Test

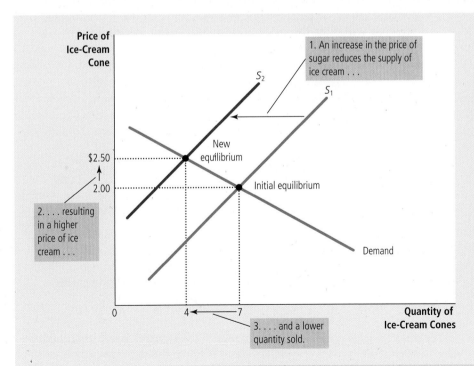

FIGURE 11

How a Decrease in Supply Affects the Equilibrium
An event that reduces quantity supplied at any given price shifts the supply curve to the left. The equilibrium price rises, and the equilibrium quantity falls. Here an increase in the price of sugar (an input) causes sellers to supply less ice cream. The supply curve shifts from *S*1 to *S*2, which causes the equilibrium price of ice cream to rise from $2.00 to $2.50 and the equilibrium quantity to fall from 7 to 4 cones.

FIGURE 12

A Shift in Both Supply and Demand

Here we observe a simultaneous increase in demand and decrease in supply. Two outcomes are possible. In panel (a), the equilibrium price rises from P_1 to P_2 and the equilibrium quantity rises from Q_1 to Q_2. In panel (b), the equilibrium price again rises from P_1 to P_2 but the equilibrium quantity falls from Q_1 to Q_2.

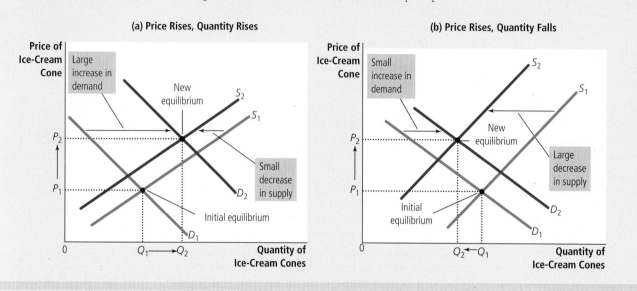

(a) Price Rises, Quantity Rises

Price of Ice-Cream Cone

Large increase in demand

New equilibrium

S_2

S_1

P_2

P_1

Small decrease in supply

D_2

Initial equilibrium

D_1

0   Q_1 ⟶ Q_2 Quantity of Ice-Cream Cones

(b) Price Rises, Quantity Falls

Price of Ice-Cream Cone

Small increase in demand

S_2

S_1

New equilibrium

P_2

Large decrease in supply

P_1

Initial equilibrium

D_2

D_1

0   Q_2 ⟵ Q_1 Quantity of Ice-Cream Cones

Summary   We have just seen three examples of how to use supply and demand curves to analyze a change in equilibrium. Whenever an event shifts the supply curve, the demand curve, or perhaps both curves, you can use these tools to predict how the event will alter the price and quantity sold in equilibrium. Table 4 shows the predicted outcome for any combination of shifts in the two curves. To make sure you understand how to use the tools of supply and demand, pick a few

TABLE 4

What Happens to Price and Quantity When Supply or Demand Shifts?
As a quick quiz, make sure you can explain at least a few of the entries in this table using a supply-and-demand diagram.

	No Change in Supply	An Increase in Supply	A Decrease in Supply
No Change in Demand	P same Q same	P down Q up	P up Q down
An Increase in Demand	P up Q up	P ambiguous Q up	P up Q ambiguous
A Decrease in Demand	P down Q down	P down Q ambiguous	P ambiguous Q down

entries in this table and make sure you can explain to yourself why the table contains the prediction that it does.

Quick Quiz *On the appropriate diagram, show what happens to the market for pizza if the price of tomatoes rises.* • *On a separate diagram, show what happens to the market for pizza if the price of hamburgers falls.*

4-5 Conclusion: How Prices Allocate Resources

This chapter has analyzed supply and demand in a single market. Although our discussion has centered on the market for ice cream, the lessons learned here apply in most other markets as well. Whenever you go to a store to buy something, you are contributing to the demand for that item. Whenever you look for a job, you are contributing to the supply of labor services. Because supply and demand are such pervasive economic phenomena, the model of supply and demand is a powerful tool for analysis. We will be using this model repeatedly in the following chapters.

One of the *Ten Principles of Economics* discussed in Chapter 1 is that markets are usually a good way to organize economic activity. Although it is still too early to judge whether market outcomes are good or bad, in this chapter we have begun to see how markets work. In any economic system, scarce resources have to be allocated among competing uses. Market economies harness the forces of supply and demand to serve that end. Supply and demand together determine the prices of the economy's many different goods and services; prices in turn are the signals that guide the allocation of resources.

For example, consider the allocation of beachfront land. Because the amount of this land is limited, not everyone can enjoy the luxury of living by the beach. Who gets this resource? The answer is whoever is willing and able to pay the price. The price of beachfront land adjusts until the quantity of land demanded exactly balances the quantity supplied. Thus, in market economies, prices are the mechanism for rationing scarce resources.

Similarly, prices determine who produces each good and how much is produced. For instance, consider farming. Because we need food to survive, it is crucial that some people work on farms. What determines who is a farmer and who is not? In a free society, there is no government planning agency making this decision and ensuring an adequate supply of food. Instead, the allocation of workers to farms is based on the job decisions of millions of workers. This decentralized system works well because these decisions depend on prices. The prices of food and the wages of farmworkers (the price of their labor) adjust to ensure that enough people choose to be farmers.

If a person had never seen a market economy in action, the whole idea might seem preposterous. Economies are enormous groups of people engaged in a multitude of interdependent activities. What prevents decentralized decision making from degenerating into chaos? What coordinates the actions of the millions of people with their varying abilities and desires? What ensures that what needs to be done is in fact done? The answer, in a word, is *prices*. If an invisible hand guides market economies, as Adam Smith famously suggested, then the price system is the baton that the invisible hand uses to conduct the economic orchestra.

"Two dollars"

"—and seventy-five cents."

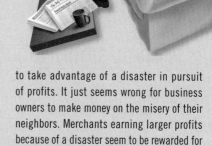

IN THE NEWS
....

Price Increases after Disasters

When a disaster such as a hurricane strikes a region, many goods experience an increase in demand or a decrease in supply, putting upward pressure on prices. Policymakers often object to these price hikes, but this opinion piece endorses the market's natural response.

Is Price Gouging Reverse Looting?

By John Carney

Four dollars for a can of coke. Five hundred dollars a night for a hotel in downtown Brooklyn. A pair of D-batteries for $6.99.

These are just a few of the examples of price hikes I or friends of mine have personally come across in the run-up and aftermath of hurricane Sandy. Price gouging, as this is often called, is a common occurrence during emergencies.

Price gouging around natural disasters is one of the things politicians on the left and right agree is a terrible, no good, very bad thing. New York Attorney General Eric Schneiderman sent out a press release warning "against price inflation of necessary goods and services during hurricane Sandy." New Jersey Governor Chris Christie issued a "forceful reminder" that

price gouging "will result in significant penalties." Hotlines have been established to allow consumers to report gouging.

New Jersey's law is very specific. Price increases of more than 10 percent during a declared state of emergency are considered excessive. A New Jersey gas station paid a $50,000 fine last year for hiking gasoline prices by 16 percent during tropical storm Irene.

New York's law may be even stricter. According to AG Schneiderman's release, all price increases on "necessary goods and items" count as gouging.

"General Business Law prohibits such increase in costs of essential items like food, water, gas, generators, batteries and flashlights, and services like transportation, during natural disasters or other events that disrupt the market," the NY AG release said.

These laws are built on the quite conventional view that it is unethical for a business

to take advantage of a disaster in pursuit of profits. It just seems wrong for business owners to make money on the misery of their neighbors. Merchants earning larger profits because of a disaster seem to be rewarded for doing nothing more than raising their prices.

"It's reverse looting," a neighbor of mine in Brooklyn said about the price of batteries at a local electronic store.

Unfortunately, ethics runs into economics in a way that can make these laws positively harmful. Price gouging can occur only when there is a shortage of the goods in demand. If there were no shortage, normal market processes would prevent sudden price spikes. A deli owner charging $4 for a can of Pepsi would discover he was just driving customers to the deli a block away, which charges a buck.

But when everyone suddenly starts buying batteries or bottles of water for fear of a blackout, shortages can arise. Sometimes

Summary

- Economists use the model of supply and demand to analyze competitive markets. In a competitive market, there are many buyers and sellers, each of whom has little or no influence on the market price.

- The demand curve shows how the quantity of a good demanded depends on the price. According to the law of demand, as the price of a good falls, the quantity demanded rises. Therefore, the demand curve slopes downward.

- In addition to price, other determinants of how much consumers want to buy include income, the prices of substitutes and complements, tastes, expectations, and

the number of buyers. If one of these factors changes, the demand curve shifts.

- The supply curve shows how the quantity of a good supplied depends on the price. According to the law of supply, as the price of a good rises, the quantity supplied rises. Therefore, the supply curve slopes upward.

- In addition to price, other determinants of how much producers want to sell include input prices, technology, expectations, and the number of sellers. If one of these factors changes, the supply curve shifts.

- The intersection of the supply and demand curves determines the market equilibrium. At the equilibrium

there simply is not enough of a particular good to satisfy a sharp spike in demand. And so the question arises: how do we decide which customers get the batteries, the groceries, the gasoline?

We could hold a lottery. Perhaps people could receive a ticket at the grocery store. Winners would get to shop at the usual prices. Losers would just go hungry. Or, more likely, they would be forced to buy the food away from the lottery winners—at elevated prices no doubt, since no one would buy food just to sell it at the same price. So the gouging would just pass from merchant to lottery winning customer.

Would you pay $4 for this?

Source: Courtesy of CNBC.

We could have some sort of rationing program. Each person could be assigned a portion of the necessary goods according to their household need. This is something the U.S. resorted to during World War II. The problem is that rationing requires an immense amount of planning—and an impossible level of knowledge. The rationing bureaucrat would have to know precisely how much of each good was available in a given area and how many people would need it. Good luck getting that in place as a hurricane bears down on your city.

We could simply sell goods on a first come, first serve basis. This is, in fact, what anti-gouging laws encourage. The result is all too familiar. People hoard goods. Store shelves are emptied. And you have to wonder, why is a first to the register race a fairer system than the alternative of market prices? Speed seems a poor proxy for justice.

Allowing prices to rise at times of extreme demand discourages overconsumption. People consider their purchases more carefully. Instead of buying a dozen batteries (or bottles of water or gallons of gas), perhaps they buy half that. The result is that goods under extreme demand are available to more customers. The market process actually results in a more equitable distribution than the anti-gouging laws.

Once we understand this, it's easy to see that merchants aren't really profiting from disaster. They are profiting from managing their prices, which has the socially beneficial effect of broadening distribution and discouraging hoarding. In short, they are being justly rewarded for performing an important public service.

One objection is that a system of free-floating, legal gouging would allow the wealthy to buy everything and leave the poor out altogether. But this concern is overrated. For the most part, price hikes during disasters do not actually put necessary goods and services out of reach of even the poorest people. They just put the budgets of the poor under additional strain. This is a problem better resolved through transfer payments to alleviate the household budgetary effects of the prices after the fact, rather than trying to control the price in the first place....

Instead of cracking down on price gougers, we should be using our experience of shortages during this time of crisis to spark a reform of our counter-productive laws. Next time disaster strikes, we should hope for a bit more gouging and a lot fewer empty store shelves. ◢

price, the quantity demanded equals the quantity supplied.

- The behavior of buyers and sellers naturally drives markets toward their equilibrium. When the market price is above the equilibrium price, there is a surplus of the good, which causes the market price to fall. When the market price is below the equilibrium price, there is a shortage, which causes the market price to rise.

- To analyze how any event influences a market, we use the supply-and-demand diagram to examine how the event affects the equilibrium price and quantity. To do this, we follow three steps. First, we decide whether the event shifts the supply curve or the demand curve (or both). Second, we decide in which direction the curve shifts. Third, we compare the new equilibrium with the initial equilibrium.

- In market economies, prices are the signals that guide economic decisions and thereby allocate scarce resources. For every good in the economy, the price ensures that supply and demand are in balance. The equilibrium price then determines how much of the good buyers choose to consume and how much sellers choose to produce.

Key Concepts

market, *p. 66*
competitive market, *p. 66*
quantity demanded, *p. 67*
law of demand, *p. 67*
demand schedule, *p. 67*
demand curve, *p. 68*
normal good, *p. 70*

inferior good, *p. 70*
substitutes, *p. 70*
complements, *p. 70*
quantity supplied, *p. 73*
law of supply, *p. 73*
supply schedule, *p. 74*
supply curve, *p. 74*

equilibrium, *p. 77*
equilibrium price, *p. 77*
equilibrium quantity, *p. 77*
surplus, *p. 77*
shortage, *p. 78*
law of supply and demand, *p. 79*

Questions for Review

1. What is a competitive market? Briefly describe a type of market that is *not* perfectly competitive.

2. What are the demand schedule and the demand curve, and how are they related? Why does the demand curve slope downward?

3. Does a change in consumers' tastes lead to a movement along the demand curve or a shift in the demand curve? Does a change in price lead to a movement along the demand curve or a shift in the demand curve? Explain your answers.

4. Popeye's income declines, and as a result, he buys more spinach. Is spinach an inferior or a normal good? What happens to Popeye's demand curve for spinach?

5. What are the supply schedule and the supply curve, and how are they related? Why does the supply curve slope upward?

6. Does a change in producers' technology lead to a movement along the supply curve or a shift in the supply curve? Does a change in price lead to a movement along the supply curve or a shift in the supply curve?

7. Define the equilibrium of a market. Describe the forces that move a market toward its equilibrium.

8. Beer and pizza are complements because they are often enjoyed together. When the price of beer rises, what happens to the supply, demand, quantity supplied, quantity demanded, and price in the market for pizza?

9. Describe the role of prices in market economies.

Quick Check Multiple Choice

1. A change in which of the following will NOT shift the demand curve for hamburgers?
   a. the price of hot dogs
   b. the price of hamburgers
   c. the price of hamburger buns
   d. the income of hamburger consumers

2. An increase in _____ will cause a movement along a given demand curve, which is called a change in

   _____.
   a. supply, demand
   b. supply, quantity demanded
   c. demand, supply
   d. demand, quantity supplied

3. Movie tickets and DVDs are substitutes. If the price of DVDs increases, what happens in the market for movie tickets?
   a. The supply curve shifts to the left.
   b. The supply curve shifts to the right.
   c. The demand curve shifts to the left.
   d. The demand curve shifts to the right.

4. The discovery of a large new reserve of crude oil will shift the _____ curve for gasoline, leading to a _____ equilibrium price.

   a. supply, higher
   b. supply, lower
   c. demand, higher
   d. demand, lower

5. If the economy goes into a recession and incomes fall, what happens in the markets for inferior goods?
   a. Prices and quantities both rise.
   b. Prices and quantities both fall.
   c. Prices rise, quantities fall.
   d. Prices fall, quantities rise.

6. Which of the following might lead to an increase in the equilibrium price of jelly and a decrease in the equilibrium quantity of jelly sold?
   a. an increase in the price of peanut better, a complement to jelly
   b. an increase in the price of Marshmallow Fluff, a substitute for jelly
   c. an increase in the price of grapes, an input into jelly
   d. an increase in consumers' incomes, as long as jelly is a normal good

Problems and Applications

1. Explain each of the following statements using supply-and-demand diagrams.
   a. "When a cold snap hits Florida, the price of orange juice rises in supermarkets throughout the country."
   b. "When the weather turns warm in New England every summer, the price of hotel rooms in Caribbean resorts plummets."
   c. "When a war breaks out in the Middle East, the price of gasoline rises and the price of a used Cadillac falls."

2. "An increase in the demand for notebooks raises the quantity of notebooks demanded but not the quantity supplied." Is this statement true or false? Explain.

3. Consider the market for minivans. For each of the events listed here, identify which of the determinants of demand or supply are affected. Also indicate whether demand or supply increases or decreases. Then draw a diagram to show the effect on the price and quantity of minivans.
   a. People decide to have more children.
   b. A strike by steelworkers raises steel prices.
   c. Engineers develop new automated machinery for the production of minivans.
   d. The price of sports utility vehicles rises.
   e. A stock market crash lowers people's wealth.

4. Consider the markets for DVDs, TV screens, and tickets at movie theaters.
   a. For each pair, identify whether they are complements or substitutes:
      • DVDs and TV screens
      • DVDs and movie tickets
      • TV screens and movie tickets
   b. Suppose a technological advance reduces the cost of manufacturing TV screens. Draw a diagram to show what happens in the market for TV screens.
   c. Draw two more diagrams to show how the change in the market for TV screens affects the markets for DVDs and movie tickets.

5. Over the past 30 years, technological advances have reduced the cost of computer chips. How do you think this has affected the market for computers? For computer software? For typewriters?

6. Using supply-and-demand diagrams, show the effect of the following events on the market for sweatshirts.
   a. A hurricane in South Carolina damages the cotton crop.
   b. The price of leather jackets falls.
   c. All colleges require morning exercise in appropriate attire.
   d. New knitting machines are invented.

7. Ketchup is a complement (as well as a condiment) for hot dogs. If the price of hot dogs rises, what happens to the market for ketchup? For tomatoes? For tomato juice? For orange juice?

8. The market for pizza has the following demand and supply schedules:

Price	Quantity Demanded	Quantity Supplied
$4	135 pizzas	26 pizzas
5	104	53
6	81	81
7	68	98
8	53	110
9	39	121

   a. Graph the demand and supply curves. What is the equilibrium price and quantity in this market?
   b. If the actual price in this market were *above* the equilibrium price, what would drive the market toward the equilibrium?
   c. If the actual price in this market were *below* the equilibrium price, what would drive the market toward the equilibrium?

9. Consider the following events: Scientists reveal that eating oranges decreases the risk of diabetes, and at the same time, farmers use a new fertilizer that makes orange trees produce more oranges. Illustrate and explain what effect these changes have on the equilibrium price and quantity of oranges.

10. Because bagels and cream cheese are often eaten together, they are complements.
   a. We observe that both the equilibrium price of cream cheese and the equilibrium quantity of bagels have risen. What could be responsible for this pattern—a fall in the price of flour or a fall in the price of milk? Illustrate and explain your answer.
   b. Suppose instead that the equilibrium price of cream cheese has risen but the equilibrium quantity of bagels has fallen. What could be responsible for this pattern—a rise in the price of flour or a rise in the price of milk? Illustrate and explain your answer.

11. Suppose that the price of basketball tickets at your college is determined by market forces. Currently, the demand and supply schedules are as follows:

Price	Quantity Demanded	Quantity Supplied
$4	10,000 tickets	8,000 tickets
8	8,000	8,000
12	6,000	8,000
16	4,000	8,000
20	2,000	8,000

a. Draw the demand and supply curves. What is unusual about this supply curve? Why might this be true?

b. What are the equilibrium price and quantity of tickets?

c. Your college plans to increase total enrollment next year by 5,000 students. The additional students will have the following demand schedule:

Price	Quantity Demanded
$4	4,000 tickets
8	3,000
12	2,000
16	1,000
20	0

Now add the old demand schedule and the demand schedule for the new students to calculate the new demand schedule for the entire college. What will be the new equilibrium price and quantity?

Go to CengageBrain.com to purchase access to the proven, critical Study Guide to accompany this text, which features additional notes and context, practice tests, and much more.

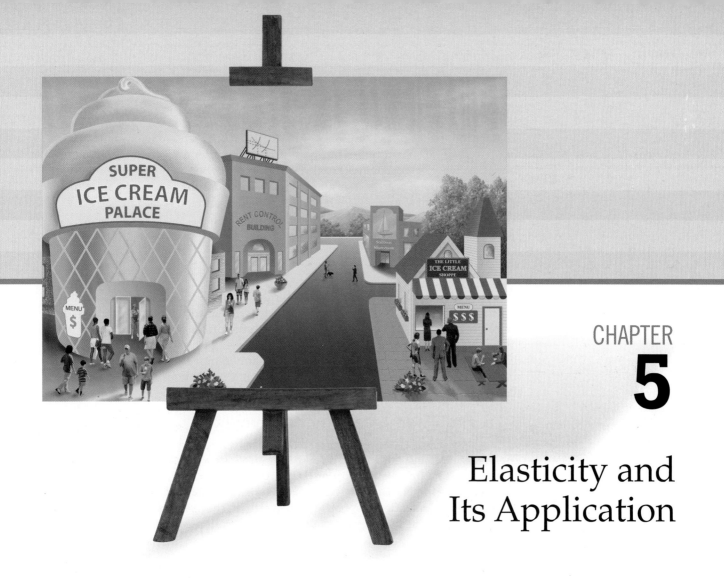

Elasticity and Its Application

Imagine that some event drives up the price of gasoline in the United States. It could be a war in the Middle East that disrupts the world supply of oil, a booming Chinese economy that boosts the world demand for oil, or a new tax on gasoline passed by Congress. How would U.S. consumers respond to the higher price?

It is easy to answer this question in broad fashion: Consumers would buy less. That follows from the law of demand that we learned in the previous chapter. But you might want a precise answer. By how much would consumption of gasoline fall? This question can be answered using a concept called *elasticity*, which we develop in this chapter.

Elasticity is a measure of how much buyers and sellers respond to changes in market conditions. When studying how some event or policy affects a market, we can discuss not only the direction of the effects but their magnitude as well. Elasticity is useful in many applications, as we see toward the end of this chapter.

Before proceeding, however, you might be curious about the answer to the gasoline question. Many studies have examined consumers' response to gasoline prices, and they typically find that the quantity demanded responds more in the long run than it does in the short run. A 10 percent increase in gasoline prices reduces gasoline consumption by about 2.5 percent after a year and about 6 percent after five years. About half of the long-run reduction in quantity demanded arises because people drive less, and half arises because they switch to more fuel-efficient cars. Both responses are reflected in the demand curve and its elasticity.

5-1 The Elasticity of Demand

When we introduced demand in Chapter 4, we noted that consumers usually buy more of a good when its price is lower, when their incomes are higher, when the prices of its substitutes are higher, or when the prices of its complements are lower. Our discussion of demand was qualitative, not quantitative. That is, we discussed the direction in which quantity demanded moves but not the size of the change. To measure how much consumers respond to changes in these variables, economists use the concept of **elasticity**.

elasticity
a measure of the responsiveness of quantity demanded or quantity supplied to a change in one of its determinants

price elasticity of demand
a measure of how much the quantity demanded of a good responds to a change in the price of that good, computed as the percentage change in quantity demanded divided by the percentage change in price

5-1a The Price Elasticity of Demand and Its Determinants

The law of demand states that a fall in the price of a good raises the quantity demanded. The **price elasticity of demand** measures how much the quantity demanded responds to a change in price. Demand for a good is said to be *elastic* if the quantity demanded responds substantially to changes in the price. Demand is said to be *inelastic* if the quantity demanded responds only slightly to changes in the price.

The price elasticity of demand for any good measures how willing consumers are to buy less of the good as its price rises. Because a demand curve reflects the many economic, social, and psychological forces that shape consumer preferences, there is no simple, universal rule for what determines a demand curve's elasticity. Based on experience, however, we can state some rules of thumb about what influences the price elasticity of demand.

Availability of Close Substitutes Goods with close substitutes tend to have more elastic demand because it is easier for consumers to switch from that good to others. For example, butter and margarine are easily substitutable. A small increase in the price of butter, assuming the price of margarine is held fixed, causes the quantity of butter sold to fall by a large amount. By contrast, because eggs are a food without a close substitute, the demand for eggs is less elastic than the demand for butter. A small increase in the price of eggs does not cause a sizable drop in the quantity of eggs sold.

Necessities versus Luxuries Necessities tend to have inelastic demands, whereas luxuries have elastic demands. When the price of a doctor's visit rises, people will not dramatically reduce the number of times they go to the doctor, although they might go somewhat less often. By contrast, when the price of sailboats rises, the quantity of sailboats demanded falls substantially. The reason is that most people view doctor visits as a necessity and sailboats as a luxury. Whether a good is a necessity or a luxury depends not on the intrinsic properties of the good but on the preferences of the buyer. For avid sailors with little concern about their health, sailboats might be a necessity with inelastic demand and doctor visits a luxury with elastic demand.

Definition of the Market The elasticity of demand in any market depends on how we draw the boundaries of the market. Narrowly defined markets tend to have more elastic demand than broadly defined markets because it is easier to find close substitutes for narrowly defined goods. For example, food, a broad category, has a fairly inelastic demand because there are no good substitutes for food. Ice cream, a narrower category, has a more elastic demand because it is easy to substitute other desserts for ice cream. Vanilla ice cream, a very narrow category, has a very elastic demand because other flavors of ice cream are almost perfect substitutes for vanilla.

Time Horizon Goods tend to have more elastic demand over longer time horizons. When the price of gasoline rises, the quantity of gasoline demanded falls only slightly in the first few months. Over time, however, people buy more fuel-efficient cars, switch to public transportation, and move closer to where they work. Within several years, the quantity of gasoline demanded falls more substantially.

5-1b Computing the Price Elasticity of Demand

Now that we have discussed the price elasticity of demand in general terms, let's be more precise about how it is measured. Economists compute the price elasticity of demand as the percentage change in the quantity demanded divided by the percentage change in the price. That is,

$$\text{Price elasticity of demand} = \frac{\text{Percentage change in quantity demanded}}{\text{Percentage change in price}}.$$

For example, suppose that a 10 percent increase in the price of an ice-cream cone causes the amount of ice cream you buy to fall by 20 percent. We calculate your elasticity of demand as

$$\text{Price elasticity of demand} = \frac{20 \text{ percent } \textit{change in quantity demanded}}{10 \text{ percent } \textit{change in price}} = 2.$$

In this example, the elasticity is 2, reflecting that the change in the quantity demanded is proportionately twice as large as the change in the price.

Because the quantity demanded of a good is negatively related to its price, the percentage change in quantity will always have the opposite sign as the percentage change in price. In this example, the percentage change in price is a *positive* 10 percent (reflecting an increase), and the percentage change in quantity demanded is a *negative* 20 percent (reflecting a decrease). For this reason, price elasticities of demand are sometimes reported as negative numbers. In this book, we follow the common practice of dropping the minus sign and reporting all price elasticities of demand as positive numbers. (Mathematicians call this the *absolute value*.) With this convention, a larger price elasticity implies a greater responsiveness of quantity demanded to changes in price.

5-1c The Midpoint Method: A Better Way to Calculate Percentage Changes and Elasticities

If you try calculating the price elasticity of demand between two points on a demand curve, you will quickly notice an annoying problem: The elasticity from point A to point B seems different from the elasticity from point B to point A. For example, consider these numbers:

Point A: Price = $4   Quantity = 120

Point B: Price = $6   Quantity = 80

$$\frac{120}{4} \quad \frac{80}{6}$$
$$30 \quad 13.33$$

Going from point A to point B, the price rises by 50 percent and the quantity falls by 33 percent, indicating that the price elasticity of demand is 33/50, or 0.66. By contrast, going from point B to point A, the price falls by 33 percent and the quantity rises by 50 percent, indicating that the price elasticity of demand is 50/33, or 1.5. This difference arises because the percentage changes are calculated from a different base.

One way to avoid this problem is to use the *midpoint method* for calculating elasticities. The standard procedure for computing a percentage change is to divide the change by the initial level. By contrast, the midpoint method computes a percentage change by dividing the change by the midpoint (or average) of the initial and final levels. For instance, $5 is the midpoint between $4 and $6. Therefore, according to the midpoint method, a change from $4 to $6 is considered a 40 percent rise because $(6 - 4) / 5 \times 100 = 40$. Similarly, a change from $6 to $4 is considered a 40 percent fall.

Because the midpoint method gives the same answer regardless of the direction of change, it is often used when calculating the price elasticity of demand between two points. In our example, the midpoint between point A and point B is:

Midpoint: Price = $5   Quantity = 100

According to the midpoint method, when going from point A to point B, the price rises by 40 percent and the quantity falls by 40 percent. Similarly, when going from point B to point A, the price falls by 40 percent and the quantity rises by 40 percent. In both directions, the price elasticity of demand equals 1.

The following formula expresses the midpoint method for calculating the price elasticity of demand between two points, denoted (Q_1, P_1) and (Q_2, P_2):

$$\text{Price elasticity of demand} = \frac{(Q_2 - Q_1)/[(Q_2 + Q_1)/2]}{(P_2 - P_1)/[(P_2 + P_1)/2]}.$$

The numerator is the percentage change in quantity computed using the midpoint method, and the denominator is the percentage change in price computed using the midpoint method. If you ever need to calculate elasticities, you should use this formula.

In this book, however, we rarely perform such calculations. For most of our purposes, what elasticity represents—the responsiveness of quantity demanded to a change in price—is more important than how it is calculated.

5-1d The Variety of Demand Curves

Economists classify demand curves according to their elasticity. Demand is considered *elastic* when the elasticity is greater than 1, which means the quantity moves proportionately more than the price. Demand is considered *inelastic* when the elasticity is less than 1, which means the quantity moves proportionately less than the price. If the elasticity is exactly 1, the percentage change in quantity equals the percentage change in price, and demand is said to have *unit elasticity*.

Because the price elasticity of demand measures how much quantity demanded responds to changes in the price, it is closely related to the slope of the demand curve. The following rule of thumb is a useful guide: The flatter the demand curve that passes through a given point, the greater the price elasticity of demand. The steeper the demand curve that passes through a given point, the smaller the price elasticity of demand.

Figure 1 shows five cases. In the extreme case of a zero elasticity, shown in panel (a), demand is *perfectly inelastic*, and the demand curve is vertical. In this

The price elasticity of demand determines whether the demand curve is steep or flat. Note that all percentage changes are calculated using the midpoint method.

FIGURE 1

The Price Elasticity of Demand

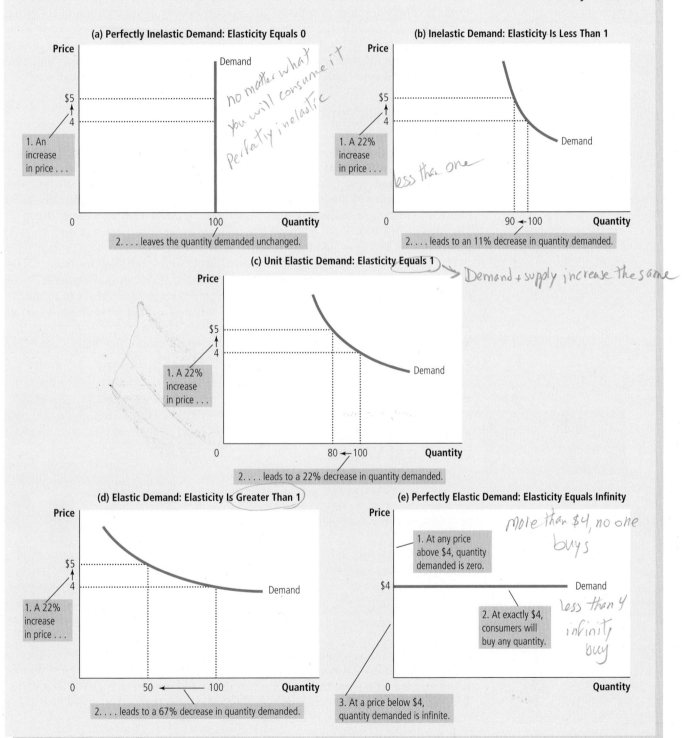

(a) Perfectly Inelastic Demand: Elasticity Equals 0

Price

Demand

$5
4

1. An increase in price . . .

0   100   Quantity

2. . . . leaves the quantity demanded unchanged.

no matter what you will consume it
perfectly inelastic

(b) Inelastic Demand: Elasticity Is Less Than 1

Price

$5
4

1. A 22% increase in price . . .

Demand

0   90 ← 100   Quantity

2. . . . leads to an 11% decrease in quantity demanded.

less than one

(c) Unit Elastic Demand: Elasticity Equals 1

Price

$5
4

1. A 22% increase in price . . .

Demand

0   80 ← 100   Quantity

2. . . . leads to a 22% decrease in quantity demanded.

Demand + supply increase the same

(d) Elastic Demand: Elasticity Is Greater Than 1

Price

$5
4

1. A 22% increase in price . . .

Demand

0   50 ← 100   Quantity

2. . . . leads to a 67% decrease in quantity demanded.

(e) Perfectly Elastic Demand: Elasticity Equals Infinity

Price

1. At any price above $4, quantity demanded is zero.

$4   Demand

2. At exactly $4, consumers will buy any quantity.

0   Quantity

3. At a price below $4, quantity demanded is infinite.

more than $4, no one buys
less than 4 infinity buy

case, regardless of the price, the quantity demanded stays the same. As the elasticity rises, the demand curve gets flatter and flatter, as shown in panels (b), (c), and (d). At the opposite extreme, shown in panel (e), demand is *perfectly elastic*. This occurs as the price elasticity of demand approaches infinity and the demand curve becomes horizontal, reflecting the fact that very small changes in the price lead to huge changes in the quantity demanded.

Finally, if you have trouble keeping straight the terms *elastic* and *inelastic,* here's a memory trick for you: *I*nelastic curves, such as in panel (a) of Figure 1, look like the letter I. This is not a deep insight, but it might help you on your next exam.

5-1e Total Revenue and the Price Elasticity of Demand

total revenue

the amount paid by buyers and received by sellers of a good, computed as the price of the good times the quantity sold

When studying changes in supply or demand in a market, one variable we often want to study is **total revenue**, the amount paid by buyers and received by sellers of a good. In any market, total revenue is $P \times Q$, the price of the good times the quantity of the good sold. We can show total revenue graphically, as in Figure 2. The height of the box under the demand curve is P, and the width is Q. The area of this box, $P \times Q$, equals the total revenue in this market. In Figure 2, where $P = \$4$ and $Q = 100$, total revenue is $\$4 \times 100$, or $\$400$.

How does total revenue change as one moves along the demand curve? The answer depends on the price elasticity of demand. If demand is inelastic, as in panel (a) of Figure 3, then an increase in the price causes an increase in total revenue. Here an increase in price from $\$4$ to $\$5$ causes the quantity demanded to fall from 100 to 90, so total revenue rises from $\$400$ to $\$450$. An increase in price raises $P \times Q$ because the fall in Q is proportionately smaller than the rise in P. In other

FYI
A Few Elasticities from the Real World

We have talked about what elasticity means, what determines it, and how it is calculated. Beyond these general ideas, you might ask for a specific number. How much, precisely, does the price of a particular good influence the quantity demanded?

To answer such a question, economists collect data from market outcomes and apply statistical techniques to estimate the price elasticity of demand. Here are some price elasticities of demand, obtained from various studies, for a range of goods:

Eggs	0.1
Healthcare	0.2
Rice	0.5
Housing	0.7
Beef	1.6
Restaurant Meals	2.3
Mountain Dew	4.4

These kinds of numbers are fun to think about, and they can be useful when comparing markets.

Nonetheless, one should take these estimates with a grain of salt. One reason is that the statistical techniques used to obtain them require some assumptions about the world, and these assumptions might not be true in practice. (The details of these techniques are beyond the scope of this book, but you will encounter them if you take a course in econometrics.) Another reason is that the price elasticity of demand need not be the same at all points on a demand curve, as we will see shortly in the case of a linear demand curve. For both reasons, you should not be surprised if different studies report different price elasticities of demand for the same good. ◢

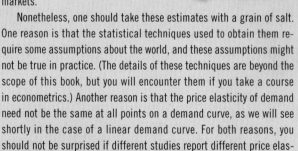

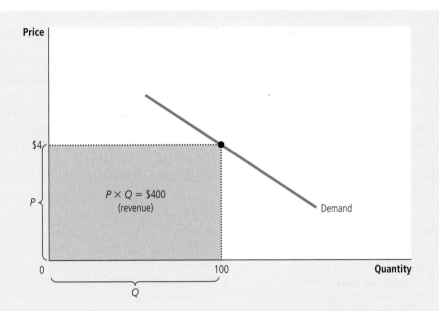

FIGURE 2

Total Revenue
The total amount paid by buyers, and received as revenue by sellers, equals the area of the box under the demand curve, $P \times Q$. Here, at a price of $4, the quantity demanded is 100 and total revenue is $400.

FIGURE 3

The impact of a price change on total revenue (the product of price and quantity) depends on the elasticity of demand. In panel (a), the demand curve is inelastic. In this case, an increase in the price leads to a decrease in quantity demanded that is proportionately smaller, so total revenue increases. Here an increase in the price from $4 to $5 causes the quantity demanded to fall from 100 to 90. Total revenue rises from $400 to $450. In panel (b), the demand curve is elastic. In this case, an increase in the price leads to a decrease in quantity demanded that is proportionately larger, so total revenue decreases. Here an increase in the price from $4 to $5 causes the quantity demanded to fall from 100 to 70. Total revenue falls from $400 to $350.

How Total Revenue Changes When Price Changes

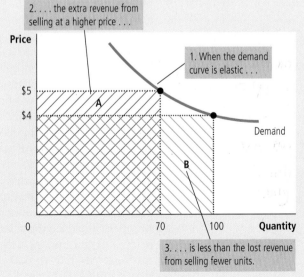

words, the extra revenue from selling units at a higher price (represented by area A in Figure 3) more than offsets the decline in revenue from selling fewer units (represented by area B).

We obtain the opposite result if demand is elastic: An increase in the price causes a decrease in total revenue. In panel (b) of Figure 3, for instance, when the price rises from $4 to $5, the quantity demanded falls from 100 to 70, so total revenue falls from $400 to $350. Because demand is elastic, the reduction in the quantity demanded is so great that it more than offsets the increase in the price. That is, an increase in price reduces $P \times Q$ because the fall in Q is proportionately greater than the rise in P. In this case, the extra revenue from selling units at a higher price (area A) is smaller than the decline in revenue from selling fewer units (area B).

The examples in this figure illustrate some general rules:

- When demand is inelastic (a price elasticity less than 1), price and total revenue move in the same direction: If the price increases, total revenue also increases.
- When demand is elastic (a price elasticity greater than 1), price and total revenue move in opposite directions: If the price increases, total revenue decreases.
- If demand is unit elastic (a price elasticity exactly equal to 1), total revenue remains constant when the price changes.

5-1f Elasticity and Total Revenue along a Linear Demand Curve

Let's examine how elasticity varies along a linear demand curve, as shown in Figure 4. We know that a straight line has a constant slope. Slope is defined as "rise over run," which here is the ratio of the change in price ("rise") to the change in quantity ("run"). This particular demand curve's slope is constant because each $1 increase in price causes the same 2-unit decrease in the quantity demanded.

Even though the slope of a linear demand curve is constant, the elasticity is not. This is true because the slope is the ratio of *changes* in the two variables, whereas the elasticity is the ratio of *percentage changes* in the two variables. You can see this by looking at the table in Figure 4, which shows the demand schedule for the linear demand curve in the graph. The table uses the midpoint method to calculate the price elasticity of demand. The table illustrates the following: *At points with a low price and high quantity, the demand curve is inelastic. At points with a high price and low quantity, the demand curve is elastic.*

The explanation for this fact comes from the arithmetic of percentage changes. When the price is low and consumers are buying a lot, a $1 price increase and 2-unit reduction in quantity demanded constitute a large percentage increase in the price and a small percentage decrease in quantity demanded, resulting in a small elasticity. By contrast, when the price is high and consumers are not buying much, the same $1 price increase and 2-unit reduction in quantity demanded constitute a small percentage increase in the price and a large percentage decrease in quantity demanded, resulting in a large elasticity.

The table also presents total revenue at each point on the demand curve. These numbers illustrate the relationship between total revenue and elasticity. When the price is $1, for instance, demand is inelastic and a price increase to $2 raises total revenue. When the price is $5, demand is elastic and a price increase to $6 reduces total revenue. Between $3 and $4, demand is exactly unit elastic and total revenue is the same at these two prices.

The slope of a linear demand curve is constant, but its elasticity is not. The demand schedule in the table was used to calculate the price elasticity of demand by the midpoint method. At points with a low price and high quantity, the demand curve is inelastic. At points with a high price and low quantity, the demand curve is elastic.

FIGURE 4

Elasticity of a Linear Demand Curve

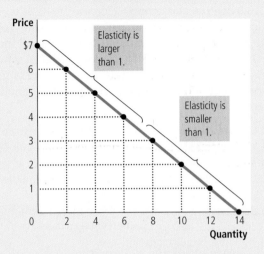

Price	Quantity	Total Revenue (Price × Quantity)	Percentage Change in Price	Percentage Change in Quantity	Elasticity	Description
$7	0	$0				
6	2	12	15	200	13.0	Elastic
5	4	20	18	67	3.7	Elastic
4	6	24	22	40	1.8	Elastic
3	8	24	29	29	1.0	Unit elastic
2	10	20	40	22	0.6	Inelastic
1	12	12	67	18	0.3	Inelastic
0	14	0	200	15	0.1	Inelastic

The linear demand curve illustrates that the price elasticity of demand need not be the same at all points on a demand curve. A constant elasticity is possible, but it is not always the case.

5-1g Other Demand Elasticities

In addition to the price elasticity of demand, economists use other elasticities to describe the behavior of buyers in a market.

The Income Elasticity of Demand The **income elasticity of demand** measures how the quantity demanded changes as consumer income changes. It is calculated as the percentage change in quantity demanded divided by the percentage change in income. That is,

$$\text{Income elasticity of demand} = \frac{\text{Percentage change in quantity demanded}}{\text{Percentage change in income}}.$$

income elasticity of demand
a measure of how much the quantity demanded of a good responds to a change in consumers' income, computed as the percentage change in quantity demanded divided by the percentage change in income

substitute= Positive
Complement =negative

As we discussed in Chapter 4, most goods are *normal goods:* Higher income raises the quantity demanded. Because quantity demanded and income move in the same direction, normal goods have positive income elasticities. A few goods, such as bus rides, are *inferior goods:* Higher income lowers the quantity demanded. Because quantity demanded and income move in opposite directions, inferior goods have negative income elasticities.

Even among normal goods, income elasticities vary substantially in size. Necessities, such as food and clothing, tend to have small income elasticities because consumers choose to buy some of these goods even when their incomes are low. Luxuries, such as caviar and diamonds, tend to have large income elasticities because consumers feel that they can do without these goods altogether if their incomes are too low.

cross-price elasticity of demand

a measure of how much the quantity demanded of one good responds to a change in the price of another good, computed as the percentage change in quantity demanded of the first good divided by the percentage change in price of the second good

on test

The Cross-Price Elasticity of Demand   The **cross-price elasticity of demand** measures how the quantity demanded of one good responds to a change in the price of another good. It is calculated as the percentage change in quantity demanded of good 1 divided by the percentage change in the price of good 2. That is,

$$\text{Cross-price elasticity of demand} = \frac{\text{Percentage change in quantity demanded of good 1}}{\text{Percentage change in the price of good 2}}.$$

Whether the cross-price elasticity is a positive or negative number depends on whether the two goods are substitutes or complements. As we discussed in Chapter 4, *substitutes* are goods that are typically used in place of one another, such as hamburgers and hot dogs. An increase in hot dog prices induces people to grill hamburgers instead. Because the price of hot dogs and the quantity of hamburgers demanded move in the same direction, the cross-price elasticity is positive. Conversely, *complements* are goods that are typically used together, such as computers and software. In this case, the cross-price elasticity is negative, indicating that an increase in the price of computers reduces the quantity of software demanded.

Quick Quiz   *Define the price elasticity of demand.* • *Explain the relationship between total revenue and the price elasticity of demand.*

5-2 The Elasticity of Supply

When we introduced supply in Chapter 4, we noted that producers of a good offer to sell more of it when the price of the good rises. To turn from qualitative to quantitative statements about quantity supplied, we once again use the concept of elasticity.

price elasticity of supply

a measure of how much the quantity supplied of a good responds to a change in the price of that good, computed as the percentage change in quantity supplied divided by the percentage change in price

5-2a The Price Elasticity of Supply and Its Determinants

The law of supply states that higher prices raise the quantity supplied. The **price elasticity of supply** measures how much the quantity supplied responds to changes in the price. Supply of a good is said to be *elastic* if the quantity supplied responds substantially to changes in the price. Supply is said to be *inelastic* if the quantity supplied responds only slightly to changes in the price.

The price elasticity of supply depends on the flexibility of sellers to change the amount of the good they produce. For example, beachfront land has an inelastic supply because it is almost impossible to produce more of it. By contrast, manu-factured goods, such as books, cars, and televisions, have elastic supplies because firms that produce them can run their factories longer in response to a higher price.

In most markets, a key determinant of the price elasticity of supply is the time period being considered. Supply is usually more elastic in the long run than in the short run. Over short periods of time, firms cannot easily change the size of their factories to make more or less of a good. Thus, in the short run, the quantity supplied is not very responsive to the price. By contrast, over longer periods, firms can build new factories or close old ones. In addition, new firms can enter a market, and old firms can exit. Thus, in the long run, the quantity supplied can respond substantially to price changes.

5-2b Computing the Price Elasticity of Supply

Now that we have a general understanding about the price elasticity of supply, let's be more precise. Economists compute the price elasticity of supply as the percentage change in the quantity supplied divided by the percentage change in the price. That is,

$$\text{Price elasticity of supply} = \frac{\text{Percentage change in quantity supplied}}{\text{Percentage change in price}}.$$

For example, suppose that an increase in the price of milk from $2.85 to $3.15 a gallon raises the amount that dairy farmers produce from 9,000 to 11,000 gallons per month. Using the midpoint method, we calculate the percentage change in price as

$$\text{Percentage change in price} = (3.15 - 2.85)/3.00 \times 100 = 10 \text{ percent}.$$

Similarly, we calculate the percentage change in quantity supplied as

$$\text{Percentage change in quantity supplied} = (11,000 - 9,000)/10,000 \times 100 = 20 \text{ percent}.$$

In this case, the price elasticity of supply is

$$\text{Price elasticity of supply} = \frac{20 \text{ percent}}{10 \text{ percent}} = 2.$$

In this example, the elasticity of 2 indicates that the quantity supplied changes proportionately twice as much as the price.

5-2c The Variety of Supply Curves

Because the price elasticity of supply measures the responsiveness of quantity supplied to the price, it is reflected in the appearance of the supply curve. Figure 5 shows five cases. In the extreme case of a zero elasticity, as shown in panel (a), supply is *perfectly inelastic* and the supply curve is vertical. In this case, the quantity supplied is the same regardless of the price. As the elasticity rises, the supply curve gets flatter, which shows that the quantity supplied responds more to changes in the price. At the opposite extreme, shown in panel (e), supply is *perfectly elastic*. This occurs as the price elasticity of supply approaches infinity and the supply curve becomes horizontal, meaning that very small changes in the price lead to very large changes in the quantity supplied.

In some markets, the elasticity of supply is not constant but varies over the supply curve. Figure 6 shows a typical case for an industry in which firms have

FIGURE 5

The Price Elasticity of Supply

The price elasticity of supply determines whether the supply curve is steep or flat. Note that all percentage changes are calculated using the midpoint method.

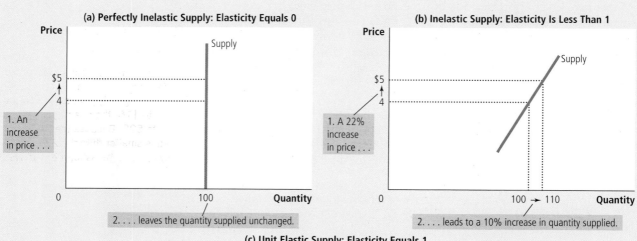

(a) Perfectly Inelastic Supply: Elasticity Equals 0

Price

Supply

$5
4

1. An increase in price . . .

0   100   Quantity

2. . . . leaves the quantity supplied unchanged.

(b) Inelastic Supply: Elasticity Is Less Than 1

Price

Supply

$5
4

1. A 22% increase in price . . .

0   100 → 110   Quantity

2. . . . leads to a 10% increase in quantity supplied.

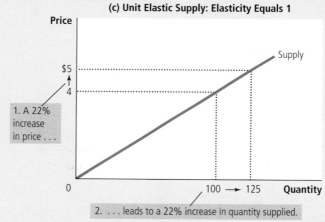

(c) Unit Elastic Supply: Elasticity Equals 1

Price

Supply

$5
4

1. A 22% increase in price . . .

0   100 → 125   Quantity

2. . . . leads to a 22% increase in quantity supplied.

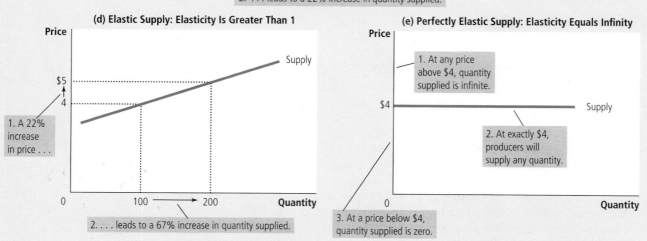

(d) Elastic Supply: Elasticity Is Greater Than 1

Price

Supply

$5
4

1. A 22% increase in price . . .

0   100 → 200   Quantity

2. . . . leads to a 67% increase in quantity supplied.

(e) Perfectly Elastic Supply: Elasticity Equals Infinity

Price

1. At any price above $4, quantity supplied is infinite.

$4   Supply

2. At exactly $4, producers will supply any quantity.

0   Quantity

3. At a price below $4, quantity supplied is zero.

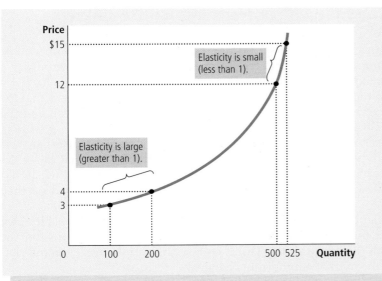

FIGURE 6

How the Price Elasticity of Supply Can Vary
Because firms often have a maximum capacity for production, the elasticity of supply may be very high at low levels of quantity supplied and very low at high levels of quantity supplied. Here an increase in price from $3 to $4 increases the quantity supplied from 100 to 200. Because the 67% increase in quantity supplied (computed using the midpoint method) is larger than the 29% increase in price, the supply curve is elastic in this range. By contrast, when the price rises from $12 to $15, the quantity supplied rises only from 500 to 525. Because the 5% increase in quantity supplied is smaller than the 22% increase in price, the supply curve is inelastic in this range.

factories with a limited capacity for production. For low levels of quantity supplied, the elasticity of supply is high, indicating that firms respond substantially to changes in the price. In this region, firms have capacity for production that is not being used, such as plants and equipment that are idle for all or part of the day. Small increases in price make it profitable for firms to begin using this idle capacity. As the quantity supplied rises, firms begin to reach capacity. Once capacity is fully used, increasing production further requires the construction of new plants. To induce firms to incur this extra expense, the price must rise substantially, so supply becomes less elastic.

Figure 6 presents a numerical example of this phenomenon. When the price rises from $3 to $4 (a 29 percent increase, according to the midpoint method), the quantity supplied rises from 100 to 200 (a 67 percent increase). Because quantity supplied changes proportionately more than the price, the supply curve has elasticity greater than 1. By contrast, when the price rises from $12 to $15 (a 22 percent increase), the quantity supplied rises from 500 to 525 (a 5 percent increase). In this case, quantity supplied moves proportionately less than the price, so the elasticity is less than 1.

Quick Quiz   *Define the price elasticity of supply. • Explain why the price elasticity of supply might be different in the long run than in the short run.*

5-3 Three Applications of Supply, Demand, and Elasticity

Can good news for farming be bad news for farmers? Why did OPEC, the international oil cartel, fail to keep the price of oil high? Does drug interdiction increase or decrease drug-related crime? At first, these questions might seem to have little in common. Yet all three questions are about markets, and all markets are subject to the forces of supply and demand. Here we apply the versatile tools of supply, demand, and elasticity to answer these seemingly complex questions.

5-3a Can Good News for Farming Be Bad News for Farmers?

Imagine yourself as a Kansas wheat farmer. Because you earn all your income from selling wheat, you devote much effort to making your land as productive as possible. You monitor weather and soil conditions, check your fields for pests and disease, and study the latest advances in farm technology. You know that the more wheat you grow, the more you will have to sell after the harvest, and the higher your income and standard of living will be.

One day, Kansas State University announces a major discovery. Researchers in its agronomy department have devised a new hybrid of wheat that raises the amount farmers can produce from each acre of land by 20 percent. How should you react to this news? Does this discovery make you better off or worse off than you were before?

Recall from Chapter 4 that we answer such questions in three steps. First, we examine whether the supply or demand curve shifts. Second, we consider the direction in which the curve shifts. Third, we use the supply-and-demand diagram to see how the market equilibrium changes.

In this case, the discovery of the new hybrid affects the supply curve. Because the hybrid increases the amount of wheat that can be produced on each acre of land, farmers are now willing to supply more wheat at any given price. In other words, the supply curve shifts to the right. The demand curve remains the same because consumers' desire to buy wheat products at any given price is not affected by the introduction of a new hybrid. Figure 7 shows an example of such a change. When the supply curve shifts from S_1 to S_2, the quantity of wheat sold increases from 100 to 110 and the price of wheat falls from \$3 to \$2.

Does this discovery make farmers better off? As a first cut to answering this question, consider what happens to the total revenue received by farmers. Farmers' total revenue is $P \times Q$, the price of the wheat times the quantity sold. The discovery affects farmers in two conflicting ways. The hybrid allows farmers to produce more wheat (Q rises), but now each bushel of wheat sells for less (P falls).

FIGURE 7

An Increase in Supply in the Market for Wheat
When an advance in farm technology increases the supply of wheat from S_1 to S_2, the price of wheat falls. Because the demand for wheat is inelastic, the increase in the quantity sold from 100 to 110 is proportionately smaller than the decrease in the price from \$3 to \$2. As a result, farmers' total revenue falls from \$300 (\$3 × 100) to \$220 (\$2 × 110).

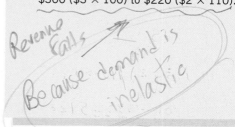

Revenue falls ↗
Because demand is inelastic

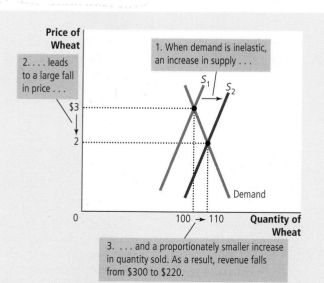

Price of Wheat

2. . . . leads to a large fall in price . . .

1. When demand is inelastic, an increase in supply . . .

S_1 S_2

\$3

2

Demand

0   100 → 110   Quantity of Wheat

3. . . . and a proportionately smaller increase in quantity sold. As a result, revenue falls from \$300 to \$220.

Whether total revenue rises or falls depends on the elasticity of demand. In practice, the demand for basic foodstuffs such as wheat is usually inelastic because these items are relatively inexpensive and have few good substitutes. When the demand curve is inelastic, as it is in Figure 7, a decrease in price causes total revenue to fall. You can see this in the figure: The price of wheat falls substantially, whereas the quantity of wheat sold rises only slightly. Total revenue falls from $300 to $220. Thus, the discovery of the new hybrid lowers the total revenue that farmers receive from the sale of their crops.

If farmers are made worse off by the discovery of this new hybrid, one might wonder why they adopt it. The answer goes to the heart of how competitive markets work. Because each farmer is only a small part of the market for wheat, she takes the price of wheat as given. For any given price of wheat, it is better to use the new hybrid to produce and sell more wheat. Yet when all farmers do this, the supply of wheat increases, the price falls, and farmers are worse off.

This example may at first seem hypothetical, but it helps to explain a major change in the U.S. economy over the past century. Two hundred years ago, most Americans lived on farms. Knowledge about farm methods was sufficiently primitive that most Americans had to be farmers to produce enough food to feed the nation's population. Yet over time, advances in farm technology increased the amount of food that each farmer could produce. This increase in food supply, together with inelastic food demand, caused farm revenues to fall, which in turn encouraged people to leave farming.

A few numbers show the magnitude of this historic change. As recently as 1950, 10 million people worked on farms in the United States, representing 17 percent of the labor force. Today, fewer than 3 million people work on farms, or 2 percent of the labor force. This change coincided with tremendous advances in farm productivity: Despite the 70 percent drop in the number of farmers, U.S. farms now produce more than twice the output of crops and livestock that they did in 1950.

This analysis of the market for farm products also helps to explain a seeming paradox of public policy: Certain farm programs try to help farmers by inducing them *not* to plant crops on all of their land. The purpose of these programs is to reduce the supply of farm products and thereby raise prices. With inelastic demand for their products, farmers as a group receive greater total revenue if they supply a smaller crop to the market. No single farmer would choose to leave her land

fallow on her own because each takes the market price as given. But if all farmers do so together, they can all be better off.

When analyzing the effects of farm technology or farm policy, it is important to keep in mind that what is good for farmers is not necessarily good for society as a whole. Improvement in farm technology can be bad for farmers because it makes farmers increasingly unnecessary, but it is surely good for consumers who pay less for food. Similarly, a policy aimed at reducing the supply of farm products may raise the incomes of farmers, but it does so at the expense of consumers.

5-3b Why Did OPEC Fail to Keep the Price of Oil High?

Many of the most disruptive events for the world's economies over the past several decades have originated in the world market for oil. In the 1970s, members of the Organization of Petroleum Exporting Countries (OPEC) decided to raise the world price of oil to increase their incomes. These countries accomplished this goal by agreeing to jointly reduce the amount of oil they supplied. As a result, the price of oil (adjusted for overall inflation) rose more than 50 percent from 1973 to 1974. Then, a few years later, OPEC did the same thing again. From 1979 to 1981, the price of oil approximately doubled.

Yet OPEC found it difficult to maintain such a high price. From 1982 to 1985, the price of oil steadily declined about 10 percent per year. Dissatisfaction and disarray soon prevailed among the OPEC countries. In 1986, cooperation among OPEC members completely broke down, and the price of oil plunged 45 percent. In 1990, the price of oil (adjusted for overall inflation) was back to where it began in 1970, and it stayed at that low level throughout most of the 1990s. (In the first decade of the 21st century, the price of oil fluctuated substantially once again, but the main driving force was changes in world demand rather than OPEC supply restrictions. Early in the decade, oil demand and prices spiked up, in part because of a large and rapidly growing Chinese economy. Prices plunged in 2008–2009 as the world economy fell into a deep recession and then started rising once again as the world economy started to recover.)

The OPEC episodes of the 1970s and 1980s show how supply and demand can behave differently in the short run and in the long run. In the short run, both the supply and demand for oil are relatively inelastic. Supply is inelastic because the quantity of known oil reserves and the capacity for oil extraction cannot be changed quickly. Demand is inelastic because buying habits do not respond immediately to changes in price. Thus, as panel (a) of Figure 8 shows, the short-run supply and demand curves are steep. When the supply of oil shifts from S_1 to S_2, the price increase from P_1 to P_2 is large.

The situation is very different in the long run. Over long periods of time, producers of oil outside OPEC respond to high prices by increasing oil exploration and by building new extraction capacity. Consumers respond with greater conservation, such as by replacing old inefficient cars with newer efficient ones. Thus, as panel (b) of Figure 8 shows, the long-run supply and demand curves are more elastic. In the long run, the shift in the supply curve from S_1 to S_2 causes a much smaller increase in the price.

This analysis shows why OPEC succeeded in maintaining a high price of oil only in the short run. When OPEC countries agreed to reduce their production of oil, they shifted the supply curve to the left. Even though each OPEC member sold less oil, the price rose by so much in the short run that OPEC incomes rose. By contrast, in the long run, when supply and demand are more elastic, the same

Figure 9. The demand curve shifts to the left from D_1 to D_2. As a result, the equilibrium quantity falls from Q_1 to Q_2, and the equilibrium price falls from P_1 to P_2. Total revenue, $P \times Q$, also falls. Thus, in contrast to drug interdiction, drug education can reduce both drug use and drug-related crime.

Advocates of drug interdiction might argue that the long-run effects of this policy are different from the short-run effects because the elasticity of demand depends on the time horizon. The demand for drugs is probably inelastic over short periods because higher prices do not substantially affect drug use by established addicts. But demand may be more elastic over longer periods because higher prices would discourage experimentation with drugs among the young and, over time, lead to fewer drug addicts. In this case, drug interdiction would increase drug-related crime in the short run while decreasing it in the long run.

Quick Quiz *How might a drought that destroys half of all farm crops be good for farmers? If such a drought is good for farmers, why don't farmers destroy their own crops in the absence of a drought?*

5-4 Conclusion

According to an old quip, even a parrot can become an economist simply by learning to say "supply and demand." These last two chapters should have convinced you that there is much truth in this statement. The tools of supply and demand allow you to analyze many of the most important events and policies that shape the economy. You are now well on your way to becoming an economist (or at least a well-educated parrot).

Summary

- The price elasticity of demand measures how much the quantity demanded responds to changes in the price. Demand tends to be more elastic if close substitutes are available, if the good is a luxury rather than a necessity, if the market is narrowly defined, or if buyers have substantial time to react to a price change.

- The price elasticity of demand is calculated as the percentage change in quantity demanded divided by the percentage change in price. If quantity demanded moves proportionately less than the price, then the elasticity is less than 1 and demand is said to be inelastic. If quantity demanded moves proportionately more than the price, then the elasticity is greater than 1 and demand is said to be elastic.

- Total revenue, the total amount paid for a good, equals the price of the good times the quantity sold. For inelastic demand curves, total revenue moves in the same direction as the price. For elastic demand curves, total revenue moves in the opposite direction as the price.

- The income elasticity of demand measures how much the quantity demanded responds to changes in consumers' income. The cross-price elasticity of demand measures how much the quantity demanded of one good responds to changes in the price of another good.

- The price elasticity of supply measures how much the quantity supplied responds to changes in the price. This elasticity often depends on the time horizon under consideration. In most markets, supply is more elastic in the long run than in the short run.

- The price elasticity of supply is calculated as the percentage change in quantity supplied divided by the percentage change in price. If quantity supplied moves proportionately less than the price, then the elasticity is less than 1 and supply is said to be inelastic. If quantity supplied moves proportionately more than the price, then the elasticity is greater than 1 and supply is said to be elastic.

- The tools of supply and demand can be applied in many different kinds of markets. This chapter uses them to analyze the market for wheat, the market for oil, and the market for illegal drugs.

Key Concepts

elasticity, *p. 90*
price elasticity of demand, *p. 90*

total revenue, *p. 94*
income elasticity of demand, *p. 97*

cross-price elasticity of demand, *p. 98*
price elasticity of supply, *p. 98*

Questions for Review

1. Define the price elasticity of demand and the income elasticity of demand.

2. List and explain the four determinants of the price elasticity of demand discussed in the chapter.

3. If the elasticity is greater than 1, is demand elastic or inelastic? If the elasticity equals zero, is demand perfectly elastic or perfectly inelastic?

4. On a supply-and-demand diagram, show equilibrium price, equilibrium quantity, and the total revenue received by producers.

5. If demand is elastic, how will an increase in price change total revenue? Explain.

6. What do we call a good with an income elasticity less than zero?

7. How is the price elasticity of supply calculated? Explain what it measures.

8. If a fixed quantity of a good is available, and no more can be made, what is the price elasticity of supply?

9. A storm destroys half the fava bean crop. Is this event more likely to hurt fava bean farmers if the demand for fava beans is very elastic or very inelastic? Explain.

Quick Check Multiple Choice

1. A life-saving medicine without any close substitutes will tend to have
   a. a small elasticity of demand.
   b. a large elasticity of demand.
   c. a small elasticity of supply.
   d. a large elasticity of supply.

2. The price of a good rises from $8 to $12, and the quantity demanded falls from 110 to 90 units. Calculated with the midpoint method, the elasticity is
   a. 1/5.
   b. 1/2.
   c. 2.
   d. 5.

3. A linear, downward-sloping demand curve is
   a. inelastic.
   b. unit elastic.
   c. elastic.
   d. inelastic at some points, and elastic at others.

4. The ability of firms to enter and exit a market over time means that, in the long run,
   a. the demand curve is more elastic.
   b. the demand curve is less elastic.
   c. the supply curve is more elastic.
   d. the supply curve is less elastic.

5. An increase in the supply of a good will decrease the total revenue producers receive if
   a. the demand curve is inelastic.
   b. the demand curve is elastic.
   c. the supply curve is inelastic.
   d. the supply curve is elastic.

6. The price of coffee rose sharply last month, while the quantity sold remained the same. Each of five people suggests an explanation:

   TOM: Demand increased, but supply was perfectly inelastic.
   DICK: Demand increased, but it was perfectly inelastic.
   HARRY: Demand increased, but supply decreased at the same time.
   LARRY: Supply decreased, but demand was unit elastic.
   MARY: Supply decreased, but demand was perfectly inelastic.

   Who could possibly be right?
   a. Tom, Dick, and Harry
   b. Tom, Dick, and Mary
   c. Tom, Harry, and Mary
   d. Dick, Harry, and Larry
   e. Dick, Harry, and Mary

Problems and Applications

1. For each of the following pairs of goods, which good would you expect to have more elastic demand and why?
   a. required textbooks or mystery novels
   b. Beethoven recordings or classical music recordings in general
   c. subway rides during the next six months or subway rides during the next five years
   d. root beer or water

2. Suppose that business travelers and vacationers have the following demand for airline tickets from New York to Boston:

Price	Quantity Demanded (business travelers)	Quantity Demanded (vacationers)
$150	2,100 tickets	1,000 tickets
200	2,000	800
250	1,900	600
300	1,800	400

   a. As the price of tickets rises from $200 to $250, what is the price elasticity of demand for (i) business travelers and (ii) vacationers? (Use the midpoint method in your calculations.)
   b. Why might vacationers have a different elasticity from business travelers?

3. Suppose the price elasticity of demand for heating oil is 0.2 in the short run and 0.7 in the long run.
   a. If the price of heating oil rises from $1.80 to $2.20 per gallon, what happens to the quantity of heating oil demanded in the short run? In the long run? (Use the midpoint method in your calculations.)
   b. Why might this elasticity depend on the time horizon?

4. A price change causes the quantity demanded of a good to decrease by 30 percent, while the total revenue of that good increases by 15 percent. Is the demand curve elastic or inelastic? Explain.

5. Cups of coffee and donuts are complements. Both have inelastic demand. A hurricane destroys half the coffee bean crop. Use appropriately labeled diagrams to answer the following questions.
   a. What happens to the price of coffee beans?
   b. What happens to the price of a cup of coffee? What happens to total expenditure on cups of coffee?
   c. What happens to the price of donuts? What happens to total expenditure on donuts?

6. Suppose that your demand schedule for DVDs is as follows:

Price	Quantity Demanded (income = $10,000)	Quantity Demanded (income = $12,000)
$8	40 DVDs	50 DVDs
10	32	45
12	24	30
14	16	20
16	8	12

   a. Use the midpoint method to calculate your price elasticity of demand as the price of DVDs increases from $8 to $10 if (i) your income is $10,000 and (ii) your income is $12,000.
   b. Calculate your income elasticity of demand as your income increases from $10,000 to $12,000 if (i) the price is $12 and (ii) the price is $16.

7. Maria has decided always to spend one-third of her income on clothing.
   a. What is her income elasticity of clothing demand?
   b. What is her price elasticity of clothing demand?
   c. If Maria's tastes change and she decides to spend only one-fourth of her income on clothing, how does her demand curve change? What is her income elasticity and price elasticity now?

8. The *New York Times* reported (Feb. 17, 1996) that subway ridership declined after a fare increase: "There were nearly 4 million fewer riders in December 1995, the first full month after the price of a token increased 25 cents to $1.50, than in the previous December, a 4.3 percent decline."
   a. Use these data to estimate the price elasticity of demand for subway rides.
   b. According to your estimate, what happens to the Transit Authority's revenue when the fare rises?
   c. Why might your estimate of the elasticity be unreliable?

9. Two drivers—Walt and Jessie—each drive up to a gas station. Before looking at the price, each places an order. Walt says, "I'd like 10 gallons of gas." Jessie says, "I'd like $10 worth of gas." What is each driver's price elasticity of demand?

10. Consider public policy aimed at smoking.
    a. Studies indicate that the price elasticity of demand for cigarettes is about 0.4. If a pack of cigarettes currently costs $2 and the government wants to reduce smoking by 20 percent, by how much should it increase the price?

b. If the government permanently increases the price of cigarettes, will the policy have a larger effect on smoking one year from now or five years from now?

c. Studies also find that teenagers have a higher price elasticity of demand than do adults. Why might this be true?

11. You are the curator of a museum. The museum is running short of funds, so you decide to increase revenue. Should you increase or decrease the price of admission? Explain.

12. Explain why the following might be true: A drought around the world raises the total revenue that farmers receive from the sale of grain, but a drought only in Kansas reduces the total revenue that Kansas farmers receive.

Go to CengageBrain.com to purchase access to the proven, critical Study Guide to accompany this text, which features additional notes and context, practice tests, and much more.

Supply, Demand, and Government Policies

Economists have two roles. As scientists, they develop and test theories to explain the world around them. As policy advisers, they use their theories to help change the world for the better. The focus of the preceding two chapters has been scientific. We have seen how supply and demand determine the price of a good and the quantity of the good sold. We have also seen how various events shift supply and demand and thereby change the equilibrium price and quantity. And we have developed the concept of elasticity to gauge the size of these changes.

This chapter offers our first look at policy. Here we analyze various types of government policy using only the tools of supply and demand. As you will see, the analysis yields some surprising insights. Policies often have effects that their architects did not intend or anticipate.

We begin by considering policies that directly control prices. For example, rent-control laws dictate a maximum rent that landlords may charge tenants. Minimum-wage laws dictate the lowest wage that firms may pay workers. Price controls are usually enacted when policymakers believe that the market price of a good or service is unfair to buyers or sellers. Yet, as we will see, these policies can generate inequities of their own.

After discussing price controls, we consider the impact of taxes. Policymakers use taxes to raise revenue for public purposes and to influence market outcomes. Although the prevalence of taxes in our economy is obvious, their effects are not. For example, when the government levies a tax on the amount that firms pay their workers, do the firms or the workers bear the burden of the tax? The answer is not at all clear—until we apply the powerful tools of supply and demand.

6-1 Controls on Prices

To see how price controls affect market outcomes, let's look once again at the market for ice cream. As we saw in Chapter 4, if ice cream is sold in a competitive market free of government regulation, the price of ice cream adjusts to balance supply and demand: At the equilibrium price, the quantity of ice cream that buyers want to buy exactly equals the quantity that sellers want to sell. To be concrete, let's suppose that the equilibrium price is $3 per cone.

Some people may not be happy with the outcome of this free-market process. The American Association of Ice-Cream Eaters complains that the $3 price is too high for everyone to enjoy a cone a day (their recommended daily allowance). Meanwhile, the National Organization of Ice-Cream Makers complains that the $3 price—the result of "cutthroat competition"—is too low and is depressing the incomes of its members. Each of these groups lobbies the government to pass laws that alter the market outcome by directly controlling the price of an ice-cream cone.

Because buyers of any good always want a lower price while sellers want a higher price, the interests of the two groups conflict. If the Ice-Cream Eaters are successful in their lobbying, the government imposes a legal maximum on the price at which ice-cream cones can be sold. Because the price is not allowed to rise above this level, the legislated maximum is called a **price ceiling**. By contrast, if the Ice-Cream Makers are successful, the government imposes a legal minimum on the price. Because the price cannot fall below this level, the legislated minimum is called a **price floor**. Let us consider the effects of these policies in turn.

price ceiling
a legal maximum on the price at which a good can be sold

price floor
a legal minimum on the price at which a good can be sold

6-1a How Price Ceilings Affect Market Outcomes

When the government, moved by the complaints and campaign contributions of the Ice-Cream Eaters, imposes a price ceiling on the market for ice cream, two outcomes are possible. In panel (a) of Figure 1, the government imposes a price ceiling of $4 per cone. In this case, because the price that balances supply and demand ($3) is below the ceiling, the price ceiling is *not binding*. Market forces naturally move the economy to the equilibrium, and the price ceiling has no effect on the price or the quantity sold.

Panel (b) of Figure 1 shows the other, more interesting, possibility. In this case, the government imposes a price ceiling of $2 per cone. Because the equilibrium price of $3 is above the price ceiling, the ceiling is a *binding constraint* on the market. The forces of supply and demand tend to move the price toward the equilibrium price, but when the market price hits the ceiling, it cannot, by law, rise any further. Thus, the market price equals the price ceiling. At this price, the quantity

In panel (a), the government imposes a price ceiling of $4. Because the price ceiling is above the equilibrium price of $3, the price ceiling has no effect, and the market can reach the equilibrium of supply and demand. In this equilibrium, quantity supplied and quantity demanded both equal 100 cones. In panel (b), the government imposes a price ceiling of $2. Because the price ceiling is below the equilibrium price of $3, the market price equals $2. At this price, 125 cones are demanded and only 75 are supplied, so there is a shortage of 50 cones.

FIGURE 1

A Market with a Price Ceiling

(a) A Price Ceiling That Is Not Binding

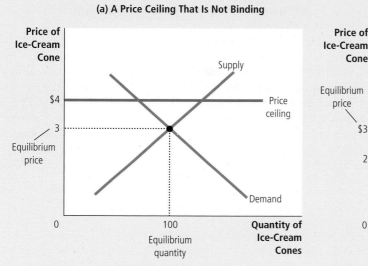

(b) A Price Ceiling That Is Binding

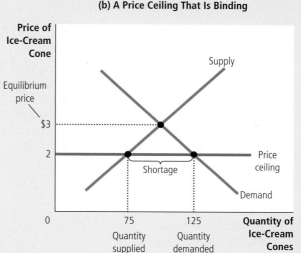

of ice cream demanded (125 cones in Figure 1) exceeds the quantity supplied (75 cones). There is a shortage: 50 people who want to buy ice cream at the going price are unable to do so.

In response to this shortage, some mechanism for rationing ice cream will naturally develop. The mechanism could be long lines: Buyers who are willing to arrive early and wait in line get a cone, but those unwilling to wait do not. Alternatively, sellers could ration ice-cream cones according to their own personal biases, selling them only to friends, relatives, or members of their own racial or ethnic group. Notice that even though the price ceiling was motivated by a desire to help buyers of ice cream, not all buyers benefit from the policy. Some buyers do get to pay a lower price, although they may have to wait in line to do so, but other buyers cannot get any ice cream at all.

This example in the market for ice cream shows a general result: *When the government imposes a binding price ceiling on a competitive market, a shortage of the good arises, and sellers must ration the scarce goods among the large number of potential buyers.* The rationing mechanisms that develop under price ceilings are rarely desirable. Long lines are inefficient because they waste buyers' time. Discrimination according to seller bias is both inefficient (because the good does not necessarily go to the buyer who values it most highly) and potentially unfair. By contrast, the rationing mechanism in a free, competitive market is both efficient and impersonal. When the market for ice cream reaches its equilibrium, anyone who wants to pay the market price can get a cone. Free markets ration goods with prices.

Lines at the Gas Pump

As we discussed in Chapter 5, in 1973 the Organization of Petroleum
Exporting Countries (OPEC) raised the price of crude oil in world oil
markets. Because crude oil is the major input used to make gasoline, the
higher oil prices reduced the supply of gasoline. Long lines at gas stations
became commonplace, and motorists often had to wait for hours to buy only a
few gallons of gas.

What was responsible for the long gas lines? Most people blame OPEC. Surely,
if OPEC had not raised the price of crude oil, the shortage of gasoline would not
have occurred. Yet economists blame U.S. government regulations that limited
the price oil companies could charge for gasoline.

Figure 2 shows what happened. As shown in panel (a), before OPEC raised the
price of crude oil, the equilibrium price of gasoline, P_1, was below the price ceiling. The price regulation, therefore, had no effect. When the price of crude oil rose,
however, the situation changed. The increase in the price of crude oil raised the
cost of producing gasoline, and this reduced the supply of gasoline. As panel (b)
shows, the supply curve shifted to the left from S_1 to S_2. In an unregulated market,
this shift in supply would have raised the equilibrium price of gasoline from P_1
to P_2, and no shortage would have resulted. Instead, the price ceiling prevented
the price from rising to the equilibrium level. At the price ceiling, producers were

---

FIGURE 2

**The Market for Gasoline with a
Price Ceiling**

Panel (a) shows the gasoline market when the price ceiling is not binding because the
equilibrium price, P_1, is below the ceiling. Panel (b) shows the gasoline market after
an increase in the price of crude oil (an input into making gasoline) shifts the supply
curve to the left from S_1 to S_2. In an unregulated market, the price would have risen
from P_1 to P_2. The price ceiling, however, prevents this from happening. At the binding
price ceiling, consumers are willing to buy Q_D, but producers of gasoline are willing to
sell only Q_S. The difference between quantity demanded and quantity supplied, Q_D-Q_S,
measures the gasoline shortage.

(a) The Price Ceiling on Gasoline Is Not Binding

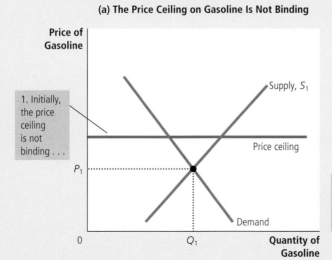

(b) The Price Ceiling on Gasoline Is Binding

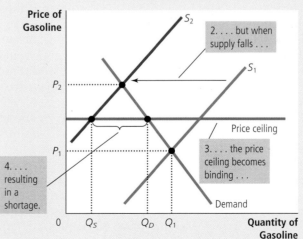

willing to sell Q_S, and consumers were willing to buy Q_D. Thus, the shift in supply caused a severe shortage at the regulated price.

Eventually, the laws regulating the price of gasoline were repealed. Lawmakers came to understand that they were partly responsible for the many hours Americans lost waiting in line to buy gasoline. Today, when the price of crude oil changes, the price of gasoline can adjust to bring supply and demand into equilibrium. ◢

case study **Rent Control in the Short Run and the Long Run**
One common example of a price ceiling is rent control. In many cities, the local government places a ceiling on rents that landlords may charge their tenants. The goal of this policy is to help the poor by making housing more affordable. Economists often criticize rent control, arguing that it is a highly inefficient way to help the poor raise their standard of living. One economist called rent control "the best way to destroy a city, other than bombing."

The adverse effects of rent control are less apparent to the general population because these effects occur over many years. In the short run, landlords have a fixed number of apartments to rent, and they cannot adjust this number quickly as market conditions change. Moreover, the number of people searching for housing in a city may not be highly responsive to rents in the short run because people take time to adjust their housing arrangements. Therefore, the short-run supply and demand for housing are relatively inelastic.

Panel (a) of Figure 3 shows the short-run effects of rent control on the housing market. As with any binding price ceiling, rent control causes a shortage.

Panel (a) shows the short-run effects of rent control: Because the supply and demand curves for apartments are relatively inelastic, the price ceiling imposed by a rent-control law causes only a small shortage of housing. Panel (b) shows the long-run effects of rent control: Because the supply and demand curves for apartments are more elastic, rent control causes a large shortage.

FIGURE 3

Rent Control in the Short Run and in the Long Run

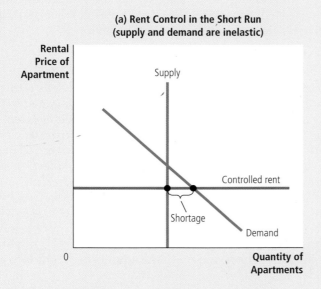

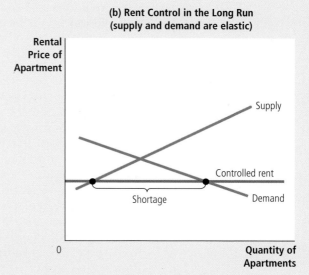

Yet because supply and demand are inelastic in the short run, the initial shortage caused by rent control is small. The primary effect in the short run is to reduce rents.

The long-run story is very different because the buyers and sellers of rental housing respond more to market conditions as time passes. On the supply side, landlords respond to low rents by not building new apartments and by failing to maintain existing ones. On the demand side, low rents encourage people to find their own apartments (rather than living with their parents or sharing apartments with roommates) and induce more people to move into a city. Therefore, both supply and demand are more elastic in the long run.

Panel (b) of Figure 3 illustrates the housing market in the long run. When rent control depresses rents below the equilibrium level, the quantity of apartments supplied falls substantially, and the quantity of apartments demanded rises substantially. The result is a large shortage of housing.

In cities with rent control, landlords use various mechanisms to ration housing. Some landlords keep long waiting lists. Others give a preference to tenants without children. Still others discriminate on the basis of race. Sometimes apartments are allocated to those willing to offer under-the-table payments to building superintendents. In essence, these bribes bring the total price of an apartment closer to the equilibrium price.

To understand fully the effects of rent control, we have to remember one of the *Ten Principles of Economics* from Chapter 1: People respond to incentives. In free markets, landlords try to keep their buildings clean and safe because desirable apartments command higher prices. By contrast, when rent control creates shortages and waiting lists, landlords lose their incentive to respond to tenants' concerns. Why should a landlord spend money to maintain and improve the property when people are waiting to get in as it is? In the end, tenants get lower rents, but they also get lower-quality housing.

Policymakers often react to the effects of rent control by imposing additional regulations. For example, various laws make racial discrimination in housing illegal and require landlords to provide minimally adequate living conditions. These laws, however, are difficult and costly to enforce. By contrast, when rent control is eliminated and a market for housing is regulated by the forces of competition, such laws are less necessary. In a free market, the price of housing adjusts to eliminate the shortages that give rise to undesirable landlord behavior. ◢

6-1b How Price Floors Affect Market Outcomes

To examine the effects of another kind of government price control, let's return to the market for ice cream. Imagine now that the government is persuaded by the pleas of the National Organization of Ice-Cream Makers whose members feel the $3 equilibrium price is too low. In this case, the government might institute a price floor. Price floors, like price ceilings, are an attempt by the government to maintain prices at other than equilibrium levels. Whereas a price ceiling places a legal maximum on prices, a price floor places a legal minimum.

When the government imposes a price floor on the ice-cream market, two outcomes are possible. If the government imposes a price floor of $2 per cone when the equilibrium price is $3, we obtain the outcome in panel (a) of Figure 4. In this case, because the equilibrium price is above the floor, the price floor is not binding. Market forces naturally move the economy to the equilibrium, and the price floor has no effect.

Panel (b) of Figure 4 shows what happens when the government imposes a price floor of $4 per cone. In this case, because the equilibrium price of $3 is below

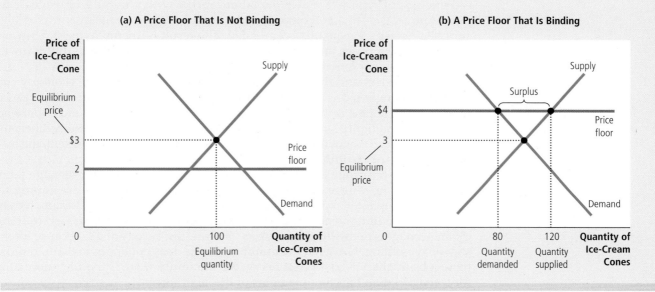

In panel (a), the government imposes a price floor of $2. Because this is below the equilibrium price of $3, the price floor has no effect. The market price adjusts to balance supply and demand. At the equilibrium, quantity supplied and quantity demanded both equal 100 cones. In panel (b), the government imposes a price floor of $4, which is above the equilibrium price of $3. Therefore, the market price equals $4. Because 120 cones are supplied at this price and only 80 are demanded, there is a surplus of 40 cones.

FIGURE 4

A Market with a Price Floor

the floor, the price floor is a binding constraint on the market. The forces of supply and demand tend to move the price toward the equilibrium price, but when the market price hits the floor, it can fall no further. The market price equals the price floor. At this floor, the quantity of ice cream supplied (120 cones) exceeds the quantity demanded (80 cones). Some people who want to sell ice cream at the going price are unable to. *Thus, a binding price floor causes a surplus.*

Just as the shortages resulting from price ceilings can lead to undesirable rationing mechanisms, so can the surpluses resulting from price floors. The sellers who appeal to the personal biases of the buyers, perhaps due to racial or familial ties, may be better able to sell their goods than those who do not. By contrast, in a free market, the price serves as the rationing mechanism, and sellers can sell all they want at the equilibrium price.

case study

The Minimum Wage

An important example of a price floor is the minimum wage. Minimum-wage laws dictate the lowest price for labor that any employer may pay. The U.S. Congress first instituted a minimum wage with the Fair Labor Standards Act of 1938 to ensure workers a minimally adequate standard of living. In 2012, the minimum wage according to federal law was $7.25 per hour. (Some states mandate minimum wages above the federal level.) Most European nations have minimum-wage laws as well, sometimes significantly higher than in the United States. For example, average income in France is 27 percent lower than it is in the United States, but the French minimum wage is 9.40 euros per hour, which is about $12 per hour.

To examine the effects of a minimum wage, we must consider the market for labor. Panel (a) of Figure 5 shows the labor market, which, like all markets, is subject to the forces of supply and demand. Workers determine the supply of labor, and firms determine the demand. If the government doesn't intervene, the wage normally adjusts to balance labor supply and labor demand.

Panel (b) of Figure 5 shows the labor market with a minimum wage. If the minimum wage is above the equilibrium level, as it is here, the quantity of labor supplied exceeds the quantity demanded. The result is unemployment. Thus, the minimum wage raises the incomes of those workers who have jobs, but it lowers the incomes of workers who cannot find jobs.

To fully understand the minimum wage, keep in mind that the economy contains not a single labor market but many labor markets for different types of workers. The impact of the minimum wage depends on the skill and experience of the worker. Highly skilled and experienced workers are not affected because their equilibrium wages are well above the minimum. For these workers, the minimum wage is not binding.

The minimum wage has its greatest impact on the market for teenage labor. The equilibrium wages of teenagers are low because teenagers are among the least skilled and least experienced members of the labor force. In addition, teenagers are often willing to accept a lower wage in exchange for on-the-job training. (Some teenagers are willing to work as "interns" for no pay at all. Because internships pay nothing, however, the minimum wage does not apply to them. If it did, these jobs might not exist.) As a result, the minimum wage is binding more often for teenagers than for other members of the labor force.

FIGURE 5

How the Minimum Wage Affects the Labor Market

Panel (a) shows a labor market in which the wage adjusts to balance labor supply and labor demand. Panel (b) shows the impact of a binding minimum wage. Because the minimum wage is a price floor, it causes a surplus: The quantity of labor supplied exceeds the quantity demanded. The result is unemployment.

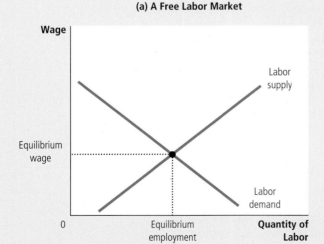

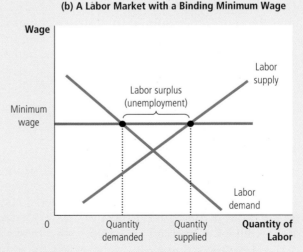

Many economists have studied how minimum-wage laws affect the teenage labor market. These researchers compare the changes in the minimum wage over time with the changes in teenage employment. Although there is some debate about how much the minimum wage affects employment, the typical study finds that a 10 percent increase in the minimum wage depresses teenage employment between 1 and 3 percent. In interpreting this estimate, note that a 10 percent increase in the minimum wage does not raise the average wage of teenagers by 10 percent. A change in the law does not directly affect those teenagers who are already paid well above the minimum, and enforcement of minimum-wage laws is not perfect. Thus, the estimated drop in employment of 1 to 3 percent is significant.

In addition to altering the quantity of labor demanded, the minimum wage alters the quantity supplied. Because the minimum wage raises the wage that teenagers can earn, it increases the number of teenagers who choose to look for jobs. Studies have found that a higher minimum wage influences which teenagers are employed. When the minimum wage rises, some teenagers who are still attending high school choose to drop out and take jobs. These new dropouts displace other teenagers who had already dropped out of school and who now become unemployed.

The minimum wage is a frequent topic of debate. Economists are about evenly divided on the issue. In a 2006 survey of Ph.D. economists, 47 percent favored eliminating the minimum wage, while 14 percent would maintain it at its current level and 38 percent would increase it.

Advocates of the minimum wage view the policy as one way to raise the income of the working poor. They correctly point out that workers who earn the minimum wage can afford only a meager standard of living. In 2012, for instance, when the minimum wage was $7.25 per hour, two adults working 40 hours a week for every week of the year at minimum-wage jobs had a total annual income of only $30,160, which was less than two-thirds of the median family income in the United States. Many advocates of the minimum wage admit that it has some adverse effects, including unemployment, but they believe that these effects are small and that, all things considered, a higher minimum wage makes the poor better off.

Opponents of the minimum wage contend that it is not the best way to combat poverty. They note that a high minimum wage causes unemployment, encourages teenagers to drop out of school, and prevents some unskilled workers from getting the on-the-job training they need. Moreover, opponents of the minimum wage point out that it is a poorly targeted policy. Not all minimum-wage workers are heads of households trying to help their families escape poverty. In fact, fewer than a third of minimum-wage earners are in families with incomes below the poverty line. Many are teenagers from middle-class homes working at part-time jobs for extra spending money. ◢

6-1c Evaluating Price Controls

One of the *Ten Principles of Economics* discussed in Chapter 1 is that markets are usually a good way to organize economic activity. This principle explains why economists usually oppose price ceilings and price floors. To economists, prices are not the outcome of some haphazard process. Prices, they contend, are the result of the millions of business and consumer decisions that lie behind the supply and demand curves. Prices have the crucial job of balancing supply and demand and, thereby, coordinating economic activity. When policymakers set prices

IN THE NEWS
·············

Venezuela versus the Market

This is what happens when political leaders replace market prices with their own.

With Venezuelan Food Shortages, Some Blame Price Controls

By William Neuman

CARACAS, Venezuela — By 6:30 a.m., a full hour and a half before the store would open, about two dozen people were already in line. They waited patiently, not for the latest iPhone, but for something far more basic: groceries.

"Whatever I can get," said Katherine Huga, 23, a mother of two, describing her shopping list. She gave a shrug of resignation. "You buy what they have."

Venezuela is one of the world's top oil producers at a time of soaring energy prices, yet shortages of staples like milk, meat and toilet paper are a chronic part of life here, often turning grocery shopping into a hit or miss proposition.

Some residents arrange their calendars around the once-a-week deliveries made to government-subsidized stores like this one, lining up before dawn to buy a single frozen chicken before the stock runs out. Or a couple of bags of flour. Or a bottle of cooking oil.

The shortages affect both the poor and the well-off, in surprising ways. A supermarket in the upscale La Castellana neighborhood recently had plenty of chicken and cheese—even quail eggs—but not a single roll of toilet paper. Only a few bags of coffee remained on a bottom shelf.

Asked where a shopper could get milk on a day when that, too, was out of stock, a manager said with sarcasm, "At Chávez's house."

At the heart of the debate is President Hugo Chávez's socialist-inspired government, which imposes strict price controls that are intended to make a range of foods and other goods more affordable for the poor. They are often the very products that are the hardest to find.

"Venezuela is too rich a country to have this," Nery Reyes, 55, a restaurant worker, said outside a government-subsidized store in the working-class Santa Rosalía neighborhood. "I'm wasting my day here standing in line to buy one chicken and some rice."

Venezuela was long one of the most prosperous countries in the region, with sophisticated manufacturing, vibrant agriculture and strong businesses, making it hard for many residents to accept such widespread scarcities. But amid the prosperity, the gap between rich and poor was extreme, a problem that Mr. Chávez and his ministers say they are trying to eliminate.

They blame unfettered capitalism for the country's economic ills and argue that controls are needed to keep prices in check in a country where inflation rose to 27.6 percent last year, one of the highest rates in the world. They say companies cause shortages on purpose, holding products off the market to push up prices. This month, the government required price cuts on fruit juice, toothpaste,

by legal decree, they obscure the signals that normally guide the allocation of society's resources.

Another one of the *Ten Principles of Economics* is that governments can sometimes improve market outcomes. Indeed, policymakers are led to control prices because they view the market's outcome as unfair. Price controls are often aimed at helping the poor. For instance, rent-control laws try to make housing affordable for everyone, and minimum-wage laws try to help people escape poverty.

Yet price controls often hurt those they are trying to help. Rent control may keep rents low, but it also discourages landlords from maintaining their buildings and makes housing hard to find. Minimum-wage laws may raise the incomes of some workers, but they also cause other workers to be unemployed.

Helping those in need can be accomplished in ways other than controlling prices. For instance, the government can make housing more affordable by paying a fraction of the rent for poor families. Unlike rent control, such rent subsidies do not reduce the quantity of housing supplied and, therefore, do not lead to housing shortages. Similarly, wage subsidies raise the living standards of the working poor without discouraging firms from hiring them. An example of a wage

disposable diapers and more than a dozen other products.

"We are not asking them to lose money, just that they make money in a rational way, that they don't rob the people," Mr. Chávez said recently.

But many economists call it a classic case of a government causing a problem rather than solving it. Prices are set so low, they say, that companies and producers cannot make a profit. So farmers grow less food, manufacturers cut back production and retailers stock less inventory. Moreover, some of the shortages are in industries, like dairy and coffee, where the government has seized private companies and is now running them, saying it is in the national interest.

In January, according to a scarcity index compiled by the Central Bank of Venezuela, the difficulty of finding basic goods on store shelves was at its worst level since 2008. While that measure has eased considerably, many products can still be hard to come by.

Datanálisis, a polling firm that regularly tracks scarcities, said that powdered milk, a staple here, could not be found in 42 percent of the stores its researchers visited in early March. Liquid milk can be even harder to find.

Other products in short supply last month, according to Datanálisis, included beef, chicken, vegetable oil and sugar. The polling firm also says that the problem is most extreme in the government-subsidized stores that were created to provide affordable food to the poor....

Francisco Rodríguez, an economist with Bank of America Merrill Lynch who studies the Venezuelan economy, said the government might score some political points with the new round of price controls. But over time, he argued, they will spell trouble for the economy.

"In the medium to long term, this is going to be a disaster," Mr. Rodriguez said.

The price controls also mean that products missing from store shelves usually show up on the black market at much higher prices, a source of outrage for many. For government supporters, that is proof of speculation. Others say it is the consequence of a misguided policy....

If there is one product that Venezuela should be able to produce in abundance it is coffee, a major crop here for centuries. Until 2009, Venezuela was a coffee exporter, but it began importing large amounts of it three years ago to make up for a decline in production.

Farmers and coffee roasters say the problem is simple: retail price controls keep prices close to or below what it costs farmers to grow and harvest the coffee. As a result, many do not invest in new plantings or fertilizer, or they cut back on the amount of land used to grow coffee. Making matters worse, the recent harvest was poor in many areas.

A group representing small- to medium-size roasters said last month that there was no domestic coffee left on the wholesale market—the earliest time of year that industry leaders could remember such supplies running out. The group announced a deal with the government to buy imported beans to keep coffee on store shelves.

Similar problems have played out with other agricultural products under price controls, like lags in production and rising imports for beef, milk and corn.

Waiting in line to buy chicken and other staples, Jenny Montero, 30, recalled how she could not find cooking oil last fall and had to switch from the fried food she prefers to soups and stews.

"It was good for me," she said drily, pushing her 14-month-old daughter in a stroller. "I lost several pounds." ◢

Source: *New York Times*, April 20, 2012.

---

subsidy is the *earned income tax credit,* a government program that supplements the incomes of low-wage workers.

Although these alternative policies are often better than price controls, they are not perfect. Rent and wage subsidies cost the government money and, therefore, require higher taxes. As we see in the next section, taxation has costs of its own.

Quick Quiz *Define* price ceiling *and* price floor *and give an example of each. Which leads to a shortage? Which leads to a surplus? Why?*

6-2 Taxes

All governments—from the federal government in Washington, D.C., to the local governments in small towns—use taxes to raise revenue for public projects, such as roads, schools, and national defense. Because taxes are such an important policy instrument, and because they affect our lives in many ways, we return to the study of taxes several times throughout this book. In this section, we begin our study of how taxes affect the economy.

To set the stage for our analysis, imagine that a local government decides to hold an annual ice-cream celebration—with a parade, fireworks, and speeches by town officials. To raise revenue to pay for the event, the town decides to place a $0.50 tax on the sale of ice-cream cones. When the plan is announced, our two lobbying groups swing into action. The American Association of Ice-Cream Eaters claims that consumers of ice cream are having trouble making ends meet, and it argues that *sellers* of ice cream should pay the tax. The National Organization of Ice-Cream Makers claims that its members are struggling to survive in a competitive market, and it argues that *buyers* of ice cream should pay the tax. The town mayor, hoping to reach a compromise, suggests that half the tax be paid by the buyers and half be paid by the sellers.

To analyze these proposals, we need to address a simple but subtle question: When the government levies a tax on a good, who actually bears the burden of the tax? The people buying the good? The people selling the good? Or if buyers and sellers share the tax burden, what determines how the burden is divided? Can the government simply legislate the division of the burden, as the mayor is suggesting, or is the division determined by more fundamental market forces? The term **tax incidence** refers to how the burden of a tax is distributed among the various people who make up the economy. As we will see, some surprising lessons about tax incidence can be learned by applying the tools of supply and demand.

tax incidence

the manner in which the burden of a tax is shared among participants in a market

6-2a How Taxes on Sellers Affect Market Outcomes

We begin by considering a tax levied on sellers of a good. Suppose the local government passes a law requiring sellers of ice-cream cones to send $0.50 to the government for each cone they sell. How does this law affect the buyers and sellers of ice cream? To answer this question, we can follow the three steps in Chapter 4 for analyzing supply and demand: (1) We decide whether the law affects the supply curve or demand curve. (2) We decide which way the curve shifts. (3) We examine how the shift affects the equilibrium price and quantity.

Step One   The immediate impact of the tax is on the sellers of ice cream. Because the tax is not levied on buyers, the quantity of ice cream demanded at any given price is the same; thus, the demand curve does not change. By contrast, the tax on sellers makes the ice-cream business less profitable at any given price, so it shifts the supply curve.

Step Two   Because the tax on sellers raises the cost of producing and selling ice cream, it reduces the quantity supplied at every price. The supply curve shifts to the left (or, equivalently, upward).

In addition to determining the direction in which the supply curve moves, we can also be precise about the size of the shift. For any market price of ice cream, the effective price to sellers—the amount they get to keep after paying the tax—is $0.50 lower. For example, if the market price of a cone happened to be $2.00, the effective price received by sellers would be $1.50. Whatever the market price, sellers will supply a quantity of ice cream as if the price were $0.50 lower than it is. Put differently, to induce sellers to supply any given quantity, the market price must now be $0.50 higher to compensate for the effect of the tax. Thus, as shown in Figure 6, the supply curve shifts *upward* from S_1 to S_2 by the exact size of the tax ($0.50).

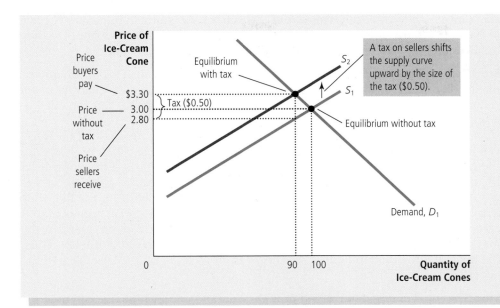

FIGURE 6

A Tax on Sellers
When a tax of $0.50 is levied on sellers, the supply curve shifts up by $0.50 from S_1 to S_2. The equilibrium quantity falls from 100 to 90 cones. The price that buyers pay rises from $3.00 to $3.30. The price that sellers receive (after paying the tax) falls from $3.00 to $2.80. Even though the tax is levied on sellers, buyers and sellers share the burden of the tax.

Step Three   Having determined how the supply curve shifts, we can now compare the initial and the new equilibriums. Figure 6 shows that the equilibrium price of ice cream rises from $3.00 to $3.30, and the equilibrium quantity falls from 100 to 90 cones. Because sellers sell less and buyers buy less in the new equilibrium, the tax reduces the size of the ice-cream market.

Implications   We can now return to the question of tax incidence: Who pays the tax? Although sellers send the entire tax to the government, buyers and sellers share the burden. Because the market price rises from $3.00 to $3.30 when the tax is introduced, buyers pay $0.30 more for each ice-cream cone than they did without the tax. Thus, the tax makes buyers worse off. Sellers get a higher price ($3.30) from buyers than they did previously, but what they get to keep after paying the tax is only $2.80 ($3.30 − $0.50 = $2.80), compared with $3.00 before the tax was implemented. Thus, the tax also makes sellers worse off.

To sum up, this analysis yields two lessons:

- Taxes discourage market activity. When a good is taxed, the quantity of the good sold is smaller in the new equilibrium.
- Buyers and sellers share the burden of taxes. In the new equilibrium, buyers pay more for the good, and sellers receive less.

6-2b How Taxes on Buyers Affect Market Outcomes

Now consider a tax levied on buyers of a good. Suppose that our local government passes a law requiring buyers of ice-cream cones to send $0.50 to the government for each ice-cream cone they buy. What are the effects of this law? Again, we apply our three steps.

Step One   The initial impact of the tax is on the demand for ice cream. The supply curve is not affected because, for any given price of ice cream, sellers have the same incentive to provide ice cream to the market. By contrast, buyers now have to pay a tax to the government (as well as the price to the sellers) whenever they buy ice cream. Thus, the tax shifts the demand curve for ice cream.

Step Two   We next determine the direction of the shift. Because the tax on buyers makes buying ice cream less attractive, buyers demand a smaller quantity of ice cream at every price. As a result, the demand curve shifts to the left (or, equivalently, downward), as shown in Figure 7.

Once again, we can be precise about the size of the shift. Because of the $0.50 tax levied on buyers, the effective price to buyers is now $0.50 higher than the market price (whatever the market price happens to be). For example, if the market price of a cone happened to be $2.00, the effective price to buyers would be $2.50. Because buyers look at their total cost including the tax, they demand a quantity of ice cream as if the market price were $0.50 higher than it actually is. In other words, to induce buyers to demand any given quantity, the market price must now be $0.50 lower to make up for the effect of the tax. Thus, the tax shifts the demand curve *downward* from D_1 to D_2 by the exact size of the tax ($0.50).

Step Three   Having determined how the demand curve shifts, we can now see the effect of the tax by comparing the initial equilibrium and the new equilibrium. You can see in Figure 7 that the equilibrium price of ice cream falls from $3.00 to $2.80, and the equilibrium quantity falls from 100 to 90 cones. Once again, the tax on ice cream reduces the size of the ice-cream market. And once again, buyers and sellers share the burden of the tax. Sellers get a lower price for their product; buyers pay a lower market price to sellers than they did previously, but the effective price (including the tax buyers have to pay) rises from $3.00 to $3.30.

FIGURE 7

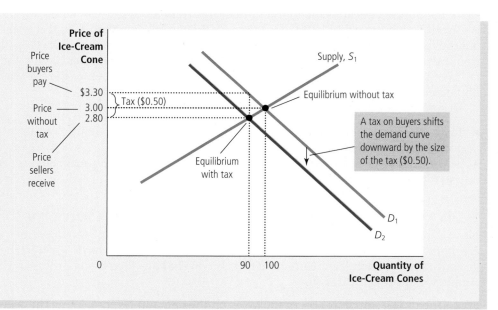

A Tax on Buyers
When a tax of $0.50 is levied on buyers, the demand curve shifts down by $0.50 from D_1 to D_2. The equilibrium quantity falls from 100 to 90 cones. The price that sellers receive falls from $3.00 to $2.80. The price that buyers pay (including the tax) rises from $3.00 to $3.30. Even though the tax is levied on buyers, buyers and sellers share the burden of the tax.

Implications   If you compare Figures 6 and 7, you will notice a surprising conclusion: *Taxes levied on sellers and taxes levied on buyers are equivalent.* In both cases, the tax places a wedge between the price that buyers pay and the price that sellers receive. The wedge between the buyers' price and the sellers' price is the same, regardless of whether the tax is levied on buyers or sellers. In either case, the wedge shifts the relative position of the supply and demand curves. In the new equilibrium, buyers and sellers share the burden of the tax. The only difference between a tax levied on sellers and a tax levied on buyers is who sends the money to the government.

The equivalence of these two taxes is easy to understand if we imagine that the government collects the $0.50 ice-cream tax in a bowl on the counter of each ice-cream store. When the government levies the tax on sellers, the seller is required to place $0.50 in the bowl after the sale of each cone. When the government levies the tax on buyers, the buyer is required to place $0.50 in the bowl every time a cone is bought. Whether the $0.50 goes directly from the buyer's pocket into the bowl, or indirectly from the buyer's pocket into the seller's hand and then into the bowl, does not matter. Once the market reaches its new equilibrium, buyers and sellers share the burden, regardless of how the tax is levied.

case study   **Can Congress Distribute the Burden of a Payroll Tax?**

If you have ever received a paycheck, you probably noticed that taxes were deducted from the amount you earned. One of these taxes is called FICA, an acronym for the Federal Insurance Contributions Act. The federal government uses the revenue from the FICA tax to pay for Social Security and Medicare, the income support and healthcare programs for the elderly. FICA is an example of a *payroll tax,* which is a tax on the wages that firms pay their workers. In 2013, the total FICA tax for the typical worker was 15.3 percent of earnings.

Who do you think bears the burden of this payroll tax—firms or workers? When Congress passed this legislation, it tried to mandate a division of the tax burden. According to the law, half of the tax is paid by firms, and half is paid by workers. That is, half of the tax is paid out of firms' revenues, and half is deducted from workers' paychecks. The amount that shows up as a deduction on your pay stub is the worker contribution.

Our analysis of tax incidence, however, shows that lawmakers cannot so easily dictate the distribution of a tax burden. To illustrate, we can analyze a payroll tax as merely a tax on a good, where the good is labor and the price is the wage. The key feature of the payroll tax is that it places a wedge between the wage that firms pay and the wage that workers receive. Figure 8 shows the outcome. When a payroll tax is enacted, the wage received by workers falls, and the wage paid by firms rises. In the end, workers and firms share the burden of the tax, much as the legislation requires. Yet this division of the tax burden between workers and firms has nothing to do with the legislated division: The division of the burden in Figure 8 is not necessarily 50-50, and the same outcome would prevail if the law levied the entire tax on workers or if it levied the entire tax on firms.

This example shows that the most basic lesson of tax incidence is often overlooked in public debate. Lawmakers can decide whether a tax comes from the

FIGURE 8

A Payroll Tax
A payroll tax places a wedge between the wage that workers receive and the wage that firms pay. Comparing wages with and without the tax, you can see that workers and firms share the tax burden. This division of the tax burden between workers and firms does not depend on whether the government levies the tax on workers, levies the tax on firms, or divides the tax equally between the two groups.

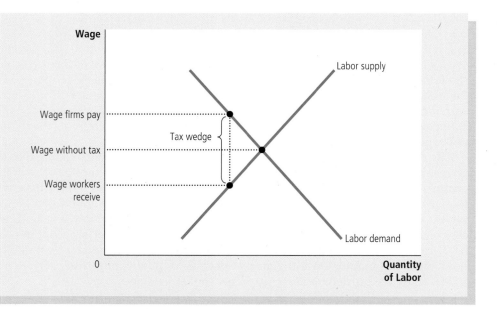

buyer's pocket or from the seller's, but they cannot legislate the true burden of a tax. Rather, tax incidence depends on the forces of supply and demand. ◢

6-2c Elasticity and Tax Incidence

When a good is taxed, buyers and sellers of the good share the burden of the tax. But how exactly is the tax burden divided? Only rarely will it be shared equally. To see how the burden is divided, consider the impact of taxation in the two markets in Figure 9. In both cases, the figure shows the initial demand curve, the initial supply curve, and a tax that drives a wedge between the amount paid by buyers and the amount received by sellers. (Not drawn in either panel of the figure is the new supply or demand curve. Which curve shifts depends on whether the tax is levied on buyers or sellers. As we have seen, this is irrelevant for the incidence of the tax.) The difference in the two panels is the relative elasticity of supply and demand.

Panel (a) of Figure 9 shows a tax in a market with very elastic supply and relatively inelastic demand. That is, sellers are very responsive to changes in the price of the good (so the supply curve is relatively flat), whereas buyers are not very responsive (so the demand curve is relatively steep). When a tax is imposed on a market with these elasticities, the price received by sellers does not fall much, so sellers bear only a small burden. By contrast, the price paid by buyers rises substantially, indicating that buyers bear most of the burden of the tax.

Panel (b) of Figure 9 shows a tax in a market with relatively inelastic supply and very elastic demand. In this case, sellers are not very responsive to changes in the price (so the supply curve is steeper), whereas buyers are very responsive (so the demand curve is flatter). The figure shows that when a tax is imposed, the price paid by buyers does not rise much, but the price received by sellers falls substantially. Thus, sellers bear most of the burden of the tax.

The two panels of Figure 9 show a general lesson about how the burden of a tax is divided: *A tax burden falls more heavily on the side of the market that is less elastic.*

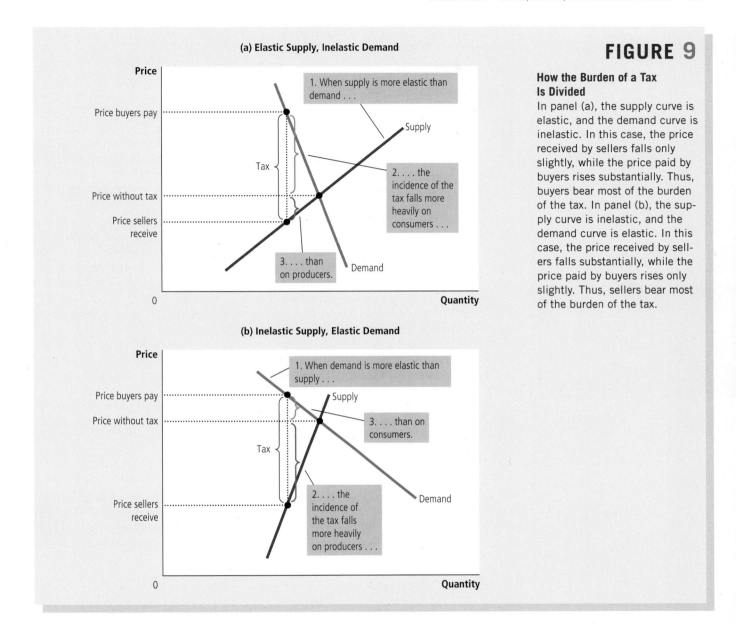

FIGURE 9

How the Burden of a Tax Is Divided

In panel (a), the supply curve is elastic, and the demand curve is inelastic. In this case, the price received by sellers falls only slightly, while the price paid by buyers rises substantially. Thus, buyers bear most of the burden of the tax. In panel (b), the supply curve is inelastic, and the demand curve is elastic. In this case, the price received by sellers falls substantially, while the price paid by buyers rises only slightly. Thus, sellers bear most of the burden of the tax.

Why is this true? In essence, the elasticity measures the willingness of buyers or sellers to leave the market when conditions become unfavorable. A small elasticity of demand means that buyers do not have good alternatives to consuming this particular good. A small elasticity of supply means that sellers do not have good alternatives to producing this particular good. When the good is taxed, the side of the market with fewer good alternatives is less willing to leave the market and must, therefore, bear more of the burden of the tax.

We can apply this logic to the payroll tax discussed in the previous case study. Most labor economists believe that the supply of labor is much less elastic than the demand. This means that workers, rather than firms, bear most of the burden of the payroll tax. In other words, the distribution of the tax burden is far from the 50-50 split that lawmakers intended.

case study   Who Pays the Luxury Tax?

In 1990, Congress adopted a new luxury tax on items such as yachts, private airplanes, furs, jewelry, and expensive cars. The goal of the tax was to raise revenue from those who could most easily afford to pay. Because only the rich could afford to buy such extravagances, taxing luxuries seemed a logical way of taxing the rich.

Yet, when the forces of supply and demand took over, the outcome was quite different from the one Congress intended. Consider, for example, the market for yachts. The demand for yachts is quite elastic. A millionaire can easily not buy a yacht; he can use the money to buy a bigger house, take a European vacation, or leave a larger bequest to his heirs. By contrast, the supply of yachts is relatively inelastic, at least in the short run. Yacht factories are not easily converted to alternative uses, and workers who build yachts are not eager to change careers in response to changing market conditions.

Our analysis makes a clear prediction in this case. With elastic demand and inelastic supply, the burden of a tax falls largely on the suppliers. That is, a tax on yachts places a burden largely on the firms and workers who build yachts because they end up getting a significantly lower price for their product. The workers, however, are not wealthy. Thus, the burden of a luxury tax falls more on the middle class than on the rich.

The mistaken assumptions about the incidence of the luxury tax quickly became apparent after the tax went into effect. Suppliers of luxuries made their congressional representatives well aware of the economic hardship they experienced, and Congress repealed most of the luxury tax in 1993. ◢

"If this boat were any more expensive, we'd be playing golf."

Quick Quiz   *In a supply-and-demand diagram, show how a tax on car buyers of $1,000 per car affects the quantity of cars sold and the price of cars. In another diagram, show how a tax on car sellers of $1,000 per car affects the quantity of cars sold and the price of cars. In both of your diagrams, show the change in the price paid by car buyers and the change in the price received by car sellers.*

6-3 Conclusion

The economy is governed by two kinds of laws: the laws of supply and demand and the laws enacted by governments. In this chapter, we have begun to see how these laws interact. Price controls and taxes are common in various markets in the economy, and their effects are frequently debated in the press and among policymakers. Even a little bit of economic knowledge can go a long way toward understanding and evaluating these policies.

In subsequent chapters, we analyze many government policies in greater detail. We examine the effects of taxation more fully and consider a broader range of policies than we considered here. Yet the basic lessons of this chapter will not change: When analyzing government policies, supply and demand are the first and most useful tools of analysis.

Summary

- A price ceiling is a legal maximum on the price of a good or service. An example is rent control. If the price ceiling is below the equilibrium price, then the price ceiling is binding, and the quantity demanded exceeds the quantity supplied. Because of the resulting shortage, sellers must in some way ration the good or service among buyers.

- A price floor is a legal minimum on the price of a good or service. An example is the minimum wage. If the price floor is above the equilibrium price, then the price floor is binding, and the quantity supplied exceeds the quantity demanded. Because of the resulting surplus, buyers' demands for the good or service must in some way be rationed among sellers.

- When the government levies a tax on a good, the equilibrium quantity of the good falls. That is, a tax on a market shrinks the size of the market.

- A tax on a good places a wedge between the price paid by buyers and the price received by sellers. When the market moves to the new equilibrium, buyers pay more for the good and sellers receive less for it. In this sense, buyers and sellers share the tax burden. The incidence of a tax (that is, the division of the tax burden) does not depend on whether the tax is levied on buyers or sellers.

- The incidence of a tax depends on the price elasticities of supply and demand. Most of the burden falls on the side of the market that is less elastic because that side of the market cannot respond as easily to the tax by changing the quantity bought or sold.

Key Concepts

price ceiling, *p. 112*   price floor, *p. 112*   tax incidence, *p. 122*

Questions for Review

1. Give an example of a price ceiling and an example of a price floor.

2. Which causes a shortage of a good—a price ceiling or a price floor? Justify your answer with a graph.

3. What mechanisms allocate resources when the price of a good is not allowed to bring supply and demand into equilibrium?

4. Explain why economists usually oppose controls on prices.

5. Suppose the government removes a tax on buyers of a good and levies a tax of the same size on sellers of

the good. How does this change in tax policy affect the price that buyers pay sellers for this good, the amount buyers are out of pocket (including any tax payments they make), the amount sellers receive (net of any tax payments they make), and the quantity of the good sold?

6. How does a tax on a good affect the price paid by buyers, the price received by sellers, and the quantity sold?

7. What determines how the burden of a tax is divided between buyers and sellers? Why?

Quick Check Multiple Choice

1. When the government imposes a binding price floor, it causes
   a. the supply curve to shift to the left.
   b. the demand curve to shift to the right.
   c. a shortage of the good to develop.
   d. a surplus of the good to develop.

2. In a market with a binding price ceiling, an increase in the ceiling will _____ the quantity supplied, _____ the quantity demanded, and reduce the _____.
   a. increase, decrease, surplus
   b. decrease, increase, surplus

   c. increase, decrease, shortage
   d. decrease, increase, shortage

3. A $1 per unit tax levied on consumers of a good is equivalent to
   a. a $1 per unit tax levied on producers of the good.
   b. a $1 per unit subsidy paid to producers of the good.
   c. a price floor that raises the good's price by $1 per unit.
   d. a price ceiling that raises the good's price by $1 per unit.

4. Which of the following would increase quantity supplied, decrease quantity demanded, and increase the price that consumers pay?
   a. the imposition of a binding price floor
   b. the removal of a binding price floor
   c. the passage of a tax levied on producers
   d. the repeal of a tax levied on producers

5. Which of the following would increase quantity supplied, increase quantity demanded, and decrease the price that consumers pay?
   a. the imposition of a binding price floor
   b. the removal of a binding price floor
   c. the passage of a tax levied on producers
   d. the repeal of a tax levied on producers

6. When a good is taxed, the burden of the tax falls mainly on consumers if
   a. the tax is levied on consumers.
   b. the tax is levied on producers.
   c. supply is inelastic, and demand is elastic.
   d. supply is elastic, and demand is inelastic.

Problems and Applications

1. Lovers of classical music persuade Congress to impose a price ceiling of $40 per concert ticket. As a result of this policy, do more or fewer people attend classical music concerts? Explain.

2. The government has decided that the free-market price of cheese is too low.
   a. Suppose the government imposes a binding price floor in the cheese market. Draw a supply-and-demand diagram to show the effect of this policy on the price of cheese and the quantity of cheese sold. Is there a shortage or surplus of cheese?
   b. Producers of cheese complain that the price floor has reduced their total revenue. Is this possible? Explain.
   c. In response to cheese producers' complaints, the government agrees to purchase all the surplus cheese at the price floor. Compared to the basic price floor, who benefits from this new policy? Who loses?

3. A recent study found that the demand and supply schedules for Frisbees are as follows:

Price per Frisbee	Quantity Demanded	Quantity Supplied
$11	1 million Frisbees	15 million Frisbees
10	2	12
9	4	9
8	6	6
7	8	3
6	10	1

   a. What are the equilibrium price and quantity of Frisbees?
   b. Frisbee manufacturers persuade the government that Frisbee production improves scientists' understanding of aerodynamics and thus is important for national security. A concerned Congress votes to impose a price floor $2 above the equilibrium price. What is the new market price? How many Frisbees are sold?
   c. Irate college students march on Washington and demand a reduction in the price of Frisbees. An even more concerned Congress votes to repeal the price floor and impose a price ceiling $1 below the former price floor. What is the new market price? How many Frisbees are sold?

4. Suppose the federal government requires beer drinkers to pay a $2 tax on each case of beer purchased. (In fact, both the federal and state governments impose beer taxes of some sort.)
   a. Draw a supply-and-demand diagram of the market for beer without the tax. Show the price paid by consumers, the price received by producers, and the quantity of beer sold. What is the difference between the price paid by consumers and the price received by producers?
   b. Now draw a supply-and-demand diagram for the beer market with the tax. Show the price paid by consumers, the price received by producers, and the quantity of beer sold. What is the difference between the price paid by consumers and the price received by producers? Has the quantity of beer sold increased or decreased?

5. A senator wants to raise tax revenue and make workers better off. A staff member proposes raising the payroll tax paid by firms and using part of the extra revenue to reduce the payroll tax paid by workers. Would this accomplish the senator's goal? Explain.

6. If the government places a $500 tax on luxury cars, will the price paid by consumers rise by more than $500, less than $500, or exactly $500? Explain.

7. Congress and the president decide that the United States should reduce air pollution by reducing its use

of gasoline. They impose a $0.50 tax on each gallon of gasoline sold.

a. Should they impose this tax on producers or consumers? Explain carefully using a supply-and-demand diagram.

b. If the demand for gasoline were more elastic, would this tax be more effective or less effective in reducing the quantity of gasoline consumed? Explain with both words and a diagram.

c. Are consumers of gasoline helped or hurt by this tax? Why?

d. Are workers in the oil industry helped or hurt by this tax? Why?

8. A case study in this chapter discusses the federal minimum-wage law.

a. Suppose the minimum wage is above the equilibrium wage in the market for unskilled labor. Using a supply-and-demand diagram of the market for unskilled labor, show the market wage, the number of workers who are employed, and the number of workers who are unemployed. Also show the total wage payments to unskilled workers.

b. Now suppose the secretary of labor proposes an increase in the minimum wage. What effect would this increase have on employment? Does the change in employment depend on the elasticity of demand, the elasticity of supply, both elasticities, or neither?

c. What effect would this increase in the minimum wage have on unemployment? Does the change in unemployment depend on the elasticity of demand, the elasticity of supply, both elasticities, or neither?

d. If the demand for unskilled labor were inelastic, would the proposed increase in the minimum wage raise or lower total wage payments to unskilled workers? Would your answer change if the demand for unskilled labor were elastic?

9. At Fenway Park, home of the Boston Red Sox, seating is limited to 39,000. Hence, the number of tickets issued is fixed at that figure. Seeing a golden opportunity to raise revenue, the City of Boston levies a per ticket tax of $5 to be paid by the ticket buyer. Boston sports fans, a famously civic-minded lot, dutifully send in the $5 per ticket. Draw a well-labeled graph showing the impact of the tax. On whom does the tax burden fall—the team's owners, the fans, or both? Why?

10. A subsidy is the opposite of a tax. With a $0.50 tax on the buyers of ice-cream cones, the government collects $0.50 for each cone purchased; with a $0.50 subsidy for the buyers of ice-cream cones, the government pays buyers $0.50 for each cone purchased.

a. Show the effect of a $0.50 per cone subsidy on the demand curve for ice-cream cones, the effective price paid by consumers, the effective price received by sellers, and the quantity of cones sold.

b. Do consumers gain or lose from this policy? Do producers gain or lose? Does the government gain or lose?

Go to CengageBrain.com to purchase access to the proven, critical Study Guide to accompany this text, which features additional notes and context, practice tests, and much more.

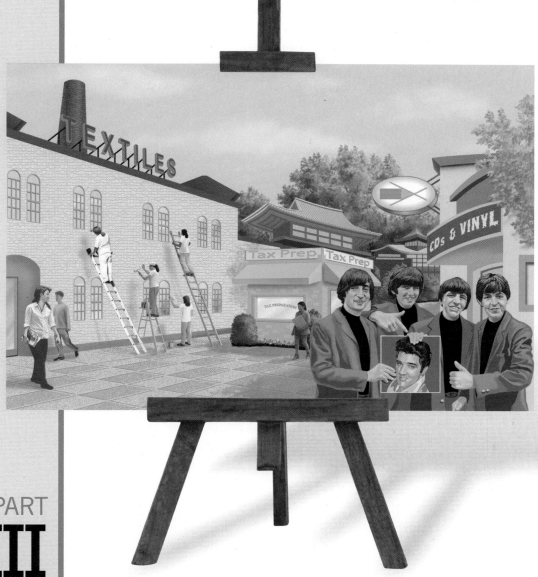

Markets and Welfare

Consumers, Producers, and the Efficiency of Markets

Positive=what is
normative=what should be

When consumers go to grocery stores to buy their turkeys for Thanksgiving dinner, they may be disappointed that the price of turkey is as high as it is. At the same time, when farmers bring to market the turkeys they have raised, they probably wish the price of turkey were even higher. These views are not surprising: Buyers always want to pay less, and sellers always want to be paid more. But is there a "right price" for turkey from the standpoint of society as a whole?

In previous chapters, we saw how, in market economies, the forces of supply and demand determine the prices of goods and services and the quantities sold. So far, however, we have described the way markets allocate scarce resources without directly addressing the question of whether these market allocations are desirable. In other words, our analysis has been *positive* (what is) rather than *normative* (what should be). We know that the price of turkey adjusts to ensure that the quantity of turkey supplied equals the

welfare economics
the study of how the allocation of resources affects economic well-being

quantity of turkey demanded. But at this equilibrium, is the quantity of turkey produced and consumed too small, too large, or just right?

In this chapter, we take up the topic of **welfare economics**, the study of how the allocation of resources affects economic well-being. We begin by examining the benefits that buyers and sellers receive from engaging in market transactions. We then examine how society can make these benefits as large as possible. This analysis leads to a profound conclusion: In any market, the equilibrium of supply and demand maximizes the total benefits received by all buyers and sellers combined.

As you may recall from Chapter 1, one of the *Ten Principles of Economics* is that markets are usually a good way to organize economic activity. The study of welfare economics explains this principle more fully. It also answers our question about the right price of turkey: The price that balances the supply and demand for turkey is, in a particular sense, the best one because it maximizes the total welfare of turkey consumers and turkey producers. No consumer or producer of turkeys aims to achieve this goal, but their joint action directed by market prices moves them toward a welfare-maximizing outcome, as if led by an invisible hand.

7-1 Consumer Surplus

We begin our study of welfare economics by looking at the benefits buyers receive from participating in a market.

7-1a Willingness to Pay

Imagine that you own a mint-condition recording of Elvis Presley's first album. Because you are not an Elvis Presley fan, you decide to sell it. One way to do so is to hold an auction.

Four Elvis fans show up for your auction: John, Paul, George, and Ringo. Each of them would like to own the album, but there is a limit to the amount that each is willing to pay for it. Table 1 shows the maximum price that each of the four possible buyers would pay. Each buyer's maximum is called his **willingness to pay**, and it measures how much that buyer values the good. Each buyer would be eager to buy the album at a price less than his willingness to pay, and he would refuse to buy the album at a price greater than his willingness to pay. At a price equal to his willingness to pay, the buyer would be indifferent about buying the good: If the price is exactly the same as the value he places on the album, he would be equally happy buying it or keeping his money.

willingness to pay
the maximum amount that a buyer will pay for a good

TABLE 1

Four Possible Buyers' Willingness to Pay

Buyer	Willingness to Pay
John	$100
Paul	80
George	70
Ringo	50

To sell your album, you begin the bidding at a low price, say, $10. Because all four buyers are willing to pay much more, the price rises quickly. The bidding stops when John bids $80 (or slightly more). At this point, Paul, George, and Ringo have dropped out of the bidding because they are unwilling to bid any more than $80. John pays you $80 and gets the album. Note that the album has gone to the buyer who values it most highly.

[handwritten: John would have paid $100, but paid $80. Paid $100 - $80 = $20 surplus for John :)]

What benefit does John receive from buying the Elvis Presley album? In a sense, John has found a real bargain: He is willing to pay $100 for the album but pays only $80 for it. We say that John receives *consumer surplus* of $20. **Consumer surplus** is the amount a buyer is willing to pay for a good minus the amount the buyer actually pays for it. *[handwritten: on test]*

[margin note]
consumer surplus
the amount a buyer is willing to pay for a good minus the amount the buyer actually pays for it

Consumer surplus measures the benefit buyers receive from participating in a market. In this example, John receives a $20 benefit from participating in the auction because he pays only $80 for a good he values at $100. Paul, George, and Ringo get no consumer surplus from participating in the auction because they left without the album and without paying anything.

Now consider a somewhat different example. Suppose that you had two identical Elvis Presley albums to sell. Again, you auction them off to the four possible buyers. To keep things simple, we assume that both albums are to be sold for the same price and that no buyer is interested in buying more than one album. Therefore, the price rises until two buyers are left.

In this case, the bidding stops when John and Paul bid $70 (or slightly higher). At this price, John and Paul are each happy to buy an album, and George and Ringo are not willing to bid any higher. John and Paul each receive consumer surplus equal to his willingness to pay minus the price. John's consumer surplus is $30, and Paul's is $10. John's consumer surplus is higher now than in the previous example because he gets the same album but pays less for it. The total consumer surplus in the market is $40.

7-1b Using the Demand Curve to Measure Consumer Surplus

Consumer surplus is closely related to the demand curve for a product. To see how they are related, let's continue our example and consider the demand curve for this rare Elvis Presley album.

We begin by using the willingness to pay of the four possible buyers to find the market demand schedule for the album. The table in Figure 1 shows the demand schedule that corresponds to Table 1. If the price is above $100, the quantity demanded in the market is 0 because no buyer is willing to pay that much. If the price is between $80 and $100, the quantity demanded is 1 because only John is willing to pay such a high price. If the price is between $70 and $80, the quantity demanded is 2 because both John and Paul are willing to pay the price. We can continue this analysis for other prices as well. In this way, the demand schedule is derived from the willingness to pay of the four possible buyers.

[handwritten: marginal = Additional]

The graph in Figure 1 shows the demand curve that corresponds to this demand schedule. Note the relationship between the height of the demand curve and the buyers' willingness to pay. At any quantity, the price given by the demand curve shows the willingness to pay of the *marginal buyer*, the buyer who would leave the market first if the price were any higher. At a quantity of 4 albums, for instance, the demand curve has a height of $50, the price that Ringo (the marginal buyer) is willing to pay for an album. At a quantity of 3 albums, the demand curve has a height of $70, the price that George (who is now the marginal buyer) is willing to pay.

FIGURE 1

The Demand Schedule and the Demand Curve

The table shows the demand schedule for the buyers (listed in Table 1) of the mint-condition copy of Elvis Presley's first album. The graph shows the corresponding demand curve. Note that the height of the demand curve reflects the buyers' willingness to pay.

Price	Buyers	Quantity Demanded
More than $100	None	0
$80 to $100	John	1
$70 to $80	John, Paul	2
$50 to $70	John, Paul, George	3
$50 or less	John, Paul, George, Ringo	4

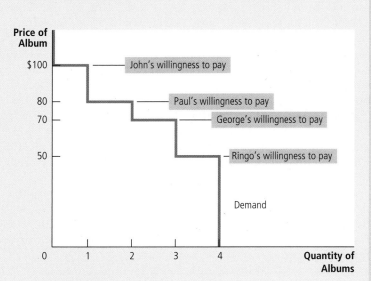

Because the demand curve reflects buyers' willingness to pay, we can also use it to measure consumer surplus. Figure 2 uses the demand curve to compute consumer surplus in our two examples. In panel (a), the price is $80 (or slightly above) and the quantity demanded is 1. Note that the area above the price and below the demand curve equals $20. This amount is exactly the consumer surplus we computed earlier when only 1 album is sold.

Panel (b) of Figure 2 shows consumer surplus when the price is $70 (or slightly above). In this case, the area above the price and below the demand curve equals the total area of the two rectangles: John's consumer surplus at this price is $30 and Paul's is $10. This area equals a total of $40. Once again, this amount is the consumer surplus we computed earlier.

The lesson from this example holds for all demand curves: *The area below the demand curve and above the price measures the consumer surplus in a market.* This is true because the height of the demand curve measures the value buyers place on the good, as measured by their willingness to pay for it. The difference between this willingness to pay and the market price is each buyer's consumer surplus. Thus, the total area below the demand curve and above the price is the sum of the consumer surplus of all buyers in the market for a good or service.

7-1c How a Lower Price Raises Consumer Surplus

Because buyers always want to pay less for the goods they buy, a lower price makes buyers of a good better off. But how much does buyers' well-being rise in response to a lower price? We can use the concept of consumer surplus to answer this question precisely.

In panel (a), the price of the good is $80 and the consumer surplus is $20. In panel (b), the price of the good is $70 and the consumer surplus is $40.

FIGURE 2

Measuring Consumer Surplus with the Demand Curve

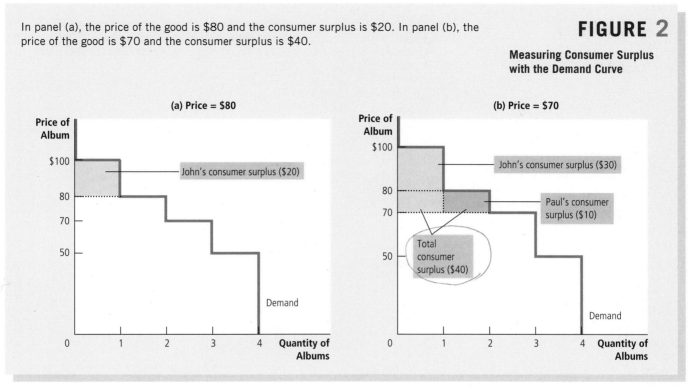

Figure 3 shows a typical demand curve. You may notice that this curve gradually slopes downward instead of taking discrete steps as in the previous two figures. In a market with many buyers, the resulting steps from each buyer dropping out are so small that they form, in essence, a smooth curve. Although this curve has a different shape, the ideas we have just developed still apply: Consumer surplus is the area above the price and below the demand curve. In panel (a), consumer surplus at a price of P_1 is the area of triangle ABC.

Now suppose that the price falls from P_1 to P_2, as shown in panel (b). The consumer surplus now equals the area ADF. The increase in consumer surplus attributable to the lower price is the area BCFD.

This increase in consumer surplus is composed of two parts. First, those buyers who were already buying Q_1 of the good at the higher price P_1 are better off because they now pay less. The increase in consumer surplus of existing buyers is the reduction in the amount they pay; it equals the area of the rectangle BCED. Second, some new buyers enter the market because they are willing to buy the good at the lower price. As a result, the quantity demanded in the market increases from Q_1 to Q_2. The consumer surplus these newcomers receive is the area of the triangle CEF.

7-1d What Does Consumer Surplus Measure?

Our goal in developing the concept of consumer surplus is to make judgments about the desirability of market outcomes. Now that you have seen what consumer surplus is, let's consider whether it is a good measure of economic well-being.

FIGURE 3

How Price Affects Consumer Surplus

In panel (a), the price is P_1, the quantity demanded is Q_1, and consumer surplus equals the area of the triangle ABC. When the price falls from P_1 to P_2, as in panel (b), the quantity demanded rises from Q_1 to Q_2 and the consumer surplus rises to the area of the triangle ADF. The increase in consumer surplus (area BCFD) occurs in part because existing consumers now pay less (area BCED) and in part because new consumers enter the market at the lower price (area CEF).

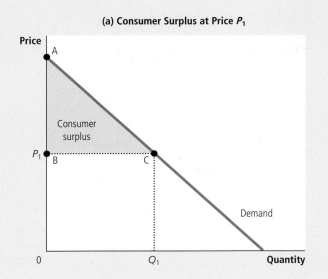

(a) Consumer Surplus at Price P_1

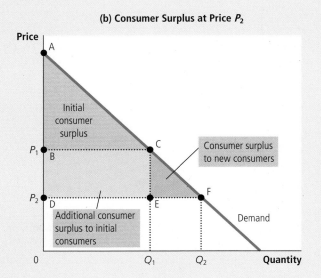

(b) Consumer Surplus at Price P_2

many buyers make smoother slope

Imagine that you are a policymaker trying to design a good economic system. Would you care about the amount of consumer surplus? Consumer surplus, the amount that buyers are willing to pay for a good minus the amount they actually pay for it, measures the benefit that buyers receive from a good *as the buyers themselves perceive it*. Thus, consumer surplus is a good measure of economic well-being if policymakers want to respect the preferences of buyers.

In some circumstances, policymakers might choose to disregard consumer surplus because they do not respect the preferences that drive buyer behavior. For example, drug addicts are willing to pay a high price for heroin. Yet we would not say that addicts get a large benefit from being able to buy heroin at a low price (even though addicts might say they do). From the standpoint of society, willingness to pay in this instance is not a good measure of the buyers' benefit, and consumer surplus is not a good measure of economic well-being, because addicts are not looking after their own best interests.

In most markets, however, consumer surplus does reflect economic well-being. Economists normally assume that buyers are rational when they make decisions. Rational people do the best they can to achieve their objectives, given their opportunities. Economists also normally assume that people's preferences should be respected. In this case, consumers are the best judges of how much benefit they receive from the goods they buy.

Quick Quiz   *Draw a demand curve for turkey. In your diagram, show a price of turkey and the consumer surplus at that price. Explain in words what this consumer surplus measures.*

7-2 Producer Surplus

We now turn to the other side of the market and consider the benefits sellers receive from participating in a market. As you will see, our analysis of sellers' welfare is similar to our analysis of buyers' welfare.

7-2a Cost and the Willingness to Sell

Imagine now that you are a homeowner and you want to get your house painted. You turn to four sellers of painting services: Mary, Frida, Georgia, and Grandma. Each painter is willing to do the work for you if the price is right. You decide to take bids from the four painters and auction off the job to the painter who will do the work for the lowest price.

Each painter is willing to take the job if the price she would receive exceeds her cost of doing the work. Here the term **cost** should be interpreted as the painters' opportunity cost: It includes the painters' out-of-pocket expenses (for paint, brushes, and so on) as well as the value that the painters place on their own time. Table 2 shows each painter's cost. Because a painter's cost is the lowest price she would accept for her work, cost is a measure of her willingness to sell her services. Each painter would be eager to sell her services at a price greater than her cost and would refuse to sell her services at a price less than her cost. At a price exactly equal to her cost, she would be indifferent about selling her services: She would be equally happy getting the job or using her time and energy for another purpose.

When you take bids from the painters, the price might start high, but it quickly falls as the painters compete for the job. Once Grandma has bid $600 (or slightly less), she is the sole remaining bidder. Grandma is happy to do the job for this price because her cost is only $500. Mary, Frida, and Georgia are unwilling to do the job for less than $600. Note that the job goes to the painter who can do the work at the lowest cost.

What benefit does Grandma receive from getting the job? Because she is willing to do the work for $500 but gets $600 for doing it, we say that she receives *producer surplus* of $100. **Producer surplus** is the amount a seller is paid minus the cost of production. Producer surplus measures the benefit sellers receive from participating in a market.

Now consider a somewhat different example. Suppose that you have two houses that need painting. Again, you auction off the jobs to the four painters. To keep things simple, let's assume that no painter is able to paint both houses and that you will pay the same amount to paint each house. Therefore, the price falls until two painters are left.

cost
the value of everything a seller must give up to produce a good

producer surplus
the amount a seller is paid for a good minus the seller's cost of providing it

[handwritten: this was on test]

[handwritten: if Grandma gets $600 her producer surplus is $100]

Seller	Cost
Mary	$900
Frida	800
Georgia	600
Grandma	500

TABLE 2

The Costs of Four Possible Sellers

In this case, the bidding stops when Georgia and Grandma each offer to do the job for a price of $800 (or slightly less). Georgia and Grandma are willing to do the work at this price, while Mary and Frida are not willing to bid a lower price. At a price of $800, Grandma receives producer surplus of $300 and Georgia receives producer surplus of $200. The total producer surplus in the market is $500.

7-2b Using the Supply Curve to Measure Producer Surplus

Just as consumer surplus is closely related to the demand curve, producer surplus is closely related to the supply curve. To see how, let's continue our example.

We begin by using the costs of the four painters to find the supply schedule for painting services. The table in Figure 4 shows the supply schedule that corresponds to the costs in Table 2. If the price is below $500, none of the four painters is willing to do the job, so the quantity supplied is zero. If the price is between $500 and $600, only Grandma is willing to do the job, so the quantity supplied is 1. If the price is between $600 and $800, Grandma and Georgia are willing to do the job, so the quantity supplied is 2, and so on. Thus, the supply schedule is derived from the costs of the four painters.

The graph in Figure 4 shows the supply curve that corresponds to this supply schedule. Note that the height of the supply curve is related to the sellers' costs. At any quantity, the price given by the supply curve shows the cost of the *marginal seller*, the seller who would leave the market first if the price were any lower. At a quantity of 4 houses, for instance, the supply curve has a height of $900, the cost that Mary (the marginal seller) incurs to provide her painting services. At a quantity of 3 houses, the supply curve has a height of $800, the cost that Frida (who is now the marginal seller) incurs.

FIGURE 4

The Supply Schedule and the Supply Curve

The table shows the supply schedule for the sellers (listed in Table 2) of painting services. The graph shows the corresponding supply curve. Note that the height of the supply curve reflects the sellers' costs.

Price	Sellers	Quantity Supplied
$900 or more	Mary, Frida, Georgia, Grandma	4
$800 to $900	Frida, Georgia, Grandma	3
$600 to $800	Georgia, Grandma	2
$500 to $600	Grandma	1
Less than $500	None	0

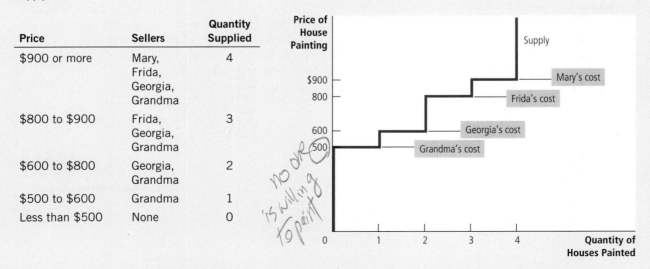

Because the supply curve reflects sellers' costs, we can use it to measure producer surplus. Figure 5 uses the supply curve to compute producer surplus in our two examples. In panel (a), we assume that the price is $600 (or slightly less). In this case, the quantity supplied is 1. Note that the area below the price and above the supply curve equals $100. This amount is exactly the producer surplus we computed earlier for Grandma.

Panel (b) of Figure 5 shows producer surplus at a price of $800 (or slightly less). In this case, the area below the price and above the supply curve equals the total area of the two rectangles. This area equals $500, the producer surplus we computed earlier for Georgia and Grandma when two houses needed painting.

The lesson from this example applies to all supply curves: *The area below the price and above the supply curve measures the producer surplus in a market.* The logic is straightforward: The height of the supply curve measures sellers' costs, and the difference between the price and the cost of production is each seller's producer surplus. Thus, the total area is the sum of the producer surplus of all sellers.

7-2c How a Higher Price Raises Producer Surplus

You will not be surprised to hear that sellers always want to receive a higher price for the goods they sell. But how much does sellers' well-being rise in response to a higher price? The concept of producer surplus offers a precise answer to this question.

Figure 6 shows a typical upward-sloping supply curve that would arise in a market with many sellers. Although this supply curve differs in shape from the previous figure, we measure producer surplus in the same way: Producer surplus

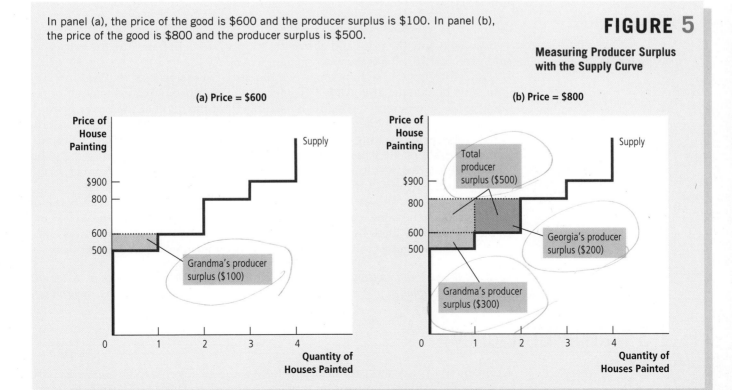

In panel (a), the price of the good is $600 and the producer surplus is $100. In panel (b), the price of the good is $800 and the producer surplus is $500.

FIGURE 5

Measuring Producer Surplus with the Supply Curve

FIGURE 6

How Price Affects Producer Surplus

In panel (a), the price is P_1, the quantity demanded is Q_1, and producer surplus equals the area of the triangle ABC. When the price rises from P_1 to P_2, as in panel (b), the quantity supplied rises from Q_1 to Q_2 and the producer surplus rises to the area of the triangle ADF. The increase in producer surplus (area BCFD) occurs in part because existing producers now receive more (area BCED) and in part because new producers enter the market at the higher price (area CEF).

(a) Producer Surplus at Price P_1

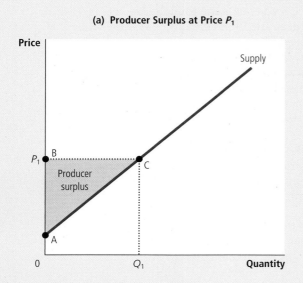

(b) Producer Surplus at Price P_2

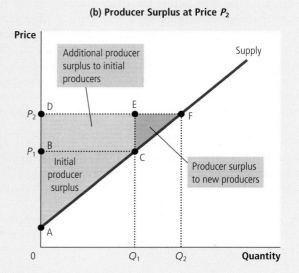

is the area below the price and above the supply curve. In panel (a), the price is P_1 and producer surplus is the area of triangle ABC.

Panel (b) shows what happens when the price rises from P_1 to P_2. Producer surplus now equals the area ADF. This increase in producer surplus has two parts. First, those sellers who were already selling Q_1 of the good at the lower price P_1 are better off because they now get more for what they sell. The increase in producer surplus for existing sellers equals the area of the rectangle BCED. Second, some new sellers enter the market because they are willing to produce the good at the higher price, resulting in an increase in the quantity supplied from Q_1 to Q_2. The producer surplus of these newcomers is the area of the triangle CEF.

As this analysis shows, we use producer surplus to measure the well-being of sellers in much the same way as we use consumer surplus to measure the well-being of buyers. Because these two measures of economic welfare are so similar, it is natural to use them together. And indeed, that is exactly what we do in the next section.

Quick Quiz   *Draw a supply curve for turkey. In your diagram, show a price of turkey and the producer surplus at that price. Explain in words what this producer surplus measures.*

7-3 Market Efficiency

Consumer surplus and producer surplus are the basic tools that economists use to study the welfare of buyers and sellers in a market. These tools can help us address a fundamental economic question: Is the allocation of resources determined by free markets desirable?

7-3a The Benevolent Social Planner

To evaluate market outcomes, we introduce into our analysis a new, hypothetical character called the benevolent social planner. The benevolent social planner is an all-knowing, all-powerful, well-intentioned dictator. The planner wants to maximize the economic well-being of everyone in society. What should this planner do? Should she just leave buyers and sellers at the equilibrium that they reach naturally on their own? Or can she increase economic well-being by altering the market outcome in some way?

To answer this question, the planner must first decide how to measure the economic well-being of a society. One possible measure is the sum of consumer and producer surplus, which we call *total surplus*. Consumer surplus is the benefit that buyers receive from participating in a market, and producer surplus is the benefit that sellers receive. It is therefore natural to use total surplus as a measure of society's economic well-being.

To better understand this measure of economic well-being, recall how we measure consumer and producer surplus. We define consumer surplus as

Consumer surplus = Value to buyers − Amount paid by buyers.

Similarly, we define producer surplus as

Producer surplus = Amount received by sellers − Cost to sellers.

When we add consumer and producer surplus together, we obtain

Total surplus = (Value to buyers − Amount paid by buyers)
+ (Amount received by sellers − Cost to sellers).

The amount paid by buyers equals the amount received by sellers, so the middle two terms in this expression cancel each other. As a result, we can write total surplus as

Total surplus = Value to buyers − Cost to sellers.

Total surplus in a market is the total value to buyers of the goods, as measured by their willingness to pay, minus the total cost to sellers of providing those goods.

If an allocation of resources maximizes total surplus, we say that the allocation exhibits **efficiency**. If an allocation is not efficient, then some of the potential gains from trade among buyers and sellers are not being realized. For example, an allocation is inefficient if a good is not being produced by the sellers with lowest cost. In this case, moving production from a high-cost producer to a low-cost producer will lower the total cost to sellers and raise total surplus. Similarly, an allocation is inefficient if a good is not being consumed by the buyers who value it most highly. In this case, moving consumption of the good from a buyer with a low valuation to a buyer with a high valuation will raise total surplus.

In addition to efficiency, the social planner might also care about **equality**—that is, whether the various buyers and sellers in the market have a similar level of economic well-being. In essence, the gains from trade in a market are like a pie to be shared among the market participants. The question of efficiency concerns whether the pie is as big as possible. The question of equality concerns how the pie is sliced and how the portions are distributed among members of society. In this chapter, we concentrate on efficiency as the social planner's goal. Keep in mind, however, that real policymakers often care about equality as well.

efficiency
the property of a resource allocation of maximizing the total surplus received by all members of society

equality
the property of distributing economic prosperity uniformly among the members of society

7-3b Evaluating the Market Equilibrium

Figure 7 shows consumer and producer surplus when a market reaches the equilibrium of supply and demand. Recall that consumer surplus equals the area above the price and under the demand curve and producer surplus equals the area below the price and above the supply curve. Thus, the total area between the supply and demand curves up to the point of equilibrium represents the total surplus in this market.

Is this equilibrium allocation of resources efficient? That is, does it maximize total surplus? To answer this question, recall that when a market is in equilibrium, the price determines which buyers and sellers participate in the market. Those buyers who value the good more than the price (represented by the segment AE on the demand curve) choose to buy the good; buyers who value it less than the price (represented by the segment EB) do not. Similarly, those sellers whose costs are less than the price (represented by the segment CE on the supply curve) choose to produce and sell the good; sellers whose costs are greater than the price (represented by the segment ED) do not.

These observations lead to two insights about market outcomes:

1. Free markets allocate the supply of goods to the buyers who value them most highly, as measured by their willingness to pay.
2. Free markets allocate the demand for goods to the sellers who can produce them at the lowest cost.

Thus, given the quantity produced and sold in a market equilibrium, the social planner cannot increase economic well-being by changing the allocation of consumption among buyers or the allocation of production among sellers.

But can the social planner raise total economic well-being by increasing or decreasing the quantity of the good? The answer is no, as stated in this third insight about market outcomes:

3. Free markets produce the quantity of goods that maximizes the sum of consumer and producer surplus.

FIGURE 7

Consumer and Producer Surplus in the Market Equilibrium
Total surplus—the sum of consumer and producer surplus—is the area between the supply and demand curves up to the equilibrium quantity.

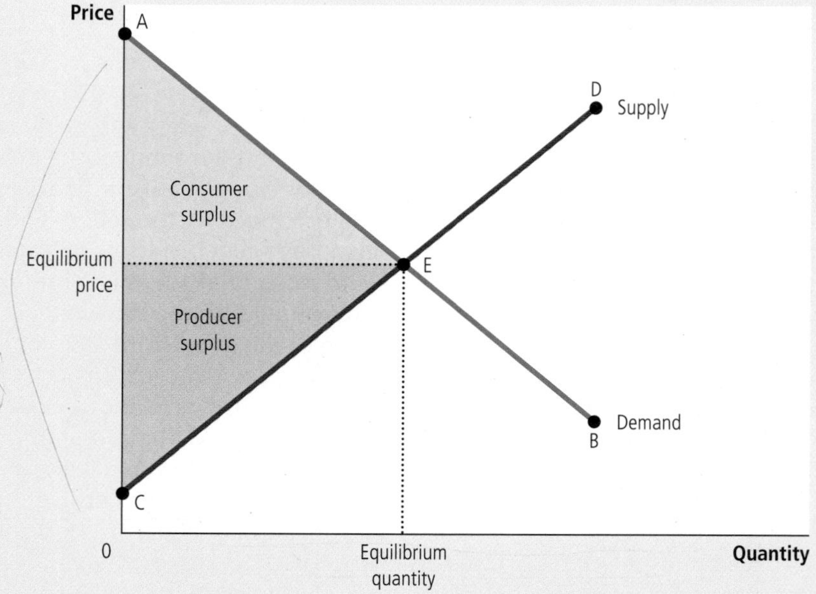

Figure 8 illustrates why this is true. To interpret this figure, keep in mind that the demand curve reflects the value to buyers and the supply curve reflects the cost to sellers. At any quantity below the equilibrium level, such as Q_1, the value to the marginal buyer exceeds the cost to the marginal seller. As a result, increasing the quantity produced and consumed raises total surplus. This continues to be true until the quantity reaches the equilibrium level. Similarly, at any quantity beyond the equilibrium level, such as Q_2, the value to the marginal buyer is less than the cost to the marginal seller. In this case, decreasing the quantity raises total surplus, and this continues to be true until quantity falls to the equilibrium level. To maximize total surplus, the social planner would choose the quantity where the supply and demand curves intersect.

Together, these three insights tell us that the market outcome makes the sum of consumer and producer surplus as large as it can be. In other words, the equilibrium outcome is an efficient allocation of resources. The benevolent social planner can, therefore, leave the market outcome just as she finds it. This policy of leaving well enough alone goes by the French expression *laissez faire*, which literally translates to "leave to do" but is more broadly interpreted as "let people do as they will."

Society is lucky that the planner doesn't need to intervene. Although it has been a useful exercise imagining what an all-knowing, all-powerful, well-intentioned dictator would do, let's face it: Such characters are hard to come by. Dictators are rarely benevolent, and even if we found someone so virtuous, she would lack crucial information.

Suppose our social planner tried to choose an efficient allocation of resources on her own, instead of relying on market forces. To do so, she would need to know the value of a particular good to every potential consumer in the market and the cost of every potential producer. And she would need this information not only for this market but for every one of the many thousands of markets in

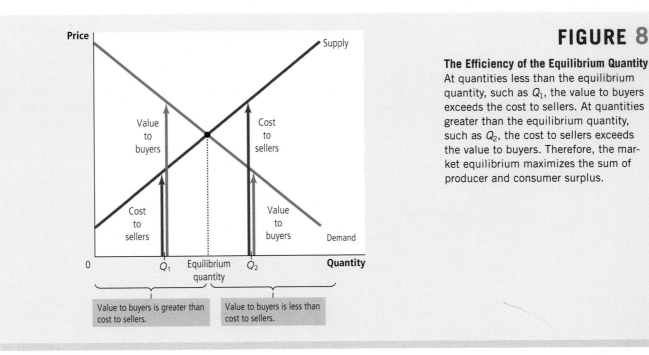

FIGURE 8

The Efficiency of the Equilibrium Quantity
At quantities less than the equilibrium quantity, such as Q_1, the value to buyers exceeds the cost to sellers. At quantities greater than the equilibrium quantity, such as Q_2, the cost to sellers exceeds the value to buyers. Therefore, the market equilibrium maximizes the sum of producer and consumer surplus.

IN THE NEWS
·················

The Invisible Hand Can Park Your Car

In many cities, finding an available parking spot on the street seems about as likely as winning the lottery. But if local governments relied more on the price system, they might be able to achieve a more efficient allocation of this scarce resource.

A Meter So Expensive, It Creates Parking Spots

By Michael Cooper and Jo Craven McGinty

SAN FRANCISCO—The maddening quest for street parking is not just a tribulation for drivers, but a trial for cities. As much as a third of the traffic in some areas has been attributed to drivers circling as they hunt for spaces. The wearying tradition takes a toll in lost time, polluted air and, when drivers despair, double-parked cars that clog traffic even more.

But San Francisco is trying to shorten the hunt with an ambitious experiment that aims to make sure that there is always at least one empty parking spot available on every block that has meters. The program, which uses new technology and the law of supply and demand, raises the price of parking on the city's most crowded blocks and lowers it on its emptiest blocks. While the new prices are still being phased in—the most expensive spots have risen to $4.50 an hour, but could reach $6—preliminary data suggests that the change may be having a positive effect in some areas.

Change can already be seen on a stretch of Drumm Street downtown near the Embarcadero and the popular restaurants at the Ferry Building. Last summer it was nearly impossible to find spots there. But after the city gradually raised the price of parking to $4.50 an hour from $3.50, high-tech sensors embedded in the street showed that spots were available a little more often—leaving a welcome space the other day for the silver Toyota Corolla driven by Victor Chew, a salesman for a commercial dishwasher company who frequently parks in the area.

"There are more spots available now," said Mr. Chew, 48. "Now I don't have to walk half a mile."

San Francisco's parking experiment is the latest major attempt to improve the uneasy relationship between cities and the internal combustion engine—a century-long saga that has seen cities build highways and tear them down, widen streets and narrow them, and make more parking available at some times and discourage it at others, all to try to make their downtowns accessible but not too congested.

The program here is being closely watched by cities around the country. With the help of a federal grant, San Francisco installed parking sensors and new meters at roughly a quarter of its 26,800 metered spots to track when and where cars are parked. And beginning last

---

the economy. The task is practically impossible, which explains why centrally planned economies never work very well.

The planner's job becomes easy, however, once she takes on a partner: Adam Smith's invisible hand of the marketplace. The invisible hand takes all the information about buyers and sellers into account and guides everyone in the market to the best outcome as judged by the standard of economic efficiency. It is, truly, a remarkable feat. That is why economists so often advocate free markets as the best way to organize economic activity.

case study **Should There Be a Market in Organs?**
Some years ago, the front page of the *Boston Globe* ran the headline "How a Mother's Love Helped Save Two Lives." The newspaper told the story of Susan Stephens, a woman whose son needed a kidney transplant. When the doctor learned that the mother's kidney was not compatible, he proposed a novel solution: If Stephens donated one of her kidneys to a stranger, her son would move to the top of the kidney waiting list. The mother accepted the deal, and soon two patients had the transplants they were waiting for.

summer, the city began tweaking its prices every two months—giving it the option of raising them 25 cents an hour, or lowering them by as much as 50 cents—in the hope of leaving each block with at least one available spot. The city also has cut prices at many of the garages and parking lots it manages, to lure cars off the street....

The program is the biggest test yet of the theories of Donald Shoup, a professor of urban planning at the University of California, Los Angeles. His 2005 book, "The High Cost of Free Parking," made him something of a cult figure to city planners—a Facebook group, The Shoupistas, has more than a thousand members. "I think the basic idea is that we will see a lot of benefits if we get the price of curbside parking right, which is the lowest price a city can charge and still have one or two vacant spaces available on every block," he said.

But raising prices is rarely popular. A chapter in Mr. Shoup's book opens with a quote from George Costanza, the "Seinfeld" character: "My father didn't pay for parking, my mother, my brother, nobody. It's like going to a prostitute. Why should I pay when, if I apply myself, maybe I can get it for free?" Some San Francisco neighborhoods recently objected to

The new San Francisco electronic parking meter helps equilibrate supply and demand.

a proposal to install meters on streets where parking is now free. And raising prices in the most desirable areas raises concerns that it will make them less accessible to the poor.

That was on the minds of some parkers on Drumm Street, where the midday occupancy rate on one block fell to 86 percent from 98 percent after prices rose. Edward Saldate, 55, a hairstylist who paid nearly $17 for close to four hours of parking there, called it "a big rip-off."

Tom Randlett, 69, an accountant, said that he was pleased to be able to find a spot there for the first time, but acknowledged that the program was "complicated on the social equity level."

Officials note that parking rates are cut as often as they are raised. And Professor Shoup said that the program would benefit many poor people, including the many San Franciscans who do not have cars, because all parking revenues are used for mass transit and any reduction in traffic will speed the buses many people here rely on. And he imagined a day when drivers will no longer attribute good parking spots to luck or karma.

"It will be taken for granted," he said, "the way you take it for granted that when you go to a store you can get fresh bananas or apples." ◢

The ingenuity of the doctor's proposal and the nobility of the mother's act cannot be doubted. But the story raises some intriguing questions. If the mother could trade a kidney for a kidney, would the hospital allow her to trade a kidney for an expensive, experimental cancer treatment that she could not otherwise afford? Should she be allowed to exchange her kidney for free tuition for her son at the hospital's medical school? Should she be able to sell her kidney so she can use the cash to trade in her old Chevy for a new Lexus?

As a matter of public policy, our society makes it illegal for people to sell their organs. In essence, in the market for organs, the government has imposed a price ceiling of zero. The result, as with any binding price ceiling, is a shortage of the good. The deal in the Stephens case did not fall under this prohibition because no cash changed hands.

Many economists believe that there would be large benefits to allowing a free market in organs. People are born with two kidneys, but they usually need only one. Meanwhile, a few people suffer from illnesses that leave them without any working kidney. Despite the obvious gains from trade, the current situation is dire: The typical patient has to wait several years for a kidney transplant, and every year thousands of people die because a compatible kidney cannot be found.

If those needing a kidney were allowed to buy one from those who have two, the price would rise to balance supply and demand. Sellers would be better off with the extra cash in their pockets. Buyers would be better off with the organ they need to save their lives. The shortage of kidneys would disappear.

Such a market would lead to an efficient allocation of resources, but critics of this plan worry about fairness. A market for organs, they argue, would benefit the rich at the expense of the poor because organs would then be allocated to those most willing and able to pay. But you can also question the fairness of the current system. Now, most of us walk around with an extra organ that we don't really need, while some of our fellow citizens are dying to get one. Is that fair? ◢

Quick Quiz   *Draw the supply and demand curves for turkey. In the equilibrium, show producer and consumer surplus. Explain why producing more turkeys would lower total surplus.*

7-4 Conclusion: Market Efficiency and Market Failure

This chapter introduced the basic tools of welfare economics—consumer and producer surplus—and used them to evaluate the efficiency of free markets. We showed that the forces of supply and demand allocate resources efficiently. That is, even though each buyer and seller in a market is concerned only about her own welfare, together they are led by an invisible hand to an equilibrium that maximizes the total benefits to buyers and sellers.

A word of warning is in order. To conclude that markets are efficient, we made several assumptions about how markets work. When these assumptions do not hold, our conclusion that the market equilibrium is efficient may no longer be true. As we close this chapter, let's consider briefly two of the most important of these assumptions.

First, our analysis assumed that markets are perfectly competitive. In actual economies, however, competition is sometimes far from perfect. In some markets, a single buyer or seller (or a small group of them) may be able to control market prices. This ability to influence prices is called *market power*. Market power can cause markets to be inefficient because it keeps the price and quantity away from the levels determined by the equilibrium of supply and demand.

Second, our analysis assumed that the outcome in a market matters only to the buyers and sellers who participate in that market. Yet sometimes the decisions of buyers and sellers affect people who are not participants in the market at all. Pollution is the classic example. The use of agricultural pesticides, for instance, affects not only the manufacturers who make them and the farmers who use them but many others who breathe air or drink water that has been polluted with these pesticides. When a market exhibits such side effects, called *externalities,* the welfare implications of market activity depend on more than just the value obtained by the buyers and the cost incurred by the sellers. Because buyers and sellers may ignore these side effects when deciding how much to consume and produce, the equilibrium in a market can be inefficient from the standpoint of society as a whole.

Market power and externalities are examples of a general phenomenon called *market failure*—the inability of some unregulated markets to allocate resources efficiently. When markets fail, public policy can potentially remedy the problem and increase economic efficiency. Microeconomists devote much effort to studying when market failure is likely and what sorts of policies are best at correcting market failures. As you continue your study of economics, you will see that the tools of welfare economics developed here are readily adapted to that endeavor.

Despite the possibility of market failure, the invisible hand of the marketplace is extraordinarily important. In many markets, the assumptions we made in this chapter work well and the conclusion of market efficiency applies directly. Moreover, we can use our analysis of welfare economics and market efficiency to shed light on the effects of various government policies. In the next two chapters, we apply the tools we have just developed to study two important policy issues—the welfare effects of taxation and of international trade.

Summary

- Consumer surplus equals buyers' willingness to pay for a good minus the amount they actually pay, and it measures the benefit buyers get from participating in a market. Consumer surplus can be computed by finding the area below the demand curve and above the price.

- Producer surplus equals the amount sellers receive for their goods minus their costs of production, and it measures the benefit sellers get from participating in a market. Producer surplus can be computed by finding the area below the price and above the supply curve.

- An allocation of resources that maximizes the sum of consumer and producer surplus is said to be efficient. Policymakers are often concerned with the efficiency, as well as the equality, of economic outcomes.

- The equilibrium of supply and demand maximizes the sum of consumer and producer surplus. That is, the invisible hand of the marketplace leads buyers and sellers to allocate resources efficiently.

- Markets do not allocate resources efficiently in the presence of market failures such as market power or externalities.

Key Concepts

welfare economics, p. 136
willingness to pay, p. 136
consumer surplus, p. 137
cost, p. 141
producer surplus, p. 141
efficiency, p. 145
equality, p. 145

Questions for Review

1. Explain how buyers' willingness to pay, consumer surplus, and the demand curve are related.

2. Explain how sellers' costs, producer surplus, and the supply curve are related.

3. In a supply-and-demand diagram, show producer and consumer surplus in the market equilibrium.

4. What is efficiency? Is it the only goal of economic policymakers?

5. Name two types of market failure. Explain why each may cause market outcomes to be inefficient.

Quick Check Multiple Choice

1. Jen values her time at $60 an hour. She spends 2 hours giving Colleen a massage. Colleen was willing to pay as much at $300 for the massage, but they negotiate a price of $200. In this transaction,
   a. consumer surplus is $20 larger than producer surplus.
   b. consumer surplus is $40 larger than producer surplus.
   c. producer surplus is $20 larger than consumer surplus.
   d. producer surplus is $40 larger than consumer surplus.

2. The demand curve for cookies is downward sloping. When the price of cookies is $2, the quantity demanded is 100. If the price rises to $3, what happens to consumer surplus?
   a. It falls by less than $100.
   b. It falls by more than $100.
   c. It rises by less than $100.
   d. It rises by more than $100.

3. John has been working as a tutor for $300 a semester. When the university raises the price it pays tutors to $400, Emily enters the market and begins tutoring as well. How much does producer surplus rise as a result of this price increase?
   a. by less than $100
   b. between $100 and $200
   c. between $200 and $300
   d. by more than $300

4. An efficient allocation of resources maximizes
   a. consumer surplus.
   b. producer surplus.
   c. consumer surplus plus producer surplus.
   d. consumer surplus minus producer surplus.

5. When a market is in equilibrium, the buyers are those with the _____ willingness to pay and the sellers are those with the _____ costs.
   a. highest, highest
   b. highest, lowest
   c. lowest, highest
   d. lowest, lowest

6. Producing a quantity larger than the equilibrium of supply and demand is inefficient because the marginal buyer's willingness to pay is
   a. negative.
   b. zero.
   c. positive but less than the marginal seller's cost.
   d. positive and greater than the marginal seller's cost.

Problems and Applications

1. Melissa buys an iPhone for $120 and gets consumer surplus of $80.
   a. What is her willingness to pay?
   b. If she had bought the iPhone on sale for $90, what would her consumer surplus have been?
   c. If the price of an iPhone were $250, what would her consumer surplus have been?

2. An early freeze in California sours the lemon crop. Explain what happens to consumer surplus in the market for lemons. Explain what happens to consumer surplus in the market for lemonade. Illustrate your answers with diagrams.

3. Suppose the demand for French bread rises. Explain what happens to producer surplus in the market for French bread. Explain what happens to producer surplus in the market for flour. Illustrate your answers with diagrams.

4. It is a hot day, and Bert is thirsty. Here is the value he places on each bottle of water:

Value of first bottle	$7
Value of second bottle	$5
Value of third bottle	$3
Value of fourth bottle	$1

   a. From this information, derive Bert's demand schedule. Graph his demand curve for bottled water.
   b. If the price of a bottle of water is $4, how many bottles does Bert buy? How much consumer surplus does Bert get from his purchases? Show Bert's consumer surplus in your graph.
   c. If the price falls to $2, how does quantity demanded change? How does Bert's consumer surplus change? Show these changes in your graph.

5. Ernie owns a water pump. Because pumping large amounts of water is harder than pumping small amounts, the cost of producing a bottle of water rises as he pumps more. Here is the cost he incurs to produce each bottle of water:

Cost of first bottle	$1
Cost of second bottle	$3
Cost of third bottle	$5
Cost of fourth bottle	$7

   a. From this information, derive Ernie's supply schedule. Graph his supply curve for bottled water.
   b. If the price of a bottle of water is $4, how many bottles does Ernie produce and sell? How much producer surplus does Ernie get from these sales? Show Ernie's producer surplus in your graph.
   c. If the price rises to $6, how does quantity supplied change? How does Ernie's producer surplus change? Show these changes in your graph.

6. Consider a market in which Bert from problem 4 is the buyer and Ernie from problem 5 is the seller.
   a. Use Ernie's supply schedule and Bert's demand schedule to find the quantity supplied and quantity demanded at prices of $2, $4, and $6. Which of these prices brings supply and demand into equilibrium?
   b. What are consumer surplus, producer surplus, and total surplus in this equilibrium?
   c. If Ernie produced and Bert consumed one fewer bottle of water, what would happen to total surplus?
   d. If Ernie produced and Bert consumed one additional bottle of water, what would happen to total surplus?

7. The cost of producing flat-screen TVs has fallen over the past decade. Let's consider some implications of this fact.
   a. Draw a supply-and-demand diagram to show the effect of falling production costs on the price and quantity of flat-screen TVs sold.
   b. In your diagram, show what happens to consumer surplus and producer surplus.
   c. Suppose the supply of flat-screen TVs is very elastic. Who benefits most from falling production costs—consumers or producers of these TVs?

8. There are four consumers willing to pay the following amounts for haircuts:

   Gloria: $7   Jay: $2   Claire: $8   Phil: $5

   There are four haircutting businesses with the following costs:

   Firm A: $3   Firm B: $6   Firm C: $4   Firm D: $2

   Each firm has the capacity to produce only one haircut. For efficiency, how many haircuts should be given? Which businesses should cut hair and which consumers should have their hair cut? How large is the maximum possible total surplus?

9. One of the largest changes in the economy over the past several decades is that technological advances have reduced the cost of making computers.
   a. Draw a supply-and-demand diagram to show what happened to price, quantity, consumer surplus, and producer surplus in the market for computers.
   b. Forty years ago, students used typewriters to prepare papers for their classes; today they use computers. Does that make computers and typewriters complements or substitutes? Use a supply-and-demand diagram to show what happened to price, quantity, consumer surplus, and producer surplus in the market for typewriters. Should typewriter producers have been happy or sad about the technological advance in computers?
   c. Are computers and software complements or substitutes? Draw a supply-and-demand diagram to show what happened to price, quantity, consumer surplus, and producer surplus in the market for software. Should software producers have been happy or sad about the technological advance in computers?
   d. Does this analysis help explain why software producer Bill Gates is one of the world's richest men?

10. A friend of yours is considering two cell phone service providers. Provider A charges $120 per month for the service regardless of the number of phone calls made. Provider B does not have a fixed service fee but instead charges $1 per minute for calls. Your friend's monthly demand for minutes of calling is given by the equation $Q^D = 150 - 50P$, where P is the price of a minute.
    a. With each provider, what is the cost to your friend of an extra minute on the phone?
    b. In light of your answer to (a), how many minutes with each provider would your friend talk on the phone?
    c. How much would she end up paying each provider every month?
    d. How much consumer surplus would she obtain with each provider? (*Hint*: Graph the demand curve and recall the formula for the area of a triangle.)
    e. Which provider would you recommend that your friend choose? Why?

11. Consider how health insurance affects the quantity of healthcare services performed. Suppose that the typical medical procedure has a cost of $100, yet a person with health insurance pays only $20 out of pocket. Her insurance company pays the remaining $80. (The insurance company recoups the $80 through premiums, but the premium a person pays does not depend on how many procedures that person chooses to undertake.)
    a. Draw the demand curve in the market for medical care. (In your diagram, the horizontal axis should represent the number of medical procedures.) Show the quantity of procedures demanded if each procedure has a price of $100.
    b. On your diagram, show the quantity of procedures demanded if consumers pay only $20 per procedure. If the cost of each procedure to society is truly $100, and if individuals have health insurance as just described, will the number of procedures performed maximize total surplus? Explain.
    c. Economists often blame the health insurance system for excessive use of medical care. Given your analysis, why might the use of care be viewed as "excessive"?
    d. What sort of policies might prevent this excessive use?

Go to CengageBrain.com to purchase access to the proven, critical Study Guide to accompany this text, which features additional notes and context, practice tests, and much more.

Application: The Costs of Taxation

Taxes are often a source of heated political debate. In 1776, the anger of the American colonists over British taxes sparked the American Revolution. More than two centuries later, the American political parties continue to debate the proper size and shape of the tax system. Yet no one would deny that some level of taxation is necessary. As Oliver Wendell Holmes, Jr., once said, "Taxes are what we pay for civilized society."

Because taxation has such a major impact on the modern economy, we return to the topic several times throughout this book as we expand the set of tools we have at our disposal. We began our study of taxes in Chapter 6. There we saw how a tax on a good affects its price and the quantity sold and how the forces of supply and demand divide the burden of a tax between buyers and sellers. In this chapter, we extend this analysis and look at how taxes affect welfare, the economic well-being of participants in a market. In other words, we see how high the price of civilized society can be.

The effects of taxes on welfare might at first seem obvious. The government enacts taxes to raise revenue and that revenue must come out of someone's pocket. As we saw in Chapter 6, both buyers and sellers are worse off when a good is taxed: A tax raises the price buyers pay and lowers the price sellers receive. Yet to understand more fully how taxes affect economic well-being, we must compare the reduced welfare of buyers and sellers to the amount of revenue the government raises. The tools of consumer and producer surplus allow us to make this comparison. Our analysis will show that the cost of taxes to buyers and sellers typically exceeds the revenue raised by the government.

8-1 The Deadweight Loss of Taxation

We begin by recalling one of the surprising lessons from Chapter 6: The impact of a tax on a market outcome is the same whether the tax is levied on buyers or sellers of a good. When a tax is levied on buyers, the demand curve shifts downward by the size of the tax; when it is levied on sellers, the supply curve shifts upward by that amount. In either case, when the tax is enacted, the price paid by buyers rises, and the price received by sellers falls. In the end, the elasticities of supply and demand determine how the tax burden is distributed between producers and consumers. This distribution is the same regardless of how it is levied.

Figure 1 shows these effects. To simplify our discussion, this figure does not show a shift in either the supply or demand curve, although one curve must shift. Which curve shifts depends on whether the tax is levied on sellers (the supply curve shifts) or buyers (the demand curve shifts). In this chapter, we can keep the analysis general and simplify the graphs by not bothering to show the shift. The key result for our purposes here is that the tax places a wedge between the price buyers pay and the price sellers receive. Because of this tax wedge, the quantity sold falls below the level that would be sold without a tax. In other words, a tax on

FIGURE 1

The Effects of a Tax
A tax on a good places a wedge between the price that buyers pay and the price that sellers receive. The quantity of the good sold falls.

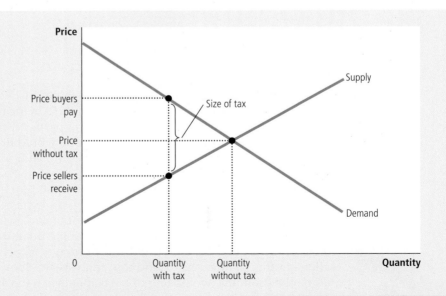

a good causes the size of the market for the good to shrink. These results should be familiar from Chapter 6.

8-1a How a Tax Affects Market Participants

Let's use the tools of welfare economics to measure the gains and losses from a tax on a good. To do this, we must take into account how the tax affects buyers, sellers, and the government. The benefit received by buyers in a market is measured by consumer surplus—the amount buyers are willing to pay for the good minus the amount they actually pay for it. The benefit received by sellers in a market is measured by producer surplus—the amount sellers receive for the good minus their costs. These are precisely the measures of economic welfare we used in Chapter 7.

What about the third interested party, the government? If T is the size of the tax and Q is the quantity of the good sold, then the government gets total tax revenue of $T \times Q$. It can use this tax revenue to provide services, such as roads, police, and public education, or to help the needy. Therefore, to analyze how taxes affect economic well-being, we use the government's tax revenue to measure the public benefit from the tax. Keep in mind, however, that this benefit actually accrues not to the government but to those on whom the revenue is spent.

Figure 2 shows that the government's tax revenue is represented by the rectangle between the supply and demand curves. The height of this rectangle is the size of the tax, T, and the width of the rectangle is the quantity of the good sold, Q. Because a rectangle's area is its height times its width, this rectangle's area is $T \times Q$, which equals the tax revenue.

Welfare without a Tax   To see how a tax affects welfare, we begin by considering welfare before the government imposes a tax. Figure 3 shows the supply-and-demand diagram and marks the key areas with the letters A through F.

Without a tax, the equilibrium price and quantity are found at the intersection of the supply and demand curves. The price is P_1, and the quantity sold is Q_1.

"You know, the idea of taxation with representation doesn't appeal to me very much, either."

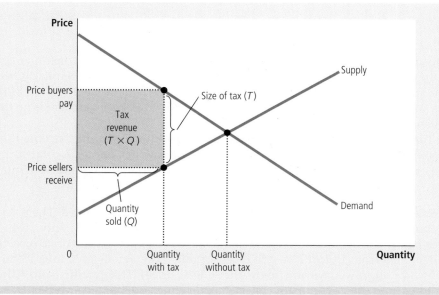

FIGURE 2

Tax Revenue
The tax revenue that the government collects equals $T \times Q$, the size of the tax T times the quantity sold Q. Thus, tax revenue equals the area of the rectangle between the supply and demand curves.

FIGURE 3

How a Tax Affects Welfare

A tax on a good reduces consumer surplus (by the area B + C) and producer surplus (by the area D + E). Because the fall in producer and consumer surplus exceeds tax revenue (area B + D), the tax is said to impose a deadweight loss (area C + E).

	Without Tax	With Tax	Change
Consumer Surplus	A + B + C	A	−(B + C)
Producer Surplus	D + E + F	F	−(D + E)
Tax Revenue	None	B + D	+(B + D)
Total Surplus	A + B + C + D + E + F	A + B + D + F	−(C + E)

The area C + E shows the fall in total surplus and is the deadweight loss of the tax.

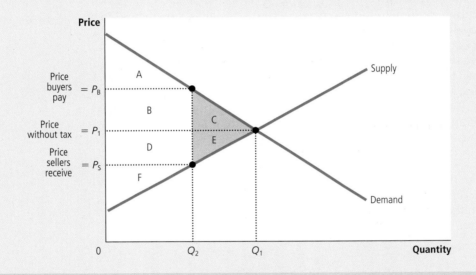

Because the demand curve reflects buyers' willingness to pay, consumer surplus is the area between the demand curve and the price, A + B + C. Similarly, because the supply curve reflects sellers' costs, producer surplus is the area between the supply curve and the price, D + E + F. In this case, because there is no tax, tax revenue equals zero.

Total surplus, the sum of consumer and producer surplus, equals the area A + B + C + D + E + F. In other words, as we saw in Chapter 7, total surplus is the area between the supply and demand curves up to the equilibrium quantity. The first column of the table in Figure 3 summarizes these conclusions.

Welfare with a Tax Now consider welfare after the tax is enacted. The price paid by buyers rises from P_1 to P_B, so consumer surplus now equals only area A (the area below the demand curve and above the buyer's price). The price received by sellers falls from P_1 to P_S, so producer surplus now equals only area F (the area above the supply curve and below the seller's price). The quantity sold falls from Q_1 to Q_2, and the government collects tax revenue equal to the area B + D.

To compute total surplus with the tax, we add consumer surplus, producer surplus, and tax revenue. Thus, we find that total surplus is area A + B + D + F. The second column of the table summarizes these results.

Changes in Welfare   We can now see the effects of the tax by comparing welfare before and after the tax is enacted. The third column of the table in Figure 3 shows the changes. The tax causes consumer surplus to fall by the area B + C and producer surplus to fall by the area D + E. Tax revenue rises by the area B + D. Not surprisingly, the tax makes buyers and sellers worse off and the government better off.

The change in total welfare includes the change in consumer surplus (which is negative), the change in producer surplus (which is also negative), and the change in tax revenue (which is positive). When we add these three pieces together, we find that total surplus in the market falls by the area C + E. *Thus, the losses to buyers and sellers from a tax exceed the revenue raised by the government.* The fall in total surplus that results when a tax (or some other policy) distorts a market outcome is called a **deadweight loss**. The area C + E measures the size of the deadweight loss.

To understand why taxes impose deadweight losses, recall one of the *Ten Principles of Economics* in Chapter 1: People respond to incentives. In Chapter 7, we saw that free markets normally allocate scarce resources efficiently. That is, in the absence of any tax, the equilibrium of supply and demand maximizes the total surplus of buyers and sellers in a market. When the government imposes a tax, it raises the price buyers pay and lowers the price sellers receive, giving buyers an incentive to consume less and sellers an incentive to produce less. As buyers and sellers respond to these incentives, the size of the market shrinks below its optimum (as shown in the figure by the movement from Q_1 to Q_2). Thus, because taxes distort incentives, they cause markets to allocate resources inefficiently.

deadweight loss
the fall in total surplus that results from a market distortion, such as a tax

8-1b Deadweight Losses and the Gains from Trade

To get some further insight into why taxes result in deadweight losses, consider an example. Imagine that Joe cleans Jane's house each week for $100. The opportunity cost of Joe's time is $80, and the value of a clean house to Jane is $120. Thus, Joe and Jane each receive a $20 benefit from their deal. The total surplus of $40 measures the gains from trade in this particular transaction.

Now suppose that the government levies a $50 tax on the providers of cleaning services. There is now no price that Jane can pay Joe that will leave both of them better off. The most Jane would be willing to pay is $120, but then Joe would be left with only $70 after paying the tax, which is less than his $80 opportunity cost. Conversely, for Joe to receive his opportunity cost of $80, Jane would need to pay $130, which is above the $120 value she places on a clean house. As a result, Jane and Joe cancel their arrangement. Joe goes without the income, and Jane lives in a dirtier house.

The tax has made Joe and Jane worse off by a total of $40 because they have each lost $20 of surplus. But note that the government collects no revenue from Joe and Jane because they decide to cancel their arrangement. The $40 is pure deadweight loss: It is a loss to buyers and sellers in a market that is not offset by an increase in government revenue. From this example, we can see the ultimate source of deadweight losses: *Taxes cause deadweight losses because they prevent buyers and sellers from realizing some of the gains from trade.*

The area of the triangle between the supply and demand curves created by the tax wedge (area C + E in Figure 3) measures these losses. This conclusion can be seen more easily in Figure 4 by recalling that the demand curve reflects the value

FIGURE 4

The Source of a Deadweight Loss

When the government imposes a tax on a good, the quantity sold falls from Q_1 to Q_2. At every quantity between Q_1 and Q_2, the potential gains from trade among buyers and sellers are not realized. These lost gains from trade create the deadweight loss.

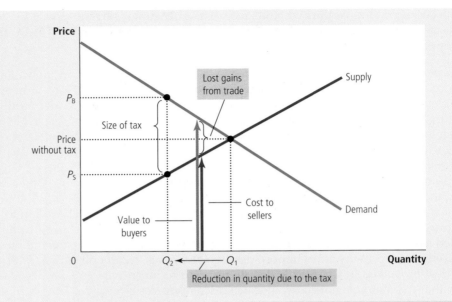

of the good to consumers and that the supply curve reflects the costs of producers. When the tax raises the price buyers pay to P_B and lowers the price sellers receive to P_S, the marginal buyers and sellers leave the market, so the quantity sold falls from Q_1 to Q_2. Yet as the figure shows, the value of the good to these buyers still exceeds the cost to these sellers. At every quantity between Q_1 and Q_2, the situation is the same as in our example with Joe and Jane. The gains from trade—the difference between buyers' value and sellers' cost—are less than the tax. As a result, these trades are not made once the tax is imposed. The deadweight loss is the surplus that is lost because the tax discourages these mutually advantageous trades.

Quick Quiz *Draw the supply and demand curves for cookies. If the government imposes a tax on cookies, show what happens to the price paid by buyers, the price received by sellers, and the quantity sold. In your diagram, show the deadweight loss from the tax. Explain the meaning of the deadweight loss.*

8-2 The Determinants of the Deadweight Loss

What determines whether the deadweight loss from a tax is large or small? The answer is the price elasticities of supply and demand, which measure how much the quantity supplied and quantity demanded respond to changes in the price.

Let's consider first how the elasticity of supply affects the size of the deadweight loss. In the top two panels of Figure 5, the demand curve and the size of the tax are the same. The only difference in these figures is the elasticity of the supply curve. In panel (a), the supply curve is relatively inelastic: Quantity supplied responds only slightly to changes in the price. In panel (b), the supply curve is relatively elastic: Quantity supplied responds substantially to changes in the

In panels (a) and (b), the demand curve and the size of the tax are the same, but the price elasticity of supply is different. Notice that the more elastic the supply curve, the larger the deadweight loss of the tax. In panels (c) and (d), the supply curve and the size of the tax are the same, but the price elasticity of demand is different. Notice that the more elastic the demand curve, the larger the deadweight loss of the tax.

FIGURE 5

Tax Distortions and Elasticities

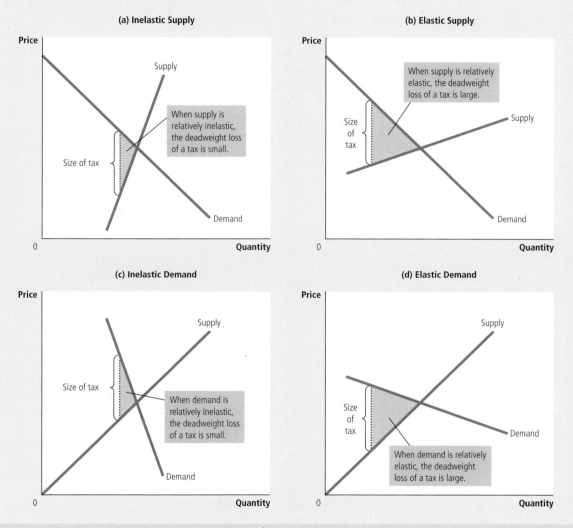

(a) Inelastic Supply

Price

Supply

When supply is relatively inelastic, the deadweight loss of a tax is small.

Size of tax

Demand

Quantity

0

(b) Elastic Supply

Price

When supply is relatively elastic, the deadweight loss of a tax is large.

Size of tax

Supply

Demand

Quantity

0

(c) Inelastic Demand

Price

Supply

Size of tax

When demand is relatively inelastic, the deadweight loss of a tax is small.

Demand

Quantity

0

(d) Elastic Demand

Price

Supply

Size of tax

Demand

When demand is relatively elastic, the deadweight loss of a tax is large.

Quantity

0

price. Notice that the deadweight loss, the area of the triangle between the supply and demand curves, is larger when the supply curve is more elastic.

Similarly, the bottom two panels of Figure 5 show how the elasticity of demand affects the size of the deadweight loss. Here the supply curve and the size of the tax are held constant. In panel (c), the demand curve is relatively inelastic, and the deadweight loss is small. In panel (d), the demand curve is more elastic, and the deadweight loss from the tax is larger.

The lesson from this figure is apparent. A tax has a deadweight loss because it induces buyers and sellers to change their behavior. The tax raises the price paid by buyers, so they consume less. At the same time, the tax lowers the price received by sellers, so they produce less. Because of these changes in behavior, the equilibrium quantity in the market shrinks below the optimal quantity. The more responsive buyers and sellers are to changes in the price, the more the equilibrium quantity shrinks. Hence, *the greater the elasticities of supply and demand, the greater the deadweight loss of a tax.*

<table><tr><td>case
study</td><td></td></tr></table>

The Deadweight Loss Debate

Supply, demand, elasticity, deadweight loss—all this economic theory is enough to make your head spin. But believe it or not, these ideas go to the heart of a profound political question: How big should the government be? The debate hinges on these concepts because the larger the deadweight loss of taxation, the larger the cost of any government program. If taxation entails large deadweight losses, then these losses are a strong argument for a leaner government that does less and taxes less. But if taxes impose small deadweight losses, then government programs are less costly than they otherwise might be.

So how big are the deadweight losses of taxation? Economists disagree on the answer to this question. To see the nature of this disagreement, consider the most important tax in the U.S. economy: the tax on labor. The Social Security tax, the Medicare tax, and much of the federal income tax are labor taxes. Many state governments also tax labor earnings. A labor tax places a wedge between the wage that firms pay and the wage that workers receive. For a typical worker, if all forms of labor taxes are added together, the *marginal tax rate* on labor income—the tax on the last dollar of earnings—is about 40 percent.

The size of the labor tax is easy to determine, but the deadweight loss of this tax is less straightforward. Economists disagree about whether this 40 percent labor tax has a small or a large deadweight loss. This disagreement arises because economists hold different views about the elasticity of labor supply.

Economists who argue that labor taxes do not greatly distort market outcomes believe that labor supply is fairly inelastic. Most people, they claim, would work full-time regardless of the wage. If so, the labor supply curve is almost vertical, and a tax on labor has a small deadweight loss.

Economists who argue that labor taxes are highly distorting believe that labor supply is more elastic. While admitting that some groups of workers may not change the quantity of labor they supply by very much in response to changes in labor taxes, these economists claim that many other groups respond more to incentives. Here are some examples:

- Many workers can adjust the number of hours they work—for instance, by working overtime. The higher the wage, the more hours they choose to work.
- Some families have second earners—often married women with children—with some discretion over whether to do unpaid work at home or paid work in the marketplace. When deciding whether to take a job, these second earners compare the benefits of being at home (including savings on the cost of child care) with the wages they could earn.
- Many of the elderly can choose when to retire, and their decisions are partly based on the wage. Once they are retired, the wage determines their incentive to work part-time.

- Some people consider engaging in illegal economic activity, such as the drug trade, or working at jobs that pay "under the table" to evade taxes. Economists call this the *underground economy*. In deciding whether to work in the underground economy or at a legitimate job, these potential criminals compare what they can earn by breaking the law with the wage they can earn legally.

"What's your position on the elasticity of labor supply?"

In each of these cases, the quantity of labor supplied responds to the wage (the price of labor). Thus, these workers' decisions are distorted when their labor earnings are taxed. Labor taxes encourage workers to work fewer hours, second earners to stay at home, the elderly to retire early, and the unscrupulous to enter the underground economy.

The debate over the distortionary effects of labor taxation persists to this day. Indeed, whenever you see two political candidates debating whether the government should provide more services or reduce the tax burden, keep in mind that part of the disagreement may rest on different views about the elasticity of labor supply and the deadweight loss of taxation. ◢

Quick Quiz *The demand for beer is more elastic than the demand for milk. Would a tax on beer or a tax on milk have a larger deadweight loss? Why?*

8-3 Deadweight Loss and Tax Revenue as Taxes Vary

Taxes rarely stay the same for long periods of time. Policymakers in local, state, and federal governments are always considering raising one tax or lowering another. Here we consider what happens to the deadweight loss and tax revenue when the size of a tax changes.

Figure 6 shows the effects of a small, medium, and large tax, holding constant the market's supply and demand curves. The deadweight loss—the reduction in total surplus that results when the tax reduces the size of a market below the optimum—equals the area of the triangle between the supply and demand curves. For the small tax in panel (a), the area of the deadweight loss triangle is quite small. But as the size of a tax rises in panels (b) and (c), the deadweight loss grows larger and larger.

Indeed, the deadweight loss of a tax rises even more rapidly than the size of the tax. This occurs because the deadweight loss is the area of a triangle, and the area of a triangle depends on the *square* of its size. If we double the size of a tax, for instance, the base and height of the triangle double, so the deadweight loss rises by a factor of 4. If we triple the size of a tax, the base and height triple, so the deadweight loss rises by a factor of 9.

The government's tax revenue is the size of the tax times the amount of the good sold. As the first three panels of Figure 6 show, tax revenue equals the area of the rectangle between the supply and demand curves. For the small tax in panel (a), tax revenue is small. As the size of a tax increases from panel (a) to panel (b), tax revenue grows. But as the size of the tax increases further from panel (b) to panel (c), tax revenue falls because the higher tax drastically reduces the size of the market. For a very large tax, no revenue would be raised because people would stop buying and selling the good altogether.

The last two panels of Figure 6 summarize these results. In panel (d), we see that as the size of a tax increases, its deadweight loss quickly gets larger. By contrast, panel (e) shows that tax revenue first rises with the size of the tax, but as the tax increases further, the market shrinks so much that tax revenue starts to fall.

FIGURE 6

How Deadweight Loss and Tax Revenue Vary with the Size of a Tax

The deadweight loss is the reduction in total surplus due to the tax. Tax revenue is the amount of the tax times the amount of the good sold. In panel (a), a small tax has a small deadweight loss and raises a small amount of revenue. In panel (b), a somewhat larger tax has a larger deadweight loss and raises a larger amount of revenue. In panel (c), a very large tax has a very large deadweight loss, but because it has reduced the size of the market so much, the tax raises only a small amount of revenue. Panels (d) and (e) summarize these conclusions. Panel (d) shows that as the size of a tax grows larger, the deadweight loss grows larger. Panel (e) shows that tax revenue first rises and then falls. This relationship is sometimes called the Laffer curve.

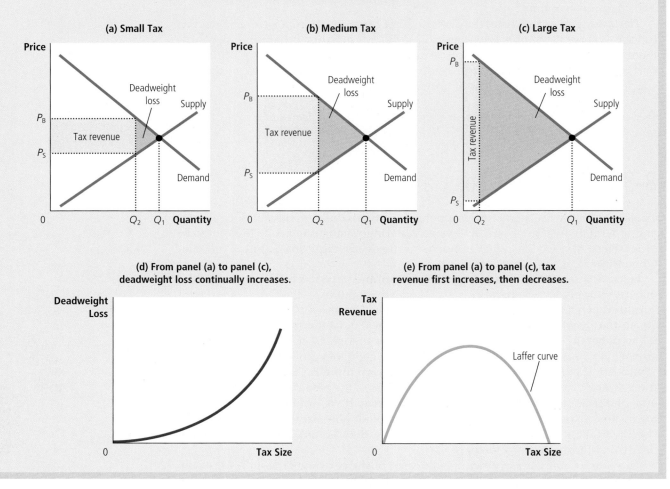

(a) Small Tax

(b) Medium Tax

(c) Large Tax

(d) From panel (a) to panel (c), deadweight loss continually increases.

(e) From panel (a) to panel (c), tax revenue first increases, then decreases.

case study

The Laffer Curve and Supply-Side Economics

One day in 1974, economist Arthur Laffer sat in a Washington restaurant with some prominent journalists and politicians. He took out a napkin and drew a figure on it to show how tax rates affect tax revenue. It looked much like panel (e) of our Figure 6. Laffer then suggested that the United States was on the downward-sloping side of this curve. Tax rates were so high, he argued, that reducing them would actually increase tax revenue.

Most economists were skeptical of Laffer's suggestion. The idea that a cut in tax rates could increase tax revenue was correct as a matter of economic theory, but there was more doubt about whether it would do so in practice. There was little evidence for Laffer's view that U.S. tax rates had in fact reached such extreme levels.

Nonetheless, the *Laffer curve* (as it became known) captured the imagination of Ronald Reagan. David Stockman, budget director in the first Reagan administration, offers the following story:

> [Reagan] had once been on the Laffer curve himself. "I came into the Big Money making pictures during World War II," he would always say. At that time the wartime income surtax hit 90 percent. "You could only make four pictures and then you were in the top bracket," he would continue. "So we all quit working after four pictures and went off to the country." High tax rates caused less work. Low tax rates caused more. His experience proved it.

When Reagan ran for president in 1980, he made cutting taxes part of his platform. Reagan argued that taxes were so high that they were discouraging hard work. He argued that lower taxes would give people the proper incentive to work, which would raise economic well-being and perhaps even tax revenue. Because the cut in tax rates was intended to encourage people to increase the quantity of labor they supplied, the views of Laffer and Reagan became known as *supply-side economics*.

Economists continue to debate Laffer's argument. Many believe that subsequent history refuted Laffer's conjecture that lower tax rates would raise tax revenue. Yet because history is open to alternative interpretations, other economists view the events of the 1980s as more favorable to the supply siders. To evaluate Laffer's hypothesis definitively, we would need to rerun history without the Reagan tax cuts and see if tax revenues were higher or lower. Unfortunately, that experiment is impossible.

Some economists take an intermediate position on this issue. They believe that while an overall cut in tax rates normally reduces revenue, some taxpayers may occasionally find themselves on the wrong side of the Laffer curve. Other things being equal, a tax cut is more likely to raise tax revenue if the cut applies to those taxpayers facing the highest tax rates. In addition, Laffer's argument may be more compelling when considering countries with much higher tax rates than the United States. In Sweden in the early 1980s, for instance, the typical worker faced a marginal tax rate of about 80 percent. Such a high tax rate provides a substantial disincentive to work. Studies have suggested that Sweden would indeed have raised more tax revenue if it had lowered its tax rates.

Economists disagree about these issues in part because there is no consensus about the size of the relevant elasticities. The more elastic supply and demand are in any market, the more taxes distort behavior, and the more likely it is that a tax cut will increase tax revenue. There is no debate, however, about the general lesson: How much revenue the government gains or loses from a tax change cannot be computed just by looking at tax rates. It also depends on how the tax change affects people's behavior. ◢

Quick Quiz *If the government doubles the tax on gasoline, can you be sure that revenue from the gasoline tax will rise? Can you be sure that the deadweight loss from the gasoline tax will rise? Explain.*

IN THE NEWS   The Tax Debate
· · · · · · · · · · · · · ·

In 2012, during and after President Obama's reelection campaign, a prominent policy debate centered on whether to increase taxes, particularly on higher-income taxpayers. In these two opinion pieces, prominent economists present both sides of the issue.

High Tax Rates Won't Slow Growth

By Peter Diamond and Emmanuel Saez

The share of pre-tax income accruing to the top 1% of earners in the U.S. has more than doubled to about 20% in 2010 from less than 10% in the 1970s. At the same time, the average federal income tax rate on top earners has declined significantly. Given the large current and projected deficits, should the top 1% be taxed more? Because U.S. income concentration is now so high, the potential tax revenue at stake is large.

But will taxable incomes of the top 1% respond to a tax increase by declining so much that revenue rises very little or even drops? In other words, are we already near or beyond the peak of the famous Laffer Curve, the revenue-maximizing tax rate?

The Laffer Curve is used to illustrate the concept of taxable income "elasticity,"—i.e., that taxable income will change in response to a change in the rate of taxation. Top earners can, of course, move taxable income between years to subject them to lower tax rates, for example, by changing the timing of charitable donations and realized capital gains. And some can convert earned income into capital gains, and avoid higher taxes in other ways. But existing studies do not show much change in actual work being done.

According to our analysis of current tax rates and their elasticity, the revenue-maximizing top federal marginal income tax rate would be in or near the range of 50%–70% (taking into account that individuals face additional taxes from Medicare and state and local taxes). Thus we conclude that raising the top tax rate is very likely to result in revenue increases at least until we reach the 50% rate that held during the first Reagan administration, and possibly until the 70% rate of the 1970s. To reduce tax avoidance opportunities, tax rates on capital gains and dividends should increase along with the basic rate. Closing loopholes and stepping up enforcement would further limit tax avoidance and evasion.

But will raising top tax rates significantly lower economic growth? In the postwar U.S., higher top tax rates tend to go with higher economic growth—not lower. Indeed, according to the U.S. Department of Commerce's Bureau of Economic Analysis, GDP annual growth per capita (to adjust for population growth) averaged 1.68% between 1980 and 2010 when top tax rates were relatively low, while growth averaged 2.23% between 1950 and 1980 when top tax rates were at or above 70%.

Neither does international evidence support a case for lower growth from higher top taxes. There is no clear correlation between economic growth since the 1970s and top tax-rate cuts across Organization for Economic Cooperation and Development countries.

For example, from 1970 to 2010, real GDP annual growth per capita averaged 1.8% and 2.03% in the U.S. and the U.K., both of which dramatically lowered their top tax rates during that period, while it averaged 1.72% and 1.89% in France and Germany, which kept high top tax rates during the period. While in no way does this prove that higher top tax rates actually encourage growth, there is not good evidence from the aggregate data supporting the view that higher rates slow growth.

One cannot evaluate the ultimate growth effects of raising more revenue without identifying what is done with the revenue. If part of the revenue is used to reduce the federal debt, more of savings go into capital investment, enhancing growth. The fact that those paying higher taxes will reduce their savings somewhat does not fully offset this effect as some of their higher taxes would come out of consumption.

If some of the additional revenue is used for public investments with a high return, such as education, infrastructure and research, it raises growth further. The neglect of public investment over the last few decades suggests that the returns could be quite high.

Large losses in efficiency come when people are limited in their ability to finance good investment opportunities. Surveys show difficulty of borrowing as an issue for start-ups. And higher education is influenced by the finances of parents, and the earnings premium for higher education is very high. Access to investment financing is a much bigger issue for low earners than for high earners. By the time Bill Gates got rich, Microsoft was not likely to have trouble financing investments. Hence, increasing tax rates on the already rich might not hurt growth as much as increasing tax rates on the soon-to-be rich.

By itself, a suitable increase in the taxation of top earners will not solve our unsustainable long-term fiscal trajectory. But that is no reason not to use this tool to contribute to addressing this problem.

Mr. Diamond is professor emeritus at MIT and a Nobel laureate in economics. Mr. Saez is a professor of economics at UC Berkeley. ◢

Taxes Are Much Higher Than You Think

By Edward C. Prescott and Lee E. Ohanian

President Obama argues that the election gave him a mandate to raise taxes on high earners, and the White House indicates that he won't compromise on this issue as the so-called fiscal cliff approaches.

But tax rates are already high—much higher than is commonly understood—and increasing them will likely further depress the economy, especially by affecting the number of hours Americans work.

Taking into account all taxes on earnings and consumer spending—including federal, state and local income taxes, Social Security and Medicare payroll taxes, excise taxes, and state and local sales taxes—Edward Prescott has shown (especially in the *Quarterly Review of the Federal Reserve Bank of Minneapolis*, 2004) that the U.S. average marginal effective tax rate is around 40%. This means that if the average worker earns $100 from additional output, he will be able to consume only an additional $60.

Research by others (including Lee Ohanian, Andrea Raffo and Richard Rogerson in the *Journal of Monetary Economics*, 2008, and Edward Prescott in the *American Economic Review*, 2002) indicates that raising tax rates further will significantly reduce U.S. economic activity and by implication will increase tax revenues only a little.

High tax rates—on both labor income and consumption—reduce the incentive to work by making consumption more expensive relative to leisure, for example. The incentive to produce goods for the market is particularly depressed when tax revenue is returned to households either as government transfers or transfers-in-kind—such as public schooling, police and fire protection, food stamps, and health care—that substitute for private consumption.

In the 1950s, when European tax rates were low, many Western Europeans, including

the French and the Germans, worked more hours per capita than did Americans. Over time, tax rates that affect earnings and consumption rose substantially in much of Western Europe. Over the decades, these have accounted for much of the nearly 30% decline in work hours in several European countries—to 1,000 hours per adult per year today from around 1,400 in the 1950s.

Changes in tax rates are also important in accounting for the increase in the number of hours worked in the Netherlands in the late 1980s, following the enactment of lower marginal income-tax rates.

In Japan, the tax rate on earnings and consumption is about the same as it is in the U.S., and the average Japanese worker in 2007 (the last nonrecession year) worked 1,363 hours—or about the same as the 1,336 worked by the average American.

All this has major implications for the U.S. Consider California, which just enacted higher rates of income and sales tax. The top California income-tax rate will be 13.3%, and the top sales-tax rate in some areas may rise as high as 10%. Combine these state taxes with a top combined federal rate of 44%, plus federal excise taxes, and the combined marginal tax rate for the highest California earners is likely to be around 60%—as high as in France, Germany and Italy.

Higher labor-income and consumption taxes also have consequences for entrepreneurship and risk-taking. A key factor driving U.S. economic growth has been the remarkable impact of entrepreneurs such as Bill Gates of Microsoft, Steve Jobs of Apple, Fred Smith of FedEx and others who took substantial risk to implement new ideas, directly and indirectly creating new economic sectors and millions of new jobs.

Entrepreneurship is much lower in Europe, suggesting that high tax rates and poorly designed regulation discourage new business creation. *The Economist* reports that between 1976 and 2007 only one continental European startup, Norway's Renewable

Energy Corporation, achieved a level of success comparable to that of Microsoft, Apple and other U.S. giants making the Financial Times Index of the world's 500 largest companies. ...

The economy now faces two serious risks: the risk of higher marginal tax rates that will depress the number of hours of work, and the risk of continuing policies such as Dodd-Frank, bailouts, and subsidies to specific industries and technologies that depress productivity growth by protecting inefficient producers and restricting the flow of resources to the most productive users.

If these two risks are realized, the U.S. will face a much more serious problem than a 2013 recession. It will face a permanent and growing decline in relative living standards....

Economic growth requires new ideas and new businesses, which in turn require a large group of talented young workers who are willing to take on the considerable risk of starting a business. This requires undoing the impediments that stand in the way of creating new economic activity—and increasing the after-tax returns to succeeding.

Mr. Prescott is a professor at Arizona State University and a Nobel laureate in economics. Mr. Ohanian is a professor of economics at UCLA.

8-4 Conclusion

In this chapter we have used the tools developed in the previous chapter to further our understanding of taxes. One of the *Ten Principles of Economics* discussed in Chapter 1 is that markets are usually a good way to organize economic activity. In Chapter 7, we used the concepts of producer and consumer surplus to make this principle more precise. Here we have seen that when the government imposes taxes on buyers or sellers of a good, society loses some of the benefits of market efficiency. Taxes are costly to market participants not only because taxes transfer resources from those participants to the government but also because they alter incentives and distort market outcomes.

The analysis presented here and in Chapter 6 should give you a good basis for understanding the economic impact of taxes, but this is not the end of the story. Microeconomists study how best to design a tax system, including how to strike the right balance between equality and efficiency. Macroeconomists study how taxes influence the overall economy and how policymakers can use the tax system to stabilize economic activity and to achieve more rapid economic growth. So as you continue your study of economics, don't be surprised when the subject of taxation comes up yet again.

Summary

- A tax on a good reduces the welfare of buyers and sellers of the good, and the reduction in consumer and producer surplus usually exceeds the revenue raised by the government. The fall in total surplus—the sum of consumer surplus, producer surplus, and tax revenue—is called the deadweight loss of the tax.

- Taxes have deadweight losses because they cause buyers to consume less and sellers to produce less, and these changes in behavior shrink the size of the market below the level that maximizes total surplus. Because

the elasticities of supply and demand measure how much market participants respond to market conditions, larger elasticities imply larger deadweight losses.

- As a tax grows larger, it distorts incentives more, and its deadweight loss grows larger. Because a tax reduces the size of the market, however, tax revenue does not continually increase. It first rises with the size of a tax, but if the tax gets large enough, tax revenue starts to fall.

Key Concept

deadweight loss, *p. 159*

Questions for Review

1. What happens to consumer and producer surplus when the sale of a good is taxed? How does the change in consumer and producer surplus compare to the tax revenue? Explain.

2. Draw a supply-and-demand diagram with a tax on the sale of a good. Show the deadweight loss. Show the tax revenue.

3. How do the elasticities of supply and demand affect the deadweight loss of a tax? Why do they have this effect?

4. Why do experts disagree about whether labor taxes have small or large deadweight losses?

5. What happens to the deadweight loss and tax revenue when a tax is increased?

Quick Check Multiple Choice

1. A tax on a good has a deadweight loss if
   a. the reduction in consumer and producer surplus is greater than the tax revenue.
   b. the tax revenue is greater than the reduction in consumer and producer surplus.
   c. the reduction in consumer surplus is greater than the reduction in producer surplus.
   d. the reduction in producer surplus is greater than the reduction in consumer surplus.

2. Jane pays Chuck $50 to mow her lawn every week. When the government levies a mowing tax of $10 on Chuck, he raises his price to $60. Jane continues to hire him at the higher price. What is the change in producer surplus, change in consumer surplus, and deadweight loss?
   a. $0, $0, $10
   b. $0, −$10, $0
   c. +$10, −$10, $10
   d. +$10, −$10, $0

3. Eggs have a supply curve that is linear and upward-sloping and a demand curve that is linear and downward sloping. If a 2 cent per egg tax is increased to 3 cents, the deadweight loss of the tax
   a. increases by less than 50 percent and may even decline.
   b. increases by exactly 50 percent.
   c. increases by more than 50 percent.
   d. The answer depends on whether supply or demand is more elastic.

4. Peanut butter has an upward-sloping supply and a downward-sloping demand curve. If a 1... per pound tax is increased to 15 cents, the government's tax revenue
   a. increases by less than 50 percent and may even decline.
   b. increases by exactly 50 percent.
   c. increases by more than 50 percent.
   d. The answer depends on whether supply or demand is more elastic.

5. The Laffer curve illustrates that, in some circumstances, the government can reduce a tax on a good and increase the
   a. deadweight loss.
   b. government's tax revenue.
   c. equilibrium quantity.
   d. price paid by consumers.

6. If a policymaker wants to raise revenue by taxing goods while minimizing the deadweight losses, he should look for goods with _____ elasticities of demand and _____ elasticities of supply.
   a. small, small
   b. small, large
   c. large, small
   d. large, large

Problems and Applications

1. The market for pizza is characterized by a downward-sloping demand curve and an upward-sloping supply curve.
   a. Draw the competitive market equilibrium. Label the price, quantity, consumer surplus, and producer surplus. Is there any deadweight loss? Explain.
   b. Suppose that the government forces each pizzeria to pay a $1 tax on each pizza sold. Illustrate the effect of this tax on the pizza market, being sure to label the consumer surplus, producer surplus, government revenue, and deadweight loss. How does each area compare to the pre-tax case?
   c. If the tax were removed, pizza eaters and sellers would be better off, but the government would lose tax revenue. Suppose that consumers and producers voluntarily transferred some of their gains to the government. Could all parties (including the government) be better off than they were with a tax? Explain using the labeled areas in your graph.

2. Evaluate the following two statements. Do you agree? Why or why not?
   a. "A tax that has no deadweight loss cannot raise any revenue for the government."
   b. "A tax that raises no revenue for the government cannot have any deadweight loss."

3. Consider the market for rubber bands.
   a. If this market has very elastic supply and very inelastic demand, how would the burden of a tax on rubber bands be shared between consumers and producers? Use the tools of consumer surplus and producer surplus in your answer.
   b. If this market has very inelastic supply and very elastic demand, how would the burden of a tax on rubber bands be shared between consumers and producers? Contrast your answer with your answer to part (a).

4. Suppose that the government imposes a tax on heating oil.
   a. Would the deadweight loss from this tax likely be greater in the first year after it is imposed or in the fifth year? Explain.
   b. Would the revenue collected from this tax likely be greater in the first year after it is imposed or in the fifth year? Explain.

5. After economics class one day, your friend suggests that taxing food would be a good way to raise revenue because the demand for food is quite inelastic. In what sense is taxing food a "good" way to raise revenue? In what sense is it not a "good" way to raise revenue?

6. Daniel Patrick Moynihan, the late senator from New York, once introduced a bill that would levy a 10,000 percent tax on certain hollow-tipped bullets.
   a. Do you expect that this tax would raise much revenue? Why or why not?
   b. Even if the tax would raise no revenue, why might Senator Moynihan have proposed it?

7. The government places a tax on the purchase of socks.
   a. Illustrate the effect of this tax on equilibrium price and quantity in the socks market. Identify the following areas both before and after the imposition of the tax: total spending by consumers, total revenue for producers, and government tax revenue.
   b. Does the price received by producers rise or fall? Can you tell whether total receipts for producers rise or fall? Explain.
   c. Does the price paid by consumers rise or fall? Can you tell whether total spending by consumers rises or falls? Explain carefully. (*Hint*: Think about elasticity.) If total consumer spending falls, does consumer surplus rise? Explain.

8. This chapter analyzed the welfare effects of a tax on a good. Consider now the opposite policy. Suppose that the government *subsidizes* a good: For each unit of the good sold, the government pays $2 to the buyer. How does the subsidy affect consumer surplus, producer surplus, tax revenue, and total surplus? Does a subsidy lead to a deadweight loss? Explain.

9. Hotel rooms in Smalltown go for $100, and 1,000 rooms are rented on a typical day.

   a. To raise revenue, the mayor decides to charge hotels a tax of $10 per rented room. After the tax is imposed, the going rate for hotel rooms rises to $108, and the number of rooms rented falls to 900. Calculate the amount of revenue this tax raises for Smalltown and the deadweight loss of the tax. (*Hint*: The area of a triangle is ½ × base × height.)
   b. The mayor now doubles the tax to $20. The price rises to $116, and the number of rooms rented falls to 800. Calculate tax revenue and deadweight loss with this larger tax. Are they double, more than double, or less than double? Explain.

10. Suppose that a market is described by the following supply and demand equations:

$$Q^S = 2P$$
$$Q^D = 300 - P$$

   a. Solve for the equilibrium price and the equilibrium quantity.
   b. Suppose that a tax of T is placed on buyers, so the new demand equation is

$$Q^D = 300 - (P + T)$$

   Solve for the new equilibrium. What happens to the price received by sellers, the price paid by buyers, and the quantity sold?
   c. Tax revenue is $T \times Q$. Use your answer to part (b) to solve for tax revenue as a function of T. Graph this relationship for T between 0 and 300.
   d. The deadweight loss of a tax is the area of the triangle between the supply and demand curves. Recalling that the area of a triangle is ½ × base × height, solve for deadweight loss as a function of T. Graph this relationship for T between 0 and 300. (*Hint*: Looking sideways, the base of the deadweight loss triangle is T, and the height is the difference between the quantity sold with the tax and the quantity sold without the tax.)
   e. The government now levies a tax on this good of $200 per unit. Is this a good policy? Why or why not? Can you propose a better policy?

Go to CengageBrain.com to purchase access to the proven, critical Study Guide to accompany this text, which features additional notes and context, practice tests, and much more.

Application: International Trade

I f you check the labels on the clothes you are wearing, you will probably find that some were made in another country. A century ago, the textile and clothing industry was a major part of the U.S. economy, but that is no longer the case. Faced with foreign competitors that can produce quality goods at low cost, many U.S. firms have found it increasingly difficult to produce and sell textiles and clothing at a profit. As a result, they have laid off their workers and shut down their factories. Today, most of the textiles and clothing that Americans consume are imported.

The story of the textile industry raises important questions for economic policy: How does international trade affect economic well-being? Who gains and who loses from free trade among countries, and how do the gains compare to the losses?

Chapter 3 introduced the study of international trade by applying the principle of comparative advantage. According to this principle, all countries can benefit from trading with one another because trade allows each country to specialize in doing what it does best. But the analysis in Chapter 3 was incomplete. It did not explain how the international marketplace achieves these gains from trade or how the gains are distributed among various economic participants.

We now return to the study of international trade and take up these questions. Over the past several chapters, we have developed many tools for analyzing how markets work: supply, demand, equilibrium, consumer surplus, producer surplus, and so on. With these tools, we can learn more about how international trade affects economic well-being.

9-1 The Determinants of Trade

Consider the market for textiles. The textile market is well suited to studying the gains and losses from international trade: Textiles are made in many countries around the world, and there is much world trade in textiles. Moreover, the textile market is one in which policymakers often consider (and sometimes implement) trade restrictions to protect domestic producers from foreign competitors. We examine here the textile market in the imaginary country of Isoland.

9-1a The Equilibrium without Trade

As our story begins, the Isolandian textile market is isolated from the rest of the world. By government decree, no one in Isoland is allowed to import or export textiles, and the penalty for violating the decree is so large that no one dares try.

Because there is no international trade, the market for textiles in Isoland consists solely of Isolandian buyers and sellers. As Figure 1 shows, the domestic price adjusts to balance the quantity supplied by domestic sellers and the quantity demanded by domestic buyers. The figure shows the consumer and producer surplus in the equilibrium without trade. The sum of consumer and producer surplus measures the total benefits that buyers and sellers receive from participating in the textile market.

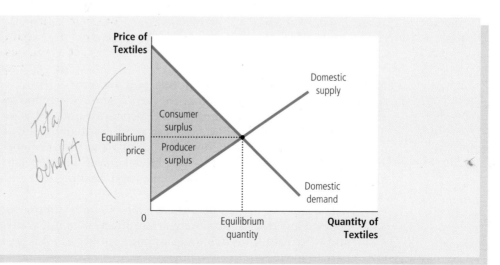

FIGURE 1

The Equilibrium without International Trade
When an economy cannot trade in world markets, the price adjusts to balance domestic supply and demand. This figure shows consumer and producer surplus in an equilibrium without international trade for the textile market in the imaginary country of Isoland.

Now suppose that, in a political upset, Isoland elects a new president. The president campaigned on a platform of "change" and promised the voters bold new ideas. Her first act is to assemble a team of economists to evaluate Isolandian trade policy. She asks them to report on three questions:

- If the government allows Isolandians to import and export textiles, what will happen to the price of textiles and the quantity of textiles sold in the domestic textile market?
- Who will gain from free trade in textiles and who will lose, and will the gains exceed the losses?
- Should a tariff (a tax on textile imports) be part of the new trade policy?

After reviewing supply and demand in their favorite textbook (this one, of course), the Isolandian economics team begins its analysis.

9-1b The World Price and Comparative Advantage

The first issue our economists take up is whether Isoland is likely to become a textile importer or a textile exporter. In other words, if free trade is allowed, will Isolandians end up buying or selling textiles in world markets?

To answer this question, the economists compare the current Isolandian price of textiles to the price of textiles in other countries. We call the price prevailing in world markets the **world price**. If the world price of textiles is higher than the domestic price, then Isoland will export textiles once trade is permitted. Isolandian textile producers will be eager to receive the higher prices available abroad and will start selling their textiles to buyers in other countries. Conversely, if the world price of textiles is lower than the domestic price, then Isoland will import textiles. Because foreign sellers offer a better price, Isolandian textile consumers will quickly start buying textiles from other countries.

In essence, comparing the world price and the domestic price before trade indicates whether Isoland has a comparative advantage in producing textiles. The domestic price reflects the opportunity cost of textiles: It tells us how much an Isolandian must give up to obtain one unit of textiles. If the domestic price is low, the cost of producing textiles in Isoland is low, suggesting that Isoland has a comparative advantage in producing textiles relative to the rest of the world. If the domestic price is high, then the cost of producing textiles in Isoland is high, suggesting that foreign countries have a comparative advantage in producing textiles.

As we saw in Chapter 3, trade among nations is ultimately based on comparative advantage. That is, trade is beneficial because it allows each nation to specialize in doing what it does best. By comparing the world price and the domestic price before trade, we can determine whether Isoland is better or worse at producing textiles than the rest of the world.

world price *the price of a good that prevails in the world market for that good*

Quick Quiz *The country Autarka does not allow international trade. In Autarka, you can buy a wool suit for 3 ounces of gold. Meanwhile, in neighboring countries, you can buy the same suit for 2 ounces of gold. If Autarka were to allow free trade, would it import or export wool suits? Why?*

9-2 The Winners and Losers from Trade

To analyze the welfare effects of free trade, the Isolandian economists begin with the assumption that Isoland is a small economy compared to the rest of the world. This small-economy assumption means that Isoland's actions have little effect on world markets. Specifically, any change in Isoland's trade policy will not affect the world price of textiles. The Isolandians are said to be *price takers* in the world economy. That is, they take the world price of textiles as given. Isoland can be an exporting country by selling textiles at this price or an importing country by buying textiles at this price.

The small-economy assumption is not necessary to analyze the gains and losses from international trade. But the Isolandian economists know from experience (and from reading Chapter 2 of this book) that making simplifying assumptions is a key part of building a useful economic model. The assumption that Isoland is a small economy simplifies the analysis, and the basic lessons do not change in the more complicated case of a large economy.

9-2a The Gains and Losses of an Exporting Country

Figure 2 shows the Isolandian textile market when the domestic equilibrium price before trade is below the world price. Once trade is allowed, the domestic price rises to equal the world price. No seller of textiles would accept less than the world price, and no buyer would pay more than the world price.

FIGURE 2   *Exporting Country*

International Trade in an Exporting Country
Once trade is allowed, the domestic price rises to equal the world price. The supply curve shows the quantity of textiles produced domestically, and the demand curve shows the quantity consumed domestically. Exports from Isoland equal the difference between the domestic quantity supplied and the domestic quantity demanded at the world price. Sellers are better off (producer surplus rises from C to B + C + D), and buyers are worse off (consumer surplus falls from A + B to A). Total surplus rises by an amount equal to area D, indicating that trade raises the economic well-being of the country as a whole.

	Before Trade	After Trade	Change
Consumer Surplus	A + B	A	−B
Producer Surplus	C	B + C + D	+(B + D)
Total Surplus	A + B + C	A + B + C + D	+D

The area D shows the increase in total surplus and represents the gains from trade.

[handwritten annotations: After trade Consumers lost B Producers gained BD D is gain]

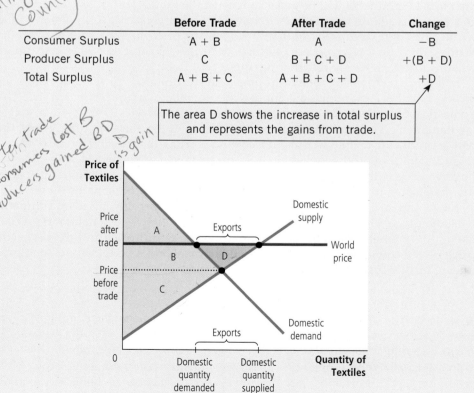

After the domestic price has risen to equal the world price, the domestic quantity supplied differs from the domestic quantity demanded. The supply curve shows the quantity of textiles supplied by Isolandian sellers. The demand curve shows the quantity of textiles demanded by Isolandian buyers. Because the domestic quantity supplied is greater than the domestic quantity demanded, Isoland sells textiles to other countries. Thus, Isoland becomes a textile exporter.

Although domestic quantity supplied and domestic quantity demanded differ, the textile market is still in equilibrium because there is now another participant in the market: the rest of the world. One can view the horizontal line at the world price as representing the rest of the world's demand for textiles. This demand curve is perfectly elastic because Isoland, as a small economy, can sell as many textiles as it wants at the world price.

Now consider the gains and losses from opening up trade. Clearly, not everyone benefits. Trade forces the domestic price to rise to the world price. Domestic producers of textiles are better off because they can now sell textiles at a higher price, but domestic consumers of textiles are worse off because they have to buy textiles at a higher price.

To measure these gains and losses, we look at the changes in consumer and producer surplus. Before trade is allowed, the price of textiles adjusts to balance domestic supply and domestic demand. Consumer surplus, the area between the demand curve and the before-trade price, is area A + B. Producer surplus, the area between the supply curve and the before-trade price, is area C. Total surplus before trade, the sum of consumer and producer surplus, is area A + B + C.

After trade is allowed, the domestic price rises to the world price. Consumer surplus is reduced to area A (the area between the demand curve and the world price). Producer surplus is increased to area B + C + D (the area between the supply curve and the world price). Thus, total surplus with trade is area A + B + C + D.

These welfare calculations show who wins and who loses from trade in an exporting country. Sellers benefit because producer surplus increases by the area B + D. Buyers are worse off because consumer surplus decreases by the area B. Because the gains of sellers exceed the losses of buyers by the area D, total surplus in Isoland increases.

This analysis of an exporting country yields two conclusions:

- When a country allows trade and becomes an exporter of a good, domestic producers of the good are better off, and domestic consumers of the good are worse off.
- Trade raises the economic well-being of a nation in the sense that the gains of the winners exceed the losses of the losers.

9-2b The Gains and Losses of an Importing Country

Now suppose that the domestic price before trade is above the world price. Once again, after trade is allowed, the domestic price must equal the world price. As Figure 3 shows, the domestic quantity supplied is less than the domestic quantity demanded. The difference between the domestic quantity demanded and the domestic quantity supplied is bought from other countries, and Isoland becomes a textile importer.

In this case, the horizontal line at the world price represents the supply of the rest of the world. This supply curve is perfectly elastic because Isoland is a small economy and, therefore, can buy as many textiles as it wants at the world price.

FIGURE 3

Importing country [handwritten annotation]

International Trade in an Importing Country
Once trade is allowed, the domestic price falls to equal the world price. The supply curve shows the amount produced domestically, and the demand curve shows the amount consumed domestically. Imports equal the difference between the domestic quantity demanded and the domestic quantity supplied at the world price. Buyers are better off (consumer surplus rises from A to A + B + D), and sellers are worse off (producer surplus falls from B + C to C). Total surplus rises by an amount equal to area D, indicating that trade raises the economic well-being of the country as a whole.

Consumers gain B D [handwritten]
Producers loose B [handwritten]
Overall gain is D [handwritten]

	Before Trade	After Trade	Change
Consumer Surplus	A	A + B + D	+(B + D)
Producer Surplus	B + C	C	−B
Total Surplus	A + B + C	A + B + C + D	+D

The area D shows the increase in total surplus and represents the gains from trade.

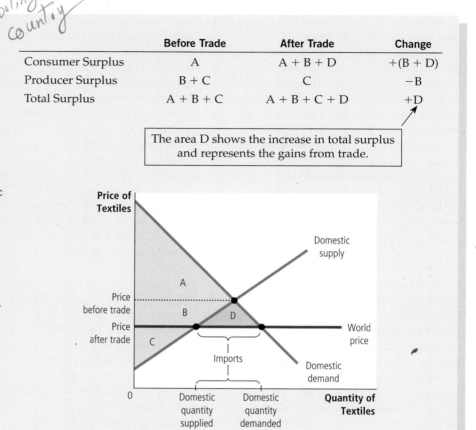

Now consider the gains and losses from trade. Once again, not everyone benefits. When trade forces the domestic price to fall, domestic consumers are better off (they can now buy textiles at a lower price), and domestic producers are worse off (they now have to sell textiles at a lower price). Changes in consumer and producer surplus measure the size of the gains and losses. Before trade, consumer surplus is area A, producer surplus is area B + C, and total surplus is area A + B + C. After trade is allowed, consumer surplus is area A + B + D, producer surplus is area C, and total surplus is area A + B + C + D.

These welfare calculations show who wins and who loses from trade in an importing country. Buyers benefit because consumer surplus increases by the area B + D. Sellers are worse off because producer surplus falls by the area B. The gains of buyers exceed the losses of sellers, and total surplus increases by the area D.

This analysis of an importing country yields two conclusions parallel to those for an exporting country:

- When a country allows trade and becomes an importer of a good, domestic consumers of the good are better off, and domestic producers of the good are worse off.
- Trade raises the economic well-being of a nation in the sense that the gains of the winners exceed the losses of the losers.

Having completed our analysis of trade, we can better understand one of the *Ten Principles of Economics* in Chapter 1: Trade can make everyone better off. If Isoland opens its textile market to international trade, the change creates winners and losers, regardless of whether Isoland ends up exporting or importing textiles. In either case, however, the gains of the winners exceed the losses of the losers, so the winners could compensate the losers and still be better off. In this sense, trade *can* make everyone better off. But *will* trade make everyone better off? Probably not. In practice, compensation for the losers from international trade is rare. Without such compensation, opening an economy to international trade is a policy that expands the size of the economic pie, while perhaps leaving some participants in the economy with a smaller slice.

We can now see why the debate over trade policy is often contentious. Whenever a policy creates winners and losers, the stage is set for a political battle. Nations sometimes fail to enjoy the gains from trade because the losers from free trade are better organized than the winners. The losers may turn their cohesiveness into political clout and lobby for trade restrictions such as tariffs or import quotas.

9-2c The Effects of a Tariff

The Isolandian economists next consider the effects of a **tariff**—a tax on imported goods. The economists quickly realize that a tariff on textiles will have no effect if Isoland becomes a textile exporter. If no one in Isoland is interested in importing textiles, a tax on textile imports is irrelevant. The tariff matters only if Isoland becomes a textile importer. Concentrating their attention on this case, the economists compare welfare with and without the tariff.

tariff
tax on goods produced abroad and sold domestically

Figure 4 shows the Isolandian market for textiles. Under free trade, the domestic price equals the world price. A tariff raises the price of imported textiles above the world price by the amount of the tariff. Domestic suppliers of textiles, who compete with suppliers of imported textiles, can now sell their textiles for the world price plus the amount of the tariff. Thus, the price of textiles—both imported and domestic—rises by the amount of the tariff and is, therefore, closer to the price that would prevail without trade.

The change in price affects the behavior of domestic buyers and sellers. Because the tariff raises the price of textiles, it reduces the domestic quantity demanded from Q_1^D to Q_2^D and raises the domestic quantity supplied from Q_1^S to Q_2^S. *Thus, the tariff reduces the quantity of imports and moves the domestic market closer to its equilibrium without trade.*

Now consider the gains and losses from the tariff. Because the tariff raises the domestic price, domestic sellers are better off, and domestic buyers are worse off. In addition, the government raises revenue. To measure these gains and losses, we look at the changes in consumer surplus, producer surplus, and government revenue. These changes are summarized in the table in Figure 4.

Before the tariff, the domestic price equals the world price. Consumer surplus, the area between the demand curve and the world price, is area A + B + C + D + E + F. Producer surplus, the area between the supply curve and the world price, is area G. Government revenue equals zero. Total surplus, the sum of consumer surplus, producer surplus, and government revenue, is area A + B + C + D + E + F + G.

Once the government imposes a tariff, the domestic price exceeds the world price by the amount of the tariff. Consumer surplus is now area A + B. Producer surplus is area C + G. Government revenue, which is the quantity of after-tariff imports times the size of the tariff, is the area E. Thus, total surplus with the tariff is area A + B + C + E + G.

FIGURE 4

The Effects of a Tariff

A tariff reduces the quantity of imports and moves a market closer to the equilibrium that would exist without trade. Total surplus falls by an amount equal to area D + F. These two triangles represent the deadweight loss from the tariff.

	Before Tariff	After Tariff	Change
Consumer Surplus	A + B + C + D + E + F	A + B	−(C + D + E + F)
Producer Surplus	G	C + G	+C
Government Revenue	None	E	+E
Total Surplus	A + B + C + D + E + F + G	A + B + C + E + G	−(D + F)

The area D + F shows the fall in total surplus and represents the deadweight loss of the tariff.

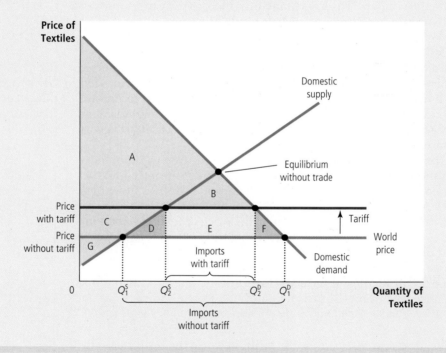

To determine the total welfare effects of the tariff, we add the change in consumer surplus (which is negative), the change in producer surplus (positive), and the change in government revenue (positive). We find that total surplus in the market decreases by the area D + F. This fall in total surplus is called the *deadweight loss* of the tariff.

A tariff causes a deadweight loss because a tariff is a type of tax. Like most taxes, it distorts incentives and pushes the allocation of scarce resources away from the optimum. In this case, we can identify two effects. First, when the tariff raises the domestic price of textiles above the world price, it encourages domestic producers to increase production from Q_1^S to Q_2^S. Even though the

Import Quotas: Another Way to Restrict Trade

Beyond tariffs, another way that nations sometimes restrict international trade is by putting limits on how much of a good can be imported. In this book, we will not analyze such a policy, other than to point out the conclusion: Import quotas are much like tariffs. Both tariffs and import quotas reduce the quantity of imports, raise the domestic price of the good, decrease the welfare of domestic consumers, increase the welfare of domestic producers, and cause deadweight losses.

There is only one difference between these two types of trade restriction: A tariff raises revenue for the government, whereas an import quota creates surplus for those who obtain the licenses to import. The profit for the holder of an import license is the difference between the domestic price (at which she sells the imported good) and the world price (at which she buys it).

Tariffs and import quotas are even more similar if the government charges a fee for the import licenses. Suppose the government sets the license fee equal to the difference between the domestic price and the world price. In this case, all the profit of license holders is paid to the government in license fees, and the import quota works exactly like a tariff. Consumer surplus, producer surplus, and government revenue are precisely the same under the two policies.

In practice, however, countries that restrict trade with import quotas rarely do so by selling the import licenses. For example, the U.S. government has at times pressured Japan to "voluntarily" limit the sale of Japanese cars in the United States. In this case, the Japanese government allocates the import licenses to Japanese firms, and the surplus from these licenses accrues to those firms. From the standpoint of U.S. welfare, this kind of import quota is worse than a U.S. tariff on imported cars. Both a tariff and an import quota raise prices, restrict trade, and cause deadweight losses, but at least the tariff produces revenue for the U.S. government rather than profit for foreign producers. ◢

---

cost of making these incremental units exceeds the cost of buying them at the world price, the tariff makes it profitable for domestic producers to manufacture them nonetheless. Second, when the tariff raises the price that domestic textile consumers have to pay, it encourages them to reduce consumption of textiles from Q_1^D to Q_2^D. Even though domestic consumers value these incremental units at more than the world price, the tariff induces them to cut back their purchases. Area D represents the deadweight loss from the overproduction of textiles, and area F represents the deadweight loss from the underconsumption of textiles. The total deadweight loss of the tariff is the sum of these two triangles.

9-2d The Lessons for Trade Policy

The team of Isolandian economists can now write to the new president:

Dear Madam President,

You asked us three questions about opening up trade. After much hard work, we have the answers.

Question: If the government allows Isolandians to import and export textiles, what will happen to the price of textiles and the quantity of textiles sold in the domestic textile market?

Answer: Once trade is allowed, the Isolandian price of textiles will be driven to equal the price prevailing around the world.

If the world price is now higher than the Isolandian price, our price will rise. The higher price will reduce the amount of textiles Isolandians consume and raise the amount of textiles that Isolandians produce. Isoland will, therefore, become a textile exporter. This occurs because, in this case, Isoland has a comparative advantage in producing textiles.

Conversely, if the world price is now lower than the Isolandian price, our price will fall. The lower price will raise the amount of textiles that Isolandians consume and lower the amount of textiles that Isolandians produce. Isoland will, therefore, become a textile importer. This occurs because, in this case, other countries have a comparative advantage in producing textiles.

Question: Who will gain from free trade in textiles and who will lose, and will the gains exceed the losses?

Answer: The answer depends on whether the price rises or falls when trade is allowed. If the price rises, producers of textiles gain, and consumers of textiles lose. If the price falls, consumers gain, and producers lose. In both cases, the gains are larger than the losses. Thus, free trade raises the total welfare of Isolandians.

Question: Should a tariff be part of the new trade policy?

Answer: A tariff has an impact only if Isoland becomes a textile importer. In this case, a tariff moves the economy closer to the no-trade equilibrium and, like most taxes, has deadweight losses. A tariff improves the welfare of domestic producers and raises revenue for the government, but these gains are more than offset by the losses suffered by consumers. The best policy, from the standpoint of economic efficiency, would be to allow trade without a tariff.

We hope you find these answers helpful as you decide on your new policy.

Your faithful servants,
Isolandian economics team

9-2e Other Benefits of International Trade

The conclusions of the Isolandian economics team are based on the standard analysis of international trade. Their analysis uses the most fundamental tools in the economist's toolbox: supply, demand, and producer and consumer surplus. It shows that there are winners and losers when a nation opens itself up to trade, but the gains to the winners exceed the losses of the losers.

The case for free trade can be made even stronger, however, because there are several other economic benefits of trade beyond those emphasized in the standard analysis. Here, in a nutshell, are some of these other benefits:

- **Increased variety of goods.** Goods produced in different countries are not exactly the same. German beer, for instance, is not the same as American beer. Free trade gives consumers in all countries greater variety from which to choose.
- **Lower costs through economies of scale.** Some goods can be produced at low cost only if they are produced in large quantities—a phenomenon called *economies of scale*. A firm in a small country cannot take full advantage of economies of scale if it can sell only in a small domestic market. Free trade gives firms access to larger world markets and allows them to realize economies of scale more fully.

IN THE NEWS   Threats to Free Trade

In 2012, as the United States and many other nations around the world were slowly recovering from a deep recession, trade restrictions proved an irresistible temptation to many policymakers.

The Return of the Protectionist Illusion

By Douglas A. Irwin

When the Great Depression struck in the early 1930s, countries imposed high tariffs, import quotas and foreign-exchange controls in the false hope that they might help revive their economies. Instead, these beggar-thy-neighbor policies led to a collapse in world trade. Today the threat of protectionism once again looms across the world.

In order to prop up the peso, Argentina is rationing foreign exchange to sharply limit spending on imports, prompting foreign retaliation. Brazil has been cracking down on automobile imports from Argentina and Mexico. A steady stream of new antidumping duties creates additional obstacles to trade.

Export restrictions have also interrupted trade flows: Indonesia and nickel ore, China and rare-earth minerals, Tanzania and maize. And subtle product regulations are increasingly invoked to block imports. Russia recently banned imports of live animals from the European Union, ostensibly for health and safety reasons, prompting vigorous objections from Brussels.

In addition to these overt measures, there are worrisome proposals on the horizon. The EU is considering a "Buy European" initiative for public procurement that would mimic, and perhaps go well beyond, "Buy American" provisions in U.S. law. These laws give preferences for domestic suppliers in government contracts, limiting trade and raising prices that taxpayers pay for government services. India is considering mandating preferences for purchases of information and communications-technology equipment, not just for government entities but for private firms, as well.

Pascal Lamy, director general of the World Trade Organization (WTO), says these and other measures restricting or potentially restricting trade are "now a matter of serious concern." EU Trade Commissioner Karel De Gucht is also worried by what he characterizes as "the sharp rise in trade-restrictive measures introduced over the last eight months."

G-20 leaders at the recent summit in Los Cabos, Mexico, claimed they too were "deeply concerned about rising instances of protectionism around the world," and reaffirmed their "standstill commitment" to avoid imposing new trade restrictions. They pledged to "roll back any new protectionist measure that may have arisen, including new export restrictions and WTO-inconsistent measures to stimulate exports."

Talk is cheap. Global Trade Alert, a monitoring service run by Simon Evenett at the University of St. Gallen, Switzerland, points out that the G-20 countries themselves have been most responsible for the protectionist creep. Many trade measures enacted by G-20 members exploit loopholes in WTO rules.

Unfortunately, President Obama has provided no leadership in trying to keep world markets open for trade. Out of fear of offending labor unions and other domestic constituencies, his administration long delayed submitting free trade agreements with Korea, Colombia and Panama for congressional approval. Instead of seeking to reinvigorate the languishing Doha round of trade negotiations at the WTO, it has been almost completely passive and allowed world-trade policies to drift.

Congress has also done little to help. Senate Republicans and Democrats teamed up late last month to maintain import restrictions for the sugar industry, defeating an amendment from Sen. Jeanne Shaheen (D., N.H.) that would have gradually eliminated them. Keeping domestic sugar prices at twice the world level helps a few sugar-cane and beet farmers at the expense of consumers and taxpayers, while leading to job losses in sugar-using industries, such as candy and confectionary manufacturing....

Any serious march backward toward protectionism would constitute a major failure of economic policy. Experience has shown that, once imposed, trade restrictions are very difficult to remove because vested interests then have a stake in perpetuating them. Protectionism also breeds foreign retaliation, making barriers doubly difficult to unwind. Now is no time to entertain dangerous illusions.

Mr. Irwin is professor of economics at Dartmouth College and author of Trade Policy Disaster: Lessons from the 1930s *(MIT Press, 2012).*

- **Increased competition.** A company shielded from foreign competitors is more likely to have market power, which in turn gives it the ability to raise prices above competitive levels. This is a type of market failure. Opening up trade fosters competition and gives the invisible hand a better chance to work its magic.

- **Enhanced flow of ideas.** The transfer of technological advances around the world is often thought to be linked to the trading of the goods that embody those advances. The best way for a poor agricultural nation to learn about the computer revolution, for instance, is to buy some computers from abroad rather than trying to make them domestically.

Thus, free international trade increases variety for consumers, allows firms to take advantage of economies of scale, makes markets more competitive, and facilitates the spread of technology. If the Isolandian economists also took these effects into account, their advice to their president would be even more forceful.

Quick Quiz *Draw a supply-and-demand diagram for wool suits in the country of Autarka. When trade is allowed, the price of a suit falls from 3 to 2 ounces of gold. In your diagram, show the change in consumer surplus, the change in producer surplus, and the change in total surplus. How would a tariff on suit imports alter these effects?*

9-3 The Arguments for Restricting Trade

The letter from the economics team starts to persuade the new president of Isoland to consider allowing trade in textiles. She notes that the domestic price is now high compared to the world price. Free trade would, therefore, cause the price of textiles to fall and hurt domestic textile producers. Before implementing the new policy, she asks Isolandian textile companies to comment on the economists' advice.

Not surprisingly, the textile companies oppose free trade in textiles. They believe that the government should protect the domestic textile industry from foreign competition. Let's consider some of the arguments they might give to support their position and how the economics team would respond.

BERRY'S WORLD reprinted by permission of United Feature Syndicate, Inc.

"You like protectionism as a 'working man.' How about as a consumer?"

IN THE NEWS

Should the Winners from Free Trade Compensate the Losers?

Politicians and pundits often say that the government should help workers made worse off by international trade by, for example, paying for their retraining. In this opinion piece, an economist makes the opposite case.

What to Expect When You're Free Trading

By Steven E. Landsburg

All economists know that when American jobs are outsourced, Americans as a group are net winners. What we lose through lower wages is more than offset by what we gain through lower prices. In other words, the winners can more than afford to compensate the losers. Does that mean they ought to? Does it create a moral mandate for taxpayer-subsidized retraining programs?...

Um, no. Even if you've just lost your job, there's something fundamentally churlish about blaming the very phenomenon that's elevated you above the subsistence level since the day you were born. If the world owes you compensation for enduring the downside of trade, what do you owe the world for enjoying the upside?

I doubt there's a human being on earth who hasn't benefited from the opportunity to trade freely with his neighbors. Imagine what your life would be like if you had to grow your own food, make your own clothes and rely on your grandmother's home remedies for health care. Access to a trained physician might reduce the demand for grandma's home remedies, but—especially at her age—she's still got plenty of reason to be thankful for having a doctor.

Some people suggest, however, that it makes sense to isolate the moral effects of a single new trading opportunity or free trade agreement. Surely we have fellow citizens who are hurt by those agreements, at least in the limited sense that they'd be better off in a world where trade flourishes, except in this one instance. What do we owe those fellow citizens?

One way to think about that is to ask what your moral instincts tell you in analogous situations. Suppose, after years of buying shampoo at your local pharmacy, you discover you can order the same shampoo for less money on the Web. Do you have an obligation to compensate your pharmacist? If you move to a cheaper apartment, should you compensate your landlord? When you eat at McDonald's, should you compensate the owners of the diner next door? Public policy should not be designed to advance moral instincts that we all reject every day of our lives.

In what morally relevant way, then, might displaced workers differ from displaced pharmacists or displaced landlords? You might argue that pharmacists and landlords have always faced cutthroat competition and therefore knew what they were getting into, while decades of tariffs and quotas have led manufacturing workers to expect a modicum of protection. That expectation led them to develop certain skills, and now it's unfair to pull the rug out from under them.

Once again, that argument does not mesh with our everyday instincts. For many decades, schoolyard bullying has been a profitable occupation. All across America, bullies have built up skills so they can take advantage of that opportunity. If we toughen the rules to make bullying unprofitable, must we compensate the bullies?

Bullying and protectionism have a lot in common. They both use force (either directly or through the power of the law) to enrich someone else at your involuntary expense. If you're forced to pay $20 an hour to an American for goods you could have bought from a Mexican for $5 an hour, you're being extorted. When a free trade agreement allows you to buy from the Mexican after all, rejoice in your liberation.

Mr. Landsburg is a professor of economics at the University of Rochester. ◢

Source: *New York Times*, January 16, 2008.

9-3a The Jobs Argument

Opponents of free trade often argue that trade with other countries destroys domestic jobs. In our example, free trade in textiles would cause the price of textiles to fall, reducing the quantity of textiles produced in Isoland and thus reducing employment in the Isolandian textile industry. Some Isolandian textile workers would lose their jobs.

Yet free trade creates jobs at the same time that it destroys them. When Isolandians buy textiles from other countries, those countries obtain the resources to buy other goods from Isoland. Isolandian workers would move from the textile

[handwritten note in margin: Answer: the trading with other countries will produce more jobs in other industries — so as whole is good for country]

industry to those industries in which Isoland has a comparative advantage. The transition may impose hardship on some workers in the short run, but it allows Isolandians as a whole to enjoy a higher standard of living.

Opponents of trade are often skeptical that trade creates jobs. They might respond that *everything* can be produced more cheaply abroad. Under free trade, they might argue, Isolandians could not be profitably employed in any industry. As Chapter 3 explains, however, the gains from trade are based on comparative advantage, not absolute advantage. Even if one country is better than another country at producing everything, each country can still gain from trading with the other. Workers in each country will eventually find jobs in an industry in which that country has a comparative advantage.

9-3b The National-Security Argument

When an industry is threatened with competition from other countries, opponents of free trade often argue that the industry is vital to national security. For example, if Isoland were considering free trade in steel, domestic steel companies might point out that steel is used to make guns and tanks. Free trade would allow Isoland to become dependent on foreign countries to supply steel. If a war later broke out and the foreign supply was interrupted, Isoland might be unable to produce enough steel and weapons to defend itself.

IN THE NEWS   Second Thoughts about Free Trade

Some economists worry about the impact of trade on the distribution of income. Even if free trade enhances efficiency, it may reduce equality.

Trouble with Trade

By Paul Krugman

While the United States has long imported oil and other raw materials from the third world, we used to import manufactured goods mainly from other rich countries like Canada, European nations and Japan.

But recently we crossed an important watershed: we now import more manufactured goods from the third world than from other advanced economies. That is, a majority of our industrial trade is now with countries that are much poorer than we are and that pay their workers much lower wages.

For the world economy as a whole—and especially for poorer nations—growing trade between high-wage and low-wage countries is a very good thing. Above all, it offers backward economies their best hope of moving up the income ladder.

But for American workers the story is much less positive. In fact, it's hard to avoid the conclusion that growing U.S. trade with third-world countries reduces the real wages of many and perhaps most workers in this country. And that reality makes the politics of trade very difficult.

Let's talk for a moment about economics.

Trade between high-wage countries tends to be a modest win for all, or almost all, concerned. When a free-trade pact made it possible to integrate the U.S. and Canadian auto industries in the 1960s, each country's industry concentrated on producing a narrower range of products at larger scale. The result was an all-round, broadly shared rise in productivity and wages.

By contrast, trade between countries at very different levels of economic development tends to create large classes of losers as well as winners.

Although the outsourcing of some high-tech jobs to India has made headlines, on balance, highly educated workers in the United States benefit from higher wages and expanded job opportunities because of trade. For example, ThinkPad notebook computers are now made by a Chinese company, Lenovo, but a lot of Lenovo's research and development is conducted in North Carolina.

Economists acknowledge that protecting key industries may be appropriate when there are legitimate concerns over national security. Yet they fear that this argument may be used too quickly by producers eager to gain at consumers' expense.

One should be wary of the national-security argument when it is made by representatives of industry rather than the defense establishment. Companies have an incentive to exaggerate their role in national defense to obtain protection from foreign competition. A nation's generals may see things very differently. Indeed, when the military is a consumer of an industry's output, it would benefit from imports. Cheaper steel in Isoland, for example, would allow the Isolandian military to accumulate a stockpile of weapons at lower cost.

9-3c The Infant-Industry Argument

New industries sometimes argue for temporary trade restrictions to help them get started. After a period of protection, the argument goes, these industries will mature and be able to compete with foreign firms.

Similarly, older industries sometimes argue that they need temporary protection to help them adjust to new conditions. For example, in 2002, President Bush imposed temporary tariffs on imported steel. He said, "I decided that imports were severely affecting our industry, an important industry." The tariff, which lasted 20 months, offered "temporary relief so that the industry could restructure itself."

But workers with less formal education either see their jobs shipped overseas or find their wages driven down by the ripple effect as other workers with similar qualifications crowd into their industries and look for employment to replace the jobs they lost to foreign competition. And lower prices at Wal-Mart aren't sufficient compensation.

All this is textbook international economics: contrary to what people sometimes assert, economic theory says that free trade normally makes a country richer, but it doesn't say that it's normally good for everyone. Still, when the effects of third-world exports on U.S. wages first became an issue in the 1990s, a number of economists—myself included—looked at the data and concluded that any negative effects on U.S. wages were modest.

The trouble now is that these effects may no longer be as modest as they were, because imports of manufactured goods from the third world have grown dramatically—from just 2.5 percent of G.D.P. in 1990 to 6 percent in 2006.

And the biggest growth in imports has come from countries with very low wages. The original "newly industrializing economies" exporting manufactured goods—South Korea, Taiwan, Hong Kong and Singapore—paid wages that were about 25 percent of U.S. levels in 1990. Since then, however, the sources of our imports have shifted to Mexico, where wages are only 11 percent of the U.S. level, and China, where they're only about 3 percent or 4 percent.

There are some qualifying aspects to this story. For example, many of those made-in-China goods contain components made in Japan and other high-wage economies. Still, there's little doubt that the pressure of globalization on American wages has increased.

So am I arguing for protectionism? No. Those who think that globalization is always and everywhere a bad thing are wrong. On the contrary, keeping world markets relatively open is crucial to the hopes of billions of people.

But I am arguing for an end to the finger-wagging, the accusation either of not understanding economics or of kowtowing to special interests that tends to be the editorial response to politicians who express skepticism about the benefits of free-trade agreements.

It's often claimed that limits on trade benefit only a small number of Americans, while hurting the vast majority. That's still true of things like the import quota on sugar. But when it comes to manufactured goods, it's at least arguable that the reverse is true. The highly educated workers who clearly benefit from growing trade with third-world economies are a minority, greatly outnumbered by those who probably lose.

As I said, I'm not a protectionist. For the sake of the world as a whole, I hope that we respond to the trouble with trade not by shutting trade down, but by doing things like strengthening the social safety net. But those who are worried about trade have a point, and deserve some respect.

Mr. Krugman is a professor of economics at Princeton University and winner of the 2008 Nobel Prize in economics.

Source: *New York Times,* December 28, 2007.

Economists are often skeptical about such claims, largely because the infant-industry argument is difficult to implement in practice. To apply protection successfully, the government would need to decide which industries will eventually be profitable and decide whether the benefits of establishing these industries exceed the costs of this protection to consumers. Yet "picking winners" is extraordinarily difficult. It is made even more difficult by the political process, which often awards protection to those industries that are politically powerful. And once a powerful industry is protected from foreign competition, the "temporary" policy is sometimes hard to remove.

In addition, many economists are skeptical about the infant-industry argument in principle. Suppose, for instance, that an industry is young and unable to compete profitably against foreign rivals, but there is reason to believe that the industry can be profitable in the long run. In this case, firm owners should be willing to incur temporary losses to obtain the eventual profits. Protection is not necessary for an infant industry to grow. History shows that start-up firms often incur temporary losses and succeed in the long run, even without protection from competition.

9-3d The Unfair-Competition Argument

A common argument is that free trade is desirable only if all countries play by the same rules. If firms in different countries are subject to different laws and regulations, then it is unfair (the argument goes) to expect the firms to compete in the international marketplace. For instance, suppose that the government of Neighborland subsidizes its textile industry by giving textile companies large tax breaks. The Isolandian textile industry might argue that it should be protected from this foreign competition because Neighborland is not competing fairly.

Would it, in fact, hurt Isoland to buy textiles from another country at a subsidized price? Certainly, Isolandian textile producers would suffer, but Isolandian textile consumers would benefit from the low price. The case for free trade is the same as before: The gains of the consumers from buying at the low price would exceed the losses of the producers. Neighborland's subsidy to its textile industry may be a bad policy, but it is the taxpayers of Neighborland who bear the burden. Isoland can benefit from the opportunity to buy textiles at a subsidized price. Rather than objecting to the foreign subsidies, perhaps Isoland should send Neighborland a thank-you note.

9-3e The Protection-as-a-Bargaining-Chip Argument

Another argument for trade restrictions concerns the strategy of bargaining. Many policymakers claim to support free trade but, at the same time, argue that trade restrictions can be useful when we bargain with our trading partners. They claim that the threat of a trade restriction can help remove a trade restriction already imposed by a foreign government. For example, Isoland might threaten to impose a tariff on textiles unless Neighborland removes its tariff on wheat. If Neighborland responds to this threat by removing its tariff, the result can be freer trade.

The problem with this bargaining strategy is that the threat may not work. If it doesn't work, the country faces a choice between two bad options. It can carry out its threat and implement the trade restriction, which would reduce its own economic welfare. Or it can back down from its threat, which would cause it to lose prestige in international affairs. Faced with this choice, the country would probably wish that it had never made the threat in the first place.

case study Trade Agreements and the World Trade Organization

A country can take one of two approaches to achieving free trade. It can take a *unilateral* approach and remove its trade restrictions on its own. This is the approach that Great Britain took in the 19th century and that Chile and South Korea have taken in recent years. Alternatively, a country can take a *multilateral* approach and reduce its trade restrictions while other countries do the same. In other words, it can bargain with its trading partners in an attempt to reduce trade restrictions around the world.

One important example of the multilateral approach is the North American Free Trade Agreement (NAFTA), which in 1993 lowered trade barriers among the United States, Mexico, and Canada. Another is the General Agreement on Tariffs and Trade (GATT), which is a continuing series of negotiations among many of the world's countries with the goal of promoting free trade. The United States helped to found GATT after World War II in response to the high tariffs imposed during the Great Depression of the 1930s. Many economists believe that the high tariffs contributed to the worldwide economic hardship of that period. GATT has successfully reduced the average tariff among member countries from about 40 percent after World War II to about 5 percent today.

The rules established under GATT are now enforced by an international institution called the World Trade Organization (WTO). The WTO was established in 1995 and has its headquarters in Geneva, Switzerland. As of 2009, 153 countries have joined the organization, accounting for more than 97 percent of world trade. The functions of the WTO are to administer trade agreements, provide a forum for negotiations, and handle disputes among member countries.

What are the pros and cons of the multilateral approach to free trade? One advantage is that the multilateral approach has the potential to result in freer trade than a unilateral approach because it can reduce trade restrictions abroad as well as at home. If international negotiations fail, however, the result could be more restricted trade than under a unilateral approach.

In addition, the multilateral approach may have a political advantage. In most markets, producers are fewer and better organized than consumers—and thus wield greater political influence. Reducing the Isolandian tariff on textiles, for example, may be politically difficult if considered by itself. The textile companies would oppose free trade, and the buyers of textiles who would benefit are so numerous that organizing their support would be difficult. Yet suppose that Neighborland promises to reduce its tariff on wheat at the same time that Isoland reduces its tariff on textiles. In this case, the Isolandian wheat farmers, who are also politically powerful, would back the agreement. Thus, the multilateral approach to free trade can sometimes win political support when a unilateral approach cannot. ◢

Quick Quiz *The textile industry of Autarka advocates a ban on the import of wool suits. Describe five arguments its lobbyists might make. Give a response to each of these arguments.*

9-4 Conclusion

Economists and the public often disagree about free trade. In 2008, the *Los Angeles Times* asked the American public, "Generally speaking, do you believe that free international trade has helped or hurt the economy, or hasn't it made a difference to the economy one way or the other?" Only 26 percent of those polled said free international trade helped, whereas 50 percent thought it hurt. (The rest thought it made no difference or were unsure.) By contrast, most economists support free international trade. They view free trade as a way of allocating production efficiently and raising living standards both at home and abroad.

Economists view the United States as an ongoing experiment that confirms the virtues of free trade. Throughout its history, the United States has allowed unrestricted trade among the states, and the country as a whole has benefited from the specialization that trade allows. Florida grows oranges, Alaska pumps oil, California makes wine, and so on. Americans would not enjoy the high standard of living they do today if people could consume only those goods and services produced in their own states. The world could similarly benefit from free trade among countries.

To better understand economists' view of trade, let's continue our parable. Suppose that the president of Isoland, after reading the latest poll results, ignores the advice of her economics team and decides not to allow free trade in textiles. The country remains in the equilibrium without international trade.

Then, one day, some Isolandian inventor discovers a new way to make textiles at very low cost. The process is quite mysterious, however, and the inventor insists on keeping it a secret. What is odd is that the inventor doesn't need traditional inputs such as cotton or wool. The only material input he needs is wheat. And even more oddly, to manufacture textiles from wheat, he hardly needs any labor input at all.

The inventor is hailed as a genius. Because everyone buys clothing, the lower cost of textiles allows all Isolandians to enjoy a higher standard of living. Workers who had previously produced textiles experience some hardship when their factories close, but they eventually find work in other industries. Some become farmers and grow the wheat that the inventor turns into textiles. Others enter new industries that emerge as a result of higher Isolandian living standards. Everyone understands that the displacement of workers in outmoded industries is an inevitable part of technological progress and economic growth.

After several years, a newspaper reporter decides to investigate this mysterious new textiles process. She sneaks into the inventor's factory and learns that the inventor is a fraud. The inventor has not been making textiles at all. Instead, he has been smuggling wheat abroad in exchange for textiles from other countries. The only thing that the inventor had discovered was the gains from international trade.

When the truth is revealed, the government shuts down the inventor's operation. The price of textiles rises, and workers return to jobs in textile factories. Living standards in Isoland fall back to their former levels. The inventor is jailed and held up to public ridicule. After all, he was no inventor. He was just an economist.

Summary

- The effects of free trade can be determined by comparing the domestic price without trade to the world price. A low domestic price indicates that the country has a comparative advantage in producing the good and that the country will become an exporter. A high domestic price indicates that the rest of the world has a comparative advantage in producing the good and that the country will become an importer.

- When a country allows trade and becomes an exporter of a good, producers of the good are better off, and consumers of the good are worse off. When a country allows trade and becomes an importer of a good, consumers are better off, and producers are worse off. In both cases, the gains from trade exceed the losses.

- A tariff—a tax on imports—moves a market closer to the equilibrium that would exist without trade and, therefore, reduces the gains from trade. Although domestic producers are better off and the government raises revenue, the losses to consumers exceed these gains.

- There are various arguments for restricting trade: protecting jobs, defending national security, helping infant industries, preventing unfair competition, and responding to foreign trade restrictions. Although some of these arguments have merit in some cases, economists believe that free trade is usually the better policy.

Key Concepts

world price, *p. 173*

tariff, *p. 177*

Questions for Review

1. What does the domestic price that prevails without international trade tell us about a nation's comparative advantage?

2. When does a country become an exporter of a good? An importer?

3. Draw the supply-and-demand diagram for an importing country. What is consumer surplus and producer surplus before trade is allowed? What is consumer surplus and producer surplus with free trade? What is the change in total surplus?

4. Describe what a tariff is and its economic effects.

5. List five arguments often given to support trade restrictions. How do economists respond to these arguments?

6. What is the difference between the unilateral and multilateral approaches to achieving free trade? Give an example of each.

Quick Check Multiple Choice

1. If a nation that does not allow international trade in steel has a domestic price of steel lower than the world price, then
   a. the nation has a comparative advantage in producing steel and would become a steel exporter if it opened up trade.
   b. the nation has a comparative advantage in producing steel and would become a steel importer if it opened up trade.
   c. the nation does not have a comparative advantage in producing steel and would become a steel exporter if it opened up trade.
   d. the nation does not have a comparative advantage in producing steel and would become a steel importer if it opened up trade.

2. When the nation of Ectenia opens itself to world trade in coffee beans, the domestic price of coffee beans falls. Which of the following describes the situation?
   a. Domestic production of coffee rises, and Ectenia becomes a coffee importer.
   b. Domestic production of coffee rises, and Ectenia becomes a coffee exporter.
   c. Domestic production of coffee falls, and Ectenia becomes a coffee importer.
   d. Domestic production of coffee falls, and Ectenia becomes a coffee exporter.

3. When a nation opens itself to trade in a good and becomes an importer,
   a. producer surplus decreases, but consumer surplus and total surplus both increase.
   b. producer surplus decreases, consumer surplus increases, and so the impact on total surplus is ambiguous.
   c. producer surplus and total surplus increase, but consumer surplus decreases.
   d. producer surplus, consumer surplus, and total surplus all increase.

4. If a nation that imports a good imposes a tariff, it will increase
   a. the domestic quantity demanded.
   b. the domestic quantity supplied.
   c. the quantity imported from abroad.
   d. all of the above.

5. Which of the following trade policies would benefit producers, hurt consumers, and increase the amount of trade?
   a. the increase of a tariff in an importing country
   b. the reduction of a tariff in an importing country

   c. starting to allow trade when the world price is greater than the domestic price
   d. starting to allow trade when the world price is less than the domestic price

6. The main difference between imposing a tariff and handing out licenses under an import quota is that a tariff increases
   a. consumer surplus.
   b. producer surplus.
   c. international trade.
   d. government revenue.

Problems and Applications

1. The world price of wine is below the price that would prevail in Canada in the absence of trade.
   a. Assuming that Canadian imports of wine are a small part of total world wine production, draw a graph for the Canadian market for wine under free trade. Identify consumer surplus, producer surplus, and total surplus in an appropriate table.
   b. Now suppose that an unusual shift of the Gulf Stream leads to an unseasonably cold summer in Europe, destroying much of the grape harvest there. What effect does this shock have on the world price of wine? Using your graph and table from part (a), show the effect on consumer surplus, producer surplus, and total surplus in Canada. Who are the winners and losers? Is Canada as a whole better or worse off?

2. Suppose that Congress imposes a tariff on imported autos to protect the U.S. auto industry from foreign competition. Assuming that the United States is a price taker in the world auto market, show the following on a diagram: the change in the quantity of imports, the loss to U.S. consumers, the gain to U.S. manufacturers, government revenue, and the deadweight loss associated with the tariff. The loss to consumers can be decomposed into three pieces: a gain to domestic producers, revenue for the government, and a deadweight loss. Use your diagram to identify these three pieces.

3. When China's clothing industry expands, the increase in world supply lowers the world price of clothing.
   a. Draw an appropriate diagram to analyze how this change in price affects consumer surplus, producer surplus, and total surplus in a nation that imports clothing, such as the United States.
   b. Now draw an appropriate diagram to show how this change in price affects consumer surplus, producer surplus, and total surplus in a nation that exports clothing, such as the Dominican Republic.

   c. Compare your answers to parts (a) and (b). What are the similarities and what are the differences? Which country should be concerned about the expansion of the Chinese textile industry? Which country should be applauding it? Explain.

4. Consider the arguments for restricting trade.
   a. Imagine that you are a lobbyist for timber, an established industry suffering from low-priced foreign competition, and you are trying to get Congress to pass trade restrictions. Which two or three of the five arguments do you think would be most persuasive to the average member of Congress? Explain your reasoning.
   b. Now assume you are an astute student of economics (not a hard assumption, we hope). Although all the arguments for restricting trade have their shortcomings, name the two or three arguments that seem to make the most economic sense to you. For each, describe the economic rationale for and against these arguments for trade restrictions.

5. The nation of Textilia does not allow imports of clothing. In its equilibrium without trade, a T-shirt costs $20, and the equilibrium quantity is 3 million T-shirts. One day, after reading Adam Smith's *The Wealth of Nations* while on vacation, the president decides to open the Textilian market to international trade. The market price of a T-shirt falls to the world price of $16. The number of T-shirts consumed in Textilia rises to 4 million, while the number of T-shirts produced declines to 1 million.
   a. Illustrate the situation just described in a graph. Your graph should show all the numbers.
   b. Calculate the change in consumer surplus, producer surplus, and total surplus that results from opening up trade. (*Hint*: Recall that the area of a triangle is ½ × base × height.)

6. China is a major producer of grains, such as wheat, corn, and rice. In 2008, the Chinese government, concerned that grain exports were driving up food prices for domestic consumers, imposed a tax on grain exports.
   a. Draw the graph that describes the market for grain in an exporting country. Use this graph as the starting point to answer the following questions.
   b. How does an export tax affect domestic grain prices?
   c. How does it affect the welfare of domestic consumers, the welfare of domestic producers, and government revenue?
   d. What happens to total welfare in China, as measured by the sum of consumer surplus, producer surplus, and tax revenue?

7. Consider a country that imports a good from abroad. For each of following statements, state whether it is true or false. Explain your answer.
   a. "The greater the elasticity of demand, the greater the gains from trade."
   b. "If demand is perfectly inelastic, there are no gains from trade."
   c. "If demand is perfectly inelastic, consumers do not benefit from trade."

8. Kawmin is a small country that produces and consumes jelly beans. The world price of jelly beans is $1 per bag, and Kawmin's domestic demand and supply for jelly beans are governed by the following equations:

   Demand: $Q^D = 8 - P$
   Supply: $Q^S = P$,

   where P is in dollars per bag and Q is in bags of jelly beans.
   a. Draw a well-labeled graph of the situation in Kawmin if the nation does not allow trade. Calculate the following (recalling that the area of a triangle is ½ × base × height): the equilibrium price and quantity, consumer surplus, producer surplus, and total surplus.
   b. Kawmin then opens the market to trade. Draw another graph to describe the new situation in the jelly bean market. Calculate the equilibrium price, quantities of consumption and production, imports, consumer surplus, producer surplus, and total surplus.
   c. After a while, the Czar of Kawmin responds to the pleas of jelly bean producers by placing a $1 per bag tariff on jelly bean imports. On a

   graph, show the effects of this tariff. Calculate the equilibrium price, quantities of consumption and production, imports, consumer surplus, producer surplus, government revenue, and total surplus.
   d. What are the gains from opening up trade? What are the deadweight losses from restricting trade with the tariff? Give numerical answers.

9. Having rejected a tariff on textiles (a tax on imports), the president of Isoland is now considering the same-sized tax on textile consumption (including both imported and domestically produced textiles).
   a. Using Figure 4, identify the quantity consumed and the quantity produced in Isoland under a textile consumption tax.
   b. Construct a table similar to that in Figure 4 for the textile consumption tax.
   c. Which raises more revenue for the government— the consumption tax or the tariff? Which has a smaller deadweight loss? Explain.

10. Assume the United States is an importer of televisions and there are no trade restrictions. U.S. consumers buy 1 million televisions per year, of which 400,000 are produced domestically and 600,000 are imported.
   a. Suppose that a technological advance among Japanese television manufacturers causes the world price of televisions to fall by $100. Draw a graph to show how this change affects the welfare of U.S. consumers and U.S. producers and how it affects total surplus in the United States.
   b. After the fall in price, consumers buy 1.2 million televisions, of which 200,000 are produced domestically and 1 million are imported. Calculate the change in consumer surplus, producer surplus, and total surplus from the price reduction.
   c. If the government responded by putting a $100 tariff on imported televisions, what would this do? Calculate the revenue that would be raised and the deadweight loss. Would it be a good policy from the standpoint of U.S. welfare? Who might support the policy?
   d. Suppose that the fall in price is attributable not to technological advance but to a $100 per television subsidy from the Japanese government to Japanese industry. How would this affect your analysis?

11. Consider a small country that exports steel. Suppose that a "pro-trade" government decides to subsidize the export of steel by paying a certain amount for each ton sold abroad. How does this export subsidy affect the domestic price of steel, the quantity of steel produced, the quantity of steel consumed, and the quantity of steel exported? How does it affect consumer surplus, producer surplus, government revenue, and total surplus? Is it a good policy from the standpoint of economic efficiency? (*Hint*: The analysis of an export subsidy is similar to the analysis of a tariff.)

Go to CengageBrain.com to purchase access to the proven, critical Study Guide to accompany this text, which features additional notes and context, practice tests, and much more.

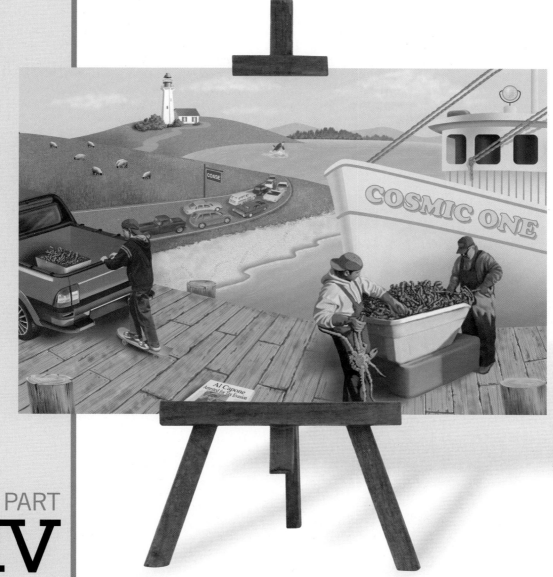

The Economics of the Public Sector

Externalities

F irms that make and sell paper also create, as a by-product of the manufacturing process, a chemical called dioxin. Scientists believe that once dioxin enters the environment, it raises the population's risk of cancer, birth defects, and other health problems.

Is the production and release of dioxin a problem for society? In Chapters 4 through 9, we examined how markets allocate scarce resources with the forces of supply and demand, and we saw that the equilibrium of supply and demand is typically an efficient allocation of resources. To use Adam Smith's famous metaphor, the "invisible hand" of the marketplace leads self-interested buyers and sellers in a market to maximize the total benefit that society derives from that market. This insight is the basis for one of the *Ten Principles of Economics* in Chapter 1: Markets are usually a good way to organize economic activity. Should we conclude, therefore, that the invisible hand prevents firms in the paper market from emitting too much dioxin?

externality
the uncompensated impact of one person's actions on the well-being of a bystander

Markets do many things well, but they do not do everything well. In this chapter, we begin our study of another of the *Ten Principles of Economics*: Government action can sometimes improve upon market outcomes. We examine why markets sometimes fail to allocate resources efficiently, how government policies can potentially improve the market's allocation, and what kinds of policies are likely to work best.

The market failures examined in this chapter fall under a general category called *externalities*. An **externality** arises when a person engages in an activity that influences the well-being of a bystander but neither pays nor receives compensation for that effect. If the impact on the bystander is adverse, it is called a *negative externality*. If it is beneficial, it is called a *positive externality*. In the presence of externalities, society's interest in a market outcome extends beyond the well-being of buyers and sellers who participate in the market to include the well-being of bystanders who are affected indirectly. Because buyers and sellers neglect the external effects of their actions when deciding how much to demand or supply, the market equilibrium is not efficient when there are externalities. That is, the equilibrium fails to maximize the total benefit to society as a whole. The release of dioxin into the environment, for instance, is a negative externality. Self-interested paper firms will not consider the full cost of the pollution they create in their production process, and consumers of paper will not consider the full cost of the pollution they contribute to as a result of their purchasing decisions. Therefore, the firms will emit too much pollution unless the government prevents or discourages them from doing so.

Externalities come in many varieties, as do the policy responses that try to deal with the market failure. Here are some examples:

- The exhaust from automobiles is a negative externality because it creates smog that other people have to breathe. As a result of this externality, drivers tend to pollute too much. The federal government attempts to solve this problem by setting emission standards for cars. It also taxes gasoline to reduce the amount that people drive.
- Restored historic buildings convey a positive externality because people who walk or ride by them can enjoy the beauty and the sense of history that these buildings provide. Building owners do not get the full benefit of restoration and, therefore, tend to discard older buildings too quickly. Many local governments respond to this problem by regulating the destruction of historic buildings and by providing tax breaks to owners who restore them.
- Barking dogs create a negative externality because neighbors are disturbed by the noise. Dog owners do not bear the full cost of the noise and, therefore, tend to take too few precautions to prevent their dogs from barking. Local governments address this problem by making it illegal to "disturb the peace."
- Research into new technologies provides a positive externality because it creates knowledge that other people can use. Because inventors cannot capture the full benefits of their inventions, they tend to devote too few resources to research. The federal government addresses this problem partially through the patent system, which gives inventors exclusive use of their inventions for a limited time.

In each of these cases, some decision maker fails to take account of the external effects of his behavior. The government responds by trying to influence this behavior to protect the interests of bystanders.

10-1 Externalities and Market Inefficiency

In this section, we use the tools of welfare economics developed in Chapter 7 to examine how externalities affect economic well-being. The analysis shows precisely why externalities cause markets to allocate resources inefficiently. Later in this chapter, we examine various ways in which private individuals and public policymakers may remedy this type of market failure.

10-1a Welfare Economics: A Recap

We begin by recalling the key lessons of welfare economics from Chapter 7. To make our analysis concrete, we consider a specific market—the market for aluminum. Figure 1 shows the supply and demand curves in the market for aluminum.

Recall from Chapter 7 that the supply and demand curves contain important information about costs and benefits. The demand curve for aluminum reflects the value of aluminum to consumers, as measured by the prices they are willing to pay. At any given quantity, the height of the demand curve shows the willingness to pay of the marginal buyer. In other words, it shows the value to the consumer of the last unit of aluminum bought. Similarly, the supply curve reflects the costs of producing aluminum. At any given quantity, the height of the supply curve shows the cost to the marginal seller. In other words, it shows the cost to the producer of the last unit of aluminum sold.

In the absence of government intervention, the price adjusts to balance the supply and demand for aluminum. The quantity produced and consumed in the market equilibrium, shown as Q_{MARKET} in Figure 1, is efficient in the sense that it maximizes the sum of producer and consumer surplus. That is, the market allocates resources in a way that maximizes the total value to the consumers who buy and use aluminum minus the total costs to the producers who make and sell aluminum.

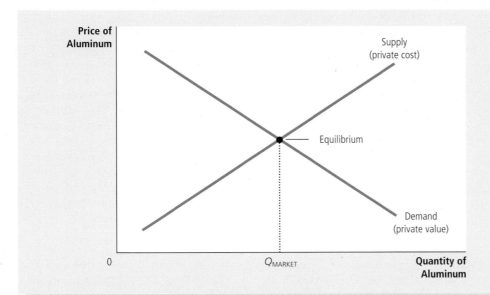

FIGURE 1

The Market for Aluminum
The demand curve reflects the value to buyers, and the supply curve reflects the costs of sellers. The equilibrium quantity, Q_{MARKET}, maximizes the total value to buyers minus the total costs of sellers. In the absence of externalities, therefore, the market equilibrium is efficient.

"All I can say is that if being a leading manufacturer means being a leading polluter, so be it."

© J.B. Handelsman/The New Yorker Collection/www.cartoonbank.com

10-1b Negative Externalities

Now let's suppose that aluminum factories emit pollution: For each unit of aluminum produced, a certain amount of smoke enters the atmosphere. Because this smoke creates a health risk for those who breathe the air, it is a negative externality. How does this externality affect the efficiency of the market outcome?

Because of the externality, the cost to *society* of producing aluminum is larger than the cost to the aluminum producers. For each unit of aluminum produced, the *social cost* includes the private costs of the aluminum producers plus the costs to those bystanders affected adversely by the pollution. Figure 2 shows the social cost of producing aluminum. The social-cost curve is above the supply curve because it takes into account the external costs imposed on society by aluminum production. The difference between these two curves reflects the cost of the pollution emitted.

What quantity of aluminum should be produced? To answer this question, we once again consider what a benevolent social planner would do. The planner wants to maximize the total surplus derived from the market—the value to consumers of aluminum minus the cost of producing aluminum. The planner understands, however, that the cost of producing aluminum includes the external costs of the pollution.

The planner would choose the level of aluminum production at which the demand curve crosses the social-cost curve. This intersection determines the optimal amount of aluminum from the standpoint of society as a whole. Below this level of production, the value of the aluminum to consumers (as measured by the height of the demand curve) exceeds the social cost of producing it (as measured by the height of the social-cost curve). The planner does not produce more than this level because the social cost of producing additional aluminum exceeds the value to consumers.

Note that the equilibrium quantity of aluminum, Q_{MARKET}, is larger than the socially optimal quantity, $Q_{OPTIMUM}$. This inefficiency occurs because the market equilibrium reflects only the private costs of production. In the market equilibrium, the marginal consumer values aluminum at less than the social cost of producing it. That is, at Q_{MARKET}, the demand curve lies below the social-cost curve.

FIGURE 2

Pollution and the Social Optimum

In the presence of a negative externality, such as pollution, the social cost of the good exceeds the private cost. The optimal quantity, $Q_{OPTIMUM}$, is therefore smaller than the equilibrium quantity, Q_{MARKET}.

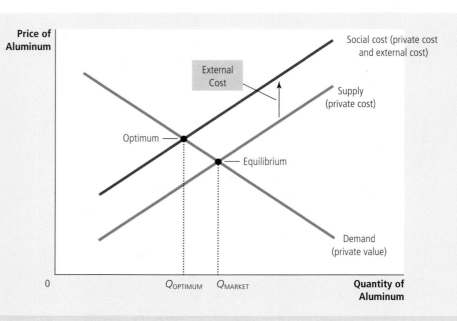

Thus, reducing aluminum production and consumption below the market equilibrium level raises total economic well-being.

How can the social planner achieve the optimal outcome? One way would be to tax aluminum producers for each ton of aluminum sold. The tax would shift the supply curve for aluminum upward by the size of the tax. If the tax accurately reflected the external cost of pollutants released into the atmosphere, the new supply curve would coincide with the social-cost curve. In the new market equilibrium, aluminum producers would produce the socially optimal quantity of aluminum.

The use of such a tax is called **internalizing the externality** because it gives buyers and sellers in the market an incentive to take into account the external effects of their actions. Aluminum producers would, in essence, take the costs of pollution into account when deciding how much aluminum to supply because the tax would make them pay for these external costs. And, because the market price would reflect the tax on producers, consumers of aluminum would have an incentive to use a smaller quantity. The policy is based on one of the *Ten Principles of Economics*: People respond to incentives. Later in this chapter, we consider in more detail how policymakers can deal with externalities.

internalizing the externality
altering incentives so that people take account of the external effects of their actions

10-1c Positive Externalities

Although some activities impose costs on third parties, others yield benefits. For example, consider education. To a large extent, the benefit of education is private: The consumer of education becomes a more productive worker and thus reaps much of the benefit in the form of higher wages. Beyond these private benefits, however, education also yields positive externalities. One externality is that a more educated population leads to more informed voters, which means better government for everyone. Another externality is that a more educated population tends to mean lower crime rates. A third externality is that a more educated population may encourage the development and dissemination of technological advances, leading to higher productivity and wages for everyone. Because of these three positive externalities, a person may prefer to have neighbors who are well educated.

The analysis of positive externalities is similar to the analysis of negative externalities. As Figure 3 shows, the demand curve does not reflect the value to society

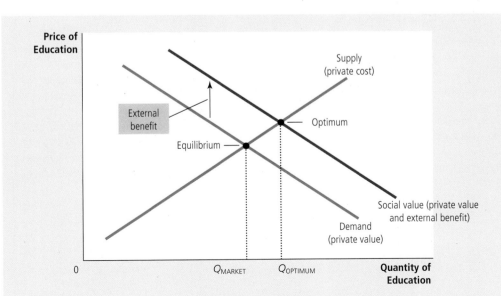

FIGURE 3

Education and the Social Optimum
In the presence of a positive externality, the social value of the good exceeds the private value. The optimal quantity, $Q_{OPTIMUM}$, is therefore larger than the equilibrium quantity, Q_{MARKET}.

IN THE NEWS
·····················

The Externalities of Country Living

An economist says urbanization gets a bum rap.

The Lorax Was Wrong: Skyscrapers Are Green

By Edward L. Glaeser

In Dr. Seuss's environmentalist fable, "The Lorax," the Once-ler, a budding textile magnate, chops down Truffula to knit "Thneeds."

Over the protests of the environmentally sensitive Lorax, the Once-ler builds a great industrial town that despoils the environment, because he "had to grow bigger." Eventually, the Once-ler overdoes it, and he chops down the last Truffula tree, destroying the source of his income. Chastened, Dr. Seuss's industrialist turns green, urging a young listener to take the last Truffula seed and plant a new forest.

Some of the lessons told by this story are correct. From a purely profit-maximizing point of view, the Once-ler is pretty inept, because he kills his golden goose. Any good management consultant would have told him to manage his growth more wisely. One aspect of the story's environmentalist message, that bad things happen when we overfish a common pool, is also correct.

But the unfortunate aspect of the story is that urbanization comes off terribly. The forests are good; the factories are bad. Not only does the story disparage the remarkable benefits that came from the mass production of clothing in 19th-century textile towns, it sends exactly the wrong message on the environment. Contrary to the story's implied message, living in cities is green, while living surrounded by forests is brown.

By building taller and taller buildings, the Once-ler was proving himself to be the real environmentalist.

Matthew Kahn, a U.C.L.A. environmental economist, and I looked across America's metropolitan areas and calculated the carbon emissions associated with a new home in different parts of the country. We estimated expected energy use from driving and public transportation, for a family of fixed size and income. We added in carbon emissions from home electricity and home heating....

In almost every metropolitan area, we found the central city residents emitted less carbon than the suburban counterparts. In New York and San Francisco, the average urban family emits more than two tons less carbon annually because it drives less. In Nashville, the city-suburb carbon gap due to driving is more than three tons. After all, density is the defining characteristic of cities. All that closeness means that people need to travel shorter distances, and that shows up clearly in the data.

While public transportation certainly uses much less energy, per rider, than driving, large carbon reductions are possible without any switch to buses or rails. Higher-density suburban areas, which are still entirely car-dependent, still involve a lot less travel than the really sprawling places. This fact offers

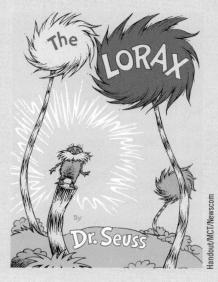

Handout/MCT/Newscom

some hope for greens eager to reduce carbon emissions, since it is a lot easier to imagine Americans driving shorter distances than giving up their cars.

But cars represent only one-third of the gap in carbon emissions between New Yorkers and their suburbanites. The gap in electricity usage between New York City and its suburbs is also about two tons. The gap in emissions from home heating is almost three tons. All told, we estimate a seven-ton difference in carbon emissions between the residents of Manhattan's urban aeries and the good burghers of Westchester County. Living surrounded by concrete is actually pretty green. Living surrounded by trees is not.

The policy prescription that follows from this is that environmentalists should be championing the growth of more and taller skyscrapers. Every new crane in New York City means less low-density development. The environmental ideal should be an apartment in downtown San Francisco, not a ranch in Marin County.

Of course, many environmentalists will still prefer to take their cue from Henry David Thoreau, who advocated living alone in the woods. They would do well to remember that Thoreau, in a sloppy chowder-cooking moment, burned down 300 acres of prime Concord woodland. Few Boston merchants did as much environmental harm, which suggests that if you want to take good care of the environment, stay away from it and live in cities.

Mr. Glaeser is an economics professor at Harvard University. ◢

Source: *New York Times,* Economix blog, March 10, 2009.

of the good. Because the social value is greater than the private value, the social-value curve lies above the demand curve. The optimal quantity is found where the social-value curve and the supply curve intersect. Hence, the socially optimal quantity is greater than the quantity that the private market would naturally reach on its own.

Once again, the government can correct the market failure by inducing market participants to internalize the externality. The appropriate response in the case of positive externalities is exactly the opposite to the case of negative externalities. To move the market equilibrium closer to the social optimum, a positive externality requires a subsidy. In fact, that is exactly the policy the government follows: Education is heavily subsidized through public schools and government scholarships.

To summarize: *Negative externalities lead markets to produce a larger quantity than is socially desirable. Positive externalities lead markets to produce a smaller quantity than is socially desirable. To remedy the problem, the government can internalize the externality by taxing goods that have negative externalities and subsidizing goods that have positive externalities.*

case study **Technology Spillovers, Industrial Policy, and Patent Protection**
A potentially important type of positive externality is called a *technology spillover*—the impact of one firm's research and production efforts on other firms' access to technological advance. For example, consider the market for industrial robots. Robots are at the frontier of a rapidly changing technology. Whenever a firm builds a robot, there is some chance that the firm will discover a new and better design. This new design may benefit not only this firm but also society as a whole because the design will enter society's pool of technological knowledge. That is, the new design may have positive externalities for other producers in the economy.

In this case, the government can internalize the externality by subsidizing the production of robots. If the government paid firms a subsidy for each robot produced, the supply curve would shift down by the amount of the subsidy, and this shift would increase the equilibrium quantity of robots. To ensure that the market equilibrium equals the social optimum, the subsidy should equal the value of the technology spillover.

How large are technology spillovers, and what do they imply for public policy? This is an important question because technological progress is the key to why living standards rise over time. Yet it is also a difficult question on which economists often disagree.

Some economists believe that technology spillovers are pervasive and that the government should encourage those industries that yield the largest spillovers. For instance, these economists argue that if making computer chips yields greater spillovers than making potato chips, the government should encourage the production of computer chips relative to the production of potato chips. The U.S. tax code does this in a limited way by offering special tax breaks for expenditures on research and development. Some nations go further by subsidizing specific industries that supposedly yield large technology spillovers. Government intervention that aims to promote technology-enhancing industries is sometimes called *industrial policy*.

Other economists are skeptical about industrial policy. Even if technology spillovers are common, the success of an industrial policy requires that the government be able to measure the size of the spillovers from different markets. This measurement problem is difficult at best. Moreover, without precise measurements, the political system may end up subsidizing industries with the most political clout rather than those that yield the largest positive externalities.

Another way to deal with technology spillovers is patent protection. The patent laws protect the rights of inventors by giving them exclusive use of their inventions for a period of time. When a firm makes a technological breakthrough, it can patent the idea and capture much of the economic benefit for itself. The patent internalizes the externality by giving the firm a *property right* over its invention. If other firms want to use the new technology, they have to obtain permission from the inventing firm and pay it a royalty. Thus, the patent system gives firms a greater incentive to engage in research and other activities that advance technology. ◢

Quick Quiz   *Give an example of a negative externality and a positive externality. Explain why market outcomes are inefficient in the presence of these externalities.*

10-2 Public Policies toward Externalities

We have discussed why externalities lead markets to allocate resources inefficiently but have mentioned only briefly how this inefficiency can be remedied. In practice, both public policymakers and private individuals respond to externalities in various ways. All of the remedies share the goal of moving the allocation of resources closer to the social optimum.

This section considers governmental solutions. As a general matter, the government can respond to externalities in one of two ways. *Command-and-control policies* regulate behavior directly. *Market-based policies* provide incentives so that private decision makers will choose to solve the problem on their own.

10-2a Command-and-Control Policies: Regulation

The government can remedy an externality by either requiring or forbidding certain behaviors. For example, it is a crime to dump poisonous chemicals into the water supply. In this case, the external costs to society far exceed the benefits to the polluter. The government therefore institutes a command-and-control policy that prohibits this act altogether.

In most cases of pollution, however, the situation is not this simple. Despite the stated goals of some environmentalists, it would be impossible to prohibit all polluting activity. For example, virtually all forms of transportation—even the horse—produce some undesirable polluting by-products. But it would not be sensible for the government to ban all transportation. Thus, instead of trying to eradicate pollution entirely, society has to weigh the costs and benefits to decide the kinds and quantities of pollution it will allow. In the United States, the Environmental Protection Agency (EPA) is the government agency with the task of developing and enforcing regulations aimed at protecting the environment.

Environmental regulations can take many forms. Sometimes the EPA dictates a maximum level of pollution that a factory may emit. Other times the EPA requires that firms adopt a particular technology to reduce emissions. In all cases, to design good rules, the government regulators need to know the details about specific industries and about the alternative technologies that those industries could adopt. This information is often difficult for government regulators to obtain.

10-2b Market-Based Policy 1: Corrective Taxes and Subsidies

Instead of regulating behavior in response to an externality, the government can use market-based policies to align private incentives with social efficiency. For instance, as we saw earlier, the government can internalize the externality by taxing activities that have negative externalities and subsidizing activities that have positive externalities. Taxes enacted to deal with the effects of negative externalities are called **corrective taxes**. They are also called *Pigovian taxes* after economist Arthur Pigou (1877–1959), an early advocate of their use. An ideal corrective tax would equal the external cost from an activity with negative externalities, and an ideal corrective subsidy would equal the external benefit from an activity with positive externalities.

Economists usually prefer corrective taxes to regulations as a way to deal with pollution because they can reduce pollution at a lower cost to society. To see why, let us consider an example.

Suppose that two factories—a paper mill and a steel mill—are each dumping 500 tons of glop into a river every year. The EPA decides that it wants to reduce the amount of pollution. It considers two solutions:

- Regulation: The EPA could tell each factory to reduce its pollution to 300 tons of glop per year.
- Corrective tax: The EPA could levy a tax on each factory of $50,000 for each ton of glop it emits.

The regulation would dictate a level of pollution, whereas the tax would give factory owners an economic incentive to reduce pollution. Which solution do you think is better?

Most economists prefer the tax. To explain this preference, they would first point out that a tax is just as effective as a regulation in reducing the overall level of pollution. The EPA can achieve whatever level of pollution it wants by setting the tax at the appropriate level. The higher the tax, the larger the reduction in pollution. If the tax is high enough, the factories will close down altogether, reducing pollution to zero.

Although regulation and corrective taxes are both capable of reducing pollution, the tax accomplishes this goal more efficiently. The regulation requires each factory to reduce pollution by the same amount. An equal reduction, however, is not necessarily the least expensive way to clean up the water. It is possible that the paper mill can reduce pollution at lower cost than the steel mill. If so, the paper mill would respond to the tax by reducing pollution substantially to avoid the tax, whereas the steel mill would respond by reducing pollution less and paying the tax.

In essence, the corrective tax places a price on the right to pollute. Just as markets allocate goods to those buyers who value them most highly, a corrective tax allocates pollution to those factories that face the highest cost of reducing it. Whatever level of pollution the EPA chooses, it can achieve this goal at the lowest total cost using a tax.

Economists also argue that corrective taxes are better for the environment. Under the command-and-control policy of regulation, the factories have no reason to reduce emission further once they have reached the target of 300 tons of glop. By contrast, the tax gives the factories an incentive to develop cleaner technologies because a cleaner technology would reduce the amount of tax the factory has to pay.

corrective tax
a tax designed to induce private decision makers to take account of the social costs that arise from a negative externality

Arthur Pigou

Corrective taxes are unlike most other taxes. As we discussed in Chapter 8, most taxes distort incentives and move the allocation of resources away from the social optimum. The reduction in economic well-being—that is, in consumer and producer surplus—exceeds the amount of revenue the government raises, resulting in a deadweight loss. By contrast, when externalities are present, society also cares about the well-being of the affected bystanders. Corrective taxes alter incentives that market participants face to account for the presence of externalities and thereby move the allocation of resources closer to the social optimum. Thus, while corrective taxes raise revenue for the government, they also enhance economic efficiency.

case study **Why Is Gasoline Taxed So Heavily?**

In many nations, gasoline is among the most heavily taxed goods. The gas tax can be viewed as a corrective tax aimed at addressing three negative externalities associated with driving:

- *Congestion:* If you have ever been stuck in bumper-to-bumper traffic, you have probably wished that there were fewer cars on the road. A gasoline tax keeps congestion down by encouraging people to take public transportation, carpool more often, and live closer to work.
- *Accidents:* Whenever people buy large cars or sport-utility vehicles, they may make themselves safer but they certainly put their neighbors at risk. According to the National Highway Traffic Safety Administration, a person driving a typical car is five times as likely to die if hit by a sport-utility vehicle than if hit by another car. The gas tax is an indirect way of making people pay when their large, gas-guzzling vehicles impose risk on others. It would induce them to take this risk into account when choosing what vehicle to purchase.

- *Pollution:* Cars cause smog. Moreover, the burning of fossil fuels such as gasoline is widely believed to be the primary cause of global warming. Experts disagree about how dangerous this threat is, but there is no doubt that the gas tax reduces the threat by reducing the use of gasoline.

So the gas tax, rather than causing deadweight losses like most taxes, actually makes the economy work better. It means less traffic congestion, safer roads, and a cleaner environment.

How high should the tax on gasoline be? Most European countries impose gasoline taxes that are much higher than those in the United States. Many observers have suggested that the United States should also tax gasoline more heavily. A 2007 study published in the *Journal of Economic Literature* summarized the research on the size of the various externalities associated with driving. It concluded that the optimal corrective tax on gasoline was $2.28 per gallon in 2005 dollars; after adjusting for inflation, that amount is equivalent to about $2.70 per gallon in 2012 dollars. By contrast, the actual tax in the United States in 2012 was only about 50 cents per gallon.

The tax revenue from a gasoline tax could be used to lower taxes that distort incentives and cause deadweight losses, such as income taxes. In addition, some of the burdensome government regulations that require automakers to produce more fuel-efficient cars would prove unnecessary. This idea, however, has never proven politically popular. ◢

10-2c Market-Based Policy 2: Tradable Pollution Permits

Returning to our example of the paper mill and the steel mill, let us suppose that, despite the advice of its economists, the EPA adopts the regulation and requires each factory to reduce its pollution to 300 tons of glop per year. Then one day, after the regulation is in place and both mills have complied, the two firms go to the EPA with a proposal. The steel mill wants to increase its emission of glop by 100 tons. The paper mill has agreed to reduce its emission by the same amount if the steel mill pays it $5 million. Should the EPA allow the two factories to make this deal?

From the standpoint of economic efficiency, allowing the deal is good policy. The deal must make the owners of the two factories better off because they are voluntarily agreeing to it. Moreover, the deal does not have any external effects because the total amount of pollution remains the same. Thus, social welfare is enhanced by allowing the paper mill to sell its pollution rights to the steel mill.

The same logic applies to any voluntary transfer of the right to pollute from one firm to another. If the EPA allows firms to make these deals, it will, in essence, have created a new scarce resource: pollution permits. A market to trade these permits will eventually develop, and that market will be governed by the forces of supply and demand. The invisible hand will ensure that this new market allocates the right to pollute efficiently. That is, the permits will end up in the hands of those firms that value them most highly, as judged by their willingness to pay. A firm's willingness to pay for the right to pollute, in turn, will depend on its cost of reducing pollution: The more costly it is for a firm to cut back on pollution, the more it will be willing to pay for a permit.

An advantage of allowing a market for pollution permits is that the initial allocation of pollution permits among firms does not matter from the standpoint of economic efficiency. Those firms that can reduce pollution at a low cost will sell whatever permits they get, and firms that can reduce pollution only at a high cost will buy whatever permits they need. As long as there is a free market for the pollution rights, the final allocation will be efficient regardless of the initial allocation.

Reducing pollution using pollution permits may seem very different from using corrective taxes, but the two policies have much in common. In both cases, firms pay for their pollution. With corrective taxes, polluting firms must pay a tax to the government. With pollution permits, polluting firms must pay to buy the permit. (Even firms that already own permits must pay to pollute: The opportunity cost of polluting is what they could have received by selling their permits on the open market.) Both corrective taxes and pollution permits internalize the externality of pollution by making it costly for firms to pollute.

The similarity of the two policies can be seen by considering the market for pollution. Both panels in Figure 4 show the demand curve for the right to pollute. This curve shows that the lower the price of polluting, the more firms will choose to pollute. In panel (a), the EPA uses a corrective tax to set a price for pollution. In this case, the supply curve for pollution rights is perfectly elastic (because firms can pollute as much as they want by paying the tax), and the position of the demand curve determines the quantity of pollution. In panel (b), the EPA sets a quantity of pollution by issuing pollution permits. In this case, the supply curve for pollution rights is perfectly inelastic (because the quantity of pollution is fixed by the number of permits), and the position of the demand curve determines the price of pollution. Hence, the EPA can achieve any point on a given demand curve either by setting a price with a corrective tax or by setting a quantity with pollution permits.

FIGURE 4

The Equivalence of Corrective Taxes and Pollution Permits

In panel (a), the EPA sets a price on pollution by levying a corrective tax, and the demand curve determines the quantity of pollution. In panel (b), the EPA limits the quantity of pollution by limiting the number of pollution permits, and the demand curve determines the price of pollution. The price and quantity of pollution are the same in the two cases.

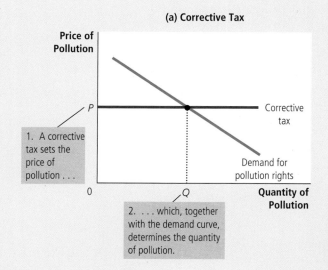

(a) Corrective Tax

1. A corrective tax sets the price of pollution . . .

2. . . . which, together with the demand curve, determines the quantity of pollution.

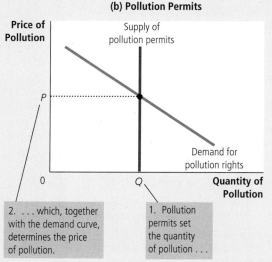

(b) Pollution Permits

1. Pollution permits set the quantity of pollution . . .

2. . . . which, together with the demand curve, determines the price of pollution.

long-run growth by nudging the economy away from consumption and borrowing and toward saving and investment.

Of course, carbon taxes also lower carbon emissions. Economic theory suggests that putting a price on pollution reduces emissions more affordably and more effectively than any other measure. This conclusion is supported by empirical evidence from previous market-based policies, like those in the 1990 amendments to the Clean Air Act that targeted sulfur dioxide emissions. British Columbia's carbon tax is only four years old, but preliminary data show that greenhouse gas emissions are down 4.5 percent even as population and gross domestic product have been growing. Sales of motor gasoline have fallen by 2 percent since 2007, compared with a 5 percent increase for Canada as a whole.

What would a British Columbia-style carbon tax look like in the United States? According to our calculations, a British Columbia-style $30 carbon tax would generate about $145 billion a year in the United States. That could be used to reduce individual and corporate income taxes by 10 percent, and afterward there would still be $35 billion left over. If recent budget deals are any guide, Congress might choose to set aside half of that remainder to reduce estate taxes (to please Republicans) and the other half to offset the impacts of higher fuel and electricity prices resulting from the carbon tax on low-income households through refundable tax credits or a targeted reduction in payroll taxes (to please Democrats).

Revenue from a carbon tax would most likely decline over time as Americans reduce their carbon emissions, but for many years to come it could pay for big reductions in existing taxes. It would also promote energy conservation and steer investment into clean technology and other productive economic activities.

Lastly, the carbon tax would actually give Americans more control over how much they pay in taxes. Households and businesses could reduce their carbon tax payments simply by reducing their use of fossil fuels. Americans would trim their carbon footprints—and their tax burdens—by investing in energy efficiency at home and at work, switching to less-polluting vehicles and pursuing countless other innovations. All of this would be driven not by government mandates but by Adam Smith's invisible hand.

A carbon tax makes sense whether you are a Republican or a Democrat, a climate change skeptic or a believer, a conservative or a conservationist (or both). We can move past the partisan fireworks over global warming by turning British Columbia's carbon tax into a made-in-America solution.

Yoram Bauman, an environmental economist, is a fellow at Sightline Institute in Seattle. Shi-Ling Hsu, a law professor at Florida State University, is the author of "The Case for a Carbon Tax."

Source: *New York Times,* July 5, 2012.

integrating different types of businesses. For example, consider an apple grower and a beekeeper who are located next to each other. Each business confers a positive externality on the other: By pollinating the flowers on the trees, the bees help the orchard produce apples. At the same time, the bees use the nectar they get from the apple trees to produce honey. Nonetheless, when the apple grower is deciding how many trees to plant and the beekeeper is deciding how many bees to keep, they neglect the positive externality. As a result, the apple grower plants too few trees and the beekeeper keeps too few bees. These externalities could be internalized if the beekeeper bought the apple orchard or if the apple grower bought the beehives: Both activities would then take place within the same firm, and this single firm could choose the optimal number of trees and bees. Internalizing externalities is one reason that some firms are involved in multiple types of businesses.

Another way for the private market to deal with external effects is for the interested parties to enter into a contract. In the foregoing example, a contract between the apple grower and the beekeeper can solve the problem of too few trees and too few bees. The contract can specify the number of trees, the number of bees, and perhaps a payment from one party to the other. By setting the right number of trees and bees, the contract can solve the inefficiency that normally arises from these externalities and make both parties better off.

10-3b The Coase Theorem

How effective is the private market in dealing with externalities? A famous result, called the **Coase theorem** after economist Ronald Coase, suggests that it can be very effective in some circumstances. According to the Coase theorem, if private

Coase theorem
the proposition that if private parties can bargain without cost over the allocation of resources, they can solve the problem of externalities on their own

parties can bargain over the allocation of resources at no cost, then the private market will always solve the problem of externalities and allocate resources efficiently.

To see how the Coase theorem works, consider an example. Suppose that Dick owns a dog named Spot. Spot barks and disturbs Jane, Dick's neighbor. Dick gets a benefit from owning the dog, but the dog confers a negative externality on Jane. Should Dick be forced to send Spot to the pound, or should Jane have to suffer sleepless nights because of Spot's barking?

Consider first what outcome is socially efficient. A social planner, considering the two alternatives, would compare the benefit that Dick gets from the dog to the cost that Jane bears from the barking. If the benefit exceeds the cost, it is efficient for Dick to keep the dog and for Jane to live with the barking. Yet if the cost exceeds the benefit, then Dick should get rid of the dog.

According to the Coase theorem, the private market will reach the efficient outcome on its own. How? Jane can simply offer to pay Dick to get rid of the dog. Dick will accept the deal if the amount of money Jane offers is greater than the benefit of keeping the dog.

By bargaining over the price, Dick and Jane can always reach the efficient outcome. For instance, suppose that Dick gets a $500 benefit from the dog and Jane bears an $800 cost from the barking. In this case, Jane can offer Dick $600 to get rid of the dog, and Dick will gladly accept. Both parties are better off than they were before, and the efficient outcome is reached.

It is possible, of course, that Jane would not be willing to offer any price that Dick would accept. For instance, suppose that Dick gets a $1,000 benefit from the dog and Jane bears an $800 cost from the barking. In this case, Dick would turn down any offer below $1,000, while Jane would not offer any amount above $800. Therefore, Dick ends up keeping the dog. Given these costs and benefits, however, this outcome is efficient.

So far, we have assumed that Dick has the legal right to keep a barking dog. In other words, we have assumed that Dick can keep Spot unless Jane pays him enough to induce him to give up the dog voluntarily. But how different would the outcome be if Jane had the legal right to peace and quiet?

According to the Coase theorem, the initial distribution of rights does not matter for the market's ability to reach the efficient outcome. For instance, suppose that Jane can legally compel Dick to get rid of the dog. Having this right works to Jane's advantage, but it probably will not change the outcome. In this case, Dick can offer to pay Jane to allow him to keep the dog. If the benefit of the dog to Dick exceeds the cost of the barking to Jane, then Dick and Jane will strike a bargain in which Dick keeps the dog.

Although Dick and Jane can reach the efficient outcome regardless of how rights are initially distributed, the distribution of rights is not irrelevant: It determines the distribution of economic well-being. Whether Dick has the right to a barking dog or Jane the right to peace and quiet determines who pays whom in the final bargain. But in either case, the two parties can bargain with each other and solve the externality problem. Dick will end up keeping the dog only if his benefit exceeds Jane's cost.

To sum up: *The Coase theorem says that private economic actors can potentially solve the problem of externalities among themselves. Whatever the initial distribution of rights, the interested parties can reach a bargain in which everyone is better off and the outcome is efficient.*

10-3c Why Private Solutions Do Not Always Work

Despite the appealing logic of the Coase theorem, private individuals on their own often fail to resolve the problems caused by externalities. The Coase theorem applies only when the interested parties have no trouble reaching and enforcing an agreement. In the real world, however, bargaining does not always work, even when a mutually beneficial agreement is possible.

Sometimes the interested parties fail to solve an externality problem because of **transaction costs**, the costs that parties incur in the process of agreeing to and following through on a bargain. In our example, imagine that Dick and Jane speak different languages so that, to reach an agreement, they need to hire a translator. If the benefit of solving the barking problem is less than the cost of the translator, Dick and Jane might choose to leave the problem unsolved. In more realistic examples, the transaction costs are the expenses not of translators but of lawyers required to draft and enforce contracts.

transaction costs
the costs that parties incur in the process of agreeing to and following through on a bargain

At other times, bargaining simply breaks down. The recurrence of wars and labor strikes shows that reaching agreement can be difficult and that failing to reach agreement can be costly. The problem is often that each party tries to hold out for a better deal. For example, suppose that Dick gets a $500 benefit from having the dog and Jane bears an $800 cost from the barking. Although it is efficient for Jane to pay Dick to find another home for the dog, there are many prices that could lead to this outcome. Dick might demand $750, and Jane might offer only $550. As they haggle over the price, the inefficient outcome with the barking dog persists.

Reaching an efficient bargain is especially difficult when the number of interested parties is large, because coordinating everyone is costly. For example, consider a factory that pollutes the water of a nearby lake. The pollution confers a negative externality on the local fishermen. According to the Coase theorem, if the pollution is inefficient, then the factory and the fishermen could reach a bargain in which the fishermen pay the factory not to pollute. If there are many fishermen, however, trying to coordinate them all to bargain with the factory may be almost impossible.

When private bargaining does not work, the government can sometimes play a role. The government is an institution designed for collective action. In this example, the government can act on behalf of the fishermen, even when it is impractical for the fishermen to act for themselves.

Quick Quiz   *Give an example of a private solution to an externality.* • *What is the Coase theorem?* • *Why are private economic participants sometimes unable to solve the problems caused by an externality?*

10-4 Conclusion

The invisible hand is powerful but not omnipotent. A market's equilibrium maximizes the sum of producer and consumer surplus. When the buyers and sellers in the market are the only interested parties, this outcome is efficient from the standpoint of society as a whole. But when there are external effects, such as pollution, evaluating a market outcome requires taking into account the well-being of third parties as well. In this case, the invisible hand of the marketplace may fail to allocate resources efficiently.

In some cases, people can solve the problem of externalities on their own. The Coase theorem suggests that the interested parties can bargain among themselves and agree on an efficient solution. Sometimes, however, an efficient outcome cannot be reached, perhaps because the large number of interested parties makes bargaining difficult.

When people cannot solve the problem of externalities privately, the government often steps in. Yet even with government intervention, society should not abandon market forces entirely. Rather, the government can address the problem by requiring decision makers to bear the full costs of their actions. Pollution permits and corrective taxes on emissions, for instance, are designed to internalize the externality of pollution. More and more, these are the policies of choice for those interested in protecting the environment. Market forces, properly redirected, are often the best remedy for market failure.

Summary

- When a transaction between a buyer and seller directly affects a third party, the effect is called an externality. If an activity yields negative externalities, such as pollution, the socially optimal quantity in a market is less than the equilibrium quantity. If an activity yields positive externalities, such as technology spillovers, the socially optimal quantity is greater than the equilibrium quantity.

- Governments pursue various policies to remedy the inefficiencies caused by externalities. Sometimes the government prevents socially inefficient activity by regulating behavior. Other times it internalizes an externality using corrective taxes. Another public policy is to issue permits. For example, the government could protect the environment by issuing a limited number of pollution permits. The result of this policy is largely the same as imposing corrective taxes on polluters.

- Those affected by externalities can sometimes solve the problem privately. For instance, when one business imposes an externality on another business, the two businesses can internalize the externality by merging. Alternatively, the interested parties can solve the problem by negotiating a contract. According to the Coase theorem, if people can bargain without cost, then they can always reach an agreement in which resources are allocated efficiently. In many cases, however, reaching a bargain among the many interested parties is difficult, so the Coase theorem does not apply.

Key Concepts

externality, *p. 196*
internalizing the externality, *p. 199*

corrective tax, *p. 203*
Coase theorem, *p. 209*

transaction costs, *p. 211*

Questions for Review

1. Give an example of a negative externality and an example of a positive externality.

2. Draw a supply-and-demand diagram to explain the effect of a negative externality that occurs as a result of a firm's production process.

3. In what way does the patent system help society solve an externality problem?

4. What are corrective taxes? Why do economists prefer them to regulations as a way to protect the environment from pollution?

5. List some of the ways that the problems caused by externalities can be solved without government intervention.

6. Imagine that you are a nonsmoker sharing a room with a smoker. According to the Coase theorem, what determines whether your roommate smokes in the room? Is this outcome efficient? How do you and your roommate reach this solution?

Quick Check Multiple Choice

1. Which of the following is an example of a positive externality?
   a. Bob mows Hillary's lawn and is paid $100 for performing the service.
   b. While mowing the lawn, Bob's lawnmower spews out smoke that Hillary's neighbor Kristen has to breathe.
   c. Hillary's newly cut lawn makes her neighborhood more attractive.
   d. Hillary's neighbors pay her if she promises to get her lawn cut on a regular basis.

2. If the production of a good yields a negative externality, then the social-cost curve lies _____ the supply curve, and the socially optimal quantity is _____ than the equilibrium quantity.
   a. above, greater
   b. above, less
   c. below, greater
   d. below, less

3. When the government levies a tax on a good equal to the external cost associated with the good's production, it _____ the price paid by consumers and makes the market outcome _____ efficient.
   a. increases, more
   b. increases, less

   c. decreases, more
   d. decreases, less

4. Which of the following statements about corrective taxes is NOT true?
   a. Economists prefer them to command-and-control regulation.
   b. They raise government revenue.
   c. They cause deadweight losses.
   d. They reduce the quantity sold in a market.

5. The government auctions off 500 units of pollution rights. They sell for $50 per unit, raising total revenue of $25,000. This policy is equivalent to a corrective tax of _____ per unit of pollution.
   a. $10
   b. $50
   c. $450
   d. $500

6. The Coase theorem does NOT apply if
   a. there is a significant externality between two parties.
   b. the court system vigorously enforces all contracts.
   c. transaction costs make negotiating difficult.
   d. both parties understand the externality fully.

Problems and Applications

1. Consider two ways to protect your car from theft. The Club (a steering wheel lock) makes it difficult for a car thief to take your car. Lojack (a tracking system) makes it easier for the police to catch the car thief who has stolen it. Which of these types of protection conveys a negative externality on other car owners? Which conveys a positive externality? Do you think there are any policy implications of your analysis?

2. Consider the market for fire extinguishers.
   a. Why might fire extinguishers exhibit positive externalities?
   b. Draw a graph of the market for fire extinguishers, labeling the demand curve, the social-value curve, the supply curve, and the social-cost curve.
   c. Indicate the market equilibrium level of output and the efficient level of output. Give an intuitive explanation for why these quantities differ.
   d. If the external benefit is $10 per extinguisher, describe a government policy that would yield the efficient outcome.

3. A local drama company proposes a new neighborhood theater in San Francisco. Before approving the building permit, the city planner completes a study of the theater's impact on the surrounding community.

   a. One finding of the study is that theaters attract traffic, which adversely affects the community. The city planner estimates that the cost to the community from the extra traffic is $5 per ticket. What kind of an externality is this? Why?
   b. Graph the market for theater tickets, labeling the demand curve, the social-value curve, the supply curve, the social-cost curve, the market equilibrium level of output, and the efficient level of output. Also show the per-unit amount of the externality.
   c. Upon further review, the city planner uncovers a second externality. Rehearsals for the plays tend to run until late at night, with actors, stagehands, and other theater members coming and going at various hours. The planner has found that the increased foot traffic improves the safety of the surrounding streets, an estimated benefit to the community of $2 per ticket. What kind of externality is this? Why?
   d. On a new graph, illustrate the market for theater tickets in the case of these two externalities. Again, label the demand curve, the social-value curve, the supply curve, the social-cost curve, the market equilibrium level of output, the efficient level of output, and the per-unit amount of both externalities.

e. Describe a government policy that would result in an efficient outcome.

4. Greater consumption of alcohol leads to more motor vehicle accidents and, thus, imposes costs on people who do not drink and drive.
   a. Illustrate the market for alcohol, labeling the demand curve, the social-value curve, the supply curve, the social-cost curve, the market equilibrium level of output, and the efficient level of output.
   b. On your graph, shade the area corresponding to the deadweight loss of the market equilibrium. (*Hint*: The deadweight loss occurs because some units of alcohol are consumed for which the social cost exceeds the social value.) Explain.

5. Many observers believe that the levels of pollution in our society are too high.
   a. If society wishes to reduce overall pollution by a certain amount, why is it efficient to have different amounts of reduction at different firms?
   b. Command-and-control approaches often rely on uniform reductions among firms. Why are these approaches generally unable to target the firms that should undertake bigger reductions?
   c. Economists argue that appropriate corrective taxes or tradable pollution rights will result in efficient pollution reduction. How do these approaches target the firms that should undertake bigger reductions?

6. The many identical residents of Whoville love drinking Zlurp. Each resident has the following willingness to pay for the tasty refreshment:

First bottle	$5
Second bottle	4
Third bottle	3
Fourth bottle	2
Fifth bottle	1
Further bottles	0

   a. The cost of producing Zlurp is $1.50, and the competitive suppliers sell it at this price. (The supply curve is horizontal.) How many bottles will each Whovillian consume? What is each person's consumer surplus?
   b. Producing Zlurp creates pollution. Each bottle has an external cost of $1. Taking this additional cost into account, what is total surplus per person in the allocation you described in part (a)?
   c. Cindy Lou Who, one of the residents of Whoville, decides on her own to reduce her consumption of Zlurp by one bottle. What happens to Cindy's welfare (her consumer surplus minus the cost of pollution she experiences)? How does Cindy's decision affect total surplus in Whoville?
   d. Mayor Grinch imposes a $1 tax on Zlurp. What is consumption per person now? Calculate consumer surplus, the external cost, government revenue, and total surplus per person.

e. Based on your calculations, would you support the mayor's policy? Why or why not?

7. Ringo loves playing rock 'n' roll music at high volume. Luciano loves opera and hates rock 'n' roll. Unfortunately, they are next-door neighbors in an apartment building with paper-thin walls.
   a. What is the externality here?
   b. What command-and-control policy might the landlord impose? Could such a policy lead to an inefficient outcome?
   c. Suppose the landlord lets the tenants do whatever they want. According to the Coase theorem, how might Ringo and Luciano reach an efficient outcome on their own? What might prevent them from reaching an efficient outcome?

8. Figure 4 shows that for any given demand curve for the right to pollute, the government can achieve the same outcome either by setting a price with a corrective tax or by setting a quantity with pollution permits. Suppose there is a sharp improvement in the technology for controlling pollution.
   a. Using graphs similar to those in Figure 4, illustrate the effect of this development on the demand for pollution rights.
   b. What is the effect on the price and quantity of pollution under each regulatory system? Explain.

9. Suppose that the government decides to issue tradable permits for a certain form of pollution.
   a. Does it matter for economic efficiency whether the government distributes or auctions the permits? Why or why not?
   b. If the government chooses to distribute the permits, does the allocation of permits among firms matter for efficiency? Explain.

10. There are three industrial firms in Happy Valley.

Firm	Initial Pollution Level	Cost of Reducing Pollution by 1 Unit
A	70 units	$20
B	80 units	$25
C	50 units	$10

   The government wants to reduce pollution to 120 units, so it gives each firm 40 tradable pollution permits.
   a. Who sells permits and how many do they sell? Who buys permits and how many do they buy? Briefly explain why the sellers and buyers are each willing to do so. What is the total cost of pollution reduction in this situation?
   b. How much higher would the costs of pollution reduction be if the permits could not be traded?

Go to CengageBrain.com to purchase access to the proven, critical Study Guide to accompany this text, which features additional notes and context, practice tests, and much more.

Public Goods and Common Resources

An old song lyric maintains that "the best things in life are free." A moment's thought reveals a long list of goods that the songwriter could have had in mind. Nature provides some of them, such as rivers, mountains, beaches, lakes, and oceans. The government provides others, such as playgrounds, parks, and parades. In each case, people do not pay a fee when they choose to enjoy the benefit of the good.

Goods without prices provide a special challenge for economic analysis. Most goods in our economy are allocated in markets, in which buyers pay for what they receive and sellers are paid for what they provide. For these goods, prices are the signals that guide the decisions of buyers and sellers, and these decisions lead to an efficient allocation of resources. When goods are available free of charge, however, the market forces that normally allocate resources in our economy are absent.

In this chapter, we examine the problems that arise for the allocation of resources when there are goods without market prices. Our analysis will shed light on one of the *Ten Principles of Economics* in Chapter 1: Governments can sometimes improve market outcomes. When a good does not have a price attached to it, private markets cannot ensure that the good is produced and consumed in the proper amounts. In such cases, government policy can potentially remedy the market failure and increase economic well-being.

11-1 The Different Kinds of Goods

How well do markets work in providing the goods that people want? The answer to this question depends on the good being considered. As we discussed in Chapter 7, a market can provide the efficient number of ice-cream cones: The price of ice-cream cones adjusts to balance supply and demand, and this equilibrium maximizes the sum of producer and consumer surplus. Yet as we discussed in Chapter 10, the market cannot be counted on to prevent aluminum manufacturers from polluting the air we breathe: Buyers and sellers in a market typically do not take into account the external effects of their decisions. Thus, markets work well when the good is ice cream, but they work badly when the good is clean air.

In thinking about the various goods in the economy, it is useful to group them according to two characteristics:

excludability
the property of a good whereby a person can be prevented from using it

- Is the good **excludable**? That is, can people be prevented from using the good?
- Is the good **rival in consumption**? That is, does one person's use of the good reduce another person's ability to use it?

rivalry in consumption
the property of a good whereby one person's use diminishes other people's use

Using these two characteristics, Figure 1 divides goods into four categories:

private goods
goods that are both excludable and rival in consumption

1. **Private goods** are both excludable and rival in consumption. Consider an ice-cream cone, for example. An ice-cream cone is excludable because it is possible to prevent someone from eating one—you just don't give it to her. An ice-cream cone is rival in consumption because if one person eats an ice-cream cone, another person cannot eat the same cone. Most goods in the economy are private goods like ice-cream cones: You don't get one unless you pay for it, and once you have it, you are the only person who benefits. When we analyzed supply and demand in Chapters 4–6 and the efficiency of markets in Chapters 7–9, we implicitly assumed that goods were both excludable and rival in consumption.

public goods
goods that are neither excludable nor rival in consumption

2. **Public goods** are neither excludable nor rival in consumption. That is, people cannot be prevented from using a public good, and one person's use of a public good does not reduce another person's ability to use it. For example, a tornado siren in a small town is a public good. Once the siren sounds, it is impossible to prevent any single person from hearing it (so it is not excludable). Moreover, when one person gets the benefit of the warning, she does not reduce the benefit to anyone else (so it is not rival in consumption).

common resources
goods that are rival in consumption but not excludable

3. **Common resources** are rival in consumption but not excludable. For example, fish in the ocean are rival in consumption: When one person catches fish, there are fewer fish for the next person to catch. Yet these fish are not an excludable good because, given the vast size of an ocean, it is difficult to stop fishermen from taking fish out of it.

		Rival in consumption? Yes	Rival in consumption? No
Excludable?	**Yes**	Private Goods • Ice-cream cones • Clothing • Congested toll roads	Club Goods • Fire protection • Cable TV • Uncongested toll roads
	No	Common Resources • Fish in the ocean • The environment • Congested nontoll roads	Public Goods • Tornado siren • National defense • Uncongested nontoll roads

FIGURE 1

Four Types of Goods
Goods can be grouped into four categories according to two characteristics: (1) A good is *excludable* if people can be prevented from using it. (2) A good is *rival in consumption* if one person's use of the good diminishes other people's use of it. This diagram gives examples of goods in each category.

4. **Club goods** are excludable but not rival in consumption. For instance, consider fire protection in a small town. It is easy to exclude someone from using this good: The fire department can just let her house burn down. Yet fire protection is not rival in consumption: Once a town has paid for the fire department, the additional cost of protecting one more house is small. (We discuss club goods again in Chapter 15, where we see that they are one type of a *natural monopoly*.)

club goods
goods that are excludable but not rival in consumption

Although Figure 1 offers a clean separation of goods into four categories, the boundaries between the categories are sometimes fuzzy. Whether goods are excludable or rival in consumption is often a matter of degree. Fish in an ocean may not be excludable because monitoring fishing is so difficult, but a large enough coast guard could make fish at least partly excludable. Similarly, although fish are generally rival in consumption, this would be less true if the population of fishermen were small relative to the population of fish. (Think of North American fishing waters before the arrival of European settlers.) For purposes of our analysis, however, it will be helpful to group goods into these four categories.

In this chapter, we examine goods that are not excludable: public goods and common resources. Because people cannot be prevented from using these goods, they are available to everyone free of charge. The study of public goods and common resources is closely related to the study of externalities. For both of these types of goods, externalities arise because something of value has no price attached to it. If one person were to provide a public good, such as a tornado siren, other people would be better off. They would receive a benefit without paying for it—a positive externality. Similarly, when one person uses a common resource such as the fish in the ocean, other people are worse off because there are fewer fish to catch. They suffer a loss but are not compensated for it—a negative externality. Because of these external effects, private decisions about consumption and production can lead to an inefficient allocation of resources, and government intervention can potentially raise economic well-being.

Quick Quiz *Define* public goods *and* common resources *and give an example of each.*

11-2 Public Goods

To understand how public goods differ from other goods and why they present problems for society, let's consider an example: a fireworks display. This good is not excludable because it is impossible to prevent someone from seeing fireworks, and it is not rival in consumption because one person's enjoyment of fireworks does not reduce anyone else's enjoyment of them.

11-2a The Free-Rider Problem

The citizens of Smalltown, U.S.A., like seeing fireworks on the Fourth of July. Each of the town's 500 residents places a $10 value on the experience for a total benefit of $5,000. The cost of putting on a fireworks display is $1,000. Because the $5,000 benefit exceeds the $1,000 cost, it is efficient for Smalltown to have a fireworks display on the Fourth of July.

Would the private market produce the efficient outcome? Probably not. Imagine that Ellen, a Smalltown entrepreneur, decided to put on a fireworks display. Ellen would surely have trouble selling tickets to the event because her potential customers would quickly figure out that they could see the fireworks even without a ticket. Because fireworks are not excludable, people have an incentive to be free riders. A **free rider** is a person who receives the benefit of a good but does not pay for it. Because people would have an incentive to be free riders rather than ticket buyers, the market would fail to provide the efficient outcome.

free rider
a person who receives the benefit of a good but avoids paying for it

One way to view this market failure is that it arises because of an externality. If Ellen puts on the fireworks display, she confers an external benefit on those who see the display without paying for it. When deciding whether to put on the display, however, Ellen does not take the external benefits into account. Even though the fireworks display is socially desirable, it is not profitable. As a result, Ellen makes the privately rational but socially inefficient decision not to put on the display.

Although the private market fails to supply the fireworks display demanded by Smalltown residents, the solution to Smalltown's problem is obvious: The local government can sponsor a Fourth of July celebration. The town council can raise everyone's taxes by $2 and use the revenue to hire Ellen to produce the fireworks. Everyone in Smalltown is better off by $8—the $10 at which residents value the fireworks minus the $2 tax bill. Ellen can help Smalltown reach the efficient outcome as a public employee even though she could not do so as a private entrepreneur.

The story of Smalltown is simplified but realistic. In fact, many local governments in the United States pay for fireworks on the Fourth of July. Moreover, the story shows a general lesson about public goods: Because public goods are not excludable, the free-rider problem prevents the private market from supplying them. The government, however, can potentially remedy the problem. If the government decides that the total benefits of a public good exceed its costs, it can provide the public good, pay for it with tax revenue, and make everyone better off.

11-2b Some Important Public Goods

There are many examples of public goods. Here we consider three of the most important.

"I like the concept if we can do it with no new taxes."

National Defense   The defense of a country from foreign aggressors is a classic example of a public good. Once the country is defended, it is impossible to prevent any single person from enjoying the benefit of this defense. Moreover, when one person enjoys the benefit of national defense, she does not reduce the benefit to anyone else. Thus, national defense is neither excludable nor rival in consumption.

National defense is also one of the most expensive public goods. In 2011, the U.S. federal government spent a total of $717 billion on national defense, more than $2,298 per person. People disagree about whether this amount is too small or too large, but almost no one doubts that some government spending for national defense is necessary. Even economists who advocate small government agree that the national defense is a public good the government should provide.

Basic Research   Knowledge is created through research. In evaluating the appropriate public policy toward knowledge creation, it is important to distinguish general knowledge from specific technological knowledge. Specific technological knowledge, such as the invention of a longer-lasting battery, a smaller microchip, or a better digital music player, can be patented. The patent gives the inventor the exclusive right to the knowledge she has created for a period of time. Anyone else who wants to use the patented information must pay the inventor for the right to do so. In other words, the patent makes the knowledge created by the inventor excludable.

By contrast, general knowledge is a public good. For example, a mathematician cannot patent a theorem. Once a theorem is proven, the knowledge is not excludable: The theorem enters society's general pool of knowledge that anyone can use without charge. The theorem is also not rival in consumption: One person's use of the theorem does not prevent any other person from using the theorem.

Profit-seeking firms spend a lot on research trying to develop new products that they can patent and sell, but they do not spend much on basic research. Their incentive, instead, is to free ride on the general knowledge created by others. As a result, in the absence of any public policy, society would devote too few resources to creating new knowledge.

The government tries to provide the public good of general knowledge in various ways. Government agencies, such as the National Institutes of Health and the National Science Foundation, subsidize basic research in medicine, mathematics, physics, chemistry, biology, and even economics. Some people justify government funding of the space program on the grounds that it adds to society's pool of knowledge. Determining the appropriate level of government support for these endeavors is difficult because the benefits are hard to measure. Moreover, the members of Congress who appropriate funds for research usually have little expertise in science and, therefore, are not in the best position to judge what lines of research will produce the largest benefits. So, while basic research is surely a public good, we should not be surprised if the public sector fails to pay for the right amount and the right kinds.

Fighting Poverty   Many government programs are aimed at helping the poor. The welfare system (officially called TANF, Temporary Assistance for Needy Families) provides a small income for some poor families. Food stamps (officially called SNAP, Supplemental Nutrition Assistance Program) subsidize the purchase of food for those with low incomes. And various government housing programs make shelter more affordable. These antipoverty programs are financed by taxes paid by families that are financially more successful.

Economists disagree among themselves about what role the government should play in fighting poverty. We discuss this debate more fully in Chapter 20, but here we note one important argument: Advocates of antipoverty programs claim that fighting poverty is a public good. Even if everyone prefers living in a society without poverty, fighting poverty is not a "good" that private actions will adequately provide.

To see why, suppose someone tried to organize a group of wealthy individuals to try to eliminate poverty. They would be providing a public good. This good would not be rival in consumption: One person's enjoyment of living in a society without poverty would not reduce anyone else's enjoyment of it. The good would not be excludable: Once poverty is eliminated, no one can be prevented from taking pleasure in this fact. As a result, there would be a tendency for people to free ride on the generosity of others, enjoying the benefits of poverty elimination without contributing to the cause.

Because of the free-rider problem, eliminating poverty through private charity will probably not work. Yet government action can solve this problem. Taxing the wealthy to raise the living standards of the poor can potentially make everyone better off. The poor are better off because they now enjoy a higher standard of living, and those paying the taxes are better off because they enjoy living in a society with less poverty.

case study

Are Lighthouses Public Goods?

Some goods can switch between being public goods and being private goods depending on the circumstances. For example, a fireworks display is a public good if performed in a town with many residents. Yet if performed at a private amusement park, such as Walt Disney World, a fireworks display is more like a private good because visitors to the park pay for admission.

Another example is a lighthouse. Economists have long used lighthouses as an example of a public good. Lighthouses mark specific locations along the coast so that passing ships can avoid treacherous waters. The benefit that the lighthouse provides to the ship captain is neither excludable nor rival in consumption, so each captain has an incentive to free ride by using the lighthouse to navigate without paying for the service. Because of this free-rider problem, private markets usually fail to provide the lighthouses that ship captains need. As a result, most lighthouses today are operated by the government.

In some cases, however, lighthouses have been closer to private goods. On the coast of England in the 19th century, for example, some lighthouses were privately owned and operated. Instead of trying to charge ship captains for the service, however, the owner of the lighthouse charged the owner of the nearby port. If the port owner did not pay, the lighthouse owner turned off the light, and ships avoided that port.

In deciding whether something is a public good, one must determine who the beneficiaries are and whether these beneficiaries can be excluded from using the good. A free-rider problem arises when the number of beneficiaries is large and exclusion of any one of them is impossible. If a lighthouse benefits many ship captains, it is a public good. Yet if it primarily benefits a single port owner, it is more like a private good. ◢

Shutterstock.com/Simon Bratt

What kind of good is this?

11-2c The Difficult Job of Cost–Benefit Analysis

So far we have seen that the government provides public goods because the private market on its own will not produce an efficient quantity. Yet deciding that the government must play a role is only the first step. The government must then determine what kinds of public goods to provide and in what quantities.

Suppose that the government is considering a public project, such as building a new highway. To judge whether to build the highway, it must compare the total benefits of all those who would use it to the costs of building and maintaining it. To make this decision, the government might hire a team of economists and engineers to conduct a study, called a **cost–benefit analysis**, to estimate the total costs and benefits of the project to society as a whole.

Cost–benefit analysts have a tough job. Because the highway will be available to everyone free of charge, there is no price with which to judge the value of the highway. Simply asking people how much they would value the highway is not reliable: Quantifying benefits is difficult using the results from a questionnaire, and respondents have little incentive to tell the truth. Those who would use the highway have an incentive to exaggerate the benefit they receive to get the highway built. Those who would be harmed by the highway have an incentive to exaggerate the costs to them to prevent the highway from being built.

The efficient provision of public goods is, therefore, intrinsically more difficult than the efficient provision of private goods. When buyers of a private good enter

cost–benefit analysis
a study that compares the costs and benefits to society of providing a public good

a market, they reveal the value they place on it through the prices they are willing to pay. At the same time, sellers reveal their costs with the prices they are willing to accept. The equilibrium is an efficient allocation of resources because it reflects all this information. By contrast, cost–benefit analysts do not have any price signals to observe when evaluating whether the government should provide a public good and how much to provide. Their findings on the costs and benefits of public projects are rough approximations at best.

case study   **How Much Is a Life Worth?**

Imagine that you have been elected to serve as a member of your local town council. The town engineer comes to you with a proposal: The town can spend $10,000 to build and operate a traffic light at a town intersection that now has only a stop sign. The benefit of the traffic light is increased safety. The engineer estimates, based on data from similar intersections, that the traffic light would reduce the risk of a fatal traffic accident over the lifetime of the traffic light from 1.6 to 1.1 percent. Should you spend the money for the new light?

To answer this question, you turn to cost–benefit analysis. But you quickly run into an obstacle: The costs and benefits must be measured in the same units if you are to compare them meaningfully. The cost is measured in dollars, but the benefit—the possibility of saving a person's life—is not directly monetary. To make your decision, you have to put a dollar value on a human life.

At first, you may be tempted to conclude that a human life is priceless. After all, there is probably no amount of money that you could be paid to voluntarily give up your life or that of a loved one. This suggests that a human life has an infinite dollar value.

For the purposes of cost–benefit analysis, however, this answer leads to nonsensical results. If we truly placed an infinite value on human life, we should place traffic lights on every street corner, and we should all drive large cars loaded with all the latest safety features. Yet traffic lights are not at every corner, and people sometimes choose to pay less for smaller cars without safety options such as side-impact air bags or antilock brakes. In both our public and private decisions, we are at times willing to risk our lives to save some money.

Once we have accepted the idea that a person's life has an implicit dollar value, how can we determine what that value is? One approach, sometimes used by courts to award damages in wrongful-death suits, is to look at the total amount of money a person would have earned if she had lived. Economists are often critical of this approach because it ignores other opportunity costs of losing one's life. It thus has the bizarre implication that the life of a retired or disabled person has no value.

A better way to value human life is to look at the risks that people are voluntarily willing to take and how much they must be paid for taking them. Mortality risk varies across jobs, for example. Construction workers in high-rise buildings face greater risk of death on the job than office workers do. By comparing wages in risky and less risky occupations, controlling for education, experience, and other determinants of wages, economists can get some sense about what value people put on their own lives. Studies using this approach conclude that the value of a human life is about $10 million.

We can now return to our original example and respond to the town engineer. The traffic light reduces the risk of fatality by 0.5 percentage points. Thus, the expected benefit from installing the traffic light is 0.005 × $10 million, or $50,000. This estimate of the benefit well exceeds the cost of $10,000, so you should approve the project. ◢

Quick Quiz *What is the* free-rider *problem? Why does the free-rider problem induce the government to provide public goods? • How should the government decide whether to provide a public good?*

11-3 Common Resources

Common resources, like public goods, are not excludable: They are available free of charge to anyone who wants to use them. Common resources are, however, rival in consumption: One person's use of the common resource reduces other people's ability to use it. Thus, common resources give rise to a new problem. Once the good is provided, policymakers need to be concerned about how much it is used. This problem is best understood from the classic parable called the **Tragedy of the Commons**.

Tragedy of the Commons
a parable that illustrates why common resources are used more than is desirable from the standpoint of society as a whole

11-3a The Tragedy of the Commons

Consider life in a small medieval town. Of the many economic activities that take place in the town, one of the most important is raising sheep. Many of the town's families own flocks of sheep and support themselves by selling the sheep's wool, which is used to make clothing.

As our story begins, the sheep spend much of their time grazing on the land surrounding the town, called the Town Common. No family owns the land. Instead, the town residents own the land collectively, and all the residents are allowed to graze their sheep on it. Collective ownership works well because land is plentiful. As long as everyone can get all the good grazing land they want, the Town Common is not rival in consumption, and allowing residents' sheep to graze for free causes no problems. Everyone in the town is happy.

As the years pass, the population of the town grows, and so does the number of sheep grazing on the Town Common. With a growing number of sheep and a fixed amount of land, the land starts to lose its ability to replenish itself. Eventually, the land is grazed so heavily that it becomes barren. With no grass left on the Town Common, raising sheep is impossible, and the town's once prosperous wool industry disappears. Many families lose their source of livelihood.

What causes the tragedy? Why do the shepherds allow the sheep population to grow so large that it destroys the Town Common? The reason is that social and private incentives differ. Avoiding the destruction of the grazing land depends on the collective action of the shepherds. If the shepherds acted together, they could reduce the sheep population to a size that the Town Common can support. Yet no single family has an incentive to reduce the size of its own flock because each flock represents only a small part of the problem.

In essence, the Tragedy of the Commons arises because of an externality. When one family's flock grazes on the common land, it reduces the quality of the land available for other families. Because people neglect this negative externality when deciding how many sheep to own, the result is an excessive number of sheep.

If the tragedy had been foreseen, the town could have solved the problem in various ways. It could have regulated the number of sheep in each family's flock, internalized the externality by taxing sheep, or auctioned off a limited number of sheep-grazing permits. That is, the medieval town could have dealt with the problem of overgrazing in the way that modern society deals with the problem of pollution.

In the case of land, however, there is a simpler solution. The town can divide the land among town families. Each family can enclose its parcel of land with a fence and then protect it from excessive grazing. In this way, the land becomes a private good rather than a common resource. This outcome in fact occurred during the enclosure movement in England in the 17th century.

The Tragedy of the Commons is a story with a general lesson: When one person uses a common resource, she diminishes other people's enjoyment of it. Because of this negative externality, common resources tend to be used excessively. The

IN THE NEWS   The Case for Toll Roads

Many economists think drivers should be charged more for using roads. Here is why.

Why You'll Love Paying for Roads That Used to Be Free

By Eric A. Morris

To end the scourge of traffic congestion, Julius Caesar banned most carts from the streets of Rome during daylight hours. It didn't work—traffic jams just shifted to dusk. Two thousand years later, we have put a man on the moon and developed garments infinitely more practical than the toga, but we seem little nearer to solving the congestion problem.

If you live in a city, particularly a large one, you probably need little convincing that traffic congestion is frustrating and wasteful. According to the Texas Transportation Institute, the average American urban traveler lost 38 hours, nearly one full work week, to congestion in 2005. And congestion is getting worse, not better; urban travelers in 1982 were delayed only 14 hours that year.

Americans want action, but unfortunately there aren't too many great ideas about what that action might be. As Anthony Downs's

excellent book *Still Stuck in Traffic: Coping With Peak-Hour Traffic Congestion* chronicles, most of the proposed solutions are too difficult to implement, won't work, or both.

Fortunately, there is one remedy which is both doable and largely guaranteed to succeed. In the space of a year or two we could have you zipping along the 405 or the LIE at the height of rush hour at a comfortable 55 miles per hour.

There's just one small problem with this silver bullet for congestion: many people seem to prefer the werewolf. Despite its merits, this policy, which is known as "congestion pricing," "value pricing," or "variable tolling," is not an easy political sell.

For decades, economists and other transportation thinkers have advocated imposing tolls that vary with congestion levels on roadways. Simply put, the more congestion, the higher the toll, until the congestion goes away.

To many people, this sounds like a scheme by mustache-twirling bureaucrats and their academic apologists to fleece drivers out of their hard-earned cash. Why should drivers have to pay to use roads their tax dollars have

already paid for? Won't the remaining free roads be swamped as drivers are forced off the tolled roads? Won't the working-class and poor be the victims here, as the tolled routes turn into "Lexus lanes"?

And besides, adopting this policy would mean listening to economists, and who wants to do that?

There's a real problem with this logic, which is that, on its own terms, it makes perfect sense (except for the listening to economists part). Opponents of tolls are certainly not stupid, and their arguments deserve serious consideration. But in the end, their concerns are largely overblown, and the benefits of tolling swamp the potential costs.

Unfortunately, it can be hard to convey this because the theory behind tolling is somewhat complex and counterintuitive. This is too bad, because variable tolling is an excellent public policy. Here's why: the basic economic theory is that when you give out something valuable—in this case, road

government can solve the problem by using regulation or taxes to reduce consumption of the common resource. Alternatively, the government can sometimes turn the common resource into a private good.

This lesson has been known for thousands of years. The ancient Greek philosopher Aristotle pointed out the problem with common resources: "What is common to many is taken least care of, for all men have greater regard for what is their own than for what they possess in common with others."

11-3b Some Important Common Resources

There are many examples of common resources. In almost all cases, the same problem arises as in the Tragedy of the Commons: Private decision makers use the common resource too much. Governments often regulate behavior or impose fees to mitigate the problem of overuse.

space—for less than its true value, shortages result.

Ultimately, there's no free lunch; instead of paying with money, you pay with the effort and time needed to acquire the good. Think of Soviet shoppers spending their lives in endless queues to purchase artificially low-priced but exceedingly scarce goods. Then think of Americans who can fulfill nearly any consumerist fantasy quickly but at a monetary cost. Free but congested roads have left us shivering on the streets of Moscow.

To consider it another way, delay is an externality imposed by drivers on their peers. By driving onto a busy road and contributing to congestion, drivers slow the speeds of others—but they never have to pay for it, at least not directly. In the end, of course, everybody pays, because as we impose congestion on others, others impose it on us. This degenerates into a game that nobody can win.

Markets work best when externalities are internalized: i.e., you pay for the hassle you inflict on others.... Using tolls to help internalize the congestion externality would somewhat reduce the number of trips made on the most congested roads at the peak usage periods; some trips would be moved to less congested times and routes, and others would be foregone entirely. This way we would cut down on the congestion costs we impose on each other.

Granted, tolls cannot fully cope with accidents and other incidents, which are major causes of delay. But pricing can largely eliminate chronic, recurring congestion. No matter how high the demand for a road, there is a level of toll that will keep it flowing freely.

To make tolling truly effective, the price must be right. Too high a price drives away too many cars and the road does not function at its capacity. Too low a price and congestion isn't licked.

The best solution is to vary the tolls in real time based on an analysis of current traffic conditions. Pilot toll projects on roads (like the I-394 in Minnesota and the I-15 in Southern California) use sensors embedded in the pavement to monitor the number and speeds of vehicles on the facility.

A simple computer program then determines the number of cars that should be allowed in. The computer then calculates the level of toll that will attract that number of cars—and no more. Prices are then updated every few minutes on electronic message signs. Hi-tech transponders and antenna arrays make waiting at toll booths a thing of the past.

The bottom line is that speeds are kept high (over 45 m.p.h.) so that throughput is higher than when vehicles are allowed to crowd all at once onto roadways at rush hour, slowing traffic to a crawl.

To maximize efficiency, economists would like to price all travel, starting with the freeways. But given that elected officials have no burning desire to lose their jobs, a more realistic option, for now, is to toll just some freeway lanes that are either new capacity or underused carpool lanes. The other lanes would be left free—and congested. Drivers will then have a choice: wait or pay. Granted, neither is ideal. But right now drivers have no choice at all.

What's the bottom line here? The state of Washington recently opened congestion-priced lanes on its State Route 167. The peak toll in the first month of operation (reached on the evening of Wednesday, May 21) was $5.75. I know, I know, you would never pay such an exorbitant amount when America has taught you that free roads are your birthright. But that money bought Washington drivers a 27-minute time savings. Is a half hour of your time worth $6?

I think I already know the answer, and it is "it depends." Most people's value of time varies widely depending on their activities on any given day. Late for picking the kids up from daycare? Paying $6 to save a half hour is an incredible bargain. Have to clean the house? The longer your trip home takes, the better. Tolling will introduce a new level of flexibility and freedom into your life, giving you the power to tailor your travel costs to fit your schedule. ◢

Source: Freakonomics blog, January 6, 2009.

Clean Air and Water   As we discussed in Chapter 10, markets do not adequately protect the environment. Pollution is a negative externality that can be remedied with regulations or with corrective taxes on polluting activities. One can view this market failure as an example of a common-resource problem. Clean air and clean water are common resources like open grazing land, and excessive pollution is like excessive grazing. Environmental degradation is a modern Tragedy of the Commons.

Congested Roads   Roads can be either public goods or common resources. If a road is not congested, then one person's use does not affect anyone else's use. In this case, use is not rival in consumption, and the road is a public good. Yet if a road is congested, then use of that road yields a negative externality. When one person drives on the road, it becomes more crowded, and other people must drive more slowly. In this case, the road is a common resource.

One way for the government to address the problem of road congestion is to charge drivers a toll. A toll is, in essence, a corrective tax on the externality of congestion. Sometimes, as in the case of local roads, tolls are not a practical solution because the cost of collecting them is too high. But several major cities, including London and Stockholm, have found increasing tolls to be a very effective way to reduce congestion.

Sometimes congestion is a problem only at certain times of day. If a bridge is heavily traveled only during rush hour, for instance, the congestion externality is largest during this time. The efficient way to deal with these externalities is to charge higher tolls during rush hour. This toll would provide an incentive for drivers to alter their schedules, reducing traffic when congestion is greatest.

Another policy that responds to the problem of road congestion, discussed in a case study in Chapter 10, is the tax on gasoline. Gasoline is a complementary good to driving: An increase in the price of gasoline tends to reduce the quantity of driving demanded. Therefore, a gasoline tax reduces road congestion. A gasoline tax, however, is an imperfect solution, because it affects other decisions besides the amount of driving on congested roads. For example, the gasoline tax discourages driving on uncongested roads, even though there is no congestion externality for these roads.

Fish, Whales, and Other Wildlife   Many species of animals are common resources. Fish and whales, for instance, have commercial value, and anyone can go to the ocean and catch whatever is available. Each person has little incentive to maintain the species for the next year. Just as excessive grazing can destroy the Town Common, excessive fishing and whaling can destroy commercially valuable marine populations.

Oceans remain one of the least regulated common resources. Two problems prevent an easy solution. First, many countries have access to the oceans, so any solution would require international cooperation among countries that hold different values. Second, because the oceans are so vast, enforcing any agreement is difficult. As a result, fishing rights have been a frequent source of international tension among normally friendly countries.

Within the United States, various laws aim to manage the use of fish and other wildlife. For example, the government charges for fishing and hunting licenses, and it restricts the lengths of the fishing and hunting seasons. Fishermen are often required to throw back small fish, and hunters can kill only a limited number of animals. All these laws reduce the use of a common resource and help maintain animal populations.

case
study

Why the Cow Is Not Extinct

Throughout history, many species of animals have been threatened with extinction. When Europeans first arrived in North America, more than 60 million buffalo roamed the continent. Yet hunting the buffalo was so popular during the 19th century that by 1900 the animal's population had fallen to about 400 before the government stepped in to protect the species. In some African countries today, the elephant faces a similar challenge, as poachers kill the animals for the ivory in their tusks.

Yet not all animals with commercial value face this threat. The cow, for example, is a valuable source of food, but no one worries that the cow will soon be extinct. Indeed, the great demand for beef seems to ensure that the species will continue to thrive.

Why does the commercial value of ivory threaten the elephant, while the commercial value of beef protects the cow? The reason is that elephants are a common resource, whereas cows are a private good. Elephants roam freely without any owners. Each poacher has a strong incentive to kill as many elephants as she can find. Because poachers are numerous, each poacher has only a slight incentive to preserve the elephant population. By contrast, cattle live on ranches that are privately owned. Each rancher makes a great effort to maintain the cattle population on her ranch because she reaps the benefit.

Governments have tried to solve the elephant's problem in two ways. Some countries, such as Kenya, Tanzania, and Uganda, have made it illegal to kill elephants and sell their ivory. Yet these laws have been hard to enforce, and the battle between the authorities and the poachers has become increasingly violent. Meanwhile, elephant populations have continued to dwindle. By contrast, other countries, such as Botswana, Malawi, Namibia, and Zimbabwe, have made elephants a private good by allowing people to kill elephants, but only those on their own property. Landowners now have an incentive to preserve the species on their own land, and as a result, elephant populations have started to rise. With private ownership and the profit motive now on its side, the African elephant might someday be as safe from extinction as the cow. ◢

Quick Quiz   *Why do governments try to limit the use of common resources?*

"Will the market protect me?"

11-4 Conclusion: The Importance of Property Rights

In this and the previous chapter, we have seen there are some "goods" that the market does not provide adequately. Markets do not ensure that the air we breathe is clean or that our country is defended from foreign aggressors. Instead, societies rely on the government to protect the environment and to provide for the national defense.

The problems we considered in these chapters arise in many different markets, but they share a common theme. In all cases, the market fails to allocate resources efficiently because *property rights* are not well established. That is, some item of value does not have an owner with the legal authority to control it. For example, although no one doubts that the "good" of clean air or national defense is valuable, no one has the right to attach a price to it and profit from its use. A factory pollutes too much because no one charges the factory for the pollution it emits. The market does not provide for national defense because no one can charge those who are defended for the benefit they receive.

When the absence of property rights causes a market failure, the government can potentially solve the problem. Sometimes, as in the sale of pollution permits, the solution is for the government to help define property rights and thereby unleash market forces. Other times, as in restricted hunting seasons, the solution is for the government to regulate private behavior. Still other times, as in the provision of national defense, the solution is for the government to use tax revenue to supply a good that the market fails to supply. In all cases, if the policy is well planned and well run, it can make the allocation of resources more efficient and thus raise economic well-being.

Summary

- Goods differ in whether they are excludable and whether they are rival in consumption. A good is excludable if it is possible to prevent someone from using it. A good is rival in consumption if one person's use of the good reduces others' ability to use the same unit of the good. Markets work best for private goods, which are both excludable and rival in consumption. Markets do not work as well for other types of goods.

- Public goods are neither rival in consumption nor excludable. Examples of public goods include fireworks displays, national defense, and the creation of fundamental knowledge. Because people are not charged for their use of the public good, they have an incentive to free ride, making private provision of the good untenable. Therefore, governments provide public goods, basing their decision about the quantity of each good on cost–benefit analysis.

- Common resources are rival in consumption but not excludable. Examples include common grazing land, clean air, and congested roads. Because people are not charged for their use of common resources, they tend to use them excessively. Therefore, governments use various methods to limit the use of common resources.

Key Concepts

excludability, *p. 216*

rivalry in consumption, *p. 216*

private goods, *p. 216*

public goods, *p. 216*

common resources, *p. 216*

club goods, *p. 217*

free rider, *p. 218*

cost–benefit analysis, *p. 221*

Tragedy of the Commons, *p. 223*

Questions for Review

1. Explain what is meant by a good being "excludable." Explain what is meant by a good being "rival in consumption." Is a slice of pizza excludable? Is it rival in consumption?

2. Define and give an example of a public good. Can the private market provide this good on its own? Explain.

3. What is cost–benefit analysis of public goods? Why is it important? Why is it hard?

4. Define and give an example of a common resource. Without government intervention, will people use this good too much or too little? Why?

Quick Check Multiple Choice

1. Which categories of goods are excludable?
   a. private goods and club goods
   b. private goods and common resources
   c. public goods and club goods
   d. public goods and common resources

2. Which categories of goods are rival in consumption?
   a. private goods and club goods
   b. private goods and common resources
   c. public goods and club goods
   d. public goods and common resources

3. Which of the following is an example of a public good?
   a. residential housing
   b. national defense
   c. restaurant meals
   d. fish in the ocean

4. Which of the following is an example of a common resource?
   a. residential housing
   b. national defense
   c. restaurant meals
   d. fish in the ocean

5. Public goods are
   a. efficiently provided by market forces.
   b. underprovided in the absence of government.
   c. overused in the absence of government.
   d. a type of natural monopoly.

6. Common resources are
   a. efficiently provided by market forces.
   b. underprovided in the absence of government.
   c. overused in the absence of government.
   d. a type of natural monopoly.

Problems and Applications

1. Think about the goods and services provided by your local government.
   a. Using the classification in Figure 1, explain which category each of the following goods falls into:
      • police protection
      • snow plowing
      • education
      • rural roads
      • city streets
   b. Why do you think the government provides items that are not public goods?

2. Both public goods and common resources involve externalities.
   a. Are the externalities associated with public goods generally positive or negative? Use examples in your answer. Is the free-market quantity of public goods generally greater or less than the efficient quantity?
   b. Are the externalities associated with common resources generally positive or negative? Use examples in your answer. Is the free-market use of common resources generally greater or less than the efficient use?

3. Charlie loves watching *Downton Abbey* on his local public TV station, but he never sends any money to support the station during its fund-raising drives.
   a. What name do economists have for people like Charlie?
   b. How can the government solve the problem caused by people like Charlie?
   c. Can you think of ways the private market can solve this problem? How does the existence of cable TV alter the situation?

4. Wireless, high-speed Internet is provided for free in the airport of the city of Communityville.
   a. At first, only a few people use the service. What type of a good is this and why?
   b. Eventually, as more people find out about the service and start using it, the speed of the connection begins to fall. Now what type of a good is the wireless Internet service?
   c. What problem might result and why? What is one possible way to correct this problem?

5. Four roommates are planning to spend the weekend in their dorm room watching old movies, and they are debating how many to watch. Here is their willingness to pay for each film:

	Judd	Joel	Gus	Tim
First film	$7	$5	$3	$2
Second film	6	4	2	1
Third film	5	3	1	0
Fourth film	4	2	0	0
Fifth film	3	1	0	0

   a. Within the dorm room, is the showing of a movie a public good? Why or why not?
   b. If it costs $8 to rent a movie, how many movies should the roommates rent to maximize total surplus?
   c. If they choose the optimal number from part (b) and then split the cost of renting the movies equally, how much surplus does each person obtain from watching the movies?
   d. Is there any way to split the cost to ensure that everyone benefits? What practical problems does this solution raise?
   e. Suppose they agree in advance to choose the efficient number and to split the cost of the movies equally. When Judd is asked his willingness to pay, will he have an incentive to tell the truth? If so, why? If not, what will he be tempted to say?
   f. What does this example teach you about the optimal provision of public goods?

6. Some economists argue that private firms will not undertake the efficient amount of basic scientific research.
   a. Explain why this might be so. In your answer, classify basic research in one of the categories shown in Figure 1.
   b. What sort of policy has the United States adopted in response to this problem?
   c. It is often argued that this policy increases the technological capability of American producers relative to that of foreign firms. Is this argument consistent with your classification of basic research in part (a)? (*Hint*: Can excludability apply to some potential beneficiaries of a public good and not others?)

7. There is often litter along highways but rarely in people's yards. Provide an economic explanation for this fact.

8. The nation of Wiknam has five million residents whose only activities are producing and consuming fish. They produce fish in two ways. Each person who works on a fish farm raises 2 fish per day. Each person who goes fishing in one of the nation's many lakes catches X fish per day. X depends on N, the number of residents (in millions) fishing in the lakes. In particular, if N million people fish in the lakes, each catches $X = 6 - N$ fish. Each resident is attracted to the job that pays more fish, so in equilibrium the two jobs must offer equal pay.
   a. Why do you suppose that X, the productivity of each fisherman, falls as N, the number of fishermen, rises? What economic term would you use to describe the fish in the town lakes? Would the same description apply to the fish from the farms? Explain.
   b. The town's Freedom Party thinks every individual should have the right to choose between fishing in the lake and farming without government interference. Under its policy, how many of the residents would fish in the lakes and how many would work on fish farms? How many fish are produced?
   c. The town's Efficiency Party thinks Wiknam should produce as many fish as it can. To achieve this goal, how many of the residents should fish in the lakes and how many should work on the farms? (*Hint*: Create a table that shows the number of fish produced—on farms, from the lake, and in total—for each N from 0 to 5.)
   d. The Efficiency Party proposes achieving its goal by taxing each person fishing in the lake by an amount equal to T fish per day. It will then distribute the proceeds equally among all Wiknam residents. (Fish are assumed to be divisible, so these rebates need not be whole numbers.) Calculate the value of T that would yield the outcome you derived in part (c).

e. Compared with the Freedom Party's hands-off policy, who benefits and who loses from the imposition of the Efficiency Party's fishing tax?

9. Many transportation systems, such as the Washington, D.C., Metro (subway), charge higher fares during rush hours than during the rest of the day. Why might they do this?

10. High-income people are willing to pay more than lower-income people to avoid the risk of death. For example, they are more likely to pay for safety features on cars. Do you think cost–benefit analysts should take this fact into account when evaluating public projects? Consider, for instance, a rich town and a poor town, both of which are considering the installation of a traffic light. Should the rich town use a higher dollar value for a human life in making this decision? Why or why not?

Go to CengageBrain.com to purchase access to the proven, critical Study Guide to accompany this text, which features additional notes and context, practice tests, and much more.

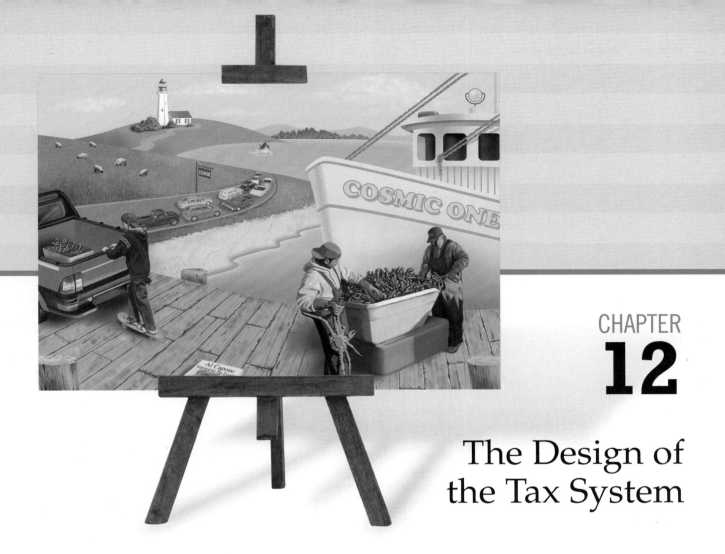

The Design of the Tax System

A l "Scarface" Capone, the notorious 1920s gangster and crime boss, was never convicted for his many violent crimes. Yet, eventually, he did go to jail—for tax evasion. He had neglected to heed Ben Franklin's observation that "in this world nothing is certain but death and taxes."

When Franklin made this claim in 1789, the average American paid less than 5 percent of his income in taxes, and that remained true for the next hundred years. Over the course of the 20th century, however, taxes became ever more important in the life of the typical U.S. citizen. Today, all taxes taken together— including personal income taxes, corporate income taxes, payroll taxes, sales taxes, and property taxes—use up more than a quarter of the average American's income. In many European countries, the tax bite is even larger.

Taxes are inevitable because we as citizens expect our government to provide us with various goods and services. The previous two chapters shed light on one of the *Ten Principles of Economics* from Chapter 1: The government can sometimes improve market outcomes. When the government remedies an externality (such as air pollution), provides a public good (such as national defense), or regulates the use of a common resource (such as fish in a public lake), it can raise economic well-being. Yet these activities are costly. For the government to perform these and its many other functions, it needs to raise revenue through taxation.

We began our study of taxation in earlier chapters, where we saw how a tax on a good affects supply and demand for that good. In Chapter 6, we saw that a tax reduces the quantity sold in a market, and we examined how the burden of a tax is shared by buyers and sellers depending on the elasticities of supply and demand. In Chapter 8, we examined how taxes affect economic well-being. We learned that taxes cause *deadweight losses:* The reduction in consumer and producer surplus resulting from a tax exceeds the revenue raised by the government.

In this chapter, we build on these lessons to discuss the design of a tax system. We begin with a financial overview of the U.S. government. When thinking about the tax system, it is useful to know some basic facts about how the U.S. government raises and spends money. We then consider the fundamental principles of taxation. Most people agree that taxes should impose as small a cost on society as possible and that the burden of taxes should be distributed fairly. That is, the tax system should be both *efficient* and *equitable.* As we will see, however, stating these goals is easier than achieving them.

12-1 A Financial Overview of the U.S. Government

How much of the nation's income does the government take as taxes? Figure 1 shows government revenue, including federal, state, and local governments, as a percentage of total income for the U.S. economy. It shows that the role of

FIGURE 1

Government Revenue as a Percentage of GDP

This figure shows revenue of the federal government and of state and local governments as a percentage of gross domestic product (GDP), which measures total income in the economy. It shows that the government plays a large role in the U.S. economy and that its role has grown over time.

Source: *Historical Statistics of the United States*; Bureau of Economic Analysis; and author's calculations.

government has grown substantially over the past century. In 1902, the government collected 7 percent of total income; in recent years, government has collected almost 30 percent. In other words, as the economy's income has grown, the government's revenue from taxation has grown even more.

Table 1 compares the tax burden for several major countries, as measured by the government's tax revenue as a percentage of the nation's total income. The United States has a low tax burden compared to most other advanced economies. Many European nations have much higher taxes, which finance a more generous social safety net, including more substantial income support for the poor and unemployed and universal government-provided healthcare.

TABLE 1

Total Government Tax Revenue as a Percentage of GDP

Source: OECD. Data are for 2011.

Denmark	48%	Canada	31
Sweden	45	Greece	31
France	44	Japan	28
Italy	43	Australia	26
Germany	37	United States	25
United Kingdom	36	Chile	21
Spain	32	Mexico	20

The overall size of government tells only part of the story. Behind the total dollar figures lie thousands of individual decisions about taxes and spending. To understand the government's finances more fully, let's look at how the total breaks down into some broad categories.

12-1a The Federal Government

The U.S. federal government collects about two-thirds of the taxes in our economy. It raises this money in a number of ways, and it finds even more ways to spend it.

Receipts   Table 2 shows the receipts of the federal government in 2011. Total receipts that year were $2,520 billion, a number so large that it is hard to comprehend. To bring this astronomical number down to earth, we can divide it by the size of the U.S. population, which was about 312 million in 2011. We then find that the average American paid $8,077 to the federal government.

TABLE 2

Receipts of the Federal Government: 2011

Source: Bureau of Economic Analysis. Columns may not sum to total due to rounding.

Tax	Amount (billions)	Amount per Person	Percent of Receipts
Individual income taxes	$1,075	$3,446	43%
Social insurance taxes	906	2,904	36
Corporate income taxes	304	974	12
Other	235	753	9
Total	$2,520	$8,077	100%

The largest source of revenue for the federal government is the individual income tax. As April 15 approaches each year, almost every American family fills out a tax form to determine how much income tax it owes the government. Each family is required to report its income from all sources: wages from working, interest on savings, dividends from corporations in which it owns shares, profits from any small businesses it operates, and so on. The family's *tax liability* (how much it owes) is then based on its total income.

A family's income tax liability is not simply proportional to its income. Instead, the law requires a more complicated calculation. Taxable income is computed as total income minus an amount based on the number of dependents (primarily children) and minus certain expenses that policymakers have deemed "deductible" (such as mortgage interest payments, state and local tax payments, and charitable giving). Then the tax liability is calculated from taxable income using a schedule such as the one shown in Table 3.

This table presents the *marginal tax rate*—the tax rate applied to each additional dollar of income. Because the marginal tax rate rises as income rises, higher-income families pay a larger percentage of their income in taxes. Note that each tax rate in the table applies only to income within the associated range, not to a person's entire income. For example, a person with an income of $1 million still pays only 10 percent of the first $8,925. (Later in this chapter we discuss the concept of the marginal tax rate more fully.)

Almost as important to the federal government as the individual income tax are payroll taxes. A *payroll tax* is a tax on the wages that a firm pays its workers. Table 2 calls this revenue *social insurance taxes* because the revenue from these taxes is earmarked to pay for Social Security and Medicare. Social Security is an income-support program designed primarily to maintain the living standards of the elderly. Medicare is the government health program for the elderly. Table 2 shows that the average American paid $2,904 in social insurance taxes in 2011.

Next in magnitude, but much smaller than either individual income taxes or social insurance taxes, is the corporate income tax. A *corporation* is a business set up to have its own legal existence, distinct and separate from its owners. The government taxes each corporation based on its profit—the amount the corporation receives for the goods or services it sells minus the costs of producing those goods or services. Notice that corporate profits are, in essence, taxed twice. They

TABLE 3

The Federal Income Tax Rates: 2013
This table shows the marginal tax rates for an unmarried taxpayer. The taxes owed by a taxpayer depend on all the marginal tax rates up to his income level. For example, a taxpayer with income of $25,000 pays 10 percent of the first $8,925 of income, and then 15 percent of the rest.

On Taxable Income . . .	The Tax Rate Is . . .
Up to $8,925	10%
From $8,925 to $36,250	15
From $36,250 to $87,850	25
From $87,850 to $183,250	28
From $183,250 to $398,350	33
From $398,350 to $400,000	35
Over $400,000	39.6

are taxed once by the corporate income tax when the corporation earns the profits; they are taxed a second time by the individual income tax when the corporation uses its profits to pay dividends to its shareholders. In part to compensate for this double taxation, policymakers have decided to tax dividend income at lower rates than other types of income: In 2013, the top marginal tax rate on dividend income was only 20 percent (plus a 3.8 percent Medicare tax), compared with the top tax rate on ordinary income of 39.6 percent (plus the same 3.8 percent).

The last category, labeled "other" in Table 2, makes up 9 percent of receipts. This category includes *excise taxes*, which are taxes on specific goods like gasoline, cigarettes, and alcoholic beverages. It also includes various small items, such as estate taxes and customs duties.

Spending   Table 4 shows the spending of the federal government in 2011. Total spending was $3,757 billion, or $12,042 per person. This table also shows how the federal government's spending was divided among major categories.

The largest category in Table 4 is for income security, a category that includes a variety of transfer payments. A *transfer payment* is a government payment not made in exchange for a good or service. Such payments include the Social Security income of the elderly and disabled, unemployment insurance payments made to workers who have lost their jobs, and welfare payments to the poor. This category made up about a third of spending by the federal government in 2011. The federal government pays some of this money to state and local governments, which administer the programs under federal guidelines.

The second largest category of spending is on health programs. This category includes Medicare (the government's health plan for the elderly), Medicaid (the federal health program for the poor), and spending on medical research, such as that conducted through the National Institutes of Health. Total health spending makes up about a quarter of the federal budget.

The next largest category of spending is national defense. This includes both the salaries of military personnel and the purchases of military equipment such as guns, fighter jets, and warships. Spending on national defense fluctuates over time as international tensions and the political climate change. Not surprisingly, spending on national defense rises substantially during wars.

TABLE 4

Spending of the Federal Government: 2011

Source: Bureau of Economic Analysis.
Columns may not sum to total due to rounding.

Category	Amount (billions)	Amount per Person	Percent of Spending
Income Security	$1,233	$3,951	33%
Health	940	3,013	25
National defense	717	2,298	19
Net interest	325	1,042	9
Other	542	1,737	14
Total	$3,757	$12,042	100%

Next on the list is net interest. When a person borrows from a bank, the bank requires the borrower to pay interest for the loan. The same is true when the government borrows from the public. The more indebted the government, the larger the amount it must spend in interest payments.

The "other" category in Table 4 consists of many less expensive functions of government. It includes, for example, the federal court system, the space program, farm-support programs, housing credit programs, as well as the salaries of members of Congress and the president.

You might have noticed that total receipts of the federal government shown in Table 2 fall short of total spending shown in Table 4 by more than $1 trillion. In such a situation, the government is said to run a **budget deficit**. When receipts exceed spending, the government is said to run a **budget surplus**. The government finances a budget deficit by borrowing from the public. That is, it sells government debt to the private sector, including both investors in the United States and those abroad. When the government runs a budget surplus, it uses the excess receipts to reduce its outstanding debts.

budget deficit
an excess of government spending over government receipts

budget surplus
an excess of government receipts over government spending

case study

The Fiscal Challenge Ahead

From 2009 to 2012, the U.S. federal government ran budget deficits that exceeded $1 trillion every year, the largest budget shortfalls since World War II. These large budget deficits were due primarily to the deep recession the economy was experiencing at the time. Recessions tend to increase government spending and reduce government revenue. Indeed, as the economy started to recover, the budget deficit started to shrink.

Yet this short-term increase in the deficit is only the tip of an ominous iceberg: Long-term projections of the government's budget show that, under current law, the government will spend vastly more than it will receive in tax revenue in the decades ahead. As a percentage of gross domestic product (GDP, the total income in the economy), taxes are projected to be about constant. But government spending as a percentage of GDP is projected to rise substantially over the next several decades.

One reason for the rise in government spending is that Social Security and Medicare provide significant benefits for the elderly, who are a growing percentage of the overall population. Over the past half century, medical advances and lifestyle improvements have greatly increased life expectancy. In 1950, a 65-year-old man could expect to live for another 13 years; now he can expect to live another 17 years. The life expectancy of a 65-year-old woman has risen from 16 years in 1950 to 20 years today. At the same time, people are having fewer children. In 1950, the typical woman had three children. Today, the number is about two. As a result of smaller families, the labor force is growing more slowly now than it has in the past.

Panel (a) of Figure 2 shows the demographic shift that is arising from the combination of longer life expectancy and lower fertility. In 1950, the elderly population equaled about 14 percent of the working-age population. Now the elderly are about 21 percent of the working-age population, and that figure will rise to about 40 percent over the next 50 years. Turning those numbers on their head, this means that in 1950 there were about 7 working-age people for every elderly person, whereas in 2050 there will be only 2.5. As a result, there will be fewer workers paying taxes to support the government benefits that each elderly person receives.

Panel (a) shows the U.S. population age 65 and older as a percentage of the population age 20 to 64. The growing elderly population will put increasing pressure on the government budget. Panel (b) shows government spending on Social Security and health programs as a percentage of GDP. The projection for future years assumes no change in current law. Unless changes in benefits are enacted, government spending on these programs will rise significantly and will require large tax increases to pay for them.

FIGURE 2

The Demographic and Fiscal Challenge

Source: Congressional Budget Office.

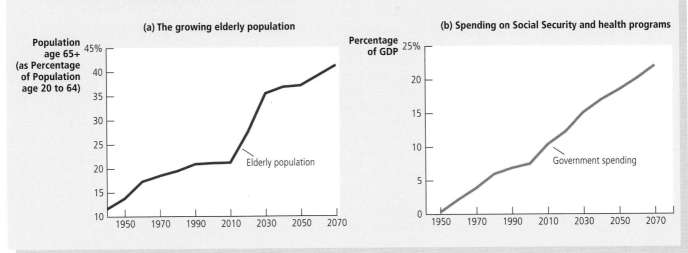

(a) The growing elderly population

(b) Spending on Social Security and health programs

A second, related trend that will affect government spending in the decades ahead is the rising cost of healthcare. The federal government provides healthcare to the elderly through the Medicare system and to the poor through Medicaid. And once the health insurance reform passed in 2010 is fully implemented, the government will start providing subsidies for health insurance to many families with low to moderate incomes. As the cost of healthcare increases, government spending on these programs will increase as well.

Policymakers have proposed various ways to stem the rise in healthcare costs, such as reducing the burden of lawsuits on the healthcare system, encouraging more competition among healthcare providers, promoting greater use of information technology, and providing better incentives to doctors to choose more cost-effective treatments. Many health economists, however, believe that such measures will have only a limited impact on reducing the government's healthcare expenditures. They argue that the main reason for rising healthcare costs is medical advances that provide new, better, but often expensive ways to extend and improve our lives. So even if these reforms are worth pursuing, spending on healthcare programs will nonetheless continue to rise.

Panel (b) of Figure 2 shows government spending on Social Security and health programs as a percentage of GDP. Spending on these programs has risen from less than 1 percent in 1950 to more than 10 percent today. The combination of a growing elderly population and rising healthcare costs is expected to continue the trend.

How our society will handle these spending increases is an open question. Simply increasing the budget deficit is not feasible. A budget deficit just pushes the cost of government spending onto a future generation of taxpayers, who will inherit a government with greater debts. In the long run, the government needs to pay for what it spends.

Some economists believe that to pay for these commitments, we will need to raise taxes substantially as a percentage of GDP. If so, the long-term trend we saw in Figure 1 will continue. Spending on Social Security and health programs is expected to rise by about 10 percentage points of GDP. Because taxes are now 30 percent of GDP, paying for these benefits would require approximately a one-third increase in all taxes.

Other economists believe that such high tax rates would impose too great a cost on younger workers. They believe that policymakers should reduce the promises now being made to the elderly of the future and that, at the same time, people should be encouraged to take a greater role in caring for themselves as they age. This might entail raising the normal retirement age, while giving people more incentive to save during their working years to prepare for their own retirement and health costs.

It is likely that the final resolution will involve a combination of measures. No one can dispute that resolving this debate is one of the great challenges ahead. ◢

12-1b State and Local Governments

State and local governments collect about 40 percent of all taxes paid. Let's look at how they obtain tax revenue and how they spend it.

Receipts   Table 5 shows the receipts of U.S. state and local governments. Total receipts for 2011 were $2,064 billion, or $6,615 per person. The table also shows how this total is broken down into different kinds of taxes.

The two most important taxes for state and local governments are sales taxes and property taxes. Sales taxes are levied as a percentage of the total amount spent at retail stores. Every time a customer buys something, he pays the storekeeper an extra amount that the storekeeper remits to the government. (Some states exclude certain items that are considered necessities, such as food and clothing.) Property taxes are levied as a percentage of the estimated value of land and structures and are paid by property owners. Together, these two taxes make up more than 40 percent of all receipts of state and local governments.

TABLE 5

Receipts of State and Local Governments: 2011

Source: Bureau of Economic Analysis. Columns may not sum to total due to rounding.

Tax	Amount (billions)	Amount per Person	Percent of Receipts
Sales taxes	$462	$1,481	22%
Property taxes	440	1,410	21
Individual income taxes	323	1,035	16
Corporate income taxes	48	154	2
Federal government	498	1,596	24
Other	293	939	14
Total	$2,064	$6,615	100%

State and local governments also levy individual and corporate income taxes. In many cases, state and local income taxes are similar to federal income taxes. In other cases, they are quite different. For example, some states tax income from wages less heavily than income earned in the form of interest and dividends. Some states do not tax income at all.

State and local governments also receive substantial funds from the federal government. To some extent, the federal government's policy of sharing its revenue with state governments redistributes funds from high-income states (which pay more taxes) to low-income states (which receive more benefits). Often, these funds are tied to specific programs that the federal government wants to subsidize.

Finally, state and local governments receive much of their receipts from various sources included in the "other" category in Table 5. These include fees for fishing and hunting licenses, tolls from roads and bridges, and fares for public buses and subways.

Spending   Table 6 shows the total spending of state and local governments in 2011 and its breakdown among the major categories.

By far the biggest single expenditure for state and local governments is education. Local governments pay for the public schools, which educate most students from kindergarten through high school. State governments contribute to the support of public universities. In 2011, education accounted for about a third of the spending of state and local governments.

The second largest category of spending is for health programs, such as Medicaid, followed by spending on public order and safety, which includes the police, firefighters, courts, and prisons. Next come income security programs, the building and maintenance of roads and highways, and interest on state and local government debt. The "other" category in Table 6 includes the many additional services provided by state and local governments, such as libraries, garbage and snow removal, and the maintenance of public parks and playgrounds.

Quick Quiz   What are the two most important sources of tax revenue for the federal government? • What are the two most important sources of tax revenue for state and local governments?

TABLE 6

Spending of State and Local Governments: 2011

Source: Bureau of Economic Analysis. Columns may not sum to total due to rounding.

Category	Amount (billions)	Amount Per Person	Percent of Spending
Education	$730	$2,340	34%
Health	481	1,542	22
Public order and safety	285	913	13
Income security	163	522	8
Highways	127	407	6
Interest	109	350	5
Other	271	869	13
Total	$2,166	$6,942	100%

12-2 Taxes and Efficiency

Now that we have seen how various levels of the U.S. government raise and spend money, let's consider how one might evaluate its tax policy and design a tax system. The primary aim of a tax system is to raise revenue for the government, but there are many ways to raise any given amount of money. When choosing among the many alternative tax systems, policymakers have two objectives: efficiency and equity.

One tax system is more efficient than another if it raises the same amount of revenue at a smaller cost to taxpayers. What are the costs of taxes to taxpayers? The most obvious cost is the tax payment itself. This transfer of money from the taxpayer to the government is an inevitable feature of any tax system. Yet taxes also impose two other costs, which well-designed tax policy tries to avoid or, at least, minimize:

- The deadweight losses that result when taxes distort the decisions that people make;
- The administrative burdens that taxpayers bear as they comply with the tax laws.

An efficient tax system is one that imposes small deadweight losses and small administrative burdens.

BERRY'S WORLD reprinted by permission of United Feature Syndicate, Inc.

© 1977 by NEA, Inc.

"I was gonna fix the place up, but if I did, the city would just raise my taxes!"

12-2a Deadweight Losses

One of the *Ten Principles of Economics* is that people respond to incentives, and this includes incentives provided by the tax system. If the government taxes ice cream, people eat less ice cream and more frozen yogurt. If the government taxes housing, people live in smaller houses and spend more of their income on other things. If the government taxes labor earnings, people work less and enjoy more leisure.

Because taxes distort incentives, they entail deadweight losses. As we first discussed in Chapter 8, the deadweight loss of a tax is the reduction in economic well-being of taxpayers in excess of the amount of revenue raised by the government. The deadweight loss is the inefficiency that a tax creates as people allocate resources according to the tax incentive rather than the true costs and benefits of the goods and services that they buy and sell.

To recall how taxes cause deadweight losses, consider an example. Suppose that Joe places an $8 value on a pizza and Jane places a $6 value on it. If there is no tax on pizza, the price of pizza will reflect the cost of making it. Let's suppose that the price of pizza is $5, so both Joe and Jane choose to buy one. Both consumers get some surplus of value over the amount paid. Joe gets consumer surplus of $3, and Jane gets consumer surplus of $1. Total surplus is $4.

Now suppose that the government levies a $2 tax on pizza and the price of pizza rises to $7. (This occurs if supply is perfectly elastic.) Joe still buys a pizza, but now he has consumer surplus of only $1. Jane now decides not to buy a pizza because its price is higher than its value to her. The government collects tax revenue of $2 on Joe's pizza. Total consumer surplus has fallen by $3 (from $4 to $1). Because total surplus has fallen by more than the tax revenue, the tax has a deadweight loss. In this case, the deadweight loss is $1.

Notice that the deadweight loss comes not from Joe, the person who pays the tax, but from Jane, the person who doesn't. The reduction of $2 in Joe's surplus exactly offsets the amount of revenue the government collects. The deadweight loss arises because the tax causes Jane to alter her behavior. When the tax raises the price of pizza, Jane is worse off, and yet there is no offsetting revenue to the government. This reduction in Jane's welfare is the deadweight loss of the tax.

case study **Should Income or Consumption Be Taxed?**

When taxes induce people to change their behavior—such as inducing Jane to buy less pizza—the taxes cause deadweight losses and make the allocation of resources less efficient. As we have already seen, much government revenue comes from the individual income tax. In a case study in Chapter 8, we discussed how this tax discourages people from working as hard as they otherwise might. Another inefficiency caused by this tax is that it discourages people from saving.

Consider a person 25 years old who is considering saving $1,000. If he puts this money in a savings account that earns 8 percent and leaves it there, he will have $21,720 when he retires at age 65. Yet if the government taxes one-fourth of his interest income each year, the effective interest rate is only 6 percent. After 40 years of earning 6 percent, the $1,000 grows to only $10,290, less than half of what it would have been without taxation. Thus, because interest income is taxed, saving is much less attractive.

Some economists advocate eliminating the current tax system's disincentive toward saving by changing the basis of taxation. Rather than taxing the amount of income that people earn, the government could tax the amount that people spend. Under this proposal, all income that is saved would not be taxed until the saving is later spent. This alternative system, called a *consumption tax,* would not distort people's saving decisions.

Various provisions of current law already make the tax system a bit like a consumption tax. Taxpayers can put a limited amount of their income into special savings accounts, such as Individual Retirement Accounts and 401(k) plans, and this income and the accumulated interest it earns escape taxation until the money is withdrawn at retirement. For people who do most of their saving through these retirement accounts, their tax bill is, in effect, based on their consumption rather than their income.

European countries tend to rely more on consumption taxes than does the United States. Most of them raise a significant amount of government revenue through a value-added tax, or a VAT. A VAT is like the retail sales tax that many U.S. states use. But rather than collecting all of the tax at the retail level when the consumer buys the final good, the government collects the tax in stages as the good is being produced (that is, as value is added by firms along the chain of production).

Various U.S. policymakers have proposed that the tax code move further in the direction of taxing consumption rather than income. In 2005, economist Alan Greenspan, then Chairman of the Federal Reserve, offered this advice to a presidential commission on tax reform: "As you know, many economists believe that a consumption tax would be best from the perspective of promoting economic growth—particularly if one were designing a tax system from scratch—because a consumption tax is likely to encourage saving and capital formation. However, getting from the current tax system to a consumption tax raises a challenging set of transition issues." ◢

12-2b Administrative Burden

If you ask the typical person on April 15 for an opinion about the tax system, you might get an earful (perhaps peppered with expletives) about the headache of filling out tax forms. The administrative burden of any tax system is part of the inefficiency it creates. This burden includes not only the time spent in early April filling out forms but also the time spent throughout the year keeping records for tax purposes and the resources the government has to use to enforce the tax laws.

Many taxpayers—especially those in higher tax brackets—hire tax lawyers and accountants to help them with their taxes. These experts in the complex tax laws fill out the tax forms for their clients and help them arrange their affairs in a way that reduces the amount of taxes owed. This behavior is legal tax avoidance, which is different from illegal tax evasion.

Critics of our tax system say that these advisers help their clients avoid taxes by abusing some of the detailed provisions of the tax code, often dubbed "loopholes." In some cases, loopholes are congressional mistakes: They arise from ambiguities or omissions in the tax laws. More often, they arise because Congress has chosen to give special treatment to specific types of behavior. For example, the U.S. federal tax code gives preferential treatment to investors in municipal bonds because Congress wanted to make it easier for state and local governments to borrow money. To some extent, this provision benefits states and localities; and to some extent, it benefits high-income taxpayers. Most loopholes are well known by those in Congress who make tax policy, but what looks like a loophole to one taxpayer may look like a justifiable tax deduction to another.

The resources devoted to complying with the tax laws are a type of deadweight loss. The government gets only the amount of taxes paid. By contrast, the taxpayer loses not only this amount but also the time and money spent documenting, computing, and avoiding taxes.

The administrative burden of the tax system could be reduced by simplifying the tax laws. Yet simplification is often politically difficult. Most people are ready to simplify the tax code by eliminating the loopholes that benefit others, but few are eager to give up the loopholes that they benefit from themselves. In the end, the complexity of the tax law results from the political process as various taxpayers with their own special interests lobby for their causes.

12-2c Marginal Tax Rates versus Average Tax Rates

When discussing the efficiency and equity of income taxes, economists distinguish between two notions of the tax rate: the average and the marginal. The **average tax rate** is total taxes paid divided by total income. The **marginal tax rate** is the amount that taxes increase from an additional dollar of income.

average tax rate
total taxes paid divided by total income

marginal tax rate
the amount that taxes increase from an additional dollar of income

For example, suppose that the government taxes 20 percent of the first $50,000 of income and 50 percent of all income above $50,000. Under this tax, a person who makes $60,000 pays a tax of $15,000: 20 percent of the first $50,000 (0.20 × $50,000 = $10,000) plus 50 percent of the next $10,000 (0.50 × $10,000 = $5,000). For this person, the average tax rate is $15,000/$60,000, or 25 percent. But the marginal tax rate is 50 percent. If the taxpayer earned an additional dollar of income, that dollar would be subject to the 50 percent tax rate, so the amount the taxpayer would owe to the government would rise by $0.50.

The marginal and average tax rates each contain a useful piece of information. If we are trying to gauge the sacrifice made by a taxpayer, the average tax rate is more appropriate because it measures the fraction of income paid in taxes. By contrast, if we are trying to gauge how much the tax system distorts incentives, the marginal tax rate is more meaningful. One of the *Ten Principles of Economics* in Chapter 1 is that rational people think at the margin. A corollary to this principle is that the marginal tax rate measures how much the tax system discourages people from working. If you are thinking of working an extra few hours, the marginal tax rate determines how much the government takes of your additional earnings. It is the marginal tax rate, therefore, that determines the deadweight loss of an income tax.

12-2d Lump-Sum Taxes

Suppose the government imposes a tax of $4,000 on everyone. That is, everyone owes the same amount, regardless of earnings or any actions that a person might take. Such a tax is called a **lump-sum tax**.

lump-sum tax
a tax that is the same amount for every person

A lump-sum tax shows clearly the difference between average and marginal tax rates. For a taxpayer with income of $20,000, the average tax rate of a $4,000 lump-sum tax is 20 percent; for a taxpayer with income of $40,000, the average tax rate is 10 percent. For both taxpayers, the marginal tax rate is zero because no tax is owed on an additional dollar of income.

A lump-sum tax is the most efficient tax possible. Because a person's decisions do not alter the amount owed, the tax does not distort incentives and, therefore, does not cause deadweight losses. Because everyone can easily compute the amount owed and because there is no benefit to hiring tax lawyers and accountants, the lump-sum tax imposes a minimal administrative burden on taxpayers.

If lump-sum taxes are so efficient, why do we rarely observe them in the real world? The reason is that efficiency is only one goal of the tax system. A lump-sum tax would take the same amount from the poor and the rich, an outcome most people would view as unfair. To understand the tax systems that we observe, we must therefore consider the other major goal of tax policy: equity.

Quick Quiz   *What is meant by the* efficiency *of a tax system? • What can make a tax system inefficient?*

12-3 Taxes and Equity

Ever since American colonists dumped imported tea into Boston harbor to protest high British taxes, tax policy has generated some of the most heated debates in American politics. The heat is rarely fueled by questions of efficiency. Instead, it arises from disagreements over how the tax burden should be distributed. Senator Russell Long once mimicked the public debate with this ditty:

> Don't tax you.
> Don't tax me.
> Tax that fella behind the tree.

Of course, if we are to rely on the government to provide some of the goods and services we want, taxes must fall on someone. In this section, we consider the equity of a tax system. How should the burden of taxes be divided among the population? How do we evaluate whether a tax system is fair? Everyone agrees that the tax system should be equitable, but there is much disagreement about how to judge the equity of a tax system.

12-3a The Benefits Principle

benefits principle
the idea that people should pay taxes based on the benefits they receive from government services

One principle of taxation, called the **benefits principle**, states that people should pay taxes based on the benefits they receive from government services. This principle tries to make public goods similar to private goods. It seems fair that a person who often goes to the movies pays more in total for movie tickets than a person who rarely goes. Similarly, a person who gets great benefit from a public good should pay more for it than a person who gets little benefit.

The gasoline tax, for instance, is sometimes justified using the benefits principle. In some states, revenues from the gasoline tax are used to build and maintain roads. Because those who buy gasoline are the same people who use the roads, the gasoline tax might be viewed as a fair way to pay for this government service.

The benefits principle can also be used to argue that wealthy citizens should pay higher taxes than poorer ones. Why? Simply because the wealthy benefit more from public services. Consider, for example, the benefits of police protection from theft. Citizens with much to protect benefit more from police than do those with less to protect. Therefore, according to the benefits principle, the wealthy should contribute more than the poor to the cost of maintaining the police force. The same argument can be used for many other public services, such as fire protection, national defense, and the court system.

It is even possible to use the benefits principle to argue for antipoverty programs funded by taxes on the wealthy. As we discussed in Chapter 11, people may prefer living in a society without poverty, suggesting that antipoverty programs are a public good. If the wealthy place a greater dollar value on this public good than members of the middle class do, perhaps just because the wealthy have more to spend, then according to the benefits principle, they should be taxed more heavily to pay for these programs.

12-3b The Ability-to-Pay Principle

Another way to evaluate the equity of a tax system is called the **ability-to-pay principle**, which states that taxes should be levied on a person according to how well that person can shoulder the burden. This principle is sometimes justified by the claim that all citizens should make an "equal sacrifice" to support the government. The magnitude of a person's sacrifice, however, depends not only on the size of his tax payment but also on his income and other circumstances. A $1,000 tax paid by a poor person may require a larger sacrifice than a $10,000 tax paid by a rich one.

The ability-to-pay principle leads to two corollary notions of equity: vertical equity and horizontal equity. **Vertical equity** states that taxpayers with a greater ability to pay should contribute a larger amount. **Horizontal equity** states that taxpayers with similar abilities to pay should contribute the same amount. These notions of equity are widely accepted, but applying them to evaluate a tax system is rarely straightforward.

Vertical Equity If taxes are based on ability to pay, then richer taxpayers should pay more than poorer taxpayers. But how much more should the rich pay? Much of the debate over tax policy concerns this question.

Consider the three tax systems in Table 7. In each case, taxpayers with higher incomes pay more. Yet the systems differ in how quickly taxes rise with income. The first system is called **proportional** because all taxpayers pay the same fraction of income. The second system is called **regressive** because high-income taxpayers pay a smaller fraction of their income, even though they pay a larger amount. The third system is called **progressive** because high-income taxpayers pay a larger fraction of their income.

Which of these three tax systems is most fair? There is no obvious answer, and economic theory does not offer any help in trying to find one. Equity, like beauty, is in the eye of the beholder.

ability-to-pay principle
the idea that taxes should be levied on a person according to how well that person can shoulder the burden

vertical equity
the idea that taxpayers with a greater ability to pay taxes should pay larger amounts

horizontal equity
the idea that taxpayers with similar abilities to pay taxes should pay the same amount

proportional tax
a tax for which high-income and low-income taxpayers pay the same fraction of income

regressive tax
a tax for which high-income taxpayers pay a smaller fraction of their income than do low-income taxpayers

progressive tax
a tax for which high-income taxpayers pay a larger fraction of their income than do low-income taxpayers

TABLE 7

Three Tax Systems

Income	Proportional Tax		Regressive Tax		Progressive Tax	
	Amount of Tax	Percent of Income	Amount of Tax	Percent of Income	Amount of Tax	Percent of Income
$50,000	$12,500	25%	$15,000	30%	$10,000	20%
100,000	25,000	25	25,000	25	25,000	25
200,000	50,000	25	40,000	20	60,000	30

case
study

How the Tax Burden Is Distributed

Much debate over tax policy concerns whether the wealthy pay their fair share. There is no objective way to make this judgment. In evaluating the issue for yourself, however, it is useful to know how much families with different incomes pay under the current tax system.

Table 8 presents some data on how federal taxes are distributed among income classes. These figures are for 2009, the most recent year available as this book was going to press, and were tabulated by the Congressional Budget Office. They include all federal taxes—individual income taxes, payroll taxes, corporate income taxes, and excise taxes—but not state and local taxes. When calculating a household's tax burden, the CBO allocates corporate income taxes to the owners of capital and payroll taxes to workers.

To construct the table, households are ranked according to their income and placed into five groups of equal size, called *quintiles*. The table also presents data on the richest 1 percent of Americans. The second column of the table shows the average income of each group. Income includes both market income (income that households have earned from their work and savings) and transfer payments from government programs, such as Social Security and welfare. The poorest one-fifth of households had average income of $23,500, and the richest one-fifth had average income of $223,500. The richest 1 percent had average income of over $1.2 million.

The third column of the table shows total taxes as a percentage of income. As you can see, the U.S. federal tax system is progressive. The poorest fifth of households paid 1.0 percent of their incomes in taxes, and the richest fifth paid 23.2 percent. The top 1 percent paid 28.9 percent of their incomes.

The fourth and fifth columns compare the distribution of income and the distribution of taxes. The poorest quintile earned 5.1 percent of all income and paid 0.3 percent of all taxes. The richest quintile earned 50.8 percent of all income and paid 67.9 percent of all taxes. The richest 1 percent (which, remember, is ½₀ the size of each quintile) earned 13.4 percent of all income and paid 22.3 percent of all taxes.

These numbers on taxes paid are a good starting point for understanding how the burden of government is distributed, but they give an incomplete picture. Money flows not only from households to the government in the form of taxes but also from the government back to households in the form of transfer payments. In some ways, transfer payments are the opposite of taxes. Including transfers as negative taxes substantially changes the distribution of the tax burden. The richest

TABLE 8

The Burden of Federal Taxes

Source: Congressional Budget Office Analysis. Figures are for 2009.

Quintile	Average Income	Taxes as a Percentage of Income	Percentage of All Income	Percentage of All Taxes
Lowest	$23,500	1.0%	5.1%	0.3%
Second	43,400	6.8	9.8	3.8
Middle	64,300	11.1	14.7	9.4
Fourth	93,800	15.1	21.1	18.3
Highest	223,500	23.2	50.8	67.9
Top 1%	1,219,700	28.9	13.4	22.3

quintile of households still pays about one-quarter of its income to the government, even after transfers are subtracted, and the top 1 percent still pays almost 30 percent. By contrast, the average tax rate for the poorest quintile becomes a sizeable negative number. That is, typical households in the bottom of the income distribution receive substantially more in transfers than they pay in taxes. The lesson is clear: To understand fully the progressivity of government policies, one must take account of both what people pay and what they receive.

Finally, it is worth noting that the numbers in Table 8 are a bit out of date. In late 2012, the U.S. Congress passed and President Obama signed a tax bill that increased taxes significantly from those that prevailed previously, particularly for taxpayers at the top of the income distribution. For individuals earning taxable income more than $400,000 and couples earning more than $450,000, the marginal income tax rate was increased from 35 to 39.6 percent. As a result, the tax system in place for 2013 and beyond is more progressive than the one shown in the table. ◢

Horizontal Equity   If taxes are based on ability to pay, then similar taxpayers should pay similar amounts of taxes. But what determines if two taxpayers are similar? Families differ in many ways. To evaluate whether a tax code is horizontally equitable, one must determine which differences are relevant for a family's ability to pay and which differences are not.

Suppose the Smith and Jones families each have income of $100,000. The Smiths have no children, but Mr. Smith has an illness that results in medical expenses of $40,000. The Joneses are in good health, but they have four children. Two of the Jones children are in college, generating tuition bills of $60,000. Would it be fair for these two families to pay the same tax because they have the same income? Would it be fair to give the Smiths a tax break to help them offset their high medical expenses? Would it be fair to give the Joneses a tax break to help them with their tuition expenses?

There are no easy answers to these questions. In practice, the U.S. tax code is filled with special provisions that alter a family's tax obligations based on its specific circumstances.

12-3c Tax Incidence and Tax Equity

Tax incidence—the study of who bears the burden of taxes—is central to evaluating tax equity. As we first saw in Chapter 6, the person who bears the burden of a tax is not always the person who gets the tax bill from the government. Because taxes alter supply and demand, they alter equilibrium prices. As a result, they affect people beyond those who, according to statute, actually pay the tax. When evaluating the vertical and horizontal equity of any tax, it is important to take these indirect effects into account.

Many discussions of tax equity ignore the indirect effects of taxes and are based on what economists mockingly call the *flypaper theory* of tax incidence. According to this theory, the burden of a tax, like a fly on flypaper, sticks wherever it first lands. This assumption, however, is rarely valid.

For example, a person not trained in economics might argue that a tax on expensive fur coats is vertically equitable because most buyers of furs are wealthy. Yet if these buyers can easily substitute other luxuries for furs, then a tax on furs might only reduce the sale of furs. In the end, the burden of the tax will fall more on those who make and sell furs than on those who buy them. Because most workers who make furs are not wealthy, the equity of a fur tax could be quite different from what the flypaper theory indicates.

IN THE NEWS | Tax Expenditures

Tax reformers and deficit hawks often suggest reducing the deductions, credits, and exclusions that narrow the tax base.

The Blur Between Spending and Taxes

By N. Gregory Mankiw

Should the government cut spending or raise taxes to deal with its long-term fiscal imbalance? As President Obama's deficit commission rolls out its final report in the coming weeks, this issue will most likely divide the political right and left. But, in many ways, the question is the wrong one. The distinction between spending and taxation is often murky and sometimes meaningless.

Imagine that there is some activity—say, snipe hunting—that members of Congress want to encourage. Senator Porkbelly proposes a government subsidy. "America needs more snipe hunters," he says. "I propose that every time an American bags a snipe, the federal government should pay him or her $100."

"No, no," says Congressman Blowhard. "The Porkbelly plan would increase the size of an already bloated government. Let's instead reduce the burden of taxation. I propose that every time an American tracks down a snipe,

the hunter should get a $100 credit to reduce his or her tax liabilities."

To be sure, government accountants may treat the Porkbelly and Blowhard plans differently. They would likely deem the subsidy to be a spending increase and the credit to be a tax cut. Moreover, the rhetoric of the two politicians about spending and taxes may appeal to different political bases.

But it hardly takes an economic genius to see how little difference there is between the two plans. Both policies enrich the nation's snipe hunters. And because the government must balance its books, at least in the long run, the gains of the snipe hunters must come at the cost of higher taxes or lower government benefits for the rest of us.

Economists call the Blowhard plan a "tax expenditure." The tax code is filled with them—although not yet one for snipe hunting. Every time a politician promises a "targeted tax cut," he or she is probably offering up a form of government spending in disguise.

Erskine B. Bowles and Alan K. Simpson, the chairmen of President Obama's deficit reduction commission, have taken at hard look

at these tax expenditures—and they don't like what they see. In their draft proposal, released earlier this month, they proposed doing away with tax expenditures, which together cost the Treasury over $1 trillion a year.

Such a drastic step would allow Mr. Bowles and Mr. Simpson to move the budget toward fiscal sustainability, while simultaneously reducing all income tax rates. Under their plan, the top tax rate would fall to 23 percent from the 35 percent in today's law (and the 39.6 percent currently advocated by Democratic leadership).

This approach has long been the basic recipe for tax reform. By broadening the tax base and lowering tax rates, we can increase government revenue and distort incentives less. That should command widespread applause across the ideological spectrum. Unfortunately, the reaction has been less enthusiastic.

Pundits on the left are suspicious of any plan that reduces marginal tax rates on the rich. But, as Mr. Bowles and Mr. Simpson point out, tax expenditures disproportionately

case study | Who Pays the Corporate Income Tax?

The corporate income tax provides a good example of the importance of tax incidence for tax policy. The corporate tax is popular among voters. After all, corporations are not people. Voters are always eager to have their taxes reduced and have some impersonal corporation pick up the tab.

But before deciding that the corporate income tax is a good way for the government to raise revenue, we should consider who bears the burden of the corporate tax. This is a difficult question on which economists disagree, but one thing is certain: *People pay all taxes.* When the government levies a tax on a corporation, the corporation is more like a tax collector than a taxpayer. The burden of the tax ultimately falls on people—the owners, customers, or workers of the corporation.

Many economists believe that workers and customers bear much of the burden of the corporate income tax. To see why, consider an example. Suppose that the

benefit those at the top of the economic ladder. According to their figures, tax expenditures increase the after-tax income of those in the bottom quintile by about 6 percent. Those in the top 1 percent of the income distribution enjoy about twice that gain. Progressives who are concerned about the gap between rich and poor should be eager to scale back tax expenditures.

Pundits on the right, meanwhile, are suspicious of anything that increases government revenue. But they should recognize that tax expenditures are best viewed as a hidden form of spending. If we eliminate tax expenditures and reduce marginal tax rates, as Mr. Bowles and Mr. Simpson propose, we are essentially doing what economic conservatives have long advocated: cutting spending and taxes.

Yet another political problem is that each tax expenditure has its own political constituency. If Congressman Blowhard ever got his way, the snipe hunters of the world would surely fight to keep their tax break.

One major tax expenditure that the Bowles–Simpson plan would curtail or eliminate is the mortgage interest deduction. Without doubt, many homeowners and the real estate industry will object. But they won't have the merits on their side.

This subsidy to homeownership is neither economically efficient nor particularly equitable. Economists have long pointed out that

The New York Times, November 21, 2010/Artist David Klein

tax subsidies to housing, together with the high taxes on corporations, cause too much of the economy's capital stock to be tied up in residential structures and too little in corporate capital. This misallocation of resources results in lower productivity and reduced real wages.

Moreover, there is nothing particularly ignoble about renting that deserves the scorn of the tax code. But let's face it: subsidizing homeowners is the same as penalizing renters. In the end, someone has to pick up the tab.

There are certain tax expenditures that I like. My personal favorite is the deduction for charitable giving. It encourages philanthropy

and, thus, private rather than governmental solutions to society's problems.

But I know that solving the long-term fiscal problem won't be easy. Everyone will have to give a little, and perhaps even more than a little. I am willing to give up my favorite tax expenditure if everyone else is willing to give up theirs.

The Bowles–Simpson proposal is not perfect, but it is far better than the status quo. The question ahead is whether we can get Senator Porkbelly and Congressman Blowhard to agree. ◢

Source: *New York Times,* November 21, 2010.

U.S. government decides to raise the tax on the income earned by car companies. At first, this tax hurts the owners of the car companies, who receive less profit. But over time, these owners will respond to the tax. Because producing cars is less profitable, they invest less in building new car factories. Instead, they invest their wealth in other ways—for example, by buying larger houses or by building factories in other industries or other countries. With fewer car factories, the supply of cars declines, as does the demand for autoworkers. Thus, a tax on corporations making cars causes the price of cars to rise and the wages of autoworkers to fall.

The corporate income tax shows how dangerous the flypaper theory of tax incidence can be. The corporate income tax is popular in part because it appears to be paid by rich corporations. Yet those who bear the ultimate burden of the tax—the customers and workers of corporations—are often not rich. If the true incidence of the corporate tax were more widely known, this tax might be less popular among voters. ◢

Bill Pugliano/Getty Images

This worker pays part of the corporate income tax.

Quick Quiz　*Explain the* benefits principle *and the* ability-to-pay principle. • *What are* vertical equity *and* horizontal equity? • *Why is studying tax incidence important for determining the equity of a tax system?*

12-4 Conclusion: The Trade-off between Equity and Efficiency

Almost everyone agrees that equity and efficiency are the two most important goals of a tax system. But these two goals often conflict, especially when equity is judged by the progressivity of the tax system. People disagree about tax policy often because they attach different weights to these goals.

The recent history of tax policy shows how political leaders differ in their views on equity and efficiency. When Ronald Reagan was elected president in 1980, the marginal tax rate on the earnings of the richest Americans was 50 percent. On interest income, the marginal tax rate was 70 percent. Reagan argued that such high tax rates greatly distorted economic incentives to work and save. In other words, he claimed that these high tax rates cost too much in terms of economic efficiency. Tax reform was, therefore, a high priority of his administration. Reagan signed into law large cuts in tax rates in 1981 and then again in 1986. When Reagan left office in 1989, the richest Americans faced a marginal tax rate of only 28 percent.

The pendulum of political debate swings both ways. When Bill Clinton ran for president in 1992, he argued that the rich were not paying their fair share of taxes. In other words, the low tax rates on the rich violated his view of vertical equity. In 1993, President Clinton signed into law a bill that raised the tax rates on the richest Americans to about 40 percent. When George W. Bush ran for president, he reprised many of Reagan's themes, and as president he reversed part of the Clinton tax increase, reducing the highest tax rate to 35 percent. Barack Obama pledged during the 2008 presidential campaign that he would raise taxes on high-income households, and starting in 2013 the top marginal tax rate was back at about 40 percent.

Economics alone cannot determine the best way to balance the goals of efficiency and equity. This issue involves political philosophy as well as economics. But economists have an important role in this debate: They can shed light on the trade-offs that society inevitably faces when designing the tax system and can help us avoid policies that sacrifice efficiency without any benefit in terms of equity.

Summary

- The U.S. government raises revenue using various taxes. The most important taxes for the federal government are individual income taxes and payroll taxes for social insurance. The most important taxes for state and local governments are sales taxes and property taxes.

- The efficiency of a tax system refers to the costs it imposes on taxpayers. There are two costs of taxes beyond the transfer of resources from the taxpayer to the government. The first is the deadweight loss that arises as taxes alter incentives and distort the allocation of resources. The second is the administrative burden of complying with the tax laws.

- The equity of a tax system concerns whether the tax burden is distributed fairly among the population.

- According to the benefits principle, it is fair for people to pay taxes based on the benefits they receive from the government. According to the ability-to-pay principle, it is fair for people to pay taxes based on their capability to handle the financial burden. When evaluating the equity of a tax system, it is important to remember a lesson from the study of tax incidence: The distribution of tax burdens is not the same as the distribution of tax bills.

- When considering changes in the tax laws, policymakers often face a trade-off between efficiency and equity. Much of the debate over tax policy arises because people give different weights to these two goals.

Key Concepts

budget deficit, *p. 238*
budget surplus, *p. 238*
average tax rate, *p. 245*
marginal tax rate, *p. 245*

lump-sum tax, *p. 245*
benefits principle, *p. 246*
ability-to-pay principle, *p. 247*
vertical equity, *p. 247*

horizontal equity, *p. 247*
proportional tax, *p. 247*
regressive tax, *p. 247*
progressive tax, *p. 247*

Questions for Review

1. Over the past century, has the government's tax revenue grown more or less slowly than the rest of the economy?

2. Explain how corporate profits are taxed twice.

3. Why is the burden of a tax to taxpayers greater than the revenue received by the government?

4. Why do some economists advocate taxing consumption rather than income?

5. What is the marginal tax rate on a lump-sum tax? How is this related to the efficiency of the tax?

6. Give two arguments why wealthy taxpayers should pay more taxes than poor taxpayers.

7. What is the concept of horizontal equity and why is it hard to apply?

Quick Check Multiple Choice

1. The two largest sources of tax revenue for the U.S. federal government are
   a. individual and corporate income taxes.
   b. individual income taxes and payroll taxes for social insurance.
   c. corporate income taxes and payroll taxes for social insurance.
   d. payroll taxes for social insurance and property taxes.

2. Andy gives piano lessons. He has an opportunity cost of $50 per lesson and charges $60. He has two students: Bob, who has a willingness to pay of $70, and Carl, who has a willingness to pay of $90. When the government puts a $20 tax on piano lessons and Andy raises his price to $80, the deadweight loss is _____ and the tax revenue is _____.
   a. $10, $20
   b. $10, $40
   c. $20, $20
   d. $20, $40

3. If the tax code exempts the first $20,000 of income from taxation and then taxes 25 percent of all income above that level, then a person who earns $50,000 has an average tax rate of _____ percent and a marginal tax rate of _____ percent.

   a. 15, 25
   b. 25, 15
   c. 25, 30
   d. 30, 25

4. A toll is a tax on those citizens who use toll roads. This policy can be viewed as an application of
   a. the benefits principle.
   b. horizontal equity.
   c. vertical equity.
   d. tax progressivity.

5. In the United States, taxpayers in the top 1 percent of the income distribution pay about _____ percent of their income in federal taxes.
   a. 5
   b. 10
   c. 20
   d. 30

6. If the corporate income tax induces businesses to reduce their capital investment, then
   a. the tax does not have any deadweight loss.
   b. corporate shareholders benefit from the tax.
   c. workers bear some of the burden of the tax.
   d. the tax achieves the goal of vertical equity.

Problems and Applications

1. In a published source or on the Internet, find out whether the U.S. federal government had a budget deficit or surplus last year. What do policymakers expect to happen over the next few years? (*Hint*: The website of the Congressional Budget Office is http://www.cbo.gov.)

2. The information in many of the tables in this chapter can be found in the *Economic Report of the President*, which appears annually. Using a recent issue of the report at your library or on the Internet, answer the following questions and provide some numbers to support your answers. (*Hint*: The website of the Government Printing Office is http://www.gpo.gov.)
   a. Figure 1 shows that government revenue as a percentage of total income has increased over time. Is this increase primarily attributable to changes in federal government revenue or in state and local government revenue?
   b. Looking at the combined revenue of the federal government and state and local governments,

   how has the composition of total revenue changed over time? Are personal income taxes more or less important? Social insurance taxes? Corporate profits taxes?
   c. Looking at the combined expenditures of the federal government and state and local governments, how have the relative shares of transfer payments and purchases of goods and services changed over time?

3. The chapter states that the elderly population in the United States is growing more rapidly than the total population. In particular, the number of workers is rising slowly, while the number of retirees is rising quickly. Concerned about the future of Social Security, some members of Congress propose a "freeze" on the program.
   a. If total expenditures were frozen, what would happen to benefits per retiree? To tax payments per worker? (Assume that Social Security taxes and receipts are balanced in each year.)

b. If benefits per retiree were frozen, what would happen to total expenditures? To tax payments per worker?

c. If tax payments per worker were frozen, what would happen to total expenditures? To benefits per retiree?

d. What do your answers to parts (a), (b), and (c) imply about the difficult decisions faced by policymakers?

4. Suppose you are a typical person in the U.S. economy. You pay 4 percent of your income in a state income tax and 15.3 percent of your labor earnings in federal payroll taxes (employer and employee shares combined). You also pay federal income taxes as in Table 3. How much tax of each type do you pay if you earn $20,000 a year? Taking all taxes into account, what are your average and marginal tax rates? What happens to your tax bill and to your average and marginal tax rates if your income rises to $40,000?

5. Some states exclude necessities, such as food and clothing, from their sales tax. Other states do not. Discuss the merits of this exclusion. Consider both efficiency and equity.

6. When someone owns an asset (such as a share of stock) that rises in value, he has an "accrued" capital gain. If he sells the asset, he "realizes" the gains that have previously accrued. Under the U.S. income tax system, realized capital gains are taxed, but accrued gains are not.
   a. Explain how individuals' behavior is affected by this rule.

b. Some economists believe that cuts in capital gains tax rates, especially temporary ones, can raise tax revenue. How might this be so?

c. Do you think it is a good rule to tax realized but not accrued capital gains? Why or why not?

7. Suppose that your state raises its sales tax from 5 percent to 6 percent. The state revenue commissioner forecasts a 20 percent increase in sales tax revenue. Is this plausible? Explain.

8. The Tax Reform Act of 1986 eliminated the deductibility of interest payments on consumer debt (mostly credit cards and auto loans) but maintained the deductibility of interest payments on mortgages and home equity loans. What do you think happened to the relative amounts of borrowing through consumer debt and home equity debt?

9. Categorize each of the following funding schemes as examples of the benefits principle or the ability-to-pay principle.
   a. Visitors to many national parks pay an entrance fee.
   b. Local property taxes support elementary and secondary schools.
   c. An airport trust fund collects a tax on each plane ticket sold and uses the money to improve airports and the air traffic control system.

Go to CengageBrain.com to purchase access to the proven, critical Study Guide to accompany this text, which features additional notes and context, practice tests, and much more.

V

Firm Behavior and the Organization of Industry

The Costs
of Production

The economy is made up of thousands of firms that produce the goods and services you enjoy every day: General Motors produces automobiles, General Electric produces lightbulbs, and General Mills produces breakfast cereals. Some firms, such as these three, are large; they employ thousands of workers and have thousands of stockholders who share in the firms' profits. Other firms, such as the local barbershop or café, are small; they employ only a few workers and are owned by a single person or family.

In previous chapters, we used the supply curve to summarize firms' production decisions. According to the law of supply, firms are willing to produce and sell a greater quantity of a good when the price of the good is higher, and this response leads to a supply curve that slopes upward. For analyzing many questions, the law of supply is all you need to know about firm behavior.

In this chapter and the ones that follow, we examine firm behavior in more detail. This topic will give you a better understanding of the decisions behind the supply curve. In addition, it will introduce you to a part of economics called *industrial organization*—the study of how firms' decisions about prices and quantities depend on the market conditions they face. The town in which you live, for instance, may have several pizzerias but only one cable television company. This raises a key question: How does the number of firms affect the prices in a market and the efficiency of the market outcome? The field of industrial organization addresses exactly this question.

Before turning to these issues, we need to discuss the costs of production. All firms, from Delta Air Lines to your local deli, incur costs as they make the goods and services that they sell. As we will see in the coming chapters, a firm's costs are a key determinant of its production and pricing decisions. In this chapter, we define some of the variables that economists use to measure a firm's costs, and we consider the relationships among these variables.

A word of warning: This topic is dry and technical. To be honest, one might even call it boring. But this material provides a crucial foundation for the fascinating topics that follow.

13-1 What Are Costs?

We begin our discussion of costs at Caroline's Cookie Factory. Caroline, the owner of the firm, buys flour, sugar, chocolate chips, and other cookie ingredients. She also buys the mixers and ovens and hires workers to run this equipment. She then sells the cookies to consumers. By examining some of the issues that Caroline faces in her business, we can learn some lessons about costs that apply to all firms in an economy.

13-1a Total Revenue, Total Cost, and Profit

We begin with the firm's objective. To understand the decisions a firm makes, we must understand what it is trying to do. It is conceivable that Caroline started her firm because of an altruistic desire to provide the world with cookies or, perhaps, out of love for the cookie business. More likely, Caroline started her business to make money. Economists normally assume that the goal of a firm is to maximize profit, and they find that this assumption works well in most cases.

total revenue
the amount a firm receives for the sale of its output

What is a firm's profit? The amount that the firm receives for the sale of its output (cookies) is called its **total revenue**. The amount that the firm pays to buy inputs (flour, sugar, workers, ovens, and so forth) is called its **total cost**. Caroline gets to keep any revenue that is not needed to cover costs. **Profit** is a firm's total revenue minus its total cost:

total cost
the market value of the inputs a firm uses in production

$$\text{Profit} = \text{Total revenue} - \text{Total cost.}$$

Caroline's objective is to make her firm's profit as large as possible.

profit
total revenue minus total cost

To see how a firm goes about maximizing profit, we must consider fully how to measure its total revenue and its total cost. Total revenue is the easy part: It equals the quantity of output the firm produces times the price at which it sells its output. If Caroline produces 10,000 cookies and sells them at $2 a cookie, her total revenue is $20,000. The measurement of a firm's total cost, however, is more subtle.

13-1b Costs as Opportunity Costs

When measuring costs at Caroline's Cookie Factory or any other firm, it is important to keep in mind one of the *Ten Principles of Economics* from Chapter 1: The cost of something is what you give up to get it. Recall that the *opportunity cost* of an item refers to all those things that must be forgone to acquire that item. When economists speak of a firm's cost of production, they include all the opportunity costs of making its output of goods and services.

While some of a firm's opportunity costs of production are obvious, others are less so. When Caroline pays $1,000 for flour, that $1,000 is an opportunity cost because Caroline can no longer use that $1,000 to buy something else. Similarly, when Caroline hires workers to make the cookies, the wages she pays are part of the firm's costs. Because these opportunity costs require the firm to pay out some money, they are called **explicit costs**. By contrast, some of a firm's opportunity costs, called **implicit costs**, do not require a cash outlay. Imagine that Caroline is skilled with computers and could earn $100 per hour working as a programmer. For every hour that Caroline works at her cookie factory, she gives up $100 in income, and this forgone income is also part of her costs. The total cost of Caroline's business is the sum of her explicit and implicit costs.

The distinction between explicit and implicit costs highlights an important difference between how economists and accountants analyze a business. Economists are interested in studying how firms make production and pricing decisions. Because these decisions are based on both explicit and implicit costs, economists include both when measuring a firm's costs. By contrast, accountants have the job of keeping track of the money that flows into and out of firms. As a result, they measure the explicit costs but usually ignore the implicit costs.

The difference between the methods of economists and accountants is easy to see in the case of Caroline's Cookie Factory. When Caroline gives up the opportunity to earn money as a computer programmer, her accountant will not count this as a cost of her cookie business. Because no money flows out of the business to pay for this cost, it never shows up on the accountant's financial statements. An economist, however, will count the forgone income as a cost because it will affect the decisions that Caroline makes in her cookie business. For example, if Caroline's wage as a computer programmer rises from $100 to $500 per hour, she might decide that running her cookie business is too costly and choose to shut down the factory to become a full-time computer programmer.

13-1c The Cost of Capital as an Opportunity Cost

An important implicit cost of almost every business is the opportunity cost of the financial capital that has been invested in the business. Suppose, for instance, that Caroline used $300,000 of her savings to buy her cookie factory from its previous owner. If Caroline had instead left this money deposited in a savings account that pays an interest rate of 5 percent, she would have earned $15,000 per year. To own her cookie factory, therefore, Caroline has given up $15,000 a year in interest income. This forgone $15,000 is one of the implicit opportunity costs of Caroline's business.

As we have already noted, economists and accountants treat costs differently, and this is especially true in their treatment of the cost of capital. An economist views the $15,000 in interest income that Caroline gives up every year as an implicit cost of her business. Caroline's accountant, however, will not show this $15,000 as a cost because no money flows out of the business to pay for it.

To further explore the difference between the methods of economists and accountants, let's change the example slightly. Suppose now that Caroline did not have the entire $300,000 to buy the factory but, instead, used $100,000 of her own savings and borrowed $200,000 from a bank at an interest rate of 5 percent. Caroline's accountant, who only measures explicit costs, will now count the

explicit costs *money*
input costs that require an outlay of money by the firm

implicit costs *no money no opportunity cost*
input costs that do not require an outlay of money by the firm

Total cost = explicit + implicit costs

Accountants only look at explicit costs
economists look at both

not earning interest on money is implicit costs

$10,000 interest paid on the bank loan every year as a cost because this amount of money now flows out of the firm. By contrast, according to an economist, the opportunity cost of owning the business is still $15,000. The opportunity cost equals the interest on the bank loan (an explicit cost of $10,000) plus the forgone interest on savings (an implicit cost of $5,000).

13-1d Economic Profit versus Accounting Profit

economic profit
total revenue minus total cost, including both explicit and implicit costs

accounting profit
total revenue minus total explicit cost

Now let's return to the firm's objective: profit. Because economists and accountants measure costs differently, they also measure profit differently. An economist measures a firm's **economic profit** as the firm's total revenue minus all the opportunity costs (explicit and implicit) of producing the goods and services sold. An accountant measures the firm's **accounting profit** as the firm's total revenue minus only the firm's explicit costs.

Figure 1 summarizes this difference. Notice that because the accountant ignores the implicit costs, accounting profit is usually larger than economic profit. For a business to be profitable from an economist's standpoint, total revenue must cover all the opportunity costs, both explicit and implicit.

Economic profit is an important concept because it is what motivates the firms that supply goods and services. As we will see, a firm making positive economic profit will stay in business. It is covering all its opportunity costs and has some revenue left to reward the firm owners. When a firm is making economic losses (that is, when economic profits are negative), the business owners are failing to earn enough revenue to cover all the costs of production. Unless conditions change, the firm owners will eventually close down the business and exit the industry. To understand business decisions, we need to keep an eye on economic profit.

Quick Quiz　*Farmer McDonald gives banjo lessons for $20 an hour. One day, he spends 10 hours planting $100 worth of seeds on his farm. What opportunity cost has he incurred? What cost would his accountant measure? If these seeds yield $200 worth of crops, does McDonald earn an accounting profit? Does he earn an economic profit?*

FIGURE 1

Economists versus Accountants
Economists include all opportunity costs when analyzing a firm, whereas accountants measure only explicit costs. Therefore, economic profit is smaller than accounting profit.

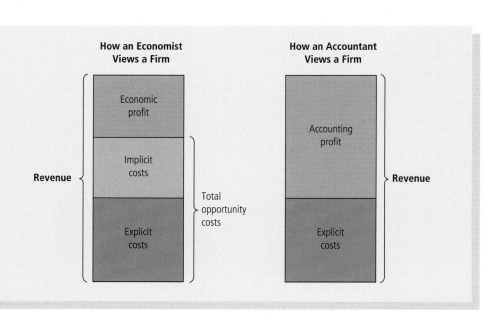

13-2 Production and Costs

Firms incur costs when they buy inputs to produce the goods and services that they plan to sell. In this section, we examine the link between a firm's production process and its total cost. Once again, we consider Caroline's Cookie Factory.

In the analysis that follows, we make an important simplifying assumption: We assume that the size of Caroline's factory is fixed and that Caroline can vary the quantity of cookies produced only by changing the number of workers she employs. This assumption is realistic in the short run but not in the long run. That is, Caroline cannot build a larger factory overnight, but she can do so over the next year or two. This analysis, therefore, describes the production decisions that Caroline faces in the short run. We examine the relationship between costs and time horizon more fully later in the chapter.

13-2a The Production Function

Table 1 shows how the quantity of cookies produced per hour at Caroline's factory depends on the number of workers. As you can see in the first two columns, if there are no workers in the factory, Caroline produces no cookies. When there is 1 worker, she produces 50 cookies. When there are 2 workers, she produces 90 cookies and so on. Panel (a) of Figure 2 presents a graph of these two columns of numbers. The number of workers is on the horizontal axis, and the number of cookies produced is on the vertical axis. This relationship between the quantity of inputs (workers) and quantity of output (cookies) is called the **production function**.

production function
the relationship between quantity of inputs used to make a good and the quantity of output of that good

Number of Workers	Output (quantity of cookies produced per hour)	Marginal Product of Labor	Cost of Factory	Cost of Workers	Total Cost of Inputs (cost of factory + cost of workers)
0	0		$30	$0	$30
		50			
1	50		30	10	40
		40			
2	90		30	20	50
		30			
3	120		30	30	60
		20			
4	140		30	40	70
		10			
5	150		30	50	80
		5			
6	155		30	60	90

TABLE 1

A Production Function and Total Cost: Caroline's Cookie Factory

FIGURE 2

Caroline's Production Function and Total-Cost Curve

The production function in panel (a) shows the relationship between the number of workers hired and the quantity of output produced. Here the number of workers hired (on the horizontal axis) is from the first column in Table 1, and the quantity of output produced (on the vertical axis) is from the second column. The production function gets flatter as the number of workers increases, reflecting diminishing marginal product. The total-cost curve in panel (b) shows the relationship between the quantity of output produced and total cost of production. Here the quantity of output produced (on the horizontal axis) is from the second column in Table 1, and the total cost (on the vertical axis) is from the sixth column. The total-cost curve gets steeper as the quantity of output increases because of diminishing marginal product.

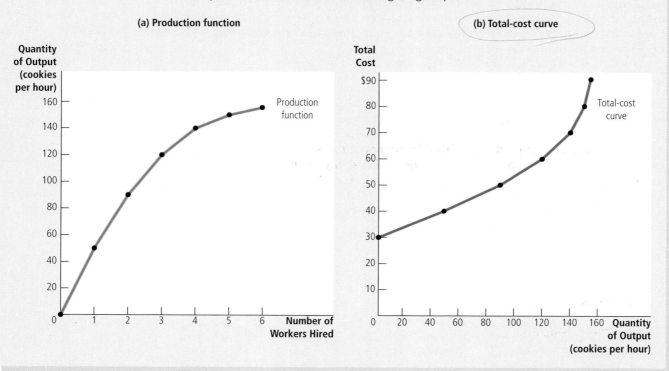

(a) Production function

(b) Total-cost curve

marginal product

the increase in output that arises from an additional unit of input

One of the *Ten Principles of Economics* introduced in Chapter 1 is that rational people think at the margin. As we will see in future chapters, this idea is the key to understanding the decisions a firm makes about how many workers to hire and how much output to produce. To take a step toward understanding these decisions, the third column in the table gives the marginal product of a worker. The **marginal product** of any input in the production process is the increase in the quantity of output obtained from one additional unit of that input. When the number of workers goes from 1 to 2, cookie production increases from 50 to 90, so the marginal product of the second worker is 40 cookies. And when the number of workers goes from 2 to 3, cookie production increases from 90 to 120, so the marginal product of the third worker is 30 cookies. In the table, the marginal product is shown halfway between two rows because it represents the change in output as the number of workers increases from one level to another.

Notice that as the number of workers increases, the marginal product declines. The second worker has a marginal product of 40 cookies, the third worker has a marginal product of 30 cookies, and the fourth worker has a marginal product of 20 cookies. This property is called **diminishing marginal product**. At first, when only a few workers are hired, they have easy access to Caroline's kitchen equipment. As the number of workers increases, additional workers have to share equipment and work in more crowded conditions. Eventually, the kitchen is so crowded that the workers start getting in each other's way. Hence, as more workers are hired, each additional worker contributes fewer additional cookies to total production.

Diminishing marginal product is also apparent in Figure 2. The production function's slope ("rise over run") tells us the change in Caroline's output of cookies ("rise") for each additional input of labor ("run"). That is, the slope of the production function measures the marginal product of a worker. As the number of workers increases, the marginal product declines, and the production function becomes flatter.

diminishing marginal product
the property whereby the marginal product of an input declines as the quantity of the input increases

13-2b From the Production Function to the Total-Cost Curve

The last three columns of Table 1 show Caroline's cost of producing cookies. In this example, the cost of Caroline's factory is $30 per hour, and the cost of a worker is $10 per hour. If she hires 1 worker, her total cost is $40 per hour. If she hires 2 workers, her total cost is $50 per hour, and so on. With this information, the table now shows how the number of workers Caroline hires is related to the quantity of cookies she produces and to her total cost of production.

Our goal in the next several chapters is to study firms' production and pricing decisions. For this purpose, the most important relationship in Table 1 is between quantity produced (in the second column) and total cost (in the sixth column). Panel (b) of Figure 2 graphs these two columns of data with the quantity produced on the horizontal axis and total cost on the vertical axis. This graph is called the *total-cost curve*.

Now compare the total-cost curve in panel (b) with the production function in panel (a). These two curves are opposite sides of the same coin. The total-cost curve gets steeper as the amount produced rises, whereas the production function gets flatter as production rises. These changes in slope occur for the same reason. High production of cookies means that Caroline's kitchen is crowded with many workers. Because the kitchen is crowded, each additional worker adds less to production, reflecting diminishing marginal product. Therefore, the production function is relatively flat. But now turn this logic around: When the kitchen is crowded, producing an additional cookie requires a lot of additional labor and is thus very costly. Therefore, when the quantity produced is large, the total-cost curve is relatively steep.

Quick Quiz   *If Farmer Jones plants no seeds on his farm, he gets no harvest. If he plants 1 bag of seeds, he gets 3 bushels of wheat. If he plants 2 bags, he gets 5 bushels. If he plants 3 bags, he gets 6 bushels. A bag of seeds costs $100, and seeds are his only cost. Use these data to graph the farmer's production function and total-cost curve. Explain their shapes.*

13-3 The Various Measures of Cost

Our analysis of Caroline's Cookie Factory demonstrated how a firm's total cost reflects its production function. From data on a firm's total cost, we can derive several related measures of cost, which will turn out to be useful when we analyze production and pricing decisions in future chapters. To see how these related measures are derived, we consider the example in Table 2. This table presents cost data on Caroline's neighbor—Conrad's Coffee Shop.

The first column of the table shows the number of cups of coffee that Conrad might produce, ranging from 0 to 10 cups per hour. The second column shows Conrad's total cost of producing coffee. Figure 3 plots Conrad's total-cost curve. The quantity of coffee (from the first column) is on the horizontal axis, and total cost (from the second column) is on the vertical axis. Conrad's total-cost curve has a shape similar to Caroline's. In particular, it becomes steeper as the quantity produced rises, which (as we have discussed) reflects diminishing marginal product.

13-3a Fixed and Variable Costs

fixed costs

costs that do not vary with the quantity of output produced

Conrad's total cost can be divided into two types. Some costs, called **fixed costs**, do not vary with the quantity of output produced. They are incurred even if the firm produces nothing at all. Conrad's fixed costs include any rent he pays because this cost is the same regardless of how much coffee he produces. Similarly, if Conrad needs to hire a full-time bookkeeper to pay bills, regardless of the quantity of coffee produced, the bookkeeper's salary is a fixed cost. The third column in Table 2 shows Conrad's fixed cost, which in this example is $3.00.

[handwritten: Avg Total Cost = $\frac{\text{Total cost}}{Q} = \frac{3.80}{2} = 1.90$]

TABLE 2

The Various Measures of Cost: Conrad's Coffee Shop

Output (cups of coffee per hour)	Total Cost	Fixed Cost	Variable Cost	Average Fixed Cost	Average Variable Cost	Average Total Cost	Marginal Cost
0	$ 3.00	$3.00	$ 0.00	—	—	—	
							$0.30
1	3.30	3.00	0.30	$3.00	$0.30	$3.30	
							0.50
2	3.80	3.00	0.80	1.50	0.40	1.90	
							0.70
3	4.50	3.00	1.50	1.00	0.50	1.50	
							0.90
4	5.40	3.00	2.40	0.75	0.60	1.35	
							1.10
5	6.50	3.00	3.50	0.60	0.70	1.30	
							1.30
6	7.80	3.00	4.80	0.50	0.80	1.30	
							1.50
7	9.30	3.00	6.30	0.43	0.90	1.33	
							1.70
8	11.00	3.00	8.00	0.38	1.00	1.38	
							1.90
9	12.90	3.00	9.90	0.33	1.10	1.43	
							2.10
10	15.00	3.00	12.00	0.30	1.20	1.50	

[handwritten notes in left margin:]

$\frac{\text{Change in Cost}}{\text{Change in Q}}$

$\frac{3.80 - 3.30}{2 - 1} =$

$\frac{0.5}{1} = 0.50$

$\frac{4.50 - 3.80}{3 - 2} =$

$\frac{0.7}{1} = 0.70$

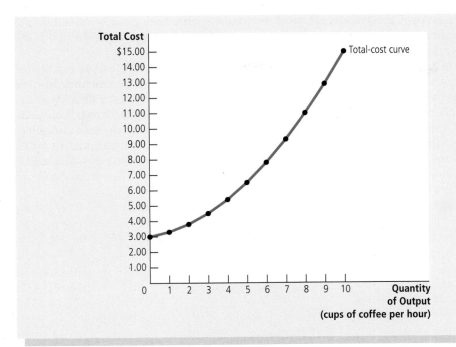

FIGURE 3

Conrad's Total-Cost Curve
Here the quantity of output produced (on the horizontal axis) is from the first column in Table 2, and the total cost (on the vertical axis) is from the second column. As in Figure 2, the total-cost curve gets steeper as the quantity of output increases because of diminishing marginal product.

Some of the firm's costs, called **variable costs**, change as the firm alters the quantity of output produced. Conrad's variable costs include the cost of coffee beans, milk, sugar, and paper cups: The more cups of coffee Conrad makes, the more of these items he needs to buy. Similarly, if Conrad has to hire more workers to make more cups of coffee, the salaries of these workers are variable costs. The fourth column of the table shows Conrad's variable cost. The variable cost is 0 if he produces nothing, $0.30 if he produces 1 cup of coffee, $0.80 if he produces 2 cups, and so on.

A firm's total cost is the sum of fixed and variable costs. In Table 2, total cost in the second column equals fixed cost in the third column plus variable cost in the fourth column.

variable costs
costs that vary with the quantity of output produced

13-3b Average and Marginal Cost

As the owner of his firm, Conrad has to decide how much to produce. One issue he will want to consider when making this decision is how the level of production affects his firm's costs. Conrad might ask his production supervisor the following two questions about the cost of producing coffee:

- How much does it cost to make the typical cup of coffee?
- How much does it cost to increase production of coffee by 1 cup?

These two questions might seem to have the same answer, but they do not. Both answers are important for understanding how firms make production decisions.

To find the cost of the typical unit produced, we divide the firm's costs by the quantity of output it produces. For example, if the firm produces 2 cups of coffee per hour, its total cost is $3.80, and the cost of the typical cup is $3.80/2, or $1.90. Total cost divided by the quantity of output is called **average total cost**. Because total cost is the sum of fixed and variable costs, average total cost can be expressed

average total cost
total cost divided by the quantity of output

average fixed cost
fixed cost divided by the quantity of output

average variable cost
variable cost divided by the quantity of output

marginal cost
the increase in total cost that arises from an extra unit of production

as the sum of average fixed cost and average variable cost. **Average fixed cost** is the fixed cost divided by the quantity of output, and **average variable cost** is the variable cost divided by the quantity of output.

Average total cost tells us the cost of the typical unit, but it does not tell us how much total cost will change as the firm alters its level of production. The last column in Table 2 shows the amount that total cost rises when the firm increases production by 1 unit of output. This number is called **marginal cost**. For example, if Conrad increases production from 2 to 3 cups, total cost rises from $3.80 to $4.50, so the marginal cost of the third cup of coffee is $4.50 minus $3.80, or $0.70. In the table, the marginal cost appears halfway between any two rows because it represents the change in total cost as quantity of output increases from one level to another.

It may be helpful to express these definitions mathematically:

$$\text{Average total cost} = \text{Total cost/Quantity}$$
$$ATC = TC/Q,$$

and

$$\text{Marginal cost} = \text{Change in total cost/Change in quantity}$$
$$MC = \Delta TC/\Delta Q.$$

Here Δ, the Greek letter delta, represents the change in a variable. These equations show how average total cost and marginal cost are derived from total cost. *Average total cost tells us the cost of a typical unit of output if total cost is divided evenly over all the units produced. Marginal cost tells us the increase in total cost that arises from producing an additional unit of output.* As we will see more fully in the next chapter, business managers like Conrad need to keep in mind the concepts of average total cost and marginal cost when deciding how much of their product to supply to the market.

13-3c Cost Curves and Their Shapes

Just as in previous chapters we found graphs of supply and demand useful when analyzing the behavior of markets, we will find graphs of average and marginal cost useful when analyzing the behavior of firms. Figure 4 graphs Conrad's costs using the data from Table 2. The horizontal axis measures the quantity the firm produces, and the vertical axis measures marginal and average costs. The graph shows four curves: average total cost (*ATC*), average fixed cost (*AFC*), average variable cost (*AVC*), and marginal cost (*MC*).

The cost curves shown here for Conrad's Coffee Shop have some features that are common to the cost curves of many firms in the economy. Let's examine three features in particular: the shape of the marginal-cost curve, the shape of the average-total-cost curve, and the relationship between marginal and average total cost.

Rising Marginal Cost   Conrad's marginal cost rises as the quantity of output produced increases. This upward slope reflects the property of diminishing marginal product. When Conrad produces a small quantity of coffee, he has few workers, and much of his equipment is not used. Because he can easily put these idle resources to use, the marginal product of an extra worker is large, and the

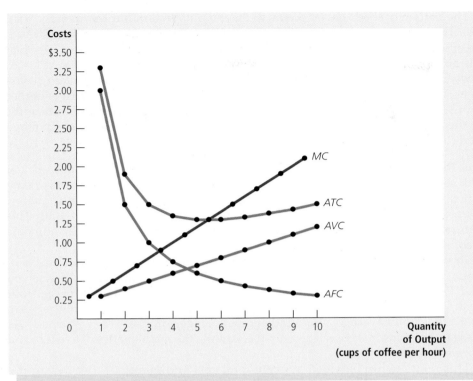

FIGURE 4

Conrad's Average-Cost and Marginal-Cost Curves
This figure shows the average total cost (*ATC*), average fixed cost (*AFC*), average variable cost (*AVC*), and marginal cost (*MC*) for Conrad's Coffee Shop. All of these curves are obtained by graphing the data in Table 2. These cost curves show three features that are typical of many firms: (1) Marginal cost rises with the quantity of output. (2) The average-total-cost curve is U-shaped. (3) The marginal-cost curve crosses the average-total-cost curve at the minimum of average total cost.

marginal cost of an extra cup of coffee is small. By contrast, when Conrad produces a large quantity of coffee, his shop is crowded with workers, and most of his equipment is fully utilized. Conrad can produce more coffee by adding workers, but these new workers have to work in crowded conditions and may have to wait to use the equipment. Therefore, when the quantity of coffee produced is already high, the marginal product of an extra worker is low, and the marginal cost of an extra cup of coffee is large.

U-Shaped Average Total Cost Conrad's average-total-cost curve is U-shaped, as shown in Figure 4. To understand why, remember that average total cost is the sum of average fixed cost and average variable cost. Average fixed cost always declines as output rises because the fixed cost is spread over a larger number of units. Average variable cost typically rises as output increases because of diminishing marginal product.

Average total cost reflects the shapes of both average fixed cost and average variable cost. At very low levels of output, such as 1 or 2 cups per hour, average total cost is very high. Even though average variable cost is low, average fixed cost is high because the fixed cost is spread over only a few units. As output increases, the fixed cost is spread over more units. Average fixed cost declines, rapidly at first and then more slowly. As a result, average total cost also declines until the firm's output reaches 5 cups of coffee per hour, when average total cost is $1.30 per cup. When the firm produces more than 6 cups per hour, however, the increase in average variable cost becomes the dominant force, and average total cost starts rising. The tug of war between average fixed cost and average variable cost generates the U-shape in average total cost.

The bottom of the U-shape occurs at the quantity that minimizes average total cost. This quantity is sometimes called the **efficient scale** of the firm. For Conrad, the efficient scale is 5 or 6 cups of coffee per hour. If he produces more or less than this amount, his average total cost rises above the minimum of $1.30. At lower levels of output, average total cost is higher than $1.30 because the fixed cost is spread over so few units. At higher levels of output, average total cost is higher than $1.30 because the marginal product of inputs has diminished significantly. At the efficient scale, these two forces are balanced to yield the lowest average total cost.

The Relationship between Marginal Cost and Average Total Cost   If you look at Figure 4 (or back at Table 2), you will see something that may be surprising at first. *Whenever marginal cost is less than average total cost, average total cost is falling. Whenever marginal cost is greater than average total cost, average total cost is rising.* This feature of Conrad's cost curves is not a coincidence from the particular numbers used in the example: It is true for all firms.

To see why, consider an analogy. Average total cost is like your cumulative grade point average. Marginal cost is like the grade you get in the next course you take. If your grade in your next course is less than your grade point average, your grade point average will fall. If your grade in your next course is higher than your grade point average, your grade point average will rise. The mathematics of average and marginal costs is exactly the same as the mathematics of average and marginal grades.

This relationship between average total cost and marginal cost has an important corollary: *The marginal-cost curve crosses the average-total-cost curve at its minimum.* Why? At low levels of output, marginal cost is below average total cost, so average total cost is falling. But after the two curves cross, marginal cost rises above average total cost. For the reason we have just discussed, average total cost must start to rise at this level of output. Hence, this point of intersection is the minimum of average total cost. As you will see in the next chapter, minimum average total cost plays a key role in the analysis of competitive firms.

13-3d Typical Cost Curves

In the examples we have studied so far, the firms have exhibited diminishing marginal product and, therefore, rising marginal cost at all levels of output. This simplifying assumption was useful because it allowed us to focus on the key features of cost curves that are useful in analyzing firm behavior. Yet actual firms are usually more complicated than this. In many firms, marginal product does not start to fall immediately after the first worker is hired. Depending on the production process, the second or third worker might have a higher marginal product than the first because a team of workers can divide tasks and work more productively than a single worker. Firms exhibiting this pattern would experience increasing marginal product for a while before diminishing marginal product set in.

Figure 5 shows the cost curves for such a firm, including average total cost (*ATC*), average fixed cost (*AFC*), average variable cost (*AVC*), and marginal cost (*MC*). At low levels of output, the firm experiences increasing marginal product, and the marginal-cost curve falls. Eventually, the firm starts to experience diminishing marginal product, and the marginal-cost curve starts to rise. This combination of increasing then diminishing marginal product also makes the average-variable-cost curve U-shaped.

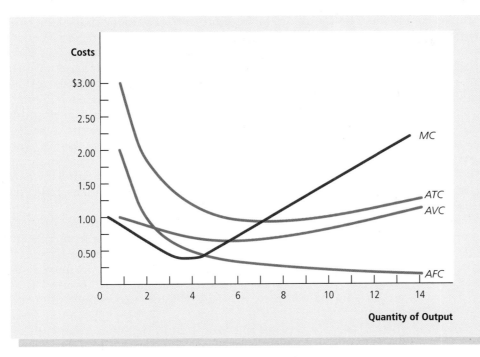

FIGURE 5

Cost Curves for a Typical Firm
Many firms experience increasing marginal product before diminishing marginal product. As a result, they have cost curves shaped like those in this figure. Notice that marginal cost and average variable cost fall for a while before starting to rise.

Despite these differences from our previous example, the cost curves shown in Figure 5 share the three properties that are most important to remember:

- Marginal cost eventually rises with the quantity of output.
- The average-total-cost curve is U-shaped.
- The marginal-cost curve crosses the average-total-cost curve at the minimum of average total cost.

Quick Quiz *Suppose Honda's total cost of producing 4 cars is $225,000 and its total cost of producing 5 cars is $250,000. What is the average total cost of producing 5 cars? What is the marginal cost of the fifth car?* • *Draw the marginal-cost curve and the average-total-cost curve for a typical firm, and explain why these curves cross where they do.*

13-4 Costs in the Short Run and in the Long Run

We noted earlier in this chapter that a firm's costs might depend on the time horizon under consideration. Let's examine more precisely why this might be the case.

13-4a The Relationship between Short-Run and Long-Run Average Total Cost

For many firms, the division of total costs between fixed and variable costs depends on the time horizon. Consider, for instance, a car manufacturer such as Ford Motor Company. Over a period of only a few months, Ford cannot adjust the number or sizes of its car factories. The only way it can produce additional cars is to hire more workers at the factories it already has. The cost of these factories is, therefore, a fixed cost in the short run. By contrast, over a period of several years, Ford can expand the size of its factories, build new factories, or close old ones. Thus, the cost of its factories is a variable cost in the long run.

Because many decisions are fixed in the short run but variable in the long run, a firm's long-run cost curves differ from its short-run cost curves. Figure 6 shows an example. The figure presents three short-run average-total-cost curves—for a small, medium, and large factory. It also presents the long-run average-total-cost curve. As the firm moves along the long-run curve, it is adjusting the size of the factory to the quantity of production.

This graph shows how short-run and long-run costs are related. The long-run average-total-cost curve is a much flatter U-shape than the short-run average-total-cost curve. In addition, all the short-run curves lie on or above the long-run curve. These properties arise because firms have greater flexibility in the long run. In essence, in the long run, the firm gets to choose which short-run curve it wants to use. But in the short run, it has to use whatever short-run curve it has, based on decisions it has made in the past.

The figure shows an example of how a change in production alters costs over different time horizons. When Ford wants to increase production from 1,000 to 1,200 cars per day, it has no choice in the short run but to hire more workers at its existing medium-sized factory. Because of diminishing marginal product, average total cost rises from $10,000 to $12,000 per car. In the long run, however, Ford can expand both the size of the factory and its workforce, and average total cost returns to $10,000.

How long does it take a firm to get to the long run? The answer depends on the firm. It can take a year or more for a major manufacturing firm, such as a car company, to build a larger factory. By contrast, a person running a coffee shop can buy another coffee maker within a few days. There is, therefore, no single answer to the question of how long it takes a firm to adjust its production facilities.

13-4b Economies and Diseconomies of Scale

The shape of the long-run average-total-cost curve conveys important information about the production processes that a firm has available for manufacturing a good. In particular, it tells us how costs vary with the scale—that is, the size—of a firm's operations. When long-run average total cost declines as output increases,

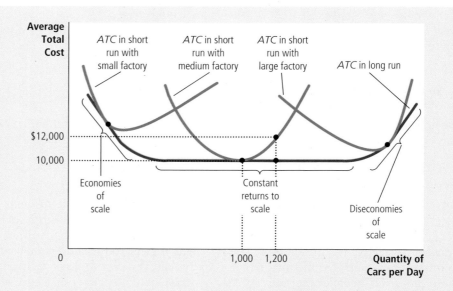

FIGURE 6

Average Total Cost in the Short and Long Runs
Because fixed costs are variable in the long run, the average-total-cost curve in the short run differs from the average-total-cost curve in the long run.

there are said to be **economies of scale**. When long-run average total cost rises as output increases, there are said to be **diseconomies of scale**. When long-run average total cost does not vary with the level of output, there are said to be **constant returns to scale**. As we can see in Figure 6, Ford has economies of scale at low levels of output, constant returns to scale at intermediate levels of output, and diseconomies of scale at high levels of output.

What might cause economies or diseconomies of scale? Economies of scale often arise because higher production levels allow *specialization* among workers, which permits each worker to become better at a specific task. For instance, if Ford hires a large number of workers and produces a large number of cars, it can reduce costs using modern assembly-line production. Diseconomies of scale can arise because of *coordination problems* that are inherent in any large organization. The more cars Ford produces, the more stretched the management team becomes, and the less effective the managers become at keeping costs down.

This analysis shows why long-run average-total-cost curves are often U-shaped. At low levels of production, the firm benefits from increased size because it can take advantage of greater specialization. Coordination problems, meanwhile, are not yet acute. By contrast, at high levels of production, the benefits of specialization have already been realized, and coordination problems become more severe as the firm grows larger. Thus, long-run average total cost is falling at low levels of production because of increasing specialization and rising at high levels of production because of the increasing prevalence of coordination problems.

economies of scale
the property whereby long-run average total cost falls as the quantity of output increases

diseconomies of scale
the property whereby long-run average total cost rises as the quantity of output increases

constant returns to scale
the property whereby long-run average total cost stays the same as the quantity of output changes

Bigger factories have more cost, but they can produce more so average Total cost falls
smaller companies Their cost is less, but each product cost is more — see video

Quick Quiz If Boeing produces 9 jets per month, its long-run total cost is $9.0 million per month. If it produces 10 jets per month, its long-run total cost is $9.5 million per month. Does Boeing exhibit economies or diseconomies of scale?

FYI

Lessons from a Pin Factory

"Jack of all trades, master of none." This well-known adage sheds light on the nature of cost curves. A person who tries to do everything usually ends up doing nothing very well. If a firm wants its workers to be as productive as they can be, it is often best to give each worker a limited task that she can master. But this organization of work is possible only if a firm employs many workers and produces a large quantity of output.

In his celebrated book *An Inquiry into the Nature and Causes of the Wealth of Nations*, Adam Smith described a visit he made to a pin factory. Smith was impressed by the specialization among the workers and the resulting economies of scale. He wrote,

One man draws out the wire, another straightens it, a third cuts it, a fourth points it, a fifth grinds it at the top for receiving the head; to make the head requires two or three distinct operations; to put it on is a peculiar business; to whiten it is another; it is even a trade by itself to put them into paper.

Smith reported that because of this specialization, the pin factory produced thousands of pins per worker every day. He conjectured that if the workers had chosen to work separately, rather than as a team of specialists, "they certainly could not each of them make twenty, perhaps not one pin a day." In other words, because of specialization, a large pin factory could achieve higher output per worker and lower average cost per pin than a small pin factory.

The specialization that Smith observed in the pin factory is prevalent in the modern economy. If you want to build a house, for instance, you could try to do all the work yourself. But most people turn to a builder, who in turn hires carpenters, plumbers, electricians, painters, and many other types of workers. These workers focus their training and experience in particular jobs, and as a result, they become better at their jobs than if they were generalists. Indeed, the use of specialization to achieve economies of scale is one reason modern societies are as prosperous as they are.

13-5 Conclusion

The purpose of this chapter has been to develop some tools to study how firms make production and pricing decisions. You should now understand what economists mean by the term *costs* and how costs vary with the quantity of output a firm produces. To refresh your memory, Table 3 summarizes some of the definitions we have encountered.

By themselves, a firm's cost curves do not tell us what decisions the firm will make. But they are a key component of that decision, as we will see in the next chapter.

TABLE 3

The Many Types of Cost: A Summary

Term	Definition	Mathematical Description
Explicit costs	Costs that require an outlay of money by the firm	
Implicit costs	Costs that do not require an outlay of money by the firm	
Fixed costs	Costs that do not vary with the quantity of output produced	FC
Variable costs	Costs that vary with the quantity of output produced	VC
Total cost	The market value of all the inputs that a firm uses in production	$TC = FC + VC$
Average fixed cost	Fixed cost divided by the quantity of output	$AFC = FC/Q$
Average variable cost	Variable cost divided by the quantity of output	$AVC = VC/Q$
Average total cost	Total cost divided by the quantity of output	$ATC = TC/Q$
Marginal cost	The increase in total cost that arises from an extra unit of production	$MC = \Delta TC/\Delta Q$

Summary

- The goal of firms is to maximize profit, which equals total revenue minus total cost.

- When analyzing a firm's behavior, it is important to include all the opportunity costs of production. Some of the opportunity costs, such as the wages a firm pays its workers, are explicit. Other opportunity costs, such as the wages the firm owner gives up by working at the firm rather than taking another job, are implicit.

- Economic profit takes both explicit and implicit costs into account, whereas accounting profit considers only explicit costs.

- A firm's costs reflect its production process. A typical firm's production function gets flatter as the quantity of an input increases, displaying the property of diminishing marginal product. As a result, a firm's total-cost curve gets steeper as the quantity produced rises.

- A firm's total costs can be divided between fixed costs and variable costs. Fixed costs are costs that do not change when the firm alters the quantity of output produced. Variable costs are costs that change when the firm alters the quantity of output produced.

- From a firm's total cost, two related measures of cost are derived. Average total cost is total cost divided by the quantity of output. Marginal cost is the amount by which total cost rises if output increases by 1 unit.

- When analyzing firm behavior, it is often useful to graph average total cost and marginal cost. For a typical firm, marginal cost rises with the quantity of output. Average total cost first falls as output increases and then rises as output increases further. The marginal-cost curve always crosses the average-total-cost curve at the minimum of average total cost.

- A firm's costs often depend on the time horizon considered. In particular, many costs are fixed in the short run but variable in the long run. As a result, when the firm changes its level of production, average total cost may rise more in the short run than in the long run.

Key Concepts

total revenue, *p. 260*
total cost, *p. 260*
profit, *p. 260*
explicit costs, *p. 261*
implicit costs, *p. 261*
economic profit, *p. 262*
accounting profit, *p. 262*

production function, *p. 263*
marginal product, *p. 264*
diminishing marginal product, *p. 265*
fixed costs, *p. 266*
variable costs, *p. 267*
average total cost, *p. 267*
average fixed cost, *p. 268*

average variable cost, *p. 268*
marginal cost, *p. 268*
efficient scale, *p. 270*
economies of scale, *p. 273*
diseconomies of scale, *p. 273*
constant returns to scale, *p. 273*

Questions for Review

1. What is the relationship between a firm's total revenue, profit, and total cost?

2. Give an example of an opportunity cost that an accountant might not count as a cost. Why would the accountant ignore this cost?

3. What is marginal product, and what does it mean if it is diminishing?

4. Draw a production function that exhibits diminishing marginal product of labor. Draw the associated total-cost curve. (In both cases, be sure to label the axes.) Explain the shapes of the two curves you have drawn.

5. Define *total cost, average total cost,* and *marginal cost.* How are they related?

6. Draw the marginal-cost and average-total-cost curves for a typical firm. Explain why the curves have the shapes that they do and why they cross where they do.

7. How and why does a firm's average-total-cost curve differ in the short run and in the long run?

8. Define *economies of scale* and explain why they might arise. Define *diseconomies of scale* and explain why they might arise.

Quick Check Multiple Choice

1. Raj opens up a lemonade stand for two hours. He spends $10 for ingredients and sells $60 worth of lemonade. In the same two hours, he could have mowed his neighbor's lawn for $40. Raj has an accounting profit of _____ and an economic profit of _____.
   a. $50, $10
   b. $90, $50
   c. $10, $50
   d. $50, $90

2. Diminishing marginal product explains why, as a firm's output increases,
   a. the production function and total-cost curve both get steeper.
   b. the production function and total-cost curve both get flatter.
   c. the production function gets steeper, while the total-cost curve gets flatter.
   d. the production function gets flatter, while the total-cost curve gets steeper.

3. A firm is producing 1,000 units at a total cost of $5,000. If it were to increase production to 1,001 units, its total cost would rise to $5,008. What does this information tell you about the firm?
   a. Marginal cost is $5, and average variable cost is $8.
   b. Marginal cost is $8, and average variable cost is $5.
   c. Marginal cost is $5, and average total cost is $8.
   d. Marginal cost is $8, and average total cost is $5.

4. A firm is producing 20 units with an average total cost of $25 and marginal cost of $15. If it were to increase production to 21 units, which of the following must occur?
   a. Marginal cost would decrease.
   b. Marginal cost would increase.
   c. Average total cost would decrease.
   d. Average total cost would increase.

5. The government imposes a $1,000 per year license fee on all pizza restaurants. Which cost curves shift as a result?
   a. average total cost and marginal cost
   b. average total cost and average fixed cost
   c. average variable cost and marginal cost
   d. average variable cost and average fixed cost

6. If a higher level of production allows workers to specialize in particular tasks, a firm will likely exhibit _____ of scale and _____ average total cost.
   a. economies, falling
   b. economies, rising
   c. diseconomies, falling
   d. diseconomies, rising

Problems and Applications

1. This chapter discusses many types of costs: opportunity cost, total cost, fixed cost, variable cost, average total cost, and marginal cost. Fill in the type of cost that best completes each sentence:
   a. What you give up for taking some action is called the _____.
   b. _____ is falling when marginal cost is below it and rising when marginal cost is above it.
   c. A cost that does not depend on the quantity produced is a(n) _____.
   d. In the ice-cream industry in the short run, _____ includes the cost of cream and sugar but not the cost of the factory.
   e. Profits equal total revenue minus _____.
   f. The cost of producing an extra unit of output is the _____.

2. Your aunt is thinking about opening a hardware store. She estimates that it would cost $500,000 per year to rent the location and buy the stock. In addition, she would have to quit her $50,000 per year job as an accountant.
   a. Define *opportunity cost*.
   b. What is your aunt's opportunity cost of running a hardware store for a year? If your aunt thinks she can sell $510,000 worth of merchandise in a year, should she open the store? Explain.

3. A commercial fisherman notices the following relationship between hours spent fishing and the quantity of fish caught:

Hours	Quantity of Fish (in pounds)
0	0
1	10
2	18
3	24
4	28
5	30

a. What is the marginal product of each hour spent fishing?
b. Use these data to graph the fisherman's production function. Explain its shape.
c. The fisherman has a fixed cost of $10 (his pole). The opportunity cost of his time is $5 per hour. Graph the fisherman's total-cost curve. Explain its shape.

4. Nimbus, Inc., makes brooms and then sells them door-to-door. Here is the relationship between the number of workers and Nimbus's output in a given day:

Workers	Output	Marginal Product	Total Cost	Average Total Cost	Marginal Cost
0	0		—	—	
1	20		—	—	
2	50		—	—	
3	90		—	—	
4	120		—	—	
5	140		—	—	
6	150		—	—	
7	155		—	—	

a. Fill in the column of marginal products. What pattern do you see? How might you explain it?
b. A worker costs $100 a day, and the firm has fixed costs of $200. Use this information to fill in the column for total cost.
c. Fill in the column for average total cost. (Recall that $ATC=TC/Q$.) What pattern do you see?

d. Now fill in the column for marginal cost. (Recall that $MC = \Delta TC/\Delta Q$.) What pattern do you see?

e. Compare the column for marginal product and the column for marginal cost. Explain the relationship.

f. Compare the column for average total cost and the column for marginal cost. Explain the relationship.

5. You are the chief financial officer for a firm that sells digital music players. Your firm has the following average-total-cost schedule:

Quantity	Average Total Cost
600 players	$300
601	301

Your current level of production is 600 devices, all of which have been sold. Someone calls, desperate to buy one of your music players. The caller offers you $550 for it. Should you accept the offer? Why or why not?

6. Consider the following cost information for a pizzeria:

Quantity	Total Cost	Variable Cost
0 dozen pizzas	$300	$0
1	350	50
2	390	90
3	420	120
4	450	150
5	490	190
6	540	240

a. What is the pizzeria's fixed cost?

b. Construct a table in which you calculate the marginal cost per dozen pizzas using the information on total cost. Also, calculate the marginal cost per dozen pizzas using the information on variable cost. What is the relationship between these sets of numbers? Comment.

7. Your cousin Vinnie owns a painting company with fixed costs of $200 and the following schedule for variable costs:

Quantity of Houses Painted per Month	1	2	3	4	5	6	7
Variable Costs	$10	$20	$40	$80	$160	$320	$640

Calculate average fixed cost, average variable cost, and average total cost for each quantity. What is the efficient scale of the painting company?

8. The city government is considering two tax proposals:

- A lump-sum tax of $300 on each producer of hamburgers.
- A tax of $1 per burger, paid by producers of hamburgers.

a. Which of the following curves—average fixed cost, average variable cost, average total cost, and marginal cost—would shift as a result of the lump-sum tax? Why? Show this in a graph. Label the graph as precisely as possible.

b. Which of these same four curves would shift as a result of the per-burger tax? Why? Show this in a new graph. Label the graph as precisely as possible.

9. Jane's Juice Bar has the following cost schedules:

Quantity	Variable Cost	Total Cost
0 vats of juice	$ 0	$ 30
1	10	40
2	25	55
3	45	75
4	70	100
5	100	130
6	135	165

a. Calculate average variable cost, average total cost, and marginal cost for each quantity.

b. Graph all three curves. What is the relationship between the marginal-cost curve and the average-total-cost curve? Between the marginal-cost curve and the average-variable-cost curve? Explain.

10. Consider the following table of long-run total costs for three different firms:

Quantity	1	2	3	4	5	6	7
Firm A	$60	$70	$80	$90	$100	$110	$120
Firm B	11	24	39	56	75	96	119
Firm C	21	34	49	66	85	106	129

Does each of these firms experience economies of scale or diseconomies of scale?

Go to CengageBrain.com to purchase access to the proven, critical Study Guide to accompany this text, which features additional notes and context, practice tests, and much more.

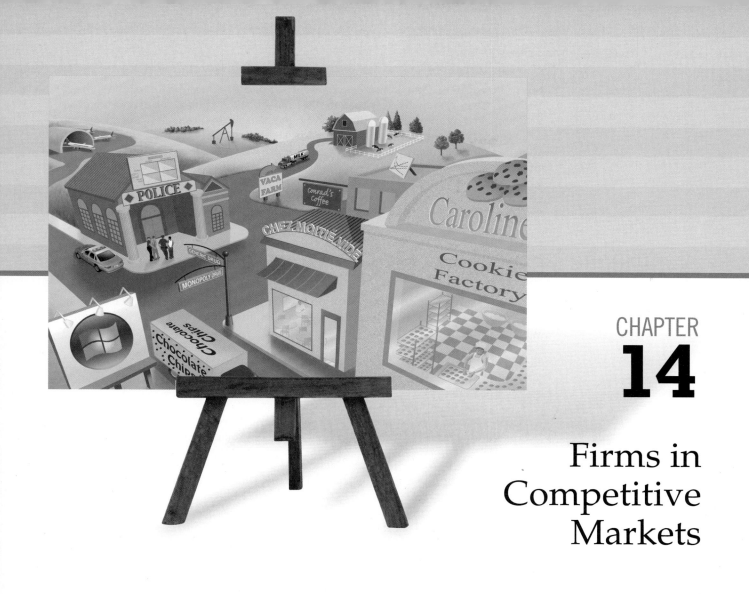

CHAPTER
14

Firms in Competitive Markets

I f your local gas station raised its price for gasoline by 20 percent, it would see a large drop in the amount of gasoline it sold. Its customers would quickly switch to buying their gasoline at other gas stations. By contrast, if your local water company raised the price of water by 20 percent, it would see only a small decrease in the amount of water it sold. People might water their lawns less often and buy more water-efficient showerheads, but they would be hard-pressed to reduce water consumption greatly and would be unlikely to find another supplier. The difference between the gasoline market and the water market is that many firms supply gasoline to the local market, but only one firm supplies water. As you might expect, this difference in market structure shapes the pricing and production decisions of the firms that operate in these markets.

In this chapter, we examine the behavior of competitive firms, such as your local gas station. You may recall that a market is competitive if each buyer and seller is small compared to the size of the market and, therefore, has little ability to influence market prices. By contrast, if a firm can influence the market price of the good it sells, it is said to have *market power*. Later in the book, we examine the behavior of firms with market power, such as your local water company.

Our analysis of competitive firms in this chapter sheds light on the decisions that lie behind the supply curve in a competitive market. Not surprisingly, we find that a market supply curve is tightly linked to firms' costs of production. Less obvious, however, is the question of which among a firm's many types of cost—fixed, variable, average, and marginal—are most relevant for its supply decisions. We see that all these measures of cost play important and interrelated roles.

14-1 What Is a Competitive Market? = Perfectly competitive Market

Our goal in this chapter is to examine how firms make production decisions in competitive markets. As a background for this analysis, we begin by reviewing what a competitive market is.

14-1a The Meaning of Competition

competitive market
a market with many buyers and sellers trading identical products so that each buyer and seller is a price taker

A **competitive market**, sometimes called a *perfectly competitive market*, has two characteristics:

- There are many buyers and many sellers in the market.
- The goods offered by the various sellers are largely the same.

As a result of these conditions, the actions of any single buyer or seller in the market have a negligible impact on the market price. Each buyer and seller takes the market price as given.

As an example, consider the market for milk. No single consumer of milk can influence the price of milk because each buys a small amount relative to the size of the market. Similarly, each dairy farmer has limited control over the price because many other sellers are offering milk that is essentially identical. Because each seller can sell all he wants at the going price, he has little reason to charge less, and if he charges more, buyers will go elsewhere. Buyers and sellers in competitive markets must accept the price the market determines and, therefore, are said to be *price takers*.

In addition to the previous two conditions for competition, a third condition is sometimes thought to characterize perfectly competitive markets:

- Firms can freely enter or exit the market.

If, for instance, anyone can decide to start a dairy farm, and if any existing dairy farmer can decide to leave the dairy business, then the dairy industry satisfies this condition. Much of the analysis of competitive firms does not need the assumption of free entry and exit because this condition is not necessary for firms to be price takers. Yet, as we see later in this chapter, when there is free entry and exit in a competitive market, it is a powerful force shaping the long-run equilibrium.

14-1b The Revenue of a Competitive Firm

A firm in a competitive market, like most other firms in the economy, tries to maximize profit (total revenue minus total cost). To see how it does this, we first consider the revenue of a competitive firm. To keep matters concrete, let's consider a specific firm: the Vaca Family Dairy Farm.

The Vaca Farm produces a quantity of milk, Q, and sells each unit at the market price, P. The farm's total revenue is $P \times Q$. For example, if a gallon of milk sells for $6 and the farm sells 1,000 gallons, its total revenue is $6,000.

Because the Vaca Farm is small compared to the world market for milk, it takes the price as given by market conditions. This means, in particular, that the price of milk does not depend on the number of gallons that the Vaca Farm produces and sells. If the Vacas double the amount of milk they produce to 2,000 gallons, the price of milk remains the same, and their total revenue doubles to $12,000. As a result, total revenue is proportional to the amount of output.

Table 1 shows the revenue for the Vaca Family Dairy Farm. The first two columns show the amount of output the farm produces and the price at which it sells its output. The third column is the farm's total revenue. The table assumes that the price of milk is $6 a gallon, so total revenue is $6 times the number of gallons.

Just as the concepts of average and marginal were useful in the preceding chapter when analyzing costs, they are also useful when analyzing revenue. To see what these concepts tell us, consider these two questions:

- How much revenue does the farm receive for the typical gallon of milk?
- How much additional revenue does the farm receive if it increases production of milk by 1 gallon?

The last two columns in Table 1 answer these questions.

The fourth column in the table shows **average revenue**, which is total revenue (from the third column) divided by the amount of output (from the first column). Average revenue tells us how much revenue a firm receives for the typical unit sold. In Table 1, you can see that average revenue equals $6, the price of a gallon of milk. This illustrates a general lesson that applies not only to competitive firms but to other firms as well. Average revenue is total revenue ($P \times Q$) divided by the quantity (Q). Therefore, *for all types of firms, average revenue equals the price of the good.*

average revenue
total revenue divided by the quantity sold

Handwritten margin notes: Since competitive market is price Taker, the price is fixed. Company raises more revenue by Producing more, not by raising the price. Because they can't. if they raise price, customers have many other choices — milk

Handwritten above table: Price does not change in Competitive market

Handwritten above Total Revenue column: Total Rev ÷ output

Quantity (Q)	Price (P)	Total Revenue (TR = P × Q)	Average Revenue (AR = TR / Q)	Marginal Revenue (MR = ΔTR / ΔQ)	
					TABLE 1
					Total, Average, and Marginal Revenue for a Competitive Firm
1 gallon	$6	$6	$6		
				$6	
2	6	12	12 ÷ 2 = 6		
				6 = 6/1 = 6	
3	6	18	18 ÷ 3 = 6		
				6	
4	6	6×4 = 24	24 ÷ 4 = 6		
				6 → change in revenue ÷ change in Q	
5	6	5×6 = 30	30 ÷ 5 = 6		6/1 = 6
				6	
6	6	6×6 = 36	36 ÷ 6 = 6		
				6	
7	6	7×6 = 42	42 ÷ 7 = 6		
				6	
8	6	8×6 = 48	48 ÷ 8 = 6		

Handwritten note by MR column: Total

marginal revenue
the change in total revenue from an additional unit sold

The fifth column shows **marginal revenue**, which is the change in total revenue from the sale of each additional unit of output. In Table 1, marginal revenue equals $6, the price of a gallon of milk. This result illustrates a lesson that applies only to competitive firms. Total revenue is $P \times Q$, and P is fixed for a competitive firm. Therefore, when Q rises by 1 unit, total revenue rises by P dollars. *For competitive firms, marginal revenue equals the price of the good.*

Quick Quiz *When a competitive firm doubles the amount it sells, what happens to the price of its output and its total revenue?*

14-2 Profit Maximization and the Competitive Firm's Supply Curve

The goal of a firm is to maximize profit, which equals total revenue minus total cost. We have just discussed the competitive firm's revenue, and in the preceding chapter, we discussed the firm's costs. We are now ready to examine how a competitive firm maximizes profit and how that decision determines its supply curve.

14-2a A Simple Example of Profit Maximization

Let's begin our analysis of the firm's supply decision with the example in Table 2. In the first column of the table is the number of gallons of milk the Vaca Family Dairy Farm produces. The second column shows the farm's total revenue, which is $6 times the number of gallons. The third column shows the farm's total cost. Total cost includes fixed costs, which are $3 in this example, and variable costs, which depend on the quantity produced.

The fourth column shows the farm's profit, which is computed by subtracting total cost from total revenue. If the farm produces nothing, it has a loss of $3 (its fixed cost). If it produces 1 gallon, it has a profit of $1. If it produces 2 gallons, it has a profit of $4 and so on. Because the Vaca family's goal is to maximize profit, it chooses to produce the quantity of milk that makes profit as large as possible. In this example, profit is maximized when the farm produces either 4 or 5 gallons of milk, for a profit of $7.

There is another way to look at the Vaca Farm's decision: The Vacas can find the profit-maximizing quantity by comparing the marginal revenue and marginal cost from each unit produced. The fifth and sixth columns in Table 2 compute marginal revenue and marginal cost from the changes in total revenue and total cost, and the last column shows the change in profit for each additional gallon produced. The first gallon of milk the farm produces has a marginal revenue of $6 and a marginal cost of $2; hence, producing that gallon increases profit by $4 (from −$3 to $1). The second gallon produced has a marginal revenue of $6 and a marginal cost of $3, so that gallon increases profit by $3 (from $1 to $4). As long as marginal revenue exceeds marginal cost, increasing the quantity produced raises profit. Once the Vaca Farm has reached 5 gallons of milk, however, the situation changes. The sixth gallon would have a marginal revenue of $6 and a marginal cost of $7, so producing it would reduce profit by $1 (from $7 to $6). As a result, the Vacas would not produce beyond 5 gallons.

One of the *Ten Principles of Economics* in Chapter 1 is that rational people think at the margin. We now see how the Vaca Family Dairy Farm can apply this principle. If marginal revenue is greater than marginal cost—as it is at 1, 2, or 3 gallons—the

[handwritten: 6 = Price of one gallon — Fixed]
[handwritten: $3 = Fixed cost Then add variable]

TABLE 2

Profit Maximization: A Numerical Example

Quantity (Q)	Total Revenue (TR)	Total Cost (TC)	Profit (TR − TC)	Marginal Revenue (MR = ΔTR / ΔQ)	Marginal Cost (MC = ΔTC / ΔQ)	Change in Profit (MR − MC)
0 gallons	$ 0	$ 3	−$3			
				$6	$2	$4
1	6	5	1			
				6	3	3
2	12	8	4			
				6	4	2
3	18	12	6			
				6	5	1
4	24	17	7			
				6	6	0
5	30	23	7			
				6	7	−1
6	36	30	6			
				6	8	−2
7	42	38	4			
				6	9	−3
8	48	47	1			

[handwritten annotations: 0−3 −$3; 3+2; 6−5 1; 5+3; 12−8 4; 8+4; 18−12 6; 12+5; "most profit"; 6−2 = $4; 6−3 = 3; 4·1=1; 4:1:1; 6−6 = 0; 6−7 = −1; 6−8 = −2; 6−9 = −3; "marginal Rev higher than marginal cost = max profit"]

Vacas should increase the production of milk because it will put more money in their pockets (marginal revenue) than it takes out (marginal cost). If marginal revenue is less than marginal cost—as it is at 6, 7, or 8 gallons—the Vacas should decrease production. If the Vacas think at the margin and make incremental adjustments to the level of production, they end up producing the profit-maximizing quantity.

14-2b The Marginal-Cost Curve and the Firm's Supply Decision

To extend this analysis of profit maximization, consider the cost curves in Figure 1. These cost curves have the three features that, as we discussed in the previous chapter, are thought to describe most firms: The marginal-cost curve (MC) is upward sloping. The average-total-cost curve (ATC) is U-shaped. And the marginal-cost curve crosses the average-total-cost curve at the minimum of average total cost. The figure also shows a horizontal line at the market price (P). The price line is horizontal because a competitive firm is a price taker: The price of the firm's output is the same regardless of the quantity that the firm decides to produce. Keep in mind that, for a competitive firm, the firm's price equals both its average revenue (AR) and its marginal revenue (MR).

We can use Figure 1 to find the quantity of output that maximizes profit. Imagine that the firm is producing at Q_1. At this level of output, the marginal-revenue curve is above the marginal-cost curve, showing that marginal revenue is greater than marginal cost. This means that if the firm were to raise production by 1 unit, the additional revenue (MR_1) would exceed the additional cost (MC_1). Profit, which equals total revenue minus total cost, would increase. Hence, if marginal revenue is greater than marginal cost, as it is at Q_1, the firm can increase profit by increasing production.

FIGURE 1

Profit Maximization for a Competitive Firm

This figure shows the marginal-cost curve (MC), the average-total-cost curve (ATC), and the average-variable-cost curve (AVC). It also shows the market price (P), which for a competitive firm equals both marginal revenue (MR) and average revenue (AR). At the quantity Q_1, marginal revenue MR_1 exceeds marginal cost MC_1, so raising production increases profit. At the quantity Q_2, marginal cost MC_2 is above marginal revenue MR_2, so reducing production increases profit. The profit-maximizing quantity Q_{MAX} is found where the horizontal line representing the price intersects the marginal-cost curve.

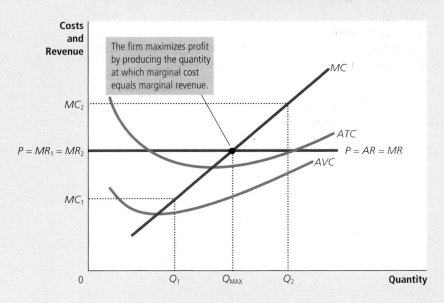

A similar argument applies when output is at Q_2. In this case, the marginal-cost curve is above the marginal-revenue curve, showing that marginal cost is greater than marginal revenue. If the firm were to reduce production by 1 unit, the costs saved (MC_2) would exceed the revenue lost (MR_2). Therefore, if marginal revenue is less than marginal cost, as it is at Q_2, the firm can increase profit by reducing production.

Where do these marginal adjustments to production end? Regardless of whether the firm begins with production at a low level (such as Q_1) or at a high level (such as Q_2), the firm will eventually adjust production until the quantity produced reaches Q_{MAX}. This analysis yields three general rules for profit maximization:

- If marginal revenue is greater than marginal cost, the firm should increase its output.
- If marginal cost is greater than marginal revenue, the firm should decrease its output.
- At the profit-maximizing level of output, marginal revenue and marginal cost are exactly equal.

These rules are the key to rational decision making by any profit-maximizing firm. They apply not only to competitive firms but, as we will see in the next chapter, to other types of firms as well.

We can now see how the competitive firm decides what quantity of its good to supply to the market. Because a competitive firm is a price taker, its marginal revenue equals the market price. For any given price, the competitive firm's profit-maximizing quantity of output is found by looking at the intersection of the price with the marginal-cost curve. In Figure 1, that quantity of output is Q_{MAX}.

Suppose that the price prevailing in this market rises, perhaps because of an increase in market demand. Figure 2 shows how a competitive firm responds to the price increase. When the price is P_1, the firm produces quantity Q_1, the quantity that equates marginal cost to the price. When the price rises to P_2, the firm finds that marginal revenue is now higher than marginal cost at the previous level of output, so the firm increases production. The new profit-maximizing quantity is Q_2, at which marginal cost equals the new, higher price. *In essence, because the firm's marginal-cost curve determines the quantity of the good the firm is willing to supply at any price, the marginal-cost curve is also the competitive firm's supply curve.* There are, however, some caveats to that conclusion, which we examine next.

14-2c The Firm's Short-Run Decision to Shut Down

So far, we have been analyzing the question of how much a competitive firm will produce. In certain circumstances, however, the firm will decide to shut down and not produce anything at all.

Here we need to distinguish between a temporary shutdown of a firm and the permanent exit of a firm from the market. A *shutdown* refers to a short-run decision not to produce anything during a specific period of time because of current market conditions. *Exit* refers to a long-run decision to leave the market. The short-run and long-run decisions differ because most firms cannot avoid their fixed costs in the short run but can do so in the long run. That is, a firm that shuts down temporarily still has to pay its fixed costs, whereas a firm that exits the market does not have to pay any costs at all, fixed or variable.

For example, consider the production decision that a farmer faces. The cost of the land is one of the farmer's fixed costs. If the farmer decides not to produce any crops one season, the land lies fallow, and he cannot recover this cost. When making the short-run decision of whether to shut down for a season, the fixed cost of land is said to be a *sunk cost*. By contrast, if the farmer decides to leave farming altogether, he can sell the land. When making the long-run decision of whether to exit the market, the cost of land is not sunk. (We return to the issue of sunk costs shortly.)

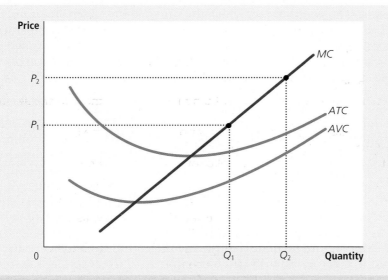

Price

P_2

P_1

MC

ATC

AVC

0 Q_1 Q_2 **Quantity**

FIGURE 2

Marginal Cost as the Competitive Firm's Supply Curve
An increase in the price from P_1 to P_2 leads to an increase in the firm's profit-maximizing quantity from Q_1 to Q_2. Because the marginal-cost curve shows the quantity supplied by the firm at any given price, it is the firm's supply curve.

[handwritten margin note: IF revenue is less than variable cost = shutdown   was on test]

Now let's consider what determines a firm's shutdown decision. If the firm shuts down, it loses all revenue from the sale of its product. At the same time, it saves the variable costs of making its product (but must still pay the fixed costs). Thus, *the firm shuts down if the revenue that it would earn from producing is less than its variable costs of production.*

A bit of mathematics can make this shutdown rule more useful. If *TR* stands for total revenue and *VC* stands for variable cost, then the firm's decision can be written as

$$\text{Shut down if } TR < VC.$$

The firm shuts down if total revenue is less than variable cost. By dividing both sides of this inequality by the quantity *Q*, we can write it as

$$\text{Shut down if } TR/Q < VC/Q.$$

[handwritten: P × Q]

The left side of the inequality, *TR/Q*, is total revenue $P \times Q$ divided by quantity *Q*, which is average revenue, most simply expressed as the good's price, *P*. The right side of the inequality, *VC/Q*, is average variable cost, *AVC*. Therefore, the firm's shutdown rule can be restated as

$$\text{Shut down if } P < AVC.$$

[handwritten margin note: Price of good   IF P < AVC shutdown]

That is, a firm chooses to shut down if the price of the good is less than the average variable cost of production. This criterion is intuitive: When choosing to produce, the firm compares the price it receives for the typical unit to the average variable cost that it must incur to produce the typical unit. If the price doesn't cover the average variable cost, the firm is better off stopping production altogether. The firm still loses money (because it has to pay fixed costs), but it would lose even more money by staying open. The firm can reopen in the future if conditions change so that price exceeds average variable cost.

[handwritten margin note: Stay in business   MC = good's price]

We now have a full description of a competitive firm's profit-maximizing strategy. If the firm produces anything, it produces the quantity at which marginal cost equals the good's price, which the firm takes as given. Yet if the price is less than average variable cost at that quantity, the firm is better off shutting down temporarily and not producing anything. These results are illustrated in Figure 3. *The competitive firm's short-run supply curve is the portion of its marginal-cost curve that lies above average variable cost.*

14-2d Spilt Milk and Other Sunk Costs *[handwritten: = spilt milk]*

Sometime in your life you may have been told, "Don't cry over spilt milk," or "Let bygones be bygones." These adages hold a deep truth about rational decision making. Economists say that a cost is a **sunk cost** when it has already been committed and cannot be recovered. Because nothing can be done about sunk costs, you should ignore them when making decisions about various aspects of life, including business strategy.

Our analysis of the firm's shutdown decision is one example of the irrelevance of sunk costs. We assume that the firm cannot recover its fixed costs by temporarily stopping production. That is, regardless of the quantity of output supplied (even if it is zero), the firm still has to pay its fixed costs. As a result, the fixed costs are sunk in the short run, and the firm should ignore them when deciding how much to produce. The firm's short-run supply curve is the part of the

sunk cost

a cost that has already been committed and cannot be recovered

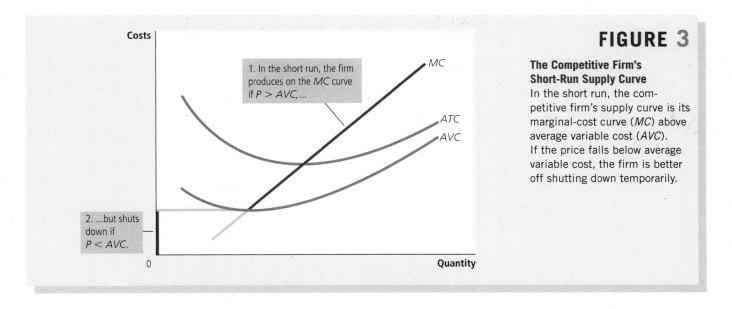

FIGURE 3

The Competitive Firm's Short-Run Supply Curve
In the short run, the competitive firm's supply curve is its marginal-cost curve (*MC*) above average variable cost (*AVC*). If the price falls below average variable cost, the firm is better off shutting down temporarily.

marginal-cost curve that lies above average variable cost, and the size of the fixed cost does not matter for this supply decision.

The irrelevance of sunk costs is also important when making personal decisions. Imagine, for instance, that you place a $15 value on seeing a newly released movie. You buy a ticket for $10, but before entering the theater, you lose the ticket. Should you buy another ticket? Or should you now go home and refuse to pay a total of $20 to see the movie? The answer is that you should buy another ticket. The benefit of seeing the movie ($15) still exceeds the opportunity cost (the $10 for the second ticket). The $10 you paid for the lost ticket is a sunk cost. As with spilt milk, there is no point in crying about it.

case study **Near-Empty Restaurants and Off-Season Miniature Golf**
Have you ever walked into a restaurant for lunch and found it almost empty? Why, you might have asked, does the restaurant even bother to stay open? It might seem that the revenue from so few customers could not possibly cover the cost of running the restaurant.

In making the decision of whether to open for lunch, a restaurant owner must keep in mind the distinction between fixed and variable costs. Many of a restaurant's costs—the rent, kitchen equipment, tables, plates, silverware, and so on—are fixed. Shutting down during lunch would not reduce these costs. In other words, these costs are sunk in the short run. When the owner is deciding whether to serve lunch, only the variable costs—the price of the additional food and the wages of the extra staff—are relevant. The owner shuts down the restaurant at lunchtime only if the revenue from the few lunchtime customers fails to cover the restaurant's variable costs.

An operator of a miniature-golf course in a summer resort community faces a similar decision. Because revenue varies substantially from season to season, the firm must decide when to open and when to close. Once again, the fixed costs—the costs of buying the land and building the course—are irrelevant in making this short-run decision. The miniature-golf course should be open for business only during those times of year when its revenue exceeds its variable costs. ◢

Staying open can be profitable, even with many tables empty.

[handwritten margin notes: "Exit", "Exit/shutdown if Revenue less than Total cost", "shutdown Revenue less than variable cost", "P < ATC Exit"]

14-2e The Firm's Long-Run Decision to Exit or Enter a Market

A firm's long-run decision to exit a market is similar to its shutdown decision. If the firm exits, it will again lose all revenue from the sale of its product, but now it will save not only its variable costs of production but also its fixed costs. Thus, *the firm exits the market if the revenue it would get from producing is less than its total costs.*

We can again make this criterion more useful by writing it mathematically. If TR stands for total revenue, and TC stands for total cost, then the firm's exit rule can be written as

$$\text{Exit if } TR < TC.$$

The firm exits if total revenue is less than total cost. By dividing both sides of this inequality by quantity Q, we can write it as

$$\text{Exit if } TR/Q < TC/Q.$$

We can simplify this further by noting that TR/Q is average revenue, which equals the price P, and that TC/Q is average total cost, ATC. Therefore, the firm's exit rule is

$$\text{Exit if } P < ATC.$$

That is, a firm chooses to exit if the price of its good is less than the average total cost of production.

A parallel analysis applies to an entrepreneur who is considering starting a firm. He will enter the market if starting a firm would be profitable, which occurs if the price of the good exceeds the average total cost of production. The entry rule is

$$\text{Enter if } P > ATC.$$

The rule for entry is exactly the opposite of the rule for exit.

We can now describe a competitive firm's long-run profit-maximizing strategy. If the firm produces anything, it chooses the quantity at which marginal cost equals the price of the good. Yet if the price is less than the average total cost at that quantity, the firm chooses to exit (or not enter) the market. These results are illustrated in Figure 4. *The competitive firm's long-run supply curve is the portion of its marginal-cost curve that lies above average total cost.*

14-2f Measuring Profit in Our Graph for the Competitive Firm

As we study exit and entry, it is useful to analyze the firm's profit in more detail. Recall that profit equals total revenue (TR) minus total cost (TC):

$$\text{Profit} = TR - TC.$$

We can rewrite this definition by multiplying and dividing the right side by Q:

$$\text{Profit} = (TR/Q - TC/Q) \times Q.$$

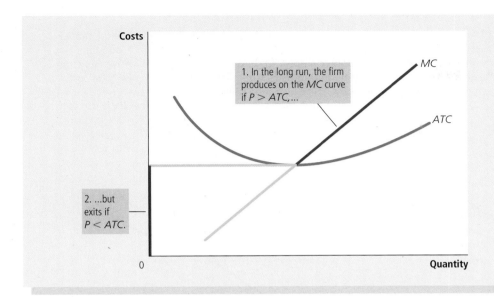

Costs

1. In the long run, the firm produces on the *MC* curve if *P* > *ATC,...*

MC

ATC

2. ...but exits if *P* < *ATC*.

0 **Quantity**

FIGURE 4

The Competitive Firm's Long-Run Supply Curve
In the long run, the competitive firm's supply curve is its marginal-cost curve (*MC*) above average total cost (*ATC*). If the price falls below average total cost, the firm is better off exiting the market.

But note that TR/Q is average revenue, which is the price, P, and TC/Q is average total cost, ATC. Therefore,

$$\text{Profit} = (P - ATC) \times Q.$$

This way of expressing the firm's profit allows us to measure profit in our graphs.

Panel (a) of Figure 5 shows a firm earning positive profit. As we have already discussed, the firm maximizes profit by producing the quantity at which price equals marginal cost. Now look at the shaded rectangle. The height of the rectangle is $P - ATC$, the difference between price and average total cost. The width of the rectangle is Q, the quantity produced. Therefore, the area of the rectangle is $(P - ATC) \times Q$, which is the firm's profit.

Similarly, panel (b) of Figure 5 shows a firm with losses (negative profit). In this case, maximizing profit means minimizing losses, a task accomplished once again by producing the quantity at which price equals marginal cost. Now consider the shaded rectangle. The height of the rectangle is $ATC - P$, and the width is Q. The area is $(ATC - P) \times Q$, which is the firm's loss. Because a firm in this situation is not making enough revenue on each unit to cover its average total cost, it would choose to exit the market in the long run.

Quick Quiz *How does a competitive firm determine its profit-maximizing level of output? Explain. • When does a profit-maximizing competitive firm decide to shut down? When does it decide to exit a market?*

14-3 The Supply Curve in a Competitive Market

Now that we have examined the supply decision of a single firm, we can discuss the supply curve for a market. There are two cases to consider. First, we examine a market with a fixed number of firms. Second, we examine a market in which

FIGURE 5

Profit as the Area between Price
and Average Total Cost

The area of the shaded box between price and average total cost represents the firm's
profit. The height of this box is price minus average total cost ($P - ATC$), and the
width of the box is the quantity of output (Q). In panel (a), price is above average total
cost, so the firm has positive profit. In panel (b), price is less than average total cost,
so the firm incurs a loss.

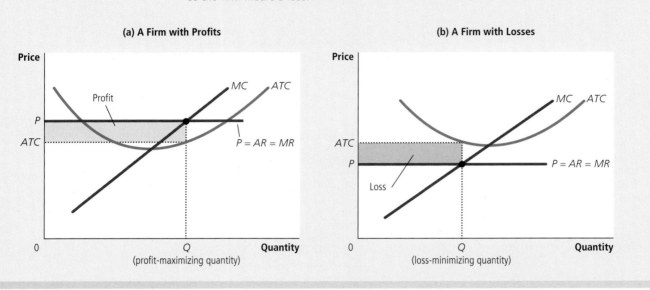

(a) A Firm with Profits   (b) A Firm with Losses

the number of firms can change as old firms exit the market and new firms enter.
Both cases are important, for each applies to a specific time horizon. Over short
periods of time, it is often difficult for firms to enter and exit, so the assumption of
a fixed number of firms is appropriate. But over long periods of time, the number
of firms can adjust to changing market conditions.

14-3a The Short Run: Market Supply with a Fixed Number of Firms

Consider first a market with 1,000 identical firms. For any given price, each firm
supplies a quantity of output so that its marginal cost equals the price, as shown in
panel (a) of Figure 6. That is, as long as price is above average variable cost, each
firm's marginal-cost curve is its supply curve. The quantity of output supplied to
the market equals the sum of the quantities supplied by each of the 1,000 individual
firms. Thus, to derive the market supply curve, we add the quantity supplied by each
firm in the market. As panel (b) of Figure 6 shows, because the firms are identical, the
quantity supplied to the market is 1,000 times the quantity supplied by each firm.

14-3b The Long Run: Market Supply with Entry and Exit

Now consider what happens if firms are able to enter or exit the market. Let's
suppose that everyone has access to the same technology for producing the good
and access to the same markets to buy the inputs for production. Therefore, all
current and potential firms have the same cost curves.

Decisions about entry and exit in a market of this type depend on the incentives facing the owners of existing firms and the entrepreneurs who could start
new firms. If firms already in the market are profitable, then new firms will have
an incentive to enter the market. This entry will expand the number of firms,

In the short run, the number of firms in the market is fixed. As a result, the market supply curve, shown in panel (b), reflects the individual firms' marginal-cost curves, shown in panel (a). Here, in a market of 1,000 firms, the quantity of output supplied to the market is 1,000 times the quantity supplied by each firm.

FIGURE 6

Short-Run Market Supply

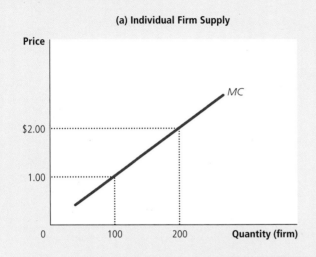

(a) Individual Firm Supply

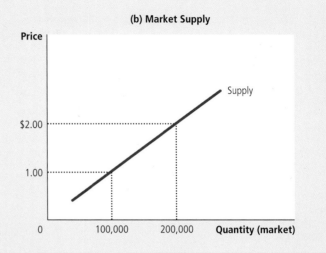

(b) Market Supply

increase the quantity of the good supplied, and drive down prices and profits. Conversely, if firms in the market are making losses, then some existing firms will exit the market. Their exit will reduce the number of firms, decrease the quantity of the good supplied, and drive up prices and profits. *At the end of this process of entry and exit, firms that remain in the market must be making zero economic profit.*

Recall that we can write a firm's profit as

$$\text{Profit} = (P - ATC) \times Q.$$

This equation shows that an operating firm has zero profit if and only if the price of the good equals the average total cost of producing that good. If price is above average total cost, profit is positive, which encourages new firms to enter. If price is less than average total cost, profit is negative, which encourages some firms to exit. *The process of entry and exit ends only when price and average total cost are driven to equality.*

This analysis has a surprising implication. We noted earlier in the chapter that competitive firms maximize profits by choosing a quantity at which price equals marginal cost. We just noted that free entry and exit force price to equal average total cost. But if price is to equal both marginal cost and average total cost, these two measures of cost must equal each other. Marginal cost and average total cost are equal, however, only when the firm is operating at the minimum of average total cost. Recall from the preceding chapter that the level of production with lowest average total cost is called the firm's *efficient scale*. Therefore, *in the long-run equilibrium of a competitive market with free entry and exit, firms must be operating at their efficient scale.*

Panel (a) of Figure 7 shows a firm in such a long-run equilibrium. In this figure, price *P* equals marginal cost *MC*, so the firm is maximizing profit. Price also equals average total cost *ATC*, so profit is zero. New firms have no incentive to enter the market, and existing firms have no incentive to leave the market.

FIGURE 7

Long-Run Market Supply

In the long run, firms will enter or exit the market until profit is driven to zero. As a result, price equals the minimum of average total cost, as shown in panel (a). The number of firms adjusts to ensure that all demand is satisfied at this price. The long-run market supply curve is horizontal at this price, as shown in panel (b).

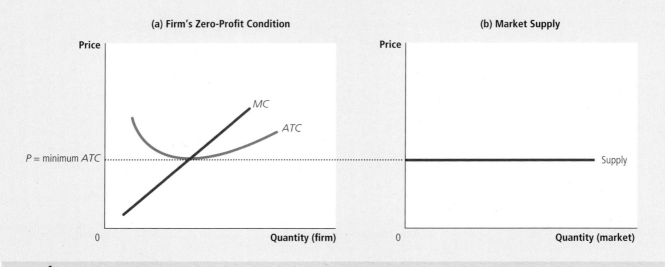

From this analysis of firm behavior, we can determine the long-run supply curve for the market. In a market with free entry and exit, there is only one price consistent with zero profit—the minimum of average total cost. As a result, the long-run market supply curve must be horizontal at this price, as illustrated by the perfectly elastic supply curve in panel (b) of Figure 7. Any price above this level would generate profit, leading to entry and an increase in the total quantity supplied. Any price below this level would generate losses, leading to exit and a decrease in the total quantity supplied. Eventually, the number of firms in the market adjusts so that price equals the minimum of average total cost, and there are enough firms to satisfy all the demand at this price.

14-3c Why Do Competitive Firms Stay in Business If They Make Zero Profit?

At first, it might seem odd that competitive firms earn zero profit in the long run. After all, people start businesses to make a profit. If entry eventually drives profit to zero, there might seem to be little reason to stay in business.

To understand the zero-profit condition more fully, recall that profit equals total revenue minus total cost and that total cost includes all the opportunity costs of the firm. In particular, total cost includes the time and money that the firm owners devote to the business. In the zero-profit equilibrium, the firm's revenue must compensate the owners for these opportunity costs.

Consider an example. Suppose that, to start his farm, a farmer had to invest $1 million, which otherwise he could have deposited in a bank and earned $50,000 a year in interest. In addition, he had to give up another job that would have paid him $30,000 a year. Then the farmer's opportunity cost of farming includes both the interest he could have earned and the forgone wages—a total of $80,000. Even if his profit is driven to zero, his revenue from farming compensates him for these opportunity costs.

If revenue (not profit) is more than opportunity cost, then staying in business even if profit is zero is a good idea

Keep in mind that accountants and economists measure costs differently. As we discussed in the previous chapter, accountants keep track of explicit costs but not implicit costs. That is, they measure costs that require an outflow of money from the firm, but they do not include the opportunity costs of production that do not involve an outflow of money. As a result, in the zero-profit equilibrium, economic profit is zero, but accounting profit is positive. Our farmer's accountant, for instance, would conclude that the farmer earned an accounting profit of $80,000, which is enough to keep the farmer in business.

14-3d A Shift in Demand in the Short Run and Long Run

Now that we have a more complete understanding of how firms make supply decisions, we can better explain how markets respond to changes in demand. Because firms can enter and exit in the long run but not in the short run, the response of a market to a change in demand depends on the time horizon. To see this, let's trace the effects of a shift in demand over time.

Suppose the market for milk begins in a long-run equilibrium. Firms are earning zero profit, so price equals the minimum of average total cost. Panel (a) of Figure 8 shows this situation. The long-run equilibrium is point A, the quantity sold in the market is Q_1, and the price is P_1.

Now suppose scientists discover that milk has miraculous health benefits. As a result, the quantity of milk demanded at every price increases, and the demand curve for milk shifts outward from D_1 to D_2, as in panel (b) of Figure 8. The short-run equilibrium moves from point A to point B; as a result, the quantity rises from Q_1 to Q_2, and the price rises from P_1 to P_2. All of the existing firms respond to the higher price by raising the amount they produce. Because each firm's supply curve reflects its marginal-cost curve, how much each firm increases production is determined by the marginal-cost curve. In the new short-run equilibrium, the price of milk exceeds average total cost, so the firms are making positive profit.

Over time, the profit generated in this market encourages new firms to enter. Some farmers may switch to producing milk instead of other farm products, for example. As the number of firms grows, the quantity supplied at every price increases, the short-run supply curve shifts to the right from S_1 to S_2, as in panel (c) of Figure 8, and this shift causes the price of milk to fall. Eventually, the price is driven back down to the minimum of average total cost, profits are zero, and firms stop entering. Thus, the market reaches a new long-run equilibrium, point C. The price of milk has returned to P_1, but the quantity produced has risen to Q_3. Each firm is again producing at its efficient scale, but because more firms are in the dairy business, the quantity of milk produced and sold is higher.

14-3e Why the Long-Run Supply Curve Might Slope Upward

So far, we have seen that entry and exit can cause the long-run market supply curve to be perfectly elastic. The essence of our analysis is that there are a large number of potential entrants, each of which faces the same costs. As a result, the long-run market supply curve is horizontal at the minimum of average total cost. When the demand for the good increases, the long-run result is an increase in the number of firms and in the total quantity supplied, without any change in the price.

There are, however, two reasons that the long-run market supply curve might slope upward. The first is that some resources used in production may be available only in limited quantities. For example, consider the market for farm products.

"We're a nonprofit organization—we don't intend to be, but we are!"

FIGURE 8

An Increase in Demand in the Short Run and Long Run

The market starts in a long-run equilibrium, shown as point A in panel (a). In this equilibrium, each firm makes zero profit, and the price equals the minimum average total cost. Panel (b) shows what happens in the short run when demand rises from D_1 to D_2. The equilibrium goes from point A to point B, price rises from P_1 to P_2, and the quantity sold in the market rises from Q_1 to Q_2. Because price now exceeds average total cost, each firm now makes a profit, which over time encourages new firms to enter the market. This entry shifts the short-run supply curve to the right from S_1 to S_2, as shown in panel (c). In the new long-run equilibrium, point C, price has returned to P_1 but the quantity sold has increased to Q_3. Profits are again zero, and price is back to the minimum of average total cost, but the market has more firms to satisfy the greater demand.

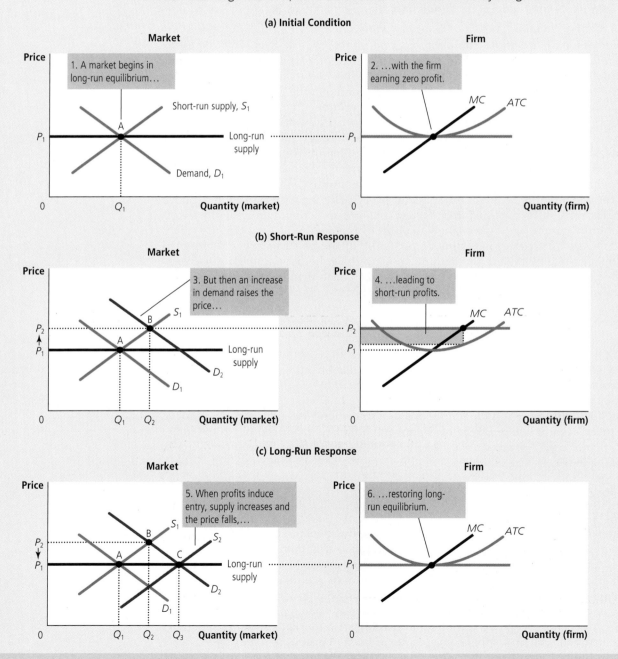

Anyone can choose to buy land and start a farm, but the quantity of land is limited. As more people become farmers, the price of farmland is bid up, which raises the costs of all farmers in the market. Thus, an increase in demand for farm products cannot induce an increase in quantity supplied without also inducing a rise in farmers' costs, which in turn means a rise in price. The result is a long-run market supply curve that is upward sloping, even with free entry into farming.

A second reason for an upward-sloping supply curve is that firms may have different costs. For example, consider the market for painters. Anyone can enter the market for painting services, but not everyone has the same costs. Costs vary in part because some people work faster than others and in part because some people have better alternative uses of their time than others. For any given price, those with lower costs are more likely to enter than those with higher costs. To increase the quantity of painting services supplied, additional entrants must be encouraged to enter the market. Because these new entrants have higher costs, the price must rise to make entry profitable for them. Thus, the long-run market supply curve for painting services slopes upward even with free entry into the market.

Notice that if firms have different costs, some firms earn profit even in the long run. In this case, the price in the market reflects the average total cost of the *marginal firm*—the firm that would exit the market if the price were any lower. This firm earns zero profit, but firms with lower costs earn positive profit. Entry does not eliminate this profit because would-be entrants have higher costs than firms already in the market. Higher-cost firms will enter only if the price rises, making the market profitable for them.

Thus, for these two reasons, a higher price may be necessary to induce a larger quantity supplied, in which case the long-run supply curve is upward sloping rather than horizontal. Nonetheless, the basic lesson about entry and exit remains true. *Because firms can enter and exit more easily in the long run than in the short run, the long-run supply curve is typically more elastic than the short-run supply curve.*

Quick Quiz   *In the long run with free entry and exit, is the price in a market equal to marginal cost, average total cost, both, or neither? Explain with a diagram.*

14-4 Conclusion: Behind the Supply Curve

We have been discussing the behavior of profit-maximizing firms that supply goods in perfectly competitive markets. You may recall from Chapter 1 that one of the *Ten Principles of Economics* is that rational people think at the margin. This chapter has applied this idea to the competitive firm. Marginal analysis has given us a theory of the supply curve in a competitive market and, as a result, a deeper understanding of market outcomes.

We have learned that when you buy a good from a firm in a competitive market, you can be assured that the price you pay is close to the cost of producing that good. In particular, if firms are competitive and profit maximizing, the price of a good equals the marginal cost of making that good. In addition, if firms can freely enter and exit the market, the price also equals the lowest possible average total cost of production.

Although we have assumed throughout this chapter that firms are price takers, many of the tools developed here are also useful for studying firms in less competitive markets. We now turn to examining the behavior of firms with market power. Marginal analysis will again be useful, but it will have quite different implications for a firm's production decisions and for the nature of market outcomes.

Summary

- Because a competitive firm is a price taker, its revenue is proportional to the amount of output it produces. The price of the good equals both the firm's average revenue and its marginal revenue.

- To maximize profit, a firm chooses a quantity of output such that marginal revenue equals marginal cost. Because marginal revenue for a competitive firm equals the market price, the firm chooses quantity so that price equals marginal cost. Thus, the firm's marginal-cost curve is its supply curve.

- In the short run when a firm cannot recover its fixed costs, the firm will choose to shut down temporarily if the price of the good is less than average variable cost. In the long run when the firm can recover both fixed

and variable costs, it will choose to exit if the price is less than average total cost.

- In a market with free entry and exit, profit is driven to zero in the long run. In this long-run equilibrium, all firms produce at the efficient scale, price equals the minimum of average total cost, and the number of firms adjusts to satisfy the quantity demanded at this price.

- Changes in demand have different effects over different time horizons. In the short run, an increase in demand raises prices and leads to profits, and a decrease in demand lowers prices and leads to losses. But if firms can freely enter and exit the market, then in the long run, the number of firms adjusts to drive the market back to the zero-profit equilibrium.

Key Concepts

competitive market, *p. 280*
average revenue, *p. 281*

marginal revenue, *p. 282*

sunk cost, *p. 286*

Questions for Review

1. What are the main characteristics of a competitive market?

2. Explain the difference between a firm's revenue and its profit. Which do firms maximize?

3. Draw the cost curves for a typical firm. Explain how a competitive firm chooses the level of output that maximizes profit. At that level of output, show on your graph the firm's total revenue and total costs.

4. Under what conditions will a firm shut down temporarily? Explain.

5. Under what conditions will a firm exit a market? Explain.

6. Does a competitive firm's price equal its marginal cost in the short run, in the long run, or both? Explain.

7. Does a competitive firm's price equal the minimum of its average total cost in the short run, in the long run, or both? Explain.

8. Are market supply curves typically more elastic in the short run or in the long run? Explain.

Quick Check Multiple Choice

1. A perfectly competitive firm
   a. chooses its price to maximize profits.
   b. sets its price to undercut other firms selling similar products.
   c. takes its price as given by market conditions.
   d. picks the price that yields the largest market share.

2. A competitive firm maximizes profit by choosing the quantity at which
   a. average total cost is at its minimum.
   b. marginal cost equals the price.
   c. average total cost equals the price.
   d. marginal cost equals average total cost.

3. A competitive firm's short-run supply curve is its _____ cost curve above its _____ cost curve.
   a. average total, marginal
   b. average variable, marginal
   c. marginal, average total
   d. marginal, average variable

4. If a profit-maximizing, competitive firm is producing a quantity at which marginal cost is between average variable cost and average total cost, it will
   a. keep producing in the short run but exit the market in the long run.

b. shut down in the short run but return to production in the long run.

c. shut down in the short run and exit the market in the long run.

d. keep producing both in the short run and in the long run.

5. In the long-run equilibrium of a competitive market with identical firms, what is the relationship between price P, marginal cost MC, and average total cost ATC?

a. $P > MC$ and $P > ATC$.

b. $P > MC$ and $P = ATC$.

c. $P = MC$ and $P > ATC$.

d. $P = MC$ and $P = ATC$.

6. Pretzel stands in New York City are a perfectly competitive industry in long-run equilibrium. One day, the city starts imposing a $100 per month tax on each stand. How does this policy affect the number of pretzels consumed in the short run and in the long run?

a. down in the short run, no change in the long run

b. up in the short run, no change in the long run

c. no change in the short run, down in the long run

d. no change in the short run, up in the long run

Problems and Applications

1. Many small boats are made of fiberglass, which is de-rived from crude oil. Suppose that the price of oil rises.

a. Using diagrams, show what happens to the cost curves of an individual boat-making firm and to the market supply curve.

b. What happens to the profits of boat makers in the short run? What happens to the number of boat makers in the long run?

2. You go out to the best restaurant in town and order a lobster dinner for $40. After eating half of the lobster, you realize that you are quite full. Your date wants you to finish your dinner because you can't take it home and because "you've already paid for it." What should you do? Relate your answer to the material in this chapter.

3. Bob's lawn-mowing service is a profit-maximizing, competitive firm. Bob mows lawns for $27 each. His total cost each day is $280, of which $30 is a fixed cost. He mows 10 lawns a day. What can you say about Bob's short-run decision regarding shutdown and his long-run decision regarding exit?

4. Consider total cost and total revenue given in the following table:

Quantity	0	1	2	3	4	5	6	7
Total cost	$8	9	10	11	13	19	27	37
Total revenue	$0	8	16	24	32	40	48	56

a. Calculate profit for each quantity. How much should the firm produce to maximize profit?

b. Calculate marginal revenue and marginal cost for each quantity. Graph them. (*Hint*: Put the points between whole numbers. For example, the marginal cost between 2 and 3 should be graphed at 2½.) At what quantity do these curves cross? How does this relate to your answer to part (a)?

c. Can you tell whether this firm is in a competitive industry? If so, can you tell whether the industry is in a long-run equilibrium?

5. Ball Bearings, Inc. faces costs of production as follows:

Quantity	Total Fixed Costs	Total Variable Costs
0	$100	$0
1	100	50
2	100	70
3	100	90
4	100	140
5	100	200
6	100	360

a. Calculate the company's average fixed costs, average variable costs, average total costs, and marginal costs at each level of production.

b. The price of a case of ball bearings is $50. Seeing that he can't make a profit, the chief executive officer (CEO) decides to shut down operations. What is the firm's profit/loss? Was this a wise decision? Explain.

c. Vaguely remembering his introductory economics course, the chief financial officer tells the CEO it is better to produce 1 case of ball bearings, because marginal revenue equals marginal cost at that quantity. What is the firm's profit/loss at that level of production? Was this the best decision? Explain.

6. Suppose the book-printing industry is competitive and begins in a long-run equilibrium.

a. Draw a diagram showing the average total cost, marginal cost, marginal revenue, and supply curve of the typical firm in the industry.

b. Hi-Tech Printing Company invents a new process that sharply reduces the cost of printing books. What happens to Hi-Tech's profits and the price of books in the short run when Hi-Tech's patent prevents other firms from using the new technology?

c. What happens in the long run when the patent expires and other firms are free to use the technology?

7. A firm in a competitive market receives $500 in total revenue and has marginal revenue of $10. What is the average revenue, and how many units were sold?

8. A profit-maximizing firm in a competitive market is currently producing 100 units of output. It has average revenue of $10, average total cost of $8, and fixed costs of $200.
   a. What is its profit?
   b. What is its marginal cost?
   c. What is its average variable cost?
   d. Is the efficient scale of the firm more than, less than, or exactly 100 units?

9. The market for fertilizer is perfectly competitive. Firms in the market are producing output but are currently incurring economic losses.
   a. How does the price of fertilizer compare to the average total cost, the average variable cost, and the marginal cost of producing fertilizer?
   b. Draw two graphs, side by side, illustrating the present situation for the typical firm and for the market.
   c. Assuming there is no change in either demand or the firms' cost curves, explain what will happen in the long run to the price of fertilizer, marginal cost, average total cost, the quantity supplied by each firm, and the total quantity supplied to the market.

10. The market for apple pies in the city of Ectenia is competitive and has the following demand schedule:

Price	Quantity Demanded
$1	1,200 pies
2	1,100
3	1,000
4	900
5	800
6	700
7	600
8	500
9	400
10	300
11	200
12	100
13	0

Each producer in the market has fixed costs of $9 and the following marginal cost:

Quantity	Marginal Cost
1 pie	$2
2	4
3	6
4	8
5	10
6	12

a. Compute each producer's total cost and average total cost for 1 to 6 pies.

b. The price of a pie is now $11. How many pies are sold? How many pies does each producer make? How many producers are there? How much profit does each producer earn?

c. Is the situation described in part (b) a long-run equilibrium? Why or why not?

d. Suppose that in the long run there is free entry and exit. How much profit does each producer earn in the long-run equilibrium? What is the market price and number of pies each producer makes? How many pies are sold? How many pie producers are operating?

11. Suppose that the U.S. textile industry is competitive and there is no international trade in textiles. In long-run equilibrium, the price per unit of cloth is $30.
   a. Describe the equilibrium using graphs for the entire market and for an individual producer.

   Now suppose that textile producers in other countries are willing to sell large quantities of cloth in the United States for only $25 per unit.

   b. Assuming that U.S. textile producers have large fixed costs, what is the short-run effect of these imports on the quantity produced by an individual producer? What is the short-run effect on profits? Illustrate your answer with a graph.

   c. What is the long-run effect on the number of U.S. firms in the industry?

12. An industry currently has 100 firms, each of which has fixed costs of $16 and average variable costs as follows:

Quantity	Average Variable Cost
1	$1
2	2
3	3
4	4
5	5
6	6

a. Compute a firm's marginal cost and average total cost for each quantity from 1 to 6.

b. The equilibrium price is currently $10. How much does each firm produce? What is the total quantity supplied in the market?

c. In the long run, firms can enter and exit the market, and all entrants have the same costs as above. As this market makes the transition to its long-run equilibrium, will the price rise or fall? Will the quantity demanded rise or fall? Will the quantity supplied by each firm rise or fall? Explain your answers.

d. Graph the long-run supply curve for this market, with specific numbers on the axes as relevant.

Go to CengageBrain.com to purchase access to the proven, critical Study Guide to accompany this text, which features additional notes and context, practice tests, and much more.

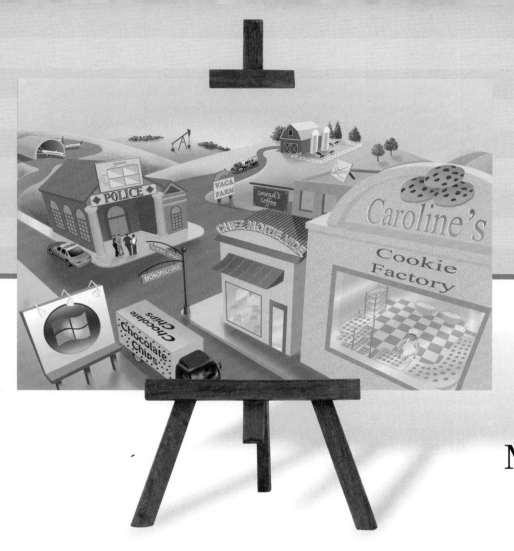

Monopoly

I f you own a personal computer, it probably uses some version of Windows, the operating system sold by the Microsoft Corporation. When Microsoft first designed Windows many years ago, it applied for and received a copyright from the government. The copyright gives Microsoft the exclusive right to make and sell copies of the Windows operating system. If a person wants to buy a copy of Windows, she has little choice but to give Microsoft the approximately $100 that the firm has decided to charge for its product. Microsoft is said to have a *monopoly* in the market for Windows.

Microsoft's business decisions are not well described by the model of firm behavior we developed in the previous chapter. In that chapter, we analyzed competitive markets, in which many firms offer essentially identical products, so each firm has little influence over the price it receives. By contrast, a monopoly such as Microsoft has no close competitors and, therefore, has the

[handwritten margin notes: Competitive markets Take the Price, then produce Quantity To supply To price equals marginal cost. Monopoly charges price that exceed marginal cost]

power to influence the market price of its product. Whereas a competitive firm is a *price taker*, a monopoly firm is a *price maker*.

In this chapter, we examine the implications of this market power. We will see that market power alters the relationship between a firm's costs and the price at which it sells its product. A competitive firm takes the price of its output as given by the market and then chooses the quantity it will supply so that price equals marginal cost. By contrast, a monopoly charges a price that exceeds marginal cost. This result is clearly true in the case of Microsoft's Windows. The marginal cost of Windows—the extra cost that Microsoft incurs by printing one more copy of the program onto a CD—is only a few dollars. The market price of Windows is many times its marginal cost.

It is not surprising that monopolies charge high prices for their products. Customers of monopolies might seem to have little choice but to pay whatever the monopoly charges. But if so, why does a copy of Windows not cost $1,000? Or $10,000? The reason is that if Microsoft were to set the price that high, fewer people would buy the product. People would buy fewer computers, switch to other operating systems, or make illegal copies. A monopoly firm can control the price of the good it sells, but because a high price reduces the quantity that its customers buy, the monopoly's profits are not unlimited.

As we examine the production and pricing decisions of monopolies, we also consider the implications of monopoly for society as a whole. Monopoly firms, like competitive firms, aim to maximize profit. But this goal has very different ramifications for competitive and monopoly firms. In competitive markets, self-interested consumers and producers reach an equilibrium that promotes general economic well-being, as if guided by an invisible hand. By contrast, because monopoly firms are unchecked by competition, the outcome in a market with a monopoly is often not in the best interest of society.

One of the *Ten Principles of Economics* in Chapter 1 is that governments can sometimes improve market outcomes. The analysis in this chapter sheds more light on this principle. As we examine the problems that monopolies raise for society, we discuss the various ways in which government policymakers might respond to these problems. The U.S. government, for example, keeps a close eye on Microsoft's business decisions. In 1994, it blocked Microsoft from buying Intuit, a leading seller of personal finance software, on the grounds that combining the two firms would concentrate too much market power. Similarly, in 1998, the U.S. Department of Justice objected when Microsoft started integrating its Internet browser into its Windows operating system, claiming that this addition would extend the firm's market power into new areas. In recent years, regulators in the United States and abroad have shifted their focus to firms with growing market power, such as Google and Samsung, but they also continue to monitor Microsoft's compliance with the antitrust laws.

15-1 Why Monopolies Arise

monopoly
a firm that is the sole seller of a product without close substitutes

A firm is a **monopoly** if it is the sole seller of its product and if its product does not have close substitutes. The fundamental cause of monopoly is *barriers to entry*: A monopoly remains the only seller in its market because other firms cannot enter the market and compete with it. Barriers to entry, in turn, have three main sources:

[handwritten margin note: there barriers reasons]

- *Monopoly resources:* A key resource required for production is owned by a single firm.

- *Government regulation:* The government gives a single firm the exclusive right to produce some good or service.
- *The production process:* A single firm can produce output at a lower cost than can a larger number of firms.

Let's briefly discuss each of these.

15-1a Monopoly Resources

The simplest way for a monopoly to arise is for a single firm to own a key resource. For example, consider the market for water in a small town in the Old West. If dozens of town residents have working wells, the competitive model discussed in the preceding chapter describes the behavior of sellers. As a result of the competition among water suppliers, the price of a gallon is driven to equal the marginal cost of pumping an extra gallon. But if there is only one well in town and it is impossible to get water from anywhere else, then the owner of the well has a monopoly on water. Not surprisingly, the monopolist has much greater market power than any single firm in a competitive market. In the case of a necessity like water, the monopolist can command quite a high price, even if the marginal cost of pumping an extra gallon is low.

A classic example of market power arising from the ownership of a key resource is DeBeers, the South African diamond company. Founded in 1888 by Cecil Rhodes, an English businessman (and benefactor for the Rhodes scholarship), DeBeers has at times controlled up to 80 percent of the production from the world's diamond mines. Because its market share is less than 100 percent, DeBeers is not exactly a monopoly, but the company has nonetheless exerted substantial influence over the market price of diamonds.

Although exclusive ownership of a key resource is a potential cause of monopoly, in practice monopolies rarely arise for this reason. Economies are large, and resources are owned by many people. Indeed, because many goods are traded internationally, the natural scope of their markets is often worldwide. There are, therefore, few examples of firms that own a resource for which there are no close substitutes.

15-1b Government-Created Monopolies

In many cases, monopolies arise because the government has given one person or firm the exclusive right to sell some good or service. Sometimes the monopoly arises from the sheer political clout of the would-be monopolist. Kings, for example, once granted exclusive business licenses to their friends and allies. At other times, the government grants a monopoly because doing so is viewed to be in the public interest.

The patent and copyright laws are two important examples. When a pharmaceutical company discovers a new drug, it can apply to the government for a patent. If the government deems the drug to be truly original, it approves the patent, which gives the company the exclusive right to manufacture and sell the drug for 20 years. Similarly, when a novelist finishes a book, she can copyright it. The copyright is a government guarantee that no one can print and sell the work without the author's permission. The copyright makes the novelist a monopolist in the sale of her novel.

The effects of patent and copyright laws are easy to see. Because these laws give one producer a monopoly, they lead to higher prices than would occur under competition. But by allowing these monopoly producers to charge higher prices and earn higher profits, the laws also encourage some desirable behavior. Drug

"Rather than a monopoly, we like to consider ourselves 'the only game in town.'"

THE WALL STREET JOURNAL—PERMISSION, CARTOON FEATURES SYNDICATE

DAVE CARPENTER

Patent and copyrights give monopolistic abilities to owners

companies are allowed to be monopolists in the drugs they discover to encourage research. Authors are allowed to be monopolists in the sale of their books to encourage them to write more and better books.

Thus, the laws governing patents and copyrights have benefits and costs. The benefits of the patent and copyright laws are the increased incentives for creative activity. These benefits are offset, to some extent, by the costs of monopoly pricing, which we examine fully later in this chapter.

15-1c Natural Monopolies

natural monopoly
a monopoly that arises because a single firm can supply a good or service to an entire market at a smaller cost than could two or more firms

An industry is a **natural monopoly** when a single firm can supply a good or service to an entire market at a lower cost than could two or more firms. A natural monopoly arises when there are economies of scale over the relevant range of output. Figure 1 shows the average total costs of a firm with economies of scale. In this case, a single firm can produce any amount of output at the least cost. That is, for any given amount of output, a larger number of firms leads to less output per firm and higher average total cost.

An example of a natural monopoly is the distribution of water. To provide water to residents of a town, a firm must build a network of pipes throughout the town. If two or more firms were to compete in the provision of this service, each firm would have to pay the fixed cost of building a network. Thus, the average total cost of water is lowest if a single firm serves the entire market.

We saw other examples of natural monopolies when we discussed public goods and common resources in Chapter 11. We noted that *club goods* are excludable but not rival in consumption. An example is a bridge used so infrequently that it is never congested. The bridge is excludable because a toll collector can prevent someone from using it. The bridge is not rival in consumption because use of the bridge by one person does not diminish the ability of others to use it. Because there is a large fixed cost of building the bridge and a negligible marginal cost of additional users, the average total cost of a trip across the bridge (the total cost divided by the number of trips) falls as the number of trips rises. Hence, the bridge is a natural monopoly.

When a firm is a natural monopoly, it is less concerned about new entrants eroding its monopoly power. Normally, a firm has trouble maintaining a monopoly

(handwritten margin note: Double fixed cost if 2 companies produce water)

FIGURE 1

Economies of Scale as a Cause of Monopoly
When a firm's average-total-cost curve continually declines, the firm has what is called a natural monopoly. In this case, when production is divided among more firms, each firm produces less, and average total cost rises. As a result, a single firm can produce any given amount at the least cost.

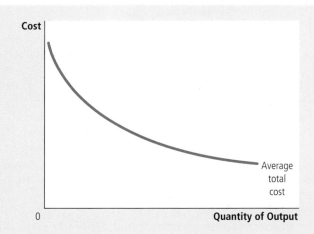

position without ownership of a key resource or protection from the government. The monopolist's profit attracts entrants into the market, and these entrants make the market more competitive. By contrast, entering a market in which another firm has a natural monopoly is unattractive. Would-be entrants know that they cannot achieve the same low costs that the monopolist enjoys because, after entry, each firm would have a smaller piece of the market.

In some cases, the size of the market is one determinant of whether an industry is a natural monopoly. Again, consider a bridge across a river. When the population is small, the bridge may be a natural monopoly. A single bridge can satisfy the entire demand for trips across the river at lowest cost. Yet as the population grows and the bridge becomes congested, satisfying the entire demand may require two or more bridges across the same river. Thus, as a market expands, a natural monopoly can evolve into a more competitive market.

[handwritten margin notes: Two entrants have to share same amount - so no one enters - Because they have to share. If too many people cross bridge, another bridge is required so monopoly → competitive]

Quick Quiz   *What are the three reasons that a market might have a monopoly? • Give two examples of monopolies and explain the reason for each.*

15-2 How Monopolies Make Production and Pricing Decisions

Now that we know how monopolies arise, we can consider how a monopoly firm decides how much of its product to make and what price to charge for it. The analysis of monopoly behavior in this section is the starting point for evaluating whether monopolies are desirable and what policies the government might pursue in monopoly markets.

15-2a Monopoly versus Competition

The key difference between a competitive firm and a monopoly is the monopoly's ability to influence the price of its output. A competitive firm is small relative to the market in which it operates and, therefore, has no power to influence the price of its output. It takes the price as given by market conditions. By contrast, because a monopoly is the sole producer in its market, it can alter the price of its good by adjusting the quantity it supplies to the market.

One way to view this difference between a competitive firm and a monopoly is to consider the demand curve that each firm faces. When we analyzed profit maximization by competitive firms in the preceding chapter, we drew the market price as a horizontal line. Because a competitive firm can sell as much or as little as it wants at this price, the competitive firm faces a horizontal demand curve, as in panel (a) of Figure 2. In effect, because the competitive firm sells a product with many perfect substitutes (the products of all the other firms in its market), the demand curve that any one firm faces is perfectly elastic.

By contrast, because a monopoly is the sole producer in its market, its demand curve is the market demand curve. Thus, the monopolist's demand curve slopes downward for all the usual reasons, as in panel (b) of Figure 2. If the monopolist raises the price of its good, consumers buy less of it. Looked at another way, if the monopolist reduces the quantity of output it produces and sells, the price of its output increases.

The market demand curve provides a constraint on a monopoly's ability to profit from its market power. A monopolist would prefer, if it were possible, to charge a high price and sell a large quantity at that high price. The market demand

FIGURE 2

Demand Curves for Competitive and Monopoly Firms

Because competitive firms are price takers, they in effect face horizontal demand curves, as in panel (a). Because a monopoly firm is the sole producer in its market, it faces the downward-sloping market demand curve, as in panel (b). As a result, the monopoly has to accept a lower price if it wants to sell more output.

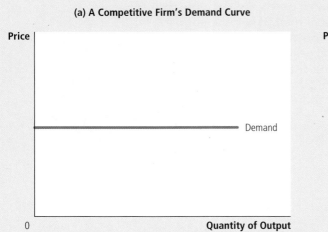

(a) A Competitive Firm's Demand Curve

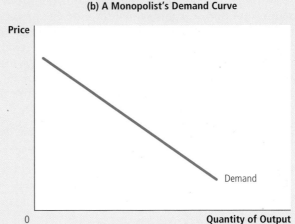

(b) A Monopolist's Demand Curve

curve makes that outcome impossible. In particular, the market demand curve describes the combinations of price and quantity that are available to a monopoly firm. By adjusting the quantity produced (or equivalently, the price charged), the monopolist can choose any point on the demand curve, but it cannot choose a point off the demand curve.

What price and quantity of output will the monopolist choose? As with competitive firms, we assume that the monopolist's goal is to maximize profit. Because the firm's profit is total revenue minus total costs, our next task in explaining monopoly behavior is to examine a monopolist's revenue.

15-2b A Monopoly's Revenue

Consider a town with a single producer of water. Table 1 shows how the monopoly's revenue might depend on the amount of water produced.

The first two columns show the monopolist's demand schedule. If the monopolist produces 1 gallon of water, it can sell that gallon for $10. If it produces 2 gallons, it must lower the price to $9 to sell both gallons. If it produces 3 gallons, it must lower the price to $8. And so on. If you graphed these two columns of numbers, you would get a typical downward-sloping demand curve.

The third column of the table presents the monopolist's *total revenue*. It equals the quantity sold (from the first column) times the price (from the second column). The fourth column computes the firm's *average revenue,* the amount of revenue the firm receives per unit sold. We compute average revenue by taking the number for total revenue in the third column and dividing it by the quantity of output in the first column. As we discussed in the previous chapter, average revenue always equals the price of the good. This is true for monopolists as well as for competitive firms.

The last column of Table 1 computes the firm's *marginal revenue,* the amount of revenue that the firm receives for each additional unit of output. We compute

TABLE 1

A Monopoly's Total, Average, and Marginal Revenue

Quantity of Water (Q)	Price (P)	Total Revenue (TR = P × Q)	Average Revenue (AR = TR / Q)	Marginal Revenue (MR = ΔTR / ΔQ)
0 gallons	$11	$ 0	—	
				$10
1	10	10	$10	
				8
2	9	18	9	
				6
3	8	24	8	
				4
4	7	28	7	
				2
5	6	30	6	
				0
6	5	30	5	
				−2
7	4	28	4	
				−4
8	3	24	3	

marginal revenue by taking the change in total revenue when output increases by 1 unit. For example, when the firm is producing 3 gallons of water, it receives total revenue of $24. Raising production to 4 gallons increases total revenue to $28. Thus, marginal revenue from the sale of the fourth gallon is $28 minus $24, or $4.

Table 1 shows a result that is important for understanding monopoly behavior: *A monopolist's marginal revenue is always less than the price of its good.* For example, if the firm raises production of water from 3 to 4 gallons, it will increase total revenue by only $4, even though it will be able to sell each gallon for $7. For a monopoly, marginal revenue is lower than price because a monopoly faces a downward-sloping demand curve. To increase the amount sold, a monopoly firm must lower the price it charges to all customers. Hence, to sell the fourth gallon of water, the monopolist will get $1 less revenue for each of the first 3 gallons. This $3 loss accounts for the difference between the price of the fourth gallon ($7) and the marginal revenue of that fourth gallon ($4).

Marginal revenue for monopolies is very different from marginal revenue for competitive firms. When a monopoly increases the amount it sells, this action has two effects on total revenue (P × Q):

- *The output effect:* More output is sold, so Q is higher, which tends to increase total revenue.
- *The price effect:* The price falls, so P is lower, which tends to decrease total revenue.

Because a competitive firm can sell all it wants at the market price, there is no price effect. When it increases production by 1 unit, it receives the market price for that unit, and it does not receive any less for the units it was already selling. That is, because the competitive firm is a price taker, its marginal revenue equals the price of its good. By contrast, when a monopoly increases production by 1 unit, it must reduce the price it charges for every unit it sells, and this cut in price reduces revenue on the units it was already selling. As a result, a monopoly's marginal revenue is less than its price.

Figure 3 graphs the demand curve and the marginal-revenue curve for a monopoly firm. (Because the firm's price equals its average revenue, the demand curve is also the average-revenue curve.) These two curves always start at the same point on the vertical axis because the marginal revenue of the first unit sold equals the price of the good. But for the reason we just discussed, the monopolist's marginal revenue on all units after the first is less than the price of the good. Thus, a monopoly's marginal-revenue curve lies below its demand curve.

You can see in Figure 3 (as well as in Table 1) that marginal revenue can even become negative. Marginal revenue is negative when the price effect on revenue is greater than the output effect. In this case, when the firm produces an extra unit of output, the price falls by enough to cause the firm's total revenue to decline, even though the firm is selling more units.

15-2c Profit Maximization

Now that we have considered the revenue of a monopoly firm, we are ready to examine how such a firm maximizes profit. Recall from Chapter 1 that one of the *Ten Principles of Economics* is that rational people think at the margin. This lesson is as true for monopolists as it is for competitive firms. Here we apply the logic of marginal analysis to the monopolist's decision about how much to produce.

Figure 4 graphs the demand curve, the marginal-revenue curve, and the cost curves for a monopoly firm. All these curves should seem familiar: The demand and marginal-revenue curves are like those in Figure 3, and the cost curves are like those we encountered in the last two chapters. These curves contain all the information we need to determine the level of output that a profit-maximizing monopolist will choose.

FIGURE 3

Demand and Marginal-Revenue Curves for a Monopoly
The demand curve shows how the quantity affects the price of the good. The marginal-revenue curve shows how the firm's revenue changes when the quantity increases by 1 unit. Because the price on *all* units sold must fall if the monopoly increases production, marginal revenue is always less than the price.

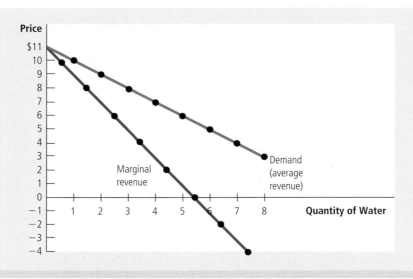

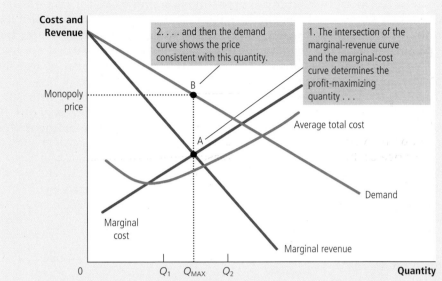

FIGURE 4

Profit Maximization for a Monopoly
A monopoly maximizes profit by choosing the quantity at which marginal revenue equals marginal cost (point A). It then uses the demand curve to find the price that will induce consumers to buy that quantity (point B).

Read this

Suppose, first, that the firm is producing at a low level of output, such as Q_1. In this case, marginal cost is less than marginal revenue. If the firm increased production by 1 unit, the additional revenue would exceed the additional costs, and profit would rise. Thus, when marginal cost is less than marginal revenue, the firm can increase profit by producing more units.

A similar argument applies at high levels of output, such as Q_2. In this case, marginal cost is greater than marginal revenue. If the firm reduced production by 1 unit, the costs saved would exceed the revenue lost. Thus, if marginal cost is greater than marginal revenue, the firm can raise profit by reducing production.

In the end, the firm adjusts its level of production until the quantity reaches Q_{MAX}, at which marginal revenue equals marginal cost. Thus, *the monopolist's profit-maximizing quantity of output is determined by the intersection of the marginal-revenue curve and the marginal-cost curve.* In Figure 4, this intersection occurs at point A.

You might recall from the previous chapter that competitive firms also choose the quantity of output at which marginal revenue equals marginal cost. In following this rule for profit maximization, competitive firms and monopolies are alike. But there is also an important difference between these types of firms: The marginal revenue of a competitive firm equals its price, whereas the marginal revenue of a monopoly is less than its price. That is,

> For a competitive firm: $P = MR = MC$.
> For a monopoly firm: $P > MR = MC$.

The equality of marginal revenue and marginal cost determines the profit-maximizing quantity for both types of firm. What differs is how the price is related to marginal revenue and marginal cost.

How does the monopoly find the profit-maximizing price for its product? The demand curve answers this question because the demand curve relates the amount that customers are willing to pay to the quantity sold. Thus, after the monopoly firm chooses the quantity of output that equates marginal revenue and marginal cost, it uses the demand curve to find the highest price it can charge for that quantity. In Figure 4, the profit-maximizing price is found at point B.

We can now see a key difference between markets with competitive firms and markets with a monopoly firm: *In competitive markets, price equals marginal cost. In monopolized markets, price exceeds marginal cost.* As we will see in a moment, this finding is crucial to understanding the social cost of monopoly.

15-2d A Monopoly's Profit

How much profit does a monopoly make? To see a monopoly firm's profit in a graph, recall that profit equals total revenue (*TR*) minus total costs (*TC*):

$$\text{Profit} = TR - TC.$$

We can rewrite this as

$$\text{Profit} = (TR/Q - TC/Q) \times Q.$$

TR/Q is average revenue, which equals the price, P, and TC/Q is average total cost, ATC. Therefore,

$$\text{Profit} = (P - ATC) \times Q.$$

This equation for profit (which also holds for competitive firms) allows us to measure the monopolist's profit in our graph.

Consider the shaded box in Figure 5. The height of the box (the segment BC) is price minus average total cost, $P - ATC$, which is the profit on the typical unit

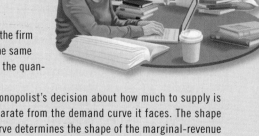

Why a Monopoly Does Not Have a Supply Curve

You may have noticed that we have analyzed the price in a monopoly market using the market demand curve and the firm's cost curves. We have not made any mention of the market supply curve. By contrast, when we analyzed prices in competitive markets beginning in Chapter 4, the two most important words were always *supply* and *demand*.

What happened to the supply curve? Although monopoly firms make decisions about what quantity to supply (in the way described in this chapter), a monopoly does not have a supply curve. A supply curve tells us the quantity that firms choose to supply at any given price. This concept makes sense when we are analyzing competitive firms, which are price takers. But a monopoly firm is a price maker, not a price taker. It is not meaningful to ask what amount such a firm would produce at

any price because the firm sets the price at the same time as it chooses the quantity to supply.

Indeed, the monopolist's decision about how much to supply is impossible to separate from the demand curve it faces. The shape of the demand curve determines the shape of the marginal-revenue curve, which in turn determines the monopolist's profit-maximizing quantity. In a competitive market, supply decisions can be analyzed without knowing the demand curve, but that is not true in a monopoly market. Therefore, we never talk about a monopoly's supply curve. ◢

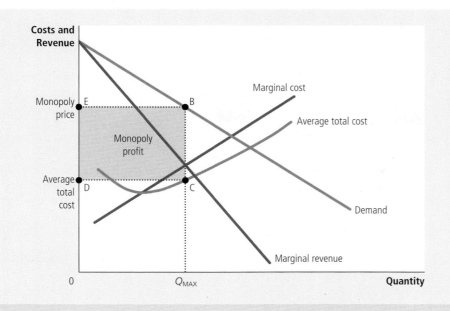

The Monopolist's Profit
The area of the box BCDE equals the profit of the monopoly firm. The height of the box (BC) is price minus average total cost, which equals profit per unit sold. The width of the box (DC) is the number of units sold.

sold. The width of the box (the segment DC) is the quantity sold, Q_{MAX}. Therefore, the area of this box is the monopoly firm's total profit.

case study   **Monopoly Drugs versus Generic Drugs**
According to our analysis, prices are determined differently in monopolized markets and competitive markets. A natural place to test this theory is the market for pharmaceutical drugs because this market takes on both market structures. When a firm discovers a new drug, patent laws give the firm a monopoly on the sale of that drug. But eventually, the firm's patent runs out, and any company can make and sell the drug. At that time, the market switches from being monopolistic to being competitive.

What should happen to the price of a drug when the patent runs out? Figure 6 shows the market for a typical drug. In this figure, the marginal cost of producing the drug is constant. (This is approximately true for many drugs.) During the life of the patent, the monopoly firm maximizes profit by producing the quantity at which marginal revenue equals marginal cost and charging a price well above marginal cost. But when the patent runs out, the profit from making the drug should encourage new firms to enter the market. As the market becomes more competitive, the price should fall to equal marginal cost.

Experience is, in fact, consistent with our theory. When the patent on a drug expires, other companies quickly enter and begin selling so-called generic products that are chemically identical to the former monopolist's brand-name product. And just as our analysis predicts, the price of the competitively produced generic drug is well below the price that the monopolist was charging.

The expiration of a patent, however, does not cause the monopolist to lose all its market power. Some consumers remain loyal to the brand-name drug, perhaps out of fear that the new generic drugs are not actually the same as the drug

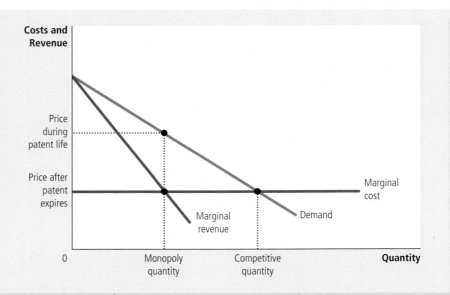

FIGURE 6

The Market for Drugs
When a patent gives a firm a monopoly over the sale of a drug, the firm charges the monopoly price, which is well above the marginal cost of making the drug. When the patent on a drug runs out, new firms enter the market, making it more competitive. As a result, the price falls from the monopoly price to marginal cost.

they have been using for years. As a result, the former monopolist can continue to charge a price above the price charged by its new competitors.

For example, one of the most widely used antidepressants is the drug fluoxetine, which is taken by millions of Americans. Because the patent on this drug expired in 2001, a consumer today has the choice between the original drug, sold under the brand name Prozac, and a generic version of the same medicine. Prozac sells for about three times the price of generic fluoxetine. This price differential can persist because some consumers are not convinced that the two pills are perfect substitutes. ◢

Quick Quiz *Explain how a monopolist chooses the quantity of output to produce and the price to charge.*

15-3 The Welfare Cost of Monopolies

Is monopoly a good way to organize a market? We have seen that a monopoly, in contrast to a competitive firm, charges a price above marginal cost. From the standpoint of consumers, this high price makes monopoly undesirable. At the same time, however, the monopoly is earning profit from charging this high price. From the standpoint of the owners of the firm, the high price makes monopoly very desirable. Is it possible that the benefits to the firm's owners exceed the costs imposed on consumers, making monopoly desirable from the standpoint of society as a whole?

We can answer this question using the tools of welfare economics. Recall from Chapter 7 that total surplus measures the economic well-being of buyers and sellers in a market. Total surplus is the sum of consumer surplus and producer surplus. Consumer surplus is consumers' willingness to pay for a good minus the amount they actually pay for it. Producer surplus is the amount producers receive for a good minus their costs of producing it. In this case, there is a single producer—the monopolist.

You can probably guess the result of this analysis. In Chapter 7, we concluded that the equilibrium of supply and demand in a competitive market is not only a natural outcome but also a desirable one. The invisible hand of the market leads to an allocation of resources that makes total surplus as large as it can be. Because a monopoly leads to an allocation of resources different from that in a competitive market, the outcome must, in some way, fail to maximize total economic well-being.

15-3a The Deadweight Loss

We begin by considering what the monopoly firm would do if it were run by a benevolent social planner. The social planner cares not only about the profit earned by the firm's owners but also about the benefits received by the firm's consumers. The planner tries to maximize total surplus, which equals producer surplus (profit) plus consumer surplus. Keep in mind that total surplus equals the value of the good to consumers minus the costs of making the good incurred by the monopoly producer.

Figure 7 analyzes how a benevolent social planner would choose the monopoly's level of output. The demand curve reflects the value of the good to consumers, as measured by their willingness to pay for it. The marginal-cost curve reflects the costs of the monopolist. Thus, *the socially efficient quantity is found where the demand curve and the marginal-cost curve intersect.* Below this quantity, the value

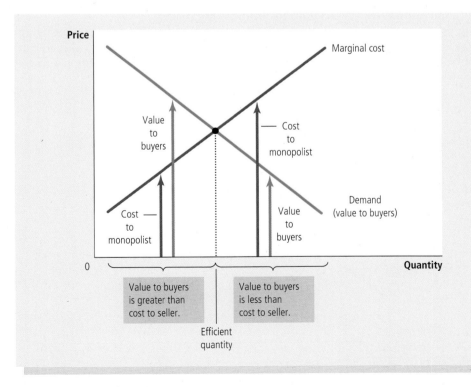

Price

Marginal cost

Value to buyers

— Cost to monopolist

Cost — to monopolist

Value to buyers

Demand (value to buyers)

0

Quantity

Value to buyers is greater than cost to seller.

Value to buyers is less than cost to seller.

Efficient quantity

FIGURE 7

The Efficient Level of Output
A benevolent social planner maximizes total surplus in the market by choosing the level of output where the demand curve and the marginal-cost curve intersect. Below this level, the value of the good to the marginal buyer (as reflected in the demand curve) exceeds the marginal cost of making the good. Above this level, the value to the marginal buyer is less than the marginal cost.

of an extra unit to consumers exceeds the cost of providing it, so increasing output would raise total surplus. Above this quantity, the cost of producing an extra unit exceeds the value of that unit to consumers, so decreasing output would raise total surplus. At the optimal quantity, the value of an extra unit to consumers exactly equals the marginal cost of production.

If the social planner were running the monopoly, the firm could achieve this efficient outcome by charging the price found at the intersection of the demand and marginal-cost curves. Thus, like a competitive firm and unlike a profit-maximizing monopoly, a social planner would charge a price equal to marginal cost. Because this price would give consumers an accurate signal about the cost of producing the good, consumers would buy the efficient quantity.

We can evaluate the welfare effects of monopoly by comparing the level of output that the monopolist chooses to the level of output that a social planner would choose. As we have seen, the monopolist chooses to produce and sell the quantity of output at which the marginal-revenue and marginal-cost curves intersect; the social planner would choose the quantity at which the demand and marginal-cost curves intersect. Figure 8 shows the comparison. *The monopolist produces less than the socially efficient quantity of output.*

We can also view the inefficiency of monopoly in terms of the monopolist's price. Because the market demand curve describes a negative relationship between the price and quantity of the good, a quantity that is inefficiently low is equivalent to a price that is inefficiently high. When a monopolist charges a price above marginal cost, some potential consumers value the good at more than its marginal cost but less than the monopolist's price. These consumers do not buy the good. Because the value these consumers place on the good is greater than the cost of providing it to them, this result is inefficient. Thus, monopoly pricing prevents some mutually beneficial trades from taking place.

The inefficiency of monopoly can be measured with a deadweight loss triangle, as illustrated in Figure 8. Because the demand curve reflects the value to consumers and the marginal-cost curve reflects the costs to the monopoly producer,

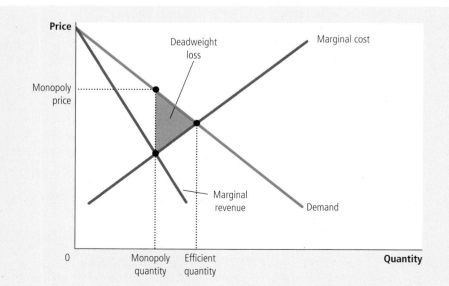

FIGURE 8

The Inefficiency of Monopoly
Because a monopoly charges a price above marginal cost, not all consumers who value the good at more than its cost buy it. Thus, the quantity produced and sold by a monopoly is below the socially efficient level. The deadweight loss is represented by the area of the triangle between the demand curve (which reflects the value of the good to consumers) and the marginal-cost curve (which reflects the costs of the monopoly producer).

the area of the deadweight loss triangle between the demand curve and the marginal-cost curve equals the total surplus lost because of monopoly pricing. It is the reduction in economic well-being that results from the monopoly's use of its market power.

The deadweight loss caused by monopoly is similar to the deadweight loss caused by a tax. Indeed, a monopolist is like a private tax collector. As we saw in Chapter 8, a tax on a good places a wedge between consumers' willingness to pay (as reflected by the demand curve) and producers' costs (as reflected by the supply curve). Because a monopoly exerts its market power by charging a price above marginal cost, it creates a similar wedge. In both cases, the wedge causes the quantity sold to fall short of the social optimum. The difference between the two cases is that the government gets the revenue from a tax, whereas a private firm gets the monopoly profit.

15-3b The Monopoly's Profit: A Social Cost?

It is tempting to decry monopolies for "profiteering" at the expense of the public. And indeed, a monopoly firm does earn a profit by virtue of its market power. According to the economic analysis of monopoly, however, the firm's profit is not in itself necessarily a problem for society.

Welfare in a monopolized market, like all markets, includes the welfare of both consumers and producers. Whenever a consumer pays an extra dollar to a producer because of a monopoly price, the consumer is worse off by a dollar and the producer is better off by the same amount. This transfer from the consumers of the good to the owners of the monopoly does not affect the market's total surplus—the sum of consumer and producer surplus. In other words, the monopoly profit itself represents not a reduction in the size of the economic pie but merely a bigger slice for producers and a smaller slice for consumers. Unless consumers are for some reason more deserving than producers—a normative judgment about equity that goes beyond the realm of economic efficiency—the monopoly profit is not a social problem.

The problem in a monopolized market arises because the firm produces and sells a quantity of output below the level that maximizes total surplus. The deadweight loss measures how much the economic pie shrinks as a result. This inefficiency is connected to the monopoly's high price: Consumers buy fewer units when the firm raises its price above marginal cost. But keep in mind that the profit earned on the units that continue to be sold is not the problem. The problem stems from the inefficiently low quantity of output. Put differently, if the high monopoly price did not discourage some consumers from buying the good, it would raise producer surplus by exactly the amount it reduced consumer surplus, leaving total surplus the same as could be achieved by a benevolent social planner.

There is, however, a possible exception to this conclusion. Suppose that a monopoly firm has to incur additional costs to maintain its monopoly position. For example, a firm with a government-created monopoly might need to hire lobbyists to convince lawmakers to continue its monopoly. In this case, the monopoly may use up some of its monopoly profits paying for these additional costs. If so, the social loss from monopoly includes both these costs and the deadweight loss resulting from reduced output.

Quick Quiz *How does a monopolist's quantity of output compare to the quantity of output that maximizes total surplus? How does this difference relate to the concept of deadweight loss?*

15-4 Price Discrimination

price discrimination

the business practice of selling the same good at different prices to different customers

So far, we have been assuming that the monopoly firm charges the same price to all customers. Yet in many cases, firms sell the same good to different customers for different prices, even though the costs of producing for the two customers are the same. This practice is called **price discrimination**.

Before discussing the behavior of a price-discriminating monopolist, we should note that price discrimination is not possible when a good is sold in a competitive market. In a competitive market, many firms are selling the same good at the market price. No firm is willing to charge a lower price to any customer because the firm can sell all it wants at the market price. And if any firm tried to charge a higher price to a customer, that customer would buy from another firm. For a firm to price discriminate, it must have some market power.

15-4a A Parable about Pricing

To understand why a monopolist would price discriminate, let's consider an example. Imagine that you are the president of Readalot Publishing Company. Readalot's best-selling author has just written a new novel. To keep things simple, let's imagine that you pay the author a flat $2 million for the exclusive rights to publish the book. Let's also assume that the cost of printing the book is zero (as it would be, for example, for an e-book). Readalot's profit, therefore, is the revenue from selling the book minus the $2 million it has paid to the author. Given these assumptions, how would you, as Readalot's president, decide the book's price?

Your first step is to estimate the demand for the book. Readalot's marketing department tells you that the book will attract two types of readers. The book will appeal to the author's 100,000 die-hard fans who are willing to pay as much as $30. In addition, the book will appeal to about 400,000 less enthusiastic readers who will pay up to $5.

If Readalot charges a single price to all customers, what price maximizes profit? There are two natural prices to consider: $30 is the highest price Readalot can charge and still get the 100,000 die-hard fans, and $5 is the highest price it can charge and still get the entire market of 500,000 potential readers. Solving Readalot's problem is a matter of simple arithmetic. At a price of $30, Readalot sells 100,000 copies, has revenue of $3 million, and makes profit of $1 million. At a price of $5, it sells 500,000 copies, has revenue of $2.5 million, and makes profit of $500,000. Thus, Readalot maximizes profit by charging $30 and forgoing the opportunity to sell to the 400,000 less enthusiastic readers.

Notice that Readalot's decision causes a deadweight loss. There are 400,000 readers willing to pay $5 for the book, and the marginal cost of providing it to them is zero. Thus, $2 million of total surplus is lost when Readalot charges the higher price. This deadweight loss is the inefficiency that arises whenever a monopolist charges a price above marginal cost.

Now suppose that Readalot's marketing department makes a discovery: These two groups of readers are in separate markets. The die-hard fans live in Australia, and the other readers live in the United States. Moreover, it is hard for readers in one country to buy books in the other.

In response to this discovery, Readalot can change its marketing strategy and increase profits. To the 100,000 Australian readers, it can charge $30 for the book. To the 400,000 American readers, it can charge $5 for the book. In this case, revenue is $3 million in Australia and $2 million in the United States, for a total of $5 million. Profit is then $3 million, which is substantially greater than the $1 million the company could earn charging the same $30 price to all customers. Not surprisingly, Readalot chooses to follow this strategy of price discrimination.

The story of Readalot Publishing is hypothetical, but it describes accurately the business practice of many publishing companies. Textbooks, for example, are often sold at a lower price in Europe than in the United States. Even more important is the price differential between hardcover books and paperbacks. When a publisher has a new novel, it initially releases an expensive hardcover edition and later releases a cheaper paperback edition. The difference in price between these two editions far exceeds the difference in printing costs. The publisher's goal is just as in our example. By selling the hardcover to die-hard fans and the paperback to less enthusiastic readers, the publisher price discriminates and raises its profit.

15-4b The Moral of the Story

Like any parable, the story of Readalot Publishing is stylized. Yet also like any parable, it teaches some general lessons. In this case, three lessons can be learned about price discrimination.

The first and most obvious lesson is that price discrimination is a rational strategy for a profit-maximizing monopolist. That is, by charging different prices to different customers, a monopolist can increase its profit. In essence, a price-discriminating monopolist charges each customer a price closer to her willingness to pay than is possible with a single price.

The second lesson is that price discrimination requires the ability to separate customers according to their willingness to pay. In our example, customers were separated geographically. But sometimes monopolists choose other differences, such as age or income, to distinguish among customers.

A corollary to this second lesson is that certain market forces can prevent firms from price discriminating. In particular, one such force is *arbitrage,* the process of buying a good in one market at a low price and selling it in another market at a higher price to profit from the price difference. In our example, if Australian bookstores could buy the book in the United States and resell it to Australian readers, the arbitrage would prevent Readalot from price discriminating, because no Australian would buy the book at the higher price.

The third lesson from our parable is the most surprising: Price discrimination can raise economic welfare. Recall that a deadweight loss arises when Readalot charges a single $30 price because the 400,000 less enthusiastic readers do not end up with the book, even though they value it at more than its marginal cost of production. By contrast, when Readalot price discriminates, all readers get the book, and the outcome is efficient. Thus, price discrimination can eliminate the inefficiency inherent in monopoly pricing.

Note that in this example the increase in welfare from price discrimination shows up as higher producer surplus rather than higher consumer surplus. Consumers are no better off for having bought the book: The price they pay exactly equals the value they place on the book, so they receive no consumer surplus. The entire increase in total surplus from price discrimination accrues to Readalot Publishing in the form of higher profit.

15-4c The Analytics of Price Discrimination

Let's consider a bit more formally how price discrimination affects economic welfare. We begin by assuming that the monopolist can price discriminate perfectly. *Perfect price discrimination* describes a situation in which the monopolist knows exactly each customer's willingness to pay and can charge each customer a different price. In this case, the monopolist charges each customer exactly her willingness to pay, and the monopolist gets the entire surplus in every transaction.

Figure 9 illustrates producer and consumer surplus with and without price discrimination. To keep things simple, this figure is drawn assuming constant per unit costs—that is, marginal cost and average total cost are constant and equal. Without price discrimination, the firm charges a single price above marginal cost, as shown in panel (a). Because some potential customers who value the good at more than marginal cost do not buy it at this high price, the monopoly causes a deadweight loss. Yet when a firm can perfectly price discriminate, as shown in panel (b), each customer who values the good at more than marginal cost buys the good and is charged her willingness to pay. All mutually beneficial trades take place, no deadweight loss occurs, and the entire surplus derived from the market goes to the monopoly producer in the form of profit.

In reality, of course, price discrimination is not perfect. Customers do not walk into stores with signs displaying their willingness to pay. Instead, firms price discriminate by dividing customers into groups: young versus old, weekday versus weekend shoppers, Americans versus Australians, and so on. Unlike those in our parable of Readalot Publishing, customers within each group differ in their willingness to pay for the product, making perfect price discrimination impossible.

How does this imperfect price discrimination affect welfare? The analysis of these pricing schemes is complicated, and it turns out that there is no general

FIGURE 9

Welfare with and without Price Discrimination

Panel (a) shows a monopoly that charges the same price to all customers. Total surplus in this market equals the sum of profit (producer surplus) and consumer surplus. Panel (b) shows a monopoly that can perfectly price discriminate. Because consumer surplus equals zero, total surplus now equals the firm's profit. Comparing these two panels, you can see that perfect price discrimination raises profit, raises total surplus, and lowers consumer surplus.

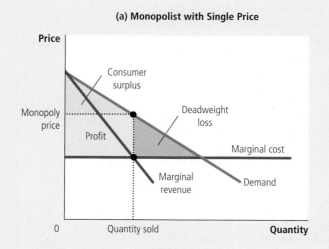

(a) Monopolist with Single Price

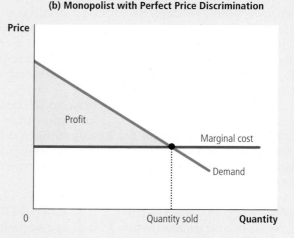

(b) Monopolist with Perfect Price Discrimination

answer to this question. Compared to the monopoly outcome with a single price, imperfect price discrimination can raise, lower, or leave unchanged total surplus in a market. The only certain conclusion is that price discrimination raises the monopoly's profit; otherwise, the firm would choose to charge all customers the same price.

15-4d Examples of Price Discrimination

Firms in our economy use various business strategies aimed at charging different prices to different customers. Now that we understand the economics of price discrimination, let's consider some examples.

Movie Tickets Many movie theaters charge a lower price for children and senior citizens than for other patrons. This fact is hard to explain in a competitive market. In a competitive market, price equals marginal cost, and the marginal cost of providing a seat for a child or senior citizen is the same as the marginal cost of providing a seat for anyone else. Yet the differential pricing is easily explained if movie theaters have some local monopoly power and if children and senior citizens have a lower willingness to pay for a ticket. In this case, movie theaters raise their profit by price discriminating.

Airline Prices Seats on airplanes are sold at many different prices. Most airlines charge a lower price for a round-trip ticket between two cities if the traveler stays over a Saturday night. At first, this seems odd. Why should it matter to the airline whether a passenger stays over a Saturday night? The reason is that this rule provides a way to separate business travelers and leisure travelers. A passenger on a business trip has a high willingness to pay and, most likely, does not want to stay over a Saturday night. By contrast, a passenger traveling for personal reasons has a lower willingness to pay and is more likely to be willing to stay over a Saturday night. Thus, the airlines can successfully price discriminate by charging a lower price for passengers who stay over a Saturday night.

"Would it bother you to hear how little I paid for this flight?"

Discount Coupons Many companies offer discount coupons to the public in newspapers, magazines, or online. A buyer simply has to clip the coupon to get $0.50 off her next purchase. Why do companies offer these coupons? Why don't they just cut the price of the product by $0.50?

The answer is that coupons allow companies to price discriminate. Companies know that not all customers are willing to spend time clipping coupons. Moreover, the willingness to clip coupons is related to the customer's willingness to pay for the good. A rich and busy executive is unlikely to spend her time clipping discount coupons out of the newspaper, and she is probably willing to pay a higher price for many goods. A person who is unemployed is more likely to clip coupons and to have a lower willingness to pay. Thus, by charging a lower price only to those customers who clip coupons, firms can successfully price discriminate.

Financial Aid Many colleges and universities give financial aid to needy students. One can view this policy as a type of price discrimination. Wealthy students have greater financial resources and, therefore, a higher willingness to pay than needy students. By charging high tuition and selectively offering financial aid, schools in effect charge prices to customers based on the value they place on going to that school. This behavior is similar to that of any price-discriminating monopolist.

Quantity Discounts   So far in our examples of price discrimination, the monopolist charges different prices to different customers. Sometimes, however, monopolists price discriminate by charging different prices to the same customer for different units that the customer buys. For example, many firms offer lower prices to customers who buy large quantities. A bakery might charge $0.50 for each donut but $5 for a dozen. This is a form of price discrimination because the customer pays a higher price for the first unit bought than for the twelfth. Quantity discounts are often a successful way of price discriminating because a customer's willingness to pay for an additional unit declines as the customer buys more units.

Quick Quiz   *Give two examples of price discrimination. • How does perfect price discrimination affect consumer surplus, producer surplus, and total surplus?*

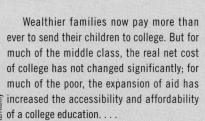

IN THE NEWS

Price Discrimination in Higher Education

Colleges and universities are increasingly charging different prices to different students, which makes data on the cost of education harder to interpret.

Misconceptions 101: Why College Costs Aren't Soaring

By Evan Soltas

© Monashee Frantz/Alamy

Conventional wisdom suggests that U.S. colleges and universities have become sharply more expensive in recent years.

"When kids do graduate, the most daunting challenge can be the cost of college," President Barack Obama said in his 2012 State of the Union address. "We can't just keep subsidizing skyrocketing tuition; we'll run out of money."

At first, the view that the cost of college is rising appears to have data on its side. Published tuition prices and fees at colleges have risen three times faster than the rate of Consumer Price Index inflation since 1978, according to the Bureau of Labor Statistics. . . .

Real tuition and fees have increased, to be sure, but hardly as significantly as the media often report or the data suggest at face value. The inflation-adjusted net price

of college has risen only modestly over the last two decades, according to data from the College Board's Annual Survey of Colleges.

What has happened is a shift toward price discrimination—offering multiple prices for the same product. Universities have offset the increase in sticker price for most families through an expansion of grant-based financial aid and scholarships. That has caused the BLS measure to rise without increasing the net cost.

Wealthier families now pay more than ever to send their children to college. But for much of the middle class, the real net cost of college has not changed significantly; for much of the poor, the expansion of aid has increased the accessibility and affordability of a college education. . . .

The nation's most selective institutions are leading the trend toward income-based price discrimination. For example, at Harvard University, the majority of students receive financial aid: In 2012, one year of undergraduate education had a sticker price of $54,496 and came with an average grant of roughly $41,000.

In other words, the cost burden of college has become significantly more progressive since the 1990s. Students from wealthier families not only now pay more for their own educations but also have come to heavily subsidize the costs of the less fortunate. ◢

Source: Bloomberg.com, November 27, 2012.

15-5 Public Policy toward Monopolies

We have seen that monopolies, in contrast to competitive markets, fail to allocate resources efficiently. Monopolies produce less than the socially desirable quantity of output and charge prices above marginal cost. Policymakers in the government can respond to the problem of monopoly in one of four ways:

- By trying to make monopolized industries more competitive.
- By regulating the behavior of the monopolies.
- By turning some private monopolies into public enterprises.
- By doing nothing at all.

15-5a Increasing Competition with Antitrust Laws

If Coca-Cola and PepsiCo wanted to merge, the deal would be closely examined by the federal government before it went into effect. The lawyers and economists in the Department of Justice might well decide that a merger between these two large soft-drink companies would make the U.S. soft-drink market substantially less competitive and, as a result, would reduce the economic well-being of the country as a whole. If so, the Department of Justice would challenge the merger in court, and if the judge agreed, the two companies would not be allowed to merge. It is precisely this kind of challenge that prevented software giant Microsoft from buying Intuit in 1994.

The government derives this power over private industry from the antitrust laws, a collection of statutes aimed at curbing monopoly power. The first and most important of these laws was the Sherman Antitrust Act, which Congress passed in 1890 to reduce the market power of the large and powerful "trusts" that were viewed as dominating the economy at the time. The Clayton Antitrust Act, passed in 1914, strengthened the government's powers and authorized private lawsuits. As the U.S. Supreme Court once put it, the antitrust laws are "a comprehensive charter of economic liberty aimed at preserving free and unfettered competition as the rule of trade."

The antitrust laws give the government various ways to promote competition. They allow the government to prevent mergers, such as our hypothetical merger between Coca-Cola and PepsiCo. They also allow the government to break up companies. For example, in 1984, the government split up AT&T, the large telecommunications company, into eight smaller companies. Finally, the antitrust laws prevent companies from coordinating their activities in ways that make markets less competitive.

Antitrust laws have costs as well as benefits. Sometimes companies merge not to reduce competition but to lower costs through more efficient joint production. These benefits from mergers are sometimes called *synergies*. For example, many U.S. banks have merged in recent years and, by combining operations, have been able to reduce administrative staff. If antitrust laws are to raise social welfare, the government must be able to determine which mergers are desirable and which are not. That is, it must be able to measure and compare the social benefit from synergies with the social costs of reduced competition. Critics of the antitrust laws are skeptical that the government can perform the necessary cost–benefit analysis with sufficient accuracy.

"But if we do merge with Amalgamated, we'll have enough resources to fight the antitrust violation caused by the merger."

15-5b Regulation

Another way the government deals with the problem of monopoly is by regulating the behavior of monopolists. This solution is common in the case of natural monopolies, such as water and electric companies. These companies are not allowed to charge any price they want. Instead, government agencies regulate their prices.

What price should the government set for a natural monopoly? This question is not as easy as it might at first appear. One might conclude that the price should equal the monopolist's marginal cost. If price equals marginal cost, customers will buy the quantity of the monopolist's output that maximizes total surplus and the allocation of resources will be efficient.

There are, however, two practical problems with marginal-cost pricing as a regulatory system. The first arises from the logic of cost curves. By definition, natural monopolies have declining average total cost. As we first discussed in Chapter 13, when average total cost is declining, marginal cost is less than average total cost. This situation is illustrated in Figure 10, which shows a firm with a large fixed cost and then constant marginal cost thereafter. If regulators were to set price equal to marginal cost, that price would be less than the firm's average total cost and the firm would lose money. Instead of charging such a low price, the monopoly firm would just exit the industry.

Regulators can respond to this problem in various ways, none of which is perfect. One way is to subsidize the monopolist. In essence, the government picks up the losses inherent in marginal-cost pricing. Yet to pay for the subsidy, the government needs to raise money through taxation, which involves its own deadweight losses. Alternatively, the regulators can allow the monopolist to charge a price higher than marginal cost. If the regulated price equals average total cost, the monopolist earns exactly zero economic profit. Yet average-cost pricing leads to deadweight losses because the monopolist's price no longer reflects the marginal cost of producing the good. In essence, average-cost pricing is like a tax on the good the monopolist is selling.

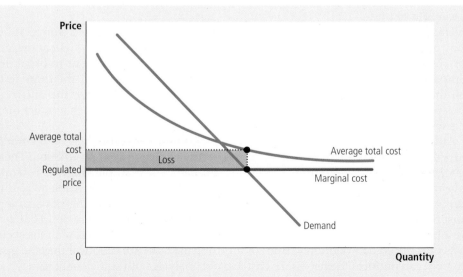

FIGURE 10

Marginal-Cost Pricing for a Natural Monopoly
Because a natural monopoly has declining average total cost, marginal cost is less than average total cost. Therefore, if regulators require a natural monopoly to charge a price equal to marginal cost, price will be below average total cost, and the monopoly will lose money.

The second problem with marginal-cost pricing as a regulatory system (and with average-cost pricing as well) is that it gives the monopolist no incentive to reduce costs. Each firm in a competitive market tries to reduce its costs because lower costs mean higher profits. But if a regulated monopolist knows that regulators will reduce prices whenever costs fall, the monopolist will not benefit from lower costs. In practice, regulators deal with this problem by allowing monopolists to keep some of the benefits from lower costs in the form of higher profit, a practice that requires some departure from marginal-cost pricing.

15-5c Public Ownership

The third policy used by the government to deal with monopoly is public ownership. That is, rather than regulating a natural monopoly that is run by a private firm, the government can run the monopoly itself. This solution is common in many European countries, where the government owns and operates utilities such as telephone, water, and electric companies. In the United States, the government runs the Postal Service. The delivery of ordinary first-class mail is often thought to be a natural monopoly.

Economists usually prefer private to public ownership of natural monopolies. The key issue is how the ownership of the firm affects the costs of production. Private owners have an incentive to minimize costs as long as they reap part of the benefit in the form of higher profit. If the firm's managers are doing a bad job of keeping costs down, the firm's owners will fire them. By contrast, if the government bureaucrats who run a monopoly do a bad job, the losers are the customers and taxpayers, whose only recourse is the political system. The bureaucrats may become a special-interest group and attempt to block cost-reducing reforms. Put simply, as a way of ensuring that firms are well run, the voting booth is less reliable than the profit motive.

15-5d Doing Nothing

Each of the foregoing policies aimed at reducing the problem of monopoly has drawbacks. As a result, some economists argue that it is often best for the government not to try to remedy the inefficiencies of monopoly pricing. Here is the assessment of economist George Stigler, who won the Nobel Prize for his work in industrial organization:

> A famous theorem in economics states that a competitive enterprise economy will produce the largest possible income from a given stock of resources. No real economy meets the exact conditions of the theorem, and all real economies will fall short of the ideal economy—a difference called "market failure." In my view, however, the degree of "market failure" for the American economy is much smaller than the "political failure" arising from the imperfections of economic policies found in real political systems.

As this quotation makes clear, determining the proper role of the government in the economy requires judgments about politics as well as economics.

Quick Quiz *Describe the ways policymakers can respond to the inefficiencies caused by monopolies. List a potential problem with each of these policy responses.*

15-6 Conclusion: The Prevalence of Monopolies

This chapter has discussed the behavior of firms that have control over the prices they charge. We have seen that these firms behave very differently from the competitive firms studied in the previous chapter. Table 2 summarizes some of the key similarities and differences between competitive and monopoly markets.

From the standpoint of public policy, a crucial result is that a monopolist produces less than the socially efficient quantity and charges a price above marginal cost. As a result, a monopoly causes deadweight losses. In some cases, these inefficiencies can be mitigated through price discrimination by the monopolist, but other times, they call for policymakers to take an active role.

How prevalent are the problems of monopoly? There are two answers to this question.

In one sense, monopolies are common. Most firms have some control over the prices they charge. They are not forced to charge the market price for their goods because their goods are not exactly the same as those offered by other firms. A Ford Taurus is not the same as a Toyota Camry. Ben and Jerry's ice cream is not the same as Breyer's. Each of these goods has a downward-sloping demand curve, which gives each producer some degree of monopoly power.

Yet firms with substantial monopoly power are rare. Few goods are truly unique. Most have substitutes that, even if not exactly the same, are similar. Ben and Jerry can raise the price of their ice cream a little without losing all their sales, but if they raise it a lot, sales will fall substantially as their customers switch to other brands.

In the end, monopoly power is a matter of degree. It is true that many firms have some monopoly power. It is also true that their monopoly power is usually limited. In such a situation, we will not go far wrong assuming that firms operate in competitive markets, even if that is not precisely the case.

TABLE 2

Competition versus Monopoly: A Summary Comparison

	Competition	Monopoly
Similarities		
Goal of firms	Maximize profits	Maximize profits
Rule for maximizing	$MR = MC$	$MR = MC$
Can earn economic profits in the short run?	Yes	Yes
Differences		
Number of firms	Many	One
Marginal revenue	$MR = P$	$MR < P$
Price	$P = MC$	$P > MC$
Produces welfare-maximizing level of output?	Yes	No
Entry in the long run?	Yes	No
Can earn economic profits in the long run?	No	Yes
Price discrimination possible?	No	Yes

Summary

- A monopoly is a firm that is the sole seller in its market. A monopoly arises when a single firm owns a key resource, when the government gives a firm the exclusive right to produce a good, or when a single firm can supply the entire market at a lower cost than many firms could.

- Because a monopoly is the sole producer in its market, it faces a downward-sloping demand curve for its product. When a monopoly increases production by 1 unit, it causes the price of its good to fall, which reduces the amount of revenue earned on all units produced. As a result, a monopoly's marginal revenue is always below the price of its good.

- Like a competitive firm, a monopoly firm maximizes profit by producing the quantity at which marginal revenue equals marginal cost. The monopoly then sets the price at which that quantity is demanded. Unlike a competitive firm, a monopoly firm's price exceeds its marginal revenue, so its price exceeds marginal cost.

- A monopolist's profit-maximizing level of output is below the level that maximizes the sum of consumer and producer surplus. That is, when the monopoly charges a price above marginal cost, some consumers who value the good more than its cost of production do not buy it. As a result, monopoly causes deadweight losses similar to those caused by taxes.

- A monopolist can often increase profits by charging different prices for the same good based on a buyer's willingness to pay. This practice of price discrimination can raise economic welfare by getting the good to some consumers who otherwise would not buy it. In the extreme case of perfect price discrimination, the deadweight loss of monopoly is completely eliminated and the entire surplus in the market goes to the monopoly producer. More generally, when price discrimination is imperfect, it can either raise or lower welfare compared to the outcome with a single monopoly price.

- Policymakers can respond to the inefficiency of monopoly behavior in four ways. They can use the antitrust laws to try to make the industry more competitive. They can regulate the prices that the monopoly charges. They can turn the monopolist into a government-run enterprise. Or, if the market failure is deemed small compared to the inevitable imperfections of policies, they can do nothing at all.

Key Concepts

monopoly, *p. 300*   natural monopoly, *p. 302*   price discrimination, *p. 314*

Questions for Review

1. Give an example of a government-created monopoly. Is creating this monopoly necessarily bad public policy? Explain.

2. Define *natural monopoly*. What does the size of a market have to do with whether an industry is a natural monopoly?

3. Why is a monopolist's marginal revenue less than the price of its good? Can marginal revenue ever be negative? Explain.

4. Draw the demand, marginal-revenue, average-total-cost, and marginal-cost curves for a monopolist. Show the profit-maximizing level of output, the profit-maximizing price, and the amount of profit.

5. In your diagram from the previous question, show the level of output that maximizes total surplus.

Show the deadweight loss from the monopoly. Explain your answer.

6. Give two examples of price discrimination. In each case, explain why the monopolist chooses to follow this business strategy.

7. What gives the government the power to regulate mergers between firms? Give a good reason and a bad reason (from the perspective of society's welfare) that two firms might want to merge.

8. Describe the two problems that arise when regulators tell a natural monopoly that it must set a price equal to marginal cost.

Quick Check Multiple Choice

1. A firm is a natural monopoly if it exhibits the following as its output increases:
   a. decreasing marginal revenue
   b. increasing marginal cost
   c. decreasing average revenue
   d. decreasing average total cost

2. For a profit-maximizing monopoly that charges the same price to all consumers, what is the relationship between price P, marginal revenue MR, and marginal cost MC?
   a. $P = MR$ and $MR = MC$.
   b. $P > MR$ and $MR = MC$.
   c. $P = MR$ and $MR > MC$.
   d. $P > MR$ and $MR > MC$.

3. If a monopoly's fixed costs increase, its price will _____ and its profit will _____.
   a. increase, decrease
   b. decrease, increase
   c. increase, stay the same
   d. stay the same, decrease

4. Compared to the social optimum, a monopoly firm chooses
   a. a quantity that is too low and a price that is too high.
   b. a quantity that is too high and a price that is too low.
   c. a quantity and a price that are both too high.
   d. a quantity and a price that are both too low.

5. The deadweight loss from monopoly arises because
   a. the monopoly firm makes higher profits than a competitive firm would.
   b. some potential consumers who forgo buying the good value it more than its marginal cost.
   c. consumers who buy the good have to pay more than marginal cost, reducing their consumer surplus.
   d. the monopoly firm chooses a quantity that fails to equate price and average revenue.

6. When a monopolist switches from charging a single price to perfect price discrimination, it reduces
   a. the quantity produced.
   b. the firm's profit.
   c. consumer surplus.
   d. total surplus.

Problems and Applications

1. A publisher faces the following demand schedule for the next novel from one of its popular authors:

Price	Quantity Demanded
$100	0 novels
90	100,000
80	200,000
70	300,000
60	400,000
50	500,000
40	600,000
30	700,000
20	800,000
10	900,000
0	1,000,000

   The author is paid $2 million to write the book, and the marginal cost of publishing the book is a constant $10 per book.
   a. Compute total revenue, total cost, and profit at each quantity. What quantity would a profit-maximizing publisher choose? What price would it charge?

   b. Compute marginal revenue. (Recall that $MR = \Delta TR/\Delta Q$.) How does marginal revenue compare to the price? Explain.
   c. Graph the marginal-revenue, marginal-cost, and demand curves. At what quantity do the marginal-revenue and marginal-cost curves cross? What does this signify?
   d. In your graph, shade in the deadweight loss. Explain in words what this means.
   e. If the author were paid $3 million instead of $2 million to write the book, how would this affect the publisher's decision regarding what price to charge? Explain.
   f. Suppose the publisher was not profit-maximizing but was concerned with maximizing economic efficiency. What price would it charge for the book? How much profit would it make at this price?

2. A small town is served by many competing supermarkets, which have the same constant marginal cost.
   a. Using a diagram of the market for groceries, show the consumer surplus, producer surplus, and total surplus.

b. Now suppose that the independent supermarkets combine into one chain. Using a new diagram, show the new consumer surplus, producer surplus, and total surplus. Relative to the competitive market, what is the transfer from consumers to producers? What is the deadweight loss?

3. Johnny Rockabilly has just finished recording his latest CD. His record company's marketing department determines that the demand for the CD is as follows:

Price	Number of CDs
$24	10,000
22	20,000
20	30,000
18	40,000
16	50,000
14	60,000

The company can produce the CD with no fixed cost and a variable cost of $5 per CD.
a. Find total revenue for quantity equal to 10,000, 20,000, and so on. What is the marginal revenue for each 10,000 increase in the quantity sold?
b. What quantity of CDs would maximize profit? What would the price be? What would the profit be?
c. If you were Johnny's agent, what recording fee would you advise Johnny to demand from the record company? Why?

4. A company is considering building a bridge across a river. The bridge would cost $2 million to build and nothing to maintain. The following table shows the company's anticipated demand over the lifetime of the bridge:

Price per Crossing	Number of Crossings, in Thousands
$8	0
7	100
6	200
5	300
4	400
3	500
2	600
1	700
0	800

a. If the company were to build the bridge, what would be its profit-maximizing price? Would that be the efficient level of output? Why or why not?
b. If the company is interested in maximizing profit, should it build the bridge? What would be its profit or loss?

c. If the government were to build the bridge, what price should it charge?
d. Should the government build the bridge? Explain.

5. Larry, Curly, and Moe run the only saloon in town. Larry wants to sell as many drinks as possible without losing money. Curly wants the saloon to bring in as much revenue as possible. Moe wants to make the largest possible profits. Using a single diagram of the saloon's demand curve and its cost curves, show the price and quantity combinations favored by each of the three partners. Explain.

6. The residents of the town Ectenia all love economics, and the mayor proposes building an economics museum. The museum has a fixed cost of $2,400,000 and no variable costs. There are 100,000 town residents, and each has the same demand for museum visits: $Q^D = 10 - P$, where P is the price of admission.
a. Graph the museum's average-total-cost curve and its marginal-cost curve. What kind of market would describe the museum?
b. The mayor proposes financing the museum with a lump-sum tax of $24 and then opening the museum to the public for free. How many times would each person visit? Calculate the benefit each person would get from the museum, measured as consumer surplus minus the new tax.
c. The mayor's antitax opponent says the museum should finance itself by charging an admission fee. What is the lowest price the museum can charge without incurring losses? (*Hint:* Find the number of visits and museum profits for prices of $2, $3, $4, and $5.)
d. For the break-even price you found in part (c), calculate each resident's consumer surplus. Compared with the mayor's plan, who is better off with this admission fee, and who is worse off? Explain.
e. What real-world considerations absent in the problem above might provide reasons to favor an admission fee?

7. Consider the relationship between monopoly pricing and price elasticity of demand.
a. Explain why a monopolist will never produce a quantity at which the demand curve is inelastic. (*Hint:* If demand is inelastic and the firm raises its price, what happens to total revenue and total costs?)
b. Draw a diagram for a monopolist, precisely labeling the portion of the demand curve that is inelastic. (*Hint:* The answer is related to the marginal-revenue curve.)
c. On your diagram, show the quantity and price that maximize total revenue.

8. You live in a town with 300 adults and 200 children, and you are thinking about putting on a play to

entertain your neighbors and make some money. A play has a fixed cost of $2,000, but selling an extra ticket has zero marginal cost. Here are the demand schedules for your two types of customers:

Price	Adults	Children
$10	0	0
9	100	0
8	200	0
7	300	0
6	300	0
5	300	100
4	300	200
3	300	200
2	300	200
1	300	200
0	300	200

a. To maximize profit, what price would you charge for an adult ticket? For a child's ticket? How much profit do you make?

b. The city council passes a law prohibiting you from charging different prices to different customers. What price do you set for a ticket now? How much profit do you make?

c. Who is worse off because of the law prohibiting price discrimination? Who is better off? (If you can, quantify the changes in welfare.)

d. If the fixed cost of the play were $2,500 rather than $2,000, how would your answers to parts (a), (b), and (c) change?

9. Only one firm produces and sells soccer balls in the country of Wiknam, and as the story begins, international trade in soccer balls is prohibited. The following equations describe the monopolist's demand, marginal revenue, total cost, and marginal cost:

$$\text{Demand: } P = 10 - Q$$
$$\text{Marginal Revenue: } MR = 10 - 2Q$$
$$\text{Total Cost: } TC = 3 + Q + 0.5Q^2$$
$$\text{Marginal Cost: } MC = 1 + Q$$

where Q is quantity and P is the price measured in Wiknamian dollars.

a. How many soccer balls does the monopolist produce? At what price are they sold? What is the monopolist's profit?

b. One day, the King of Wiknam decrees that henceforth there will be free trade—either imports or exports— of soccer balls at the world price of $6. The firm is now a price taker in a competitive market. What happens to domestic production of soccer balls? To domestic consumption? Does Wiknam export or import soccer balls?

c. In our analysis of international trade in Chapter 9, a country becomes an exporter when the price without trade is below the world price and an importer when the price without trade is above the world price. Does that conclusion hold in your answers to parts (a) and (b)? Explain.

d. Suppose that the world price was not $6 but, instead, happened to be exactly the same as the domestic price without trade as determined in part (a). Would allowing trade have changed anything in the Wiknamian economy? Explain. How does the result here compare with the analysis in Chapter 9?

10. Based on market research, a film production company in Ectenia obtains the following information about the demand and production costs of its new DVD:

$$\text{Demand: } P = 1,000 - 10Q$$
$$\text{Total Revenue: } TR = 1,000Q - 10Q^2$$
$$\text{Marginal Revenue: } MR = 1,000 - 20Q$$
$$\text{Marginal Cost: } MC = 100 + 10Q$$

where Q indicates the number of copies sold and P is the price in Ectenian dollars.

a. Find the price and quantity that maximize the company's profit.

b. Find the price and quantity that would maximize social welfare.

c. Calculate the deadweight loss from monopoly.

d. Suppose, in addition to the costs above, the director of the film has to be paid. The company is considering four options:
   i. a flat fee of 2,000 Ectenian dollars.
   ii. 50 percent of the profits.
   iii. 150 Ectenian dollars per unit sold.
   iv. 50 percent of the revenue.

For each option, calculate the profit-maximizing price and quantity. Which, if any, of these compensation schemes would alter the deadweight loss from monopoly? Explain.

11. Many schemes for price discriminating involve some cost. For example, discount coupons take up the time and resources of both the buyer and the seller. This question considers the implications of costly price discrimination. To keep things simple, let's assume that our monopolist's production costs are simply proportional to output so that average total cost and marginal cost are constant and equal to each other.

a. Draw the cost, demand, and marginal-revenue curves for the monopolist. Show the price the monopolist would charge without price discrimination.

b. In your diagram, mark the area equal to the monopolist's profit and call it X. Mark the area equal to consumer surplus and call it Y. Mark the area equal to the deadweight loss and call it Z.

c. Now suppose that the monopolist can perfectly price discriminate. What is the monopolist's profit? (Give your answer in terms of X, Y, and Z.)

d. What is the change in the monopolist's profit from price discrimination? What is the change in total surplus from price discrimination? Which change is larger? Explain. (Give your answer in terms of X, Y, and Z.)

e. Now suppose that there is some cost of price discrimination. To model this cost, let's assume that the monopolist has to pay a fixed cost C to price discriminate. How would a monopolist make the decision whether to pay this fixed cost? (Give your answer in terms of X, Y, Z, and C.)

f. How would a benevolent social planner, who cares about total surplus, decide whether the monopolist should price discriminate? (Give your answer in terms of X, Y, Z, and C.)

g. Compare your answers to parts (e) and (f). How does the monopolist's incentive to price discriminate differ from the social planner's? Is it possible that the monopolist will price discriminate even though doing so is not socially desirable?

Go to CengageBrain.com to purchase access to the proven, critical Study Guide to accompany this text, which features additional notes and context, practice tests, and much more.

CHAPTER

16

Monopolistic Competition

Price Makers

Y ou walk into a bookstore to buy a book to read during your next vacation. On the store's shelves you find a Sue Grafton mystery, a Stephen King thriller, a David McCullough history, a Stephenie Meyer vampire romance, and many other choices. When you pick out a book and buy it, what kind of market are you participating in?

On the one hand, the market for books seems competitive. As you look over the shelves at your bookstore, you find many authors and many publishers vying for your attention. A buyer in this market has thousands of competing products from which to choose. And because anyone can enter the industry by writing and publishing a book, the book business is not very profitable. For every highly paid novelist, there are hundreds of struggling ones.

On the other hand, the market for books seems monopolistic. Because each book is unique, publishers have some latitude in choosing what price to charge. The sellers in this market are price makers rather than price takers.

329

And indeed, the price of books greatly exceeds marginal cost. The price of a typical hardcover novel, for instance, is about $25, whereas the cost of printing one additional copy of the novel is less than $5.

The market for novels fits neither the competitive nor the monopoly model. Instead, it is best described by the model of *monopolistic competition*, the subject of this chapter. The term "monopolistic competition" might at first seem to be an oxymoron, like "jumbo shrimp." But as we will see, monopolistically competitive industries are monopolistic in some ways and competitive in others. The model describes not only the publishing industry but also the market for many other goods and services.

16-1 Between Monopoly and Perfect Competition

The previous two chapters analyzed markets with many competitive firms and markets with a single monopoly firm. In Chapter 14, we saw that the price in a perfectly competitive market always equals the marginal cost of production. We also saw that, in the long run, entry and exit drive economic profit to zero, so the price also equals average total cost. In Chapter 15, we saw how monopoly firms can use their market power to keep prices above marginal cost, leading to a positive economic profit for the firm and a deadweight loss for society. Competition and monopoly are extreme forms of market structure. Competition occurs when there are many firms in a market offering essentially identical products; monopoly occurs when there is only one firm in a market.

Although the cases of perfect competition and monopoly illustrate some important ideas about how markets work, most markets in the economy include elements of both these cases and, therefore, are not completely described by either of them. The typical firm in the economy faces competition, but the competition is not so rigorous that it makes the firm a price taker like the firms analyzed in Chapter 14. The typical firm also has some degree of market power, but its market power is not so great that the firm can be described exactly by the monopoly model presented in Chapter 15. In other words, many industries fall somewhere between the polar cases of perfect competition and monopoly. Economists call this situation *imperfect competition*.

oligopoly
a market structure in which only a few sellers offer similar or identical products

One type of imperfectly competitive market is an **oligopoly**, a market with only a few sellers, each offering a product that is similar or identical to the products offered by other sellers in the market. Economists measure a market's domination by a small number of firms with a statistic called the *concentration ratio*, which is the percentage of total output in the market supplied by the four largest firms. In the U.S. economy, most industries have a four-firm concentration ratio under 50 percent, but in some industries, the biggest firms play a more dominant role. Highly concentrated industries include the market for electric lamp bulbs (which has a concentration ratio of 75 percent), breakfast cereal (80 percent), aircraft manufacturing (81 percent), household laundry equipment (98 percent), and cigarettes (98 percent). These industries are best described as oligopolies. In the next chapter we see that the small number of firms in oligopolies makes strategic interactions among them a key part of the analysis. That is, in choosing how much to produce and what price to charge, each firm in an oligopoly is concerned not only with what its competitors are doing but also with how its competitors would react to what it might do.

monopolistic competition
a market structure in which many firms sell products that are similar but not identical

A second type of imperfectly competitive market is called **monopolistic competition**. This describes a market structure in which there are many firms selling products that are similar but not identical. In a monopolistically competitive market, each firm has a monopoly over the product it makes, but many other firms make similar products that compete for the same customers.

To be more precise, monopolistic competition describes a market with the following attributes:

- *Many sellers:* There are many firms competing for the same group of customers.
- *Product differentiation:* Each firm produces a product that is at least slightly different from those of other firms. Thus, rather than being a price taker, each firm faces a downward-sloping demand curve.
- *Free entry and exit:* Firms can enter or exit the market without restriction. Thus, the number of firms in the market adjusts until economic profits are driven to zero.

A moment's thought reveals a long list of markets with these attributes: books, DVDs, computer games, restaurants, piano lessons, cookies, clothing, and so on.

Monopolistic competition, like oligopoly, is a market structure that lies between the extreme cases of perfect competition and monopoly. But oligopoly and monopolistic competition are quite different. Oligopoly departs from the perfectly competitive ideal of Chapter 14 because there are only a few sellers in the market. The small number of sellers makes rigorous competition less likely and strategic interactions among them vitally important. By contrast, a monopolistically competitive market has many sellers, each of which is small compared to the market. It departs from the perfectly competitive ideal because each of the sellers offers a somewhat different product.

Figure 1 summarizes the four types of market structure. The first question to ask about any market is how many firms there are. If there is only one firm, the market is a monopoly. If there are only a few firms, the market is an oligopoly. If there are many firms, we need to ask another question: Do the firms sell identical or differentiated products? If the many firms sell differentiated products, the market is monopolistically competitive. If the many firms sell identical products, the market is perfectly competitive.

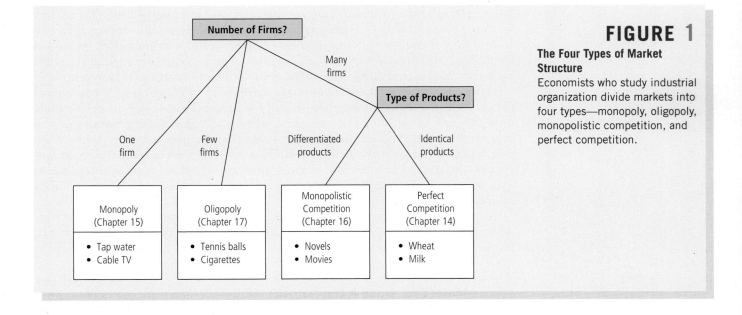

FIGURE 1

The Four Types of Market Structure
Economists who study industrial organization divide markets into four types—monopoly, oligopoly, monopolistic competition, and perfect competition.

Because reality is never as clear-cut as theory, at times you may find it hard to decide what structure best describes a market. There is, for instance, no magic number that separates "few" from "many" when counting the number of firms. (Do the approximately dozen companies that now sell cars in the United States make this market an oligopoly, or is the market more competitive? The answer is open to debate.) Similarly, there is no sure way to determine when products are differentiated and when they are identical. (Are different brands of milk really the same? Again, the answer is debatable.) When analyzing actual markets, economists have to keep in mind the lessons learned from studying all types of market structure and then apply each lesson as it seems appropriate.

Now that we understand how economists define the various types of market structure, we can continue our analysis of each of them. In this chapter we examine monopolistic competition. In the next chapter we analyze oligopoly.

Quick Quiz   *Define* oligopoly *and* monopolistic competition *and give an example of each.*

16-2 Competition with Differentiated Products

To understand monopolistically competitive markets, we first consider the decisions facing an individual firm. We then examine what happens in the long run as firms enter and exit the industry. Next, we compare the equilibrium under monopolistic competition to the equilibrium under perfect competition that we examined in Chapter 14. Finally, we consider whether the outcome in a monopolistically competitive market is desirable from the standpoint of society as a whole.

16-2a The Monopolistically Competitive Firm in the Short Run

Each firm in a monopolistically competitive market is, in many ways, like a monopoly. Because its product is different from those offered by other firms, it faces a downward-sloping demand curve. (By contrast, a perfectly competitive firm faces a horizontal demand curve at the market price.) Thus, the monopolistically competitive firm follows a monopolist's rule for profit maximization: It chooses to produce the quantity at which marginal revenue equals marginal cost and then uses its demand curve to find the price at which it can sell that quantity.

Figure 2 shows the cost, demand, and marginal-revenue curves for two typical firms, each in a different monopolistically competitive industry. In both panels of this figure, the profit-maximizing quantity is found at the intersection of the marginal-revenue and marginal-cost curves. The two panels in this figure show different outcomes for the firm's profit. In panel (a), price exceeds average total cost, so the firm makes a profit. In panel (b), price is below average total cost. In this case, the firm is unable to make a positive profit, so the best the firm can do is to minimize its losses.

All this should seem familiar. A monopolistically competitive firm chooses its quantity and price just as a monopoly does. In the short run, these two types of market structure are similar.

16-2b The Long-Run Equilibrium

The situations depicted in Figure 2 do not last long. When firms are making profits, as in panel (a), new firms have an incentive to enter the market. This entry

Monopolistic competitors, like monopolists, maximize profit by producing the quantity at which marginal revenue equals marginal cost. The firm in panel (a) makes a profit because, at this quantity, price is above average total cost. The firm in panel (b) makes losses because, at this quantity, price is less than average total cost.

FIGURE 2

Monopolistic Competitors in the Short Run

(a) Firm Makes Profit

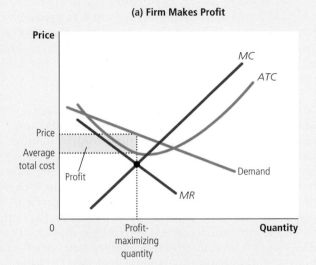

(b) Firm Makes Losses

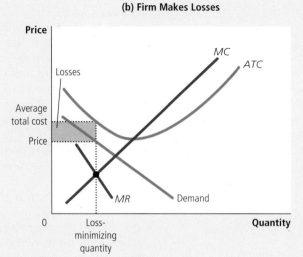

"GIVEN THE DOWNWARD SLOPE OF OUR DEMAND CURVE, AND THE EASE WITH WHICH OTHER FIRMS CAN ENTER THE INDUSTRY, WE CAN STRENGTHEN OUR PROFIT POSITION ONLY BY EQUATING MARGINAL COST AND MARGINAL REVENUE. ORDER MORE JELLY BEANS."

ScienceCartoonsPlus.com

increases the number of products from which customers can choose and, therefore, reduces the demand faced by each firm already in the market. In other words, profit encourages entry, and entry shifts the demand curves faced by the incumbent firms to the left. As the demand for incumbent firms' products falls, these firms experience declining profit.

Conversely, when firms are making losses, as in panel (b), firms in the market have an incentive to exit. As firms exit, customers have fewer products from which to choose. This decrease in the number of firms expands the demand faced by those firms that stay in the market. In other words, losses encourage exit, and exit shifts the demand curves of the remaining firms to the right. As the demand for the remaining firms' products rises, these firms experience rising profits (that is, declining losses).

This process of entry and exit continues until the firms in the market are making exactly zero economic profit. Figure 3 depicts the long-run equilibrium. Once the market reaches this equilibrium, new firms have no incentive to enter, and existing firms have no incentive to exit.

Notice that the demand curve in Figure 3 just barely touches the average-total-cost curve. Mathematically, we say the two curves are *tangent* to each other. These two curves must be tangent once entry and exit have driven profit to zero. Because profit per unit sold is the difference between price (found on the demand curve) and average total cost, the maximum profit is zero only if these two curves touch each other without crossing. Also note that this point of tangency occurs at the same quantity where marginal revenue equals marginal cost. That these two points line up is not a coincidence: It is required because this particular quantity maximizes profit and the maximum profit is exactly zero in the long run.

To sum up, two characteristics describe the long-run equilibrium in a monopolistically competitive market:

- As in a monopoly market, price exceeds marginal cost. This conclusion arises because profit maximization requires marginal revenue to equal marginal cost

FIGURE 3

A Monopolistic Competitor in the Long Run

In a monopolistically competitive market, if firms are making profits, new firms enter, and the demand curves for the incumbent firms shift to the left. Similarly, if firms are making losses, some of the firms in the market exit and the demand curves of the remaining firms shift to the right. Because of these shifts in demand, monopolistically competitive firms eventually find themselves in the long-run equilibrium shown here. In this long-run equilibrium, price equals average total cost and each firm earns zero profit.

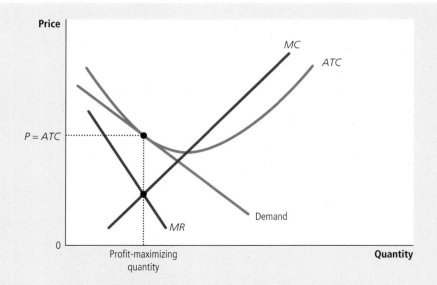

and because the downward-sloping demand curve makes marginal revenue less than the price.
- As in a competitive market, price equals average total cost. This conclusion arises because free entry and exit drive economic profit to zero.

The second characteristic shows how monopolistic competition differs from monopoly. Because a monopoly is the sole seller of a product without close substitutes, it can earn positive economic profit, even in the long run. By contrast, because there is free entry into a monopolistically competitive market, the economic profit of a firm in this type of market is driven to zero.

16-2c Monopolistic versus Perfect Competition

Figure 4 compares the long-run equilibrium under monopolistic competition to the long-run equilibrium under perfect competition. (Chapter 14 discussed the equilibrium with perfect competition.) There are two noteworthy differences between monopolistic and perfect competition: excess capacity and the markup.

Excess Capacity   As we have just seen, the process of entry and exit drives each firm in a monopolistically competitive market to a point of tangency between its demand and average-total-cost curves. Panel (a) of Figure 4 shows that the quantity of output at this point is smaller than the quantity that minimizes average total cost. Thus, under monopolistic competition, firms produce on the downward-sloping

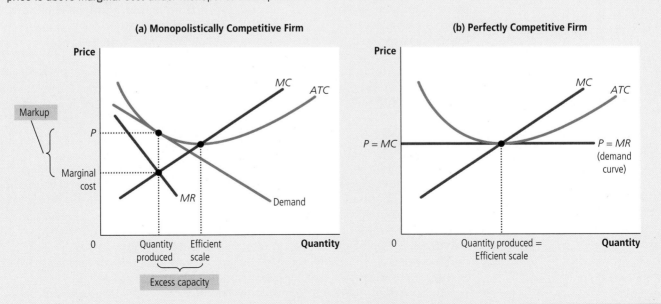

Panel (a) shows the long-run equilibrium in a monopolistically competitive market, and panel (b) shows the long-run equilibrium in a perfectly competitive market. Two differences are notable. (1) The perfectly competitive firm produces at the efficient scale, where average total cost is minimized. By contrast, the monopolistically competitive firm produces at less than the efficient scale. (2) Price equals marginal cost under perfect competition, but price is above marginal cost under monopolistic competition.

FIGURE 4

Monopolistic versus Perfect Competition

(a) Monopolistically Competitive Firm

(b) Perfectly Competitive Firm

portion of their average-total-cost curves. In this way, monopolistic competition contrasts starkly with perfect competition. As panel (b) of Figure 4 shows, free entry in competitive markets drives firms to produce at the minimum of average total cost.

The quantity that minimizes average total cost is called the *efficient scale* of the firm. In the long run, perfectly competitive firms produce at the efficient scale, whereas monopolistically competitive firms produce below this level. Firms are said to have *excess capacity* under monopolistic competition. In other words, a monopolistically competitive firm, unlike a perfectly competitive firm, could increase the quantity it produces and lower the average total cost of production. The firm forgoes this opportunity because it would need to cut its price to sell the additional output. It is more profitable for a monopolistic competitor to continue operating with excess capacity.

Markup over Marginal Cost   A second difference between perfect competition and monopolistic competition is the relationship between price and marginal cost. For a perfectly competitive firm, such as the one shown in panel (b) of Figure 4, price equals marginal cost. For a monopolistically competitive firm, such as the one shown in panel (a), price exceeds marginal cost because the firm always has some market power.

How is this markup over marginal cost consistent with free entry and zero profit? The zero-profit condition ensures only that price equals average total cost. It does *not* ensure that price equals marginal cost. Indeed, in the long-run equilibrium, monopolistically competitive firms operate on the declining portion of their average-total-cost curves, so marginal cost is below average total cost. Thus, for price to equal average total cost, price must be above marginal cost.

In this relationship between price and marginal cost, we see a key behavioral difference between perfect competitors and monopolistic competitors. Imagine that you were to ask a firm the following question: "Would you like to see another customer come through your door ready to buy from you at your current price?" A perfectly competitive firm would answer that it didn't care. Because price exactly equals marginal cost, the profit from an extra unit sold is zero. By contrast, a monopolistically competitive firm is always eager to get another customer. Because its price exceeds marginal cost, an extra unit sold at the posted price means more profit.

According to an old quip, monopolistically competitive markets are those in which sellers send Christmas cards to the buyers. Trying to attract more customers makes sense only if price exceeds marginal cost.

16-2d Monopolistic Competition and the Welfare of Society

Is the outcome in a monopolistically competitive market desirable from the standpoint of society as a whole? Can policymakers improve on the market outcome? In previous chapters we evaluated markets from the standpoint of efficiency— that is, whether society is getting the most it can out of its scarce resources. We learned that competitive markets lead to efficient outcomes, unless there are externalities, whereas monopoly markets lead to deadweight losses. Monopolistically competitive markets are more complex than either of these polar cases, so evaluating welfare in these markets is a more subtle exercise.

One source of inefficiency is the markup of price over marginal cost. Because of the markup, some consumers who value the good at more than the marginal cost of production (but less than the price) will be deterred from buying it. Thus, a monopolistically competitive market has the normal deadweight loss of monopoly pricing.

This outcome is undesirable compared with the efficient quantity that arises when price equals marginal cost, but policymakers don't have an easy way to fix the problem. To enforce marginal-cost pricing, they would need to regulate all firms that produce differentiated products. Because such products are so common in the economy, the administrative burden of such regulation would be overwhelming.

Moreover, regulating monopolistic competitors entails all the problems of regulating natural monopolies. In particular, because monopolistic competitors are making zero profits already, requiring them to lower their prices to equal marginal cost would cause them to make losses. To keep these firms in business, the government would need to help them cover these losses. Rather than raise taxes to pay for these subsidies, policymakers often decide it is better to live with the inefficiency of monopolistic pricing.

Another way in which monopolistic competition may be socially inefficient is that the number of firms in the market may not be "ideal." That is, there may be too much or too little entry. One way to think about this problem is in terms of the externalities associated with entry. Whenever a new firm considers entering the market with a new product, it takes into account only the profit it would make. Yet its entry would also have the following two effects that are external to the firm:

- *The product-variety externality:* Because consumers get some consumer surplus from the introduction of a new product, entry of a new firm conveys a positive externality on consumers.
- *The business-stealing externality:* Because other firms lose customers and profits from the entry of a new competitor, entry of a new firm imposes a negative externality on existing firms.

Thus, in a monopolistically competitive market, there are positive and negative externalities associated with the entry of new firms. Depending on which externality is larger, a monopolistically competitive market could have either too few or too many products.

Both of these externalities are closely related to the conditions for monopolistic competition. The product-variety externality arises because new firms offer products that differ from those of the existing firms. The business-stealing externality arises because firms post a price above marginal cost and, therefore, are always eager to sell additional units. Conversely, because perfectly competitive firms produce identical goods and charge a price equal to marginal cost, neither of these externalities exists under perfect competition.

In the end, we can conclude only that monopolistically competitive markets do not have all the desirable welfare properties of perfectly competitive markets. That is, the invisible hand does not ensure that total surplus is maximized under monopolistic competition. Yet because the inefficiencies are subtle, hard to measure, and hard to fix, there is no easy way for public policy to improve the market outcome.

Quick Quiz   *List the three key attributes of monopolistic competition. • Draw and explain a diagram to show the long-run equilibrium in a monopolistically competitive market. How does this equilibrium differ from that in a perfectly competitive market?*

IN THE NEWS
··············

Insufficient Variety as a Market Failure

In the presence of large fixed costs, the market may insufficiently serve customers with unusual preferences.

If the Shoe Doesn't Fit

By Joel Waldfogel

Last week, Nike unveiled a shoe designed specifically for American Indians. The sneaker has both a native-theme design and—more importantly—a wider shape to accommodate the distinctly shaped feet of American Indians. With diabetes and related conditions near epidemic levels in some tribes, American Indian leaders were happy to welcome this comfortable product. If anything, what seems odd is that it took so long. After all, free-market economists have told us for decades that we should rely on market decisions, not the government, to meet our needs, because it's the market that satisfies everyone's every desire.

And yet it turns out that it's the Indians' long wait for a good sneaker that's typical. For small groups with preferences outside the norm, the market often fails to deliver, as I argue in my new book, *The Tyranny of the Market: Why You Can't Always Get What You Want.*

John Stuart Mill pointed out that voting gives rise to a tyranny of the majority. If we vote on what color shirts to make—or whether to make wide or narrow shoes—then the majority gets what it prefers, and the minority does not. The market, on the other hand, is supposed to work differently. As Milton Friedman eloquently put it in 1962, "the characteristic feature of action through political channels is that it tends to require or enforce substantial conformity. The great advantage of the market is that it permits wide diversity. Each man can vote, as it were, for the color of tie he wants and get it; he does not have to see what color the majority wants and then, if he is in the minority, submit." This is a wonderful argument. Except that for many products and for many people, it's wrong.

Two simple conditions that prevail in many markets mean that individual taste alone doesn't determine individual satisfaction. These conditions are (1) big setup costs and (2) preferences that differ across groups; when they're present, an individual's

satisfaction is a function of how many people share his or her tastes. In other words, in these cases, markets share some of the objectionable features of government. They give bigger groups more and better options.

In my research, I've discovered that this phenomenon is widespread. Ten years ago, I started studying radio-station listening patterns. I noticed that people listened to the radio more in metro areas of the United States with relatively large populations. This is not terribly surprising. In larger cities, more stations can attract enough listeners and advertising revenue to cover their costs and stay on the air. With more to choose from on the dial, residents tune in more. So, in this situation of high fixed costs (each station needs a following to keep broadcasting), people help one another by making more options viable.

But who benefits whom? When I looked at black and white listeners separately, I noticed something surprising. Blacks listen more in cities

16-3 Advertising

It is nearly impossible to go through a typical day in a modern economy without being bombarded with advertising. Whether you are surfing the Internet, posting on Facebook, reading a newspaper, watching television, or driving down the highway, some firm will try to convince you to buy its product. Such behavior is a natural feature of monopolistic competition (as well as some oligopolistic industries). When firms sell differentiated products and charge prices above marginal cost, each firm has an incentive to advertise to attract more buyers to its particular product.

The amount of advertising varies substantially across products. Firms that sell highly differentiated consumer goods, such as over-the-counter drugs, perfumes, soft drinks, razor blades, breakfast cereals, and dog food, typically spend between 10 and 20 percent of revenue on advertising. Firms that sell industrial products, such as drill presses and communications satellites, typically spend very little on advertising. And firms that sell homogeneous products, such as wheat, peanuts, and crude oil, spend nothing at all.

with larger black populations, and whites listen more in cities with larger white populations. Black listening does *not* increase where there's a higher white population, and white listening does not increase with a higher black population. Which means that while overall people help each other by increasing the number of stations on the dial, blacks do not help whites, and whites do not help blacks. Similar patterns arise for Hispanics and non-Hispanics.

A closer look at the data—necessary only because I'm a middle-aged white economist—showed why this was happening. Blacks and whites don't listen to the same radio stations. The black-targeted formats account for about two-thirds of black listening and only 3 percent of white listening. Similarly, the formats that attract the largest white audiences, like country, attract almost no blacks. This means that if you dropped Larry the Cable Guy and a few thousand of his friends from a helicopter (with parachutes) into a metro area, you'd create more demand for country and perhaps album-rock stations, which would be nice for white listeners. But the influx wouldn't help black listeners at all.

In this example, different population groups don't help each other, but they don't hurt each other, either. Sometimes, though, the effect that groups have on each other

AP Photos/Don Ryan

through the market is actually negative. Industries like daily newspapers offer essentially one product per market. Because the paper can be pitched to appeal to one group or another, the larger one group is, the less the product is tailored to anyone else. This is the tyranny of the majority translated almost literally from politics into markets.

This brings us back to Nike's new shoe. Foot Locker is full of options that fit me and most other Americans. But American Indians make up just 1.5 percent of the U.S. population, and with feet on average three sizes wider, they need different-sized shoes. If we had all voted in a national election on whether the Ministry of Shoes should make wide or typical-width shoes, we surely would have chosen the latter. That's why Friedman

condemned government allocation. And yet the market made the same choice. If Nike's announcement looks like a solution to this problem of ignored minority preference, it really isn't. The company took too many years to bring the shoe on line, and according to the Associated Press, the new sneaker "represents less of a financial opportunity than a goodwill and branding effort."

The tyranny of the market arises elsewhere. With drug development costs near $1 billion, if you are going to be sick, hope that your disease is common enough to attract the interest of drug makers. If you want to fly from your town to Chicago, hope that your city is big enough to fill a plane every day.

When you're not so lucky, you benefit when the government steps in on your behalf, with subsidies for research on drugs for rare diseases or for air service to small locales. For a generation, influential economists have argued for letting the market decide a wide array of questions, to protect your freedom to choose whatever you want. This is true—if everyone agrees with you.

Mr. Waldfogel is a professor of economics at the University of Pennsylvania. ◢

Source: *Slate*, Thursday, October 4, 2007.

For the economy as a whole, about 2 percent of total firm revenue is spent on advertising. This spending takes many forms, including ads on websites, television, radio, and billboards, and in newspapers, magazines, the yellow pages, and direct mail.

16-3a The Debate over Advertising

Is society wasting the resources it devotes to advertising? Or does advertising serve a valuable purpose? Assessing the social value of advertising is difficult and often generates heated argument among economists. Let's consider both sides of the debate.

The Critique of Advertising   Critics of advertising argue that firms advertise to manipulate people's tastes. Much advertising is psychological rather than informational. Consider, for example, the typical television commercial for some brand of soft drink. The commercial most likely does not tell the viewer about the product's price or quality. Instead, it might show a group of happy people at a party on a beach on a beautiful sunny day. In their hands are cans of the soft drink. The goal of the commercial is to convey a subconscious (if not subtle) message: "You too can have many friends and be happy, if you drink our product." Critics of advertising argue that such a commercial creates a desire that otherwise might not exist.

Critics also argue that advertising impedes competition. Advertising often tries to convince consumers that products are more different than they truly are. By increasing the perception of product differentiation and fostering brand loyalty, advertising makes buyers less concerned with price differences among similar goods, thereby making the demand for a particular brand less elastic. When a firm faces a less elastic demand curve, it can increase its profits by charging a larger markup over marginal cost.

The Defense of Advertising   Defenders of advertising argue that firms use advertising to provide information to customers. Advertising conveys the prices of the goods offered for sale, the existence of new products, and the locations of retail outlets. This information allows customers to make better choices about what to buy and, thus, enhances the ability of markets to allocate resources efficiently.

Defenders also argue that advertising fosters competition. Because advertising allows customers to be more fully informed about all the firms in the market, customers can more easily take advantage of price differences. Thus, each firm has less market power. In addition, advertising allows new firms to enter more easily because it gives entrants a means to attract customers from existing firms.

Over time, policymakers have come to accept the view that advertising can make markets more competitive. One important example is the regulation of advertising for certain professions, such as lawyers, doctors, and pharmacists. In the past, these groups succeeded in getting state governments to prohibit advertising in their fields on the grounds that advertising was "unprofessional." In recent years, however, the courts have concluded that the primary effect of these restrictions on advertising was to curtail competition. They have, therefore, overturned many of the laws that prohibit advertising by members of these professions.

case study   **Advertising and the Price of Eyeglasses**

What effect does advertising have on the price of a good? On the one hand, advertising might make consumers view products as being more different than they otherwise would. If so, it would make markets less competitive and firms' demand curves less elastic, and this would lead firms to charge higher prices. On the other hand, advertising might make it easier for consumers to find the firms offering the best prices. In this case, it would make markets more competitive and firms' demand curves more elastic, which would lead to lower prices.

In an article published in the *Journal of Law and Economics* in 1972, economist Lee Benham tested these two views of advertising. In the United States during the 1960s, the various state governments had vastly different rules about advertising by optometrists. Some states allowed advertising for eyeglasses and eye examinations. Many states, however, prohibited it. For example, the Florida law read as follows:

> It is unlawful for any person, firm, or corporation to … advertise either directly or indirectly by any means whatsoever any definite or indefinite price or credit terms on prescriptive or corrective lens, frames, complete prescriptive or corrective glasses, or any optometric service…. This section is passed in the interest of public health, safety, and welfare, and its provisions shall be liberally construed to carry out its objects and purposes.

Professional optometrists enthusiastically endorsed these restrictions on advertising.

Benham used the differences in state law as a natural experiment to test the two views of advertising. The results were striking. In those states that prohibited advertising, the average price paid for a pair of eyeglasses was $33, or $248 in 2012 dollars. In states that did not restrict advertising, the average price was $26, or $196 in 2012 dollars. Thus, advertising reduced average prices by more than 20 percent. In the market for eyeglasses, and probably in many other markets as well, advertising fosters competition and leads to lower prices for consumers. ◢

16-3b Advertising as a Signal of Quality

Many types of advertising contain little apparent information about the product being advertised. Consider a firm introducing a new breakfast cereal. The firm might saturate the airwaves with advertisements showing some actor eating the cereal and exclaiming how wonderful it tastes. How much information does the advertisement really provide?

The answer is more than you might think. Defenders of advertising argue that even advertising that appears to contain little hard information may in fact tell consumers something about product quality. The willingness of the firm to spend a large amount of money on advertising can itself be a *signal* to consumers about the quality of the product being offered.

Consider the problem facing two firms—Post and Kellogg. Each company has just come up with a recipe for a new cereal, which it would sell for $3 a box. To keep things simple, let's assume that the marginal cost of making cereal is zero, so the $3 is all profit. Each company knows that if it spends $10 million on advertising, it will get 1 million consumers to try its new cereal. And each company knows that if consumers like the cereal, they will buy it not once but many times.

First consider Post's decision. Based on market research, Post knows that its cereal tastes like shredded newspaper with sugar on top. Advertising would sell one box to each of 1 million consumers, but consumers would quickly learn that the cereal is not very good and stop buying it. Post decides it is not worth spending $10 million on advertising to get only $3 million in sales. So it does not bother to advertise. It sends its cooks back to the test kitchen to develop another recipe.

Kellogg, on the other hand, knows that its cereal is great. Each person who tries it will buy a box a month for the next year. Thus, the $10 million in advertising will bring in $36 million in sales. Advertising is profitable here because Kellogg has a good product that consumers will buy repeatedly. Thus, Kellogg chooses to advertise.

Now that we have considered the behavior of the two firms, let's consider the behavior of consumers. We began by asserting that consumers are inclined to try a new cereal that they see advertised. But is this behavior rational? Should a consumer try a new cereal just because the seller has chosen to advertise it?

In fact, it may be completely rational for consumers to try new products that they see advertised. In our story, consumers decide to try Kellogg's new cereal because Kellogg advertises. Kellogg chooses to advertise because it knows that its cereal is quite good, while Post chooses not to advertise because it knows that its cereal is not good at all. By its willingness to spend money on advertising, Kellogg signals to consumers the quality of its cereal. Each consumer thinks,

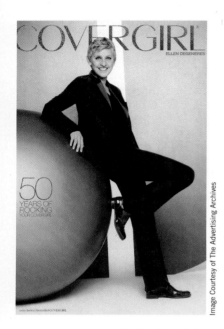

Is it rational for consumers to be impressed that Ellen DeGeneres is endorsing this product?

quite sensibly, "Boy, if the Kellogg Company is willing to spend so much money advertising this new cereal, it must be really good."

What is most surprising about this theory of advertising is that the content of the advertisement is irrelevant. Kellogg signals the quality of its product by its willingness to spend money on advertising. What the advertisements say is not as important as the fact that consumers know ads are expensive. By contrast, cheap advertising cannot be effective at signaling quality to consumers. In our example, if an advertising campaign cost less than $3 million, both Post and Kellogg would use it to market their new cereals. Because both good and bad cereals would be advertised, consumers could not infer the quality of a new cereal from the fact that it is advertised. Over time, consumers would learn to ignore such cheap advertising.

This theory can explain why firms pay famous actors large amounts of money to make advertisements that, on the surface, appear to convey no information at all. The information is not in the advertisement's content but simply in its existence and expense.

16-3c Brand Names

Advertising is closely related to the existence of brand names. In many markets, there are two types of firms. Some firms sell products with widely recognized brand names, while other firms sell generic substitutes. For example, in a typical drugstore, you can find Bayer aspirin on the shelf next to generic aspirin. In a typical grocery store, you can find Pepsi next to less familiar colas. Most often, the firm with the brand name spends more on advertising and charges a higher price for its product.

Just as there is disagreement about the economics of advertising, there is disagreement about the economics of brand names. Let's consider both sides of the debate.

Critics argue that brand names cause consumers to perceive differences that do not really exist. In many cases, the generic good is almost indistinguishable from the brand-name good. Consumers' willingness to pay more for the brand-name good, these critics assert, is a form of irrationality fostered by advertising. Economist Edward Chamberlin, one of the early developers of the theory of monopolistic competition, concluded from this argument that brand names were bad for the economy. He proposed that the government discourage their use by refusing to enforce the exclusive trademarks that companies use to identify their products.

More recently, economists have defended brand names as a useful way for consumers to ensure that the goods they buy are of high quality. There are two related arguments. First, brand names provide consumers with *information* about quality when quality cannot be easily judged in advance of purchase. Second, brand names give firms an *incentive* to maintain high quality because firms have a financial stake in maintaining the reputation of their brand names.

To see how these arguments work in practice, consider a famous brand name: McDonald's hamburgers. Imagine that you are driving through an unfamiliar town and want to stop for lunch. You see a McDonald's and a local restaurant next to it. Which do you choose? The local restaurant may in fact offer better food at lower prices, but you have no way of knowing that. By contrast, McDonald's offers a consistent product across many cities. Its brand name is useful to you as a way of judging the quality of what you are about to buy.

The McDonald's brand name also ensures that the company has an incentive to maintain quality. For example, if some customers were to become ill from

bad food sold at a McDonald's, the news would be disastrous for the company. McDonald's would lose much of the valuable reputation that it has built up with years of expensive advertising. As a result, it would lose sales and profit not just in the outlet that sold the bad food but in its many outlets throughout the country. By contrast, if some customers were to become ill from bad food at a local restaurant, that restaurant might have to close down, but the lost profits would be much smaller. Hence, McDonald's has a greater incentive to ensure that its food is safe.

The debate over brand names thus centers on the question of whether consumers are rational in preferring brand names to generic substitutes. Critics argue that brand names are the result of an irrational consumer response to advertising. Defenders argue that consumers have good reason to pay more for brand-name products because they can be more confident in the quality of these products.

Quick Quiz *How might advertising make markets less competitive? How might it make markets more competitive? • Give the arguments for and against brand names.*

16-4 Conclusion

Monopolistic competition is true to its name: It is a hybrid of monopoly and competition. Like a monopoly, each monopolistic competitor faces a downward-sloping demand curve and, as a result, charges a price above marginal cost. As in a perfectly competitive market, there are many firms, and entry and exit drive the profit of each monopolistic competitor toward zero in the long run. Table 1 summarizes these lessons.

Because monopolistically competitive firms produce differentiated products, each firm advertises to attract customers to its own brand. To some extent, advertising manipulates consumers' tastes, promotes irrational brand loyalty, and impedes competition. To a larger extent, advertising provides information, establishes brand names of reliable quality, and fosters competition.

The theory of monopolistic competition seems to describe many markets in the economy. It is somewhat disappointing, therefore, that the theory does not yield simple and compelling advice for public policy. From the standpoint of the economic theorist, the allocation of resources in monopolistically competitive markets is not perfect. Yet from the standpoint of a practical policymaker, there may be little that can be done to improve it.

TABLE 1

Monopolistic Competition:
Between Perfect Competition
and Monopoly

	Market Structure		
	Perfect Competition	Monopolistic Competition	Monopoly
Features that all three market structures share			
Goal of firms	Maximize profits	Maximize profits	Maximize profits
Rule for maximizing profit	$MR = MC$	$MR = MC$	$MR = MC$
Can earn economic profits in the short run?	Yes	Yes	Yes
Features that monopolistic competition shares with monopoly			
Price taker?	Yes	No	No
Price	$P = MC$	$P > MC$	$P > MC$
Produces welfare-maximizing level of output?	Yes	No	No
Features that monopolistic competition shares with competition			
Number of firms	Many	Many	One
Entry in the long run?	Yes	Yes	No
Can earn economic profits in the long run?	No	No	Yes

Summary

- A monopolistically competitive market is character-ized by three attributes: many firms, differentiated products, and free entry.

- The long-run equilibrium in a monopolistically competi-tive market differs from that in a perfectly competitive market in two related ways. First, each firm in a monopolistically competitive market has excess capacity. That is, it chooses a quantity that puts it on the down-ward-sloping portion of the average-total-cost curve. Second, each firm charges a price above marginal cost.

- Monopolistic competition does not have all the desirable properties of perfect competition. There is the standard deadweight loss of monopoly caused by the markup of price over marginal cost. In addition, the number of firms (and thus the variety of products) can be too large or too small. In practice, the ability of policymakers to correct these inefficiencies is limited.

- The product differentiation inherent in monopolistic competition leads to the use of advertising and brand names. Critics of advertising and brand names argue that firms use them to manipulate consumers' tastes and to reduce competition. Defenders of advertising and brand names argue that firms use them to inform consumers and to compete more vigorously on price and product quality.

Key Concepts

oligopoly, *p. 330*   monopolistic competition, *p. 330*

Questions for Review

1. Describe the three attributes of monopolistic competition. How is monopolistic competition like monopoly? How is it like perfect competition?

2. Draw a diagram depicting a firm that is making a profit in a monopolistically competitive market. Now show what happens to this firm as new firms enter the industry.

3. Draw a diagram of the long-run equilibrium in a monopolistically competitive market. How is price related to average total cost? How is price related to marginal cost?

4. Does a monopolistic competitor produce too much or too little output compared to the most efficient level? What practical considerations make it difficult for policymakers to solve this problem?

5. How might advertising reduce economic well-being? How might advertising increase economic well-being?

6. How might advertising with no apparent informational content in fact convey information to consumers?

7. Explain two benefits that might arise from the existence of brand names.

Quick Check Multiple Choice

1. Which of the following conditions does NOT describe a firm in a monopolistically competitive market?
   a. It makes a product different from its competitors.
   b. It takes its price as given by market conditions.
   c. It maximizes profit both in the short run and in the long run.
   d. It has the freedom to enter or exit in the long run.

2. Which of the following goods best fits the definition of monopolistic competition?
   a. wheat
   b. tap water
   c. crude oil
   d. soft drinks

3. A monopolistically competitive firm will increase its production if
   a. marginal revenue is greater than marginal cost.
   b. marginal revenue is greater than average total cost.
   c. price is greater than marginal cost.
   d. price is greater than average total cost.

4. New firms will enter a monopolistically competitive market if
   a. marginal revenue is greater than marginal cost.
   b. marginal revenue is greater than average total cost.
   c. price is greater than marginal cost.
   d. price is greater than average total cost.

5. What is true of a monopolistically competitive market in long-run equilibrium?
   a. Price is greater than marginal cost.
   b. Price is equal to marginal revenue.
   c. Firms make positive economic profits.
   d. Firms produce at the minimum of average total cost.

6. If advertising makes consumers more loyal to particular brands, it could _____ the elasticity of demand and _____ the markup of price over marginal cost.
   a. increase, increase
   b. increase, decrease
   c. decrease, increase
   d. decrease, decrease

Problems and Applications

1. Among monopoly, oligopoly, monopolistic competition, and perfect competition, how would you classify the markets for each of the following drinks?
   a. tap water
   b. bottled water
   c. cola
   d. beer

2. Classify the following markets as perfectly competitive, monopolistic, or monopolistically competitive, and explain your answers.
   a. wooden no. 2 pencils
   b. copper
   c. local electricity service
   d. peanut butter
   e. lipstick

3. For each of the following characteristics, say whether it describes a perfectly competitive firm, a monopolistically competitive firm, both, or neither.
   a. sells a product differentiated from that of its competitors
   b. has marginal revenue less than price
   c. earns economic profit in the long run
   d. produces at the minimum of average total cost in the long run
   e. equates marginal revenue and marginal cost
   f. charges a price above marginal cost

4. For each of the following characteristics, say whether it describes a monopoly firm, a monopolistically competitive firm, both, or neither.
   a. faces a downward-sloping demand curve
   b. has marginal revenue less than price
   c. faces the entry of new firms selling similar products
   d. earns economic profit in the long run
   e. equates marginal revenue and marginal cost
   f. produces the socially efficient quantity of output

5. You are hired as the consultant to a monopolistically competitive firm. The firm reports the following information about its price, marginal cost, and average total cost. Can the firm possibly be maximizing profit? If not, what should it do to increase profit? If the firm is profit maximizing, is the firm in a long-run equilibrium? If not, what will happen to restore long-run equilibrium?
   a. $P < MC, P > ATC$
   b. $P > MC, P < ATC$
   c. $P = MC, P > ATC$
   d. $P > MC, P = ATC$

6. Sparkle is one firm of many in the market for toothpaste, which is in long-run equilibrium.
   a. Draw a diagram showing Sparkle's demand curve, marginal-revenue curve, average-total-cost curve, and marginal-cost curve. Label Sparkle's profit-maximizing output and price.
   b. What is Sparkle's profit? Explain.
   c. On your diagram, show the consumer surplus derived from the purchase of Sparkle toothpaste. Also show the deadweight loss relative to the efficient level of output.
   d. If the government forced Sparkle to produce the efficient level of output, what would happen to the firm? What would happen to Sparkle's customers?

7. Consider a monopolistically competitive market with N firms. Each firm's business opportunities are described by the following equations:

   Demand: $Q = 100/N - P$
   Marginal Revenue: $MR = 100/N - 2Q$
   Total Cost: $TC = 50 + Q^2$
   Marginal Cost: $MC = 2Q$

   a. How does N, the number of firms in the market, affect each firm's demand curve? Why?
   b. How many units does each firm produce? (The answers to this and the next two questions depend on N.)

   c. What price does each firm charge?
   d. How much profit does each firm make?
   e. In the long run, how many firms will exist in this market?

8. The market for peanut butter in Nutville is monopolistically competitive and in long-run equilibrium. One day, consumer advocate Skippy Jif discovers that all brands of peanut butter in Nutville are identical. Thereafter, the market becomes perfectly competitive and again reaches its long-run equilibrium. Using an appropriate diagram, explain whether each of the following variables increases, decreases, or stays the same for a typical firm in the market.
   a. price
   b. quantity
   c. average total cost
   d. marginal cost
   e. profit

9. For each of the following pairs of firms, explain which firm would be more likely to engage in advertising.
   a. a family-owned farm or a family-owned restaurant
   b. a manufacturer of forklifts or a manufacturer of cars
   c. a company that invented a very comfortable razor or a company that invented a less comfortable razor

10. Sleek Sneakers Co. is one of many firms in the market for shoes.
   a. Assume that Sleek is currently earning short-run economic profit. On a correctly labeled diagram, show Sleek's profit-maximizing output and price, as well as the area representing profit.
   b. What happens to Sleek's price, output, and profit in the long run? Explain this change in words, and show it on a new diagram.
   c. Suppose that over time consumers become more focused on stylistic differences among shoe brands. How would this change in attitudes affect each firm's price elasticity of demand? In the long run, how will this change in demand affect Sleek's price, output, and profit?
   d. At the profit-maximizing price you identified in part (c), is Sleek's demand curve elastic or inelastic? Explain.

Go to CengageBrain.com to purchase access to the proven, critical Study Guide to accompany this text, which features additional notes and context, practice tests, and much more.

Oligopoly

If you go to a store to buy tennis balls, you will probably come home with one of four brands: Wilson, Penn, Dunlop, or Spalding. These four companies make almost all the tennis balls sold in the United States. Together these firms determine the quantity of tennis balls produced and, given the market demand curve, the price at which tennis balls are sold.

The market for tennis balls is an example of an **oligopoly**. The essence of an oligopolistic market is that there are only a few sellers. As a result, the actions of any one seller in the market can have a large impact on the profits of all the other sellers. Oligopolistic firms are interdependent in a way that competitive firms are not. Our goal in this chapter is to see how this interdependence shapes the firms' behavior and what problems it raises for public policy.

oligopoly
a market structure in which only a few sellers offer similar or identical products

game theory
the study of how people behave in strategic situations

The analysis of oligopoly offers an opportunity to introduce **game theory**, the study of how people behave in strategic situations. By "strategic" we mean a situation in which a person, when choosing among alternative courses of action, must consider how others might respond to the action she takes. Strategic thinking is crucial not only in checkers, chess, and tic-tac-toe but also in many business decisions. Because oligopolistic markets have only a small number of firms, each firm must act strategically. Each firm knows that its profit depends not only on how much it produces but also on how much the other firms produce. In making its production decision, each firm in an oligopoly should consider how its decision might affect the production decisions of all the other firms in the market.

Game theory is not necessary for understanding competitive or monopoly markets. In a market that is either perfectly competitive or monopolistically competitive, each firm is so small compared to the market that strategic interactions with other firms are not important. In a monopolized market, strategic interactions are absent because the market has only one firm. But, as we will see, game theory is useful for understanding oligopolies and many other situations in which a small number of players interact with one another. Game theory helps explain the strategies that people choose, whether they are playing tennis or selling tennis balls.

17-1 Markets with Only a Few Sellers

Because an oligopolistic market has only a small group of sellers, a key feature of oligopoly is the tension between cooperation and self-interest. The oligopolists are best off when they cooperate and act like a monopolist—producing a small quantity of output and charging a price above marginal cost. Yet because each oligopolist cares only about its own profit, there are powerful incentives at work that hinder a group of firms from maintaining the cooperative outcome.

17-1a A Duopoly Example

To understand the behavior of oligopolies, let's consider an oligopoly with only two members, called a *duopoly*. Duopoly is the simplest type of oligopoly. Oligopolies with three or more members face the same problems as duopolies, so we do not lose much by starting with the simpler case.

Imagine a town in which only two residents—Jack and Jill—own wells that produce water safe for drinking. Each Saturday, Jack and Jill decide how many gallons of water to pump, bring the water to town, and sell it for whatever price the market will bear. To keep things simple, suppose that Jack and Jill can pump as much water as they want without cost. That is, the marginal cost of water equals zero.

Table 1 shows the town's demand schedule for water. The first column shows the total quantity demanded, and the second column shows the price. If the two well owners sell a total of 10 gallons of water, water goes for $110 a gallon. If they sell a total of 20 gallons, the price falls to $100 a gallon. And so on. If you graphed these two columns of numbers, you would get a standard downward-sloping demand curve.

The last column in Table 1 shows the total revenue from the sale of water. It equals the quantity sold times the price. Because there is no cost to pumping water, the total revenue of the two producers equals their total profit.

TABLE 1

The Demand Schedule for Water

Quantity	Price	Total Revenue (and total profit)
0 gallons	$120	$ 0
10	110	1,100
20	100	2,000
30	90	2,700
40	80	3,200
50	70	3,500
60	60	3,600
70	50	3,500
80	40	3,200
90	30	2,700
100	20	2,000
110	10	1,100
120	0	0

Let's now consider how the organization of the town's water industry affects the price of water and the quantity of water sold.

17-1b Competition, Monopolies, and Cartels

Before considering the price and quantity of water that would result from the duopoly of Jack and Jill, let's discuss briefly what the outcome would be if the water market were either perfectly competitive or monopolistic. These two polar cases are natural benchmarks.

If the market for water were perfectly competitive, the production decisions of each firm would drive price equal to marginal cost. Because we have assumed that the marginal cost of pumping additional water is zero, the equilibrium price of water under perfect competition would be zero as well. The equilibrium quantity would be 120 gallons. The price of water would reflect the cost of producing it, and the efficient quantity of water would be produced and consumed.

Now consider how a monopoly would behave. Table 1 shows that total profit is maximized at a quantity of 60 gallons and a price of $60 a gallon. A profit-maximizing monopolist, therefore, would produce this quantity and charge this price. As is standard for monopolies, price would exceed marginal cost. The result would be inefficient, because the quantity of water produced and consumed would fall short of the socially efficient level of 120 gallons.

What outcome should we expect from our duopolists? One possibility is that Jack and Jill get together and agree on the quantity of water to produce and the price to charge for it. Such an agreement among firms over production and price is called **collusion**, and the group of firms acting in unison is called a **cartel**. Once a cartel is formed, the market is in effect served by a monopoly and we can apply our analysis from Chapter 15. That is, if Jack and Jill were to collude, they would agree on the monopoly outcome because that outcome maximizes the total profit that they can get from the market. Our two producers would produce

collusion
an agreement among firms in a market about quantities to produce or prices to charge

cartel
a group of firms acting in unison

a total of 60 gallons, which would be sold at a price of $60 a gallon. Once again, price exceeds marginal cost, and the outcome is socially inefficient.

A cartel must agree not only on the total level of production but also on the amount produced by each member. In our case, Jack and Jill must agree on how to split the monopoly production of 60 gallons. Each member of the cartel will want a larger share of the market because a larger market share means larger profit. If Jack and Jill agreed to split the market equally, each would produce 30 gallons, the price would be $60 a gallon, and each would get a profit of $1,800.

IN THE NEWS   Public Price Fixing

If a group of producers coordinates their prices in secret meetings, they can be sent to jail for criminal violations of antitrust laws. But what if they discuss the same topic in public?

Market Talk

By Alistair Lindsay

Most companies have antitrust compliance policies. They typically—and quite rightly—identify a number of things that officers and employees should not do, on pain of criminal liability, eye-watering fines and unlimited damages actions. All make clear that companies must not agree with their competitors to fix prices. This is a bright-line rule. But it raises an important question: Can companies coordinate price increases without infringing the cartel rules?

In markets where competitors need to publish their prices to win business—for example, many retail markets—it is perfectly lawful to shadow a rival's increases, so long as each seller acts entirely independently in setting its charges. The very definition of an oligopoly is a market involving a small number of suppliers that set their own commercial strategies but take account of their competitors. One competitor may emerge as a leader, with others taking their cue on when to raise prices and by how much.

When prices are privately negotiated—as in many industrials markets—it is common for a customer to volunteer information about a rival's prices to obtain leverage: *"You've quoted £100 per ton, but X is offering £95 and I'm going to them unless you can do better."* A company that receives this information obtains valuable intelligence about what its rivals are charging, but it does not infringe cartel rules. . . .

Companies also sometimes signal to one another in their communications with investors, whether deliberately or not. A competitor which informs the markets, say, that it expects a price war to end in February is providing relevant information to actual and potential owners of its stock. But of course its rivals read the same reports and can change their strategies accordingly. So a statement to the market can serve as just as much of a signal to competitors as a statement made during a cartel meeting. . . .

Signaling through investor communications raises difficult questions for cartel enforcement. The enforcers want to protect consumers from the adverse effects of blatant signaling, but not at the price of losing transparency in financial markets. For example, it is highly relevant to an investor to know an airline's predicted growth of per-mile passenger revenue for the next quarter. But a rival airline might use the announced figure as a benchmark when setting its own fares for the next quarter.

As things stand, cartel authorities have focused their efforts in such situations on blocking mergers in markets where signaling is prevalent, arguing that consolidation in such markets can further dampen competition by making coordination easier or more successful. However, they have not taken high-profile action alleging cartel infringements against companies for announcements made to investors.

If there is no justification for a particular announcement other than to signal to competitors, cartel authorities should seek to intervene. For in this case the public announcement is analytically the same as a private discussion directly with the rivals, and there is scope for consumers to be seriously harmed. But most announcements do serve legitimate purposes, such as keeping investors informed. In these cases, intervention by the cartel authorities seems too complex, given the disparate policy objectives in play. ◢

17-1c The Equilibrium for an Oligopoly

Oligopolists would like to form cartels and earn monopoly profits, but that is often impossible. Squabbling among cartel members over how to divide the profit in the market can make agreement among members difficult. In addition, antitrust laws prohibit explicit agreements among oligopolists as a matter of public policy. Even talking about pricing and production restrictions with competitors can be a criminal offense. Let's therefore consider what happens if Jack and Jill decide separately how much water to produce.

At first, one might expect Jack and Jill to reach the monopoly outcome on their own, because this outcome maximizes their joint profit. In the absence of a binding agreement, however, the monopoly outcome is unlikely. To see why, imagine that Jack expects Jill to produce only 30 gallons (half of the monopoly quantity). Jack would reason as follows:

"I could produce 30 gallons as well. In this case, a total of 60 gallons of water would be sold at a price of $60 a gallon. My profit would be $1,800 (30 gallons × $60 a gallon). Alternatively, I could produce 40 gallons. In this case, a total of 70 gallons of water would be sold at a price of $50 a gallon. My profit would be $2,000 (40 gallons × $50 a gallon). Even though total profit in the market would fall, my profit would be higher, because I would have a larger share of the market."

Of course, Jill might reason the same way. If so, Jack and Jill would each bring 40 gallons to town. Total sales would be 80 gallons, and the price would fall to $40. Thus, if the duopolists individually pursue their own self-interest when deciding how much to produce, they produce a total quantity greater than the monopoly quantity, charge a price lower than the monopoly price, and earn total profit less than the monopoly profit.

Although the logic of self-interest increases the duopoly's output above the monopoly level, it does not push the duopolists all the way to the competitive allocation. Consider what happens when each duopolist produces 40 gallons. The price is $40, and each duopolist makes a profit of $1,600. In this case, Jack's self-interested logic leads to a different conclusion:

"Right now, my profit is $1,600. Suppose I increase my production to 50 gallons. In this case, a total of 90 gallons of water would be sold, and the price would be $30 a gallon. Then my profit would be only $1,500. Rather than increasing production and driving down the price, I am better off keeping my production at 40 gallons."

The outcome in which Jack and Jill each produce 40 gallons looks like some sort of equilibrium. In fact, this outcome is called a Nash equilibrium. (It is named after economic theorist John Nash, whose life was portrayed in the book and movie *A Beautiful Mind*.) A **Nash equilibrium** is a situation in which economic actors interacting with one another each choose their best strategy given the strategies the others have chosen. In this case, given that Jill is producing 40 gallons, the best strategy for Jack is to produce 40 gallons. Similarly, given that Jack is producing 40 gallons, the best strategy for Jill is to produce 40 gallons. Once they reach this Nash equilibrium, neither Jack nor Jill has an incentive to make a different decision.

This example illustrates the tension between cooperation and self-interest. Oligopolists would be better off cooperating and reaching the monopoly outcome. Yet because they pursue their own self-interest, they do not end up reaching the monopoly outcome and maximizing their joint profit. Each oligopolist is tempted to raise production and capture a larger share of the market. As each of them tries to do this, total production rises, and the price falls.

Nash equilibrium
a situation in which economic actors interacting with one another each choose their best strategy given the strategies that all the other actors have chosen

At the same time, self-interest does not drive the market all the way to the competitive outcome. Like monopolists, oligopolists are aware that increasing the amount they produce reduces the price of their product, which in turn affects profits. Therefore, they stop short of following the competitive firm's rule of producing up to the point where price equals marginal cost.

In summary, *when firms in an oligopoly individually choose production to maximize profit, they produce a quantity of output greater than the level produced by monopoly and less than the level produced by perfect competition. The oligopoly price is less than the monopoly price but greater than the competitive price (which equals marginal cost).*

17-1d How the Size of an Oligopoly Affects the Market Outcome

We can use the insights from this analysis of duopoly to discuss how the size of an oligopoly is likely to affect the outcome in a market. Suppose, for instance, that John and Joan suddenly discover water sources on their property and join Jack and Jill in the water oligopoly. The demand schedule in Table 1 remains the same, but now more producers are available to satisfy this demand. How would an increase in the number of sellers from two to four affect the price and quantity of water in the town?

If the sellers of water could form a cartel, they would once again try to maximize total profit by producing the monopoly quantity and charging the monopoly price. Just as when there were only two sellers, the members of the cartel would need to agree on production levels for each member and find some way to enforce the agreement. As the cartel grows larger, however, this outcome is less likely. Reaching and enforcing an agreement becomes more difficult as the size of the group increases.

If the oligopolists do not form a cartel—perhaps because the antitrust laws prohibit it—they must each decide on their own how much water to produce. To see how the increase in the number of sellers affects the outcome, consider the decision facing each seller. At any time, each well owner has the option to raise production by one gallon. In making this decision, the well owner weighs the following two effects:

- *The output effect:* Because price is above marginal cost, selling one more gallon of water at the going price will raise profit.
- *The price effect:* Raising production will increase the total amount sold, which will lower the price of water and lower the profit on all the other gallons sold.

If the output effect is larger than the price effect, the well owner will increase production. If the price effect is larger than the output effect, the owner will not raise production. (In fact, in this case, it is profitable to reduce production.) Each oligopolist continues to increase production until these two marginal effects exactly balance, taking the other firms' production as given.

Now consider how the number of firms in the industry affects the marginal analysis of each oligopolist. The larger the number of sellers, the less each seller is concerned about her own impact on the market price. That is, as the oligopoly grows in size, the magnitude of the price effect falls. When the oligopoly grows very large, the price effect disappears altogether. That is, the production decision of an individual firm no longer affects the market price. In this extreme case, each firm takes the market price as given when deciding how much to produce. It increases production as long as price is above marginal cost.

We can now see that a large oligopoly is essentially a group of competitive firms. A competitive firm considers only the output effect when deciding how much to produce: Because a competitive firm is a price taker, the price effect is absent. Thus, *as the number of sellers in an oligopoly grows larger, an oligopolistic market looks more and more like a competitive market. The price approaches marginal cost, and the quantity produced approaches the socially efficient level.*

This analysis of oligopoly offers a new perspective on the effects of international trade. Imagine that Toyota and Honda are the only automakers in Japan, Volkswagen and BMW are the only automakers in Germany, and Ford and General Motors are the only automakers in the United States. If these nations prohibited international trade in autos, each would have an auto oligopoly with only two members, and the market outcome would likely depart substantially from the competitive ideal. With international trade, however, the car market is a world market, and the oligopoly in this example has six members. Allowing free trade increases the number of producers from which each consumer can choose, and this increased competition keeps prices closer to marginal cost. Thus, the theory of oligopoly provides another reason, in addition to the theory of comparative advantage discussed in Chapter 3, why all countries can benefit from free trade.

Quick Quiz *If the members of an oligopoly could agree on a total quantity to produce, what quantity would they choose? • If the oligopolists do not act together but instead make production decisions individually, do they produce a total quantity more or less than in your answer to the previous question? Why?*

17-2 The Economics of Cooperation

As we have seen, oligopolies would like to reach the monopoly outcome. Doing so, however, requires cooperation, which at times is difficult to establish and maintain. In this section we look more closely at the problems that arise when cooperation among actors is desirable but difficult. To analyze the economics of cooperation, we need to learn a little about game theory.

In particular, we focus on a "game" called the **prisoners' dilemma**, which provides insight into why cooperation is difficult. Many times in life, people fail to cooperate with one another even when cooperation would make them all better off. An oligopoly is just one example. The story of the prisoners' dilemma contains a general lesson that applies to any group trying to maintain cooperation among its members.

prisoners' dilemma
a particular "game" between two captured prisoners that illustrates why cooperation is difficult to maintain even when it is mutually beneficial

17-2a The Prisoners' Dilemma

The prisoners' dilemma is a story about two criminals who have been captured by the police. Let's call them Bonnie and Clyde. The police have enough evidence to convict Bonnie and Clyde of the minor crime of carrying an unregistered gun, so that each would spend a year in jail. The police also suspect that the two criminals have committed a bank robbery together, but they lack hard evidence to convict them of this major crime. The police question Bonnie and Clyde in separate rooms and offer each of them the following deal:

"Right now, we can lock you up for 1 year. If you confess to the bank robbery and implicate your partner, however, we'll give you immunity and you can go free. Your partner will get 20 years in jail. But if you both confess to the crime, we won't need your testimony and we can avoid the cost of a trial, so you will each get an intermediate sentence of 8 years."

If Bonnie and Clyde, heartless bank robbers that they are, care only about their own sentences, what would you expect them to do? Figure 1 shows their choices. Each prisoner has two strategies: confess or remain silent. The sentence each prisoner gets depends on the strategy he or she chooses and the strategy chosen by his or her partner in crime.

Consider first Bonnie's decision. She reasons as follows: "I don't know what Clyde is going to do. If he remains silent, my best strategy is to confess, since then I'll go free rather than spending a year in jail. If he confesses, my best strategy is still to confess, since then I'll spend 8 years in jail rather than 20. So, regardless of what Clyde does, I am better off confessing."

dominant strategy
a strategy that is best for a player in a game regardless of the strategies chosen by the other players

In the language of game theory, a strategy is called a **dominant strategy** if it is the best strategy for a player to follow regardless of the strategies pursued by other players. In this case, confessing is a dominant strategy for Bonnie. She spends less time in jail if she confesses, regardless of whether Clyde confesses or remains silent.

Now consider Clyde's decision. He faces the same choices as Bonnie, and he reasons in much the same way. Regardless of what Bonnie does, Clyde can reduce his jail time by confessing. In other words, confessing is also a dominant strategy for Clyde.

In the end, both Bonnie and Clyde confess, and both spend 8 years in jail. This outcome is a Nash equilibrium: Each criminal is choosing the best strategy available, given the strategy the other is following. Yet, from their standpoint, the outcome is terrible. If they had *both* remained silent, both of them would have been better off, spending only 1 year in jail on the gun charge. Because each pursues his or her own interests, the two prisoners together reach an outcome that is worse for each of them.

You might have thought that Bonnie and Clyde would have foreseen this situation and planned ahead. But even with advanced planning, they would still run into problems. Imagine that, before the police captured Bonnie and Clyde, the two criminals had made a pact not to confess. Clearly, this agreement would make them both better off *if* they both lived up to it, because they would each spend only 1 year in jail. But would the two criminals in fact remain silent, simply

FIGURE 1

The Prisoners' Dilemma
In this game between two criminals suspected of committing a crime, the sentence that each receives depends both on his or her decision whether to confess or remain silent and on the decision made by the other.

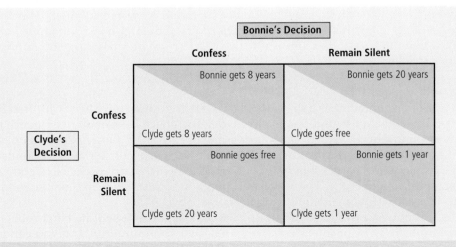

because they had agreed to? Once they are being questioned separately, the logic of self-interest takes over and leads them to confess. Cooperation between the two prisoners is difficult to maintain, because cooperation is individually irrational.

17-2b Oligopolies as a Prisoners' Dilemma

What does the prisoners' dilemma have to do with markets and imperfect competition? It turns out that the game oligopolists play in trying to reach the monopoly outcome is similar to the game that the two prisoners play in the prisoners' dilemma.

Consider again the choices facing Jack and Jill. After prolonged negotiation, the two suppliers of water agree to keep production at 30 gallons so that the price will be kept high and together they will earn the maximum profit. After they agree on production levels, however, each of them must decide whether to cooperate and live up to this agreement or to ignore it and produce at a higher level. Figure 2 shows how the profits of the two producers depend on the strategies they choose.

Suppose you are Jack. You might reason as follows: "I could keep production at 30 gallons as we agreed, or I could raise my production and sell 40 gallons. If Jill lives up to the agreement and keeps her production at 30 gallons, then I earn profit of $2,000 by selling 40 gallons and $1,800 by selling 30 gallons. In this case, I am better off with the higher-level production. If Jill fails to live up to the agreement and produces 40 gallons, then I earn $1,600 by selling 40 gallons and $1,500 by selling 30 gallons. Once again, I am better off with higher production. So, regardless of what Jill chooses to do, I am better off reneging on our agreement and producing at the higher level."

Producing 40 gallons is a dominant strategy for Jack. Of course, Jill reasons in exactly the same way, and so both produce at the higher level of 40 gallons. The result is the inferior outcome (from Jack and Jill's standpoint) with low profits for each of the two producers.

This example illustrates why oligopolies have trouble maintaining monopoly profits. The monopoly outcome is jointly rational, but each oligopolist has an incentive to cheat. Just as self-interest drives the prisoners in the prisoners' dilemma to confess, self-interest makes it difficult for the oligopolists to maintain the cooperative outcome with low production, high prices, and monopoly profits.

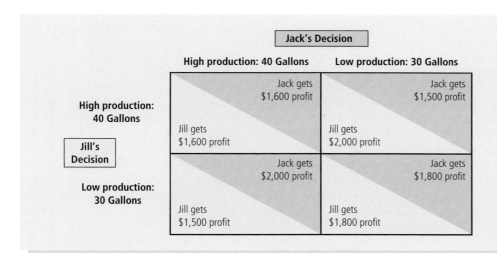

FIGURE 2

Jack and Jill's Oligopoly Game
In this game between Jack and Jill, the profit that each earns from selling water depends on both the quantity he or she chooses to sell and the quantity the other chooses to sell.

case study

OPEC and the World Oil Market

Our story about the town's market for water is fictional, but if we change water to crude oil, and Jack and Jill to Iran and Iraq, the story is close to being true. Much of the world's oil is produced by a few countries, mostly in the Middle East. These countries together make up an oligopoly. Their decisions about how much oil to pump are much the same as Jack and Jill's decisions about how much water to pump.

The countries that produce most of the world's oil have formed a cartel, called the Organization of Petroleum Exporting Countries (OPEC). As originally formed in 1960, OPEC included Iran, Iraq, Kuwait, Saudi Arabia, and Venezuela. By 1973, eight other nations had joined: Qatar, Indonesia, Libya, the United Arab Emirates, Algeria, Nigeria, Ecuador, and Gabon. These countries control about three-fourths of the world's oil reserves. Like any cartel, OPEC tries to raise the price of its product through a coordinated reduction in quantity produced. OPEC tries to set production levels for each of the member countries.

The problem that OPEC faces is much the same as the problem that Jack and Jill face in our story. The OPEC countries would like to maintain a high price for oil. But each member of the cartel is tempted to increase its production to get a larger share of the total profit. OPEC members frequently agree to reduce production but then cheat on their agreements.

OPEC was most successful at maintaining cooperation and high prices in the period from 1973 to 1985. The price of crude oil rose from $3 a barrel in 1972 to $11 in 1974 and then to $35 in 1981. But in the mid-1980s, member countries began arguing about production levels, and OPEC became ineffective at maintaining cooperation. By 1986 the price of crude oil had fallen back to $13 a barrel.

In recent years, the members of OPEC have continued to meet regularly, but they have been less successful at reaching and enforcing agreements. As a result, fluctuations in oil prices have been driven more by the natural forces of supply and demand than by the cartel's artificial restrictions on production. While this lack of cooperation among OPEC nations has reduced the profits of the oil-producing nations below what they might have been, it has benefited consumers around the world. ◢

17-2c Other Examples of the Prisoners' Dilemma

We have seen how the prisoners' dilemma can be used to understand the problem facing oligopolies. The same logic applies to many other situations as well. Here we consider two examples in which self-interest prevents cooperation and leads to an inferior outcome for the parties involved.

Arms Races In the decades after World War II, the world's two superpowers—the United States and the Soviet Union—were engaged in a prolonged competition over military power. This topic motivated some of the early work on game theory. The game theorists pointed out that an arms race is much like the prisoners' dilemma.

To see why, consider the decisions of the United States and the Soviet Union about whether to build new weapons or to disarm. Each country prefers to have more arms than the other because a larger arsenal would give it more influence in world affairs. But each country also prefers to live in a world safe from the other country's weapons.

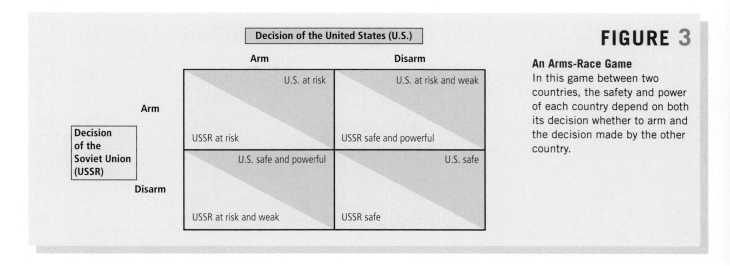

FIGURE 3

An Arms-Race Game
In this game between two countries, the safety and power of each country depend on both its decision whether to arm and the decision made by the other country.

Figure 3 shows the deadly game. If the Soviet Union chooses to arm, the United States is better off doing the same to prevent the loss of power. If the Soviet Union chooses to disarm, the United States is better off arming because doing so would make it more powerful. For each country, arming is a dominant strategy. Thus, each country chooses to continue the arms race, resulting in the inferior outcome with both countries at risk.

Throughout the Cold War era from about 1945 to 1991, the United States and the Soviet Union attempted to solve this problem through negotiation and agreements over arms control. The problems that the two countries faced were similar to those that oligopolists encounter in trying to maintain a cartel. Just as oligopolists argue over production levels, the United States and the Soviet Union argued over the amount of arms that each country would be allowed. And just as cartels have trouble enforcing production levels, the United States and the Soviet Union each feared that the other country would cheat on any agreement. In both arms races and oligopolies, the relentless logic of self-interest drives the participants toward the noncooperative outcome, which is worse for both parties.

Common Resources   In Chapter 11 we saw that people tend to overuse common resources. One can view this problem as an example of the prisoners' dilemma.

Imagine that two oil companies—Exxon and Texaco—own adjacent oil fields. Under the fields is a common pool of oil worth $12 million. Drilling a well to recover the oil costs $1 million. If each company drills one well, each will get half of the oil and earn a $5 million profit ($6 million in revenue minus $1 million in costs).

Because the pool of oil is a common resource, the companies will not use it efficiently. Suppose that either company could drill a second well. If one company has two of the three wells, that company gets two-thirds of the oil, which yields a profit of $6 million. The other company gets one-third of the oil, for a profit of $3 million. Yet if each company drills a second well, the two companies again split the oil. In this case, each bears the cost of a second well, so profit is only $4 million for each company.

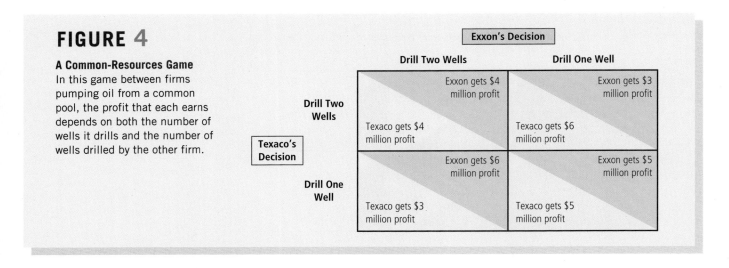

FIGURE 4

A Common-Resources Game
In this game between firms pumping oil from a common pool, the profit that each earns depends on both the number of wells it drills and the number of wells drilled by the other firm.

Figure 4 shows the game. Drilling two wells is a dominant strategy for each company. Once again, the self-interest of the two players leads them to an inferior outcome.

17-2d The Prisoners' Dilemma and the Welfare of Society

The prisoners' dilemma describes many of life's situations, and it shows that cooperation can be difficult to maintain, even when cooperation would make both players in the game better off. Clearly, this lack of cooperation is a problem for those involved in these situations. But is lack of cooperation a problem from the standpoint of society as a whole? The answer depends on the circumstances.

In some cases, the noncooperative equilibrium is bad for society as well as the players. In the arms-race game in Figure 3, both the United States and the Soviet Union end up at risk. In the common-resources game in Figure 4, the extra wells dug by Texaco and Exxon are pure waste. In both cases, society would be better off if the two players could reach the cooperative outcome.

By contrast, in the case of oligopolists trying to maintain monopoly profits, lack of cooperation is desirable from the standpoint of society as a whole. The monopoly outcome is good for the oligopolists, but it is bad for the consumers of the product. As we first saw in Chapter 7, the competitive outcome is best for society because it maximizes total surplus. When oligopolists fail to cooperate, the quantity they produce is closer to this optimal level. Put differently, the invisible hand guides markets to allocate resources efficiently only when markets are competitive, and markets are competitive only when firms in the market fail to cooperate with one another.

Similarly, consider the case of the police questioning two suspects. Lack of cooperation between the suspects is desirable, for it allows the police to convict more criminals. The prisoners' dilemma is a dilemma for the prisoners, but it can be a boon to everyone else.

17-2e Why People Sometimes Cooperate

The prisoners' dilemma shows that cooperation is difficult. But is it impossible? Not all prisoners, when questioned by the police, decide to turn in their partners in crime. Cartels sometimes manage to maintain collusive arrangements, despite the incentive for individual members to defect. Very often, players can solve the prisoners' dilemma because they play the game not once but many times.

To see why cooperation is easier to enforce in repeated games, let's return to our duopolists, Jack and Jill, whose choices were given in Figure 2. Jack and Jill would like to agree to maintain the monopoly outcome in which each produces 30 gallons. Yet, if Jack and Jill are to play this game only once, neither has any incentive to live up to this agreement. Self-interest drives each of them to renege and choose the dominant strategy of 40 gallons.

Now suppose that Jack and Jill know that they will play the same game every week. When they make their initial agreement to keep production low, they can also specify what happens if one party reneges. They might agree, for instance, that once one of them reneges and produces 40 gallons, both of them will produce 40 gallons forever after. This penalty is easy to enforce, for if one party is producing at a high level, the other has every reason to do the same.

The threat of this penalty may be all that is needed to maintain cooperation. Each person knows that defecting would raise his or her profit from $1,800 to $2,000. But this benefit would last for only one week. Thereafter, profit would fall to $1,600 and stay there. As long as the players care enough about future profits, they will choose to forgo the one-time gain from defection. Thus, in a game of repeated prisoners' dilemma, the two players may well be able to reach the cooperative outcome.

case study **The Prisoners' Dilemma Tournament**

Imagine that you are playing a game of prisoners' dilemma with a person being "questioned" in a separate room. Moreover, imagine that you are going to play not once but many times. Your score at the end of the game is the total number of years in jail. You would like to make this score as small as possible. What strategy would you play? Would you begin by confessing or remaining silent? How would the other player's actions affect your subsequent decisions about confessing?

Repeated prisoners' dilemma is a complicated game. To encourage cooperation, players must penalize each other for not cooperating. Yet the strategy described earlier for Jack and Jill's water cartel—defect forever as soon as the other player defects—is not very forgiving. In a game repeated many times, a strategy that allows players to return to the cooperative outcome after a period of noncooperation may be preferable.

To see what strategies work best, political scientist Robert Axelrod held a tournament. People entered by sending computer programs designed to play repeated prisoners' dilemma. Each program then played the game against all the other programs. The "winner" was the program that received the fewest total years in jail.

The winner turned out to be a simple strategy called *tit-for-tat*. According to tit-for-tat, a player should start by cooperating and then do whatever the other player did last time. Thus, a tit-for-tat player cooperates until the other player defects; then she defects until the other player cooperates again. In other words, this strategy starts out friendly, penalizes unfriendly players, and forgives them if warranted. To Axelrod's surprise, this simple strategy did better than all the more complicated strategies that people had sent in.

The tit-for-tat strategy has a long history. It is essentially the biblical strategy of "an eye for an eye, a tooth for a tooth." The prisoners' dilemma tournament suggests that this may be a good rule of thumb for playing some of the games of life. ◢

Quick Quiz   *Tell the story of the prisoners' dilemma. Write down a table showing the prisoners' choices and explain what outcome is likely. • What does the prisoners' dilemma teach us about oligopolies?*

17-3 Public Policy toward Oligopolies

One of the *Ten Principles of Economics* in Chapter 1 is that governments can sometimes improve market outcomes. This principle applies directly to oligopolistic markets. As we have seen, cooperation among oligopolists is undesirable from the standpoint of society as a whole because it leads to production that is too low and prices that are too high. To move the allocation of resources closer to the social optimum, policymakers should try to induce firms in an oligopoly to compete rather than cooperate. Let's consider how policymakers do this and then examine the controversies that arise in this area of public policy.

17-3a Restraint of Trade and the Antitrust Laws

One way that policy discourages cooperation is through the common law. Normally, freedom of contract is an essential part of a market economy. Businesses and households use contracts to arrange mutually advantageous trades. In doing this, they rely on the court system to enforce contracts. Yet, for many centuries, judges in England and the United States have deemed agreements among competitors to reduce quantities and raise prices to be contrary to the public good. They have therefore refused to enforce such agreements.

The Sherman Antitrust Act of 1890 codified and reinforced this policy:

> Every contract, combination in the form of trust or otherwise, or conspiracy, in restraint of trade or commerce among the several States, or with foreign nations, is declared to be illegal. . . . Every person who shall monopolize, or attempt to monopolize, or combine or conspire with any person or persons to monopolize any part of the trade or commerce among the several States, or with foreign nations, shall be deemed guilty of a misdemeanor, and on conviction thereof, shall be punished by fine not exceeding fifty thousand dollars, or by imprisonment not exceeding one year, or by both said punishments, in the discretion of the court.

The Sherman Act elevated agreements among oligopolists from unenforceable contracts to criminal conspiracies.

The Clayton Act of 1914 further strengthened the antitrust laws. According to this law, if a person could prove that she was damaged by an illegal arrangement to restrain trade, that person could sue and recover three times the damages she sustained. The purpose of this unusual rule of triple damages is to encourage private lawsuits against conspiring oligopolists.

Today, both the U.S. Justice Department and private parties have the authority to bring legal suits to enforce the antitrust laws. As we discussed in Chapter 15, these laws are used to prevent mergers that would lead to excessive market power in any single firm. In addition, these laws are used to prevent oligopolists from acting together in ways that would make their markets less competitive.

case study

An Illegal Phone Call
Firms in oligopolies have a strong incentive to collude in order to reduce production, raise price, and increase profit. The great 18th-century economist Adam Smith was well aware of this potential market failure. In *The Wealth of Nations* he wrote, "People of the same trade seldom meet together, but the conversation ends in a conspiracy against the public, or in some diversion to raise prices."

To see a modern example of Smith's observation, consider the following excerpt of a phone conversation between two airline executives in the early 1980s. The call was reported in the *New York Times* on February 24, 1983. Robert Crandall was president of American Airlines, and Howard Putnam was president of Braniff Airways, a major airline at the time.

CRANDALL: I think it's dumb as hell . . . to sit here and pound the @#$% out of each other and neither one of us making a #$%& dime.
PUTNAM: Do you have a suggestion for me?
CRANDALL: Yes, I have a suggestion for you. Raise your $%*& fares 20 percent. I'll raise mine the next morning.
PUTNAM: Robert, we . . .
CRANDALL: You'll make more money, and I will, too.
PUTNAM: We can't talk about pricing!
CRANDALL: Oh @#$%, Howard. We can talk about any &*#@ thing we want to talk about.

Putnam was right: The Sherman Antitrust Act prohibits competing executives from even talking about fixing prices. When Putnam gave a tape of this conversation to the Justice Department, the Justice Department filed suit against Crandall.

Two years later, Crandall and the Justice Department reached a settlement in which Crandall agreed to various restrictions on his business activities, including his contacts with officials at other airlines. The Justice Department said that the terms of settlement would "protect competition in the airline industry, by preventing American and Crandall from any further attempts to monopolize passenger airline service on any route through discussions with competitors about the prices of airline services." ◢

17-3b Controversies over Antitrust Policy

Over time, much controversy has centered on what kinds of behavior the antitrust laws should prohibit. Most commentators agree that price-fixing agreements among competing firms should be illegal. Yet the antitrust laws have been used to condemn some business practices whose effects are not obvious. Here we consider three examples.

Resale Price Maintenance One example of a controversial business practice is *resale price maintenance*. Imagine that Superduper Electronics sells Blu-ray disc players to retail stores for $100. If Superduper requires the retailers to charge customers $150, it is said to engage in resale price maintenance. Any retailer that charged less than $150 would violate its contract with Superduper.

At first, resale price maintenance might seem anticompetitive and, therefore, detrimental to society. Like an agreement among members of a cartel, it prevents the retailers from competing on price. For this reason, the courts have at times viewed resale price maintenance as a violation of the antitrust laws.

Yet some economists defend resale price maintenance on two grounds. First, they deny that it is aimed at reducing competition. To the extent that Superduper Electronics has any market power, it can exert that power through the wholesale price, rather than through resale price maintenance. Moreover, Superduper has no incentive to discourage competition among its retailers. Indeed, because a cartel of retailers sells less than a group of competitive retailers, Superduper would be worse off if its retailers were a cartel.

Second, economists believe that resale price maintenance has a legitimate goal. Superduper may want its retailers to provide customers a pleasant showroom and a knowledgeable sales force. Yet, without resale price maintenance, some customers would take advantage of one store's service to learn about the Blu-ray player's special features and then buy the item at a discount retailer that does not provide this service. To some extent, good service is a public good among the retailers that sell Superduper products. As we discussed in Chapter 11, when one person provides a public good, others are able to enjoy it without paying for it. In this case, discount retailers would free ride on the service provided by other retailers, leading to less service than is desirable. Resale price maintenance is one way for Superduper to solve this free-rider problem.

The example of resale price maintenance illustrates an important principle: *Business practices that appear to reduce competition may in fact have legitimate purposes.* This principle makes the application of the antitrust laws all the more difficult. The economists, lawyers, and judges in charge of enforcing these laws must determine what kinds of behavior public policy should prohibit as impeding competition and reducing economic well-being. Often that job is not easy.

Predatory Pricing Firms with market power normally use that power to raise prices above the competitive level. But should policymakers ever be concerned that firms with market power might charge prices that are too low? This question is at the heart of a second debate over antitrust policy.

Imagine that a large airline, call it Coyote Air, has a monopoly on some route. Then Roadrunner Express enters and takes 20 percent of the market, leaving Coyote with 80 percent. In response to this competition, Coyote starts slashing its fares. Some antitrust analysts argue that Coyote's move could be anticompetitive: The price cuts may be intended to drive Roadrunner out of the market so Coyote can recapture its monopoly and raise prices again. Such behavior is called *predatory pricing*.

Although predatory pricing is a common claim in antitrust suits, some economists are skeptical of this argument and believe that predatory pricing is rarely, if ever, a profitable business strategy. Why? For a price war to drive out a rival, prices have to be driven below cost. Yet if Coyote starts selling cheap tickets at a loss, it had better be ready to fly more planes, because low fares will attract more customers. Roadrunner, meanwhile, can respond to Coyote's predatory move by cutting back on flights. As a result, Coyote ends up bearing more than 80 percent of the losses, putting Roadrunner in a good position to survive the price war. As in the old Roadrunner–Coyote cartoons, the predator suffers more than the prey.

Economists continue to debate whether predatory pricing should be a concern for antitrust policymakers. Various questions remain unresolved. Is predatory pricing ever a profitable business strategy? If so, when? Are the courts capable of telling which price cuts are competitive and thus good for consumers and which are predatory? There are no simple answers.

Tying A third example of a controversial business practice is *tying*. Suppose that Makemoney Movies produces two new films—*The Avengers* and *Hamlet*. If Makemoney offers theaters the two films together at a single price, rather than separately, the studio is said to be tying its two products.

When the practice of tying movies was challenged, the Supreme Court banned it. The court reasoned as follows: Imagine that *The Avengers* is a blockbuster, whereas *Hamlet* is an unprofitable art film. Then the studio could use the high demand for *The Avengers* to force theaters to buy *Hamlet*. It seemed that the studio could use tying as a mechanism for expanding its market power.

Many economists are skeptical of this argument. Imagine that theaters are willing to pay $20,000 for *The Avengers* and nothing for *Hamlet*. Then the most that a theater would pay for the two movies together is $20,000—the same as it would pay for *The Avengers* by itself. Forcing the theater to accept a worthless movie as part of the deal does not increase the theater's willingness to pay. Makemoney cannot increase its market power simply by bundling the two movies together.

Why, then, does tying exist? One possibility is that it is a form of price discrimination. Suppose there are two theaters. City Theater is willing to pay $15,000 for *The Avengers* and $5,000 for *Hamlet*. Country Theater is just the opposite: It is willing to pay $5,000 for *The Avengers* and $15,000 for *Hamlet*. If Makemoney charges separate prices for the two films, its best strategy is to charge $15,000 for each film, and each theater chooses to show only one film. Yet if Makemoney offers the two movies as a bundle, it can charge each theater $20,000 for the movies. Thus, if different theaters value the films differently, tying may allow the studio to increase profit by charging a combined price closer to the buyers' total willingness to pay.

Tying remains a controversial business practice. The Supreme Court's argument that tying allows a firm to extend its market power to other goods is not well founded, at least in its simplest form. Yet economists have proposed more elaborate theories for how tying can impede competition. Given our current economic knowledge, it is unclear whether tying has adverse effects for society as a whole.

case study **The Microsoft Case**

The most important and controversial antitrust case in recent years has been the U.S. government's suit against the Microsoft Corporation, filed in 1998. Certainly, the case did not lack drama. It pitted one of the world's richest men (Bill Gates) against one of the world's most powerful regulatory agencies (the U.S. Justice Department). Testifying for the government was a prominent economist (MIT professor Franklin Fisher). Testifying for Microsoft was an equally prominent economist (MIT professor Richard Schmalensee). At stake was the future of one of the world's most valuable companies (Microsoft) in one of the economy's fastest-growing industries (computer software).

A central issue in the Microsoft case involved tying—in particular, whether Microsoft should be allowed to integrate its Internet browser into its Windows operating system. The government claimed that Microsoft was bundling these two products together to expand its market power in computer operating systems into the unrelated market of Internet browsers. Allowing Microsoft to incorporate such products into its operating system, the government argued, would deter other software companies from entering the market and offering new products.

Microsoft responded by pointing out that putting new features into old products is a natural part of technological progress. Cars today include CD players and air conditioners, which were once sold separately, and cameras come with built-in flashes. The same is true with operating systems. Over time, Microsoft has added many features to Windows that were previously stand-alone products. This has made computers more reliable and easier to use because consumers can be confident that the pieces work together. The integration of Internet technology, Microsoft argued, was the natural next step.

One point of disagreement concerned the extent of Microsoft's market power. Noting that more than 80 percent of new personal computers used a Microsoft operating system, the government argued that the company had substantial monopoly power, which it was trying to expand. Microsoft replied that the software market is always changing and that Microsoft's Windows was constantly being challenged by competitors, such as the Apple Mac and Linux operating systems. It also argued that the low price it charged for Windows—about $50, or only 3 percent of the price of a typical computer—was evidence that its market power was severely limited.

Like many large antitrust suits, the Microsoft case became a legal morass. In November 1999, after a long trial, Judge Penfield Jackson ruled that Microsoft had great monopoly power and that it had illegally abused that power. In June 2000, after hearings on possible remedies, he ordered that Microsoft be broken up into two companies—one that sold the operating system and one that sold applications software. A year later, an appeals court overturned Jackson's breakup order and handed the case to a new judge. In September 2001, the Justice Department announced that it no longer sought a breakup of the company and wanted to settle the case quickly.

A settlement was finally reached in November 2002. Microsoft accepted some restrictions on its business practices, and the government accepted that a browser would remain part of the Windows operating system. But the settlement did not end Microsoft's antitrust troubles. In recent years, the company has contended with several private antitrust suits, as well as suits brought by the European Union alleging a variety of anticompetitive behaviors. ◢

"Me? A monopolist? Now just wait a minute . . ."

Quick Quiz *What kind of agreement is illegal for businesses to make? * Why are the antitrust laws controversial?*

17-4 Conclusion

Oligopolies would like to act like monopolies, but self-interest drives them toward competition. Where oligopolies end up on this spectrum depends on the number of firms in the oligopoly and how cooperative the firms are. The story of the prisoners' dilemma shows why oligopolies can fail to maintain cooperation, even when cooperation is in their best interest.

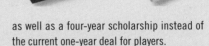

IN THE NEWS
....

Should the N.C.A.A. Be Taken to Court?

Colleges and universities regularly meet to discuss the deals they offer student athletes. This op-ed questions whether this coordination might violate the antitrust laws.

The College Sports Cartel

By Joe Nocera

Twice a year in Vienna, the members of the Organization of Petroleum Exporting Countries gather to decide on the short-term direction of oil prices. Sometimes, O.P.E.C. agrees to cut back on oil production, pushing up the price of oil. Other times, it decides to boost production. Always, the goal is to fix the price of oil, rather than allow it to be set by the competitive marketplace. Indeed, collusion and price-fixing are the main reasons cartels exist—and why they are illegal in America.

Yet, in Indianapolis a few weeks from now, a home-grown cartel will hold its annual meeting, where it, too, will be working to collude and fix prices. This cartel is the National Collegiate Athletic Association. The N.C.A.A. would have you believe that it is the great protector of amateur athletics, preventing college athletes from being tainted by the river of money pouring over college sports.

Victims of a cartel?

In fact, the N.C.A.A.'s real role is to oversee the collusion of university athletic departments, whose goal is to maximize revenue and suppress the wages of its captive labor force, a k a the players. . . .

Sports leagues can't exist without at least some collusion. As Andy Schwarz, an economist and litigation consultant, puts it, "If steel companies got together to decide when and where to produce steel, that would violate the antitrust laws. But if sports teams in a league get together to decide when and where to play games, that's generally allowed." Major League Baseball has long had an antitrust exemption; other professional leagues have salary caps, which are legal because they have been agreed to by the players.

The N.C.A.A. has neither an antitrust exemption nor a player's union to negotiate with. In other words, it lacks some of the legal protections that shield professional sports from antitrust suits. What it has, instead, is a work force full of young adults dreaming of becoming pros and willing to sign any document, no matter how onerous, if it will help them reach that goal. The document the N.C.A.A. forces them to sign completely stacks the deck against them.

Recently, Mark Emmert, the president of the N.C.A.A., tried to make the rules a tad less onerous. He got the N.C.A.A. board of directors to approve an optional $2,000 stipend

as well as a four-year scholarship instead of the current one-year deal for players.

And how did the cartel react to these modest changes? It rose up in revolt. Enough universities signed an override petition to temporarily ice the new stipend. The same thing happened with the four-year scholarship.

A lawyer in Fort Worth, Christian Dennie, who specializes in sports law, got ahold of an internal N.C.A.A. document outlining some of the objections. One is especially worth repeating: "The new coach may have a completely different style of offense/defense that the student athlete no longer fits into," wrote Indiana State. Four-year scholarships might mean that the school would be stuck with "someone that is of no 'athletic' usefulness to the program." Thus does at least one school show how it truly views its "student athletes." . . .

How can it be that the N.C.A.A. can define amateurism in one moment as allowing a $2,000 stipend and in the next moment as forbidding such a stipend? How can it justify rolling back a change that would truly help student athletes, such as the four-year scholarship, simply because coaches want to continue to have life-or-death power over their charges? How can the labor force that generates so much money for everyone else be kept in shackles by the N.C.A.A.?

The N.C.A.A. claims it has the legal right to do all the above and more. And maybe it does. But it certainly would be worthwhile to see someone challenge its cartel behavior in court. The inevitable rollback of the $2,000 stipend and the four-year scholarship would be an awfully good place to start. ◢

Source: New York Times, December 31, 2011.

Policymakers regulate the behavior of oligopolists through the antitrust laws. The proper scope of these laws is the subject of ongoing controversy. Although price fixing among competing firms clearly reduces economic welfare and should be illegal, some business practices that appear to reduce competition may have legitimate if subtle purposes. As a result, policymakers need to be careful when they use the substantial powers of the antitrust laws to place limits on firm behavior.

Summary

- Oligopolists maximize their total profits by forming a cartel and acting like a monopolist. Yet, if oligopolists make decisions about production levels individually, the result is a greater quantity and a lower price than under the monopoly outcome. The larger the number of firms in the oligopoly, the closer the quantity and price will be to the levels that would prevail under perfect competition.

- The prisoners' dilemma shows that self-interest can prevent people from maintaining cooperation, even when cooperation is in their mutual interest. The logic of the prisoners' dilemma applies in many situations, including arms races, common-resource problems, and oligopolies.

- Policymakers use the antitrust laws to prevent oligopolies from engaging in behavior that reduces competition. The application of these laws can be controversial, because some behavior that can appear to reduce competition may in fact have legitimate business purposes.

Key Concepts

oligopoly, *p. 347*

game theory, *p. 348*

collusion, *p. 349*

cartel, *p. 349*

Nash equilibrium, *p. 351*

prisoners' dilemma, *p. 353*

dominant strategy, *p. 354*

Questions for Review

1. If a group of sellers could form a cartel, what quantity and price would they try to set?

2. Compare the quantity and price of an oligopoly to those of a monopoly.

3. Compare the quantity and price of an oligopoly to those of a competitive market.

4. How does the number of firms in an oligopoly affect the outcome in its market?

5. What is the prisoners' dilemma, and what does it have to do with oligopoly?

6. Give two examples other than oligopoly that show how the prisoners' dilemma helps to explain behavior.

7. What kinds of behavior do the antitrust laws prohibit?

Quick Check Multiple Choice

1. The key feature of an oligopolistic market is that
   a. each firm produces a different product from other firms.
   b. a single firm chooses a point on the market demand curve.
   c. each firm takes the market price as given.
   d. a small number of firms are acting strategically.

2. If an oligopolistic industry organizes itself as a cooperative cartel, it will produce a quantity of output that is _____ the competitive level and _____ the monopoly level.
   a. less than, more than
   b. more than, less than
   c. less than, equal to
   d. equal to, more than

3. If an oligopoly does not cooperate and each firm chooses its own quantity, the industry will produce a quantity of output that is _____ the competitive level and _____ the monopoly level.
   a. less than, more than
   b. more than, less than
   c. less than, equal to
   d. equal to, more than

4. As the number of firms in an oligopoly grows large, the industry approaches a level of output that is _____ the competitive level and _____ the monopoly level.
   a. less than, more than
   b. more than, less than
   c. less than, equal to
   d. equal to, more than

5. The prisoners' dilemma is a two-person game illustrating that
   a. the cooperative outcome could be worse for both people than the Nash equilibrium.
   b. even if the cooperative outcome is better than the Nash equilibrium for one person, it might be worse for the other.
   c. even if cooperation is better than the Nash equilibrium, each person might have an incentive not to cooperate.
   d. rational, self-interested individuals will naturally avoid the Nash equilibrium because it is worse for both of them.

6. The antitrust laws aim to
   a. facilitate cooperation among firms in oligopolistic industries.
   b. encourage mergers to take advantage of economies of scale.
   c. discourage firms from moving production facilities overseas.
   d. prevent firms from acting in ways that reduce competition.

Problems and Applications

1. A large share of the world supply of diamonds comes from Russia and South Africa. Suppose that the marginal cost of mining diamonds is constant at $1,000 per diamond and the demand for diamonds is described by the following schedule:

Price	Quantity
$8,000	5,000 diamonds
7,000	6,000
6,000	7,000
5,000	8,000
4,000	9,000
3,000	10,000
2,000	11,000
1,000	12,000

   a. If there were many suppliers of diamonds, what would be the price and quantity?
   b. If there were only one supplier of diamonds, what would be the price and quantity?
   c. If Russia and South Africa formed a cartel, what would be the price and quantity? If the countries split the market evenly, what would be South Africa's production and profit? What would happen to South Africa's profit if it increased its production by $1,000 while Russia stuck to the cartel agreement?
   d. Use your answers to part (c) to explain why cartel agreements are often not successful.

2. The *New York Times* (Nov. 30, 1993) reported that "the inability of OPEC to agree last week to cut production has sent the oil market into turmoil . . . [leading to] the lowest price for domestic crude oil since June 1990."
   a. Why were the members of OPEC trying to agree to cut production?
   b. Why do you suppose OPEC was unable to agree on cutting production? Why did the oil market go into "turmoil" as a result?
   c. The newspaper also noted OPEC's view "that producing nations outside the organization, like Norway and Britain, should do their share and cut production." What does the phrase "do their share" suggest about OPEC's desired relationship with Norway and Britain?

3. This chapter discusses companies that are oligopolists in the market for the goods they sell. Many of the same ideas apply to companies that are oligopolists in the market for the inputs they buy.
   a. If sellers who are oligopolists try to increase the price of goods they sell, what is the goal of buyers who are oligopolists?
   b. Major league baseball team owners have an oligopoly in the market for baseball players. What is the owners' goal regarding players' salaries? Why is this goal difficult to achieve?
   c. Baseball players went on strike in 1994 because they would not accept the salary cap that the owners wanted to impose. If the owners were already colluding over salaries, why did they feel the need for a salary cap?

4. Consider trade relations between the United States and Mexico. Assume that the leaders of the two countries believe the payoffs to alternative trade policies are as follows:

United States' Decision

		Low Tariffs	High Tariffs
Mexico's Decision	**Low Tariffs**	U.S. gains $25 billion / Mexico gains $25 billion	U.S. gains $30 billion / Mexico gains $10 billion
	High Tariffs	U.S. gains $10 billion / Mexico gains $30 billion	U.S. gains $20 billion / Mexico gains $20 billion

a. What is the dominant strategy for the United States? For Mexico? Explain.
b. Define *Nash equilibrium*. What is the Nash equilibrium for trade policy?
c. In 1993, the U.S. Congress ratified the North American Free Trade Agreement, in which the United States and Mexico agreed to reduce trade barriers simultaneously. Do the perceived payoffs shown here justify this approach to trade policy? Explain.
d. Based on your understanding of the gains from trade (discussed in Chapters 3 and 9), do you think that these payoffs actually reflect a nation's welfare under the four possible outcomes?

5. Synergy and Dynaco are the only two firms in a specific high-tech industry. They face the following payoff matrix as they decide upon the size of their research budget:

Synergy's Decision

		Large Budget	Small Budget
Dynaco's Decision	**Large Budget**	Synergy gains $20 million / Dynaco gains $30 million	Synergy gains zero / Dynaco gains $70 million
	Small Budget	Synergy gains $30 million / Dynaco gains zero	Synergy gains $40 million / Dynaco gains $50 million

a. Does Synergy have a dominant strategy? Explain.
b. Does Dynaco have a dominant strategy? Explain.
c. Is there a Nash equilibrium for this scenario? Explain. (*Hint*: Look closely at the definition of Nash equilibrium.)

6. You and a classmate are assigned a project on which you will receive one combined grade. You each want to receive a good grade, but you also want to avoid hard work. In particular, here is the situation:
• If both of you work hard, you both get an A, which gives each of you 40 units of happiness.

• If only one of you works hard, you both get a B, which gives each of you 30 units of happiness.
• If neither of you works hard, you both get a D, which gives each of you 10 units of happiness.
• Working hard costs 25 units of happiness.
a. Fill in the payoffs in the following decision box:

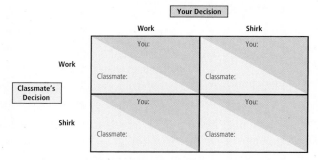

b. What is the likely outcome? Explain your answer.
c. If you get this classmate as your partner on a series of projects throughout the year, rather than only once, how might that change the outcome you predicted in part (b)?
d. Another classmate cares more about good grades: She gets 50 units of happiness for a B, and 80 units of happiness for an A. If this classmate were your partner (but your preferences were unchanged), how would your answers to parts (a) and (b) change? Which of the two classmates would you prefer as a partner? Would she also want you as a partner?

7. A case study in the chapter describes a phone conversation between the presidents of American Airlines and Braniff Airways. Let's analyze the game between the two companies. Suppose that each company can charge either a high price for tickets or a low price. If one company charges $300, it earns low profit if the other company also charges $300 and high profit if the other company charges $600. On the other hand, if the company charges $600, it earns very low profit if the other company charges $300 and medium profit if the other company also charges $600.
a. Draw the decision box for this game.
b. What is the Nash equilibrium in this game? Explain.
c. Is there an outcome that would be better than the Nash equilibrium for both airlines? How could it be achieved? Who would lose if it were achieved?

8. Two athletes of equal ability are competing for a prize of $10,000. Each is deciding whether to take a dangerous performance-enhancing drug. If one athlete takes the drug, and the other does not, the one who takes the drug wins the prize. If both or neither take the drug, they tie and split the prize. Taking the drug imposes health risks that are equivalent to a loss of X dollars.
a. Draw a 2 × 2 payoff matrix describing the decisions the athletes face.

b. For what X is taking the drug the Nash equilibrium?

c. Does making the drug safer (that is, lowering X) make the athletes better or worse off? Explain.

9. Little Kona is a small coffee company that is considering entering a market dominated by Big Brew. Each company's profit depends on whether Little Kona enters and whether Big Brew sets a high price or a low price:

		Big Brew	
		High Price	**Low Price**
Little Kona	**Enter**	Brew makes $3 million / Kona makes $2 million	Brew makes $1 million / Kona loses $1 million
	Don't Enter	Brew makes $7 million / Kona makes zero	Brew makes $2 million / Kona makes zero

a. Does either player in this game have a dominant strategy?

b. Does your answer to part (a) help you figure out what the other player should do? What is the Nash equilibrium? Is there only one?

c. Big Brew threatens Little Kona by saying, "If you enter, we're going to set a low price, so you had better stay out." Do you think Little Kona should believe the threat? Why or why not?

d. If the two firms could collude and agree on how to split the total profits, what outcome would they pick?

Go to CengageBrain.com to purchase access to the proven, critical Study Guide to accompany this text, which features additional notes and context, practice tests, and much more.

PART
VI

The Economics of Labor Markets

The Markets for the Factors of Production

When you finish school, your income will be determined largely by what kind of job you take. If you become a computer programmer, you will earn more than if you become a gas station attendant. This fact is not surprising, but it is not obvious why it is true. No law requires that computer programmers be paid more than gas station attendants. No ethical principle says that programmers are more deserving. What then determines which job will pay you the higher wage?

Your income, of course, is a small piece of a larger economic picture. In 2012, the total income of all U.S. residents was about $15 trillion. People earned this income in various ways. Workers earned about two-thirds of it in the form of wages and fringe benefits. The rest went to landowners and to the owners of *capital*—the economy's stock of equipment and structures—in the form of rent, profit, and interest. What determines how much goes to workers? To landowners? To the owners of capital? Why do some workers earn higher wages than others, some landowners higher rental income than others, and some capital owners greater profit than others? Why, in particular, do computer programmers earn more than gas station attendants?

The answers to these questions, like most in economics, hinge on supply and demand. The supply and demand for labor, land, and capital determine the prices paid to workers, landowners, and capital owners. To understand why some people have higher incomes than others, therefore, we need to look more deeply at the markets for the services they provide. That is our job in this and the next two chapters.

This chapter provides the basic theory for the analysis of factor markets. As you may recall from Chapter 2, the **factors of production** are the inputs used to produce goods and services. Labor, land, and capital are the three most important factors of production. When a computer firm produces a new software program, it uses programmers' time (labor), the physical space on which its offices are located (land), and an office building and computer equipment (capital). Similarly, when a gas station sells gas, it uses attendants' time (labor), the physical space (land), and the gas tanks and pumps (capital).

In many ways factor markets resemble the markets for goods and services we analyzed in previous chapters, but they are different in one important way: The demand for a factor of production is a *derived demand*. That is, a firm's demand for a factor of production is derived from its decision to supply a good in another market. The demand for computer programmers is inseparably linked to the supply of computer software, and the demand for gas station attendants is inseparably linked to the supply of gasoline.

In this chapter, we analyze factor demand by considering how a competitive, profit-maximizing firm decides how much of any factor to buy. We begin our analysis by examining the demand for labor. Labor is the most important factor of production, because workers receive most of the total income earned in the U.S. economy. Later in the chapter, we will see that our analysis of the labor market also applies to the markets for the other factors of production.

The basic theory of factor markets developed in this chapter takes a large step toward explaining how the income of the U.S. economy is distributed among workers, landowners, and owners of capital. Chapter 19 builds on this analysis to examine in more detail why some workers earn more than others. Chapter 20 examines how much income inequality results from the functioning of factor markets and then considers what role the government should and does play in altering the income distribution.

factors of production
the inputs used to produce goods and services

18-1 The Demand for Labor

Labor markets, like other markets in the economy, are governed by the forces of supply and demand. This is illustrated in Figure 1. In panel (a), the supply and demand for apples determine the price of apples. In panel (b), the supply and demand for apple pickers determine the price, or wage, of apple pickers.

As we have already noted, labor markets are different from most other markets because labor demand is a derived demand. Most labor services, rather than being final goods ready to be enjoyed by consumers, are inputs into the production of other goods. To understand labor demand, we need to focus on the firms that hire the labor and use it to produce goods for sale. By examining the link between the production of goods and the demand for labor to make those goods, we gain insight into the determination of equilibrium wages.

The basic tools of supply and demand apply to goods and to labor services. Panel (a) shows how the supply and demand for apples determine the price of apples. Panel (b) shows how the supply and demand for apple pickers determine the wage of apple pickers.

FIGURE 1

The Versatility of Supply and Demand

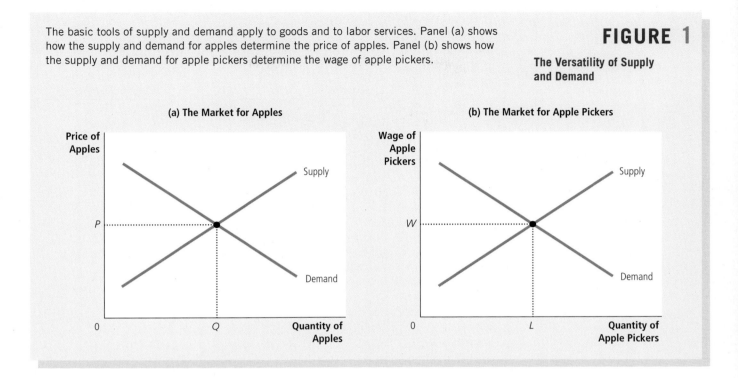

(a) The Market for Apples

(b) The Market for Apple Pickers

18-1a The Competitive Profit-Maximizing Firm

Let's look at how a typical firm, such as an apple producer, decides what quantity of labor to demand. The firm owns an apple orchard and each week must decide how many apple pickers to hire to harvest its crop. After the firm makes its hiring decision, the workers pick as many apples as they can. The firm then sells the apples, pays the workers, and keeps what is left as profit.

We make two assumptions about our firm. First, we assume that our firm is *competitive* both in the market for apples (where the firm is a seller) and in the market for apple pickers (where the firm is a buyer). A competitive firm is a price taker. Because there are many other firms selling apples and hiring apple pickers, a single firm has little influence over the price it gets for apples or the wage it pays apple pickers. The firm takes the price and the wage as given by market conditions. It only has to decide how many apples to sell and how many workers to hire.

Second, we assume that the firm is *profit maximizing*. Thus, the firm does not directly care about the number of workers it has or the number of apples it produces. It cares only about profit, which equals the total revenue from the sale of apples minus the total cost of producing them. The firm's supply of apples and its demand for workers are derived from its primary goal of maximizing profit.

18-1b The Production Function and the Marginal Product of Labor

To make its hiring decision, the firm must consider how the size of its workforce affects the amount of output produced. In other words, it must consider how the number of apple pickers affects the quantity of apples it can harvest and sell. Table 1 gives a numerical example. In the first column is the number of workers. In the second column is the quantity of apples the workers harvest each week.

TABLE 1

How the Competitive Firm Decides How Much Labor to Hire

Labor L	Output Q	Marginal Product of Labor $MPL = \Delta Q / \Delta L$	Value of the Marginal Product of Labor $VMPL = P \times MPL$	Wage W	Marginal Profit $\Delta Profit = VMPL - W$
0 workers	0 bushels				
		100 bushels	$1,000	$500	$500
1	100				
		80	800	500	300
2	180				
		60	600	500	100
3	240				
		40	400	500	−100
4	280				
		20	200	500	−300
5	300				

production function
the relationship between the quantity of inputs used to make a good and the quantity of output of that good

These two columns of numbers describe the firm's ability to produce. Recall that economists use the term **production function** to describe the relationship between the quantity of inputs used in production and the quantity of output from production. Here the "input" is the apple pickers and the "output" is the apples. The other inputs—the trees themselves, the land, the firm's trucks and tractors, and so on—are held fixed for now. This firm's production function shows that if the firm hires 1 worker, that worker will pick 100 bushels of apples per week. If the firm hires 2 workers, the 2 workers together will pick 180 bushels per week. And so on.

Figure 2 graphs the data on labor and output presented in Table 1. The number of workers is on the horizontal axis, and the amount of output is on the vertical axis. This figure illustrates the production function.

One of the *Ten Principles of Economics* introduced in Chapter 1 is that rational people think at the margin. This idea is the key to understanding how firms decide what quantity of labor to hire. To take a step toward this decision, the third column in Table 1 gives the **marginal product of labor**, the increase in the amount of output from an additional unit of labor. When the firm increases the number of workers from 1 to 2, for example, the amount of apples produced rises from 100 to 180 bushels. Therefore, the marginal product of the second worker is 80 bushels.

marginal product of labor
the increase in the amount of output from an additional unit of labor

diminishing marginal product
the property whereby the marginal product of an input declines as the quantity of the input increases

Notice that as the number of workers increases, the marginal product of labor declines. That is, the production process exhibits **diminishing marginal product**. At first, when only a few workers are hired, they can pick the low-hanging fruit. As the number of workers increases, additional workers have to climb higher up the ladders to find apples to pick. Hence, as more and more workers are hired, each additional worker contributes less to the production of apples. For this reason, the production function in Figure 2 becomes flatter as the number of workers rises.

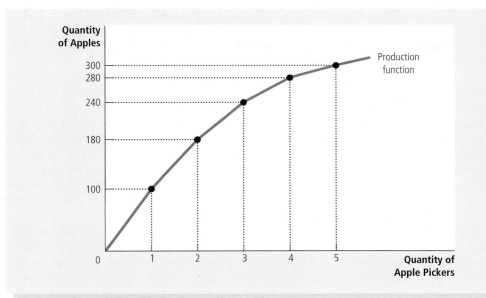

FIGURE 2

The Production Function
The production function shows how an input into production (apple pickers) influences the output from production (apples). As the quantity of the input increases, the production function gets flatter, reflecting the property of diminishing marginal product.

18-1c The Value of the Marginal Product and the Demand for Labor

Our profit-maximizing firm is concerned not about apples themselves but rather about the money it can make by producing and selling them. As a result, when deciding how many workers to hire to pick apples, the firm considers how much profit each worker would bring in. Because profit is total revenue minus total cost, the profit from an additional worker is the worker's contribution to revenue minus the worker's wage.

To find the worker's contribution to revenue, we must convert the marginal product of labor (which is measured in bushels of apples) into the *value* of the marginal product (which is measured in dollars). We do this using the price of apples. To continue our example, if a bushel of apples sells for $10 and if an additional worker produces 80 bushels of apples, then the worker produces $800 of revenue.

The **value of the marginal product** of any input is the marginal product of that input multiplied by the market price of the output. The fourth column in Table 1 shows the value of the marginal product of labor in our example, assuming the price of apples is $10 per bushel. Because the market price is constant for a competitive firm while the marginal product declines with more workers, the value of the marginal product diminishes as the number of workers rises. Economists sometimes call this column of numbers the firm's *marginal revenue product:* It is the extra revenue the firm gets from hiring an additional unit of a factor of production.

Now consider how many workers the firm will hire. Suppose that the market wage for apple pickers is $500 per week. In this case, as you can see in Table 1, the first worker that the firm hires is profitable: The first worker yields $1,000 in revenue, or $500 in profit. Similarly, the second worker yields $800 in additional revenue, or $300 in profit. The third worker produces $600 in additional revenue,

value of the marginal product
the marginal product of an input times the price of the output

or $100 in profit. After the third worker, however, hiring workers is unprofitable. The fourth worker would yield only $400 of additional revenue. Because the worker's wage is $500, hiring the fourth worker would mean a $100 reduction in profit. Thus, the firm hires only three workers.

It is instructive to consider the firm's decision graphically. Figure 3 graphs the value of the marginal product. This curve slopes downward because the marginal product of labor diminishes as the number of workers rises. The figure also includes a horizontal line at the market wage. To maximize profit, the firm hires workers up to the point where these two curves cross. Below this level of employment, the value of the marginal product exceeds the wage, so hiring another worker would increase profit. Above this level of employment, the value of the marginal product is less than the wage, so the marginal worker is unprofitable. Thus, *a competitive, profit-maximizing firm hires workers up to the point at which the value of the marginal product of labor equals the wage.*

Having explained the profit-maximizing hiring strategy for a competitive firm, we can now offer a theory of labor demand. Recall that a firm's labor-demand curve tells us the quantity of labor that a firm demands at any given wage. We have just seen in Figure 3 that the firm makes that decision by choosing the quantity of labor at which the value of the marginal product equals the wage. As a result, *the value-of-marginal-product curve is the labor-demand curve for a competitive, profit-maximizing firm.*

18-1d What Causes the Labor-Demand Curve to Shift?

We now understand that the labor-demand curve reflects the value of the marginal product of labor. With this insight in mind, let's consider a few of the things that might cause the labor-demand curve to shift.

The Output Price   The value of the marginal product is marginal product times the price of the firm's output. Thus, when the output price changes, the value of the marginal product changes, and the labor-demand curve shifts. An increase in

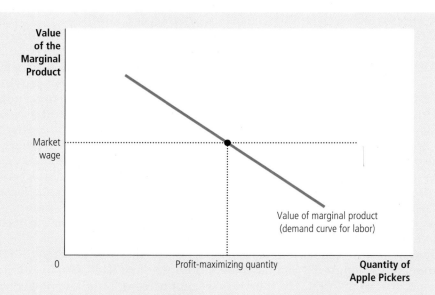

FIGURE 3

The Value of the Marginal Product of Labor

This figure shows how the value of the marginal product (the marginal product times the price of the output) depends on the number of workers. The curve slopes downward because of diminishing marginal product. For a competitive, profit-maximizing firm, this value-of-marginal-product curve is also the firm's labor-demand curve.

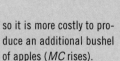

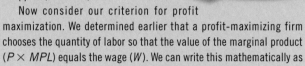

Input Demand and Output Supply: Two Sides of the Same Coin

In Chapter 14, we saw how a competitive, profit-maximizing firm decides how much of its output to sell: It chooses the quantity of output at which the price of the good equals the marginal cost of production. We have just seen how such a firm decides how much labor to hire: It chooses the quantity of labor at which the wage equals the value of the marginal product. Because the production function links the quantity of inputs to the quantity of output, you should not be surprised to learn that the firm's decision about input demand is closely linked to its decision about output supply. In fact, these two decisions are two sides of the same coin.

To see this relationship more fully, let's consider how the marginal product of labor (*MPL*) and marginal cost (*MC*) are related. Suppose an additional worker costs $500 and has a marginal product of 50 bushels of apples. In this case, producing 50 more bushels costs $500; the marginal cost of a bushel is $500/50, or $10. More generally, if *W* is the wage, and an extra unit of labor produces *MPL* units of output, then the marginal cost of a unit of output is $MC = W/MPL$.

This analysis shows that diminishing marginal product is closely related to increasing marginal cost. When our apple orchard grows crowded with workers, each additional worker adds less to the production of apples (*MPL* falls). Similarly, when the apple firm is producing a large quantity of apples, the orchard is already crowded with workers, so it is more costly to produce an additional bushel of apples (*MC* rises).

Now consider our criterion for profit maximization. We determined earlier that a profit-maximizing firm chooses the quantity of labor so that the value of the marginal product ($P \times MPL$) equals the wage (*W*). We can write this mathematically as

$$P \times MPL = W.$$

If we divide both sides of this equation by *MPL*, we obtain

$$P = W/MPL.$$

We just noted that W/MPL equals marginal cost, *MC*. Therefore, we can substitute to obtain

$$P = MC.$$

This equation states that the price of the firm's output equals the marginal cost of producing a unit of output. Thus, *when a competitive firm hires labor up to the point at which the value of the marginal product equals the wage, it also produces up to the point at which the price equals marginal cost*. Our analysis of labor demand in this chapter is just another way of looking at the production decision we first saw in Chapter 14. ◢

the price of apples, for instance, raises the value of the marginal product of each worker who picks apples and, therefore, increases labor demand from the firms that supply apples. Conversely, a decrease in the price of apples reduces the value of the marginal product and decreases labor demand.

Technological Change   Between 1960 and 2012, the output a typical U.S. worker produced in an hour rose by 192 percent. Why? The most important reason is technological progress: Scientists and engineers are constantly figuring out new and better ways of doing things. This has profound implications for the labor market. Technological advance typically raises the marginal product of labor, which in turn increases the demand for labor and shifts the labor-demand curve to the right.

It is also possible for technological change to reduce labor demand. The invention of a cheap industrial robot, for instance, could conceivably reduce the marginal product of labor, shifting the labor-demand curve to the left. Economists call this *labor-saving* technological change. History suggests, however, that most technological progress is instead *labor-augmenting*. Such technological advance explains persistently rising employment in the face of rising wages: Even though wages (adjusted for inflation) increased by 152 percent in the last half century, firms nonetheless increased the amount of labor they employed by 88 percent.

The Supply of Other Factors The quantity available of one factor of production can affect the marginal product of other factors. A fall in the supply of ladders, for instance, will reduce the marginal product of apple pickers and thus the demand for apple pickers. We consider this linkage among the factors of production more fully later in the chapter.

Quick Quiz *Define* marginal product of labor *and* value of the marginal product of labor. • *Describe how a competitive, profit-maximizing firm decides how many workers to hire.*

18-2 The Supply of Labor

Having analyzed labor demand in detail, let's turn to the other side of the market and consider labor supply. A formal model of labor supply is included in Chapter 21, where we develop the theory of household decision making. Here we discuss briefly and informally the decisions that lie behind the labor-supply curve.

18-2a The Trade-off between Work and Leisure

One of the *Ten Principles of Economics* in Chapter 1 is that people face trade-offs. Probably no trade-off is more obvious or more important in a person's life than the trade-off between work and leisure. The more hours you spend working, the fewer hours you have to watch TV, enjoy dinner with friends, or pursue your favorite hobby. The trade-off between labor and leisure lies behind the labor-supply curve.

Another of the *Ten Principles of Economics* is that the cost of something is what you give up to get it. What do you give up to get an hour of leisure? You give up an hour of work, which in turn means an hour of wages. Thus, if your wage is $15 per hour, the opportunity cost of an hour of leisure is $15. And when you get a raise to $20 per hour, the opportunity cost of enjoying leisure goes up.

The labor-supply curve reflects how workers' decisions about the labor-leisure trade-off respond to a change in that opportunity cost. An upward-sloping labor-supply curve means that an increase in the wage induces workers to increase the quantity of labor they supply. Because time is limited, more work means less leisure. That is, workers respond to the increase in the opportunity cost of leisure by taking less of it.

It is worth noting that the labor-supply curve need not be upward sloping. Imagine you got that raise from $15 to $20 per hour. The opportunity cost of leisure is now greater, but you are also richer than you were before. You might decide that with your extra wealth you can now afford to enjoy more leisure. That is, at the higher wage, you might choose to work fewer hours. If so, your labor-supply curve would slope backward. In Chapter 21, we discuss this possibility in terms of conflicting effects on your labor-supply decision (called the *income* and *substitution effects*). For now, we ignore the possibility of backward-sloping labor supply and assume that the labor-supply curve is upward sloping.

18-2b What Causes the Labor-Supply Curve to Shift?

The labor-supply curve shifts whenever people change the amount they want to work at a given wage. Let's now consider some of the events that might cause such a shift.

"I really didn't enjoy working five days a week, fifty weeks a year for forty years, but I needed the money."

© Peter C. Vey/ The New Yorker Collection/www.cartoonbank.com

Changes in Tastes In 1950, 34 percent of women were employed at paid jobs or looking for work. In 2012, the number had risen to 58 percent. There are many explanations for this development, but one of them is changing tastes, or attitudes toward work. Sixty years ago, it was the norm for women to stay at home and raise children. Today, the typical family size is smaller, and more mothers choose to work. The result is an increase in the supply of labor.

Changes in Alternative Opportunities The supply of labor in any one labor market depends on the opportunities available in other labor markets. If the wage earned by pear pickers suddenly rises, some apple pickers may choose to switch occupations, causing the supply of labor in the market for apple pickers to fall.

Immigration Movement of workers from region to region, or country to country, is another important source of shifts in labor supply. When immigrants come to the United States, for instance, the supply of labor in the United States increases, and the supply of labor in the immigrants' home countries falls. In fact, much of the policy debate about immigration centers on its effect on labor supply and, thereby, equilibrium wages in the labor market.

Quick Quiz *Who has a greater opportunity cost of enjoying leisure—a janitor or a brain surgeon? Explain. Can this help explain why doctors work such long hours?*

18-3 Equilibrium in the Labor Market

So far we have established two facts about how wages are determined in competitive labor markets:

- The wage adjusts to balance the supply and demand for labor.
- The wage equals the value of the marginal product of labor.

At first, it might seem surprising that the wage can do both of these things at once. In fact, there is no real puzzle here, but understanding why there is no puzzle is an important step toward understanding wage determination.

Figure 4 shows the labor market in equilibrium. The wage and the quantity of labor have adjusted to balance supply and demand. When the market is in this equilibrium, each firm has bought as much labor as it finds profitable at the equilibrium wage. That is, each firm has followed the rule for profit maximization: It has hired workers until the value of the marginal product equals the wage. Hence, the wage must equal the value of the marginal product of labor once it has brought supply and demand into equilibrium.

This brings us to an important lesson: *Any event that changes the supply or demand for labor must change the equilibrium wage and the value of the marginal product by the same amount because these must always be equal.* To see how this works, let's consider some events that shift these curves.

18-3a Shifts in Labor Supply

Suppose that immigration increases the number of workers willing to pick apples. As Figure 5 shows, the supply of labor shifts to the right from S_1 to S_2. At the initial wage W_1, the quantity of labor supplied now exceeds the quantity demanded.

FIGURE 4

Equilibrium in a Labor Market
Like all prices, the price of labor
(the wage) depends on supply
and demand. Because the
demand curve reflects the value
of the marginal product of labor,
in equilibrium workers receive
the value of their marginal
contribution to the production
of goods and services.

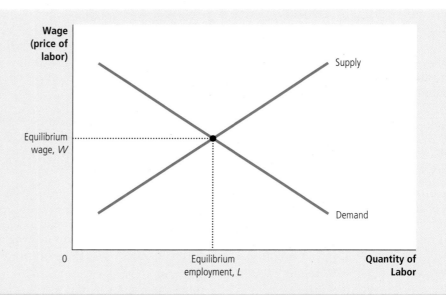

FIGURE 5

A Shift in Labor Supply
When labor supply increases
from S_1 to S_2, perhaps because
of an immigration of new workers, the equilibrium wage falls
from W_1 to W_2. At this lower
wage, firms hire more labor, so
employment rises from L_1 to L_2.
The change in the wage reflects
a change in the value of the
marginal product of labor: With
more workers, the added output
from an extra worker is smaller.

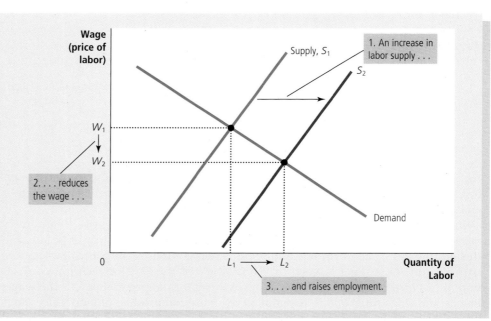

This surplus of labor puts downward pressure on the wage of apple pickers, and
the fall in the wage from W_1 to W_2 in turn makes it profitable for firms to hire more
workers. As the number of workers employed in each apple orchard rises, the
marginal product of a worker falls, and so does the value of the marginal product.
In the new equilibrium, both the wage and the value of the marginal product of
labor are lower than they were before the influx of new workers.

An episode from Israel, studied by MIT economist Joshua Angrist, illustrates
how a shift in labor supply can alter the equilibrium in a labor market. During

most of the 1980s, many thousands of Palestinians regularly commuted from their homes in the Israeli-occupied West Bank and Gaza Strip to jobs in Israel, primarily in the construction and agriculture industries. In 1988, however, political unrest in these occupied areas induced the Israeli government to take steps that, as a by-product, reduced this supply of workers. Curfews were imposed, work permits were checked more thoroughly, and a ban on overnight stays of Palestinians in Israel was enforced more rigorously. The economic impact of these steps was exactly as theory predicts: The number of Palestinians with jobs in Israel fell by half, while those who continued to work in Israel enjoyed wage increases of about 50 percent. With a reduced number of Palestinian workers in Israel, the value of the marginal product of the remaining workers was much higher.

18-3b Shifts in Labor Demand

Now suppose that an increase in the popularity of apples causes their price to rise. This price increase does not change the marginal product of labor for any given number of workers, but it does raise the *value* of the marginal product. With a higher price for apples, hiring more apple pickers is now profitable. As Figure 6 shows, when the demand for labor shifts to the right from D_1 to D_2, the equilibrium wage rises from W_1 to W_2, and equilibrium employment rises from L_1 to L_2. Once again, the wage and the value of the marginal product of labor move together.

This analysis shows that prosperity for firms in an industry is often linked to prosperity for workers in that industry. When the price of apples rises, apple producers make greater profit, and apple pickers earn higher wages. When the price of apples falls, apple producers earn smaller profit, and apple pickers earn lower wages. This lesson is well known to workers in industries with highly volatile prices. Workers in oil fields, for instance, know from experience that their earnings are closely linked to the world price of crude oil.

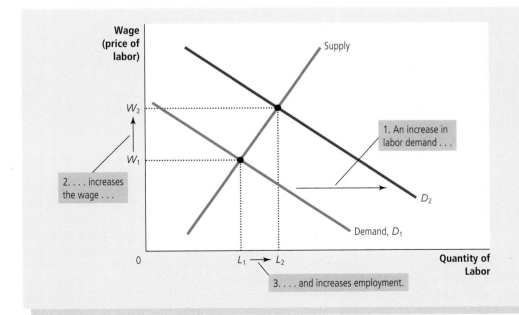

FIGURE 6

A Shift in Labor Demand
When labor demand increases from D_1 to D_2, perhaps because of an increase in the price of the firm's output, the equilibrium wage rises from W_1 to W_2, and employment rises from L_1 to L_2. The change in the wage reflects a change in the value of the marginal product of labor: With a higher output price, the added output from an extra worker is more valuable.

The Economics of Immigration

Here is an interview with Pia Orrenius, a senior economist at the Federal Reserve Bank of Dallas who studies immigration.

Q: What can you tell us about the size of the immigrant population in the United States?

A: Immigrants make up about 13 percent of the overall population, which means about 40 million foreign-born live in the United States. The commonly accepted estimate for the undocumented portion of the foreign-born population is 11 million. Immigrants come from all parts of the world, but we've seen big changes in their origins. In the 1950s and 1960s, 75 percent of immigrants were from Europe. Today, about 80 percent are from Latin America and Asia. Inflows are also much larger today, with 1 million to 2 million newcomers entering each year. Still, 2010–2011 immigration was below the levels experienced prior to the Great Recession of 2007–2009, when the housing bust led to a significant decline in illegal immigration.

What's interesting about the United States is how our economy has been able to absorb immigrants and put them to work.

Pia Orrenius

U.S. immigrants are much more likely to be working compared with immigrants in other developed countries. This is partly because we don't set high entry-level wages or have cumbersome hiring and firing rules. In this type of flexible system, there are more job openings. Workers have more opportunities. Of course, entry-level wages are also lower, but immigrants at least get their foot in the door.

Being in the workforce allows immigrants to interact with the rest of society. They learn the language faster, pay taxes and become stakeholders.

Q: Where do immigrants fit into the U.S. economy?

A: U.S. immigrants are diverse in economic terms. We rely on them to fill both high- and low-skilled jobs. Some immigrants do medium-skilled work, but more than anything else they're found on the low and the high ends of the education distribution.

The economic effects of immigration are different depending on which group you're talking about. We have an extremely important group of high-skilled immigrants. We rely on them to fill high-level jobs in health, science, technology, and engineering. Each year, over one-third of Ph.D.s in science and engineering is awarded to students who were

Courtesy of Federal Reserve Bank of Dallas, Southwest Economy, March/April 2006

From these examples, you should now have a good understanding of how wages are set in competitive labor markets. Labor supply and labor demand together determine the equilibrium wage, and shifts in the supply or demand curve for labor cause the equilibrium wage to change. At the same time, profit maximization by the firms that demand labor ensures that the equilibrium wage always equals the value of the marginal product of labor.

case study

Productivity and Wages

One of the *Ten Principles of Economics* in Chapter 1 is that our standard of living depends on our ability to produce goods and services. We can now see how this principle works in the market for labor. In particular, our analysis of labor demand shows that wages equal productivity as measured by the value of the marginal product of labor. Put simply, highly productive workers are highly paid, and less productive workers are less highly paid.

This lesson is key to understanding why workers today are better off than workers in previous generations. Table 2 presents some data on growth in productivity

born abroad. Moreover, research shows that foreign-born workers in STEM fields [science, technology, engineering, and mathematics] are more innovative and entrepreneurial than their U.S.-born counterparts.

High-skilled immigration has many economic benefits—it boosts productivity growth and contributes positively to government finances. People tend to focus on undocumented or low-skilled immigrants when discussing immigration and often do not recognize the tremendous contributions of high-skilled immigrants.

Q: What about the low-skilled immigration?

A: With low-skilled immigration, the economic benefits of the added labor, such as lower prices for consumers, have to be balanced against the fiscal impact, which is likely negative. The fiscal impact is the difference between what families contribute in taxes and what they use up in the form of publicly provided services.

What makes the fiscal issue more difficult is the distribution of the burden. The federal government reaps much of the revenue from immigrants who work and pay employment taxes. State and local governments realize less of that benefit and have to pay more of

the costs associated with low-skilled immigration—usually health care and educational expenses.

Q: Does it matter whether the immigration is legal or not?

A: Illegal immigration has helped fuel the U.S. economy for many years. Five percent of the U.S. workforce is made up of unauthorized workers; the outcome of decades of robust labor demand and, until recently, lax enforcement. Nevertheless, from an economic perspective, it makes more sense to differentiate among immigrants of various skill levels than it does to focus on legal status.

The economic benefits of low-skilled immigrants aren't typically going to depend on how they entered the United States. Illegal immigrants may pay less in taxes, but they're also ineligible for public programs. So being illegal doesn't mean these immigrants have a worse fiscal impact. In fact, a low-skilled illegal immigrant likely creates less fiscal burden than a low-skilled legal immigrant because the undocumented get almost no government benefits.

Q: How does immigration affect jobs and earnings for the native-born population?

A: Labor economists have looked long and hard at this question, namely how

immigration has affected the wages of Americans, particularly the low-skilled who lack a high school degree. The reason we worry about this is that the real wages of less-educated U.S. men have been falling since the late 1970s.

The studies tend to show that little of the decline is due to immigration. The consensus seems to be that wages overall are about 1 to 3 percent lower today as a result of immigration, although some scholars find larger effects for low-skilled workers. Still, labor economists think it's a bit of a puzzle that they haven't been able to systematically identify larger adverse wage effects.

The reason may be the way the economy is constantly adjusting to the inflow of immigrants. On a geographical basis, for example, a large influx of immigrants into an area tends to encourage an inflow of capital or a change in technology or production processes which puts new workers to use. So you have an increase in labor supply, but you also have an increase in labor demand, and the wage effects are ameliorated. ◢

Source: This interview, updated for this edition by Dr. Orrenius, was originally published in *Southwest Economy*, March/April 2006.

TABLE 2

Productivity and Wage Growth in the United States

Time Period	Growth Rate of Productivity	Growth Rate of Real Wages
1959–2012	2.1%	1.8%
1959–1973	2.8	2.8
1973–1995	1.4	1.1
1995–2012	2.3	1.9

Source: Bureau of Labor Statistics. Growth in productivity is measured here as the annualized rate of change in output per hour in the nonfarm business sector. Growth in real wages is measured as the annualized change in compensation per hour in the nonfarm business sector divided by the implicit price deflator for that sector. These productivity data measure average productivity—the quantity of output divided by the quantity of labor—rather than marginal productivity, but average and marginal productivity are thought to move closely together.

and growth in real wages (that is, wages adjusted for inflation). From 1959 to 2012, productivity as measured by output per hour of work grew about 2.1 percent per year. Real wages grew at 1.8 percent—almost the same rate. With a growth rate of 2 percent per year, productivity and real wages double about every 35 years.

Productivity growth varies over time. Table 2 also shows the data for three shorter periods that economists have identified as having very different productivity experiences. Around 1973, the U.S. economy experienced a significant slowdown in productivity growth that lasted until 1995. The cause of the productivity slowdown is not well understood, but the link between productivity and real wages is exactly as standard theory predicts. The slowdown in productivity growth from 2.8 to 1.4 percent per year coincided with a slowdown in real wage growth from 2.8 to 1.1 percent per year.

Productivity growth picked up again around 1995, and many observers hailed the arrival of the "new economy." This productivity acceleration is most often attributed to the spread of computers and information technology. As theory predicts, growth in real wages picked up as well. From 1995 to 2012, productivity grew by 2.3 percent per year, and real wages grew by 1.9 percent per year.

The bottom line: Both theory and history confirm the close connection between productivity and real wages. ◢

Quick Quiz *How does an immigration of workers affect labor supply, labor demand, the marginal product of labor, and the equilibrium wage?*

FYI

Monopsony

On the preceding pages, we built our analysis of the labor market with the tools of supply and demand. In doing so, we assumed that the labor market was competitive. That is, we assumed that there were many buyers and sellers of labor, so each buyer or seller had a negligible effect on the wage.

Yet imagine the labor market in a small town dominated by a single, large employer. That employer can exert a large influence on the going wage, and it may well use that market power to alter the outcome. Such a market in which there is a single buyer is called a *monopsony*.

A monopsony (a market with one buyer) is in many ways similar to a monopoly (a market with one seller). Recall from Chapter 15 that a monopoly firm produces less of the good than would a competitive firm; by reducing the quantity offered for sale, the monopoly firm moves along the product's demand curve, raising the price and also its profits.

Similarly, a monopsony firm in a labor market hires fewer workers than would a competitive firm; by reducing the number of jobs available, the monopsony firm moves along the labor supply curve, reducing the wage it pays and raising its profits. Thus, both monopolists and monopsonists reduce economic activity in a market below the socially optimal level. In both cases, the existence of market power distorts the outcome and causes deadweight losses.

This book does not present the formal model of monopsony because monopsonies are rare. In most labor markets, workers have many possible employers, and firms compete with one another to attract workers. In this case, the model of supply and demand is the best one to use. ◢

18-4 The Other Factors of Production: Land and Capital

We have seen how firms decide how much labor to hire and how these decisions determine workers' wages. At the same time that firms are hiring workers, they are also deciding about other inputs to production. For example, our apple-producing firm might have to choose the size of its apple orchard and the number of ladders for its apple pickers. We can think of the firm's factors of production as falling into three categories: labor, land, and capital.

The meaning of the terms *labor* and *land* is clear, but the definition of *capital* is somewhat tricky. Economists use the term **capital** to refer to the stock of equipment and structures used for production. That is, the economy's capital represents the accumulation of goods produced in the past that are being used in the present to produce new goods and services. For our apple firm, the capital stock includes the ladders used to climb the trees, the trucks used to transport the apples, the buildings used to store the apples, and even the trees themselves.

capital
the equipment and structures used to produce goods and services

18-4a Equilibrium in the Markets for Land and Capital

What determines how much the owners of land and capital earn for their contribution to the production process? Before answering this question, we need to distinguish between two prices: the purchase price and the rental price. The *purchase price* of land or capital is the price a person pays to own that factor of production indefinitely. The *rental price* is the price a person pays to use that factor for a limited period of time. It is important to keep this distinction in mind because, as we will see, these prices are determined by somewhat different economic forces.

Having defined these terms, we can now apply the theory of factor demand that we developed for the labor market to the markets for land and capital. Because the wage is the rental price of labor, much of what we have learned about wage determination applies also to the rental prices of land and capital. As Figure 7 illustrates, the rental price of land, shown in panel (a), and the rental price of capital, shown in panel (b), are determined by supply and demand. Moreover, the demand for land and capital is determined just like the demand for labor. That

Supply and demand determine the compensation paid to the owners of land, as shown in panel (a), and the compensation paid to the owners of capital, as shown in panel (b). The demand for each factor, in turn, depends on the value of the marginal product of that factor.

FIGURE 7

The Markets for Land and Capital

(a) The Market for Land

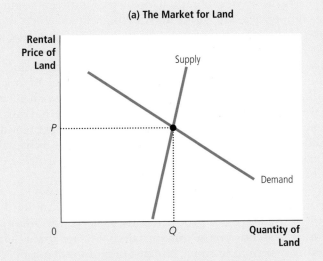

(b) The Market for Capital

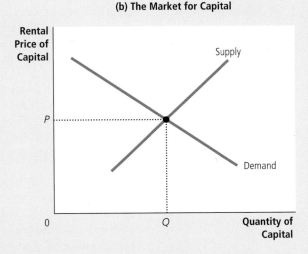

FYI

What Is Capital Income?

Labor income is an easy concept to understand: It is the paycheck that workers get from their employers. The income earned by capital, however, is less obvious.

In our analysis, we have been implicitly assuming that households own the economy's stock of capital—ladders, drill presses, warehouses, and so on—and rent it to the firms that use it. Capital income, in this case, is the rent that households receive for the use of their capital. This assumption simplified our analysis of how capital owners are compensated, but it is not entirely realistic. In fact, firms usually own the capital they use, and therefore, they receive the earnings from this capital.

These earnings from capital, however, are paid to households eventually in a variety of forms. Some of the earnings are paid in the form of interest to those households that have lent money to firms. Bondholders and bank depositors are two examples of recipients of interest. Thus, when you receive interest on your bank account, that income is part of the economy's capital income.

In addition, some of the earnings from capital are paid to households in the form of dividends. Dividends are payments by a firm to the firm's stockholders. A stockholder is a person who has bought a share in the ownership of the firm and, therefore, is entitled to share in the firm's profits.

A firm does not have to pay out all its earnings to households in the form of interest and dividends. Instead, it can retain some earnings within the firm and use these earnings to buy additional capital. Unlike dividends, these retained earnings do not yield a direct cash payment to the firm's stockholders, but the stockholders benefit from them nonetheless. Because retained earnings increase the amount of capital the firm owns, they tend to increase future earnings and, thereby, the value of the firm's stock.

These institutional details are interesting and important, but they do not alter our conclusion about the income earned by the owners of capital. Capital is paid according to the value of its marginal product, regardless of whether this income is transmitted to households in the form of interest or dividends or whether it is kept within firms as retained earnings.

is, when our apple-producing firm is deciding how much land and how many ladders to rent, it follows the same logic as when deciding how many workers to hire. For both land and capital, the firm increases the quantity hired until the value of the factor's marginal product equals the factor's price. Thus, the demand curve for each factor reflects the marginal productivity of that factor.

We can now explain how much income goes to labor, how much goes to landowners, and how much goes to the owners of capital. As long as the firms using the factors of production are competitive and profit-maximizing, each factor's rental price must equal the value of the marginal product for that factor. *Labor, land, and capital each earn the value of their marginal contribution to the production process.*

Now consider the purchase price of land and capital. The rental price and the purchase price are related: Buyers are willing to pay more for a piece of land or capital if it produces a valuable stream of rental income. And as we have just seen, the equilibrium rental income at any point in time equals the value of that factor's marginal product. Therefore, the equilibrium purchase price of a piece of land or capital depends on both the current value of the marginal product and the value of the marginal product expected to prevail in the future.

18-4b Linkages among the Factors of Production

We have seen that the price paid for any factor of production—labor, land, or capital—equals the value of the marginal product of that factor. The marginal product of any factor, in turn, depends on the quantity of that factor that is available. Because of diminishing marginal product, a factor in abundant supply has a low marginal product and thus a low price, and a factor in scarce supply has a high marginal product and a high price. As a result, when the supply of a factor falls, its equilibrium price rises.

When the supply of any factor changes, however, the effects are not limited to the market for that factor. In most situations, factors of production are used together in a way that makes the productivity of each factor depend on the quantities of the other factors available for use in the production process. As a result, when some event changes the supply of any one factor of production, it will typically affect not only the earnings of that factor but also the earnings of all the factors as well.

For example, suppose a hurricane destroys many of the ladders that workers use to pick apples from the orchards. What happens to the earnings of the various factors of production? Most obviously, when the supply of ladders falls, the equilibrium rental price of ladders rises. Those owners who were lucky enough to avoid damage to their ladders now earn a higher return when they rent out their ladders to the firms that produce apples.

Yet the effects of this event do not stop at the ladder market. Because there are fewer ladders with which to work, the workers who pick apples have a smaller marginal product. Thus, the reduction in the supply of ladders reduces the demand for the labor of apple pickers, and this shift in demand causes the equilibrium wage to fall.

This story shows a general lesson: *An event that changes the supply of any factor of production can alter the earnings of all the factors.* The change in earnings of any factor can be found by analyzing the impact of the event on the value of the marginal product of that factor.

Workers who survived
the plague were lucky in
more ways than one.

case study   The Economics of the Black Death

In 14th-century Europe, the bubonic plague wiped out about one-third of the population within a few years. This event, called the *Black Death*, provides a grisly natural experiment to test the theory of factor markets that we have just developed. Consider the effects of the Black Death on those who were lucky enough to survive. What do you think happened to the wages earned by workers and the rents earned by landowners?

To answer this question, let's examine the effects of a reduced population on the marginal product of labor and the marginal product of land. With a smaller supply of workers, the marginal product of labor rises. (This is diminishing marginal product working in reverse.) Thus, we would expect the Black Death to raise wages.

Because land and labor are used together in production, a smaller supply of workers also affects the market for land, the other major factor of production in medieval Europe. With fewer workers available to farm the land, an additional unit of land produced less additional output. In other words, the marginal product of land fell. Thus, we would expect the Black Death to lower rents.

In fact, both predictions are consistent with the historical evidence. Wages approximately doubled during this period, and rents declined 50 percent or more. The Black Death led to economic prosperity for the peasant classes and reduced incomes for the landed classes. ◢

Quick Quiz   *What determines the income of the owners of land and capital? • How would an increase in the quantity of capital affect the incomes of those who already own capital? How would it affect the incomes of workers?*

18-5 Conclusion

This chapter explained how labor, land, and capital are compensated for the roles they play in the production process. The theory developed here is called the *neoclassical theory of distribution*. According to the neoclassical theory, the amount paid to each factor of production depends on the supply and demand for that factor. The demand, in turn, depends on that particular factor's marginal productivity. In equilibrium, each factor of production earns the value of its marginal contribution to the production of goods and services.

The neoclassical theory of distribution is widely accepted. Most economists begin with the neoclassical theory when trying to explain how the U.S. economy's $15 trillion of income is distributed among the economy's various members. In the following two chapters, we consider the distribution of income in more detail. As you will see, the neoclassical theory provides the framework for this discussion.

Even at this point, you can use the theory to answer the question that began this chapter: Why are computer programmers paid more than gas station attendants? It is because programmers can produce a good of greater market value than can gas station attendants. People are willing to pay dearly for a good computer game, but they are willing to pay little to have their gas pumped and their windshield washed. The wages of these workers reflect the market prices of the goods they produce. If people suddenly got tired of using computers and decided to spend more time driving, the prices of these goods would change, and so would the equilibrium wages of these two groups of workers.

Summary

- The economy's income is distributed in the markets for the factors of production. The three most important factors of production are labor, land, and capital.

- The demand for factors, such as labor, is a derived demand that comes from firms that use the factors to produce goods and services. Competitive, profit-maximizing firms hire each factor up to the point at which the value of the factor's marginal product equals its price.

- The supply of labor arises from individuals' trade-off between work and leisure. An upward-sloping labor-supply curve means that people respond to an increase in the wage by working more hours and enjoying less leisure.

- The price paid to each factor adjusts to balance the supply and demand for that factor. Because factor demand reflects the value of the marginal product of that factor, in equilibrium each factor is compensated according to its marginal contribution to the production of goods and services.

- Because factors of production are used together, the marginal product of any one factor depends on the quantities of all factors that are available. As a result, a change in the supply of one factor alters the equilibrium earnings of all the factors.

Key Concepts

factors of production, *p. 374*
production function, *p. 376*

marginal product of labor, *p. 376*
diminishing marginal product, *p. 376*

value of the marginal product, *p. 377*
capital, *p. 387*

Questions for Review

1. Explain how a firm's production function is related to its marginal product of labor, how a firm's marginal product of labor is related to the value of its marginal product, and how a firm's value of marginal product is related to its demand for labor.

2. Give two examples of events that could shift the demand for labor, and explain why they do so.

3. Give two examples of events that could shift the supply of labor, and explain why they do so.

4. Explain how the wage can adjust to balance the supply and demand for labor while simultaneously equaling the value of the marginal product of labor.

5. If the population of the United States suddenly grew because of a large wave of immigration, what would happen to wages? What would happen to the rents earned by the owners of land and capital?

Quick Check Multiple Choice

1. Approximately what percentage of U.S. national income is paid to workers, as opposed to owners of capital and land?
   a. 30 percent
   b. 50 percent
   c. 70 percent
   d. 90 percent

2. If firms are competitive and profit-maximizing, the demand curve for labor is determined by
   a. the opportunity cost of workers' time.
   b. the value of the marginal product of labor.
   c. offsetting income and substitution effects.
   d. the value of the marginal product of capital.

3. A bakery operating in competitive markets sells its output for $20 per cake and hires labor at $10 per hour. To maximize profit, it should hire labor until the marginal product of labor is
   a. 1/2 cake per hour.
   b. 2 cakes per hour.
   c. 10 cakes per hour.
   d. 15 cakes per hour.

4. A technological advance that increases the marginal product of labor shifts the labor- _____ curve to the _____.
   a. demand, left
   b. demand, right
   c. supply, left
   d. supply, right

5. Around 1973, the U.S. economy experienced a significant _____ in productivity growth, coupled with a(n) _____ in the growth of real wages.
   a. acceleration, acceleration
   b. acceleration, slowdown
   c. slowdown, acceleration
   d. slowdown, slowdown

6. A storm destroys several factories, thereby reducing the stock of capital. What effect does this event have on factor markets?
   a. Wages and the rental price of capital both rise.
   b. Wages and the rental price of capital both fall.
   c. Wages rise, and the rental price of capital falls.
   d. Wages fall, and the rental price of capital rises.

Problems and Applications

1. Suppose that the president proposes a new law aimed at reducing healthcare costs: All Americans are required to eat one apple daily.
   a. How would this apple-a-day law affect the demand and equilibrium price of apples?
   b. How would the law affect the marginal product and the value of the marginal product of apple pickers?
   c. How would the law affect the demand and equilibrium wage for apple pickers?

2. Show the effect of each of the following events on the market for labor in the computer manufacturing industry.
   a. Congress buys personal computers for all U.S. college students.
   b. More college students major in engineering and computer science.
   c. Computer firms build new manufacturing plants.

3. Suppose that labor is the only input used by a perfectly competitive firm. The firm's production function is as follows:

Days of Labor	Units of Output
0 days	0 units
1	7
2	13
3	19
4	25
5	28
6	29
7	29

   a. Calculate the marginal product for each additional worker.
   b. Each unit of output sells for $10. Calculate the value of the marginal product of each worker.
   c. Compute the demand schedule showing the number of workers hired for all wages from zero to $100 a day.
   d. Graph the firm's demand curve.
   e. What happens to this demand curve if the price of output rises from $10 to $12 per unit?

4. Smiling Cow Dairy can sell all the milk it wants for $4 a gallon, and it can rent all the robots it wants to milk the cows at a capital rental price of $100 a day. It faces the following production schedule:

Number of Robots	Total Product
0	0 gallons
1	50
2	85
3	115
4	140
5	150
6	155

   a. In what kind of market structure does the firm sell its output? How can you tell?
   b. In what kind of market structure does the firm rent robots? How can you tell?
   c. Calculate the marginal product and the value of the marginal product for each additional robot.
   d. How many robots should the firm rent? Explain.

5. The nation of Ectenia has twenty competitive apple orchards, which sell apples at the world price of $2 per apple. The following equations describe the production function and the marginal product of labor in each orchard:

$$Q = 100L - L^2$$
$$MPL = 100 - 2L$$

where Q is the number of apples produced in a day, L is the number of workers, and MPL is the marginal product of labor.

   a. What is each orchard's labor demand as a function of the daily wage W? What is the market's labor demand?
   b. Ectenia has 200 workers who supply their labor inelastically. Solve for the wage W. How many workers does each orchard hire? How much profit does each orchard owner make?
   c. Calculate what happens to the income of workers and orchard owners if the world price of apples doubles to $4 per apple.
   d. Now suppose the price is back at $2 per apple, but a hurricane destroys half the orchards. Calculate how the hurricane affects the income of each worker and of each remaining orchard owner. What happens to the income of Ectenia as a whole?

6. Your enterprising uncle opens a sandwich shop that employs seven people. The employees are paid $6 per hour, and a sandwich sells for $3. If your uncle is maximizing his profit, what is the value of the marginal product of the last worker he hired? What is that worker's marginal product?

7. Leadbelly Co. sells pencils in a perfectly competitive product market and hires workers in a perfectly competitive labor market. Assume that the market wage rate for workers is $150 per day.

   a. What rule should Leadbelly follow to hire the profit-maximizing amount of labor?
   b. At the profit-maximizing level of output, the marginal product of the last worker hired is 30 boxes of pencils per day. Calculate the price of a box of pencils.
   c. Draw a diagram of the labor market for pencil workers (as in Figure 4 of this chapter) next to a diagram of the labor supply and demand for Leadbelly Co. (as in Figure 3). Label the equilibrium wage and quantity of labor for both the market and the firm. How are these diagrams related?
   d. Suppose some pencil workers switch to jobs in the growing computer industry. On the side-by-side diagrams from part (c), show how this change affects the equilibrium wage and quantity of labor for both the pencil market and for Leadbelly. How does this change affect the marginal product of labor at Leadbelly?

8. During the 1980s, 1990s, and the first decade of the 21st century, the United States experienced a significant inflow of capital from abroad. For example, Toyota, BMW, and other foreign car companies built auto plants in the United States.

a. Using a diagram of the U.S. capital market, show the effect of this inflow on the rental price of capital in the United States and on the quantity of capital in use.

b. Using a diagram of the U.S. labor market, show the effect of the capital inflow on the average wage paid to U.S. workers.

9. Policymakers sometimes propose laws requiring firms to give workers certain fringe benefits, such as health insurance or paid parental leave. Let's consider the effects of such a policy on the labor market.

a. Suppose that a law required firms to give each worker $3 of fringe benefits for every hour that the worker is employed by the firm. How does this law affect the marginal profit that a firm earns from each worker at a given cash wage? How does the law affect the demand curve for labor? Draw your answer on a graph with the cash wage on the vertical axis.

b. If there is no change in labor supply, how would this law affect employment and wages?

c. Why might the labor-supply curve shift in response to this law? Would this shift in labor supply raise or lower the impact of the law on wages and employment?

d. As discussed in Chapter 6, the wages of some workers, particularly the unskilled and inexperienced, are kept above the equilibrium level by minimum-wage laws. What effect would a fringe-benefit mandate have for these workers?

Go to CengageBrain.com to purchase access to the proven, critical Study Guide to accompany this text, which features additional notes and context, practice tests, and much more.

Earnings and Discrimination

I n the United States today, the typical physician earns about $200,000 a year, the typical police officer about $60,000, and the typical fast-food cook about $20,000. These examples illustrate the large differences in earnings that are so common in our economy. The differences explain why some people live in mansions, ride in limousines, and vacation on the French Riviera, while other people live in small apartments, ride the bus, and vacation in their own backyards.

Why do earnings vary so much from person to person? Chapter 18, which developed the basic neoclassical theory of the labor market, offers an answer to this question. There we saw that wages are governed by labor supply and labor demand. Labor demand, in turn, reflects the marginal productivity of labor. In equilibrium, each worker is paid the value of her marginal contribution to the economy's production of goods and services.

This theory of the labor market, though widely accepted by economists, is only the beginning of the story. To understand the wide variation in earnings that we observe, we must go beyond this general framework and examine more precisely what determines the supply and demand for different types of labor. That is our goal in this chapter.

19-1 Some Determinants of Equilibrium Wages

Workers differ from one another in many ways. Jobs also have differing characteristics—both in terms of the wages they pay and in terms of their nonmonetary attributes. In this section, we consider how the characteristics of jobs and workers affect labor supply, labor demand, and equilibrium wages.

19-1a Compensating Differentials

When a worker is deciding whether to take a job, the wage is only one of many job attributes that the worker takes into account. Some jobs are easy, fun, and safe, while others are hard, dull, and dangerous. The better the job as gauged by these nonmonetary characteristics, the more people there are who are willing to do the job at any given wage. In other words, the supply of labor for easy, fun, and safe jobs is greater than the supply of labor for hard, dull, and dangerous jobs. As a result, "good" jobs will tend to have lower equilibrium wages than "bad" jobs.

For example, imagine you are looking for a summer job in a local beach community. Two kinds of jobs are available. You can take a job as a beach-badge checker, or you can take a job as a garbage collector. The beach-badge checkers take leisurely strolls along the beach during the day and check to make sure the tourists have bought the required beach permits. The garbage collectors wake up before dawn to drive dirty, noisy trucks around town to pick up garbage. Which job would you want? Most people would prefer the beach job if the wages were the same. To induce people to become garbage collectors, the town has to offer higher wages to garbage collectors than to beach-badge checkers.

Economists use the term **compensating differential** to refer to a difference in wages that arises from nonmonetary characteristics of different jobs. Compensating differentials are prevalent in the economy. Here are some examples:

- Coal miners are paid more than other workers with similar levels of education. Their higher wage compensates them for the dirty and dangerous nature of coal mining, as well as the long-term health problems that coal miners experience.
- Workers who work the night shift at factories are paid more than similar workers who work the day shift. The higher wage compensates them for having to work at night and sleep during the day, a lifestyle that most people find undesirable.
- Professors are paid less than lawyers and doctors, who have similar amounts of education. The higher wages of lawyers and doctors compensate them for missing out on the great intellectual and personal satisfaction that professors' jobs offer. (Indeed, teaching economics is so much fun that it is surprising that economics professors are paid anything at all!)

19-1b Human Capital

As we discussed in the previous chapter, the word *capital* usually refers to an economy's stock of equipment and structures. The capital stock includes the farmer's

compensating differential
a difference in wages that arises to offset the nonmonetary characteristics of different jobs

Robert Mankoff/The New Yorker Collection/
www.cartoonbank.com

"On the one hand, I know I could make more money if I left public service for the private sector, but, on the other hand, I couldn't chop off heads."

tractor, the manufacturer's factory, and the teacher's chalkboard. The essence of capital is that it is a factor of production that itself has been produced.

There is another type of capital that, while less tangible than physical capital, is just as important to the economy's production. **Human capital** is the accumulation of investments in people. The most important type of human capital is education. Like all forms of capital, education represents an expenditure of resources at one time to raise productivity in the future. But unlike an investment in other forms of capital, an investment in education is tied to a specific person, and this linkage is what makes it human capital.

Not surprisingly, workers with more human capital earn more on average than those with less human capital. College graduates in the United States, for example, earn almost twice as much as those workers who end their education with a high school diploma. This large difference has been documented in many countries around the world. It tends to be even larger in less developed countries, where educated workers are in scarce supply.

From the perspective of supply and demand it is easy to see why education raises wages. Firms—the demanders of labor—are willing to pay more for highly educated workers because these workers have higher marginal products. Workers—the suppliers of labor—are willing to pay the cost of becoming educated only if there is a reward for doing so. In essence, the difference in wages between highly educated workers and less educated workers may be considered a compensating differential for the cost of becoming educated.

human capital
the accumulation of investments in people, such as education and on-the-job training

case study — The Increasing Value of Skills

"The rich get richer, and the poor get poorer." Like many adages, this one is not always true, but it has been in recent years. Many studies have documented that the earnings gap between workers with high skills and workers with low skills has increased over the past several decades.

Table 1 presents data on the average earnings of college graduates and of high school graduates without any additional education. These data show the increase in the financial reward from education. In 1975, a man on average earned 42 percent more with a college degree than without one; by 2011, this figure had risen to 75 percent. For a woman, the reward for attending college rose from a 35 percent increase in earnings in 1975 to an 81 percent increase in 2011. The incentive to stay in school is as great today as it has ever been.

Why has the gap in earnings between skilled and unskilled workers widened in recent years? No one knows for sure, but economists have proposed two hypotheses to explain this trend. Both hypotheses suggest that the demand for skilled labor has risen over time relative to the demand for unskilled labor. The shift in demand has led to a corresponding change in the wages of both groups, which in turn has led to greater inequality.

The first hypothesis is that international trade has altered the relative demand for skilled and unskilled labor. In recent years, the amount of trade with other countries has increased substantially. As a percentage of total U.S. production of goods and services, imports have risen from 5 percent in 1970 to 18 percent in 2011, and exports have risen from 6 percent in 1970 to 14 percent in 2011. Because unskilled labor is plentiful and cheap in many foreign countries, the United States tends to import goods produced with unskilled labor and export goods produced with skilled labor. Thus, when international trade expands, the domestic demand for skilled labor rises and the domestic demand for unskilled labor falls.

TABLE 1

Average Annual Earnings by Educational Attainment
College graduates have always earned more than workers without the benefit of college, but the salary gap has grown even larger over the past few decades.

	1975	2011
Men		
High school, no college	$48,720	$46,038
College graduates	$69,146	$80,508
Percent extra for college grads	+42%	+75%
Women		
High school, no college	$28,066	$32,249
College graduates	$37,804	$58,229
Percent extra for college grads	+35%	+81%

Note: Earnings data are adjusted for inflation and are expressed in 2011 dollars. Data apply to full-time, year-round workers age 18 and over. Data for college graduates exclude workers with additional schooling beyond college, such as a master's degree or Ph.D.

Source: U.S. Census Bureau and author's calculations.

IN THE NEWS ········· Higher Education as an Investment

Is a college degree a good investment compared with, say, stocks and bonds? According to the Hamilton Project, a research effort run by a prominent Washington think tank, the answer is a resounding "yes."

Regardless of the Cost, College Still Matters

By Michael Greenstone and Adam Looney

As America continues its recovery from the Great Recession, there is an ongoing debate in the media and among policymakers about the value of a college degree in today's economic climate. One issue that is receiving a significant amount of attention is the rising cost of college. Indeed, tuition has increased by almost 50 percent in the last 30 years, prompting some people to ask whether college is still worth the price of admission.

In this month's analysis, The Hamilton Project confirms its previous findings that the returns to college attendance are much higher than other investments, such as stocks, bonds, and real estate. We also find that the returns

to college have been largely constant over the last 35 years, indicating that the rising tuition costs have been offset by the increased earnings premium for college graduates. . . .

In most respects, a college degree has never been more valuable. Recent college graduates earn more money and have an easier time finding employment than their peers who only have a high school diploma. What may be less intuitive is that these gaps have been growing in recent years. A young college graduate earned about $4,000 more per year in the 1980s, adjusting for inflation, than someone of the same age who did not attend college (averaged across the entire population, not just those in the workforce). Over the last three decades, that figure has climbed to $12,000 per year.

Differences in employment rates between college graduates and non-graduates have

not demonstrated as clear of a trend over this period, with one key exception. In recent years—particularly in the aftermath of the Great Recession—college has become an increasingly important determinant of one's employment status. Today, a college graduate is almost 20 percentage points more likely to be employed than someone with only a high school diploma. This "employment gap" between college and high school graduates is the largest in our nation's history. . . .

While the evidence is clear about the life-long value of more education, skeptics are increasingly pointing to rising tuition costs to claim that college is not as sound of an investment as it once was. And it is true that tuition has increased significantly over the past few decades. In 1980, it cost an average of about

The second hypothesis is that changes in technology have altered the relative demand for skilled and unskilled labor. Consider, for instance, the introduction of computers. Computers raise the demand for skilled workers who can use the new machines and reduce the demand for the unskilled workers whose jobs are replaced by the computers. For example, many companies now rely more on computer databases, and less on filing cabinets, to keep business records. This change raises the demand for computer programmers and reduces the demand for filing clerks. Thus, as more firms use computers, the demand for skilled labor rises and the demand for unskilled labor falls.

Economists have found it difficult to gauge the validity of these two hypotheses. It is possible that both are true: Increasing international trade and technological change may share responsibility for the increasing income inequality we have observed in recent decades. In the next chapter, we discuss the issue of increasing inequality in more detail. ◢

19-1c Ability, Effort, and Chance

Why do major league baseball players get paid more than minor league players? Certainly, the higher wage is not a compensating differential. Playing in the major leagues is not a less pleasant job than playing in the minor leagues; in fact, the opposite is true. The major leagues do not require more years of schooling or

$56,000 (adjusting for inflation) to attend a university for four years. This figure includes tuition, fees, and the "opportunity cost," or income one foregoes to attend school instead of holding a job. (This figure excludes room and board: one must eat and sleep whether she is in college or not.) In 2010, four years of college cost more than $82,000, a nearly 50 percent increase over that 30-year period.

This increase in tuition is based on calculations from the National Center for Education Statistics but it may overstate the rise in the costs of college. First, this rise in tuition does not account for recent increases in financial aid. Thus, while the sticker price of college may have gone up, it is unclear to what extent the cost to students and their families has increased. Indeed, according to the College Board, the actual cost of a four-year degree has remained relatively constant over the last 15 years.

Regardless of the magnitude of the exact increase in tuition, a sole focus on the cost of college is misleading because it only tells half of the story. Specifically, the monetary benefits of a college degree have increased dramatically over the last few decades. An individual who entered college in 1980 could expect to earn about $260,000 more over the course of her life compared to someone who received only a high school diploma. In contrast, for someone starting college in 2010, the expected lifetime increase in earnings relative to a high school graduate was more than $450,000. These estimates are adjusted both for inflation and the fact that most of this additional income will come much later in a graduate's life.

Even if we assume that all students actually pay tuition at the published rates, the bottom line is this: while college may be 50 percent more expensive now than it was 30 years ago, the increase to lifetime earnings that a college degree brings is 75 percent higher. In short, the cost of college is growing, but the benefits of college—and, by extension, the cost of not going to college—are growing even faster.

The returns to an investment in a college education, therefore, are high. The Hamilton Project estimated that investing in a four-year degree yields a return of above 15 percent. While this is down slightly from almost 18 percent in the late '90s, attending college remains one of the best ways one can invest her money. The return to college is more than double the average return over the last 60 years experienced in the stock market (6.8 percent), and more than five times the return to investments in corporate bonds (2.9 percent), gold (2.3 percent), long-term government bonds (2.2 percent), or housing (0.4 percent).

The cost of college can be daunting for many families, but it is precisely because college is such a sound investment that there is an important role for government to ensure that loan programs are plentiful and accessible. The nation and the economy are strengthened when college attendance is determined by students' abilities, not their families' financial background. Indeed, it is not just the direct recipients of these loans that benefit from the increased number of Americans who are able to go to college. One recent study showed that even individuals with only a high school diploma earn more when they live in cities populated with more college graduates. More education is not just good for individuals; it's a good investment for the broader community. ◢

Source: The Hamilton Project at the Brookings Institution, October 5, 2012.

more experience. To a large extent, players in the major leagues earn more just because they have greater natural ability.

Natural ability is important for workers in all occupations. Because of heredity and upbringing, people differ in their physical and mental attributes. Some people are strong, others weak. Some people are smart, others less so. Some people are outgoing, others awkward in social situations. These and many other personal characteristics determine how productive workers are and, therefore, play a role in determining the wages they earn.

Closely related to ability is effort. Some people work hard; others are lazy. We should not be surprised to find that those who work hard are more productive and earn higher wages. To some extent, firms reward workers directly by paying people based on what they produce. Salespeople, for instance, are often paid a percentage of the sales they make. At other times, hard work is rewarded less directly in the form of a higher annual salary or a bonus.

Chance also plays a role in determining wages. If a person attended a trade school to learn how to repair televisions with vacuum tubes and then found this skill made obsolete by the invention of solid-state electronics, she would end up earning a low wage compared to others with similar years of training. The low wage of this worker is due to chance—a phenomenon that economists recognize but do not shed much light on.

How important are ability, effort, and chance in determining wages? It is hard to say because these factors are difficult to measure. But indirect evidence suggests that they are very important. When labor economists study wages, they relate a worker's wage to those variables that can be measured, such as years of schooling, years of experience, age, and job characteristics. All these measured variables affect a worker's wage as theory predicts, but they account for less than half of the variation in wages in our economy. Because so much of the variation in wages is left unexplained, omitted variables, including ability, effort, and chance, must play an important role.

case study

The Benefits of Beauty

People differ in many ways, one of which is physical attractiveness. The actor Ryan Gosling, for instance, is a handsome man. In part for this reason, his movies attract large audiences. Not surprisingly, the large audiences mean a large income for Mr. Gosling.

How prevalent are the economic benefits of beauty? Labor economists Daniel Hamermesh and Jeff Biddle tried to answer this question in a study published in the December 1994 issue of the *American Economic Review*. Hamermesh and Biddle examined data from surveys of individuals in the United States and Canada. The interviewers who conducted the survey were asked to rate each respondent's physical appearance. Hamermesh and Biddle then examined how much the wages of the respondents depended on the standard determinants—education, experience, and so on—and how much they depended on physical appearance.

Hamermesh and Biddle found that beauty pays. People who are deemed more attractive than average earn 5 percent more than people of average looks, and people of average looks earn 5 to 10 percent more than people considered less attractive than average. Similar results were found for men and women.

What explains these differences in wages? There are several ways to interpret the "beauty premium."

One interpretation is that good looks are themselves a type of innate ability determining productivity and wages. Some people are born with the physical attributes of a movie star; other people are not. Good looks are useful in any job in which workers present themselves to the public—such as acting, sales, and waiting on tables. In this case, an attractive worker is more valuable to the firm than an unattractive worker. The firm's willingness to pay more to attractive workers reflects its customers' preferences.

A second interpretation is that reported beauty is an indirect measure of other types of ability. How attractive a person appears depends on more than just heredity. It also depends on dress, hairstyle, personal demeanor, and other attributes that a person can control. Perhaps a person who successfully projects an attractive image in a survey interview is more likely to be an intelligent person who succeeds at other tasks as well.

A third interpretation is that the beauty premium is a type of discrimination, a topic to which we return later. ◢

Good looks pay.

19-1d An Alternative View of Education: Signaling

Earlier we discussed the human-capital view of education, according to which schooling raises workers' wages because it makes them more productive. Although this view is widely accepted, some economists have proposed an alternative theory, which emphasizes that firms use educational attainment as a way of sorting between high-ability and low-ability workers. According to this alternative view, when people earn a college degree, for instance, they do not become more productive, but they do *signal* their high ability to prospective employers. Because it is easier for high-ability people to earn a college degree than it is for low-ability people, more high-ability people get college degrees. As a result, it is rational for firms to interpret a college degree as a signal of ability.

The signaling theory of education is similar to the signaling theory of advertising discussed in Chapter 16. In the signaling theory of advertising, the advertisement itself contains no real information, but the firm signals the quality of its product to consumers by its willingness to spend money on advertising. In the signaling theory of education, schooling has no real productivity benefit, but the worker signals her innate productivity to employers by her willingness to spend years at school. In both cases, an action is being taken not for its intrinsic benefit but because the willingness to take that action conveys private information to someone observing it.

Thus, we now have two views of education: the human-capital theory and the signaling theory. Both views can explain why more educated workers tend to earn more than less educated workers. According to the human-capital view, education makes workers more productive; according to the signaling view, education is correlated with natural ability. But the two views have radically different predictions for the effects of policies that aim to increase educational attainment. According to the human-capital view, increasing educational levels for all workers would raise all workers' productivity and thereby their wages. According to the signaling view, education does not enhance productivity, so raising all workers' educational levels would not affect wages.

Most likely, the truth lies somewhere between these two extremes. The benefits to education are probably a combination of the productivity-enhancing effects of human capital and the productivity-revealing effects of signaling. The relative size of these two effects is an open question.

19-1e The Superstar Phenomenon

Although most actors earn little and often take jobs as waiters to support themselves, Leonardo DiCaprio earns millions of dollars for each film he makes. Similarly, while most people who play tennis do it for free as a hobby, Maria Sharapova earns millions on the pro tour. DiCaprio and Sharapova are superstars in their fields, and their great public appeal is reflected in astronomical incomes.

Why do DiCaprio and Sharapova earn so much? It is not surprising that incomes differ within occupations. Good carpenters earn more than mediocre carpenters, and good plumbers earn more than mediocre plumbers. People vary in ability and effort, and these differences lead to differences in income. Yet the best carpenters and plumbers do not earn the many millions that are common among the best actors and athletes. What explains the difference?

To understand the tremendous incomes of DiCaprio and Sharapova, we must examine the special features of the markets in which they sell their services. Superstars arise in markets that have two characteristics:

- Every customer in the market wants to enjoy the good supplied by the best producer.
- The good is produced with a technology that makes it possible for the best producer to supply every customer at low cost.

If Leonardo DiCaprio is the best actor around, then everyone will want to see his next movie; seeing twice as many movies by an actor half as talented is not a good substitute. Moreover, it is *possible* for everyone to enjoy a performance by Leonardo DiCaprio. Because it is easy to make multiple copies of a film, DiCaprio can provide his service to millions of people simultaneously. Similarly, because tennis matches are broadcast on television, millions of fans can enjoy the extraordinary athletic skills of Maria Sharapova.

We can now see why there are no superstar carpenters and plumbers. Other things being equal, everyone prefers to employ the best carpenter, but a carpenter, unlike a movie actor, can provide her services to only a limited number of customers. Although the best carpenter will be able to command a somewhat higher wage than the average carpenter, the average carpenter will still be able to earn a good living.

19-1f Above-Equilibrium Wages: Minimum-Wage Laws, Unions, and Efficiency Wages

Most analyses of wage differences among workers are based on the equilibrium model of the labor market—that is, wages are assumed to adjust to balance labor supply and labor demand. But this assumption does not always apply. For some workers, wages are set above the level that brings supply and demand into equilibrium. Let's consider three reasons this might be so.

One reason for above-equilibrium wages is minimum-wage laws, as we first saw in Chapter 6. Most workers in the economy are not affected by these laws because their equilibrium wages are well above the legal minimum. But for some workers, especially the least skilled and experienced, minimum-wage laws raise wages above the level they would earn in an unregulated labor market.

A second reason that wages might rise above their equilibrium level is the market power of labor unions. A **union** is a worker association that bargains with employers over wages and working conditions. Unions often raise wages above the level that would prevail in their absence perhaps because they can threaten

union
a worker association that bargains with employers over wages and working conditions

to withhold labor from the firm by calling a **strike**. Studies suggest that union workers earn about 10 to 20 percent more than similar, nonunion workers.

A third reason for above-equilibrium wages is suggested by the theory of **efficiency wages**. This theory holds that a firm can find it profitable to pay high wages because doing so increases the productivity of its workers. In particular, high wages may reduce worker turnover, increase worker effort, and raise the quality of workers who apply for jobs at the firm. If this theory is correct, then some firms may choose to pay their workers more than they would normally earn.

Above-equilibrium wages, whether caused by minimum-wage laws, unions, or efficiency wages, have similar effects on the labor market. In particular, pushing a wage above the equilibrium level raises the quantity of labor supplied and reduces the quantity of labor demanded. The result is a surplus of labor, or unemployment. The study of unemployment and the public policies aimed to deal with it is usually considered a topic within macroeconomics, so it goes beyond the scope of this chapter. But it would be a mistake to ignore these issues completely when analyzing earnings. Although most wage differences can be understood while maintaining the assumption of equilibrium in the labor market, above-equilibrium wages play a role in some cases.

strike
the organized withdrawal of labor from a firm by a union

efficiency wages
above-equilibrium wages paid by firms to increase worker productivity

Quick Quiz *Define* compensating differential *and give an example.* • *Give two reasons why more educated workers earn more than less educated workers.*

19-2 The Economics of Discrimination

Another source of differences in wages is discrimination. **Discrimination** occurs when the marketplace offers different opportunities to similar individuals who differ only by race, ethnic group, sex, age, or other personal characteristics. Discrimination reflects some people's prejudice against certain groups in society. Discrimination is an emotionally charged topic that often generates heated debate, but economists try to study the topic objectively to separate myth from reality.

discrimination
the offering of different opportunities to similar individuals who differ only by race, ethnic group, sex, age, or other personal characteristics

19-2a Measuring Labor-Market Discrimination

How much does discrimination in labor markets affect the earnings of different groups of workers? This question is important, but answering it is not easy.

There is no doubt that different groups of workers earn substantially different wages, as Table 2 demonstrates. The median black man in the United States is paid

	White	Black	Percent by Which Earnings Are Lower for Black Workers
Men	$50,070	$39,483	21%
Women	$37,719	$33,501	11%
Percent by Which Earnings Are Lower for Women Workers	25%	15%	

Note: Earnings data are for the year 2011 and apply to full-time, year-round workers age 14 and over.

Source: U.S. Census Bureau.

TABLE 2

Median Annual Earnings by Race and Sex

21 percent less than the median white man, and the median black woman is paid 11 percent less than the median white woman. The differences by sex are also significant. The median white woman is paid 25 percent less than the median white man, and the median black woman is paid 15 percent less than the median black man. Taken at face value, these differentials look like evidence that employers discriminate against blacks and women.

Yet there is a potential problem with this inference. Even in a labor market free of discrimination, different people have different wages. People differ in the amount of human capital they have and in the kinds of work they are able and willing to do. The wage differences we observe in an economy are, to some extent, attributable to the determinants of equilibrium wages we discussed in the preceding section. Simply observing differences in wages among broad groups—whites and blacks, men and women—does not prove that employers discriminate.

Consider, for example, the role of human capital. In 2011, among men age 25 and older, 32 percent of the white population had a college degree, compared with 18 percent of the black population. Among women age 25 and older, 31 percent of the white population had a college degree, compared with 21 percent of the black population. Thus, at least some of the difference between the wages of whites and the wages of blacks can be traced to differences in educational attainment.

Moreover, human capital may be more important in explaining wage differentials than years of schooling suggest. Historically, public schools in predominantly black areas have been of lower quality—as measured by expenditure, class size, and so on—than public schools in predominantly white areas. If we could measure the quality as well as the quantity of education, the differences in human capital among these groups would seem even larger.

Human capital acquired in the form of job experience can also help explain wage differences. In particular, women are more likely to interrupt their careers to raise children. Among the population aged 25 to 34 (when many people have small children at home), only 75 percent of women are in the labor force, compared to 90 percent of men. As a result, female workers, especially at older ages, tend to have less job experience than male workers.

Yet another source of wage differences is compensating differentials. Men and women do not always choose the same type of work, and this fact may help explain some of the earnings differential between men and women. For example, women are more likely to be secretaries, and men are more likely to be truck drivers. The relative wages of secretaries and truck drivers depend in part on the working conditions of each job. Because these nonmonetary aspects are hard to measure, it is difficult to gauge the practical importance of compensating differentials in explaining the wage differences that we observe.

In the end, the study of wage differences among groups does not establish any clear conclusion about the prevalence of discrimination in U.S. labor markets. Most economists believe that some of the observed wage differentials are attributable to discrimination, but there is no consensus about how much. The only conclusion about which economists are in consensus is a negative one: Because the differences in average wages among groups in part reflect differences in human capital and job characteristics, they do not by themselves say anything about how much discrimination there is in the labor market.

Of course, differences in human capital among groups of workers may also reflect a kind of discrimination. The less rigorous curriculums historically offered to female students, for instance, can be considered a discriminatory practice. Similarly, the inferior schools historically available to black students may be traced to prejudice on the part of city councils and school boards. But this kind of discrimination occurs long before the worker enters the labor market. In this case, the disease is political, even if the symptom is economic.

case study

Is Emily More Employable than Lakisha?

Although measuring the extent of discrimination from labor-market outcomes is hard, some compelling evidence for the existence of such discrimination comes from a creative "field experiment." Economists Marianne Bertrand and Sendhil Mullainathan answered more than 1,300 help-wanted ads run in Boston and Chicago newspapers by sending in nearly 5,000 fake résumés. Half of the résumés had names that were common in the African-American community, such as Lakisha Washington or Jamal Jones. The other half had names that were more common among the white population, such as Emily Walsh and Greg Baker. Otherwise, the résumés were similar. The results of this experiment were published in the *American Economic Review* in September 2004.

The researchers found large differences in how employers responded to the two groups of résumés. Job applicants with white names received about 50 percent more calls from interested employers than applicants with African-American names. The study found that this discrimination occurred for all types of employers, including those who claimed to be an "Equal Opportunity Employer" in their help-wanted ads. The researchers concluded that "racial discrimination is still a prominent feature of the labor market." ◢

19-2b Discrimination by Employers

Let's now turn from measurement to the economic forces that lie behind discrimination in labor markets. If one group in society receives a lower wage than another group, even after controlling for human capital and job characteristics, who is to blame for this differential?

The answer is not obvious. It might seem natural to blame employers for discriminatory wage differences. After all, employers make the hiring decisions that determine labor demand and wages. If some groups of workers earn lower wages than they should, then it seems that employers are responsible. Yet many economists are skeptical of this easy answer. They believe that competitive, market economies provide a natural antidote to employer discrimination. That antidote is called the profit motive.

Imagine an economy in which workers are differentiated by their hair color. Blondes and brunettes have the same skills, experience, and work ethic. Yet because of discrimination, employers prefer to hire workers with brunette hair. Thus, the demand for blondes is lower than it otherwise would be. As a result, blondes earn a lower wage than brunettes.

How long can this wage differential persist? In this economy, there is an easy way for a firm to beat out its competitors: It can hire blonde workers. By hiring blondes, a firm pays lower wages and thus has lower costs than firms that hire brunettes. Over time, more and more "blonde" firms enter the market to take advantage of this cost advantage. The existing "brunette" firms have higher costs and, therefore, begin to lose money when faced with the new competitors. These losses induce the brunette firms to go out of business. Eventually, the entry of blonde firms and the exit of brunette firms cause the demand for blonde workers to rise and the demand for brunette workers to fall. This process continues until the wage differential disappears.

Put simply, business owners who care only about making money are at an advantage when competing against those who also care about discriminating. As a result, firms that do not discriminate tend to replace those that do. In this way, competitive markets have a natural remedy for employer discrimination.

case study

Segregated Streetcars and the Profit Motive

In the early 20th century, streetcars in many southern cities were segregated by race. White passengers sat in the front of the streetcars, and black passengers sat in the back. What do you suppose caused and maintained this discriminatory practice? And how was this practice viewed by the firms that ran the streetcars?

In a 1986 article in the *Journal of Economic History*, economic historian Jennifer Roback looked at these questions. Roback found that the segregation of races on streetcars was the result of laws that required such segregation. Before these laws were passed, racial discrimination in seating was rare. It was far more common to segregate smokers and nonsmokers.

Moreover, the firms that ran the streetcars often opposed the laws requiring racial segregation. Providing separate seating for different races raised the firms' costs and reduced their profits. One railroad company manager complained to the city council that, under the segregation laws, "the company has to haul around a good deal of empty space."

Here is how Roback describes the situation in one southern city:

The railroad company did not initiate the segregation policy and was not at all eager to abide by it. State legislation, public agitation, and a threat to arrest the president of the railroad were all required to induce them to separate the races on their cars.... There is no indication that the management was motivated by belief in civil rights or racial equality. The evidence indicates their primary motives were economic; separation was costly.... Officials of the company may or may not have disliked blacks, but they were not willing to forgo the profits necessary to indulge such prejudice.

The story of southern streetcars illustrates a general lesson: Business owners are usually more interested in making profits than in discriminating against a particular group. When firms engage in discriminatory practices, the ultimate source of the discrimination often lies not with the firms themselves but elsewhere. In this particular case, the streetcar companies segregated whites and blacks because discriminatory laws, which the companies opposed, required them to do so. ◢

19-2c Discrimination by Customers and Governments

The profit motive is a strong force acting to eliminate discriminatory wage differentials, but there are limits to its corrective abilities. Two important limiting factors are customer preferences and government policies.

To see how customer preferences for discrimination can affect wages, consider again our imaginary economy with blondes and brunettes. Suppose that restaurant owners discriminate against blondes when hiring waiters. As a result, blonde waiters earn lower wages than brunette waiters. In this case, a restaurant can open up with blonde waiters and charge lower prices. If customers care only about the quality and price of their meals, the discriminatory firms will be driven out of business, and the wage differential will disappear.

On the other hand, it is possible that customers prefer being served by brunette waiters. If this discriminatory preference is strong, the entry of blonde restaurants need not succeed in eliminating the wage differential between brunettes and blondes. That is, if customers have discriminatory preferences, a competitive market is consistent with a discriminatory wage differential. An economy with such discrimination would contain two types of restaurants. Blonde restaurants hire blondes, have lower costs, and charge lower prices. Brunette restaurants hire brunettes, have higher costs, and charge higher prices. Customers who did not care about the hair color of their waiters would be attracted to the lower prices at the blonde restaurants. Bigoted customers would go to the brunette restaurants and would pay for their discriminatory preference in the form of higher prices.

Another way for discrimination to persist in competitive markets is for the government to mandate discriminatory practices. If, for instance, the government passed a law stating that blondes could wash dishes in restaurants but could not work as waiters, then a wage differential could persist in a competitive market. The example of segregated streetcars in the previous case study is one example of government-mandated discrimination. Similarly, before South Africa abandoned its formal policy of racial segregation called apartheid in 1990, blacks were prohibited from working in some jobs. Discriminatory governments pass such laws to suppress the normal equalizing force of free and competitive markets.

To sum up: *Competitive markets contain a natural remedy for employer discrimination. The entry of firms that care only about profit tends to eliminate discriminatory wage differentials. These wage differentials persist in competitive markets only when customers are willing to pay to maintain the discriminatory practice or when the government mandates it.*

case study   **Discrimination in Sports**
As we have seen, measuring discrimination is often difficult. To determine whether one group of workers is discriminated against, a researcher must correct for differences in the productivity between that group and other workers in the economy. Yet in most firms, it is difficult to measure a particular worker's contribution to the production of goods and services.

One type of firm in which such measurements are easier is the sports team. Professional teams have many objective measures of productivity. In baseball, for instance, we can measure a player's batting average, the frequency of home runs, the number of stolen bases, and so on.

Studies of sports teams suggest that racial discrimination has, in fact, been common and that much of the blame lies with customers. One study, published in the *Journal of Labor Economics* in 1988, examined the salaries of basketball players and found that black players earned 20 percent less than white players of comparable ability. The study also found that attendance at basketball games was larger for teams with a greater proportion of white players. One interpretation of these facts is that, at least at the time of the study, customer discrimination made black players less profitable than white players for team owners. In the presence of such customer discrimination, a discriminatory wage gap can persist, even if team owners care only about profit.

A similar situation once existed for baseball players. A study using data from the late 1960s showed that black players earned less than comparable white

Gender Differences

Economic research is shedding light on why men and women choose different career paths.

The Difference between Men and Women, Revisited: It's about Competition

By Hal R. Varian

Gender differences are a topic of endless discussion for parents, teachers and social scientists. . . . A noteworthy case in point is a recent National Bureau of Economic Research working paper by a Stanford economist, Muriel Niederle, and Lise Vesterlund, a University of Pittsburgh economist, titled, "Do Women Shy Away From Competition? Do Men Compete Too Much?"

It is widely noted that women are not well represented in high-paying corporate jobs, or in mathematics, science and engineering jobs. As the authors observe, the "standard economic explanations for such occupational differences include preferences, ability and discrimination."

To this list the authors add a new factor: attitudes toward competitive environments. If men prefer more competitive environments than women, then there will be more men represented in areas where competition is intense.

Of course, discussions of gender differences of any sort can only be statements about averages; it is clear that there are women who thrive in competitive environments and men who do not. Furthermore, attitudes toward competition may be ingrained or a result of factors like social stereotyping.

Is there any evidence that the hypothesis is true? Do men really prefer more competitive environments than women? One could cite anecdote after anecdote, but the authors took a much more direct approach: they ran an experiment.

By using an experiment, the authors were able to determine not only whether men and women differ in their willingness to compete, but more important, whether they differ in their willingness to compete conditioned on their actual performance.

The economists asked 80 subjects, divided into groups of two women and two men, to add up sets of five two-digit

players. Moreover, fewer fans attended games pitched by blacks than games pitched by whites, even though black pitchers had better records than white pitchers. Studies of more recent salaries in baseball, however, have found no evidence of discriminatory wage differentials.

Another study, published in the *Quarterly Journal of Economics* in 1990, examined the market prices of old baseball cards. This study found similar evidence of discrimination. The cards of black hitters sold for 10 percent less than the cards of comparable white hitters, and the cards of black pitchers sold for 13 percent less than the cards of comparable white pitchers. These results suggest customer discrimination among baseball fans. ◢

Quick Quiz *Why is it hard to establish whether a group of workers is being discriminated against? • Explain how profit-maximizing firms tend to eliminate discriminatory wage differentials. • How might a discriminatory wage differential persist?*

19-3 Conclusion

In competitive markets, workers earn a wage equal to the value of their marginal contribution to the production of goods and services. There are, however, many things that affect the value of the marginal product. Firms pay more for workers who are more talented, more diligent, more experienced, and more educated

numbers for five minutes. The subjects performed the task first on a piece-rate basis (50 cents for each correct answer) and then as a tournament (the person with the most correct answers in each group received $2 per correct answer, while other participants received nothing). Note that a subject with a 25 percent chance of being a winner in the tournament received the same average payment as in the piece-rate system.

All participants were told how many problems they got right, but not their relative performance. After completing the two tasks, the subjects were asked to choose whether they preferred a piece-rate system or a tournament for the third set of problems.

There were several interesting findings in this experiment. First, there were no differences between men and women in their performance under either compensation system. Despite this, twice as many men selected the tournament as women (75 percent versus 35 percent).

Even if one accounts for performance by comparing only men and women with the same number of correct answers, the women have a 38 percent lower probability of choosing the tournament compensation.

Why were the men much more likely to choose the tournament? Perhaps it was because they felt more confident about their abilities. The data support this hypothesis, with 75 percent of the men believing that they won their four-player tournament, while 43 percent of the women thought they were best in their group.

Though both groups were overconfident about their performance, the men were much more so.... The results of this experiment are consistent with the finding by a Berkeley finance professor, Terry Odean, that men trade stocks excessively, apparently because they (wrongly) feel that they have exceptional ability to pick winners. Women trade less, but do better on average, because they are more likely to follow a buy-and-hold strategy.

The authors summarized their experimental results by saying, "From a payoff-maximizing perspective, high-performing women enter the tournament too rarely, and low-performing men enter the tournament too often." The low-performing men and the high-performing women are both hurt by this behavior but, in this experiment at least, the costs to the women who did not choose the tournament when they should have exceeded the costs to the men who should have avoided the tournament.

One should not read too much into one study. But if it is really true that women choose occupations that involve less competition, then one may well ask why. Sociobiologists may suggest that such differences come from genetic propensities; sociologists may argue for differences in social roles and expectations; developmental psychologists may emphasize child-rearing practices. Whatever the cause, Ms. Niederle and Ms. Vesterlund have certainly raised a host of interesting and important questions.

Mr. Varian is a professor emeritus at the University of California at Berkeley and Chief Economist at Google. ◢

Source: *New York Times*, March 9, 2006.

because these workers are more productive. Firms pay less to those workers against whom customers discriminate because these workers contribute less to revenue.

The theory of the labor market we have developed in the last two chapters explains why some workers earn higher wages than other workers. The theory does not say that the resulting distribution of income is equal, fair, or desirable in any way. That is the topic we take up in Chapter 20.

Summary

- Workers earn different wages for many reasons. To some extent, wage differentials compensate workers for job attributes. Other things being equal, workers in hard, unpleasant jobs are paid more than workers in easy, pleasant jobs.

- Workers with more human capital are paid more than workers with less human capital. The return to accumulating human capital is high and has increased over the past several decades.

- Although years of education, experience, and job characteristics affect earnings as theory predicts, there is much variation in earnings that cannot be explained by things that economists can measure. The unexplained variation in earnings is largely attributable to natural ability, effort, and chance.

- Some economists have suggested that more educated workers earn higher wages not because education raises productivity but because workers with high natural ability use education as a way to signal their high ability to employers. If this signaling theory is correct, then increasing the educational attainment of all workers would not raise the overall level of wages.

- Wages are sometimes pushed above the level that brings supply and demand into balance. Three reasons for above-equilibrium wages are minimum-wage laws, unions, and efficiency wages.

- Some differences in earnings are attributable to discrimination based on race, sex, or other factors. Measuring the amount of discrimination is difficult, however, because one must correct for differences in human capital and job characteristics.

- Competitive markets tend to limit the impact of discrimination on wages. If the wages of a group of workers are lower than those of another group for reasons not related to marginal productivity, then nondiscriminatory firms will be more profitable than discriminatory firms. Profit-maximizing behavior, therefore, can reduce discriminatory wage differentials. Discrimination persists in competitive markets, however, if customers are willing to pay more to discriminatory firms or if the government passes laws requiring firms to discriminate.

Key Concepts

compensating differential, *p. 396*
human capital, *p. 397*

union, *p. 402*
strike, *p. 403*

efficiency wages, *p. 403*
discrimination, *p. 403*

Questions for Review

1. Why are coal miners paid more than other workers with similar amounts of education?

2. In what sense is education a type of capital?

3. How might education raise a worker's wage without raising the worker's productivity?

4. What conditions lead to highly compensated superstars? Would you expect to see superstars in dentistry? In music? Explain.

5. Give three reasons a worker's wage might be above the level that balances supply and demand.

6. What difficulties arise in deciding whether a group of workers has a lower wage because of discrimination?

7. Do the forces of economic competition tend to exacerbate or ameliorate discrimination based on race?

8. Give an example of how discrimination might persist in a competitive market.

Quick Check Multiple Choice

1. Ricky leaves his job as a high school math teacher and returns to school to study the latest developments in computer programming, after which he takes a higher-paying job at a software firm. This is an example of
   a. a compensating differential.
   b. human capital.
   c. signaling.
   d. efficiency wages.

2. Lucy and Ethel work at a local department store. Lucy, who greets customers as they arrive, is paid less than Ethel, who cleans the bathrooms. This is an example of
   a. a compensating differential.
   b. human capital.
   c. signaling.
   d. efficiency wages.

3. Fred runs a small manufacturing company. He pays his employees about twice what other firms in the area pay, even though he could pay less and still recruit all the workers he wants. He believes that higher wages make his workers more loyal and hard-working. This is an example of
   a. a compensating differential.
   b. human capital.
   c. signaling.
   d. efficiency wages.

4. A business consulting firm hires Vivian because she was a math major in college. Her new job does not require any of the mathematics she learned, but the firm believes that anyone who can graduate with a math degree must be very smart. This is an example of
   a. a compensating differential.
   b. human capital.
   c. signaling.
   d. efficiency wages.

5. Measuring how much discrimination affects labor market outcomes is difficult because
   a. data on wages are crucial but not readily available.
   b. firms misreport the wages they pay to hide discriminatory practices.
   c. workers differ in their attributes and the types of jobs they have.
   d. the same minimum-wage law applies to workers in all groups.

6. The forces of competition in markets with free entry and exit tend to eliminate wage differentials that arise from discrimination by
   a. employers.
   b. customers.
   c. government.
   d. all of the above.

Problems and Applications

1. College students sometimes work as summer interns for private firms or the government. Many of these positions pay little or nothing.
   a. What is the opportunity cost of taking such a job?
   b. Explain why students are willing to take these jobs.
   c. If you were to compare the earnings later in life of workers who had worked as interns and those who had taken summer jobs that paid more, what would you expect to find?

2. As explained in Chapter 6, a minimum-wage law distorts the market for low-wage labor. To reduce this distortion, some economists advocate a two-tiered minimum-wage system, with a regular minimum wage for adult workers and a lower, "subminimum" wage for teenage workers. Give two reasons a single minimum wage might distort the labor market for teenage workers more than it would the market for adult workers.

3. A basic finding of labor economics is that workers who have more experience in the labor force are paid more than workers who have less experience (holding constant the amount of formal education). Why might this be so? Some studies have also found that experience at the same job (called *job tenure*) has an extra positive influence on wages. Explain why this might occur.

4. At some colleges and universities, economics professors receive higher salaries than professors in some other fields.
   a. Why might this be true?
   b. Some other colleges and universities have a policy of paying equal salaries to professors in all fields. At some of these schools, economics professors have lighter teaching loads than professors in some other fields. What role do the differences in teaching loads play?

5. Imagine that someone offered you a choice: You could spend 4 years studying at the world's best university, but you would have to keep your attendance there a secret. Or you could be awarded an official degree from the world's best university, but you couldn't actually attend. Which choice do you think would enhance your future earnings more? What does your answer say about the debate over signaling versus human capital in the role of education?

6. When recording devices were first invented more than 100 years ago, musicians could suddenly supply their music to large audiences at low cost. How do you suppose this development affected the income of the best musicians? How do you suppose it affected the income of average musicians?

7. A current debate in education is whether teachers should be paid on a standard pay scale based solely upon their years of training and teaching experience, or whether part of their salary should be based upon their performance (called "merit pay").
   a. Why might merit pay be desirable?
   b. Who might be opposed to a system of merit pay?
   c. What is a potential challenge of merit pay?
   d. A related issue: Why might a school district decide to pay teachers significantly more than the salaries offered by surrounding districts?

8. When Alan Greenspan (who would later become chairman of the Federal Reserve) ran an economic consulting firm in the 1960s, he primarily hired female economists. He once told the *New York Times*, "I always valued men and women equally, and I found that because others did not, good women economists were cheaper than men." Is Greenspan's behavior profit-maximizing? Is it admirable or despicable? If more employers were like Greenspan, what would happen to the wage differential between men and women? Why might other economic consulting firms at the time not have followed Greenspan's business strategy?

9. This chapter considers the economics of discrimination by employers, customers, and governments. Now consider discrimination by workers. Suppose that some brunette workers do not like working with blonde workers. Can this worker discrimination explain lower wages for blonde workers? If such a wage differential existed, what would a profit-maximizing entrepreneur do? If there were many such entrepreneurs, what would happen over time?

Go to CengageBrain.com to purchase access to the proven, critical Study Guide to accompany this text, which features additional notes and context, practice tests, and much more.

Income Inequality and Poverty

The great British Prime Minister Winston Churchill once summarized alternative economic systems as follows: "The inherent vice of capitalism is the unequal sharing of blessings. The inherent virtue of socialism is the equal sharing of miseries." Churchill's quip draws attention to two important facts. First, nations that use market mechanisms to allocate resources usually achieve greater prosperity than those that do not. This is the result of Adam Smith's invisible hand in action. Second, the prosperity that market economies produce is not shared equally. Incomes can differ greatly between those at the top and those at the bottom of the economic ladder. The gap between rich and poor is a fascinating and important topic of study—for the comfortable rich, for the struggling poor, and for the aspiring and worried middle class.

From the previous two chapters, you should have some understanding about why different people have different incomes. A person's earnings depend on the supply and demand for that person's labor, which in turn depend on natural ability, human capital, compensating differentials, discrimination, and so on. Because labor earnings make up about two-thirds of the total income in the U.S. economy, the factors that determine wages are also largely responsible for determining how the economy's total income is distributed among the various members of society. In other words, they determine who is rich and who is poor.

In this chapter, we discuss the distribution of income—a topic that raises some fundamental questions about the role of economic policy. One of the *Ten Principles of Economics* in Chapter 1 is that governments can sometimes improve market outcomes. This possibility is particularly important when considering the distribution of income. The invisible hand of the marketplace acts to allocate resources efficiently, but it does not necessarily ensure that resources are allocated fairly. As a result, many economists—though not all—believe that the government should redistribute income to achieve greater equality. In doing so, however, the government runs into another of the *Ten Principles of Economics*: People face trade-offs. When the government enacts policies to make the distribution of income more equal, it distorts incentives, alters behavior, and makes the allocation of resources less efficient.

Our discussion of the distribution of income proceeds in three steps. First, we assess how much inequality there is in our society. Second, we consider some different views about what role the government should play in altering the distribution of income. Third, we discuss various public policies aimed at helping society's poorest members.

20-1 The Measurement of Inequality

We begin our study of the distribution of income by addressing four questions of measurement:

- How much inequality is there in our society?
- How many people live in poverty?
- What problems arise in measuring the amount of inequality?
- How often do people move between income classes?

These measurement questions are the natural starting point from which to discuss public policies aimed at changing the distribution of income.

20-1a U.S. Income Inequality

Imagine that you lined up all the families in the economy according to their annual income. Then you divided the families into five equal groups: the bottom fifth, the second fifth, the middle fifth, the fourth fifth, and the top fifth. Table 1 shows the income ranges for each of these groups, as well as for the top 5 percent. You can use this table to find where your family lies in the income distribution.

For examining differences in the income distribution over time, economists find it useful to present the income data as in Table 2. This table shows the share of total income that each group of families received in selected years. In 2011, the bottom fifth of all families received 3.8 percent of all income, and the top fifth of

"As far as I'm concerned, they can do what they want with the minimum wage, just as long as they keep their hands off the maximum wage."

TABLE 1

The Distribution of Income in
the United States: 2011

Group	Annual Family Income
Bottom Fifth	Under $27,218
Second Fifth	$27,218 – $48,502
Middle Fifth	$48,502 – $75,000
Fourth Fifth	$75,000 – $115,866
Top Fifth	$115,866 and over
Top 5 percent	$205,200 and over

Source: U.S. Bureau of the Census.

TABLE 2

Income Inequality in the
United States
This table shows the
percentage of total before-tax
income received by families
in each fifth of the income
distribution and by those
families in the top 5 percent.

Year	Bottom Fifth	Second Fifth	Middle Fifth	Fourth Fifth	Top Fifth	Top 5%
2011	3.8%	9.3%	15.1%	23.0%	48.9%	21.3%
2010	3.8	9.5	15.4	23.5	48.8	20.0
2000	4.3	9.8	15.5	22.8	47.4	20.8
1990	4.6	10.8	16.6	23.8	44.3	17.4
1980	5.2	11.5	17.5	24.3	41.5	15.3
1970	5.5	12.2	17.6	23.8	40.9	15.6
1960	4.8	12.2	17.8	24.0	41.3	15.9
1950	4.5	12.0	17.4	23.4	42.7	17.3
1935	4.1	9.2	14.1	20.9	51.7	26.5

Source: U.S. Bureau of the Census.

all families received 48.9 percent of all income. In other words, even though the top and bottom fifths include the same number of families, the top fifth has more than twelve times as much income as the bottom fifth.

The last column in the table shows the share of total income received by the very richest families. In 2011, the top 5 percent of families received 21.3 percent of all income, which was greater than the total income of the poorest 40 percent.

Table 2 also shows the distribution of income in various years beginning in 1935. At first glance, the distribution of income appears to have been remarkably stable over time. Throughout the past several decades, the bottom fifth of families has received about 4 to 5 percent of income, while the top fifth has received about 40 to 50 percent of income. Closer inspection of the table reveals some trends in the degree of inequality. From 1935 to 1970, the distribution gradually became more equal. The share of the bottom fifth rose from 4.1 to 5.5 percent, and the share of the top fifth fell from 51.7 percent to 40.9 percent. In more recent years, this trend has reversed itself. From 1970 to 2011, the share of the bottom fifth fell from 5.5 percent to 3.8 percent and the share of the top fifth rose from 40.9 to 48.9 percent.

In Chapter 19, we discussed some explanations for this recent rise in inequality. Increases in international trade with low-wage countries and changes in technology have tended to reduce the demand for unskilled labor and raise the demand for skilled labor. As a result, the wages of unskilled workers have fallen relative to the wages of skilled workers, and this change in relative wages has increased inequality in family incomes.

20-1b Inequality around the World

How does the amount of inequality in the United States compare to that in other countries? This question is interesting, but answering it is problematic. For some countries, data are not available. Even when they are, not every country collects data in the same way; for example, some countries collect data on individual incomes, whereas other countries collect data on family incomes, and still others collect data on expenditure rather than income. As a result, whenever we find a difference between two countries, we can never be sure whether it reflects a true difference in the economies or merely a difference in the way data are collected.

With this warning in mind, consider Figure 1, which compares inequality in the twenty-five most populous countries. The inequality measure is the ratio of

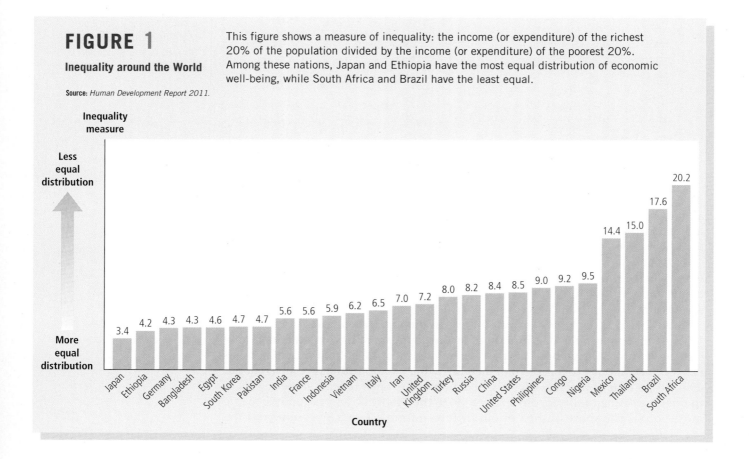

FIGURE 1

Inequality around the World

Source: *Human Development Report 2011.*

This figure shows a measure of inequality: the income (or expenditure) of the richest 20% of the population divided by the income (or expenditure) of the poorest 20%. Among these nations, Japan and Ethiopia have the most equal distribution of economic well-being, while South Africa and Brazil have the least equal.

Inequality
measure

Less
equal
distribution

More
equal
distribution

3.4 4.2 4.3 4.3 4.6 4.7 4.7 5.6 5.6 5.9 6.2 6.5 7.0 7.2 8.0 8.2 8.4 8.5 9.0 9.2 9.5 14.4 15.0 17.6 20.2

Japan, Ethiopia, Germany, Bangladesh, Egypt, South Korea, Pakistan, India, France, Indonesia, Vietnam, Italy, Iran, United Kingdom, Turkey, Russia, China, United States, Philippines, Congo, Nigeria, Mexico, Thailand, Brazil, South Africa

Country

the income received by the richest fifth of the population to the income of the poorest fifth. The most equality is found in Japan, where the top fifth receives 3.4 times as much income as the bottom fifth. The least equality is found in South Africa, where the top group receives 20.1 times as much income as the bottom group. All countries have significant disparities between rich and poor, but the degree of inequality varies substantially around the world.

When countries are ranked by inequality, the United States ends up with a bit more inequality than the typical country. The United States has greater income disparity than most other economically advanced countries, such as Japan and Germany. But the United States has a more equal income distribution than some developing countries, such as South Africa and Brazil.

20-1c The Poverty Rate

A commonly used gauge of the distribution of income is the poverty rate. The **poverty rate** is the percentage of the population whose family income falls below an absolute level called the **poverty line**. The poverty line is set by the federal government at roughly three times the cost of providing an adequate diet. This line is adjusted every year to account for changes in the level of prices, and it depends on family size.

To get some idea about what the poverty rate tells us, consider the data for 2011. In that year, the median family in the United States had an income of $60,974, and the poverty line for a family of four was $23,021. The poverty rate was 15.0 percent. In other words, 15.0 percent of the U.S. population were members of families with incomes below the poverty line for their family size.

Figure 2 shows the poverty rate since 1959, when the official data begin. You can see that the poverty rate fell from 22.4 percent in 1959 to a low of 11.1 percent in 1973. This decline is not surprising, because average income in the economy (adjusted for inflation) rose more than 50 percent during this period. Because the poverty line is an absolute rather than a relative standard, more families are pushed above the poverty line as economic growth pushes the entire income distribution upward. As John F. Kennedy once put it, a rising tide lifts all boats.

poverty rate
the percentage of the population whose family income falls below an absolute level called the poverty line

poverty line
an absolute level of income set by the federal government for each family size below which a family is deemed to be in poverty

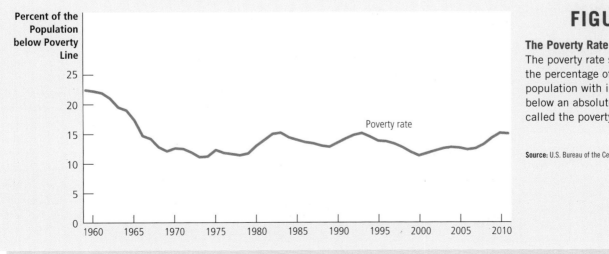

FIGURE 2

The Poverty Rate
The poverty rate shows the percentage of the population with incomes below an absolute level called the poverty line.

Source: U.S. Bureau of the Census.

Since the early 1970s, however, the economy's rising tide has left some boats behind. Despite continued growth in average income, the poverty rate has not declined below the level reached in 1973. This lack of progress in reducing poverty in recent decades is closely related to the increasing inequality we saw in Table 2. Although economic growth has raised the income of the typical family, the increase in inequality has prevented the poorest families from sharing in this greater economic prosperity.

Poverty is an economic malady that affects all groups within the population, but it does not affect all groups with equal frequency. Table 3 shows the poverty rates for several groups, and it reveals three striking facts:

- Poverty is correlated with race. Blacks and Hispanics are about three times more likely to live in poverty than are whites.
- Poverty is correlated with age. Children are more likely than average to be members of poor families, and the elderly are less likely than average to be poor.
- Poverty is correlated with family composition. Families headed by a female adult without a spouse present are about five times as likely to live in poverty as families headed by a married couple.

These three facts have described American society for many years, and they show which people are most likely to be poor. These effects also work together: Among black and Hispanic children in female-headed households, about half live in poverty.

20-1d Problems in Measuring Inequality

Although data on the income distribution and the poverty rate give us some idea about the degree of inequality in our society, interpreting these data is not always straightforward. The data are based on households' annual incomes. What people care about, however, is not their incomes but their ability to

---

TABLE 3

Who Is Poor?
This table shows that the poverty rate varies greatly among different groups within the population.

Group	Poverty Rate
All persons	15.0%
White, not Hispanic	9.8
Black	27.6
Hispanic	25.3
Asian	12.3
Children (under age 18)	21.9
Elderly (over age 64)	8.7
Married-couple families	6.2
Female household, no spouse present	31.2

Source: U.S. Bureau of the Census. Data are for 2011.

maintain a good standard of living. For at least three reasons, data on the income distribution and the poverty rate give an incomplete picture of inequality in living standards.

In-Kind Transfers Measurements of the distribution of income and the poverty rate are based on families' *money* income. Through various government programs, however, the poor receive many nonmonetary items, including food stamps, housing vouchers, and medical services. Transfers to the poor given in the form of goods and services rather than cash are called **in-kind transfers**. Standard measurements of the degree of inequality do not take account of these in-kind transfers.

Because in-kind transfers are received mostly by the poorest members of society, the failure to include in-kind transfers as part of income greatly affects the measured poverty rate. According to a study by the Census Bureau, if in-kind transfers were included in income at their market value, the number of families in poverty would be about 10 percent lower than the standard data indicate.

The Economic Life Cycle Incomes vary predictably over people's lives. A young worker, especially one in school, has a low income. Income rises as the worker gains maturity and experience, peaks at around age 50, and then falls sharply when the worker retires at around age 65. This regular pattern of income variation is called the **life cycle**.

Because people can borrow and save to smooth out life cycle changes in income, their standard of living in any year depends more on lifetime income than on that year's income. The young often borrow, perhaps to go to school or to buy a house, and then repay these loans later when their incomes rise. People have their highest saving rates when they are middle-aged. Because people can save in anticipation of retirement, the large declines in incomes at retirement need not lead to similar declines in the standard of living. This normal life cycle pattern causes inequality in the distribution of annual income, but it does not necessarily represent true inequality in living standards.

Transitory versus Permanent Income Incomes vary over people's lives not only because of predictable life cycle variation but also because of random and transitory forces. One year a frost kills off the Florida orange crop, and Florida orange growers see their incomes fall temporarily. At the same time, the Florida frost drives up the price of oranges, and California orange growers see their incomes temporarily rise. The next year the reverse might happen.

Just as people can borrow and save to smooth out life cycle variation in income, they can also borrow and save to smooth out transitory variation in income. To the extent that a family saves in good years and borrows (or depletes its savings) in bad years, transitory changes in income need not affect its standard of living. A family's ability to buy goods and services depends largely on its **permanent income**, which is its normal, or average, income.

To gauge inequality of living standards, the distribution of permanent income is more relevant than the distribution of annual income. Many economists believe that people base their consumption on their permanent income; as a result, inequality in consumption is one gauge of inequality of permanent income. Because permanent income and consumption are less affected by transitory changes in income, they are more equally distributed than is current income.

in-kind transfers
transfers to the poor given in the form of goods and services rather than cash

life cycle
the regular pattern of income variation over a person's life

permanent income
a person's normal income

case study **Alternative Measures of Inequality**

A 2008 study by Michael Cox and Richard Alm of the Federal Reserve Bank of Dallas shows how different measures of inequality lead to dramatically different results. Cox and Alm compared American households in the top fifth of the income distribution to those in the bottom fifth to see how far apart they are.

According to Cox and Alm, the richest fifth of U.S. households in 2006 had an average income of $149,963, while the poorest fifth had an average income of $9,974. Thus, the top group had about 15 times as much income as the bottom group.

The gap between rich and poor shrinks a bit if taxes are taken into account. Because the tax system is progressive, the top group paid a higher percentage of its income in taxes than did the bottom group. Cox and Alm found that the richest fifth had 14 times as much after-tax income as the poorest fifth.

The gap shrinks more substantially if one looks at consumption rather than income. Households having an unusually good year are more likely to be in the top group and are likely to save a high fraction out of their incomes. Households having an unusually bad year are more likely to be in the bottom group and are more likely to consume out of their savings. According to Cox and Alms, the consumption of the richest fifth was only 3.9 times as much as the consumption of the poorest fifth.

The consumption gap becomes smaller still if one corrects for differences in the number of people in the household. Because larger families are more likely to have two earners, they are more likely to find themselves near the top of the income distribution. But they also have more mouths to feed. Cox and Alms reported that households in the top fifth had an average of 3.1 people, while those in the bottom fifth had an average of 1.7 people. As a result, consumption per person in the richest fifth of households was only 2.1 times consumption per person in the poorest fifth.

These data show that inequality in material standards of living is much smaller than inequality in annual income. ◢

20-1e Economic Mobility

People sometimes speak of "the rich" and "the poor" as if these groups consisted of the same families year after year. In fact, this is not at all the case. Economic mobility, the movement of people between income classes, is significant in the U.S. economy. Movements up the income ladder can be due to good luck or hard work, and movements down the ladder can be due to bad luck or laziness. Some of this mobility reflects transitory variation in income, while some reflects more persistent changes in income.

Because family income changes over time, temporary poverty is more common than the poverty rate suggests, but persistent poverty is less common. In a typical 10-year period, about one in four families falls below the poverty line in at least 1 year. Yet fewer than 3 percent of families are poor for 8 or more years. Because it is likely that the temporarily poor and the persistently poor face different problems, policies that aim to combat poverty need to distinguish between these groups.

Another way to gauge economic mobility is the persistence of economic success from generation to generation. Economists who have studied this topic find that having an above-average income carries over from parents to children, but the persistence is far from perfect, indicating substantial mobility among income classes. If a father earns 20 percent above his generation's average income, his son will most likely earn 8 percent above his generation's average income. There is only a small correlation between the income of a grandfather and the income of his grandson.

One result of this intergenerational economic mobility is that the U.S. economy is filled with self-made millionaires (as well as with heirs who have squandered the fortunes they inherited). According to one study, about four out of five millionaires made their money on their own, often by starting and building a business or by climbing the corporate ladder. Only one in five millionaires inherited his fortune.

Quick Quiz   *What does the poverty rate measure? • Describe three potential problems in interpreting the measured poverty rate.*

20-2 The Political Philosophy of Redistributing Income

We have just seen how the economy's income is distributed and have considered some of the problems in interpreting measured inequality. This discussion was *positive* in the sense that it merely described the world as it is. We now turn to the *normative* question facing policymakers: What should the government do about economic inequality?

This question is not just about economics. Economic analysis alone cannot tell us whether policymakers should try to make our society more egalitarian. Our views on this question are, to a large extent, a matter of political philosophy. Yet because the government's role in redistributing income is central to so many debates over economic policy, here we digress from economic science to consider a bit of political philosophy.

20-2a Utilitarianism

A prominent school of thought in political philosophy is **utilitarianism**. The founders of utilitarianism are the English philosophers Jeremy Bentham (1748–1832) and John Stuart Mill (1806–1873). To a large extent, the goal of utilitarians is to apply the logic of individual decision making to questions concerning morality and public policy.

The starting point of utilitarianism is the notion of **utility**—the level of happiness or satisfaction that a person receives from his circumstances. Utility is a measure of well-being and, according to utilitarians, is the ultimate objective of all public and private actions. The proper goal of the government, they claim, is to maximize the sum of utility achieved by everyone in society.

The utilitarian case for redistributing income is based on the assumption of *diminishing marginal utility*. It seems reasonable that an extra dollar of income provides a poor person with more additional utility than an extra dollar would provide to a rich person. In other words, as a person's income rises, the extra well-being derived from an additional dollar of income falls. This plausible assumption, together with the utilitarian goal of maximizing total utility, implies that the government should try to achieve a more equal distribution of income.

The argument is simple. Imagine that Peter and Paul are the same, except that Peter earns $80,000 and Paul earns $20,000. In this case, taking a dollar from Peter to pay Paul will reduce Peter's utility and raise Paul's utility. But because of diminishing marginal utility, Peter's utility falls by less than Paul's utility rises. Thus, this redistribution of income raises total utility, which is the utilitarian's objective.

At first, this utilitarian argument might seem to imply that the government should continue to redistribute income until everyone in society has exactly the same income. Indeed, that would be the case if the total amount of income—$100,000 in our example—were fixed. But in fact, it is not. Utilitarians reject complete equalization of incomes because they accept one of the *Ten Principles of Economics* presented in Chapter 1: People respond to incentives.

utilitarianism
the political philosophy according to which the government should choose policies to maximize the total utility of everyone in society

utility
a measure of happiness or satisfaction

To take from Peter to pay Paul, the government must pursue policies that redistribute income. The U.S. federal income tax and welfare system are examples. Under these policies, people with high incomes pay high taxes, and people with low incomes receive income transfers. These income transfers are phased out: As a person earns more, he receives less from the government. Yet when the government uses higher income taxes and phased-out transfers to take away additional income a person might earn, both Peter and Paul have less incentive to work hard. As they work less, society's income falls, and so does total utility. The utilitarian government has to balance the gains from greater equality against the losses from distorted incentives. To maximize total utility, therefore, the government stops short of making society fully egalitarian.

A famous parable sheds light on the utilitarian's logic. Imagine that Peter and Paul are thirsty travelers trapped at different places in the desert. Peter's oasis has a lot of water; Paul's has only a little. If the government could transfer water from one oasis to the other without cost, it would maximize total utility from water by equalizing the amount in the two places. But suppose that the government has only a leaky bucket. As it tries to move water from one place to the other, some of the water is lost in transit. In this case, a utilitarian government might still try to move some water from Peter to Paul, depending on the size of Paul's thirst and the size of the bucket's leak. But with only a leaky bucket at its disposal, a utilitarian government will stop short of trying to reach complete equality.

20-2b Liberalism

A second way of thinking about inequality might be called **liberalism**. Philosopher John Rawls develops this view in his book *A Theory of Justice*. This book was first published in 1971, and it quickly became a classic in political philosophy.

Rawls begins with the premise that a society's institutions, laws, and policies should be just. He then takes up the natural question: How can we, the members of society, ever agree on what justice means? It might seem that every person's point of view is inevitably based on his particular circumstances—whether he is talented or less talented, diligent or lazy, educated or less educated, born to a wealthy family or a poor one. Could we ever *objectively* determine what a just society would be?

To answer this question, Rawls proposes the following thought experiment. Imagine that before any of us is born, we all get together in the beforelife (the pre-birth version of the afterlife) for a meeting to design the rules that will govern society. At this point, we are all ignorant about the station in life each of us will end up filling. In Rawls's words, we are sitting in an "original position" behind a "veil of ignorance." In this original position, Rawls argues, we can choose a just set of rules for society because we must consider how those rules will affect every person. As Rawls puts it, "Since all are similarly situated and no one is able to design principles to favor his particular conditions, the principles of justice are the result of fair agreement or bargain." Designing public policies and institutions in this way allows us to be objective about what policies are just.

Rawls then considers what public policy designed behind this veil of ignorance would try to achieve. In particular, he considers what income distribution a person would consider fair if that person did not know whether he would end up at the top, bottom, or middle of the distribution. Rawls argues that a person in the original position would be especially concerned about the possibility of being at the *bottom* of the income distribution. In designing public policies, therefore, we should aim to raise the welfare of the worst-off person in society. That is, rather than maximizing the sum of everyone's utility, as a utilitarian would do, Rawls would maximize the minimum utility. Rawls's rule is called the **maximin criterion**.

liberalism
the political philosophy according to which the government should choose policies deemed just, as evaluated by an impartial observer behind a "veil of ignorance"

maximin criterion
the claim that the government should aim to maximize the well-being of the worst-off person in society

Because the maximin criterion emphasizes the least fortunate person in society, it justifies public policies aimed at equalizing the distribution of income. By transferring income from the rich to the poor, society raises the well-being of the least fortunate. The maximin criterion would not, however, lead to a completely egalitarian society. If the government promised to equalize incomes completely, people would have no incentive to work hard, society's total income would fall substantially, and the least fortunate person would be worse off. Thus, the maximin criterion still allows disparities in income because such disparities can improve incentives and thereby raise society's ability to help the poor. Nonetheless, because Rawls's philosophy puts weight on only the least fortunate members of society, it calls for more income redistribution than does utilitarianism.

Rawls's views are controversial, but the thought experiment he proposes has much appeal. In particular, this thought experiment allows us to consider the redistribution of income as a form of **social insurance**. That is, from the perspective of the original position behind the veil of ignorance, income redistribution is like an insurance policy. Homeowners buy fire insurance to protect themselves from the risk of their house burning down. Similarly, when we as a society choose policies that tax the rich to supplement the incomes of the poor, we are all insuring ourselves against the possibility that we might have been members of poor families. Because people dislike risk, we should be happy to have been born into a society that provides us this insurance.

social insurance
government policy aimed at protecting people against the risk of adverse events

It is not at all clear, however, that rational people behind the veil of ignorance would truly be so averse to risk as to follow the maximin criterion. Indeed, because a person in the original position might end up anywhere in the distribution of outcomes, he might treat all possible outcomes equally when designing public policies. In this case, the best policy behind the veil of ignorance would be to maximize the average utility of members of society, and the resulting notion of justice would be more utilitarian than Rawlsian.

20-2c Libertarianism

A third view of inequality is called **libertarianism**. The two views we have considered so far—utilitarianism and liberalism—both view the total income of society as a shared resource that a social planner can freely redistribute to achieve some social goal. By contrast, libertarians argue that society itself earns no income—only individual members of society earn income. According to libertarians, the government should not take from some individuals and give to others to achieve any particular distribution of income.

libertarianism
the political philosophy according to which the government should punish crimes and enforce voluntary agreements but not redistribute income

For instance, philosopher Robert Nozick writes the following in his famous 1974 book *Anarchy, State, and Utopia*:

> We are not in the position of children who have been given portions of pie by someone who now makes last minute adjustments to rectify careless cutting. There is no *central* distribution, no person or group entitled to control all the resources, jointly deciding how they are to be doled out. What each person gets, he gets from others who give to him in exchange for something, or as a gift. In a free society, diverse persons control different resources, and new holdings arise out of the voluntary exchanges and actions of persons.

Whereas utilitarians and liberals try to judge what amount of inequality is desirable in a society, Nozick denies the validity of this very question.

The libertarian alternative to evaluating economic *outcomes* is to evaluate the *process* by which these outcomes arise. When the distribution of income is achieved unfairly—for instance, when one person steals from another—the government has the right and duty to remedy the problem. But as long as the process determining the distribution of income is just, the resulting distribution is fair, no matter how unequal.

Nozick criticizes Rawls's liberalism by drawing an analogy between the distribution of income in society and the distribution of grades in a course. Suppose you were asked to judge the fairness of the grades in the economics course you are now taking. Would you imagine yourself behind a veil of ignorance and choose a grade distribution without knowing the talents and efforts of each student? Or would you ensure that the process of assigning grades to students is fair without regard for whether the resulting distribution is equal or unequal? For the case of grades at least, the libertarian emphasis on process over outcomes is compelling.

Libertarians conclude that equality of opportunities is more important than equality of incomes. They believe that the government should enforce individual rights to ensure that everyone has the same opportunity to use his talents and achieve success. Once these rules of the game are established, the government has no reason to alter the resulting distribution of income.

Quick Quiz   *Pam earns more than Pauline. Someone proposes taxing Pam to supplement Pauline's income. How would a utilitarian, a liberal, and a libertarian each evaluate this proposal?*

20-3 Policies to Reduce Poverty

As we have just seen, political philosophers hold various views about what role the government should take in altering the distribution of income. Political debate among the larger population of voters reflects a similar disagreement. Despite these continuing debates, most people believe that, at the very least, the government should try to help those most in need. According to a popular metaphor, the government should provide a "safety net" to prevent any citizen from falling too far.

Poverty is one of the most difficult problems that policymakers face. Poor families are more likely than the overall population to experience homelessness, drug dependence, health problems, teenage pregnancy, illiteracy, unemployment, and low educational attainment. Members of poor families are both more likely to commit crimes and more likely to be victims of crimes. Although it is hard to separate the causes of poverty from the effects, there is no doubt that poverty is associated with various economic and social ills.

Suppose that you were a policymaker in the government and your goal was to reduce the number of people living in poverty. How would you achieve this goal? Here we examine some of the policy options that you might consider. Each of these options helps some people escape poverty, but none of them is perfect, and deciding upon the best combination to use is not easy.

20-3a Minimum-Wage Laws

Laws setting a minimum wage that employers can pay workers are a perennial source of debate. Advocates view the minimum wage as a way of helping the working poor without any cost to the government. Critics view it as hurting those it is intended to help.

The minimum wage is easily understood using the tools of supply and demand, as we first saw in Chapter 6. For workers with low levels of skill and experience, a high minimum wage forces the wage above the level that balances supply and demand. It therefore raises the cost of labor to firms and reduces the quantity of labor that those firms demand. The result is higher unemployment among those groups of workers affected by the minimum wage. Those workers who remain employed benefit from a higher wage, but those who might have been employed at a lower wage are worse off.

The magnitude of these effects depends crucially on the elasticity of labor demand. Advocates of a high minimum wage argue that the demand for unskilled labor is relatively inelastic so that a high minimum wage depresses employment only slightly. Critics of the minimum wage argue that labor demand is more elastic, especially in the long run when firms can adjust employment and production more fully. They also note that many minimum-wage workers are teenagers from middle-class families so that a high minimum wage is imperfectly targeted as a policy for helping the poor.

20-3b Welfare

One way for the government to raise the living standards of the poor is to supplement their incomes. The primary way the government does this is through the welfare system. **Welfare** is a broad term that encompasses various government programs. Temporary Assistance for Needy Families (TANF) is a program that assists families with children and no adult able to support the family. In a typical family receiving such assistance, the father is absent and the mother is at home raising small children. Another welfare program is Supplemental Security Income (SSI), which provides assistance to the poor who are sick or disabled. Note that for both of these welfare programs, a poor person cannot qualify for assistance simply by having a low income. He must also establish some additional "need," such as small children or a disability.

welfare
government programs that supplement the incomes of the needy

A common criticism of welfare programs is that they create incentives for people to become "needy." For example, these programs may encourage families to break up, for many families qualify for financial assistance only if the father is absent. The programs may also encourage illegitimate births, for many poor, single women qualify for assistance only if they have children. Because poor, single mothers are such a large part of the poverty problem and because welfare programs seem to raise the number of poor, single mothers, critics of the welfare system assert that these policies exacerbate the very problems they are supposed to cure. As a result of these arguments, the welfare system was revised in a 1996 law that limited the amount of time recipients could stay on welfare.

How severe are these potential problems with the welfare system? No one knows for sure. Proponents of the welfare system point out that being a poor, single mother on welfare is a difficult existence at best, and they are skeptical that many people would be encouraged to pursue such a life if it were not thrust upon them. Moreover, trends over time do not support the view that the decline of the two-parent family is largely a symptom of the welfare system, as the system's critics sometimes claim. Since the early 1970s, welfare benefits (adjusted for inflation) have declined, yet the percentage of children living with only one parent has risen.

20-3c Negative Income Tax

Whenever the government chooses a system to collect taxes, it affects the distribution of income. This is clearly true in the case of a progressive income tax, whereby high-income families pay a larger percentage of their income in taxes than do low-income families. As we discussed in Chapter 12, equity across income groups is an important criterion in the design of a tax system.

negative income tax
a tax system that collects revenue from high-income households and gives subsidies to low-income households

Many economists have advocated supplementing the income of the poor using a **negative income tax**. According to this policy, every family would report its income to the government. High-income families would pay a tax based on their incomes. Low-income families would receive a subsidy. In other words, they would "pay" a "negative tax."

For example, suppose the government used the following formula to compute a family's tax liability:

$$\text{Taxes owed} = (\tfrac{1}{3} \text{ of income}) - \$10,000.$$

In this case, a family that earned $60,000 would pay $10,000 in taxes and a family that earned $90,000 would pay $20,000 in taxes. A family that earned $30,000 would owe nothing. And a family that earned $15,000 would "owe" −$5,000. In other words, the government would send this family a check for $5,000.

Under a negative income tax, poor families would receive financial assistance without having to demonstrate need. The only qualification required to receive assistance would be a low income. Depending on one's point of view, this feature can be either an advantage or a disadvantage. On the one hand, a negative income tax does not encourage illegitimate births and the breakup of families, as critics of the welfare system believe current policy does. On the other hand, a negative income tax would subsidize not only the unfortunate but also those who are simply lazy and, in some people's eyes, undeserving of government support.

One actual tax provision that works much like a negative income tax is the Earned Income Tax Credit (EITC). This credit allows poor working families to receive income tax refunds greater than the taxes they paid during the year. Because the EITC applies only to the working poor, it does not discourage recipients from working, as other antipoverty programs may. For the same reason, however, it also does not help alleviate poverty due to unemployment, sickness, or other inability to work.

20-3d In-Kind Transfers

Another way to help the poor is to provide them directly with some of the goods and services they need to raise their living standards. For example, charities provide the needy with food, clothing, shelter, and toys at Christmas. The government gives poor families food stamps, which are government vouchers that can be used to buy food at stores; the stores then redeem the vouchers for money. The government also gives many poor people healthcare through a program called Medicaid.

Is it better to help the poor with these in-kind transfers or with direct cash payments? There is no clear answer.

Advocates of in-kind transfers argue that such transfers ensure that the poor get what they need most. Among the poorest members of society, alcohol and drug addiction is more common than it is in society as a whole. By providing the poor with food and shelter, society can be more confident that it is not helping to support such addictions. This is one reason in-kind transfers are more politically popular than cash payments to the poor.

Advocates of cash payments, on the other hand, argue that in-kind transfers are inefficient and disrespectful. The government does not know what goods and services the poor need most. Many of the poor are ordinary people down on their luck. Despite their misfortune, they are in the best position to decide how to raise their own living standards. Rather than giving the poor in-kind transfers of goods and services that they may not want, it may be better to give them cash and allow them to buy what they think they need most.

20-3e Antipoverty Programs and Work Incentives

Many policies aimed at helping the poor can have the unintended effect of discouraging the poor from escaping poverty on their own. To see why, consider the following example. Suppose that a family needs an income of $20,000 to maintain a reasonable standard of living. And suppose that, out of concern for the poor, the government promises to guarantee every family that income. Whatever a family earns, the government makes up the difference between that income and $20,000. What effect would you expect this policy to have?

The incentive effects of this policy are obvious: Any person who would make under $20,000 by working has little incentive to find and keep a job. For every dollar that the person would earn, the government would reduce the income supplement by a dollar. In effect, the government taxes 100 percent of additional earnings. An effective marginal tax rate of 100 percent is surely a policy with a large deadweight loss.

The adverse effects of this high effective tax rate can persist over time. A person discouraged from working loses the on-the-job training that a job might offer. In addition, his children miss the lessons learned by observing a parent with a full-time job, and this may adversely affect their own ability to find and hold a job.

Although the antipoverty program we have been discussing is hypothetical, it is not as unrealistic as might first appear. Welfare, Medicaid, food stamps, and the EITC are all programs aimed at helping the poor, and they are all tied to family income. As a family's income rises, the family becomes ineligible for these programs. When all these programs are taken together, it is common for families to face effective marginal tax rates that are very high. Sometimes the effective marginal tax rates even exceed 100 percent so that poor families are worse off when they earn more. By trying to help the poor, the government discourages those families from working. According to critics of antipoverty programs, these programs alter work attitudes and create a "culture of poverty."

It might seem that there is an easy solution to this problem: Reduce benefits to poor families more gradually as their incomes rise. For example, if a poor family loses 30 cents of benefits for every dollar it earns, then it faces an effective marginal tax rate of 30 percent. This effective tax reduces work effort to some extent, but it does not eliminate the incentive to work completely.

The problem with this solution is that it greatly increases the cost of programs to combat poverty. If benefits are phased out gradually as a poor family's income rises, then families just above the poverty level will also be eligible for substantial benefits. The more gradual the phase-out, the more families are eligible, and the more the program costs. Thus, policymakers face a trade-off between burdening the poor with high effective marginal tax rates and burdening taxpayers with costly programs to reduce poverty.

There are various other ways to reduce the work disincentive of antipoverty programs. One is to require any person collecting benefits to accept a government-provided job—a system sometimes called *workfare*. Another possibility is to provide benefits for only a limited period of time. This route was taken in the 1996 welfare reform bill, which imposed a 5-year lifetime limit on welfare recipients. When President Clinton signed the bill, he explained his policy as follows: "Welfare should be a second chance, not a way of life."

Quick Quiz *List three policies aimed at helping the poor, and discuss the pros and cons of each.*

IN THE NEWS
....

International Differences in Income Redistribution

Many nations have more generous social safety nets than the United States, but they also have very different tax systems.

Combating Inequality May Require Broader Tax

By Eduardo Porter

Rarely have we experienced such a confluence of arguments in favor of raising taxes on the rich. After a hard-won re-election fought mainly over taxes and spending, President Obama arguably has a mandate from voters to tap the wealthy to address our budget woes.

What's more, raising more money from the wealthy might go a long way toward righting our lopsided economy—which delivered 93 percent of our income growth in the first two years of the economic recovery to the richest 1 percent of families, and only 7 percent to the rest of us.

Yet while raising more taxes from the winners in the globalized economy is a start, and may help us dig out of our immediate fiscal hole, it is unlikely to be enough to address our long-term needs. The experience of many other developed countries suggests that paying for a government that could help the poor and the middle class cope in our brave new globalized world will require more money from the middle class itself.

Many Americans may find this hard to believe, but the United States already has one of the most progressive tax systems in the developed world, according to several studies, raising proportionately more revenue from the wealthy than other advanced countries do. Taxes on American households do more to redistribute resources and reduce inequality than the tax codes of most other rich nations.

But taxation provides only half the picture of public finance. Despite the progressivity of our taxes, according to a study of public finances across the industrial countries in the Organization for Economic Co-operation and Development, we also have one of the least effective governments at combating income inequality. There is one main reason: our tax code does not raise enough money.

This paradox underscores two crucial lessons we could learn from the experience of our peers around the globe. The first is that the government's success at combating income inequality is determined less by the progressivity of either the tax code or the benefits than by the amount of tax revenue that the government can spend on programs that benefit the middle class and the poor.

The second is that very progressive tax codes are not very effective at raising money. The corollary—suggested by Peter Lindert of the University of California, Davis in his 2004 book "Growing Public"—is that insisting on highly progressive taxes that draw most revenue from the rich may result in more inequality than if we relied on a flatter, more "regressive" tax schedule to raise money from everybody and pay for a government that could help every American family attain a decent standard of living.

Consider government aid for families. According to the O.E.C.D. study, our Temporary Assistance for Needy Families is the most progressive program of cash benefits for families among 22 advanced countries, accurately targeted to serve the poor.

But American family cash benefits are the least effective at reducing inequality. The reason is that they are so meager. The entire budget for cash assistance for families in the United States amounts to one-tenth of 1 percent of the nation's economic output. The average across the O.E.C.D. nations is 11 times bigger. Even including tax breaks and direct government services, we spend a much smaller share of our economic output

20-4 Conclusion

People have long reflected on the distribution of income in society. Plato, the ancient Greek philosopher, concluded that in an ideal society the income of the richest person would be no more than four times the income of the poorest person. Although the measurement of inequality is difficult, it is clear that our society has much more inequality than Plato recommended.

One of the *Ten Principles of Economics* discussed in Chapter 1 is that governments can sometimes improve market outcomes. There is little consensus, however, about how this principle should be applied to the distribution of income.

on family assistance than almost any other advanced nation.

The same pattern can be found across a range of government programs. The reason is always the same: their relatively small size. Over all, government cash benefits in the United States—including pensions, disability, unemployment insurance and the like—contribute about 10 percent to household income, on average, according to the study. The average across industrial nations is twice that.

Our budget reveals a core philosophical difference with other advanced countries. In the big-government social democracies like those of Western Europe, government is expected to guarantee a set of universal public services—from health care to child care to pensions—that are considered basic rights of citizenry. To pay for this minimum welfare package, everybody is expected to contribute proportionately into the pot.

Government in the United States has a different goal. Benefits are narrower. Social Security and Medicare follow a universal service template, but only for older Americans. Other social spending is aimed carefully to benefit the poor. Financed through a more progressive tax code, it looks more like charity than a universal right. On top of that, our philosophical stance virtually ensures a small government.

Progressive taxes make it hard to raise money because they distort people's behavior. They encourage taxpayers to reduce their tax liability rather than to increase their pretax income. High corporate taxes encourage companies to avoid them. High taxes on capital income also encourage avoidance and capital flight. High income tax rates on top earners can discourage work and investment, too. So trying to raise a lot of money with our progressive tax code would probably not achieve the goal and could damage economic growth.

Big-government social democracies, by contrast, rely on flatter taxes to finance their public spending, like gas taxes and value-added taxes on consumption. The Nordic countries, for instance, have very low tax rates on capital income relative to income from work. And they have relatively high taxes on consumption. In Denmark, consumption tax revenue amounts to about 11 percent of the nation's economy. In the United States, sales taxes and excise taxes on cigarettes and other items amount to roughly 4 percent.

Liberal Democrats have long opposed them because they fall much more heavily on the poor, who spend a larger share of their incomes than the rich. But these taxes have one big positive feature: they are difficult to avoid and produce fewer disincentives to work or invest. That means they can be used to raise much more revenue.

Public finances are under strain today on both sides of the Atlantic, as governments struggle to cope with our long global recession and the aging of the baby boom generation. In Southern Europe, the pressure to pare back universal welfare systems is intense. In the United States, political leaders on both sides of the partisan divide have realized that even our relatively meager package of social goods cannot be sustained with our slim tax take.

But the United States has one option that most of Europe's flailing economies do not. Its tax revenue is so low, comparatively, that it has more space to raise it. A more efficient, flatter tax schedule would allow us to do so without hindering economic activity.

Bruce Bartlett, a tax expert who served in the administrations of Ronald Reagan and George H. W. Bush, told me last week that he thought federal tax revenue could increase to 22 percent of the nation's economic output, well above its historical average of 18.5 percent, without causing economic harm. If President Obama tries to go down this road, however, he may have to build a flatter tax code.

"We should reform the tax system, no question," William Gale, a tax policy expert at the Brookings Institution and co-director of the nonpartisan Tax Policy Center, wrote in an e-mail. "We are going to need to move beyond the current set of tax instruments to raise the needed revenues—a VAT and/or a carbon tax seem like the obvious ways to go." And Mr. Bartlett also pointed out: "We can't get all the revenue we need from the rich. Eventually, everyone will have to pay more." ◢

Source: *New York Times*, November 28, 2012.

Philosophers and policymakers today do not agree on how much income inequality is desirable, or even whether public policy should aim to alter the distribution of income. Much of public debate reflects this disagreement. Whenever taxes are raised, for instance, lawmakers argue over how much of the tax hike should fall on the rich, the middle class, and the poor.

Another of the *Ten Principles of Economics* is that people face trade-offs. This principle is important to keep in mind when thinking about economic inequality. Policies that penalize the successful and reward the unsuccessful reduce the incentive to succeed. Thus, policymakers face a trade-off between equality and efficiency. The more equally the pie is divided, the smaller the pie becomes. This is the one lesson concerning the distribution of income about which almost everyone agrees.

Summary

- Data on the distribution of income show a wide disparity in U.S. society. The richest fifth of families earns more than twelve times as much income as the poorest fifth.

- Because in-kind transfers, the economic life cycle, transitory income, and economic mobility are so important for understanding variation in income, it is difficult to gauge the degree of inequality in our society using data on the distribution of income in a single year. When these other factors are taken into account, they tend to suggest that economic well-being is more equally distributed than is annual income.

- Political philosophers differ in their views about the role of government in altering the distribution of income. Utilitarians (such as John Stuart Mill) would choose the distribution of income to maximize the sum of utility of everyone in society. Liberals (such as John Rawls) would determine the distribution of income as if we were behind a "veil of ignorance" that prevented us from knowing our stations in life. Libertarians (such as Robert Nozick) would have the government enforce individual rights to ensure a fair process but then not be concerned about inequality in the resulting distribution of income.

- Various policies aim to help the poor—minimum-wage laws, welfare, negative income taxes, and in-kind transfers. While these policies help some families escape poverty, they also have unintended side effects. Because financial assistance declines as income rises, the poor often face very high effective marginal tax rates, which discourage poor families from escaping poverty on their own.

Key Concepts

poverty rate, *p. 417*
poverty line, *p. 417*
in-kind transfers, *p. 419*
life cycle, *p. 419*
permanent income, *p. 419*

utilitarianism, *p. 421*
utility, *p. 421*
liberalism, *p. 422*
maximin criterion, *p. 422*
social insurance, *p. 423*

libertarianism, *p. 423*
welfare, *p. 425*
negative income tax, *p. 425*

Questions for Review

1. Does the richest fifth of the U.S. population earn closer to three, six, or twelve times the income of the poorest fifth?

2. What has happened to the income share of the richest fifth of the U.S. population over the past 40 years?

3. What groups in the U.S. population are most likely to live in poverty?

4. When gauging the amount of inequality, why do transitory and life cycle variations in income cause difficulties?

5. How would a utilitarian, a liberal, and a libertarian each determine how much income inequality is permissible?

6. What are the pros and cons of in-kind (rather than cash) transfers to the poor?

7. Describe how antipoverty programs can discourage the poor from working. How might you reduce this disincentive? What are the disadvantages of your proposed policy?

Quick Check Multiple Choice

1. In the United States, the poorest fifth of the population earns about _____ percent of all income, while the richest fifth earns about _____ percent.
   a. 2, 65
   b. 4, 45
   c. 10, 35
   d. 15, 25

2. When income inequality is compared across countries, one finds that the United States
   a. is one of the most equal nations in the world.
   b. is one of the least equal nations in the world.
   c. has more equality than most advanced nations but less equality than many developing countries.
   d. has less equality than most advanced nations but more equality than many developing countries.

3. A utilitarian believes that the redistribution of income from the rich to the poor is worthwhile as long as
   a. the worst-off members of society benefit from it.
   b. those contributing to the system are in favor of it.
   c. each person's income, after taxes and transfers, reflects his marginal product.
   d. the distortionary effect on work incentives is not too large.

4. Rawls's thought experiment of the "original position" behind the "veil of ignorance" is meant to draw attention to the fact that
   a. most of the poor do not know how to find better jobs and escape poverty.
   b. the station of life each of us was born into is largely a matter of luck.
   c. the rich have so much money that they don't know how to spend it all.
   d. outcomes are efficient only if everyone begins with equal opportunity.

5. A negative income tax is a policy under which
   a. individuals with low income get transfers from the government.
   b. the government raises tax revenue without distorting incentives.
   c. everyone pays less than under a conventional income tax.
   d. some taxpayers are on the wrong side of the Laffer curve.

6. If the benefits from an antipoverty program are phased out as an individual's income increases, then the program will
   a. encourage greater work effort from the poor.
   b. lead to an excess supply of labor among unskilled workers.
   c. increase the effective marginal tax rate that the poor face.
   d. cost the government more than a program that benefits everyone.

Problems and Applications

1. Table 2 shows that income inequality in the United States has increased since 1970. Some factors contributing to this increase were discussed in Chapter 19. What are they?

2. Table 3 shows that the percentage of children in families with income below the poverty line far exceeds the percentage of the elderly in such families. How might the allocation of government money across different social programs have contributed to this phenomenon? (*Hint:* See Chapter 12.)

3. This chapter discusses the importance of economic mobility.
   a. What policies might the government pursue to increase economic mobility *within* a generation?
   b. What policies might the government pursue to increase economic mobility *across* generations?
   c. Do you think we should reduce spending on current welfare programs to increase spending on programs that enhance economic mobility? What are some of the advantages and disadvantages of doing so?

4. Consider two communities. In one community, ten families have incomes of $100,000 each and ten families have incomes of $20,000 each. In the other community, ten families have incomes of $200,000 each and ten families have incomes of $22,000 each.
   a. In which community is the distribution of income more unequal? In which community is the problem of poverty likely to be worse?
   b. Which distribution of income would Rawls prefer? Explain.
   c. Which distribution of income do you prefer? Explain.
   d. Why might someone have the opposite preference?

5. This chapter uses the analogy of a "leaky bucket" to explain one constraint on the redistribution of income.
   a. What elements of the U.S. system for redistributing income create the leaks in the bucket? Be specific.
   b. Do you think that Republicans or Democrats generally believe that the bucket used for redistributing income is leakier? How does that belief affect their views about the amount of income redistribution that the government should undertake?

6. Suppose there are two possible income distributions in a society of ten people. In the first distribution, nine people have incomes of $30,000 and one person has an income of $10,000. In the second distribution, all ten people have incomes of $25,000.
   a. If the society had the first income distribution, what would be the utilitarian argument for redistributing income?
   b. Which income distribution would Rawls consider more equitable? Explain.
   c. Which income distribution would Nozick consider more equitable? Explain.

7. The poverty rate would be substantially lower if the market value of in-kind transfers were added to family income. The largest in-kind transfer is

Medicaid, the government health program for the poor. Let's say the program costs $10,000 per recipient family.

a. If the government gave each recipient family a $10,000 check instead of enrolling them in the Medicaid program, do you think that most of these families would spend that money to purchase health insurance? Why? (Recall that the poverty level for a family of four is about $23,000.)

b. How does your answer to part (a) affect your view about whether we should determine the poverty rate by valuing in-kind transfers at the price the government pays for them? Explain.

c. How does your answer to part (a) affect your view about whether we should provide assistance to the poor in the form of cash transfers or in-kind transfers? Explain.

8. Consider two of the income security programs in the United States: TANF and the EITC.

a. When a woman with children and very low income earns an extra dollar, she receives less in TANF benefits. What do you think is the effect of this feature of TANF on the labor supply of low-income women? Explain.

b. The EITC provides greater benefits as low-income workers earn more income (up to a point). What do you think is the effect of this program on the labor supply of low-income individuals? Explain.

c. What are the disadvantages of eliminating TANF and allocating the savings to the EITC?

Go to CengageBrain.com to purchase access to the proven, critical Study Guide to accompany this text, which features additional notes and context, practice tests, and much more.

Topics for
Further Study

The Theory of Consumer Choice

W hen you walk into a store, you are confronted with thousands of goods that you might buy. Because your financial resources are limited, however, you cannot buy everything that you want. You therefore consider the prices of the various goods offered for sale and buy a bundle of goods that, given your resources, best suits your needs and desires.

In this chapter, we develop a theory that describes how consumers make decisions about what to buy. Thus far in this book, we have summarized consumers' decisions with the demand curve. As we have seen, the demand curve for a good reflects consumers' willingness to pay for it. When the price of a good rises, consumers are willing to pay for fewer units, so the quantity demanded falls. We now look more deeply at the decisions that lie behind the demand curve. The theory of consumer choice presented in this chapter provides a more complete understanding of demand, just as the theory of the competitive firm in Chapter 14 provides a more complete understanding of supply.

One of the *Ten Principles of Economics* discussed in Chapter 1 is that people face trade-offs. The theory of consumer choice examines the trade-offs that people face in their role as consumers. When a consumer buys more of one good, she can afford less of other goods. When she spends more time enjoying leisure and less time working, she has lower income and can afford less consumption. When she spends more of her income in the present and saves less of it, she must accept a lower level of consumption in the future. The theory of consumer choice examines how consumers facing these trade-offs make decisions and how they respond to changes in their environment.

After developing the basic theory of consumer choice, we apply it to three questions about household decisions. In particular, we ask:

- Do all demand curves slope downward?
- How do wages affect labor supply?
- How do interest rates affect household saving?

At first, these questions might seem unrelated. But as we will see, we can use the theory of consumer choice to address each of them.

21-1 The Budget Constraint: What the Consumer Can Afford

Most people would like to increase the quantity or quality of the goods they consume—to take longer vacations, drive fancier cars, or eat at better restaurants. People consume less than they desire because their spending is *constrained*, or limited, by their income. We begin our study of consumer choice by examining this link between income and spending.

To keep things simple, we examine the decision facing a consumer who buys only two goods: pizza and Pepsi. Of course, real people buy thousands of different kinds of goods. Assuming there are only two goods greatly simplifies the problem without altering the basic insights about consumer choice.

We first consider how the consumer's income constrains the amount she spends on pizza and Pepsi. Suppose the consumer has an income of $1,000 per month and she spends her entire income on pizza and Pepsi. The price of a pizza is $10, and the price of a liter of Pepsi is $2.

The table in Figure 1 shows some of the many combinations of pizza and Pepsi that the consumer can buy. The first row in the table shows that if the consumer spends all her income on pizza, she can eat 100 pizzas during the month, but she would not be able to buy any Pepsi at all. The second row shows another possible consumption bundle: 90 pizzas and 50 liters of Pepsi. And so on. Each consumption bundle in the table costs exactly $1,000.

The graph in Figure 1 illustrates the consumption bundles that the consumer can choose. The vertical axis measures the number of liters of Pepsi, and the horizontal axis measures the number of pizzas. Three points are marked on this figure. At point A, the consumer buys no Pepsi and consumes 100 pizzas. At point B, the consumer buys no pizza and consumes 500 liters of Pepsi. At point C, the consumer buys 50 pizzas and 250 liters of Pepsi. Point C, which is exactly at the middle of the line from A to B, is the point at which the consumer spends an equal amount ($500) on pizza and Pepsi. These are only three of the many combinations of pizza and Pepsi that the consumer can choose. All the points on the line from A to B are possible. This line, called the **budget constraint**, shows the consumption

budget constraint
the limit on the consumption bundles that a consumer can afford

The budget constraint shows the various bundles of goods that the consumer can buy for a given income. Here the consumer buys bundles of pizza and Pepsi. The table and graph show what the consumer can afford if her income is $1,000, the price of pizza is $10, and the price of Pepsi is $2.

FIGURE 1

The Consumer's Budget Constraint

Number of Pizzas	Liters of Pepsi	Spending on Pizza	Spending on Pepsi	Total Spending
100×10	0	$1,000	$ 0	$1,000
90 ×10	50 ×2	900	100	1,000
80	100×2	800	200	1,000
70	150	700	300	1,000
60	200	600	400	1,000
50	250	500	500	1,000
40	300	400	600	1,000
30	350	300	700	1,000
20	400	200	800	1,000
10	450	100	900	1,000
0	500	0	1,000	1,000

Trade off between Pizza and Pepsi (handwritten)

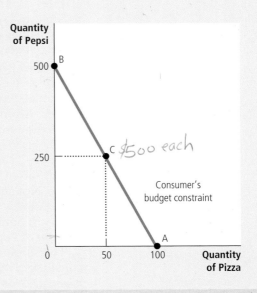

C $500 each (handwritten)

500/100 = 5 slope is 5 Liters per pizza (handwritten)

5 liter per Pizza (handwritten)

5 pepsi = 1 Pizza (handwritten)

(5×2) = $10 (handwritten)

opportunity cost of one Pizza is 5 Pepsi (handwritten)

bundles that the consumer can afford. In this case, it shows the trade-off between pizza and Pepsi that the consumer faces.

The slope of the budget constraint measures the rate at which the consumer can trade one good for the other. Recall that the slope between two points is calculated as the change in the vertical distance divided by the change in the horizontal distance ("rise over run"). From point A to point B, the vertical distance is 500 liters, and the horizontal distance is 100 pizzas. Thus, the slope is 5 liters per pizza. (Actually, because the budget constraint slopes downward, the slope is a negative number. But for our purposes we can ignore the minus sign.)

Notice that the slope of the budget constraint equals the *relative price* of the two goods—the price of one good compared to the price of the other. A pizza costs five times as much as a liter of Pepsi, so the opportunity cost of a pizza is 5 liters of Pepsi. The budget constraint's slope of 5 reflects the trade-off the market is offering the consumer: 1 pizza for 5 liters of Pepsi.

Quick Quiz *Draw the budget constraint for a person with income of $1,000 if the price of Pepsi is $5 and the price of pizza is $10. What is the slope of this budget constraint?*

21-2 Preferences: What the Consumer Wants

Our goal in this chapter is to see how consumers make choices. The budget constraint is one piece of the analysis: It shows the combinations of goods the consumer can afford given her income and the prices of the goods. The consumer's choices, however, depend not only on her budget constraint but also on her preferences regarding the two goods. Therefore, the consumer's preferences are the next piece of our analysis.

21-2a Representing Preferences with Indifference Curves

The consumer's preferences allow her to choose among different bundles of pizza and Pepsi. If you offer the consumer two different bundles, she chooses the bundle that best suits her tastes. If the two bundles suit her tastes equally well, we say that the consumer is *indifferent* between the two bundles.

Just as we have represented the consumer's budget constraint graphically, we can also represent her preferences graphically. We do this with indifference curves. An **indifference curve** shows the various bundles of consumption that make the consumer equally happy. In this case, the indifference curves show the combinations of pizza and Pepsi with which the consumer is equally satisfied.

Figure 2 shows two of the consumer's many indifference curves. The consumer is indifferent among combinations A, B, and C because they are all on the same curve. Not surprisingly, if the consumer's consumption of pizza is reduced, say, from point A to point B, consumption of Pepsi must increase to keep her equally happy. If consumption of pizza is reduced again, from point B to point C, the amount of Pepsi consumed must increase yet again.

The slope at any point on an indifference curve equals the rate at which the consumer is willing to substitute one good for the other. This rate is called the **marginal rate of substitution** (*MRS*). In this case, the marginal rate of substitution measures how much Pepsi the consumer requires to be compensated for a one-unit reduction in pizza consumption. Notice that because the indifference curves are not straight lines, the marginal rate of substitution is not the same at all points on a given indifference curve. The rate at which a consumer is willing to trade one good for the other depends on the amounts of the goods she is already consuming. That is, the rate at which a consumer is willing to trade pizza for Pepsi depends on whether she is hungrier or thirstier, which in turn depends on how much pizza and Pepsi she is consuming.

The consumer is equally happy at all points on any given indifference curve, but she prefers some indifference curves to others. Because she prefers more

indifference curve ~~on Test~~
a curve that shows consumption bundles that give the consumer the same level of satisfaction

marginal rate of substitution
the rate at which a consumer is willing to trade one good for another

FIGURE 2

The Consumer's Preferences
The consumer's preferences are represented with indifference curves, which show the combinations of pizza and Pepsi that make the consumer equally satisfied. Because the consumer prefers more of a good, points on a higher indifference curve (I_2 here) are preferred to points on a lower indifference curve (I_1). The marginal rate of substitution (*MRS*) shows the rate at which the consumer is willing to trade Pepsi for pizza. It measures the quantity of Pepsi the consumer must be given in exchange for 1 pizza.

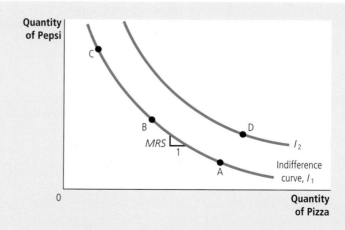

consumption to less, higher indifference curves are preferred to lower ones. In Figure 2, any point on curve I_2 is preferred to any point on curve I_1.

A consumer's set of indifference curves gives a complete ranking of the consumer's preferences. That is, we can use the indifference curves to rank any two bundles of goods. For example, the indifference curves tell us that point D is preferred to point A because point D is on a higher indifference curve than point A. (That conclusion may be obvious, however, because point D offers the consumer both more pizza and more Pepsi.) The indifference curves also tell us that point D is preferred to point C because point D is on a higher indifference curve. Even though point D has less Pepsi than point C, it has more than enough extra pizza to make the consumer prefer it. By seeing which point is on the higher indifference curve, we can use the set of indifference curves to rank any combination of pizza and Pepsi.

21-2b Four Properties of Indifference Curves

Because indifference curves represent a consumer's preferences, they have certain properties that reflect those preferences. Here we consider four properties that describe most indifference curves:

- *Property 1: Higher indifference curves are preferred to lower ones.* People usually prefer to consume more goods rather than less. This preference for greater quantities is reflected in the indifference curves. As Figure 2 shows, higher indifference curves represent larger quantities of goods than lower indifference curves. Thus, the consumer prefers being on higher indifference curves.
- *Property 2: Indifference curves are downward sloping.* The slope of an indifference curve reflects the rate at which the consumer is willing to substitute one good for the other. In most cases, the consumer likes both goods. Therefore, if the quantity of one good is reduced, the quantity of the other good must increase for the consumer to be equally happy. For this reason, most indifference curves slope downward.
- *Property 3: Indifference curves do not cross.* To see why this is true, suppose that two indifference curves did cross, as in Figure 3. Then, because point A is on the same indifference curve as point B, the two points would make the consumer equally happy. In addition, because point B is on the same

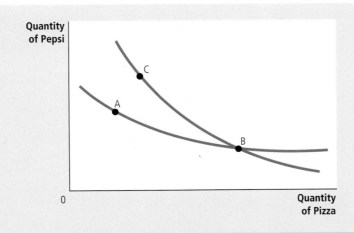

Quantity of Pepsi

C

A

B

0

Quantity of Pizza

FIGURE 3

The Impossibility of Intersecting Indifference Curves
A situation like this can never happen. According to these indifference curves, the consumer would be equally satisfied at points A, B, and C, even though point C has more of both goods than point A.

indifference curve as point C, these two points would make the consumer equally happy. But these conclusions imply that points A and C would also make the consumer equally happy, even though point C has more of both goods. This contradicts our assumption that the consumer always prefers more of both goods to less. Thus, indifference curves cannot cross.

- *Property 4: Indifference curves are bowed inward.* The slope of an indifference curve is the marginal rate of substitution—the rate at which the consumer is willing to trade off one good for the other. The marginal rate of substitution usually depends on the amount of each good the consumer is currently consuming. In particular, because people are more willing to trade away goods that they have in abundance and less willing to trade away goods of which they have little, the indifference curves are bowed inward. As an example, consider Figure 4. At point A, because the consumer has a lot of Pepsi and only a little pizza, she is very hungry but not very thirsty. To induce the consumer to give up 1 pizza, she has to be given 6 liters of Pepsi: The marginal rate of substitution is 6 liters per pizza. By contrast, at point B, the consumer has little Pepsi and a lot of pizza, so she is very thirsty but not very hungry. At this point, she would be willing to give up 1 pizza to get 1 liter of Pepsi: The marginal rate of substitution is 1 liter per pizza. Thus, the bowed shape of the indifference curve reflects the consumer's greater willingness to give up a good that she already has in large quantity.

21-2c Two Extreme Examples of Indifference Curves

The shape of an indifference curve tells us about the consumer's willingness to trade one good for the other. When the goods are easy to substitute for each other, the indifference curves are less bowed; when the goods are hard to substitute, the indifference curves are very bowed. To see why this is true, let's consider the extreme cases.

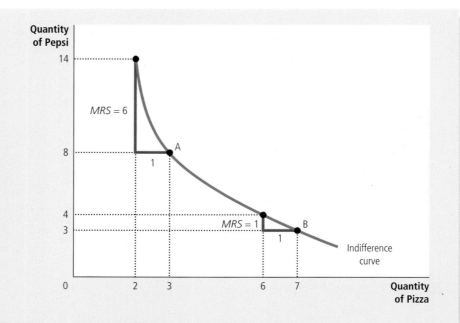

FIGURE 4

Bowed Indifference Curves
Indifference curves are usually bowed inward. This shape implies that the marginal rate of substitution (*MRS*) depends on the quantity of the two goods the consumer is consuming. At point A, the consumer has little pizza and much Pepsi, so she requires a lot of extra Pepsi to induce her to give up one of the pizzas: The marginal rate of substitution is 6 liters of Pepsi per pizza. At point B, the consumer has much pizza and little Pepsi, so she requires only a little extra Pepsi to induce her to give up one of the pizzas: The marginal rate of substitution is 1 liter of Pepsi per pizza.

Perfect Substitutes Suppose that someone offered you bundles of nickels and dimes. How would you rank the different bundles?

Most likely, you would care only about the total monetary value of each bundle. If so, you would always be willing to trade 2 nickels for 1 dime, regardless of the number of nickels and dimes in the bundle. Your marginal rate of substitution between nickels and dimes would be a fixed number—2.

We can represent your preferences over nickels and dimes with the indifference curves in panel (a) of Figure 5. Because the marginal rate of substitution is constant, the indifference curves are straight lines. In this extreme case of straight indifference curves, we say that the two goods are **perfect substitutes**.

perfect substitutes
two goods with straight-line indifference curves

Perfect Complements Suppose now that someone offered you bundles of shoes. Some of the shoes fit your left foot, others your right foot. How would you rank these different bundles?

In this case, you might care only about the number of pairs of shoes. In other words, you would judge a bundle based on the number of pairs you could assemble from it. A bundle of 5 left shoes and 7 right shoes yields only 5 pairs. Getting 1 more right shoe has no value if there is no left shoe to go with it.

We can represent your preferences for right and left shoes with the indifference curves in panel (b) of Figure 5. In this case, a bundle with 5 left shoes and 5 right shoes is just as good as a bundle with 5 left shoes and 7 right shoes. It is also just as good as a bundle with 7 left shoes and 5 right shoes. The indifference curves, therefore, are right angles. In this extreme case of right-angle indifference curves, we say that the two goods are **perfect complements**.

perfect complements
two goods with right-angle indifference curves

In the real world, of course, most goods are neither perfect substitutes (like nickels and dimes) nor perfect complements (like right shoes and left shoes). More typically, the indifference curves are bowed inward, but not so bowed that they become right angles.

When two goods are easily substitutable, such as nickels and dimes, the indifference curves are straight lines, as shown in panel (a). When two goods are strongly complementary, such as left shoes and right shoes, the indifference curves are right angles, as shown in panel (b).

FIGURE 5

Perfect Substitutes and Perfect Complements

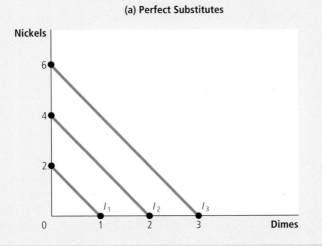

(a) Perfect Substitutes

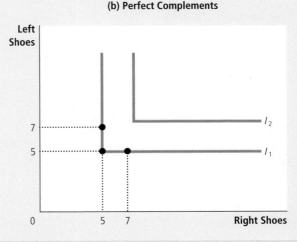

(b) Perfect Complements

Quick Quiz   *Draw some indifference curves for pizza and Pepsi. Explain the four properties of these indifference curves.*

21-3 Optimization: What the Consumer Chooses

The goal of this chapter is to understand how a consumer makes choices. We have the two pieces necessary for this analysis: the consumer's budget constraint (how much she can afford to spend) and the consumer's preferences (what she wants to spend it on). Now we put these two pieces together and consider the consumer's decision about what to buy.

21-3a The Consumer's Optimal Choices

Consider once again our pizza and Pepsi example. The consumer would like to end up with the best possible combination of pizza and Pepsi for her—that is, the combination on her highest possible indifference curve. But the consumer must also end up on or below her budget constraint, which measures the total resources available to her.

Figure 6 shows the consumer's budget constraint and three of her many indifference curves. The highest indifference curve that the consumer can reach (I_2 in the figure) is the one that just barely touches her budget constraint. The point at which this indifference curve and the budget constraint touch is called the *optimum*. The consumer would prefer point A, but she cannot afford that point because it lies above her budget constraint. The consumer can afford point B, but that point is on a lower indifference curve and, therefore, provides the consumer less satisfaction. The optimum represents the best combination of pizza and Pepsi available to the consumer.

Notice that, at the optimum, the slope of the indifference curve equals the slope of the budget constraint. We say that the indifference curve is *tangent* to the budget constraint. The slope of the indifference curve is the marginal rate of

FIGURE 6

The Consumer's Optimum
The consumer chooses the point on her budget constraint that lies on the highest indifference curve. At this point, called the optimum, the marginal rate of substitution equals the relative price of the two goods. Here the highest indifference curve the consumer can reach is I_2. The consumer prefers point A, which lies on indifference curve I_3, but she cannot afford this bundle of pizza and Pepsi. By contrast, point B is affordable, but because it lies on a lower indifference curve, the consumer does not prefer it.

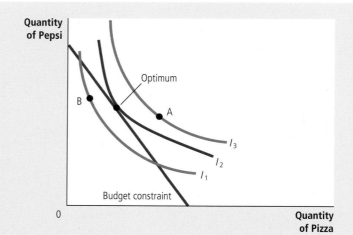

substitution between pizza and Pepsi, and the slope of the budget constraint is the relative price of pizza and Pepsi. Thus, *the consumer chooses consumption of the two goods so that the marginal rate of substitution equals the relative price.*

In Chapter 7, we saw how market prices reflect the marginal value that consumers place on goods. This analysis of consumer choice shows the same result in another way. In making her consumption choices, the consumer takes as given the relative price of the two goods and then chooses an optimum at which her marginal rate of substitution equals this relative price. The relative price is the rate at which the *market* is willing to trade one good for the other, whereas the marginal rate of substitution is the rate at which the *consumer* is willing to trade one good for the other. At the consumer's optimum, the consumer's valuation of the two goods (as measured by the marginal rate of substitution) equals the market's valuation (as measured by the relative price). As a result of this consumer optimization, market prices of different goods reflect the value that consumers place on those goods.

FYI

Utility: An Alternative Way to Describe Preferences and Optimization

We have used indifference curves to represent the consumer's preferences. Another common way to represent preferences is with the concept of *utility*. Utility is an abstract measure of the satisfaction or happiness that a consumer receives from a bundle of goods. Economists say that a consumer prefers one bundle of goods to another if one provides more utility than the other.

Indifference curves and utility are closely related. Because the consumer prefers points on higher indifference curves, bundles of goods on higher indifference curves provide higher utility. Because the consumer is equally happy with all points on the same indifference curve, all these bundles provide the same utility. You can think of an indifference curve as an "equal-utility" curve.

The *marginal utility* of any good is the increase in utility that the consumer gets from an additional unit of that good. Most goods are assumed to exhibit *diminishing marginal utility:* The more of the good the consumer already has, the lower the marginal utility provided by an extra unit of that good.

The marginal rate of substitution between two goods depends on their marginal utilities. For example, if the marginal utility of good X is twice the marginal utility of good Y, then a person would need 2 units of good Y to compensate for losing 1 unit of good X, and the marginal rate of substitution equals 2. More generally, the marginal rate of substitution (and thus the slope of the indifference curve) equals the marginal utility of one good divided by the marginal utility of the other good.

Utility analysis provides another way to describe consumer optimization. Recall that, at the consumer's optimum, the marginal rate of substitution equals the ratio of prices. That is,

$$MRS = P_X / P_Y.$$

Because the marginal rate of substitution equals the ratio of marginal utilities, we can write this condition for optimization as

$$MU_X / MU_Y = P_X / P_Y.$$

Now rearrange this expression to become

$$MU_X / P_X = MU_Y / P_Y.$$

This equation has a simple interpretation: At the optimum, the marginal utility per dollar spent on good X equals the marginal utility per dollar spent on good Y. (Why? If this equality did not hold, the consumer could increase utility by spending less on the good that provided lower marginal utility per dollar and more on the good that provided higher marginal utility per dollar.)

When economists discuss the theory of consumer choice, they sometimes express the theory using different words. One economist might say that the goal of the consumer is to maximize utility. Another economist might say that the goal of the consumer is to end up on the highest possible indifference curve. The first economist would conclude that at the consumer's optimum, the marginal utility per dollar is the same for all goods, whereas the second would conclude that the indifference curve is tangent to the budget constraint. In essence, these are two ways of saying the same thing. ◢

21-3b How Changes in Income Affect the Consumer's Choices

Now that we have seen how the consumer makes a consumption decision, let's examine how this decision responds to changes in the consumer's income. To be specific, suppose that income increases. With higher income, the consumer can afford more of both goods. The increase in income, therefore, shifts the budget constraint outward, as in Figure 7. Because the relative price of the two goods has not changed, the slope of the new budget constraint is the same as the slope of the initial budget constraint. That is, an increase in income leads to a parallel shift in the budget constraint.

The expanded budget constraint allows the consumer to choose a better combination of pizza and Pepsi, one that is on a higher indifference curve. Given the shift in the budget constraint and the consumer's preferences as represented by her indifference curves, the consumer's optimum moves from the point labeled "initial optimum" to the point labeled "new optimum."

Notice that, in Figure 7, the consumer chooses to consume more Pepsi and more pizza. The logic of the model does not require increased consumption of both goods in response to increased income, but this situation is the most common. As you may recall from Chapter 4, if a consumer wants more of a good when her income rises, economists call it a **normal good**. The indifference curves in Figure 7 are drawn under the assumption that both pizza and Pepsi are normal goods.

Figure 8 shows an example in which an increase in income induces the consumer to buy more pizza but less Pepsi. If a consumer buys less of a good when her income rises, economists call it an **inferior good**. Figure 8 is drawn under the assumption that pizza is a normal good and Pepsi is an inferior good.

Although most goods are normal goods, there are some inferior goods in the world. One example is bus rides. As income increases, consumers are more likely

normal good
a good for which an increase in income raises the quantity demanded

inferior good
a good for which an increase in income reduces the quantity demanded

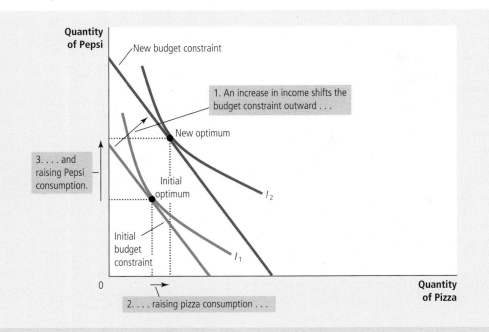

FIGURE 7

An Increase in Income
When the consumer's income rises, the budget constraint shifts outward. If both goods are normal goods, the consumer responds to the increase in income by buying more of both of them. Here the consumer buys more pizza and more Pepsi.

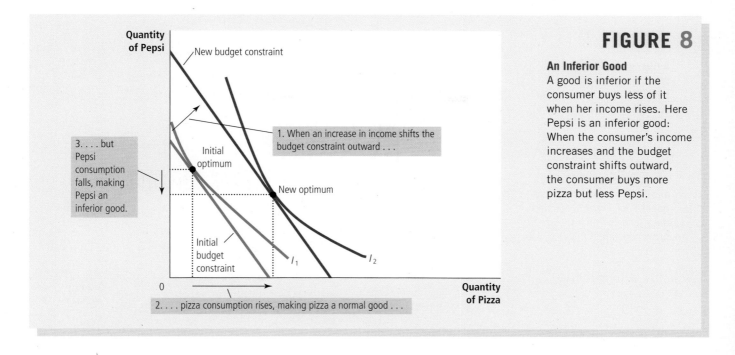

FIGURE 8

An Inferior Good
A good is inferior if the consumer buys less of it when her income rises. Here Pepsi is an inferior good: When the consumer's income increases and the budget constraint shifts outward, the consumer buys more pizza but less Pepsi.

to own cars or take taxis and less likely to ride the bus. Bus rides, therefore, are an inferior good.

21-3c How Changes in Prices Affect the Consumer's Choices

Let's now use this model of consumer choice to consider how a change in the price of one of the goods alters the consumer's choices. Suppose, in particular, that the price of Pepsi falls from $2 to $1 per liter. It is no surprise that the lower price expands the consumer's set of buying opportunities. In other words, a fall in the price of any good shifts the budget constraint outward.

Figure 9 considers more specifically how the fall in price affects the budget constraint. If the consumer spends her entire $1,000 income on pizza, then the price of Pepsi is irrelevant. Thus, point A in the figure stays the same. Yet if the consumer spends her entire income of $1,000 on Pepsi, she can now buy 1,000 rather than only 500 liters. Thus, the end point of the budget constraint moves from point B to point D.

Notice that in this case the outward shift in the budget constraint changes its slope. (This differs from what happened previously when prices stayed the same but the consumer's income changed.) As we have discussed, the slope of the budget constraint reflects the relative price of pizza and Pepsi. Because the price of Pepsi has fallen to $1 from $2, while the price of pizza has remained $10, the consumer can now trade a pizza for 10 rather than 5 liters of Pepsi. As a result, the new budget constraint has a steeper slope.

How such a change in the budget constraint alters the consumption of both goods depends on the consumer's preferences. For the indifference curves drawn in this figure, the consumer buys more Pepsi and less pizza.

FIGURE 9

A Change in Price
When the price of Pepsi falls, the consumer's budget constraint shifts outward and changes slope. The consumer moves from the initial optimum to the new optimum, which changes her purchases of both pizza and Pepsi. In this case, the quantity of Pepsi consumed rises, and the quantity of pizza consumed falls.

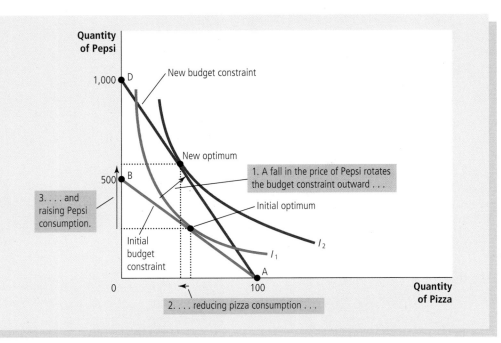

Quantity of Pepsi

1,000 ● D   New budget constraint

New optimum

500 ● B   1. A fall in the price of Pepsi rotates the budget constraint outward . . .

3. . . . and raising Pepsi consumption.

Initial optimum

Initial budget constraint

● A

I_1

I_2

0   ← 100   Quantity of Pizza

2. . . . reducing pizza consumption . . .

21-3d Income and Substitution Effects

income effect
the change in consumption that results when a price change moves the consumer to a higher or lower indifference curve

substitution effect
the change in consumption that results when a price change moves the consumer along a given indifference curve to a point with a new marginal rate of substitution

The impact of a change in the price of a good on consumption can be decomposed into two effects: an **income effect** and a **substitution effect**. To see what these two effects are, consider how our consumer might respond when she learns that the price of Pepsi has fallen. She might reason in the following ways:

- "Great news! Now that Pepsi is cheaper, my income has greater purchasing power. I am, in effect, richer than I was. Because I am richer, I can buy both more pizza and more Pepsi." (This is the income effect.)
- "Now that the price of Pepsi has fallen, I get more liters of Pepsi for every pizza that I give up. Because pizza is now relatively more expensive, I should buy less pizza and more Pepsi." (This is the substitution effect.)

Which statement do you find more compelling?

In fact, both of these statements make sense. The decrease in the price of Pepsi makes the consumer better off. If pizza and Pepsi are both normal goods, the consumer will want to spread this improvement in her purchasing power over both goods. This income effect tends to make the consumer buy more pizza and more Pepsi. Yet at the same time, consumption of Pepsi has become less expensive relative to consumption of pizza. This substitution effect tends to make the consumer choose less pizza and more Pepsi.

Now consider the result of these two effects working at the same time. The consumer certainly buys more Pepsi because the income and substitution effects both act to increase purchases of Pepsi. But it is ambiguous whether the consumer buys more pizza, because the income and substitution effects work in opposite directions. This conclusion is summarized in Table 1.

Good	Income Effect	Substitution Effect	Total Effect
Pepsi	Consumer is richer, so she buys more Pepsi.	Pepsi is relatively cheaper, so consumer buys more Pepsi.	Income and substitution effects act in the same direction, so consumer buys more Pepsi.
Pizza	Consumer is richer, so she buys more pizza.	Pizza is relatively more expensive, so consumer buys less pizza.	Income and substitution effects act in opposite directions, so the total effect on pizza consumption is ambiguous.

TABLE 1

Income and Substitution Effects When the Price of Pepsi Falls

We can interpret the income and substitution effects using indifference curves. *The income effect is the change in consumption that results from the movement to a higher indifference curve. The substitution effect is the change in consumption that results from being at a point on an indifference curve with a different marginal rate of substitution.*

Figure 10 shows graphically how to decompose the change in the consumer's decision into the income effect and the substitution effect. When the price of Pepsi falls, the consumer moves from the initial optimum, point A, to the new optimum, point C. We can view this change as occurring in two steps. First, the consumer moves *along* the initial indifference curve, I_1, from point A to point B. The consumer is equally happy at these two points, but at point B, the marginal

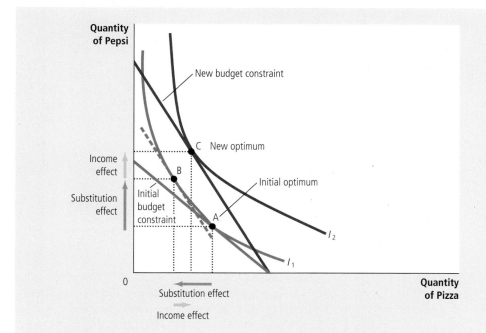

FIGURE 10

Income and Substitution Effects The effect of a change in price can be broken down into an income effect and a substitution effect. The substitution effect—the movement along an indifference curve to a point with a different marginal rate of substitution—is shown here as the change from point A to point B along indifference curve I_1. The income effect—the shift to a higher indifference curve—is shown here as the change from point B on indifference curve I_1 to point C on indifference curve I_2.

rate of substitution reflects the new relative price. (The dashed line through point B is parallel to the new budget constraint and thus reflects the new relative price.) Next, the consumer *shifts* to the higher indifference curve, I_2, by moving from point B to point C. Even though point B and point C are on different indifference curves, they have the same marginal rate of substitution. That is, the slope of the indifference curve I_1 at point B equals the slope of the indifference curve I_2 at point C.

The consumer never actually chooses point B, but this hypothetical point is useful to clarify the two effects that determine the consumer's decision. Notice that the change from point A to point B represents a pure change in the marginal rate of substitution without any change in the consumer's welfare. Similarly, the change from point B to point C represents a pure change in welfare without any change in the marginal rate of substitution. Thus, the movement from A to B shows the substitution effect, and the movement from B to C shows the income effect.

21-3e Deriving the Demand Curve

We have just seen how changes in the price of a good alter the consumer's budget constraint and, therefore, the quantities of the two goods that she chooses to buy. The demand curve for any good reflects these consumption decisions. Recall that a demand curve shows the quantity demanded of a good for any given price. We can view a consumer's demand curve as a summary of the optimal decisions that arise from her budget constraint and indifference curves.

For example, Figure 11 considers the demand for Pepsi. Panel (a) shows that when the price of a liter falls from $2 to $1, the consumer's budget constraint shifts outward. Because of both income and substitution effects, the consumer increases

FIGURE 11

Deriving the Demand Curve

Panel (a) shows that when the price of Pepsi falls from $2 to $1, the consumer's optimum moves from point A to point B, and the quantity of Pepsi consumed rises from 250 to 750 liters. The demand curve in panel (b) reflects this relationship between the price and the quantity demanded.

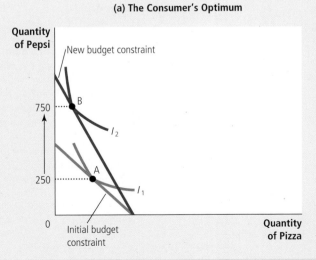

(a) The Consumer's Optimum

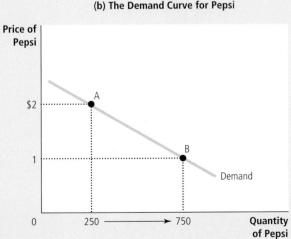

(b) The Demand Curve for Pepsi

her purchases of Pepsi from 250 to 750 liters. Panel (b) shows the demand curve that results from this consumer's decisions. In this way, the theory of consumer choice provides the theoretical foundation for the consumer's demand curve.

It may be comforting to know that the demand curve arises naturally from the theory of consumer choice, but this exercise by itself does not justify developing the theory. There is no need for a rigorous, analytic framework just to establish that people respond to changes in prices. The theory of consumer choice is, however, useful in studying various decisions that people make as they go about their lives, as we see in the next section.

Quick Quiz   *Draw a budget constraint and indifference curves for pizza and Pepsi. Show what happens to the budget constraint and the consumer's optimum when the price of pizza rises. In your diagram, decompose the change into an income effect and a substitution effect.*

21-4 Three Applications

Now that we have developed the basic theory of consumer choice, let's use it to shed light on three questions about how the economy works. These three questions might at first seem unrelated. But because each question involves household decision making, we can address it with the model of consumer behavior we have just developed.

21-4a Do All Demand Curves Slope Downward?

Normally, when the price of a good rises, people buy less of it. This usual behavior, called the *law of demand*, is reflected in the downward slope of the demand curve.

As a matter of economic theory, however, demand curves can sometimes slope upward. In other words, consumers can sometimes violate the law of demand and buy *more* of a good when the price rises. To see how this can happen, consider Figure 12. In this example, the consumer buys two goods—meat and potatoes. Initially, the consumer's budget constraint is the line from point A to point B. The optimum is point C. When the price of potatoes rises, the budget constraint shifts inward and is now the line from point A to point D. The optimum is now point E. Notice that a rise in the price of potatoes has led the consumer to buy a larger quantity of potatoes.

Why is the consumer responding in a seemingly perverse way? In this example, potatoes are a strongly inferior good. When the price of potatoes rises, the consumer is poorer. The income effect makes the consumer want to buy less meat and more potatoes. At the same time, because the potatoes have become more expensive relative to meat, the substitution effect makes the consumer want to buy more meat and fewer potatoes. In this particular case, however, the income effect is so strong that it exceeds the substitution effect. In the end, the consumer responds to the higher price of potatoes by buying less meat and more potatoes.

Economists use the term **Giffen good** to describe a good that violates the law of demand. (The term is named for economist Robert Giffen, who first noted this possibility.) In this example, potatoes are a Giffen good. Giffen goods are inferior goods for which the income effect dominates the substitution effect. Therefore, they have demand curves that slope upward.

Giffen good
a good for which an increase in the price raises the quantity demanded

FIGURE 12

A Giffen Good
In this example, when the price of potatoes rises, the consumer's optimum shifts from point C to point E. In this case, the consumer responds to a higher price of potatoes by buying less meat and more potatoes.

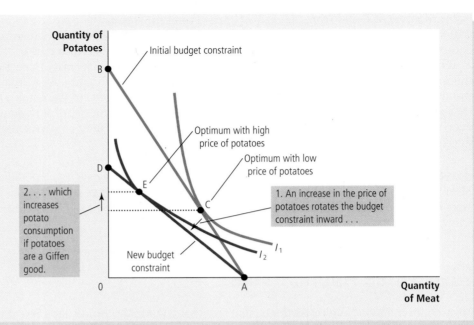

Quantity of Potatoes

Initial budget constraint

Optimum with high price of potatoes

Optimum with low price of potatoes

1. An increase in the price of potatoes rotates the budget constraint inward . . .

2. . . . which increases potato consumption if potatoes are a Giffen good.

New budget constraint

Quantity of Meat

<table>
<tr><td>case study</td><td></td></tr>
</table>

The Search for Giffen Goods

Have any actual Giffen goods ever been observed? Some historians suggest that potatoes were a Giffen good during the Irish potato famine of the 19th century. Potatoes were such a large part of people's diet that when the price of potatoes rose, it had a large income effect. People responded to their reduced living standard by cutting back on the luxury of meat and buying more of the staple food of potatoes. Thus, it is argued that a higher price of potatoes actually raised the quantity of potatoes demanded.

A recent study by Robert Jensen and Nolan Miller has produced similar but more concrete evidence for the existence of Giffen goods. These two economists conducted a field experiment for five months in the Chinese province of Hunan. They gave randomly selected households vouchers that subsidized the purchase of rice, a staple in local diets, and used surveys to measure how consumption of rice responded to changes in the price. They found strong evidence that poor households exhibited Giffen behavior. Lowering the price of rice with the subsidy voucher caused households to reduce their consumption of rice, and removing the subsidy had the opposite effect. Jensen and Miller wrote, "To the best of our knowledge, this is the first rigorous empirical evidence of Giffen behavior."

Thus, the theory of consumer choice allows demand curves to slope upward, and sometimes that strange phenomenon actually occurs. As a result, the law of demand we first saw in Chapter 4 is not completely reliable. It is safe to say, however, that Giffen goods are very rare.

21-4b How Do Wages Affect Labor Supply?

So far, we have used the theory of consumer choice to analyze how a person allocates income between two goods. We can use the same theory to analyze how a person allocates time. People spend some of their time enjoying leisure and some of it working so they can afford to buy consumption goods. The essence of the time-allocation problem is the trade-off between leisure and consumption.

Consider the decision facing Carrie, a freelance software designer. Carrie is awake for 100 hours per week. She spends some of this time enjoying leisure—riding her bike, watching television, and studying economics. She spends the rest of this time at her computer developing software. For every hour she works developing software, she earns $50, which she spends on consumption goods—food, clothing, and music downloads. Her wage ($50) reflects the trade-off Carrie faces between leisure and consumption. For every hour of leisure she gives up, she works one more hour and gets $50 of consumption.

Figure 13 shows Carrie's budget constraint. If she spends all 100 hours enjoying leisure, she has no consumption. If she spends all 100 hours working, she earns a weekly consumption of $5,000 but has no time for leisure. If she works a normal 40-hour week, she enjoys 60 hours of leisure and has weekly consumption of $2,000.

Figure 13 uses indifference curves to represent Carrie's preferences for consumption and leisure. Here consumption and leisure are the two "goods" between which Carrie is choosing. Because Carrie always prefers more leisure and more consumption, she prefers points on higher indifference curves to points on lower ones. At a wage of $50 per hour, Carrie chooses a combination of consumption and leisure represented by the point labeled "optimum." This is the point on the budget constraint that is on the highest possible indifference curve, I_2.

Now consider what happens when Carrie's wage increases from $50 to $60 per hour. Figure 14 shows two possible outcomes. In each case, the budget constraint, shown in the left graphs, shifts outward from BC_1 to BC_2. In the process, the budget constraint becomes steeper, reflecting the change in relative price: At the higher wage, Carrie earns more consumption for every hour of leisure that she gives up.

Carrie's preferences, as represented by her indifference curves, determine how her choice regarding consumption and leisure responds to the higher wage. In both panels, consumption rises. Yet the response of leisure to the change in the wage is different in the two cases. In panel (a), Carrie responds to the higher wage by enjoying less leisure. In panel (b), Carrie responds by enjoying more leisure.

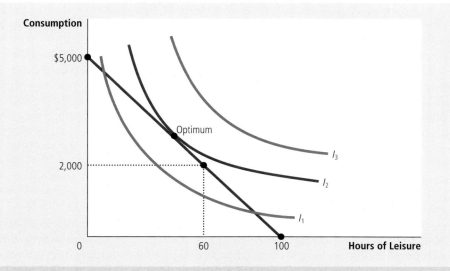

FIGURE 13

The Work-Leisure Decision
This figure shows Carrie's budget constraint for deciding how much to work, her indifference curves for consumption and leisure, and her optimum.

FIGURE 14

An Increase in the Wage

The two panels of this figure show how a person might respond to an increase in the wage. The graphs on the left show the consumer's initial budget constraint, BC_1, and new budget constraint, BC_2, as well as the consumer's optimal choices over consumption and leisure. The graphs on the right show the resulting labor-supply curve. Because hours worked equal total hours available minus hours of leisure, any change in leisure implies an opposite change in the quantity of labor supplied. In panel (a), when the wage rises, consumption rises and leisure falls, resulting in a labor-supply curve that slopes upward. In panel (b), when the wage rises, both consumption and leisure rise, resulting in a labor-supply curve that slopes backward.

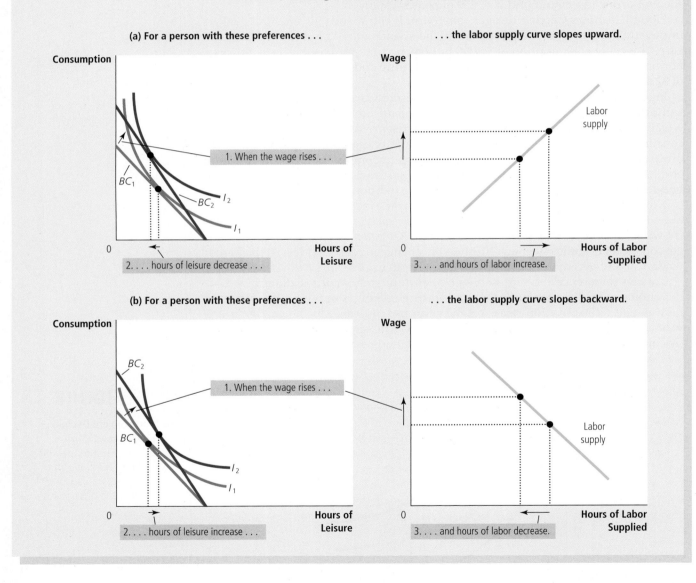

(a) For a person with these preferences . . .

. . . the labor supply curve slopes upward.

Consumption

Wage

Labor supply

BC_1

1. When the wage rises . . .

BC_2 I_2

I_1

0   Hours of Leisure

2. . . . hours of leisure decrease . . .

0   Hours of Labor Supplied

3. . . . and hours of labor increase.

(b) For a person with these preferences . . .

. . . the labor supply curve slopes backward.

Consumption

Wage

BC_2

1. When the wage rises . . .

BC_1

I_2

I_1

Labor supply

0   Hours of Leisure

2. . . . hours of leisure increase . . .

0   Hours of Labor Supplied

3. . . . and hours of labor decrease.

Carrie's decision between leisure and consumption determines her supply of labor because the more leisure she enjoys, the less time she has left to work. In each panel of Figure 14, the right graph shows the labor-supply curve implied by Carrie's decision. In panel (a), a higher wage induces Carrie to enjoy less leisure and work more, so the labor-supply curve slopes upward. In panel (b), a higher wage induces Carrie to enjoy more leisure and work less, so the labor-supply curve slopes "backward."

At first, the backward-sloping labor-supply curve is puzzling. Why would a person respond to a higher wage by working less? The answer comes from considering the income and substitution effects of a higher wage.

Consider first the substitution effect. When Carrie's wage rises, leisure becomes more costly relative to consumption, and this encourages Carrie to substitute away from leisure and toward consumption. In other words, the substitution effect induces Carrie to work more in response to higher wages, which tends to make the labor-supply curve slope upward.

Now consider the income effect. When Carrie's wage rises, she moves to a higher indifference curve. She is now better off than she was. As long as consumption and leisure are both normal goods, she tends to want to use this increase in well-being to enjoy both higher consumption and greater leisure. In other words, the income effect induces her to work less, which tends to make the labor-supply curve slope backward.

In the end, economic theory does not give a clear prediction about whether an increase in the wage induces Carrie to work more or less. If the substitution effect is greater than the income effect for Carrie, she works more. If the income effect is greater than the substitution effect, she works less. The labor-supply curve, therefore, could be either upward or backward sloping.

<table>
<tr><td>case
study</td><td>**Income Effects on Labor Supply: Historical Trends, Lottery Winners,
and the Carnegie Conjecture**</td></tr>
</table>

The idea of a backward-sloping labor-supply curve might at first seem like a mere theoretical curiosity, but in fact it is not. Evidence indicates that the labor-supply curve, considered over long periods, does in fact slope backward. A hundred years ago, many people worked six days a week. Today, five-day workweeks are the norm. At the same time that the length of the workweek has been falling, the wage of the typical worker (adjusted for inflation) has been rising.

Here is how economists explain this historical pattern: Over time, advances in technology raise workers' productivity and, thereby, the demand for labor. This increase in labor demand raises equilibrium wages. As wages rise, so does the reward for working. Yet rather than responding to this increased incentive by working more, most workers choose to take part of their greater prosperity in the form of more leisure. In other words, the income effect of higher wages dominates the substitution effect.

Further evidence that the income effect on labor supply is strong comes from a very different kind of data: winners of lotteries. Winners of large prizes in the lottery see large increases in their incomes and, as a result, large outward shifts in their budget constraints. Because the winners' wages have not changed, however, the *slopes* of their budget constraints remain the same. There is, therefore, no substitution effect. By examining the behavior of lottery winners, we can isolate the income effect on labor supply.

The results from studies of lottery winners are striking. Of those winners who win more than $50,000, almost 25 percent quit working within a year and another 9 percent reduce the number of hours they work. Of those winners who win more than $1 million, almost 40 percent stop working. The income effect on labor supply of winning such a large prize is substantial.

"No more 9 to 5 for me."

Similar results were found in a 1993 study, published in the *Quarterly Journal of Economics,* of how receiving a bequest affects a person's labor supply. The study found that a single person who inherits more than $150,000 is four times as likely to stop working as a single person who inherits less than $25,000. This finding would not have surprised the 19th-century industrialist Andrew Carnegie. Carnegie warned that "the parent who leaves his son enormous wealth generally deadens the talents and energies of the son, and tempts him to lead a less useful and less worthy life than he otherwise would." That is, Carnegie viewed the income effect on labor supply to be substantial and, from his paternalistic perspective, regrettable. During his life and at his death, Carnegie gave much of his vast fortune to charity. ◢

21-4c How Do Interest Rates Affect Household Saving?

An important decision that every person faces is how much income to consume today and how much to save for the future. We can use the theory of consumer choice to analyze how people make this decision and how the amount they save depends on the interest rate their savings will earn.

Consider the decision facing Saul, a worker planning for retirement. To keep things simple, let's divide Saul's life into two periods. In the first period, Saul is young and working. In the second period, he is old and retired. When young, Saul earns $100,000. He divides this income between current consumption and saving. When he is old, Saul will consume what he has saved, including the interest that his savings have earned.

Suppose the interest rate is 10 percent. Then for every dollar that Saul saves when young, he can consume $1.10 when old. We can view "consumption when young" and "consumption when old" as the two goods that Saul must choose between. The interest rate determines the relative price of these two goods.

Figure 15 shows Saul's budget constraint. If he saves nothing, he consumes $100,000 when young and nothing when old. If he saves everything, he

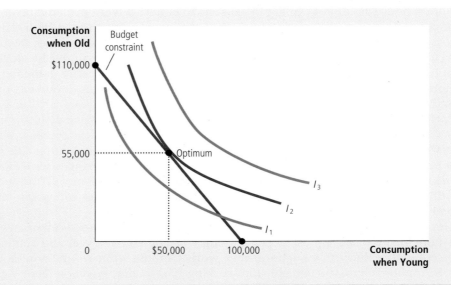

FIGURE 15

The Consumption–Saving Decision
This figure shows the budget constraint for a person deciding how much to consume in the two periods of his life, the indifference curves representing his preferences, and the optimum.

consumes nothing when young and $110,000 when old. The budget constraint shows these and all the intermediate possibilities.

Figure 15 uses indifference curves to represent Saul's preferences for consumption in the two periods. Because Saul prefers more consumption in both periods, he prefers points on higher indifference curves to points on lower ones. Given his preferences, Saul chooses the optimal combination of consumption in both periods of life, which is the point on the budget constraint that is on the highest possible indifference curve. At this optimum, Saul consumes $50,000 when young and $55,000 when old.

Now consider what happens when the interest rate increases from 10 percent to 20 percent. Figure 16 shows two possible outcomes. In both cases, the budget constraint shifts outward and becomes steeper. At the new, higher interest rate, Saul gets more consumption when old for every dollar of consumption that he gives up when young.

The two panels show the results given different preferences by Saul. In both cases, consumption when old rises. Yet the response of consumption when young to the change in the interest rate is different in the two cases. In panel (a), Saul responds to the higher interest rate by consuming less when young. In panel (b), Saul responds by consuming more when young.

Saul's saving is his income when young minus the amount he consumes when young. In panel (a), an increase in the interest rate reduces consumption when young, so saving must rise. In panel (b), an increase in the interest rate induces Saul to consume more when young, so saving must fall.

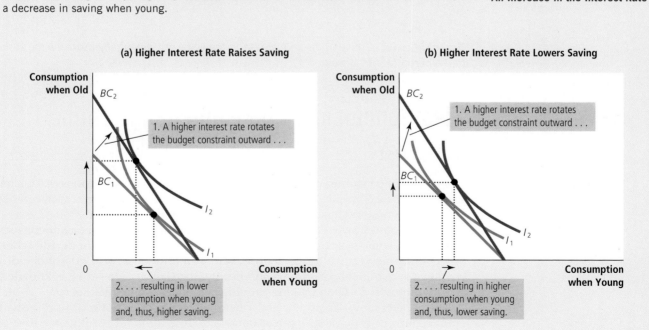

In both panels, an increase in the interest rate shifts the budget constraint outward. In panel (a), consumption when young falls, and consumption when old rises. The result is an increase in saving when young. In panel (b), consumption in both periods rises. The result is a decrease in saving when young.

FIGURE 16

An Increase in the Interest Rate

(a) Higher Interest Rate Raises Saving

Consumption when Old

BC_2

1. A higher interest rate rotates the budget constraint outward . . .

BC_1

I_2

I_1

0

Consumption when Young

2. . . . resulting in lower consumption when young and, thus, higher saving.

(b) Higher Interest Rate Lowers Saving

Consumption when Old

BC_2

1. A higher interest rate rotates the budget constraint outward . . .

BC_1

I_2

I_1

0

Consumption when Young

2. . . . resulting in higher consumption when young and, thus, lower saving.

The case shown in panel (b) might at first seem odd: Saul responds to an increase in the return to saving by saving less. Yet this behavior is not as peculiar as it might seem. We can understand it by considering the income and substitution effects of a higher interest rate.

Consider first the substitution effect. When the interest rate rises, consumption when old becomes less costly relative to consumption when young. Therefore, the substitution effect induces Saul to consume more when old and less when young. In other words, the substitution effect induces Saul to save more.

Now consider the income effect. When the interest rate rises, Saul moves to a higher indifference curve. He is now better off than he was. As long as consumption in both periods consists of normal goods, he tends to want to use this increase in well-being to enjoy higher consumption in both periods. In other words, the income effect induces him to save less.

The result depends on both the income and substitution effects. If the substitution effect of a higher interest rate is greater than the income effect, Saul saves more. If the income effect is greater than the substitution effect, Saul saves less. Thus, the theory of consumer choice says that an increase in the interest rate could either encourage or discourage saving.

This ambiguous result is interesting from the standpoint of economic theory, but it is disappointing from the standpoint of economic policy. It turns out that an important issue in tax policy hinges in part on how saving responds to interest rates. Some economists have advocated reducing the taxation of interest and other capital income. They argue that such a policy change would raise the after-tax interest rate that savers can earn and thereby encourage people to save more. Other economists have argued that because of offsetting income and substitution effects, such a tax change might not increase saving and could even reduce it. Unfortunately, research has not led to a consensus about how interest rates affect saving. As a result, there remains disagreement among economists about whether changes in tax policy aimed to encourage saving would, in fact, have the intended effect.

Quick Quiz   *Explain how an increase in the wage can potentially decrease the amount that a person wants to work.*

21-5 Conclusion: Do People Really Think This Way?

The theory of consumer choice describes how people make decisions. As we have seen, it has broad applicability. It can explain how a person chooses between pizza and Pepsi, work and leisure, consumption and saving, and so on.

At this point, however, you might be tempted to treat the theory of consumer choice with some skepticism. After all, you are a consumer. You decide what to buy every time you walk into a store. And you know that you do not decide by writing down budget constraints and indifference curves. Doesn't this knowledge about your own decision making provide evidence against the theory?

The answer is no. The theory of consumer choice does not try to present a literal account of how people make decisions. It is a model. And as we first discussed in Chapter 2, models are not intended to be completely realistic.

The best way to view the theory of consumer choice is as a metaphor for how consumers make decisions. No consumer (except an occasional economist) goes through the explicit optimization envisioned in the theory. Yet consumers are aware that their choices are constrained by their financial resources. And given those constraints, they do the best they can to achieve the highest level of satisfaction. The theory of consumer choice tries to describe this implicit, psychological process in a way that permits explicit, economic analysis.

Just as the proof of the pudding is in the eating, the test of a theory is in its applications. In the last section of this chapter, we applied the theory of consumer choice to three practical issues about the economy. If you take more advanced courses in economics, you will see that this theory provides the framework for much additional analysis.

Summary

- A consumer's budget constraint shows the possible combinations of different goods she can buy given her income and the prices of the goods. The slope of the budget constraint equals the relative price of the goods.

- The consumer's indifference curves represent her preferences. An indifference curve shows the various bundles of goods that make the consumer equally happy. Points on higher indifference curves are preferred to points on lower indifference curves. The slope of an indifference curve at any point is the consumer's marginal rate of substitution—the rate at which the consumer is willing to trade one good for the other.

- The consumer optimizes by choosing the point on her budget constraint that lies on the highest indifference curve. At this point, the slope of the indifference curve (the marginal rate of substitution between the goods) equals the slope of the budget constraint (the relative price of the goods), and the consumer's valuation of the two goods (measured by the marginal rate of substitution) equals the market's valuation (measured by the relative price).

- When the price of a good falls, the impact on the consumer's choices can be broken down into an income effect and a substitution effect. The income effect is the change in consumption that arises because a lower price makes the consumer better off. The substitution effect is the change in consumption that arises because a price change encourages greater consumption of the good that has become relatively cheaper. The income effect is reflected in the movement from a lower to a higher indifference curve, whereas the substitution effect is reflected by a movement along an indifference curve to a point with a different slope.

- The theory of consumer choice can be applied in many situations. It explains why demand curves can potentially slope upward, why higher wages could either increase or decrease the quantity of labor supplied, and why higher interest rates could either increase or decrease saving.

Key Concepts

budget constraint, *p. 436*
indifference curve, *p. 438*
marginal rate of substitution, *p. 438*
perfect substitutes, *p. 441*

perfect complements, *p. 441*
normal good, *p. 444*
inferior good, *p. 444*
income effect, *p. 446*

substitution effect, *p. 446*
Giffen good, *p. 449*

Questions for Review

1. A consumer has income of $3,000. Wine costs $3 per glass, and cheese costs $6 per pound. Draw the consumer's budget constraint with wine on the vertical axis. What is the slope of this budget constraint?

2. Draw a consumer's indifference curves for wine and cheese. Describe and explain four properties of these indifference curves.

3. Pick a point on an indifference curve for wine and cheese and show the marginal rate of substitution. What does the marginal rate of substitution tell us?

4. Show a consumer's budget constraint and indifference curves for wine and cheese. Show the optimal consumption choice. If the price of wine is $3 per glass and the price of cheese is $6 per pound, what is the marginal rate of substitution at this optimum?

5. A person who consumes wine and cheese gets a raise, so her income increases from $3,000 to $4,000. Show what happens if both wine and cheese are normal goods. Now show what happens if cheese is an inferior good.

6. The price of cheese rises from $6 to $10 per pound, while the price of wine remains $3 per glass. For a consumer with a constant income of $3,000, show what happens to consumption of wine and cheese. Decompose the change into income and substitution effects.

7. Can an increase in the price of cheese possibly induce a consumer to buy more cheese? Explain.

Quick Check Multiple Choice

1. Emilio buys pizza for $10 and soda for $2. He has income of $100. His budget constraint will experience a parallel outward shift if which of the following events occur?
   a. The price of pizza falls to $5, the price of soda falls to $1, and his income falls to $50.
   b. The price of pizza rises to $20, the price of soda rises to $4, and his income remains the same.
   c. The price of pizza falls to $8, the price of soda falls to $1, and his income rises to $120.
   d. The price of pizza rises to $20, the price of soda rises to $4, and his income rises to $400.

2. At any point on an indifference curve, the slope of the curve measures the consumer's
   a. income.
   b. willingness to trade one good for the other.
   c. perception of the two goods as substitutes or complements.
   d. elasticity of demand.

3. Matthew and Susan are both optimizing consumers in the markets for shirts and hats, where they pay $100 for a shirt and $50 for hat. Matthew buys 4 shirts and 16 hats, while Susan buys 6 shirts and 12 hats. From this information, we can infer that Matthew's marginal rate of substitution is _____ hats per shirt, while Susan's is _____.
   a. 2, 1
   b. 2, 2
   c. 4, 1
   d. 4, 2

4. Charlie buys only milk and cereal. Milk is a normal good, while cereal is an inferior good. When the price of milk rises, Charlie buys
   a. less of both goods.
   b. more milk and less cereal.
   c. less milk and more cereal.
   d. less milk, but the impact on cereal is ambiguous.

5. If the price of pasta increases and a consumer buys more pasta, we can infer that
   a. pasta is a normal good, and the income effect is greater than the substitution effect.
   b. pasta is a normal good, and the substitution effect is greater than the income effect.
   c. pasta is an inferior good, and the income effect is greater than the substitution effect.
   d. pasta is an inferior good, and the substitution effect is greater than the income effect.

6. The labor-supply curve slopes upward if
   a. leisure is a normal good.
   b. consumption is a normal good.
   c. the income effect on leisure is greater than the substitution effect.
   d. the substitution effect on leisure is greater than the income effect.

Problems and Applications

1. Jennifer divides her income between coffee and croissants (both of which are normal goods). An early frost in Brazil causes a large increase in the price of coffee in the United States.
   a. Show the effect of the frost on Jennifer's budget constraint.
   b. Show the effect of the frost on Jennifer's optimal consumption bundle assuming that the substitution effect outweighs the income effect for croissants.
   c. Show the effect of the frost on Jennifer's optimal consumption bundle assuming that the income effect outweighs the substitution effect for croissants.

2. Compare the following two pairs of goods:
   - Coke and Pepsi
   - Skis and ski bindings
   a. In which case are the two goods complements? In which case are they substitutes?
   b. In which case do you expect the indifference curves to be fairly straight? In which case do you expect the indifference curves to be very bowed?
   c. In which case will the consumer respond more to a change in the relative price of the two goods?

3. You consume only soda and pizza. One day, the price of soda goes up, the price of pizza goes down, and you are just as happy as you were before the price changes.
   a. Illustrate this situation on a graph.
   b. How does your consumption of the two goods change? How does your response depend on income and substitution effects?
   c. Can you afford the bundle of soda and pizza you consumed before the price changes?

4. Mario consumes only cheese and crackers.
   a. Could cheese and crackers both be inferior goods for Mario? Explain.
   b. Suppose that cheese is a normal good for Mario while crackers are an inferior good. If the price of cheese falls, what happens to Mario's consumption of crackers? What happens to his consumption of cheese? Explain.

5. Jim buys only milk and cookies.
   a. In year 1, Jim earns $100, milk costs $2 per quart, and cookies cost $4 per dozen. Draw Jim's budget constraint.
   b. Now suppose that all prices increase by 10 percent in year 2 and that Jim's salary increases by 10 percent as well. Draw Jim's new budget constraint. How would Jim's optimal combination of milk and cookies in year 2 compare to his optimal combination in year 1?

6. State whether each of the following statements is true or false. Explain your answers.
   a. "All Giffen goods are inferior goods."
   b. "All inferior goods are Giffen goods."

7. A college student has two options for meals: eating at the dining hall for $6 per meal, or eating a Cup O' Soup for $1.50 per meal. Her weekly food budget is $60.
   a. Draw the budget constraint showing the trade-off between dining hall meals and Cups O' Soup. Assuming that she spends equal amounts on both goods, draw an indifference curve showing the optimum choice. Label the optimum as point A.
   b. Suppose the price of a Cup O' Soup now rises to $2. Using your diagram from part (a), show the consequences of this change in price. Assume that our student now spends only 30 percent of her income on dining hall meals. Label the new optimum as point B.
   c. What happened to the quantity of Cups O' Soup consumed as a result of this price change? What does this result say about the income and substitution effects? Explain.
   d. Use points A and B to draw a demand curve for Cup O' Soup. What is this type of good called?

8. Consider your decision about how many hours to work.
   a. Draw your budget constraint assuming that you pay no taxes on your income. On the same diagram, draw another budget constraint assuming that you pay 15 percent tax.
   b. Show how the tax might lead to more hours of work, fewer hours, or the same number of hours. Explain.

9. Sarah is awake for 100 hours per week. Using one diagram, show Sarah's budget constraints if she earns $6 per hour, $8 per hour, and $10 per hour. Now draw indifference curves such that Sarah's labor-supply curve is upward sloping when the wage is between $6 and $8 per hour, and backward sloping when the wage is between $8 and $10 per hour.

10. Draw the indifference curve for someone deciding how to allocate time between work and leisure. Suppose the wage increases. Is it possible that the person's consumption would fall? Is this plausible? Discuss. (*Hint*: Think about income and substitution effects.)

11. Consider a couple's decision about how many children to have. Assume that over a lifetime a couple has 200,000 hours of time to either work or raise children. The wage is $10 per hour. Raising a child takes 20,000 hours of time.
   a. Draw the budget constraint showing the trade-off between lifetime consumption and the number of children. (Ignore the fact that children come only in whole numbers!) Show indifference curves and an optimum choice.
   b. Suppose the wage increases to $12 per hour. Show how the budget constraint shifts. Using income and substitution effects, discuss the impact of the change on the number of children and lifetime consumption.
   c. We observe that, as societies get richer and wages rise, people typically have fewer children. Is this fact consistent with this model? Explain.

12. Economist George Stigler once wrote that, according to consumer theory, "if consumers do not buy less of a commodity when their incomes rise, they will surely buy less when the price of the commodity rises." Explain this statement using the concepts of income and substitution effects.

13. Five consumers have the following marginal utility of apples and pears:

	Marginal Utility of Apples	Marginal Utility of Pears
Claire	6	12
Phil	6	6
Haley	6	3
Alex	3	6
Luke	3	12

The price of an apple is $1, and the price of a pear is $2. Which, if any, of these consumers are optimizing over their choice of fruit? For those who are not, how should they change their spending?

Go to CengageBrain.com to purchase access to the proven, critical Study Guide to accompany this text, which features additional notes and context, practice tests, and much more.

Frontiers of
Microeconomics

Economics is a study of the choices that people make and the resulting interactions they have with one another. This study has many facets, as we have seen in the preceding chapters. Yet it would be a mistake to think that all the facets we have seen make up a finished jewel, perfect and unchanging. Like all scientists, economists are always on the lookout for new areas to study and new phenomena to explain. This final chapter on microeconomics offers an assortment of three topics at the discipline's frontier to show how economists are trying to expand their understanding of human behavior and society.

The first topic is the economics of *asymmetric information*. In many different situations, some people are better informed than others, and the imbalance in information affects the choices they make and how they deal with one another. Thinking about this asymmetry can shed light on many aspects of the world, from the market for used cars to the custom of gift giving.

The second topic we examine in this chapter is *political economy*. Throughout this book, we have seen many examples in which markets fail and government policy can potentially improve matters. But "potentially" is a necessary qualifier: Whether this potential is realized depends on how well our political institutions work. The field of political economy uses the tools of economics to understand the functioning of government.

The third topic in this chapter is *behavioral economics*. This field brings some of the insights from psychology into the study of economic issues. It offers a view of human behavior that is more subtle and complex than the one found in conventional economic theory, a view that may be more realistic.

This chapter covers a lot of ground. To do so, it offers not full helpings of these three topics but, instead, a taste of each. One goal of this chapter is to show a few of the directions economists are heading in their effort to expand knowledge of how the economy works. Another is to whet your appetite for more courses in economics.

22-1 Asymmetric Information

"I know something you don't know." This statement is a common taunt among children, but it also conveys a deep truth about how people sometimes interact with one another. Many times in life, one person knows more about what is going on than another. A difference in access to knowledge that is relevant to an interaction is called an *information asymmetry*.

Examples abound. A worker knows more than his employer about how much effort he puts into his job. A seller of a used car knows more than the buyer about the car's condition. The first is an example of a *hidden action,* whereas the second is an example of a *hidden characteristic*. In each case, the uninformed party (the employer, the car buyer) would like to know the relevant information, but the informed party (the worker, the car seller) may have an incentive to conceal it.

Because asymmetric information is so prevalent, economists have devoted much effort in recent decades to studying its effects. Let's discuss some of the insights that this study has revealed.

22-1a Hidden Actions: Principals, Agents, and Moral Hazard

moral hazard
the tendency of a person who is imperfectly monitored to engage in dishonest or otherwise undesirable behavior

agent
a person who is performing an act for another person, called the principal

principal
a person for whom another person, called the agent, is performing some act

Moral hazard is a problem that arises when one person, called the **agent**, is performing some task on behalf of another person, called the **principal**. If the principal cannot perfectly monitor the agent's behavior, the agent tends to undertake less effort than the principal considers desirable. The phrase *moral hazard* refers to the risk, or "hazard," of inappropriate or otherwise "immoral" behavior by the agent. In such a situation, the principal tries various ways to encourage the agent to act more responsibly.

The employment relationship is the classic example. The employer is the principal, and the worker is the agent. The moral-hazard problem is the temptation of imperfectly monitored workers to shirk their responsibilities. Employers can respond to this problem in various ways:

- *Better monitoring.* Employers may plant hidden video cameras to record workers' behavior. The aim is to catch irresponsible actions that might occur when supervisors are absent.

- *High wages.* According to *efficiency-wage theories* (discussed in Chapter 19), some employers may choose to pay their workers a wage above the level that balances supply and demand in the labor market. A worker who earns an above-equilibrium wage is less likely to shirk because if he is caught and fired, he might not be able to find another high-paying job.

- *Delayed payment.* Firms can delay part of a worker's compensation, so if the worker is caught shirking and is fired, he suffers a larger penalty. One example of delayed compensation is the year-end bonus. Similarly, a firm may choose to pay its workers more later in their lives. Thus, the wage increases that workers get as they age may reflect not just the benefits of experience but also a response to moral hazard.

Employers can use any combination of these various mechanisms to reduce the problem of moral hazard.

There are also many examples of moral hazard beyond the workplace. A homeowner with fire insurance will likely buy too few fire extinguishers

FYI

Corporate Management

Much production in the modern economy takes place within corporations. Like other firms, corporations buy inputs in markets for the factors of production and sell their output in markets for goods and services. Also like other firms, they are guided in their decisions by the objective of profit maximization. But a large corporation has to deal with some issues that do not arise in, say, a small family-owned business.

What is distinctive about a corporation? From a legal standpoint, a corporation is an organization that is granted a charter recognizing it as a separate legal entity, with its own rights and responsibilities distinct from those of its owners and employees. From an economic standpoint, the most important feature of the corporate form of organization is the separation of ownership and control. One group of people, called the shareholders, own the corporation and share in its profits. Another group of people, called the managers, are employed by the corporation to make decisions about how to deploy the corporation's resources.

The separation of ownership and control creates a principal-agent problem. In this case, the shareholders are the principals and the managers are the agents. The chief executive officer and other managers, who are in the best position to know the available business opportunities, are charged with the task of maximizing profits for the shareholders. But ensuring that they carry out this task is not always easy. The managers may have goals of their own, such as taking life easy, having a plush office and a private jet, throwing lavish parties, or presiding over a large business empire. The managers' goals may not always coincide with the shareholders' goal of profit maximization.

The corporation's board of directors is responsible for hiring and firing the top management. The board monitors the managers' performance, and it designs their compensation packages. These packages often include incentives aimed at aligning the interests of shareholders with the interests of management. Managers might be given bonuses based on performance or options to buy the company's stock, which are more valuable if the company performs well.

Note, however, that the directors are themselves agents of the shareholders. The existence of a board overseeing management only shifts the principal-agent problem. The issue then becomes how to ensure that the board of directors fulfills its own legal obligation of acting in the best interest of the shareholders. If the directors become too friendly with management, they may not provide the required oversight.

The corporation's principal-agent problem became big news around 2005. The top managers of several prominent companies, such as Enron, Tyco, and WorldCom, were found to be engaging in activities that enriched themselves at the expense of their shareholders. In these cases, the actions were so extreme as to be criminal, and the corporate managers were not just fired but also sent to prison. Some shareholders sued directors for failing to monitor management sufficiently.

Fortunately, criminal activity by corporate managers is rare. But in some ways, it is only the tip of the iceberg. Whenever ownership and control are separated, as they are in most large corporations, there is an inevitable tension between the interests of shareholders and the interests of management.

because the homeowner bears the cost of the extinguisher while the insurance company receives much of the benefit. A family may live near a river with a high risk of flooding because the family enjoys the scenic views, while the government bears the cost of disaster relief after a flood. Many regulations are aimed at addressing the problem: An insurance company may require homeowners to buy fire extinguishers, and the government may prohibit building homes on land with high risk of flooding. But the insurance company does not have perfect information about how cautious homeowners are, and the government does not have perfect information about the risk that families undertake when choosing where to live. As a result, the problem of moral hazard persists.

22-1b Hidden Characteristics: Adverse Selection and the Lemons Problem

adverse selection

the tendency for the mix of unobserved attributes to become undesirable from the standpoint of an uninformed party

Adverse selection is a problem that arises in markets in which the seller knows more about the attributes of the good being sold than the buyer does. In such a situation, the buyer runs the risk of being sold a good of low quality. That is, the "selection" of goods sold may be "adverse" from the standpoint of the uninformed buyer.

The classic example of adverse selection is the market for used cars. Sellers of used cars know their vehicles' defects while buyers often do not. Because owners of the worst cars are more likely to sell them than are the owners of the best cars, buyers are apprehensive about getting a "lemon." As a result, many people avoid buying vehicles in the used car market. This lemons problem can explain why a used car only a few weeks old sells for thousands of dollars less than a new car of the same type. A buyer of the used car might surmise that the seller is getting rid of the car quickly because the seller knows something about it that the buyer does not.

A second example of adverse selection occurs in the labor market. According to another efficiency-wage theory, workers vary in their abilities, and they may know their own abilities better than do the firms that hire them. When a firm cuts the wage it pays, the more talented workers are more likely to quit, knowing they are better able to find other employment. Conversely, a firm may choose to pay an above-equilibrium wage to attract a better mix of workers.

A third example of adverse selection occurs in markets for insurance. For example, buyers of health insurance know more about their own health problems than do insurance companies. Because people with greater hidden health problems are more likely to buy health insurance than are other people, the price of health insurance reflects the costs of a sicker-than-average person. As a result, people in average health may observe the high price of insurance and decide not to buy it.

When markets suffer from adverse selection, the invisible hand does not necessarily work its magic. In the used car market, owners of good cars may choose to keep them rather than sell them at the low price that skeptical buyers are willing to pay. In the labor market, wages may be stuck above the level that balances supply and demand, resulting in unemployment. In insurance markets, buyers with low risk may choose to remain uninsured because the policies they are offered fail to reflect their true characteristics. Advocates of government-provided health insurance sometimes point to the problem of adverse selection as one reason not to trust the private market to provide the right amount of health insurance on its own.

22-1c Signaling to Convey Private Information

Although asymmetric information is sometimes a motivation for public policy, it also motivates some individual behavior that otherwise might be hard to explain. Markets respond to problems of asymmetric information in many ways. One of them is **signaling**, which refers to actions taken by an informed party for the sole purpose of credibly revealing his private information.

We have seen examples of signaling in previous chapters. As we saw in Chapter 16, firms may spend money on advertising to signal to potential customers that they have high-quality products. As we saw in Chapter 20, students may earn college degrees merely to signal to potential employers that they are high-ability individuals, rather than to increase their productivity. These two examples of signaling (advertising, education) may seem very different, but below the surface, they are much the same: In both cases, the informed party (the firm, the student) uses the signal to convince the uninformed party (the customer, the employer) that the informed party is offering something of high quality.

What does it take for an action to be an effective signal? Obviously, it must be costly. If a signal were free, everyone would use it and it would convey no information. For the same reason, there is another requirement: The signal must be less costly, or more beneficial, to the person with the higher-quality product. Otherwise, everyone would have the same incentive to use the signal and the signal would reveal nothing.

Consider again our two examples. In the advertising case, a firm with a good product reaps a larger benefit from advertising because customers who try the product once are more likely to become repeat customers. Thus, it is rational for the firm with a good product to pay for the cost of the signal (advertising), and it is rational for the customer to use the signal as a piece of information about the product's quality. In the education case, a talented person can get through school more easily than a less talented one. Thus, it is rational for the talented person to pay for the cost of the signal (education), and it is rational for the employer to use the signal as a piece of information about the person's talent.

The world is replete with instances of signaling. Magazine ads sometimes include the phrase "as seen on TV." Why does a firm selling a product in a magazine choose to stress this fact? One possibility is that the firm is trying to convey its willingness to pay for an expensive signal (a spot on television) in the hope that you will infer that its product is of high quality. For the same reason, graduates of elite schools are always sure to put that fact on their résumés.

signaling
an action taken by an informed party to reveal private information to an uninformed party

---

case study **Gifts as Signals**

A man is debating what to give his girlfriend for her birthday. "I know," he says to himself, "I'll give her cash. After all, I don't know her tastes as well as she does, and with cash, she can buy anything she wants."

But when he hands her the money, she is offended. Convinced he doesn't really love her, she breaks off the relationship.

What's the economics behind this story?

In some ways, gift giving is a strange custom. As the man in our story suggests, people typically know their own preferences better than others do, so we might expect everyone to prefer cash to in-kind transfers. If your employer substituted merchandise of his choosing for your paycheck, you would likely object to this

"Now we'll see how much he loves me."

means of payment. But your reaction is very different when someone who (you hope) loves you does the same thing.

One interpretation of gift giving is that it reflects asymmetric information and signaling. The man in our story has private information that the girlfriend would like to know: Does he really love her? Choosing a good gift for her is a signal of his love. Certainly, the act of picking out a gift, rather than giving cash, has the right characteristics to be a signal. It is costly (it takes time), and its cost depends on private information (how much he loves her). If he really loves her, choosing a good gift is easy because he is thinking about her all the time. If he doesn't love her, finding the right gift is more difficult. Thus, giving a gift that suits the girlfriend is one way for him to convey the private information of his love for her. Giving cash shows that he isn't even bothering to try.

The signaling theory of gift giving is consistent with another observation: People care most about the custom when the strength of affection is most in question. Thus, giving cash to a girlfriend or boyfriend is usually a bad move. But when college students receive a check from their parents, they are less often offended. The parents' love is less likely to be in doubt, so the recipient probably won't interpret the cash gift as a signal of lack of affection. ◢

22-1d Screening to Uncover Private Information

When an informed party takes actions to reveal private information, the phenomenon is called signaling. When an uninformed party takes actions to induce the informed party to reveal private information, the phenomenon is called **screening**.

screening
an action taken by an uninformed party to induce an informed party to reveal information

Some screening is common sense. A person buying a used car may ask that it be checked by an auto mechanic before the sale. A seller who refuses this request reveals his private information that the car is a lemon. The buyer may decide to offer a lower price or to look for another car.

Other examples of screening are more subtle. For example, consider a firm that sells car insurance. The firm would like to charge a low premium to safe drivers and a high premium to risky drivers. But how can it tell them apart? Drivers know whether they are safe or risky, but the risky ones won't admit it. A driver's history is one piece of information (which insurance companies in fact use), but because of the intrinsic randomness of car accidents, history is an imperfect indicator of future risk.

The insurance company might be able to sort out the two kinds of drivers by offering different insurance policies that would induce the drivers to separate themselves. One policy would have a high premium and cover the full cost of any accidents that occur. Another policy would have low premiums but would have, say, a $1,000 deductible. (That is, the driver would be responsible for the first $1,000 of damage, and the insurance company would cover the remaining risk.) Notice that the deductible is more of a burden for risky drivers because they are more likely to have an accident. Thus, with a large enough deductible, the low-premium policy with a deductible would attract the safe drivers, while the high-premium policy without a deductible would attract the risky drivers. Faced with these two policies, the two kinds of drivers would reveal their private information by choosing different insurance policies.

22-1e Asymmetric Information and Public Policy

We have examined two kinds of asymmetric information: moral hazard and adverse selection. And we have seen how individuals may respond to the problem with signaling or screening. Now let's consider what the study of asymmetric information suggests about the proper scope of public policy.

The tension between market success and market failure is central in microeconomics. We learned in Chapter 7 that the equilibrium of supply and demand is efficient in the sense that it maximizes the total surplus that society can obtain in a market. Adam Smith's invisible hand seemed to reign supreme. This conclusion was then tempered with the study of externalities (Chapter 10), public goods (Chapter 11), imperfect competition (Chapters 15 through 17), and poverty (Chapter 20). In those chapters, we saw that government can sometimes improve market outcomes.

The study of asymmetric information gives us a new reason to be wary of markets. When some people know more than others, the market may fail to put resources to their best use. People with high-quality used cars may have trouble selling them because buyers will be afraid of getting a lemon. People with few health problems may have trouble getting low-cost health insurance because insurance companies lump them together with those who have significant (but hidden) health problems.

Asymmetric information may call for government action in some cases, but three facts complicate the issue. First, as we have seen, the private market can sometimes deal with information asymmetries on its own using a combination of signaling and screening. Second, the government rarely has more information than the private parties. Even if the market's allocation of resources is not ideal, it may be the best that can be achieved. That is, when there are information asymmetries, policymakers may find it hard to improve upon the market's admittedly imperfect outcome. Third, the government is itself an imperfect institution—a topic we take up in the next section.

Quick Quiz   *A person who buys a life insurance policy pays a certain amount per year and receives for his family a much larger payment in the event of his death. Would you expect buyers of life insurance to have higher or lower death rates than the average person? How might this be an example of moral hazard? Of adverse selection? How might a life insurance company deal with these problems?*

22-2 Political Economy

As we have seen, markets left on their own do not always reach a desirable allocation of resources. When we judge the market's outcome to be either inefficient or inequitable, there may be a role for the government to step in and improve the situation. Yet before we embrace an activist government, we need to consider one more fact: The government is also an imperfect institution. The field of **political economy** (sometimes called the field of *public choice*) uses the methods of economics to study how government works.

political economy
the study of government using the analytic methods of economics

22-2a The Condorcet Voting Paradox

Most advanced societies rely on democratic principles to set government policy. When a city is deciding between two locations to build a new park, for example, we have a simple way to choose: The majority gets its way. Yet for most policy issues, the number of possible outcomes far exceeds two. A new park could be placed in many possible locations. In this case, as the 18th-century French political theorist Marquis de Condorcet famously noted, democracy might run into some problems trying to choose the best outcome.

For example, suppose there are three possible outcomes, labeled A, B, and C, and there are three voter types with the preferences shown in Table 1. The mayor of our town wants to aggregate these individual preferences into preferences for society as a whole. How should he do it?

At first, he might try some pairwise votes. If he asks voters to choose first between B and C, voter types 1 and 2 will vote for B, giving B the majority. If he then asks voters to choose between A and B, voter types 1 and 3 will vote for A, giving A the majority. Observing that A beats B, and B beats C, the mayor might conclude that A is the voters' clear choice.

But wait: Suppose the mayor then asks voters to choose between A and C. In this case, voter types 2 and 3 vote for C, giving C the majority. That is, under pairwise majority voting, A beats B, B beats C, and C beats A. Normally, we expect preferences to exhibit a property called *transitivity:* If A is preferred to B, and B is preferred to C, then we would expect A to be preferred to C. The **Condorcet paradox** is that democratic outcomes do not always obey this property. Pairwise voting might produce transitive preferences for society in some cases, but as our example in the table shows, it cannot be counted on to do so.

One implication of the Condorcet paradox is that the order in which things are voted on can affect the result. If the mayor suggests choosing first between A and B and then comparing the winner to C, the town ends up choosing C. But if the voters choose first between B and C and then compare the winner to A, the town ends up with A. And if the voters choose first between A and C and then compare the winner to B, the town ends up with B.

The Condorcet paradox teaches two lessons. The narrow lesson is that when there are more than two options, setting the agenda (that is, deciding the order in which items are voted on) can have a powerful influence over the outcome of a democratic election. The broad lesson is that majority voting by itself does not tell us what outcome a society really wants.

Condorcet paradox
the failure of majority rule to produce transitive preferences for society

22-2b Arrow's Impossibility Theorem

Since political theorists first noticed Condorcet's paradox, they have spent much energy studying existing voting systems and proposing new ones. For example, as an alternative to pairwise majority voting, the mayor of our town could ask each voter to rank the possible outcomes. For each voter, we could give 1 point for last place, 2 points for second to last, 3 points for third to last, and so on. The outcome that receives the most total points wins. With the preferences in Table 1, outcome B is the winner. (You can do the arithmetic yourself.) This voting method

TABLE 1

The Condorcet Paradox
If voters have these preferences over outcomes A, B, and C, then in pairwise majority voting, A beats B, B beats C, and C beats A.

	Voter Type		
	Type 1	Type 2	Type 3
Percent of Electorate	35	45	20
First choice	A	B	C
Second choice	B	C	A
Third choice	C	A	B

is called a *Borda count* for the 18th-century French mathematician and political theorist who devised it. It is often used in polls that rank sports teams.

Is there a perfect voting system? Economist Kenneth Arrow took up this question in his 1951 book *Social Choice and Individual Values*. Arrow started by defining what a perfect voting system would be. He assumes that individuals in society have preferences over the various possible outcomes: A, B, C, and so on. He then assumes that society wants a voting system to choose among these outcomes that satisfies several properties:

- *Unanimity:* If everyone prefers A to B, then A should beat B.
- *Transitivity:* If A beats B, and B beats C, then A should beat C.
- *Independence of irrelevant alternatives:* The ranking between any two outcomes A and B should not depend on whether some third outcome C is also available.
- *No dictators:* There is no person who always gets his way, regardless of everyone else's preferences.

These all seem like desirable properties of a voting system. Yet Arrow proved, mathematically and incontrovertibly, that *no voting system can satisfy all these properties*. This amazing result is called **Arrow's impossibility theorem.**

The mathematics needed to prove Arrow's theorem is beyond the scope of this book, but we can get some sense of why the theorem is true from a couple of examples. We have already seen the problem with the method of majority rule. The Condorcet paradox shows that majority rule fails to produce a ranking of outcomes that always satisfies transitivity.

As another example, the Borda count fails to satisfy the independence of irrelevant alternatives. Recall that, using the preferences in Table 1, outcome B wins with a Borda count. But suppose that suddenly C disappears as an alternative. If the Borda count method is applied only to outcomes A and B, then A wins. (Once again, you can do the arithmetic on your own.) Thus, eliminating alternative C changes the ranking between A and B. This change occurs because the result of the Borda count depends on the number of points that A and B receive, and the number of points depends on whether the irrelevant alternative, C, is also available.

Arrow's impossibility theorem is a deep and disturbing result. It doesn't say that we should abandon democracy as a form of government. But it does say that no matter what voting system society adopts for aggregating the preferences of its members, it will in some way be flawed as a mechanism for social choice.

Arrow's impossibility theorem
a mathematical result showing that, under certain assumed conditions, there is no scheme for aggregating individual preferences into a valid set of social preferences

22-2c The Median Voter Is King

Despite Arrow's theorem, voting is how most societies choose their leaders and public policies, often by majority rule. The next step in studying government is to examine how governments run by majority rule work. That is, in a democratic society, who determines what policy is chosen? In some cases, the theory of democratic government yields a surprisingly simple answer.

Let's consider an example. Imagine that society is deciding how much money to spend on some public good, such as the army or the national parks. Each voter has his own most preferred budget, and he always prefers outcomes closer to his most preferred value to outcomes farther away. Thus, we can line up voters from those who prefer the smallest budget to those who prefer the largest. Figure 1 is an example. Here there are 100 voters, and the budget size varies from zero to $20 billion. Given these preferences, what outcome would you expect democracy to produce?

FIGURE 1

The Median Voter Theorem: An Example
This bar chart shows how 100 voters' most preferred budgets are distributed over five options, ranging from zero to $20 billion. If society makes its choice by majority rule, the median voter (who here prefers $10 billion) determines the outcome.

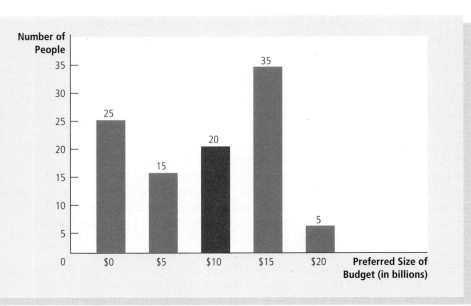

median voter theorem
a mathematical result showing that if voters are choosing a point along a line and each voter wants the point closest to his most preferred point, then majority rule will pick the most preferred point of the median voter

According to a famous result called the **median voter theorem**, majority rule will produce the outcome most preferred by the median voter. The *median voter* is the voter exactly in the middle of the distribution. In this example, if you take the line of voters ordered by their preferred budgets and count 50 voters from either end of the line, you will find that the median voter wants a budget of $10 billion. By contrast, the average preferred outcome (calculated by adding the preferred outcomes and dividing by the number of voters) is $9 billion, and the modal outcome (the one preferred by the greatest number of voters) is $15 billion.

The median voter rules the day because his preferred outcome beats any other proposal in a two-way race. In our example, more than half the voters want $10 billion or more, and more than half want $10 billion or less. If someone proposes, say, $8 billion instead of $10 billion, everyone who prefers $10 billion or more will vote with the median voter. Similarly, if someone proposes $12 billion instead of $10 billion, everyone who wants $10 billion or less will vote with the median voter. In either case, the median voter has more than half the voters on his side.

What about the Condorcet voting paradox? It turns out that when the voters are picking a point along a line and each voter aims for his own most preferred point, the Condorcet paradox cannot arise. The median voter's most preferred outcome beats all challengers.

One implication of the median voter theorem is that if two political parties are each trying to maximize their chance of election, they will both move their positions toward the median voter. Suppose, for example, that the Democratic Party advocates a budget of $15 billion, while the Republican Party advocates a budget of $10 billion. The Democratic position is more popular in the sense that $15 billion has more proponents than any other single choice. Nonetheless, the Republicans get more than 50 percent of the vote: They will attract the 20 voters who want $10 billion, the 15 voters who want $5 billion, and the 25 voters who want zero. If the Democrats want to win, they will move their platform toward the median voter. Thus, this theory can explain why the parties in a two-party system are similar to each other: They are both moving toward the median voter.

Another implication of the median voter theorem is that minority views are not given much weight. Imagine that 40 percent of the population want a lot of money spent on the national parks and 60 percent want nothing spent. In this case, the median voter's preference is zero, regardless of the intensity of the minority's view. Such is the logic of democracy. Rather than reaching a compromise that takes into account everyone's preferences, majority rule looks only to the person in the exact middle of the distribution.

22-2d Politicians Are People Too

When economists study consumer behavior, they assume that consumers buy the bundle of goods and services that gives them the greatest level of satisfaction. When economists study firm behavior, they assume that firms produce the quantity of goods and services that yields the greatest level of profits. What should they assume when they study people involved in the practice of politics?

Politicians also have objectives. It would be nice to assume that political leaders are always looking out for the well-being of society as a whole, that they are aiming for an optimal combination of efficiency and equality. Nice, perhaps, but not realistic. Self-interest is as powerful a motive for political actors as it is for consumers and firm owners. Some politicians, motivated by a desire for reelection, are willing to sacrifice the national interest to solidify their base of voters. Others are motivated by simple greed. If you have any doubt, you should look at the world's poor nations, where corruption among government officials is a common impediment to economic development.

This book is not the place to develop a theory of political behavior. But when thinking about economic policy, remember that this policy is made not by a benevolent king (or even by benevolent economists) but by real people with their own all-too-human desires. Sometimes they are motivated to further the national interest, but sometimes they are motivated by their own political and financial ambitions. We shouldn't be surprised when economic policy fails to resemble the ideals derived in economics textbooks.

www.CartoonStock.com/Chris Wildt

"Isn't that the real genius of democracy? . . . The VOTERS are ultimately to blame."

Quick Quiz   *A public school district is deciding on the school budget and the resulting student–teacher ratio. A poll finds that 20 percent of the voters want a ratio of 9:1, 25 percent want a ratio of 10:1, 15 percent want a ratio of 11:1, and 40 percent want a ratio of 12:1. If the district uses majority-rule voting, what outcome would you expect the district to end up with? Explain.*

22-3 Behavioral Economics

Economics is a study of human behavior, but it is not the only field that can make that claim. The social science of psychology also sheds light on the choices that people make in their lives. The fields of economics and psychology usually proceed independently, in part because they address a different range of questions. But recently, a field called **behavioral economics** has emerged in which economists are making use of basic psychological insights. Let's consider some of these insights here.

behavioral economics
the subfield of economics that integrates the insights of psychology

22-3a People Aren't Always Rational

Economic theory is populated by a particular species of organism, sometimes called *Homo economicus*. Members of this species are always rational. As firm owners, they maximize profits. As consumers, they maximize utility (or equivalently, pick the point on the highest indifference curve). Given the constraints they face, they rationally weigh all the costs and benefits and always choose the best possible course of action.

Real people, however, are *Homo sapiens*. Although in many ways they resemble the rational, calculating people assumed in economic theory, they are far more complex. They can be forgetful, impulsive, confused, emotional, and shortsighted. These imperfections of human reasoning are the bread and butter of psychologists, but until recently, economists have neglected them.

Herbert Simon, one of the first social scientists to work at the boundary of economics and psychology, suggested that humans should be viewed not as rational maximizers but as *satisficers*. Rather than always choosing the best course of action, they make decisions that are merely good enough. Similarly, other economists have suggested that humans are only "near rational" or that they exhibit "bounded rationality."

Studies of human decision making have tried to detect systematic mistakes that people make. Here are a few of the findings:

- *People are overconfident.* Imagine that you were asked some numerical questions, such as the number of African countries in the United Nations, the height of the tallest mountain in North America, and so on. Instead of being asked for a single estimate, however, you were asked to give a 90 percent confidence interval—a range such that you were 90 percent confident the true number falls within it. When psychologists run experiments like this, they find that most people give ranges that are too small: The true number falls within their intervals far less than 90 percent of the time. That is, most people are too sure of their own abilities.
- *People give too much weight to a small number of vivid observations.* Imagine that you are thinking about buying a car of brand X. To learn about its reliability, you read *Consumer Reports,* which has surveyed 1,000 owners of car X. Then you run into a friend who owns car X, and he tells you that his car is a lemon. How do you treat your friend's observation? If you think rationally, you will realize that he has only increased your sample size from 1,000 to 1,001, which does not provide much new information. But because your friend's story is so vivid, you may be tempted to give it more weight in your decision making than you should.
- *People are reluctant to change their minds.* People tend to interpret evidence to confirm beliefs they already hold. In one study, subjects were asked to read and evaluate a research report on whether capital punishment deters crime. After reading the report, those who initially favored the death penalty said they were surer in their view, and those who initially opposed the death penalty also said they were surer in their view. The two groups interpreted the same evidence in exactly opposite ways.

Think about decisions you have made in your own life. Do you exhibit some of these traits?

A hotly debated issue is whether deviations from rationality are important for understanding economic phenomena. An intriguing example arises in the study of 401(k) plans, the tax-advantaged retirement savings accounts that some firms offer their workers. In some firms, workers can choose to participate in the plan by filling out a simple form. In other firms, workers are automatically enrolled and can opt out of the plan by filling out a simple form. It turns out many more workers participate in the second case than in the first. If workers were perfectly rational maximizers, they would choose the optimal amount of retirement saving, regardless of the default offered by their employer. In fact, workers' behavior appears to exhibit substantial inertia. Understanding their behavior seems easier once we abandon the model of rational man.

Why, you might ask, is economics built on the rationality assumption when psychology and common sense cast doubt on it? One answer is that the assumption, even if not exactly true, may be true enough that it yields reasonably accurate models of behavior. For example, when we studied the differences between competitive and monopoly firms, the assumption that firms rationally maximize profit yielded many important and valid insights. Incorporating complex psychological deviations from rationality into the story might have added realism, but it also would have muddied the waters and made those insights harder to find. Recall from Chapter 2 that economic models are not meant to replicate reality but are supposed to show the essence of the problem at hand as an aid to understanding.

Another reason economists so often assume rationality may be that economists are themselves not rational maximizers. Like most people, they are overconfident and they are reluctant to change their minds. Their choice among alternative theories of human behavior may exhibit excessive inertia. Moreover, economists may be content with a theory that is not perfect but is good enough. The model of rational man may be the theory of choice for a satisficing social scientist.

case study   Left-Digit Bias

You may have noticed that prices often end in .99. In some ways, this phenomenon is odd. Why charge $4.99, instead of an even $5.00? If people were truly rational, sellers wouldn't have a good reason to focus on prices ending in .99. But in fact, it turns out that sellers are smart for using this approach to pricing. Various studies suggest that buyers are excessively sensitive to a price's left-most digit. Even though $4.99 is only one penny less than $5.00, buyers may not perceive it that way. Because adding the extra penny changes the left-most digit from a 4 to a 5, the change may exert a surprisingly large impact on consumer behavior. An irrational focus on the left-most digit is called *left-digit bias.*

In one study, participants were given the choice of buying two different pens, a cheap one and a better, more expensive one. When the pens were priced at $2.00 and $3.99, 44 percent bought the higher-priced pen. When the prices were $1.99 and $4.00, only 18 percent bought the more expensive one. Such a large change in behavior in response to such tiny changes in the prices seems hard to square with standard models of rationality. But it is easier to understand if one imagines a consumer that focuses excessively on the left-most digit. To such a consumer, the prices would look like $2 and $3 in the first scenario and $1 and $4 in the second, and so the changes from the first to the second scenario would appear larger than they really are.

Another study of left-digit bias examined how the number of miles on a used car's odometer affected the price at which the car sold. The study examined data on millions of used cars sold at auction. Not surprisingly, cars that had been driven more miles sold for less. But the effect was not smooth. For example, when the odometer reading increased from 78,000 to 79,000 (leaving the left-most digit the same), the price of the car fell by about $10. But when the odometer reading

Why not add a penny to this price?

increased from 79,000 to 80,000 (increasing the left-most digit), the price fell by $210. The prices of used cars jumped down at every 10,000 mile mark, when the left-most digit on the odometer changed.

When looking at either prices or odometers, buyers seem to be irrationally influenced by the left-most digit. ◢

22-3b People Care about Fairness

Another insight about human behavior is best illustrated with an experiment called the *ultimatum game*. The game works like this: Two volunteers (who are otherwise strangers to each other) are told that they are going to play a game and could win a total of $100. Before they play, they learn the rules. The game begins with a coin toss, which is used to assign the volunteers to the roles of player A and player B. Player A's job is to propose a division of the $100 prize between himself and the other player. After player A makes his proposal, player B decides whether to accept or reject it. If he accepts it, both players are paid according to the proposal. If player B rejects the proposal, both players walk away with nothing. In either case, the game then ends.

Before proceeding, stop and think about what you would do in this situation. If you were player A, what division of the $100 would you propose? If you were player B, what proposals would you accept?

Conventional economic theory assumes in this situation that people are rational wealth maximizers. This assumption leads to a simple prediction: Player A should propose that he gets $99 and player B gets $1, and player B should accept the proposal. After all, once the proposal is made, player B is better off accepting it as long as he gets something out of it. Moreover, because player A knows that accepting the proposal is in player B's interest, player A has no reason to offer him more than $1. In the language of game theory (discussed in Chapter 17), the 99–1 split is the Nash equilibrium.

Yet when experimental economists ask real people to play the ultimatum game, the results differ from this prediction. People in player B's role usually reject proposals that give them only $1 or a similarly small amount. Anticipating this, people in the role of player A usually propose giving player B much more than $1. Some people will offer a 50–50 split, but it is more common for player A to propose giving player B an amount such as $30 or $40, keeping the larger share for himself. In this case, player B usually accepts the proposal.

What's going on here? The natural interpretation is that people are driven in part by some innate sense of fairness. A 99–1 split seems so wildly unfair to many people that they reject it, even to their own detriment. By contrast, a 70–30 split is still unfair, but it is not so unfair that it induces people to abandon their normal self-interest.

Throughout our study of household and firm behavior, the innate sense of fairness has not played any role. But the results of the ultimatum game suggest that perhaps it should. For example, in Chapters 18 and 19, we discussed how wages were determined by labor supply and labor demand. Some economists have suggested that the perceived fairness of what a firm pays its workers should also enter the picture. Thus, when a firm has an especially profitable year, workers (like player B) may expect to be paid a fair share of the prize, even if the standard equilibrium does not dictate it. The firm (like player A) might well decide to give workers more than the equilibrium wage for fear that the workers might otherwise try to punish the firm with reduced effort, strikes, or even vandalism.

22-3c People Are Inconsistent over Time

Imagine some dreary task, such as doing your laundry, shoveling snow off your driveway, or filling out your income tax forms. Now consider the following questions:

1. Would you prefer (A) to spend 50 minutes doing the task right now or (B) to spend 60 minutes doing the task tomorrow?
2. Would you prefer (A) to spend 50 minutes doing the task in 90 days or (B) to spend 60 minutes doing the task in 91 days?

When asked questions like these, many people choose B for question 1 and A for question 2. When looking ahead to the future (as in question 2), they minimize the amount of time spent on the dreary task. But faced with the prospect of doing the task immediately (as in question 1), they choose to put it off.

In some ways, this behavior is not surprising: Everyone procrastinates from time to time. But from the standpoint of the theory of rational man, it is puzzling. Suppose that in response to question 2, a person chooses to spend 50 minutes in 90 days. Then, when the 90th day arrives, we allow him to change his mind. In effect, he then faces question 1, so he opts for doing the task the next day. But why should the mere passage of time affect the choices he makes?

Many times in life, people make plans for themselves, but then they fail to follow through. A smoker promises himself that he will quit, but within a few hours of smoking his last cigarette, he craves another and breaks his promise. A person trying to lose weight promises that he will stop eating dessert, but when the waiter brings the dessert cart, the promise is forgotten. In both cases, the desire for instant gratification induces the decision maker to abandon his past plans.

Some economists believe that the consumption–saving decision is an important instance in which people exhibit this inconsistency over time. For many people, spending provides a type of instant gratification. Saving, like passing up the cigarette or the dessert, requires a sacrifice in the present for a reward in the distant future. And just as many smokers wish they could quit and many overweight individuals wish they ate less, many consumers wish they saved more of their income. According to one survey, 76 percent of Americans said they were not saving enough for retirement.

An implication of this inconsistency over time is that people should try to find ways to commit their future selves to following through on their plans. A smoker trying to quit may throw away his cigarettes, and a person on a diet may put a lock on the refrigerator. What can a person who saves too little do? He should find some way to lock up his money before he spends it. Some retirement accounts, such as 401(k) plans, do exactly that. A worker can agree to have some money taken out of his paycheck before he ever sees it. The money is deposited in an account that can be used before retirement only with a penalty. Perhaps that is one reason these retirement accounts are so popular: They protect people from their own desires for instant gratification.

Quick Quiz *Describe at least three ways in which human decision making differs from that of the rational individual of conventional economic theory.*

Can Brain Science Improve Economics?

Some scholars believe that studying the biology of the brain may improve our understanding of economic behavior.

The Neuroeconomics Revolution

By Robert J. Shiller

Economics is at the start of a revolution that is traceable to an unexpected source: medical schools and their research facilities. Neuroscience—the science of how the brain, that physical organ inside one's head, really works—is beginning to change the way we think about how people make decisions. These findings will inevitably change the way we think about how economies function. In short, we are at the dawn of "neuroeconomics."

Efforts to link neuroscience to economics have occurred mostly in just the last few years, and the growth of neuroeconomics is still in its early stages. But its nascence follows a pattern: revolutions in science tend to come from completely unexpected places. A field of science can turn barren if no fundamentally new approaches to research are on the horizon. Scholars can become so trapped in their methods—in the language and assumptions of the accepted approach to their

discipline—that their research becomes repetitive or trivial.

Then something exciting comes along from someone who was never involved with these methods—some new idea that attracts young scholars and a few iconoclastic old scholars, who are willing to learn a different science and its different research methods. At a certain moment in this process, a scientific revolution is born.

The neuroeconomic revolution has passed some key milestones quite recently, notably the publication last year of neuroscientist Paul Glimcher's book *Foundations of Neuroeconomic Analysis*—a pointed variation on the title of Paul Samuelson's 1947 classic work, *Foundations of Economic Analysis*, which helped to launch an earlier revolution in economic theory. And Glimcher himself now holds an appointment at New York University's economics department (he also works at NYU's Center for Neural Science).

To most economists, however, Glimcher might as well have come from outer space. After all, his doctorate is from the University of Pennsylvania School of Medicine's

neuroscience department. Moreover, neuroeconomists like him conduct research that is well beyond their conventional colleagues' intellectual comfort zone, for they seek to advance some of the core concepts of economics by linking them to specific brain structures.

Much of modern economic and financial theory is based on the assumption that people are rational, and thus that they systematically maximize their own happiness, or as economists call it, their "utility." When Samuelson took on the subject in his 1947 book, he did not look into the brain, but relied instead on "revealed preference." People's objectives are revealed only by observing their economic activities. Under Samuelson's guidance, generations of economists have based their research not on any physical structure underlying thought and behavior, but only on the assumption of rationality.

As a result, Glimcher is skeptical of prevailing economic theory, and is seeking a physical basis for it in the brain. He wants

22-4 Conclusion

This chapter has examined the frontier of microeconomics. You may have noticed that we have sketched out ideas rather than fully developing them. This is no accident. One reason is that you might study these topics in more detail in advanced courses. Another reason is that these topics remain active areas of research and, therefore, are still being fleshed out.

To see how these topics fit into the broader picture, recall the *Ten Principles of Economics* from Chapter 1. One principle states that markets are usually a good way to organize economic activity. Another principle states that governments can sometimes improve market outcomes. As you study economics, you can more

to transform "soft" utility theory into "hard" utility theory by discovering the brain mechanisms that underlie it.

In particular, Glimcher wants to identify brain structures that process key elements of utility theory when people face uncertainty: "(1) subjective value, (2) probability, (3) the product of subjective value and probability (expected subjective value), and (4) a neuro-computational mechanism that selects the element from the choice set that has the highest 'expected subjective value'. . . ."

While Glimcher and his colleagues have uncovered tantalizing evidence, they have yet to find most of the fundamental brain structures. Maybe that is because such structures simply do not exist, and the whole utility-maximization theory is wrong, or at least in need of fundamental revision. If so, that finding alone would shake economics to its foundations.

Another direction that excites neuroscientists is how the brain deals with ambiguous situations, when probabilities are not known, and when other highly relevant information is not available. It has already been discovered that the brain regions used to deal with problems when probabilities are clear are different from those used when probabilities are unknown. This research might help us to understand how people handle uncertainty and risk in, say, financial markets at a time of crisis.

A neuroeconomist at work

John Maynard Keynes thought that most economic decision-making occurs in ambiguous situations in which probabilities are not known. He concluded that much of our business cycle is driven by fluctuations in "animal spirits," something in the mind—and not understood by economists.

Of course, the problem with economics is that there are often as many interpretations of any crisis as there are economists. An economy is a remarkably complex structure, and fathoming it depends on understanding its laws, regulations, business practices and customs, and balance sheets, among many other details.

Yet it is likely that one day we will know much more about how economies work —or fail

to work—by understanding better the physical structures that underlie brain functioning. Those structures—networks of neurons that communicate with each other via axons and dendrites—underlie the familiar analogy of the brain to a computer—networks of transistors that communicate with each other via electric wires. The economy is the next analogy: a network of people who communicate with each other via electronic and other connections.

The brain, the computer, and the economy: all three are devices whose purpose is to solve fundamental information problems in coordinating the activities of individual units—the neurons, the transistors, or individual people. As we improve our understanding of the problems that any one of these devices solves—and how it overcomes obstacles in doing so—we learn something valuable about all three.

Mr. Shiller is an economics professor at Yale University. ◢

Source: Project Syndicate, November 21, 2011.

fully appreciate the truth of these principles as well as the caveats that go with them. The study of asymmetric information should make you more wary of market outcomes. The study of political economy should make you more wary of government solutions. And the study of behavioral economics should make you wary of any institution that relies on human decision making, including both the market and the government.

If there is a unifying theme to these topics, it is that life is messy. Information is imperfect, government is imperfect, and people are imperfect. Of course, you knew this long before you started studying economics, but economists need to understand these imperfections as precisely as they can if they are to explain, and perhaps even improve, the world around them.

Summary

- In many economic transactions, information is asymmetric. When there are hidden actions, principals may be concerned that agents suffer from the problem of moral hazard. When there are hidden characteristics, buyers may be concerned about the problem of adverse selection among the sellers. Private markets sometimes deal with asymmetric information with signaling and screening.

- Although government policy can sometimes improve market outcomes, governments are themselves imperfect institutions. The Condorcet paradox shows that majority rule fails to produce transitive preferences for society, and Arrow's impossibility theorem shows that

no voting system will be perfect. In many situations, democratic institutions will produce the outcome desired by the median voter, regardless of the preferences of the rest of the electorate. Moreover, the individuals who set government policy may be motivated by self-interest rather than the national interest.

- The study of psychology and economics reveals that human decision making is more complex than is assumed in conventional economic theory. People are not always rational, they care about the fairness of economic outcomes (even to their own detriment), and they can be inconsistent over time.

Key Concepts

moral hazard, *p. 462*
agent, *p. 462*
principal, *p. 462*
adverse selection, *p. 464*

signaling, *p. 465*
screening, *p. 466*
political economy, *p. 467*
Condorcet paradox, *p. 468*

Arrow's impossibility theorem, *p. 469*
median voter theorem, *p. 470*
behavioral economics, *p. 471*

Questions for Review

1. What is moral hazard? List three things an employer might do to reduce the severity of this problem.

2. What is adverse selection? Give an example of a market in which adverse selection might be a problem.

3. Define *signaling* and *screening* and give an example of each.

4. What unusual property of voting did Condorcet notice?

5. Explain why majority rule respects the preferences of the median voter rather than the average voter.

6. Describe the ultimatum game. What outcome from this game would conventional economic theory predict? Do experiments confirm this prediction? Explain.

Quick Check Multiple Choice

1. Because Elaine has a family history of significant medical problems, she buys health insurance, whereas her friend Jerry, who has a healthier family, goes without. This is an example of
   a. moral hazard.
   b. adverse selection.
   c. signaling.
   d. screening.

2. George has a life insurance policy that pays his family $1 million if he dies. As a result, he does not hesitate to enjoy his favorite hobby of bungee jumping. This is an example of
   a. moral hazard.
   b. adverse selection.
   c. signaling.
   d. screening.

3. Before selling anyone a health insurance policy, the Kramer Insurance Company requires that applicants undergo a medical examination. Those with significant preexisting medical problems are charged more. This is an example of
   a. moral hazard.
   b. adverse selection.
   c. signaling.
   d. screening.

4. The Condorcet paradox illustrates Arrow's impossibility theorem by showing that pairwise majority voting
   a. is inconsistent with the principle of unanimity.
   b. leads to social preferences that are not transitive.
   c. violates the independence of irrelevant alternatives.
   d. makes one person in effect a dictator.

5. Two political candidates are vying for town mayor, and the key issue is how much to spend on the annual Fourth of July fireworks. Among the 100 voters, 40 want to spend $30,000, 30 want to spend $10,000, and 30 want to spend nothing at all. What is the winning position on this issue?
   a. $10,000
   b. $15,000
   c. $20,000
   d. $30,000

6. The experiment called the ultimatum game illustrates that people
   a. are overconfident in their own abilities.
   b. play the Nash equilibrium in strategic situations.
   c. care about fairness, even to their own detriment.
   d. make inconsistent decisions over time.

Problems and Applications

1. Each of the following situations involves moral hazard. In each case, identify the principal and the agent and explain why there is asymmetric information. How does the action described reduce the problem of moral hazard?
   a. Landlords require tenants to pay security deposits.
   b. Firms compensate top executives with options to buy company stock at a given price in the future.
   c. Car insurance companies offer discounts to customers who install antitheft devices in their cars.

2. Suppose that the Live-Long-and-Prosper Health Insurance Company charges $5,000 annually for a family insurance policy. The company's president suggests that the company raise the annual price to $6,000 to increase its profits. If the firm followed this suggestion, what economic problem might arise? Would the firm's pool of customers tend to become more or less healthy on average? Would the company's profits necessarily increase?

3. A case study in this chapter describes how a boyfriend can signal his love to a girlfriend by giving an appropriate gift. Do you think saying "I love you" can also serve as a signal? Why or why not?

4. Some AIDS activists believe that health insurance companies should not be allowed to ask applicants if they are infected with the HIV virus that causes AIDS. Would this rule help or hurt those who are HIV-positive? Would it help or hurt those who are not HIV-positive? Would it exacerbate or mitigate the problem of adverse selection in the market for health insurance? Do you think it would increase or decrease the number of people without health insurance? In your opinion, would this be a good policy? Explain your answers to each question.

5. Ken walks into an ice-cream parlor.

   WAITER: "We have vanilla and chocolate today."

   KEN: "I'll take vanilla."

   WAITER: "I almost forgot. We also have strawberry."

   KEN: "In that case, I'll take chocolate."

What standard property of decision making is Ken violating? (*Hint*: Reread the section on Arrow's impossibility theorem.)

6. Three friends are choosing a restaurant for dinner. Here are their preferences:

	Rachel	Ross	Joey
First choice	Italian	Italian	Chinese
Second choice	Chinese	Chinese	Mexican
Third choice	Mexican	Mexican	French
Fourth choice	French	French	Italian

   a. If the three friends use a Borda count to make their decision, where do they go to eat?
   b. On their way to their chosen restaurant, they see that the Mexican and French restaurants are closed, so they use a Borda count again to decide between the remaining two restaurants. Where do they decide to go now?
   c. How do your answers to parts (a) and (b) relate to Arrow's impossibility theorem?

7. Three friends are choosing a TV show to watch. Here are their preferences:

	Chandler	Phoebe	Monica
First choice	*NCIS*	*Glee*	*Homeland*
Second choice	*Glee*	*Homeland*	*NCIS*
Third choice	*Homeland*	*NCIS*	*Glee*

   a. If the three friends try using a Borda count to make their choice, what would happen?
   b. Monica suggests a vote by majority rule. She proposes that first they choose between *NCIS* and *Glee*, and then they choose between the winner of the first vote and *Homeland*. If they all vote their preferences honestly, what outcome would occur?
   c. Should Chandler agree to Monica's suggestion? What voting system would he prefer?
   d. Phoebe and Monica convince Chandler to go along with Monica's proposal. In round one, Chandler dishonestly says he prefers *Glee* over *NCIS*. Why might he do this?

8. Five roommates are planning to spend the weekend in their dorm room watching movies, and they are debating how many movies to watch. Here is their willingness to pay:

	Quentin	Spike	Ridley	Martin	Steven
First film	$14	$10	$8	$4	$2
Second film	12	8	4	2	0
Third film	10	6	2	0	0
Fourth film	6	2	0	0	0
Fifth film	2	0	0	0	0

Buying a DVD costs $15, which the roommates split equally, so each pays $3 per movie.
   a. What is the efficient number of movies to watch (that is, the number that maximizes total surplus)?
   b. From the standpoint of each roommate, what is the preferred number of movies?
   c. What is the preference of the median roommate?
   d. If the roommates held a vote on the efficient outcome versus the median voter's preference, how would each person vote? Which outcome would get a majority?
   e. If one of the roommates proposed a different number of movies, could his proposal beat the winner from part (d) in a vote?

   f. Can majority rule be counted on to reach efficient outcomes in the provision of public goods?

9. Two ice-cream stands are deciding where to set up along a 1-mile beach. The people are uniformly located along the beach, and each person sitting on the beach buys exactly 1 ice-cream cone per day from the nearest stand. Each ice-cream seller wants the maximum number of customers. Where along the beach will the two stands locate? Of which result in this chapter does this outcome remind you?

10. The government is considering two ways to help the needy: giving them cash or giving them free meals at soup kitchens.
   a. Give an argument, based on the standard theory of the rational consumer, for giving cash.
   b. Give an argument, based on asymmetric information, for why the soup kitchen may be better than the cash handout.
   c. Give an argument, based on behavioral economics, for why the soup kitchen may be better than the cash handout.

Go to CengageBrain.com to purchase access to the proven, critical Study Guide to accompany this text, which features additional notes and context, practice tests, and much more.

The Data of Macroeconomics

Measuring a Nation's Income

When you finish school and start looking for a full-time job, your experience will, to a large extent, be shaped by prevailing economic conditions. In some years, firms throughout the economy are expanding their production of goods and services, employment is rising, and jobs are easy to find. In other years, firms are cutting back production, employment is declining, and finding a good job takes a long time. Not surprisingly, any college graduate would rather enter the labor force in a year of economic expansion than in a year of economic contraction.

Because the health of the overall economy profoundly affects all of us, changes in economic conditions are widely reported by the media. Indeed, it is hard to pick up a newspaper, check an online news service, or turn on the TV without seeing some newly reported statistic about the economy. The statistic might measure the total income of everyone in the economy (gross domestic product, or GDP), the rate at which average prices are rising or falling (inflation/deflation), the percentage of the labor force that is out of work (unemployment), total spending at stores (retail sales), or the imbalance of trade between the United States and the rest of the world (the trade deficit). All these statistics are *macroeconomic*. Rather than telling us about a particular household, firm, or market, they tell us something about the entire economy.

As you may recall from Chapter 2, economics is divided into two branches: microeconomics and macroeconomics. **Microeconomics** is the study of how individual households and firms make decisions and how they interact with one another in markets. **Macroeconomics** is the study of the economy as a whole. The goal of macroeconomics is to explain the economic changes that affect many households, firms, and markets simultaneously. Macroeconomists address diverse questions: Why is average income high in some countries while it is low in others? Why do prices sometimes rise rapidly while at other times they are more stable? Why do production and employment expand in some years and contract in others? What, if anything, can the government do to promote rapid growth in incomes, low inflation, and stable employment? These questions are all macroeconomic in nature because they concern the workings of the entire economy.

Because the economy as a whole is a collection of many households and many firms interacting in many markets, microeconomics and macroeconomics are closely linked. The basic tools of supply and demand, for instance, are as central to macroeconomic analysis as they are to microeconomic analysis. Yet studying the economy in its entirety raises some new and intriguing challenges.

In this and the next chapter, we discuss some of the data that economists and policymakers use to monitor the performance of the overall economy. These data reflect the economic changes that macroeconomists try to explain. This chapter considers *gross domestic product*, which measures the total income of a nation. GDP is the most closely watched economic statistic because it is thought to be the best single measure of a society's economic well-being.

microeconomics
the study of how households and firms make decisions and how they interact in markets

macroeconomics
the study of economy-wide phenomena, including inflation, unemployment, and economic growth

23-1 The Economy's Income and Expenditure

If you were to judge how a person is doing economically, you might first look at her income. A person with a high income can more easily afford life's necessities and luxuries. It is no surprise that people with higher incomes enjoy higher standards of living—better housing, better healthcare, fancier cars, more opulent vacations, and so on.

The same logic applies to a nation's overall economy. When judging whether the economy is doing well or poorly, it is natural to look at the total income that everyone in the economy is earning. That is the task of GDP.

GDP measures two things at once: the total income of everyone in the economy and the total expenditure on the economy's output of goods and services. GDP can perform the trick of measuring both total income and total expenditure because these two things are really the same. *For an economy as a whole, income must equal expenditure.*

Why is this true? An economy's income is the same as its expenditure because every transaction has two parties: a buyer and a seller. Every dollar of spending by some buyer is a dollar of income for some seller. Suppose, for instance, that Karen pays Doug $100 to mow her lawn. In this case, Doug is a seller of a service and Karen is a buyer. Doug earns $100 and Karen spends $100. Thus, the transaction contributes equally to the economy's income and to its expenditure. GDP, whether measured as total income or total expenditure, rises by $100.

Another way to see the equality of income and expenditure is with the circular-flow diagram in Figure 1. As you may recall from Chapter 2, this diagram describes all the transactions between households and firms in a simple economy. It simplifies matters by assuming that all goods and services are bought by households and that households spend all of their income. In this economy, when households buy goods and services from firms, these expenditures flow through the markets for goods and services. When the firms in turn use the money they receive from sales to pay workers' wages, landowners' rent, and firm owners' profit, this income flows through the markets for the factors of production. Money continuously flows from households to firms and then back to households.

GDP measures this flow of money. We can compute it for this economy in one of two ways: by adding up the total expenditure by households or by adding up the total income (wages, rent, and profit) paid by firms. Because all expenditure in the economy ends up as someone's income, GDP is the same regardless of how we compute it.

The actual economy is, of course, more complicated than the one illustrated in Figure 1. Households do not spend all of their income; they pay some of it to the government in taxes, and they save some for use in the future. In addition, households do not buy all goods and services produced in the economy; some goods and services are bought by governments, and some are bought by firms that plan

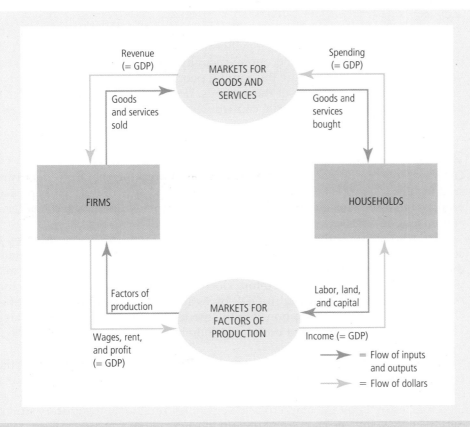

FIGURE 1

The Circular-Flow Diagram
Households buy goods and services from firms, and firms use their revenue from sales to pay wages to workers, rent to landowners, and profit to firm owners. GDP equals the total amount spent by households in the market for goods and services. It also equals the total wages, rent, and profit paid by firms in the markets for the factors of production.

to use them in the future to produce their own output. Yet the basic lesson remains the same: Regardless of whether a household, government, or firm buys a good or service, the transaction has a buyer and a seller. Thus, for the economy as a whole, expenditure and income are always the same.

Quick Quiz   *What two things does GDP measure? How can it measure two things at once?*

23-2 The Measurement of GDP

Having discussed the meaning of gross domestic product in general terms, let's be more precise about how this statistic is measured. Here is a definition of GDP that focuses on GDP as a measure of total expenditure:

gross domestic product (GDP)
the market value of all final goods and services produced within a country in a given period of time

- **Gross domestic product (GDP)** is the market value of all final goods and services produced within a country in a given period of time.

This definition might seem simple enough. But in fact, many subtle issues arise when computing an economy's GDP. Let's therefore consider each phrase in this definition with some care.

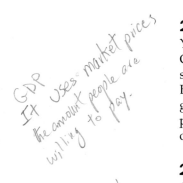

GDP
It uses market prices
the amount people are willing to pay.

23-2a "GDP Is the Market Value . . ."
You have probably heard the adage "You can't compare apples and oranges." Yet GDP does exactly that. GDP adds together many different kinds of products into a single measure of the value of economic activity. To do this, it uses market prices. Because market prices measure the amount people are willing to pay for different goods, they reflect the value of those goods. If the price of an apple is twice the price of an orange, then an apple contributes twice as much to GDP as does an orange.

23-2b ". . . of All . . ."
GDP tries to be comprehensive. It includes all items produced in the economy and sold legally in markets. GDP measures the market value of not just apples and oranges but also pears and grapefruit, books and movies, haircuts and healthcare, and on and on.

all items produced
goods + services

GDP also includes the market value of the housing services provided by the economy's stock of housing. For rental housing, this value is easy to calculate—the rent equals both the tenant's expenditure and the landlord's income. Yet many people own their homes and, therefore, do not pay rent. The government includes this owner-occupied housing in GDP by estimating its rental value. In effect, GDP is based on the assumption that the owner is renting the house to herself. The imputed rent is included both in the homeowner's expenditure and in her income, so it adds to GDP.

There are some products, however, that GDP excludes because measuring them is so difficult. GDP excludes most items produced and sold illicitly, such as illegal drugs. It also excludes most items that are produced and consumed at home and, therefore, never enter the marketplace. Vegetables you buy at the grocery store are part of GDP; vegetables you grow in your garden are not.

Exception = Illegal items, vegetable
in my garden

[handwritten: Seemingly absurd or self-contradictory]

These exclusions from GDP can at times lead to paradoxical results. For example, when Karen pays Doug to mow her lawn, that transaction is part of GDP. But suppose Doug and Karen marry. Even though Doug may continue to mow Karen's lawn, the value of the mowing is now left out of GDP because Doug's service is no longer sold in a market. Thus, their marriage reduces GDP.

23-2c "... Final ..."

When International Paper makes paper, which Hallmark then uses to make a greeting card, the paper is called an *intermediate good* and the card is called a *final good*. GDP includes only the value of final goods. This is done because the value of intermediate goods is already included in the prices of the final goods. Adding the market value of the paper to the market value of the card would be double counting. That is, it would (incorrectly) count the paper twice.

An important exception to this principle arises when an intermediate good is produced and, rather than being used, is added to a firm's inventory of goods for use or sale at a later date. In this case, the intermediate good is taken to be "final" for the moment and its value as inventory investment is included as part of GDP. Thus, additions to inventory add to GDP, and when the goods in inventory are later used or sold, the reductions in inventory subtract from GDP.

[handwritten: GDP only includes value of final goods, not intermediate good. Intermediate is already in final good. Would be double counting.]

[handwritten: If intermediate good sits for now, it counts toward GDP. if added to Final product, it's subtracted then.]

23-2d "... Goods and Services ..."

GDP includes both tangible goods (food, clothing, cars) and intangible services (haircuts, housecleaning, doctor visits). When you buy a CD by your favorite band, you are buying a good, and the purchase price is part of GDP. When you pay to hear a concert by the same band, you are buying a service, and the ticket price is also part of GDP.

[handwritten: Tangible + intangible]

23-2e "... Produced ..."

GDP includes goods and services currently produced. It does not include transactions involving items produced in the past. When Ford produces and sells a new car, the value of the car is included in GDP. When one person sells a used car to another person, the value of the used car is not included in GDP.

[handwritten: Past does not count. used cars don't count]

23-2f "... Within a Country ..."

GDP measures the value of production within the geographic confines of a country. When a Canadian citizen works temporarily in the United States, her production is part of U.S. GDP. When an American citizen owns a factory in Haiti, the production at her factory is not part of U.S. GDP. (It is part of Haiti's GDP.) Thus, items are included in a nation's GDP if they are produced domestically, regardless of the nationality of the producer.

[handwritten: Produced domestically, the nationality of producer doesn't matter.]

23-2g "... In a Given Period of Time."

GDP measures the value of production that takes place within a specific interval of time. Usually, that interval is a year or a quarter (three months). GDP measures the economy's flow of income, as well as its flow of expenditure, during that interval.

When the government reports the GDP for a quarter, it usually presents GDP "at an annual rate." This means that the figure reported for quarterly GDP is the amount of income and expenditure during the quarter multiplied by 4. The government uses this convention so that quarterly and annual figures on GDP can be compared more easily.

[handwritten: annual]

In addition, when the government reports quarterly GDP, it presents the data after they have been modified by a statistical procedure called *seasonal adjustment*. The unadjusted data show clearly that the economy produces more goods and services during some times of the year than during others. (As you might guess, December's holiday shopping season is a high point.) When monitoring the condition of the economy, economists and policymakers often want to look beyond these regular seasonal changes. Therefore, government statisticians adjust the quarterly data to take out the seasonal cycle. The GDP data reported in the news are always seasonally adjusted.

Now let's repeat the definition of GDP:

- Gross domestic product (GDP) is the market value of all final goods and services produced within a country in a given period of time.

This definition focuses on GDP as total expenditure in the economy. But don't forget that every dollar spent by a buyer of a good or service becomes a dollar of income to the seller of that good or service. Therefore, in addition to applying this definition, the government adds up total income in the economy. The two ways of calculating GDP give almost exactly the same answer. (Why "almost"? The two measures should be precisely the same, but data sources are not perfect. The difference between the two calculations of GDP is called the *statistical discrepancy*.)

It should be apparent that GDP is a sophisticated measure of the value of economic activity. In advanced courses in macroeconomics, you will learn more about the subtleties that arise in its calculation. But even now you can see that each phrase in this definition is packed with meaning.

Quick Quiz   *Which contributes more to GDP—the production of a pound of hamburger or the production of a pound of caviar? Why?*

23-3 The Components of GDP

Spending in the economy takes many forms. At any moment, the Smith family may be having lunch at Burger King; Ford may be building a car factory; the Navy may be procuring a submarine; and British Airways may be buying an airplane from Boeing. GDP includes all of these various forms of spending on domestically produced goods and services.

To understand how the economy is using its scarce resources, economists study the composition of GDP among various types of spending. To do this, GDP (which we denote as *Y*) is divided into four components: consumption (*C*), investment (*I*), government purchases (*G*), and net exports (*NX*):

$$Y = C + I + G + NX.$$

This equation is an *identity*—an equation that must be true because of how the variables in the equation are defined. In this case, because each dollar of expenditure included in GDP is placed into one of the four components of GDP, the total of the four components must be equal to GDP. Let's look at each of these four components more closely.

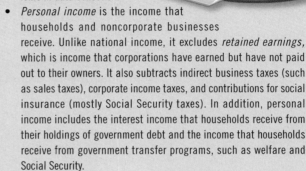

FYI

Other Measures of Income

When the U.S. Department of Commerce computes the nation's GDP every three months, it also computes various other measures of income to get a more complete picture of what's happening in the economy. These other measures differ from GDP by excluding or including certain categories of income. What follows is a brief description of five of these income measures, ordered from largest to smallest.

- *Gross national product* (GNP) is the total income earned by a nation's permanent residents (called *nationals*). It differs from GDP in that it includes income that our citizens earn abroad and excludes income that foreigners earn here. For example, when a Canadian citizen works temporarily in the United States, her production is part of U.S. GDP, but it is not part of U.S. GNP. (It is part of Canada's GNP.) For most countries, including the United States, domestic residents are responsible for most domestic production, so GDP and GNP are quite close.
- *Net national product* (NNP) is the total income of a nation's residents (GNP) minus losses from depreciation. *Depreciation* is the wear and tear on the economy's stock of equipment and structures, such as trucks rusting and old computer models becoming obsolete. In the national income accounts prepared by the Department of Commerce, depreciation is called the "consumption of fixed capital."
- *National income* is the total income earned by a nation's residents in the production of goods and services. It is almost identical to net national product. These two measures differ because of the

statistical discrepancy that arises from problems in data collection.

- *Personal income* is the income that households and noncorporate businesses receive. Unlike national income, it excludes *retained earnings*, which is income that corporations have earned but have not paid out to their owners. It also subtracts indirect business taxes (such as sales taxes), corporate income taxes, and contributions for social insurance (mostly Social Security taxes). In addition, personal income includes the interest income that households receive from their holdings of government debt and the income that households receive from government transfer programs, such as welfare and Social Security.
- *Disposable personal income* is the income that households and noncorporate businesses have left after satisfying all their obligations to the government. It equals personal income minus personal taxes and certain nontax payments (such as traffic tickets).

Although the various measures of income differ in detail, they almost always tell the same story about economic conditions. When GDP grows rapidly, these other measures of income usually grow rapidly. And when GDP falls, these other measures usually fall as well. For monitoring fluctuations in the overall economy, it does not matter much which measure of income we use. ◢

23-3a Consumption

Consumption is spending by households on goods and services, with the exception of purchases of new housing. Goods include durable goods, such as automobiles and appliances, and nondurable goods, such as food and clothing. Services include such intangible items as haircuts and medical care. Household spending on education is also included in consumption of services (although one might argue that it would fit better in the next component).

consumption
spending by households on goods and services, with the exception of purchases of new housing

23-3b Investment *To be used in future*

Investment is the purchase of goods that will be used in the future to produce more goods and services. It is the sum of purchases of capital equipment, inventories, and structures. Investment in structures includes expenditure on new housing. By convention, the purchase of a new house is the one form of household spending categorized as investment rather than consumption.

As mentioned earlier in this chapter, the treatment of inventory accumulation is noteworthy. When Apple produces a computer and adds it to its inventory instead of selling it, Apple is assumed to have "purchased" the computer for itself. That is,

investment
spending on capital equipment, inventories, and structures, including household purchases of new housing

the national income accountants treat the computer as part of Apple's investment spending. (If Apple later sells the computer out of inventory, Apple's inventory investment will then be negative, offsetting the positive expenditure of the buyer.) Inventories are treated this way because one aim of GDP is to measure the value of the economy's production, and goods added to inventory are part of that period's production.

Notice that GDP accounting uses the word *investment* differently from how you might hear the term in everyday conversation. When you hear the word *investment*, you might think of financial investments, such as stocks, bonds, and mutual funds—topics that we study later in this book. By contrast, because GDP measures expenditure on goods and services, here the word *investment* means purchases of goods (such as capital equipment, structures, and inventories) used to produce other goods and services in the future.

23-3c Government Purchases

government purchases
spending on goods and services by local, state, and federal governments

on Test

Government purchases include spending on goods and services by local, state, and federal governments. It includes the salaries of government workers as well as expenditures on public works. Recently, the U.S. national income accounts have switched to the longer label *government consumption expenditure and gross investment,* but in this book, we will use the traditional and shorter term *government purchases.*

The meaning of government purchases requires a bit of clarification. When the government pays the salary of an Army general or a schoolteacher, that salary is part of government purchases. But when the government pays a Social Security benefit to a person who is elderly or an unemployment insurance benefit to a worker who was recently laid off, the story is very different: These are called *transfer payments* because they are not made in exchange for a currently produced good or service. Transfer payments alter household income, but they do not reflect the economy's production. (From a macroeconomic standpoint, transfer payments are like negative taxes.) Because GDP is intended to measure income from, and expenditure on, the production of goods and services, transfer payments are not counted as part of government purchases.

23-3d Net Exports   *Exports $-$ Imports $=$ net exports*
    minus

net exports
spending on domestically produced goods by foreigners (exports) minus spending on foreign goods by domestic residents (imports)

When we buy used cars = 40,000 consumption
minus
40,000 Import
$0= no affect

Net exports equal the foreign purchases of domestically produced goods (exports) minus the domestic purchases of foreign goods (imports). A domestic firm's sale to a buyer in another country, such as Boeing's sale of an airplane to British Airways, increases net exports.

The *net* in *net exports* refers to the fact that imports are subtracted from exports. This subtraction is made because other components of GDP include imports of goods and services. For example, suppose that a household buys a $40,000 car from Volvo, the Swedish carmaker. This transaction increases consumption by $40,000 because car purchases are part of consumer spending. It also reduces net exports by $40,000 because the car is an import. In other words, net exports include goods and services produced abroad (with a minus sign) because these goods and services are included in consumption, investment, and government purchases (with a plus sign). Thus, when a domestic household, firm, or government buys a good or service from abroad, the purchase reduces net exports, but because it also raises consumption, investment, or government purchases, it does not affect GDP.

TABLE 1

GDP and Its Components
This table shows total GDP for the U.S. economy in 2012 and the breakdown of GDP among its four components. When reading this table, recall the identity $Y = C + I + G + NX$.

	Total (in billions of dollars)	Per Person (in dollars)	Percent of Total
Gross domestic product, Y	$15,676	$49,923	100%
Consumption, C	11,119	35,411	71
Investment, I	2,059	6,557	13
Government purchases, G	3,064	9,758	20
Net exports, NX	–567	–1,806	–4

Source: U.S. Department of Commerce. Parts may not sum to totals due to rounding.

case study

The Components of U.S. GDP

Table 1 shows the composition of U.S. GDP in 2012. In this year, the GDP of the United States was over $15 trillion. Dividing this number by the 2012 U.S. population of 314 million yields GDP per person (sometimes called GDP per capita). In 2012 the income and expenditure of the average American was $49,923.

Consumption made up 71 percent of GDP, or $35,411 per person. Investment was $6,557 per person. Government purchases were $9,758 per person. Net exports were –$1,806 per person. This number is negative because Americans spent more on foreign goods than foreigners spent on American goods.

These data come from the Bureau of Economic Analysis, the part of the U.S. Department of Commerce that produces the national income accounts. You can find more recent data on GDP on its website, http://www.bea.gov. ◢

Quick Quiz *List the four components of expenditure. Which is the largest?*

23-4 Real versus Nominal GDP

As we have seen, GDP measures the total spending on goods and services in all markets in the economy. If total spending rises from one year to the next, at least one of two things must be true: (1) the economy is producing a larger output of goods and services, or (2) goods and services are being sold at higher prices. When studying changes in the economy over time, economists want to separate these two effects. In particular, they want a measure of the total quantity of goods and services the economy is producing that is not affected by changes in the prices of those goods and services.

To do this, economists use a measure called *real GDP*. Real GDP answers a hypothetical question: What would be the value of the goods and services produced this year if we valued these goods and services at the prices that prevailed in some specific year in the past? By evaluating current production using prices that are fixed at past levels, real GDP shows how the economy's overall production of goods and services changes over time.

[handwritten margin notes:]
IF GDP goes up:
1 - producing larger output
or
2 - or prices are higher

Real:
Keep prices same so we can see if amount went up

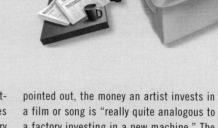

IN THE NEWS
....

The BEA Changes the Definitions of Investment and GDP

In 2013, the Bureau of Economic Analysis announced that it would expand the definitions of investment and GDP to include the production of various forms of intellectual property. This article discusses the change. Because the new data were not yet available as this book was going to press, all the data presented here use the traditional, narrower definitions.

Yes, Lady Gaga's Songs Contribute to GDP

By Osagie Imasogie and Thaddeus J. Kobylarz

The U.S. government recently announced a welcome revision to the way it estimates gross domestic product. Starting July 31, the Bureau of Economic Analysis will record expenditures for "R&D and for entertainment, literary and artistic originals as fixed investment," grouping them with expenditures for software into a new investment category called "intellectual property products."

What does this mean for GDP? Until this change, as Wellesley economist Daniel Sichel recently told NPR, "If Lady Gaga did a concert and sold concert tickets, the concert tickets would count as GDP," but the money she spent writing and recording an album wouldn't. That didn't make sense, because as Mr. Sichel pointed out, the money an artist invests in a film or song is "really quite analogous to a factory investing in a new machine." The same is clearly true of money invested in R&D for new drugs or smartphones.

Taken together, these new revisions are even more significant than the 1999 revision that added expenditures for computer software to the national accounts. Why? First, by expanding the list of intellectual-property investments used to calculate GDP to

---

To see more precisely how real GDP is constructed, let's consider an example.

23-4a A Numerical Example

Table 2 shows some data for an economy that produces only two goods: hot dogs and hamburgers. The table shows the prices and quantities produced of the two goods in the years 2013, 2014, and 2015.

To compute total spending in this economy, we would multiply the quantities of hot dogs and hamburgers by their prices. In the year 2013, 100 hot dogs are sold at a price of $1 per hot dog, so expenditure on hot dogs equals $100. In the same year, 50 hamburgers are sold for $2 per hamburger, so expenditure on hamburgers also equals $100. Total expenditure in the economy—the sum of expenditure on hot dogs and expenditure on hamburgers—is $200. This amount, the production of goods and services valued at current prices, is called **nominal GDP**.

The table shows the calculation of nominal GDP for these three years. Total spending rises from $200 in 2013 to $600 in 2014 and then to $1,200 in 2015. Part of this rise is attributable to the increase in the quantities of hot dogs and hamburgers, and part is attributable to the increase in the prices of hot dogs and hamburgers.

To obtain a measure of the amount produced that is not affected by changes in prices, we use **real GDP**, which is the production of goods and services valued at constant prices. We calculate real GDP by first designating one year as a *base year*. We then use the prices of hot dogs and hamburgers in the base year to compute the value of goods and services in all the years. In other words, the prices in the base year provide the basis for comparing quantities in different years.

Suppose that we choose 2013 to be the base year in our example. We can then use the prices of hot dogs and hamburgers in 2013 to compute the value of goods

nominal GDP
the production of goods and services valued at current prices

real GDP
the production of goods and services valued at constant prices

include R&D and the arts and entertainment industry, the present U.S. economy is shown to be roughly 3%—or $400 billion—larger than thought. (That doesn't mean we'll see a dramatic increase in GDP after July; the GDP figures going back to 1929 will also be adjusted, lessening the impact of the change on current growth rates.)

Second, the revision reflects the economy's quiet transformation from one based principally on industry to one decidedly based on knowledge and information. Third, this revision opens the door to further changes in the GDP calculation methodology, since the Bureau of Economic Analysis has in essence conceded that the GDP indicator, as now defined, has fallen behind today's economic realities.

This change is more than an arcane issue of interest only to economists. Government GDP figures are used to determine fundamental policy matters that affect everyday citizens' lives, such as budget decisions and

funding for federal programs. GDP numbers also constitute a shorthand for evaluating the performance of the national economy.

A clear goal of the BEA's decision is to better reflect the role of intellectual property as a key contributor to the national economy. This change in the measurement of GDP will affect both policy decisions regarding intellectual property and how we perceive ourselves as a society.

Right now there are pivotal cases before the U.S. Supreme Court on the legitimate scope and subject matter of patent protection, including in the growing field of genetics where at least 25% of all human genes have already been patented by private companies. Crucial decisions similarly confront us on the educational funding and direction, particularly in relation to science, technology, engineering and math and early childhood education.

In the past two decades, intellectual property has emerged as the principal driver of

economic growth in the U.S. and other developed countries. IP is now, in many respects, the new global currency. This is largely the result of America's successful effort to internationalize its views regarding the economic importance of IP protection, notwithstanding the continuing challenge of piracy. In short, America's place as a world economic leader depends on its ability to cultivate a sufficiently creative "mint" by which to generate, and profit from, this new global currency.

The government's new GDP measure suggests that economists are rightly adjusting to this new landscape. Whereas traditionalists have long counted land, labor and capital as the primary factors of production, economists are increasingly recognizing the productive significance of more intangible factors. This includes IP and, more generally, intellectual capital. ◢

Source: *The Wall Street Journal*, May 28, 2013.

TABLE 2

Real and Nominal GDP
This table shows how to calculate real GDP, nominal GDP, and the GDP deflator for a hypothetical economy that produces only hot dogs and hamburgers.

Prices and Quantities

Year	Price of Hot Dogs	Quantity of Hot Dogs	Price of Hamburgers	Quantity of Hamburgers
2013	$1	100	$2	50
2014	$2	150	$3	100
2015	$3	200	$4	150

Calculating Nominal GDP

2013	($1 per hot dog × 100 hot dogs) + ($2 per hamburger × 50 hamburgers) = $200
2014	($2 per hot dog × 150 hot dogs) + ($3 per hamburger × 100 hamburgers) = $600
2015	($3 per hot dog × 200 hot dogs) + ($4 per hamburger × 150 hamburgers) = $1,200

Calculating Real GDP (base year 2013)

2013	($1 per hot dog × 100 hot dogs) + ($2 per hamburger × 50 hamburgers) = $200
2014	($1 per hot dog × 150 hot dogs) + ($2 per hamburger × 100 hamburgers) = $350
2015	($1 per hot dog × 200 hot dogs) + ($2 per hamburger × 150 hamburgers) = $500

Calculating the GDP Deflator

2013	($200 / $200) × 100 = 100
2014	($600 / $350) × 100 = 171
2015	($1,200 / $500) × 100 = 240

[Handwritten annotations: "Both Price + Quantity went up" "NOT affected by Price" near Nominal GDP section; "current price" above Calculating Nominal GDP; "Same price over 3 years" and "constant price / Take one year as base year" near Calculating Real GDP section.]

In base year
Real + nominal are the same

Real GDP shows what quantity really went up
not affected by price

Real is better
Economist use Real

and services produced in 2013, 2014, and 2015. Table 2 shows these calculations. To compute real GDP for 2013, we use the prices of hot dogs and hamburgers in 2013 (the base year) and the quantities of hot dogs and hamburgers produced in 2013. (Thus, for the base year, real GDP always equals nominal GDP.) To compute real GDP for 2014, we use the prices of hot dogs and hamburgers in 2013 (the base year) and the quantities of hot dogs and hamburgers produced in 2014. Similarly, to compute real GDP for 2015, we use the prices in 2013 and the quantities in 2015. When we find that real GDP has risen from $200 in 2013 to $350 in 2014 and then to $500 in 2015, we know that the increase is attributable to an increase in the quantities produced because the prices are being held fixed at base-year levels.

To sum up: *Nominal GDP uses current prices to place a value on the economy's production of goods and services. Real GDP uses constant base-year prices to place a value on the economy's production of goods and services.* Because real GDP is not affected by changes in prices, changes in real GDP reflect only changes in the amounts being produced. Thus, real GDP is a measure of the economy's production of goods and services.

Our goal in computing GDP is to gauge how well the overall economy is performing. Because real GDP measures the economy's production of goods and services, it reflects the economy's ability to satisfy people's needs and desires. Thus, real GDP is a better gauge of economic well-being than is nominal GDP. When economists talk about the economy's GDP, they usually mean real GDP rather than nominal GDP. And when they talk about growth in the economy, they measure that growth as the percentage change in real GDP from one period to another.

23-4b The GDP Deflator

As we have just seen, nominal GDP reflects both the quantities of goods and services the economy is producing and the prices of those goods and services. By contrast, by holding prices constant at base-year levels, real GDP reflects only the quantities produced. From these two statistics, we can compute a third, called the GDP deflator, which reflects only the prices of goods and services.

The **GDP deflator** is calculated as follows:

GDP deflator
a measure of the price level calculated as the ratio of nominal GDP to real GDP times 100

Deflator is only prices of Goods + services

$$\text{GDP deflator} = \frac{\text{Nominal GDP}}{\text{Real GDP}} \times 100.$$

Because nominal GDP and real GDP must be the same in the base year, the GDP deflator for the base year always equals 100. The GDP deflator for subsequent years measures the change in nominal GDP from the base year that cannot be attributable to a change in real GDP.

The GDP deflator measures the current level of prices relative to the level of prices in the base year. To see why this is true, consider a couple of simple examples. First, imagine that the quantities produced in the economy rise over time but prices remain the same. In this case, both nominal and real GDP rise at the same rate, so the GDP deflator is constant. Now suppose, instead, that prices rise over time but the quantities produced stay the same. In this second case, nominal GDP rises but real GDP remains the same, so the GDP deflator rises. Notice that, in both cases, the GDP deflator reflects what's happening to prices, not quantities.

Let's now return to our numerical example in Table 2. The GDP deflator is computed at the bottom of the table. For the year 2013, nominal GDP is $200 and real GDP is $200, so the GDP deflator is 100. (The deflator is always 100 in the base year.) For the year 2014, nominal GDP is $600 and real GDP is $350, so the GDP deflator is 171.

Economists use the term *inflation* to describe a situation in which the economy's overall price level is rising. The *inflation rate* is the percentage change in some measure of the price level from one period to the next. Using the GDP deflator, the inflation rate between two consecutive years is computed as follows:

$$\text{Inflation rate in year 2} = \frac{\text{GDP deflator in year 2} - \text{GDP deflator in year 1}}{\text{GDP deflator in year 1}} \times 100.$$

Because the GDP deflator rose in year 2014 from 100 to 171, the inflation rate is $100 \times (171 - 100)/100$, or 71 percent. In 2015, the GDP deflator rose to 240 from 171 the previous year, so the inflation rate is $100 \times (240 - 171)/171$, or 40 percent.

The GDP deflator is one measure that economists use to monitor the average level of prices in the economy and thus the rate of inflation. The GDP deflator gets its name because it can be used to take inflation out of nominal GDP—that is, to "deflate" nominal GDP for the rise that is due to increases in prices. We examine another measure of the economy's price level, called the consumer price index, in the next chapter, where we also describe the differences between the two measures.

case study | **Real GDP over Recent History**
Now that we know how real GDP is defined and measured, let's look at what this macroeconomic variable tells us about the recent history of the United States. Figure 2 shows quarterly data on real GDP for the U.S. economy since 1965.

The most obvious feature of these data is that real GDP grows over time. The real GDP of the U.S. economy in 2012 was almost four times its 1965 level. Put differently, the output of goods and services produced in the United States has

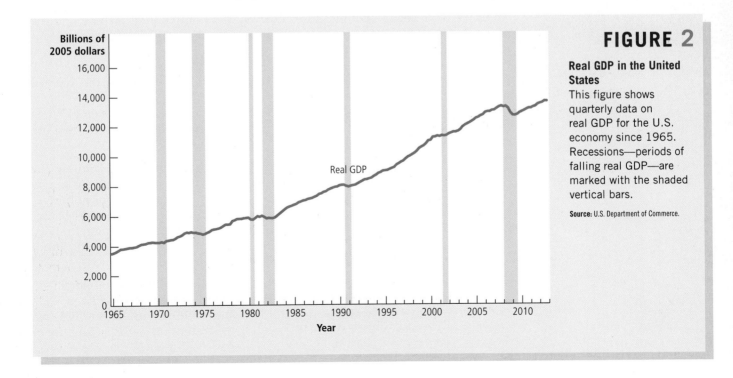

FIGURE 2

Real GDP in the United States
This figure shows quarterly data on real GDP for the U.S. economy since 1965. Recessions—periods of falling real GDP—are marked with the shaded vertical bars.

Source: U.S. Department of Commerce.

grown on average about 3 percent per year. This continued growth in real GDP enables most Americans to enjoy greater economic prosperity than their parents and grandparents did.

A second feature of the GDP data is that growth is not steady. The upward climb of real GDP is occasionally interrupted by periods during which GDP declines, called *recessions*. Figure 2 marks recessions with shaded vertical bars. (There is no ironclad rule for when the official business cycle dating committee will declare that a recession has occurred, but an old rule of thumb is two consecutive quarters of falling real GDP.) Recessions are associated not only with lower incomes but also with other forms of economic distress: rising unemployment, falling profits, increased bankruptcies, and so on.

Much of macroeconomics is aimed at explaining the long-run growth and short-run fluctuations in real GDP. As we will see in the coming chapters, we need different models for these two purposes. Because the short-run fluctuations represent deviations from the long-run trend, we first examine the behavior of key macroeconomic variables, including real GDP, in the long run. Then in later chapters, we build on this analysis to explain short-run fluctuations. ◢

Quick Quiz   *Define* real GDP *and* nominal GDP. *Which is a better measure of economic well-being? Why?*

23-5 Is GDP a Good Measure of Economic Well-Being?

Earlier in this chapter, GDP was called the best single measure of the economic well-being of a society. Now that we know what GDP is, we can evaluate this claim.

As we have seen, GDP measures both the economy's total income and the economy's total expenditure on goods and services. Thus, GDP per person tells us the income and expenditure of the average person in the economy. Because most people would prefer to receive higher income and enjoy higher expenditure, GDP per person seems a natural measure of the economic well-being of the average individual.

Yet some people dispute the validity of GDP as a measure of well-being. When Senator Robert Kennedy was running for president in 1968, he gave a moving critique of such economic measures:

> [Gross domestic product] does not allow for the health of our children, the quality of their education, or the joy of their play. It does not include the beauty of our poetry or the strength of our marriages, the intelligence of our public debate or the integrity of our public officials. It measures neither our courage, nor our wisdom, nor our devotion to our country. It measures everything, in short, except that which makes life worthwhile, and it can tell us everything about America except why we are proud that we are Americans.

Much of what Robert Kennedy said is correct. Why, then, do we care about GDP?

The answer is that a large GDP does in fact help us to lead good lives. GDP does not measure the health of our children, but nations with larger GDP can afford better healthcare for their children. GDP does not measure the quality of their education, but nations with larger GDP can afford better educational systems. GDP does not measure the beauty of our poetry, but nations with larger GDP can afford to teach more of their citizens to read and enjoy poetry. GDP does not take account of our intelligence, integrity, courage, wisdom, or devotion to country, but all of these laudable attributes are easier to foster when people are less concerned about being able to afford the material necessities of life. In short, GDP does not directly measure those things that make life worthwhile, but it does measure our ability to obtain many of the inputs into a worthwhile life.

GDP is not, however, a perfect measure of well-being. Some things that contribute to a good life are left out of GDP. One is leisure. Suppose, for instance, that everyone in the economy suddenly started working every day of the week, rather than enjoying leisure on weekends. More goods and services would be produced, and GDP would rise. Yet despite the increase in GDP, we should not conclude that everyone would be better off. The loss from reduced leisure would offset the gain from producing and consuming a greater quantity of goods and services.

Because GDP uses market prices to value goods and services, it excludes the value of almost all activity that takes place outside markets. In particular, GDP omits the value of goods and services produced at home. When a chef prepares a delicious meal and sells it at her restaurant, the value of that meal is part of GDP. But if the chef prepares the same meal for her family, the value she has added to the raw ingredients is left out of GDP. Similarly, child care provided in day-care centers is part of GDP, whereas child care by parents at home is not. Volunteer work also contributes to the well-being of those in society, but GDP does not reflect these contributions.

Another thing that GDP excludes is the quality of the environment. Imagine that the government eliminated all environmental regulations. Firms could then produce goods and services without considering the pollution they create, and GDP might rise. Yet well-being would most likely fall. The deterioration in the quality of air and water would more than offset the gains from greater production.

GDP also says nothing about the distribution of income. A society in which 100 people have annual incomes of $50,000 has GDP of $5 million and, not surprisingly, GDP per person of $50,000. So does a society in which 10 people earn $500,000 and 90 suffer with nothing at all. Few people would look at those two situations and call them equivalent. GDP per person tells us what happens to the average person, but behind the average lies a large variety of personal experiences.

In the end, we can conclude that GDP is a good measure of economic well-being for most—but not all—purposes. It is important to keep in mind what GDP includes and what it leaves out.

GDP reflects the factory's production, but not the harm it inflicts on the environment.

case study   International Differences in GDP and the Quality of Life

One way to gauge the usefulness of GDP as a measure of economic well-being is to examine international data. Rich and poor countries have vastly different levels of GDP per person. If a large GDP leads to a higher standard of living, then we should observe GDP to be strongly correlated with various measures of the quality of life. And, in fact, we do.

Table 3 shows twelve of the world's most populous countries ranked in order of GDP per person. The table also shows life expectancy, the average years of schooling among adults, and the percentage of the population that reports

IN THE NEWS

....

The Underground Economy

The gross domestic product misses many transactions that take place in the underground economy.

Searching for the Hidden Economy

By Doug Campbell

Here is the brief, unremarkable story of how I recently came to participate in the underground economy:

Midafternoon on the iciest day this past winter, a man knocked at my front door. "Shovel your walk?" he asked. "Only $5."

Outside, it was a bone-chilling 15 degrees. "Sold," I said. A half-hour later I handed over a five-dollar bill and thanked him for saving me the trouble.

Officially, this was an unofficial transaction—off the books, with no taxes paid or safety regulations followed. (At least, I assume this hired hand didn't bother to report that income or register with the proper authorities.) As such, it was technically illegal. And, of course, it's the sort of thing that happens all the time.

International Differences in the Underground Economy

Country	Underground Economy as a Percentage of GDP
Bolivia	68 percent
Zimbabwe	63
Peru	61
Thailand	54
Mexico	33
Argentina	29
Sweden	18
Australia	13
United Kingdom	12
Japan	11
Switzerland	9
United States	8

Source: Friedrich Schneider. Figures are for 2002.

The size of the official U.S. economy, as measured by Gross Domestic Product (GDP), was almost $12 trillion in 2004. Measurements of the unofficial economy—not including illegal activities like drug dealing and prostitution—differ substantially. But it's generally agreed to be significant, somewhere between 6 percent and 20 percent of GDP. At the midpoint, this would be about $1.5 trillion a year.

Broadly defined, the underground, gray, informal, or shadow economy involves otherwise legal transactions that go unreported or unrecorded. That's a wide net, capturing everything from babysitting fees, to bartering home repairs with a neighbor, to failing to report pay from moonlighting gigs. The "underground" label tends to make it sound much more sinister than it really is.

TABLE 3

GDP and the Quality of Life

The table shows GDP per person and three other measures of the quality of life for twelve major countries.

Country	Real GDP per Person	Life Expectancy	Average Years of Schooling	Satisfied with Water Quality (% of population)
United States	$43,017	79 years	12 years	90
Germany	35,854	80	12	95
Japan	32,295	83	12	88
Russia	14, 561	69	10	53
Mexico	13,245	77	9	68
Brazil	10,162	74	7	83
China	7,746	74	8	73
Indonesia	3,716	69	6	87
India	3,468	65	4	63
Pakistan	2,550	65	5	55
Nigeria	2,069	52	5	47
Bangladesh	1,529	69	5	70

Source: *Human Development Report 2011*, United Nations. Real GDP is for 2011, expressed in 2005 dollars. Average years of schooling is among adults 25 years and older.

Criminal activities make up a large portion of what could be termed the total underground economy. Many studies have been done on the economics of drug dealing, prostitution, and gambling. But because money from crime is almost never recovered, many policymakers are more interested in portions of the underground economy that otherwise would be legal if not hidden from authorities. Things like shoveling walks.

Despite its intrigue, the informal economy's importance and consequences remain in debate. The reason: "You're trying to measure a phenomenon whose entire purpose is to hide itself from observation," says Ed Feige, an economist at the University of Wisconsin.

This uncertainty poses problems for policymakers. Without knowing the precise size, scope, and causes of the underground economy, how can they decide what—if anything—to do about it?

Was the man who shoveled my walk engaging in a socially positive or negative activity? Was I? Suffice it to say, some economists have dedicated their entire careers to answering questions about the underground

A Shadowy Enterprise?

economy—and still there is nothing close to a consensus about its size or description. . . .

Economists generally agree that the shadow economy is worse in developing nations, whose webs of bureaucratic red tape and corruption are notorious. For instance, [economist Friedrich] Schneider in 2003 published "shadow economy" estimates (defined broadly as all market-based, legal production of goods and services deliberately concealed from the authorities) for countries including: Zimbabwe, estimated at a whopping 63.2 percent of GDP, Thailand's at 54.1 percent, and Bolivia's at 68.3 percent. Among former Soviet bloc nations, Georgia led the way with a

68 percent of GDP shadow economy, and together those nations had an average 40.1 percent of GDP underground. This contrasts with an average of 16.7 percent among Western nations. . . .

In his 2003 book, *Reefer Madness: Sex, Drugs and Cheap Labor in the American Black Market*, investigative writer Eric Schlosser invokes Adam Smith's "invisible hand" theory that men pursuing their own self-interest will generate benefits for society as a whole. This invisible hand has produced a fairly sizable underground economy, and we cannot understand our entire economic system without understanding how the hidden underbelly functions, too. "The underground is a good measure of the progress and the health of nations," Schlosser writes. "When much is wrong, much needs to be hidden." Schlosser's implication was that much is wrong in the United States. If he had taken a more global view, he might have decided relatively little is hidden here. ◢

Source: "Region Focus," Federal Reserve Bank of Richmond, Spring 2005.

being satisfied with the quality of water they have available. These data show a clear pattern. In rich countries, such as the United States, Germany, and Japan, people can expect to live to about 80 and have 12 years of schooling; about 9 out of 10 people are satisfied with the quality of water they have to drink. In poor countries, such as Bangladesh, Nigeria, and Pakistan, people typically die 10 to 20 years earlier and have less than half as much schooling; about a third to a half of the population is unsatisfied with the quality of water locally available.

Data on other aspects of the quality of life tell a similar story. Countries with low GDP per person tend to have more infants with low birth weight, higher rates of infant mortality, higher rates of maternal mortality, and higher rates of child malnutrition. In countries with low GDP per person, fewer school-age children are actually in school, those who are in school must learn with fewer teachers per student, and illiteracy among adults is more common. These countries also tend to have fewer televisions, fewer telephones, fewer paved roads, fewer households with electricity, and fewer opportunities to access the Internet. International data leave no doubt that a nation's GDP per person is closely associated with its citizens' standard of living. ◢

Quick Quiz   *Why should policymakers care about GDP?*

Measuring Macroeconomic Well-Being

Can we do better than using gross domestic product?

Nations Seek Success Beyond GDP

By Mark Whitehouse

Money isn't everything. But in measuring the success of nations, it isn't easy to find a substitute.

Political leaders are increasingly expressing dissatisfaction with gross domestic product—a monetary measure of all the goods and services a country produces—as a gauge of a nation's success in raising living standards.

In November, British Prime Minister David Cameron announced plans to build measures of national well-being that would take into account factors such as peoples' life satisfaction, following a similar effort by French President Nicolas Sarkozy.

Their efforts cut to the core of what economics is supposed to be about: What makes us better off? How can we all have more of it? Anyone hoping for a clear-cut answer, though, is likely to be disappointed.

"There is more to life than GDP, but it will be hard to come up with a single measure to replace it and we are not sure that a single measure is the answer," said Paul Allin, director of the Measuring National Well-Being Project at the U.K.'s Office of National Statistics. "Maybe we live in a multidimensional world and we have to get used to handling a reasonable number of bits of information."

After a session on creating a national success indicator at the annual meeting of the American Economic Association on Friday, Carol Graham, fellow at the Brookings Institution, summed up the situation thus: "It's like a new science. There's still a lot of work to be done."

For much of the past four decades, economists have puzzled over a paradox that cast doubt on GDP as the world's main indicator of success.

People in richer countries didn't appear to be any happier than people in poor countries. In research beginning in the 1970s, University of Pennsylvania economist Richard Easterlin found no evidence of a link between countries' income—as measured by GDP per person—and peoples' reported levels of happiness.

More recent research suggests GDP isn't quite so bad. Using more data and different statistical techniques, three economists at the University of Pennsylvania's Wharton School—Daniel Sacks, Betsey Stevenson and Justin Wolfers—found that a given percentage increase in GDP per person tends to coincide with a similar increase in reported well-being. The correlation held across different countries and over time.

Still, for measuring the success of policy, GDP is far from ideal. Making everybody work 120 hours a week could radically boost a country's GDP per capita, but it wouldn't make people happier. Removing pollution limits could boost GDP per hour worked, but wouldn't necessarily lead to a world we'd want to live in.

One approach is to enhance GDP with other objective factors such as inequality, leisure and life expectancy. In a paper presented Saturday at the American Economic Association meeting, Stanford economists Peter Klenow and Charles Jones found that doing so can make a big difference.

By their calculation, accounting for longer life expectancy, additional leisure time and lower levels of inequality makes living standards in France and Germany look almost the same as those in the U.S., which otherwise leads the pack by a large margin.

Mr. Klenow points out that the calculation is fraught with difficulties. For one, many

23-6 Conclusion

This chapter has discussed how economists measure the total income of a nation. Measurement is, of course, only a starting point. Much of macroeconomics is aimed at revealing the long-run and short-run determinants of a nation's GDP. Why, for example, is GDP higher in the United States and Japan than in India and Nigeria? What can the governments of the poorest countries do to promote more rapid GDP growth? Why does GDP in the United States rise rapidly in some years and fall in others? What can U.S. policymakers do to reduce

countries have poor data on crucial factors such as life expectancy.

For the purpose of comparing well-being across countries, asking people how they feel might be better than monetary measures. Angus Deaton, an economist at Princeton University, notes that placing values on the extremely different goods and services consumed in the U.S. and, say, Tajikistan, can be impossible to do in a comparable way. Just asking people about their situation could be much easier and no less accurate.

Surveys already play a meaningful role in the way many countries assess their performance, from consumer confidence in the U.S. to the Netherlands's Life Situation Index, which accounts for factors such as relationships and community involvement.

As part of its effort to gauge well-being, the U.K. plans to add more subjective questions to its household surveys.

But surveys can also send misleading policy signals. Mr. Wolfers, for example, has found that surveys of women's subjective well-being in the U.S. suggest that they are less happy than they were four decades ago, despite improvements in wages, education and other objective measures. That, he says, doesn't mean the feminist movement should be reversed. Rather, it could be related to rising expectations or greater frankness among the women interviewed.

Peoples' true preferences are often revealed more by what they do than by what they say. Surveys suggest people with children tend to be less happy than those without, yet people keep having children—and nobody would advocate mass sterilization to improve overall well-being.

"What we care about in the world is not just happiness," says Mr. Wolfers. "If you measure just one part of what makes for a full life you're going to end up harming the other parts."

For the time being, that leaves policy makers to choose the measures of success that seem most appropriate for the task at hand. That's not ideal, but it's the best economics has to offer. ◢

Happily ever after

More wealth doesn't always translate into greater quality of life, when factors such as leisure and length of life are included.

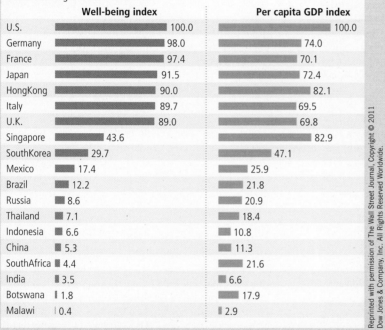

	Well-being index	Per capita GDP index
U.S.	100.0	100.0
Germany	98.0	74.0
France	97.4	70.1
Japan	91.5	72.4
HongKong	90.0	82.1
Italy	89.7	69.5
U.K.	89.0	69.8
Singapore	43.6	82.9
SouthKorea	29.7	47.1
Mexico	17.4	25.9
Brazil	12.2	21.8
Russia	8.6	20.9
Thailand	7.1	18.4
Indonesia	6.6	10.8
China	5.3	11.3
SouthAfrica	4.4	21.6
India	3.5	6.6
Botswana	1.8	17.9
Malawi	0.4	2.9

Note: 2000 data.
Source: Peter Klenow and Charles Jones, Stanford University

Source: *The Wall Street Journal,* January 10, 2011.

the severity of these fluctuations in GDP? These are the questions we will take up shortly.

At this point, it is important to acknowledge the significance of just measuring GDP. We all get some sense of how the economy is doing as we go about our lives. But the economists who study changes in the economy and the policymakers who formulate economic policies need more than this vague sense—they need concrete data on which to base their judgments. Quantifying the behavior of the economy with statistics such as GDP is, therefore, the first step to developing a science of macroeconomics.

Summary

- Because every transaction has a buyer and a seller, the total expenditure in the economy must equal the total income in the economy.

- Gross domestic product (GDP) measures an economy's total expenditure on newly produced goods and services and the total income earned from the production of these goods and services. More precisely, GDP is the market value of all final goods and services produced within a country in a given period of time.

- GDP is divided among four components of expenditure: consumption, investment, government purchases, and net exports. Consumption includes spending on goods and services by households, with the exception of purchases of new housing. Investment includes spending on new equipment and structures, including households' purchases of new housing. Government purchases include spending on goods

and services by local, state, and federal governments. Net exports equal the value of goods and services produced domestically and sold abroad (exports) minus the value of goods and services produced abroad and sold domestically (imports).

- Nominal GDP uses current prices to value the economy's production of goods and services. Real GDP uses constant base-year prices to value the economy's production of goods and services. The GDP deflator—calculated from the ratio of nominal to real GDP—measures the level of prices in the economy.

- GDP is a good measure of economic well-being because people prefer higher to lower incomes. But it is not a perfect measure of well-being. For example, GDP excludes the value of leisure and the value of a clean environment.

Key Concepts

microeconomics, *p. 484*
macroeconomics, *p. 484*
gross domestic product (GDP), *p. 486*
consumption, *p. 489*

investment, *p. 489*
government purchases, *p. 490*
net exports, *p. 490*
nominal GDP, *p. 492*

real GDP, *p. 492*
GDP deflator, *p. 494*

Questions for Review

1. Explain why an economy's income must equal its expenditure.

2. Which contributes more to GDP—the production of an economy car or the production of a luxury car? Why?

3. A farmer sells wheat to a baker for $2. The baker uses the wheat to make bread, which is sold for $3. What is the total contribution of these transactions to GDP?

4. Many years ago, Peggy paid $500 to put together a record collection. Today, she sold her albums at a garage sale for $100. How does this sale affect current GDP?

5. List the four components of GDP. Give an example of each.

6. Why do economists use real GDP rather than nominal GDP to gauge economic well-being?

7. In the year 2013, the economy produces 100 loaves of bread that sell for $2 each. In the year 2014, the economy produces 200 loaves of bread that sell for $3 each. Calculate nominal GDP, real GDP, and the GDP deflator for each year. (Use 2013 as the base year.) By what percentage does each of these three statistics rise from one year to the next?

8. Why is it desirable for a country to have a large GDP? Give an example of something that would raise GDP and yet be undesirable.

Quick Check Multiple Choice

1. If the price of a hot dog is $2 and the price of a hamburger is $4, then 30 hot dogs contribute as much to GDP as _____ hamburgers.
   a. 5
   b. 15
   c. 30
   d. 60

2. Angus the sheep farmer sells wool to Barnaby the knitter for $20. Barnaby makes two sweaters, each of which has a market price of $40. Collette buys one of them, while the other remains on the shelf of Barnaby's store to be sold later. What is GDP here?
   a. $40
   b. $60
   c. $80
   d. $100

3. Which of the following does NOT add to U.S. GDP?
   a. Air France buys a plane from Boeing, the U.S. aircraft manufacturer.
   b. General Motors builds a new auto factory in North Carolina.
   c. The city of New York pays a salary to a policeman.
   d. The federal government sends a Social Security check to your grandmother.

4. An American buys a pair of shoes manufactured in Italy. How do the U.S. national income accounts treat the transaction?
   a. Net exports and GDP both rise.
   b. Net exports and GDP both fall.
   c. Net exports fall, while GDP is unchanged.
   d. Net exports are unchanged, while GDP rises.

5. Which is the largest component of GDP?
   a. consumption
   b. investment
   c. government purchases
   d. net exports

6. If all quantities produced rise by 10 percent and all prices fall by 10 percent, which of the following occurs?
   a. Real GDP rises by 10 percent, while nominal GDP falls by 10 percent.
   b. Real GDP rises by 10 percent, while nominal GDP is unchanged.
   c. Real GDP is unchanged, while nominal GDP rises by 10 percent.
   d. Real GDP is unchanged, while nominal GDP falls by 10 percent.

Problems and Applications

1. What components of GDP (if any) would each of the following transactions affect? Explain.
   a. A family buys a new refrigerator.
   b. Aunt Jane buys a new house.
   c. Ford sells a Mustang from its inventory.
   d. You buy a pizza.
   e. California repaves Highway 101.
   f. Your parents buy a bottle of French wine.
   g. Honda expands its factory in Marysville, Ohio.

2. The government purchases component of GDP does not include spending on transfer payments such as Social Security. Thinking about the definition of GDP, explain why transfer payments are excluded.

3. As the chapter states, GDP does not include the value of used goods that are resold. Why would including such transactions make GDP a less informative measure of economic well-being?

4. Below are some data from the land of milk and honey.

Year	Price of Milk	Quantity of Milk	Price of Honey	Quantity of Honey
2013	$1	100 quarts	$2	50 quarts
2014	$1	200	$2	100
2015	$2	200	$4	100

   a. Compute nominal GDP, real GDP, and the GDP deflator for each year, using 2013 as the base year.
   b. Compute the percentage change in nominal GDP, real GDP, and the GDP deflator in 2014 and 2015 from the preceding year. For each year, identify the variable that does not change. Explain why your answer makes sense.

   c. Did economic well-being rise more in 2014 or 2015? Explain.

5. Consider an economy that produces only chocolate bars. In year 1, the quantity produced is 3 bars and the price is $4. In year 2, the quantity produced is 4 bars and the price is $5. In year 3, the quantity produced is 5 bars and the price is $6. Year 1 is the base year.
   a. What is nominal GDP for each of these three years?
   b. What is real GDP for each of these years?
   c. What is the GDP deflator for each of these years?
   d. What is the percentage growth rate of real GDP from year 2 to year 3?
   e. What is the inflation rate as measured by the GDP deflator from year 2 to year 3?
   f. In this one-good economy, how might you have answered parts (d) and (e) without first answering parts (b) and (c)?

6. Consider the following data on U.S. GDP:

Year	Nominal GDP (in billions of dollars)	GDP Deflator (base year 2005)
2012	15,676	115.4
2002	10,642	92.2

   a. What was the growth rate of nominal GDP between 2002 and 2012? (*Hint*: The growth rate of a variable X over an N-year period is calculated as $100 \times [(X_{final}/X_{initial})^{1/N} - 1]$.)
   b. What was the growth rate of the GDP deflator between 2002 and 2012?
   c. What was real GDP in 2002 measured in 2005 prices?

d. What was real GDP in 2012 measured in 2005 prices?

e. What was the growth rate of real GDP between 2002 and 2012?

f. *Was* the growth rate of nominal GDP higher or lower than the growth rate of real GDP? Explain.

7. Revised estimates of U.S. GDP are usually released by the government near the end of each month. Find a newspaper article that reports on the most recent release, or read the news release yourself at http://www.bea.gov, the website of the U.S. Bureau of Economic Analysis. Discuss the recent changes in real and nominal GDP and in the components of GDP.

8. A farmer grows wheat, which she sells to a miller for $100. The miller turns the wheat into flour, which she sells to a baker for $150. The baker turns the wheat into bread, which she sells to consumers for $180. Consumers eat the bread.

a. What is GDP in this economy? Explain.

b. *Value added* is defined as the value of a producer's output minus the value of the intermediate goods that the producer buys to make the output. Assuming there are no intermediate goods beyond those described above, calculate the value added of each of the three producers.

c. What is total value added of the three producers in this economy? How does it compare to the economy's GDP? Does this example suggest another way of calculating GDP?

9. Goods and services that are not sold in markets, such as food produced and consumed at home, are generally not included in GDP. Can you think of how this might cause the numbers in the second column of Table 3 to be misleading in a comparison of the economic well-being of the United States and India? Explain.

10. The participation of women in the U.S. labor force has risen dramatically since 1970.

a. How do you think this rise affected GDP?

b. Now imagine a measure of well-being that includes time spent working in the home and taking leisure. How would the change in this measure of well-being compare to the change in GDP?

c. Can you think of other aspects of well-being that are associated with the rise in women's labor-force participation? Would it be practical to construct a measure of well-being that includes these aspects?

11. One day, Barry the Barber, Inc., collects $400 for haircuts. Over this day, his equipment depreciates in value by $50. Of the remaining $350, Barry sends $30 to the government in sales taxes, takes home $220 in wages, and retains $100 in his business to add new equipment in the future. From the $220 that Barry takes home, he pays $70 in income taxes. Based on this information, compute Barry's contribution to the following measures of income.

a. gross domestic product

b. net national product

c. national income

d. personal income

e. disposable personal income

Go to CengageBrain.com to purchase access to the proven, critical Study Guide to accompany this text, which features additional notes and context, practice tests, and much more.

Measuring the Cost of Living

In 1931, as the U.S. economy was suffering through the Great Depression, the New York Yankees paid famed baseball player Babe Ruth a salary of $80,000. At the time, this pay was extraordinary, even among the stars of baseball. According to one story, a reporter asked Ruth whether he thought it was right that he made more than President Herbert Hoover, who had a salary of only $75,000. Ruth replied, "I had a better year."

In 2012, the median salary earned by a player on the New York Yankees was $1.9 million, and shortstop Alex Rodriguez was paid $30 million. At first, this fact might lead you to think that baseball has become vastly more lucrative over the past eight decades. But as everyone knows, the prices of goods and services have also risen. In 1931, a nickel would buy an ice-cream cone and a quarter would buy a ticket at the local movie theater. Because prices were so much lower in Babe Ruth's day than they are today, it is not clear whether Ruth enjoyed a higher or lower standard of living than today's players.

In the preceding chapter, we looked at how economists use gross domestic product (GDP) to measure the quantity of goods and services that the economy is producing. This chapter examines how economists measure the overall cost of living. To compare Babe Ruth's salary of $80,000 to salaries from today, we need to find some way of turning dollar figures into meaningful measures of purchasing power. That is exactly the job of a statistic called the *consumer price index*. After seeing how the consumer price index is constructed, we discuss how we can use such a price index to compare dollar figures from different points in time.

The consumer price index is used to monitor changes in the cost of living over time. When the consumer price index rises, the typical family has to spend more money to maintain the same standard of living. Economists use the term *inflation* to describe a situation in which the economy's overall price level is rising. The *inflation rate* is the percentage change in the price level from the previous period. The preceding chapter showed how economists can measure inflation using the GDP deflator. The inflation rate you are likely to hear on the nightly news, however, is calculated from the consumer price index, which better reflects the goods and services bought by consumers.

As we will see in the coming chapters, inflation is a closely watched aspect of macroeconomic performance and is a key variable guiding macroeconomic policy. This chapter provides the background for that analysis by showing how economists measure the inflation rate using the consumer price index and how this statistic can be used to compare dollar figures from different times.

24-1 The Consumer Price Index

consumer price index (CPI)
a measure of the overall cost of the goods and services bought by a typical consumer

The **consumer price index (CPI)** is a measure of the overall cost of the goods and services bought by a typical consumer. Each month, the Bureau of Labor Statistics (BLS), which is part of the Department of Labor, computes and reports the consumer price index. In this section, we discuss how the consumer price index is calculated and what problems arise in its measurement. We also consider how this index compares to the GDP deflator, another measure of the overall level of prices, which we examined in the preceding chapter.

24-1a How the CPI Is Calculated

When the BLS calculates the consumer price index and the inflation rate, it uses data on the prices of thousands of goods and services. To see exactly how these statistics are constructed, let's consider a simple economy in which consumers buy only two goods: hot dogs and hamburgers. Table 1 shows the five steps that the BLS follows.

1. *Fix the basket.* Determine which prices are most important to the typical consumer. If the typical consumer buys more hot dogs than hamburgers, then the price of hot dogs is more important than the price of hamburgers and, therefore, should be given greater weight in measuring the cost of living. The BLS sets these weights by surveying consumers to find the basket of goods and services bought by the typical consumer. In the example in the table, the typical consumer buys a basket of 4 hot dogs and 2 hamburgers.
2. *Find the prices.* Find the prices of each of the goods and services in the basket at each point in time. The table shows the prices of hot dogs and hamburgers for three different years.

3. *Compute the basket's cost.* Use the data on prices to calculate the cost of the basket of goods and services at different times. The table shows this calculation for each of the three years. Notice that only the prices in this calculation change. By keeping the basket of goods the same (4 hot dogs and 2 hamburgers), we are isolating the effects of price changes from the effects of any quantity changes that might be occurring at the same time.

4. *Choose a base year and compute the index.* Designate one year as the base year. The base year is the benchmark against which other years are compared. (The choice of base year is arbitrary, as the index is used to measure *changes* in the cost of living.) Once the base year is chosen, the index is calculated as follows:

$$\text{Consumer price index} = \frac{\text{Price of basket of goods and services in current year}}{\text{Price of basket in base year}} \times 100.$$

That is, the price of the basket of goods and services in each year is divided by the price of the basket in the base year, and this ratio is then multiplied by 100. The resulting number is the consumer price index.

In the example in Table 1, 2013 is the base year. In this year, the basket of hot dogs and hamburgers costs $8. Therefore, to calculate the consumer price index, the price of the basket in each year is divided by $8 and multiplied

TABLE 1

Calculating the Consumer Price Index and the Inflation Rate: An Example

This table shows how to calculate the consumer price index and the inflation rate for a hypothetical economy in which consumers buy only hot dogs and hamburgers.

Step 1: Survey Consumers to Determine a Fixed Basket of Goods

Basket = 4 hot dogs, 2 hamburgers

Step 2: Find the Price of Each Good in Each Year

Year	Price of Hot Dogs	Price of Hamburgers
2013	$1	$2
2014	2	3
2015	3	4

Step 3: Compute the Cost of the Basket of Goods in Each Year

2013	($1 per hot dog × 4 hot dogs) + ($2 per hamburger × 2 hamburgers) = $8 per basket
2014	($2 per hot dog × 4 hot dogs) + ($3 per hamburger × 2 hamburgers) = $14 per basket
2015	($3 per hot dog × 4 hot dogs) + ($4 per hamburger × 2 hamburgers) = $20 per basket

Step 4: Choose One Year as a Base Year (2013) and Compute the Consumer Price Index in Each Year

2013	($8 / $8) × 100 = 100
2014	($14 / $8) × 100 = 175
2015	($20 / $8) × 100 = 250

Step 5: Use the Consumer Price Index to Compute the Inflation Rate from Previous Year

2014	(175 − 100) / 100 × 100 = 75%
2015	(250 − 175) / 175 × 100 = 43%

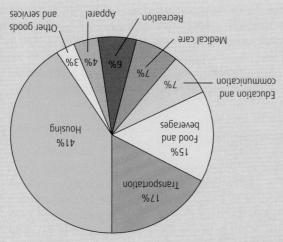

FIGURE 1

The Typical Basket of Goods and Services
This figure shows how the typical consumer divides spending among various categories of goods and services. The Bureau of Labor Statistics calls each percentage the "relative importance" of the category.

Source: Bureau of Labor Statistics.

Pie chart categories: Housing 41%, Transportation 17%, Food and beverages 15%, Education and communication 7%, Medical care 7%, Recreation 6%, Apparel 4%, Other goods and services 3%.

FYI

What Is in the CPI's Basket?

When constructing the consumer price index, the Bureau of Labor Statistics tries to include all the goods and services that the typical consumer buys. Moreover, it tries to weight these goods and services according to how much consumers buy of each item.

Figure 1 shows the breakdown of consumer spending into the major categories of goods and services. By far the largest category is housing, which makes up 41 percent of the typical consumer's budget. This category includes the cost of shelter (32 percent), fuel and other utilities (5 percent), and household furnishings and operation (4 percent). The next largest category, at 17 percent, is transportation, which includes spending on cars, gasoline, buses, subways, and so on. The next category, at 15 percent, is food and beverages; this includes food at home (8 percent), food away from home (6 percent), and alcoholic beverages (1 percent). Next are medical care, recreation, and education and communication, each at about 7 percent. This last category includes tuition (3 percent), telephone service (2 percent), information technology such as personal computers and internet service (1 percent), and educational books and supplies such as this textbook (0.3 percent). Apparel, which includes clothing, footwear, and jewelry, makes up 4 percent of the typical consumer's budget.

Also included in the figure, at 3 percent of spending, is a category for other goods and services. This is a catchall for consumer purchases (such as cigarettes, haircuts, and funeral expenses) that do not naturally fit into the other categories. ■

by 100. The consumer price index is always 100 in the base year. (The index is 100 in 2013.) The consumer price index is 175 in 2014. This means that the price of the basket in 2014 is 175 percent of its price in the base year. Put differently, a basket of goods that costs $100 in the base year costs $175 in 2014. Similarly, the consumer price index is 250 in 2015, indicating that the price level in 2015 is 250 percent of the price level in the base year.

5. *Compute the inflation rate.* Use the consumer price index to calculate the **inflation rate**, which is the percentage change in the price index from the preceding period. That is, the inflation rate between two consecutive years is computed as follows:

$$\text{Inflation rate in year 2} = \frac{\text{CPI in Year 2} - \text{CPI in Year 1}}{\text{CPI in Year 1}} \times 100.$$

As shown at the bottom of Table 1, the inflation rate in our example is 75 percent in 2014 and 43 percent in 2015.

inflation rate
the percentage change in the price index from the preceding period

Although this example simplifies the real world by including only two goods, it shows how the BLS computes the consumer price index and the inflation rate. The BLS collects and processes data on the prices of thousands of goods and services every month and, by following the five foregoing steps, determines how quickly the cost of living for the typical consumer is rising. When the BLS makes its monthly announcement of the consumer price index, you can usually hear the number on the evening television news or see it in the next day's newspaper.

In addition to the consumer price index for the overall economy, the BLS calculates several other price indexes. It reports the index for specific metropolitan areas within the country (such as Boston, New York, and Los Angeles) and for some narrow categories of goods and services (such as food, clothing, and energy). It also calculates the **producer price index** (PPI), which measures the cost of a basket of goods and services bought by firms rather than consumers. Because firms eventually pass on their costs to consumers in the form of higher consumer prices, changes in the producer price index are often thought to be useful in predicting changes in the consumer price index.

producer price index
a measure of the cost of a basket of goods and services bought by firms

24-1b Problems in Measuring the Cost of Living

The goal of the consumer price index is to measure changes in the cost of living. In other words, the consumer price index tries to gauge how much incomes must rise to maintain a constant standard of living. The consumer price index, however, is not a perfect measure of the cost of living. Three problems with the index are widely acknowledged but difficult to solve.

The first problem is called *substitution bias*. When prices change from one year to the next, they do not all change proportionately: Some prices rise more than others. Consumers respond to these differing price changes by buying less of the goods whose prices have risen by relatively large amounts and by buying more of the goods whose prices have risen less or perhaps even have fallen. That is, consumers substitute toward goods that have become relatively less expensive. If a price index is computed assuming a fixed basket of goods, it ignores the possibility of consumer substitution and, therefore, overstates the increase in the cost of living from one year to the next.

Let's consider a simple example. Imagine that in the base year, apples are cheaper than pears, so consumers buy more apples than pears. When the BLS constructs the basket of goods, it will include more apples than pears. Suppose that next year pears are cheaper than apples. Consumers will naturally respond to the price changes by buying more pears and fewer apples. Yet when computing the consumer price index, the BLS uses a fixed basket, which in essence assumes that consumers continue buying the now expensive apples in the same quantities as before. For this reason, the index will measure a much larger increase in the cost of living than consumers actually experience.

The second problem with the consumer price index is the *introduction of new goods*. When a new good is introduced, consumers have more variety from which to choose, and this in turn reduces the cost of maintaining the same level of economic well-being. To see why, consider a hypothetical situation: Suppose you could choose between a $100 gift certificate at a large store that offered a wide array of goods and a $100 gift certificate at a small store with the same prices but a more limited selection. Which would you prefer? Most people would pick the store with greater variety. In essence, the increased set of possible choices makes each dollar more valuable. The same is true with the evolution of the economy

over time: As new goods are introduced, consumers have more choices, and each dollar is worth more. Yet because the consumer price index is based on a fixed basket of goods and services, it does not reflect the increase in the value of the dollar that arises from the introduction of new goods.

Again, let's consider an example. When the iPod was introduced in 2001, consumers found it more convenient to listen to their favorite music. Devices to play music were available previously, but they were not nearly as portable and versatile. The iPod was a new option that increased consumers' set of opportunities. For any given number of dollars, the introduction of the iPod made people better off; conversely, achieving the same level of economic well-being required a smaller number of dollars. A perfect cost-of-living index would have reflected the introduction

---

IN THE NEWS

Monitoring Inflation in the Internet Age

The web is providing alternative ways to collect data on the overall level of prices.

Do We Need Google to Measure Inflation?

By Annie Lowrey

At some 23,000 retailers and businesses in 90 U.S. cities, hundreds of government workers find and mark down prices on very precise products. And I'm not kidding when I say "very precise."

Say the relevant worker is finding the price for a motel room. She might write a report like this: *Occupancy*—two adults; *Type of accommodation*—deluxe room; *Room classification/location*—ocean view, room 306; *Time of stay*—weekend; *Length of stay*—one night; *Bathroom facilities*—one full bathroom; *Kitchen facilities*—none; *Television*—one, includes free movie channel; *Telephone*—one telephone, free local calls; *Air-conditioned*—yes; *Meals included*—breakfast; *Parking*—free self parking; *Transportation*—Transportation to airport, no charge; *Recreation facilities*—an indoor and an outdoor pool, a private beach, three tennis courts, and an exercise room.

This mind-numbingly tedious process goes on for a dizzying panoply of items: wine, takeaway meals, bedroom furniture, surgical procedures, pet dogs, college tuition, cigarettes, haircuts, funerals. When all of the prices are marked down, the workers submit forms that are collated, checked, and input into massive spreadsheets. Then the government boils all those numbers down to one. It weights certain prices, taking into account that consumers spend more on rent than cereal, for instance. It considers product improvements and changes in spending habits. Then it comes up with a master number showing how much a customer's spending needed to increase to buy the same goods, month-on-month. That number is the Consumer Price Index, the government's main gauge of inflation.

Each month, the Bureau of Labor Statistics goes through all that hassle because knowing the rate of inflation is such an important measure of economic health—and it's important to the government's own budget. High inflation? Savers panic, watching the spending power of their accounts erode. Deflation? Everyone saves, awaiting cheaper prices in a few months. And wildly changing inflation makes it difficult for businesses and consumers to make economic decisions.

Moreover, the government needs to know the rate of inflation to index to certain payments, like Social Security benefits or interest payments on TIPS bonds.

But just because the government expends so much energy determining the rate of inflation does not mean it is tallying it in the smartest or most accurate way. The reigning methodology is, well, clunky. It costs Washington around $234 million a year to get all those people to go and bear witness to a $1.57 price increase in a packet of tube socks and then to massage those individual data points down to one number. Moreover, there is a weekslong lag between the checkers tallying up the numbers and the government announcing the changes. The inflation measure comes out only 12 times a year, though prices change, sometimes dramatically, all the time. Plus, the methodology is archaic, given that we live in the Internet age. Prices are easily available online and a lot of shopping happens on the Web rather than in stores.

But there might be a better way. In the last few months, economists have come up

of the iPod with a decrease in the cost of living. The consumer price index, however, did not decrease in response to the introduction of the iPod. Eventually, the BLS revised the basket of goods to include the iPod, and subsequently, the index reflected changes in iPod prices. But the reduction in the cost of living associated with the initial introduction of the iPod never showed up in the index.

The third problem with the consumer price index is *unmeasured quality change.* If the quality of a good deteriorates from one year to the next while its price remains the same, the value of a dollar falls, because you are getting a lesser good for the same amount of money. Similarly, if the quality rises from one year to the next, the value of a dollar rises. The BLS does its best to account for quality change. When the quality of a good in the basket changes—for example, when a car model has

with new methods for calculating inflation at Internet speed—nimbler, cheaper, faster, and perhaps even more accurate than Washington's. The first comes from the Massachusetts Institute of Technology. In 2007, economists Roberto Rigobon and Alberto Cavallo started tracking prices online and inputting them into a massive database. Then, last month, they unveiled the Billion Prices Project, an inflation measure based on 5 million items sold by 300 online retailers in 70 countries. (For the United States, the BPP collects about 500,000 prices.)

The BPP's inflation measure is markedly different from the government's. The economists just average all the prices culled online, meaning the basket of goods is whatever you can buy on the Web. (Some things, like books, are most often bought online. Some items, like cats, are not.) Plus, the researchers do not weight certain items' prices, even if they tend to make up a bigger proportion of household spending.

Still, thus far, the BPP has tracked the CPI closely. And the online-based measure has additional advantages. It comes out daily, giving a better sense of inflation's direction. It also lets researchers examine minute, day-to-day price changes. For instance, this month Rigobon and Cavallo noted that Black Friday discounts "had a smaller effect on average prices in 2010 than in 2009," contrary to reports of deeper discounting this year.

"I wonder how much this costs online."

And it has already produced some academic insights. For instance, Cavallo found that retailers change prices less often, but more, percentage-wise, than economists previously thought.

A second inflation measure comes from Web behemoth Google and is a pet project of the company's chief economist, Hal Varian. As reported by the *Financial Times*, earlier this year, Varian decided to use Google's vast database of Web prices to construct the "Google Price Index," a constantly updated measure of price changes and inflation. (The idea came to him when he was searching for a pepper grinder online.) Google has not yet decided whether it will publish the price index, and has not released its methodology. But Varian said that his preliminary index tracked CPI closely, though it did show periods of deflation—the worrisome incidence of prices actually falling—where the CPI did not.

The new indices lead to the big question of whether the government *needs* to update its methods to account for changes in the economy—taking new pricing trends into consideration, rejiggering its formula, updating more frequently. The answer might be yes. (Economists have reformed the CPI before.) But the CPI and its Stone Age method of calculation boasts one huge benefit: It's a stable, tested measure, consistent over time, since its methodology doesn't change much. Moreover, and somewhat remarkably, the Google and Billion Prices Project indices actually seem to confirm the accuracy of the old-fashioned CPI, tracking it closely rather than showing it to be off-base.

Ultimately, there is a good argument for *more* inflation measures, not just better or newer ones. The government already calculates a number of rates of inflation to give a fuller picture of price changes, the value of money, and the economy. Most notably, the BLS publishes a "core inflation" number, a measure of inflation outside volatile food and energy prices. There are dozens of other measures, as well. The new Web-based yardsticks provide even more alternatives and opportunities to examine the accuracy of the CPI—and to make new findings. That means, for now, those detective-like government rubes painstakingly checking prices on clipboards get to stay in work.

Source: *Slate*, December 20, 2010.

more horsepower or gets better gas mileage from one year to the next—the Bureau adjusts the price of the good to account for the quality change. It is, in essence, trying to compute the price of a basket of goods of constant quality. Despite these efforts, changes in quality remain a problem because quality is so hard to measure.

There is still much debate among economists about how severe these measurement problems are and what should be done about them. Several studies written during the 1990s concluded that the consumer price index overstated inflation by about 1 percentage point per year. In response to this criticism, the BLS adopted several technical changes to improve the CPI, and many economists believe the bias is now only about half as large as it once was. The issue is important because many government programs use the consumer price index to adjust for changes in the overall level of prices. Recipients of Social Security, for instance, get annual increases in benefits that are tied to the consumer price index. Some economists have suggested modifying these programs to correct for the measurement problems by, for instance, reducing the magnitude of the automatic benefit increases.

24-1c The GDP Deflator versus the Consumer Price Index

In the preceding chapter, we examined another measure of the overall level of prices in the economy—the GDP deflator. The GDP deflator is the ratio of nominal GDP to real GDP. Because nominal GDP is current output valued at current prices and real GDP is current output valued at base-year prices, the GDP deflator reflects the current level of prices relative to the level of prices in the base year.

Economists and policymakers monitor both the GDP deflator and the consumer price index to gauge how quickly prices are rising. Usually, these two statistics tell a similar story. Yet two important differences can cause them to diverge.

The first difference is that the GDP deflator reflects the prices of all goods and services *produced domestically*, whereas the consumer price index reflects the prices of all goods and services *bought by consumers*. For example, suppose that the price of an airplane produced by Boeing and sold to the Air Force rises. Even though the plane is part of GDP, it is not part of the basket of goods and services bought by a typical consumer. Thus, the price increase shows up in the GDP deflator but not in the consumer price index.

As another example, suppose that Volvo raises the price of its cars. Because Volvos are made in Sweden, the car is not part of U.S. GDP. But U.S. consumers buy Volvos, so the car is part of the typical consumer's basket of goods. Hence, a price increase in an imported consumption good, such as a Volvo, shows up in the consumer price index but not in the GDP deflator.

This first difference between the consumer price index and the GDP deflator is particularly important when the price of oil changes. The United States produces some oil, but much of the oil we use is imported. As a result, oil and oil products such as gasoline and heating oil make up a much larger share of consumer spending than of GDP. When the price of oil rises, the consumer price index rises by much more than does the GDP deflator.

The second and subtler difference between the GDP deflator and the consumer price index concerns how various prices are weighted to yield a single number for the overall level of prices. The consumer price index compares the price of a *fixed* basket of goods and services to the price of the basket in the base year. Only occasionally does the BLS change the basket of goods. By contrast, the GDP deflator compares the price of *currently produced* goods and

"The price may seem a little high, but you have to remember that's in today's dollars."

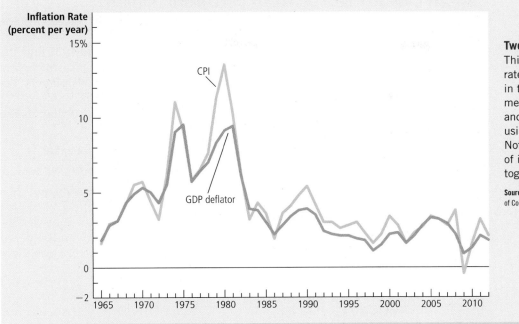

FIGURE 2

Two Measures of Inflation
This figure shows the inflation rate—the percentage change in the level of prices—as measured by the GDP deflator and the consumer price index using annual data since 1965. Notice that the two measures of inflation generally move together.

Source: U.S. Department of Labor; U.S. Department of Commerce.

services to the price of the same goods and services in the base year. Thus, the group of goods and services used to compute the GDP deflator changes automatically over time. This difference is not important when all prices are changing proportionately. But if the prices of different goods and services are changing by varying amounts, the way we weight the various prices matters for the overall inflation rate.

Figure 2 shows the inflation rate as measured by both the GDP deflator and the consumer price index for each year since 1965. You can see that sometimes the two measures diverge. When they do diverge, it is possible to go behind these numbers and explain the divergence with the two differences we have discussed. For example, in 1979 and 1980, CPI inflation spiked up more than the GDP deflator largely because oil prices more than doubled during these two years. Yet divergence between these two measures is the exception rather than the rule. In the 1970s, both the GDP deflator and the consumer price index show high rates of inflation. In the late 1980s, 1990s, and the first decade of the 2000s, both measures show low rates of inflation.

Quick Quiz *Explain briefly what the CPI measures and how it is constructed.*
• *Identify one reason why the CPI is an imperfect measure of the cost of living.*

24-2 Correcting Economic Variables for the Effects of Inflation

The purpose of measuring the overall level of prices in the economy is to allow us to compare dollar figures from different times. Now that we know how price indexes are calculated, let's see how we might use such an index to compare a dollar figure from the past to a dollar figure in the present.

24-2a Dollar Figures from Different Times

We first return to the issue of Babe Ruth's salary. Was his salary of $80,000 in 1931 high or low compared to the salaries of today's players?

To answer this question, we need to know the level of prices in 1931 and the level of prices today. Part of the increase in baseball salaries compensates players for higher prices today. To compare Ruth's salary to those of today's players, we need to inflate Ruth's salary to turn 1931 dollars into today's dollars.

The formula for turning dollar figures from year T into today's dollars is the following:

$$\text{Amount in today's dollars} = \text{Amount in year } T \text{ dollars} \times \frac{\text{Price level today}}{\text{Price level in year } T}.$$

A price index such as the consumer price index measures the price level and thus determines the size of the inflation correction.

Let's apply this formula to Ruth's salary. Government statistics show a consumer price index of 15.2 for 1931 and 229.5 for 2012. Thus, the overall level of prices has risen by a factor of 15.1 (calculated from 229.5/15.2). We can use these numbers to measure Ruth's salary in 2012 dollars, as follows:

$$\text{Salary in 2012 dollars} = \text{Salary in 1931 dollars} \times \frac{\text{Price level in 2012}}{\text{Price level in 1931}}$$

$$= \$80,000 \times \frac{229.5}{15.2}$$

$$= \$1,207,894.$$

We find that Babe Ruth's 1931 salary is equivalent to a salary today of over $1.2 million. That is a good income, but it is a third less than the median Yankee salary today and only 4 percent of what the Yankees pay A-Rod. Various forces, including overall economic growth and the increasing income shares earned by superstars, have substantially raised the living standards of the best athletes.

Let's also examine President Hoover's 1931 salary of $75,000. To translate that figure into 2012 dollars, we again multiply the ratio of the price levels in the two years. We find that Hoover's salary is equivalent to $75,000 × (229.5/15.2), or $1,132,401, in 2012 dollars. This is well above President Barack Obama's salary of $400,000. It seems that President Hoover did have a pretty good year after all.

24-2b Indexation

As we have just seen, price indexes are used to correct for the effects of inflation when comparing dollar figures from different times. This type of correction shows up in many places in the economy. When some dollar amount is automatically corrected for changes in the price level by law or contract, the amount is said to be **indexed** for inflation.

For example, many long-term contracts between firms and unions include partial or complete indexation of the wage to the consumer price index. Such a provision is called a *cost-of-living allowance*, or COLA. A COLA automatically raises the wage when the consumer price index rises.

Indexation is also a feature of many laws. Social Security benefits, for example, are adjusted every year to compensate the elderly for increases in prices. The brackets

indexation
the automatic correction by law or contract of a dollar amount for the effects of inflation

FYI

Mr. Index Goes to Hollywood

What is the most popular movie of all time? The answer might surprise you.

Movie popularity is usually gauged by box office receipts. By that measure, *Avatar* is the number 1 movie of all time with domestic

"Frankly, my dear, I don't care much for the effects of inflation."

receipts of $761 million, followed by *Titanic* ($659 million) and *Marvel's The Avengers* ($623 million). But this ranking ignores an obvious but important fact: Prices, including those of movie tickets, have been rising over time. Inflation gives an advantage to newer films.

When we correct box office receipts for the effects of inflation, the story is very different. The number 1 movie is now *Gone with the Wind* ($1,604 million), followed by *Star Wars* ($1,414 million) and *The Sound of Music* ($1,131 million). *Avatar* falls to number 14.

Gone with the Wind was released in 1939, before everyone had televisions in their homes. In the 1930s, about 90 million Americans went to the cinema each week, compared to about 25 million today. But the movies from that era don't show up in conventional popularity rankings because ticket prices were only a quarter. And indeed, in the ranking based on nominal box office receipts, *Gone with the Wind* does not make the top 50 films. Scarlett and Rhett fare a lot better once we correct for the effects of inflation. ◢

of the federal income tax—the income levels at which the tax rates change—are also indexed for inflation. There are, however, many ways in which the tax system is not indexed for inflation, even when perhaps it should be. We discuss these issues more fully when we discuss the costs of inflation later in this book.

24-2c Real and Nominal Interest Rates

Correcting economic variables for the effects of inflation is particularly important, and somewhat tricky, when we look at data on interest rates. The very concept of an interest rate necessarily involves comparing amounts of money at different points in time. When you deposit your savings in a bank account, you give the bank some money now, and the bank returns your deposit with interest in the future. Similarly, when you borrow from a bank, you get some money now, but you will have to repay the loan with interest in the future. In both cases, to fully understand the deal between you and the bank, it is crucial to acknowledge that future dollars could have a different value than today's dollars. That is, you have to correct for the effects of inflation.

Let's consider an example. Suppose Sally Saver deposits $1,000 in a bank account that pays an annual interest rate of 10 percent. A year later, after Sally has accumulated $100 in interest, she withdraws her $1,100. Is Sally $100 richer than she was when she made the deposit a year earlier?

The answer depends on what we mean by "richer." Sally does have $100 more than she had before. In other words, the number of dollars in her possession has risen by 10 percent. But Sally does not care about the amount of money itself: She cares about what she can buy with it. If prices have risen while her money was in the bank, each dollar now buys less than it did a year ago. In this case, her purchasing power—the amount of goods and services she can buy—has not risen by 10 percent.

To keep things simple, let's suppose that Sally is a movie fan and buys only DVDs. When Sally made her deposit, a DVD at her local movie store cost $10. Her deposit of $1,000 was equivalent to 100 DVDs. A year later, after getting her 10 percent interest, she has $1,100. How many DVDs can she buy now? It depends on what has happened to the price of a DVD. Here are some examples:

- Zero inflation: If the price of a DVD remains at $10, the amount she can buy has risen from 100 to 110 DVDs. The 10 percent increase in the number of dollars means a 10 percent increase in her purchasing power.
- Six percent inflation: If the price of a DVD rises from $10 to $10.60, then the number of DVDs she can buy has risen from 100 to approximately 104. Her purchasing power has increased by about 4 percent.
- Ten percent inflation: If the price of a DVD rises from $10 to $11, she can still buy only 100 DVDs. Even though Sally's dollar wealth has risen, her purchasing power is the same as it was a year earlier.
- Twelve percent inflation: If the price of a DVD increases from $10 to $11.20, the number of DVDs she can buy has fallen from 100 to approximately 98. Even with her greater number of dollars, her purchasing power has decreased by about 2 percent.

And if Sally were living in an economy with deflation—falling prices—another possibility could arise:

- Two percent deflation: If the price of a DVD falls from $10 to $9.80, then the number of DVDs she can buy rises from 100 to approximately 112. Her purchasing power increases by about 12 percent.

These examples show that the higher the rate of inflation, the smaller the increase in Sally's purchasing power. If the rate of inflation exceeds the rate of interest, her purchasing power actually falls. And if there is deflation (that is, a negative rate of inflation), her purchasing power rises by more than the rate of interest.

To understand how much a person earns in a savings account, we need to consider both the interest rate and the change in prices. The interest rate that measures the change in dollar amounts is called the **nominal interest rate**, and the interest rate corrected for inflation is called the **real interest rate**. The nominal interest rate, the real interest rate, and inflation are related approximately as follows:

nominal interest rate
the interest rate as usually reported without a correction for the effects of inflation

real interest rate
the interest rate corrected for the effects of inflation

$$\text{Real interest rate} = \text{Nominal interest rate} - \text{Inflation rate}.$$

The real interest rate is the difference between the nominal interest rate and the rate of inflation. The nominal interest rate tells you how fast the number of dollars in your bank account rises over time, while the real interest rate tells you how fast the purchasing power of your bank account rises over time.

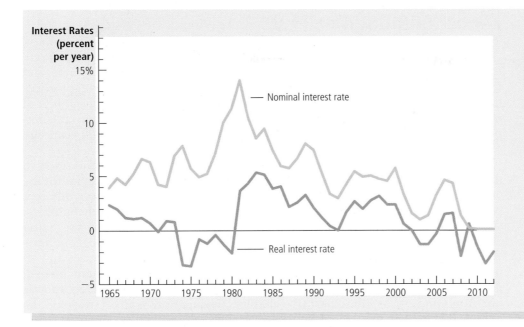

FIGURE 3

Real and Nominal Interest Rates
This figure shows nominal and real interest rates using annual data since 1965. The nominal interest rate is the rate on a three-month Treasury bill. The real interest rate is the nominal interest rate minus the inflation rate as measured by the consumer price index. Notice that nominal and real interest rates often do not move together.

Source: U.S. Department of Labor; U.S. Department of Treasury.

case study

Interest Rates in the U.S. Economy

Figure 3 shows real and nominal interest rates in the U.S. economy since 1965. The nominal interest rate in this figure is the rate on three-month Treasury bills (although data on other interest rates would be similar). The real interest rate is computed by subtracting the rate of inflation from this nominal interest rate. Here the inflation rate is measured as the percentage change in the consumer price index.

One feature of this figure is that the nominal interest rate almost always exceeds the real interest rate. This reflects the fact that the U.S. economy has experienced rising consumer prices in almost every year during this period. By contrast, if you look at data for the U.S. economy during the late 19th century or for the Japanese economy in some recent years, you will find periods of deflation. During deflation, the real interest rate exceeds the nominal interest rate.

The figure also shows that because inflation is variable, real and nominal interest rates do not always move together. For example, in the late 1970s, nominal interest rates were high. But because inflation was very high, real interest rates were low. Indeed, during much of the 1970s, real interest rates were negative, for inflation eroded people's savings more quickly than nominal interest payments increased them. By contrast, in the late 1990s, nominal interest rates were lower than they had been two decades earlier. But because inflation was much lower, real interest rates were higher. In the coming chapters, we will examine the economic forces that determine both real and nominal interest rates. ◢

Quick Quiz *Henry Ford paid his workers $5 a day in 1914. If the consumer price index was 10 in 1914 and 230 in 2012, how much is the Ford paycheck worth in 2012 dollars?*

24-3 Conclusion

"A nickel ain't worth a dime anymore," baseball player Yogi Berra once observed. Indeed, throughout recent history, the real values behind the nickel, the dime, and the dollar have not been stable. Persistent increases in the overall level of prices have been the norm. Such inflation reduces the purchasing power of each unit of money over time. When comparing dollar figures from different times, it is important to keep in mind that a dollar today is not the same as a dollar 20 years ago or, most likely, 20 years from now.

This chapter has discussed how economists measure the overall level of prices in the economy and how they use price indexes to correct economic variables for the effects of inflation. Price indexes allow us to compare dollar figures from different points in time and, therefore, get a better sense of how the economy is changing.

The discussion of price indexes in this chapter, together with the preceding chapter's discussion of GDP, is only a first step in the study of macroeconomics. We have not yet examined what determines a nation's GDP or the causes and effects of inflation. To do that, we need to go beyond issues of measurement. Indeed, that is our next task. Having explained how economists measure macroeconomic quantities and prices in the past two chapters, we are now ready to develop the models that explain movements in these variables.

Here is our strategy in the upcoming chapters. First, we look at the long-run determinants of real GDP and related variables, such as saving, investment, real interest rates, and unemployment. Second, we look at the long-run determinants of the price level and related variables, such as the money supply, inflation, and nominal interest rates. Last of all, having seen how these variables are determined in the long run, we examine the more complex question of what causes short-run fluctuations in real GDP and the price level. In all of these chapters, the measurement issues we have just discussed will provide the foundation for the analysis.

Summary

- The consumer price index shows the cost of a basket of goods and services relative to the cost of the same basket in the base year. The index is used to measure the overall level of prices in the economy. The percentage change in the consumer price index measures the inflation rate.

- The consumer price index is an imperfect measure of the cost of living for three reasons. First, it does not take into account consumers' ability to substitute toward goods that become relatively cheaper over time. Second, it does not take into account increases in the purchasing power of the dollar due to the introduction of new goods. Third, it is distorted by unmeasured changes in the quality of goods and services. Because of these measurement problems, the CPI overstates true inflation.

- Like the consumer price index, the GDP deflator measures the overall level of prices in the economy. The two price indexes usually move together, but there are important differences. The GDP deflator differs from the CPI because it includes goods and services produced rather than goods and services consumed. As a result,

imported goods affect the consumer price index but not the GDP deflator. In addition, while the consumer price index uses a fixed basket of goods, the GDP deflator automatically changes the group of goods and services over time as the composition of GDP changes.

- Dollar figures from different times do not represent a valid comparison of purchasing power. To compare a dollar figure from the past to a dollar figure today, the older figure should be inflated using a price index.

- Various laws and private contracts use price indexes to correct for the effects of inflation. The tax laws, however, are only partially indexed for inflation.

- A correction for inflation is especially important when looking at data on interest rates. The nominal interest rate is the interest rate usually reported; it is the rate at which the number of dollars in a savings account increases over time. By contrast, the real interest rate takes into account changes in the value of the dollar over time. The real interest rate equals the nominal interest rate minus the rate of inflation.

Key Concepts

consumer price index (CPI), *p. 506*
inflation rate, *p. 508*

producer price index, *p. 509*
indexation, *p. 514*

nominal interest rate, *p. 516*
real interest rate, *p. 516*

Questions for Review

1. Which do you think has a greater effect on the consumer price index: a 10 percent increase in the price of chicken or a 10 percent increase in the price of caviar? Why?

2. Describe the three problems that make the consumer price index an imperfect measure of the cost of living.

3. If the price of imported French wine rises, is the consumer price index or the GDP deflator affected more? Why?

4. Over a long period of time, the price of a candy bar rose from $0.20 to $1.20. Over the same period, the consumer price index rose from 150 to 300. Adjusted for overall inflation, how much did the price of the candy bar change?

5. Explain the meaning of *nominal interest rate* and *real interest rate*. How are they related?

Quick Check Multiple Choice

1. The consumer price index measures approximately the same economic phenomenon as
   a. nominal GDP.
   b. real GDP.
   c. the GDP deflator.
   d. the unemployment rate.

2. The largest component in the basket of goods and services used to compute the CPI is
   a. food and beverages.
   b. housing.
   c. medical care.
   d. apparel.

3. If a Pennsylvania gun manufacturer raises the price of rifles it sells to the U.S. Army, its price hikes will increase
   a. both the CPI and the GDP deflator.
   b. neither the CPI nor the GDP deflator.
   c. the CPI but not the GDP deflator.
   d. the GDP deflator but not the CPI.

4. Because consumers can sometimes substitute cheaper goods for those that have risen in price,
   a. the CPI overstates inflation.
   b. the CPI understates inflation.
   c. the GDP deflator overstates inflation.
   d. the GDP deflator understates inflation.

5. If the consumer price index is 200 in year 1980 and 300 today, then $600 in 1980 has the same purchasing power as _____ today.
   a. $400
   b. $500
   c. $700
   d. $900

6. You deposit $2,000 in a savings account, and a year later you have $2,100. Meanwhile, the consumer price index rises from 200 to 204. In this case, the nominal interest rate is _____ percent, and the real interest rate is _____ percent.
   a. 1, 5
   b. 3, 5
   c. 5, 1
   d. 5, 3

Problems and Applications

1. Suppose that the year you were born someone bought $100 of goods and services for your baby shower. How much would you guess it would cost today to buy a similar amount of goods and services?

   Now find data on the consumer price index and compute the answer based on it. (You can find the BLS's inflation calculator here: http://www.bls.gov/data/inflation_calculator.htm.)

2. The residents of Vegopia spend all of their income on cauliflower, broccoli, and carrots. In 2013, they spend a total of $200 for 100 heads of cauliflower, $75 for 50 bunches of broccoli, and $50 for 500 carrots. In 2014, they spend a total of $225 for 75 heads of cauliflower, $120 for 80 bunches of broccoli, and $100 for 500 carrots.
   a. Calculate the price of one unit of each vegetable in each year.
   b. Using 2013 as the base year, calculate the CPI for each year.
   c. What is the inflation rate in 2014?

3. Suppose that people consume only three goods, as shown in this table:

	Tennis Balls	Golf Balls	Bottles of Gatorade
2014 price	$2	$4	$1
2014 quantity	100	100	200
2015 price	$2	$6	$2
2015 quantity	100	100	200

   a. What is the percentage change in the price of each of the three goods?
   b. Using a method similar to the consumer price index, compute the percentage change in the overall price level.
   c. If you were to learn that a bottle of Gatorade increased in size from 2014 to 2015, should that information affect your calculation of the inflation rate? If so, how?
   d. If you were to learn that Gatorade introduced new flavors in 2015, should that information affect your calculation of the inflation rate? If so, how?

4. Go to the website of the BLS (http://www.bls.gov) and find data on the consumer price index. By how much has the index including all items risen over the past year? For which categories of spending have prices risen the most? The least? Have any categories experienced price declines? Can you explain any of these facts?

5. A small nation of ten people idolizes the TV show *American Idol*. All they produce and consume are karaoke machines and CDs, in the following amounts:

	Karaoke Machines		CDs	
	Quantity	Price	Quantity	Price
2014	10	$40	30	$10
2015	12	60	50	12

   a. Using a method similar to the consumer price index, compute the percentage change in the overall price level. Use 2014 as the base year and fix the basket at 1 karaoke machine and 3 CDs.

   b. Using a method similar to the GDP deflator, compute the percentage change in the overall price level. Also use 2014 as the base year.
   c. Is the inflation rate in 2015 the same using the two methods? Explain why or why not.

6. Which of the problems in the construction of the CPI might be illustrated by each of the following situations? Explain.
   a. the invention of the cell phone
   b. the introduction of air bags in cars
   c. increased personal computer purchases in response to a decline in their price
   d. more scoops of raisins in each package of Raisin Bran
   e. greater use of fuel-efficient cars after gasoline prices increase

7. The *New York Times* cost $0.15 in 1970 and $2.00 in 2011. The average wage in manufacturing was $3.36 per hour in 1970 and $23.09 in 2011.
   a. By what percentage did the price of a newspaper rise?
   b. By what percentage did the wage rise?
   c. In each year, how many minutes did a worker have to work to earn enough to buy a newspaper?
   d. Did workers' purchasing power in terms of newspapers rise or fall?

8. The chapter explains that Social Security benefits are increased each year in proportion to the increase in the CPI, even though most economists believe that the CPI overstates actual inflation.
   a. If the elderly consume the same market basket as other people, does Social Security provide the elderly with an improvement in their standard of living each year? Explain.
   b. In fact, the elderly consume more healthcare compared to younger people, and healthcare costs have risen faster than overall inflation. What would you do to determine whether the elderly are actually better off from year to year?

9. Suppose that a borrower and a lender agree on the nominal interest rate to be paid on a loan. Then inflation turns out to be higher than they both expected.
   a. Is the real interest rate on this loan higher or lower than expected?
   b. Does the lender gain or lose from this unexpectedly high inflation? Does the borrower gain or lose?
   c. Inflation during the 1970s was much higher than most people had expected when the decade began. How did this affect homeowners who obtained fixed-rate mortgages during the 1960s? How did it affect the banks that lent the money?

Go to CengageBrain.com to purchase access to the proven, critical Study Guide to accompany this text, which features additional notes and context, practice tests, and much more.

The Real Economy
in the Long Run

25

Production and Growth

When you travel around the world, you see tremendous variation in the standard of living. The average income in a rich country, such as the United States, Japan, or Germany, is more than ten times the average income in a poor country, such as India, Indonesia, or Nigeria. These large differences in income are reflected in large differences in the quality of life. People in richer countries have better nutrition, safer housing, better healthcare, and longer life expectancy as well as more automobiles, more telephones, and more televisions.

Even within a country, there are large changes in the standard of living over time. In the United States over the past century, average income as measured by real GDP (gross domestic product) per person has grown by about 2 percent per year. Although 2 percent might seem small, this rate of growth implies that average income doubles every 35 years. Because of this growth, most Americans enjoy much greater economic prosperity than did their parents, grandparents, and great-grandparents.

523

Growth rates vary substantially from country to country. In recent history, some East Asian countries, such as Singapore, South Korea, and Taiwan, have experienced economic growth of about 7 percent per year; at this rate, average income doubles every 10 years. Over the past two decades, China has enjoyed an even higher rate of growth—about 12 percent per year, according to some estimates. A country experiencing such rapid growth can, in one generation, go from being among the poorest in the world to being among the richest. By contrast, in some nations in sub-Saharan Africa, average income has been stagnant for many years. Zimbabwe has had one of the worst growth experiences: From 1991 to 2011, income per person fell by a total of 38 percent.

What explains these diverse experiences? How can rich countries maintain their high standard of living? What policies should poor countries pursue to promote more rapid growth and join the developed world? These are among the most important questions in macroeconomics. As the Nobel-Prize-winning economist Robert Lucas put it, "The consequences for human welfare in questions like these are simply staggering: Once one starts to think about them, it is hard to think about anything else."

In the previous two chapters, we discussed how economists measure macroeconomic quantities and prices. We can now begin to study the forces that determine these variables. As we have seen, an economy's GDP measures both the total income earned in the economy and the total expenditure on the economy's output of goods and services. The level of real GDP is a good gauge of economic prosperity, and the growth of real GDP is a good gauge of economic progress. In this chapter we focus on the long-run determinants of the level and growth of real GDP. Later, we study the short-run fluctuations of real GDP around its long-run trend.

We proceed here in three steps. First, we examine international data on real GDP per person. These data will give you some sense of how much the level and growth of living standards vary around the world. Second, we examine the role of *productivity*—the amount of goods and services produced for each hour of a worker's time. In particular, we see that a nation's standard of living is determined by the productivity of its workers, and we consider the factors that determine a nation's productivity. Third, we consider the link between productivity and the economic policies that a nation pursues.

25-1 Economic Growth around the World

As a starting point for our study of long-run growth, let's look at the experiences of some of the world's economies. Table 1 shows data on real GDP per person for thirteen countries. For each country, the data cover more than a century of history. The first and second columns of the table present the countries and time periods. (The time periods differ somewhat from country to country because of differences in data availability.) The third and fourth columns show estimates of real GDP per person about a century ago and for a recent year.

The data on real GDP per person show that living standards vary widely from country to country. Income per person in the United States, for instance, is about six times that in China and about fourteen times that in India. The poorest countries have average levels of income not seen in the developed world for many decades. The typical citizen of India in 2010 had less real income than the typical

TABLE 1

The Variety of Growth Experiences

Country	Period	Real GDP per Person at Beginning of Period[a]	Real GDP per Person at End of Period[a]	Growth Rate (per year)
Japan	1890–2010	$1,517	$34,810	2.65%
Brazil	1900–2010	785	10,980	2.43
Mexico	1900–2010	1,169	14,350	2.31
China	1900–2010	723	7,520	2.15
Germany	1870–2010	2,204	38,410	2.06
Canada	1870–2010	2,397	38,370	2.00
United States	1870–2010	4,044	47,210	1.77
Argentina	1900–2010	2,314	15,470	1.74
India	1900–2010	681	3,330	1.45
United Kingdom	1870–2010	4,853	35,620	1.43
Indonesia	1900–2010	899	4,180	1.41
Pakistan	1900–2010	744	2,760	1.20
Bangladesh	1900–2010	629	1,800	0.96

[a]Real GDP is measured in 2010 dollars.

Source: Robert J. Barro and Xavier Sala-i-Martin, *Economic Growth* (New York: McGraw-Hill, 1995), Tables 10.2 and 10.3; *World Development Indicators* online; and author's calculations.

resident of England in 1870. The typical person in Bangladesh in 2010 had less than half the real income of a typical American a century ago.

The last column of the table shows each country's growth rate. The growth rate measures how rapidly real GDP per person grew in the typical year. In the United States, for example, where real GDP per person was $4,044 in 1870 and $47,210 in 2010, the growth rate was 1.77 percent per year. This means that if real GDP per person, beginning at $4,044, were to increase by 1.77 percent for each of 140 years, it would end up at $47,210. Of course, real GDP per person did not rise exactly 1.77 percent every year: Some years it rose by more, other years it rose by less, and in still other years it fell. The growth rate of 1.77 percent per year ignores short-run fluctuations around the long-run trend and represents an average rate of growth for real GDP per person over many years.

The countries in Table 1 are ordered by their growth rate from the most to the least rapid. Japan tops the list, with a growth rate of 2.65 percent per year. A hundred years ago, Japan was not a rich country. Japan's average income was only somewhat higher than Mexico's, and it was well behind Argentina's. The standard of living in Japan in 1890 was less than half of that in India today. But because of its spectacular growth, Japan is now an economic superpower, with average income more than twice that of Mexico and Argentina and similar to that of Germany, Canada, and the United Kingdom. At the bottom of the list of countries are Pakistan and Bangladesh, which have experienced growth of 1.2 percent per year or less over the past century. As a result, the typical resident of these countries continues to live in abject poverty.

Because of differences in growth rates, the ranking of countries by income changes substantially over time. As we have seen, Japan is a country that has risen relative to others. One country that has fallen behind is the United Kingdom. In 1870, the United Kingdom was the richest country in the world, with average income about 20 percent higher than that of the United States and more than twice Canada's. Today, average income in the United Kingdom is 25 percent below that of the United States and 7 percent below Canada's.

These data show that the world's richest countries have no guarantee they will stay the richest and that the world's poorest countries are not doomed to forever remain in poverty. But what explains these changes over time? Why do some countries zoom ahead while others lag behind? These are precisely the questions that we take up next.

Quick Quiz   *What has been the approximate long-run growth rate of real GDP per person in the United States? Name a country that has had faster growth and a country that has had slower growth.*

25-2 Productivity: Its Role and Determinants

Explaining why living standards vary so much around the world is, in one sense, very easy. The answer can be summarized in a single word—*productivity*. But in another sense, the international variation in living standards is deeply puzzling.

FYI

Are You Richer Than the Richest American?

American Heritage magazine once published a list of the richest Americans of all time. The number 1 spot went to John D. Rockefeller, the oil entrepreneur who lived from 1839 to 1937. According to the magazine's calculations, his wealth would today be the equivalent of about $200 billion, almost three times that of Bill Gates, the software entrepreneur who is today's richest American.

Despite his great wealth, Rockefeller did not enjoy many of the conveniences that we now take for granted. He couldn't watch television, play video games, surf the Internet, or send e-mail. During the heat of summer, he couldn't cool his home with air-conditioning. For much of his life, he couldn't travel by car or plane, and he couldn't use a telephone to call friends or family. If he became ill, he couldn't take advantage of many medicines, such as antibiotics, that doctors today routinely use to prolong and enhance life.

John D. Rockefeller

Now consider: How much money would someone have to pay you to give up for the rest of your life all the modern conveniences that Rockefeller lived without? Would you do it for $200 billion? Perhaps not. And if you wouldn't, is it fair to say that you are better off than John D. Rockefeller, allegedly the richest American ever?

The preceding chapter discussed how standard price indexes, which are used to compare sums of money from different points in time, fail to fully reflect the introduction of new goods in the economy. As a result, the rate of inflation is overestimated. The flip side of this observation is that the rate of real economic growth is underestimated. Pondering Rockefeller's life shows how significant this problem might be. Because of tremendous technological advances, the average American today is arguably "richer" than the richest American a century ago, even if that fact is lost in standard economic statistics. ◢

To explain why incomes are so much higher in some countries than in others, we must look at the many factors that determine a nation's productivity.

25-2a Why Productivity Is So Important

Let's begin our study of productivity and economic growth by developing a simple model based loosely on Daniel Defoe's famous novel *Robinson Crusoe* about a sailor stranded on a desert island. Because Crusoe lives alone, he catches his own fish, grows his own vegetables, and makes his own clothes. We can think of Crusoe's activities—his production and consumption of fish, vegetables, and clothing—as a simple economy. By examining Crusoe's economy, we can learn some lessons that also apply to more complex and realistic economies.

What determines Crusoe's standard of living? In a word, **productivity**, the quantity of goods and services produced from each unit of labor input. If Crusoe is good at catching fish, growing vegetables, and making clothes, he lives well. If he is bad at doing these things, he lives poorly. Because Crusoe gets to consume only what he produces, his living standard is tied to his productivity.

productivity
the quantity of goods and services produced from each unit of labor input

In the case of Crusoe's economy, it is easy to see that productivity is the key determinant of living standards and that growth in productivity is the key determinant of growth in living standards. The more fish Crusoe can catch per hour, the more he eats at dinner. If Crusoe finds a better place to catch fish, his productivity rises. This increase in productivity makes Crusoe better off: He can eat the extra fish, or he can spend less time fishing and devote more time to making other goods he enjoys.

Productivity's key role in determining living standards is as true for nations as it is for stranded sailors. Recall that an economy's GDP measures two things at once: the total income earned by everyone in the economy and the total expenditure on the economy's output of goods and services. GDP can measure these two things simultaneously because, for the economy as a whole, they must be equal. Put simply, an economy's income is the economy's output.

Like Crusoe, a nation can enjoy a high standard of living only if it can produce a large quantity of goods and services. Americans live better than Nigerians because American workers are more productive than Nigerian workers. The Japanese have enjoyed more rapid growth in living standards than Argentineans because Japanese workers have experienced more rapid growth in productivity. Indeed, one of the *Ten Principles of Economics* in Chapter 1 is that a country's standard of living depends on its ability to produce goods and services.

Hence, to understand the large differences in living standards we observe across countries or over time, we must focus on the production of goods and services. But seeing the link between living standards and productivity is only the first step. It leads naturally to the next question: Why are some economies so much better at producing goods and services than others?

25-2b How Productivity Is Determined

Although productivity is uniquely important in determining Robinson Crusoe's standard of living, many factors determine Crusoe's productivity. Crusoe will be better at catching fish, for instance, if he has more fishing poles, if he has been trained in the best fishing techniques, if his island has a plentiful fish supply, or if he invents a better fishing lure. Each of these determinants of Crusoe's productivity—which we can call *physical capital, human capital, natural resources,* and *technological knowledge*—has a counterpart in more complex and realistic economies. Let's consider each factor in turn.

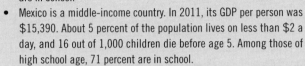

FYI

A Picture Is Worth a Thousand Statistics

George Bernard Shaw once said, "It is the mark of a truly intelligent person to be moved by statistics." Most of us, however, have trouble being moved by data on GDP—until we see with our own eyes what these statistics represent.

The three photos on these pages show a typical family from each of three countries—the United Kingdom, Mexico, and Mali. Each family was photographed outside their home, together with all their material possessions.

These nations have very different standards of living, as judged by these photos, GDP, or other statistics.

- The United Kingdom is an advanced economy. In 2011, its GDP per person was $36,010. A negligible share of the population lives in extreme poverty, defined here as less than $2 a day. A baby born in the United Kingdom can expect a relatively healthy childhood: Only 5 out of 1,000 children die before reaching age 5. Educational attainment is high: Among children of high school age, 98 percent are in school.

- Mexico is a middle-income country. In 2011, its GDP per person was $15,390. About 5 percent of the population lives on less than $2 a day, and 16 out of 1,000 children die before age 5. Among those of high school age, 71 percent are in school.

- Mali is a poor country. In 2011, its GDP per person was only $1,040. Extreme poverty is the norm: More than three-quarters of the population lives on less than $2 per day. Life is often cut short: 176 out of 1,000 children die before age 5. And educational attainment in Mali is low: Among those of high school age, only 31 percent are in school.

Economists who study economic growth try to understand what causes such large differences in the standard of living. ◢

A Typical Family in the United Kingdom

David Reed - from MATERIAL WORLD

A Typical Family in Mexico

A Typical Family in Mali

Physical Capital per Worker   Workers are more productive if they have tools with which to work. The stock of equipment and structures used to produce goods and services is called **physical capital**, or just *capital*. For example, when woodworkers make furniture, they use saws, lathes, and drill presses. More tools allow the woodworkers to produce their output more quickly and more accurately: A worker with only basic hand tools can make less furniture each week than a worker with sophisticated and specialized woodworking equipment.

physical capital
the stock of equipment and structures that are used to produce goods and services

As you may recall, the inputs used to produce goods and services—labor, capital, and so on—are called the *factors of production*. An important feature of capital is that it is a *produced* factor of production. That is, capital is an input into the production process that in the past was an output from the production process. The woodworker uses a lathe to make the leg of a table. Earlier, the lathe itself was the output of a firm that manufactures lathes. The lathe manufacturer in turn used other equipment to make its product. Thus, capital is a factor of production used to produce all kinds of goods and services, including more capital.

Human Capital per Worker   A second determinant of productivity is human capital. **Human capital** is the economist's term for the knowledge and skills that workers acquire through education, training, and experience. Human capital includes the skills accumulated in early childhood programs, grade school, high school, college, and on-the-job training for adults in the labor force.

human capital
the knowledge and skills that workers acquire through education, training, and experience

Education, training, and experience are less tangible than lathes, bulldozers, and buildings, but human capital is like physical capital in many ways. Like physical capital, human capital raises a nation's ability to produce goods and services. Also like physical capital, human capital is a produced factor of production. Producing human capital requires inputs in the form of teachers, libraries, and student time. Indeed, students can be viewed as "workers" who have the important job of producing the human capital that will be used in future production.

Natural Resources per Worker   A third determinant of productivity is **natural resources**. Natural resources are inputs into production that are provided by nature, such as land, rivers, and mineral deposits. Natural resources take two forms: renewable and nonrenewable. A forest is an example of a renewable resource. When one tree is cut down, a seedling can be planted in its place to be harvested in the future. Oil is an example of a nonrenewable resource. Because oil is produced by nature over many millions of years, there is only a limited supply. Once the supply of oil is depleted, it is impossible to create more.

natural resources
the inputs into the production of goods and services that are provided by nature, such as land, rivers, and mineral deposits

Differences in natural resources are responsible for some of the differences in standards of living around the world. The historical success of the United States was driven in part by the large supply of land well suited for agriculture. Today, some countries in the Middle East, such as Kuwait and Saudi Arabia, are rich simply because they happen to be on top of some of the largest pools of oil in the world.

Although natural resources can be important, they are not necessary for an economy to be highly productive in producing goods and services. Japan, for instance, is one of the richest countries in the world, despite having few natural resources. International trade makes Japan's success possible. Japan imports many of the natural resources it needs, such as oil, and exports its manufactured goods to economies rich in natural resources.

technological knowledge
society's understanding of the best ways to produce goods and services

Technological Knowledge   A fourth determinant of productivity is **technological knowledge**—the understanding of the best ways to produce goods and services. A hundred years ago, most Americans worked on farms because farm technology required a high input of labor to feed the entire population. Today, thanks to advances in farming technology, a small fraction of the population can produce enough food to feed the entire country. This technological change made labor available to produce other goods and services.

Technological knowledge takes many forms. Some technology is common knowledge—after one person uses it, everyone becomes aware of it. For example, once Henry Ford successfully introduced assembly-line production, other carmakers quickly followed suit. Other technology is proprietary—it is known only by the company that discovers it. Only the Coca-Cola Company, for instance, knows the secret recipe for making its famous soft drink. Still other technology is proprietary for a short time. When a pharmaceutical company discovers a new drug, the patent system gives that company a temporary right to be its exclusive manufacturer. When the patent expires, however, other companies are allowed to make the drug. All these forms of technological knowledge are important for the economy's production of goods and services.

It is worthwhile to distinguish between technological knowledge and human capital. Although they are closely related, there is an important difference. Technological knowledge refers to society's understanding about how the world works. Human capital refers to the resources expended transmitting this understanding to the labor force. To use a relevant metaphor, technological knowledge is the quality of society's textbooks, whereas human capital is the amount of time that the population has devoted to reading them. Workers' productivity depends on both.

FYI
The Production Function

Economists often use a *production function* to describe the relationship between the quantity of inputs used in production and the quantity of output from production. For example, suppose Y denotes the quantity of output, L the quantity of labor, K the quantity of physical capital, H the quantity of human capital, and N the quantity of natural resources. Then we might write

$$Y = AF(L, K, H, N),$$

where $F(\ )$ is a function that shows how the inputs are combined to produce output. A is a variable that reflects the available production technology. As technology improves, A rises, so the economy produces more output from any given combination of inputs.

Many production functions have a property called *constant returns to scale*. If a production function has constant returns to scale, then doubling all inputs causes the amount of output to double as well. Mathematically, we write that a production function has constant returns to scale if, for any positive number x,

$$xY = AF(xL, xK, xH, xN).$$

A doubling of all inputs would be represented in this equation by $x = 2$. The right side shows the inputs doubling, and the left side shows output doubling.

Production functions with constant returns to scale have an interesting and useful implication. To see this implication, set $x = 1/L$ so that the preceding equation becomes

$$Y/L = AF(1, K/L, H/L, N/L).$$

Notice that Y/L is output per worker, which is a measure of productivity. This equation says that labor productivity depends on physical capital per worker (K/L), human capital per worker (H/L), and natural resources per worker (N/L). Productivity also depends on the state of technology, as reflected by the variable A. Thus, this equation provides a mathematical summary of the four determinants of productivity we have just discussed. ◢

Are Natural Resources a Limit to Growth?

Today, the world's population is almost 7 billion, more than four times what it was a century ago. At the same time, many people are enjoying a much higher standard of living than did their great-grandparents. A perennial debate concerns whether this growth in population and living standards can continue in the future.

Many commentators have argued that natural resources will eventually limit how much the world's economies can grow. At first, this argument might seem hard to ignore. If the world has only a fixed supply of nonrenewable natural resources, how can population, production, and living standards continue to grow over time? Eventually, won't supplies of oil and minerals start to run out? When these shortages start to occur, won't they stop economic growth and, perhaps, even force living standards to fall?

Despite the apparent appeal of such arguments, most economists are less concerned about such limits to growth than one might guess. They argue that technological progress often yields ways to avoid these limits. If we compare the economy today to the economy of the past, we see various ways in which the use of natural resources has improved. Modern cars have better gas mileage. New houses have better insulation and require less energy to heat and cool. More efficient oil rigs waste less oil in the process of extraction. Recycling allows some nonrenewable resources to be reused. The development of alternative fuels, such as ethanol instead of gasoline, allows us to substitute renewable for nonrenewable resources.

Seventy years ago, some conservationists were concerned about the excessive use of tin and copper. At the time, these were crucial commodities: Tin was used to make many food containers, and copper was used to make telephone wire. Some people advocated mandatory recycling and rationing of tin and copper so that supplies would be available for future generations. Today, however, plastic has replaced tin as a material for making many food containers, and phone calls often travel over fiber-optic cables, which are made from sand. Technological progress has made once crucial natural resources less necessary.

But are all these efforts enough to permit continued economic growth? One way to answer this question is to look at the prices of natural resources. In a market economy, scarcity is reflected in market prices. If the world were running out of natural resources, then the prices of those resources would be rising over time. But in fact, the opposite is more often true. Natural resource prices exhibit substantial short-run fluctuations, but over long spans of time, the prices of most natural resources (adjusted for overall inflation) are stable or falling. It appears that our ability to conserve these resources is growing more rapidly than their supplies are dwindling. Market prices give no reason to believe that natural resources are a limit to economic growth. ◢

Quick Quiz *List and describe four determinants of a country's productivity.*

25-3 Economic Growth and Public Policy

So far, we have determined that a society's standard of living depends on its ability to produce goods and services and that its productivity in turn depends on physical capital per worker, human capital per worker, natural resources per worker, and technological knowledge. Let's now turn to the question faced by policymakers around the world: What can government policy do to raise productivity and living standards?

25-3a Saving and Investment

Because capital is a produced factor of production, a society can change the amount of capital it has. If today the economy produces a large quantity of new capital goods, then tomorrow it will have a larger stock of capital and be able to produce more goods and services. Thus, one way to raise future productivity is to invest more current resources in the production of capital.

One of the *Ten Principles of Economics* presented in Chapter 1 is that people face trade-offs. This principle is especially important when considering the accumulation of capital. Because resources are scarce, devoting more resources to producing capital requires devoting fewer resources to producing goods and services for current consumption. That is, for society to invest more in capital, it must consume less and save more of its current income. The growth that arises from capital accumulation is not a free lunch: It requires that society sacrifice consumption of goods and services in the present to enjoy higher consumption in the future.

The next chapter examines in more detail how the economy's financial markets coordinate saving and investment. It also examines how government policies influence the amount of saving and investment that takes place. At this point, it is important to note that encouraging saving and investment is one way that a government can encourage growth and, in the long run, raise the economy's standard of living.

25-3b Diminishing Returns and the Catch-Up Effect

Suppose that a government pursues policies that raise the nation's saving rate—the percentage of GDP devoted to saving rather than consumption. What happens? With the nation saving more, fewer resources are needed to make consumption goods, and more resources are available to make capital goods. As a result, the capital stock increases, leading to rising productivity and more rapid growth in GDP. But how long does this higher rate of growth last? Assuming that the saving rate remains at its new, higher level, does the growth rate of GDP stay high indefinitely or only for a period of time?

The traditional view of the production process is that capital is subject to **diminishing returns:** As the stock of capital rises, the extra output produced from an additional unit of capital falls. In other words, when workers already have a large quantity of capital to use in producing goods and services, giving them an additional unit of capital increases their productivity only slightly. This is illustrated in Figure 1, which shows how the amount of capital per worker determines the amount of output per worker, holding constant all the other determinants of output.

diminishing returns
the property whereby the benefit from an extra unit of an input declines as the quantity of the input increases

Because of diminishing returns, an increase in the saving rate leads to higher growth only for a while. As the higher saving rate allows more capital to be accumulated, the benefits from additional capital become smaller over time, and so growth slows down. *In the long run, the higher saving rate leads to a higher level of productivity and income but not to higher growth in these variables.* Reaching this long run, however, can take quite a while. According to studies of international data on economic growth, increasing the saving rate can lead to substantially higher growth for a period of several decades.

The property of diminishing returns to capital has another important implication: Other things being equal, it is easier for a country to grow fast if it starts out

FIGURE 1

Illustrating the Production Function
This figure shows how the amount of capital per worker influences the amount of output per worker. Other determinants of output, including human capital, natural resources, and technology, are held constant. The curve becomes flatter as the amount of capital increases because of diminishing returns to capital.

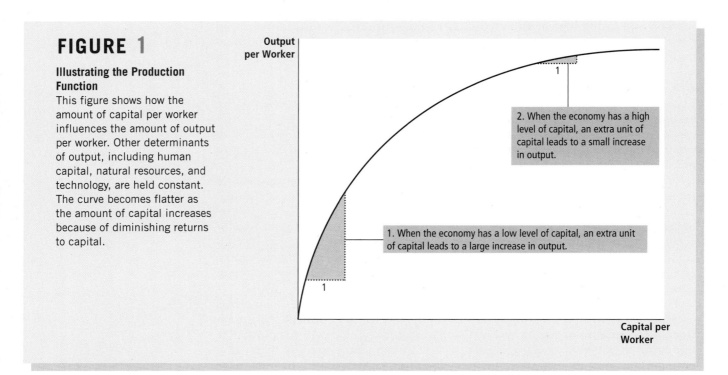

Output per Worker

2. When the economy has a high level of capital, an extra unit of capital leads to a small increase in output.

1. When the economy has a low level of capital, an extra unit of capital leads to a large increase in output.

Capital per Worker

catch-up effect
the property whereby countries that start off poor tend to grow more rapidly than countries that start off rich

relatively poor. This effect of initial conditions on subsequent growth is sometimes called the **catch-up effect**. In poor countries, workers lack even the most rudimentary tools and, as a result, have low productivity. Thus, small amounts of capital investment can substantially raise these workers' productivity. By contrast, workers in rich countries have large amounts of capital with which to work, and this partly explains their high productivity. Yet with the amount of capital per worker already so high, additional capital investment has a relatively small effect on productivity. Studies of international data on economic growth confirm this catch-up effect: Controlling for other variables, such as the percentage of GDP devoted to investment, poor countries tend to grow at faster rates than rich countries.

This catch-up effect can help explain some otherwise puzzling facts. Here's an example: From 1960 to 1990, the United States and South Korea devoted a similar share of GDP to investment. Yet over this time, the United States experienced only mediocre growth of about 2 percent, while South Korea experienced spectacular growth of more than 6 percent. The explanation is the catch-up effect. In 1960, South Korea had GDP per person less than one-tenth the U.S. level, in part because previous investment had been so low. With a small initial capital stock, the benefits to capital accumulation were much greater in South Korea, and this gave South Korea a higher subsequent growth rate.

This catch-up effect shows up in other aspects of life. When a school gives an end-of-year award to the "Most Improved" student, that student is usually one who began the year with relatively poor performance. Students who began the year not studying find improvement easier than students who always worked hard. Note that it is good to be "Most Improved," given the starting point, but it is even better to be "Best Student." Similarly, economic growth over the last several decades has been much more rapid in South Korea than in the United States, but GDP per person is still higher in the United States.

25-3c Investment from Abroad

So far, we have discussed how policies aimed at increasing a country's saving rate can increase investment and, thereby, long-term economic growth. Yet saving by domestic residents is not the only way for a country to invest in new capital. The other way is investment by foreigners.

Investment from abroad takes several forms. Ford Motor Company might build a car factory in Mexico. A capital investment that is owned and operated by a foreign entity is called *foreign direct investment*. Alternatively, an American might buy stock in a Mexican corporation (that is, buy a share in the ownership of the corporation); the Mexican corporation can use the proceeds from the stock sale to build a new factory. An investment that is financed with foreign money but operated by domestic residents is called *foreign portfolio investment*. In both cases, Americans provide the resources necessary to increase the stock of capital in Mexico. That is, American saving is being used to finance Mexican investment.

When foreigners invest in a country, they do so because they expect to earn a return on their investment. Ford's car factory increases the Mexican capital stock and, therefore, increases Mexican productivity and Mexican GDP. Yet Ford takes some of this additional income back to the United States in the form of profit. Similarly, when an American investor buys Mexican stock, the investor has a right to a portion of the profit that the Mexican corporation earns.

Investment from abroad, therefore, does not have the same effect on all measures of economic prosperity. Recall that gross domestic product (GDP) is the income earned within a country by both residents and nonresidents, whereas gross national product (GNP) is the income earned by residents of a country both at home and abroad. When Ford opens its car factory in Mexico, some of the income the factory generates accrues to people who do not live in Mexico. As a result, foreign investment in Mexico raises the income of Mexicans (measured by GNP) by less than it raises the production in Mexico (measured by GDP).

Nonetheless, investment from abroad is one way for a country to grow. Even though some of the benefits from this investment flow back to the foreign owners, this investment does increase the economy's stock of capital, leading to higher productivity and higher wages. Moreover, investment from abroad is one way for poor countries to learn the state-of-the-art technologies developed and used in richer countries. For these reasons, many economists who advise governments in less developed economies advocate policies that encourage investment from abroad. Often, this means removing restrictions that governments have imposed on foreign ownership of domestic capital.

An organization that tries to encourage the flow of capital to poor countries is the World Bank. This international organization obtains funds from the world's advanced countries, such as the United States, and uses these resources to make loans to less developed countries so that they can invest in roads, sewer systems, schools, and other types of capital. It also offers the countries advice about how the funds might best be used. The World Bank, together with its sister organization, the International Monetary Fund, was set up after World War II. One lesson from the war was that economic distress often leads to political turmoil, international tensions, and military conflict. Thus, every country has an interest in promoting economic prosperity around the world. The World Bank and the International Monetary Fund were established to achieve that common goal.

25-3d Education

Education—investment in human capital—is at least as important as investment in physical capital for a country's long-run economic success. In the United States, each year of schooling has historically raised a person's wage by an average of about 10 percent. In less developed countries, where human capital is especially scarce, the gap between the wages of educated and uneducated workers is even larger. Thus, one way government policy can enhance the standard of living is to provide good schools and to encourage the population to take advantage of them.

Investment in human capital, like investment in physical capital, has an opportunity cost. When students are in school, they forgo the wages they could have earned as members of the labor force. In less developed countries, children often drop out of school at an early age, even though the benefit of additional schooling is very high, simply because their labor is needed to help support the family.

Some economists have argued that human capital is particularly important for economic growth because human capital conveys positive externalities. An *externality* is the effect of one person's actions on the well-being of a bystander. An educated person, for instance, might generate new ideas about how best to produce goods and services. If these ideas enter society's pool of knowledge so that everyone can use them, then the ideas are an external benefit of education. In this case, the return from schooling for society is even greater than the return for the individual. This argument would justify the large subsidies to human-capital investment that we observe in the form of public education.

One problem facing some poor countries is the *brain drain*—the emigration of many of the most highly educated workers to rich countries, where these workers can enjoy a higher standard of living. If human capital does have positive externalities, then this brain drain makes those people left behind even poorer. This problem offers policymakers a dilemma. On the one hand, the United States and other rich countries have the best systems of higher education, and it would seem natural for poor countries to send their best students abroad to earn higher degrees. On the other hand, those students who have spent time abroad may choose not to return home, and this brain drain will reduce the poor nation's stock of human capital even further.

25-3e Health and Nutrition

The term *human capital* usually refers to education, but it can also be used to describe another type of investment in people: expenditures that lead to a healthier population. Other things being equal, healthier workers are more productive. The right investments in the health of the population provide one way for a nation to increase productivity and raise living standards.

According to the late economic historian Robert Fogel, improved health from better nutrition has been a significant factor in long-run economic growth. Fogel estimated that in Great Britain in 1780, about one in five people were so malnourished that they were incapable of manual labor. Among those who could work, insufficient caloric intake substantially reduced the work effort they could put forth. As nutrition improved, so did workers' productivity.

Fogel studied these historical trends in part by looking at the height of the population. Short stature can be an indicator of malnutrition, especially during gestation and the early years of life. Fogel found that as nations develop economically, people eat more and the population gets taller. From 1775 to 1975, the average caloric intake in Great Britain rose by 26 percent and the height of the average man rose by 3.6 inches. Similarly, during the spectacular economic growth in South Korea from 1962 to 1995, caloric consumption rose by 44 percent and average male height rose by 2 inches. Of course, a person's height is determined by a combination of genetics and environment. But because the genetic makeup of a population is slow to change, such increases in average height are most likely due to changes in the environment—nutrition being the obvious explanation.

Moreover, studies have found that height is an indicator of productivity. Looking at data on a large number of workers at a point in time, researchers have found that taller workers tend to earn more. Because wages reflect a worker's productivity, this finding suggests that taller workers tend to be more productive. The effect of height on wages is especially pronounced in poorer countries, where malnutrition is a bigger risk.

Fogel won the Nobel Prize in Economics in 1993 for his work in economic history, which includes not only his studies of nutrition but also his studies of American slavery and the role of railroads in the development of the American economy. In the lecture he gave when he was awarded the prize, he surveyed the evidence on health and economic growth. He concluded that "improved gross nutrition accounts for roughly 30 percent of the growth of per capita income in Britain between 1790 and 1980."

Today, malnutrition is fortunately rare in developed nations such as Great Britain and the United States. (Obesity is a more widespread problem.) But for people in developing nations, poor health and inadequate nutrition remain obstacles to higher productivity and improved living standards. The United Nations estimates that almost a third of the population in sub-Saharan Africa is undernourished.

The causal link between health and wealth runs in both directions. Poor countries are poor in part because their populations are not healthy, and their populations are not healthy in part because they are poor and cannot afford adequate healthcare and nutrition. It is a vicious circle. But this fact opens the possibility of a virtuous circle: Policies that lead to more rapid economic growth would naturally improve health outcomes, which in turn would further promote economic growth.

25-3f Property Rights and Political Stability

Another way policymakers can foster economic growth is by protecting property rights and promoting political stability. This issue goes to the very heart of how market economies work.

Production in market economies arises from the interactions of millions of individuals and firms. When you buy a car, for instance, you are buying the output of a car dealer, a car manufacturer, a steel company, an iron ore mining company, and so on. This division of production among many firms allows the economy's factors of production to be used as effectively as possible. To achieve this outcome, the economy has to coordinate transactions among these firms, as well as between firms and consumers. Market economies achieve this coordination through market prices. That is, market prices are the instrument with which the invisible hand of the marketplace brings supply and demand into balance in each of the many thousands of markets that make up the economy.

An important prerequisite for the price system to work is an economy-wide respect for *property rights*. Property rights refer to the ability of people to exercise authority over the resources they own. A mining company will not make the effort to mine iron ore if it expects the ore to be stolen. The company mines the ore only if it is confident that it will benefit from the ore's subsequent sale. For this reason, courts serve an important role in a market economy: They enforce property rights. Through the criminal justice system, the courts discourage theft. In addition, through the civil justice system, the courts ensure that buyers and sellers live up to their contracts.

Those of us in developed countries tend to take property rights for granted, but those living in less developed countries understand that a lack of property rights can be a major problem. In many countries, the system of justice does not work well. Contracts are hard to enforce, and fraud often goes unpunished. In more extreme cases, the government not only fails to enforce property rights but actually infringes upon them. To do business in some countries, firms are expected to bribe government officials. Such corruption impedes the coordinating power of markets. It also discourages domestic saving and investment from abroad.

One threat to property rights is political instability. When revolutions and coups are common, there is doubt about whether property rights will be respected in the future. If a revolutionary government might confiscate the capital of some businesses, as was often true after communist revolutions, domestic residents

IN THE NEWS
. . . .

Does Food Aid Help or Hurt?

Economic policies often have unintended consequences. Here is an example.

Food Aid to Developing Nations May Increase Armed Conflict

By Justin Lahart

The country is torn by conflict. The people are hungry.

Our natural response is to send food, but in practice that can be problematic. For decades, aid workers, journalists and others have documented cases where food aid has been misappropriated by armed groups who use it to feed their soldiers and buy weapons. Convoy trucks and other equipment are often captured.

Such reports are, in the end, merely anecdotal, and may only represent extreme, outlying cases. Moreover, there are chicken-and-egg problems such as the question of

whether the food aid heightened the conflict, or whether the brewing conflict brought in the food aid.

But Harvard's Nathan Nunn and Yale's Nancy Qian devised a way to sidestep such issues and more directly measure what is happening. Their results are sobering.

The flow of American food aid, the economists found, has a lot to do with the wheat crop. In bumper years, the U.S. government accumulates wheat as part of its price support program. In the following year, the surplus is shipped to developing countries as food aid. This allowed the economists to tease out the effects of the flow of food to 134 developing countries from 1972 through 2006.

They found that an increase in food aid raises the incidence, onset and duration of armed civil conflict in a recipient country.

The problem is particularly acute in countries where there are few roads—giving aid convoys fewer opportunities to circumvent problems—and ones where there are stark ethnic divisions.

The economists note that food, because it is bulky and needs to be transported across territories a country may have little control over, is an especially attractive target for armed groups. As a result, they say, "our results should not be extrapolated as evidence of the impacts of foreign aid in general." ◢

Source: *The Wall Street Journal*, Real Time Economics blog, January 30, 2012.

have less incentive to save, invest, and start new businesses. At the same time, foreigners have less incentive to invest in the country. Even the threat of revolution can act to depress a nation's standard of living.

Thus, economic prosperity depends in part on political prosperity. A country with an efficient court system, honest government officials, and a stable constitution will enjoy a higher economic standard of living than a country with a poor court system, corrupt officials, and frequent revolutions and coups.

25-3g Free Trade

Some of the world's poorest countries have tried to achieve more rapid economic growth by pursuing *inward-oriented policies*. These policies attempt to increase productivity and living standards within the country by avoiding interaction with the rest of the world. Domestic firms often advance the infant-industry argument, claiming they need protection from foreign competition to thrive and grow. Together with a general distrust of foreigners, this argument has at times led policymakers in less developed countries to impose tariffs and other trade restrictions.

Most economists today believe that poor countries are better off pursuing *outward-oriented policies* that integrate these countries into the world economy. International trade in goods and services can improve the economic well-being of a country's citizens. Trade is, in some ways, a type of technology. When a country exports wheat and imports textiles, the country benefits as if it had invented a technology for turning wheat into textiles. A country that eliminates trade restrictions will, therefore, experience the same kind of economic growth that would occur after a major technological advance.

The adverse impact of inward orientation becomes clear when one considers the small size of many less developed economies. The total GDP of Argentina, for instance, is about that of Houston, Texas. Imagine what would happen if the Houston city council were to prohibit city residents from trading with people living outside the city limits. Without being able to take advantage of the gains from trade, Houston would need to produce all the goods it consumes. It would also have to produce all its own capital goods, rather than importing state-of-the-art equipment from other cities. Living standards in Houston would fall immediately, and the problem would likely only get worse over time. This is precisely what happened when Argentina pursued inward-oriented policies throughout much of the 20th century. In contrast, countries that pursued outward-oriented policies, such as South Korea, Singapore, and Taiwan, enjoyed high rates of economic growth.

The amount that a nation trades with others is determined not only by government policy but also by geography. Countries with natural seaports find trade easier than countries without this resource. It is not a coincidence that many of the world's major cities, such as New York, San Francisco, and Hong Kong, are located next to oceans. Similarly, because landlocked countries find international trade more difficult, they tend to have lower levels of income than countries with easy access to the world's waterways. For example, countries with more than 80 percent of their population living within 100 kilometers of a coast have an average GDP per person about four times as large as countries with less than 20 percent of their population living near a coast. The critical importance of access to the sea helps explain why the African continent, which contains many landlocked countries, is so poor.

25-3h Research and Development

The primary reason that living standards are higher today than they were a century ago is that technological knowledge has advanced. The telephone, the transistor, the computer, and the internal combustion engine are among the thousands of innovations that have improved the ability to produce goods and services.

Most technological advances come from private research by firms and individual inventors, but there is also a public interest in promoting these efforts. To a large extent, knowledge is a *public good:* That is, once one person discovers an idea, the idea enters society's pool of knowledge and other people can freely use it. Just as government has a role in providing a public good such as national defense, it also has a role in encouraging the research and development of new technologies.

The U.S. government has long played a role in the creation and dissemination of technological knowledge. A century ago, the government sponsored research about farming methods and advised farmers how best to use their land. More recently, the U.S. government, through the Air Force and NASA, has supported aerospace research; as a result, the United States is a leading maker of rockets and planes. The government continues to encourage advances in knowledge with research grants from the National Science Foundation and the National Institutes of Health and with tax breaks for firms engaging in research and development.

Yet another way in which government policy encourages research is through the patent system. When a person or firm invents a new product, such as a new drug, the inventor can apply for a patent. If the product is deemed truly original, the government awards the patent, which gives the inventor the exclusive right to make the product for a specified number of years. In essence, the patent gives the inventor a property right over her invention, turning her new idea from a public good into a private good. By allowing inventors to profit from their inventions—even if only temporarily—the patent system enhances the incentive for individuals and firms to engage in research.

25-3i Population Growth

Economists and other social scientists have long debated how population affects a society. The most direct effect is on the size of the labor force: A large population means more workers to produce goods and services. The tremendous size of the Chinese population is one reason China is such an important player in the world economy.

At the same time, however, a large population means more people to consume those goods and services. So while a large population means a larger total output of goods and services, it need not mean a higher standard of living for a typical citizen. Indeed, both large and small nations are found at all levels of economic development.

Beyond these obvious effects of population size, population growth interacts with the other factors of production in ways that are more subtle and open to debate.

Stretching Natural Resources Thomas Robert Malthus (1766–1834), an English minister and early economic thinker, is famous for his book called *An Essay on the Principle of Population as It Affects the Future Improvement of Society.* In it, he offered what may be history's most chilling forecast. Malthus argued that an ever-increasing population would continually strain society's ability to provide for itself. As a result, mankind was doomed to forever live in poverty.

Malthus's logic was simple. He began by noting that "food is necessary to the existence of man" and that "the passion between the sexes is necessary and will remain nearly in its present state." He concluded that "the power of population is infinitely greater than the power in the earth to produce subsistence for man." According to Malthus, the only check on population growth was "misery and vice." Attempts by charities or governments to alleviate poverty were counterproductive, he argued, because they merely allowed the poor to have more children, placing even greater strains on society's productive capabilities.

Malthus may have correctly described the world at the time when he lived, but fortunately, his dire forecast was far off the mark. The world population has increased about sixfold over the past two centuries, but living standards around the world are on average much higher. As a result of economic growth, chronic hunger and malnutrition are less common now than they were in Malthus's day. Modern famines occur from time to time but are more often the result of an unequal income distribution or political instability than inadequate food production.

Where did Malthus go wrong? As we discussed in a case study earlier in this chapter, growth in human ingenuity has offset the effects of a larger population. Pesticides, fertilizers, mechanized farm equipment, new crop varieties, and other technological advances that Malthus never imagined have allowed each farmer to feed ever greater numbers of people. Even with more mouths to feed, fewer farmers are necessary because each farmer is much more productive.

Thomas Robert Malthus

Diluting the Capital Stock   Whereas Malthus worried about the effects of population on the use of natural resources, some modern theories of economic growth emphasize its effects on capital accumulation. According to these theories, high population growth reduces GDP per worker because rapid growth in the number of workers forces the capital stock to be spread more thinly. In other words, when population growth is rapid, each worker is equipped with less capital. A smaller quantity of capital per worker leads to lower productivity and lower GDP per worker.

This problem is most apparent in the case of human capital. Countries with high population growth have large numbers of school-age children. This places a larger burden on the educational system. It is not surprising, therefore, that educational attainment tends to be low in countries with high population growth.

The differences in population growth around the world are large. In developed countries, such as the United States and those in Western Europe, the population has risen only about 1 percent per year in recent decades and is expected to rise even more slowly in the future. By contrast, in many poor African countries, population grows at about 3 percent per year. At this rate, the population doubles every 23 years. This rapid population growth makes it harder to provide workers with the tools and skills they need to achieve high levels of productivity.

Rapid population growth is not the main reason that less developed countries are poor, but some analysts believe that reducing the rate of population growth would help these countries raise their standards of living. In some countries, this goal is accomplished directly with laws that regulate the number of children families may have. China, for instance, allows only one child per family; couples who violate this rule are subject to substantial fines. In countries with greater freedom, the goal of reduced population growth is accomplished less directly by increasing awareness of birth control techniques.

Another way in which a country can influence population growth is to apply one of the *Ten Principles of Economics:* People respond to incentives. Bearing a child, like any decision, has an opportunity cost. When the opportunity cost rises, people will choose to have smaller families. In particular, women with the opportunity to receive a good education and desirable employment tend to want fewer children than those with fewer opportunities outside the home. Hence, policies that foster equal treatment of women may be one way for less developed economies to reduce the rate of population growth and, perhaps, raise their standards of living.

Promoting Technological Progress Rapid population growth may depress economic prosperity by reducing the amount of capital each worker has, but it

IN THE NEWS One Economist's Answer

This article offers one perspective on the profound question of why some nations thrive while others do not.

What Makes a Nation Rich?

By Daron Acemoglu

We are the rich, the haves, the developed. And most of the rest—in Africa, South Asia, and South America, the Somalias and Bolivias and Bangladeshes of the world—are the nots. It's always been this way, a globe divided by wealth and poverty, health and sickness, food and famine, though the extent of inequality across nations today is unprecedented: The average citizen of the United States is ten times as prosperous as the average Guatemalan, more than twenty times as prosperous as the average North Korean, and more than forty times as prosperous as those living in Mali, Ethiopia, Congo, or Sierra Leone.

The question social scientists have unsuccessfully wrestled with for centuries is, Why? But the question they should have been asking is, How? Because inequality is not predetermined. Nations are not like children—they are not born rich or poor. Their governments make them that way.

You can chart the search for a theory of inequality to the French political philosopher Montesquieu, who in the mid-eighteenth century came up with a very simple explanation: People in hot places are inherently lazy. Other no less sweeping explanations soon followed: Could it be that Max Weber's Protestant work ethic is the true driver of economic success? Or perhaps the richest countries are those that were former British colonies? Or maybe it's as simple as tracing which nations have the largest populations of European descent? The problem with all of these theories is that while they superficially fit some specific cases, others radically disprove them.

It's the same with the theories put forth today. Economist Jeffrey Sachs, director of Columbia University's Earth Institute, attributes the relative success of nations to geography and weather: In the poorest parts of the world, he argues, nutrient-starved tropical soil makes agriculture a challenge, and tropical climates foment disease, particularly malaria. Perhaps if we were to fix these problems, teach the citizens of these nations better farming techniques, eliminate malaria, or at the very least equip them with artemisinin to fight this deadly disease, we could eliminate poverty. Or better yet, perhaps we just move these people and abandon their inhospitable land altogether.

Jared Diamond, the famous ecologist and best-selling author, has a different theory: The origin of world inequality stems from the historical endowment of plant and animal species and the advancement of technology. In Diamond's telling, the cultures that first learned to plant crops were the first to learn how to use a plow, and thus were first to adopt other technologies, the engine of every successful economy. Perhaps then the solution to world inequality rests in technology—wiring the developing world with Internet and cell phones.

And yet while Sachs and Diamond offer good insight into certain aspects of poverty, they share something in common with Montesquieu and others who followed: They ignore incentives. People need incentives to invest and prosper; they need to know that if they work hard, they can make money and actually keep that money. And the key to ensuring those incentives is sound institutions—the rule of law and security and a governing system that offers opportunities to achieve and innovate. That's what determines the haves from the have-nots—not geography or weather or technology or disease or ethnicity.

Put simply: Fix incentives and you will fix poverty. And if you wish to fix institutions, you have to fix governments.

How do we know that institutions are so central to the wealth and poverty of nations? Start in Nogales, a city cut in half by the Mexican-American border fence. There is no difference in geography between the two halves of Nogales. The weather is the same. The winds are the same, as are the soils. The types of diseases prevalent in the area given its geography and climate are the same, as

may also have some benefits. Some economists have suggested that world population growth has been an engine of technological progress and economic prosperity. The mechanism is simple: If there are more people, then there are more scientists, inventors, and engineers to contribute to technological advance, which benefits everyone.

Economist Michael Kremer has provided some support for this hypothesis in an article titled "Population Growth and Technological Change: One Million B.C. to 1990," which was published in the *Quarterly Journal of Economics* in 1993.

---

is the ethnic, cultural, and linguistic background of the residents. By logic, both sides of the city should be identical economically.

And yet they are far from the same.

On one side of the border fence, in Santa Cruz County, Arizona, the median household income is $30,000. A few feet away, it's $10,000. On one side, most of the teenagers are in public high school, and the majority of the adults are high school graduates. On the other side, few of the residents have gone to high school, let alone college. Those in Arizona enjoy relatively good health and Medicare for those over sixty-five, not to mention an efficient road network, electricity, telephone service, and a dependable sewage and public-health system. None of those things are a given across the border. There, the roads are bad, the infant-mortality rate high, electricity and phone service expensive and spotty.

The key difference is that those on the north side of the border enjoy law and order and dependable government services—they can go about their daily activities and jobs without fear for their life or safety or property rights. On the other side, the inhabitants have institutions that perpetuate crime, graft, and insecurity.

Nogales may be the most obvious example, but it's far from the only one. Take Singapore, a once-impoverished tropical island that became the richest nation in Asia after British colonialists enshrined property rights and encouraged trade. Or China, where decades of stagnation and famine were reversed only after Deng Xiaoping began introducing private-property rights in agriculture, and later in industry. Or Botswana,

whose economy has flourished over the past forty years while the rest of Africa has withered, thanks to strong tribal institutions and farsighted nation building by its early elected leaders.

Now look at the economic and political failures. You can begin in Sierra Leone, where a lack of functioning institutions and an overabundance of diamonds have fueled decades of civil war and strife and corruption that continue unchecked today. Or take communist North Korea, a geographical, ethnic, and cultural mirror of its capitalist neighbor to the south, yet ten times poorer. Or Egypt, cradle of one of the world's great civilizations yet stagnant economically ever since its colonization by the Ottomans and then the Europeans, only made worse by its post-independence

Daron Acemoglu

governments, which have restricted all economic activities and markets. In fact, the theory can be used to shed light on the patterns of inequality for much of the world.

If we know why nations are poor, the resulting question is what can we do to help them. Our ability to impose institutions from the outside is limited, as the recent U.S. experiences in Afghanistan and Iraq demonstrate. But we are not helpless, and in many instances, there is a lot to be done. Even the most repressed citizens of the world will stand up to tyrants when given the opportunity. We saw this recently in Iran and a few years ago in Ukraine during the Orange Revolution.

The U.S. must not take a passive role in encouraging these types of movements. Our foreign policy should encourage them by punishing repressive regimes through trade embargoes and diplomacy.... At the micro-level, we can help foreign citizens by educating them and arming them with the modern tools of activism, most notably the Internet, and perhaps even encryption technology and cell-phone platforms that can evade firewalls and censorship put in place by repressive governments, such as those in China or Iran, that fear the power of information.

There's no doubt that erasing global inequality, which has been with us for millennia and has expanded to unprecedented levels over the past century and a half, won't be easy. But by accepting the role of failed governments and institutions in causing poverty, we have a fighting chance of reversing it.

Mr. Acemoglu is an economics professor at the Massachusetts Institute of Technology. ◢

Source: *Esquire*, November 18, 2009.

Kremer begins by noting that over the broad span of human history, world growth rates have increased with world population. For example, world growth was more rapid when the world population was 1 billion (which occurred around the year 1800) than when the population was only 100 million (around 500 B.C.). This fact is consistent with the hypothesis that a larger population induces more technological progress.

Kremer's second piece of evidence comes from comparing regions of the world. The melting of the polar icecaps at the end of the Ice Age around 10,000 B.C. flooded the land bridges and separated the world into several distinct regions that could not communicate with one another for thousands of years. If technological progress is more rapid when there are more people to discover things, then larger regions should have experienced more rapid growth.

According to Kremer, that is exactly what happened. The most successful region of the world in 1500 (when Columbus reestablished contact) comprised the "Old World" civilizations of the large Eurasia-Africa region. Next in technological development were the Aztec and Mayan civilizations in the Americas, followed by the hunter-gatherers of Australia, and then the primitive people of Tasmania, who lacked even fire-making and most stone and bone tools.

The smallest isolated region was Flinders Island, a tiny island between Tasmania and Australia. With the smallest population, Flinders Island had the fewest opportunities for technological advance and, indeed, seemed to regress. Around 3000 B.C., human society on Flinders Island died out completely. A large population, Kremer concludes, is a prerequisite for technological advance.

Quick Quiz *Describe three ways a government policymaker can try to raise the growth in living standards in a society. Are there any drawbacks to these policies?*

25-4 Conclusion: The Importance of Long-Run Growth

In this chapter, we have discussed what determines the standard of living in a nation and how policymakers can endeavor to raise it through policies that promote economic growth. Most of this chapter is summarized in one of the *Ten Principles of Economics:* A country's standard of living depends on its ability to produce goods and services. Policymakers who want to encourage growth in living standards must aim to increase their nation's productive ability by encouraging rapid accumulation of the factors of production and ensuring that these factors are employed as effectively as possible.

Economists differ in their views of the role of government in promoting economic growth. At the very least, government can lend support to the invisible hand by maintaining property rights and political stability. More controversial is whether government should target and subsidize specific industries that might be especially important for technological progress. There is no doubt that these issues are among the most important in economics. The success of one generation's policymakers in learning and heeding the fundamental lessons about economic growth determines what kind of world the next generation will inherit.

Summary

- Economic prosperity, as measured by GDP per person, varies substantially around the world. The average income in the world's richest countries is more than ten times that in the world's poorest countries. Because growth rates of real GDP also vary substantially, the relative positions of countries can change dramatically over time.

- The standard of living in an economy depends on the economy's ability to produce goods and services. Productivity, in turn, depends on the physical capital, human capital, natural resources, and technological knowledge available to workers.

- Government policies can try to influence the economy's growth rate in many ways: by encouraging saving and investment, encouraging investment from abroad, fostering education, promoting good health, maintaining property rights and political stability, allowing free trade, and promoting the research and development of new technologies.

- The accumulation of capital is subject to diminishing returns: The more capital an economy has, the less additional output the economy gets from an extra unit of capital. As a result, although higher saving leads to higher growth for a period of time, growth eventually slows down as capital, productivity, and income rise. Also because of diminishing returns, the return to capital is especially high in poor countries. Other things being equal, these countries can grow faster because of the catch-up effect.

- Population growth has a variety of effects on economic growth. On the one hand, more rapid population growth may lower productivity by stretching the supply of natural resources and by reducing the amount of capital available for each worker. On the other hand, a larger population may enhance the rate of technological progress because there are more scientists and engineers.

Key Concepts

productivity, *p. 527*
physical capital, *p. 530*
human capital, *p. 530*

natural resources, *p. 530*
technological knowledge, *p. 530*
diminishing returns, *p. 533*

catch-up effect, *p. 534*

Questions for Review

1. What does the level of a nation's GDP measure? What does the growth rate of GDP measure? Would you rather live in a nation with a high level of GDP and a low growth rate or in a nation with a low level of GDP and a high growth rate?

2. List and describe four determinants of productivity.

3. In what way is a college degree a form of capital?

4. Explain how higher saving leads to a higher standard of living. What might deter a policymaker from trying to raise the rate of saving?

5. Does a higher rate of saving lead to higher growth temporarily or indefinitely?

6. Why would removing a trade restriction, such as a tariff, lead to more rapid economic growth?

7. How does the rate of population growth influence the level of GDP per person?

8. Describe two ways the U.S. government tries to encourage advances in technological knowledge.

Quick Check Multiple Choice

1. Over the past century, real GDP per person in the United States has grown about _____ percent per year, which means it doubles about every _____ years.
   a. 2, 14
   b. 2, 35
   c. 5, 14
   d. 5, 35

2. The world's rich countries, such as Japan and Germany, have income per person that is about _____ times the income per person in the world's poor countries, such as Pakistan and India.
   a. 3
   b. 6
   c. 12
   d. 36

3. Most economists are _____ that natural resources will eventually limit economic growth. As evidence, they note that the prices of most natural resources, adjusted for overall inflation, have tended to _____ over time.
   a. concerned, rise
   b. concerned, fall
   c. not concerned, rise
   d. not concerned, fall

4. Because capital is subject to diminishing returns, higher saving and investment does not lead to higher
   a. income in the long run.
   b. income in the short run.
   c. growth in the long run.
   d. growth in the short run.

5. When the Japanese car maker Toyota expands one of its car factories in the United States, what is the likely impact of this event on the GDP and GNP of the United States?
   a. GDP rises and GNP falls.
   b. GNP rises and GDP falls.
   c. GDP shows a larger increase than GNP.
   d. GNP shows a larger increase than GDP.

6. Thomas Robert Malthus believed that population growth would
   a. put stress on the economy's ability to produce food, dooming humans to remain in poverty.
   b. spread the capital stock too thinly across the labor force, lowering each worker's productivity.
   c. promote technological progress, because there would be more scientists and inventors.
   d. eventually decline to sustainable levels, as birth control improved and people had smaller families.

Problems and Applications

1. Most countries, including the United States, import substantial amounts of goods and services from other countries. Yet the chapter says that a nation can enjoy a high standard of living only if it can produce a large quantity of goods and services itself. Can you reconcile these two facts?

2. Suppose that society decided to reduce consumption and increase investment.
   a. How would this change affect economic growth?
   b. What groups in society would benefit from this change? What groups might be hurt?

3. Societies choose what share of their resources to devote to consumption and what share to devote to investment. Some of these decisions involve private spending; others involve government spending.
   a. Describe some forms of private spending that represent consumption and some forms that represent investment. The national income accounts include tuition as a part of consumer spending. In your opinion, are the resources you devote to your education a form of consumption or a form of investment?
   b. Describe some forms of government spending that represent consumption and some forms that represent investment. In your opinion, should we view government spending on health programs as a form of consumption or investment? Would you distinguish between health programs for the young and health programs for the elderly?

4. What is the opportunity cost of investing in capital? Do you think a country can "overinvest" in capital? What is the opportunity cost of investing in human capital? Do you think a country can "overinvest" in human capital? Explain.

5. In the 1990s and the first decade of the 2000s, investors from the Asian economies of Japan and China made significant direct and portfolio investments in the United States. At the time, many Americans were unhappy that this investment was occurring.
   a. In what way was it better for the United States to receive this foreign investment than not to receive it?
   b. In what way would it have been better still for Americans to have made this investment?

6. In many developing nations, young women have lower enrollment rates in secondary school than do young men. Describe several ways in which greater educational opportunities for young women could lead to faster economic growth in these countries.

7. International data show a positive correlation between income per person and the health of the population.
   a. Explain how higher income might cause better health outcomes.
   b. Explain how better health outcomes might cause higher income.
   c. How might the relative importance of your two hypotheses be relevant for public policy?

8. The great 18th-century economist Adam Smith wrote, "Little else is requisite to carry a state to the highest degree of opulence from the lowest barbarism but peace, easy taxes, and a tolerable administration of justice: all the rest being brought about by the natural course of things." Explain how each of the three conditions Smith describes would promote economic growth.

Go to CengageBrain.com to purchase access to the proven, critical Study Guide to accompany this text, which features additional notes and context, practice tests, and much more.

Saving, Investment, and the Financial System

I magine that you have just graduated from college (with a degree in economics, of course) and you decide to start your own business—an economic forecasting firm. Before you make any money selling your forecasts, you have to incur substantial costs to set up your business. You have to buy computers with which to make your forecasts, as well as desks, chairs, and filing cabinets to furnish your new office. Each of these items is a type of capital that your firm will use to produce and sell its services.

How do you obtain the funds to invest in these capital goods? Perhaps you are able to pay for them out of your past savings. More likely, however, like most entrepreneurs, you do not have enough money of your own to finance the start of your business. As a result, you have to get the money you need from other sources.

There are various ways to finance these capital investments. You could borrow the money, perhaps from a bank or from a friend or relative. In this case, you would promise not only to return the money at a later date but also to pay interest for the use of the money. Alternatively, you could convince someone to provide the money you need for your business in exchange for a share of your future profits, whatever they might happen to be. In either case, your investment in computers and office equipment is being financed by someone else's saving.

financial system

the group of institutions in the economy that help to match one person's saving with another person's investment

The **financial system** consists of the institutions that help to match one person's saving with another person's investment. As we discussed in the previous chapter, saving and investment are key ingredients to long-run economic growth: When a country saves a large portion of its gross domestic product (GDP), more resources are available for investment in capital, and higher capital raises a country's productivity and living standard. The previous chapter, however, did not explain how the economy coordinates saving and investment. At any time, some people want to save some of their income for the future and others want to borrow to finance investments in new and growing businesses. What brings these two groups of people together? What ensures that the supply of funds from those who want to save balances the demand for funds from those who want to invest?

This chapter examines how the financial system works. First, we discuss the large variety of institutions that make up the financial system in our economy. Second, we discuss the relationship between the financial system and some key macroeconomic variables—notably saving and investment. Third, we develop a model of the supply and demand for funds in financial markets. In the model, the interest rate is the price that adjusts to balance supply and demand. The model shows how various government policies affect the interest rate and, thereby, society's allocation of scarce resources.

26-1 Financial Institutions in the U.S. Economy

At the broadest level, the financial system moves the economy's scarce resources from savers (people who spend less than they earn) to borrowers (people who spend more than they earn). Savers save for various reasons—to put a child through college in several years or to retire comfortably in several decades. Similarly, borrowers borrow for various reasons—to buy a house in which to live or to start a business with which to make a living. Savers supply their money to the financial system with the expectation that they will get it back with interest at a later date. Borrowers demand money from the financial system with the knowledge that they will be required to pay it back with interest at a later date.

The financial system is made up of various financial institutions that help coordinate savers and borrowers. As a prelude to analyzing the economic forces that drive the financial system, let's discuss the most important of these institutions. Financial institutions can be grouped into two categories: financial markets and financial intermediaries. We consider each category in turn.

financial markets

financial institutions through which savers can directly provide funds to borrowers

26-1a Financial Markets

Financial markets are the institutions through which a person who wants to save can directly supply funds to a person who wants to borrow. The two most important financial markets in our economy are the bond market and the stock market.

bond

a certificate of indebtedness

The Bond Market   When Intel, the giant maker of computer chips, wants to borrow to finance construction of a new factory, it can borrow directly from the public. It does this by selling bonds. A **bond** is a certificate of indebtedness that specifies the obligations of the borrower to the holder of the bond. Put simply, a bond is an IOU. It identifies the time at which the loan will be repaid, called the *date of maturity,* and the rate of interest that will be paid periodically until the loan matures. The buyer of a bond gives his money to Intel in exchange for this promise of interest and eventual repayment of the amount borrowed (called the *principal*). The buyer can hold the bond until maturity, or he can sell the bond at an earlier date to someone else.

There are literally millions of different bonds in the U.S. economy. When large corporations, the federal government, or state and local governments need to borrow to finance the purchase of a new factory, a new jet fighter, or a new school, they usually do so by issuing bonds. If you look at *The Wall Street Journal* or the business section of your local newspaper, you will find a listing of the prices and interest rates on some of the most important bond issues. These bonds differ according to three significant characteristics.

The first characteristic is a bond's *term*—the length of time until the bond matures. Some bonds have short terms, such as a few months, while others have terms as long as 30 years. (The British government has even issued a bond that never matures, called a *perpetuity*. This bond pays interest forever, but the principal is never repaid.) The interest rate on a bond depends, in part, on its term. Long-term bonds are riskier than short-term bonds because holders of long-term bonds have to wait longer for repayment of principal. If a holder of a long-term bond needs his money earlier than the distant date of maturity, he has no choice but to sell the bond to someone else, perhaps at a reduced price. To compensate for this risk, long-term bonds usually pay higher interest rates than short-term bonds.

The second important characteristic of a bond is its *credit risk*—the probability that the borrower will fail to pay some of the interest or principal. Such a failure to pay is called a *default*. Borrowers can (and sometimes do) default on their loans by declaring bankruptcy. When bond buyers perceive that the probability of default is high, they demand a higher interest rate as compensation for this risk. Because the U.S. government is considered a safe credit risk, government bonds tend to pay low interest rates. By contrast, financially shaky corporations raise money by issuing *junk bonds,* which pay very high interest rates. Buyers of bonds can judge credit risk by checking with various private agencies, such as Standard & Poor's, which rate the credit risk of different bonds.

The third important characteristic of a bond is its *tax treatment*—the way the tax laws treat the interest earned on the bond. The interest on most bonds is taxable income; that is, the bond owner has to pay a portion of the interest in income taxes. By contrast, when state and local governments issue bonds, called *municipal bonds,* the bond owners are not required to pay federal income tax on the interest income. Because of this tax advantage, bonds issued by state and local governments typically pay a lower interest rate than bonds issued by corporations or the federal government.

The Stock Market Another way for Intel to raise funds to build a new semiconductor factory is to sell stock in the company. **Stock** represents ownership in a firm and is, therefore, a claim to the profits that the firm makes. For example, if Intel sells a total of 1,000,000 shares of stock, then each share represents ownership of 1/1,000,000 of the business.

stock
a claim to partial ownership in a firm

The sale of stock to raise money is called *equity finance,* whereas the sale of bonds is called *debt finance.* Although corporations use both equity and debt finance to raise money for new investments, stocks and bonds are very different. The owner of shares of Intel stock is a part owner of Intel, while the owner of an Intel bond is a creditor of the corporation. If Intel is very profitable, the stockholders enjoy the benefits of these profits, whereas the bondholders get only the interest on their bonds. And if Intel runs into financial difficulty, the bondholders are paid what they are due before stockholders receive anything at all. Compared to bonds, stocks offer the holder both higher risk and potentially higher return.

After a corporation issues stock by selling shares to the public, these shares trade among stockholders on organized stock exchanges. In these transactions, the corporation itself receives no money when its stock changes hands. The most important stock exchanges in the U.S. economy are the New York Stock Exchange and the NASDAQ (National Association of Securities Dealers Automated Quotation system). Most of the world's countries have their own stock exchanges on which the shares of local companies trade.

The prices at which shares trade on stock exchanges are determined by the supply of and demand for the stock in these companies. Because stock represents ownership in a corporation, the demand for a stock (and thus its price) reflects people's perception of the corporation's future profitability. When people become optimistic about a company's future, they raise their demand for its stock and thereby bid up the price of a share of stock. Conversely, when people's expectations of a company's prospects decline, the price of a share falls.

Various stock indexes are available to monitor the overall level of stock prices. A *stock index* is computed as an average of a group of stock prices. The most famous stock index is the Dow Jones Industrial Average, which has been computed regularly since 1896. It is now based on the prices of the stocks of thirty major U.S. companies, such as General Electric, Microsoft, Coca-Cola, Boeing, AT&T, and Wal-Mart. Another well-known stock index is the Standard & Poor's 500 Index, which is based on the prices of the stocks of 500 major companies. Because stock prices reflect expected profitability, these stock indexes are watched closely as possible indicators of future economic conditions.

26-1b Financial Intermediaries

financial intermediaries
financial institutions through which savers can indirectly provide funds to borrowers

Financial intermediaries are financial institutions through which savers can indirectly provide funds to borrowers. The term *intermediary* reflects the role of these institutions in standing between savers and borrowers. Here we consider two of the most important financial intermediaries: banks and mutual funds.

Banks If the owner of a small grocery store wants to finance an expansion of his business, he probably takes a strategy quite different from that of Intel. Unlike Intel, a small grocer would find it difficult to raise funds in the bond and stock markets. Most buyers of stocks and bonds prefer to buy those issued by larger, more familiar companies. The small grocer, therefore, most likely finances his business expansion with a loan from a local bank.

Banks are the financial intermediaries with which people are most familiar. A primary job of banks is to take in deposits from people who want to save and use these deposits to make loans to people who want to borrow. Banks pay depositors interest on their deposits and charge borrowers slightly higher interest on their loans. The difference between these rates of interest covers the banks' costs and returns some profit to the owners of the banks.

Besides being financial intermediaries, banks play a second important role in the economy: They facilitate purchases of goods and services by allowing

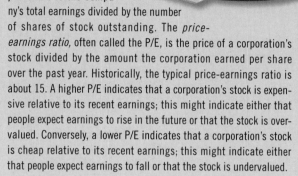

When following the stock of any company, you should keep an eye on three key numbers. These numbers are reported on the financial pages of some newspapers, and you can easily obtain them online as well (such as at Yahoo! Finance):

- **Price.** The single most important piece of information about a stock is the price of a share. News services usually present several prices. The "last" price is the price at which the stock more recently traded. The "previous close" is the price of the last transaction that occurred before the stock exchange closed in its previous day of trading. A news service may also give the "high" and "low" prices over the past day of trading and, sometimes, over the past year as well. It may also report the change from the previous day's closing price.
- **Dividend.** Corporations pay out some of their profits to their stockholders; this amount is called the *dividend*. (Profits not paid out are called *retained earnings* and are used by the corporation for additional investment.) News services often report the dividend paid over the previous year for each share of stock. They sometimes report the *dividend yield*, which is the dividend expressed as a percentage of the stock's price.
- **Price-earnings ratio.** A corporation's earnings, or accounting profit, is the amount of revenue it receives for the sale of its products

minus its costs of production as measured by its accountants. *Earnings per share* is the company's total earnings divided by the number of shares of stock outstanding. The *price-earnings ratio*, often called the P/E, is the price of a corporation's stock divided by the amount the corporation earned per share over the past year. Historically, the typical price-earnings ratio is about 15. A higher P/E indicates that a corporation's stock is expensive relative to its recent earnings; this might indicate either that people expect earnings to rise in the future or that the stock is overvalued. Conversely, a lower P/E indicates that a corporation's stock is cheap relative to its recent earnings; this might indicate either that people expect earnings to fall or that the stock is undervalued.

Why do news services report all these data? Many people who invest their savings in stock follow these numbers closely when deciding which stocks to buy and sell. By contrast, other stockholders follow a buy-and-hold strategy: They buy the stock of well-run companies, hold it for long periods of time, and do not respond to the daily fluctuations.

people to write checks against their deposits and to access those deposits with debit cards. In other words, banks help create a special asset that people can use as a *medium of exchange*. A medium of exchange is an item that people can easily use to engage in transactions. A bank's role in providing a medium of exchange distinguishes it from many other financial institutions. Stocks and bonds, like bank deposits, are a possible *store of value* for the wealth that people have accumulated in past saving, but access to this wealth is not as easy, cheap, and immediate as just writing a check or swiping a debit card. For now, we ignore this second role of banks, but we will return to it when we discuss the monetary system later in the book.

Mutual Funds A financial intermediary of increasing importance in the U.S. economy is the mutual fund. A **mutual fund** is an institution that sells shares to the public and uses the proceeds to buy a selection, or *portfolio*, of various types of stocks, bonds, or both stocks and bonds. The shareholder of the mutual fund accepts all the risk and return associated with the portfolio. If the value of the portfolio rises, the shareholder benefits; if the value of the portfolio falls, the shareholder suffers the loss.

The primary advantage of mutual funds is that they allow people with small amounts of money to diversify their holdings. Buyers of stocks and bonds are

mutual fund
an institution that sells shares to the public and uses the proceeds to buy a portfolio of stocks and bonds

ARLO AND JANIS by Jimmy Johnson

ARLO AND JANIS REPRINTED BY PERMISSION OF UNITED FEATURE SYNDICATE, INC.

well advised to heed the adage: Don't put all your eggs in one basket. Because the value of any single stock or bond is tied to the fortunes of one company, holding a single kind of stock or bond is very risky. By contrast, people who hold a diverse portfolio of stocks and bonds face less risk because they have only a small stake in each company. Mutual funds make this diversification easy. With only a few hundred dollars, a person can buy shares in a mutual fund and, indirectly, become the part owner or creditor of hundreds of major companies. For this service, the company operating the mutual fund charges shareholders a fee, usually between 0.5 and 2.0 percent of assets each year.

A second advantage claimed by mutual fund companies is that mutual funds give ordinary people access to the skills of professional money managers. The managers of most mutual funds pay close attention to the developments and prospects of the companies in which they buy stock. These managers buy the stock of companies they view as having a profitable future and sell the stock of companies with less promising prospects. This professional management, it is argued, should increase the return that mutual fund depositors earn on their savings.

Financial economists, however, are often skeptical of this argument. With thousands of money managers paying close attention to each company's prospects, the price of a company's stock is usually a good reflection of the company's true value. As a result, it is hard to "beat the market" by buying good stocks and selling bad ones. In fact, mutual funds called *index funds,* which buy all the stocks in a given stock index, perform somewhat better on average than mutual funds that take advantage of active trading by professional money managers. The explanation for the superior performance of index funds is that they keep costs low by buying and selling very rarely and by not having to pay the salaries of professional money managers.

26-1c Summing Up

The U.S. economy contains a large variety of financial institutions. In addition to the bond market, the stock market, banks, and mutual funds, there are also pension funds, credit unions, insurance companies, and even the local loan shark. These institutions differ in many ways. When analyzing the macroeconomic role of the financial system, however, it is more important to keep in mind that, despite their differences, these financial institutions all serve the same goal: directing the resources of savers into the hands of borrowers.

Quick Quiz   *What is stock? What is a bond? How are they different? How are they similar?*

Should Students Sell Equity in Themselves?

An economist suggests a new way to finance higher education.

The College Graduate as Collateral

By Luigi Zingales

Academic economists like to make fun of businesspeople: they want competition when they enter a new market but are quick to lobby for subsidies and barriers to competitors once they get in. Yet scholars like me are no better. We work in the least competitive and most subsidized industry of all: higher education.

We criticize predatory loans by mortgage brokers, when student loans can be just as abusive. To avoid the next credit bubble and debt crisis, we need to eliminate government subsidies and link tuition financing to the incomes of college graduates.

Nearly eight million students received Pell grants in 2010, costing $28 billion. In addition, the federal direct loan program, which allows nonaffluent students to get government-guaranteed loans at low interest rates, cost taxpayers $13 billion in 2010–11. Total subsidies to university education amount to $43 billion a year, including around $2 billion in Congressional earmarks—and that does not even include tax subsidies (for college funds); tax breaks (for university endowments, for example); and subsidies dedicated to research.

Just as subsidies for homeownership have increased the price of houses, so have education subsidies contributed to the soaring price of college. Between 1977 and 2009 the real average cost of university tuition more than doubled.

These subsidies also distort the credit market. Since the government guarantees student loans, lenders have no incentive to lend wisely. All the burden of making the right decision falls on the borrowers.

Unfortunately, 18-year-olds aren't particularly good at judging the profitability of an investment without expert advice, and when they do get such advice, it generally counsels taking the largest possible loan. The stock of student loans has reached $1 trillion, while the percentage of borrowers in default jumped to 8.8 percent in 2009 from 6.7 percent in 2007.

Last but not least, these subsidized loans keep afloat colleges that do not add much value for their students, preventing people from accumulating useful skills.

I do not want to suggest that helping underprivileged students attend college is bad. A true free-market system equalizes opportunities, if not for fairness, at least for efficiency: talent should not be wasted.

The best way to fix this inefficiency is to address the root of the problem: most bright students do not have any collateral and cannot easily pledge their future income. Yet the venture-capital industry has shown that the private sector can do a good job at financing new ventures with no collateral. So why can't they finance bright students?

Investors could finance students' education with equity rather than debt. In exchange for their capital, the investors would receive a fraction of a student's future income—or, even better, a fraction of the increase in her income that derives from college attendance. (This increase can be easily calculated as the difference between the actual income and the average income of high school graduates in the same area.)

This is not a modern form of indentured servitude, but a voluntary form of taxation, one that would make only the beneficiaries of a college education—not all taxpayers—pay for the costs of it.

The cost of enforcing contracts contingent on future income is very large, but there

is an effective solution: piggybacking on the tax collection system. The Internal Revenue Service could perform collection services on behalf of private lenders, and at no cost to taxpayers. (In Australia, such a system has been in place since the 1980s. The national tax agency enforces repayment of loans contingent on income, though the payments of the wealthiest graduates are capped, and therefore less affluent graduates need to be charged more to make the program viable than in the system I am proposing.)...

Equity contracts would diversify the risk of failure, with highly compensated superstars helping to finance the educations of less successful college graduates. They will also avoid pushing graduates into lucrative jobs just to pay off debt. Most important, these contracts would provide financiers with an incentive to counsel students wisely, as financiers would profit from good educational investments and lose from bad ones. This would create more informed demand for the schools, exerting pressure on them to contain costs and improve quality.

The most important effect of these equity contracts would be to show that it is possible to intervene to help the disadvantaged without turning that help into an undue subsidy for the producers (universities) and the creation of a privileged class (professors like me) at the expense of everybody else (students and taxpayers). After all, how can we scholars criticize crony capitalism when we benefit from it?

Mr. Zingales is a professor of economics at the University of Chicago. ◢

Source: *New York Times*, June 14, 2012.

26-2 Saving and Investment in the National Income Accounts

Events that occur within the financial system are central to understanding developments in the overall economy. As we have just seen, the institutions that make up this system—the bond market, the stock market, banks, and mutual funds—have the role of coordinating the economy's saving and investment. And as we saw in the previous chapter, saving and investment are important determinants of long-run growth in GDP and living standards. As a result, macroeconomists need to understand how financial markets work and how various events and policies affect them.

As a starting point for an analysis of financial markets, we discuss in this section the key macroeconomic variables that measure activity in these markets. Our emphasis here is not on behavior but on accounting. *Accounting* refers to how various numbers are defined and added up. A personal accountant might help an individual add up his income and expenses. A national income accountant does the same thing for the economy as a whole. The national income accounts include, in particular, GDP and the many related statistics.

The rules of national income accounting include several important identities. Recall that an *identity* is an equation that must be true because of the way the variables in the equation are defined. Identities are useful to keep in mind, for they clarify how different variables are related to one another. Here we consider some accounting identities that shed light on the macroeconomic role of financial markets.

26-2a Some Important Identities

Recall that GDP is both total income in an economy and the total expenditure on the economy's output of goods and services. GDP (denoted as Y) is divided into four components of expenditure: consumption (C), investment (I), government purchases (G), and net exports (NX). We write

$$Y = C + I + G + NX.$$

This equation is an identity because every dollar of expenditure that shows up on the left side also shows up in one of the four components on the right side. Because of the way each of the variables is defined and measured, this equation must always hold.

In this chapter, we simplify our analysis by assuming that the economy we are examining is closed. A *closed economy* is one that does not interact with other economies. In particular, a closed economy does not engage in international trade in goods and services, nor does it engage in international borrowing and lending. Actual economies are *open economies*—that is, they interact with other economies around the world. Nonetheless, assuming a closed economy is a useful simplification with which we can learn some lessons that apply to all economies. Moreover, this assumption applies perfectly to the world economy (for interplanetary trade is not yet common).

Because a closed economy does not engage in international trade, imports and exports are exactly zero. Therefore, net exports (NX) are also zero. In this case, we can write

$$Y = C + I + G.$$

This equation states that GDP is the sum of consumption, investment, and government purchases. Each unit of output sold in a closed economy is consumed, invested, or bought by the government.

To see what this identity can tell us about financial markets, subtract C and G from both sides of this equation. We obtain

$$Y - C - G = I.$$

The left side of this equation $(Y-C-G)$ is the total income in the economy that remains after paying for consumption and government purchases: This amount is called **national saving**, or just **saving**, and is denoted by S. Substituting S for $Y - C - G$, we can write the last equation as

$$S = I.$$

This equation states that saving equals investment.

To understand the meaning of national saving, it is helpful to manipulate the definition a bit more. Let T denote the amount that the government collects from households in taxes minus the amount it pays back to households in the form of transfer payments (such as Social Security and welfare). We can then write national saving in either of two ways:

$$S = Y - C - G$$

or

$$S = (Y - T - C) + (T - G).$$

These equations are the same because the two T's in the second equation cancel each other, but each reveals a different way of thinking about national saving. In particular, the second equation separates national saving into two pieces: private saving $(Y - T - C)$ and public saving $(T - G)$.

Consider each of these two pieces. **Private saving** is the amount of income that households have left after paying their taxes and paying for their consumption. In particular, because households receive income of Y, pay taxes of T, and spend C on consumption, private saving is $Y - T - C$. **Public saving** is the amount of tax revenue that the government has left after paying for its spending. The government receives T in tax revenue and spends G on goods and services. If T exceeds G, the government runs a **budget surplus** because it receives more money than it spends. This surplus of $T - G$ represents public saving. If the government spends more than it receives in tax revenue, then G is larger than T. In this case, the government runs a **budget deficit**, and public saving $T - G$ is a negative number.

Now consider how these accounting identities are related to financial markets. The equation $S = I$ reveals an important fact: *For the economy as a whole, saving must be equal to investment.* Yet this fact raises some important questions: What mechanisms lie behind this identity? What coordinates those people who are deciding how much to save and those people who are deciding how much to invest? The answer is the financial system. The bond market, the stock market, banks, mutual funds, and other financial markets and intermediaries stand between the two sides of the $S = I$ equation. They take in the nation's saving and direct it to the nation's investment.

national saving (saving)
the total income in the economy that remains after paying for consumption and government purchases

private saving
the income that households have left after paying for taxes and consumption

public saving
the tax revenue that the government has left after paying for its spending

budget surplus
an excess of tax revenue over government spending

budget deficit
a shortfall of tax revenue from government spending

26-2b The Meaning of Saving and Investment

The terms *saving* and *investment* can sometimes be confusing. Most people use these terms casually and sometimes interchangeably. By contrast, the macroeconomists who put together the national income accounts use these terms carefully and distinctly.

Consider an example. Suppose that Larry earns more than he spends and deposits his unspent income in a bank or uses it to buy some stock or a bond from a corporation. Because Larry's income exceeds his consumption, he adds to the nation's saving. Larry might think of himself as "investing" his money, but a macroeconomist would call Larry's act saving rather than investment.

In the language of macroeconomics, investment refers to the purchase of new capital, such as equipment or buildings. When Moe borrows from the bank to build himself a new house, he adds to the nation's investment. (Remember, the purchase of a new house is the one form of household spending that is investment rather than consumption.) Similarly, when the Curly Corporation sells some stock and uses the proceeds to build a new factory, it also adds to the nation's investment.

Although the accounting identity $S = I$ shows that saving and investment are equal for the economy as a whole, this does not have to be true for every individual household or firm. Larry's saving can be greater than his investment, and he can deposit the excess in a bank. Moe's saving can be less than his investment, and he can borrow the shortfall from a bank. Banks and other financial institutions make these individual differences between saving and investment possible by allowing one person's saving to finance another person's investment.

Quick Quiz   *Define* private saving, public saving, national saving, *and* investment. *How are they related?*

26-3 The Market for Loanable Funds

Having discussed some of the important financial institutions in our economy and the macroeconomic role of these institutions, we are ready to build a model of financial markets. Our purpose in building this model is to explain how financial markets coordinate the economy's saving and investment. The model also gives us a tool with which we can analyze various government policies that influence saving and investment.

market for loanable funds
the market in which those who want to save supply funds and those who want to borrow to invest demand funds

To keep things simple, we assume that the economy has only one financial market, called the **market for loanable funds**. All savers go to this market to deposit their saving, and all borrowers go to this market to take out their loans. Thus, the term *loanable funds* refers to all income that people have chosen to save and lend out, rather than use for their own consumption, and to the amount that investors have chosen to borrow to fund new investment projects. In the market for loanable funds, there is one interest rate, which is both the return to saving and the cost of borrowing.

The assumption of a single financial market, of course, is not literally true. As we have seen, the economy has many types of financial institutions. But as we discussed in Chapter 2, the art in building an economic model is simplifying the world in order to explain it. For our purposes here, we can ignore the diversity of financial institutions and assume that the economy has a single financial market.

26-3a Supply and Demand for Loanable Funds

The economy's market for loanable funds, like other markets in the economy, is governed by supply and demand. To understand how the market for loanable funds operates, therefore, we first look at the sources of supply and demand in that market.

The supply of loanable funds comes from people who have some extra income they want to save and lend out. This lending can occur directly, such as when a household buys a bond from a firm, or it can occur indirectly, such as when a household makes a deposit in a bank, which in turn uses the funds to make loans. In both cases, *saving is the source of the supply of loanable funds*.

The demand for loanable funds comes from households and firms who wish to borrow to make investments. This demand includes families taking out mortgages to buy new homes. It also includes firms borrowing to buy new equipment or build factories. In both cases, *investment is the source of the demand for loanable funds*.

The interest rate is the price of a loan. It represents the amount that borrowers pay for loans and the amount that lenders receive on their saving. Because a high interest rate makes borrowing more expensive, the quantity of loanable funds demanded falls as the interest rate rises. Similarly, because a high interest rate makes saving more attractive, the quantity of loanable funds supplied rises as the interest rate rises. In other words, the demand curve for loanable funds slopes downward, and the supply curve for loanable funds slopes upward.

Figure 1 shows the interest rate that balances the supply and demand for loanable funds. In the equilibrium shown, the interest rate is 5 percent, and the quantity of loanable funds demanded and the quantity of loanable funds supplied both equal $1,200 billion.

The adjustment of the interest rate to the equilibrium level occurs for the usual reasons. If the interest rate were lower than the equilibrium level, the quantity of loanable funds supplied would be less than the quantity of loanable funds demanded. The resulting shortage of loanable funds would encourage lenders to

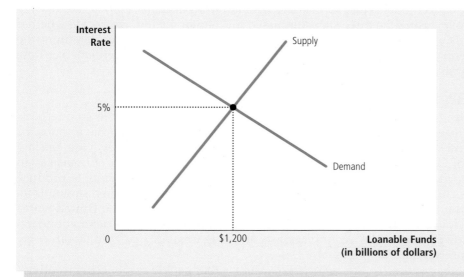

FIGURE 1

The Market for Loanable Funds
The interest rate in the economy adjusts to balance the supply and demand for loanable funds. The supply of loanable funds comes from national saving, including both private saving and public saving. The demand for loanable funds comes from firms and households that want to borrow for purposes of investment. Here the equilibrium interest rate is 5 percent, and $1,200 billion of loanable funds are supplied and demanded.

raise the interest rate they charge. A higher interest rate would encourage saving (thereby increasing the quantity of loanable funds supplied) and discourage borrowing for investment (thereby decreasing the quantity of loanable funds demanded). Conversely, if the interest rate were higher than the equilibrium level, the quantity of loanable funds supplied would exceed the quantity of loanable funds demanded. As lenders competed for the scarce borrowers, interest rates would be driven down. In this way, the interest rate approaches the equilibrium level at which the supply and demand for loanable funds exactly balance.

Recall that economists distinguish between the real interest rate and the nominal interest rate. The nominal interest rate is the interest rate as usually reported—the monetary return to saving and the monetary cost of borrowing. The real interest rate is the nominal interest rate corrected for inflation; it equals the nominal interest rate minus the inflation rate. Because inflation erodes the value of money over time, the real interest rate more accurately reflects the real return to saving and the real cost of borrowing. Therefore, the supply and demand for loanable funds depend on the real (rather than nominal) interest rate, and the equilibrium in Figure 1 should be interpreted as determining the real interest rate in the economy. For the rest of this chapter, when you see the term *interest rate*, you should remember that we are talking about the real interest rate.

This model of the supply and demand for loanable funds shows that financial markets work much like other markets in the economy. In the market for milk, for instance, the price of milk adjusts so that the quantity of milk supplied balances the quantity of milk demanded. In this way, the invisible hand coordinates the behavior of dairy farmers and the behavior of milk drinkers. Once we realize that saving represents the supply of loanable funds and investment represents the demand, we can see how the invisible hand coordinates saving and investment. When the interest rate adjusts to balance supply and demand in the market for loanable funds, it coordinates the behavior of people who want to save (the suppliers of loanable funds) and the behavior of people who want to invest (the demanders of loanable funds).

We can now use this analysis of the market for loanable funds to examine various government policies that affect the economy's saving and investment. Because this model is just supply and demand in a particular market, we analyze any policy using the three steps discussed in Chapter 4. First, we decide whether the policy shifts the supply curve or the demand curve. Second, we determine the direction of the shift. Third, we use the supply-and-demand diagram to see how the equilibrium changes.

26-3b Policy 1: Saving Incentives

American families save a smaller fraction of their incomes than their counterparts in many other countries, such as Japan and Germany. Although the reasons for these international differences are unclear, many U.S. policymakers view the low level of U.S. saving as a major problem. One of the *Ten Principles of Economics* in Chapter 1 is that a country's standard of living depends on its ability to produce goods and services. And as we discussed in the preceding chapter, saving is an important long-run determinant of a nation's productivity. If the United States could somehow raise its saving rate to the level that prevails in other countries, the growth rate of GDP would increase, and over time, U.S. citizens would enjoy a higher standard of living.

Another of the *Ten Principles of Economics* is that people respond to incentives. Many economists have used this principle to suggest that the low saving rate in the United States is at least partly attributable to tax laws that discourage saving. The U.S. federal government, as well as many state governments, collects revenue by taxing income, including interest and dividend income. To see the effects of this policy, consider a 25-year-old who saves $1,000 and buys a 30-year bond that pays an interest rate of 9 percent. In the absence of taxes, the $1,000 grows to $13,268 when the individual reaches age 55. Yet if that interest is taxed at a rate of, say, 33 percent, the after-tax interest rate is only 6 percent. In this case, the $1,000 grows to only $5,743 over the 30 years. The tax on interest income substantially reduces the future payoff from current saving and, as a result, reduces the incentive for people to save.

In response to this problem, many economists and lawmakers have proposed reforming the tax code to encourage greater saving. For example, one proposal is to expand eligibility for special accounts, such as Individual Retirement Accounts, that allow people to shelter some of their saving from taxation. Let's consider the effect of such a saving incentive on the market for loanable funds, as illustrated in Figure 2. We analyze this policy following our three steps.

First, which curve would this policy affect? Because the tax change would alter the incentive for households to save *at any given interest rate,* it would affect the quantity of loanable funds supplied at each interest rate. Thus, the supply of loanable funds would shift. The demand for loanable funds would remain the same because the tax change would not directly affect the amount that borrowers want to borrow at any given interest rate.

Second, which way would the supply curve shift? Because saving would be taxed less heavily than under current law, households would increase their saving by consuming a smaller fraction of their income. Households would use this additional saving to increase their deposits in banks or to buy more bonds. The supply of loanable funds would increase, and the supply curve would shift to the right from S_1 to S_2, as shown in Figure 2.

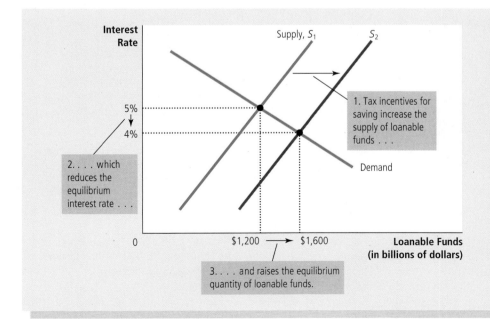

FIGURE 2

Saving Incentives Increase the Supply of Loanable Funds
A change in the tax laws to encourage Americans to save more would shift the supply of loanable funds to the right from S_1 to S_2. As a result, the equilibrium interest rate would fall, and the lower interest rate would stimulate investment. Here the equilibrium interest rate falls from 5 percent to 4 percent, and the equilibrium quantity of loanable funds saved and invested rises from $1,200 billion to $1,600 billion.

Finally, we can compare the old and new equilibria. In the figure, the increased supply of loanable funds reduces the interest rate from 5 percent to 4 percent. The lower interest rate raises the quantity of loanable funds demanded from $1,200 billion to $1,600 billion. That is, the shift in the supply curve moves the market equilibrium along the demand curve. With a lower cost of borrowing, households and firms are motivated to borrow more to finance greater investment. Thus, *if a reform of the tax laws encouraged greater saving, the result would be lower interest rates and greater investment.*

This analysis of the effects of increased saving is widely accepted among economists, but there is less consensus about what kinds of tax changes should be enacted. Many economists endorse tax reform aimed at increasing saving to stimulate investment and growth. Yet others are skeptical that these tax changes would have much effect on national saving. These skeptics also doubt the equity of the proposed reforms. They argue that, in many cases, the benefits of the tax changes would accrue primarily to the wealthy, who are least in need of tax relief.

26-3c Policy 2: Investment Incentives

Suppose that Congress passed a tax reform aimed at making investment more attractive. In essence, this is what Congress does when it institutes an *investment tax credit,* which it does from time to time. An investment tax credit gives a tax advantage to any firm building a new factory or buying a new piece of equipment. Let's consider the effect of such a tax reform on the market for loanable funds, as illustrated in Figure 3.

First, would the law affect supply or demand? Because the tax credit would reward firms that borrow and invest in new capital, it would alter investment at any given interest rate and, thereby, change the demand for loanable funds. By contrast, because the tax credit would not affect the amount that households save at any given interest rate, it would not affect the supply of loanable funds.

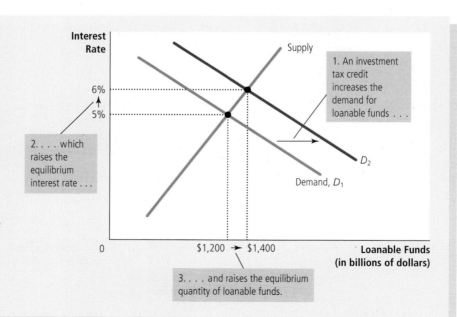

FIGURE 3

Investment Incentives Increase the Demand for Loanable Funds
If the passage of an investment tax credit encouraged firms to invest more, the demand for loanable funds would increase. As a result, the equilibrium interest rate would rise, and the higher interest rate would stimulate saving. Here, when the demand curve shifts from D_1 to D_2, the equilibrium interest rate rises from 5 percent to 6 percent, and the equilibrium quantity of loanable funds saved and invested rises from $1,200 billion to $1,400 billion.

1. An investment tax credit increases the demand for loanable funds . . .

2. . . . . which raises the equilibrium interest rate . . .

3. . . . and raises the equilibrium quantity of loanable funds.

Second, which way would the demand curve shift? Because firms would have an incentive to increase investment at any interest rate, the quantity of loanable funds demanded would be higher at any given interest rate. Thus, the demand curve for loanable funds would move to the right, as shown by the shift from D_1 to D_2 in the figure.

Third, consider how the equilibrium would change. In Figure 3, the increased demand for loanable funds raises the interest rate from 5 percent to 6 percent, and the higher interest rate in turn increases the quantity of loanable funds supplied from $1,200 billion to $1,400 billion, as households respond by increasing the amount they save. This change in household behavior is represented here as a movement along the supply curve. Thus, *if a reform of the tax laws encouraged greater investment, the result would be higher interest rates and greater saving.*

26-3d Policy 3: Government Budget Deficits and Surpluses

A perpetual topic of political debate is the status of the government budget. Recall that a *budget deficit* is an excess of government spending over tax revenue. Governments finance budget deficits by borrowing in the bond market, and the accumulation of past government borrowing is called the *government debt*. A *budget surplus*, an excess of tax revenue over government spending, can be used to repay some of the government debt. If government spending exactly equals tax revenue, the government is said to have a *balanced budget*.

Imagine that the government starts with a balanced budget and then, because of an increase in government spending, starts running a budget deficit. We can analyze the effects of the budget deficit by following our three steps in the market for loanable funds, as illustrated in Figure 4.

First, which curve shifts when the government starts running a budget deficit? Recall that national saving—the source of the supply of loanable funds—is composed of private saving and public saving. A change in the government budget

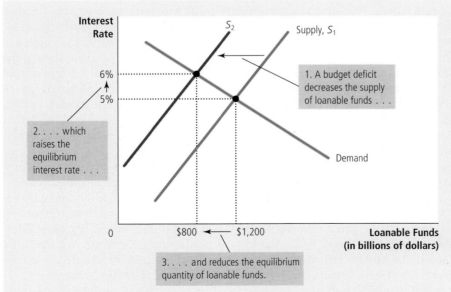

FIGURE 4

The Effect of a Government Budget Deficit
When the government spends more than it receives in tax revenue, the resulting budget deficit lowers national saving. The supply of loanable funds decreases, and the equilibrium interest rate rises. Thus, when the government borrows to finance its budget deficit, it crowds out households and firms that otherwise would borrow to finance investment. Here, when the supply shifts from S_1 to S_2, the equilibrium interest rate rises from 5 percent to 6 percent, and the equilibrium quantity of loanable funds saved and invested falls from $1,200 billion to $800 billion.

Interest Rate

S_2

Supply, S_1

6%

5%

1. A budget deficit decreases the supply of loanable funds . . .

2. . . . which raises the equilibrium interest rate . . .

Demand

0

$800

$1,200

Loanable Funds (in billions of dollars)

3. . . . and reduces the equilibrium quantity of loanable funds.

balance represents a change in public saving and, thereby, in the supply of loanable funds. Because the budget deficit does not influence the amount that households and firms want to borrow to finance investment at any given interest rate, it does not alter the demand for loanable funds.

Second, which way does the supply curve shift? When the government runs a budget deficit, public saving is negative, and this reduces national saving. In other words, when the government borrows to finance its budget deficit, it reduces the supply of loanable funds available to finance investment by households and firms. Thus, a budget deficit shifts the supply curve for loanable funds to the left from S_1 to S_2, as shown in Figure 4.

Third, we can compare the old and new equilibria. In the figure, when the budget deficit reduces the supply of loanable funds, the interest rate rises from 5 percent to 6 percent. This higher interest rate then alters the behavior of the households and firms that participate in the loan market. In particular, many demanders of loanable funds are discouraged by the higher interest rate. Fewer families buy new homes, and fewer firms choose to build new factories. The fall in investment because of government borrowing is called **crowding out** and is represented in Figure 4 by the movement along the demand curve from a quantity of $1,200 billion in loanable funds to a quantity of $800 billion. That is, when the government borrows to finance its budget deficit, it crowds out private borrowers who are trying to finance investment.

Thus, the most basic lesson about budget deficits follows directly from their effects on the supply and demand for loanable funds: *When the government reduces national saving by running a budget deficit, the interest rate rises, and investment falls.* Because investment is important for long-run economic growth, government budget deficits reduce the economy's growth rate.

Why, you might ask, does a budget deficit affect the supply of loanable funds, rather than the demand for them? After all, the government finances a budget deficit by selling bonds, thereby borrowing from the private sector. Why does increased borrowing from the government shift the supply curve, whereas increased borrowing by private investors shifts the demand curve? To answer this question, we need to examine more precisely the meaning of "loanable funds." The model as presented here takes this term to mean the *flow of resources available to fund private investment*; thus, a government budget deficit reduces the supply of loanable funds. If, instead, we had defined the term "loanable funds" to mean the *flow of resources available from private saving,* then the government budget deficit would increase demand rather than reduce supply. Changing the interpretation of the term would cause a semantic change in how we described the model, but the bottom line from the analysis would be the same: In either case, a budget deficit increases the interest rate, thereby crowding out private borrowers who are relying on financial markets to fund private investment projects.

So far, we have examined a budget deficit that results from an increase in government spending, but a budget deficit that results from a tax cut has similar effects. A tax cut reduces public saving $T - G$. Private saving, $Y - T - C$, might increase because of lower T, but as long as households respond to the lower taxes by consuming more, C increases, so private saving rises by less than public saving declines. Thus, national saving ($S = Y - C - G$), the sum of public and private saving, declines. Once again, the budget deficit reduces the supply of loanable funds, drives up the interest rate, and crowds out borrowers trying to finance capital investments.

Now that we understand the impact of budget deficits, we can turn the analysis around and see that government budget surpluses have the opposite effects. When the government collects more in tax revenue than it spends, it saves the difference

crowding out

a decrease in investment that results from government borrowing

by retiring some of the outstanding government debt. This budget surplus, or public saving, contributes to national saving. Thus, *a budget surplus increases the supply of
loanable funds, reduces the interest rate, and stimulates investment*. Higher investment, in
turn, means greater capital accumulation and more rapid economic growth.

case study   **The History of U.S. Government Debt**

How indebted is the U.S. government? The answer to this question
varies substantially over time. Figure 5 shows the debt of the U.S. federal
government expressed as a percentage of U.S. GDP. It shows that the government debt has fluctuated from zero in 1836 to 107 percent of GDP in 1945.

The behavior of the debt-to-GDP ratio is one gauge of what's happening with
the government's finances. Because GDP is a rough measure of the government's
tax base, a declining debt-to-GDP ratio indicates that the government indebtedness is shrinking relative to its ability to raise tax revenue. This suggests that the
government is, in some sense, living within its means. By contrast, a rising debt-
to-GDP ratio means that the government indebtedness is increasing relative to its
ability to raise tax revenue. It is often interpreted as meaning that fiscal policy—
government spending and taxes—cannot be sustained forever at current levels.

The debt of the U.S. federal government, expressed here as a percentage of GDP, has varied
throughout history. Wartime spending is typically associated with substantial increases in
government debt.

FIGURE 5

The U.S. Government Debt

Source: U.S. Department of Treasury; U.S. Department
of Commerce; and T. S. Berry, "Production and Population
since 1789," Bostwick Paper No. 6, Richmond, 1988.

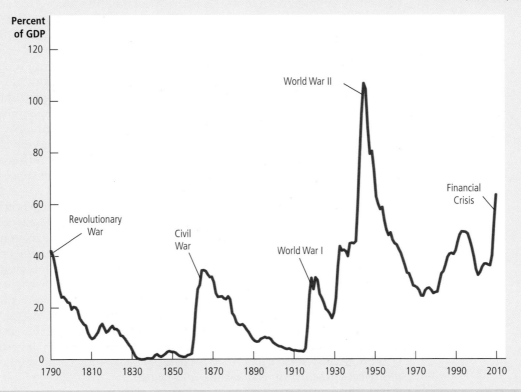

Throughout history, the primary cause of fluctuations in government debt has been war. When wars occur, government spending on national defense rises substantially to pay for soldiers and military equipment. Taxes sometimes rise as well but typically by much less than the increase in spending. The result is a budget deficit and increasing government debt. When the war is over, government spending declines and the debt-to-GDP ratio starts declining as well.

There are two reasons to believe that debt financing of war is an appropriate policy. First, it allows the government to keep tax rates smooth over time. Without debt financing, tax rates would have to rise sharply during wars, and this would cause a substantial decline in economic efficiency. Second, debt financing of wars shifts part of the cost of wars to future generations, who will have to pay off the government debt. This is arguably a fair distribution of the burden, for future generations get some of the benefit when one generation fights a war to defend the nation against foreign aggressors.

One large increase in government debt that cannot be explained by war is the increase that occurred beginning around 1980. When President Ronald Reagan took office in 1981, he was committed to smaller government and lower taxes. Yet he found cutting government spending to be more difficult politically than cutting taxes. The result was the beginning of a period of large budget deficits that continued not only through Reagan's time in office but also for many years thereafter. As a result, government debt rose from 26 percent of GDP in 1980 to 50 percent of GDP in 1993.

Because government budget deficits reduce national saving, investment, and long-run economic growth, the rise in government debt during the 1980s troubled many economists and policymakers. When Bill Clinton moved into the Oval Office in 1993, deficit reduction was his first major goal. Similarly, when the Republicans took control of Congress in 1995, deficit reduction was high on their legislative agenda. Both of these efforts substantially reduced the size of the government budget deficit. In addition, a booming economy in the late 1990s brought in even more tax revenue. Eventually, the federal budget turned from deficit to surplus, and the debt-to-GDP ratio declined significantly for several years.

This fall in the debt-to-GDP ratio, however, stopped during the presidency of George W. Bush, as the budget surplus turned back into a budget deficit. There were three reasons for this change. First, President Bush signed into law several major tax cuts, which he had promised during the 2000 presidential campaign. Second, in 2001, the economy experienced a *recession* (a reduction in economic activity), which automatically decreased tax revenue and increased government spending. Third, there were increases in government spending on homeland security following the September 11, 2001 attacks and on the subsequent wars in Iraq and Afghanistan.

Truly dramatic increases in the debt-to-GDP ratio started occurring in 2008, as the economy experienced a financial crisis and a deep recession. (The accompanying FYI box addresses this topic briefly, but we will study it more fully in coming chapters.) The recession automatically increased the budget deficit, and several policy measures passed by the Bush and Obama administrations aimed at combating the recession reduced tax revenue and increased government spending even more. From 2009 to 2012, the federal government's budget deficit averaged about 9 percent of GDP, levels not seen since World War II. The borrowing to finance these deficits led to the substantial increase in the debt-to-GDP ratio shown in Figure 5. ◢

Quick Quiz   *If more Americans adopted a "live for today" approach to life, how would this affect saving, investment, and the interest rate?*

FYI

Financial Crises

In 2008 and 2009, the U.S. economy and many other major economies around the world experienced a financial crisis, which in turn led to a deep downturn in economic activity. We will examine these events in detail later in this book. But because this chapter introduces the financial system, let's discuss briefly the key elements of financial crises.

The first element of a financial crisis is a large decline in some asset prices. In 2008 and 2009, that asset was real estate. The price of housing, after experiencing a boom earlier in the decade, fell by about 30 percent over just a few years. Such a large decline in real estate prices had not been seen in the United States since the 1930s.

The second element of a financial crisis is insolvencies at financial institutions. In 2008 and 2009, many banks and other financial firms had in effect placed bets on real estate prices by holding mortgages backed by that real estate. When house prices fell, large numbers of homeowners stopped repaying their loans. These defaults pushed several financial institutions toward bankruptcy.

The third element of a financial crisis is a decline in confidence in financial institutions. Although some deposits in banks are insured by government policies, not all are. As insolvencies mounted, every financial institution became a possible candidate for the next bankruptcy. Individuals and firms with uninsured deposits in those institutions pulled out their money. Facing a rash of withdrawals, banks started selling off assets (sometimes at reduced "fire-sale" prices) and cut back on new lending.

The fourth element of a financial crisis is a credit crunch. With many financial institutions facing difficulties, would-be borrowers had trouble getting loans, even if they had profitable investment projects. In essence, the financial system had trouble performing its normal function of directing the resources of savers into the hands of borrowers with the best investment opportunities.

The fifth element of a financial crisis is an economic downturn. With people unable to obtain financing for new investment projects, the overall demand for goods and services declined. As a result, for reasons we discuss more fully later in the book, national income fell and unemployment rose.

The sixth and final element of a financial crisis is a vicious circle. The economic downturn reduced the profitability of many companies and the value of many assets. Thus, we started over again at step one, and the problems in the financial system and the economic downturn reinforced each other.

Financial crises, such as the one of 2008 and 2009, can have severe consequences. Fortunately, they do end. Financial institutions eventually get back on their feet, perhaps with some help from government policy, and they return to their normal function of financial intermediation. ◢

26-4 Conclusion

"Neither a borrower nor a lender be," Polonius advises his son in Shakespeare's *Hamlet*. If everyone followed this advice, this chapter would have been unnecessary.

Few economists would agree with Polonius. In our economy, people borrow and lend often, and usually for good reason. You may borrow one day to start your own business or to buy a home. And people may lend to you in the hope that the interest you pay will allow them to enjoy a more prosperous retirement. The financial system has the job of coordinating all this borrowing and lending activity.

In many ways, financial markets are like other markets in the economy. The price of loanable funds—the interest rate—is governed by the forces of supply and demand, just as other prices in the economy are. And we can analyze shifts in supply or demand in financial markets as we do in other markets. One of the *Ten Principles of Economics* introduced in Chapter 1 is that markets are usually a good way to organize economic activity. This principle applies to financial markets as well. When financial markets bring the supply and demand for loanable funds into balance, they help allocate the economy's scarce resources to their most efficient uses.

In one way, however, financial markets are special. Financial markets, unlike most other markets, serve the important role of linking the present and the future. Those who supply loanable funds—savers—do so because they want to convert some of their current income into future purchasing power. Those who demand loanable funds—borrowers—do so because they want to invest today in order to have additional capital in the future to produce goods and services. Thus, well-functioning financial markets are important not only for current generations but also for future generations who will inherit many of the resulting benefits.

Summary

- The U.S. financial system is made up of many types of financial institutions, such as the bond market, the stock market, banks, and mutual funds. All these institutions act to direct the resources of households that want to save some of their income into the hands of households and firms that want to borrow.

- National income accounting identities reveal some important relationships among macroeconomic variables. In particular, for a closed economy, national saving must equal investment. Financial institutions are the mechanism through which the economy matches one person's saving with another person's investment.

- The interest rate is determined by the supply and demand for loanable funds. The supply of loanable funds comes from households that want to save some of their income and lend it out. The demand for loanable funds comes from households and firms that want to borrow for investment. To analyze how any policy or event affects the interest rate, one must consider how it affects the supply and demand for loanable funds.

- National saving equals private saving plus public saving. A government budget deficit represents negative public saving and, therefore, reduces national saving and the supply of loanable funds available to finance investment. When a government budget deficit crowds out investment, it reduces the growth of productivity and GDP.

Key Concepts

financial system, *p. 548*
financial markets, *p. 548*
bond, *p. 548*
stock, *p. 549*
financial intermediaries, *p. 550*

mutual fund, *p. 551*
national saving (saving), *p. 555*
private saving, *p. 555*
public saving, *p. 555*
budget surplus, *p. 555*

budget deficit, *p. 555*
market for loanable funds, *p. 556*
crowding out, *p. 562*

Questions for Review

1. What is the role of the financial system? Name and describe two markets that are part of the financial system in the U.S. economy. Name and describe two financial intermediaries.

2. Why is it important for people who own stocks and bonds to diversify their holdings? What type of financial institution makes diversification easier?

3. What is national saving? What is private saving? What is public saving? How are these three variables related?

4. What is investment? How is it related to national saving in a closed economy?

5. Describe a change in the tax code that might increase private saving. If this policy were implemented, how would it affect the market for loanable funds?

6. What is a government budget deficit? How does it affect interest rates, investment, and economic growth?

Quick Check Multiple Choice

1. Nina wants to buy and operate an ice-cream truck but doesn't have the financial resources to start the business. She borrows $5,000 from her friend Max, to whom she promises an interest rate of 7 percent, and gets another $10,000 from her friend David, to whom she promises a third of her profits. What best describes this situation?
   a. Max is a stockholder, and Nina is a bondholder.
   b. Max is a stockholder, and David is a bondholder.
   c. David is a stockholder, and Nina is a bondholder.
   d. David is a stockholder, and Max is a bondholder.

2. If the government collects more in tax revenue than it spends, and households consume more than they get in after-tax income, then
   a. private and public saving are both positive.
   b. private and public saving are both negative.
   c. private saving is positive, but public saving is negative.
   d. private saving is negative, but public saving is positive.

3. A closed economy has income of $1,000, government spending of $200, taxes of $150, and investment of $250. What is private saving?
   a. $100
   b. $200
   c. $300
   d. $400

4. If a popular TV show on personal finance convinces more Americans about the importance of saving for retirement, the _____ curve for loanable funds would shift, driving the equilibrium interest rate _____.
   a. supply, up
   b. supply, down
   c. demand, up
   d. demand, down

5. If the business community becomes more optimistic about the profitability of capital, the _____ curve for loanable funds would shift, driving the equilibrium interest rate _____.
   a. supply, up
   b. supply, down
   c. demand, up
   d. demand, down

6. From 2008 to 2012, the ratio of government debt to GDP in the United States
   a. increased markedly.
   b. decreased markedly.
   c. was stable at a historically high level.
   d. was stable at a historically low level.

Problems and Applications

1. For each of the following pairs, which bond would you expect to pay a higher interest rate? Explain.
   a. a bond of the U.S. government or a bond of an Eastern European government
   b. a bond that repays the principal in year 2020 or a bond that repays the principal in year 2040
   c. a bond from Coca-Cola or a bond from a software company you run in your garage
   d. a bond issued by the federal government or a bond issued by New York State

2. Many workers hold large amounts of stock issued by the firms at which they work. Why do you suppose companies encourage this behavior? Why might a person *not* want to hold stock in the company where he works?

3. Explain the difference between saving and investment as defined by a macroeconomist. Which of the following situations represent investment? Saving? Explain.
   a. Your family takes out a mortgage and buys a new house.
   b. You use your $200 paycheck to buy stock in AT&T.
   c. Your roommate earns $100 and deposits it in his account at a bank.
   d. You borrow $1,000 from a bank to buy a car to use in your pizza delivery business.

4. Suppose GDP is $8 trillion, taxes are $1.5 trillion, private saving is $0.5 trillion, and public saving is $0.2 trillion. Assuming this economy is closed, calculate consumption, government purchases, national saving, and investment.

5. Economists in Funlandia, a closed economy, have collected the following information about the economy for a particular year:

$Y = 10,000$
$C = 6,000$
$T = 1,500$
$G = 1,700$

The economists also estimate that the investment function is:

$$I = 3,300 - 100r,$$

where r is the country's real interest rate, expressed as a percentage. Calculate private saving, public saving, national saving, investment, and the equilibrium real interest rate.

6. Suppose that Intel is considering building a new chip-making factory.
   a. Assuming that Intel needs to borrow money in the bond market, why would an increase in interest rates affect Intel's decision about whether to build the factory?
   b. If Intel has enough of its own funds to finance the new factory without borrowing, would an increase in interest rates still affect Intel's decision about whether to build the factory? Explain.

7. Three students have each saved $1,000. Each has an investment opportunity in which he or she can invest up to $2,000. Here are the rates of return on the students' investment projects:

Harry	5 percent
Ron	8 percent
Hermione	20 percent

   a. If borrowing and lending is prohibited, so each student uses only personal saving to finance his or her own investment project, how much will each student have a year later when the project pays its return?
   b. Now suppose their school opens up a market for loanable funds in which students can borrow and lend among themselves at an interest rate r. What would determine whether a student would choose to be a borrower or lender in this market?

   c. Among these three students, what would be the quantity of loanable funds supplied and quantity demanded at an interest rate of 7 percent? At 10 percent?
   d. At what interest rate would the loanable funds market among these three students be in equilibrium? At this interest rate, which student(s) would borrow and which student(s) would lend?
   e. At the equilibrium interest rate, how much does each student have a year later after the investment projects pay their return and loans have been repaid? Compare your answers to those you gave in part (a). Who benefits from the existence of the loanable funds market—the borrowers or the lenders? Is anyone worse off?

8. Suppose the government borrows $20 billion more next year than this year.
   a. Use a supply-and-demand diagram to analyze this policy. Does the interest rate rise or fall?
   b. What happens to investment? To private saving? To public saving? To national saving? Compare the size of the changes to the $20 billion of extra government borrowing.
   c. How does the elasticity of supply of loanable funds affect the size of these changes?
   d. How does the elasticity of demand for loanable funds affect the size of these changes?
   e. Suppose households believe that greater government borrowing today implies higher taxes to pay off the government debt in the future. What does this belief do to private saving and the supply of loanable funds today? Does it increase or decrease the effects you discussed in parts (a) and (b)?

9. This chapter explains that investment can be increased both by reducing taxes on private saving and by reducing the government budget deficit.
   a. Why is it difficult to implement both of these policies at the same time?
   b. What would you need to know about private saving to judge which of these two policies would be a more effective way to raise investment?

Go to CengageBrain.com to purchase access to the proven, critical Study Guide to accompany this text, which features additional notes and context, practice tests, and much more.

The Basic Tools
of Finance

Sometime in your life, you will have to deal with the economy's financial system. You will deposit your savings in a bank account, or you will take out a mortgage to buy a house. After you have a job, you will decide whether to invest the funds in your retirement account in stocks, bonds, or other financial instruments. If you try to put together your own portfolio, you will have to decide between buying stocks in established companies such as General Electric or newer ones such as Facebook. And whenever you watch the evening news, you will hear reports about whether the stock market is up or down, together with the often feeble attempts to explain why the market behaves as it does.

If you reflect for a moment on the many financial decisions you will make during your life, you will see two related elements in almost all of them: time and risk. As we saw in the preceding two chapters, the financial system coordinates the economy's saving and investment, which in turn are crucial determinants of economic growth. Most fundamentally, the financial system concerns decisions and actions we undertake today that will affect our lives in the future. But the future is unknown. When a person decides to allocate some saving, or a firm decides to undertake an investment, the decision is based on a guess about the likely result. The actual result, however, could end up being very different from what was expected.

This chapter introduces some tools that help us understand the decisions that people make as they participate in financial markets. The field of **finance** develops these tools in great detail, and you may choose to take courses that focus on this topic. But because the financial system is so important to the functioning of the economy, many of the basic insights of finance are central to understanding how the economy works. The tools of finance can also help you think through some of the decisions that you will make in your own life.

This chapter takes up three topics. First, we discuss how to compare sums of money at different points in time. Second, we discuss how to manage risk. Third, we build on our analysis of time and risk to examine what determines the value of an asset, such as a share of stock.

finance
the field that studies how people make decisions regarding the allocation of resources over time and the handling of risk

27-1 Present Value: Measuring the Time Value of Money

Imagine that someone offers to give you $100 today or $100 in 10 years. Which would you choose? This is an easy question. Getting $100 today is better because you can always deposit the money in a bank, still have it in 10 years, and earn interest on the $100 along the way. The lesson: Money today is more valuable than the same amount of money in the future.

Now consider a harder question: Imagine that someone offers you $100 today or $200 in 10 years. Which would you choose? To answer this question, you need some way to compare sums of money from different points in time. Economists do this with a concept called present value. The **present value** of any future sum of money is the amount today that would be needed, at current interest rates, to produce that future sum.

To learn how to use the concept of present value, let's work through a couple of simple examples:

present value
the amount of money today that would be needed, using prevailing interest rates, to produce a given future amount of money

Question: If you put $100 in a bank account today, how much will it be worth in N years? That is, what will be the **future value** of this $100?

Answer: Let's use r to denote the interest rate expressed in decimal form (so an interest rate of 5 percent means $r = 0.05$). Suppose that interest is paid annually and that it remains in the bank account to earn more interest—a process called **compounding**. Then the $100 will become

future value
the amount of money in the future that an amount of money today will yield, given prevailing interest rates

compounding
the accumulation of a sum of money in, say, a bank account, where the interest earned remains in the account to earn additional interest in the future

$(1 + r) \times \$100$	after 1 year,
$(1 + r) \times (1 + r) \times \$100 = (1 + r)^2 \times \$100$	after 2 years,
$(1 + r) \times (1 + r) \times (1 + r) \times \$100 = (1 + r)^3 \times \$100$	after 3 years, . . .
$(1 + r)^N \times \$100$	after N years.

For example, if we are investing at an interest rate of 5 percent for 10 years, then the future value of the $100 will be $(1.05)^{10} \times \$100$, or $163.

Question: Now suppose you are going to be paid $200 in N years. What is the *present value* of this future payment? That is, how much would you have to deposit in a bank right now to yield $200 in N years?

Answer: To answer this question, just turn the previous answer on its head. In the last question, we computed a future value from a present value by *multiplying* by the factor $(1 + r)^N$. To compute a present value from a future value, we *divide* by the factor $(1 + r)^N$. Thus, the present value of $200 in N years is $200/$(1 + r)^N$. If that amount is deposited in a bank today, after N years it will become $(1 + r)^N \times [\$200/(1 + r)^N]$, which equals $200. For instance, if the interest rate is 5 percent, the present value of $200 to be paid in 10 years is $200/(1.05)^{10}$, or $123. This means that $123 deposited today in a bank account that earned 5 percent would produce $200 after 10 years.

This illustrates the general formula:

- If r is the interest rate, then an amount X to be received in N years has a present value of $X/(1 + r)^N$.

Because the possibility of earning interest reduces the present value below the amount X, the process of finding a present value of a future sum of money is called *discounting*. This formula shows precisely how much future sums should be discounted.

Let's now return to our earlier question: Should you choose $100 today or $200 in 10 years? Based on our calculation of present value using an interest rate of 5 percent, you should prefer the $200 in 10 years. The future $200 has a present value of $123, which is greater than $100. You are better off waiting for the future sum.

Notice that the answer to our question depends on the interest rate. If the interest rate were 8 percent, then the $200 in 10 years would have a present value of $200/(1.08)^{10}$, which is only $93. In this case, you should take the $100 today. Why should the interest rate matter for your choice? The answer is that the higher the interest rate, the more you can earn by depositing your money in a bank, so the more attractive getting $100 today becomes.

The concept of present value is useful in many applications, including the decisions that companies face when evaluating investment projects. For instance, imagine that General Motors is thinking about building a new factory. Suppose that the factory will cost $100 million today and will yield the company $200 million in 10 years. Should General Motors undertake the project? You can see that this decision is exactly like the one we have been studying. To make its decision, the company will compare the present value of the $200 million return to the $100 million cost.

The company's decision, therefore, will depend on the interest rate. If the interest rate is 5 percent, then the present value of the $200 million return from the factory is $123 million, and the company will choose to pay the $100 million cost. By contrast, if the interest rate is 8 percent, then the present value of the return is only $93 million, and the company will decide to forgo the project. Thus, the concept of present value helps explain why investment—and thus the quantity of loanable funds demanded—declines when the interest rate rises.

Here is another application of present value: Suppose you win a million-dollar lottery and are given a choice between $20,000 a year for 50 years (totaling $1,000,000) or an immediate payment of $400,000. Which would you choose? To make the right choice, you need to calculate the present value of the stream of payments. Let's suppose the interest rate is 7 percent. After performing 50 calculations similar to those above (one calculation for each payment) and adding up the results, you would learn that the present value of this million-dollar prize at a 7 percent interest rate is only $276,000. You are better off picking the immediate

FYI

The Magic of Compounding and the Rule of 70

Suppose you observe that one country has an average growth rate of 1 percent per year, while another has an average growth rate of 3 percent per year. At first, this might not seem like a big deal. What difference can 2 percent make?

The answer is: a big difference. Growth rates that seem small when written in percentage terms are large after they are compounded for many years.

Consider an example. Suppose that two college graduates— Marshall and Lily—both take their first jobs at the age of 22 earning $30,000 a year. Marshall lives in an economy where all incomes grow at 1 percent per year, while Lily lives in one where incomes grow at 3 percent per year. Straightforward calculations show what happens. Forty years later, when both are 62 years old, Marshall earns $45,000 a year, while Lily earns $98,000. Because of that difference of 2 percentage points in the growth rate, Lily's salary is more than twice Marshall's.

An old rule of thumb, called the *rule of 70*, is helpful in understanding growth rates and the effects of compounding. According to the rule of 70, if some variable grows at a rate of *x* percent per year, then that variable doubles in approximately 70/*x* years. In Marshall's economy, incomes grow at 1 percent per year, so it takes about 70 years for incomes to double. In Lily's economy, incomes grow at 3 percent per year, so it takes about 70/3, or 23, years for incomes to double.

The rule of 70 applies not only to a growing economy but also to a growing savings account. Here is an example: In 1791, Ben Franklin died and left $5,000 to be invested for a period of 200 years to benefit medical students and scientific research. If this money had earned 7 percent per year (which would, in fact, have been possible), the investment would have doubled in value every 10 years. Over 200 years, it would have doubled 20 times. At the end of 200 years of compounding, the investment would have been worth $2^{20} \times \$5,000$, which is about $5 billion. (In fact, Franklin's $5,000 grew to only $2 million over 200 years because some of the money was spent along the way.)

As these examples show, growth rates and interest rates compounded over many years can lead to some spectacular results. That is probably why Albert Einstein once called compounding "the greatest mathematical discovery of all time." ◢

payment of $400,000. The million dollars may seem like more money, but the future cash flows, once discounted to the present, are worth far less.

Quick Quiz   *The interest rate is 7 percent. What is the present value of $150 to be received in 10 years?*

27-2 Managing Risk

Life is full of gambles. When you go skiing, you risk breaking your leg in a fall. When you drive to work, you risk a car accident. When you put some of your savings in the stock market, you risk a fall in stock prices. The rational response to this risk is not necessarily to avoid it at any cost but to take it into account in your decision making. Let's consider how a person might do that.

27-2a Risk Aversion

risk aversion
a dislike of uncertainty

Most people are **risk averse**. This means more than that people dislike bad things happening to them. It means that they dislike bad things more than they like comparable good things.

For example, suppose a friend offers you the following opportunity. She will toss a coin. If it comes up heads, she will pay you $1,000. But if it comes up tails, you will have to pay her $1,000. Would you accept the bargain? You wouldn't if you were risk averse. For a risk-averse person, the pain of losing the $1,000 would exceed the pleasure from winning $1,000.

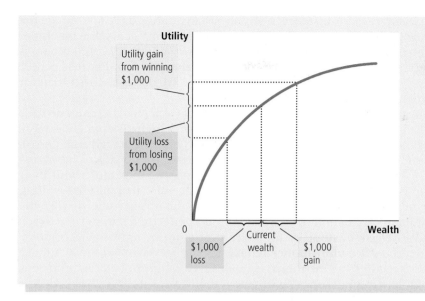

Economists have developed models of risk aversion using the concept of *utility*, which is a person's subjective measure of well-being or satisfaction. Every level of wealth provides a certain amount of utility, as shown by the utility function in Figure 1. But the function exhibits the property of diminishing marginal utility: The more wealth a person has, the less utility she gets from an additional dollar. Thus, in the figure, the utility function gets flatter as wealth increases. Because of diminishing marginal utility, the utility lost from losing the $1,000 bet is more than the utility gained from winning it. As a result, people are risk averse.

Risk aversion provides the starting point for explaining various things we observe in the economy. Let's consider three of them: insurance, diversification, and the risk-return trade-off.

27-2b The Markets for Insurance

One way to deal with risk is to buy insurance. The general feature of insurance contracts is that a person facing a risk pays a fee to an insurance company, which in return agrees to accept all or part of the risk. There are many types of insurance. Car insurance covers the risk of your being in an auto accident, fire insurance covers the risk that your house will burn down, health insurance covers the risk that you might need expensive medical treatment, and life insurance covers the risk that you will die and leave your family without your income. There is also insurance against the risk of living too long: For a fee paid today, an insurance company will pay you an *annuity*—a regular income every year until you die.

In a sense, every insurance contract is a gamble. It is possible that you will not be in an auto accident, that your house will not burn down, and that you will not need expensive medical treatment. In most years, you will pay the insurance company the premium and get nothing in return except peace of mind. Indeed, the insurance company is counting on the fact that most people will not make claims on their policies; otherwise, it couldn't pay out large claims to the unlucky few and still stay in business.

From the standpoint of the economy as a whole, the role of insurance is not to eliminate the risks inherent in life but to spread them around more efficiently.

Consider fire insurance, for instance. Owning fire insurance does not reduce the risk of losing your home in a fire. But if that unlucky event occurs, the insurance company compensates you. The risk, rather than being borne by you alone, is shared among the thousands of insurance-company shareholders. Because people are risk averse, it is easier for 10,000 people to bear 1/10,000 of the risk than for one person to bear the entire risk herself.

The markets for insurance suffer from two types of problems that impede their ability to spread risk. One problem is *adverse selection:* A high-risk person is more likely to apply for insurance than a low-risk person because a high-risk person would benefit more from insurance protection. A second problem is *moral hazard:* After people buy insurance, they have less incentive to be careful about their risky behavior because the insurance company will cover much of the resulting losses. Insurance companies are aware of these problems, but they cannot fully guard against them. An insurance company cannot perfectly distinguish between high-risk and low-risk customers, and it cannot monitor all of its customers' risky behavior. The price of insurance reflects the actual risks that the insurance company will face after the insurance is bought. The high price of insurance is why some people, especially those who know themselves to be low-risk, decide against buying it and, instead, endure some of life's uncertainty on their own.

27-2c Diversification of Firm-Specific Risk

In 2002, Enron, a large and once widely respected company, went bankrupt amid accusations of fraud and accounting irregularities. Several of the company's top executives were prosecuted and ended up going to prison. The saddest part of the story, however, involved thousands of lower-level employees. Not only did they lose their jobs but many lost their life savings as well. The employees had about two-thirds of their retirement funds in Enron stock, which became worthless.

If there is one piece of practical advice that finance offers to risk-averse people, it is this: "Don't put all your eggs in one basket." You may have heard this before, but finance has turned this folk wisdom into a science. It goes by the name **diversification**.

diversification

the reduction of risk achieved by replacing a single risk with a large number of smaller, unrelated risks

The market for insurance is one example of diversification. Imagine a town with 10,000 homeowners, each facing the risk of a house fire. If someone starts an insurance company and each person in town becomes both a shareholder and a policyholder of the company, they all reduce their risk through diversification. Each person now faces 1/10,000 of the risk of 10,000 possible fires, rather than the entire risk of a single fire in her own home. Unless the entire town catches fire at the same time, the downside that each person faces is much smaller.

When people use their savings to buy financial assets, they can also reduce risk through diversification. A person who buys stock in a company is placing a bet on the future profitability of that company. That bet is often quite risky because companies' fortunes are hard to predict. Microsoft evolved from a start-up by some geeky teenagers into one of the world's most valuable companies in only a few years; Enron went from one of the world's most respected companies to an almost worthless one in only a few months. Fortunately, a shareholder need not tie her own fortune to that of any single company. Risk can be reduced by placing a large number of small bets, rather than a small number of large ones.

Figure 2 shows how the risk of a portfolio of stocks depends on the number of stocks in the portfolio. Risk is measured here with a statistic called the *standard deviation,* which you may have learned about in a math or statistics class. The standard deviation measures the volatility of a variable—that is, how much

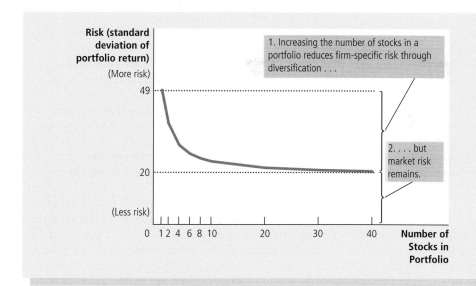

FIGURE 2

Diversification Reduces Risk
This figure shows how the risk of a portfolio, measured here with a statistic called the *standard deviation*, depends on the number of stocks in the portfolio. The investor is assumed to put an equal percentage of her portfolio in each of the stocks. Increasing the number of stocks reduces, but does not eliminate, the amount of risk in a stock portfolio.

Source: Adapted from Meir Statman, "How Many Stocks Make a Diversified Portfolio?" *Journal of Financial and Quantitative Analysis* 22 (September 1987): 353–364.

the variable is likely to fluctuate. The higher the standard deviation of a portfolio's return, the more volatile its return is likely to be, and the riskier it is that someone holding the portfolio will fail to get the return that she expected.

The figure shows that the risk of a stock portfolio falls substantially as the number of stocks increases. For a portfolio with a single stock, the standard deviation is 49 percent. Going from 1 stock to 10 stocks eliminates about half the risk. Going from 10 to 20 stocks reduces the risk by another 10 percent. As the number of stocks continues to increase, risk continues to fall, although the reductions in risk after 20 or 30 stocks are small.

Notice that it is impossible to eliminate all risk by increasing the number of stocks in the portfolio. Diversification can eliminate **firm-specific risk**—the uncertainty associated with the specific companies. But diversification cannot eliminate **market risk**—the uncertainty associated with the entire economy, which affects all companies traded on the stock market. For example, when the economy goes into a recession, most companies experience falling sales, reduced profit, and low stock returns. Diversification reduces the risk of holding stocks, but it does not eliminate it.

firm-specific risk
risk that affects only a single company

market risk
risk that affects all companies in the stock market

27-2d The Trade-off between Risk and Return

One of the *Ten Principles of Economics* in Chapter 1 is that people face trade-offs. The trade-off that is most relevant for understanding financial decisions is the trade-off between risk and return.

As we have seen, there are risks inherent in holding stocks, even in a diversified portfolio. But risk-averse people are willing to accept this uncertainty because they are compensated for doing so. Historically, stocks have offered much higher rates of return than alternative financial assets, such as bonds and bank savings accounts. Over the past two centuries, stocks offered an average real return of about 8 percent per year, while short-term government bonds paid a real return of only 3 percent per year.

When deciding how to allocate their savings, people have to decide how much risk they are willing to undertake to earn a higher return. For example, consider a person choosing how to allocate her portfolio between two asset classes:

- The first asset class is a diversified group of risky stocks, with an average return of 8 percent and a standard deviation of 20 percent. (You may recall from a math or statistics class that a normal random variable stays within two standard deviations of its average about 95 percent of the time. Thus, while actual returns are centered around 8 percent, they typically vary from a gain of 48 percent to a loss of 32 percent.)
- The second asset class is a safe alternative, with a return of 3 percent and a standard deviation of zero. The safe alternative can be either a bank savings account or a government bond.

Figure 3 illustrates the trade-off between risk and return. Each point in this figure represents a particular allocation of a portfolio between risky stocks and the safe asset. The figure shows that the more the individual puts into stocks, the greater both the risk and the return are.

Acknowledging the risk-return trade-off does not, by itself, tell us what a person should do. The choice of a particular combination of risk and return depends on a person's risk aversion, which reflects her own preferences. But it is important for stockholders to recognize that the higher average return that they enjoy comes at the price of higher risk.

Quick Quiz *Describe three ways that a risk-averse person might reduce the risk she faces.*

27-3 Asset Valuation

Now that we have developed a basic understanding of the two building blocks of finance—time and risk—let's apply this knowledge. This section considers a simple question: What determines the price of a share of stock? As with most prices, the answer is supply and demand. But that is not the end of the story. To

FIGURE 3

The Trade-off between Risk and Return
When people increase the percentage of their savings that they have invested in stocks, they increase the average return they can expect to earn, but they also increase the risks they face.

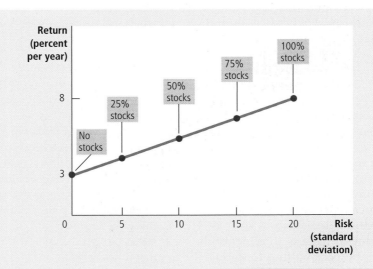

understand stock prices, we need to think more deeply about what determines a person's willingness to pay for a share of stock.

27-3a Fundamental Analysis

Let's imagine that you have decided to put 60 percent of your savings into stock, and to achieve diversification, you have decided to buy twenty different stocks. If you open up the newspaper, you will find thousands of stocks listed. How should you pick the twenty for your portfolio?

When you buy stock, you are buying shares in a business. To decide which businesses you want to own, it is natural to consider two things: the value of that share of the business and the price at which the shares are being sold. If the price is less than the value, the stock is said to be *undervalued*. If the price is more than the value, the stock is said to be *overvalued*. If the price and the value are equal, the stock is said to be *fairly valued*. When choosing twenty stocks for your portfolio, you should prefer undervalued stocks. In these cases, you are getting a bargain by paying less than the business is worth.

This is easier said than done. Learning the price is easy: You can just look it up. Determining the value of the business is the hard part. The term **fundamental analysis** refers to the detailed analysis of a company to estimate its value. Many Wall Street firms hire stock analysts to conduct such fundamental analysis and offer advice about which stocks to buy.

fundamental analysis
the study of a company's accounting statements and future prospects to determine its value

The value of a stock to a stockholder is what she gets out of owning it, which includes the present value of the stream of dividend payments and the final sale price. Recall that *dividends* are the cash payments that a company makes to its shareholders. A company's ability to pay dividends, as well as the value of the stock when the stockholder sells her shares, depends on the company's ability to earn profits. Its profitability, in turn, depends on a large number of factors: the demand for its product, how much competition it faces, how much capital it has in place, whether its workers are unionized, how loyal its customers are, what kinds of government regulations and taxes it faces, and so on. The goal of fundamental analysis is to take all these factors into account to determine how much a share of stock in the company is worth.

If you want to rely on fundamental analysis to pick a stock portfolio, there are three ways to do it. One way is to do all the necessary research yourself, such as by reading through companies' annual reports. A second way is to rely on the advice of Wall Street analysts. A third way is to buy shares in a mutual fund, which has a manager who conducts fundamental analysis and makes the decision for you.

27-3b The Efficient Markets Hypothesis

There is another way to choose twenty stocks for your portfolio: Pick them randomly by, for instance, putting the stock pages on your bulletin board and throwing darts at the page. This may sound crazy, but there is reason to believe that it won't lead you too far astray. That reason is called the **efficient markets hypothesis**.

efficient markets hypothesis
the theory that asset prices reflect all publicly available information about the value of an asset

To understand this theory, the starting point is to acknowledge that each company listed on a major stock exchange is followed closely by many money managers, such as the individuals who run mutual funds. Every day, these managers monitor news stories and conduct fundamental analysis to try to determine the stock's value. Their job is to buy a stock when its price falls below its fundamental value and to sell it when its price rises above its fundamental value.

The second piece to the efficient markets hypothesis is that the equilibrium of supply and demand sets the market price. This means that, at the market price, the number of shares being offered for sale exactly equals the number of shares that people want to buy. In other words, at the market price, the number of people who think the stock is overvalued exactly balances the number of people who think it's undervalued. As judged by the typical person in the market, all stocks are fairly valued all the time.

According to this theory, the stock market exhibits **informational efficiency**: It reflects all available information about the value of the asset. Stock prices change when information changes. When good news about the company's prospects becomes public, the value and the stock price both rise. When the company's prospects deteriorate, the value and price both fall. But at any moment in time, the market price is the best guess of the company's value based on available information.

One implication of the efficient markets hypothesis is that stock prices should follow a **random walk**. This means that changes in stock prices are impossible to predict from available information. If, based on publicly available information, a person could predict that a stock price would rise by 10 percent tomorrow, then the stock market must be failing to incorporate that information today. According to this theory, the only thing that can move stock prices is news that changes the market's perception of the company's value. But news must be unpredictable—otherwise, it wouldn't really be news. For the same reason, changes in stock prices should be unpredictable.

If the efficient markets hypothesis is correct, then there is little point in spending many hours studying the business page to decide which twenty stocks to add to your portfolio. If prices reflect all available information, no stock is a better buy than any other. The best you can do is to buy a diversified portfolio.

informational efficiency
the description of asset prices that rationally reflect all available information

random walk
the path of a variable whose changes are impossible to predict

case study — Random Walks and Index Funds

The efficient markets hypothesis is a theory about how financial markets work. The theory is probably not completely true: As we discuss in the next section, there is reason to doubt that stockholders are always rational and that stock prices are informationally efficient at every moment. Nonetheless, the efficient markets hypothesis does much better as a description of the world than you might think.

There is much evidence that stock prices, even if not exactly a random walk, are very close to it. For example, you might be tempted to buy stocks that have recently risen and avoid stocks that have recently fallen (or perhaps just the opposite). But statistical studies have shown that following such trends (or bucking them) fails to outperform the market. The correlation between how well a stock does one year and how well it does the following year is almost exactly zero.

Some of the best evidence in favor of the efficient markets hypothesis comes from the performance of index funds. An index fund is a mutual fund that buys all the stocks in a given stock index. The performance of these funds can be compared with that of actively managed mutual funds, where a professional portfolio manager picks stocks based on extensive research and alleged expertise. In essence, an index fund buys all stocks, whereas active funds are supposed to buy only the best stocks.

In practice, active managers usually fail to beat index funds. For example, in the 10-year period ending January 2013, 84 percent of stock mutual funds performed worse than a broadly based index fund holding all stocks traded on U.S. stock exchanges. Over this period, the average annual return on stock funds fell short of the return on the index fund by 1.21 percentage points. Most active portfolio managers failed to beat the market because they trade more frequently, incurring more trading costs, and because they charge greater fees as compensation for their alleged expertise.

What about the 16 percent of managers who did beat the market? Perhaps they are smarter than average, or perhaps they were luckier. If you have 5,000 people flipping coins ten times, on average about 5 will flip ten heads; these 5 might

claim an exceptional coin-flipping skill, but they would have trouble replicating the feat. Similarly, studies have shown that mutual fund managers with a history of superior performance usually fail to maintain it in subsequent periods.

The efficient markets hypothesis says that it is impossible to beat the market. The accumulation of many studies of financial markets confirms that beating the market is, at best, extremely difficult. Even if the efficient markets hypothesis is not an exact description of the world, it contains a large element of truth. ◢

27-3c Market Irrationality

The efficient markets hypothesis assumes that people buying and selling stock rationally process the information they have about the stock's underlying value. But is the stock market really that rational? Or do stock prices sometimes deviate from reasonable expectations of their true value?

There is a long tradition suggesting that fluctuations in stock prices are partly psychological. In the 1930s, economist John Maynard Keynes suggested that asset markets are driven by the "animal spirits" of investors—irrational waves of optimism and pessimism. In the 1990s, as the stock market soared to new heights, Fed Chairman Alan Greenspan questioned whether the boom reflected "irrational exuberance." Stock prices did subsequently fall, but whether the exuberance of the 1990s was irrational given the information available at the time remains debatable. Whenever the price of an asset rises above what appears to be its fundamental value, the market is said to be experiencing a *speculative bubble*.

The possibility of speculative bubbles in the stock market arises in part because the value of the stock to a stockholder depends not only on the stream of dividend payments but also on the final sale price. Thus, a person might be willing to pay more than a stock is worth today if she expects another person to pay even more for it tomorrow. When you evaluate a stock, you have to estimate not only the value of the business but also what other people will think the business is worth in the future.

There is much debate among economists about the frequency and importance of departures from rational pricing. Believers in market irrationality point out (correctly) that the stock market often moves in ways that are hard to explain on the basis of news that might alter a rational valuation. Believers in the efficient markets hypothesis point out (correctly) that it is impossible to know the correct, rational valuation of a company, so one should not quickly jump to the conclusion that any particular valuation is irrational. Moreover, if the market were irrational, a rational person should be able to take advantage of this fact; yet as the previous case study discussed, beating the market is nearly impossible.

Quick Quiz   Fortune *magazine regularly publishes a list of the "most respected" companies. According to the efficient markets hypothesis, if you restrict your stock portfolio to these companies, will you earn a better-than-average return? Explain.*

IN THE NEWS
················

Is the Efficient Markets Hypothesis Kaput?

In 2008 and 2009, the U.S. economy experienced a financial crisis that started with a substantial decline in house prices and widespread defaults on mortgages. Some observers say the crisis should cause us to reject the efficient markets hypothesis. Economist Jeremy Siegel is not convinced.

Efficient Market Theory and the Crisis

By Jeremy Siegel

Financial journalist and best-selling author Roger Lowenstein didn't mince words in a piece for the *Washington Post* this summer: "The upside of the current Great Recession is that it could drive a stake through the heart of the academic nostrum known as the efficient-market hypothesis." In a similar vein, the highly respected money manager and financial analyst Jeremy Grantham wrote in his quarterly letter last January: "The incredibly inaccurate efficient market theory [caused] a lethally dangerous combination of asset bubbles, lax controls, pernicious incentives and wickedly complicated instruments [that] led to our current plight."

But is the Efficient Market Hypothesis (EMH) really responsible for the current crisis? The answer is no. The EMH, originally put forth by Eugene Fama of the University of Chicago in the 1960s, states that the prices of securities reflect all known information that impacts their value. The hypothesis does not claim that the market price is always right. On the contrary, it implies that the prices in the market are mostly wrong, but at any given moment it is not at all easy to say whether they are too high or too low. The fact that the best and brightest on Wall Street made so many mistakes shows how hard it is to beat the market.

This does not mean the EMH can be used as an excuse by the CEOs of the failed financial firms or by the regulators who did not see the risks that subprime mortgage-backed securities posed to the financial stability of the economy. Regulators wrongly believed that financial firms were offsetting their credit risks, while the banks and credit rating agencies were fooled by faulty models that underestimated the risk in real estate.

After the 1982 recession, the U.S. and world economies entered into a long period where the fluctuations in variables such as gross domestic product, industrial production, and employment were significantly lower than they had been since World War II. Economists called this period the "Great Moderation" and attributed the increased stability to better monetary policy, a larger service sector and better inventory control, among other factors.

The economic response to the Great Moderation was predictable: risk premiums shrank and individuals and firms took on more leverage. Housing prices were boosted by historically low nominal and real interest rates and the development of the securitized subprime lending market.

According to data collected by Prof. Robert Shiller of Yale University, in the 61 years from 1945 through 2006 the maximum cumulative decline in the average price of homes was 2.84% in 1991. If this low volatility of home prices persisted into the future, a mortgage security composed of a nationally diversified portfolio of loans comprising the first 80% of a home's value would have never come close to defaulting. The credit quality of home buyers was secondary because it was thought that underlying collateral—the home—could always cover the principal in the event the homeowner defaulted. These models led credit agencies to rate these subprime mortgages as "investment grade."

But this assessment was faulty. From 2000 through 2006, national home prices rose by 88.7%, far more than the 17.5% gain in the consumer price index or the paltry 1% rise in median household income. Never before have home prices jumped that far ahead of prices and incomes.

This should have sent up red flags and cast doubts on using models that looked only at historical declines to judge future risk. But these flags were ignored as Wall Street was reaping large profits bundling and selling the securities while Congress was happy that more Americans could enjoy the "American Dream" of home ownership. Indeed, through government-sponsored enterprises such as Fannie Mae and Freddie Mac, Washington helped fuel the subprime boom.

Neither the rating agencies' mistakes nor the overleveraging by the financial firms in the subprime securities is the fault of the Efficient Market Hypothesis. The fact that the yields on these mortgages were high despite their investment-grade rating indicated that the market was rightly suspicious of the quality of the securities, and this should have served as a warning to prospective buyers.

With few exceptions (Goldman Sachs being one), financial firms ignored these warnings. CEOs failed to exercise their authority to monitor overall risk of the firm and instead put their faith in technicians whose narrow models could not capture the big picture. . . .

Our crisis wasn't due to blind faith in the Efficient Market Hypothesis. The fact that risk premiums were low does not mean they were non-existent and that market prices were right. Despite the recent recession, the Great Moderation is real and our economy is inherently more stable.

But this does not mean that risks have disappeared. To use an analogy, the fact that automobiles today are safer than they were years ago does not mean that you can drive at 120 mph. A small bump on the road, perhaps insignificant at lower speeds, will easily flip the best-engineered car. Our financial firms drove too fast, our central bank failed to stop them, and the housing deflation crashed the banks and the economy.

Mr. Siegel is a professor of finance at the Wharton School of the University of Pennsylvania. ◢

27-4 Conclusion

This chapter has developed some of the basic tools that people should (and often do) use as they make financial decisions. The concept of present value reminds us that a dollar in the future is less valuable than a dollar today, and it gives us a way to compare sums of money at different points in time. The theory of risk management reminds us that the future is uncertain and that risk-averse people can take precautions to guard against this uncertainty. The study of asset valuation tells us that the stock price of any company should reflect its expected future profitability.

Although most of the tools of finance are well established, there is more controversy about the validity of the efficient markets hypothesis and whether stock prices are, in practice, rational estimates of a company's true worth. Rational or not, the large movements in stock prices that we observe have important macroeconomic implications. Stock market fluctuations often go hand in hand with fluctuations in the economy more broadly. We revisit the stock market when we study economic fluctuations later in the book.

Summary

- Because savings can earn interest, a sum of money today is more valuable than the same sum of money in the future. A person can compare sums from different times using the concept of present value. The present value of any future sum is the amount that would be needed today, given prevailing interest rates, to produce that future sum.

- Because of diminishing marginal utility, most people are risk averse. Risk-averse people can reduce risk by buying insurance, diversifying their holdings, and choosing a portfolio with lower risk and lower return.

- The value of an asset equals the present value of the cash flows the owner will receive. For a share of stock, these cash flows include the stream of dividends and the final sale price. According to the efficient markets hypothesis, financial markets process available information rationally, so a stock price always equals the best estimate of the value of the underlying business. Some economists question the efficient markets hypothesis, however, and believe that irrational psychological factors also influence asset prices.

Key Concepts

finance, *p. 570*
present value, *p. 570*
future value, *p. 570*
compounding, *p. 570*

risk aversion, *p. 572*
diversification, *p. 574*
firm-specific risk, *p. 575*
market risk, *p. 575*

fundamental analysis, *p. 577*
efficient markets hypothesis, *p. 577*
informational efficiency, *p. 578*
random walk, *p. 578*

Questions for Review

1. The interest rate is 7 percent. Use the concept of present value to compare $200 to be received in 10 years and $300 to be received in 20 years.

2. What benefit do people get from the market for insurance? What two problems impede the insurance market from working perfectly?

3. What is diversification? Does a stockholder get a greater benefit from diversification going from 1 to 10 stocks or going from 100 to 120 stocks?

4. Comparing stocks and government bonds, which type of asset has more risk? Which pays a higher average return?

5. What factors should a stock analyst think about in determining the value of a share of stock?

6. Describe the efficient markets hypothesis and give a piece of evidence consistent with this hypothesis.

7. Explain the view of those economists who are skeptical of the efficient markets hypothesis.

Quick Check Multiple Choice

1. If the interest rate is zero, then $100 to be paid in 10 years has a present value that is
   a. less than $100.
   b. exactly $100.
   c. more than $100.
   d. indeterminate.

2. If the interest rate is 10 percent, then the future value in 2 years of $100 today is
   a. $80.
   b. $83.
   c. $120.
   d. $121.

3. If the interest rate is 10 percent, then the present value of $100 to be paid in 2 years is
   a. $80.
   b. $83.
   c. $120.
   d. $121.

4. The ability of insurance to spread risk is limited by
   a. risk aversion and moral hazard.
   b. risk aversion and adverse selection.
   c. moral hazard and adverse selection.
   d. risk aversion only.

5. The benefit of diversification when constructing a portfolio is that it can eliminate
   a. speculative bubbles.
   b. risk aversion.
   c. firm-specific risk.
   d. market risk.

6. According to the efficient markets hypothesis,
   a. changes in stock prices are impossible to predict from public information.
   b. excessive diversification can reduce an investor's expected portfolio returns.
   c. the stock market moves based on the changing animal spirits of investors.
   d. actively managed mutual funds should give higher returns than index funds.

Problems and Applications

1. According to an old myth, Native Americans sold the island of Manhattan about 400 years ago for $24. If they had invested this amount at an interest rate of 7 percent per year, how much, approximately, would they have today?

2. A company has an investment project that would cost $10 million today and yield a payoff of $15 million in 4 years.
   a. Should the firm undertake the project if the interest rate is 11 percent? 10 percent? 9 percent? 8 percent?
   b. Can you figure out the exact cutoff for the interest rate between profitability and nonprofitability?

3. Bond A pays $8,000 in 20 years. Bond B pays $8,000 in 40 years. (To keep things simple, assume these are zero-coupon bonds, which means the $8,000 is the only payment the bondholder receives.)
   a. If the interest rate is 3.5 percent, what is the value of each bond today? Which bond is worth more? Why? (*Hint*: You can use a calculator, but the rule of 70 should make the calculation easy.)
   b. If the interest rate increases to 7 percent, what is the value of each bond? Which bond has a larger percentage change in value?
   c. Based on the example above, complete the two blanks in this sentence: "The value of a bond

   [rises/falls] when the interest rate increases, and bonds with a longer time to maturity are [more/less] sensitive to changes in the interest rate."

4. Your bank account pays an interest rate of 8 percent. You are considering buying a share of stock in XYZ Corporation for $110. After 1, 2, and 3 years, it will pay a dividend of $5. You expect to sell the stock after 3 years for $120. Is XYZ a good investment? Support your answer with calculations.

5. For each of the following kinds of insurance, give an example of behavior that can be called *moral hazard* and another example of behavior that can be called *adverse selection*.
   a. health insurance
   b. car insurance

6. Which kind of stock would you expect to pay the higher average return: stock in an industry that is very sensitive to economic conditions (such as an automaker) or stock in an industry that is relatively insensitive to economic conditions (such as a water company)? Why?

7. A company faces two kinds of risk. A firm-specific risk is that a competitor might enter its market and take

some of its customers. A market risk is that the economy might enter a recession, reducing sales. Which of these two risks would more likely cause the company's shareholders to demand a higher return? Why?

8. When company executives buy and sell stock based on private information they obtain as part of their jobs, they are engaged in *insider trading*.
   a. Give an example of inside information that might be useful for buying or selling stock.
   b. Those who trade stocks based on inside information usually earn very high rates of return. Does this fact violate the efficient markets hypothesis?
   c. Insider trading is illegal. Why do you suppose that is?

9. Jamal has a utility function $U = W^{1/2}$, where W is his wealth in millions of dollars and U is the utility he obtains from that wealth. In the final stage of a game show, the host offers Jamal a choice between (A) $4 million for sure, or (B) a gamble that pays $1 million with probability 0.6 and $9 million with probability 0.4.
   a. Graph Jamal's utility function. Is he risk averse? Explain.
   b. Does A or B offer Jamal a higher expected prize? Explain your reasoning with appropriate calculations. (*Hint:* The expected value of a random variable is the weighted average of the possible outcomes, where the probabilities are the weights.)
   c. Does A or B offer Jamal a higher expected utility? Again, show your calculations.
   d. Should Jamal pick A or B? Why?

Go to CengageBrain.com to purchase access to the proven, critical Study Guide to accompany this text, which features additional notes and context, practice tests, and much more.

28

Unemployment

osing a job can be the most distressing economic event in a person's life. Most people rely on their labor earnings to maintain their standard of living, and many people also get a sense of personal accomplishment from working. A job loss means a lower living standard in the present, anxiety about the future, and reduced self-esteem. It is not surprising, therefore, that politicians campaigning for office often speak about how their proposed policies will help create jobs.

In previous chapters, we have seen some of the forces that determine the level and growth of a country's standard of living. A country that saves and invests a high fraction of its income, for instance, enjoys more rapid growth in its capital stock and GDP than a similar country that saves and invests less. An even more obvious determinant of a country's standard of living is the amount of unemployment it typically experiences. People who would like to work but cannot find a job are not contributing to the economy's production of goods and services. Although some degree of unemployment is inevitable in a complex economy with thousands of firms and millions of workers, the amount of unemployment varies substantially over time and across countries. When a country keeps its workers as fully employed as possible, it achieves a higher level of GDP than it would if it left many of its workers idle.

This chapter begins our study of unemployment. The problem of unemployment is usefully divided into two categories: the long-run problem and the short-run problem. The economy's *natural rate of unemployment* refers to the amount of unemployment that the economy normally experiences. *Cyclical unemployment* refers to the year-to-year fluctuations in unemployment around its natural rate, and it is closely associated with the short-run ups and downs of economic activity. Cyclical unemployment has its own explanation, which we defer until we study short-run economic fluctuations later in this book. In this chapter, we discuss the determinants of an economy's natural rate of unemployment. As we will see, the designation *natural* does not imply that this rate of unemployment is desirable. Nor does it imply that it is constant over time or impervious to economic policy. It just means that this unemployment does not go away on its own even in the long run.

We begin the chapter by looking at some of the relevant facts that describe unemployment. In particular, we examine three questions: How does the government measure the economy's rate of unemployment? What problems arise in interpreting the unemployment data? How long are the unemployed typically without work?

We then turn to the reasons economies always experience some unemployment and the ways in which policymakers can help the unemployed. We discuss four explanations for the economy's natural rate of unemployment: job search, minimum-wage laws, unions, and efficiency wages. As we will see, long-run unemployment does not arise from a single problem that has a single solution. Instead, it reflects a variety of related problems. As a result, there is no easy way for policymakers to reduce the economy's natural rate of unemployment and, at the same time, to alleviate the hardships experienced by the unemployed.

28-1 Identifying Unemployment

Let's start by examining more precisely what the term *unemployment* means.

28-1a How Is Unemployment Measured?

Measuring unemployment is the job of the Bureau of Labor Statistics (BLS), which is part of the Department of Labor. Every month, the BLS produces data on unemployment and on other aspects of the labor market, including types of employment, length of the average workweek, and the duration of unemployment. These data come from a regular survey of about 60,000 households, called the Current Population Survey.

Based on the answers to survey questions, the BLS places each adult (age 16 and older) in each surveyed household into one of three categories:

- *Employed:* This category includes those who worked as paid employees, worked in their own business, or worked as unpaid workers in a family member's business. Both full-time and part-time workers are counted. This category also includes those who were not working but who had jobs from which they were temporarily absent because of, for example, vacation, illness, or bad weather.

- *Unemployed:* This category includes those who were not employed, were available for work, and had tried to find employment during the previous four weeks. It also includes those waiting to be recalled to a job from which they had been laid off.
- *Not in the labor force:* This category includes those who fit neither of the first two categories, such as full-time students, homemakers, and retirees.

Figure 1 shows the breakdown into these categories for 2012.

Once the BLS has placed all the individuals covered by the survey in a category, it computes various statistics to summarize the state of the labor market. The BLS defines the **labor force** as the sum of the employed and the unemployed:

$$\text{Labor force} = \text{Number of employed} + \text{Number of unemployed}.$$

The BLS defines the **unemployment rate** as the percentage of the labor force that is unemployed:

$$\text{Unemployment rate} = \frac{\text{Number of unemployed}}{\text{Labor force}} \times 100.$$

The BLS computes unemployment rates for the entire adult population and for more narrowly defined groups such as blacks, whites, men, women, and so on.

The BLS uses the same survey to produce data on labor-force participation. The **labor-force participation rate** measures the percentage of the total adult population of the United States that is in the labor force:

$$\text{Labor-force participation rate} = \frac{\text{Labor force}}{\text{Adult population}} \times 100.$$

labor force
the total number of workers, including both the employed and the unemployed

unemployment rate
the percentage of the labor force that is unemployed

labor-force participation rate
the percentage of the adult population that is in the labor force

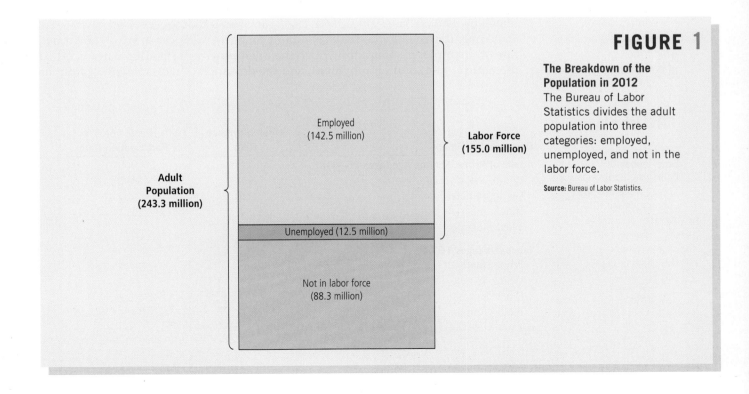

FIGURE 1

The Breakdown of the Population in 2012
The Bureau of Labor Statistics divides the adult population into three categories: employed, unemployed, and not in the labor force.

Source: Bureau of Labor Statistics.

This statistic tells us the fraction of the population that has chosen to participate in the labor market. The labor-force participation rate, like the unemployment rate, is computed for both the entire adult population and more specific groups.

To see how these data are computed, consider the figures for 2012. In that year, 142.5 million people were employed, and 12.5 million people were unemployed. The labor force was

$$\text{Labor force} = 142.5 + 12.5 = 155.0 \text{ million.}$$

The unemployment rate was

$$\text{Unemployment rate} = (12.5/155.0) \times 100 = 8.1 \text{ percent.}$$

Because the adult population was 243.3 million, the labor-force participation rate was

$$\text{Labor-force participation rate} = (155.0/243.3) \times 100 = 63.7 \text{ percent.}$$

Hence, in 2012, almost two-thirds of the U.S. adult population were participating in the labor market, and 8.1 percent of those labor-market participants were without work.

Table 1 shows the statistics on unemployment and labor-force participation for various groups within the U.S. population. Three comparisons are most apparent. First, women of prime working age (25 to 54 years old) have lower rates of labor-force participation than men, but once in the labor force, men and women have similar rates of unemployment. Second, prime-age blacks have similar rates of labor-force participation as prime-age whites, but they have much higher rates of unemployment. Third, teenagers have much lower rates of labor-force participation and much higher rates of unemployment than older workers. More generally, these data show that labor-market experiences vary widely among groups within the economy.

The BLS data on the labor market also allow economists and policymakers to monitor changes in the economy over time. Figure 2 shows the unemployment rate in the United States since 1960. The figure shows that the economy always has some unemployment and that the amount changes from year to year. The normal rate of unemployment around which the unemployment rate fluctuates is called the **natural rate of unemployment**, and the deviation of unemployment from its

natural rate of unemployment
the normal rate of unemployment around which the unemployment rate fluctuates

TABLE 1

The Labor-Market Experiences of Various Demographic Groups
This table shows the unemployment rate and the labor-force participation rate of various groups in the U.S. population for 2012.

Demographic Group	Unemployment Rate	Labor-Force Participation Rate
Adults of Prime Working Age (ages 25–54)		
White, male	6.2%	90.0%
White, female	6.4	74.7
Black, male	12.7	80.5
Black, female	11.3	76.2
Teenagers (ages 16–19)		
White, male	24.5	36.7
White, female	18.4	37.1
Black, male	41.3	25.6
Black, female	35.6	28.2

Source: Bureau of Labor Statistics.

This graph uses annual data on the U.S. unemployment rate to show the percentage of the labor force without a job. The natural rate of unemployment is the normal level of unemployment around which the unemployment rate fluctuates.

Source: U.S. Department of Labor, Congressional Budget Office.

FIGURE 2

Unemployment Rate since 1960

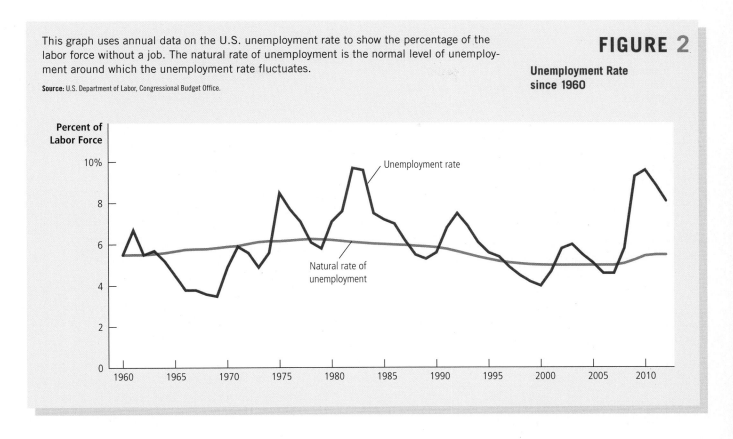

natural rate is called **cyclical unemployment**. The natural rate of unemployment shown in the figure is a series estimated by economists at the Congressional Budget Office. For 2012, they estimated a natural rate of 5.5 percent, well below the actual unemployment rate of 8.1 percent. Later in this book, we discuss short-run economic fluctuations, including the year-to-year fluctuations in unemployment around its natural rate. In the rest of this chapter, however, we ignore the short-run fluctuations and examine why there is always some unemployment in market economies.

cyclical unemployment
the deviation of unemployment from its natural rate

case study

Labor-Force Participation of Men and Women in the U.S. Economy
    Women's role in American society has changed dramatically over the past century. Social commentators have pointed to many causes for this change. In part, it is attributable to new technologies, such as the washing machine, clothes dryer, refrigerator, freezer, and dishwasher, which have reduced the amount of time required to complete routine household tasks. In part, it is attributable to improved birth control, which has reduced the number of children born to the typical family. This change in women's role is also partly attributable to changing political and social attitudes, which in turn may have been facilitated by the advances in technology and birth control. Together these developments have had a profound impact on society in general and on the economy in particular.

    Nowhere is that impact more obvious than in data on labor-force participation. Figure 3 shows the labor-force participation rates of men and women in the

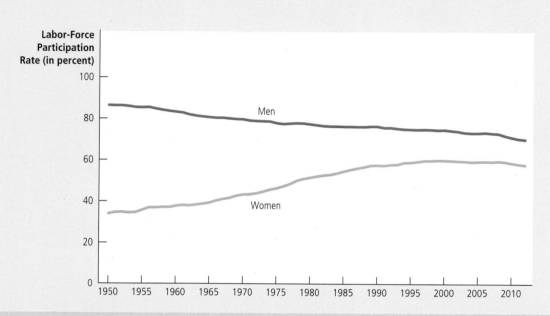

FIGURE 3

**Labor-Force Participation
Rates for Men and Women
since 1950**

This figure shows the percentage of adult men and women who are members of the labor force. It shows that, over the past 60 years, women have entered the labor force and men have left it.

Source: U.S. Department of Labor.

United States since 1950. Just after World War II, men and women had very different roles in society. Only 33 percent of women were working or looking for work, in contrast to 87 percent of men. Over the past 60 years, this difference in participation rates has gradually diminished, as growing numbers of women have entered the labor force and some men have left it. Data for 2012 show that 58 percent of women were in the labor force, in contrast to 70 percent of men. As measured by labor-force participation, men and women are now playing a more equal role in the economy.

The increase in women's labor-force participation is easy to understand, but the fall in men's may seem puzzling. There are several reasons for this decline. First, young men now stay in school longer than their fathers and grandfathers did. Second, older men now retire earlier and live longer. Third, with more women employed, more fathers now stay at home to raise their children. Full-time students, retirees, and stay-at-home dads are all counted as being out of the labor force. ◢

28-1b Does the Unemployment Rate Measure What We Want It To?

Measuring the amount of unemployment in the economy might seem a straight-forward task, but it is not. While it is easy to distinguish between a person with a full-time job and a person who is not working at all, it is much harder to distinguish between a person who is unemployed and a person who is not in the labor force.

Movements into and out of the labor force are, in fact, common. More than one-third of the unemployed are recent entrants into the labor force. These entrants include young workers looking for their first jobs. They also include, in greater numbers, older workers who had previously left the labor force but have now returned to look for work. Moreover, not all unemployment ends with the job seeker finding a job. Almost half of all spells of unemployment end when the unemployed person leaves the labor force.

Because people move into and out of the labor force so often, statistics on unemployment are difficult to interpret. On the one hand, some of those who report being unemployed may not, in fact, be trying hard to find a job. They may be calling themselves unemployed because they want to qualify for a government program that gives financial assistance to the unemployed or because they are working but paid "under the table" to avoid taxes on their earnings. It may be more accurate to view these individuals as out of the labor force or, in some cases, employed. On the other hand, some of those who report being out of the labor force may want to work. These individuals may have tried to find a job and may have given up after an unsuccessful search. Such individuals, called **discouraged workers**, do not show up in unemployment statistics, even though they are truly workers without jobs.

Because of these and other problems, the BLS calculates several other measures of labor underutilization, in addition to the official unemployment rate. These alternative measures are presented in Table 2. In the end, it is best to view the official unemployment rate as a useful but imperfect measure of joblessness.

discouraged workers
individuals who would like to work but have given up looking for a job

TABLE 2

Alternative Measures of Labor Underutilization
The table shows various measures of joblessness for the U.S. economy. The data are for January 2013.

Source: U.S. Department of Labor.

Measure and Description		Rate
U-1	Persons unemployed 15 weeks or longer, as a percent of the civilian labor force (includes only very long-term unemployed)	4.2%
U-2	Job losers and persons who have completed temporary jobs, as a percent of the civilian labor force (excludes job leavers)	4.3
U-3	Total unemployed, as a percent of the civilian labor force (official unemployment rate)	7.9
U-4	Total unemployed, plus discouraged workers, as a percent of the civilian labor force plus discouraged workers	8.4
U-5	Total unemployed plus all marginally attached workers, as a percent of the civilian labor force plus all marginally attached workers	9.3
U-6	Total unemployed, plus all marginally attached workers, plus total employed part-time for economic reasons, as a percent of the civilian labor force plus all marginally attached workers	14.4

Note: The Bureau of Labor Statistics defines terms as follows:
- *Marginally attached workers* are persons who currently are neither working nor looking for work but indicate that they want and are available for a job and have looked for work sometime in the recent past.
- *Discouraged workers* are marginally attached workers who have given a job-market-related reason for not currently looking for a job.
- *Persons employed part-time for economic reasons* are those who want and are available for full-time work but have had to settle for a part-time schedule.

28-1c How Long Are the Unemployed without Work?

In judging how serious the problem of unemployment is, one question to consider is whether unemployment is typically a short-term or long-term condition. If unemployment is short-term, one might conclude that it is not a big problem. Workers may require a few weeks between jobs to find the openings that best suit their tastes and skills. Yet if unemployment is long-term, one might conclude that it is a serious problem. Workers unemployed for many months are more likely to suffer economic and psychological hardship.

Because the duration of unemployment can affect our view about how big a problem unemployment is, economists have devoted much energy to studying data on the duration of unemployment spells. In this work, they have uncovered a result that is important, subtle, and seemingly contradictory: *Most spells of unemployment are short, and most unemployment observed at any given time is long-term.*

To see how this statement can be true, consider an example. Suppose that you visited the government's unemployment office every week for a year to survey the unemployed. Each week you find that there are four unemployed workers. Three of these workers are the same individuals for the whole year, while the fourth person changes every week. Based on this experience, would you say that unemployment is typically short-term or long-term?

Some simple calculations help answer this question. In this example, you meet a total of 55 unemployed people over the course of a year; 52 of them are unemployed for one week, and 3 are unemployed for the full year. This means that 52/55, or 95 percent, of unemployment spells end in one week. Yet whenever you walk into the unemployment office, three of the four people you meet will be unemployed for the entire year. So, even though 95 percent of unemployment spells end in one week, 75 percent of the unemployment observed at any moment is attributable to those individuals who are unemployed for a full year. In this example, as in the world, most spells of unemployment are short, and most unemployment observed at any given time is long-term.

This subtle conclusion implies that economists and policymakers must be careful when interpreting data on unemployment and when designing policies to help the unemployed. Most people who become unemployed will soon find jobs. Yet most of the economy's unemployment problem is attributable to the relatively few workers who are jobless for long periods of time.

28-1d Why Are There Always Some People Unemployed?

We have discussed how the government measures the amount of unemployment, the problems that arise in interpreting unemployment statistics, and the findings of labor economists on the duration of unemployment. You should now have a good idea about what unemployment is.

This discussion, however, has not explained why economies experience unemployment. In most markets in the economy, prices adjust to bring quantity supplied and quantity demanded into balance. In an ideal labor market, wages would adjust to balance the quantity of labor supplied and the quantity of labor demanded. This adjustment of wages would ensure that all workers are always fully employed.

Of course, reality does not resemble this ideal. There are always some workers without jobs, even when the overall economy is doing well. In other words, the unemployment rate never falls to zero; instead, it fluctuates around the natural rate of unemployment. To understand this natural rate, the remaining sections of this chapter examine the reasons actual labor markets depart from the ideal of full employment.

The Jobs Number

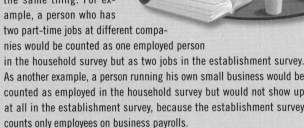

When the Bureau of Labor Statistics announces the unemployment rate at the beginning of every month, it also announces the number of jobs the economy has gained or lost. As an indicator of short-run economic trends, the jobs number gets as much attention as the unemployment rate.

Where does the jobs number come from? You might guess that it comes from the same survey of 60,000 households that yields the unemployment rate. And indeed the household survey does produce data on total employment. The jobs number that gets the most attention, however, comes from a separate survey of 160,000 business establishments, which have over 40 million workers on their payrolls. The results from the establishment survey are announced at the same time as the results from the household survey.

Both surveys yield information about total employment, but the results are not always the same. One reason is that the establishment survey has a larger sample, which makes it more reliable. Another reason is that the surveys are not measuring exactly the same thing. For example, a person who has two part-time jobs at different companies would be counted as one employed person in the household survey but as two jobs in the establishment survey. As another example, a person running his own small business would be counted as employed in the household survey but would not show up at all in the establishment survey, because the establishment survey counts only employees on business payrolls.

The establishment survey is closely watched for its data on jobs, but it says nothing about unemployment. To measure the number of unemployed, we need to know how many people without jobs are trying to find them. The household survey is the only source of that information.

To preview our conclusions, we will find that there are four ways to explain unemployment in the long run. The first explanation is that it takes time for workers to search for the jobs that are best suited for them. The unemployment that results from the process of matching workers and jobs is sometimes called **frictional unemployment**, and it is often thought to explain relatively short spells of unemployment.

The next three explanations for unemployment suggest that the number of jobs available in some labor markets may be insufficient to give a job to everyone who wants one. This occurs when the quantity of labor supplied exceeds the quantity demanded. Unemployment of this sort is sometimes called **structural unemployment**, and it is often thought to explain longer spells of unemployment. As we will see, this kind of unemployment results when wages are, for some reason, set above the level that brings supply and demand into equilibrium. We will examine three possible reasons for an above-equilibrium wage: minimum-wage laws, unions, and efficiency wages.

frictional unemployment
unemployment that results because it takes time for workers to search for the jobs that best suit their tastes and skills

structural unemployment
unemployment that results because the number of jobs available in some labor markets is insufficient to provide a job for everyone who wants one

Quick Quiz *How is the unemployment rate measured? • How might the unemployment rate overstate the amount of joblessness? How might it understate the amount of joblessness?*

28-2 Job Search

One reason economies always experience some unemployment is job search. **Job search** is the process of matching workers with appropriate jobs. If all workers and all jobs were the same, so that all workers were equally well suited for all jobs, job search would not be a problem. Laid-off workers would quickly find new jobs that were well suited for them. But in fact, workers differ in their tastes and skills, jobs differ in their attributes, and information about job candidates and job vacancies is disseminated slowly among the many firms and households in the economy.

job search
the process by which workers find appropriate jobs given their tastes and skills

28-2a Why Some Frictional Unemployment Is Inevitable

Frictional unemployment is often the result of changes in the demand for labor among different firms. When consumers decide that they prefer Dell to Apple computers, Dell increases employment and Apple lays off workers. The former Apple workers must now search for new jobs, and Dell must decide which new workers to hire for the various jobs that have opened up. The result of this transition is a period of unemployment.

Similarly, because different regions of the country produce different goods, employment can rise in one region while falling in another. Consider, for instance, what happens when the world price of oil falls. Oil-producing firms in Alaska respond to the lower price by cutting back on production and employment. At the same time, cheaper gasoline stimulates car sales, so auto-producing firms in Michigan raise production and employment. Just the opposite happens when the world price of oil rises. Changes in the composition of demand among industries or regions are called *sectoral shifts*. Because it takes time for workers to search for jobs in the new sectors, sectoral shifts temporarily cause unemployment.

Frictional unemployment is inevitable simply because the economy is always changing. A century ago, the four industries with the largest employment in the United States were cotton goods, woolen goods, men's clothing, and lumber. Today, the four largest industries are autos, aircraft, communications, and electrical components. As this transition took place, jobs were created in some firms and destroyed in others. The result of this process has been higher productivity and higher living standards. But along the way, workers in declining industries found themselves out of work and searching for new jobs.

Data show that at least 10 percent of U.S. manufacturing jobs are destroyed every year. In addition, more than 3 percent of workers leave their jobs in a typical month, sometimes because they realize that the jobs are not a good match for their tastes and skills. Many of these workers, especially younger ones, find new jobs at higher wages. This churning of the labor force is normal in a well-functioning and dynamic market economy, but the result is some amount of frictional unemployment.

28-2b Public Policy and Job Search

Even if some frictional unemployment is inevitable, the precise amount is not. The faster information spreads about job openings and worker availability, the more rapidly the economy can match workers and firms. The Internet, for instance, may help facilitate job search and reduce frictional unemployment. In addition, public policy may play a role. If policy can reduce the time it takes unemployed workers to find new jobs, it can reduce the economy's natural rate of unemployment.

Government programs try to facilitate job search in various ways. One way is through government-run employment agencies, which give out information about job vacancies. Another way is through public training programs, which aim to ease workers' transition from declining to growing industries and to help disadvantaged groups escape poverty. Advocates of these programs believe that they make the economy operate more efficiently by keeping the labor force more fully employed and that they reduce the inequities inherent in a constantly changing market economy.

Critics of these programs question whether the government should get involved with the process of job search. They argue that it is better to let the private market match workers and jobs. In fact, most job search in our economy takes place without intervention by the government. Newspaper ads, Internet job sites, college placement offices, headhunters, and word of mouth all help spread information about job openings and job candidates. Similarly, much worker education is done privately, either through schools or through on-the-job training. These critics contend that the government is no better—and most likely worse—at disseminating the right information to the right workers and deciding what kinds of worker training would be most valuable. They claim that these decisions are best made privately by workers and employers.

28-2c Unemployment Insurance

One government program that increases the amount of frictional unemployment, without intending to do so, is **unemployment insurance**. This program is designed to offer workers partial protection against job loss. The unemployed who quit their jobs, were fired for cause, or just entered the labor force are not eligible. Benefits are paid only to the unemployed who were laid off because their previous employers no longer needed their skills. The terms of the program vary over time and across states, but a typical worker covered by unemployment insurance in the United States receives 50 percent of his former wages for 26 weeks.

While unemployment insurance reduces the hardship of unemployment, it also increases the amount of unemployment. The explanation is based on one of the *Ten Principles of Economics* in Chapter 1: People respond to incentives. Because unemployment benefits stop when a worker takes a new job, the unemployed devote less effort to job search and are more likely to turn down unattractive job offers. In addition, because unemployment insurance makes unemployment less onerous, workers are less likely to seek guarantees of job security when they negotiate with employers over the terms of employment.

Many studies by labor economists have examined the incentive effects of unemployment insurance. One study examined an experiment run by the state of Illinois in 1985. When unemployed workers applied to collect unemployment insurance benefits, the state randomly selected some of them and offered each a $500 bonus if they found new jobs within 11 weeks. This group was then compared to a control group not offered the incentive. The average spell of unemployment for the group offered the bonus was 7 percent shorter than the average spell for the control group. This experiment shows that the design of the unemployment insurance system influences the effort that the unemployed devote to job search.

Several other studies examined search effort by following a group of workers over time. Unemployment insurance benefits, rather than lasting forever, usually run out after 6 months or 1 year. These studies found that when the unemployed become ineligible for benefits, the probability of their finding a new job rises markedly. Thus, receiving unemployment insurance benefits does reduce the search effort of the unemployed.

Even though unemployment insurance reduces search effort and raises unemployment, we should not necessarily conclude that the policy is bad. The program does achieve its primary goal of reducing the income uncertainty that workers face. In addition, when workers turn down unattractive job offers, they have the opportunity to look for jobs that better suit their tastes and skills. Some economists argue that unemployment insurance improves the ability of the economy to match each worker with the most appropriate job.

The study of unemployment insurance shows that the unemployment rate is an imperfect measure of a nation's overall level of economic well-being. Most economists agree that eliminating unemployment insurance would reduce the amount of unemployment in the economy. Yet economists disagree on whether economic well-being would be enhanced or diminished by this change in policy.

unemployment insurance *a government program that partially protects workers' incomes when they become unemployed*

Quick Quiz *How would an increase in the world price of oil affect the amount of frictional unemployment? Is this unemployment undesirable? What public policies might affect the amount of unemployment caused by this price change?*

Why Has Employment Declined?

In this opinion column, an economist argues that rising government benefits are one reason for recent declines in the employment–population ratio.

The Wages of Unemployment

By Richard Vedder

From the mid-17th century to the late 20th century, the American economy grew roughly 3.5% a year. That growth rate has since declined significantly. When the final figures are in for 2012, the annual rate of real output growth for the first dozen years of this century is likely to be about 1.81%.

What accounts for the slowdown? An important part of the answer is simple: Americans aren't working as much today. And this trend reflects more than the recession and sluggish economy of the past few years.

The national income accounts suggest that about 70% of U.S. output is attributable to the labor of human beings. Yet there has been a decline in the proportion of working-age Americans who are employed.

In recent decades there was a steady rise in the employment-to-population ratio: For every 100 working-age Americans, there were

eight more workers in 2000 than in 1960. The increase entirely reflects higher female participation in the labor force. Yet in the years since 2000, more than two-thirds of that increase in working-age population employed was erased.

The decline matters more than you may suppose. If today the country had the same proportion of persons of working age employed as it did in 2000, the U.S. would have almost 14 million more people contributing to the economy. Even assuming that these additional workers would be 25% less productive on average than the existing labor force, U.S. gross domestic product would still be more than 5% higher ($800 billion, or about $2,600 more per person) than it actually is. The annual growth rate of GDP would be 2.2%, not 1.81%. The retreat from working, in short, has had a real impact.

Why are Americans working less? While there are a number of factors, the phenomenon is due mainly to a variety of public policies that have reduced the incentives to be employed. These policies include:

• *Food stamps.* Above all else, people work to eat. If the government provides food, then the imperative to work is severely reduced. Since the food-stamp program's beginning in the 1960s, it has grown considerably, but especially so in the 21st century: There are over 30 million more Americans receiving food stamps today than in 2000.

The sharp rise in food-stamp beneficiaries predated the financial crisis of 2008: From 2000 to 2007, the number of beneficiaries rose from 17.1 million to 26.3 million, according to the Department of Agriculture. That number has leaped to 47.5 million in October 2012. The average benefit per person jumped in 2009 from $102 to $125 per month.

To be sure, we would expect the number of people on food stamps to increase with rising unemployment, poverty and falling incomes in late 2008 extending into 2009 and perhaps even into 2010 (even though the recession

28-3 Minimum-Wage Laws

Having seen how frictional unemployment results from the process of matching workers and jobs, let's now examine how structural unemployment results when the number of jobs is insufficient for the number of workers.

To understand structural unemployment, we begin by reviewing how minimum-wage laws can cause unemployment. Although minimum wages are not the predominant reason for unemployment in our economy, they have an important effect on certain groups with particularly high unemployment rates. Moreover, the analysis of minimum wages is a natural place to start because, as we will see, it can be used to understand some of the other reasons for structural unemployment.

Figure 4 reviews the basic economics of a minimum wage. When a minimum-wage law forces the wage to remain above the level that balances supply and

was officially over in late 2009). But more is going on here.

Compare 2010 with October 2012, the last month for which food-stamp data have been reported. The unemployment rate fell to 7.8% from 9.6%, and real GDP was rising steadily if not vigorously. Food-stamp usage should have peaked and probably even begun to decline. Yet the number of recipients rose by 7,223,000. In a period of falling unemployment and rising output, the number of food-stamp recipients grew nearly 10,000 a day. Congress should find out why.

• *Social Security disability payments.* The health of Americans has improved, and the decline in the number of relatively dangerous industrial production and mining jobs should have led to a smaller proportion of Americans unable to work because of disability. Yet the opposite is the case.

Barely three million Americans received work-related disability checks from Social Security in 1990, a number that had changed only modestly in the preceding decade or two. Since then, the number of people drawing disability checks has soared, passing five million by 2000, 6.5 million by 2005, and rising to nearly 8.6 million today. In a series of papers, David Autor of MIT has shown that the disability program is ineffective, inefficient, and growing at an unsustainable rate. And

news media have reported cases of rampant fraud.

• *Pell grants.* Paying people to go to college instead of to work is traditionally justified on the grounds that higher education builds "human capital" that is vital for the country's economic future. But a study Christopher Denhart, Jonathan Robe and I did for the Center for College Affordability and Productivity shows that nearly half of four-year college graduates today work in jobs that the Labor Department has determined do not require a college degree. For example, over one million "retail sales persons" and 115,000 "janitors and cleaners" are college graduates.

In 2000, fewer than 3.9 million young men and women received Pell Grant awards to attend college. The number rose one-third, to 5.2 million by 2005, and increased a million more by 2008. In the next three years, however, the number grew over 50%, to an estimated 9.7 million. That is nearly six million more than a decade earlier. The result is fewer people in the work force. Meanwhile the mismatch grows between the number of college graduates and the jobs that require a college education.

• *Extended unemployment benefits.* Since the 1930s, the unemployment-insurance system has been designed to lend a short-term, temporary helping hand to folks losing their jobs, allowing them some breathing room to look for new positions. Yet the traditional

26-week benefit has been continuously extended over the past four years—many persons out of work a year or more are still receiving benefits.

True enough, the economy isn't growing very much. But if you pay people to stay at home, many will do so rather than seek employment or accept jobs where the pay doesn't meet their expectations.

These government programs are not the only players in this game. For example, a more worker-oriented immigration policy in recent decades would have measurably raised the rate of economic growth and increased the employment-to-population ratio. Taxes are part of the story too: Today's higher marginal tax rates on work-related income could well lead to further reductions in work effort by those taxed, as well as to slower economic growth.

Most Americans recognize the need to reduce government spending to rein in the national debt. But there is another reason to cut government spending for specific programs: If more people have less incentive to stay out of the work force, they might seek jobs and help spur economic growth.

Mr. Vedder is professor emeritus of economics at Ohio University.

demand, it raises the quantity of labor supplied and reduces the quantity of labor demanded compared to the equilibrium level. There is a surplus of labor. Because there are more workers willing to work than there are jobs, some workers are unemployed.

While minimum-wage laws are one reason unemployment exists in the U.S. economy, they do not affect everyone. The vast majority of workers have wages well above the legal minimum, so the law does not prevent most wages from adjusting to balance supply and demand. Minimum-wage laws matter most for the least skilled and least experienced members of the labor force, such as teenagers. Their equilibrium wages tend to be low and, therefore, are more likely to fall below the legal minimum. It is only among these workers that minimum-wage laws explain the existence of unemployment.

Figure 4 is drawn to show the effects of a minimum-wage law, but it also illustrates a more general lesson: *If the wage is kept above the equilibrium level for any*

FIGURE 4

Unemployment from a Wage above the Equilibrium Level
In this labor market, the wage at which supply and demand balance is W_E. At this equilibrium wage, the quantity of labor supplied and the quantity of labor demanded both equal L_E. By contrast, if the wage is forced to remain above the equilibrium level, perhaps because of a minimum-wage law, the quantity of labor supplied rises to L_S and the quantity of labor demanded falls to L_D. The resulting surplus of labor, $L_S - L_D$, represents unemployment.

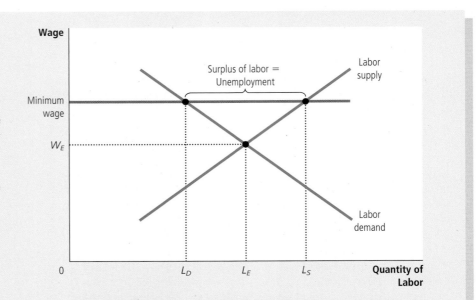

reason, the result is unemployment. Minimum-wage laws are just one reason wages may be "too high." In the remaining two sections of this chapter, we consider two other reasons wages may be kept above the equilibrium level: unions and efficiency wages. The basic economics of unemployment in these cases is the same as that shown in Figure 4, but these explanations of unemployment can apply to many more of the economy's workers.

At this point, however, we should stop and notice that the structural unemployment that arises from an above-equilibrium wage is, in an important sense, different from the frictional unemployment that arises from the process of job search. The need for job search is not due to the failure of wages to balance labor supply and labor demand. When job search is the explanation for unemployment, workers are *searching* for the jobs that best suit their tastes and skills. By contrast, when the wage is above the equilibrium level, the quantity of labor supplied exceeds the quantity of labor demanded, and workers are unemployed because they are *waiting* for jobs to open up.

Quick Quiz   *Draw the supply curve and the demand curve for a labor market in which the wage is fixed above the equilibrium level. Show the quantity of labor supplied, the quantity demanded, and the amount of unemployment.*

28-4 Unions and Collective Bargaining

union

a worker association that bargains with employers over wages, benefits, and working conditions

A **union** is a worker association that bargains with employers over wages, benefits, and working conditions. Only 11 percent of U.S. workers now belong to unions, but unions played a much larger role in the U.S. labor market in the past. In the 1940s and 1950s, when union membership was at its peak, about a third of the U.S. labor force was unionized.

Moreover, for a variety of historical reasons, unions continue to play a large role in many European countries. In Belgium, Norway, and Sweden, for instance, more than half of workers belong to unions. In France and Germany, a majority

Who Earns the Minimum Wage?

In 2012, the Department of Labor released a study of which workers reported earnings at or below the minimum wage in 2011, when the minimum wage was $7.25 per hour. (A reported wage below the minimum is possible because some workers are exempt from the statute, because enforcement is imperfect, and because some workers round down when reporting their wages on surveys.) Here is a summary of the findings:

- Of those workers paid an hourly rate, about 4 percent of men and 6 percent of women reported wages at or below the prevailing federal minimum.
- Minimum-wage workers tend to be young. About half of all hourly paid workers earning the minimum wage or less were under age 25, and about one-fourth were age 16–19. Among employed teenagers, 23 percent earned the minimum wage or less, compared with 3 percent of workers age 25 and older.
- Minimum-wage workers tend to be less educated. Among hourly paid workers age 16 and older, about 11 percent of those without a high school diploma earned the minimum wage or less, compared with about 5 percent of those who earned a high school diploma (but did not attend college) and about 2 percent for those who had obtained a college degree.

- Minimum-wage workers are more likely to be working part-time. Among part-time workers (those who usually work less than 35 hours per week), 13 percent were paid the minimum wage or less, compared to 2 percent of full-time workers.
- The industry with the highest proportion of workers with reported hourly wages at or below the minimum wage was leisure and hospitality (22 percent). About one-half of all workers paid at or below the minimum wage were employed in this industry, primarily in food services and drinking establishments. For many of these workers, tips supplement the hourly wages received.
- The proportion of hourly paid workers earning the prevailing federal minimum wage or less has changed substantially over time. It trended downward from 13 percent in 1979, when data collection first began on a regular basis, to 2 percent in 2006. It then increased to 5 percent in 2011. This recent increase is in part attributable to a legislated increase in the minimum wage from $5.15 per hour in 2006 to $7.25 per hour in 2011. ◢

of workers have wages set by collective bargaining by law, even though only some of these workers are themselves union members. In these cases, wages are not determined by the equilibrium of supply and demand in competitive labor markets.

28-4a The Economics of Unions

A union is a type of cartel. Like any cartel, a union is a group of sellers acting together in the hope of exerting their joint market power. Most workers in the U.S. economy discuss their wages, benefits, and working conditions with their employers as individuals. By contrast, workers in a union do so as a group. The process by which unions and firms agree on the terms of employment is called **collective bargaining**.

When a union bargains with a firm, it asks for higher wages, better benefits, and better working conditions than the firm would offer in the absence of a union. If the union and the firm do not reach agreement, the union can organize a withdrawal of labor from the firm, called a **strike**. Because a strike reduces production, sales, and profit, a firm facing a strike threat is likely to agree to pay higher wages than it otherwise would. Economists who study the effects of unions typically find that union workers earn about 10 to 20 percent more than similar workers who do not belong to unions.

When a union raises the wage above the equilibrium level, it raises the quantity of labor supplied and reduces the quantity of labor demanded, resulting in

collective bargaining
the process by which unions and firms agree on the terms of employment

strike
the organized withdrawal of labor from a firm by a union

unemployment. Workers who remain employed at the higher wage are better off, but those who were previously employed and are now unemployed are worse off. Indeed, unions are often thought to cause conflict between different groups of workers—between the *insiders* who benefit from high union wages and the *outsiders* who do not get the union jobs.

The outsiders can respond to their status in one of two ways. Some of them remain unemployed and wait for the chance to become insiders and earn the high union wage. Others take jobs in firms that are not unionized. Thus, when unions raise wages in one part of the economy, the supply of labor increases in other parts of the economy. This increase in labor supply, in turn, reduces wages in industries that are not unionized. In other words, workers in unions reap the benefit of collective bargaining, while workers not in unions bear some of the cost.

The role of unions in the economy depends in part on the laws that govern union organization and collective bargaining. Normally, explicit agreements among members of a cartel are illegal. When firms selling similar products agree to set high prices, the agreement is considered a "conspiracy in restraint of trade," and the government prosecutes the firms in civil and criminal court for violating the antitrust laws. By contrast, unions are exempt from these laws. The policymakers who wrote the antitrust laws believed that workers needed greater market power as they bargained with employers. Indeed, various laws are designed to encourage the formation of unions. In particular, the Wagner Act of 1935 prevents employers from interfering when workers try to organize unions and requires employers to bargain with unions in good faith. The National Labor Relations Board (NLRB) is the government agency that enforces workers' right to unionize.

Legislation affecting the market power of unions is a perennial topic of political debate. State lawmakers sometimes debate *right-to-work laws,* which give workers in a unionized firm the right to choose whether to join the union. In the absence of such laws, unions can insist during collective bargaining that firms make union membership a requirement for employment. At times, lawmakers in Washington have debated a proposed law that would prevent firms from hiring permanent replacements for workers who are on strike. This law would make strikes more costly for firms, thereby increasing the market power of unions. These and similar policy decisions will help determine the future of the union movement.

28-4b Are Unions Good or Bad for the Economy?

Economists disagree about whether unions are good or bad for the economy as a whole. Let's consider both sides of the debate.

Critics argue that unions are merely a type of cartel. When unions raise wages above the level that would prevail in competitive markets, they reduce the quantity of labor demanded, cause some workers to be unemployed, and reduce the wages in the rest of the economy. The resulting allocation of labor is, critics argue, both inefficient and inequitable. It is inefficient because high union wages reduce employment in unionized firms below the efficient, competitive level. It is inequitable because some workers benefit at the expense of other workers.

Advocates contend that unions are a necessary antidote to the market power of the firms that hire workers. The extreme case of this market power is the "company town," where a single firm does most of the hiring in a geographical region. In a company town, if workers do not accept the wages and working

"Gentlemen, nothing stands in the way of a final accord except that management wants profit maximization and the union wants more moola."

conditions that the firm offers, they have little choice but to move or stop working. In the absence of a union, therefore, the firm could use its market power to pay lower wages and offer worse working conditions than would prevail if it had to compete with other firms for the same workers. In this case, a union may balance the firm's market power and protect the workers from being at the mercy of the firm's owners.

Advocates of unions also claim that unions are important for helping firms respond efficiently to workers' concerns. Whenever a worker takes a job, the worker and the firm must agree on many attributes of the job in addition to the wage: hours of work, overtime, vacations, sick leave, health benefits, promotion schedules, job security, and so on. By representing workers' views on these issues, unions allow firms to provide the right mix of job attributes. Even if unions have the adverse effect of pushing wages above the equilibrium level and causing unemployment, they have the benefit of helping firms keep a happy and productive workforce.

In the end, there is no consensus among economists about whether unions are good or bad for the economy. Like many institutions, their influence is probably beneficial in some circumstances and adverse in others.

Quick Quiz *How does a union in the auto industry affect wages and employment at General Motors and Ford? How does it affect wages and employment in other industries?*

28-5 The Theory of Efficiency Wages

A fourth reason economies always experience some unemployment—in addition to job search, minimum-wage laws, and unions—is suggested by the theory of **efficiency wages**. According to this theory, firms operate more efficiently if wages are above the equilibrium level. Therefore, it may be profitable for firms to keep wages high even in the presence of a surplus of labor.

efficiency wages
above-equilibrium wages paid by firms to increase worker productivity

In some ways, the unemployment that arises from efficiency wages is similar to the unemployment that arises from minimum-wage laws and unions. In all three cases, unemployment is the result of wages above the level that balances the quantity of labor supplied and the quantity of labor demanded. Yet there is also an important difference. Minimum-wage laws and unions prevent firms from lowering wages in the presence of a surplus of workers. Efficiency-wage theory states that such a constraint on firms is unnecessary in many cases because firms may be better off keeping wages above the equilibrium level.

Why should firms want to keep wages high? This decision may seem odd at first, for wages are a large part of firms' costs. Normally, we expect profit-maximizing firms to want to keep costs—and therefore wages—as low as possible. The novel insight of efficiency-wage theory is that paying high wages might be profitable because they might raise the efficiency of a firm's workers.

There are several types of efficiency-wage theory. Each type suggests a different explanation for why firms may want to pay high wages. Let's now consider four of these types.

28-5a Worker Health

The first and simplest type of efficiency-wage theory emphasizes the link between wages and worker health. Better-paid workers eat a more nutritious diet, and workers who eat a better diet are healthier and more productive.

A firm may find it more profitable to pay high wages and have healthy, productive workers than to pay lower wages and have less healthy, less productive workers.

This type of efficiency-wage theory can be relevant for explaining unemployment in less developed countries where inadequate nutrition can be a problem. In these countries, firms may fear that cutting wages would, in fact, adversely influence their workers' health and productivity. In other words, nutrition concerns may explain why firms maintain above-equilibrium wages despite a surplus of labor. Worker health concerns are far less relevant for firms in rich countries such as the United States, where the equilibrium wages for most workers are well above the level needed for an adequate diet.

28-5b Worker Turnover

A second type of efficiency-wage theory emphasizes the link between wages and worker turnover. Workers quit jobs for many reasons: to take jobs in other firms, to move to other parts of the country, to leave the labor force, and so on. The frequency with which they quit depends on the entire set of incentives they face, including the benefits of leaving and the benefits of staying. The more a firm pays its workers, the less often its workers will choose to leave. Thus, a firm can reduce turnover among its workers by paying them a high wage.

Why do firms care about turnover? The reason is that it is costly for firms to hire and train new workers. Moreover, even after they are trained, newly hired workers are not as productive as experienced workers. Firms with higher turnover, therefore, will tend to have higher production costs. Firms may find it profitable to pay wages above the equilibrium level to reduce worker turnover.

28-5c Worker Quality

A third type of efficiency-wage theory emphasizes the link between wages and worker quality. All firms want workers who are talented, and they try to pick the best applicants to fill job openings. But because firms cannot perfectly gauge the quality of applicants, hiring has a degree of randomness to it. When a firm pays a high wage, it attracts a better pool of workers to apply for its jobs and thereby increases the quality of its workforce. If the firm responded to a surplus of labor by reducing the wage, the most competent applicants—who are more likely to have better alternative opportunities than less competent applicants—may choose not to apply. If this influence of the wage on worker quality is strong enough, it may be profitable for the firm to pay a wage above the level that balances supply and demand.

28-5d Worker Effort

A fourth and final type of efficiency-wage theory emphasizes the link between wages and worker effort. In many jobs, workers have some discretion over how hard to work. As a result, firms monitor the efforts of their workers, and workers caught shirking their responsibilities are fired. But not all shirkers are caught immediately because monitoring workers is costly and imperfect. A firm in such a circumstance is always looking for ways to deter shirking.

One solution is paying wages above the equilibrium level. High wages make workers more eager to keep their jobs and, thereby, give workers an incentive to put forward their best effort. If the wage were at the level that balanced supply and demand, workers would have less reason to work hard because if they were fired, they could quickly find new jobs at the same wage. Therefore, firms raise wages above the equilibrium level, providing an incentive for workers not to shirk their responsibilities.

case study

Henry Ford and the Very Generous $5-a-Day Wage

Henry Ford was an industrial visionary. As founder of the Ford Motor Company, he was responsible for introducing modern techniques of production. Rather than building cars with small teams of skilled craftsmen, Ford built cars on assembly lines in which unskilled workers were taught to perform the same simple tasks over and over again. The output of this assembly process was the Model T Ford, one of the most famous early automobiles.

In 1914, Ford introduced another innovation: the $5 workday. This might not seem like much today, but back then $5 was about twice the going wage. It was also far above the wage that balanced supply and demand. When the new $5-a-day wage was announced, long lines of job seekers formed outside the Ford factories. The number of workers willing to work at this wage far exceeded the number of workers Ford needed.

Ford's high-wage policy had many of the effects predicted by efficiency-wage theory. Turnover fell, absenteeism fell, and productivity rose. Workers were so much more efficient that Ford's production costs were lower despite higher wages. Thus, paying a wage above the equilibrium level was profitable for the firm. An historian of the early Ford Motor Company wrote, "Ford and his associates freely declared on many occasions that the high-wage policy turned out to be good business. By this they meant that it had improved the discipline of the workers, given them a more loyal interest in the institution, and raised their personal efficiency." Henry Ford himself called the $5-a-day wage "one of the finest cost-cutting moves we ever made."

Why did it take Henry Ford to introduce this efficiency wage? Why were other firms not already taking advantage of this seemingly profitable business strategy? According to some analysts, Ford's decision was closely linked to his use of the assembly line. Workers organized in an assembly line are highly interdependent. If one worker is absent or works slowly, other workers are less able to complete their own tasks. Thus, while assembly lines made production more efficient, they also raised the importance of low worker turnover, high worker effort, and high worker quality. As a result, paying efficiency wages may have been a better strategy for the Ford Motor Company than for other businesses at the time. ◢

Quick Quiz *Give four explanations for why firms might find it profitable to pay wages above the level that balances quantity of labor supplied and quantity of labor demanded.*

28-6 Conclusion

In this chapter, we discussed the measurement of unemployment and the reasons economies always experience some degree of unemployment. We have seen how job search, minimum-wage laws, unions, and efficiency wages can all help explain why some workers do not have jobs. Which of these four explanations for the natural rate of unemployment are the most important for the U.S. economy and other economies around the world? Unfortunately, there is no easy way to tell. Economists differ in which of these explanations of unemployment they consider most important.

The analysis of this chapter yields an important lesson: Although the economy will always have some unemployment, its natural rate does change over time. Many events and policies can alter the amount of unemployment the economy typically experiences. As the information revolution changes the process of job search, as Congress adjusts the minimum wage, as workers form or quit unions, and as firms change their reliance on efficiency wages, the natural rate of unemployment evolves. Unemployment is not a simple problem with a simple solution. But how we choose to organize our society can profoundly influence how prevalent a problem it is.

Summary

- The unemployment rate is the percentage of those who would like to work who do not have jobs. The Bureau of Labor Statistics calculates this statistic monthly based on a survey of thousands of households.

- The unemployment rate is an imperfect measure of joblessness. Some people who call themselves unemployed may actually not want to work, and some people who would like to work have left the labor force after an unsuccessful search and therefore are not counted as unemployed.

- In the U.S. economy, most people who become unemployed find work within a short period of time. Nonetheless, most unemployment observed at any given time is attributable to the few people who are unemployed for long periods of time.

- One reason for unemployment is the time it takes workers to search for jobs that best suit their tastes and skills. This frictional unemployment is increased

as a result of unemployment insurance, a government policy designed to protect workers' incomes.

- A second reason our economy always has some unemployment is minimum-wage laws. By raising the wage of unskilled and inexperienced workers above the equilibrium level, minimum-wage laws raise the quantity of labor supplied and reduce the quantity demanded. The resulting surplus of labor represents unemployment.

- A third reason for unemployment is the market power of unions. When unions push the wages in unionized industries above the equilibrium level, they create a surplus of labor.

- A fourth reason for unemployment is suggested by the theory of efficiency wages. According to this theory, firms find it profitable to pay wages above the equilibrium level. High wages can improve worker health, lower worker turnover, raise worker quality, and increase worker effort.

Key Concepts

labor force, *p. 587*
unemployment rate, *p. 587*
labor-force participation
  rate, *p. 587*
natural rate of unemployment, *p. 588*

cyclical unemployment, *p. 589*
discouraged workers, *p. 591*
frictional unemployment, *p. 593*
structural unemployment, *p. 593*
job search, *p. 593*

unemployment insurance, *p. 595*
union, *p. 598*
collective bargaining, *p. 599*
strike, *p. 599*
efficiency wages, *p. 601*

Questions for Review

1. What are the three categories into which the Bureau of Labor Statistics divides everyone? How does the BLS compute the labor force, the unemployment rate, and the labor-force participation rate?

2. Is unemployment typically short-term or long-term? Explain.

3. Why is frictional unemployment inevitable? How might the government reduce the amount of frictional unemployment?

4. Are minimum-wage laws a better explanation for structural unemployment among teenagers or among college graduates? Why?

5. How do unions affect the natural rate of unemployment?

6. What claims do advocates of unions make to argue that unions are good for the economy?

7. Explain four ways in which a firm might increase its profits by raising the wages it pays.

Quick Check Multiple Choice

1. The population of Ectenia is 100 people: 40 work full-time, 20 work half-time but would prefer to work full-time, 10 are looking for a job, 10 would like to work but are so discouraged they have given up looking, 10 are not interested in working because they are full-time students, and 10 are retired. What is the number of unemployed?
   a. 10
   b. 20
   c. 30
   d. 40

2. Using the numbers in the preceding question, what is the size of Ectenia's labor force?
   a. 50
   b. 60
   c. 70
   d. 80

3. The main policy goal of the unemployment insurance system is to reduce the
   a. search effort of the unemployed.
   b. income uncertainty that workers face.
   c. role of unions in wage setting.
   d. amount of frictional unemployment.

4. According to the most recent data, among workers who are paid at an hourly rate, about _____ percent have jobs that pay at or below the minimum wage.
   a. 2
   b. 5
   c. 15
   d. 40

5. Unionized workers are paid about _____ percent more than similar nonunion workers.
   a. 2
   b. 5
   c. 15
   d. 40

6. According to the theory of efficiency wages,
   a. firms may find it profitable to pay above-equilibrium wages.
   b. an excess supply of labor puts downward pressure on wages.
   c. sectoral shifts are the main source of frictional unemployment.
   d. right-to-work laws reduce the bargaining power of unions.

Problems and Applications

1. The Bureau of Labor Statistics announced that in January 2013, of all adult Americans, 143,322,000 were employed, 12,332,000 were unemployed, and 89,008,000 were not in the labor force. Use this information to calculate:
   a. the adult population
   b. the labor force
   c. the labor-force participation rate
   d. the unemployment rate

2. Go to the website of the Bureau of Labor Statistics (http://www.bls.gov). What is the national unemployment rate right now? Find the unemployment rate for the demographic group that best fits a description of you (for example, based on age, sex, and race). Is it higher or lower than the national average? Why do you think this is so?

3. Between January 2010 and January 2013, U.S. employment increased by 4.9 million workers, but the number of unemployed workers declined by only 2.7 million. How are these numbers consistent with each other? Why might one expect a reduction in the number of people counted as unemployed to be smaller than the increase in the number of people employed?

4. Economists use labor-market data to evaluate how well an economy is using its most valuable resource—its people. Two closely watched statistics are the unemployment rate and the employment–population ratio (calculated as the percentage of the adult population that is employed). Explain what happens to each of these in the following scenarios. In your opinion, which statistic is the more meaningful gauge of how well the economy is doing?
   a. An auto company goes bankrupt and lays off its workers, who immediately start looking for new jobs.
   b. After an unsuccessful search, some of the laid-off workers quit looking for new jobs.
   c. Numerous students graduate from college but cannot find work.
   d. Numerous students graduate from college and immediately begin new jobs.
   e. A stock market boom induces newly enriched 60-year-old workers to take early retirement.
   f. Advances in healthcare prolong the life of many retirees.

5. Are the following workers more likely to experience short-term or long-term unemployment? Explain.
   a. a construction worker laid off because of bad weather
   b. a manufacturing worker who loses his job at a plant in an isolated area
   c. a stagecoach-industry worker laid off because of competition from railroads
   d. a short-order cook who loses his job when a new restaurant opens across the street
   e. an expert welder with little formal education who loses his job when the company installs automatic welding machinery

6. Using a diagram of the labor market, show the effect of an increase in the minimum wage on the wage paid to workers, the number of workers supplied, the number of workers demanded, and the amount of unemployment.

7. Consider an economy with two labor markets—one for manufacturing workers and one for service workers. Suppose initially that neither is unionized.
   a. If manufacturing workers formed a union, what impact would you predict on the wages and employment in manufacturing?
   b. How would these changes in the manufacturing labor market affect the supply of labor in the market for service workers? What would happen to the equilibrium wage and employment in this labor market?

8. Structural unemployment is sometimes said to result from a mismatch between the job skills that employers want and the job skills that workers have. To explore this idea, consider an economy with two industries: auto manufacturing and aircraft manufacturing.
   a. If workers in these two industries require similar amounts of training, and if workers at the beginning of their careers could choose which industry to train for, what would you expect to happen to the wages in these two industries? How long would this process take? Explain.
   b. Suppose that one day the economy opens itself to international trade and, as a result, starts importing autos and exporting aircraft. What would happen to demand for labor in these two industries?
   c. Suppose that workers in one industry cannot be quickly retrained for the other. How would these shifts in demand affect equilibrium wages both in the short run and in the long run?
   d. If for some reason wages fail to adjust to the new equilibrium levels, what would occur?

9. Suppose that Congress passes a law requiring employers to provide employees some benefit (such as healthcare) that raises the cost of an employee by $4 per hour.
   a. What effect does this employer mandate have on the demand for labor? (In answering this and the following questions, be quantitative when you can.)
   b. If employees place a value on this benefit exactly equal to its cost, what effect does this employer mandate have on the supply of labor?
   c. If the wage can freely adjust to balance supply and demand, how does this law affect the wage and the level of employment? Are employers better or worse off? Are employees better or worse off?
   d. Suppose that, before the mandate, the wage in this market was $3 above the minimum wage. In this case, how does the employer mandate affect the wage, the level of employment, and the level of unemployment?
   e. Now suppose that workers do not value the mandated benefit at all. How does this alternative assumption change your answers to parts (b) and (c)?

Go to CengageBrain.com to purchase access to the proven, critical Study Guide to accompany this text, which features additional notes and context, practice tests, and much more.

Money and Prices in the Long Run

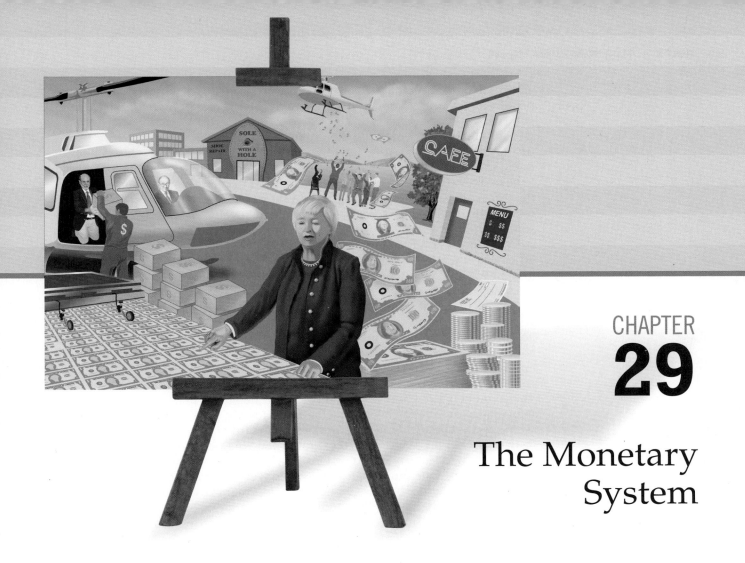

The Monetary System

When you walk into a restaurant to buy a meal, you get something of value—a full stomach. To pay for this service, you might hand the restaurateur several worn-out pieces of greenish paper decorated with strange symbols, government buildings, and the portraits of famous dead Americans. Or you might hand her a single piece of paper with the name of a bank and your signature. Or you might show her a plastic card and sign a paper slip. Whether you pay by cash, check, or debit card, the restaurateur is happy to work hard to satisfy your gastronomical desires in exchange for these pieces of paper, which, in and of themselves, are worthless.

Anyone who has lived in a modern economy is familiar with this social custom. Even though paper money has no intrinsic value, the restaurateur is confident that, in the future, some third person will accept it in exchange for something that the restaurateur does value. And that third person is confident that some fourth person will accept the money, with the knowledge that yet a fifth person will accept the money . . . and so on. To the restaurateur and to other people in our society, your cash, check, or debit card receipt represents a claim to goods and services in the future.

The social custom of using money for transactions is extraordinarily useful in a large, complex society. Imagine, for a moment, that there was no item in the economy widely accepted in exchange for goods and services. People would have to rely on *barter*—the exchange of one good or service for another—to obtain the things they need. To get your restaurant meal, for instance, you would have to offer the restaurateur something of immediate value. You could offer to wash some dishes, mow her lawn, or give her your family's secret recipe for meat loaf. An economy that relies on barter will have trouble allocating its scarce resources efficiently. In such an economy, trade is said to require the *double coincidence of wants*—the unlikely occurrence that two people each have a good or service that the other wants.

The existence of money makes trade easier. The restaurateur does not care whether you can produce a valuable good or service for her. She is happy to accept your money, knowing that other people will do the same for her. Such a convention allows trade to be roundabout. The restaurateur accepts your money and uses it to pay her chef; the chef uses her paycheck to send her child to day care; the day care center uses this tuition to pay a teacher; and the teacher hires you to mow her lawn. As money flows from person to person in the economy, it facilitates production and trade, thereby allowing each person to specialize in what she does best and raising everyone's standard of living.

In this chapter, we begin to examine the role of money in the economy. We discuss what money is, the various forms that money takes, how the banking system helps create money, and how the government controls the quantity of money in circulation. Because money is so important in the economy, we devote much effort in the rest of this book to learning how changes in the quantity of money affect various economic variables, including inflation, interest rates, production, and employment. Consistent with our long-run focus in the previous four chapters, in the next chapter we examine the long-run effects of changes in the quantity of money. The short-run effects of monetary changes are a more complex topic, which we take up later in the book. This chapter provides the background for all of this further analysis.

29-1 The Meaning of Money

What is money? This might seem like an odd question. When you read that billionaire Bill Gates has a lot of money, you know what that means: He is so rich that he can buy almost anything he wants. In this sense, the term *money* is used to mean *wealth*.

money
the set of assets in an economy that people regularly use to buy goods and services from other people

Economists, however, use the word in a more specific sense: **Money** is the set of assets in the economy that people regularly use to buy goods and services from each other. The cash in your wallet is money because you can use it to buy a meal at a restaurant or a shirt at a store. By contrast, if you happened to own a large share of Microsoft Corporation, as Bill Gates does, you would be wealthy, but this asset is not considered a form of money. You could not buy a meal or a shirt with this wealth without first obtaining some cash. According to the economist's definition, money includes only those few types of wealth that are regularly accepted by sellers in exchange for goods and services.

29-1a The Functions of Money

Medium of exchange
unit of account
store of value

Money has three functions in the economy: It is a *medium of exchange*, a *unit of account*, and a *store of value*. These three functions together distinguish money from other assets in the economy, such as stocks, bonds, real estate, art, and even baseball cards. Let's examine each of these functions of money in turn.

A **medium of exchange** is an item that buyers give to sellers when they purchase goods and services. When you go to a store to buy a shirt, the store gives you the shirt and you give the store your money. This transfer of money from buyer to seller allows the transaction to take place. When you walk into a store, you are confident that the store will accept your money for the items it is selling because money is the commonly accepted medium of exchange.

A **unit of account** is the yardstick people use to post prices and record debts. When you go shopping, you might observe that a shirt costs $30 and a hamburger costs $3. Even though it would be accurate to say that the price of a shirt is 10 hamburgers and the price of a hamburger is $1/10$ of a shirt, prices are never quoted in this way. Similarly, if you take out a loan from a bank, the size of your future loan repayments will be measured in dollars, not in a quantity of goods and services. When we want to measure and record economic value, we use money as the unit of account.

A **store of value** is an item that people can use to transfer purchasing power from the present to the future. When a seller accepts money today in exchange for a good or service, that seller can hold the money and become a buyer of another good or service at another time. Money is not the only store of value in the economy: A person can also transfer purchasing power from the present to the future by holding nonmonetary assets such as stocks and bonds. The term *wealth* is used to refer to the total of all stores of value, including both money and nonmonetary assets.

Economists use the term **liquidity** to describe the ease with which an asset can be converted into the economy's medium of exchange. Because money is the economy's medium of exchange, it is the most liquid asset available. Other assets vary widely in their liquidity. Most stocks and bonds can be sold easily with small cost, so they are relatively liquid assets. By contrast, selling a house, a Rembrandt painting, or a 1948 Joe DiMaggio baseball card requires more time and effort, so these assets are less liquid.

When people decide how to allocate their wealth, they have to balance the liquidity of each possible asset against the asset's usefulness as a store of value. Money is the most liquid asset, but it is far from perfect as a store of value. When prices rise, the value of money falls. In other words, when goods and services become more expensive, each dollar in your wallet can buy less. This link between the price level and the value of money is key to understanding how money affects the economy, a topic we start to explore in the next chapter.

medium of exchange
an item that buyers give to sellers when they want to purchase goods and services

unit of account
the yardstick people use to post prices and record debts

store of value
an item that people can use to transfer purchasing power from the present to the future

liquidity
the ease with which an asset can be converted into the economy's medium of exchange

29-1b The Kinds of Money

When money takes the form of a commodity with intrinsic value, it is called *Gold* **commodity money**. The term *intrinsic value* means that the item would have value even if it were not used as money. One example of commodity money is gold. Gold has intrinsic value because it is used in industry and in the making of jewelry. Although today we no longer use gold as money, historically gold was a common form of money because it is relatively easy to carry, measure, and verify for impurities. When an economy uses gold as money (or uses paper money that is convertible into gold on demand), it is said to be operating under a *gold standard*.

commodity money
money that takes the form of a commodity with intrinsic value

[handwritten margin notes: Commodity money = Gold / Cigarettes; decree = order; fiat money = Monopoly money]

Another example of commodity money is cigarettes. In prisoner-of-war camps during World War II, prisoners traded goods and services with one another using cigarettes as the store of value, unit of account, and medium of exchange. Similarly, as the Soviet Union was breaking up in the late 1980s, cigarettes started replacing the ruble as the preferred currency in Moscow. In both cases, even non-smokers were happy to accept cigarettes in an exchange, knowing that they could use the cigarettes to buy other goods and services.

Money without intrinsic value is called **fiat money**. A *fiat* is an order or decree, and fiat money is established as money by government decree. For example, compare the paper dollars in your wallet (printed by the U.S. government) and the paper dollars from a game of Monopoly (printed by the Parker Brothers game company). Why can you use the first to pay your bill at a restaurant but not the second? The answer is that the U.S. government has decreed its dollars to be valid money. Each paper dollar in your wallet reads: "This note is legal tender for all debts, public and private."

Although the government is central to establishing and regulating a system of fiat money (by prosecuting counterfeiters, for example), other factors are also required for the success of such a monetary system. To a large extent, the acceptance of fiat money depends as much on expectations and social convention as on government decree. The Soviet government in the 1980s never abandoned the ruble as the official currency. Yet the people of Moscow preferred to accept cigarettes (or even American dollars) in exchange for goods and services because they were more confident that these alternative monies would be accepted by others in the future.

fiat money

money without intrinsic value that is used as money because of government decree

---

IN THE NEWS

Why Gold?

For many centuries, when societies have used a form of commodity money, the most common choice has been the gold standard. This outcome may have a sound scientific basis.

A Chemist Explains Why Gold Beat Out Lithium, Osmium, Einsteinium . . .

By Jacob Goldstein and David Kestenbaum

The periodic table lists 118 different chemical elements. And yet, for thousands of years, humans have really, really liked one of them in particular: gold. Gold has been used as money for millennia, and its price has been going through the roof.

Why gold? Why not osmium, lithium, or ruthenium?

We went to an expert to find out: Sanat Kumar, a chemical engineer at Columbia University. We asked him to take the periodic table, and start eliminating anything that wouldn't work as money.

The periodic table looks kind of like a bingo card. Each square has a different element in it—one for carbon, another for gold, and so on.

Sanat starts with the far-right column of the table. The elements there have a really appealing characteristic: They're not going to change. They're chemically stable.

But there's also a big drawback: They're gases. You could put all your gaseous money in a jar, but if you opened the jar, you'd be broke. So Sanat crosses out the right-hand column.

Then he swings over to the far left-hand column, and points to one of the elements there: Lithium.

"If you expose lithium to air, it will cause a huge fire that can burn through concrete walls," he says.

Money that spontaneously bursts into flames is clearly a bad idea. In fact, you don't want your money undergoing any kind of spontaneous chemical reactions. And it turns out that a lot of the elements in the periodic table are pretty reactive.

Not all of them burst into flames. But sometimes they corrode, start to fall apart.

29-1c Money in the U.S. Economy

As we will see, the quantity of money circulating in the economy, called the *money stock*, has a powerful influence on many economic variables. But before we consider why that is true, we need to ask a preliminary question: What is the quantity of money? In particular, suppose you were given the task of measuring how much money there is in the U.S. economy. What would you include in your measure?

The most obvious asset to include is **currency**—the paper bills and coins in the hands of the public. Currency is clearly the most widely accepted medium of exchange in our economy. There is no doubt that it is part of the money stock.

Yet currency is not the only asset that you can use to buy goods and services. Many stores also accept personal checks. Wealth held in your checking account is almost as convenient for buying things as wealth held in your wallet. To measure the money stock, therefore, you might want to include **demand deposits**—balances in bank accounts that depositors can access on demand simply by writing a check or swiping a debit card at a store.

Once you start to consider balances in checking accounts as part of the money stock, you are led to consider the large variety of other accounts that people hold at banks and other financial institutions. Bank depositors usually cannot write checks against the balances in their savings accounts, but they can easily transfer funds from savings into checking accounts. In addition, depositors in money market mutual funds can often write checks against their balances. Thus, these other accounts should plausibly be part of the U.S. money stock.

[margin note, handwritten] Money stock = quantity of money circulating in economy

currency
the paper bills and coins in the hands of the public

demand deposits
balances in bank accounts that depositors can access on demand by writing a check

---

So Sanat crosses out another 38 elements, because they're too reactive.

Then we ask him about those two weird rows at the bottom of the table. They're always broken out separately from the main table, and they have some great names — promethium, einsteinium.

But it turns out they're radioactive—put some einsteinium in your pocket, and a year later, you'll be dead.

So we're down from 118 elements to 30, and we've come up with a list of three key requirements:

1. Not a gas.
2. Doesn't corrode or burst into flames.
3. Doesn't kill you.

Now Sanat adds a new requirement: You want the thing you pick to be rare. This lets him cross off a lot of the boxes near the top of the table, because the elements clustered there tend to be more abundant.

At the same time, you don't want to pick an element that's too rare. So osmium—which

In Gold We Trust.

apparently comes to earth via meteorites—gets the axe.

That leaves us with just five elements: rhodium, palladium, silver, platinum and gold. And all of them, as it happens, are considered precious metals.

But even here we can cross things out. Silver has been widely used as money, of

course. But it's reactive—it tarnishes. So Sanat says it's not the best choice.

Early civilizations couldn't have used rhodium or palladium, because they weren't discovered until the early 1800s.

That leaves platinum and gold, both of which can be found in rivers and streams.

But if you were in the ancient world and wanted to make platinum coins, you would have needed some sort of magic furnace from the future. The melting point for platinum is over 3,000 degrees Fahrenheit.

Gold happens to melt at a much lower temperature, which made it much easier for pre-industrial people to work with.

So we ask Sanat: If we could run the clock back and start history again, could things go a different way, or would gold emerge again as the element of choice?

"For the earth, with every parameter we have, gold is the sweet spot," he says. "It would come out no other way." ◢

Source: *NPR Morning Edition*, February 15, 2011.

FIGURE 1

Two Measures of the Money Stock for the U.S. Economy
The two most widely followed measures of the money stock are M1 and M2. This figure shows the size of each measure in January 2013.

Source: Federal Reserve.

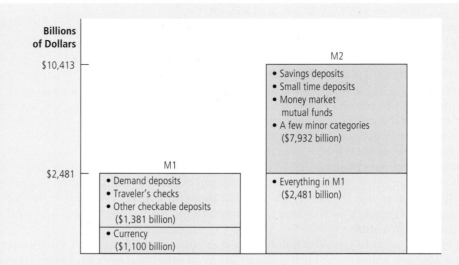

Billions of Dollars

M2
- Savings deposits
- Small time deposits
- Money market mutual funds
- A few minor categories
  ($7,932 billion)

$10,413

M1
- Demand deposits
- Traveler's checks
- Other checkable deposits
  ($1,381 billion)
- Currency
  ($1,100 billion)

$2,481

- Everything in M1
  ($2,481 billion)

In a complex economy such as ours, it is not easy to draw a line between assets that can be called "money" and assets that cannot. The coins in your pocket clearly are part of the money stock, and the Empire State Building clearly is not, but there are many assets in between these extremes for which the choice is less clear. Because different analysts can reasonably disagree about where to draw the dividing line between monetary and nonmonetary assets, various measures of the money stock are available for the U.S. economy. Figure 1 shows the two most commonly used measures of the money stock, designated M1 and M2. M2 includes more assets in its measure of money than does M1.

For our purposes in this book, we need not dwell on the differences between the various measures of money. None of our discussion will hinge on the distinction between M1 and M2. The important point is that the money stock for the U.S. economy includes not just currency but also deposits in banks and other financial institutions that can be readily accessed and used to buy goods and services.

FYI

Why Credit Cards Aren't Money

It might seem natural to include credit cards as part of the economy's stock of money. After all, people use credit cards to make many of their purchases. Aren't credit cards, therefore, a medium of exchange?

At first this argument may seem persuasive, but credit cards are excluded from all measures of the quantity of money. The reason is that credit cards are not really a method of payment but a method of *deferring* payment. When you buy a meal with a credit card, the bank that issued the card pays the restaurant what it is due. At a later date, you will repay the bank (perhaps with interest). When the time comes to pay your credit card bill, you will probably do so by writing a check against your checking account. The balance in this checking account is part of the economy's stock of money.

Notice that credit cards are different from debit cards, which automatically withdraw funds from a bank account to pay for items bought.

Rather than allowing the user to postpone payment for a purchase, a debit card allows the user immediate access to deposits in a bank account. In this sense, a debit card is more similar to a check than to a credit card. The account balances that lie behind debit cards are included in measures of the quantity of money.

Even though credit cards are not considered a form of money, they are nonetheless important for analyzing the monetary system. People who have credit cards can pay many of their bills together at the end of the month, rather than sporadically as they make purchases. As a result, people who have credit cards probably hold less money on average than people who do not have credit cards. Thus, the introduction and increased popularity of credit cards may reduce the amount of money that people choose to hold.

case study
Where Is All the Currency?
One puzzle about the money stock of the U.S. economy concerns the amount of currency. In January 2013, there was $1.1 trillion of currency outstanding. To put this number in perspective, we can divide it by 245 million, the number of adults (age 16 and older) in the United States. This calculation implies that the average adult holds about $4,490 of currency. Most people are surprised to learn that our economy has so much currency because they carry far less than this in their wallets.

Who is holding all this currency? No one knows for sure, but there are two plausible explanations.

The first explanation is that much of the currency is held abroad. In foreign countries without a stable monetary system, people often prefer U.S. dollars to domestic assets. It is, in fact, not unusual to see U.S. dollars used overseas as the medium of exchange, unit of account, and store of value.

The second explanation is that much of the currency is held by drug dealers, tax evaders, and other criminals. For most people in the U.S. economy, currency is not a particularly good way to hold wealth. Not only can currency be lost or stolen, but it also does not earn interest, whereas a bank deposit does. Thus, most people hold only small amounts of currency. By contrast, criminals may avoid putting their wealth in banks because a bank deposit gives police a paper trail they can use to trace illegal activities. For criminals, currency may be the best store of value available. ◢

Quick Quiz   *List and describe the three functions of money.*

29-2 The Federal Reserve System

Whenever an economy uses a system of fiat money, as the U.S. economy does, some agency must be responsible for regulating the system. In the United States, that agency is the **Federal Reserve**, often simply called the **Fed**. If you look at the top of a dollar bill, you will see that it is called a "Federal Reserve Note." The Fed is an example of a **central bank**—an institution designed to oversee the banking system and regulate the quantity of money in the economy. Other major central banks around the world include the Bank of England, the Bank of Japan, and the European Central Bank.

Federal Reserve (Fed)
the central bank of the United States

central bank
an institution designed to oversee the banking system and regulate the quantity of money in the economy

29-2a The Fed's Organization

The Federal Reserve was created in 1913 after a series of bank failures in 1907 convinced Congress that the United States needed a central bank to ensure the health of the nation's banking system. Today, the Fed is run by its board of governors, which has seven members appointed by the president and confirmed by the Senate. The governors have 14-year terms. Just as federal judges are given lifetime appointments to insulate them from politics, Fed governors are given long terms to give them independence from short-term political pressures when they formulate monetary policy.

Among the seven members of the board of governors, the most important is the chairman. The chairman directs the Fed staff, presides over board meetings, and testifies regularly about Fed policy in front of congressional committees. The president appoints the chairman to a 4-year term. As this book was going to press, the chairman of the Fed was Ben Bernanke, a former economics professor who was appointed to the Fed job by President George W. Bush in 2005 and reappointed by President Barack Obama in 2009.

The Federal Reserve System is made up of the Federal Reserve Board in Washington, D.C., and twelve regional Federal Reserve Banks located in major cities around the country. The presidents of the regional banks are chosen by each bank's board of directors, whose members are typically drawn from the region's banking and business community.

The Fed has two related jobs. The first is to regulate banks and ensure the health of the banking system. This task is largely the responsibility of the regional Federal Reserve Banks. In particular, the Fed monitors each bank's financial condition and facilitates bank transactions by clearing checks. It also acts as a bank's bank. That is, the Fed makes loans to banks when banks themselves want to borrow. When financially troubled banks find themselves short of cash, the Fed acts as a *lender of last resort*—a lender to those who cannot borrow anywhere else—to maintain stability in the overall banking system.

The Fed's second and more important job is to control the quantity of money that is made available in the economy, called the **money supply**. Decisions by policymakers concerning the money supply constitute **monetary policy**. At the Fed, monetary policy is made by the Federal Open Market Committee (FOMC). The FOMC meets about every 6 weeks in Washington, D.C., to discuss the condition of the economy and consider changes in monetary policy.

money supply
the quantity of money available in the economy

monetary policy
the setting of the money supply by policymakers in the central bank

29-2b The Federal Open Market Committee

The FOMC is made up of the seven members of the board of governors and five of the twelve regional bank presidents. All twelve regional presidents attend each FOMC meeting, but only five get to vote. The five with voting rights rotate among the twelve regional presidents over time. The president of the New York Fed always gets a vote, however, because New York is the traditional financial center of the U.S. economy and because all Fed purchases and sales of government bonds are conducted at the New York Fed's trading desk.

Through the decisions of the FOMC, the Fed has the power to increase or decrease the number of dollars in the economy. In simple metaphorical terms, you can imagine the Fed printing dollar bills and dropping them around the country by helicopter. Similarly, you can imagine the Fed using a giant vacuum cleaner to suck dollar bills out of people's wallets. Although in practice the Fed's methods for changing the money supply are more complex and subtle than this, the helicopter-vacuum metaphor is a good first step to understanding the meaning of monetary policy.

Later in this chapter, we discuss how the Fed actually changes the money supply, but it is worth noting here that the Fed's primary tool is the *open-market operation*—the purchase and sale of U.S. government bonds. (Recall that a U.S. government bond is a certificate of indebtedness of the federal government.) If the FOMC decides to increase the money supply, the Fed creates dollars and uses them to buy government bonds from the public in the nation's bond markets. After the purchase, these dollars are in the hands of the public. Thus, an open-market purchase of bonds by the Fed increases the money supply. Conversely, if the FOMC decides to decrease the money supply, the Fed sells government bonds from its portfolio to the public in the nation's bond markets. After the sale, the dollars the Fed receives for the bonds are out of the hands of the public. Thus, an open-market sale of bonds by the Fed decreases the money supply.

Central banks are important institutions because changes in the money supply can profoundly affect the economy. One of the *Ten Principles of Economics* in Chapter 1 is that prices rise when the government prints too much money. Another of the *Ten Principles of Economics* is that society faces a short-run trade-off between inflation and unemployment. The power of the Fed rests on these principles. For reasons we discuss more fully in the coming chapters, the Fed's policy decisions are key determinants of the economy's rate of inflation in the long run and the economy's employment and production in the short run. Indeed, the chairman of the Fed has been called the second most powerful person in the United States.

Quick Quiz *What are the primary responsibilities of the Federal Reserve? If the Fed wants to increase the supply of money, how does it usually do so?*

29-3 Banks and the Money Supply

So far, we have introduced the concept of "money" and discussed how the Federal Reserve controls the supply of money by buying and selling government bonds in open-market operations. This explanation of the money supply is correct, but it is not complete. In particular, it omits the central role that banks play in the monetary system.

Recall that the amount of money you hold includes both currency (the bills in your wallet and coins in your pocket) and demand deposits (the balance in your checking account). Because demand deposits are held in banks, the behavior of banks can influence the quantity of demand deposits in the economy and, therefore, the money supply. This section examines how banks affect the money supply and, in doing so, how they complicate the Fed's job of controlling the money supply.

"I've heard a lot about money, and now I'd like to try some."

29-3a The Simple Case of 100-Percent-Reserve Banking

To see how banks influence the money supply, let's first imagine a world without any banks at all. In this simple world, currency is the only form of money. To be concrete, let's suppose that the total quantity of currency is $100. The supply of money is, therefore, $100.

Now suppose that someone opens a bank, appropriately called First National Bank. First National Bank is only a depository institution—that is, it accepts deposits but does not make loans. The purpose of the bank is to give depositors a safe place to keep their money. Whenever a person deposits some money, the bank keeps the money in its vault until the depositor withdraws it, writes a check, or uses a debit card to access her balance. Deposits that banks have received but have not loaned out are called **reserves**. In this imaginary economy, all deposits are held as reserves, so this system is called *100-percent-reserve banking*.

reserves
deposits that banks have received but have not loaned out

We can express the financial position of First National Bank with a *T-account*, which is a simplified accounting statement that shows changes in a bank's assets and liabilities. Here is the T-account for First National Bank if the economy's entire $100 of money is deposited in the bank:

First National Bank

Assets		Liabilities	
Reserves	$100.00	Deposits	$100.00

On the left side of the T-account are the bank's assets of $100 (the reserves it holds in its vaults). On the right side are the bank's liabilities of $100 (the amount it owes to its depositors). Because the assets and liabilities exactly balance, this accounting statement is sometimes called a *balance sheet*.

Now consider the money supply in this imaginary economy. Before First National Bank opens, the money supply is the $100 of currency that people are holding. After the bank opens and people deposit their currency, the money supply is the $100 of demand deposits. (There is no longer any currency outstanding, for it is all in the bank vault.) Each deposit in the bank reduces currency and raises demand deposits by exactly the same amount, leaving the money supply unchanged. Thus, *if banks hold all deposits in reserve, banks do not influence the supply of money.*

29-3b Money Creation with Fractional-Reserve Banking

Eventually, the bankers at First National Bank may start to reconsider their policy of 100-percent-reserve banking. Leaving all that money idle in their vaults seems unnecessary. Why not lend some of it out and earn a profit by charging interest on the loans? Families buying houses, firms building new factories, and students paying for college would all be happy to pay interest to borrow some of that money for a while. First National Bank has to keep some reserves so that currency is available if depositors want to make withdrawals. But if the flow of new deposits is roughly the same as the flow of withdrawals, First National needs to keep only a fraction of its deposits in reserve. Thus, First National adopts a system called **fractional-reserve banking**.

fractional-reserve banking
a banking system in which banks hold only a fraction of deposits as reserves

The fraction of total deposits that a bank holds as reserves is called the **reserve ratio**. This ratio is influenced by both government regulation and bank policy. As we discuss more fully later in the chapter, the Fed sets a minimum amount of reserves that banks must hold, called a *reserve requirement*. In addition, banks may hold reserves above the legal minimum, called *excess reserves*, so they can be more confident that they will not run short of cash. For our purpose here, we take the reserve ratio as given to examine how fractional-reserve banking influences the money supply.

reserve ratio
the fraction of deposits that banks hold as reserves

Let's suppose that First National has a reserve ratio of 1/10, or 10 percent. This means that it keeps 10 percent of its deposits in reserve and loans out the rest. Now let's look again at the bank's T-account:

First National Bank

Assets		Liabilities	
Reserves	$10.00	Deposits	$100.00
Loans	90.00		

First National still has $100 in liabilities because making the loans did not alter the bank's obligation to its depositors. But now the bank has two kinds of assets: It has $10 of reserves in its vault, and it has loans of $90. (These loans are liabilities of the people borrowing from First National, but they are assets of the bank because the borrowers will later repay the loans.) In total, First National's assets still equal its liabilities.

Once again consider the supply of money in the economy. Before First National makes any loans, the money supply is the $100 of deposits. Yet when First National lends out some of these deposits, the money supply increases. The depositors still have demand deposits totaling $100, but now the borrowers hold $90 in currency. The money supply (which equals currency plus demand deposits) equals $190. Thus, *when banks hold only a fraction of deposits in reserve, the banking system creates money.* Loan out and make interest money

At first, this creation of money by fractional-reserve banking may seem too good to be true: It appears that the bank has created money out of thin air. To make this feat seem less miraculous, note that when First National Bank loans out some of its reserves and creates money, it does not create any wealth. Loans from First National give the borrowers some currency and thus the ability to buy goods and services. Yet the borrowers are also taking on debts, so the loans do not make them any richer. In other words, as a bank creates the asset of money, it also creates a corresponding liability for those who borrowed the created money. At the end of this process of money creation, the economy is more liquid in the sense that there is more of the medium of exchange, but the economy is no wealthier than before.

29-3c The Money Multiplier

The creation of money does not stop with First National Bank. Suppose the borrower from First National uses the $90 to buy something from someone who then deposits the currency in Second National Bank. Here is the T-account for Second National Bank:

Second National Bank

Assets		Liabilities	
Reserves	$ 9.00	Deposits	$90.00
Loans	81.00		

After the deposit, this bank has liabilities of $90. If Second National also has a reserve ratio of 10 percent, it keeps assets of $9 in reserve and makes $81 in loans. In this way, Second National Bank creates an additional $81 of money. If this $81 is eventually deposited in Third National Bank, which also has a reserve ratio of 10 percent, this bank keeps $8.10 in reserve and makes $72.90 in loans. Here is the T-account for Third National Bank:

Third National Bank

Assets		Liabilities	
Reserves	$ 8.10	Deposits	$81.00
Loans	72.90		

The process goes on and on. Each time that money is deposited and a bank loan is made, more money is created.

How much money is eventually created in this economy? Let's add it up:

Original deposit	= $100.00
First National lending	= $ 90.00 (= .9 × $100.00)
Second National lending	= $ 81.00 (= .9 × $90.00)
Third National lending	= $ 72.90 (= .9 × $81.00)
•	•
•	•
•	•
Total money supply	= $1,000.00

money multiplier

the amount of money the banking system generates with each dollar of reserves

It turns out that even though this process of money creation can continue forever, it does not create an infinite amount of money. If you laboriously add the infinite sequence of numbers in the preceding example, you find the $100 of reserves generates $1,000 of money. The amount of money the banking system generates with each dollar of reserves is called the **money multiplier**. In this imaginary economy, where the $100 of reserves generates $1,000 of money, the money multiplier is 10.

What determines the size of the money multiplier? It turns out that the answer is simple: *The money multiplier is the reciprocal of the reserve ratio.* If R is the reserve ratio for all banks in the economy, then each dollar of reserves generates $1/R$ dollars of money. In our example, $R = 1/10$, so the money multiplier is 10.

This reciprocal formula for the money multiplier makes sense. If a bank holds $1,000 in deposits, then a reserve ratio of $1/10$ (10 percent) means that the bank must hold $100 in reserves. The money multiplier just turns this idea around: If the banking system as a whole holds a total of $100 in reserves, it can have only $1,000 in deposits. In other words, if R is the ratio of reserves to deposits at each bank (that is, the reserve ratio), then the ratio of deposits to reserves in the banking system (that is, the money multiplier) must be $1/R$.

This formula shows how the amount of money banks create depends on the reserve ratio. If the reserve ratio were only $1/20$ (5 percent), then the banking system would have 20 times as much in deposits as in reserves, implying a money multiplier of 20. Each dollar of reserves would generate $20 of money. Similarly, if the reserve ratio were $1/4$ (25 percent), deposits would be 4 times reserves, the money multiplier would be 4, and each dollar of reserves would generate $4 of money. Thus, *the higher the reserve ratio, the less of each deposit banks loan out, and the smaller the money multiplier.* In the special case of 100-percent-reserve banking, the reserve ratio is 1, the money multiplier is 1, and banks do not make loans or create money.

29-3d Bank Capital, Leverage, and the Financial Crisis of 2008–2009

In the previous sections, we have seen a very simplified explanation of how banks work. The reality of modern banking, however, is a bit more complicated, and this complex reality played a leading role in the financial crisis of 2008 and 2009. Before looking at that crisis, we need to learn a bit more about how banks actually function.

In the bank balance sheets you have seen so far, a bank accepts deposits and either uses those deposits to make loans or holds them as reserves. More realistically, a bank gets financial resources not only from accepting deposits but also, like other companies, from issuing equity and debt. The resources that a bank obtains from issuing equity to its owners are called **bank capital**. A bank uses these financial resources in various ways to generate profit for its owners. It not only makes loans and holds reserves but also buys financial securities, such as stocks and bonds.

Here is a more realistic example of a bank's balance sheet:

bank capital

the resources a bank's owners have put into the institution

More Realistic National Bank

Assets		Liabilities and Owners' Equity	
Reserves	$200	Deposits	$800
Loans	700	Debt	150
Securities	100	Capital (owners' equity)	50

[handwritten annotation: Stocks + Bonds ← (pointing to Securities)]

On the right side of this balance sheet are the bank's liabilities and capital (also known as *owners' equity*). This bank obtained $50 of resources from its owners. It also took in $800 of deposits and issued $150 of debt. The total of $1,000 was put to use in three ways; these are listed on the left side of the balance sheet, which shows the bank's assets. This bank held $200 in reserves, made $700 in bank loans, and used $100 to buy financial securities, such as government or corporate bonds. The bank decides how to allocate its resources among asset classes based on their risk and return, as well as on any regulations (such as reserve requirements) that restrict the bank's choices.

By the rules of accounting, the reserves, loans, and securities on the left side of the balance sheet must always equal, in total, the deposits, debt, and capital on the right side of the balance sheet. There is no magic in this equality. It occurs because the value of the owners' equity is, by definition, the value of the bank's assets (reserves, loans, and securities) minus the value of its liabilities (deposits and debt). Therefore, the left- and right-hand sides of the balance sheet always sum to the same total.

Many businesses in the economy rely on **leverage**, the use of borrowed money to supplement existing funds for investment purposes. Indeed, whenever anyone uses debt to finance an investment project, she is applying leverage. Leverage is particularly important for banks, however, because borrowing and lending are at the heart of what they do. To fully understand banking, therefore, it is crucial to understand how leverage works.

leverage
the use of borrowed money to supplement existing funds for purposes of investment

The **leverage ratio** is the ratio of the bank's total assets to bank capital. In this example, the leverage ratio is $1,000/$50, or 20. A leverage ratio of 20 means that for every dollar of capital that the bank owners have contributed, the bank has $20 of assets. Of the $20 of assets, $19 are financed with borrowed money—either by taking in deposits or issuing debt.

leverage ratio
the ratio of assets to bank capital

You may have learned in a science class that a lever can amplify a force: A boulder that you cannot move with your arms alone will move more easily if you use a lever. A similar result occurs with bank leverage. To see how this amplification works, let's continue with this numerical example. Suppose that the bank's assets were to rise in value by 5 percent because, say, some of the securities the bank was holding rose in price. Then the $1,000 of assets would now be worth $1,050. Because the depositors and debt holders are still owed $950, the bank capital rises from $50 to $100. Thus, when the leverage rate is 20, a 5-percent increase in the value of assets increases the owners' equity by 100 percent.

The same principle works on the downside, but with troubling consequences. Suppose that some people who borrowed from the bank default on their loans, reducing the value of the bank's assets by 5 percent, to $950. Because the depositors and debt holders have the legal right to be paid before the bank owners, the value of the owners' equity falls to zero. Thus, when the leverage ratio is 20, a 5-percent fall in the value of the bank assets leads to a 100-percent fall in bank capital. If the value of assets were to fall by more than 5 percent, the bank's assets would fall below its liabilities. In this case, the bank would be *insolvent*, and it would be unable to pay off its debt holders and depositors in full.

Bank regulators require banks to hold a certain amount of capital. The goal of such a **capital requirement** is to ensure that banks will be able to pay off their depositors (without having to resort to government-provided deposit insurance funds). The amount of capital required depends on the kind of assets a bank holds. If the bank holds safe assets such as government bonds, regulators require less capital than if the bank holds risky assets such as loans to borrowers whose credit is of dubious quality.

capital requirement
a government regulation specifying a minimum amount of bank capital

[Handwritten margin notes: Bank loans money - People don't pay back - depositors want their money back, bank doesn't have enough money, borrows from Fed - Fed takes it From public fund - now public is part owner of banks]

Economic turmoil can result when banks find themselves with too little capital to satisfy capital requirements. An example of this phenomenon occurred in 2008 and 2009, when many banks realized they had incurred sizable losses on some of their assets—specifically, mortgage loans and securities backed by mortgage loans. The shortage of capital induced the banks to reduce lending, a phenomenon sometimes called a *credit crunch*, which in turn contributed to a severe downturn in economic activity. (This event is discussed more fully in Chapter 33.) To address this problem, the U.S. Treasury, working together with the Federal Reserve, put many billions of dollars of public funds into the banking system to increase the amount of bank capital. As a result, it temporarily made the U.S. taxpayer a part owner of many banks. The goal of this unusual policy was to recapitalize the banking system so that bank lending could return to a more normal level, which in fact occurred by late 2009.

29-4 The Fed's Tools of Monetary Control

As we have already discussed, the Federal Reserve is responsible for controlling the supply of money in the economy. Now that we understand how banking works, we are in a better position to understand how the Fed carries out this job. Because banks create money in a system of fractional-reserve banking, the Fed's control of the money supply is indirect. When the Fed decides to change the money supply, it must consider how its actions will work through the banking system.

The Fed has a variety of tools in its monetary toolbox. We can group the tools into two groups: those that influence the quantity of reserves and those that influence the reserve ratio and thereby the money multiplier.

29-4a How the Fed Influences the Quantity of Reserves

The first way the Fed can change the money supply is by changing the quantity of reserves. The Fed alters the quantity of reserves in the economy either by buying or selling bonds in open-market operations or by making loans to banks (or by some combination of the two). Let's consider each of these in turn.

open-market operations
the purchase and sale of U.S. government bonds by the Fed

Open-Market Operations   As we noted earlier, the Fed conducts **open-market operations** when it buys or sells government bonds. To increase the money supply, the Fed instructs its bond traders at the New York Fed to buy bonds from the public in the nation's bond markets. The dollars the Fed pays for the bonds increase the number of dollars in the economy. Some of these new dollars are held as currency, and some are deposited in banks. Each new dollar held as currency increases the money supply by exactly $1. Each new dollar deposited in a bank increases the money supply by more than a dollar because it increases reserves and, thereby, the amount of money that the banking system can create.

To reduce the money supply, the Fed does just the opposite: It sells government bonds to the public in the nation's bond markets. The public pays for these bonds with its holdings of currency and bank deposits, directly reducing the amount of money in circulation. In addition, as people make withdrawals from banks to buy these bonds from the Fed, banks find themselves with a smaller quantity of reserves. In response, banks reduce the amount of lending, and the process of money creation reverses itself.

Open-market operations are easy to conduct. In fact, the Fed's purchases and sales of government bonds in the nation's bond markets are similar to the transactions that any individual might undertake for her own portfolio. (Of course, when two individuals engage in a purchase or sale with each other, money changes hands, but the amount of money in circulation remains the same.) In addition, the Fed can use open-market operations to change the money supply by a small or large amount on any day without major changes in laws or bank regulations. Therefore, open-market operations are the tool of monetary policy that the Fed uses most often.

Fed Lending to Banks The Fed can also increase the quantity of reserves in the economy by lending reserves to banks. Banks borrow from the Fed when they feel they do not have enough reserves on hand, either to satisfy bank regulators, meet depositor withdrawals, make new loans, or for some other business reason.

There are various ways banks can borrow from the Fed. Traditionally, banks borrow from the Fed's *discount window* and pay an interest rate on that loan called the **discount rate**. When the Fed makes such a loan to a bank, the banking system has more reserves than it otherwise would, and these additional reserves allow the banking system to create more money.

The Fed can alter the money supply by changing the discount rate. A higher discount rate discourages banks from borrowing reserves from the Fed. Thus, an increase in the discount rate reduces the quantity of reserves in the banking system, which in turn reduces the money supply. Conversely, a lower discount rate encourages banks to borrow from the Fed, increasing the quantity of reserves and the money supply.

In recent years, the Fed has set up new mechanisms for banks to borrow from it. For example, under the *Term Auction Facility*, the Fed sets a quantity of funds it wants to lend to banks, and eligible banks then bid to borrow those funds. The loans go to the highest eligible bidders—that is, to the banks that have acceptable collateral and are offering to pay the highest interest rate. Unlike at the discount window, where the Fed sets the price of a loan and the banks determine the quantity of borrowing, at the Term Auction Facility the Fed sets the quantity of borrowing and competitive bidding among banks determines the price. The more funds the Fed makes available through this and similar facilities, the greater the quantity of reserves and the larger the money supply.

The Fed uses such lending not only to control the money supply but also to help financial institutions when they are in trouble. For example, when the stock market crashed by 22 percent on October 19, 1987, many Wall Street brokerage firms found themselves temporarily in need of funds to finance the high volume of stock trading. The next morning, before the stock market opened, Fed Chairman Alan Greenspan announced the Fed's "readiness to serve as a source of liquidity to support the economic and financial system." Many economists believe that Greenspan's reaction to the stock crash was an important reason it had few repercussions.

Similarly, in 2008 and 2009, a fall in housing prices throughout the United States led to a sharp rise in the number of homeowners defaulting on their mortgage loans, and many financial institutions holding those mortgages ran into trouble. In an attempt to prevent these events from having broader economic ramifications, the Fed provided many billions of dollars of loans to financial institutions in distress.

discount rate
the interest rate on the loans that the Fed makes to banks

29-4b How the Fed Influences the Reserve Ratio

In addition to influencing the quantity of reserves, the Fed changes the money supply by influencing the reserve ratio and thereby the money multiplier. The Fed can influence the reserve ratio either through regulating the quantity of reserves banks must hold or through the interest rate that the Fed pays banks on their reserves. Again, we consider each of these monetary policy tools in turn.

Reserve Requirements   One way the Fed can influence the reserve ratio is by altering **reserve requirements**, the regulations that set the minimum amount of reserves that banks must hold against their deposits. Reserve requirements influence how much money the banking system can create with each dollar of reserves. An increase in reserve requirements means that banks must hold more reserves and, therefore, can loan out less of each dollar that is deposited. As a result, an increase in reserve requirements raises the reserve ratio, lowers the money multiplier, and decreases the money supply. Conversely, a decrease in reserve requirements lowers the reserve ratio, raises the money multiplier, and increases the money supply.

> **reserve requirements**
> *regulations on the minimum amount of reserves that banks must hold against deposits*

The Fed changes reserve requirements only rarely because such changes disrupt the business of banking. When the Fed increases reserve requirements, for instance, some banks find themselves short of reserves, even though they have seen no change in deposits. As a result, they have to curtail lending until they build their level of reserves to the new required level. Moreover, in recent years, this particular tool has become less effective because many banks hold excess reserves (that is, more reserves than are required).

Paying Interest on Reserves   Traditionally, banks did not earn any interest on the reserves they held. In October 2008, however, the Fed began paying *interest on reserves*. That is, when a bank holds reserves on deposit at the Fed, the Fed now pays the bank interest on those deposits. This change gives the Fed another tool with which to influence the economy. The higher the interest rate on reserves, the more reserves banks will choose to hold. Thus, an increase in the interest rate on reserves will tend to increase the reserve ratio, lower the money multiplier, and lower the money supply. Because the Fed has paid interest on reserves for a relatively short time, it is not yet clear how important this new instrument will be in the conduct of monetary policy.

29-4c Problems in Controlling the Money Supply

The Fed's various tools—open-market operations, bank lending, reserve requirements, and interest on reserves—have powerful effects on the money supply. Yet the Fed's control of the money supply is not precise. The Fed must wrestle with two problems, each of which arises because much of the money supply is created by our system of fractional-reserve banking.

The first problem is that the Fed does not control the amount of money that households choose to hold as deposits in banks. The more money households deposit, the more reserves banks have, and the more money the banking system can create. The less money households deposit, the less reserves banks have, and the less money the banking system can create. To see why this is a problem, suppose that one day people begin to lose confidence in the banking system and, therefore, decide to withdraw deposits and hold more currency. When this happens, the banking system loses reserves and creates less money. The money supply falls, even without any Fed action.

The second problem of monetary control is that the Fed does not control the amount that bankers choose to lend. When money is deposited in a bank, it creates more money only when the bank loans it out. Because banks can choose to hold excess reserves instead, the Fed cannot be sure how much money the banking system will create. For instance, suppose that one day bankers become more cautious about economic conditions and decide to make fewer loans and hold greater reserves. In this case, the banking system creates less money than it otherwise would. Because of the bankers' decision, the money supply falls.

Hence, in a system of fractional-reserve banking, the amount of money in the economy depends in part on the behavior of depositors and bankers. Because the Fed cannot control or perfectly predict this behavior, it cannot perfectly control the money supply. Yet if the Fed is vigilant, these problems need not be large. The Fed collects data on deposits and reserves from banks every week, so it quickly becomes aware of any changes in depositor or banker behavior. It can, therefore, respond to these changes and keep the money supply close to whatever level it chooses.

case study
Bank Runs and the Money Supply

Most likely you have never witnessed a bank run in real life, but you may have seen one depicted in movies such as *Mary Poppins* or *It's a Wonderful Life*. A bank run occurs when depositors suspect that a bank may go bankrupt and, therefore, "run" to the bank to withdraw their deposits. The United States has not seen a major bank run in recent history, but in the United Kingdom, a bank called Northern Rock experienced a run in 2007 and, as a result, was eventually taken over by the government.

Bank runs are a problem for banks under fractional-reserve banking. Because a bank holds only a fraction of its deposits in reserve, it cannot satisfy withdrawal requests from all depositors. Even if the bank is in fact *solvent* (meaning that its assets exceed its liabilities), it will not have enough cash on hand to allow all depositors immediate access to all of their money. When a run occurs, the bank is forced to close its doors until some bank loans are repaid or until some lender of last resort (such as the Fed) provides it with the currency it needs to satisfy depositors.

Bank runs complicate the control of the money supply. An important example of this problem occurred during the Great Depression in the early 1930s. After a wave of bank runs and bank closings, households and bankers became more cautious. Households withdrew their deposits from banks, preferring to hold their money in the form of currency. This decision reversed the process of money creation, as bankers responded to falling reserves by reducing bank loans. At the same time, bankers increased their reserve ratios so that they would have enough cash on hand to meet their depositors' demands in any future bank runs. The higher reserve ratio reduced the money multiplier, which further reduced the money supply. From 1929 to 1933, the money supply fell by 28 percent, without the Fed taking any deliberate contractionary action. Many economists point to this massive fall in the money supply to explain the high unemployment and falling prices that prevailed during this period. (In future chapters, we examine the mechanisms by which changes in the money supply affect unemployment and prices.)

Today, bank runs are not a major problem for the U.S. banking system or the Fed. The federal government now guarantees the safety of deposits at most banks, primarily through the Federal Deposit Insurance Corporation (FDIC). Depositors do not make runs on their banks because they are confident that, even if their bank goes bankrupt, the FDIC will make good on the deposits. The policy of government deposit insurance has costs: Bankers whose deposits are guaranteed may have too little incentive to avoid bad risks when making loans. But one benefit of deposit insurance is a more stable banking system. As a result, most people see bank runs only in the movies. ◢

A not-so-wonderful bank run

RKO/THE KOBAL COLLECTION/ PICTURE DESK

IN THE NEWS

Bernanke on the Fed's Toolbox

During the financial crisis of 2008 and 2009, the Federal Reserve helped rescue various banks and other financial institutions and, in doing so, substantially expanded the quantity of bank reserves. Most of these newly created reserves were held as excess reserves. Here, the chairman of the Fed explains its plans to unwind the process. As this book was going to press, the Fed had not yet implemented this exit strategy, but the plans to do so remained much the same.

The Fed's Exit Strategy

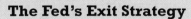

By Ben Bernanke

The depth and breadth of the global recession has required a highly accommodative monetary policy. Since the onset of the financial crisis nearly two years ago, the Federal Reserve has reduced the interest-rate target for overnight lending between banks (the federal-funds rate) nearly to zero. We have also greatly expanded the size of the Fed's balance sheet through purchases of longer-term securities and through targeted lending programs aimed at restarting the flow of credit.

These actions have softened the economic impact of the financial crisis. They have also improved the functioning of key credit markets, including the markets for interbank lending, commercial paper, consumer and small-business credit, and residential mortgages.

My colleagues and I believe that accommodative policies will likely be warranted for an extended period. At some point, however, as economic recovery takes hold, we will need to tighten monetary policy to prevent the emergence of an inflation problem down the road. The Federal Open Market Committee, which is responsible for setting U.S. monetary policy, has devoted considerable time to issues relating to an exit strategy. We are confident we have the necessary tools to withdraw policy accommodation, when that becomes appropriate, in a smooth and timely manner.

The exit strategy is closely tied to the management of the Federal Reserve balance sheet. When the Fed makes loans or acquires securities, the funds enter the banking system and ultimately appear in the reserve accounts held at the Fed by banks and other depository institutions. These reserve balances now total about $800 billion, much more than normal. And given the current economic conditions, banks have generally held their reserves as balances at the Fed.

But as the economy recovers, banks should find more opportunities to lend out their reserves. That would produce faster growth in broad money (for example, M1 or M2) and easier credit conditions, which could ultimately result in inflationary pressures—unless we adopt countervailing policy measures. When the time comes to tighten monetary policy, we must either eliminate these large reserve balances or, if they remain, neutralize any potential undesired effects on the economy.

To some extent, reserves held by banks at the Fed will contract automatically, as improving financial conditions lead to reduced use of our short-term lending facilities, and ultimately to their wind down. Indeed, short-term credit extended by the Fed to financial institutions and other market participants has already fallen to less than $600 billion as of mid-July from about $1.5 trillion at the end of 2008. In addition, reserves could be reduced by about $100 billion to $200 billion each year over the next few years as securities held by the Fed mature or are prepaid. However, reserves likely would remain quite high for several years unless additional policies are undertaken.

Even if our balance sheet stays large for a while, we have two broad means of tightening monetary policy at the appropriate time: paying interest on reserve balances and taking various actions that reduce the stock of reserves. We could use either of these approaches alone; however, to ensure effectiveness, we likely would use both in combination.

Congress granted us authority last fall to pay interest on balances held by banks at the

Fed. Currently, we pay banks an interest rate of 0.25%. When the time comes to tighten policy, we can raise the rate paid on reserve balances as we increase our target for the federal-funds rate.

Banks generally will not lend funds in the money market at an interest rate lower than the rate they can earn risk-free at the Federal Reserve. Moreover, they should compete to borrow any funds that are offered in private markets at rates below the interest rate on reserve balances because, by so doing, they can earn a spread without risk.

Thus the interest rate that the Fed pays should tend to put a floor under short-term market rates, including our policy target, the federal-funds rate. Raising the rate paid on reserve balances also discourages excessive growth in money or credit, because banks will not want to lend out their reserves at rates below what they can earn at the Fed.

Considerable international experience suggests that paying interest on reserves effectively manages short-term market rates. For example, the European Central Bank allows banks to place excess reserves in an interest-paying deposit facility. Even as that central bank's liquidity operations substantially increased its balance sheet, the overnight interbank rate remained at or above its deposit rate. In addition, the Bank of Japan and the Bank of Canada have also used their ability to pay interest on reserves to maintain a floor under short-term market rates.

Despite this logic and experience, the federal-funds rate has dipped somewhat below the rate paid by the Fed, especially in October and November 2008, when the Fed first began to pay interest on reserves. This pattern partly reflected temporary factors, such as banks' inexperience with the new system.

Fed Chairman Ben Bernanke

Chip Somodevilla/Getty Images

However, this pattern appears also to have resulted from the fact that some large lenders in the federal-funds market, notably government-sponsored enterprises such as Fannie Mae and Freddie Mac, are ineligible to receive interest on balances held at the Fed, and thus they have an incentive to lend in that market at rates below what the Fed pays banks.

Under more normal financial conditions, the willingness of banks to engage in the simple arbitrage noted above will tend to limit the gap between the federal-funds rate and the rate the Fed pays on reserves. If that gap persists, the problem can be addressed by supplementing payment of interest on reserves with steps to reduce reserves and drain excess liquidity from markets—the second means of tightening monetary policy. Here are four options for doing this.

First, the Federal Reserve could drain bank reserves and reduce the excess liquidity at other institutions by arranging large-scale reverse repurchase agreements with financial market participants, including banks, government-sponsored enterprises and other institutions. Reverse repurchase agreements involve the sale by the Fed of securities from its portfolio with an agreement to buy the securities back at a slightly higher price at a later date.

Second, the Treasury could sell bills and deposit the proceeds with the Federal Reserve. When purchasers pay for the securities, the Treasury's account at the Federal Reserve rises and reserve balances decline.

The Treasury has been conducting such operations since last fall under its Supplementary Financing Program. Although the Treasury's operations are helpful, to protect the independence of monetary policy, we must take care to ensure that we can achieve our policy objectives without reliance on the Treasury.

Third, using the authority Congress gave us to pay interest on banks' balances at the Fed, we can offer term deposits to banks—analogous to the certificates of deposit that banks offer their customers. Bank funds held in term deposits at the Fed would not be available for the federal funds market.

Fourth, if necessary, the Fed could reduce reserves by selling a portion of its holdings of long-term securities into the open market.

Each of these policies would help to raise short-term interest rates and limit the growth of broad measures of money and credit, thereby tightening monetary policy.

Overall, the Federal Reserve has many effective tools to tighten monetary policy when the economic outlook requires us to do so. As my colleagues and I have stated, however, economic conditions are not likely to warrant tighter monetary policy for an extended period. We will calibrate the timing and pace of any future tightening, together with the mix of tools to best foster our dual objectives of maximum employment and price stability. ◢

Source: *The Wall Street Journal,* July 21, 2009.

29-4d The Federal Funds Rate

If you read about U.S. monetary policy in the newspaper, you will find much discussion of the federal funds rate. This raises several questions:

federal funds rate
the interest rate at which banks make overnight loans to one another

Q: What is the federal funds rate?

A: The **federal funds rate** is the short-term interest rate that banks charge one another for loans. If one bank finds itself short of reserves while another bank has excess reserves, the second bank can lend some reserves to the first. The loans are temporary—typically overnight. The price of the loan is the federal funds rate.

Q: How is the federal funds rate different from the discount rate?

A: The discount rate is the interest rate banks pay to borrow directly from the Fed through the discount window. Borrowing reserves from another bank in the federal funds market is an alternative to borrowing reserves from the Fed, and a bank short of reserves will typically do whichever is cheaper. In practice, the discount rate and the federal funds rate move closely together.

Q: Does the federal funds rate matter only for banks?

A: Not at all. Although only banks borrow directly in the federal funds market, the economic impact of this market is much broader. Because different parts of the financial system are highly interconnected, interest rates on different kinds of loans are strongly correlated with one another. So when the federal funds rate rises or falls, other interest rates often move in the same direction.

Q: What does the Fed have to do with the federal funds rate?

A: In recent years, the Fed has set a target goal for the federal funds rate. When the FOMC meets approximately every 6 weeks, it decides whether to raise or lower that target.

Q: How can the Fed make the federal funds rate hit the target it sets?

A: Although the actual federal funds rate is set by supply and demand in the market for loans among banks, the Fed can use open-market operations to influence that market. For example, when the Fed buys bonds in open-market operations, it injects reserves into the banking system. With more reserves in the system, fewer banks find themselves in need of borrowing reserves to meet reserve requirements. The fall in demand for borrowing reserves decreases the price of such borrowing, which is the federal funds rate. Conversely, when the Fed sells bonds and withdraws reserves from the banking system, more banks find themselves short of reserves, and they bid up the price of borrowing reserves. Thus, open-market purchases lower the federal funds rate, and open-market sales raise the federal funds rate.

Q: But don't these open-market operations affect the money supply?

A: Yes, absolutely. When the Fed announces a change in the federal funds rate, it is committing itself to the open-market operations necessary to make that change happen, and these open-market operations will alter the supply of money. Decisions by the FOMC to change the target for the federal funds rate are also decisions to change the money supply. They are two sides of the same coin. Other things being equal, a decrease in the target for the federal funds rate means an expansion in the money supply, and an increase in the target for the federal funds rate means a contraction in the money supply.

Quick Quiz *Describe how banks create money.* • *If the Fed wanted to use all of its policy tools to decrease the money supply, what would it do?*

29-5 Conclusion

Some years ago, a book made the best-seller list with the title *Secrets of the Temple: How the Federal Reserve Runs the Country*. Although no doubt an exaggeration, this title did highlight the important role of the monetary system in our daily lives. Whenever we buy or sell anything, we are relying on the extraordinarily useful social convention called "money." Now that we know what money is and what determines its supply, we can discuss how changes in the quantity of money affect the economy. We begin to address that topic in the next chapter.

Summary

- The term *money* refers to assets that people regularly use to buy goods and services.

- Money serves three functions. As a medium of exchange, it is the item used to make transactions. As a unit of account, it provides the way in which prices and other economic values are recorded. As a store of value, it offers a way to transfer purchasing power from the present to the future.

- Commodity money, such as gold, is money that has intrinsic value: It would be valued even if it were not used as money. Fiat money, such as paper dollars, is money without intrinsic value: It would be worthless if it were not used as money.

- In the U.S. economy, money takes the form of currency and various types of bank deposits, such as checking accounts.

- The Federal Reserve, the central bank of the United States, is responsible for regulating the U.S. monetary system. The Fed chairman is appointed by the president and confirmed by Congress every 4 years. The chairman is the head of the Federal Open Market Committee, which meets about every 6 weeks to consider changes in monetary policy.

- Bank depositors provide resources to banks by depositing their funds into bank accounts. These deposits are part of a bank's liabilities. Bank owners also provide resources (called bank capital) for the bank. Because of leverage (the use of borrowed funds for investment), a small change in the value of a bank's assets can lead to a large change in the value of the bank's capital. To protect depositors, bank regulators require banks to hold a certain minimum amount of capital.

- The Fed controls the money supply primarily through open-market operations: The purchase of government bonds increases the money supply, and the sale of government bonds decreases the money supply. The Fed also uses other tools to control the money supply. It can expand the money supply by decreasing the discount rate, increasing its lending to banks, lowering reserve requirements, or decreasing the interest rate on reserves. It can contract the money supply by increasing the discount rate, decreasing its lending to banks, raising reserve requirements, or increasing the interest rate on reserves.

- When individuals deposit money in banks and banks loan out some of these deposits, the quantity of money in the economy increases. Because the banking system influences the money supply in this way, the Fed's control of the money supply is imperfect.

- The Fed has in recent years set monetary policy by choosing a target for the federal funds rate, a short-term interest rate at which banks make loans to one another. As the Fed achieves its target, it adjusts the money supply.

Key Concepts

money, *p. 610*
medium of exchange, *p. 611*
unit of account, *p. 611*
store of value, *p. 611*
liquidity, *p. 611*
commodity money, *p. 611*
fiat money, *p. 612*
currency, *p. 613*
demand deposits, *p. 613*

Federal Reserve (Fed), *p. 615*
central bank, *p. 615*
money supply, *p. 616*
monetary policy, *p. 616*
reserves, *p. 617*
fractional-reserve banking, *p. 618*
reserve ratio, *p. 618*
money multiplier, *p. 620*
bank capital, *p. 620*

leverage, *p. 621*
leverage ratio, *p. 621*
capital requirement, *p. 621*
open-market operations, *p. 622*
discount rate, *p. 623*
reserve requirements, *p. 624*
federal funds rate, *p. 628*

Questions for Review

1. What distinguishes money from other assets in the economy?

2. What is commodity money? What is fiat money? Which kind do we use?

3. What are demand deposits and why should they be included in the stock of money?

4. Who is responsible for setting monetary policy in the United States? How is this group chosen?

5. If the Fed wants to increase the money supply with open-market operations, what does it do?

6. Why don't banks hold 100 percent reserves? How is the amount of reserves banks hold related to the amount of money the banking system creates?

7. Bank A has a leverage ratio of 10, while Bank B has a leverage ratio of 20. Similar losses on bank loans at the two banks cause the value of their assets to fall by 7 percent. Which bank shows a larger change in bank capital? Does either bank remain solvent? Explain.

8. What is the discount rate? What happens to the money supply when the Fed raises the discount rate?

9. What are reserve requirements? What happens to the money supply when the Fed raises reserve requirements?

10. Why can't the Fed control the money supply perfectly?

Quick Check Multiple Choice

1. The money supply includes all of the following EXCEPT
   a. metal coins.
   b. paper currency.
   c. lines of credit accessible with credit cards.
   d. bank balances accessible with debit cards.

2. Chloe takes $100 of currency from her wallet and deposits it into her checking account. If the bank adds the entire $100 to reserves, the money supply _____, but if the bank lends out some of the $100, the money supply _____.
   a. increases, increases even more
   b. increases, increases by less
   c. is unchanged, increases
   d. decreases, decreases by less

3. If the reserve ratio is ¼ and the central bank increases the quantity of reserves in the banking system by $120, the money supply increases by
   a. $90.
   b. $150.
   c. $160.
   d. $480.

4. A bank has capital of $200 and a leverage ratio of 5. If the value of the bank's assets decline by 10 percent, then its capital will be reduced to
   a. $100.
   b. $150.
   c. $180.
   d. $185.

5. Which of the following actions by the Fed would reduce the money supply?
   a. an open-market purchase of government bonds
   b. a reduction in banks' reserve requirements
   c. an increase in the interest rate paid on reserves
   d. a decrease in the discount rate on Fed lending

6. In a system of fractional-reserve banking, even without any action by the central bank, the money supply declines if households choose to hold _____ currency or if banks choose to hold _____ excess reserves.
   a. more, more
   b. more, less
   c. less, more
   d. less, less

Problems and Applications

1. Which of the following are considered money in the U.S. economy? Which are not? Explain your answers by discussing each of the three functions of money.
   a. a U.S. penny
   b. a Mexican peso
   c. a Picasso painting
   d. a plastic credit card

2. Your uncle repays a $100 loan from Tenth National Bank (TNB) by writing a $100 check from his TNB checking account. Use T-accounts to show the effect of this transaction on your uncle and on TNB. Has your uncle's wealth changed? Explain.

3. Beleaguered State Bank (BSB) holds $250 million in deposits and maintains a reserve ratio of 10 percent.
   a. Show a T-account for BSB.
   b. Now suppose that BSB's largest depositor withdraws $10 million in cash from her account. If BSB decides to restore its reserve ratio by reducing the amount of loans outstanding, show its new T-account.
   c. Explain what effect BSB's action will have on other banks.
   d. Why might it be difficult for BSB to take the action described in part (b)? Discuss another way for BSB to return to its original reserve ratio.

4. You take $100 you had kept under your mattress and deposit it in your bank account. If this $100 stays in the banking system as reserves and if banks hold reserves equal to 10 percent of deposits, by how much does the total amount of deposits in the banking system increase? By how much does the money supply increase?

5. Happy Bank starts with $200 in bank capital. It then takes in $800 in deposits. It keeps 12.5 percent (1/8th) of deposits in reserve. It uses the rest of its assets to make bank loans.
   a. Show the balance sheet of Happy Bank.
   b. What is Happy Bank's leverage ratio?
   c. Suppose that 10 percent of the borrowers from Happy Bank default and these bank loans become worthless. Show the bank's new balance sheet.
   d. By what percentage do the bank's total assets decline? By what percentage does the bank's capital decline? Which change is larger? Why?

6. The Fed conducts a $10 million open-market purchase of government bonds. If the required reserve ratio is 10 percent, what is the largest possible increase in the money supply that could result? Explain. What is the smallest possible increase? Explain.

7. Assume that the reserve requirement is 5 percent. All other things being equal, will the money supply expand more if the Fed buys $2,000 worth of bonds or if someone deposits in a bank $2,000 that she had been hiding in her cookie jar? If one creates more, how much more does it create? Support your thinking.

8. Suppose that the reserve requirement for checking deposits is 10 percent and that banks do not hold any excess reserves.
   a. If the Fed sells $1 million of government bonds, what is the effect on the economy's reserves and money supply?
   b. Now suppose the Fed lowers the reserve requirement to 5 percent, but banks choose to hold another 5 percent of deposits as excess reserves. Why might banks do so? What is the overall change in the money multiplier and the money supply as a result of these actions?

9. Assume that the banking system has total reserves of $100 billion. Assume also that required reserves are 10 percent of checking deposits and that banks hold no excess reserves and households hold no currency.
   a. What is the money multiplier? What is the money supply?
   b. If the Fed now raises required reserves to 20 percent of deposits, what are the change in reserves and the change in the money supply?

10. Assume that the reserve requirement is 20 percent. Also assume that banks do not hold excess reserves and there is no cash held by the public. The Fed decides that it wants to expand the money supply by $40 million.
    a. If the Fed is using open-market operations, will it buy or sell bonds?
    b. What quantity of bonds does the Fed need to buy or sell to accomplish the goal? Explain your reasoning.

11. The economy of Elmendyn contains 2,000 $1 bills.
    a. If people hold all money as currency, what is the quantity of money?
    b. If people hold all money as demand deposits and banks maintain 100 percent reserves, what is the quantity of money?
    c. If people hold equal amounts of currency and demand deposits and banks maintain 100 percent reserves, what is the quantity of money?
    d. If people hold all money as demand deposits and banks maintain a reserve ratio of 10 percent, what is the quantity of money?
    e. If people hold equal amounts of currency and demand deposits and banks maintain a reserve ratio of 10 percent, what is the quantity of money?

Go to CengageBrain.com to purchase access to the proven, critical Study Guide to accompany this text, which features additional notes and context, practice tests, and much more.

Money Growth and Inflation

Today, if you want to buy an ice-cream cone, you need at least a couple of dollars, but that has not always been the case. In the 1930s, my grandmother ran a sweet shop in Trenton, New Jersey, where she sold ice-cream cones in two sizes. A cone with a small scoop of ice cream cost 3 cents. Hungry customers could buy a large scoop for a nickel.

You may not be surprised at the increase in the price of ice cream. In most modern economies, most prices tend to rise over time. This increase in the overall level of prices is called *inflation*. Earlier in the book, we examined how economists measure the inflation rate as the percentage change in the consumer price index (CPI), the GDP deflator, or some other index of the overall price level. These price indexes show that, in the United States over the past 80 years, prices have risen on average 3.6 percent per year. Accumulated over so many years, a 3.6 percent annual inflation rate leads to a seventeenfold increase in the price level.

Inflation may seem natural and inevitable to a person who grew up in the United States during recent decades, but in fact, it is not inevitable at all. There were long periods in the 19th century during which most prices fell—a phenomenon called *deflation*. The average level of prices in the U.S. economy was 23 percent lower in 1896 than in 1880, and this deflation was a major issue in the presidential election of 1896. Farmers, who had accumulated large debts, suffered when the fall in crop prices reduced their incomes and thus their ability to pay off their debts. They advocated government policies to reverse the deflation.

Although inflation has been the norm in more recent history, there has been substantial variation in the rate at which prices rise. From 2002 to 2012, prices rose at an average rate of 2.5 percent per year. By contrast, in the 1970s, prices rose by 7.8 percent per year, which meant the price level more than doubled over the decade. The public often views such high rates of inflation as a major economic problem. In fact, when President Jimmy Carter ran for reelection in 1980, challenger Ronald Reagan pointed to high inflation as one of the failures of Carter's economic policy.

International data show an even broader range of inflation experiences. In 2012, while the U.S. inflation rate was 2.1 percent, inflation was −0.1 percent in Japan, 5.1 percent in Russia, 9.3 percent in India, and 21.1 percent in Venezuela. And even the high inflation rates in India and Venezuela are moderate by some standards. In February 2008, the central bank of Zimbabwe announced the inflation rate in its economy had reached 24,000 percent; some independent estimates put the figure even higher. An extraordinarily high rate of inflation such as this is called *hyperinflation*.

What determines whether an economy experiences inflation and, if so, how much? This chapter answers this question by developing the *quantity theory of money*. Chapter 1 summarized this theory as one of the *Ten Principles of Economics:* Prices rise when the government prints too much money. This insight has a long and venerable tradition among economists. The quantity theory was discussed by the famous 18th-century philosopher and economist David Hume and was advocated more recently by the prominent economist Milton Friedman. This theory can explain moderate inflations, such as those we have experienced in the United States, as well as hyperinflations.

After developing a theory of inflation, we turn to a related question: Why is inflation a problem? At first glance, the answer to this question may seem obvious: Inflation is a problem because people don't like it. In the 1970s, when the United States experienced a relatively high rate of inflation, opinion polls placed inflation as the most important issue facing the nation. President Ford echoed this sentiment in 1974 when he called inflation "public enemy number one." Ford wore a "WIN" button on his lapel—for Whip Inflation Now.

But what, exactly, are the costs that inflation imposes on a society? The answer may surprise you. Identifying the various costs of inflation is not as straightforward as it first appears. As a result, although all economists decry hyperinflation, some economists argue that the costs of moderate inflation are not nearly as large as the public believes.

30-1 The Classical Theory of Inflation

We begin our study of inflation by developing the quantity theory of money. This theory is often called "classical" because it was developed by some of the earliest economic thinkers. Most economists today rely on this theory to explain the long-run determinants of the price level and the inflation rate.

30-1a The Level of Prices and the Value of Money

Suppose we observe that over some period of time the price of an ice-cream cone rises from a nickel to a dollar. What conclusion should we draw from the fact that people are willing to give up so much more money in exchange for a cone? It is possible that people have come to enjoy ice cream more (perhaps because some chemist has developed a miraculous new flavor). Yet that is probably not the case. It is more likely that people's enjoyment of ice cream has stayed roughly the same and that, over time, the money used to buy ice cream has become less valuable. Indeed, the first insight about inflation is that it is more about the value of money than about the value of goods.

This insight helps point the way toward a theory of inflation. When the CPI and other measures of the price level rise, commentators are often tempted to look at the many individual prices that make up these price indexes, "The CPI rose by 3 percent last month, led by a 20 percent rise in the price of coffee and a 30 percent rise in the price of heating oil." Although this approach does contain some interesting information about what's happening in the economy, it also misses a key point: Inflation is an economy-wide phenomenon that concerns, first and foremost, the value of the economy's medium of exchange.

The economy's overall price level can be viewed in two ways. So far, we have viewed the price level as the price of a basket of goods and services. When the price level rises, people have to pay more for the goods and services they buy. Alternatively, we can view the price level as a measure of the value of money. A rise in the price level means a lower value of money because each dollar in your wallet now buys a smaller quantity of goods and services.

It may help to express these ideas mathematically. Suppose P is the price level as measured, for instance, by the CPI or the GDP deflator. Then P measures the number of dollars needed to buy a basket of goods and services. Now turn this idea around: The quantity of goods and services that can be bought with $1 equals $1/P$. In other words, if P is the price of goods and services measured in terms of money, $1/P$ is the value of money measured in terms of goods and services.

This mathematics is simplest to understand in an economy that produces only a single good, say, ice-cream cones. In that case, P would be the price of a cone. When the price of a cone (P) is $2, then the value of a dollar ($1/P$) is half a cone. When the price (P) rises to $3, the value of a dollar ($1/P$) falls to a third of a cone. The actual economy produces thousands of goods and services, so we use a price index rather than the price of a single good. But the logic remains the same: When the overall price level rises, the value of money falls.

"So what's it going to be? The same size as last year or the same price as last year?"

30-1b Money Supply, Money Demand, and Monetary Equilibrium

What determines the value of money? The answer to this question, like many in economics, is supply and demand. Just as the supply and demand for bananas determines the price of bananas, the supply and demand for money determines the value of money. Thus, our next step in developing the quantity theory of money is to consider the determinants of money supply and money demand.

First consider money supply. In the preceding chapter, we discussed how the Federal Reserve (Fed), together with the banking system, determines the supply of money. When the Fed sells bonds in open-market operations, it receives dollars in exchange and contracts the money supply. When the Fed buys government bonds, it pays out dollars and expands the money supply. In addition, if any of these dollars are deposited in banks, which hold some as reserves and loan out the rest, the money multiplier swings into action, and these open-market operations can have an even greater effect on the money supply. For our purposes in this chapter, we ignore the complications introduced by the banking system and simply take the quantity of money supplied as a policy variable that the Fed controls.

Now consider money demand. Most fundamentally, the demand for money reflects how much wealth people want to hold in liquid form. Many factors influence the quantity of money demanded. The amount of currency that people hold in their wallets, for instance, depends on how much they rely on credit cards and on whether an automatic teller machine is easy to find. And as we will emphasize in Chapter 34, the quantity of money demanded depends on the interest rate that a person could earn by using the money to buy an interest-bearing bond rather than leaving it in a wallet or low-interest checking account.

Although many variables affect the demand for money, one variable stands out in importance: the average level of prices in the economy. People hold money because it is the medium of exchange. Unlike other assets, such as bonds or stocks, people can use money to buy the goods and services on their shopping lists. How much money they choose to hold for this purpose depends on the prices of those goods and services. The higher the prices are, the more money the typical transaction requires, and the more money people will choose to hold in their wallets and checking accounts. That is, a higher price level (a lower value of money) increases the quantity of money demanded.

What ensures that the quantity of money the Fed supplies balances the quantity of money people demand? The answer, it turns out, depends on the time horizon being considered. Later in this book, we examine the short-run answer and learn that interest rates play a key role. The long- run answer, however, is much simpler. *In the long run, money supply and money demand are brought into equilibrium by the overall level of prices.* If the price level is above the equilibrium level, people will want to hold more money than the Fed has created, so the price level must fall to balance supply and demand. If the price level is below the equilibrium level, people will want to hold less money than the Fed has created, and the price level must rise to balance supply and demand. At the equilibrium price level, the quantity of money that people want to hold exactly balances the quantity of money supplied by the Fed.

Figure 1 illustrates these ideas. The horizontal axis of this graph shows the quantity of money. The left vertical axis shows the value of money $1/P$, and the right vertical axis shows the price level P. Notice that the price-level axis on the right is inverted: A low price level is shown near the top of this axis, and a high price level is shown near the bottom. This inverted axis illustrates that when the value of money is high (as shown near the top of the left axis), the price level is low (as shown near the top of the right axis).

The two curves in this figure are the supply and demand curves for money. The supply curve is vertical because the Fed has fixed the quantity of money available. The demand curve for money is downward sloping, indicating that when the value of money is low (and the price level is high), people demand a larger quantity of it to buy goods and services. At the equilibrium, shown in the figure as point A, the quantity of money demanded balances the quantity of money supplied. This equilibrium of money supply and money demand determines the value of money and the price level.

The horizontal axis shows the quantity of money. The left vertical axis shows the value of money, and the right vertical axis shows the price level. The supply curve for money is vertical because the quantity of money supplied is fixed by the Fed. The demand curve for money is downward sloping because people want to hold a larger quantity of money when each dollar buys less. At the equilibrium, point A, the value of money (on the left axis) and the price level (on the right axis) have adjusted to bring the quantity of money supplied and the quantity of money demanded into balance.

FIGURE 1

How the Supply and Demand for Money Determine the Equilibrium Price Level

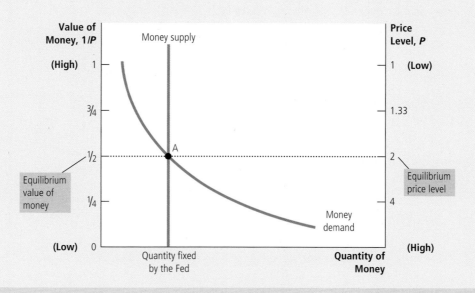

30-1c The Effects of a Monetary Injection

Let's now consider the effects of a change in monetary policy. To do so, imagine that the economy is in equilibrium and then, suddenly, the Fed doubles the supply of money by printing some dollar bills and dropping them around the country from helicopters. (Or, less dramatically and more realistically, the Fed could inject money into the economy by buying some government bonds from the public in open-market operations.) What happens after such a monetary injection? How does the new equilibrium compare to the old one?

Figure 2 shows what happens. The monetary injection shifts the supply curve to the right from MS_1 to MS_2, and the equilibrium moves from point A to point B. As a result, the value of money (shown on the left axis) decreases from ½ to ¼, and the equilibrium price level (shown on the right axis) increases from 2 to 4. In other words, when an increase in the money supply makes dollars more plentiful, the result is an increase in the price level that makes each dollar less valuable.

This explanation of how the price level is determined and why it might change over time is called the **quantity theory of money**. According to the quantity theory, the quantity of money available in an economy determines the value of money, and growth in the quantity of money is the primary cause of inflation. As economist Milton Friedman once put it, "Inflation is always and everywhere a monetary phenomenon."

quantity theory of money
a theory asserting that the quantity of money available determines the price level and that the growth rate in the quantity of money available determines the inflation rate

FIGURE 2

An Increase in the Money Supply

When the Fed increases the supply of money, the money supply curve shifts from MS_1 to MS_2. The value of money (on the left axis) and the price level (on the right axis) adjust to bring supply and demand back into balance. The equilibrium moves from point A to point B. Thus, when an increase in the money supply makes dollars more plentiful, the price level increases, making each dollar less valuable.

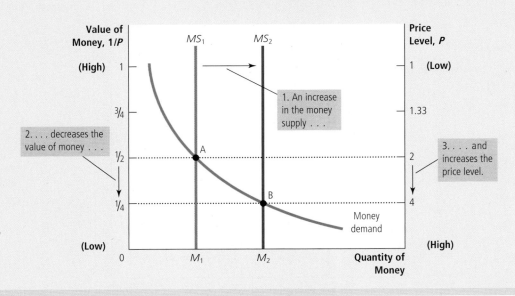

30-1d A Brief Look at the Adjustment Process

So far, we have compared the old equilibrium and the new equilibrium after an injection of money. How does the economy move from the old to the new equilibrium? A complete answer to this question requires an understanding of short-run fluctuations in the economy, which we examine later in this book. Here, we briefly consider the adjustment process that occurs after a change in the money supply.

The immediate effect of a monetary injection is to create an excess supply of money. Before the injection, the economy was in equilibrium (point A in Figure 2). At the prevailing price level, people had exactly as much money as they wanted. But after the helicopters drop the new money and people pick it up off the streets, people have more dollars in their wallets than they want. At the prevailing price level, the quantity of money supplied now exceeds the quantity demanded.

People try to get rid of this excess supply of money in various ways. They might use it to buy goods and services. Or they might use this excess money to make loans to others by buying bonds or by depositing the money in a bank savings account. These loans allow other people to buy goods and services. In either case, the injection of money increases the demand for goods and services.

The economy's ability to supply goods and services, however, has not changed. As we saw in the chapter on production and growth, the economy's output of goods and services is determined by the available labor, physical capital, human capital, natural resources, and technological knowledge. None of these is altered by the injection of money.

Thus, the greater demand for goods and services causes the prices of goods and services to increase. The increase in the price level, in turn, increases the quantity of money demanded because people are using more dollars for every transaction. Eventually, the economy reaches a new equilibrium (point B in Figure 2) at which the quantity of money demanded again equals the quantity of money supplied. In this way, the overall price level for goods and services adjusts to bring money supply and money demand into balance.

30-1e The Classical Dichotomy and Monetary Neutrality

We have seen how changes in the money supply lead to changes in the average level of prices of goods and services. How do monetary changes affect other economic variables, such as production, employment, real wages, and real interest rates? This question has long intrigued economists, including David Hume in the 18th century.

Hume and his contemporaries suggested that economic variables should be divided into two groups. The first group consists of **nominal variables**—variables measured in monetary units. The second group consists of **real variables**—variables measured in physical units. For example, the income of corn farmers is a nominal variable because it is measured in dollars, whereas the quantity of corn they produce is a real variable because it is measured in bushels. Nominal GDP is a nominal variable because it measures the dollar value of the economy's output of goods and services; real GDP is a real variable because it measures the total quantity of goods and services produced and is not influenced by the current prices of those goods and services. The separation of real and nominal variables is now called the **classical dichotomy**. (A *dichotomy* is a division into two groups, and *classical* refers to the earlier economic thinkers.)

Applying the classical dichotomy is tricky when we turn to prices. Most prices are quoted in units of money and, therefore, are nominal variables. When we say that the price of corn is $2 a bushel or that the price of wheat is $1 a bushel, both prices are nominal variables. But what about a *relative* price—the price of one thing compared to another? In our example, we could say that the price of a bushel of corn is 2 bushels of wheat. This relative price is not measured in terms of money. When comparing the prices of any two goods, the dollar signs cancel, and the resulting number is measured in physical units. Thus, while dollar prices are nominal variables, relative prices are real variables.

This lesson has many applications. For instance, the real wage (the dollar wage adjusted for inflation) is a real variable because it measures the rate at which people exchange goods and services for a unit of labor. Similarly, the real interest rate (the nominal interest rate adjusted for inflation) is a real variable because it measures the rate at which people exchange goods and services today for goods and services in the future.

Why separate variables into these groups? The classical dichotomy is useful because different forces influence real and nominal variables. According to classical analysis, nominal variables are influenced by developments in the economy's monetary system, whereas money is largely irrelevant for explaining real variables.

This idea was implicit in our discussion of the real economy in the long run. In previous chapters, we examined how real GDP, saving, investment, real interest rates, and unemployment are determined without mentioning the existence of money. In that analysis, the economy's production of goods and services depends

nominal variables
variables measured in monetary units

real variables
variables measured in physical units

classical dichotomy
the theoretical separation of nominal and real variables

on productivity and factor supplies, the real interest rate balances the supply and demand for loanable funds, the real wage balances the supply and demand for labor, and unemployment results when the real wage is for some reason kept above its equilibrium level. These conclusions have nothing to do with the quantity of money supplied.

Changes in the supply of money, according to classical analysis, affect nominal variables but not real ones. When the central bank doubles the money supply, the price level doubles, the dollar wage doubles, and all other dollar values double. Real variables, such as production, employment, real wages, and real interest rates, are unchanged. The irrelevance of monetary changes for real variables is called **monetary neutrality**.

An analogy helps explain monetary neutrality. As the unit of account, money is the yardstick we use to measure economic transactions. When a central bank doubles the money supply, all prices double, and the value of the unit of account falls by half. A similar change would occur if the government were to reduce the length of the yard from 36 to 18 inches: With the new, shorter yardstick, all *measured* distances (nominal variables) would double, but the *actual* distances (real variables) would remain the same. The dollar, like the yard, is merely a unit of measurement, so a change in its value should not have real effects.

Is monetary neutrality realistic? Not completely. A change in the length of the yard from 36 to 18 inches would not matter in the long run, but in the short run, it would lead to confusion and mistakes. Similarly, most economists today believe that over short periods of time—within the span of a year or two—monetary changes affect real variables. Hume himself also doubted that monetary neutrality would apply in the short run. (We will study short-run non-neutrality later in the book, and this topic will help explain why the Fed changes the money supply over time.)

Yet classical analysis is right about the economy in the long run. Over the course of a decade, monetary changes have significant effects on nominal variables (such as the price level) but only negligible effects on real variables (such as real GDP). When studying long-run changes in the economy, the neutrality of money offers a good description of how the world works.

monetary neutrality
the proposition that changes in the money supply do not affect real variables

30-1f Velocity and the Quantity Equation

We can obtain another perspective on the quantity theory of money by considering the following question: How many times per year is the typical dollar bill used to pay for a newly produced good or service? The answer to this question is given by a variable called the **velocity of money**. In physics, the term *velocity* refers to the speed at which an object travels. In economics, the velocity of money refers to the speed at which the typical dollar bill travels around the economy from wallet to wallet.

velocity of money
the rate at which money changes hands

To calculate the velocity of money, we divide the nominal value of output (nominal GDP) by the quantity of money. If P is the price level (the GDP deflator), Y the quantity of output (real GDP), and M the quantity of money, then velocity is

$$V = (P \times Y) / M.$$

To see why this makes sense, imagine a simple economy that produces only pizza. Suppose that the economy produces 100 pizzas in a year, that a pizza sells for $10, and that the quantity of money in the economy is $50. Then the velocity of money is

$$V = (\$10 \times 100) / \$50$$
$$= 20.$$

In this economy, people spend a total of $1,000 per year on pizza. For this $1,000 of spending to take place with only $50 of money, each dollar bill must change hands on average 20 times per year.

With slight algebraic rearrangement, this equation can be rewritten as

$$M \times V = P \times Y.$$

This equation states that the quantity of money (M) times the velocity of money (V) equals the price of output (P) times the amount of output (Y). It is called the **quantity equation** because it relates the quantity of money (M) to the nominal value of output ($P \times Y$). The quantity equation shows that an increase in the quantity of money in an economy must be reflected in one of the other three variables: The price level must rise, the quantity of output must rise, or the velocity of money must fall.

In many cases, it turns out that the velocity of money is relatively stable. For example, Figure 3 shows nominal GDP, the quantity of money (as measured by M2), and the velocity of money for the U.S. economy since 1960. During the period, the money supply and nominal GDP both increased about thirtyfold. By contrast, the velocity of money, although not exactly constant, has not changed dramatically. Thus, for some purposes, the assumption of constant velocity may be a good approximation.

quantity equation
the equation $M \times V = P \times Y$, which relates the quantity of money, the velocity of money, and the dollar value of the economy's output of goods and services

This figure shows the nominal value of output as measured by nominal GDP, the quantity of money as measured by M2, and the velocity of money as measured by their ratio. For comparability, all three series have been scaled to equal 100 in 1960. Notice that nominal GDP and the quantity of money have grown dramatically over this period, while velocity has been relatively stable.

FIGURE 3

Nominal GDP, the Quantity of Money, and the Velocity of Money

Source: U.S. Department of Commerce; Federal Reserve Board.

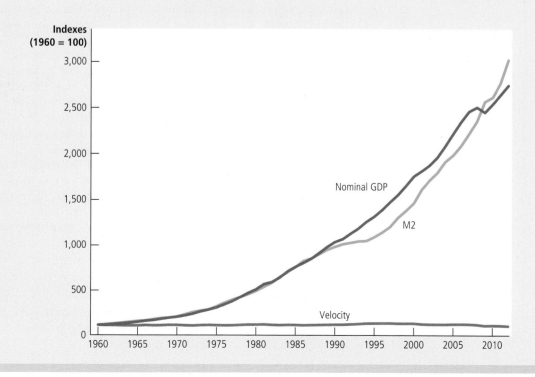

We now have all the elements necessary to explain the equilibrium price level and inflation rate. They are as follows:

1. The velocity of money is relatively stable over time.
2. Because velocity is stable, when the central bank changes the quantity of money (M), it causes proportionate changes in the nominal value of output ($P \times Y$).
3. The economy's output of goods and services (Y) is primarily determined by factor supplies (labor, physical capital, human capital, and natural resources) and the available production technology. In particular, because money is neutral, money does not affect output.
4. With output (Y) determined by factor supplies and technology, when the central bank alters the money supply (M) and induces proportional changes in the nominal value of output ($P \times Y$), these changes are reflected in changes in the price level (P).
5. Therefore, when the central bank increases the money supply rapidly, the result is a high rate of inflation.

These five steps are the essence of the quantity theory of money.

case study   **Money and Prices during Four Hyperinflations**

Although earthquakes can wreak havoc on a society, they have the beneficial by-product of providing much useful data for seismologists. These data can shed light on alternative theories and, thereby, help society predict and deal with future threats. Similarly, hyperinflations offer monetary economists a natural experiment they can use to study the effects of money on the economy.

Hyperinflations are interesting in part because the changes in the money supply and price level are so large. Indeed, hyperinflation is generally defined as inflation that exceeds 50 percent *per month*. This means that the price level increases more than a hundredfold over the course of a year.

The data on hyperinflation show a clear link between the quantity of money and the price level. Figure 4 graphs data from four classic hyperinflations that occurred during the 1920s in Austria, Hungary, Germany, and Poland. Each graph shows the quantity of money in the economy and an index of the price level. The slope of the money line represents the rate at which the quantity of money was growing, and the slope of the price line represents the inflation rate. The steeper the lines, the higher the rates of money growth or inflation.

Notice that in each graph the quantity of money and the price level are almost parallel. In each instance, growth in the quantity of money is moderate at first and so is inflation. But over time, the quantity of money in the economy starts growing faster and faster. At about the same time, inflation also takes off. Then when the quantity of money stabilizes, the price level stabilizes as well. These episodes illustrate well one of the *Ten Principles of Economics*: Prices rise when the government prints too much money. ◢

30-1g The Inflation Tax

If inflation is so easy to explain, why do countries experience hyperinflation? That is, why do the central banks of these countries choose to print so much money that its value is certain to fall rapidly over time?

This figure shows the quantity of money and the price level during four hyperinflations. (Note that these variables are graphed on *logarithmic* scales. This means that equal vertical distances on the graph represent equal *percentage* changes in the variable.) In each case, the quantity of money and the price level move closely together. The strong association between these two variables is consistent with the quantity theory of money, which states that growth in the money supply is the primary cause of inflation.

FIGURE 4

Money and Prices during Four Hyperinflations

Source: Adapted from Thomas J. Sargent, "The End of Four Big Inflations," in Robert Hall, ed., *Inflation* (Chicago: University of Chicago Press, 1983), pp. 41–93.

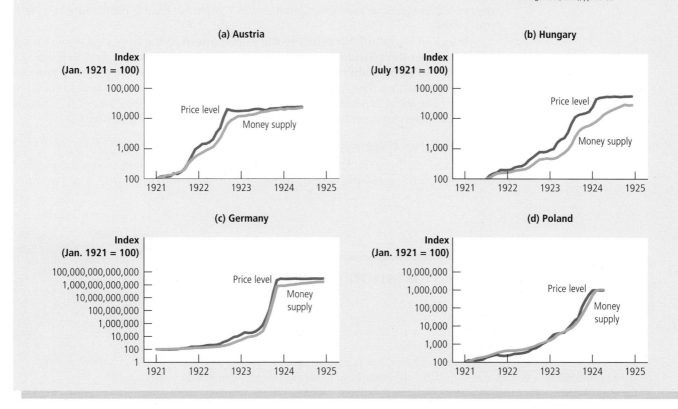

The answer is that the governments of these countries are using money creation as a way to pay for their spending. When the government wants to build roads, pay salaries to its soldiers, or give transfer payments to the poor or elderly, it first has to raise the necessary funds. Normally, the government does this by levying taxes, such as income and sales taxes, and by borrowing from the public by selling government bonds. Yet the government can also pay for spending simply by printing the money it needs.

When the government raises revenue by printing money, it is said to levy an **inflation tax**. The inflation tax is not exactly like other taxes, however, because no one receives a bill from the government for this tax. Instead, the inflation tax is subtler. When the government prints money, the price level rises, and the dollars in your wallet are less valuable. Thus, *the inflation tax is like a tax on everyone who holds money.*

inflation tax
the revenue the government raises by creating money

The importance of the inflation tax varies from country to country and over time. In the United States in recent years, the inflation tax has been a trivial source of revenue: It has accounted for less than 3 percent of government revenue. During the 1770s, however, the Continental Congress of the fledgling United States relied heavily on the inflation tax to pay for military spending. Because the new government had a limited ability to raise funds through regular taxes or borrowing, printing dollars was the easiest way to pay the American soldiers. As the quantity theory predicts, the result was a high rate of inflation: Prices measured in terms of the continental dollar rose more than a hundredfold over a few years.

Almost all hyperinflations follow the same pattern as the hyperinflation during the American Revolution. The government has high spending, inadequate tax revenue, and limited ability to borrow. As a result, it turns to the printing press to pay for its spending. The massive increases in the quantity of money lead to massive inflation. The inflation ends when the government institutes fiscal reforms—such as cuts in government spending—that eliminate the need for the inflation tax.

30-1h The Fisher Effect

According to the principle of monetary neutrality, an increase in the rate of money growth raises the rate of inflation but does not affect any real variable.

FYI

Hyperinflation in Zimbabwe

During the first decade of the 2000s, the nation of Zimbabwe experienced one of history's most extreme examples of hyperinflation. In many ways, the story is common: Large government budget deficits led to the creation of large quantities of money and high rates of inflation. The hyperinflation ended in April 2009 when the Zimbabwe central bank stopped printing the Zimbabwe dollar, and the nation started using foreign currencies such as the U.S. dollar and the South African rand as the medium of exchange.

Estimates vary about how high inflation in Zimbabwe got, but the magnitude of the problem is well documented by the denomination of the notes being issued by the central bank. Before the hyperinflation started, the Zimbabwe dollar was worth a bit more than one U.S. dollar, so the denominations of the paper currency were similar to those one would find in the United States. A person might carry, for example, a 10-dollar note in his wallet. In January 2008, however, after years of high inflation, the Reserve Bank of Zimbabwe issued notes worth 10 million Zimbabwe dollars, which was then equivalent to about 4 U.S. dollars. But even that did not prove to be large enough. A year later, the central bank announced it would issue notes worth 10 trillion Zimbabwe dollars, then worth about 3 U.S. dollars.

As prices rose and the central bank printed ever-larger denominations of money, the older, smaller-denomination currency lost value and became almost worthless. One indication of this phenomenon can be found on this sign from a public restroom in Zimbabwe: ◢

© Eugene Baron

An important application of this principle concerns the effect of money on interest rates. Interest rates are important variables for macroeconomists to understand because they link the economy of the present and the economy of the future through their effects on saving and investment.

To understand the relationship between money, inflation, and interest rates, recall the distinction between the nominal interest rate and the real interest rate. The *nominal interest rate* is the interest rate you hear about at your bank. If you have a savings account, for instance, the nominal interest rate tells you how fast the number of dollars in your account will rise over time. The *real interest rate* corrects the nominal interest rate for the effect of inflation to tell you how fast the purchasing power of your savings account will rise over time. The real interest rate is the nominal interest rate minus the inflation rate:

$$\text{Real interest rate} = \text{Nominal interest rate} - \text{Inflation rate.}$$

For example, if the bank posts a nominal interest rate of 7 percent per year and the inflation rate is 3 percent per year, then the real value of the deposits grows by 4 percent per year.

We can rewrite this equation to show that the nominal interest rate is the sum of the real interest rate and the inflation rate:

$$\text{Nominal interest rate} = \text{Real interest rate} + \text{Inflation rate.}$$

This way of looking at the nominal interest rate is useful because different economic forces determine each of the two terms on the right side of this equation. As we discussed earlier in the book, the supply and demand for loanable funds determine the real interest rate. And according to the quantity theory of money, growth in the money supply determines the inflation rate.

Let's now consider how the growth in the money supply affects interest rates. In the long run over which money is neutral, a change in money growth should not affect the real interest rate. The real interest rate is, after all, a real variable. For the real interest rate not to be affected, the nominal interest rate must adjust one-for-one to changes in the inflation rate. Thus, *when the Fed increases the rate of money growth, the long-run result is both a higher inflation rate and a higher nominal interest rate*. This adjustment of the nominal interest rate to the inflation rate is called the **Fisher effect**, after Irving Fisher (1867–1947), the economist who first studied it.

Keep in mind that our analysis of the Fisher effect has maintained a long-run perspective. The Fisher effect need not hold in the short run because inflation may be unanticipated. A nominal interest rate is a payment on a loan, and it is typically set when the loan is first made. If a jump in inflation catches the borrower and lender by surprise, the nominal interest rate they agreed on will fail to reflect the higher inflation. But if inflation remains high, people will eventually come to expect it, and loan agreements will reflect this expectation. To be precise, therefore, the Fisher effect states that the nominal interest rate adjusts to expected inflation. Expected inflation moves with actual inflation in the long run, but that is not necessarily true in the short run.

The Fisher effect is crucial for understanding changes over time in the nominal interest rate. Figure 5 shows the nominal interest rate and the inflation rate in the U.S. economy since 1960. The close association between these two variables is clear. The nominal interest rate rose from the early 1960s through the 1970s

Fisher effect
the one-for-one adjustment of the nominal interest rate to the inflation rate

FIGURE 5

**The Nominal Interest Rate
and the Inflation Rate**

Source: U.S. Department of Treasury;
U.S. Department of Labor.

This figure uses annual data since 1960 to show the nominal interest rate on three-month Treasury bills and the inflation rate as measured by the CPI. The close association between these two variables is evidence for the Fisher effect: When the inflation rate rises, so does the nominal interest rate.

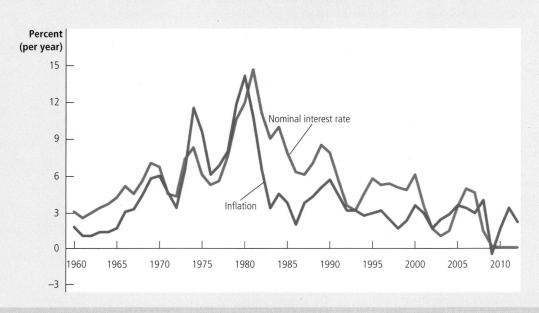

because inflation was also rising during this time. Similarly, the nominal interest rate fell from the early 1980s through the 1990s because the Fed got inflation under control. In recent years, both the nominal interest rate and the inflation rate have been low by historical standards.

Quick Quiz   *The government of a country increases the growth rate of the money supply from 5 percent per year to 50 percent per year. What happens to prices? What happens to nominal interest rates? Why might the government be doing this?*

30-2 The Costs of Inflation

In the late 1970s, when the U.S. inflation rate reached about 10 percent per year, inflation dominated debates over economic policy. And even though inflation has been low over the past 20 years, it remains a closely watched macroeconomic variable. One study found that *inflation* is the economic term mentioned most often in U.S. newspapers (ahead of second-place finisher *unemployment* and third-place finisher *productivity*).

Inflation is closely watched and widely discussed because it is thought to be a serious economic problem. But is that true? And if so, why?

30-2a A Fall in Purchasing Power? The Inflation Fallacy

If you ask the typical person why inflation is bad, he will tell you that the answer is obvious: Inflation robs him of the purchasing power of his hard-earned dollars. When prices rise, each dollar of income buys fewer goods and services. Thus, it might seem that inflation directly lowers living standards.

Yet further thought reveals a fallacy in this answer. When prices rise, buyers of goods and services pay more for what they buy. At the same time, however, sellers of goods and services get more for what they sell. Because most people earn their incomes by selling their services, such as their labor, inflation in incomes goes hand in hand with inflation in prices. Thus, *inflation does not in itself reduce people's real purchasing power*.

People believe the inflation fallacy because they do not appreciate the principle of monetary neutrality. A worker who receives an annual raise of 10 percent tends to view that raise as a reward for his own talent and effort. When an inflation rate of 6 percent reduces the real value of that raise to only 4 percent, the worker might feel that he has been cheated of what is rightfully his due. In fact, as we discussed in the chapter on production and growth, real incomes are determined by real variables, such as physical capital, human capital, natural resources, and the available production technology. Nominal incomes are determined by those factors and the overall price level. If the Fed were to lower the inflation rate from 6 percent to zero, our worker's annual raise would fall from 10 percent to 4 percent. He might feel less robbed by inflation, but his real income would not rise more quickly.

If nominal incomes tend to keep pace with rising prices, why then is inflation a problem? It turns out that there is no single answer to this question. Instead, economists have identified several costs of inflation. Each of these costs shows some way in which persistent growth in the money supply does, in fact, have some effect on real variables.

30-2b Shoeleather Costs

As we have discussed, inflation is like a tax on the holders of money. The tax itself is not a cost to society: It is only a transfer of resources from households to the government. Yet most taxes give people an incentive to alter their behavior to avoid paying the tax, and this distortion of incentives causes deadweight losses for society as a whole. Like other taxes, the inflation tax also causes deadweight losses because people waste scarce resources trying to avoid it.

How can a person avoid paying the inflation tax? Because inflation erodes the real value of the money in your wallet, you can avoid the inflation tax by holding less money. One way to do this is to go to the bank more often. For example, rather than withdrawing $200 every four weeks, you might withdraw $50 once a week. By making more frequent trips to the bank, you can keep more of your wealth in your interest-bearing savings account and less in your wallet, where inflation erodes its value.

The cost of reducing your money holdings is called the **shoeleather cost** of inflation because making more frequent trips to the bank causes your shoes to wear out more quickly. Of course, this term is not to be taken literally: The actual cost of reducing your money holdings is not the wear and tear on your shoes but the time and convenience you must sacrifice to keep less money on hand than you would if there were no inflation.

The shoeleather costs of inflation may seem trivial. Indeed, they are in the U.S. economy, which has had only moderate inflation in recent years. But this cost

shoeleather cost
the resources wasted when inflation encourages people to reduce their money holdings

is magnified in countries experiencing hyperinflation. Here is a description of one person's experience in Bolivia during its hyperinflation (as reported in the August 13, 1985, issue of *The Wall Street Journal*):

> When Edgar Miranda gets his monthly teacher's pay of 25 million pesos, he hasn't a moment to lose. Every hour, pesos drop in value. So, while his wife rushes to market to lay in a month's supply of rice and noodles, he is off with the rest of the pesos to change them into black-market dollars.
>
> Mr. Miranda is practicing the First Rule of Survival amid the most out-of-control inflation in the world today. Bolivia is a case study of how runaway inflation undermines a society. Price increases are so huge that the figures build up almost beyond comprehension. In one six-month period, for example, prices soared at an annual rate of 38,000 percent. By official count, however, last year's inflation reached 2,000 percent, and this year's is expected to hit 8,000 percent—though other estimates range many times higher. In any event, Bolivia's rate dwarfs Israel's 370 percent and Argentina's 1,100 percent—two other cases of severe inflation.
>
> It is easier to comprehend what happens to the thirty-eight-year-old Mr. Miranda's pay if he doesn't quickly change it into dollars. The day he was paid 25 million pesos, a dollar cost 500,000 pesos. So he received $50. Just days later, with the rate at 900,000 pesos, he would have received $27.

As this story shows, the shoeleather costs of inflation can be substantial. With the high inflation rate, Mr. Miranda does not have the luxury of holding the local money as a store of value. Instead, he is forced to convert his pesos quickly into goods or into U.S. dollars, which offer a more stable store of value. The time and effort that Mr. Miranda expends to reduce his money holdings are a waste of resources. If the monetary authority pursued a low-inflation policy, Mr. Miranda would be happy to hold pesos, and he could put his time and effort to more productive use. In fact, shortly after this article was written, the Bolivian inflation rate was reduced substantially with a more restrictive monetary policy.

30-2c Menu Costs

Most firms do not change the prices of their products every day. Instead, firms often announce prices and leave them unchanged for weeks, months, or even years. One survey found that the typical U.S. firm changes its prices about once a year.

Firms change prices infrequently because there are costs of changing prices. Costs of price adjustment are called **menu costs**, a term derived from a restaurant's cost of printing a new menu. Menu costs include the costs of deciding on new prices, printing new price lists and catalogs, sending these new price lists and catalogs to dealers and customers, advertising the new prices, and even dealing with customer annoyance over price changes.

Inflation increases the menu costs that firms must bear. In the current U.S. economy, with its low inflation rate, annual price adjustment is an appropriate business strategy for many firms. But when high inflation makes firms' costs rise rapidly, annual price adjustment is impractical. During hyperinflations, for example, firms must change their prices daily or even more often just to keep up with all the other prices in the economy.

30-2d Relative-Price Variability and the Misallocation of Resources

Suppose that the Eatabit Eatery prints a new menu with new prices every January and then leaves its prices unchanged for the rest of the year. If there is

menu costs
the costs of changing prices

no inflation, Eatabit's relative prices—the prices of its meals compared to other prices in the economy—would be constant over the course of the year. By contrast, if the inflation rate is 12 percent per year, Eatabit's relative prices will automatically fall by 1 percent each month. The restaurant's relative prices will be high in the early months of the year, just after it has printed a new menu, and low in the later months. And the higher the inflation rate, the greater is this automatic variability. Thus, because prices change only once in a while, inflation causes relative prices to vary more than they otherwise would.

Why does this matter? The reason is that market economies rely on relative prices to allocate scarce resources. Consumers decide what to buy by comparing the quality and prices of various goods and services. Through these decisions, they determine how the scarce factors of production are allocated among industries and firms. When inflation distorts relative prices, consumer decisions are distorted and markets are less able to allocate resources to their best use.

30-2e Inflation-Induced Tax Distortions

Almost all taxes distort incentives, cause people to alter their behavior, and lead to a less efficient allocation of the economy's resources. Many taxes, however, become even more problematic in the presence of inflation. The reason is that lawmakers often fail to take inflation into account when writing the tax laws. Economists who have studied the tax code conclude that inflation tends to raise the tax burden on income earned from savings.

One example of how inflation discourages saving is the tax treatment of *capital gains*—the profits made by selling an asset for more than its purchase price. Suppose that in 1980 you used some of your savings to buy stock in Apple Inc. for $10 and that in 2010 you sold the stock for $50. According to the tax law, you have earned a capital gain of $40, which you must include in your income when computing how much income tax you owe. But suppose the overall price level doubled from 1980 to 2010. In this case, the $10 you invested in 1980 is equivalent (in terms of purchasing power) to $20 in 2010. When you sell your stock for $50, you have a real gain (an increase in purchasing power) of only $30. The tax code, however, does not take account of inflation and assesses you a tax on a gain of $40. Thus, inflation exaggerates the size of capital gains and inadvertently increases the tax burden on this type of income.

Another example is the tax treatment of interest income. The income tax treats the *nominal* interest earned on savings as income, even though part of the nominal interest rate merely compensates for inflation. To see the effects of this policy, consider the numerical example in Table 1. The table compares two economies, both of which tax interest income at a rate of 25 percent. In Economy A, inflation is zero and the nominal and real interest rates are both 4 percent. In this case, the 25 percent tax on interest income reduces the real interest rate from 4 percent to 3 percent. In Economy B, the real interest rate is again 4 percent but the inflation rate is 8 percent. As a result of the Fisher effect, the nominal interest rate is 12 percent. Because the income tax treats this entire 12 percent interest as income, the government takes 25 percent of it, leaving an after-tax nominal interest rate of only 9 percent and an after-tax real interest rate of only 1 percent. In this case, the 25 percent tax on interest income reduces the real interest rate from 4 percent to 1 percent. Because the after-tax real interest rate provides the incentive to save, saving is much less attractive in the economy with inflation (Economy B) than in the economy with stable prices (Economy A).

TABLE 1

How Inflation Raises the Tax Burden on Saving
In the presence of zero inflation, a 25 percent tax on interest income reduces the real interest rate from 4 percent to 3 percent. In the presence of 8 percent inflation, the same tax reduces the real interest rate from 4 percent to 1 percent.

	Economy A (price stability)	Economy B (inflation)
Real interest rate	4%	4%
Inflation rate	0	8
Nominal interest rate (real interest rate + inflation rate)	4	12
Reduced interest due to 25 percent tax (0.25 × nominal interest rate)	1	3
After-tax nominal interest rate (0.75 × nominal interest rate)	3	9
After-tax real interest rate (after-tax nominal interest rate − inflation rate)	3	1

The taxes on nominal capital gains and on nominal interest income are two examples of how the tax code interacts with inflation. There are many others. Because of these inflation-induced tax changes, higher inflation tends to discourage people from saving. Recall that the economy's saving provides the resources for investment, which in turn is a key ingredient to long-run economic growth. Thus, when inflation raises the tax burden on saving, it tends to depress the economy's long-run growth rate. There is, however, no consensus among economists about the size of this effect.

One solution to this problem, other than eliminating inflation, is to index the tax system. That is, the tax laws could be rewritten to take account of the effects of inflation. In the case of capital gains, for example, the tax code could adjust the purchase price using a price index and assess the tax only on the real gain. In the case of interest income, the government could tax only real interest income by excluding that portion of the interest income that merely compensates for inflation. To some extent, the tax laws have moved in the direction of indexation. For example, the income levels at which income tax rates change are adjusted automatically each year based on changes in the CPI. Yet many other aspects of the tax laws—such as the tax treatment of capital gains and interest income—are not indexed.

In an ideal world, the tax laws would be written so that inflation would not alter anyone's real tax liability. In the world in which we live, however, tax laws are far from perfect. More complete indexation would probably be desirable, but it would further complicate a tax code that many people already consider too complex.

30-2f Confusion and Inconvenience

Imagine that we took a poll and asked people the following question: "This year the yard is 36 inches. How long do you think it should be next year?" Assuming we could get people to take us seriously, they would tell us that the yard should stay the same length—36 inches. Anything else would just complicate life needlessly.

What does this finding have to do with inflation? Recall that money, as the economy's unit of account, is what we use to quote prices and record debts. In other words, money is the yardstick with which we measure economic transactions. The job of the Fed is a bit like the job of the Bureau of Standards—to ensure the reliability of a commonly used unit of measurement. When the Fed increases the money supply and creates inflation, it erodes the real value of the unit of account.

It is difficult to judge the costs of the confusion and inconvenience that arise from inflation. Earlier, we discussed how the tax code incorrectly measures real incomes in the presence of inflation. Similarly, accountants incorrectly measure firms' earnings when prices are rising over time. Because inflation causes dollars at different times to have different real values, computing a firm's profit—the difference between its revenue and costs—is more complicated in an economy with inflation. Therefore, to some extent, inflation makes investors less able to sort successful from unsuccessful firms, which in turn impedes financial markets in their role of allocating the economy's saving to alternative types of investment.

30-2g A Special Cost of Unexpected Inflation: Arbitrary Redistributions of Wealth

So far, the costs of inflation we have discussed occur even if inflation is steady and predictable. Inflation has an additional cost, however, when it comes as a surprise. Unexpected inflation redistributes wealth among the population in a way that has nothing to do with either merit or need. These redistributions occur because many loans in the economy are specified in terms of the unit of account—money.

Consider an example. Suppose that Sam Student takes out a $20,000 loan at a 7 percent interest rate from Bigbank to attend college. In 10 years, the loan will come due. After his debt has compounded for 10 years at 7 percent, Sam will owe Bigbank $40,000. The real value of this debt will depend on inflation over the decade. If Sam is lucky, the economy will have a hyperinflation. In this case, wages and prices will rise so high that Sam will be able to pay the $40,000 debt out of pocket change. By contrast, if the economy goes through a major deflation, then wages and prices will fall, and Sam will find the $40,000 debt a greater burden than he anticipated.

This example shows that unexpected changes in prices redistribute wealth among debtors and creditors. A hyperinflation enriches Sam at the expense of Bigbank because it diminishes the real value of the debt; Sam can repay the loan in dollars that are less valuable than he anticipated. Deflation enriches Bigbank at Sam's expense because it increases the real value of the debt; in this case, Sam has to repay the loan in dollars that are more valuable than he anticipated. If inflation were predictable, then Bigbank and Sam could take inflation into account when setting the nominal interest rate. (Recall the Fisher effect.) But if inflation is hard to predict, it imposes risk on Sam and Bigbank that both would prefer to avoid.

This cost of unexpected inflation is important to consider together with another fact: Inflation is especially volatile and uncertain when the average rate of inflation is high. This is seen most simply by examining the experience of different countries. Countries with low average inflation, such as Germany in the late 20th century, tend to have stable inflation. Countries with high average inflation, such as many countries in Latin America, tend to have unstable inflation. There are no known examples of economies with high, stable inflation. This relationship between the level and volatility of inflation points to another cost of inflation. If a country pursues a high-inflation monetary policy, it will have to bear not only the costs of high expected inflation but also the arbitrary redistributions of wealth associated with unexpected inflation.

30-2h Inflation Is Bad, but Deflation May Be Worse

In recent U.S. history, inflation has been the norm. But the level of prices has fallen at times, such as during the late 19th century and early 1930s. From 1998 to 2012, Japan experienced a 4-percent decline in its overall price level. So as we conclude our discussion of the costs of inflation, we should briefly consider the costs of deflation as well.

Some economists have suggested that a small and predictable amount of deflation may be desirable. Milton Friedman pointed out that deflation would lower the nominal interest rate (recall the Fisher effect) and that a lower nominal interest rate would reduce the cost of holding money. The shoeleather costs of holding money would, he argued, be minimized by a nominal interest rate close to zero, which in turn would require deflation equal to the real interest rate. This prescription for moderate deflation is called the *Friedman rule*.

Yet there are also costs of deflation. Some of these mirror the costs of inflation. For example, just as a rising price level induces menu costs and relative-price variability, so does a falling price level. Moreover, in practice, deflation is rarely as steady and predictable as Friedman recommended. More often, it comes as a surprise, resulting in the redistribution of wealth toward creditors and away from debtors. Because debtors are often poorer, these redistributions in wealth are particularly painful.

Perhaps most important, deflation often arises because of broader macroeconomic difficulties. As we will see in future chapters, falling prices result when some event, such as a monetary contraction, reduces the overall demand for goods and services in the economy. This fall in aggregate demand can lead to falling incomes and rising unemployment. In other words, deflation is often a symptom of deeper economic problems.

---

case study   ***The Wizard of Oz* and the Free-Silver Debate**

As a child, you probably saw the movie *The Wizard of Oz*, based on a children's book written in 1900. The movie and book tell the story of a young girl, Dorothy, who finds herself lost in a strange land far from home. You probably did not know, however, that some scholars believe that the story is actually an allegory about U.S. monetary policy in the late 19th century.

From 1880 to 1896, the price level in the U.S. economy fell by 23 percent. Because this event was unanticipated, it led to a major redistribution of wealth. Most farmers in the western part of the country were debtors. Their creditors were the bankers in the east. When the price level fell, it caused the real value of these debts to rise, which enriched the banks at the expense of the farmers.

According to Populist politicians of the time, the solution to the farmers' problem was the free coinage of silver. During this period, the United States was operating with a gold standard. The quantity of gold determined the money supply and, thereby, the price level. The free-silver advocates wanted silver, as well as gold, to be used as money. If adopted, this proposal would have increased the money supply, pushed up the price level, and reduced the real burden of the farmers' debts.

The debate over silver was heated, and it was central to the politics of the 1890s. A common election slogan of the Populists was "We Are Mortgaged. All but Our Votes." One prominent advocate of free silver was William Jennings Bryan, the Democratic nominee for president in 1896. He is remembered in part for a speech at the Democratic Party's nominating convention in which he said, "You shall not press down upon the brow of labor this crown of thorns. You shall not crucify mankind upon a cross of gold." Rarely since then have politicians waxed so poetic about alternative approaches to monetary policy. Nonetheless, Bryan lost the election to Republican William McKinley, and the United States remained on the gold standard.

L. Frank Baum, author of the book *The Wonderful Wizard of Oz,* was a midwestern journalist. When he sat down to write a story for children, he made the characters represent protagonists in the major political battle of his time. Here is how economic historian Hugh Rockoff, writing in the *Journal of Political Economy* in 1990, interprets the story:

An early debate over monetary policy

DOROTHY:	Traditional American values
TOTO:	Prohibitionist party, also called the Teetotalers
SCARECROW:	Farmers
TIN WOODSMAN:	Industrial workers
COWARDLY LION:	William Jennings Bryan
MUNCHKINS:	Citizens of the East
WICKED WITCH OF THE EAST:	Grover Cleveland
WICKED WITCH OF THE WEST:	William McKinley
WIZARD:	Marcus Alonzo Hanna, chairman of the Republican Party
OZ:	Abbreviation for ounce of gold
YELLOW BRICK ROAD:	Gold standard

At the end of Baum's story, Dorothy does find her way home, but it is not by just following the yellow brick road. After a long and perilous journey, she learns that the wizard is incapable of helping her or her friends. Instead, Dorothy finally discovers the magical power of her *silver* slippers. (When the book was made into a movie in 1939, Dorothy's slippers were changed from silver to ruby. The Hollywood filmmakers were more interested in showing off the new technology of Technicolor than in telling a story about 19th-century monetary policy.)

The Populists lost the debate over the free coinage of silver, but they eventually got the monetary expansion and inflation that they wanted. In 1898, prospectors discovered gold near the Klondike River in the Canadian Yukon. Increased supplies of gold also arrived from the mines of South Africa. As a result, the money supply and the price level started to rise in the United States and in other countries operating on the gold standard. Within 15 years, prices in the United States were back to the levels that had prevailed in the 1880s, and farmers were better able to handle their debts. ◢

Quick Quiz   *List and describe six costs of inflation.*

30-3 Conclusion

This chapter discussed the causes and costs of inflation. The primary cause of inflation is growth in the quantity of money. When the central bank creates money in large quantities, the value of money falls quickly. To maintain stable prices, the central bank must maintain strict control over the money supply.

The costs of inflation are subtler. They include shoeleather costs, menu costs, increased variability of relative prices, unintended changes in tax liabilities, confusion and inconvenience, and arbitrary redistributions of wealth. Are these costs, in total, large or small? All economists agree that they become huge during hyperinflation. But during periods of moderate inflation—when prices rise by less than 10 percent per year—the size of these costs is more open to debate.

Although this chapter presented many of the most important lessons about inflation, the discussion is incomplete. When the central bank reduces the rate of money growth, prices rise less rapidly, as the quantity theory suggests. Yet as the economy makes the transition to this lower inflation rate, the change in monetary policy will have disruptive effects on production and employment. That is, even though monetary policy is neutral in the long run, it has profound effects on real variables in the short run. Later in this book we will examine the reasons for short-run monetary non-neutrality to enhance our understanding of the causes and effects of inflation.

Summary

- The overall level of prices in an economy adjusts to bring money supply and money demand into balance. When the central bank increases the supply of money, it causes the price level to rise. Persistent growth in the quantity of money supplied leads to continuing inflation.

- The principle of monetary neutrality asserts that changes in the quantity of money influence nominal variables but not real variables. Most economists believe that monetary neutrality approximately describes the behavior of the economy in the long run.

- A government can pay for some of its spending simply by printing money. When countries rely heavily on this "inflation tax," the result is hyperinflation.

- One application of the principle of monetary neutrality is the Fisher effect. According to the Fisher effect, when the inflation rate rises, the nominal interest rate rises by the same amount so that the real interest rate remains the same.

- Many people think that inflation makes them poorer because it raises the cost of what they buy. This view is a fallacy, however, because inflation also raises nominal incomes.

- Economists have identified six costs of inflation: shoeleather costs associated with reduced money holdings, menu costs associated with more frequent adjustment of prices, increased variability of relative prices, unintended changes in tax liabilities due to nonindexation of the tax code, confusion and inconvenience resulting from a changing unit of account, and arbitrary redistributions of wealth between debtors and creditors. Many of these costs are large during hyperinflation, but the size of these costs for moderate inflation is less clear.

Key Concepts

quantity theory of money, *p. 637*
nominal variables, *p. 639*
real variables, *p. 639*
classical dichotomy, *p. 639*

monetary neutrality, *p. 640*
velocity of money, *p. 640*
quantity equation, *p. 641*
inflation tax, *p. 643*

Fisher effect, *p. 645*
shoeleather costs, *p. 647*
menu costs, *p. 648*

Questions for Review

1. Explain how an increase in the price level affects the real value of money.

2. According to the quantity theory of money, what is the effect of an increase in the quantity of money?

3. Explain the difference between nominal and real variables and give two examples of each. According to the principle of monetary neutrality, which variables are affected by changes in the quantity of money?

4. In what sense is inflation like a tax? How does thinking about inflation as a tax help explain hyperinflation?

5. According to the Fisher effect, how does an increase in the inflation rate affect the real interest rate and the nominal interest rate?

6. What are the costs of inflation? Which of these costs do you think are most important for the U.S. economy?

7. If inflation is less than expected, who benefits—debtors or creditors? Explain.

Quick Check Multiple Choice

1. The classical principle of monetary neutrality states that changes in the money supply do not influence _____ variables and is thought most applicable in the _____ run.
   a. nominal, short
   b. nominal, long
   c. real, short
   d. real, long

2. If nominal GDP is $400, real GDP is $200, and the money supply is $100, then
   a. the price level is ½, and velocity is 2.
   b. the price level is ½, and velocity is 4.
   c. the price level is 2, and velocity is 2.
   d. the price level is 2, and velocity is 4.

3. According to the quantity theory of money, which variable in the quantity equation is most stable over long periods of time?
   a. money
   b. velocity
   c. price level
   d. output

4. Hyperinflations occur when the government runs a large budget _____, which the central

bank finances with a substantial monetary _____.
   a. deficit, contraction
   b. deficit, expansion
   c. surplus, contraction
   d. surplus, expansion

5. According to the quantity theory of money and the Fisher effect, if the central bank increases the rate of money growth,
   a. inflation and the nominal interest rate both increase.
   b. inflation and the real interest rate both increase.
   c. the nominal interest rate and the real interest rate both increase.
   d. inflation, the real interest rate, and the nominal interest rate all increase.

6. If an economy always has inflation of 10 percent per year, which of the following costs of inflation will it NOT suffer?
   a. shoeleather costs from reduced holdings of money
   b. menu costs from more frequent price adjustment
   c. distortions from the taxation of nominal capital gains
   d. arbitrary redistributions between debtors and creditors

Problems and Applications

1. Suppose that this year's money supply is $500 billion, nominal GDP is $10 trillion, and real GDP is $5 trillion.
   a. What is the price level? What is the velocity of money?
   b. Suppose that velocity is constant and the economy's output of goods and services rises by 5 percent each year. What will

happen to nominal GDP and the price level next year if the Fed keeps the money supply constant?
   c. What money supply should the Fed set next year if it wants to keep the price level stable?
   d. What money supply should the Fed set next year if it wants an inflation of 10 percent?

2. Suppose that changes in bank regulations expand the availability of credit cards so that people need to hold less cash.
   a. How does this event affect the demand for money?
   b. If the Fed does not respond to this event, what will happen to the price level?
   c. If the Fed wants to keep the price level stable, what should it do?

3. It is sometimes suggested that the Fed should try to achieve zero inflation. If we assume that velocity is constant, does this zero-inflation goal require that the rate of money growth equal zero? If yes, explain why. If no, explain what the rate of money growth should equal.

4. Suppose that a country's inflation rate increases sharply. What happens to the inflation tax on the holders of money? Why is wealth that is held in savings accounts *not* subject to a change in the inflation tax? Can you think of any way holders of savings accounts are hurt by the increase in the inflation rate?

5. Let's consider the effects of inflation in an economy composed of only two people: Bob, a bean farmer, and Rita, a rice farmer. Bob and Rita both always consume equal amounts of rice and beans. In 2013, the price of beans was $1 and the price of rice was $3.
   a. Suppose that in 2014 the price of beans was $2 and the price of rice was $6. What was inflation? Was Bob better off, worse off, or unaffected by the changes in prices? What about Rita?
   b. Now suppose that in 2014 the price of beans was $2 and the price of rice was $4. What was inflation? Was Bob better off, worse off, or unaffected by the changes in prices? What about Rita?
   c. Finally, suppose that in 2014 the price of beans was $2 and the price of rice was $1.50. What was inflation? Was Bob better off, worse off, or unaffected by the changes in prices? What about Rita?
   d. What matters more to Bob and Rita—the overall inflation rate or the relative price of rice and beans?

6. If the tax rate is 40 percent, compute the before-tax real interest rate and the after-tax real interest rate in each of the following cases.
   a. The nominal interest rate is 10 percent, and the inflation rate is 5 percent.
   b. The nominal interest rate is 6 percent, and the inflation rate is 2 percent.
   c. The nominal interest rate is 4 percent, and inflation rate is 1 percent.

7. Recall that money serves three functions in the economy. What are those functions? How does inflation affect the ability of money to serve each of these functions?

8. Suppose that people expect inflation to equal 3 percent, but in fact, prices rise by 5 percent. Describe how this unexpectedly high inflation rate would help or hurt the following:
   a. the government
   b. a homeowner with a fixed-rate mortgage
   c. a union worker in the second year of a labor contract
   d. a college that has invested some of its endowment in government bonds

9. Explain whether the following statements are true, false, or uncertain.
   a. "Inflation hurts borrowers and helps lenders, because borrowers must pay a higher rate of interest."
   b. "If prices change in a way that leaves the overall price level unchanged, then no one is made better or worse off."
   c. "Inflation does not reduce the purchasing power of most workers."

Go to CengageBrain.com to purchase access to the proven, critical Study Guide to accompany this text, which features additional notes and context, practice tests, and much more.

The Macroeconomics
of Open Economies

Open-Economy Macroeconomics: Basic Concepts

When you decide to buy a car, you may compare the latest models offered by Ford and Toyota. When you take your next vacation, you may consider spending it on a beach in Florida or in Mexico. When you start saving for your retirement, you may choose between a mutual fund that buys stock in U.S. companies and one that buys stock in foreign companies. In all these cases, you are participating not just in the U.S. economy but in economies around the world.

Openness to international trade yields clear benefits: Trade allows people to produce what they produce best and to consume the great variety of goods and services produced around the world. Indeed, one of the *Ten Principles of Economics* highlighted in Chapter 1 is that trade can make everyone better off. International trade can raise living standards in all countries by allowing each country to specialize in producing those goods and services in which it has a comparative advantage.

So far, our development of macroeconomics has largely ignored the economy's interaction with other economies around the world. For most questions in macroeconomics, international issues are peripheral. For instance, when we discuss the natural rate of unemployment and the causes of inflation, the effects of international trade can safely be ignored. Indeed, to keep their models simple, macroeconomists often assume a **closed economy**—an economy that does not interact with other economies.

Yet when macroeconomists study an **open economy**—an economy that interacts freely with other economies around the world—they encounter a whole set of new issues. This chapter and the next provide an introduction to open-economy macroeconomics. We begin in this chapter by discussing the key macroeconomic variables that describe an open economy's interactions in world markets. You may have noticed mention of these variables—exports, imports, the trade balance, and exchange rates—when reading news reports or watching the nightly news. Our first job is to understand what these data mean. In the next chapter, we develop a model to explain how these variables are determined and how they are affected by various government policies.

closed economy
an economy that does not interact with other economies in the world

open economy
an economy that interacts freely with other economies around the world

31-1 The International Flows of Goods and Capital

An open economy interacts with other economies in two ways: It buys and sells goods and services in world product markets, and it buys and sells capital assets such as stocks and bonds in world financial markets. Here we discuss these two activities and the close relationship between them.

31-1a The Flow of Goods: Exports, Imports, and Net Exports

Exports are domestically produced goods and services that are sold abroad, and **imports** are foreign-produced goods and services that are sold domestically. When Boeing, the U.S. aircraft manufacturer, builds a plane and sells it to Air France, the sale is an export for the United States and an import for France. When Volvo, the Swedish car manufacturer, makes a car and sells it to a U.S. resident, the sale is an import for the United States and an export for Sweden.

The **net exports** of any country are the difference between the value of its exports and the value of its imports:

Net exports = Value of country's exports − Value of country's imports.

The Boeing sale raises U.S. net exports, and the Volvo sale reduces U.S. net exports. Because net exports tell us whether a country is, in total, a seller or a buyer in world markets for goods and services, net exports are also called the **trade balance**. If net exports are positive, exports are greater than imports, indicating that the country sells more goods and services abroad than it buys from other countries. In this case, the country is said to run a **trade surplus**. If net exports are negative, exports are less than imports, indicating that the country sells fewer goods and services abroad than it buys from other

exports
goods and services that are produced domestically and sold abroad

imports
goods and services that are produced abroad and sold domestically

net exports
the value of a nation's exports minus the value of its imports; also called the trade balance

trade balance
the value of a nation's exports minus the value of its imports; also called net exports

trade surplus
an excess of exports over imports

countries. In this case, the country is said to run a **trade deficit**. If net exports are zero, its exports and imports are exactly equal, and the country is said to have **balanced trade**.

In the next chapter, we develop a theory that explains an economy's trade balance, but even at this early stage, it is easy to think of many factors that might influence a country's exports, imports, and net exports. Those factors include the following:

- The tastes of consumers for domestic and foreign goods.
- The prices of goods at home and abroad.
- The exchange rates at which people can use domestic currency to buy foreign currencies.
- The incomes of consumers at home and abroad.
- The cost of transporting goods from country to country.
- Government policies toward international trade.

As these variables change, so does the amount of international trade.

trade deficit
an excess of imports over exports

balanced trade
a situation in which exports equal imports

"But we're not just talking about buying a car—we're talking about confronting this country's trade deficit with Japan."

case study **The Increasing Openness of the U.S. Economy**
One dramatic change in the U.S. economy over the past six decades has been the increasing importance of international trade and finance. This change is illustrated in Figure 1, which shows the total value of goods and services exported to other countries and imported from other countries expressed as a percentage of gross domestic product (GDP). In the 1950s, imports and exports of goods and services were typically between 4 and 5 percent of GDP. In recent years, they have been about three times that level. The trading partners of the United States include a diverse group of countries. As of 2012, the largest

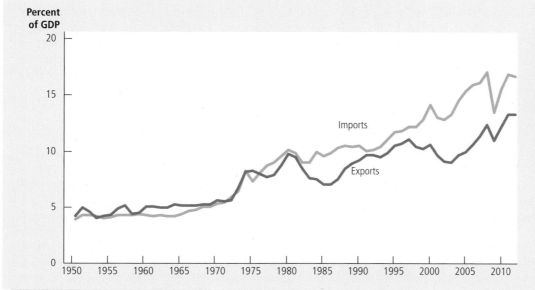

FIGURE 1

The Internationalization of the U.S. Economy
This figure shows exports and imports of the U.S. economy as a percentage of U.S. GDP since 1950. The substantial increases over time show the increasing importance of international trade and finance.

Source: U.S. Department of Commerce.

trading partner, as measured by imports and exports combined, was Canada, followed by China, Mexico, Japan, Germany, and the United Kingdom.

The increase in international trade over the past several decades is partly due to improvements in transportation. In 1950, the average merchant ship carried less than 10,000 tons of cargo; today, many ships carry more than 100,000 tons. The long-distance jet was introduced in 1958, and the wide-body jet in 1967, making air transport far cheaper than it had been. Because of these developments, goods that once had to be produced locally can now be traded around the world. Cut flowers grown in Israel are flown to the United States to be sold. Fresh fruits and vegetables that can grow only in summer in the United States can now be consumed in winter as well because they can be shipped from countries in the Southern Hemisphere.

The increase in international trade has also been influenced by advances in telecommunications, which have allowed businesses to reach overseas customers more easily. For example, the first transatlantic telephone cable was not laid

IN THE NEWS

The Changing Nature of U.S. Exports

International trade can show up in surprising places.

Jeremy Lin and America's "New Exports"

By Austan Goolsbee

Linsanity swept the nation last week. The undrafted Harvard graduate Jeremy Lin seemed to transform himself from bench-warmer to MVP candidate in a matter of days. New York Knicks #17 jerseys became the biggest seller in the NBA and interest in Mr. Lin surged world-wide.

That same week we learned that China's president-to-be, Xi Jinping, is an NBA fan. After meeting President Obama at the White House, Mr. Xi traveled to Iowa and then attended a Lakers game in Los Angeles. Mr. Obama, for his part, visited a Boeing 787 plant to tout exports as an engine of growth.

Though seemingly unrelated, these three events together highlighted one of the more promising ways out of our economic doldrums: growing exports—with exports broadly

defined to include things like entertainment royalties, tourism, travel and services.

While U.S. economic conditions have improved in recent months, anxiety lingers and the slumps in housing and consumer spending remain. Exports, however, have grown impressively and have plenty of room to keep expanding.

During our last economic expansion, we focused on the home market while the other advanced economies' exports grew three times faster than ours did. Big emerging markets grew even more.

Today, growing exports are a natural opportunity for us and one of the last areas of bipartisan agreement in Washington. And exports are not confined to traditional manufactured goods.

When a foreign visitor comes to America on vacation and, like Mr. Xi, buys an NBA ticket in Los Angeles or a lunch in Muscatine, Iowa, those count in official statistics as exports. If a fan in Indonesia watches an NBA game or buys a Jeremy Lin jersey, the royalties

count as an export. Many services increase our exports: tuition paid by foreign students, fares paid on U.S. airlines by foreign fliers, ad sales on Google from foreign companies.

These things add up. Last year, according to the Bureau of Economic Analysis (BEA), the U.S. exported $2.1 trillion of goods and services (the most ever) and more than $600 billion of that came from services.

Think of them as the New Exports. We already export far more of them than any other country. We export more educations than computers and more tourism than aerospace products or machinery. Unlike our massive trade deficit in goods, we run major trade surpluses in the New Exports—$179 billion of surplus in 2011 and probably more in 2012, according to the BEA. This supports millions of jobs across America.

until 1956. As recently as 1966, the technology allowed only 138 simultaneous conversations between North America and Europe. Today, because e-mail is such a common form of business communication, it is almost as easy to communicate with a customer across the world as it is to communicate with one across town.

Technological progress has also fostered international trade by changing the kinds of goods that economies produce. When bulky raw materials (such as steel) and perishable goods (such as foodstuffs) were a large part of the world's output, transporting goods was often costly and sometimes impossible. By contrast, goods produced with modern technology are often light and easy to transport. Consumer electronics, for instance, have low weight for every dollar of value, which makes them easy to produce in one country and sell in another. An even more extreme example is the film industry. Once a studio in Hollywood makes a movie, it can send copies of the film around the world at almost zero cost. And indeed, movies are a major export of the United States.

Promoting the New Exports requires more than just the conventional prying open of foreign markets and reducing tariff and regulatory barriers to our goods. It involves fighting restrictions on Internet commerce and enforcing intellectual-property rules. It also involves some less confrontational (and often easier) strategies such as improving foreigners' opinions of America so they want to come visit or send their children to school here, and then expanding student and tourist visas to enable them to do so.

Modest investments can facilitate major private-sector economic gains. Take tourists coming from countries like Brazil. In a recent survey, 94 % of Brazilians said it was either difficult or nearly impossible to get here. To obtain a visa, they must undergo a multi-stage ordeal that includes traveling to a personal interview in a city with a U.S. consulate—of which there are only four in all of Brazil. Start to finish, the process can take up to five months.

Last month President Obama called for speeding up the visa process to promote tourism here. The U.S. Travel Association estimates that adding a consular official costs, with overhead, around $280,000 per year. Since the average Brazilian traveler to the U.S. spends around $5,000, the association estimates that a single official can generate as much as $50 million of travel exports for U.S. business (not to mention more than $1 million in visa fees to the U.S. government).

Supporting New Exports doesn't require diplomatic battles with China or shepherding new trade agreements through Congress.

Jeremy Lin: Export Promoter.

These are exports that other countries want us to have and that we have missed by our own short-sightedness. Last week we extended the payroll tax cut to help the economy. We have given tax incentives to encourage companies to invest. Why not also use short-run government incentives to encourage New Exports, such as limited-time discounts on airline taxes, visa-application costs and airport-landing fees?

As a Chicago Bulls fan, I find the resurgent Knicks irritating. Still, I will root for more Linsanity because with every game watched in Asia, jersey sold in Europe or visit to an NBA game by a foreign tourist, this young man is doing more than just helping his team. He's demonstrating a way for our economy to grow. Playing for a .500 team, Mr. Lin probably won't be up there cutting down the nets in celebration at the end of the year. He was an economics major, though, so if it's any consolation to him, he's already helped cut down the trade deficit.

Mr. Goolsbee is a professor of economics at the University of Chicago. He was formerly an economic adviser to President Obama.

The government's trade policies have also been a factor in increasing international trade. As we discussed earlier in this book, economists have long believed that free trade between countries is mutually beneficial. Over time, most policymakers around the world have come to accept these conclusions. International agreements, such as the North American Free Trade Agreement (NAFTA) and the General Agreement on Tariffs and Trade (GATT), have gradually lowered tariffs, import quotas, and other trade barriers. The pattern of increasing trade illustrated in Figure 1 is a phenomenon that most economists and policymakers endorse and encourage. ◢

31-1b The Flow of Financial Resources: Net Capital Outflow

So far, we have been discussing how residents of an open economy participate in world markets for goods and services. In addition, residents of an open economy participate in world financial markets. A U.S. resident with $25,000 could use that money to buy a car from Toyota, or she could instead use that money to buy stock in the Toyota Corporation. The first transaction would represent a flow of goods, whereas the second would represent a flow of capital.

The term **net capital outflow** refers to the difference between the purchase of foreign assets by domestic residents and the purchase of domestic assets by foreigners:

> **net capital outflow**
> *the purchase of foreign assets by domestic residents minus the purchase of domestic assets by foreigners*

$$\text{Net capital outflow} = \text{Purchase of foreign assets by domestic residents}$$
$$- \text{Purchase of domestic assets by foreigners.}$$

When a U.S. resident buys stock in Telmex, the Mexican telecommunications company, the purchase increases the first term on the right side of this equation and, therefore, increases U.S. net capital outflow. When a Japanese resident buys a bond issued by the U.S. government, the purchase increases the second term on the right side of this equation and, therefore, decreases U.S. net capital outflow.

The flow of capital between the U.S. economy and the rest of the world takes two forms. If McDonald's opens up a fast-food outlet in Russia, that is an example of *foreign direct investment*. Alternatively, if an American buys stock in a Russian corporation, that is an example of *foreign portfolio investment*. In the first case, the American owner (McDonald's Corporation) actively manages the investment, whereas in the second case, the American owner (the stockholder) has a more passive role. In both cases, U.S. residents are buying assets located in another country, so both purchases increase U.S. net capital outflow.

The net capital outflow (sometimes called *net foreign investment*) can be either positive or negative. When it is positive, domestic residents are buying more foreign assets than foreigners are buying domestic assets. Capital is said to be flowing out of the country. When the net capital outflow is negative, domestic residents are buying less foreign assets than foreigners are buying domestic assets. Capital is said to be flowing into the country. That is, when net capital outflow is negative, a country is experiencing a capital inflow.

We develop a theory to explain net capital outflow in the next chapter. Here let's consider briefly some of the more important variables that influence net capital outflow:

- The real interest rates paid on foreign assets.
- The real interest rates paid on domestic assets.
- The perceived economic and political risks of holding assets abroad.
- The government policies that affect foreign ownership of domestic assets.

For example, consider U.S. investors deciding whether to buy Mexican government bonds or U.S. government bonds. (Recall that a bond is, in effect, an IOU of the issuer.) To make this decision, U.S. investors compare the real interest rates offered on the two bonds. The higher a bond's real interest rate, the more attractive it is. While making this comparison, however, U.S. investors must also take into account the risk that one of these governments might default on its debt (that is, not pay interest or principal when it is due), as well as any restrictions that the Mexican government has imposed, or might impose in the future, on foreign investors in Mexico.

31-1c The Equality of Net Exports and Net Capital Outflow

We have seen that an open economy interacts with the rest of the world in two ways—in world markets for goods and services and in world financial markets. Net exports and net capital outflow each measure a type of imbalance in these markets. Net exports measure an imbalance between a country's exports and its imports. Net capital outflow measures an imbalance between the amount of foreign assets bought by domestic residents and the amount of domestic assets bought by foreigners.

An important but subtle fact of accounting states that, for an economy as a whole, net capital outflow (*NCO*) must always equal net exports (*NX*):

$$NCO = NX.$$

This equation holds because every transaction that affects one side of this equation affects the other side by exactly the same amount. This equation is an *identity*— an equation that must hold because of how the variables in the equation are defined and measured.

To see why this accounting identity is true, let's consider an example. Imagine that you are a computer programmer residing in the United States. One day, you write some software and sell it to a Japanese consumer for 10,000 yen. The sale of software is an export of the United States, so it increases U.S. net exports. What else happens to ensure that this identity holds? The answer depends on what you do with the 10,000 yen you are paid.

First, let's suppose that you simply stuff the yen in your mattress. (We might say you have a yen for yen.) In this case, you are using some of your income to invest in the Japanese economy. That is, a domestic resident (you) has acquired a foreign asset (the Japanese currency). The increase in U.S. net exports is matched by an increase in the U.S. net capital outflow.

More realistically, however, if you want to invest in the Japanese economy, you won't do so by holding on to Japanese currency. More likely, you would use the 10,000 yen to buy stock in a Japanese corporation, or you might buy a Japanese government bond. Yet the result of your decision is much the same: A domestic resident ends up acquiring a foreign asset. The increase in U.S. net capital outflow (the purchase of the Japanese stock or bond) exactly equals the increase in U.S. net exports (the sale of software).

Let's now change the example. Suppose that instead of using the 10,000 yen to buy a Japanese asset, you use them to buy a good made in Japan, such as a Nintendo Wii. As a result of the Wii purchase, U.S. imports increase. Together, the software export and the Wii import represent balanced trade. Because exports and imports increase by the same amount, net exports are unchanged. In this case, no American ends up acquiring a foreign asset and no foreigner ends up acquiring a U.S. asset, so there is also no impact on U.S. net capital outflow.

A final possibility is that you go to a local bank to exchange your 10,000 yen for U.S. dollars. But this doesn't change the situation because the bank now has to do something with the 10,000 yen. It can buy Japanese assets (a U.S. net capital outflow); it can buy a Japanese good (a U.S. import); or it can sell the yen to another American who wants to make such a transaction. In the end, U.S. net exports must equal U.S. net capital outflow.

This example all started when a U.S. programmer sold some software abroad, but the story is much the same when Americans buy goods and services from other countries. For example, if Walmart buys $50 million of clothing from China and sells it to American consumers, something must happen to that $50 million. One possibility is that China could use the $50 million to invest in the U.S. economy. This capital inflow from China might take the form of Chinese purchases of U.S. government bonds. In this case, the purchase of the clothing reduces U.S. net exports, and the sale of bonds reduces U.S. net capital outflow. Alternatively, China could use the $50 million to buy a plane from Boeing, the U.S. aircraft manufacturer. In this case, the U.S. import of clothing balances the U.S. export of aircraft, so net exports and net capital outflow are both unchanged. In all cases, the transactions have the same effect on net exports and net capital outflow.

We can summarize these conclusions for the economy as a whole.

- When a nation is running a trade surplus ($NX > 0$), it is selling more goods and services to foreigners than it is buying from them. What is it doing with the foreign currency it receives from the net sale of goods and services abroad? It must be using it to buy foreign assets. Capital is flowing out of the country ($NCO > 0$).
- When a nation is running a trade deficit ($NX < 0$), it is buying more goods and services from foreigners than it is selling to them. How is it financing the net purchase of these goods and services in world markets? It must be selling assets abroad. Capital is flowing into the country ($NCO < 0$).

The international flow of goods and services and the international flow of capital are two sides of the same coin.

31-1d Saving, Investment, and Their Relationship to the International Flows

A nation's saving and investment are crucial to its long-run economic growth. As we have seen earlier in this book, saving and investment are equal in a closed economy. But matters are not as simple in an open economy. Let's now consider how saving and investment are related to the international flows of goods and capital as measured by net exports and net capital outflow.

As you may recall, the term *net exports* appeared earlier in the book when we discussed the components of GDP. The economy's GDP (Y) is divided among four components: consumption (C), investment (I), government purchases (G), and net exports (NX). We write this as

$$Y = C + I + G + NX.$$

Total expenditure on the economy's output of goods and services is the sum of expenditure on consumption, investment, government purchases, and net exports. Because each dollar of expenditure is placed into one of these four components, this equation is an accounting identity: It must be true because of the way the variables are defined and measured.

Recall that national saving is the income of the nation that is left after paying for current consumption and government purchases. National saving (S) equals $Y - C - G$. If we rearrange the equation to reflect this fact, we obtain

$$Y - C - G = I + NX$$
$$S = I + NX.$$

Because net exports (NX) also equal net capital outflow (NCO), we can write this equation as

$$S = \quad I \quad + \quad NCO$$

$$\text{Saving} = \frac{\text{Domestic}}{\text{investment}} + \frac{\text{Net capital}}{\text{outflow}}.$$

This equation shows that a nation's saving must equal its domestic investment plus its net capital outflow. In other words, when a U.S. citizen saves a dollar of her income for the future, that dollar can be used to finance the accumulation of domestic capital or it can be used to finance the purchase of foreign capital.

This equation should look somewhat familiar. Earlier in the book, when we analyzed the role of the financial system, we considered this identity for the special case of a closed economy. In a closed economy, net capital outflow is zero ($NCO = 0$), so saving equals investment ($S = I$). By contrast, an open economy has two uses for its saving: domestic investment and net capital outflow.

As before, we can view the financial system as standing between the two sides of this identity. For example, suppose the Garcia family decides to save some of its income for retirement. This decision contributes to national saving, the left side of our equation. If the Garcias deposit their saving in a mutual fund, the mutual fund may use some of the deposit to buy stock issued by General Motors, which uses the proceeds to build a factory in Ohio. In addition, the mutual fund may use some of the Garcias' deposit to buy stock issued by Toyota, which uses the proceeds to build a factory in Osaka. These transactions show up on the right side of the equation. From the standpoint of U.S. accounting, the General Motors expenditure on a new factory is domestic investment, and the purchase of Toyota stock by a U.S. resident is net capital outflow. Thus, all saving in the U.S. economy shows up as investment in the U.S. economy or as U.S. net capital outflow.

The bottom line is that saving, investment, and international capital flows are inextricably linked. When a nation's saving exceeds its domestic investment, its net capital outflow is positive, indicating that the nation is using some of its saving to buy assets abroad. When a nation's domestic investment exceeds its saving, its net capital outflow is negative, indicating that foreigners are financing some of this investment by purchasing domestic assets.

31-1e Summing Up

Table 1 summarizes many of the ideas presented so far in this chapter. It describes the three possibilities for an open economy: a country with a trade deficit, a country with balanced trade, and a country with a trade surplus.

Consider first a country with a trade surplus. By definition, a trade surplus means that the value of exports exceeds the value of imports. Because net exports are exports minus imports, net exports NX are greater than zero. As a result, income $Y = C + I + G + NX$ must be greater than domestic spending $C + I + G$. But if income Y is more than spending $C + I + G$, then saving $S = Y - C - G$ must

TABLE 1

International Flows of Goods and Capital: Summary
This table shows the three possible outcomes for an open economy.

Trade Deficit	Balanced Trade	Trade Surplus
Exports < Imports	Exports = Imports	Exports > Imports
Net Exports < 0	Net Exports = 0	Net Exports > 0
$Y < C + I + G$	$Y = C + I + G$	$Y > C + I + G$
Saving < Investment	Saving = Investment	Saving > Investment
Net Capital Outflow < 0	Net Capital Outflow = 0	Net Capital Outflow > 0

be more than investment I. Because the country is saving more than it is investing, it must be sending some of its saving abroad. That is, the net capital outflow must be greater than zero.

Similar logic applies to a country with a trade deficit (such as the U.S. economy in recent years). By definition, a trade deficit means that the value of exports is less than the value of imports. Because net exports are exports minus imports, net exports NX are negative. Thus, income $Y = C + I + G + NX$ must be less than domestic spending $C + I + G$. But if income Y is less than spending $C + I + G$, then saving $S = Y - C - G$ must be less than investment I. Because the country is investing more than it is saving, it must be financing some domestic investment by selling assets abroad. That is, the net capital outflow must be negative.

A country with balanced trade falls between these cases. Exports equal imports, so net exports are zero. Income equals domestic spending, and saving equals investment. The net capital outflow equals zero.

case study

Is the U.S. Trade Deficit a National Problem?

You may have heard the press call the United States "the world's largest debtor." The nation earned that description by borrowing heavily in world financial markets during the past three decades to finance large trade deficits. Why did the United States do this, and should this event give Americans reason to worry?

To answer these questions, let's see what the macroeconomic accounting identities tell us about the U.S. economy. Panel (a) of Figure 2 shows national saving and domestic investment as a percentage of GDP since 1960. Panel (b) shows net capital outflow (that is, the trade balance) as a percentage of GDP. Notice that, as the identities require, net capital outflow always equals national saving minus domestic investment. The figure shows that both national saving and domestic investment, as a percentage of GDP, fluctuate substantially over time. Before 1980, they tended to fluctuate together, so the net capital outflow was typically small— between −1 and 1 percent of GDP. Since 1980, national saving has often fallen well below domestic investment, leading to sizable trade deficits and substantial inflows of capital. That is, the net capital outflow is often a large negative number.

To understand the fluctuations in Figure 2, we need to go beyond these data and discuss the policies and events that influence national saving and domestic investment. History shows that there is no single cause of trade deficits. Rather, they can arise under a variety of circumstances. Here are three prominent historical episodes.

Unbalanced fiscal policy: From 1980 to 1987, the flow of capital into the United States went from 0.5 to 3.1 percent of GDP. This 2.6 percentage point change is largely attributable to a fall in national saving of 3.2 percentage points.

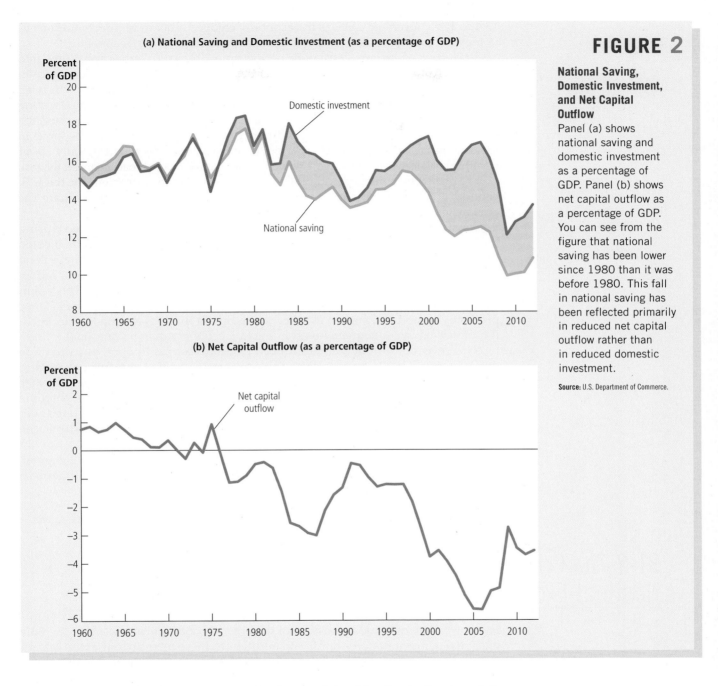

(a) National Saving and Domestic Investment (as a percentage of GDP)

(b) Net Capital Outflow (as a percentage of GDP)

FIGURE 2

National Saving, Domestic Investment, and Net Capital Outflow
Panel (a) shows national saving and domestic investment as a percentage of GDP. Panel (b) shows net capital outflow as a percentage of GDP. You can see from the figure that national saving has been lower since 1980 than it was before 1980. This fall in national saving has been reflected primarily in reduced net capital outflow rather than in reduced domestic investment.

Source: U.S. Department of Commerce.

This decline in national saving, in turn, is often explained by the decline in public saving—that is, the increase in the government budget deficit. These budget deficits arose because President Ronald Reagan cut taxes and increased defense spending, while he found his proposed cuts in nondefense spending harder to enact.

An investment boom: A different story explains the trade deficits that arose during the following decade. From 1991 to 2000, the capital flow into the United States went from 0.5 to 3.8 percent of GDP. None of this 3.3 percentage point change is attributable to a decline in saving; in fact, saving increased over this time, as the government's budget switched from deficit to surplus. But investment went from

13.4 to 17.8 percent of GDP, as the economy enjoyed a boom in information technology and many firms were eager to make these high-tech investments.

An economic downturn: During the period from 2000 to 2012, the capital flow into the United States remained large. The consistency of this variable, however, stands in stark contrast to the remarkable changes in saving and investment, both of which fell by about 4.5 percentage points. Investment fell because tough economic times starting in 2008 made additional capital less profitable, while national saving fell because the government began running extraordinarily large budget deficits in response to the downturn. At the end of this period, national saving was financing only about two-thirds of domestic investment, while flows of capital from abroad financed the rest.

Are these trade deficits and international capital flows a problem for the U.S. economy? There is no easy answer to this question. One has to evaluate the circumstances and the possible alternatives.

Consider first a trade deficit induced by a fall in saving, as occurred during the 1980s. Lower saving means that the nation is putting away less of its income to provide for its future. Once national saving has fallen, however, there is no reason to deplore the resulting trade deficits. If national saving fell without inducing a trade deficit, investment in the United States would have to fall. This fall in investment, in turn, would adversely affect the growth in the capital stock, labor productivity, and real wages. In other words, given that U.S. saving has declined, it is better to have foreigners invest in the U.S. economy than no one at all.

Now consider a trade deficit induced by an investment boom, like the trade deficits of the 1990s. In this case, the economy is borrowing from abroad to finance the purchase of new capital goods. If this additional capital provides a good return in the form of higher production of goods and services, then the economy should be able to handle the debt that is being accumulated. On the other hand, if the investment projects fail to yield the expected returns, the debts will look less desirable, at least with the benefit of hindsight.

Just as an individual can go into debt in either a prudent or a profligate manner, so can a nation. A trade deficit is not a problem in itself, but it can sometimes be a symptom of a problem. ◢

Quick Quiz *Define* net exports *and* net capital outflow. *Explain how they are related.*

31-2 The Prices for International Transactions: Real and Nominal Exchange Rates

So far, we have discussed measures of the flow of goods and services and the flow of capital across a nation's border. In addition to these quantity variables, macroeconomists also study variables that measure the prices at which these international transactions take place. Just as the price in any market serves the important role of coordinating buyers and sellers in that market, international prices help coordinate the decisions of consumers and producers as they interact in world markets. Here we discuss the two most important international prices: the nominal and real exchange rates.

nominal exchange rate
the rate at which a person can trade the currency of one country for the currency of another

31-2a Nominal Exchange Rates

The **nominal exchange rate** is the rate at which a person can trade the currency of one country for the currency of another. For example, when you go to a bank, you might see a posted exchange rate of 80 yen per dollar. If you give the bank 1 U.S. dollar, you will receive 80 Japanese yen in return; and if you give the bank 80 Japanese yen, you will receive 1 U.S. dollar. (In actuality, the bank will post slightly different prices for buying and selling yen. The difference gives the bank some profit for offering this service. For our purposes here, we can ignore these differences.)

An exchange rate can always be expressed in two ways. If the exchange rate is 80 yen per dollar, it is also 1/80(= 0.0125) dollar per yen. Throughout this book, we always express the nominal exchange rate as units of foreign currency per U.S. dollar, such as 80 yen per dollar.

If the exchange rate changes so that a dollar buys more foreign currency, that change is called an **appreciation** of the dollar. If the exchange rate changes so that a dollar buys less foreign currency, that change is called a **depreciation** of the dollar. For example, when the exchange rate rises from 80 to 90 yen per dollar, the dollar is said to appreciate. At the same time, because a Japanese yen now

appreciation
an increase in the value of a currency as measured by the amount of foreign currency it can buy

depreciation
a decrease in the value of a currency as measured by the amount of foreign currency it can buy

---

FYI   The Euro

You may have once heard of, or perhaps even seen, currencies such as the French franc, the German mark, or the Italian lira. These types of money no longer exist. During the 1990s, many European nations decided to give up their national currencies and use a common currency called the *euro*. The euro started circulating on January 1, 2002, when twelve nations began using it as their official money. As of 2013, there were seventeen nations using the euro. Several European nations, such as the United Kingdom, Sweden, and Denmark, have declined joining and have kept their own currencies.

Monetary policy for the euro area is set by the European Central Bank (ECB), with representatives from all of the participating countries. The ECB issues the euro and controls the supply of this money, much as the Federal Reserve controls the supply of dollars in the U.S. economy.

Why did these countries adopt a common currency? One benefit of a common currency is that it makes trade easier. Imagine that each of the fifty U.S. states had a different currency. Every time you crossed a state border, you would need to change your money and perform the kind of exchange-rate calculations discussed in the text. This would be inconvenient, and it might deter you from buying goods and services outside your own state. The countries of Europe decided that as their economies became more integrated, it would be better to avoid this inconvenience.

To some extent, the adoption of a common currency in Europe was a political decision based on concerns beyond the scope of standard economics.

PETER STONE / ALAMY

Some advocates of the euro wanted to reduce nationalistic feelings and to make Europeans appreciate more fully their shared history and destiny. A single money for most of the continent, they argued, would help achieve this goal.

There are, however, costs of choosing a common currency. If the nations of Europe have only one money, they can have only one monetary policy. If they disagree about what monetary policy is best, they will have to reach some kind of agreement, rather than each going its own way. Because adopting a single money has both benefits and costs, there is debate among economists about whether Europe's adoption of the euro was a good decision.

From 2010 to 2012, the euro question heated up as several European nations dealt with a variety of economic difficulties. Greece, in particular, had run up a large government debt and found itself facing possible default. As a result, it had to raise taxes and cut back government spending substantially. Some observers suggested that dealing with these problems would have been easier if the government had an additional tool—a national monetary policy. The possibility of Greece's leaving the euro area and reintroducing its own currency was even discussed. As this book was going to press, however, that outcome looked unlikely. ◢

buys less of the U.S. currency, the yen is said to depreciate. When the exchange rate falls from 80 to 70 yen per dollar, the dollar is said to depreciate, and the yen is said to appreciate.

At times, you may have heard the media report that the dollar is either "strong" or "weak." These descriptions usually refer to recent changes in the nominal exchange rate. When a currency appreciates, it is said to *strengthen* because it can then buy more foreign currency. Similarly, when a currency depreciates, it is said to *weaken*.

For any country, there are many nominal exchange rates. The U.S. dollar can be used to buy Japanese yen, British pounds, Mexican pesos, and so on. When economists study changes in the exchange rate, they often use indexes that average these many exchange rates. Just as the consumer price index turns the many prices in the economy into a single measure of the price level, an exchange rate index turns these many exchange rates into a single measure of the international value of a currency. So when economists talk about the dollar appreciating or depreciating, they often are referring to an exchange rate index that takes into account many individual exchange rates.

31-2b Real Exchange Rates

real exchange rate

the rate at which a person can trade the goods and services of one country for the goods and services of another

The **real exchange rate** is the rate at which a person can trade the goods and services of one country for the goods and services of another. For example, if you go shopping and find that a pound of Swiss cheese is twice as expensive as a pound of American cheese, the real exchange rate is ½ pound of Swiss cheese per pound of American cheese. Notice that, like the nominal exchange rate, we express the real exchange rate as units of the foreign item per unit of the domestic item. But in this instance, the item is a good rather than a currency.

Real and nominal exchange rates are closely related. To see how, consider an example. Suppose that a bushel of American rice sells for $100 and a bushel of Japanese rice sells for 16,000 yen. What is the real exchange rate between American and Japanese rice? To answer this question, we must first use the nominal exchange rate to convert the prices into a common currency. If the nominal exchange rate is 80 yen per dollar, then a price for American rice of $100 per bushel is equivalent to 8,000 yen per bushel. American rice is half as expensive as Japanese rice. The real exchange rate is ½ bushel of Japanese rice per bushel of American rice.

We can summarize this calculation for the real exchange rate with the following formula:

$$\text{Real exchange rate} = \frac{\text{Nominal exchange rate} \times \text{Domestic price}}{\text{Foreign price}}.$$

Using the numbers in our example, the formula applies as follows:

$$\text{Real exchange rate} = \frac{(80 \text{ yen/dollar}) \times (\$100/\text{bushel of American rice})}{16,000 \text{ yen/bushel of Japanese rice}}$$

$$= \frac{8,000 \text{ yen/bushel of American rice}}{16,000 \text{ yen/bushel of Japanese rice}}$$

$$= \text{½ bushel of Japanese rice/bushel of American rice}.$$

Thus, the real exchange rate depends on the nominal exchange rate and on the prices of goods in the two countries measured in the local currencies.

Why does the real exchange rate matter? As you might guess, the real exchange rate is a key determinant of how much a country exports and imports. When Uncle Ben's, Inc., is deciding whether to buy U.S. rice or Japanese rice to put into its boxes, it will ask which rice is cheaper. The real exchange rate gives the answer. As another example, imagine that you are deciding whether to take a seaside vacation in Miami, Florida, or in Cancún, Mexico. You might ask your travel agent the price of a hotel room in Miami (measured in dollars), the price of a hotel room in Cancún (measured in pesos), and the exchange rate between pesos and dollars. If you decide where to vacation by comparing costs, you are basing your decision on the real exchange rate.

When studying an economy as a whole, macroeconomists focus on overall prices rather than the prices of individual items. That is, to measure the real exchange rate, they use price indexes, such as the consumer price index, which measure the price of a basket of goods and services. By using a price index for a U.S. basket (P), a price index for a foreign basket (P^*), and the nominal exchange rate between the U.S. dollar and foreign currencies (e), we can compute the overall real exchange rate between the United States and other countries as follows:

$$\text{Real exchange rate} = (e \times P)/P^*.$$

This real exchange rate measures the price of a basket of goods and services available domestically relative to a basket of goods and services available abroad.

As we examine more fully in the next chapter, a country's real exchange rate is a key determinant of its net exports of goods and services. A depreciation (fall) in the U.S. real exchange rate means that U.S. goods have become cheaper relative to foreign goods. This change encourages consumers both at home and abroad to buy more U.S. goods and fewer goods from other countries. As a result, U.S. exports rise and U.S. imports fall; both of these changes raise U.S. net exports. Conversely, an appreciation (rise) in the U.S. real exchange rate means that U.S. goods have become more expensive compared to foreign goods, so U.S. net exports fall.

Quick Quiz   *Define nominal exchange rate and real exchange rate, and explain how they are related.* • *If the nominal exchange rate goes from 100 to 120 yen per dollar, has the dollar appreciated or depreciated?*

31-3 A First Theory of Exchange-Rate Determination: Purchasing-Power Parity

Exchange rates vary substantially over time. In 1970, a U.S. dollar could be used to buy 3.65 German marks or 627 Italian lira. In 1998, as both Germany and Italy were getting ready to adopt the euro as their common currency, a U.S. dollar bought 1.76 German marks or 1,737 Italian lira. In other words, over this period, the value of the dollar fell by more than half compared to the mark, while it more than doubled compared to the lira.

What explains these large and opposite changes? Economists have developed many models to explain how exchange rates are determined, each emphasizing just some of the many forces at work. Here we develop the simplest theory of exchange rates, called **purchasing-power parity**. This theory states that a unit of any given currency should be able to buy the same quantity of goods in all countries. Many economists believe that purchasing-power parity describes the forces that determine exchange rates in the long run. We now consider the logic on which this long-run theory of exchange rates is based, as well as the theory's implications and limitations.

31-3a The Basic Logic of Purchasing-Power Parity

The theory of purchasing-power parity is based on a principle called the *law of one price*. This law asserts that a good must sell for the same price in all locations. Otherwise, there would be opportunities for profit left unexploited. For example, suppose that coffee beans sold for less in Seattle than in Dallas. A person could buy coffee in Seattle for, say, $4 a pound and then sell it in Dallas for $5 a pound, making a profit of $1 per pound from the difference in price. The process of taking advantage of price differences for the same item in different markets is called *arbitrage*. In our example, as people took advantage of this arbitrage opportunity, they would increase the demand for coffee in Seattle and increase the supply in Dallas. The price of coffee would rise in Seattle (in response to greater demand) and fall in Dallas (in response to greater supply). This process would continue until, eventually, the prices were the same in the two markets.

Now consider how the law of one price applies to the international marketplace. If a dollar (or any other currency) could buy more coffee in the United States than in Japan, international traders could profit by buying coffee in the United States and selling it in Japan. This export of coffee from the United States to Japan would drive up the U.S. price of coffee and drive down the Japanese price. Conversely, if a dollar could buy more coffee in Japan than in the United States, traders could buy coffee in Japan and sell it in the United States. This import of coffee into the United States from Japan would drive down the U.S. price of coffee and drive up the Japanese price. In the end, the law of one price tells us that a dollar must buy the same amount of coffee in all countries.

This logic leads us to the theory of purchasing-power parity. According to this theory, a currency must have the same purchasing power in all countries. That is, a U.S. dollar must buy the same quantity of goods in the United States and Japan, and a Japanese yen must buy the same quantity of goods in Japan and the United States. Indeed, the name of this theory describes it well. *Parity* means equality, and *purchasing power* refers to the value of money in terms of the quantity of goods it can buy. *Purchasing-power parity* states that a unit of a currency must have the same real value in every country.

31-3b Implications of Purchasing-Power Parity

What does the theory of purchasing-power parity say about exchange rates? It tells us that the nominal exchange rate between the currencies of two countries depends on the price levels in those countries. If a dollar buys the same quantity of goods in the United States (where prices are measured in dollars) as in Japan (where prices are measured in yen), then the number of yen per dollar must reflect the prices of goods in the United States and Japan. For example, if a pound of coffee costs 500 yen in Japan and $5 in the United States, then the nominal exchange rate must be 100 yen per dollar (500 yen/$5 = 100 yen per dollar). Otherwise, the purchasing power of the dollar would not be the same in the two countries.

To see more fully how this works, it is helpful to use just a bit of mathematics. Suppose that P is the price of a basket of goods in the United States (measured in dollars), P^* is the price of a basket of goods in Japan (measured in yen), and e is the nominal exchange rate (the number of yen a dollar can buy). Now consider the quantity of goods a dollar can buy at home and abroad. At home, the price level is P, so the purchasing power of $1 at home is $1/P$. That is, a dollar can buy $1/P$ quantity of goods. Abroad, a dollar can be exchanged into e units of foreign currency, which in turn have purchasing power e/P^*. For the purchasing power of a dollar to be the same in the two countries, it must be the case that

$$1/P = e/P^*.$$

With rearrangement, this equation becomes

$$1 = eP/P^*.$$

Notice that the left side of this equation is a constant and the right side is the real exchange rate. Thus, *if the purchasing power of the dollar is always the same at home and abroad, then the real exchange rate—the relative price of domestic and foreign goods—cannot change.*

To see the implication of this analysis for the nominal exchange rate, we can rearrange the last equation to solve for the nominal exchange rate:

$$e = P^*/P.$$

That is, the nominal exchange rate equals the ratio of the foreign price level (measured in units of the foreign currency) to the domestic price level (measured in units of the domestic currency). *According to the theory of purchasing-power parity, the nominal exchange rate between the currencies of two countries must reflect the price levels in those countries.*

A key implication of this theory is that nominal exchange rates change when price levels change. As we saw in the preceding chapter, the price level in any country adjusts to bring the quantity of money supplied and the quantity of money demanded into balance. Because the nominal exchange rate depends on the price levels, it also depends on the money supply and money demand in each country. When a central bank in any country increases the money supply and causes the price level to rise, it also causes that country's currency to depreciate relative to other currencies in the world. In other words, *when the central bank prints large quantities of money, that money loses value both in terms of the goods and services it can buy and in terms of the amount of other currencies it can buy.*

We can now answer the question that began this section: Why did the U.S. dollar lose value compared to the German mark and gain value compared to the Italian lira? The answer is that Germany pursued a less inflationary monetary policy than the United States, and Italy pursued a more inflationary monetary policy. From 1970 to 1998, inflation in the United States was 5.3 percent per year. By contrast, inflation was 3.5 percent in Germany and 9.6 percent in Italy. As U.S. prices rose relative to German prices, the value of the dollar fell relative to the mark. Similarly, as U.S. prices fell relative to Italian prices, the value of the dollar rose relative to the lira.

Germany and Italy now have a common currency—the euro. This means that the two countries share a single monetary policy and that the inflation rates in the two countries will be closely linked. But the historical lessons of the lira and the mark will apply to the euro as well. Whether the U.S. dollar buys more or fewer euros 20 years from now than it does today depends on whether the European Central Bank produces more or less inflation in Europe than the Federal Reserve does in the United States.

case study

The Nominal Exchange Rate during a Hyperinflation

Macroeconomists can only rarely conduct controlled experiments. Most often, they must glean what they can from the natural experiments that history gives them. One natural experiment is hyperinflation—the high inflation that arises when a government turns to the printing press to pay for large amounts of government spending. Because hyperinflations are so extreme, they illustrate some basic economic principles with clarity.

Consider the German hyperinflation of the early 1920s. Figure 3 shows the German money supply, the German price level, and the nominal exchange rate (measured as U.S. cents per German mark) for that period. Notice that these series move closely together. When the supply of money starts growing quickly, the price level also takes off, and the German mark depreciates. When the money supply stabilizes, so do the price level and the exchange rate.

FIGURE 3

Money, Prices, and the Nominal Exchange Rate during the German Hyperinflation

Source: Adapted from Thomas J. Sargent, "The End of Four Big Inflations," in Robert Hall, ed., *Inflation* (Chicago: University of Chicago Press, 1983), pp. 41–93.

This figure shows the money supply, the price level, and the nominal exchange rate (measured as U.S. cents per mark) for the German hyperinflation from January 1921 to December 1924. Notice how similarly these three variables move. When the quantity of money started growing quickly, the price level followed and the mark depreciated relative to the dollar. When the German central bank stabilized the money supply, the price level and exchange rate stabilized as well.

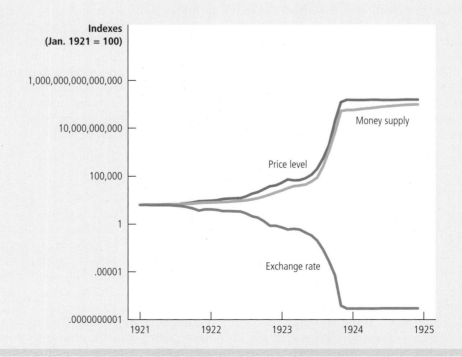

The pattern shown in this figure appears during every hyperinflation. It leaves no doubt that there is a fundamental link among money, prices, and the nominal exchange rate. The quantity theory of money discussed in the previous chapter explains how the money supply affects the price level. The theory of purchasing-power parity discussed here explains how the price level affects the nominal exchange rate. ◢

31-3c Limitations of Purchasing-Power Parity

Purchasing-power parity provides a simple model of how exchange rates are determined. For understanding many economic phenomena, the theory works well. In particular, it can explain many long-term trends, such as the depreciation of the U.S. dollar against the German mark and the appreciation of the U.S. dollar against the Italian lira. It can also explain the major changes in exchange rates that occur during hyperinflations.

Yet the theory of purchasing-power parity is not completely accurate. That is, exchange rates do not always move to ensure that a dollar has the same real value in all countries all the time. There are two reasons the theory of purchasing-power parity does not always hold in practice.

The first reason is that many goods are not easily traded. Imagine, for instance, that haircuts are more expensive in Paris than in New York. International travelers might avoid getting their haircuts in Paris, and some haircutters might move from New York to Paris. Yet such arbitrage would be too limited to eliminate the differences in prices. Thus, the deviation from purchasing-power parity might persist, and a dollar (or euro) would continue to buy less of a haircut in Paris than in New York.

The second reason that purchasing-power parity does not always hold is that even tradable goods are not always perfect substitutes when they are produced in different countries. For example, some consumers prefer German cars, and others prefer American cars. Moreover, consumer tastes can change over time. If German cars suddenly become more popular, the increase in demand will drive up the price of German cars compared to American cars. Despite this difference in prices in the two markets, there might be no opportunity for profitable arbitrage because consumers do not view the two cars as equivalent.

Thus, both because some goods are not tradable and because some tradable goods are not perfect substitutes for their foreign counterparts, purchasing-power parity is not a perfect theory of exchange-rate determination. For these reasons, real exchange rates fluctuate over time. Nonetheless, the theory of purchasing-power parity does provide a useful first step in understanding exchange rates. The basic logic is persuasive: As the real exchange rate drifts from the level predicted by purchasing-power parity, people have greater incentive to move goods across national borders. Even if the forces of purchasing-power parity do not completely fix the real exchange rate, they provide a reason to expect that changes in the real exchange rate are most often small or temporary. As a result, large and persistent movements in nominal exchange rates typically reflect changes in price levels at home and abroad.

case study

The Hamburger Standard

When economists apply the theory of purchasing-power parity to explain exchange rates, they need data on the prices of a basket of goods available in different countries. One analysis of this sort is conducted by *The Economist,* an

You can find a Big Mac almost anywhere you look.

international newsmagazine. The magazine occasionally collects data on a basket of goods consisting of "two all-beef patties, special sauce, lettuce, cheese, pickles, onions, on a sesame seed bun." It's called the "Big Mac" and is sold by McDonald's around the world.

Once we have the prices of Big Macs in two countries denominated in the local currencies, we can compute the exchange rate predicted by the theory of purchasing-power parity. The predicted exchange rate is the one that makes the cost of the Big Mac the same in the two countries. For instance, if the price of a Big Mac is $3 in the United States and 300 yen in Japan, purchasing-power parity would predict an exchange rate of 100 yen per dollar.

How well does purchasing-power parity work when applied using Big Mac prices? Here are some examples from January 2013, when the price of a Big Mac was $4.37 in the United States:

Country	Price of a Big Mac	Predicted Exchange Rate	Actual Exchange Rate
Indonesia	27,939 rupiah	6,393 rupiah/$	9,767 rupiah/$
South Korea	3,700 won	847 won/$	1,085 won/$
Japan	320 yen	72 yen/$	91 yen/$
Sweden	48.4 krona	11.1 krona/$	6.4 krona/$
Mexico	37 pesos	8.5 pesos/$	12.7 pesos/$
Euro area	3.59 euros	0.82 euros/$	0.74 euros/$
Britain	2.69 pounds	0.62 pound/$	0.63 pound/$

You can see that the predicted and actual exchange rates are not exactly the same. After all, international arbitrage in Big Macs is not easy. Yet the two exchange rates are usually in the same ballpark. Purchasing-power parity is not a precise theory of exchange rates, but it often provides a reasonable first approximation. ◢

Quick Quiz   *Over the past 20 years, Mexico has had high inflation and Japan has had low inflation. What do you predict has happened to the number of Mexican pesos a person can buy with a Japanese yen?*

31-4 Conclusion

The purpose of this chapter has been to develop some basic concepts that macroeconomists use to study open economies. You should now understand how a nation's trade balance is related to the international flow of capital and how national saving can differ from domestic investment in an open economy. You should understand that when a nation is running a trade surplus, it must be sending capital abroad, and that when it is running a trade deficit, it must be experiencing a capital inflow. You should also understand the meaning of the nominal and real exchange rates, as well as the implications and limitations of purchasing-power parity as a theory of how exchange rates are determined.

The macroeconomic variables defined here offer a starting point for analyzing an open economy's interactions with the rest of the world. In the next chapter, we develop a model that can explain what determines these variables. We can then discuss how various events and policies affect a country's trade balance and the rate at which nations make exchanges in world markets.

Summary

- Net exports are the value of domestic goods and services sold abroad (exports) minus the value of foreign goods and services sold domestically (imports). Net capital outflow is the acquisition of foreign assets by domestic residents (capital outflow) minus the acquisition of domestic assets by foreigners (capital inflow). Because every international transaction involves an exchange of an asset for a good or service, an economy's net capital outflow always equals its net exports.

- An economy's saving can be used either to finance investment at home or to buy assets abroad. Thus, national saving equals domestic investment plus net capital outflow.

- The nominal exchange rate is the relative price of the currency of two countries, and the real exchange rate

is the relative price of the goods and services of two countries. When the nominal exchange rate changes so that each dollar buys more foreign currency, the dollar is said to *appreciate* or *strengthen*. When the nominal exchange rate changes so that each dollar buys less foreign currency, the dollar is said to *depreciate* or *weaken*.

- According to the theory of purchasing-power parity, a dollar (or a unit of any other currency) should be able to buy the same quantity of goods in all countries. This theory implies that the nominal exchange rate between the currencies of two countries should reflect the price levels in those countries. As a result, countries with relatively high inflation should have depreciating currencies, and countries with relatively low inflation should have appreciating currencies.

Key Concepts

closed economy, *p. 660*
open economy, *p. 660*
exports, *p. 660*
imports, *p. 660*
net exports, *p. 660*

trade balance, *p. 660*
trade surplus, *p. 660*
trade deficit, *p. 661*
balanced trade, *p. 661*
net capital outflow, *p. 664*

nominal exchange rate, *p. 670*
appreciation, *p. 671*
depreciation, *p. 671*
real exchange rate, *p. 672*
purchasing-power parity, *p. 674*

Questions for Review

1. Define *net exports* and *net capital outflow*. Explain how and why they are related.

2. Explain the relationship among saving, investment, and net capital outflow.

3. If a Japanese car costs 500,000 yen, a similar American car costs $10,000, and a dollar can buy 100 yen, what are the nominal and real exchange rates?

4. Describe the economic logic behind the theory of purchasing-power parity.

5. If the Fed started printing large quantities of U.S. dollars, what would happen to the number of Japanese yen a dollar could buy? Why?

Quick Check Multiple Choice

1. Comparing the U.S. economy today to that of 1950, one finds that today, as a percentage of GDP,
   a. exports and imports are both higher.
   b. exports and imports are both lower.
   c. exports are higher, and imports are lower.
   d. exports are lower, and imports are higher.

2. In an open economy, national saving equals domestic investment
   a. plus the net outflow of capital abroad.
   b. minus the net exports of goods and services.

   c. plus the government's budget deficit.
   d. minus foreign portfolio investment.

3. If the value of a nation's imports exceeds the value of its exports, which of the following is NOT true?
   a. Net exports are negative.
   b. GDP is less than the sum of consumption, investment, and government purchases.
   c. Domestic investment is greater than national saving.
   d. The nation is experiencing a net outflow of capital.

4. If a nation's currency doubles in value on foreign exchange markets, the currency is said to _____, reflecting a change in the _____ exchange rate.
   a. appreciate, nominal
   b. appreciate, real
   c. depreciate, nominal
   d. depreciate, real

5. If a cup of coffee costs 2 euros in Paris and $6 in New York and purchasing-power parity holds, what is the exchange rate?
   a. ¼ euro per dollar
   b. ⅓ euro per dollar

c. 3 euros per dollar
d. 4 euros per dollar

6. The theory of purchasing-power parity says that higher inflation in a nation causes the nation's currency to _____, leaving the _____ exchange rate unchanged.
   a. appreciate, nominal
   b. appreciate, real
   c. depreciate, nominal
   d. depreciate, real

Problems and Applications

1. How would the following transactions affect U.S. exports, imports, and net exports?
   a. An American art professor spends the summer touring museums in Europe.
   b. Students in Paris flock to see the latest movie from Hollywood.
   c. Your uncle buys a new Volvo.
   d. The student bookstore at Oxford University in England sells a copy of this textbook.
   e. A Canadian citizen shops at a store in northern Vermont to avoid Canadian sales taxes.

2. Would each of the following transactions be included in net exports or net capital outflow? Be sure to say whether it would represent an increase or a decrease in that variable.
   a. An American buys a Sony TV.
   b. An American buys a share of Sony stock.
   c. The Sony pension fund buys a bond from the U.S. Treasury.
   d. A worker at a Sony plant in Japan buys some Georgia peaches from an American farmer.

3. Describe the difference between foreign direct investment and foreign portfolio investment. Who is more likely to engage in foreign direct investment—a corporation or an individual investor? Who is more likely to engage in foreign portfolio investment?

4. How would the following transactions affect U.S. net capital outflow? Also, state whether each involves direct investment or portfolio investment.
   a. An American cellular phone company establishes an office in the Czech Republic.
   b. Harrods of London sells stock to the General Electric pension fund.
   c. Honda expands its factory in Marysville, Ohio.
   d. A Fidelity mutual fund sells its Volkswagen stock to a French investor.

5. Would each of the following groups be happy or unhappy if the U.S. dollar appreciated? Explain.
   a. Dutch pension funds holding U.S. government bonds
   b. U.S. manufacturing industries
   c. Australian tourists planning a trip to the United States
   d. an American firm trying to purchase property overseas

6. What is happening to the U.S. real exchange rate in each of the following situations? Explain.
   a. The U.S. nominal exchange rate is unchanged, but prices rise faster in the United States than abroad.
   b. The U.S. nominal exchange rate is unchanged, but prices rise faster abroad than in the United States.
   c. The U.S. nominal exchange rate declines, and prices are unchanged in the United States and abroad.
   d. The U.S. nominal exchange rate declines, and prices rise faster abroad than in the United States.

7. A can of soda costs $0.75 in the United States and 12 pesos in Mexico. What is the peso-dollar exchange rate if purchasing-power parity holds? If a monetary expansion caused all prices in Mexico to double, so that soda rose to 24 pesos, what would happen to the peso-dollar exchange rate?

8. Assume that American rice sells for $100 per bushel, Japanese rice sells for 16,000 yen per bushel, and the nominal exchange rate is 80 yen per dollar.
   a. Explain how you could make a profit from this situation. What would be your profit per bushel of rice? If other people were to exploit the same opportunity, what would happen to the price of rice in Japan and the price of rice in the United States?
   b. Suppose that rice is the only commodity in the world. What would happen to the real exchange rate between the United States and Japan?

9. A case study in the chapter analyzed purchasing-power parity for several countries using the price of Big Macs. Here are data for a few more countries:

Country	Price of a Big Mac	Predicted Exchange Rate	Actual Exchange Rate
Chile	2,050 pesos	____ pesos/$	472 pesos/$
Hungary	830 forints	____ forints/$	217 forints/$
Czech Republic	70 korunas	____korunas/$	18.9 korunas/$
Brazil	11.25 real	____ real/$	1.99 real/$
Canada	5.41 C$	____ C$/$	1.00 C$/$

a. For each country, compute the predicted exchange rate of the local currency per U.S. dollar. (Recall that the U.S. price of a Big Mac was $4.37.)
b. According to purchasing-power parity, what is the predicted exchange rate between the Hungarian forint and the Canadian dollar? What is the actual exchange rate?
c. How well does the theory of purchasing-power parity explain exchange rates?

10. Purchasing-power parity holds between the nations of Ectenia and Wiknam, where the only commodity is Spam.
a. In 2000 a can of Spam costs 2 dollars in Ectenia and 6 pesos in Wiknam. What is the exchange rate between Ectenian dollars and Wiknamian pesos?
b. Over the next 20 years, inflation is 3.5 percent per year in Ectenia and 7 percent per year in Wiknam. What will happen over this period to the price of Spam and the exchange rate? (*Hint*: Recall the rule of 70 from Chapter 27.)
c. Which of these two nations will likely have a higher nominal interest rate? Why?
d. A friend of yours suggests a get-rich-quick scheme: Borrow from the nation with the lower nominal interest rate, invest in the nation with the higher nominal interest rate, and profit from the interest-rate differential. Do you see any potential problems with this idea? Explain.

Go to CengageBrain.com to purchase access to the proven, critical Study Guide to accompany this text, which features additional notes and context, practice tests, and much more.

A Macroeconomic Theory of the Open Economy

O ver the past three decades, the United States has persistently imported more goods and services than it has exported. That is, U.S. net exports have been negative. While economists debate whether these trade deficits are a problem for the U.S. economy, the nation's business community often has a strong opinion. Many business leaders claim that the trade deficits reflect unfair competition: Foreign firms are allowed to sell their products in U.S. markets, they contend, while foreign governments impede U.S. firms from selling U.S. products abroad.

Imagine that you are the president and you want to end these trade deficits. What should you do? Should you try to limit imports, perhaps by imposing a quota on textiles from China or cars from Japan? Or should you try to influence the nation's trade deficit in some other way?

To understand the factors that determine a country's trade balance and how government policies can affect it, we need a macroeconomic theory that explains how an open economy works. The preceding chapter introduced some of the key macroeconomic variables that describe an economy's relationship with other economies, including net exports, net capital outflow, and the real and nominal exchange rates. This chapter develops a model that identifies the forces that determine these variables and shows how these variables are related to one another.

To develop this macroeconomic model of an open economy, we build on our previous analysis in two ways. First, the model takes the economy's GDP as given. We assume that the economy's output of goods and services, as measured by real GDP, is determined by the supplies of the factors of production and by the available production technology that turns these inputs into output. Second, the model takes the economy's price level as given. We assume that the price level adjusts to bring the supply and demand for money into balance. In other words, this chapter takes as a starting point the lessons learned in previous chapters about the determination of the economy's output and price level.

The goal of the model in this chapter is to highlight the forces that determine the economy's trade balance and exchange rate. In one sense, the model is simple: It applies the tools of supply and demand to an open economy. Yet the model is also more complicated than others we have seen because it involves looking simultaneously at two related markets: the market for loanable funds and the market for foreign-currency exchange. After we develop this model of the open economy, we use it to examine how various events and policies affect the economy's trade balance and exchange rate. We will then be able to determine the government policies that are most likely to reverse the trade deficits that the U.S. economy has experienced over the past three decades.

32-1 Supply and Demand for Loanable Funds and for Foreign-Currency Exchange

To understand the forces at work in an open economy, we focus on supply and demand in two markets. The first is the market for loanable funds, which coordinates the economy's saving, investment, and flow of loanable funds abroad (called the net capital outflow). The second is the market for foreign-currency exchange, which coordinates people who want to exchange the domestic currency for the currency of other countries. In this section, we discuss supply and demand in each of these markets. In the next section, we put these markets together to explain the overall equilibrium for an open economy.

32-1a The Market for Loanable Funds

When we first analyzed the role of the financial system in Chapter 26, we made the simplifying assumption that the financial system consists of only one market, called the *market for loanable funds*. All savers go to this market to deposit their saving, and all borrowers go to this market to get their loans. In this market, there is one interest rate, which is both the return to saving and the cost of borrowing.

To understand the market for loanable funds in an open economy, the place to start is the identity discussed in the preceding chapter:

$$S \quad = \quad I \quad + \quad NCO$$

$$\text{Saving} = \frac{\text{Domestic}}{\text{investment}} + \frac{\text{Net capital}}{\text{outflow}}.$$

Whenever a nation saves a dollar of its income, it can use that dollar to finance the purchase of domestic capital or to finance the purchase of an asset abroad. The two sides of this identity represent the two sides of the market for loanable funds. The supply of loanable funds comes from national saving (S), and the demand for loanable funds comes from domestic investment (I) and net capital outflow (NCO).

Loanable funds should be interpreted as the domestically generated flow of resources available for capital accumulation. The purchase of a capital asset adds to the demand for loanable funds, regardless of whether that asset is located at home (I) or abroad (NCO). Because net capital outflow can be either positive or negative, it can either add to or subtract from the demand for loanable funds that arises from domestic investment. When $NCO > 0$, the country is experiencing a net outflow of capital; the net purchase of capital overseas adds to the demand for domestically generated loanable funds. When $NCO < 0$, the country is experiencing a net inflow of capital; the capital resources coming from abroad reduce the demand for domestically generated loanable funds.

As we learned in our earlier discussion of the market for loanable funds, the quantity of loanable funds supplied and the quantity of loanable funds demanded depend on the real interest rate. A higher real interest rate encourages people to save and, therefore, raises the quantity of loanable funds supplied. A higher interest rate also makes borrowing to finance capital projects more costly; thus, it discourages investment and reduces the quantity of loanable funds demanded.

In addition to influencing national saving and domestic investment, the real interest rate in a country affects that country's net capital outflow. To see why, consider two mutual funds—one in the United States and one in Germany—deciding whether to buy a U.S. government bond or a German government bond. Each mutual fund manager would make this decision in part by comparing the real interest rates in the United States and Germany. When the U.S. real interest rate rises, the U.S. bond becomes more attractive to both mutual funds. Thus, an increase in the U.S. real interest rate discourages Americans from buying foreign assets and encourages foreigners to buy U.S. assets. For both reasons, a high U.S. real interest rate reduces U.S. net capital outflow.

We illustrate the market for loanable funds on the familiar supply-and-demand diagram in Figure 1. As in our earlier analysis of the financial system, the supply curve slopes upward because a higher interest rate increases the quantity of loanable funds supplied, and the demand curve slopes downward because a higher interest rate decreases the quantity of loanable funds demanded. Unlike the situation in our previous discussion, however, the demand side of the market now represents both domestic investment and net capital outflow. That is, in an open economy, the demand for loanable funds comes not only from those who want loanable funds to buy domestic capital goods but also from those who want loanable funds to buy foreign assets.

The interest rate adjusts to bring the supply and demand for loanable funds into balance. If the interest rate were below the equilibrium level, the quantity of

FIGURE 1

The Market for Loanable Funds
The interest rate in an open economy, as in a closed economy, is determined by the supply and demand for loanable funds. National saving is the source of the supply of loanable funds. Domestic investment and net capital outflow are the sources of the demand for loanable funds. At the equilibrium interest rate, the amount that people want to save exactly balances the amount that people want to borrow for the purpose of buying domestic capital and foreign assets.

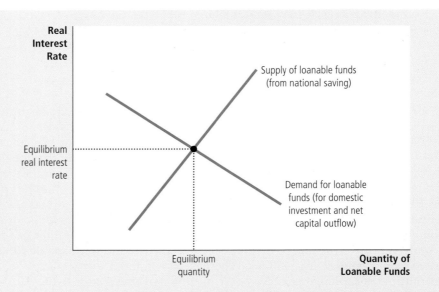

loanable funds supplied would be less than the quantity demanded. The resulting shortage of loanable funds would push the interest rate upward. Conversely, if the interest rate were above the equilibrium level, the quantity of loanable funds supplied would exceed the quantity demanded. The surplus of loanable funds would drive the interest rate downward. At the equilibrium interest rate, the supply of loanable funds exactly balances the demand. That is, *at the equilibrium interest rate, the amount that people want to save exactly balances the desired quantities of domestic investment and net capital outflow.*

32-1b The Market for Foreign-Currency Exchange

The second market in our model of the open economy is the market for foreign-currency exchange. Participants in this market trade U.S. dollars in exchange for foreign currencies. To understand the market for foreign-currency exchange, we begin with another identity from the last chapter:

$$NCO = NX$$

Net capital outflow = Net exports.

This identity states that the imbalance between the purchase and sale of capital assets abroad (NCO) equals the imbalance between exports and imports of goods and services (NX). For example, when the U.S. economy is running a trade surplus ($NX > 0$), foreigners are buying more U.S. goods and services than Americans are buying foreign goods and services. What are Americans doing with the foreign currency they are getting from this net sale of goods and services abroad? They must be buying foreign assets, so U.S. capital is flowing abroad ($NCO > 0$). Conversely, if the United States is running a trade deficit ($NX < 0$), Americans are spending more on foreign goods and services than they are earning from selling abroad. Some of this spending must be financed by selling American assets abroad, so foreign capital is flowing into the United States ($NCO < 0$).

Our model of the open economy treats the two sides of this identity as representing the two sides of the market for foreign-currency exchange. Net capital outflow represents the quantity of dollars supplied for the purpose of buying foreign assets. For example, when a U.S. mutual fund wants to buy a Japanese government bond, it needs to change dollars into yen, so it supplies dollars in the market for foreign-currency exchange. Net exports represent the quantity of dollars demanded for the purpose of buying U.S. net exports of goods and services. For example, when a Japanese airline wants to buy a plane made by Boeing, it needs to change its yen into dollars, so it demands dollars in the market for foreign-currency exchange.

What price balances the supply and demand in the market for foreign-currency exchange? The answer is the real exchange rate. As we saw in the preceding chapter, the real exchange rate is the relative price of domestic and foreign goods and, therefore, is a key determinant of net exports. When the U.S. real exchange rate appreciates, U.S. goods become more expensive relative to foreign goods, making U.S. goods less attractive to consumers both at home and abroad. As a result, exports from the United States fall, and imports into the United States rise. For both reasons, net exports fall. Hence, an appreciation of the real exchange rate reduces the quantity of dollars demanded in the market for foreign-currency exchange.

Figure 2 shows supply and demand in the market for foreign-currency exchange. The demand curve slopes downward for the reason we just discussed:

The real exchange rate is determined by the supply and demand for foreign-currency exchange. The supply of dollars to be exchanged into foreign currency comes from net capital outflow. Because net capital outflow does not depend on the real exchange rate, the supply curve is vertical. The demand for dollars comes from net exports. Because a lower real exchange rate stimulates net exports (and thus increases the quantity of dollars demanded to pay for these net exports), the demand curve is downward sloping. At the equilibrium real exchange rate, the number of dollars people supply to buy foreign assets exactly balances the number of dollars people demand to buy net exports.

FIGURE 2

The Market for Foreign-Currency Exchange

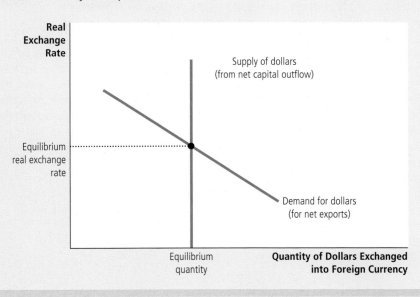

A higher real exchange rate makes U.S. goods more expensive and reduces the quantity of dollars demanded to buy those goods. The supply curve is vertical because the quantity of dollars supplied for net capital outflow does not depend on the real exchange rate. (As discussed earlier, net capital outflow depends on the real interest rate. When discussing the market for foreign-currency exchange, we take the real interest rate and net capital outflow as given.)

It might seem strange at first that net capital outflow does not depend on the exchange rate. After all, a higher exchange value of the U.S. dollar not only makes foreign goods less expensive for American buyers but also makes foreign assets less expensive. One might guess that this would make foreign assets more attractive. But remember that an American investor will eventually want to turn the foreign asset, as well as any profits earned on it, back into dollars. For example, a high value of the dollar makes it less expensive for an American to buy stock in a Japanese company, but when that stock pays dividends, those will be in yen. As these yen are exchanged for dollars, the high value of the dollar means that the dividend will buy fewer dollars. Thus, changes in the exchange rate influence both the cost of buying foreign assets and the benefit of owning them, and these two effects offset each other. For these reasons, our model of the open economy posits that net capital outflow does not depend on the real exchange rate, as represented by the vertical supply curve in Figure 2.

The real exchange rate moves to ensure equilibrium in this market. That is, it adjusts to balance the supply and demand for dollars just as the price of any good adjusts to balance supply and demand for that good. If the real exchange rate were below the equilibrium level, the quantity of dollars supplied would be

FYI

Purchasing-Power Parity as a Special Case

An alert reader of this book might ask: Why are we developing a theory of the exchange rate here? Didn't we already do that in the preceding chapter?

As you may recall, the preceding chapter developed a theory of the exchange rate called *purchasing-power parity*. This theory asserts that a dollar (or any other currency) must buy the same quantity of goods and services in every country. As a result, the real exchange rate is fixed, and all changes in the nominal exchange rate between two currencies reflect changes in the price levels in the two countries.

The model of the exchange rate developed here is related to the theory of purchasing-power parity. According to the theory of purchasing-power parity, international trade responds quickly to international price differences. If goods were cheaper in one country than in another, they would be exported from the first country and imported into the second until the price difference disappeared. In other words, the theory of purchasing-power parity assumes that net exports are highly responsive to small changes in the real exchange rate. If net exports were in fact so responsive, the demand curve in Figure 2 would be horizontal.

Thus, the theory of purchasing-power parity can be viewed as a special case of the model considered here. In that special case, the demand curve for foreign-currency exchange, rather than being downward sloping, is horizontal at the level of the real exchange rate that ensures parity of purchasing power at home and abroad.

While this special case is a good place to start when studying exchange rates, it is far from the end of the story. In practice, foreign and domestic goods are not always perfect substitutes, and there are costs that impede trade. This chapter, therefore, concentrates on the more realistic case in which the demand curve for foreign-currency exchange is downward sloping. This allows for the possibility that the real exchange rate changes over time, as in fact it often does in the real world.

less than the quantity demanded. The resulting shortage of dollars would push the value of the dollar upward. Conversely, if the real exchange rate were above the equilibrium level, the quantity of dollars supplied would exceed the quantity demanded. The surplus of dollars would drive the value of the dollar downward. *At the equilibrium real exchange rate, the demand for dollars by foreigners arising from the U.S. net exports of goods and services exactly balances the supply of dollars from Americans arising from U.S. net capital outflow.*

Quick Quiz   *Describe the sources of supply and demand in the market for loanable funds and the market for foreign-currency exchange.*

32-2 Equilibrium in the Open Economy

So far, we have discussed supply and demand in two markets: the market for loanable funds and the market for foreign-currency exchange. Let's now consider how these markets are related to each other.

32-2a Net Capital Outflow: The Link between the Two Markets

We begin by recapping what we've learned so far in this chapter. We have been discussing how the economy coordinates four important macroeconomic variables: national saving (S), domestic investment (I), net capital outflow (NCO), and net exports (NX). Keep in mind the following identities:

$$S = I + NCO$$

and

$$NCO = NX.$$

In the market for loanable funds, supply comes from national saving (S), demand comes from domestic investment (I) and net capital outflow (NCO), and the real interest rate balances supply and demand. In the market for foreign-currency exchange, supply comes from net capital outflow (NCO), demand comes from net exports (NX), and the real exchange rate balances supply and demand.

Net capital outflow is the variable that links these two markets. In the market for loanable funds, net capital outflow is a piece of demand. An American who wants to buy an asset abroad must finance this purchase by obtaining resources in the U.S. market for loanable funds. In the market for foreign-currency exchange, net capital outflow is the source of supply. An American who wants to buy an asset in another country must supply dollars to exchange them for the currency of that country.

The key determinant of net capital outflow, as we have discussed, is the real interest rate. When the U.S. interest rate is high, owning U.S. assets is more attractive, and U.S. net capital outflow is low. Figure 3 shows this negative relationship between the interest rate and net capital outflow. This net-capital-outflow curve is the link between the market for loanable funds and the market for foreign-currency exchange.

FIGURE 3

How Net Capital Outflow Depends on the Interest Rate
Because a higher domestic real interest rate makes domestic assets more attractive, it reduces net capital outflow. Note the position of zero on the horizontal axis: Net capital outflow can be positive or negative. A negative value of net capital outflow means that the economy is experiencing a net inflow of capital.

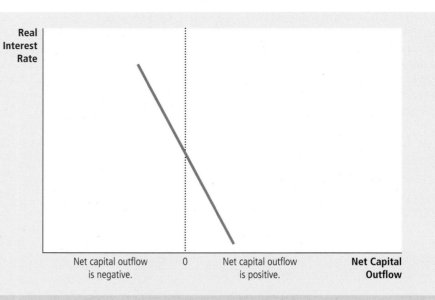

32-2b Simultaneous Equilibrium in Two Markets

We can now put all the pieces of our model together in Figure 4. This figure shows how the market for loanable funds and the market for foreign-currency exchange jointly determine the important macroeconomic variables of an open economy.

Panel (a) of the figure shows the market for loanable funds (taken from Figure 1). As before, national saving is the source of the supply of loanable funds. Domestic investment and net capital outflow are the source of the demand for loanable funds. The equilibrium real interest rate (r_1) brings the quantity of loanable funds supplied and the quantity of loanable funds demanded into balance.

Panel (b) of the figure shows net capital outflow (taken from Figure 3). It shows how the interest rate from panel (a) determines net capital outflow. A higher interest rate at home makes domestic assets more attractive, and this in turn reduces net capital outflow. Therefore, the net-capital-outflow curve in panel (b) slopes downward.

Panel (c) of the figure shows the market for foreign-currency exchange (taken from Figure 2). Because foreign assets must be purchased with foreign currency, the quantity of net capital outflow from panel (b) determines the supply of dollars to be exchanged into foreign currencies. The real exchange rate does not affect net capital outflow, so the supply curve is vertical. The demand for dollars comes from net exports. Because a depreciation of the real exchange rate increases net exports, the demand curve for foreign-currency exchange slopes downward. The equilibrium real exchange rate (E_1) brings into balance the quantity of dollars supplied and the quantity of dollars demanded in the market for foreign-currency exchange.

The two markets shown in Figure 4 determine two relative prices: the real interest rate and the real exchange rate. The real interest rate determined in panel (a) is the price of goods and services in the present relative to goods and services in the future. The real exchange rate determined in panel (c) is the price of domestic goods and services relative to foreign goods and services. These two

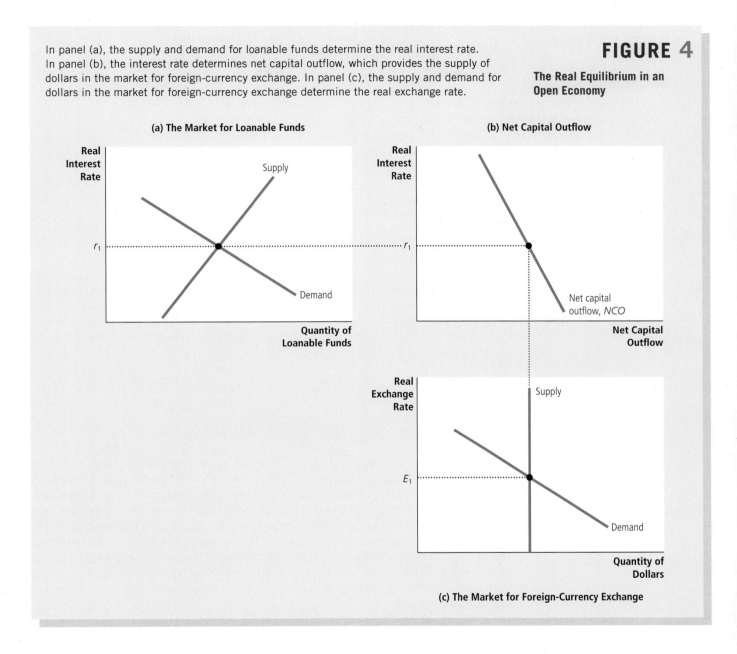

In panel (a), the supply and demand for loanable funds determine the real interest rate. In panel (b), the interest rate determines net capital outflow, which provides the supply of dollars in the market for foreign-currency exchange. In panel (c), the supply and demand for dollars in the market for foreign-currency exchange determine the real exchange rate.

FIGURE 4

The Real Equilibrium in an Open Economy

relative prices adjust simultaneously to balance supply and demand in these two markets. As they do so, they determine national saving, domestic investment, net capital outflow, and net exports. In a moment, we will use this model to see how all these variables change when some policy or event causes one of these curves to shift.

Quick Quiz *In the model of the open economy just developed, two markets determine two relative prices. What are the markets? What are the two relative prices?*

Disentangling Supply and Demand

Suppose the owner of an apple orchard decides to consume some of his own apples. Does this decision represent an increase in the demand for apples or a decrease in the supply? Either answer is defensible, and as long as we are careful in our subsequent analysis, nothing important will hinge on which answer we choose. Sometimes how we divide things between supply and demand is a bit arbitrary.

In the macroeconomic model of the open economy developed in this chapter, the division of transactions between "supply" and "demand" is also a bit arbitrary. This is true both in the market for loanable funds and in the market for foreign-currency exchange.

Consider first the market for loanable funds. The model treats the net capital outflow as part of the demand for loanable funds. Yet instead of writing $S = I + NCO$, we could just as easily have written $S - NCO = I$. When the equation is rewritten in this way, a capital outflow looks like a reduction in the supply of loanable funds. Either way would have worked. The first interpretation ($S = I + NCO$) emphasizes loanable funds generated domestically whether used at home or abroad.

The second interpretation ($S - NCO = I$) emphasizes loanable funds available for domestic investment whether generated at home or abroad. The difference is more semantic than substantive.

Similarly, consider the market for foreign-currency exchange. In our model, net exports are the source of the demand for dollars, and net capital outflow is the source of the supply. Thus, when a U.S. resident imports a car made in Japan, our model treats that transaction as a decrease in the quantity of dollars demanded (because net exports fall) rather than an increase in the quantity of dollars supplied. Similarly, when a Japanese citizen buys a U.S. government bond, our model treats that transaction as a decrease in the quantity of dollars supplied (because net capital outflow falls) rather than an increase in the quantity of dollars demanded. This definition of terms may seem somewhat unnatural at first, but it will prove useful when analyzing the effects of various policies. ◢

32-3 How Policies and Events Affect an Open Economy

Having developed a model to explain how key macroeconomic variables are determined in an open economy, we can now use the model to analyze how changes in policy and other events alter the economy's equilibrium. As we proceed, keep in mind that our model is just supply and demand in two markets: the market for loanable funds and the market for foreign-currency exchange. When using the model to analyze any event, we can apply the three steps outlined in Chapter 4. First, we determine which of the supply and demand curves the event affects. Second, we determine which way the curves shift. Third, we use the supply-and-demand diagrams to examine how these shifts alter the economy's equilibrium.

32-3a Government Budget Deficits

When we first discussed the supply and demand for loanable funds earlier in the book, we examined the effects of government budget deficits, which occur when government spending exceeds government revenue. Because a government budget deficit represents *negative* public saving, it reduces national saving (the sum of public and private saving). Thus, a government budget deficit reduces the supply of loanable funds, drives up the interest rate, and crowds out investment.

Now let's consider the effects of a budget deficit in an open economy. First, which curve in our model shifts? As in a closed economy, the initial impact of the budget deficit is on national saving and, therefore, on the supply curve for loanable funds. Second, which way does this supply curve shift? Again as in a closed economy, a budget deficit represents *negative* public saving, so it reduces national saving and shifts the supply curve for loanable funds to the left. This is shown as the shift from S_1 to S_2 in panel (a) of Figure 5.

Our third and final step is to compare the old and new equilibria. Panel (a) shows the impact of a U.S. budget deficit on the U.S. market for loanable funds. With fewer funds available for borrowers in U.S. financial markets, the interest rate rises from r_1 to r_2 to balance supply and demand. Faced with a higher interest rate, borrowers in the market for loanable funds choose to borrow less. This

When the government runs a budget deficit, it reduces the supply of loanable funds from S_1 to S_2 in panel (a). The interest rate rises from r_1 to r_2 to balance the supply and demand for loanable funds. In panel (b), the higher interest rate reduces net capital outflow. Reduced net capital outflow, in turn, reduces the supply of dollars in the market for foreign-currency exchange from S_1 to S_2 in panel (c). This fall in the supply of dollars causes the real exchange rate to appreciate from E_1 to E_2. The appreciation of the exchange rate pushes the trade balance toward deficit.

FIGURE 5

The Effects of a Government Budget Deficit

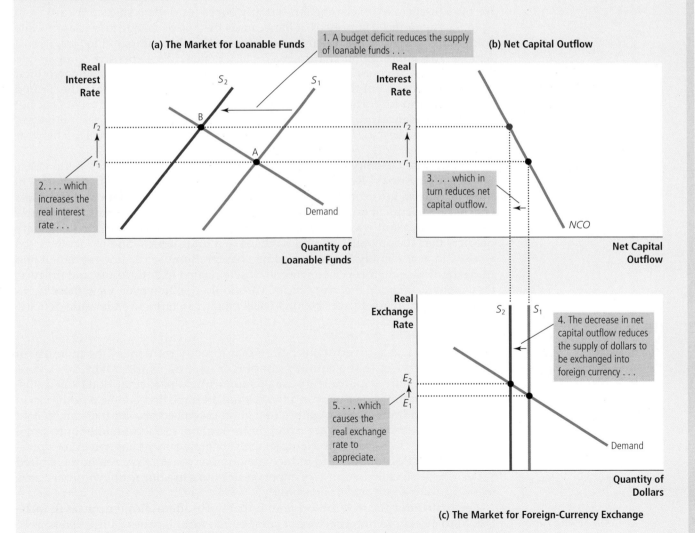

change is represented in the figure as the movement from point A to point B along the demand curve for loanable funds. In particular, households and firms reduce their purchases of capital goods. As in a closed economy, budget deficits crowd out domestic investment.

In an open economy, however, the reduced supply of loanable funds has additional effects. Panel (b) shows that the increase in the interest rate from r_1 to r_2 reduces net capital outflow. [This fall in net capital outflow is also part of the decrease in the quantity of loanable funds demanded in the movement from point A to point B in panel (a).] Because saving kept at home now earns higher rates of return, investing abroad is less attractive, and domestic residents buy fewer foreign assets. Higher interest rates also attract foreign investors, who want to earn the higher returns on U.S. assets. Thus, when budget deficits raise interest rates, both domestic and foreign behavior cause U.S. net capital outflow to fall.

Panel (c) shows how budget deficits affect the market for foreign-currency exchange. Because net capital outflow is reduced, Americans need less foreign currency to buy foreign assets and, therefore, supply fewer dollars in the market for foreign-currency exchange. The supply curve for dollars shifts leftward from S_1 to S_2. The reduced supply of dollars causes the real exchange rate to appreciate from E_1 to E_2. That is, the dollar becomes more valuable compared to foreign currencies. This appreciation, in turn, makes U.S. goods more expensive compared to foreign goods. Because people both in the United States and abroad switch their purchases away from the more expensive U.S. goods, exports from the United States fall, and imports into the United States rise. For both reasons, U.S. net exports fall. Hence, *in an open economy, government budget deficits raise real interest rates, crowd out domestic investment, cause the currency to appreciate, and push the trade balance toward deficit.*

An important example of this lesson occurred in the United States in the 1980s. Shortly after Ronald Reagan was elected president in 1980, the fiscal policy of the U.S. federal government changed dramatically. The president and Congress enacted large cuts in taxes, but they did not cut government spending by nearly as much. The result was a large budget deficit. Our model of the open economy predicts that such a policy should have led to a trade deficit, and in fact it did, as we saw in a case study in the preceding chapter. Because the budget deficit and trade deficit during this period were so closely related in both theory and practice, they were nicknamed the *twin deficits*. We should not, however, view these twins as identical, for many factors beyond fiscal policy can influence the trade deficit.

32-3b Trade Policy

trade policy

a government policy that directly influences the quantity of goods and services that a country imports or exports

A **trade policy** is a government policy that directly influences the quantity of goods and services that a country imports or exports. Trade policy takes various forms, usually with the purpose of supporting a particular domestic industry. One common trade policy is a *tariff,* a tax on imported goods. Another is an *import quota,* a limit on the quantity of a good produced abroad that can be sold domestically. Trade policies are common throughout the world, although sometimes they are disguised. For example, the U.S. government has sometimes pressured Japanese automakers to reduce the number of cars they sell in the United States. These so-called voluntary export restrictions are not really voluntary and, in essence, are a form of import quota.

Let's consider the macroeconomic impact of trade policy. Suppose that the U.S. auto industry, concerned about competition from Japanese automakers, convinces the U.S. government to impose a quota on the number of cars that can be imported from Japan. In making their case, lobbyists for the auto industry assert that the trade restriction would shrink the size of the U.S. trade deficit. Are they right? Our model, as illustrated in Figure 6, offers an answer.

The first step in analyzing the trade policy is to determine which curve shifts. The initial impact of the import restriction is, not surprisingly, on imports. Because net exports equal exports minus imports, the policy also affects net exports. And because net exports are the source of demand for dollars in the market for foreign-currency exchange, the policy affects the demand curve in this market.

When the U.S. government imposes a quota on the import of Japanese cars, nothing happens in the market for loanable funds in panel (a) or to net capital outflow in panel (b). The only effect is a rise in net exports (exports minus imports) for any given real exchange rate. As a result, the demand for dollars in the market for foreign-currency exchange rises, as shown by the shift from D_1 to D_2 in panel (c). This increase in the demand for dollars causes the value of the dollar to appreciate from E_1 to E_2. This appreciation of the dollar tends to reduce net exports, offsetting the direct effect of the import quota on the trade balance.

FIGURE 6

The Effects of an Import Quota

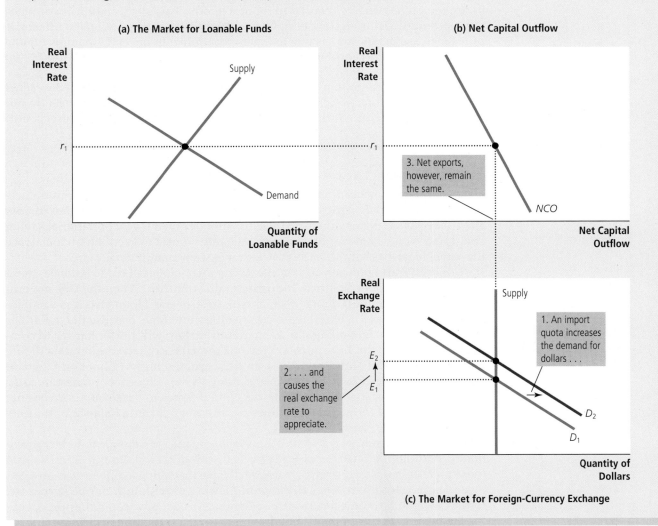

(a) The Market for Loanable Funds

(b) Net Capital Outflow

(c) The Market for Foreign-Currency Exchange

The second step is to determine which way this demand curve shifts. Because the quota restricts the number of Japanese cars sold in the United States, it reduces imports at any given real exchange rate. Net exports, which equal exports minus imports, will therefore *rise* for any given real exchange rate. Because foreigners need dollars to buy U.S. net exports, there is an increased demand for dollars in the market for foreign-currency exchange. This increase in the demand for dollars is shown in panel (c) of Figure 6 as the shift from D_1 to D_2.

The third step is to compare the old and new equilibria. As we can see in panel (c), the increase in the demand for dollars causes the real exchange rate to appreciate from E_1 to E_2. Because nothing has happened in the market for loanable funds in panel (a), there is no change in the real interest rate. Because there is no change in the real interest rate, there is also no change in net capital outflow, shown in panel (b). And because there is no change in net capital outflow, there can be no change in net exports, even though the import quota has reduced imports.

It might seem puzzling that net exports stay the same while imports fall. This puzzle is resolved by noting the change in the real exchange rate: When the dollar appreciates in value in the market for foreign-currency exchange, domestic goods become more expensive relative to foreign goods. This appreciation encourages imports and discourages exports, and both of these changes work to offset the direct increase in net exports due to the import quota. In the end, an import quota reduces both imports and exports, but net exports (exports minus imports) are unchanged.

We have thus come to a surprising implication: *Trade policies do not affect the trade balance.* That is, policies that directly influence exports or imports do not alter net exports. This conclusion seems less surprising if one recalls the accounting identity:

$$NX = NCO = S - I.$$

Net exports equal net capital outflow, which equals national saving minus domestic investment. Trade policies do not alter the trade balance because they do not alter national saving or domestic investment. For given levels of national saving and domestic investment, the real exchange rate adjusts to keep the trade balance the same, regardless of the trade policies the government puts in place.

Although trade policies do not affect a country's overall trade balance, these policies do affect specific firms, industries, and countries. When the U.S. government imposes an import quota on Japanese cars, General Motors has less competition from abroad and will sell more cars. At the same time, because the dollar has appreciated in value, Boeing, the U.S. aircraft maker, will find it harder to compete with Airbus, the European aircraft maker. U.S. exports of aircraft will fall, and U.S. imports of aircraft will rise. In this case, the import quota on Japanese cars will increase net exports of cars and decrease net exports of planes. In addition, it will increase net exports from the United States to Japan and decrease net exports from the United States to Europe. The overall trade balance of the U.S. economy, however, stays the same.

The effects of trade policies are, therefore, more microeconomic than macroeconomic. Although advocates of trade policies sometimes claim (incorrectly) that these policies can alter a country's trade balance, they are usually more motivated by concerns about particular firms or industries. One should not be surprised, for instance, to hear an executive from General Motors advocating import quotas for Japanese cars. Economists usually oppose such trade policies. Free trade allows economies to specialize in doing what they do best, making residents of all countries better off. Trade restrictions interfere with these gains from trade and, thus, reduce overall economic well-being.

32-3c Political Instability and Capital Flight

In 1994, political instability in Mexico, including the assassination of a prominent political leader, made world financial markets nervous. People began to view Mexico as a much less stable country than they had previously thought. They decided to pull some of their assets out of Mexico to move these funds to the United States and other "safe havens." Such a large and sudden movement of funds out of a country is called **capital flight**. To see the implications of capital flight for the Mexican economy, we again follow our three steps for analyzing a change in equilibrium, but this time, we apply our model of the open economy from the perspective of Mexico rather than the United States.

capital flight
a large and sudden reduction in the demand for assets located in a country

Consider first which curves in our model capital flight affects. When investors around the world observe political problems in Mexico, they decide to sell some of their Mexican assets and use the proceeds to buy U.S. assets. This act increases Mexican net capital outflow and, therefore, affects both markets in our model. Most obviously, it affects the net-capital-outflow curve, and this in turn influences the supply of pesos in the market for foreign-currency exchange. In addition, because the demand for loanable funds comes from both domestic investment and net capital outflow, capital flight affects the demand curve in the market for loanable funds.

Now consider which way these curves shift. When net capital outflow increases, there is greater demand for loanable funds to finance these purchases of capital assets abroad. Thus, as panel (a) of Figure 7 shows, the demand curve for loanable funds shifts to the right from D_1 to D_2. In addition, because net capital outflow is higher for any interest rate, the net-capital-outflow curve also shifts to the right from NCO_1 to NCO_2, as in panel (b).

To see the effects of capital flight on the Mexican economy, we compare the old and new equilibria. Panel (a) of Figure 7 shows that the increased demand for loanable funds causes the interest rate in Mexico to rise from r_1 to r_2. Panel (b) shows that Mexican net capital outflow increases. (Although the rise in the interest rate does make Mexican assets more attractive, this only partly off-sets the impact of capital flight on net capital outflow.) Panel (c) shows that the increase in net capital outflow raises the supply of pesos in the market for foreign-currency exchange from S_1 to S_2. That is, as people try to get out of Mexican assets, there is a large supply of pesos to be converted into dollars. This increase in sup-ply causes the peso to depreciate from E_1 to E_2. Thus, *capital flight from Mexico increases Mexican interest rates and decreases the value of the Mexican peso in the market for foreign-currency exchange.* This is exactly what was observed in 1994. From November 1994 to March 1995, the interest rate on short-term Mexican govern-ment bonds rose from 14 percent to 70 percent, and the peso depreciated in value from 29 to 15 U.S. cents per peso.

These price changes that result from capital flight influence some key macro-economic quantities. The depreciation of the currency makes exports cheaper and imports more expensive, pushing the trade balance toward surplus. At the same time, the increase in the interest rate reduces domestic investment, which slows capital accumulation and economic growth.

Capital flight has its largest impact on the country from which capital is flee-ing, but it also affects other countries. When capital flows out of Mexico into the United States, for instance, it has the opposite effect on the U.S. economy as it has on the Mexican economy. In particular, the rise in Mexican net capital outflow

FIGURE 7

The Effects of Capital Flight

If people decide that Mexico is a risky place to keep their savings, they will move their capital to safer havens such as the United States, resulting in an increase in Mexican net capital outflow. Consequently, the demand for loanable funds in Mexico rises from D_1 to D_2, as shown in panel (a), and this drives up the Mexican real interest rate from r_1 to r_2. Because net capital outflow is higher for any interest rate, that curve also shifts to the right from NCO_1 to NCO_2 in panel (b). At the same time, in the market for foreign-currency exchange, the supply of pesos rises from S_1 to S_2, as shown in panel (c). This increase in the supply of pesos causes the peso to depreciate from E_1 to E_2, so the peso becomes less valuable compared to other currencies.

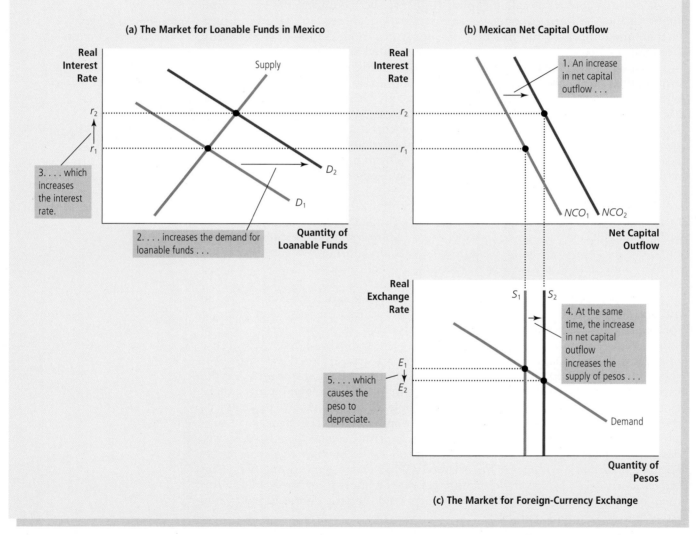

(a) The Market for Loanable Funds in Mexico

(b) Mexican Net Capital Outflow

(c) The Market for Foreign-Currency Exchange

coincides with a fall in U.S. net capital outflow. As the peso depreciates in value and Mexican interest rates rise, the dollar appreciates in value and U.S. interest rates fall. The size of this impact on the U.S. economy is small, however, because the economy of the United States is so large compared to that of Mexico.

The events that we have been describing in Mexico could happen to any economy in the world, and, in fact, they do from time to time. In 1997, the world learned that the banking systems of several Asian economies, including

Thailand, South Korea, and Indonesia, were at or near the point of bankruptcy, and this news induced capital to flee from these nations. In 1998, the Russian government defaulted on its debt, inducing international investors to take whatever money they could and run. A similar (but more complicated) set of events unfolded in Argentina in 2002. In each of these cases of capital flight, the results were much as our model predicts: rising interest rates and a falling currency.

case study

Capital Flows from China

According to our analysis of capital flight, a nation that experiences an outflow of capital sees its currency weaken in foreign exchange markets, and this depreciation in turn increases the nation's net exports. The country into which the capital is flowing sees its currency strengthen, and this appreciation pushes its trade balance toward deficit.

With these lessons in mind, consider this question: Suppose a nation's government, as a matter of policy, encourages capital to flow to another country, perhaps by making foreign investments itself. What effects would this policy have? The answer is much the same: Other things being equal, it leads to a weaker currency and a trade surplus for the nation encouraging the capital outflows and a stronger currency and a trade deficit for the recipient of those capital flows.

This analysis sheds light on one of the ongoing policy disputes between the United States and China. In recent years, the Chinese government has tried to depress the value of its currency—the renminbi—in foreign exchange markets to promote its export industries. It does this by accumulating foreign assets, including substantial amounts of U.S government bonds. As of the end of 2012, China's total reserves of foreign assets were about $3 trillion.

The U.S. government has at times objected to China's interventions in foreign-exchange markets. By holding down the value of the renminbi, the policy makes Chinese goods less expensive, which in turn contributes to the U.S. trade deficit and hurts American producers who make products that compete with imports from China. Because of these effects, the U.S. government has encouraged China to stop influencing the exchange value of its currency with government-sponsored capital flows. Some members of Congress have even gone so far as to advocate tariffs on Chinese imports unless China ceases its "currency manipulation."

Yet the impact of the Chinese policy on the U.S. economy is not all bad. American consumers of Chinese imports benefit from lower prices. In addition, the inflow of capital from China lowers U.S. interest rates, which in turn increases investment in the U.S. economy. To some extent, the Chinese government is financing U.S. economic growth. The Chinese policy of investing in the U.S. economy creates winners and losers among Americans. All things considered, the net impact on the U.S. economy is probably small.

The harder question concerns the motives behind the policy: Why are the Chinese leaders interested in producing for export and investing abroad, rather than producing for domestic consumption and investing at home? There is no obvious answer. One possibility is that China wants to accumulate a reserve of foreign assets on which it can draw in emergencies—a kind of national "rainy-day fund." Another possibility is that the policy is simply misguided. ◢

Quick Quiz *Suppose that Americans decided to spend a smaller fraction of their incomes. What would be the effect on saving, investment, interest rates, the real exchange rate, and the trade balance?*

Is a Strong Currency Always in a Nation's Interest?

An economist tries to decode the political rhetoric about the exchange rate.

Needed: Plain Talk About the Dollar

By Christina D. Romer

At a recent news conference, Ben S. Bernanke, the Federal Reserve chairman, was asked about the falling dollar. He parried the question, saying that the Treasury secretary was the government's spokesman on the exchange rate—and, of course, that the United States favors a strong dollar.

Listening to that statement, I flashed back to one of my first experiences as an adviser to Barack Obama. In November 2008, I was sharing a cab in Chicago with Larry Summers, the former Treasury secretary and a fellow economic adviser to the president-elect. To help prepare me for the interviews and the hearings to come, Larry graciously asked me questions and critiqued my answers.

When he asked about the exchange rate for the dollar, I began: "The exchange rate is a price much like any other price, and is determined by market forces."

"Wrong!" Larry boomed. "The exchange rate is the purview of the Treasury. The United States is in favor of a strong dollar."

For the record, my initial answer was much more reasonable. Our exchange rate is just a price—the price of the dollar in terms of other currencies. It is not controlled by anyone. And a high price for the dollar, which is what we mean by a strong dollar, is not always desirable.

Some countries, like China, essentially fix the price of their currency. But since the early 1970s, the United States has let the dollar's value move in response to changes in the supply and demand of dollars in the foreign exchange market. The Treasury no more determines the price of the dollar than the Department of Energy determines the price of gasoline. Both departments have a small reserve that they can use to combat market instability, but neither has the resources or the mandate to hold the relevant price away from its market equilibrium value for very long.

In practice, all that "the exchange rate is the purview of the Treasury" means is that no official other than the Treasury secretary is supposed to talk about it (and even he isn't supposed to say very much). That strikes me as a shame. Perhaps if government officials could talk about the exchange rate forthrightly, there would be more understanding of the issues and more rational policy discussions.

Such discussions would start with some basic economics. The desire to trade with other countries or invest in them is what gives rise to the market for foreign exchange. You need euros to travel in Spain or to buy a German government bond, so you need a way to exchange currencies.

The supply of dollars to the foreign exchange market comes from Americans who want to buy goods, services or assets from abroad. The demand for dollars comes from foreigners who want to buy from the United States.

Anything that increases the demand for dollars or reduces the supply drives up the dollar's price. Anything that lowers the demand for dollars or raises the supply causes the dollar to weaken.

Consider two examples. Suppose American entrepreneurs create many products that foreigners want to buy, and start many companies they want to invest in. That will increase the demand for dollars and so cause the dollar's price to rise. Such innovation will also make Americans want to buy more goods and assets in the United States—and fewer abroad. The supply of dollars to the foreign exchange market will fall, further strengthening the dollar. This example describes very

32-4 Conclusion

International economics is a topic of increasing importance. More and more, American citizens are buying goods produced abroad and producing goods to be sold overseas. Through mutual funds and other financial institutions, they borrow and lend in world financial markets. As a result, a full analysis of the U.S. economy requires an understanding of how the U.S. economy interacts with other economies in the world. This chapter has provided a basic model for thinking about the macroeconomics of open economies.

The study of international economics is valuable, but we should be careful not to exaggerate its importance. Policymakers and commentators are often quick

well the conditions of the late 1990s—when the dollar was indeed strong.

Now suppose the United States runs a large budget deficit that causes domestic interest rates to rise. Higher American interest rates make both foreigners and Americans want to buy more American bonds and fewer foreign bonds. Thus the demand for dollars increases and the supply decreases. The price of the dollar will again rise.

This example describes conditions in the early 1980s, when President Ronald Reagan's tax cuts and military buildup led to large deficits. Those deficits, along with the anti-inflationary policies of the Fed, where Paul A. Volcker was then the chairman, led to high American interest rates. The dollar was very strong in this period.

Both developments—brilliant American innovation and troublesome American budget deficits—caused the dollar to strengthen. Yet one is clearly a positive for the American economy, the other a negative. The point is that there is no universal good or bad direction for the dollar to move. The desirability of any shift in the exchange rate depends on why the dollar is moving.

It also depends on the state of the economy. At full employment, a strong dollar is good for standards of living. A high price for the dollar means that our currency buys a lot in foreign countries.

But in a depressed economy, it isn't so clear that a strong dollar is desirable. A weaker dollar means that our goods are cheaper relative to foreign goods. That

Christina Romer

stimulates our exports and reduces our imports. Higher net exports raise domestic production and employment. Foreign goods are more expensive, but more Americans are working. Given the desperate need for jobs, on net we are almost surely better off with a weaker dollar for a while.

Fed policy is determined by inflation and unemployment in the United States. But if Mr. Bernanke could discuss the exchange rate openly, he would probably tell you that one way any monetary expansion helps a distressed economy is by weakening the dollar. That is taught in every introductory economics course, yet the Fed is asked to pretend it isn't true.

Likewise, fiscal policy is determined by domestic considerations. But trimming our

budget deficit, as we should over the coming years, would also weaken the dollar. And that, in turn, would blunt the negative impact of deficit reduction on employment and output in the short run.

Strangely, every politician seems to understand that it would be desirable for the dollar to weaken against one particular currency: the Chinese renminbi. For years, China has deliberately accumulated United States Treasury bonds to keep the dollar's value high in renminbi terms. The United States would export more and grow faster if China allowed the dollar's price to fall. Congress routinely threatens retaliation if China doesn't take steps that amount to weakening the dollar.

But in the very next breath, the same members of Congress shout about the importance of a strong dollar. If a decline in its value relative to the renminbi would be beneficial, a fall relative to the currency of many countries would help even more in the current situation.

To say this openly risks being branded not just an extremist but possibly un-American. Perhaps it is time for a more adult conversation. The exchange rate is the purview of market economics, not of the Treasury or strong-dollar ideologues.

Ms. Romer is an economics professor at University of California at Berkeley and was chair of the President Obama's Council of Economic Advisers from 2009 to 2010. ◢

Source: *The New York Times,* May 22, 2011.

to blame foreigners for problems facing the U.S. economy. By contrast, economists more often view these problems as homegrown. For example, politicians often discuss foreign competition as a threat to American living standards, while economists are more likely to lament the low level of national saving. Low saving impedes growth in capital, productivity, and living standards, regardless of whether the economy is open or closed. Foreigners are a convenient target for politicians because blaming foreigners provides a way to avoid responsibility without insulting any domestic constituency. Whenever you hear popular discussions of international trade and finance, therefore, it is especially important to try to separate myth from reality. The tools you have learned in the past two chapters should help in that endeavor.

Summary

- Two markets are central to the macroeconomics of open economies: the market for loanable funds and the market for foreign-currency exchange. In the market for loanable funds, the real interest rate adjusts to balance the supply of loanable funds (from national saving) and the demand for loanable funds (for domestic investment and net capital outflow). In the market for foreign-currency exchange, the real exchange rate adjusts to balance the supply of dollars (from net capital outflow) and the demand for dollars (for net exports). Because net capital outflow is part of the demand for loanable funds and because it provides the supply of dollars for foreign-currency exchange, it is the variable that connects these two markets.

- A policy that reduces national saving, such as a government budget deficit, reduces the supply of loanable funds and drives up the interest rate. The higher interest rate reduces net capital outflow, which reduces the supply of dollars in the market for foreign-currency exchange. The dollar appreciates, and net exports fall.

- Although restrictive trade policies, such as tariffs or quotas on imports, are sometimes advocated as a way to alter the trade balance, they do not necessarily have that effect. A trade restriction increases net exports for any given exchange rate and, therefore, increases the demand for dollars in the market for foreign-currency exchange. As a result, the dollar appreciates in value, making domestic goods more expensive relative to foreign goods. This appreciation offsets the initial impact of the trade restriction on net exports.

- When investors change their attitudes about holding assets of a country, the ramifications for the country's economy can be profound. In particular, political instability can lead to capital flight, which tends to increase interest rates and cause the currency to depreciate.

Key Concepts

trade policy, *p. 694*   capital flight, *p. 697*

Questions for Review

1. Describe supply and demand in the market for loanable funds and the market for foreign-currency exchange. How are these markets linked?

2. Why are budget deficits and trade deficits sometimes called the twin deficits?

3. Suppose that a textile workers' union encourages people to buy only American-made clothes.

What would this policy do to the trade balance and the real exchange rate? What is the impact on the textile industry? What is the impact on the auto industry?

4. What is capital flight? When a country experiences capital flight, what is the effect on its interest rate and exchange rate?

Quick Check Multiple Choice

1. Holding other things constant, an increase in a nation's interest rate reduces
   a. national saving and domestic investment.
   b. national saving and the net capital outflow.
   c. domestic investment and the net capital outflow.
   d. national saving only.

2. Holding other things constant, an appreciation of a nation's currency causes
   a. exports to rise and imports to fall.
   b. exports to fall and imports to rise.

   c. both exports and imports to rise.
   d. both exports and imports to fall.

3. The government in an open economy cuts spending to reduce the budget deficit. As a result, the interest rate _____, leading to a capital _____ and a real exchange rate _____.
   a. falls, outflow, appreciation
   b. falls, outflow, depreciation
   c. falls, inflow, appreciation
   d. rises, inflow, appreciation

4. The nation of Ectenia has long banned the export of its highly prized puka shells. A newly elected president, however, removes the export ban. This change in policy will cause the nation's currency to _____, making the goods Ectenia imports _____ expensive.
   a. appreciate, less
   b. appreciate, more
   c. depreciate, less
   d. depreciate, more

5. A civil war abroad causes foreign investors to seek a safe haven for their funds in the United States, leading to _____ U.S. interest rates and a _____ U.S. dollar.
   a. higher, weaker
   b. higher, stronger

   c. lower, weaker
   d. lower, stronger

6. If business leaders in Great Britain become more confident in their economy, their optimism will induce them to increase investment, causing the British pound to _____ and pushing the British trade balance toward _____.
   a. appreciate, deficit
   b. appreciate, surplus
   c. depreciate, deficit
   d. depreciate, surplus

Problems and Applications

1. Japan generally runs a significant trade surplus. Do you think this is most related to high foreign demand for Japanese goods, low Japanese demand for foreign goods, a high Japanese saving rate relative to Japanese investment, or structural barriers against imports into Japan? Explain your answer.

2. Suppose that Congress is considering an investment tax credit, which subsidizes domestic investment.
   a. How does this policy affect national saving, domestic investment, net capital outflow, the interest rate, the exchange rate, and the trade balance?
   b. Representatives of several large exporters oppose the policy. Why might that be the case?

3. The chapter notes that the rise in the U.S. trade deficit during the 1980s was due largely to the rise in the U.S. budget deficit. On the other hand, the popular press sometimes claims that the increased trade deficit resulted from a decline in the quality of U.S. products relative to foreign products.
   a. Assume that U.S. products did decline in relative quality during the 1980s. How did this affect net exports *at any given exchange rate?*
   b. Draw a three-panel diagram to show the effect of this shift in net exports on the U.S. real exchange rate and trade balance.
   c. Is the claim in the popular press consistent with the model in this chapter? Does a decline in the quality of U.S. products have any effect on our standard of living? (*Hint*: When we sell our goods to foreigners, what do we receive in return?)

4. An economist discussing trade policy in *The New Republic* wrote: "One of the benefits of the United States removing its trade restrictions [is] the gain to U.S. industries that produce goods for export. Export industries would find it easier to sell their goods abroad—even if other countries didn't follow our example and reduce their trade barriers." Explain in words why U.S. *export* industries would benefit from a reduction in restrictions on *imports* to the United States.

5. Suppose the French suddenly develop a strong taste for California wines. Answer the following questions in words and with a diagram.
   a. What happens to the demand for dollars in the market for foreign-currency exchange?
   b. What happens to the value of dollars in the market for foreign-currency exchange?
   c. What happens to the quantity of net exports?

6. A senator renounces his past support for protectionism: "The U.S. trade deficit must be reduced, but import quotas only annoy our trading partners. If we subsidize U.S. exports instead, we can reduce the deficit by increasing our competitiveness." Using a three-panel diagram, show the effect of an export subsidy on net exports and the real exchange rate. Do you agree with the senator?

7. Suppose the United States decides to subsidize the export of U.S. agricultural products, but it does not increase taxes or decrease any other government spending to offset this expenditure. Using a three-panel diagram, show what happens to national saving, domestic investment, net capital outflow, the interest rate, the exchange rate, and the trade balance. Also explain in words how this U.S. policy affects the amount of imports, exports, and net exports.

8. Suppose that real interest rates increase across Europe. Explain how this development will affect U.S. net capital outflow. Then explain how it will affect U.S. net exports by using a formula from the chapter and by drawing a diagram. What will happen to the U.S. real interest rate and real exchange rate?

9. Suppose that Americans decide to increase their saving.
   a. If the elasticity of U.S. net capital outflow with respect to the real interest rate is very high, will this increase in private saving have a large or small effect on U.S. domestic investment?
   b. If the elasticity of U.S. exports with respect to the real exchange rate is very low, will this increase in private saving have a large or small effect on the U.S. real exchange rate?

Go to CengageBrain.com to purchase access to the proven, critical Study Guide to accompany this text, which features additional notes and context, practice tests, and much more.

Short-Run Economic Fluctuations

33

Aggregate Demand and Aggregate Supply

E conomic activity fluctuates from year to year. In most years, the production of goods and services rises. Because of increases in the labor force, increases in the capital stock, and advances in technological knowledge, the economy can produce more and more over time. This growth allows everyone to enjoy a higher standard of living. On average, over the past half century, the production of the U.S. economy as measured by real GDP has grown by about 3 percent per year.

In some years, however, the economy experiences contraction rather than growth. Firms find themselves unable to sell all the goods and services they have to offer, so they cut back on production. Workers are laid off, unemployment rises, and factories are left idle. With the economy producing fewer goods and services, real GDP and other measures of income fall. Such a period of falling incomes and rising unemployment is called a **recession** if it is relatively mild and a **depression** if it is more severe.

recession
a period of declining real incomes and rising unemployment

depression
a severe recession

An example of such a downturn occurred in 2008 and 2009. From the fourth quarter of 2007 to the second quarter of 2009, real GDP for the U.S. economy fell by 4.7 percent. The rate of unemployment rose from 4.4 percent in May 2007 to 10.0 percent in October 2009—the highest level in more than a quarter century. Not surprisingly, students graduating during this time found that desirable jobs were hard to find.

What causes short-run fluctuations in economic activity? What, if anything, can public policy do to prevent periods of falling incomes and rising unemployment? When recessions and depressions occur, how can policymakers reduce their length and severity? These are the questions we take up now.

The variables that we study are largely those we have seen in previous chapters. They include GDP, unemployment, interest rates, and the price level. Also familiar are the policy instruments of government spending, taxes, and the money supply. What differs from our earlier analysis is the time horizon. So far, our goal has been to explain the behavior of these variables in the long run. Our goal now is to explain their short-run deviations from long-run trends. In other words, instead of focusing on the forces that explain economic growth from generation to generation, we are now interested in the forces that explain economic fluctuations from year to year.

There remains some debate among economists about how best to analyze short-run fluctuations, but most economists use the *model of aggregate demand and aggregate supply*. Learning how to use this model for analyzing the short-run effects of various events and policies is the primary task ahead. This chapter introduces the model's two pieces: the aggregate-demand curve and the aggregate-supply curve. Before turning to the model, however, let's look at some of the key facts that describe the ups and downs of the economy.

33-1 Three Key Facts about Economic Fluctuations

Short-run fluctuations in economic activity have occurred in all countries throughout history. As a starting point for understanding these year-to-year fluctuations, let's discuss some of their most important properties.

33-1a Fact 1: Economic Fluctuations Are Irregular and Unpredictable

Fluctuations in the economy are often called *the business cycle*. As this term suggests, economic fluctuations correspond to changes in business conditions. When real GDP grows rapidly, business is good. During such periods of economic expansion, most firms find that customers are plentiful and that profits are growing. When real GDP falls during recessions, businesses have trouble. During such periods of economic contraction, most firms experience declining sales and dwindling profits.

The term *business cycle* is somewhat misleading because it suggests that economic fluctuations follow a regular, predictable pattern. In fact, economic fluctuations are not at all regular, and they are almost impossible to predict with much accuracy. Panel (a) of Figure 1 shows the real GDP of the U.S. economy since 1965. The shaded areas represent times of recession. As the figure shows, recessions do not come at regular intervals. Sometimes recessions are close together, such as the recessions of 1980 and 1982. Sometimes the economy goes many years without a recession. The longest period in U.S. history without a recession was the economic expansion from 1991 to 2001.

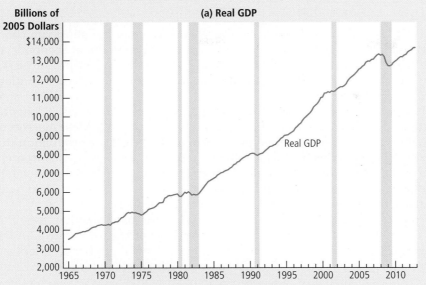

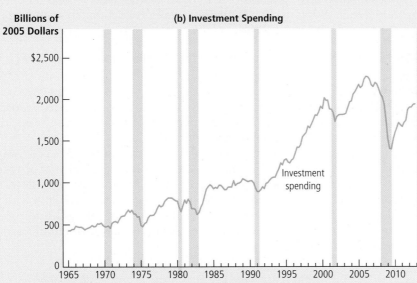

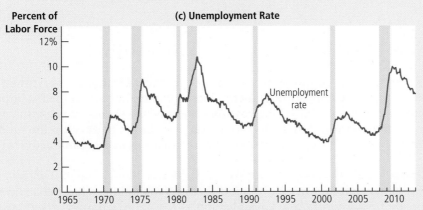

FIGURE 1

A Look at Short-Run Economic Fluctuations

This figure shows real GDP in panel (a), investment spending in panel (b), and unemployment in panel (c) for the U.S. economy using quarterly data since 1965. Recessions are shown as the shaded areas. Notice that real GDP and investment spending decline during recessions, while unemployment rises.

Source: U.S. Department of Commerce; U.S. Department of Labor.

33-1b Fact 2: Most Macroeconomic Quantities Fluctuate Together

Real GDP is the variable most commonly used to monitor short-run changes in the economy because it is the most comprehensive measure of economic activity. Real GDP measures the value of all final goods and services produced within a given period of time. It also measures the total income (adjusted for inflation) of everyone in the economy.

It turns out, however, that for monitoring short-run fluctuations, it does not really matter which measure of economic activity one looks at. Most macroeconomic variables that measure some type of income, spending, or production fluctuate closely together. When real GDP falls in a recession, so do personal income, corporate profits, consumer spending, investment spending, industrial production, retail sales, home sales, auto sales, and so on. Because recessions are economy-wide phenomena, they show up in many sources of macroeconomic data.

Although many macroeconomic variables fluctuate together, they fluctuate by different amounts. In particular, as panel (b) of Figure 1 shows, investment spending varies greatly over the business cycle. Even though investment averages about one-seventh of GDP, declines in investment account for about two-thirds of the declines in GDP during recessions. In other words, when economic conditions deteriorate, much of the decline is attributable to reductions in spending on new factories, housing, and inventories.

"You're fired. Pass it on."

33-1c Fact 3: As Output Falls, Unemployment Rises

Changes in the economy's output of goods and services are strongly correlated with changes in the economy's utilization of its labor force. In other words, when real GDP declines, the rate of unemployment rises. This fact is hardly surprising: When firms choose to produce a smaller quantity of goods and services, they lay off workers, expanding the pool of unemployed.

Panel (c) of Figure 1 shows the unemployment rate in the U.S. economy since 1965. Once again, the shaded areas in the figure indicate periods of recession. The figure shows clearly the impact of recessions on unemployment. In each of the recessions, the unemployment rate rises substantially. When the recession ends and real GDP starts to expand, the unemployment rate gradually declines. The unemployment rate never approaches zero; instead, it fluctuates around its natural rate of about 5 or 6 percent.

Quick Quiz   *List and discuss three key facts about economic fluctuations.*

33-2 Explaining Short-Run Economic Fluctuations

Describing what happens to economies as they fluctuate over time is easy. Explaining what causes these fluctuations is more difficult. Indeed, compared to the topics we have studied in previous chapters, the theory of economic fluctuations remains controversial. In this chapter, we begin to develop the model that most economists use to explain short-run fluctuations in economic activity.

33-2a The Assumptions of Classical Economics

In previous chapters, we developed theories to explain what determines most important macroeconomic variables in the long run. Chapter 25 explained the level and growth of productivity and real GDP. Chapters 26 and 27 explained how the financial system works and how the real interest rate adjusts to balance saving and investment. Chapter 28 explained why there is always some unemployment in the economy. Chapters 29 and 30 explained the monetary system and how changes in the money supply affect the price level, the inflation rate, and the nominal interest rate. Chapters 31 and 32 extended this analysis to open economies to explain the trade balance and the exchange rate.

All of this previous analysis was based on two related ideas: the classical dichotomy and monetary neutrality. Recall that the classical dichotomy is the separation of variables into real variables (those that measure quantities or relative prices) and nominal variables (those measured in terms of money). According to classical macroeconomic theory, changes in the money supply affect nominal variables but not real variables. As a result of this monetary neutrality, Chapters 25 through 28 were able to examine the determinants of real variables (real GDP, the real interest rate, and unemployment) without introducing nominal variables (the money supply and the price level).

In a sense, money does not matter in a classical world. If the quantity of money in the economy were to double, everything would cost twice as much, and everyone's income would be twice as high. But so what? The change would be *nominal* (by the standard meaning of "nearly insignificant"). The things that people *really* care about—whether they have a job, how many goods and services they can afford, and so on—would be exactly the same.

This classical view is sometimes described by the saying, "Money is a veil." That is, nominal variables may be the first things we see when we observe an economy because economic variables are often expressed in units of money. But what's important are the real variables and the economic forces that determine them. According to classical theory, to understand these real variables, we need to look behind the veil.

33-2b The Reality of Short-Run Fluctuations

Do these assumptions of classical macroeconomic theory apply to the world in which we live? The answer to this question is of central importance to understanding how the economy works. *Most economists believe that classical theory describes the world in the long run but not in the short run.*

Consider again the impact of money on the economy. Most economists believe that, beyond a period of several years, changes in the money supply affect prices and other nominal variables but do not affect real GDP, unemployment, or other real variables—just as classical theory says. When studying year-to-year changes in the economy, however, the assumption of monetary neutrality is no longer appropriate. In the short run, real and nominal variables are highly intertwined, and changes in the money supply can temporarily push real GDP away from its long-run trend.

Even the classical economists themselves, such as David Hume, realized that classical economic theory did not hold in the short run. From his vantage point in 18th-century England, Hume observed that when the money supply expanded after gold discoveries, it took some time for prices to rise, and in the meantime, the economy enjoyed higher employment and production.

To understand how the economy works in the short run, we need a new model. This new model can be built using many of the tools we developed in previous chapters, but it must abandon the classical dichotomy and the neutrality of money. We can no longer separate our analysis of real variables such as

The Social Influences of Economic Downturns

The U.S. economy experienced a deep recession in 2008 and 2009. This event led some observers to ask how such events affect society more broadly.

Recession Can Change a Way of Life

By Tyler Cowen

As job losses mount and bailout costs run into the trillions, the social costs of the economic downturn become clearer. The primary question, to be sure, is what can be done to shorten or alleviate these bad times. But there is also a broader set of questions about how this downturn is changing our lives, in ways beyond strict economics.

All recessions have cultural and social effects, but in major downturns the changes can be profound. The Great Depression, for example, may be regarded as a social and cultural era as well as an economic one. And the current crisis is also likely to enact changes in various areas, from our entertainment habits to our health.

First, consider entertainment. Many studies have shown that when a job is harder to find or less lucrative, people spend more time on self-improvement and relatively inexpensive amusements. During the Depression of the 1930s, that meant listening to the radio and playing parlor and board games, sometimes in lieu of a glamorous night on the town. These stay-at-home tendencies persisted through at least the 1950s.

In today's recession, we can also expect to turn to less expensive activities—and maybe to keep those habits for years. They may take the form of greater interest in free content on the Internet and the simple pleasures of a daily walk, instead of expensive vacations and N.B.A. box seats.

In any recession, the poor suffer the most pain. But in cultural influence, it may well be the rich who lose the most in the current crisis. This downturn is bringing a larger-than-usual decline in consumption by the wealthy.

The shift has been documented by Jonathan A. Parker and Annette Vissing-Jorgensen, finance professors at Northwestern University, in their recent paper, "Who Bears Aggregate Fluctuations and How? Estimates and Implications for Consumption Inequality." Of course, people who held much wealth in real estate or stocks have taken heavy losses. But most important, the paper says, the labor incomes of high earners have declined more than in past recessions, as seen in the financial sector.

Popular culture's catering to the wealthy may also decline in this downturn. We can

---

model of aggregate demand and aggregate supply
the model that most economists use to explain short-run fluctuations in economic activity around its long-run trend

aggregate-demand curve
a curve that shows the quantity of goods and services that households, firms, the government, and customers abroad want to buy at each price level

output and employment from our analysis of nominal variables such as money and the price level. Our new model focuses on how real and nominal variables interact.

33-2c The Model of Aggregate Demand and Aggregate Supply

Our model of short-run economic fluctuations focuses on the behavior of two variables. The first variable is the economy's output of goods and services, as measured by real GDP. The second is the average level of prices, as measured by the CPI or the GDP deflator. Notice that output is a real variable, whereas the price level is a nominal variable. By focusing on the relationship between these two variables, we are departing from the classical assumption that real and nominal variables can be studied separately.

We analyze fluctuations in the economy as a whole with the **model of aggregate demand and aggregate supply**, which is illustrated in Figure 2. On the vertical axis is the overall price level in the economy. On the horizontal axis is the overall quantity of goods and services produced in the economy. The **aggregate-demand curve** shows the quantity of goods and services that

expect a shift away from the lionizing of fancy restaurants, for example, and toward more use of public libraries. Such changes tend to occur in downturns, but this time they may be especially pronounced.

Recessions and depressions, of course, are not good for mental health. But it is less widely known that in the United States and other affluent countries, physical health seems to improve, on average, during a downturn. Sure, it's stressful to miss a paycheck, but eliminating the stresses of a job may have some beneficial effects. Perhaps more important, people may take fewer car trips, thus lowering the risk of accidents, and spend less on alcohol and tobacco. They also have more time for exercise and sleep, and tend to choose home cooking over fast food.

In a 2003 paper, "Healthy Living in Hard Times," Christopher J. Ruhm, an economist at the University of North Carolina at Greensboro, found that the death rate falls as unemployment rises. In the United States, he found, a 1 percent increase in the unemployment rate, on average, decreases the death rate by 0.5 percent.

David Potts studied the social history of Australia in the 1930s in his 2006 book, "The Myth of the Great Depression." Australia's suicide rate spiked in 1930, but overall health improved and death rates declined; after 1930, suicide rates declined as well.

While he found in interviews that many people reminisced fondly about those depression years, we shouldn't rush to conclude that depressions are happy times.

Many of their reports are likely illusory, as documented by the Harvard psychologist Daniel Gilbert in his best-selling book "Stumbling on Happiness." According to Professor Gilbert, people often have rosy memories of very trying periods, which may include extreme poverty or fighting in a war.

In today's context, we are also suffering fear and anxiety for the rather dubious consolation of having some interesting memories for the distant future.

But this downturn will likely mean a more prudent generation to come. That is implied by the work of two professors, Ulrike Malmendier of the University of California, Berkeley, and Stefan Nagel of the Stanford Business School, in a 2007 paper, "Depression Babies: Do Macroeconomic Experiences Affect Risk-Taking?"

A generation that grows up in a period of low stock returns is likely to take an unusually cautious approach to investing, even decades later, the paper found. Similarly, a generation that grows up with high inflation will be more cautious about buying bonds decades later.

In other words, today's teenagers stand less chance of making foolish decisions in the stock market down the road. They are likely to forgo some good business opportunities, but also to make fewer mistakes.

When all is said and done, something terrible has happened in the United States economy, and no one should wish for such an event. But a deeper look at the downturn, and the social changes it is bringing, shows a more complex picture.

In addition to trying to get out of the recession—our first priority—many of us will be making do with less and relying more on ourselves and our families. The social changes may well be the next big story of this recession.

Mr. Cowen is an economics professor at George Mason University. ◢

Source: *New York Times*, February 1, 2009.

---

households, firms, the government, and customers abroad want to buy at each price level. The **aggregate-supply curve** shows the quantity of goods and services that firms produce and sell at each price level. According to this model, the price level and the quantity of output adjust to bring aggregate demand and aggregate supply into balance.

It is tempting to view the model of aggregate demand and aggregate supply as nothing more than a large version of the model of market demand and market supply introduced in Chapter 4. In fact, this model is quite different. When we consider demand and supply in a specific market—ice cream, for instance—the behavior of buyers and sellers depends on the ability of resources to move from one market to another. When the price of ice cream rises, the quantity demanded falls because buyers will use their incomes to buy products other than ice cream. Similarly, a higher price of ice cream raises the quantity supplied because firms that produce ice cream can increase production by hiring workers away from other parts of the economy. This *microeconomic* substitution from one market to another is impossible for the economy as a whole. After all, the quantity that our model is trying to explain—real GDP—measures the *total* quantity of goods and services produced by *all* firms in *all* markets. To understand why the aggregate-demand

aggregate-supply curve
a curve that shows the quantity of goods and services that firms choose to produce and sell at each price level

FIGURE 2

Aggregate Demand and Aggregate Supply
Economists use the model of aggregate demand and aggregate supply to analyze economic fluctuations. On the vertical axis is the overall level of prices. On the horizontal axis is the economy's total output of goods and services. Output and the price level adjust to the point at which the aggregate-supply and aggregate-demand curves intersect.

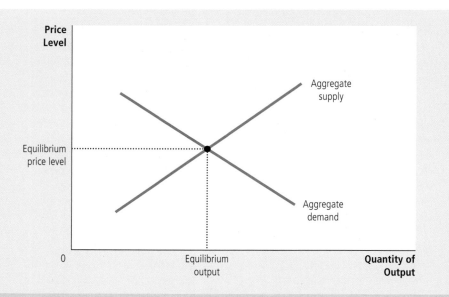

curve slopes downward and why the aggregate-supply curve slopes upward, we need a *macroeconomic* theory that explains the total quantity of goods and services demanded and the total quantity of goods and services supplied. Developing such a theory is our next task.

Quick Quiz   *How does the economy's behavior in the short run differ from its behavior in the long run? • Draw the model of aggregate demand and aggregate supply. What variables are on the two axes?*

33-3 The Aggregate-Demand Curve

The aggregate-demand curve tells us the quantity of all goods and services demanded in the economy at any given price level. As Figure 3 illustrates, the aggregate-demand curve slopes downward. This means that, other things being equal, a decrease in the economy's overall level of prices (from, say, P_1 to P_2) raises the quantity of goods and services demanded (from Y_1 to Y_2). Conversely, an increase in the price level reduces the quantity of goods and services demanded.

33-3a Why the Aggregate-Demand Curve Slopes Downward

Why does a change in the price level move the quantity of goods and services demanded in the opposite direction? To answer this question, it is useful to recall that an economy's GDP (which we denote as Y) is the sum of its consumption (C), investment (I), government purchases (G), and net exports (NX):

$$Y = C + I + G + NX.$$

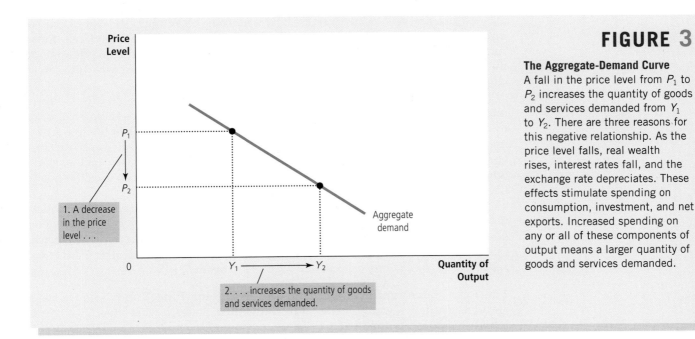

FIGURE 3

The Aggregate-Demand Curve
A fall in the price level from P_1 to P_2 increases the quantity of goods and services demanded from Y_1 to Y_2. There are three reasons for this negative relationship. As the price level falls, real wealth rises, interest rates fall, and the exchange rate depreciates. These effects stimulate spending on consumption, investment, and net exports. Increased spending on any or all of these components of output means a larger quantity of goods and services demanded.

Each of these four components contributes to the aggregate demand for goods and services. For now, we assume that government spending is fixed by policy. The other three components of spending—consumption, investment, and net exports—depend on economic conditions and, in particular, on the price level. Therefore, to understand the downward slope of the aggregate-demand curve, we must examine how the price level affects the quantity of goods and services demanded for consumption, investment, and net exports.

The Price Level and Consumption: The Wealth Effect   Consider the money that you hold in your wallet and your bank account. The nominal value of this money is fixed: One dollar is always worth one dollar. Yet the *real* value of a dollar is not fixed. If a candy bar costs one dollar, then a dollar is worth one candy bar. If the price of a candy bar falls to 50 cents, then one dollar is worth two candy bars. Thus, when the price level falls, the dollars you are holding rise in value, which increases your real wealth and your ability to buy goods and services.

This logic gives us the first reason the aggregate-demand curve slopes downward. *A decrease in the price level raises the real value of money and makes consumers wealthier, which in turn encourages them to spend more. The increase in consumer spending means a larger quantity of goods and services demanded. Conversely, an increase in the price level reduces the real value of money and makes consumers poorer, which in turn reduces consumer spending and the quantity of goods and services demanded.*

The Price Level and Investment: The Interest-Rate Effect   The price level is one determinant of the quantity of money demanded. When the price level is lower, households do not need to hold as much money to buy the goods and services they want. Therefore, when the price level falls, households try to reduce their holdings of money by lending some of it out. For instance, a household might use its excess money to buy interest-bearing bonds. Or it might deposit its excess money in an interest-bearing savings account, and the bank would use these funds to make more loans. In either case, as households try to convert some of their money into interest-bearing assets, they drive down interest rates. (The next chapter analyzes this process in more detail.)

Interest rates, in turn, affect spending on goods and services. Because a lower interest rate makes borrowing less expensive, it encourages firms to borrow more to invest in new plants and equipment, and it encourages households to borrow more to invest in new housing. (A lower interest rate might also stimulate consumer spending, especially spending on large durable purchases such as cars, which are often bought on credit.) Thus, a lower interest rate increases the quantity of goods and services demanded.

This logic gives us a second reason the aggregate-demand curve slopes downward. *A lower price level reduces the interest rate, encourages greater spending on investment goods, and thereby increases the quantity of goods and services demanded. Conversely, a higher price level raises the interest rate, discourages investment spending, and decreases the quantity of goods and services demanded.*

The Price Level and Net Exports: The Exchange-Rate Effect   As we have just discussed, a lower price level in the United States lowers the U.S. interest rate. In response to the lower interest rate, some U.S. investors will seek higher returns by investing abroad. For instance, as the interest rate on U.S. government bonds falls, a mutual fund might sell U.S. government bonds to buy German government bonds. As the mutual fund tries to convert its dollars into euros to buy the German bonds, it increases the supply of dollars in the market for foreign-currency exchange.

The increased supply of dollars to be turned into euros causes the dollar to depreciate relative to the euro. This leads to a change in the real exchange rate—the relative price of domestic and foreign goods. Because each dollar buys fewer units of foreign currencies, foreign goods become more expensive relative to domestic goods.

The change in relative prices affects spending, both at home and abroad. Because foreign goods are now more expensive, Americans buy less from other countries, causing U.S. imports of goods and services to decrease. At the same time, because U.S. goods are now cheaper, foreigners buy more from the United States, so U.S. exports increase. Net exports equal exports minus imports, so both of these changes cause U.S. net exports to increase. Thus, the fall in the real exchange value of the dollar leads to an increase in the quantity of goods and services demanded.

This logic yields a third reason the aggregate-demand curve slopes downward. *When a fall in the U.S. price level causes U.S. interest rates to fall, the real value of the dollar declines in foreign exchange markets. This depreciation stimulates U.S. net exports and thereby increases the quantity of goods and services demanded. Conversely, when the U.S. price level rises and causes U.S. interest rates to rise, the real value of the dollar increases, and this appreciation reduces U.S. net exports and the quantity of goods and services demanded.*

Summing Up   There are three distinct but related reasons a fall in the price level increases the quantity of goods and services demanded:

1. Consumers are wealthier, which stimulates the demand for consumption goods.
2. Interest rates fall, which stimulates the demand for investment goods.
3. The currency depreciates, which stimulates the demand for net exports.

The same three effects work in reverse: When the price level rises, decreased wealth depresses consumer spending, higher interest rates depress investment spending, and a currency appreciation depresses net exports.

Here is a thought experiment to hone your intuition about these effects. Imagine that one day you wake up and notice that, for some mysterious reason, the prices of all goods and services have fallen by half, so the dollars you are holding are worth twice as much. In real terms, you now have twice as much money as you had when you went to bed the night before. What would you do with the extra money? You could spend it at your favorite restaurant, increasing consumer spending. You could lend it out (by buying a bond or depositing it in your bank), reducing interest rates and increasing investment spending. Or you could invest it overseas (by buying shares in an international mutual fund), reducing the real exchange value of the dollar and increasing net exports. Whichever of these three responses you choose, the fall in the price level leads to an increase in the quantity of goods and services demanded. This is what the downward slope of the aggregate-demand curve represents.

It is important to keep in mind that the aggregate-demand curve (like all demand curves) is drawn holding "other things equal." In particular, our three explanations of the downward-sloping aggregate-demand curve assume that the money supply is fixed. That is, we have been considering how a change in the price level affects the demand for goods and services, holding the amount of money in the economy constant. As we will see, a change in the quantity of money shifts the aggregate-demand curve. At this point, just keep in mind that the aggregate-demand curve is drawn for a given quantity of the money supply.

33-3b Why the Aggregate-Demand Curve Might Shift

The downward slope of the aggregate-demand curve shows that a fall in the price level raises the overall quantity of goods and services demanded. Many other factors, however, affect the quantity of goods and services demanded at a given price level. When one of these other factors changes, the quantity of goods and services demanded at every price level changes and the aggregate-demand curve shifts.

Let's consider some examples of events that shift aggregate demand. We can categorize them according to the component of spending that is most directly affected.

Shifts Arising from Changes in Consumption   Suppose Americans suddenly become more concerned about saving for retirement and, as a result, reduce their current consumption. Because the quantity of goods and services demanded at any price level is lower, the aggregate-demand curve shifts to the left. Conversely, imagine that a stock market boom makes people wealthier and less concerned about saving. The resulting increase in consumer spending means a greater quantity of goods and services demanded at any given price level, so the aggregate-demand curve shifts to the right.

Thus, any event that changes how much people want to consume at a given price level shifts the aggregate-demand curve. One policy variable that has this effect is the level of taxation. When the government cuts taxes, it encourages people to spend more, so the aggregate-demand curve shifts to the right. When the government raises taxes, people cut back on their spending and the aggregate-demand curve shifts to the left.

Shifts Arising from Changes in Investment   Any event that changes how much firms want to invest at a given price level also shifts the aggregate-demand curve. For instance, imagine that the computer industry introduces a faster line of computers and many firms decide to invest in new computer systems. Because the quantity of goods and services demanded at any price level is higher, the aggregate-demand curve shifts to the right. Conversely, if firms become pessimistic about future business conditions, they may cut back on investment spending, shifting the aggregate-demand curve to the left.

Tax policy can also influence aggregate demand through investment. For example, an investment tax credit (a tax rebate tied to a firm's investment spending) increases the quantity of investment goods that firms demand at any given interest rate and therefore shifts the aggregate-demand curve to the right. The repeal of an investment tax credit reduces investment and shifts the aggregate-demand curve to the left.

Another policy variable that can influence investment and aggregate demand is the money supply. As we discuss more fully in the next chapter, an increase in the money supply lowers the interest rate in the short run. This decrease in the interest rate makes borrowing less costly, which stimulates investment spending and thereby shifts the aggregate-demand curve to the right. Conversely, a decrease in the money supply raises the interest rate, discourages investment spending, and thereby shifts the aggregate-demand curve to the left. Many economists believe that throughout U.S. history, changes in monetary policy have been an important source of shifts in aggregate demand.

Shifts Arising from Changes in Government Purchases   The most direct way that policymakers shift the aggregate-demand curve is through government purchases. For example, suppose Congress decides to reduce purchases of new weapons systems. Because the quantity of goods and services demanded at any price level is lower, the aggregate-demand curve shifts to the left. Conversely, if state governments start building more highways, the result is a greater quantity of goods and services demanded at any price level, so the aggregate-demand curve shifts to the right.

Shifts Arising from Changes in Net Exports   Any event that changes net exports for a given price level also shifts aggregate demand. For instance, when Europe experiences a recession, it buys fewer goods from the United States. This reduces U.S. net exports at every price level and shifts the aggregate-demand curve for the U.S. economy to the left. When Europe recovers from its recession, it starts buying U.S. goods again and the aggregate-demand curve shifts to the right.

Net exports can also change because international speculators cause movements in the exchange rate. Suppose, for instance, that these speculators lose confidence in foreign economies and want to move some of their wealth into the U.S. economy. In doing so, they bid up the value of the U.S. dollar in the foreign exchange market. This appreciation of the dollar makes U.S. goods more expensive compared to foreign goods, which depresses net exports and shifts the aggregate-demand curve to the left. Conversely, speculation that causes a depreciation of the dollar stimulates net exports and shifts the aggregate-demand curve to the right.

Summing Up   In the next chapter, we analyze the aggregate-demand curve in more detail. There we examine more precisely how the tools of monetary and fiscal policy can shift aggregate demand and whether policymakers should use these tools for that purpose. At this point, however, you should have some idea about why the aggregate-demand curve slopes downward and what kinds of events and policies can shift this curve. Table 1 summarizes what we have learned so far.

TABLE 1

The Aggregate-Demand
Curve: Summary

Why Does the Aggregate-Demand Curve Slope Downward?

1. *The Wealth Effect:* A lower price level increases real wealth, which stimulates spending on consumption.
2. *The Interest-Rate Effect:* A lower price level reduces the interest rate, which stimulates spending on investment.
3. *The Exchange-Rate Effect:* A lower price level causes the real exchange rate to depreciate, which stimulates spending on net exports.

Why Might the Aggregate-Demand Curve Shift?

1. *Shifts Arising from Changes in Consumption:* An event that causes consumers to spend more at a given price level (a tax cut, a stock market boom) shifts the aggregate-demand curve to the right. An event that causes consumers to spend less at a given price level (a tax hike, a stock market decline) shifts the aggregate-demand curve to the left.
2. *Shifts Arising from Changes in Investment:* An event that causes firms to invest more at a given price level (optimism about the future, a fall in interest rates due to an increase in the money supply) shifts the aggregate-demand curve to the right. An event that causes firms to invest less at a given price level (pessimism about the future, a rise in interest rates due to a decrease in the money supply) shifts the aggregate-demand curve to the left.
3. *Shifts Arising from Changes in Government Purchases:* An increase in government purchases of goods and services (greater spending on defense or highway construction) shifts the aggregate-demand curve to the right. A decrease in government purchases on goods and services (a cutback in defense or highway spending) shifts the aggregate-demand curve to the left.
4. *Shifts Arising from Changes in Net Exports:* An event that raises spending on net exports at a given price level (a boom overseas, speculation that causes an exchange-rate depreciation) shifts the aggregate-demand curve to the right. An event that reduces spending on net exports at a given price level (a recession overseas, speculation that causes an exchange-rate appreciation) shifts the aggregate-demand curve to the left.

Quick Quiz *Explain the three reasons the aggregate-demand curve slopes downward.* • *Give an example of an event that would shift the aggregate-demand curve. Which way would this event shift the curve?*

33-4 The Aggregate-Supply Curve

The aggregate-supply curve tells us the total quantity of goods and services that firms produce and sell at any given price level. Unlike the aggregate-demand curve, which always slopes downward, the aggregate-supply curve shows a relationship that depends crucially on the time horizon examined. *In the long run, the aggregate-supply curve is vertical, whereas in the short run, the aggregate-supply curve slopes upward.* To understand short-run economic fluctuations, and how the short-run behavior of the economy deviates from its long-run behavior, we need to examine both the long-run aggregate-supply curve and the short-run aggregate-supply curve.

33-4a Why the Aggregate-Supply Curve Is Vertical in the Long Run

What determines the quantity of goods and services supplied in the long run? We implicitly answered this question earlier in the book when we analyzed the process of economic growth. *In the long run, an economy's production of goods and services (its real GDP) depends on its supplies of labor, capital, and natural resources and on the available technology used to turn these factors of production into goods and services.*

When we analyzed these forces that govern long-run growth, we did not need to make any reference to the overall level of prices. We examined the price level in a separate chapter, where we saw that it was determined by the quantity of money. We learned that if two economies were identical except that one had twice as much money in circulation, the price level would be twice as high in the economy with more money. But since the amount of money does not affect technology or the supplies of labor, capital, and natural resources, the output of goods and services in the two economies would be the same.

Because the price level does not affect the long-run determinants of real GDP, the long-run aggregate-supply curve is vertical, as in Figure 4. In other words, in the long run, the economy's labor, capital, natural resources, and technology determine the total quantity of goods and services supplied, and this quantity supplied is the same regardless of what the price level happens to be.

The vertical long-run aggregate-supply curve is a graphical representation of the classical dichotomy and monetary neutrality. As we have already discussed, classical macroeconomic theory is based on the assumption that real variables do not depend on nominal variables. The long-run aggregate-supply curve is consistent with this idea because it implies that the quantity of output (a real variable) does not depend on the level of prices (a nominal variable). As noted earlier, most economists believe this principle works well when studying the economy over a period of many years but not when studying year-to-year changes. Thus, *the aggregate-supply curve is vertical only in the long run.*

FIGURE 4

The Long-Run Aggregate-Supply Curve
In the long run, the quantity of output supplied depends on the economy's quantities of labor, capital, and natural resources and on the technology for turning these inputs into output. Because the quantity supplied does not depend on the overall price level, the long-run aggregate-supply curve is vertical at the natural level of output.

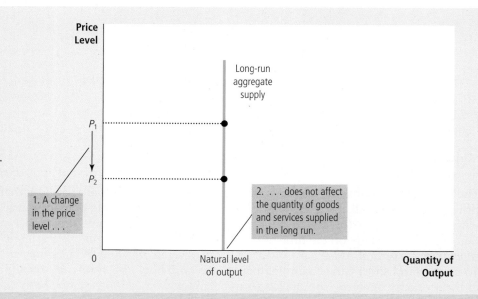

33-4b Why the Long-Run Aggregate-Supply Curve Might Shift

Because classical macroeconomic theory predicts the quantity of goods and services produced by an economy in the long run, it also explains the position of the long-run aggregate-supply curve. The long-run level of production is sometimes called *potential output* or *full-employment output*. To be more precise, we call it the **natural level of output** because it shows what the economy produces when unemployment is at its natural, or normal, rate. The natural level of output is the rate of production toward which the economy gravitates in the long run.

Any change in the economy that alters the natural level of output shifts the long-run aggregate-supply curve. Because output in the classical model depends on labor, capital, natural resources, and technological knowledge, we can categorize shifts in the long-run aggregate-supply curve as arising from these four sources.

natural level of output
the production of goods and services that an economy achieves in the long run when unemployment is at its normal rate

Shifts Arising from Changes in Labor   Imagine that an economy experiences an increase in immigration. Because there would be a greater number of workers, the quantity of goods and services supplied would increase. As a result, the long-run aggregate-supply curve would shift to the right. Conversely, if many workers left the economy to go abroad, the long-run aggregate-supply curve would shift to the left.

The position of the long-run aggregate-supply curve also depends on the natural rate of unemployment, so any change in the natural rate of unemployment shifts the long-run aggregate-supply curve. For example, if Congress were to raise the minimum wage substantially, the natural rate of unemployment would rise and the economy would produce a smaller quantity of goods and services. As a result, the long-run aggregate-supply curve would shift to the left. Conversely, if a reform of the unemployment insurance system were to encourage unemployed workers to search harder for new jobs, the natural rate of unemployment would fall and the long-run aggregate-supply curve would shift to the right.

Shifts Arising from Changes in Capital   An increase in the economy's capital stock increases productivity and, thereby, the quantity of goods and services supplied. As a result, the long-run aggregate-supply curve shifts to the right. Conversely, a decrease in the economy's capital stock decreases productivity and the quantity of goods and services supplied, shifting the long-run aggregate-supply curve to the left.

Notice that the same logic applies regardless of whether we are discussing physical capital such as machines and factories or human capital such as college degrees. An increase in either type of capital will raise the economy's ability to produce goods and services and, thus, shift the long-run aggregate-supply curve to the right.

Shifts Arising from Changes in Natural Resources   An economy's production depends on its natural resources, including its land, minerals, and weather. The discovery of a new mineral deposit shifts the long-run aggregate-supply curve to the right. A change in weather patterns that makes farming more difficult shifts the long-run aggregate-supply curve to the left.

In many countries, crucial natural resources are imported. A change in the availability of these resources can also shift the aggregate-supply curve. For example, as we discuss later in this chapter, events occurring in the world oil market have historically been an important source of shifts in aggregate supply for the United States and other oil-importing nations.

Shifts Arising from Changes in Technological Knowledge Perhaps the most important reason that the economy today produces more than it did a generation ago is that our technological knowledge has advanced. The invention of the computer, for instance, has allowed us to produce more goods and services from any given amounts of labor, capital, and natural resources. As computer use has spread throughout the economy, it has shifted the long-run aggregate-supply curve to the right.

Although not literally technological, many other events act like changes in technology. For instance, opening up international trade has effects similar to inventing new production processes because it allows a country to specialize in higher-productivity industries; therefore, it also shifts the long-run aggregate-supply curve to the right. Conversely, if the government passes new regulations preventing firms from using some production methods, perhaps to address worker safety or environmental concerns, the result is a leftward shift in the long-run aggregate-supply curve.

Summing Up Because the long-run aggregate-supply curve reflects the classical model of the economy we developed in previous chapters, it provides a new way to describe our earlier analysis. Any policy or event that raised real GDP in previous chapters can now be described as increasing the quantity of goods and services supplied and shifting the long-run aggregate-supply curve to the right. Any policy or event that lowered real GDP in previous chapters can now be described as decreasing the quantity of goods and services supplied and shifting the long-run aggregate-supply curve to the left.

33-4c Using Aggregate Demand and Aggregate Supply to Depict Long-Run Growth and Inflation

Having introduced the economy's aggregate-demand curve and the long-run aggregate-supply curve, we now have a new way to describe the economy's long-run trends. Figure 5 illustrates the changes that occur in an economy from decade to decade. Notice that both curves are shifting. Although many forces influence the economy in the long run and can in theory cause such shifts, the two most important forces in practice are technology and monetary policy. Technological progress enhances an economy's ability to produce goods and services, and the resulting increases in output are reflected in continual shifts of the long-run aggregate-supply curve to the right. At the same time, because the Federal Reserve (Fed) increases the money supply over time, the aggregate-demand curve also shifts to the right. As the figure illustrates, the result is continuing growth in output (as shown by increasing Y) and continuing inflation (as shown by increasing P). This is just another way of representing the classical analysis of growth and inflation we conducted in earlier chapters.

The purpose of developing the model of aggregate demand and aggregate supply, however, is not to dress our previous long-run conclusions in new clothing. Instead, it is to provide a framework for short-run analysis, as we will see in a moment. As we develop the short-run model, we keep the analysis simple by omitting the continuing growth and inflation shown by the shifts in Figure 5. But always remember that long-run trends are the background on which short-run fluctuations are superimposed. *The short-run fluctuations in output and the price level that we will be studying should be viewed as deviations from the long-run trends of output growth and inflation.*

As the economy becomes better able to produce goods and services over time, primarily because of technological progress, the long-run aggregate-supply curve shifts to the right. At the same time, as the Fed increases the money supply, the aggregate-demand curve also shifts to the right. In this figure, output grows from Y_{1990} to Y_{2000} and then to Y_{2010} and the price level rises from P_{1990} to P_{2000} and then to P_{2010}. Thus, the model of aggregate demand and aggregate supply offers a new way to describe the classical analysis of growth and inflation.

FIGURE 5

Long-Run Growth and Inflation in the Model of Aggregate Demand and Aggregate Supply

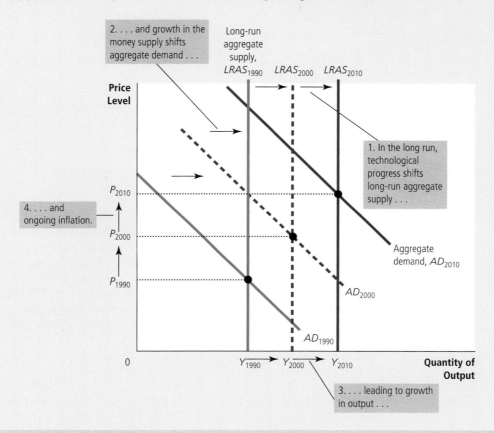

2. . . . and growth in the money supply shifts aggregate demand . . .

Long-run aggregate supply, $LRAS_{1990}$ $LRAS_{2000}$ $LRAS_{2010}$

Price Level

1. In the long run, technological progress shifts long-run aggregate supply . . .

4. . . . and ongoing inflation.

P_{2010}

P_{2000}

P_{1990}

Aggregate demand, AD_{2010}

AD_{2000}

AD_{1990}

0   Y_{1990} Y_{2000} Y_{2010} Quantity of Output

3. . . . leading to growth in output . . .

33-4d Why the Aggregate-Supply Curve Slopes Upward in the Short Run

The key difference between the economy in the short run and in the long run is the behavior of aggregate supply. The long-run aggregate-supply curve is vertical because, in the long run, the overall level of prices does not affect the economy's ability to produce goods and services. By contrast, in the short run, the price level *does* affect the economy's output. That is, over a period of a year or two, an increase in the overall level of prices in the economy tends to raise the quantity of goods and services supplied, and a decrease in the level of prices tends to reduce the quantity of goods and services supplied. As a result, the short-run aggregate-supply curve slopes upward, as shown in Figure 6.

Why do changes in the price level affect output in the short run? Macro-economists have proposed three theories for the upward slope of the short-run

FIGURE 6

The Short-Run Aggregate-Supply Curve
In the short run, a fall in the price level from P_1 to P_2 reduces the quantity of output supplied from Y_1 to Y_2. This positive relationship could be due to sticky wages, sticky prices, or misperceptions. Over time, wages, prices, and perceptions adjust, so this positive relationship is only temporary.

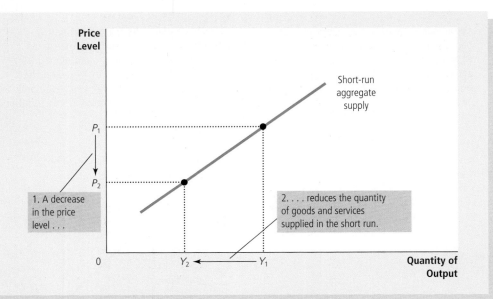

aggregate-supply curve. In each theory, a specific market imperfection causes the supply side of the economy to behave differently in the short run than it does in the long run. The following theories differ in their details, but they share a common theme: *The quantity of output supplied deviates from its long-run, or natural, level when the actual price level in the economy deviates from the price level that people expected to prevail.* When the price level rises above the level that people expected, output rises above its natural level, and when the price level falls below the expected level, output falls below its natural level.

The Sticky-Wage Theory The first explanation of the upward slope of the short-run aggregate-supply curve is the sticky-wage theory. This theory is the simplest of the three approaches to aggregate supply, and some economists believe it highlights the most important reason why the economy in the short run differs from the economy in the long run. Therefore, it is the theory of short-run aggregate supply that we emphasize in this book.

According to this theory, the short-run aggregate-supply curve slopes upward because nominal wages are slow to adjust to changing economic conditions. In other words, wages are "sticky" in the short run. To some extent, the slow adjustment of nominal wages is attributable to long-term contracts between workers and firms that fix nominal wages, sometimes for as long as 3 years. In addition, this prolonged adjustment may be attributable to slowly changing social norms and notions of fairness that influence wage setting.

An example helps explain how sticky nominal wages can result in a short-run aggregate-supply curve that slopes upward. Imagine that a year ago a firm expected the price level today to be 100, and based on this expectation, it signed a contract with its workers agreeing to pay them, say, $20 an hour. In fact, the price level, P, turns out to be only 95. Because prices have fallen below expectations, the firm gets 5 percent less than expected for each unit of its product that it sells. The cost of labor used to make the output, however, is stuck at $20 per hour. Production is now less profitable, so the firm hires fewer workers and reduces the quantity of output supplied. Over time, the labor contract will expire, and the firm can renegotiate with its workers for a lower wage (which they may accept because prices are lower), but in the meantime, employment and production will remain below their long-run levels.

The same logic works in reverse. Suppose the price level turns out to be 105 and the wage remains stuck at $20. The firm sees that the amount it is paid for each unit sold is up by 5 percent, while its labor costs are not. In response, it hires more workers and increases the quantity of output supplied. Eventually, the workers will demand higher nominal wages to compensate for the higher price level, but for a while, the firm can take advantage of the profit opportunity by increasing employment and production above their long-run levels.

In short, according to the sticky-wage theory, the short-run aggregate-supply curve slopes upward because nominal wages are based on expected prices and do not respond immediately when the actual price level turns out to be different from what was expected. This stickiness of wages gives firms an incentive to produce less output when the price level turns out lower than expected and to produce more when the price level turns out higher than expected.

The Sticky-Price Theory   Some economists have advocated another approach to explaining the upward slope of the short-run aggregate-supply curve, called the sticky-price theory. As we just discussed, the sticky-wage theory emphasizes that nominal wages adjust slowly over time. The sticky-price theory emphasizes that the prices of some goods and services also adjust sluggishly in response to changing economic conditions. This slow adjustment of prices occurs in part because there are costs to adjusting prices, called *menu costs*. These menu costs include the cost of printing and distributing catalogs and the time required to change price tags. As a result of these costs, prices as well as wages may be sticky in the short run.

To see how sticky prices explain the aggregate-supply curve's upward slope, suppose that each firm in the economy announces its prices in advance based on the economic conditions it expects to prevail over the coming year. Suppose further that after prices are announced, the economy experiences an unexpected contraction in the money supply, which (as we have learned) will reduce the overall price level in the long run. Although some firms can reduce their prices immediately in response to an unexpected change in economic conditions, other firms may not want to incur additional menu costs. As a result, they may temporarily lag behind in reducing their prices. Because these lagging firms have prices that are too high, their sales decline. Declining sales, in turn, cause these firms to cut back on production and employment. In other words, because not all prices adjust instantly to changing economic conditions, an unexpected fall in the price level leaves some firms with higher-than-desired prices, and these higher-than-desired prices depress sales and induce firms to reduce the quantity of goods and services they produce.

Similar reasoning applies when the money supply and price level turn out to be above what firms expected when they originally set their prices. While some firms raise their prices immediately in response to the new economic environment, other firms lag behind, keeping their prices at the lower-than-desired levels. These low prices attract customers, which induces these firms to increase employment and production. Thus, during the time these lagging firms are operating with outdated prices, there is a positive association between the overall price level and the quantity of output. This positive association is represented by the upward slope of the short-run aggregate-supply curve.

The Misperceptions Theory   A third approach to explaining the upward slope of the short-run aggregate-supply curve is the misperceptions theory. According to this theory, changes in the overall price level can temporarily mislead suppliers about what is happening in the individual markets in which they sell their output. As a result of these short-run misperceptions, suppliers respond to changes in the level of prices, and this response leads to an upward-sloping aggregate-supply curve.

To see how this might work, suppose the overall price level falls below the level that suppliers expected. When suppliers see the prices of their products fall, they may mistakenly believe that their *relative* prices have fallen; that is, they may believe that their prices have fallen compared to other prices in the economy. For example, wheat farmers may notice a fall in the price of wheat before they notice a fall in the prices of the many items they buy as consumers. They may infer from this observation that the reward to producing wheat is temporarily low, and they may respond by reducing the quantity of wheat they supply. Similarly, workers may notice a fall in their nominal wages before they notice that the prices of the goods they buy are also falling. They may infer that the reward for working is temporarily low and respond by reducing the quantity of labor they supply. In both cases, a lower price level causes misperceptions about relative prices, and these misperceptions induce suppliers to respond to the lower price level by decreasing the quantity of goods and services supplied.

Similar misperceptions arise when the price level is above what was expected. Suppliers of goods and services may notice the price of their output rising and infer, mistakenly, that their relative prices are rising. They would conclude that it is a good time to produce. Until their misperceptions are corrected, they respond to the higher price level by increasing the quantity of goods and services supplied. This behavior results in a short-run aggregate-supply curve that slopes upward.

Summing Up   There are three alternative explanations for the upward slope of the short-run aggregate-supply curve: (1) sticky wages, (2) sticky prices, and (3) misperceptions about relative prices. Economists debate which of these theories is correct, and it is very possible each contains an element of truth. For our purposes in this book, the similarities of the theories are more important than the differences. All three theories suggest that output deviates in the short run from its natural level when the actual price level deviates from the price level that people had expected to prevail. We can express this mathematically as follows:

$$\begin{pmatrix}\text{Quantity} \\ \text{of output} \\ \text{supplied}\end{pmatrix} = \begin{pmatrix}\text{Natural} \\ \text{level of} \\ \text{output}\end{pmatrix} + a\begin{pmatrix}\text{Actual} \\ \text{price} \\ \text{level}\end{pmatrix} - \begin{pmatrix}\text{Expected} \\ \text{price} \\ \text{level}\end{pmatrix}$$

where a is a number that determines how much output responds to unexpected changes in the price level.

Notice that each of the three theories of short-run aggregate supply emphasizes a problem that is likely to be temporary. Whether the upward slope of the aggregate-supply curve is attributable to sticky wages, sticky prices, or misperceptions, these conditions will not persist forever. Over time, nominal wages will become unstuck, prices will become unstuck, and misperceptions about relative prices will be corrected. In the long run, it is reasonable to assume that wages and prices are flexible rather than sticky and that people are not confused about relative prices. Thus, while we have several good theories to explain why the short-run aggregate-supply curve slopes upward, they are all consistent with a long-run aggregate-supply curve that is vertical.

33-4e Why the Short-Run Aggregate-Supply Curve Might Shift

The short-run aggregate-supply curve tells us the quantity of goods and services supplied in the short run for any given level of prices. This curve is similar to the long-run aggregate-supply curve, but it is upward sloping rather than vertical because of sticky wages, sticky prices, and misperceptions. Thus, when thinking about what shifts the short-run aggregate-supply curve, we have to consider all those variables that shift the long-run aggregate-supply curve. In addition, we have to consider a new variable—the expected price level—that influences the wages that are stuck, the prices that are stuck, and the perceptions about relative prices that may be flawed.

Let's start with what we know about the long-run aggregate-supply curve. As we discussed earlier, shifts in the long-run aggregate-supply curve normally arise from changes in labor, capital, natural resources, or technological knowledge. These same variables shift the short-run aggregate-supply curve. For example, when an increase in the economy's capital stock increases productivity, the economy is able to produce more output, so both the long-run and short-run aggregate-supply curves shift to the right. When an increase in the minimum wage raises the natural rate of unemployment, the economy has fewer employed workers and thus produces less output, so both the long-run and short-run aggregate-supply curves shift to the left.

The important new variable that affects the position of the short-run aggregate-supply curve is the price level that people expected to prevail. As we have discussed, the quantity of goods and services supplied depends, in the short run, on sticky wages, sticky prices, and misperceptions. Yet wages, prices, and perceptions are set based on the expected price level. So when people change their expectations of the price level, the short-run aggregate-supply curve shifts.

To make this idea more concrete, let's consider a specific theory of aggregate supply—the sticky-wage theory. According to this theory, when workers and firms expect the price level to be high, they are likely to reach a bargain with a higher level of nominal wages. Higher wages raise firms' costs, and for any given actual price level, higher costs reduce the quantity of goods and services supplied. Thus, when the expected price level rises, wages are higher, costs increase, and firms produce a smaller quantity of goods and services at any given actual price level. Thus, the short-run aggregate-supply curve shifts to the left. Conversely, when the expected price level falls, wages are lower, costs decline, firms increase output at any given price level, and the short-run aggregate-supply curve shifts to the right.

A similar logic applies in each theory of aggregate supply. The general lesson is the following: *An increase in the expected price level reduces the quantity of goods and services supplied and shifts the short-run aggregate-supply curve to the left. A decrease in the expected price level raises the quantity of goods and services supplied and shifts the short-run aggregate-supply curve to the right.* As we will see in the next section, the influence of expectations on the position of the short-run aggregate-supply curve plays a key role in explaining how the economy makes the transition from the short run to the long run. In the short run, expectations are fixed and the economy finds itself at the intersection of the aggregate-demand curve and the short-run aggregate-supply curve. In the long run, if people observe that the price level is different from what they expected, their expectations adjust and the short-run aggregate-supply curve shifts. This shift ensures that the economy eventually finds itself at the intersection of the aggregate-demand curve and the long-run aggregate-supply curve.

You should now have some understanding about why the short-run aggregate-supply curve slopes upward and what events and policies can cause this curve to shift. Table 2 summarizes our discussion.

TABLE 2

The Short-Run
Aggregate-Supply
Curve: Summary

Why Does the Short-Run Aggregate-Supply Curve Slope Upward?

1. *The Sticky-Wage Theory:* An unexpectedly low price level raises the real wage, which causes firms to hire fewer workers and produce a smaller quantity of goods and services.
2. *The Sticky-Price Theory:* An unexpectedly low price level leaves some firms with higher-than-desired prices, which depresses their sales and leads them to cut back production.
3. *The Misperceptions Theory:* An unexpectedly low price level leads some suppliers to think their relative prices have fallen, which induces a fall in production.

Why Might the Short-Run Aggregate-Supply Curve Shift?

1. *Shifts Arising from Changes in Labor:* An increase in the quantity of labor available (perhaps due to a fall in the natural rate of unemployment) shifts the aggregate-supply curve to the right. A decrease in the quantity of labor available (perhaps due to a rise in the natural rate of unemployment) shifts the aggregate-supply curve to the left.
2. *Shifts Arising from Changes in Capital:* An increase in physical or human capital shifts the aggregate-supply curve to the right. A decrease in physical or human capital shifts the aggregate-supply curve to the left.
3. *Shifts Arising from Changes in Natural Resources:* An increase in the availability of natural resources shifts the aggregate-supply curve to the right. A decrease in the availability of natural resources shifts the aggregate-supply curve to the left.
4. *Shifts Arising from Changes in Technology:* An advance in technological knowledge shifts the aggregate-supply curve to the right. A decrease in the available technology (perhaps due to government regulation) shifts the aggregate-supply curve to the left.
5. *Shifts Arising from Changes in the Expected Price Level:* A decrease in the expected price level shifts the short-run aggregate-supply curve to the right. An increase in the expected price level shifts the short-run aggregate-supply curve to the left.

Quick Quiz   *Explain why the long-run aggregate-supply curve is vertical. • Explain three theories for why the short-run aggregate-supply curve slopes upward. • What variables shift both the long-run and short-run aggregate-supply curves? • What variable shifts the short-run aggregate-supply curve but not the long-run aggregate-supply curve?*

33-5 Two Causes of Economic Fluctuations

Now that we have introduced the model of aggregate demand and aggregate supply, we have the basic tools we need to analyze fluctuations in economic activity. In particular, we can use what we have learned about aggregate demand and aggregate supply to examine the two basic causes of short-run fluctuations: shifts in aggregate demand and shifts in aggregate supply.

To keep things simple, we assume the economy begins in long-run equilibrium, as shown in Figure 7. Output and the price level are determined in the long run by the intersection of the aggregate-demand curve and the long-run aggregate-supply curve, shown as point A in the figure. At this point, output is at its natural level. Because the economy is always in a short-run equilibrium, the short-run aggregate-supply curve passes through this point as well, indicating that the expected price level has adjusted to this long-run equilibrium. That is, when an economy is in its long-run equilibrium, the expected price level must equal the

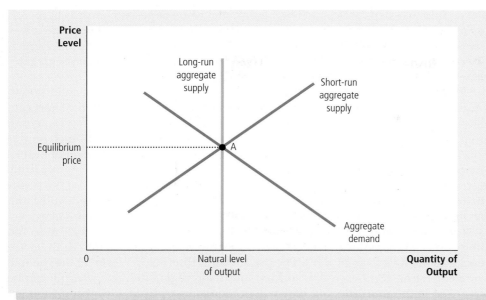

FIGURE 7

The Long-Run Equilibrium
The long-run equilibrium of the economy is found where the aggregate-demand curve crosses the long-run aggregate-supply curve (point A). When the economy reaches this long-run equilibrium, the expected price level will have adjusted to equal the actual price level. As a result, the short-run aggregate-supply curve crosses this point as well.

actual price level so that the intersection of aggregate demand with short-run aggregate supply is the same as the intersection of aggregate demand with long-run aggregate supply.

33-5a The Effects of a Shift in Aggregate Demand

Suppose that a wave of pessimism suddenly overtakes the economy. The cause might be a scandal in the White House, a crash in the stock market, or the outbreak of war overseas. Because of this event, many people lose confidence in the future and alter their plans. Households cut back on their spending and delay major purchases, and firms put off buying new equipment.

What is the macroeconomic impact of such a wave of pessimism? In answering this question, we can follow the three steps we used in Chapter 4 when analyzing supply and demand in specific markets. First, we determine whether the event affects aggregate demand or aggregate supply. Second, we determine the direction that the curve shifts. Third, we use the diagram of aggregate demand and aggregate supply to compare the initial and the new equilibrium. The new wrinkle is that we need to add a fourth step: We have to keep track of a new short-run equilibrium, a new long-run equilibrium, and the transition between them. Table 3 summarizes the four steps to analyzing economic fluctuations.

TABLE 3

Four Steps for Analyzing Macroeconomic Fluctuations

1. Decide whether the event shifts the aggregate-demand curve or the aggregate-supply curve (or perhaps both).
2. Decide the direction in which the curve shifts.
3. Use the diagram of aggregate demand and aggregate supply to determine the impact on output and the price level in the short run.
4. Use the diagram of aggregate demand and aggregate supply to analyze how the economy moves from its new short-run equilibrium to its long-run equilibrium.

The first two steps are easy. First, because the wave of pessimism affects spending plans, it affects the aggregate-demand curve. Second, because households and firms now want to buy a smaller quantity of goods and services for any given price level, the event reduces aggregate demand. As Figure 8 shows, the aggregate-demand curve shifts to the left from AD_1 to AD_2.

With this figure, we can perform step three: By comparing the initial and the new equilibrium, we can see the effects of the fall in aggregate demand. In the short run, the economy moves along the initial short-run aggregate-supply curve, AS_1, going from point A to point B. As the economy moves between these two points, output falls from Y_1 to Y_2 and the price level falls from P_1 to P_2. The falling level of output indicates that the economy is in a recession. Although not shown in the figure, firms respond to lower sales and production by reducing employment. Thus, the pessimism that caused the shift in aggregate demand is, to some extent, self-fulfilling: Pessimism about the future leads to falling incomes and rising unemployment.

Now comes step four—the transition from the short-run equilibrium to the long-run equilibrium. Because of the reduction in aggregate demand, the price level initially falls from P_1 to P_2. The price level is thus below the level that people were expecting (P_1) before the sudden fall in aggregate demand. People can be surprised in the short run, but they will not remain surprised. Over time, their expectations catch up with this new reality, and the expected price level falls as well. The fall in the expected price level alters wages, prices, and perceptions, which in turn influences the position of the short-run aggregate-supply curve. For example, according to the sticky-wage theory, once workers and firms come to expect a lower level of prices, they start to strike bargains for lower nominal wages; the reduction in labor costs encourages firms to hire more workers and expand production at any given level of prices. Thus, the fall in the expected price level shifts the short-run aggregate-supply curve to the right from AS_1 to AS_2 in Figure 8. This shift allows the economy to approach point C, where the new aggregate-demand curve (AD_2) crosses the long-run aggregate-supply curve.

FIGURE 8

A Contraction in Aggregate Demand
A fall in aggregate demand is represented with a leftward shift in the aggregate-demand curve from AD_1 to AD_2. In the short run, the economy moves from point A to point B. Output falls from Y_1 to Y_2, and the price level falls from P_1 to P_2. Over time, as the expected price level adjusts, the short-run aggregate-supply curve shifts to the right from AS_1 to AS_2, and the economy reaches point C, where the new aggregate-demand curve crosses the long-run aggregate-supply curve. In the long run, the price level falls to P_3, and output returns to its natural level, Y_1.

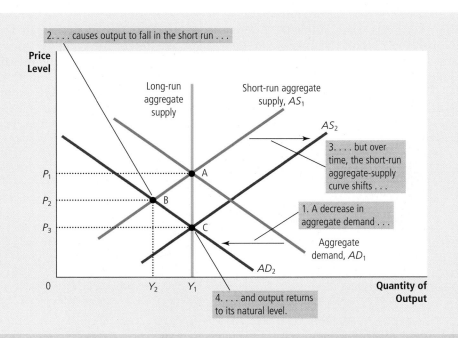

In the new long-run equilibrium, point C, output is back to its natural level. The economy has corrected itself: The decline in output is reversed in the long run, even without action by policymakers. Although the wave of pessimism has reduced aggregate demand, the price level has fallen sufficiently (to P_3) to offset the shift in the aggregate-demand curve, and people have come to expect this new lower price level as well. Thus, in the long run, the shift in aggregate demand is reflected fully in the price level and not at all in the level of output. In other words, the long-run effect of a shift in aggregate demand is a nominal change (the price level is lower) but not a real change (output is the same).

What should policymakers do when faced with a sudden fall in aggregate demand? In this analysis, we assumed they did nothing. Another possibility is that, as soon as the economy heads into recession (moving from point A to point B), policymakers could take action to increase aggregate demand. As we noted earlier, an increase in government spending or an increase in the money supply would increase the quantity of goods and services demanded at any price and, therefore, would shift the aggregate-demand curve to the right. If policymakers act with sufficient speed and precision, they can offset the initial shift in aggregate demand, return the aggregate-demand curve to AD_1, and bring the economy back to point A. If the policy is successful, the painful period of depressed output and employment can be reduced in length and severity. The next chapter discusses in more detail the ways in which monetary and fiscal policy influence aggregate demand, as well as some of the practical difficulties in using these policy instruments.

To sum up, this story about shifts in aggregate demand has three important lessons:

- In the short run, shifts in aggregate demand cause fluctuations in the economy's output of goods and services.
- In the long run, shifts in aggregate demand affect the overall price level but do not affect output.
- Because policymakers influence aggregate demand, they can potentially mitigate the severity of economic fluctuations.

FYI

Monetary Neutrality Revisited

According to classical economic theory, money is neutral. That is, changes in the quantity of money affect nominal variables such as the price level but not real variables such as output. Earlier in this chapter, we noted that most economists accept this conclusion as a description of how the economy works in the long run but not in the short run. With the model of aggregate demand and aggregate supply, we can illustrate this conclusion and explain it more fully.

Suppose that the Fed reduces the quantity of money in the economy. What effect does this change have? As we discussed, the money supply is one determinant of aggregate demand. The reduction in the money supply shifts the aggregate-demand curve to the left.

The analysis looks just like Figure 8. Even though the cause of the shift in aggregate demand is different, we would observe the same effects on output and the price level. In the short run, both output and the price level fall. The economy experiences a recession. But over time, the expected price level falls as well. Firms and workers respond to their new expectations by, for instance, agreeing to lower nominal wages. As they do so, the short-run aggregate-supply curve shifts to the right. Eventually, the economy finds itself back on the long-run aggregate-supply curve.

Figure 8 shows when money matters for real variables and when it does not. In the long run, money is neutral, as represented by the movement of the economy from point A to point C. But in the short run, a change in the money supply has real effects, as represented by the movement of the economy from point A to point B. An old saying summarizes the analysis: "Money is a veil, but when the veil flutters, real output sputters." ◢

> **case study**
>
> ### Two Big Shifts in Aggregate Demand: The Great Depression and World War II

At the beginning of this chapter, we established three key facts about economic fluctuations by looking at data since 1965. Let's now take a longer look at U.S. economic history. Figure 9 shows data since 1900 on the percentage change in real GDP over the previous 3 years. In an average three-year period, real GDP grows about 10 percent—a bit more than 3 percent per year. The business cycle, however, causes fluctuations around this average. Two episodes jump out as being particularly significant: the large drop in real GDP in the early 1930s and the large increase in real GDP in the early 1940s. Both of these events are attributable to shifts in aggregate demand.

The economic calamity of the early 1930s is called the *Great Depression*, and it is by far the largest economic downturn in U.S. history. Real GDP fell by 27 percent from 1929 to 1933, and unemployment rose from 3 percent to 25 percent. At the same time, the price level fell by 22 percent over these 4 years. Many other countries experienced similar declines in output and prices during this period.

Economic historians continue to debate the causes of the Great Depression, but most explanations center on a large decline in aggregate demand. What caused aggregate demand to contract? Here is where the disagreement arises.

Many economists place primary blame on the decline in the money supply: From 1929 to 1933, the money supply fell by 28 percent. As you may recall from our discussion of the monetary system, this decline in the money supply was due to problems in the banking system. As households withdrew their money from financially shaky banks and bankers became more cautious and started holding greater reserves, the process of money creation under fractional-reserve banking

FIGURE 9

U.S. Real GDP Growth since 1900

Source: Louis D. Johnston and Samuel H. Williamson, "What was GDP Then?" http://www.measuringworth.com/usgdp/; Department of Commerce (Bureau of Economic Analysis).

Over the course of U.S. economic history, two fluctuations stand out as especially large. During the early 1930s, the economy went through the Great Depression, when the production of goods and services plummeted. During the early 1940s, the United States entered World War II and the economy experienced rapidly rising production. Both of these events are usually explained by large shifts in aggregate demand.

went into reverse. The Fed, meanwhile, failed to offset this fall in the money multiplier with expansionary open-market operations. As a result, the money supply declined. Many economists blame the Fed's failure to act for the Great Depression's severity.

Other economists have suggested alternative reasons for the collapse in aggregate demand. For example, stock prices fell about 90 percent during this period, depressing household wealth and thereby consumer spending. In addition, the banking problems may have prevented some firms from obtaining the financing they wanted for new projects and business expansions, reducing investment spending. It is possible that all these forces may have acted together to contract aggregate demand during the Great Depression.

The second significant episode in Figure 9—the economic boom of the early 1940s—is easier to explain. The obvious cause of this event was World War II. As the United States entered the war overseas, the federal government had to devote more resources to the military. Government purchases of goods and services increased almost fivefold from 1939 to 1944. This huge expansion in aggregate demand almost doubled the economy's production of goods and services and led to a 20 percent increase in the price level (although widespread government price controls limited the rise in prices). Unemployment fell from 17 percent in 1939 to about 1 percent in 1944—the lowest level in U.S. history. ◢

The outcome of a massive decrease in aggregate demand

case study   The Recession of 2008–2009

In 2008 and 2009, the U.S. economy experienced a financial crisis and a severe downturn in economic activity. In many ways, it was the worst macroeconomic event in more than half a century.

The story of this downturn begins a few years earlier with a substantial boom in the housing market. The boom was, in part, fueled by low interest rates. In the aftermath of the recession of 2001, the Fed lowered interest rates to historically low levels. Low interest rates helped the economy recover, but by making it less expensive to get a mortgage and buy a home, they also contributed to a rise in housing prices.

In addition to low interest rates, various developments in the mortgage market made it easier for *subprime borrowers*—those borrowers with a higher risk of default based on their income and credit history—to get loans to buy homes. One development was *securitization*, the process by which a financial institution (specifically, a mortgage originator) makes loans and then (with the help of an investment bank) bundles them together into financial instruments called *mortgage-backed securities*. These mortgage-backed securities were then sold to other institutions (such as banks and insurance companies), which may not have fully appreciated the risks in these securities. Some economists blame inadequate regulation for these high-risk loans. Others blame misguided government policy: Some policies encouraged this high-risk lending to make the goal of homeownership more attainable for low-income families. Together, these many forces drove up housing demand and housing prices. From 1995 to 2006, average housing prices in the United States more than doubled.

The high price of housing, however, proved unsustainable. From 2006 to 2009, housing prices nationwide fell about 30 percent. Such price fluctuations should not necessarily be a problem in a market economy. After all, price movements are how markets equilibrate supply and demand. In this case, however, the price decline had two related repercussions that caused a sizable fall in aggregate demand.

The first repercussion was a substantial rise in mortgage defaults and home foreclosures. During the housing boom, many homeowners had bought their homes with mostly borrowed money and minimal down payments. When housing prices declined, these homeowners were *underwater* (they owed more on their mortgages than their homes were worth). Many of these homeowners stopped

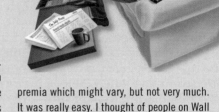

IN THE NEWS

What Have We Learned?

Since the financial crisis and deep recession of 2008–2009, economists have asked themselves how this episode should change the field of macroeconomics.

Olivier Blanchard's Five Lessons for Economists From the Financial Crisis

By David Wessel

What did the worst financial crisis and deepest recession in 75 years teach academic economists and policymakers on whose watch it happened? At a recent London School of Economics forum, convened to honor Bank of England Governor Mervyn King, Olivier Blanchard offered some answers.

Mr. Blanchard, 64 years old, is well positioned to offer such reconsideration. An internationally prominent macroeconomist, he spent 25 years on the MIT faculty before becoming chief economist at the International Monetary Fund in September 2008, just before the collapse of Lehman Brothers.

Here are Mr. Blanchard's five lessons in his own words, lightly edited by The Wall Street Journal's David Wessel:

#1: Humility is in order.

The Great Moderation [the economically tranquil period from 1987 to 2007] convinced too many of us that the large-economy crisis—a financial crisis, a banking crisis—was a thing of the past. It wasn't going to happen again, except maybe in emerging markets. History was marching on.

My generation, which was born after World War II, lived with the notion that the world

was getting to be a better and better place. We knew how to do things better, not only in economics but in other fields as well. What we have learned is that's not true. History repeats itself. We should have known.

#2: The financial system matters— a lot.

It's not the first time that we're confronted with what [former U.S. Defense Secretary Donald] Rumsfeld called "unknown unknowns," things that happened that we hadn't thought about. There is another example in macroeconomics:

The oil shocks of the 1970s during which we were students and we hadn't thought about it. It took a few years, more than a few years, for economists to understand what was going on. After a few years, we concluded that we could think of the oil shock as yet another macroeconomic shock. We did not need to understand the plumbing. We didn't need to understand the details of the oil market. When there's an increase in the price of energy or materials, we can just integrate it into our macro models— the implications of energy prices on inflation and so on.

This is different. What we have learned about the financial system is that the problem is in the plumbing and that we have to understand the plumbing. Before I came to the Fund, I thought of the financial system as a set of arbitrage equations. Basically the Federal Reserve would choose one interest rate, and then the expectations hypothesis would give all the rates everywhere else with

premia which might vary, but not very much. It was really easy. I thought of people on Wall Street as basically doing this for me so I didn't have to think about it.

What we have learned is that that's not the case. In the financial system, a myriad of distortions or small shocks build on each other. When there are enough small shocks, enough distortions, things can go very bad. This has fundamental implications for macroeconomics. We do macro on the assumption that we can look at aggregates in some way and then just have them interact in simple models. I still think that's the way to go, but this shows the limits of that approach. When it comes to the financial system, it's very clear that the details of the plumbing matter.

#3 Interconnectedness matters.

This crisis started in the U.S. and across the ocean in a matter of days and weeks. Each crisis, even in small islands, potentially has effects on the rest of the world. The complexity of the cross border claims by creditors and by debtors clearly is something that many of us had not fully realized: the cross border movements triggered by the risk-on/risk-off movements, which countries are safe havens, and when and why? Understanding this has become absolutely essential. What happens in one part of the world cannot be ignored by the rest of the world. The fact that we all

repaying their loans. The banks servicing the mortgages responded to these defaults by taking the houses away in foreclosure procedures and then selling them off. The banks' goal was to recoup whatever they could from the bad loans. As you might have expected from your study of supply and demand, the increase in the number of homes for sale exacerbated the downward spiral of house prices. As house prices fell, spending on the construction of housing also collapsed.

spend so much time thinking about Cyprus in the last few days is an example of that.

It's also true on the trade side. We used to think if one country was doing badly, then exports to that country would do badly and therefore the exporting countries would do badly. In our models, the effect was relatively small. One absolutely striking fact of the crisis is the collapse of trade in 2009. Output went down. Trade collapsed. Countries which felt they were not terribly exposed through trade turned out to be enormously exposed.

#4 We don't know if Macro-prudential tools work.

It's very clear that the traditional monetary and fiscal tools are just not good enough to deal with the very specific problems in the financial system. This has led to the development of macro-prudential tools, which may or may not become the third leg of macroeconomic policies.

[Macro-prudential tools allow a central bank to restrain lending in specific sectors without raising interest rates for the whole economy, such as increasing the minimum down payment required to get a mortgage, which reduces the loan-to-value ratio.] In principle, they can address specific issues in the financial sector. If there is a problem somewhere you can target the tool at the problem and not use the policy interest rate, which basically is kind of an atomic bomb without any precision.

The big question here is: How reliable are these tools? How much can they be used? The answer—from some experiments before the crisis with loan-to-value ratios and during the crisis with variations in cyclical bank capital ratios or loan-to-value ratios or capital controls, such as in Brazil—is this: They work but they don't work great. People and

Olivier Blanchard

AP Photo/IMF/Eugene Salazar

institutions find ways around them. In the process of reducing the problem somewhere you tend to create distortions elsewhere.

#5 Central bank independence wasn't designed for what central banks are now asked to do.

There is two-way interaction between monetary policy and macro-prudential tools. When Ben Bernanke does expansionary monetary policy, quantitative easing, and interest rates on many assets are close to zero, there's a tendency by many players to take risks to increase their rate of return. Some of this risk actually we want them to take. Some we don't want them to take. That is the interaction of monetary policy on the financial system.

You also have it the other way around. If you use Macro-prudential tools to, say, slow down the building in the housing sector you

have an effect on aggregate demand, which is going to decrease output.

The question is: How do you organize the use of these tools? It makes sense to have them under the same roof. In practice this means the central bank. But that poses questions not only about coordination between the two functions, but also about central bank independence.

One of the major achievements of the last 20 years is that most central banks have become independent of elected governments. Independence was given because the mandate and the tools were very clear. The mandate was primarily inflation, which can be observed over time. The tool was some short-term interest rate that could be used by the central bank to try to achieve the inflation target. In this case, you can give some independence to the institution in charge of this because the objective is perfectly well defined, and everybody can basically observe how well the central bank does.

If you think now of central banks as having a much larger set of responsibilities and a much larger set of tools, then the issue of central bank independence becomes much more difficult. Do you actually want to give the central bank the independence to choose loan-to-value ratios without any supervision from the political process? Isn't this going to lead to a democratic deficit in a way in which the central bank becomes too powerful? I'm sure there are ways out. Perhaps there could be independence with respect to some dimensions of monetary policy—the traditional ones—and some supervision for the rest or some interaction with a political process. ◢

A second repercussion was that the various financial institutions that owned mortgage-backed securities suffered huge losses. In essence, by borrowing large sums to buy high-risk mortgages, these companies had bet that house prices would keep rising; when this bet turned bad, they found themselves at or near the point of bankruptcy. Because of these large losses, many financial institutions did not have funds to loan out and the ability of the financial system to channel resources to those who could best use them was impaired. Even creditworthy customers found themselves unable to borrow to finance investment spending.

As a result of all these events, the economy experienced a large contractionary shift in aggregate demand. Real GDP and employment both fell sharply. The introduction to this chapter has already cited the figures, but they are worth repeating: Real GDP declined by 4.7 percent between the fourth quarter of 2007 and the second quarter of 2009, and the rate of unemployment rose from 4.4 percent in May 2007 to 10.0 percent in October 2009. This experience served as a vivid reminder that deep economic downturns and personal hardship they cause are not a relic of history but a constant risk in the modern economy.

As the crisis unfolded, the U.S. government responded in a variety of ways. Three policy actions—all aimed in part at returning aggregate demand to its previous level—are most noteworthy. First, the Fed cut its target for the federal funds rate from 5.25 percent in September 2007 to about zero in December 2008. The Fed also started buying mortgage-backed securities and other private loans in open-market operations. By purchasing these instruments from the banking system, the Fed provided banks with additional funds in the hope that the banks would makes loans more readily available.

Second, in an even more unusual move in October 2008, Congress appropriated $700 billion for the Treasury to use to rescue the financial system. The goal was to stem the financial crisis on Wall Street and make loans easier to obtain. Much of these funds were used for equity injections into banks. That is, the Treasury put funds into the banking system, which the banks could use to make loans; in exchange for these funds, the U.S. government became a part owner of these banks, at least temporarily.

Finally, when Barack Obama became president in January 2009, his first major initiative was a large increase in government spending. After a relatively brief congressional debate over the form of the legislation, the new president signed a $787 billion stimulus bill on February 17, 2009. This policy move is discussed more fully in the next chapter when we consider the impact of fiscal policy on aggregate demand.

The recovery from this recession officially began in June 2009. But it was, by historical standards, only a meager recovery. From 2010 through 2012, real GDP growth averaged 2.1 percent per year, below the average rate of growth of about 3 percent. Unemployment fell from its peak but remained high: In April 2013, it was 7.5 percent, about 3 percentage points higher than it was before the downturn began.

Which, if any, of the many policy moves were most important for ending the recession? And what other policies might have promoted a more robust recovery? These are surely questions that macroeconomic historians will debate in the years to come. ◢

33-5b The Effects of a Shift in Aggregate Supply

Imagine once again an economy in its long-run equilibrium. Now suppose that suddenly some firms experience an increase in their costs of production. For example, bad weather in farm states might destroy some crops, driving up the cost of producing food products. Or a war in the Middle East might interrupt the shipping of crude oil, driving up the cost of producing oil products.

To analyze the macroeconomic impact of such an increase in production costs, we follow the same four steps as we always do. First, which curve is affected? Because production costs affect the firms that supply goods and services, changes in production costs alter the position of the aggregate-supply curve. Second, in which direction does the curve shift? Because higher production costs make selling goods and services less profitable, firms now supply a smaller quantity of output for any given price level. Thus, as Figure 10 shows, the short-run aggregate-supply curve shifts to the left, from AS_1 to AS_2. (Depending on the event, the long-run aggregate-supply curve might also shift. To keep things simple, however, we will assume that it does not.)

The figure allows us to perform step three of comparing the initial and the new equilibrium. In the short run, the economy goes from point A to point B, moving along the existing aggregate-demand curve. The output of the economy falls from Y_1 to Y_2, and the price level rises from P_1 to P_2. Because the economy is experiencing both *stagnation* (falling output) and *inflation* (rising prices), such an event is sometimes called **stagflation**.

Now consider step four—the transition from the short-run equilibrium to the long-run equilibrium. According to the sticky-wage theory, the key issue is how stagflation affects nominal wages. Firms and workers may at first respond to the higher level of prices by raising their expectations of the price level and setting higher nominal wages. In this case, firms' costs will rise yet again, and the short-run aggregate-supply curve will shift farther to the left, making the problem of stagflation even worse. This phenomenon of higher prices leading to higher wages, in turn leading to even higher prices, is sometimes called a *wage-price spiral*.

At some point, this spiral of ever-rising wages and prices will slow. The low level of output and employment will put downward pressure on workers' wages because workers have less bargaining power when unemployment is high. As nominal wages fall, producing goods and services becomes more profitable and the short-run aggregate-supply curve shifts to the right. As it shifts back toward

stagflation
a period of falling output and rising prices

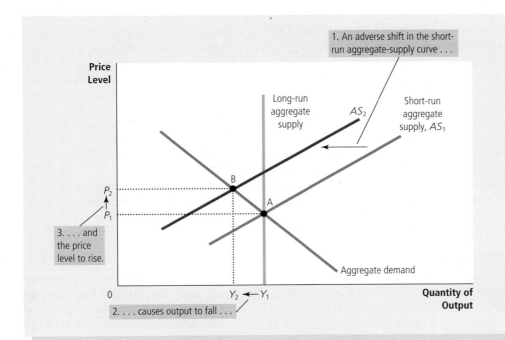

FIGURE 10

An Adverse Shift in Aggregate Supply
When some event increases firms' costs, the short-run aggregate-supply curve shifts to the left from AS_1 to AS_2. The economy moves from point A to point B. The result is stagflation: Output falls from Y_1 to Y_2, and the price level rises from P_1 to P_2.

FIGURE 11

Accommodating an Adverse Shift in Aggregate Supply
Faced with an adverse shift in aggregate supply from AS_1 to AS_2, policymakers who can influence aggregate demand might try to shift the aggregate-demand curve to the right from AD_1 to AD_2. The economy would move from point A to point C. This policy would prevent the supply shift from reducing output in the short run, but the price level would permanently rise from P_1 to P_3.

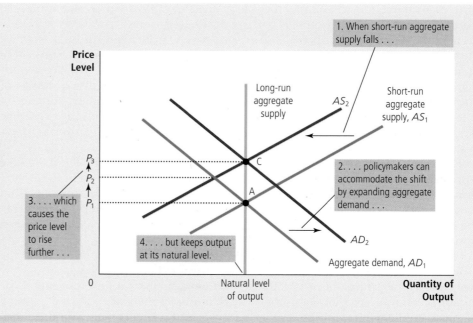

1. When short-run aggregate supply falls . . .

2. . . . policymakers can accommodate the shift by expanding aggregate demand . . .

3. . . . which causes the price level to rise further . . .

4. . . . but keeps output at its natural level.

AS_1, the price level falls and the quantity of output approaches its natural level. In the long run, the economy returns to point A, where the aggregate-demand curve crosses the long-run aggregate-supply curve.

This transition back to the initial equilibrium assumes, however, that aggregate demand is held constant throughout the process. In the real world, that may not be the case. Policymakers who control monetary and fiscal policy might attempt to offset some of the effects of the shift in the short-run aggregate-supply curve by shifting the aggregate-demand curve. This possibility is shown in Figure 11. In this case, changes in policy shift the aggregate-demand curve to the right, from AD_1 to AD_2—exactly enough to prevent the shift in aggregate supply from affecting output. The economy moves directly from point A to point C. Output remains at its natural level, and the price level rises from P_1 to P_3. In this case, policymakers are said to *accommodate* the shift in aggregate supply. An accommodative policy accepts a permanently higher level of prices to maintain a higher level of output and employment.

To sum up, this story about shifts in aggregate supply has two important lessons:

- Shifts in aggregate supply can cause stagflation—a combination of recession (falling output) and inflation (rising prices).
- Policymakers who can influence aggregate demand can potentially mitigate the adverse impact on output but only at the cost of exacerbating the problem of inflation.

case study

Oil and the Economy

Some of the largest economic fluctuations in the U.S. economy since 1970 have originated in the oil fields of the Middle East. Crude oil is a key input into the production of many goods and services, and much of the world's oil comes from Saudi Arabia, Kuwait, and other

Middle Eastern countries. When some event (usually political in origin) reduces the supply of crude oil flowing from this region, the price of oil rises around the world. Firms in the United States that produce gasoline, tires, and many other products experience rising costs, and they find it less profitable to supply their output of goods and services at any given price level. The result is a leftward shift in the aggregate-supply curve, which in turn leads to stagflation.

The first episode of this sort occurred in the mid-1970s. The countries with large oil reserves got together as members of OPEC, the Organization of Petroleum Exporting Countries. OPEC is a *cartel*—a group of sellers that attempts to thwart competition and reduce production to raise prices. And indeed, oil prices rose substantially. From 1973 to 1975, oil approximately doubled in price. Oil-importing countries around the world experienced simultaneous inflation and recession. The U.S. inflation rate as measured by the CPI exceeded 10 percent for the first time in decades. Unemployment rose from 4.9 percent in 1973 to 8.5 percent in 1975.

Almost the same thing happened a few years later. In the late 1970s, the OPEC countries again restricted the supply of oil to raise the price. From 1978 to 1981, the price of oil more than doubled. Once again, the result was stagflation. Inflation, which had subsided somewhat after the first OPEC event, again rose above 10 percent per year. But because the Fed was not willing to

FYI

The Origins of the Model of Aggregate Demand and Aggregate Supply

Now that we have a preliminary understanding of the model of aggregate demand and aggregate supply, it is worthwhile to step back from it and consider its history. How did this model of short-run fluctuations develop? The answer is that this model, to a large extent, is a by-product of the Great Depression of the 1930s. Economists and policymakers at the time were puzzled about what had caused this calamity and were uncertain about how to deal with it.

In 1936, economist John Maynard Keynes published a book titled *The General Theory of Employment, Interest, and Money*, which attempted to explain short-run economic fluctuations in general and the Great Depression in particular. Keynes's primary message was that recessions and depressions can occur because of inadequate aggregate demand for goods and services.

Keynes had long been a critic of classical economic theory—the theory we examined earlier in the book—because it could explain only the long-run effects of policies. A few years before offering *The General Theory*,

John Maynard Keynes

KEYSTONE/HULTON ARCHIVE/GETTY IMAGES

Keynes had written the following about classical economics:

> The long run is a misleading guide to current affairs. In the long run we are all dead. Economists set themselves too easy, too useless a task if in tempestuous seasons they can only tell us when the storm is long past, the ocean will be flat.

Keynes's message was aimed at policymakers as well as economists. As the world's economies suffered with high unemployment, Keynes advocated policies to increase aggregate demand, including government spending on public works.

In the next chapter, we examine in detail how policymakers can use the tools of monetary and fiscal policy to influence aggregate demand. The analysis in the next chapter, as well as in this one, owes much to the legacy of John Maynard Keynes. ◢

Changes in Middle East oil production are one source of U.S. economic fluctuations.

accommodate such a large rise in inflation, a recession was soon to follow. Unemployment rose from about 6 percent in 1978 and 1979 to about 10 percent a few years later.

The world market for oil can also be a source of favorable shifts in aggregate supply. In 1986, squabbling broke out among members of OPEC. Member countries reneged on their agreements to restrict oil production. In the world market for crude oil, prices fell by about half. This fall in oil prices reduced costs to U.S. firms, which now found it more profitable to supply goods and services at any given price level. As a result, the aggregate-supply curve shifted to the right. The U.S. economy experienced the opposite of stagflation: Output grew rapidly, unemployment fell, and the inflation rate reached its lowest level in many years.

In recent years, the world market for oil has not been as important a source of economic fluctuations. Part of the reason is that conservation efforts, changes in technology, and the availability of alternative energy sources have reduced the economy's dependence on oil. The amount of oil used to produce a unit of real GDP has declined about 40 percent since the OPEC shocks of the 1970s. As a result, the economic impact of any change in oil prices is smaller today than it was in the past. ◢

Quick Quiz *Suppose that the election of a popular presidential candidate suddenly increases people's confidence in the future. Use the model of aggregate demand and aggregate supply to analyze the effect on the economy.*

33-6 Conclusion

This chapter has achieved two goals. First, we have discussed some of the important facts about short-run fluctuations in economic activity. Second, we have introduced a basic model to explain those fluctuations, called the model of aggregate demand and aggregate supply. We continue our study of this model in the next chapter to understand more fully what causes fluctuations in the economy and how policymakers might respond to these fluctuations.

Summary

- All societies experience short-run economic fluctuations around long-run trends. These fluctuations are irregular and largely unpredictable. When recessions do occur, real GDP and other measures of income, spending, and production fall, and unemployment rises.

- Classical economic theory is based on the assumption that nominal variables such as the money supply and the price level do not influence real variables such as output and employment. Most economists believe that this assumption is accurate in the long run but not in the short run. Economists analyze short-run economic fluctuations using the model of aggregate demand and aggregate supply. According to this model, the output of goods and services and the overall level of prices adjust to balance aggregate demand and aggregate supply.

YASSER AL-ZAYYAT/AFP/Getty Images

- The aggregate-demand curve slopes downward for three reasons. The first is the wealth effect: A lower price level raises the real value of households' money holdings, which stimulates consumer spending. The second is the interest-rate effect: A lower price level reduces the quantity of money households demand; as households try to convert money into interest-bearing assets, interest rates fall, which stimulates investment spending. The third is the exchange-rate effect: As a lower price level reduces interest rates, the dollar depreciates in the market for foreign-currency exchange, which stimulates net exports.

- Any event or policy that raises consumption, investment, government purchases, or net exports at a given price level increases aggregate demand. Any event or policy that reduces consumption, investment, government purchases, or net exports at a given price level decreases aggregate demand.

- The long-run aggregate-supply curve is vertical. In the long run, the quantity of goods and services supplied depends on the economy's labor, capital, natural resources, and technology but not on the overall level of prices.

- Three theories have been proposed to explain the upward slope of the short-run aggregate-supply curve. According to the sticky-wage theory, an unexpected fall in the price level temporarily raises real wages, which induces firms to reduce employment and production. According to the sticky-price theory, an unexpected fall in the price level leaves some firms with prices that are temporarily too high, which reduces

their sales and causes them to cut back production. According to the misperceptions theory, an unexpected fall in the price level leads suppliers to mistakenly believe that their relative prices have fallen, which induces them to reduce production. All three theories imply that output deviates from its natural level when the actual price level deviates from the price level that people expected.

- Events that alter the economy's ability to produce output, such as changes in labor, capital, natural resources, or technology, shift the short-run aggregate-supply curve (and may shift the long-run aggregate-supply curve as well). In addition, the position of the short-run aggregate-supply curve depends on the expected price level.

- One possible cause of economic fluctuations is a shift in aggregate demand. When the aggregate-demand curve shifts to the left, for instance, output and prices fall in the short run. Over time, as a change in the expected price level causes wages, prices, and perceptions to adjust, the short-run aggregate-supply curve shifts to the right. This shift returns the economy to its natural level of output at a new, lower price level.

- A second possible cause of economic fluctuations is a shift in aggregate supply. When the short-run aggregate-supply curve shifts to the left, the effect is falling output and rising prices—a combination called stagflation. Over time, as wages, prices, and perceptions adjust, the short-run aggregate-supply curve shifts back to the right, returning the price level and output to their original levels.

Key Concepts

recession, *p. 707*
depression, *p. 707*
model of aggregate demand and
  aggregate supply, *p. 712*

aggregate-demand curve, *p. 712*
aggregate-supply curve, *p. 713*

natural level of output, *p. 721*
stagflation, *p. 737*

Questions for Review

1. Name two macroeconomic variables that decline when the economy goes into a recession. Name one macroeconomic variable that rises during a recession.

2. Draw a diagram with aggregate demand, short-run aggregate supply, and long-run aggregate supply. Be careful to label the axes correctly.

3. List and explain the three reasons the aggregate-demand curve slopes downward.

4. Explain why the long-run aggregate-supply curve is vertical.

5. List and explain the three theories for why the short-run aggregate-supply curve slopes upward.

6. What might shift the aggregate-demand curve to the left? Use the model of aggregate demand and aggregate supply to trace through the short-run and long-run effects of such a shift on output and the price level.

7. What might shift the aggregate-supply curve to the left? Use the model of aggregate demand and aggregate supply to trace through the short-run and long-run effects of such a shift on output and the price level.

Quick Check Multiple Choice

1. When the economy goes into a recession, real GDP _____ and unemployment _____.
   a. rises, rises
   b. rises, falls
   c. falls, rises
   d. falls, falls

2. A sudden crash in the stock market shifts
   a. the aggregate-demand curve.
   b. the short-run aggregate-supply curve, but not the long-run aggregate-supply curve.
   c. the long-run aggregate-supply curve, but not the short-run aggregate-supply curve.
   d. both the short-run and the long-run aggregate-supply curves.

3. A change in the expected price level shifts
   a. the aggregate-demand curve.
   b. the short-run aggregate-supply curve, but not the long-run aggregate-supply curve.
   c. the long-run aggregate-supply curve, but not the short-run aggregate-supply curve.
   d. both the short-run and the long-run aggregate-supply curves.

4. An increase in the aggregate demand for goods and services has a larger impact on output _____ and a larger impact on the price level _____.
   a. in the short run, in the long run
   b. in the long run, in the short run
   c. in the short run, also in the short run
   d. in the long run, also in the long run

5. Stagflation is caused by
   a. a leftward shift in the aggregate-demand curve.
   b. a rightward shift in the aggregate-demand curve.
   c. a leftward shift in the aggregate-supply curve.
   d. a rightward shift in the aggregate-supply curve.

6. The idea that economic downturns result from an inadequate aggregate demand for goods and services is derived from the work of which economist?
   a. Adam Smith
   b. David Hume
   c. David Ricardo
   d. John Maynard Keynes

Problems and Applications

1. Suppose the economy is in a long-run equilibrium.
   a. Draw a diagram to illustrate the state of the economy. Be sure to show aggregate demand, short-run aggregate supply, and long-run aggregate supply.
   b. Now suppose that a stock market crash causes aggregate demand to fall. Use your diagram to show what happens to output and the price level in the short run. What happens to the unemployment rate?
   c. Use the sticky-wage theory of aggregate supply to explain what will happen to output and the price level in the long run (assuming there is no change in policy). What role does the expected price level play in this adjustment? Be sure to illustrate your analysis in a graph.

2. Explain whether each of the following events will increase, decrease, or have no effect on long-run aggregate supply.
   a. The United States experiences a wave of immigration.
   b. Congress raises the minimum wage to $10 per hour.
   c. Intel invents a new and more powerful computer chip.
   d. A severe hurricane damages factories along the East Coast.

3. Suppose an economy is in long-run equilibrium.
   a. Use the model of aggregate demand and aggregate supply to illustrate the initial equilibrium (call it point A). Be sure to include both short-run and long-run aggregate supply.
   b. The central bank raises the money supply by 5 percent. Use your diagram to show what happens to output and the price level as the economy moves from the initial to the new short-run equilibrium (call it point B).
   c. Now show the new long-run equilibrium (call it point C). What causes the economy to move from point B to point C?
   d. According to the sticky-wage theory of aggregate supply, how do nominal wages at point A compare to nominal wages at point B? How do nominal wages at point A compare to nominal wages at point C?
   e. According to the sticky-wage theory of aggregate supply, how do real wages at point A compare to real wages at point B? How do real wages at point A compare to real wages at point C?
   f. Judging by the impact of the money supply on nominal and real wages, is this analysis consistent with the proposition that money has real effects in the short run but is neutral in the long run?

4. In 1939, with the U.S. economy not yet fully recovered from the Great Depression, President Roosevelt proclaimed that Thanksgiving would fall a week earlier than usual so that the shopping period before Christmas would be longer. Explain what President Roosevelt might have been trying to achieve, using the model of aggregate demand and aggregate supply.

5. Explain why the following statements are false.
   a. "The aggregate-demand curve slopes downward because it is the horizontal sum of the demand curves for individual goods."
   b. "The long-run aggregate-supply curve is vertical because economic forces do not affect long-run aggregate supply."
   c. "If firms adjusted their prices every day, then the short-run aggregate-supply curve would be horizontal."
   d. "Whenever the economy enters a recession, its long-run aggregate-supply curve shifts to the left."

6. For each of the three theories for the upward slope of the short-run aggregate-supply curve, carefully explain the following:
   a. how the economy recovers from a recession and returns to its long-run equilibrium without any policy intervention
   b. what determines the speed of that recovery

7. The economy begins in long-run equilibrium. Then one day, the president appoints a new chairman of the Fed. This new chairman is well known for her view that inflation is not a major problem for an economy.
   a. How would this news affect the price level that people would expect to prevail?
   b. How would this change in the expected price level affect the nominal wage that workers and firms agree to in their new labor contracts?
   c. How would this change in the nominal wage affect the profitability of producing goods and services at any given price level?
   d. How does this change in profitability affect the short-run aggregate-supply curve?
   e. If aggregate demand is held constant, how does this shift in the aggregate-supply curve affect the price level and the quantity of output produced?
   f. Do you think this Fed chairman was a good appointment?

8. Explain whether each of the following events shifts the short-run aggregate-supply curve, the aggregate-demand curve, both, or neither. For each event that does shift a curve, draw a diagram to illustrate the effect on the economy.
   a. Households decide to save a larger share of their income.
   b. Florida orange groves suffer a prolonged period of below-freezing temperatures.
   c. Increased job opportunities overseas cause many people to leave the country.

9. For each of the following events, explain the short-run and long-run effects on output and the price level, assuming policymakers take no action.
   a. The stock market declines sharply, reducing consumers' wealth.
   b. The federal government increases spending on national defense.
   c. A technological improvement raises productivity.
   d. A recession overseas causes foreigners to buy fewer U.S. goods.

10. Suppose firms become very optimistic about future business conditions and invest heavily in new capital equipment.
    a. Draw an aggregate-demand/aggregate-supply diagram to show the short-run effect of this optimism on the economy. Label the new levels of prices and real output. Explain in words why the aggregate quantity of output *supplied* changes.
    b. Now use the diagram from part (a) to show the new long-run equilibrium of the economy. (For now, assume there is no change in the long-run aggregate-supply curve.) Explain in words why the aggregate quantity of output *demanded* changes between the short run and the long run.
    c. How might the investment boom affect the long-run aggregate-supply curve? Explain.

Go to CengageBrain.com to purchase access to the proven, critical Study Guide to accompany this text, which features additional notes and context, practice tests, and much more.

The Influence of Monetary and Fiscal Policy on Aggregate Demand

I magine that you are a member of the Federal Open Market Committee, the group at the Federal Reserve that sets monetary policy. You observe that the president and Congress have agreed to raise taxes. How should the Fed respond to this change in fiscal policy? Should it expand the money supply, contract the money supply, or leave the money supply the same?

To answer this question, you need to consider the impact of monetary and fiscal policy on the economy. In the preceding chapter, we used the model of aggregate demand and aggregate supply to explain short-run economic fluctuations. We saw that shifts in the aggregate-demand curve or the aggregate-supply curve cause fluctuations in the economy's overall output of goods and services and its overall level of prices. As we noted in the previous chapter, monetary and fiscal policy can each influence aggregate demand. Thus, a change in one of these policies can lead to short-run fluctuations in output and prices. Policymakers will want to anticipate this effect and, perhaps, adjust the other policy in response.

In this chapter, we examine in more detail how the government's policy tools influence the position of the aggregate-demand curve. These tools include monetary policy (the supply of money set by the central bank) and fiscal policy (the levels of government spending and taxation set by the president and Congress). We have previously discussed the long-run effects of these policies. In Chapters 25 and 26, we saw how fiscal policy affects saving, investment, and long-run economic growth. In Chapters 29 and 30, we saw how monetary policy influences the price level in the long run. We now look at how these policy tools can shift the aggregate-demand curve and thereby affect macroeconomic variables in the short run.

As we have already learned, many factors influence aggregate demand besides monetary and fiscal policy. In particular, desired spending by households and firms determines the overall demand for goods and services. When desired spending changes, aggregate demand shifts. If policymakers do not respond, such shifts in aggregate demand cause short-run fluctuations in output and employment. As a result, monetary and fiscal policymakers sometimes use the policy levers at their disposal to try to offset these shifts in aggregate demand and stabilize the economy. Here we discuss the theory behind these policy actions and some of the difficulties that arise in using this theory in practice.

34-1 How Monetary Policy Influences Aggregate Demand

The aggregate-demand curve shows the total quantity of goods and services demanded in the economy for any price level. The preceding chapter discussed three reasons why the aggregate-demand curve slopes downward:

- *The wealth effect:* A lower price level raises the real value of households' money holdings, which are part of their wealth. Higher real wealth stimulates consumer spending and thus increases the quantity of goods and services demanded.
- *The interest-rate effect:* A lower price level reduces the amount of money people want to hold. As people try to lend out their excess money holdings, the interest rate falls. The lower interest rate stimulates investment spending and thus increases the quantity of goods and services demanded.
- *The exchange-rate effect:* When a lower price level reduces the interest rate, investors move some of their funds overseas in search of higher returns. This movement of funds causes the real value of the domestic currency to fall in the market for foreign-currency exchange. Domestic goods become less expensive relative to foreign goods. This change in the real exchange rate stimulates spending on net exports and thus increases the quantity of goods and services demanded.

These three effects occur simultaneously to increase the quantity of goods and services demanded when the price level falls and to decrease it when the price level rises.

Although all three effects work together to explain the downward slope of the aggregate-demand curve, they are not of equal importance. Because money holdings are a small part of household wealth, the wealth effect is the least important of the three. In addition, because exports and imports represent only a small fraction of U.S. GDP, the exchange-rate effect is not large for the U.S. economy. (This effect is more important for smaller countries, which typically export and import a higher fraction of their GDP.) *For the U.S. economy, the most important reason for the downward slope of the aggregate-demand curve is the interest-rate effect.*

To better understand aggregate demand, we now examine the short-run determination of interest rates in more detail. Here we develop the **theory of liquidity preference**. This theory of interest rates helps explain the downward slope of the aggregate-demand curve, as well as how monetary and fiscal policy can shift this curve. By shedding new light on aggregate demand, the theory of liquidity preference expands our understanding of what causes short-run economic fluctuations and what policymakers can potentially do about them.

theory of liquidity preference
Keynes's theory that the interest rate adjusts to bring money supply and money demand into balance

34-1a The Theory of Liquidity Preference

In his classic book *The General Theory of Employment, Interest, and Money,* John Maynard Keynes proposed the theory of liquidity preference to explain the factors that determine an economy's interest rate. The theory is, in essence, an application of supply and demand. According to Keynes, the interest rate adjusts to balance the supply of and demand for money.

You may recall that economists distinguish between two interest rates: The *nominal interest rate* is the interest rate as usually reported, and the *real interest rate* is the interest rate corrected for the effects of inflation. When there is no inflation, the two rates are the same. But when borrowers and lenders expect prices to rise over the course of the loan, they agree to a nominal interest rate that exceeds the real interest rate by the expected rate of inflation. The higher nominal interest rate compensates for the fact that they expect the loan to be repaid in less valuable dollars.

Which interest rate are we now trying to explain with the theory of liquidity preference? The answer is both. In the analysis that follows, we hold constant the expected rate of inflation. This assumption is reasonable for studying the economy in the short run, because expected inflation is typically stable over short periods of time. In this case, nominal and real interest rates differ by a constant. When the nominal interest rate rises or falls, the real interest rate that people expect to earn rises or falls as well. For the rest of this chapter, when we refer to changes in the interest rate, you should envision the real and nominal interest rates moving in the same direction.

Let's now develop the theory of liquidity preference by considering the supply and demand for money and how each depends on the interest rate.

Money Supply   The first piece of the theory of liquidity preference is the supply of money. As we first discussed in Chapter 29, the money supply in the U.S. economy is controlled by the Federal Reserve. The Fed alters the money supply primarily by changing the quantity of reserves in the banking system through the purchase and sale of government bonds in open-market operations. When the Fed buys government bonds, the dollars it pays for the bonds are typically deposited in banks, and these dollars are added to bank reserves. When the Fed sells government bonds, the dollars it receives for the bonds are withdrawn from the banking system, and bank reserves fall. These changes in bank reserves, in turn, lead to changes in banks' ability to make loans and create money. Thus, by buying and selling bonds in open-market operations, the Fed alters the quantity of money in the economy.

[handwritten margin notes: Fed bring interest down = Banks borrow more. From Fed = banks have more money = money supply increases and vice versa]

In addition to open-market operations, the Fed can influence the money supply using a variety of other tools. One option is for the Fed to change how much it lends to banks. For example, a decrease in the discount rate (the interest rate at which banks can borrow reserves from the Fed) encourages more bank borrowing, which increases bank reserves and thereby the money supply. Conversely, an increase in the discount rate discourages bank borrowing, which decreases bank reserves and the money supply. The Fed also alters the money supply by changing reserve requirements (the amount of reserves banks must hold against deposits) and by changing the interest rate it pays banks on the reserves they are holding.

These details of monetary control are important for the implementation of Fed policy, but they are not crucial for the analysis in this chapter. Our goal here is to examine how changes in the money supply affect the aggregate demand for goods and services. For this purpose, we can ignore the details of how Fed policy is implemented and assume that the Fed controls the money supply directly. In other words, the quantity of money supplied in the economy is fixed at whatever level the Fed decides to set it.

Because the quantity of money supplied is fixed by Fed policy, it does not depend on other economic variables. In particular, it does not depend on the interest rate. Once the Fed has made its policy decision, the quantity of money supplied is the same, regardless of the prevailing interest rate. We represent a fixed money supply with a vertical supply curve, as in Figure 1.

FIGURE 1

Equilibrium in the Money Market

According to the theory of liquidity preference, the interest rate adjusts to bring the quantity of money supplied and the quantity of money demanded into balance. If the interest rate is above the equilibrium level (such as at r_1), the quantity of money people want to hold (M_1^d) is less than the quantity the Fed has created, and this surplus of money puts downward pressure on the interest rate. Conversely, if the interest rate is below the equilibrium level (such as at r_2), the quantity of money people want to hold (M_2^d) is greater than the quantity the Fed has created, and this shortage of money puts upward pressure on the interest rate. Thus, the forces of supply and demand in the market for money push the interest rate toward the equilibrium interest rate, at which people are content holding the quantity of money the Fed has created.

[handwritten margin notes: shift in Money Demand — Price goes up I need more money — income goes up demand goes up]

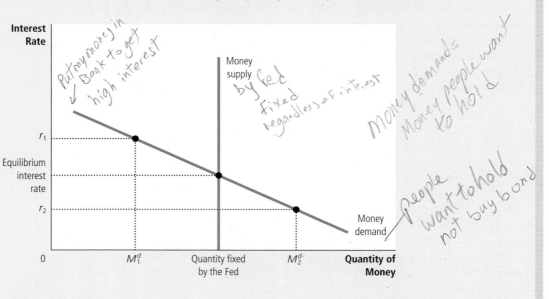

[handwritten annotations on figure: Put my money in Bank to get high interest; by fed fixed regardless of interest; Money demands Money people want to hold; people want to hold not buy bond]

Money Demand   The second piece of the theory of liquidity preference is the demand for money. As a starting point for understanding money demand, recall that any asset's *liquidity* refers to the ease with which that asset can be converted into the economy's medium of exchange. Because money is the economy's medium of exchange, it is by definition the most liquid asset available. The liquidity of money explains the demand for it: People choose to hold money instead of other assets that offer higher rates of return because money can be used to buy goods and services.

Although many factors determine the quantity of money demanded, the one emphasized by the theory of liquidity preference is the interest rate. The reason is that the interest rate is the opportunity cost of holding money. That is, when you hold wealth as cash in your wallet, instead of as an interest-bearing bond, you lose the interest you could have earned. An increase in the interest rate raises the cost of holding money and, as a result, reduces the quantity of money demanded. A decrease in the interest rate reduces the cost of holding money and raises the quantity demanded. Thus, as shown in Figure 1, the money-demand curve slopes downward.

Equilibrium in the Money Market   According to the theory of liquidity preference, the interest rate adjusts to balance the supply and demand for money. There is one interest rate, called the *equilibrium interest rate,* at which the quantity of money demanded exactly balances the quantity of money supplied. If the interest rate is at any other level, people will try to adjust their portfolios of assets and, as a result, drive the interest rate toward the equilibrium.

For example, suppose that the interest rate is above the equilibrium level, such as r_1 in Figure 1. In this case, the quantity of money that people want to hold, M_1^d, is less than the quantity of money that the Fed has supplied. Those people who are holding the surplus of money will try to get rid of it by buying interest-bearing bonds or by depositing it in interest-bearing bank accounts. Because bond issuers and banks prefer to pay lower interest rates, they respond to this surplus of money by lowering the interest rates they offer. As the interest rate falls, people become more willing to hold money until, at the equilibrium interest rate, people are happy to hold exactly the amount of money the Fed has supplied.

Conversely, at interest rates below the equilibrium level, such as r_2 in Figure 1, the quantity of money that people want to hold, M_2^d, is greater than the quantity of money that the Fed has supplied. As a result, people try to increase their holdings of money by reducing their holdings of bonds and other interest-bearing assets. As people cut back on their holdings of bonds, bond issuers find that they have to offer higher interest rates to attract buyers. Thus, the interest rate rises and approaches the equilibrium level.

34-1b The Downward Slope of the Aggregate-Demand Curve

Having seen how the theory of liquidity preference explains the economy's equilibrium interest rate, we now consider the theory's implications for the aggregate demand for goods and services. As a warm-up exercise, let's begin by using the theory to reexamine a topic we already understand—the interest-rate effect and the downward slope of the aggregate-demand curve. In particular, suppose that the overall level of prices in the economy rises. What happens to the interest

[handwritten margin notes:] the higher the interest, the more people buy bonds and vice versa. where money supplied by fed and money demand by people to hold meet is equilibrium

FYI

Interest Rates in the Long Run and the Short Run

In an earlier chapter, we said that the interest rate adjusts to balance the supply of loanable funds (national saving) and the demand for loanable funds (desired investment). Here we just said that the interest rate adjusts to balance the supply of and demand for money. Can we reconcile these two theories?

To answer this question, we need to focus on three macroeconomic variables: the economy's output of goods and services, the interest rate, and the price level. According to the classical macroeconomic theory we developed earlier in the book, these variables are determined as follows:

1. *Output* is determined by the supplies of capital and labor and the available production technology for turning capital and labor into output. (We call this the natural level of output.)
2. For any given level of output, the *interest rate* adjusts to balance the supply and demand for loanable funds.
3. Given output and the interest rate, the *price level* adjusts to balance the supply and demand for money. Changes in the supply of money lead to proportionate changes in the price level.

These are three of the essential propositions of classical economic theory. Most economists believe that these propositions do a good job of describing how the economy works *in the long run.*

Yet these propositions do not hold in the short run. As we discussed in the preceding chapter, many prices are slow to adjust to changes in the money supply; this fact is reflected in a short-run aggregate-supply curve that is upward sloping rather than vertical. As a result, *in the short run,* the overall price level cannot, by itself, move to balance the supply of and demand for money. This stickiness of the price level requires the interest rate to move to bring the money market into equilibrium. These changes in the interest rate, in turn, affect the aggregate demand for goods and services. As aggregate demand fluctuates, the economy's output of goods and services moves away from the level determined by factor supplies and technology.

To think about the operation of the economy in the short run (day to day, week to week, month to month, or quarter to quarter), it is best to keep in mind the following logic:

1. The *price level* is stuck at some level (based on previously formed expectations) and, in the short run, is relatively unresponsive to changing economic conditions.
2. For any given (stuck) price level, the *interest rate* adjusts to balance the supply of and demand for money.
3. The interest rate that balances the money market influences the quantity of goods and services demanded and thus the level of *output.*

Notice that this precisely reverses the order of analysis used to study the economy in the long run.

The two different theories of the interest rate are useful for different purposes. When thinking about the long-run determinants of the interest rate, it is best to keep in mind the loanable-funds theory, which highlights the importance of an economy's saving propensities and investment opportunities. By contrast, when thinking about the short-run determinants of the interest rate, it is best to keep in mind the liquidity-preference theory, which highlights the importance of monetary policy. ◢

rate that balances the supply and demand for money, and how does that change affect the quantity of goods and services demanded?

As we discussed in Chapter 30, the price level is one determinant of the quantity of money demanded. At higher prices, more money is exchanged every time a good or service is sold. As a result, people will choose to hold a larger quantity of money. That is, a higher price level increases the quantity of money demanded for any given interest rate. Thus, an increase in the price level from P_1 to P_2 shifts the money-demand curve to the right from MD_1 to MD_2, as shown in panel (a) of Figure 2.

Notice how this shift in money demand affects the equilibrium in the money market. For a fixed money supply, the interest rate must rise to balance money supply and money demand. Because the higher price level has increased the amount of money people want to hold, it has shifted the money demand curve to the right. Yet the quantity of money supplied is unchanged, so the interest rate must rise from r_1 to r_2 to discourage the additional demand.

An increase in the price level from P_1 to P_2 shifts the money-demand curve to the right, as in panel (a). This increase in money demand causes the interest rate to rise from r_1 to r_2. Because the interest rate is the cost of borrowing, the increase in the interest rate reduces the quantity of goods and services demanded from Y_1 to Y_2. This negative relationship between the price level and quantity demanded is represented with a downward-sloping aggregate-demand curve, as in panel (b).

FIGURE 2

The Money Market and the Slope of the Aggregate-Demand Curve

(a) The Money Market

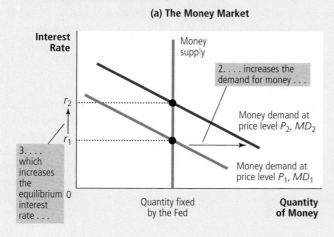

(b) The Aggregate-Demand Curve

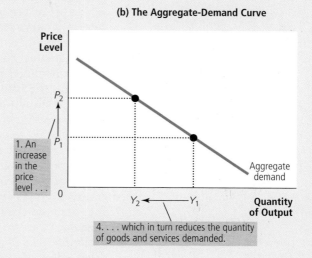

This increase in the interest rate has ramifications not only for the money market but also for the quantity of goods and services demanded, as shown in panel (b). At a higher interest rate, the cost of borrowing and the return to saving are greater. Fewer households choose to borrow to buy a new house, and those who do buy smaller houses, so the demand for residential investment falls. Fewer firms choose to borrow to build new factories and buy new equipment, so business investment falls. Thus, when the price level rises from P_1 to P_2, increasing money demand from MD_1 to MD_2 and raising the interest rate from r_1 to r_2, the quantity of goods and services demanded falls from Y_1 to Y_2.

This analysis of the interest-rate effect can be summarized in three steps: (1) A higher price level raises money demand. (2) Higher money demand leads to a higher interest rate. (3) A higher interest rate reduces the quantity of goods and services demanded. The same logic works for a decline in the price level: A lower price level reduces money demand, which leads to a lower interest rate, and this in turn increases the quantity of goods and services demanded. The result of this analysis is a negative relationship between the price level and the quantity of goods and services demanded, as illustrated by a downward-sloping aggregate-demand curve.

34-1c Changes in the Money Supply

So far, we have used the theory of liquidity preference to explain more fully how the total quantity of goods and services demanded in the economy changes as the price level changes. That is, we have examined movements along a downward-sloping aggregate-demand curve. The theory also sheds light, however, on some of the other events that alter the quantity of goods and services demanded. Whenever the quantity of goods and services demanded changes *for any given price level*, the aggregate-demand curve shifts.

One important variable that shifts the aggregate-demand curve is monetary policy. To see how monetary policy affects the economy in the short run, suppose that the Fed increases the money supply by buying government bonds in open-market operations. (Why the Fed might do this will become clear later, after we understand the effects of such a move.) Let's consider how this monetary injection influences the equilibrium interest rate for a given price level. This will tell us what the injection does to the position of the aggregate-demand curve.

As panel (a) of Figure 3 shows, an increase in the money supply shifts the money-supply curve to the right from MS_1 to MS_2. Because the money-demand curve has not changed, the interest rate falls from r_1 to r_2 to balance money supply and money demand. That is, the interest rate must fall to induce people to hold the additional money the Fed has created, restoring equilibrium in the money market.

Once again, the interest rate influences the quantity of goods and services demanded, as shown in panel (b) of Figure 3. The lower interest rate reduces the cost of borrowing and the return to saving. Households spend more on new homes, stimulating the demand for residential investment. Firms spend more on new factories and new equipment, stimulating business investment. As a result, the quantity of goods and services demanded at a given price level, $\bar{P}$, rises from Y_1 to Y_2. Of course, there is nothing special about $\bar{P}$: The monetary injection raises the quantity of goods and services demanded at every price level. Thus, the entire aggregate-demand curve shifts to the right.

To sum up: *When the Fed increases the money supply, it lowers the interest rate and increases the quantity of goods and services demanded for any given price level, shifting the aggregate-demand curve to the right. Conversely, when the Fed contracts the money supply, it raises the interest rate and reduces the quantity of goods and services demanded for any given price level, shifting the aggregate-demand curve to the left.*

FIGURE 3

A Monetary Injection

In panel (a), an increase in the money supply from MS_1 to MS_2 reduces the equilibrium interest rate from r_1 to r_2. Because the interest rate is the cost of borrowing, the fall in the interest rate raises the quantity of goods and services demanded at a given price level from Y_1 to Y_2. Thus, in panel (b), the aggregate-demand curve shifts to the right from AD_1 to AD_2.

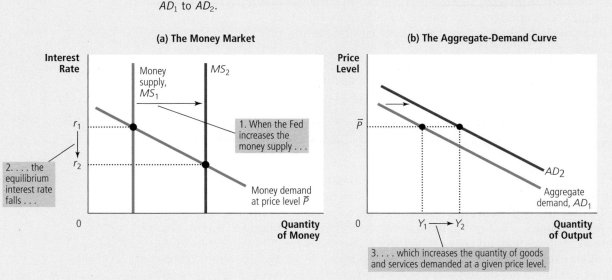

(a) The Money Market

Interest Rate

Money supply, MS_1 MS_2

r_1

r_2

1. When the Fed increases the money supply . . .

2. . . . the equilibrium interest rate falls . . .

Money demand at price level $\bar{P}$

0   Quantity of Money

(b) The Aggregate-Demand Curve

Price Level

$\bar{P}$

AD_2

Aggregate demand, AD_1

0     $Y_1 \rightarrow Y_2$ Quantity of Output

3. . . . which increases the quantity of goods and services demanded at a given price level.

34-1d The Role of Interest-Rate Targets in Fed Policy

How does the Federal Reserve affect the economy? Our discussion here and earlier in the book has treated the money supply as the Fed's policy instrument. When the Fed buys government bonds in open-market operations, it increases the money supply and expands aggregate demand. When the Fed sells government bonds in open-market operations, it decreases the money supply and contracts aggregate demand.

Discussions of Fed policy often treat the interest rate, rather than the money supply, as the Fed's policy instrument. Indeed, in recent years, the Federal Reserve has conducted policy by setting a target for the *federal funds rate*—the interest rate that banks charge one another for short-term loans. This target is reevaluated every six weeks at meetings of the Federal Open Market Committee (FOMC). The FOMC has chosen to set a target for the federal funds rate, rather than for the money supply, as it did at times in the past.

There are several related reasons for the Fed's decision to use the federal funds rate as its target. One is that the money supply is hard to measure with sufficient precision. Another is that money demand fluctuates over time. For any given money supply, fluctuations in money demand would lead to fluctuations in interest rates, aggregate demand, and output. By contrast, when the Fed announces a target for the federal funds rate, it essentially accommodates the day-to-day shifts in money demand by adjusting the money supply accordingly.

The Fed's decision to target an interest rate does not fundamentally alter our analysis of monetary policy. The theory of liquidity preference illustrates an important

FYI

The Zero Lower Bound

As we have just seen, monetary policy works through interest rates. This conclusion raises a question: What if the Fed's target interest rate has fallen as far as it can? In the recession of 2008 and 2009, the federal funds rate fell to about zero. In this situation, what, if anything, can monetary policy do to stimulate the economy?

Some economists describe this situation as a *liquidity trap*. According to the theory of liquidity preference, expansionary monetary policy works by reducing interest rates and stimulating investment spending. But if interest rates have already fallen almost to zero, then perhaps monetary policy is no longer effective. Nominal interest rates cannot fall below zero: Rather than making a loan at a negative nominal interest rate, a person would just hold cash. In this environment, expansionary monetary policy raises the supply of money, making the public's asset portfolio more liquid, but because interest rates can't fall any further, the extra liquidity might not have any effect. Aggregate demand, production, and employment may be "trapped" at low levels.

Other economists are skeptical about the relevance of liquidity traps and believe that a central bank continues to have tools to expand the economy, even after its interest rate target hits its lower bound of zero. One possibility is that the central bank could raise inflation expectations by committing itself to future monetary expansion. Even if nominal interest rates cannot fall any further, higher expected inflation can lower real interest rates by making them negative, which would stimulate investment spending.

A second possibility is that the central bank could conduct expansionary open-market operations with a larger variety of financial instruments than it normally uses. For example, it could buy mortgages and corporate debt and thereby lower the interest rates on these kinds of loans. The Federal Reserve actively pursued this last option in the aftermath of the financial crisis of 2008 and 2009. This type of unconventional monetary policy is sometimes called *quantitative easing* because it increases the quantity of bank reserves.

Some economists have suggested that the possibility of hitting the zero lower bound for interest rates justifies setting the target rate of inflation well above zero. Under zero inflation, the real interest rate, like the nominal interest, can never fall below zero. But if the normal rate of inflation is, say, 4 percent, then the central bank can easily push the real interest rate to negative 4 percent by lowering the nominal interest rate toward zero. Thus, moderate inflation gives monetary policymakers more room to stimulate the economy when needed, reducing the risk of hitting up against the zero lower bound and having the economy fall into a liquidity trap. ◢

principle: *Monetary policy can be described either in terms of the money supply or in terms of the interest rate.* When the FOMC sets a target for the federal funds rate of, say, 6 percent, the Fed's bond traders are told: "Conduct whatever open-market operations are necessary to ensure that the equilibrium interest rate is 6 percent." In other words, when the Fed sets a target for the interest rate, it commits itself to adjusting the money supply to make the equilibrium in the money market hit that target.

As a result, changes in monetary policy can be viewed either in terms of changing the interest rate target or in terms of changing the money supply. When you read in the newspaper that "the Fed has lowered the federal funds rate from 6 to 5 percent," you should understand that this occurs only because the Fed's bond traders are doing what it takes to make it happen. To lower the federal funds rate, the Fed's bond traders buy government bonds, and this purchase increases the money supply and lowers the equilibrium interest rate (just as in Figure 3). Similarly, when the FOMC raises the target for the federal funds rate, the bond traders sell government bonds, and this sale decreases the money supply and raises the equilibrium interest rate.

The lessons from this analysis are simple: *Changes in monetary policy aimed at expanding aggregate demand can be described either as increasing the money supply or as lowering the interest rate. Changes in monetary policy aimed at contracting aggregate demand can be described either as decreasing the money supply or as raising the interest rate.*

case study **Why the Fed Watches the Stock Market (and Vice Versa)**

"The stock market has predicted nine out of the past five recessions." So quipped Paul Samuelson, the famed economist (and textbook author). Samuelson was surely right that the stock market is highly volatile and can give wrong signals about the economy. But fluctuations in stock prices are often a sign of broader economic developments. The economic boom of the 1990s, for example, appeared not only in rapid GDP growth and falling unemployment but also in rising stock prices, which increased about fourfold during this decade. Similarly, the deep recession of 2008 and 2009 was reflected in falling stock prices: From November 2007 to March 2009, the stock market lost about half its value.

How should the Fed respond to stock market fluctuations? The Fed has no reason to care about stock prices in themselves, but it does have the job of monitoring and responding to developments in the overall economy, and the stock market is a piece of that puzzle. When the stock market booms, households become wealthier, and this increased wealth stimulates consumer spending. In addition, a rise in stock prices makes it more attractive for firms to sell new shares of stock, and this stimulates investment spending. For both reasons, a booming stock market expands the aggregate demand for goods and services.

As we discuss more fully later in the chapter, one of the Fed's goals is to stabilize aggregate demand, because greater stability in aggregate demand means greater stability in output and the price level. To promote stability, the Fed might respond to a stock market boom by keeping the money supply lower and interest rates higher than it otherwise would. The contractionary effects of higher interest rates would offset the expansionary effects of higher stock prices. In fact, this analysis does describe Fed behavior: Real interest rates were kept high by historical standards during the stock market boom of the late 1990s.

The opposite occurs when the stock market falls. Spending on consumption and investment tends to decline, depressing aggregate demand and pushing the economy toward recession. To stabilize aggregate demand, the Fed would increase the money supply and lower interest rates. And indeed, that is what it typically does. For example, on October 19, 1987, the stock market fell by

22.6 percent—one of the biggest one-day drops in history. The Fed responded to the market crash by increasing the money supply and lowering interest rates. The federal funds rate fell from 7.7 percent at the beginning of October to 6.6 percent at the end of the month. In part because of the Fed's quick action, the economy avoided a recession. Similarly, as we discussed in a case study in the preceding chapter, the Fed also reduced interest rates during the economic downturn and stock market decline of 2008 and 2009, but this time monetary policy was not sufficient to avert a deep recession.

While the Fed keeps an eye on the stock market, stock market participants also keep an eye on the Fed. Because the Fed can influence interest rates and economic activity, it can alter the value of stocks. For example, when the Fed raises interest rates by reducing the money supply, it makes owning stocks less attractive for two reasons. First, a higher interest rate means that bonds, the alternative to stocks, are earning a higher return. Second, the Fed's tightening of monetary policy reduces the demand for goods and services, which reduces profits. As a result, stock prices often fall when the Fed raises interest rates. ◢

Quick Quiz *Use the theory of liquidity preference to explain how a decrease in the money supply affects the equilibrium interest rate. How does this change in monetary policy affect the aggregate-demand curve?*

34-2 How Fiscal Policy Influences Aggregate Demand

The government can influence the behavior of the economy not only with monetary policy but also with fiscal policy. **Fiscal policy** refers to the government's choices regarding the overall level of government purchases and taxes. Earlier in the book, we examined how fiscal policy influences saving, investment, and growth in the long run. In the short run, however, the primary effect of fiscal policy is on the aggregate demand for goods and services.

fiscal policy
the setting of the level of government spending and taxation by government policymakers

34-2a Changes in Government Purchases

When policymakers change the money supply or the level of taxes, they shift the aggregate-demand curve indirectly by influencing the spending decisions of firms or households. By contrast, when the government alters its own purchases of goods and services, it shifts the aggregate-demand curve directly.

Suppose, for instance, that the U.S. Department of Defense places a $20 billion order for new fighter planes with Boeing, the large aircraft manufacturer. This order raises the demand for the output produced by Boeing, which induces the company to hire more workers and increase production. Because Boeing is part of the economy, the increase in the demand for Boeing planes means an increase in the total quantity of goods and services demanded at each price level. As a result, the aggregate-demand curve shifts to the right.

By how much does this $20 billion order from the government shift the aggregate-demand curve? At first, one might guess that the aggregate-demand curve shifts to the right by exactly $20 billion. It turns out, however, that this is not the case. There are two macroeconomic effects that cause the size of the shift in aggregate demand to differ from the change in government purchases. The first—the multiplier effect—suggests the shift in aggregate demand could be *larger* than $20 billion. The second—the crowding-out effect—suggests the shift in aggregate demand could be *smaller* than $20 billion. We now discuss each of these effects in turn.

34-2b The Multiplier Effect

When the government buys $20 billion of goods from Boeing, that purchase has repercussions. The immediate impact of the higher demand from the government is to raise employment and profits at Boeing. Then, as the workers see higher earnings and the firm owners see higher profits, they respond to this increase in income by raising their own spending on consumer goods. As a result, the government purchase from Boeing raises the demand for the products of many other firms in the economy. Because each dollar spent by the government can raise the aggregate demand for goods and services by more than a dollar, government purchases are said to have a **multiplier effect** on aggregate demand.

multiplier effect
the additional shifts in aggregate demand that result when expansionary fiscal policy increases income and thereby increases consumer spending

This multiplier effect continues even after this first round. When consumer spending rises, the firms that produce these consumer goods hire more people and experience higher profits. Higher earnings and profits stimulate consumer spending once again and so on. Thus, there is positive feedback as higher demand leads to higher income, which in turn leads to even higher demand. Once all these effects are added together, the total impact on the quantity of goods and services demanded can be much larger than the initial impulse from higher government spending.

Figure 4 illustrates the multiplier effect. The increase in government purchases of $20 billion initially shifts the aggregate-demand curve to the right from AD_1 to AD_2 by exactly $20 billion. But when consumers respond by increasing their spending, the aggregate-demand curve shifts still further to AD_3.

This multiplier effect arising from the response of consumer spending can be strengthened by the response of investment to higher levels of demand. For instance, Boeing might respond to the higher demand for planes by deciding to buy more equipment or build another plant. In this case, higher government demand spurs higher demand for investment goods. This positive feedback from demand to investment is sometimes called the *investment accelerator*.

FIGURE 4

The Multiplier Effect
An increase in government purchases of $20 billion can shift the aggregate-demand curve to the right by more than $20 billion. This multiplier effect arises because increases in aggregate income stimulate additional spending by consumers.

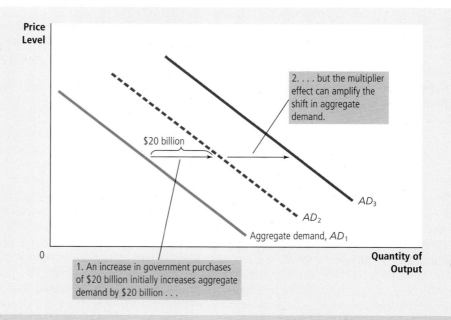

Price Level

2. . . . but the multiplier effect can amplify the shift in aggregate demand.

$20 billion

AD_3

AD_2

Aggregate demand, AD_1

Quantity of Output

0

1. An increase in government purchases of $20 billion initially increases aggregate demand by $20 billion . . .

34-2c A Formula for the Spending Multiplier

Some simple algebra permits us to derive a formula for the size of the multiplier effect that arises when an increase in government purchases induces increases in consumer spending. An important number in this formula is the *marginal propensity to consume (MPC)*—the fraction of extra income that a household consumes rather than saves. For example, suppose that the marginal propensity to consume is ¾. This means that for every extra dollar that a household earns, the household spends $0.75 (¾ of the dollar) and saves $0.25. With an *MPC* of ¾, when the workers and owners of Boeing earn $20 billion from the government contract, they increase their consumer spending by ¾ × $20 billion, or $15 billion.

To gauge the impact on aggregate demand of a change in government purchases, we follow the effects step-by-step. The process begins when the government spends $20 billion, which implies that national income (earnings and profits) also rises by this amount. This increase in income in turn raises consumer spending by *MPC* × $20 billion, which in turn raises the income for the workers and owners of the firms that produce the consumption goods. This second increase in income again raises consumer spending, this time by *MPC* × (*MPC* × $20 billion). These feedback effects go on and on.

To find the total impact on the demand for goods and services, we add up all these effects:

$$
\begin{aligned}
\text{Change in government purchases} &= \quad\quad\quad \$20 \text{ billion} \\
\text{First change in consumption} &= MPC \;\times \$20 \text{ billion} \\
\text{Second change in consumption} &= MPC^2 \times \$20 \text{ billion} \\
\text{Third change in consumption} &= MPC^3 \times \$20 \text{ billion}
\end{aligned}
$$

$$
\begin{aligned}
\text{Total change in demand} \\
&= (1 + MPC + MPC^2 + MPC^3 + \ldots) \times \$20 \text{ billion.}
\end{aligned}
$$

Here "..." represents an infinite number of similar terms. Thus, we can write the multiplier as follows:

$$\text{Multiplier} = 1 + MPC + MPC^2 + MPC^3 + \ldots.$$

This multiplier tells us the demand for goods and services that each dollar of government purchases generates.

To simplify this equation for the multiplier, recall from math class that this expression is an infinite geometric series. For x between -1 and $+1$,

$$1 + x + x^2 + x^3 + \ldots = 1/(1 - x).$$

In our case, $x = MPC$. Thus,

$$\text{Multiplier} = 1/(1 - MPC).$$

$1/(1 - 3/4) = 4$

$20 \times 4 = 80$

For example, if *MPC* is ¾, the multiplier is 1/(1 − ¾), which is 4. In this case, the $20 billion of government spending generates $80 billion of demand for goods and services.

This formula for the multiplier shows that the size of the multiplier depends on the marginal propensity to consume. While an *MPC* of ¾ leads to a multiplier of 4, an *MPC* of ½ leads to a multiplier of only 2. Thus, a larger *MPC* means a larger multiplier. To see why this is true, remember that the multiplier arises because higher income induces greater spending on consumption. With a larger *MPC*, consumption responds more to a change in income, and so the multiplier is larger.

34-2d Other Applications of the Multiplier Effect

Because of the multiplier effect, a dollar of government purchases can generate more than a dollar of aggregate demand. The logic of the multiplier effect, however, is not restricted to changes in government purchases. Instead, it applies to any event that alters spending on any component of GDP—consumption, investment, government purchases, or net exports.

For example, suppose that a recession overseas reduces the demand for U.S. net exports by $10 billion. This reduced spending on U.S. goods and services depresses U.S. national income, which reduces spending by U.S. consumers. If the marginal propensity to consume is ¾ and the multiplier is 4, then the $10 billion fall in net exports leads to a $40 billion contraction in aggregate demand.

As another example, suppose that a stock market boom increases households' wealth and stimulates their spending on goods and services by $20 billion. This extra consumer spending increases national income, which in turn generates even more consumer spending. If the marginal propensity to consume is ¾ and the multiplier is 4, then the initial impulse of $20 billion in consumer spending translates into an $80 billion increase in aggregate demand.

The multiplier is an important concept in macroeconomics because it shows how the economy can amplify the impact of changes in spending. A small initial change in consumption, investment, government purchases, or net exports can end up having a large effect on aggregate demand and, therefore, the economy's production of goods and services.

34-2e The Crowding-Out Effect

The multiplier effect seems to suggest that when the government buys $20 billion of planes from Boeing, the resulting expansion in aggregate demand is necessarily larger than $20 billion. Yet another effect works in the opposite direction. While an increase in government purchases stimulates the aggregate demand for goods and services, it also causes the interest rate to rise, which reduces investment spending and puts downward pressure on aggregate demand. The reduction in aggregate demand that results when a fiscal expansion raises the interest rate is called the **crowding-out effect**.

crowding-out effect
the offset in aggregate demand that results when expansionary fiscal policy raises the interest rate and thereby reduces investment spending

To see why crowding out occurs, let's consider what happens in the money market when the government buys planes from Boeing. As we have discussed, this increase in demand raises the incomes of the workers and owners of this firm (and because of the multiplier effect, of other firms as well). As incomes rise, households plan to buy more goods and services and, as a result, choose to hold more of their wealth in liquid form. That is, the increase in income caused by the fiscal expansion raises the demand for money.

The effect of the increase in money demand is shown in panel (a) of Figure 5. Because the Fed has not changed the money supply, the vertical supply curve remains the same. When the higher level of income shifts the money-demand curve to the right from MD_1 to MD_2, the interest rate must rise from r_1 to r_2 to keep supply and demand in balance.

The increase in the interest rate, in turn, reduces the quantity of goods and services demanded. In particular, because borrowing is more expensive, the demand for residential and business investment goods declines. That is, as the increase in government purchases increases the demand for goods and services, it may also crowd out investment. This crowding-out effect partially offsets the impact of government purchases on aggregate demand, as illustrated in panel (b) of Figure 5. The increase in government purchases initially shifts the aggregate-demand curve from AD_1 to AD_2, but once crowding out takes place, the aggregate-demand curve drops back to AD_3.

To sum up: *When the government increases its purchases by $20 billion, the aggregate demand for goods and services could rise by more or less than $20 billion depending on the*

Panel (a) shows the money market. When the government increases its purchases of goods and services, the resulting increase in income raises the demand for money from MD_1 to MD_2, and this causes the equilibrium interest rate to rise from r_1 to r_2. Panel (b) shows the effects on aggregate demand. The initial impact of the increase in government purchases shifts the aggregate-demand curve from AD_1 to AD_2. Yet because the interest rate is the cost of borrowing, the increase in the interest rate tends to reduce the quantity of goods and services demanded, particularly for investment goods. This crowding out of investment partially offsets the impact of the fiscal expansion on aggregate demand. In the end, the aggregate-demand curve shifts only to AD_3.

FIGURE 5

The Crowding-Out Effect

(a) The Money Market

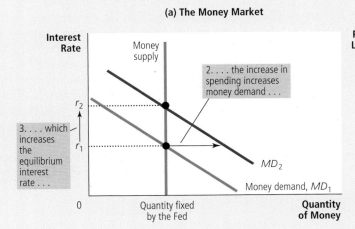

(b) The Shift in Aggregate Demand

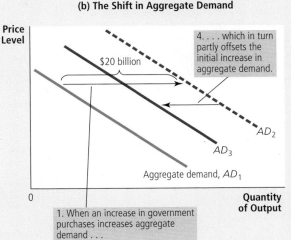

sizes of the multiplier and crowding-out effects. The multiplier effect makes the shift in aggregate demand greater than $20 billion. The crowding-out effect pushes the aggregate-demand curve in the opposite direction and, if large enough, could result in an aggregate-demand shift of less than $20 billion.

34-2f Changes in Taxes

The other important instrument of fiscal policy, besides the level of government purchases, is the level of taxation. When the government cuts personal income taxes, for instance, it increases households' take-home pay. Households will save some of this additional income, but they will also spend some of it on consumer goods. Because it increases consumer spending, the tax cut shifts the aggregate-demand curve to the right. Similarly, a tax increase depresses consumer spending and shifts the aggregate-demand curve to the left.

The size of the shift in aggregate demand resulting from a tax change is also affected by the multiplier and crowding-out effects. When the government cuts taxes and stimulates consumer spending, earnings and profits rise, which further stimulates consumer spending. This is the multiplier effect. At the same time, higher income leads to higher money demand, which tends to raise interest rates. Higher interest rates make borrowing more costly, which reduces investment spending. This is the crowding-out effect. Depending on the size of the multiplier and crowding-out effects, the shift in aggregate demand could be larger or smaller than the tax change that causes it.

In addition to the multiplier and crowding-out effects, there is another important determinant of the size of the shift in aggregate demand that results from a tax change: households' perceptions about whether the tax change is permanent or temporary. For example, suppose that the government announces a tax cut of

FYI
....

**How Fiscal Policy Might
Affect Aggregate Supply**

So far, our discussion of fiscal policy has stressed how changes in government purchases and changes in taxes influence the quantity of goods and services demanded. Most economists believe that the short-run macroeconomic effects of fiscal policy work primarily through aggregate demand. Yet fiscal policy can potentially influence the quantity of goods and services supplied as well.

For instance, consider the effects of tax changes on aggregate supply. One of the *Ten Principles of Economics* in Chapter 1 is that people respond to incentives. When government policymakers cut tax rates, workers get to keep more of each dollar they earn, so they have a greater incentive to work and produce goods and services. If they respond to this incentive, the quantity of goods and services supplied will be greater at each price level, and the aggregate-supply curve will shift to the right.

Some economists, called *supply siders*, have argued that the influence of tax cuts on aggregate supply is large. According to some supply siders, the influence is so large that a cut in tax rates will stimulate enough additional production and income that tax revenue will actually increase. This is certainly a theoretical possibility, but most economists do not consider it the normal case. While the supply-side effects of taxes are important to consider, they are usually not large enough to cause tax revenue to rise when tax rates fall.

Like changes in taxes, changes in government purchases can also potentially affect aggregate supply. Suppose, for instance, that the government increases expenditure on a form of government-provided capital, such as roads. Roads are used by private businesses to make deliveries to their customers; an increase in the quantity of roads increases these businesses' productivity. Hence, when the government spends more on roads, it increases the quantity of goods and services supplied at any given price level and, thus, shifts the aggregate-supply curve to the right. This effect on aggregate supply is probably more important in the long run than in the short run, however, because it takes time for the government to build new roads and put them into use. ◢

$1,000 per household. In deciding how much of this $1,000 to spend, households must ask themselves how long this extra income will last. If they expect the tax cut to be permanent, they will view it as adding substantially to their financial resources and, therefore, increase their spending by a large amount. In this case, the tax cut will have a large impact on aggregate demand. By contrast, if households expect the tax change to be temporary, they will view it as adding only slightly to their financial resources and, therefore, will increase their spending by only a small amount. In this case, the tax cut will have a small impact on aggregate demand.

An extreme example of a temporary tax cut was the one announced in 1992. In that year, President George H. W. Bush faced a lingering recession and an upcoming reelection campaign. He responded to these circumstances by announcing a reduction in the amount of income tax that the federal government was withholding from workers' paychecks. Because legislated income tax rates did not change, however, every dollar of reduced withholding in 1992 meant an extra dollar of taxes due on April 15, 1993, when income tax returns for 1992 were to be filed. Thus, this "tax cut" actually represented only a short-term loan from the government. Not surprisingly, the impact of the policy on consumer spending and aggregate demand was relatively small.

Quick Quiz   *Suppose that the government reduces spending on highway construction by $10 billion. Which way does the aggregate-demand curve shift? Explain why the shift might be larger than $10 billion. Explain why the shift might be smaller than $10 billion.*

34-3 Using Policy to Stabilize the Economy

We have seen how monetary and fiscal policy can affect the economy's aggregate demand for goods and services. These theoretical insights raise some important policy questions: Should policymakers use these instruments to control aggregate demand and stabilize the economy? If so, when? If not, why not?

34-3a The Case for Active Stabilization Policy

Let's return to the question that began this chapter: When the president and Congress raise taxes, how should the Federal Reserve respond? As we have seen, the level of taxation is one determinant of the position of the aggregate-demand curve. When the government raises taxes, aggregate demand will fall, depressing production and employment in the short run. If the Federal Reserve wants to prevent this adverse effect of the fiscal policy, it can expand aggregate demand by increasing the money supply. A monetary expansion would reduce interest rates, stimulate investment spending, and expand aggregate demand. If monetary policy is set appropriately, the combined changes in monetary and fiscal policy could leave the aggregate demand for goods and services unaffected.

This analysis is exactly the sort followed by members of the Federal Open Market Committee. They know that monetary policy is an important determinant of aggregate demand. They also know that there are other important determinants as well, including fiscal policy set by the president and Congress. As a result, the FOMC watches the debates over fiscal policy with a keen eye.

This response of monetary policy to the change in fiscal policy is an example of a more general phenomenon: the use of policy instruments to stabilize aggregate demand and, as a result, production and employment. Economic stabilization has been an explicit goal of U.S. policy since the Employment Act of 1946. This act states that "it is the continuing policy and responsibility of the federal government to . . . promote full employment and production." In essence, the government has chosen to hold itself accountable for short-run macroeconomic performance.

The Employment Act has two implications. The first, more modest, implication is that the government should avoid being a cause of economic fluctuations. Thus, most economists advise against large and sudden changes in monetary and fiscal policy, for such changes are likely to cause fluctuations in aggregate demand. Moreover, when large changes do occur, it is important that monetary and fiscal policymakers be aware of and respond to each others' actions.

The second, more ambitious, implication of the Employment Act is that the government should respond to changes in the private economy to stabilize aggregate demand. The act was passed not long after the publication of Keynes's *The General Theory of Employment, Interest, and Money*, which has been one of the most influential books ever written about economics. In it, Keynes emphasized the key role of aggregate demand in explaining short-run economic fluctuations. Keynes claimed that the government should actively stimulate aggregate demand when aggregate demand appeared insufficient to maintain production at its full-employment level.

Keynes (and his many followers) argued that aggregate demand fluctuates because of largely irrational waves of pessimism and optimism. He used the term "animal spirits" to refer to these arbitrary changes in attitude. When pessimism reigns, households reduce consumption spending and firms reduce investment spending. The result is reduced aggregate demand, lower production, and higher unemployment. Conversely, when optimism reigns, households and firms increase spending. The result is higher aggregate demand, higher production, and inflationary pressure. Notice that these changes in attitude are, to some extent, self-fulfilling.

In principle, the government can adjust its monetary and fiscal policy in response to these waves of optimism and pessimism and, thereby, stabilize the economy. For example, when people are excessively pessimistic, the Fed can expand the money supply to lower interest rates and expand aggregate demand. When they are excessively optimistic, it can contract the money supply to raise interest rates and dampen aggregate demand. Former Fed Chairman William McChesney Martin described this view of monetary policy very simply: "The Federal Reserve's job is to take away the punch bowl just as the party gets going."

case
study **Keynesians in the White House**

When a reporter in 1961 asked President John F. Kennedy why he advocated a tax cut, Kennedy replied, "To stimulate the economy. Don't you remember your Economics 101?" Kennedy's policy was, in fact, based on the analysis of fiscal policy we have developed in this chapter. His goal was to enact a tax cut, which would raise consumer spending, expand aggregate demand, and increase the economy's production and employment.

In choosing this policy, Kennedy was relying on his team of economic advisers. This team included such prominent economists as James Tobin and Robert Solow, who later would win Nobel Prizes for their contributions to economics. As students in the 1940s, these economists had closely studied John Maynard Keynes's *General Theory*, which was then only a few years old. When the Kennedy advisers proposed cutting taxes, they were putting Keynes's ideas into action.

Although tax changes can have a potent influence on aggregate demand, they have other effects as well. In particular, by changing the incentives that

IN THE NEWS
• • • • • • • • • • • • • •

How Large Is the Fiscal Policy Multiplier?

In the global economic downturn of 2008 and 2009, governments around the world turned to fiscal policy to prop up aggregate demand. This episode ignited a debate about the size of the multipliers, which remains a topic of much research.

Much Ado about Multipliers

It is the biggest peacetime fiscal expansion in history. Across the globe countries have countered the recession by cutting taxes and by boosting government spending. The G20 group of economies, whose leaders meet this week in Pittsburgh, have introduced stimulus packages worth an average of 2% of GDP this year and 1.6% of GDP in 2010. Co-ordinated action on this scale might suggest a consensus about the effects of fiscal stimulus. But economists are in fact deeply divided about how well, or indeed whether, such stimulus works.

The debate hinges on the scale of the "fiscal multiplier." This measure, first formalised in 1931 by Richard Kahn, a student of John Maynard Keynes, captures how effectively tax

cuts or increases in government spending stimulate output. A multiplier of one means that a $1 billion increase in government spending will increase a country's GDP by $1 billion.

The size of the multiplier is bound to vary according to economic conditions. For an economy operating at full capacity, the fiscal multiplier should be zero. Since there are no spare resources, any increase in government demand would just replace spending elsewhere. But in a recession, when workers and factories lie idle, a fiscal boost can increase overall demand. And if the initial stimulus triggers a cascade of expenditure among consumers and businesses, the multiplier can be well above one.

The multiplier is also likely to vary according to the type of fiscal action. Government spending on building a bridge may have a

bigger multiplier than a tax cut if consumers save a portion of their tax windfall. A tax cut targeted at poorer people may have a bigger impact on spending than one for the affluent, since poorer folk tend to spend a higher share of their income.

Crucially, the overall size of the fiscal multiplier also depends on how people react to higher government borrowing. If the government's actions bolster confidence and revive animal spirits, the multiplier could rise as demand goes up and private investment is "crowded in." But if interest rates climb in response to government borrowing then some private investment that would otherwise have occurred could get "crowded out." And if consumers expect higher future taxes in order to finance new government borrowing, they could spend less today. All that would reduce the fiscal multiplier, potentially to below zero.

people face, taxes can alter the aggregate supply of goods and services. Part of the Kennedy proposal was an investment tax credit, which gives a tax break to firms that invest in new capital. Higher investment would not only stimulate aggregate demand immediately but also increase the economy's productive capacity over time. Thus, the short-run goal of increasing production through higher aggregate demand was coupled with a long-run goal of increasing production through higher aggregate supply. And indeed, when the tax cut Kennedy proposed was finally enacted in 1964, it helped usher in a period of robust economic growth.

Since the 1964 tax cut, policymakers have from time to time used fiscal policy as a tool for controlling aggregate demand. For example, when President Barack Obama moved into the Oval Office in 2009, he faced an economy in the midst of a recession. One of his first policy initiatives was a stimulus bill that included substantial increases in government spending. The accompanying In the News box discusses some of the debate over this policy initiative. ◢

Different assumptions about the impact of higher government borrowing on interest rates and private spending explain wild variations in the estimates of multipliers from today's stimulus spending. Economists in the Obama administration, who assume that the federal funds rate stays constant for a four-year period, expect a multiplier of 1.6 for government purchases and 1.0 for tax cuts from America's fiscal stimulus. An alternative assessment by John Cogan, Tobias Cwik, John Taylor and Volker Wieland uses models in which interest rates and taxes rise more quickly in response to higher public borrowing. Their multipliers are much smaller. They think America's stimulus will boost GDP by only one-sixth as much as the Obama team expects.

When forward-looking models disagree so dramatically, careful analysis of previous fiscal stimuli ought to help settle the debate. Unfortunately, it is extremely tricky to isolate the impact of changes in fiscal policy. One approach is to use microeconomic case studies to examine consumer behaviour in response to specific tax rebates and cuts. These studies, largely based on tax changes in America, find that permanent cuts have

a bigger impact on consumer spending than temporary ones and that consumers who find it hard to borrow, such as those close to their credit-card limit, tend to spend more of their tax windfall. But case studies do not measure the overall impact of tax cuts or spending increases on output.

An alternative approach is to try to tease out the statistical impact of changes in government spending or tax cuts on GDP. The difficulty here is to isolate the effects of fiscal-stimulus measures from the rises in social-security spending and falls in tax revenues that naturally accompany recessions. This empirical approach has narrowed the range of estimates in some areas. It has also yielded interesting cross-country comparisons. Multipliers are bigger in closed economies than open ones (because less of the stimulus leaks abroad via imports). They have traditionally been bigger in rich countries than emerging ones (where investors tend to take fright more quickly, pushing interest rates up). But overall economists find as big a range of multipliers from empirical estimates as they do from theoretical models.

To add to the confusion, the post-war experiences from which statistical analyses are drawn differ in vital respects from the current situation. Most of the evidence on multipliers for government spending is based on military outlays, but today's stimulus packages are heavily focused on infrastructure. Interest rates in many rich countries are now close to zero, which may increase the potency of, as well as the need for, fiscal stimulus. Because of the financial crisis relatively more people face borrowing constraints, which would increase the effectiveness of a tax cut. At the same time, highly indebted consumers may now be keen to cut their borrowing, leading to a lower multiplier. And investors today have more reason to be worried about rich countries' fiscal positions than those of emerging markets.

Add all this together and the truth is that economists are flying blind. They can make relative judgments with some confidence. Temporary tax cuts pack less punch than permanent ones, for instance. Fiscal multipliers will probably be lower in heavily indebted economies than in prudent ones. But policymakers looking for precise estimates are deluding themselves. ◢

Source: *The Economist*, September 24, 2009.

34-3b The Case against Active Stabilization Policy

Some economists argue that the government should avoid active use of monetary and fiscal policy to try to stabilize the economy. They claim that these policy instruments should be set to achieve long-run goals, such as rapid economic growth and low inflation, and that the economy should be left to deal with short-run fluctuations on its own. These economists may admit that monetary and fiscal policy can stabilize the economy in theory, but they doubt whether it can do so in practice.

The primary argument against active monetary and fiscal policy is that these policies affect the economy with a long lag. As we have seen, monetary policy works by changing interest rates, which in turn influence investment spending. But many firms make investment plans far in advance. Thus, most economists believe that it takes at least six months for changes in monetary policy to have much effect on output and employment. Moreover, once these effects occur, they can last for several years. Critics of stabilization policy argue that because of this lag, the Fed should not try to fine-tune the economy. They claim that the Fed often reacts too late to changing economic conditions and, as a result, ends up being a cause of rather than a cure for economic fluctuations. These critics advocate a passive monetary policy, such as slow and steady growth in the money supply.

Fiscal policy also works with a lag, but unlike the lag in monetary policy, the lag in fiscal policy is largely attributable to the political process. In the United States, most changes in government spending and taxes must go through congressional committees in both the House and the Senate, be passed by both legislative bodies, and then be signed by the president. Completing this process can take months or, in some cases, years. By the time the change in fiscal policy is passed and ready to implement, the condition of the economy may well have changed.

These lags in monetary and fiscal policy are a problem in part because economic forecasting is so imprecise. If forecasters could accurately predict the condition of the economy a year in advance, then monetary and fiscal policymakers could look ahead when making policy decisions. In this case, policymakers could stabilize the economy despite the lags they face. In practice, however, major recessions and depressions arrive without much advance warning. The best that policymakers can do is to respond to economic changes as they occur.

34-3c Automatic Stabilizers

All economists—both advocates and critics of stabilization policy—agree that the lags in implementation reduce the efficacy of policy as a tool for short-run stabilization. The economy would be more stable, therefore, if policymakers could find a way to avoid some of these lags. In fact, they have. **Automatic stabilizers** are changes in fiscal policy that stimulate aggregate demand when the economy goes into a recession without policymakers having to take any deliberate action.

The most important automatic stabilizer is the tax system. When the economy goes into a recession, the amount of taxes collected by the government falls automatically because almost all taxes are closely tied to economic activity. The personal income tax depends on households' incomes, the payroll tax depends on workers' earnings, and the corporate income tax depends on firms' profits. Because incomes, earnings, and profits all fall in a recession, the government's tax revenue falls as well. This automatic tax cut stimulates aggregate demand and, thereby, reduces the magnitude of economic fluctuations.

Government spending also acts as an automatic stabilizer. In particular, when the economy goes into a recession and workers are laid off, more people apply for unemployment insurance benefits, welfare benefits, and other forms of income support. This automatic increase in government spending stimulates aggregate demand at exactly the time when aggregate demand is insufficient to maintain

automatic stabilizers
changes in fiscal policy that stimulate aggregate demand when the economy goes into a recession without policymakers having to take any deliberate action

full employment. Indeed, when the unemployment insurance system was first en-acted in the 1930s, economists who advocated this policy did so in part because of its power as an automatic stabilizer.

The automatic stabilizers in the U.S. economy are not sufficiently strong to prevent recessions completely. Nonetheless, without these automatic stabilizers, output and employment would probably be more volatile than they are. For this reason, many economists oppose a constitutional amendment that would require the federal gov-ernment always to run a balanced budget, as some politicians have proposed. When the economy goes into a recession, taxes fall, government spending rises, and the government's budget moves toward deficit. If the government faced a strict balanced-budget rule, it would be forced to look for ways to raise taxes or cut spending in a recession. In other words, a strict balanced-budget rule would eliminate the automatic stabilizers inherent in our current system of taxes and government spending.

Quick Quiz *Suppose a wave of negative "animal spirits" overruns the economy, and people become pessimistic about the future. What happens to aggregate demand? If the Fed wants to stabilize aggregate demand, how should it alter the money supply? If it does this, what happens to the interest rate? Why might the Fed choose not to respond in this way?*

34-4 Conclusion

Before policymakers make any change in policy, they need to consider all the effects of their decisions. Earlier in the book, we examined classical models of the economy, which describe the long-run effects of monetary and fiscal policy. There we saw how fiscal policy influences saving, investment, and long-run growth and how monetary policy influences the price level and the inflation rate.

In this chapter, we examined the short-run effects of monetary and fiscal policy. We saw how these policy instruments can change the aggregate demand for goods and services and alter the economy's production and employment in the short run. When Congress reduces government spending to balance the budget, it needs to consider both the long-run effects on saving and growth and the short-run effects on aggregate demand and employment. When the Fed reduces the growth rate of the money supply, it must take into account the long-run effect on inflation as well as the short-run effect on production. In all parts of government, policymakers must keep in mind both long-run and short-run goals.

Summary

- In developing a theory of short-run economic fluctuations, Keynes proposed the theory of liquidity preference to explain the determinants of the interest rate. According to this theory, the interest rate adjusts to balance the supply and demand for money.

- An increase in the price level raises money demand and increases the interest rate that brings the money market into equilibrium. Because the interest rate represents the cost of borrowing, a higher interest rate reduces investment and, thereby, the quantity of goods and services demanded. The downward-sloping aggregate-demand curve expresses this negative relationship between the price level and the quantity demanded.

- Policymakers can influence aggregate demand with monetary policy. An increase in the money supply reduces the equilibrium interest rate for any given price level. Because a lower interest rate stimulates investment spending, the aggregate-demand curve shifts to the right. Conversely, a decrease in the money supply raises the equilibrium interest rate for any given price level and shifts the aggregate-demand curve to the left.

- Policymakers can also influence aggregate demand with fiscal policy. An increase in government purchases

or a cut in taxes shifts the aggregate-demand curve to the right. A decrease in government purchases or an increase in taxes shifts the aggregate-demand curve to the left.

- When the government alters spending or taxes, the resulting shift in aggregate demand can be larger or smaller than the fiscal change. The multiplier effect tends to amplify the effects of fiscal policy on aggregate demand. The crowding-out effect tends to dampen the effects of fiscal policy on aggregate demand.

- Because monetary and fiscal policy can influence aggregate demand, the government sometimes uses these policy instruments in an attempt to stabilize the economy. Economists disagree about how active the government should be in this effort. According to advocates of active stabilization policy, changes in attitudes by households and firms shift aggregate demand; if the government does not respond, the result is undesirable and unnecessary fluctuations in output and employment. According to critics of active stabilization policy, monetary and fiscal policy work with such long lags that attempts at stabilizing the economy often end up being destabilizing.

Key Concepts

theory of liquidity preference, *p. 747*
fiscal policy, *p. 755*

multiplier effect, *p. 756*
crowding-out effect, *p. 758*

automatic stabilizers, *p. 764*

Questions for Review

1. What is the theory of liquidity preference? How does it help explain the downward slope of the aggregate-demand curve?

2. Use the theory of liquidity preference to explain how a decrease in the money supply affects the aggregate-demand curve.

3. The government spends $3 billion to buy police cars. Explain why aggregate demand might increase by more than $3 billion. Explain why aggregate demand might increase by less than $3 billion.

4. Suppose that survey measures of consumer confidence indicate a wave of pessimism is sweeping the country.

If policymakers do nothing, what will happen to aggregate demand? What should the Fed do if it wants to stabilize aggregate demand? If the Fed does nothing, what might Congress do to stabilize aggregate demand?

5. Give an example of a government policy that acts as an automatic stabilizer. Explain why the policy has this effect.

Quick Check Multiple Choice

1. If the central bank wants to expand aggregate demand, it can _____ the money supply, which would _____ the interest rate.
   a. increase, increase
   b. increase, decrease
   c. decrease, increase
   d. decrease, decrease

2. If the government wants to contract aggregate demand, it can _____ government purchases or _____ taxes.
   a. increase, increase
   b. increase, decrease
   c. decrease, increase
   d. decrease, decrease

3. The Federal Reserve's target rate for the federal funds rate
   a. is an extra policy tool for the central bank, in addition to and independent of the money supply.
   b. commits the Fed to set a particular money supply so that it hits the announced target.
   c. is a goal that is rarely achieved, because the Fed can determine only the money supply.
   d. matters to banks that borrow and lend federal funds but does not influence aggregate demand.

4. With the economy in a recession because of inadequate aggregate demand, the government increases its purchases by $1,200. Suppose the central bank adjusts the money supply to hold the interest rate constant, investment spending is fixed, and the marginal propensity to consume is 2/3. How large is the increase in aggregate demand?
   a. $400
   b. $800
   c. $1,800
   d. $3,600

5. If the central bank in the preceding question instead holds the money supply constant and allows the interest rate to adjust, the change in aggregate demand resulting from the increase in government purchases will be
   a. larger.
   b. the same.
   c. smaller but still positive.
   d. negative.

6. Which of the following is an example of an automatic stabilizer? When the economy goes into a recession,
   a. more people become eligible for unemployment insurance benefits.
   b. stock prices decline, particularly for firms in cyclical industries.
   c. Congress begins hearings about a possible stimulus package.
   d. the Federal Reserve changes its target for the federal funds rate.

Problems and Applications

1. Explain how each of the following developments would affect the supply of money, the demand for money, and the interest rate. Illustrate your answers with diagrams.
   a. The Fed's bond traders buy bonds in open-market operations.
   b. An increase in credit-card availability reduces the cash people hold.
   c. The Federal Reserve reduces banks' reserve requirements.
   d. Households decide to hold more money to use for holiday shopping.
   e. A wave of optimism boosts business investment and expands aggregate demand.

2. The Federal Reserve expands the money supply by 5 percent.
   a. Use the theory of liquidity preference to illustrate in a graph the impact of this policy on the interest rate.
   b. Use the model of aggregate demand and aggregate supply to illustrate the impact of this change in the interest rate on output and the price level in the short run.
   c. When the economy makes the transition from its short-run equilibrium to its long-run equilibrium, what will happen to the price level?

d. How will this change in the price level affect the demand for money and the equilibrium interest rate?

e. Is this analysis consistent with the proposition that money has real effects in the short run but is neutral in the long run?

3. Suppose a computer virus disables the nation's automatic teller machines, making withdrawals from bank accounts less convenient. As a result, people want to keep more cash on hand, increasing the demand for money.

a. Assume the Fed does not change the money supply. According to the theory of liquidity preference, what happens to the interest rate? What happens to aggregate demand?

b. If instead the Fed wants to stabilize aggregate demand, how should it change the money supply?

c. If it wants to accomplish this change in the money supply using open-market operations, what should it do?

4. Consider two policies—a tax cut that will last for only one year and a tax cut that is expected to be permanent. Which policy will stimulate greater spending by consumers? Which policy will have the greater impact on aggregate demand? Explain.

5. The economy is in a recession with high unemployment and low output.

a. Draw a graph of aggregate demand and aggregate supply to illustrate the current situation. Be sure to include the aggregate-demand curve, the short-run aggregate-supply curve, and the long-run aggregate-supply curve.

b. Identify an open-market operation that would restore the economy to its natural rate.

c. Draw a graph of the money market to illustrate the effect of this open-market operation. Show the resulting change in the interest rate.

d. Draw a graph similar to the one in part (a) to show the effect of the open-market operation on output and the price level. Explain in words why the policy has the effect that you have shown in the graph.

6. In the early 1980s, new legislation allowed banks to pay interest on checking deposits, which they could not do previously.

a. If we define money to include checking deposits, what effect did this legislation have on money demand? Explain.

b. If the Federal Reserve had maintained a constant money supply in the face of this change, what would have happened to the interest rate? What would have happened to aggregate demand and aggregate output?

c. If the Federal Reserve had maintained a constant market interest rate (the interest rate on nonmonetary assets) in the face of this change, what change in the money supply would have been necessary? What would have happened to aggregate demand and aggregate output?

7. Suppose economists observe that an increase in government spending of $10 billion raises the total demand for goods and services by $30 billion.

a. If these economists ignore the possibility of crowding out, what would they estimate the marginal propensity to consume (MPC) to be?

b. Now suppose the economists allow for crowding out. Would their new estimate of the MPC be larger or smaller than their initial one?

8. Suppose the government reduces taxes by $20 billion, that there is no crowding out, and that the marginal propensity to consume is ¾.

a. What is the initial effect of the tax reduction on aggregate demand?

b. What additional effects follow this initial effect? What is the total effect of the tax cut on aggregate demand?

c. How does the total effect of this $20 billion tax cut compare to the total effect of a $20 billion increase in government purchases? Why?

d. Based on your answer to part (c), can you think of a way in which the government can increase aggregate demand without changing the government's budget deficit?

9. An economy is operating with output $400 billion below its natural level, and fiscal policymakers want to close this recessionary gap. The central bank agrees to adjust the money supply to hold the interest rate constant, so there is no crowding out. The marginal propensity to consume is ⅘, and the price level is completely fixed in the short run. In what direction and by how much would government spending need to change to close the recessionary gap? Explain your thinking.

10. Suppose government spending increases. Would the effect on aggregate demand be larger if the Federal Reserve held the money supply constant in response or if the Fed were committed to maintaining a fixed interest rate? Explain.

11. In which of the following circumstances is expansionary fiscal policy more likely to lead to a short-run increase in investment? Explain.

a. When the investment accelerator is large or when it is small?

b. When the interest sensitivity of investment is large or when it is small?

Go to CengageBrain.com to purchase access to the proven, critical Study Guide to accompany this text, which features additional notes and context, practice tests, and much more.

The Short-Run Trade-off between Inflation and Unemployment

Two closely watched indicators of economic performance are inflation and unemployment. When the Bureau of Labor Statistics releases data on these variables each month, policymakers are eager to hear the news. Some commentators have added together the inflation rate and the unemployment rate to produce a *misery index,* which purports to measure the health of the economy.

How are these two measures of economic performance related to each other? Earlier in the book, we discussed the long-run determinants of unemployment and the long-run determinants of inflation. We saw that the natural rate of unemployment depends on various features of the labor market, such as minimum-wage laws, the market power of unions, the role of efficiency wages, and the effectiveness of job search. By contrast, the inflation rate depends primarily on growth in the money supply, which a nation's central bank controls. In the long run, therefore, inflation and unemployment are largely unrelated problems.

In the short run, just the opposite is true. One of the *Ten Principles of Economics* discussed in Chapter 1 is that society faces a short-run trade-off between inflation and unemployment. If monetary and fiscal policymakers expand aggregate demand and move the economy up along the short-run aggregate-supply curve, they can expand output and lower unemployment for a while, but only at the cost of a more rapidly rising price level. If policymakers contract aggregate demand and move the economy down the short-run aggregate-supply curve, they can lower inflation, but only at the cost of temporarily lower output and higher unemployment.

In this chapter, we examine the inflation–unemployment trade-off more closely. The relationship between inflation and unemployment has attracted the attention of some of the most brilliant economists of the last half century. The best way to understand this relationship is to see how thinking about it has evolved. As we will see, the history of thought regarding inflation and unemployment since the 1950s is inextricably connected to the history of the U.S. economy. These two histories will show why the trade-off between inflation and unemployment holds in the short run, why it does not hold in the long run, and what issues the trade-off raises for economic policymakers.

35-1 The Phillips Curve

Phillips curve
a curve that shows the short-run trade-off between inflation and unemployment

"Probably the single most important macroeconomic relationship is the Phillips curve." These are the words of economist George Akerlof from the lecture he gave when he received the Nobel Prize in 2001. The **Phillips curve** is the short-run relationship between inflation and unemployment. We begin our story with the discovery of the Phillips curve and its migration to America.

35-1a Origins of the Phillips Curve

In 1958, economist A. W. Phillips published an article in the British journal *Economica* that would make him famous. The article was titled "The Relationship between Unemployment and the Rate of Change of Money Wages in the United Kingdom, 1861–1957." In it, Phillips showed a negative correlation between the rate of unemployment and the rate of inflation. That is, Phillips showed that years with low unemployment tend to have high inflation, and years with high unemployment tend to have low inflation. (Phillips examined inflation in nominal wages rather than inflation in prices. For our purposes, the distinction is not important because these two measures of inflation usually move together.) Phillips concluded that two important macroeconomic variables—inflation and unemployment—were linked in a way that economists had not previously appreciated.

Although Phillips's discovery was based on data for the United Kingdom, researchers quickly extended his finding to other countries. Two years after Phillips published his article, economists Paul Samuelson and Robert Solow published an article in the *American Economic Review* called "Analytics of Anti-Inflation Policy" in which they showed a similar negative correlation between inflation and unemployment in data for the United States. They reasoned that this correlation arose because low unemployment was associated with high aggregate demand, which in turn put upward pressure on wages and prices throughout the economy. Samuelson and Solow dubbed the

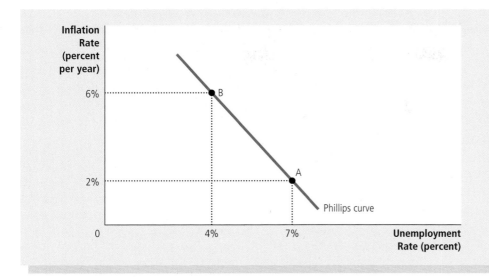

FIGURE 1

The Phillips Curve
The Phillips curve illustrates a negative association between the inflation rate and the unemployment rate. At point A, inflation is low and unemployment is high. At point B, inflation is high and unemployment is low.

negative association between inflation and unemployment the *Phillips curve*. Figure 1 shows an example of a Phillips curve like the one found by Samuelson and Solow.

As the title of their paper suggests, Samuelson and Solow were interested in the Phillips curve because they believed it held important lessons for policymakers. In particular, they suggested that the Phillips curve offers policymakers a menu of possible economic outcomes. By altering monetary and fiscal policy to influence aggregate demand, policymakers could choose any point on this curve. Point A offers high unemployment and low inflation. Point B offers low unemployment and high inflation. Policymakers might prefer both low inflation and low unemployment, but the historical data as summarized by the Phillips curve indicate that this combination is impossible. According to Samuelson and Solow, policymakers face a trade-off between inflation and unemployment, and the Phillips curve illustrates that trade-off.

35-1b Aggregate Demand, Aggregate Supply, and the Phillips Curve

The model of aggregate demand and aggregate supply provides an easy explanation for the menu of possible outcomes described by the Phillips curve. *The Phillips curve shows the combinations of inflation and unemployment that arise in the short run as shifts in the aggregate-demand curve move the economy along the short-run aggregate-supply curve.* As we saw in the preceding two chapters, an increase in the aggregate demand for goods and services leads, in the short run, to a larger output of goods and services and a higher price level. Larger output means greater employment and, thus, a lower rate of unemployment. In addition, a higher price level translates into a higher rate of inflation. Thus, shifts in aggregate demand push inflation and unemployment in opposite directions in the short run—a relationship illustrated by the Phillips curve.

To see more fully how this works, let's consider an example. To keep the numbers simple, imagine that the price level (as measured, for instance, by the consumer price index) equals 100 in the year 2020. Figure 2 shows two possible

FIGURE 2

How the Phillips Curve Is Related to the Model of Aggregate Demand and Aggregate Supply

This figure assumes a price level of 100 for the year 2020 and charts possible outcomes for the year 2021. Panel (a) shows the model of aggregate demand and aggregate supply. If aggregate demand is low, the economy is at point A; output is low (15,000), and the price level is low (102). If aggregate demand is high, the economy is at point B; output is high (16,000), and the price level is high (106). Panel (b) shows the implications for the Phillips curve. Point A, which arises when aggregate demand is low, has high unemployment (7 percent) and low inflation (2 percent). Point B, which arises when aggregate demand is high, has low unemployment (4 percent) and high inflation (6 percent).

(a) The Model of Aggregate Demand and Aggregate Supply

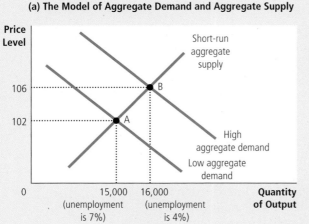

(b) The Phillips Curve

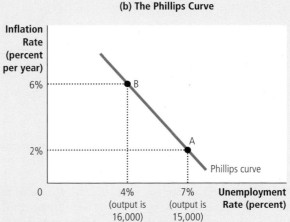

outcomes that might occur in the year 2021 depending of the strength of aggregate demand. One outcome occurs if aggregate demand is high, and the other occurs if aggregate demand is low. Panel (a) shows these two outcomes using the model of aggregate demand and aggregate supply. Panel (b) illustrates the same two outcomes using the Phillips curve.

Panel (a) of the figure shows what happens to output and the price level in the year 2021. If the aggregate demand for goods and services is low, the economy experiences outcome A. The economy produces output of 15,000, and the price level is 102. By contrast, if aggregate demand is high, the economy experiences outcome B. Output is 16,000, and the price level is 106. This is an example of a familiar conclusion: Higher aggregate demand moves the economy to an equilibrium with higher output and a higher price level.

Panel (b) shows what these two possible outcomes mean for unemployment and inflation. Because firms need more workers when they produce a greater output of goods and services, unemployment is lower in outcome B than in outcome A. In this example, when output rises from 15,000 to 16,000, unemployment falls from 7 percent to 4 percent. Moreover, because the price level is higher at outcome B than at outcome A, the inflation rate (the percentage change in the price level from the previous year) is also higher. In particular, since the price level was 100 in the year 2020, outcome A has an inflation rate of 2 percent and outcome B has an inflation rate of 6 percent. The two possible outcomes for the economy can be compared either in terms of output and the price level (using the model of aggregate demand and aggregate supply) or in terms of unemployment and inflation (using the Phillips curve).

Because monetary and fiscal policy can shift the aggregate-demand curve, they can move an economy along the Phillips curve. Increases in the money supply, increases in government spending, or cuts in taxes expand aggregate demand and move the economy to a point on the Phillips curve with lower unemployment and higher inflation. Decreases in the money supply, cuts in government spending, or increases in taxes contract aggregate demand and move the economy to a point on the Phillips curve with lower inflation and higher unemployment. In this sense, the Phillips curve offers policymakers a menu of combinations of inflation and unemployment.

Quick Quiz *Draw the Phillips curve. Use the model of aggregate demand and aggregate supply to show how policy can move the economy from a point on this curve with high inflation to a point with low inflation.*

35-2 Shifts in the Phillips Curve: The Role of Expectations

Although the Phillips curve seems to offer policymakers a menu of possible inflation–unemployment outcomes, it raises a crucial question: Does this menu of choices remain the same over time? In other words, is the downward-sloping Phillips curve a stable relationship on which policymakers can rely? Economists took up this issue in the late 1960s, shortly after Samuelson and Solow had introduced the Phillips curve into the macroeconomic policy debate.

35-2a The Long-Run Phillips Curve

In 1968, economist Milton Friedman published a paper in the *American Economic Review* based on an address he had recently given as president of the American Economic Association. The paper, titled "The Role of Monetary Policy," contained sections on "What Monetary Policy Can Do" and "What Monetary Policy Cannot Do." Friedman argued that one thing monetary policy cannot do, other than for a short time, is lower unemployment by raising inflation. At about the same time, another economist, Edmund Phelps, also published a paper denying the existence of a long-run trade-off between inflation and unemployment.

Friedman and Phelps based their conclusions on classical principles of macro-economics. Classical theory points to growth in the money supply as the primary determinant of inflation. But classical theory also states that monetary growth does not affect real variables such as output and employment; it merely alters all prices and nominal incomes proportionately. In particular, monetary growth does not influence those factors that determine the economy's unemployment rate, such as the market power of unions, the role of efficiency wages, or the process of job search. Friedman and Phelps concluded that there is no reason to think that the rate of inflation would, in the long run, be related to the rate of unemployment.

Here, in his own words, is Friedman's view about what the Federal Reserve (Fed) can hope to accomplish for the economy in the long run:

> The monetary authority controls nominal quantities—directly, the quantity of its own liabilities [currency plus bank reserves]. In principle, it can use this control to peg a nominal quantity—an exchange rate, the price level, the

nominal level of national income, the quantity of money by one definition or another—or to peg the change in a nominal quantity—the rate of inflation or deflation, the rate of growth or decline in nominal national income, the rate of growth of the quantity of money. It cannot use its control over nominal quantities to peg a real quantity—the real rate of interest, the rate of unemployment, the level of real national income, the real quantity of money, the rate of growth of real national income, or the rate of growth of the real quantity of money.

According to Friedman, monetary policymakers face a long-run Phillips curve that is vertical, as in Figure 3. If the Fed increases the money supply slowly, the inflation rate is low and the economy finds itself at point A. If the Fed increases the money supply quickly, the inflation rate is high and the economy finds itself at point B. In either case, the unemployment rate tends toward its normal level, called the *natural rate of unemployment*. The vertical long-run Phillips curve illustrates the conclusion that unemployment does not depend on money growth and inflation in the long run.

The vertical long-run Phillips curve is, in essence, one expression of the classical idea of monetary neutrality. Previously, we expressed monetary neutrality with a vertical long-run aggregate-supply curve. Figure 4 shows that the vertical long-run Phillips curve and the vertical long-run aggregate-supply curve are two sides of the same coin. In panel (a) of this figure, an increase in the money supply shifts the aggregate-demand curve to the right from AD_1 to AD_2. As a result of this shift, the long-run equilibrium moves from point A to point B. The price level rises from P_1 to P_2, but because the aggregate-supply curve is vertical, output remains the same. In panel (b), more rapid growth in the money supply raises the inflation rate by moving the economy from point A to point B. But because the Phillips curve is vertical, the rate of unemployment is the same at these two points. Thus, the vertical long-run aggregate-supply curve and the vertical long-run Phillips curve both imply that monetary policy influences nominal variables (the price level and the inflation rate) but not real variables (output and unemployment). In the long run, regardless of the monetary

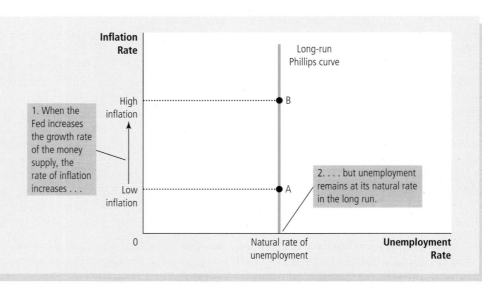

FIGURE 3

The Long-Run Phillips Curve
According to Friedman and Phelps, there is no trade-off between inflation and unemployment in the long run. Growth in the money supply determines the inflation rate. Regardless of the inflation rate, the unemployment rate gravitates toward its natural rate. As a result, the long-run Phillips curve is vertical.

Panel (a) shows the model of aggregate demand and aggregate supply with a vertical aggregate-supply curve. When expansionary monetary policy shifts the aggregate-demand curve to the right from AD_1 to AD_2, the equilibrium moves from point A to point B. The price level rises from P_1 to P_2, while output remains the same. Panel (b) shows the long-run Phillips curve, which is vertical at the natural rate of unemployment. In the long run, expansionary monetary policy moves the economy from lower inflation (point A) to higher inflation (point B) without changing the rate of unemployment.

FIGURE 4

How the Long-Run Phillips Curve Is Related to the Model of Aggregate Demand and Aggregate Supply

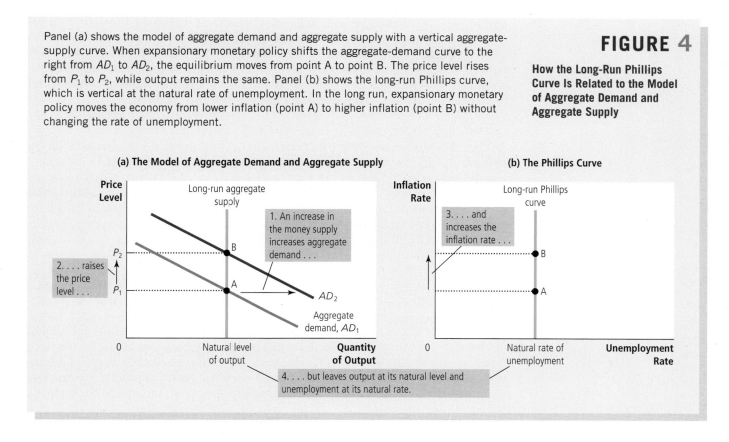

policy pursued by the Fed, output is at its natural level and unemployment is at its natural rate.

35-2b The Meaning of "Natural"

What is so "natural" about the natural rate of unemployment? Friedman and Phelps used this adjective to describe the unemployment rate toward which the economy gravitates in the long run. Yet the natural rate of unemployment is not necessarily the socially desirable rate of unemployment. Nor is the natural rate of unemployment constant over time.

For example, suppose that a newly formed union uses its market power to raise the real wages of some workers above the equilibrium level. The result is an excess supply of workers and, therefore, a higher natural rate of unemployment. This unemployment is natural not because it is good but because it is beyond the influence of monetary policy. More rapid money growth would reduce neither the market power of the union nor the level of unemployment; it would lead only to more inflation.

Although monetary policy cannot influence the natural rate of unemployment, other types of policy can. To reduce the natural rate of unemployment, policy-makers should look to policies that improve the functioning of the labor market. Earlier in the book, we discussed how various labor-market policies, such as minimum-wage laws, collective-bargaining laws, unemployment insurance, and job-training programs, affect the natural rate of unemployment. A policy change that reduced the natural rate of unemployment would shift the long-run Phillips curve to the left. In addition, because lower unemployment means more workers are producing goods and services, the quantity of goods and services supplied would be larger at any given price level and the long-run aggregate-supply curve would shift to the right. The economy could then enjoy lower unemployment and higher output for any given rate of money growth and inflation.

35-2c Reconciling Theory and Evidence

At first, Friedman and Phelps's conclusion that there is no long-run trade-off between inflation and unemployment might not seem persuasive. Their argument was based on an appeal to *theory,* specifically classical theory's prediction of monetary neutrality. By contrast, the negative correlation between inflation and unemployment documented by Phillips, Samuelson, and Solow was based on actual *evidence* from the real world. Why should anyone believe that policymakers faced a vertical Phillips curve when the world seemed to offer a downward-sloping one? Shouldn't the findings of Phillips, Samuelson, and Solow lead us to reject monetary neutrality?

Friedman and Phelps were well aware of these questions, and they offered a way to reconcile classical macroeconomic theory with the finding of a downward-sloping Phillips curve in data from the United Kingdom and the United States. They claimed that a negative relationship between inflation and unemployment exists in the short run but that it cannot be used by policymakers as a menu of outcomes in the long run. Policymakers can pursue expansionary monetary policy to achieve lower unemployment for a while, but eventually, unemployment returns to its natural rate and more expansionary monetary policy leads only to higher inflation.

Friedman and Phelps's work was the basis of our discussion of the difference between the short-run and long-run aggregate-supply curves in Chapter 33. As you may recall, the long-run aggregate-supply curve is vertical, indicating that the price level does not influence quantity supplied in the long run. But the short-run aggregate-supply curve is upward sloping, indicating that an increase in the price level raises the quantity of goods and services that firms supply. According to the sticky-wage theory of aggregate supply, for instance, nominal wages are set in advance based on the price level that workers and firms expected to prevail. When prices are higher than expected, firms have an incentive to increase production and employment; when prices are less than expected, firms reduce production and employment. Yet because the expected price level and nominal wages will eventually adjust, the positive relationship between the actual price level and quantity supplied exists only in the short run.

Friedman and Phelps applied this same logic to the Phillips curve. Just as the aggregate-supply curve slopes upward only in the short run, the trade-off between inflation and unemployment holds only in the short run. And just as the long-run aggregate-supply curve is vertical, the long-run Phillips curve is also vertical. Once again, expectations are the key for understanding how the short run and the long run are related.

Friedman and Phelps introduced a new variable into the analysis of the inflation–unemployment trade-off: *expected inflation*. Expected inflation measures how much people expect the overall price level to change. Because the expected price level affects nominal wages, expected inflation is one factor that determines the position of the short-run aggregate-supply curve. In the short run, the Fed can take expected inflation (and, thus, the short-run aggregate-supply curve) as already determined. When the money supply changes, the aggregate-demand curve shifts and the economy moves along a given short-run aggregate-supply curve. In the short run, therefore, monetary changes lead to unexpected fluctuations in output, prices, unemployment, and inflation. In this way, Friedman and Phelps explained the downward-sloping Phillips curve that Phillips, Samuelson, and Solow had documented.

The Fed's ability to create unexpected inflation by increasing the money supply exists only in the short run. In the long run, people come to expect whatever inflation rate the Fed chooses to produce and nominal wages will adjust to keep pace with inflation. As a result, the long-run aggregate-supply curve is vertical. Changes in aggregate demand, such as those due to changes in the money supply, affect neither the economy's output of goods and services nor the number of workers that firms need to hire to produce those goods and services. Friedman and Phelps concluded that unemployment returns to its natural rate in the long run.

35-2d The Short-Run Phillips Curve

The analysis of Friedman and Phelps can be summarized in the following equation:

$$\text{Unemployment rate} = \text{Natural rate of unemployment} - a \left(\text{Actual inflation} - \text{Expected inflation} \right).$$

This equation (which is, in essence, another expression of the aggregate-supply equation we have seen previously) relates the unemployment rate to the natural rate of unemployment, actual inflation, and expected inflation. In the short run, expected inflation is given, so higher actual inflation is associated with lower unemployment. (The variable a is a parameter that measures how much unemployment responds to unexpected inflation.) In the long run, people come to expect whatever inflation the Fed produces, so actual inflation equals expected inflation, and unemployment is at its natural rate.

This equation implies there can be no stable short-run Phillips curve. Each short-run Phillips curve reflects a particular expected rate of inflation. (To be precise, if you graph the equation, you'll find that the downward-sloping short-run Phillips curve intersects the vertical long-run Phillips curve at the expected rate of inflation.) When expected inflation changes, the short-run Phillips curve shifts.

According to Friedman and Phelps, it is dangerous to view the Phillips curve as a menu of options available to policymakers. To see why, imagine an economy that starts with low inflation, with an equally low rate of expected inflation, and with unemployment at its natural rate. In Figure 5, the economy is at point A. Now suppose that policymakers try to take advantage of the trade-off between inflation and unemployment by using monetary or fiscal policy to expand aggregate demand. In the short run, when expected inflation is given, the economy goes from point A to point B. Unemployment falls below its natural rate, and the actual inflation rate rises above expected inflation. As the economy moves from point A to point B, policymakers might think they have achieved permanently lower unemployment at the cost of higher inflation—a bargain that, if possible, might be worth making.

FIGURE 5

How Expected Inflation Shifts the Short-Run Phillips Curve

The higher the expected rate of inflation, the higher the curve representing the short-run trade-off between inflation and unemployment. At point A, expected inflation and actual inflation are equal at a low rate and unemployment is at its natural rate. If the Fed pursues an expansionary monetary policy, the economy moves from point A to point B in the short run. At point B, expected inflation is still low, but actual inflation is high. Unemployment is below its natural rate. In the long run, expected inflation rises, and the economy moves to point C. At point C, expected inflation and actual inflation are both high, and unemployment is back to its natural rate.

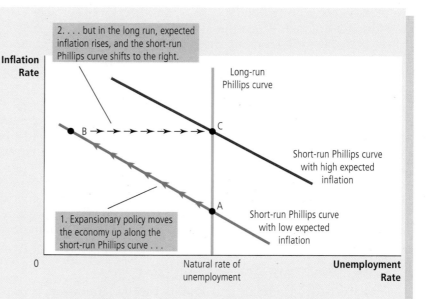

This situation, however, will not persist. Over time, people get used to this higher inflation rate, and they raise their expectations of inflation. When expected inflation rises, firms and workers start taking higher inflation into account when setting wages and prices. The short-run Phillips curve then shifts to the right, as shown in the figure. The economy ends up at point C, with higher inflation than at point A but with the same level of unemployment. Thus, Friedman and Phelps concluded that policymakers face only a temporary trade-off between inflation and unemployment. In the long run, expanding aggregate demand more rapidly will yield higher inflation without any reduction in unemployment.

35-2e The Natural Experiment for the Natural-Rate Hypothesis

Friedman and Phelps had made a bold prediction in 1968: If policymakers try to take advantage of the Phillips curve by choosing higher inflation to reduce unemployment, they will succeed at reducing unemployment only temporarily. This view—that unemployment eventually returns to its natural rate, regardless of the rate of inflation—is called the **natural-rate hypothesis**. A few years after Friedman and Phelps proposed this hypothesis, monetary and fiscal policymakers inadvertently created a natural experiment to test it. Their laboratory was the U.S. economy.

Before we examine the outcome of this test, however, let's look at the data that Friedman and Phelps had when they made their prediction in 1968. Figure 6 shows the unemployment and inflation rates for the period from 1961 to 1968. These data trace out an almost perfect Phillips curve. As inflation rose over these eight years, unemployment fell. The economic data from this era seemed to confirm that policymakers faced a trade-off between inflation and unemployment.

The apparent success of the Phillips curve in the 1960s made the prediction of Friedman and Phelps all the bolder. In 1958, Phillips had suggested a negative

natural-rate hypothesis
the claim that unemployment eventually returns to its normal, or natural, rate, regardless of the rate of inflation

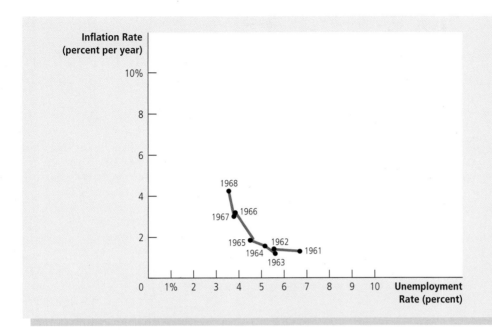

FIGURE 6

The Phillips Curve in the 1960s
This figure uses annual data from 1961 to 1968 on the unemployment rate and on the inflation rate (as measured by the GDP deflator) to show the negative relationship between inflation and unemployment.

Source: U.S. Department of Labor; U.S. Department of Commerce.

association between inflation and unemployment. In 1960, Samuelson and Solow had shown that it existed in U.S. data. Another decade of data had confirmed the relationship. To some economists at the time, it seemed ridiculous to claim that the historically reliable Phillips curve would start shifting once policymakers tried to take advantage of it.

In fact, that is exactly what happened. Beginning in the late 1960s, the government followed policies that expanded the aggregate demand for goods and services. In part, this expansion was due to fiscal policy: Government spending rose as the Vietnam War heated up. In part, it was due to monetary policy: Because the Fed was trying to hold down interest rates in the face of expansionary fiscal policy, the money supply (as measured by M2) rose about 13 percent per year during the period from 1970 to 1972, compared to 7 percent per year in the early 1960s. As a result, inflation stayed high (about 5 to 6 percent per year in the late 1960s and early 1970s, compared to about 1 to 2 percent per year in the early 1960s). But as Friedman and Phelps had predicted, unemployment did not stay low.

Figure 7 displays the history of inflation and unemployment from 1961 to 1973. It shows that the simple negative relationship between these two variables started to break down around 1970. In particular, as inflation remained high in the early 1970s, people's expectations of inflation caught up with reality, and the unemployment rate reverted to the 5 percent to 6 percent range that had prevailed in the early 1960s. Notice that the history illustrated in Figure 7 resembles the theory of a shifting short-run Phillips curve shown in Figure 5. By 1973, policymakers had learned that Friedman and Phelps were right: There is no trade-off between inflation and unemployment in the long run.

Quick Quiz   *Draw the short-run Phillips curve and the long-run Phillips curve. Explain why they are different.*

FIGURE 7

The Breakdown of the Phillips Curve
This figure shows annual data from 1961 to 1973 on the unemployment rate and on the inflation rate (as measured by the GDP deflator). The Phillips curve of the 1960s breaks down in the early 1970s, just as Friedman and Phelps had predicted. Notice that the points labeled A, B, and C in this figure correspond roughly to the points in Figure 5.

Source: U.S. Department of Labor; U.S. Department of Commerce.

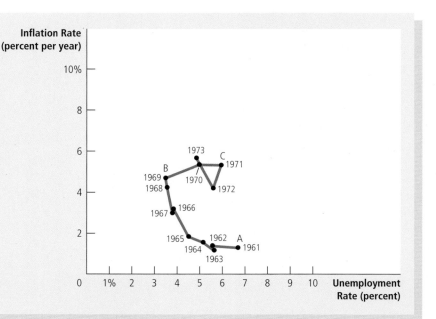

35-3 Shifts in the Phillips Curve: The Role of Supply Shocks

Friedman and Phelps had suggested in 1968 that changes in expected inflation shift the short-run Phillips curve, and the experience of the early 1970s convinced most economists that Friedman and Phelps were right. Within a few years, however, the economics profession would turn its attention to a different source of shifts in the short-run Phillips curve: shocks to aggregate supply.

This time, the change in focus came not from two American economics professors but from a group of Arab sheiks. In 1974, the Organization of Petroleum Exporting Countries (OPEC) began to exert its market power as a cartel in the world oil market to increase its members' profits. The countries of OPEC, such as Saudi Arabia, Kuwait, and Iraq, restricted the amount of crude oil they pumped and sold on world markets. Within a few years, this reduction in supply caused the world price of oil to almost double.

A large increase in the world price of oil is an example of a supply shock. A **supply shock** is an event that directly affects firms' costs of production and thus the prices they charge; it shifts the economy's aggregate-supply curve and, as a result, the Phillips curve. For example, when an oil price increase raises the cost of producing gasoline, heating oil, tires, and many other products, it reduces the quantity of goods and services supplied at any given price level. As panel (a) of Figure 8 shows, this reduction in supply is represented by the leftward shift in the aggregate-supply curve from AS_1 to AS_2. Output falls from Y_1 to Y_2, and the price level rises from P_1 to P_2. The combination of falling output (stagnation) and rising prices (inflation) is sometimes called *stagflation*.

This shift in aggregate supply is associated with a similar shift in the short-run Phillips curve, shown in panel (b). Because firms need fewer workers to produce the smaller output, employment falls and unemployment rises. Because the price level is higher, the inflation rate—the percentage change in the price level from

supply shock
an event that directly alters firms' costs and prices, shifting the economy's aggregate-supply curve and thus the Phillips curve

Panel (a) shows the model of aggregate demand and aggregate supply. When the aggregate-supply curve shifts to the left from AS_1 to AS_2, the equilibrium moves from point A to point B. Output falls from Y_1 to Y_2, and the price level rises from P_1 to P_2. Panel (b) shows the short-run trade-off between inflation and unemployment. The adverse shift in aggregate supply moves the economy from a point with lower unemployment and lower inflation (point A) to a point with higher unemployment and higher inflation (point B). The short-run Phillips curve shifts to the right from PC_1 to PC_2. Policymakers now face a worse set of options for inflation and unemployment.

FIGURE 8

An Adverse Shock to Aggregate Supply

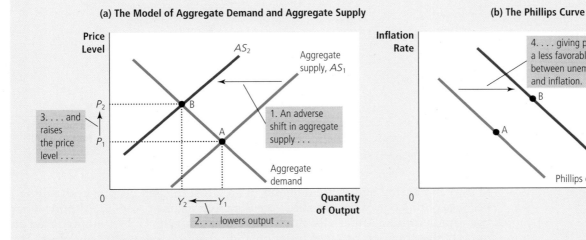

(a) The Model of Aggregate Demand and Aggregate Supply

(b) The Phillips Curve

the previous year—is also higher. Thus, the shift in aggregate supply leads to higher unemployment and higher inflation. The short-run trade-off between inflation and unemployment shifts to the right from PC_1 to PC_2.

Confronted with an adverse shift in aggregate supply, policymakers face a difficult choice between fighting inflation and fighting unemployment. If they contract aggregate demand to fight inflation, they will raise unemployment further. If they expand aggregate demand to fight unemployment, they will raise inflation further. In other words, policymakers face a less favorable trade-off between inflation and unemployment than they did before the shift in aggregate supply: They have to live with a higher rate of inflation for a given rate of unemployment, a higher rate of unemployment for a given rate of inflation, or some combination of higher unemployment and higher inflation.

Faced with such an adverse shift in the Phillips curve, policymakers will ask whether the shift is temporary or permanent. The answer depends on how people adjust their expectations of inflation. If people view the rise in inflation due to the supply shock as a temporary aberration, expected inflation will not change and the Phillips curve will soon revert to its former position. But if people believe the shock will lead to a new era of higher inflation, then expected inflation will rise and the Phillips curve will remain at its new, less desirable position.

In the United States during the 1970s, expected inflation did rise substantially. This rise in expected inflation was partly attributable to the Fed's decision to accommodate the supply shock with higher money growth. (Recall that policymakers are said to *accommodate* an adverse supply shock when they respond

FIGURE 9

The Supply Shocks of the 1970s
This figure shows annual data from 1972 to 1981 on the unemployment rate and on the inflation rate (as measured by the GDP deflator). In the periods 1973–1975 and 1978–1981, increases in world oil prices led to higher inflation and higher unemployment.

Source: U.S. Department of Labor; U.S. Department of Commerce.

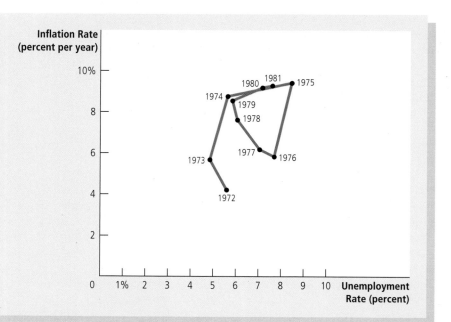

to it by increasing aggregate demand in an effort to keep output from falling.) Because of this policy decision, the recession that resulted from the supply shock was smaller than it otherwise might have been, but the U.S. economy faced an unfavorable trade-off between inflation and unemployment for many years. The problem was compounded in 1979 when OPEC once again started to exert its market power, more than doubling the price of oil. Figure 9 shows inflation and unemployment in the U.S. economy during this period.

In 1980, after two OPEC supply shocks, the U.S. economy had an inflation rate of more than 9 percent and an unemployment rate of about 7 percent. This combination of inflation and unemployment was not at all near the trade-off that seemed possible in the 1960s. (In the 1960s, the Phillips curve suggested that an unemployment rate of 7 percent would be associated with an inflation rate of only 1 percent. Inflation of more than 9 percent was unthinkable.) With the misery index in 1980 near a historic high, the public was widely dissatisfied with the performance of the economy. Largely because of this dissatisfaction, President Jimmy Carter lost his bid for reelection in November 1980 and was replaced by Ronald Reagan. Something had to be done, and soon it would be.

Quick Quiz *Give an example of a favorable shock to aggregate supply. Use the model of aggregate demand and aggregate supply to explain the effects of such a shock. How does it affect the Phillips curve?*

35-4 The Cost of Reducing Inflation

In October 1979, as OPEC was imposing adverse supply shocks on the world's economies for the second time in a decade, Fed Chairman Paul Volcker decided that the time for action had come. Volcker had been appointed chairman by President Carter only two months earlier, and he had taken the job knowing that inflation had reached unacceptable levels. As guardian of the nation's monetary system, he felt he had little choice but to pursue a policy of disinflation. *Disinflation* is a reduction in the rate of inflation, and it should not be confused with *deflation*, a reduction in the price level. To draw an analogy to a car's motion, disinflation is like slowing down, whereas deflation is like going in reverse. Chairman Volcker, along with many other Americans, wanted the economy's rising level of prices to slow down.

Volcker had no doubt that the Fed could reduce inflation through its ability to control the quantity of money. But what would be the short-run cost of disinflation? The answer to this question was much less certain.

35-4a The Sacrifice Ratio

To reduce the inflation rate, the Fed has to pursue contractionary monetary policy. Figure 10 shows some of the effects of such a decision. When the Fed slows the rate at which the money supply is growing, it contracts aggregate demand. The fall in aggregate demand, in turn, reduces the quantity of goods and services that firms produce, and this fall in production leads to a rise in unemployment. The economy begins at point A in the figure and moves along the short-run Phillips curve to point B, which has lower inflation and higher unemployment. Over time, as people come to understand that prices are rising more slowly, expected inflation falls, and the short-run Phillips curve shifts downward. The economy moves from point B to point C. Inflation is lower than it was initially at point A, and unemployment is back at its natural rate.

Thus, if a nation wants to reduce inflation, it must endure a period of high unemployment and low output. In Figure 10, this cost is represented by the movement of the economy through point B as it travels from point A to point C. The size of this cost depends on the slope of the Phillips curve and how quickly expectations of inflation adjust to the new monetary policy.

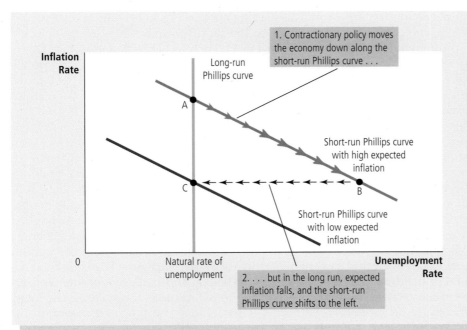

FIGURE 10

Disinflationary Monetary Policy in the Short Run and Long Run
When the Fed pursues contractionary monetary policy to reduce inflation, the economy moves along a short-run Phillips curve from point A to point B. Over time, expected inflation falls, and the short-run Phillips curve shifts downward. When the economy reaches point C, unemployment is back at its natural rate.

sacrifice ratio

the number of percentage points of annual output lost in the process of reducing inflation by 1 percentage point

Many studies have examined the data on inflation and unemployment to estimate the cost of reducing inflation. The findings of these studies are often summarized in a statistic called the **sacrifice ratio**. The sacrifice ratio is the number of percentage points of annual output lost in the process of reducing inflation by 1 percentage point. A typical estimate of the sacrifice ratio is 5. That is, for each percentage point that inflation is reduced, 5 percent of annual output must be sacrificed in the transition.

Such estimates surely must have made Paul Volcker apprehensive as he confronted the task of reducing inflation. Inflation was running at almost 10 percent per year. To reach moderate inflation of, say, 4 percent per year would mean reducing inflation by 6 percentage points. If each percentage point costs 5 percent of the economy's annual output, then reducing inflation by 6 percentage points would require sacrificing 30 percent of annual output.

According to studies of the Phillips curve and the cost of disinflation, this sacrifice could be paid in various ways. An immediate reduction in inflation would depress output by 30 percent for a single year, but that outcome was surely too harsh even for an inflation hawk like Paul Volcker. It would be better, many argued, to spread out the cost over several years. If the reduction in inflation took place over five years, for instance, then output would have to average only 6 percent below trend during that period to add up to a sacrifice of 30 percent. An even more gradual approach would be to reduce inflation slowly over a decade so that output would have to be only 3 percent below trend. Whatever path was chosen, however, it seemed that reducing inflation would not be easy.

35-4b Rational Expectations and the Possibility of Costless Disinflation

Just as Paul Volcker was pondering how costly reducing inflation might be, a group of economics professors was leading an intellectual revolution that would challenge the conventional wisdom on the sacrifice ratio. This group included such prominent economists as Robert Lucas, Thomas Sargent, and Robert Barro. Their revolution was based on a new approach to economic theory and policy called **rational expectations**. According to the theory of rational expectations, people optimally use all the information they have, including information about government policies, when forecasting the future.

rational expectations

the theory that people optimally use all the information they have, including information about government policies, when forecasting the future

This new approach has had profound implications for many areas of macroeconomics, but none is more important than its application to the trade-off between inflation and unemployment. As Friedman and Phelps had first emphasized, expected inflation is an important variable that explains why there is a trade-off between inflation and unemployment in the short run but not in the long run. How quickly the short-run trade-off disappears depends on how quickly people adjust their expectations of inflation. Proponents of rational expectations expanded upon the Friedman-Phelps analysis to argue that when economic policies change, people adjust their expectations of inflation accordingly. The studies of inflation and unemployment that had tried to estimate the sacrifice ratio had failed to take account of the direct effect of the policy regime on expectations. As a result, estimates of the sacrifice ratio were, according to the rational-expectations theorists, unreliable guides for policy.

In a 1981 paper titled "The End of Four Big Inflations," Thomas Sargent described this new view as follows:

> An alternative "rational expectations" view denies that there is any inherent momentum to the present process of inflation. This view maintains that firms and workers have now come to expect high rates of inflation in the future and that they strike inflationary bargains in light of these expectations. However, it is held that people expect high rates of inflation in the future precisely because the government's current and prospective monetary and fiscal policies warrant those expectations. . . . An implication of this view is that inflation can be stopped much more quickly than advocates of the "momentum" view have indicated and that their estimates of the length of time and the costs of stopping inflation in terms of forgone output are erroneous. . . . This is not to say that it would be easy to eradicate inflation. On the contrary, it would require more than a few temporary restrictive fiscal and monetary actions. It would require a change in the policy regime. . . . How costly such a move would be in terms of forgone output and how long it would be in taking effect would depend partly on how resolute and evident the government's commitment was.

According to Sargent, the sacrifice ratio could be much smaller than suggested by previous estimates. Indeed, in the most extreme case, it could be zero: If the government made a credible commitment to a policy of low inflation, people would be rational enough to lower their expectations of inflation immediately. The short-run Phillips curve would shift downward, and the economy would reach low inflation quickly without the cost of temporarily high unemployment and low output.

35-4c The Volcker Disinflation

As we have seen, when Paul Volcker faced the prospect of reducing inflation from its peak of about 10 percent, the economics profession offered two conflicting predictions. One group of economists offered estimates of the sacrifice ratio and concluded that reducing inflation would have great cost in terms of lost output and high unemployment. Another group offered the theory of rational expectations and concluded that reducing inflation could be much less costly and, perhaps, could even have no cost at all. Who was right?

Figure 11 shows inflation and unemployment from 1979 to 1987. As you can see, Volcker did succeed at reducing inflation. Inflation came down from almost 10 percent in 1981 and 1982 to about 4 percent in 1983 and 1984. Credit for this reduction in inflation goes completely to monetary policy. Fiscal policy at this time was acting in the opposite direction: The increases in the budget deficit during the Reagan administration were expanding aggregate demand, which tends to raise inflation. The fall in inflation from 1981 to 1984 is attributable to the tough anti-inflation policies of Fed Chairman Paul Volcker.

The figure shows that the Volcker disinflation did come at the cost of high unemployment. In 1982 and 1983, the unemployment rate was about 10 percent—about 4 percentage points above its level when Paul Volcker was appointed Fed chairman. At the same time, the production of goods and services as measured by real GDP was well below its trend level. The Volcker disinflation produced a recession that was, at the time, the deepest the United States had experienced since the Great Depression of the 1930s.

FIGURE 11

The Volcker Disinflation
This figure shows annual data from 1979 to 1987 on the unemployment rate and on the inflation rate (as measured by the GDP deflator). The reduction in inflation during this period came at the cost of very high unemployment in 1982 and 1983. Note that the points labeled A, B, and C in this figure correspond roughly to the points in Figure 10.

Source: U.S. Department of Labor; U.S. Department of Commerce.

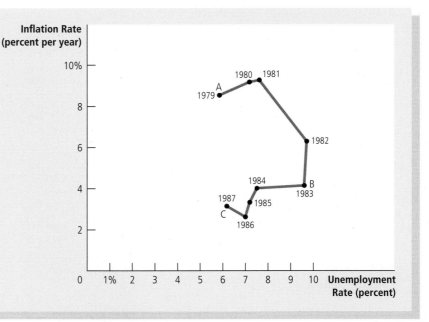

Does this episode refute the possibility of costless disinflation as suggested by the rational-expectations theorists? Some economists have argued that the answer to this question is a resounding yes. Indeed, the pattern of disinflation shown in Figure 11 is similar to the pattern predicted in Figure 10. To make the transition from high inflation (point A in both figures) to low inflation (point C), the economy had to experience a painful period of high unemployment (point B).

Yet there are two reasons not to reject the conclusions of the rational-expectations theorists so quickly. First, even though the Volcker disinflation did impose a cost of temporarily high unemployment, the cost was not as large as many economists had predicted. Most estimates of the sacrifice ratio based on the Volcker disinflation are smaller than estimates that had been obtained from previous data. Perhaps Volcker's tough stand on inflation did have some direct effect on expectations, as the rational-expectations theorists claimed.

Second, and more important, even though Volcker announced that he would aim monetary policy to lower inflation, much of the public did not believe him. Because few people thought Volcker would reduce inflation as quickly as he did, expected inflation did not fall immediately; as a result, the short-run Phillips curve did not shift down as quickly as it might have. Some evidence for this hypothesis comes from the forecasts made by commercial forecasting firms: Their forecasts of inflation fell more slowly in the 1980s than did actual inflation. Thus, the Volcker disinflation does not necessarily refute the rational-expectations view that credible disinflation can be costless. It does show, however, that policymakers cannot count on people to immediately believe them when they announce a policy of disinflation.

35-4d The Greenspan Era

Since the OPEC inflation of the 1970s and the Volcker disinflation of the 1980s, the U.S. economy has experienced relatively mild fluctuations in inflation and unemployment. Figure 12 shows inflation and unemployment from 1984 to 2005. This period is called the Greenspan era, after Alan Greenspan who in 1987 followed Paul Volcker as chairman of the Fed.

This period began with a favorable supply shock. In 1986, OPEC members started arguing over production levels, and their long-standing agreement to restrict supply broke down. Oil prices fell by about half. As the figure shows, this favorable supply shock led to falling inflation and falling unemployment from 1984 to 1986.

Throughout the Greenspan era, the Fed was careful to avoid repeating the policy mistakes of the 1960s, when excessive aggregate demand pushed unemployment below the natural rate and raised inflation. When unemployment fell and inflation rose in 1989 and 1990, the Fed raised interest rates and contracted aggregate demand, leading to a small recession in 1991 and 1992. Unemployment then rose above most estimates of the natural rate, and inflation fell once again.

The rest of the 1990s witnessed a period of economic prosperity. Inflation gradually drifted downward, approaching zero by the end of the decade. Unemployment also drifted downward, leading many observers to believe that the natural rate of unemployment had fallen. Part of the credit for this good economic performance goes to Alan Greenspan and his colleagues at the Fed, for low inflation can be achieved only with prudent monetary policy. But good luck in the form of favorable supply shocks is also part of the story.

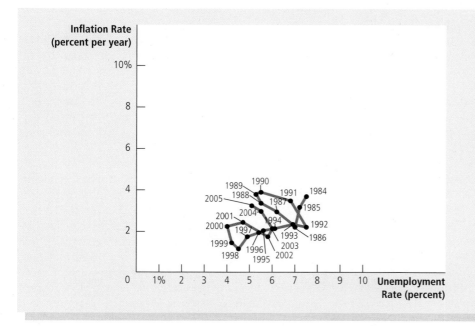

FIGURE 12

The Greenspan Era
This figure shows annual data from 1984 to 2005 on the unemployment rate and on the inflation rate (as measured by the GDP deflator). During most of this period, Alan Greenspan was chairman of the Federal Reserve. Fluctuations in inflation and unemployment were relatively small.

Source: U.S. Department of Labor; U.S. Department of Commerce.

In 2001, however, the economy ran into problems. The end of the dot-com stock market bubble, the 9/11 terrorist attacks, and corporate accounting scandals all depressed aggregate demand. Unemployment rose as the economy experienced its first recession in a decade. But a combination of expansionary monetary and fiscal policies helped end the downturn, and by early 2005, unemployment was close to most estimates of the natural rate.

In 2005, President Bush nominated Ben Bernanke to follow Alan Greenspan as the chairman of the Fed. Bernanke was sworn in on February 1, 2006. In 2009, Bernanke was reappointed by President Obama. At the time of his initial nomination, Bernanke said, "My first priority will be to maintain continuity with the policies and policy strategies established during the Greenspan years."

35-4e A Financial Crisis Takes Us for a Ride along the Phillips Curve

Ben Bernanke may have hoped to continue the policies of the Greenspan era and to enjoy the relative calm of those years, but his wishes would not be fulfilled. During his first few years on the job, the new Fed chairman faced some significant and daunting economic challenges.

As we have seen in previous chapters, the main challenge arose from problems in the housing market and financial system. From 1995 to 2006, the U.S. housing market boomed and average U.S. house prices more than doubled. But this housing boom proved unsustainable, and from 2006 to 2009 house prices fell by about one-third. This large fall led to declines in household wealth and difficulties in many financial institutions that had bet (through the purchase of mortgage-backed securities) that house prices would continue to rise. The resulting financial crisis resulted in a large decline in aggregate demand and a steep increase in unemployment.

We have already looked at the story of the crisis and the policy responses to it in many previous chapters, but Figure 13 shows the implications of these events

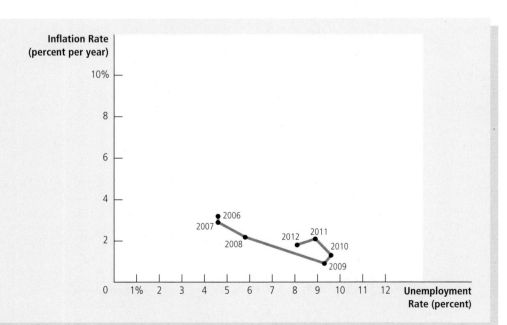

FIGURE 13

The Phillips Curve during and after the Recession of 2008–2009

This figure shows annual data from 2006 to 2012 on the unemployment rate and on the inflation rate (as measured by the GDP deflator). A financial crisis caused aggregate demand to plummet, leading to much higher unemployment and pushing inflation down to a very low level.

Source: U.S. Department of Labor; U.S. Department of Commerce.

for inflation and unemployment. From 2007 to 2009, as the decline in aggregate demand raised unemployment, it also reduced the rate of inflation from about 3 percent to about 1 percent. From 2010 to 2012, as the economy slowly recovered, unemployment fell and the rate of inflation rose from about 1 percent to about 2 percent. In essence, the economy first rode down the Phillips curve and then rode back up.

One notable feature of this period is that the very low inflation of 2009 and 2010 does not appear to have reduced expected inflation and shifted the short-run Phillips curve downward. Instead, expected inflation appears to have remained steady at about 2 percent, which kept the short-run Phillips curve relatively stable. A common explanation for this phenomenon is that the Fed had, over the previous 20 years, established a lot of credibility in its commitment to keep inflation at about 2 percent. As a result, expected inflation and the position of the short-run Phillips curve reacted less to the dramatic short-run events.

Quick Quiz   *What is the sacrifice ratio? How might the credibility of the Fed's commitment to reduce inflation affect the sacrifice ratio?*

35-5 Conclusion

This chapter has examined how economists' thinking about inflation and unemployment has evolved. We have discussed the ideas of many of the best economists of the 20th century: from the Phillips curve of Phillips, Samuelson, and Solow, to the natural-rate hypothesis of Friedman and Phelps, to the rational-expectations theory of Lucas, Sargent, and Barro. Five members of this group have already won Nobel Prizes for their work in economics, and more may well be so honored in the years to come.

Although the trade-off between inflation and unemployment has generated much intellectual turmoil over the past half century, certain principles have developed that today command consensus. Here is how Milton Friedman expressed the relationship between inflation and unemployment in 1968:

> There is always a temporary tradeoff between inflation and unemployment; there is no permanent tradeoff. The temporary tradeoff comes not from inflation per se, but from unanticipated inflation, which generally means, from a rising rate of inflation. The widespread belief that there is a permanent tradeoff is a sophisticated version of the confusion between "high" and "rising" that we all recognize in simpler forms. A rising rate of inflation may reduce unemployment, a high rate will not.
>
> But how long, you will say, is "temporary"? … I can at most venture a personal judgment, based on some examination of the historical evidence, that the initial effects of a higher and unanticipated rate of inflation last for something like two to five years.

Today, almost a half century later, this statement still summarizes the view of most macroeconomists.

Summary

- The Phillips curve describes a negative relationship between inflation and unemployment. By expanding aggregate demand, policymakers can choose a point on the Phillips curve with higher inflation and lower unemployment. By contracting aggregate demand, policymakers can choose a point on the Phillips curve with lower inflation and higher unemployment.

- The trade-off between inflation and unemployment described by the Phillips curve holds only in the short run. In the long run, expected inflation adjusts to changes in actual inflation, and the short-run Phillips curve shifts. As a result, the long-run Phillips curve is vertical at the natural rate of unemployment.

- The short-run Phillips curve also shifts because of shocks to aggregate supply. An adverse supply shock, such as an increase in world oil prices, gives policymakers a less favorable trade-off between inflation and unemployment. That is, after an adverse supply shock, policymakers have to accept a higher rate of inflation for any given rate of unemployment or a higher rate of unemployment for any given rate of inflation.

- When the Fed contracts growth in the money supply to reduce inflation, it moves the economy along the short-run Phillips curve, which results in temporarily high unemployment. The cost of disinflation depends on how quickly expectations of inflation fall. Some economists argue that a credible commitment to low inflation can reduce the cost of disinflation by inducing a quick adjustment of expectations.

Key Concepts

Phillips curve, *p. 770*
natural-rate hypothesis, *p. 778*

supply shock, *p. 780*
sacrifice ratio, *p. 784*

rational expectations, *p. 784*

Questions for Review

1. Draw the short-run trade-off between inflation and unemployment. How might the Fed move the economy from one point on this curve to another?

2. Draw the long-run trade-off between inflation and unemployment. Explain how the short-run and long-run trade-offs are related.

3. What is "natural" about the natural rate of unemployment? Why might the natural rate of unemployment differ across countries?

4. Suppose a drought destroys farm crops and drives up the price of food. What is the effect on the short-run trade-off between inflation and unemployment?

5. The Fed decides to reduce inflation. Use the Phillips curve to show the short-run and long-run effects of this policy. How might the short-run costs be reduced?

Quick Check Multiple Choice

1. When the Federal Reserve increases the money supply, it _____ aggregate demand and moves the economy along the Phillips curve to a point with _____ inflation and _____ unemployment.
   a. expands, higher, higher
   b. expands, higher, lower
   c. expands, lower, higher
   d. contracts, lower, higher

2. If the Federal Reserve increases the rate of money growth and maintains it at the new higher rate, eventually expected inflation will _____ and the short-run Phillips curve will shift _____.
   a. decrease, downward
   b. decrease, upward

   c. increase, downward
   d. increase, upward

3. When an adverse supply shock shifts the short-run aggregate-supply curve to the left, it also
   a. moves the economy along the short-run Phillips curve to a point with higher inflation and lower unemployment.
   b. moves the economy along the short-run Phillips curve to a point with lower inflation and higher unemployment.
   c. shifts the short-run Phillips curve to the right.
   d. shifts the short-run Phillips curve to the left.

4. Advocates of the theory of rational expectations believe that
   a. the sacrifice ratio can be much smaller if policy-makers make a credible commitment to low inflation.
   b. if disinflation catches people by surprise, it will have minimal impact on unemployment.
   c. wage and price setters never expect the central bank to follow through on its announcements.
   d. expected inflation depends on the rates of inflation that people have recently observed.

5. From one year to the next, inflation falls from 5 to 4 percent, while unemployment rises from 6 to 7 percent. Which of the following events could be responsible for this change?
   a. The central bank increases the growth rate of the money supply.
   b. The government cuts spending and raises taxes to reduce the budget deficit.
   c. Newly discovered oil reserves cause world oil prices to plummet.
   d. The appointment of a new Fed chairman increases expected inflation.

6. From one year to the next, inflation rises from 4 to 5 percent, while unemployment rises from 6 to 7 percent. Which of the following events could be responsible for this change?
   a. The central bank increases the growth rate of the money supply.
   b. The government cuts spending and raises taxes to reduce the budget deficit.
   c. Newly discovered oil reserves cause world oil prices to plummet.
   d. The appointment of a new Fed chairman increases expected inflation.

Problems and Applications

1. Suppose the natural rate of unemployment is 6 percent. On one graph, draw two Phillips curves that describe the four situations listed here. Label the point that shows the position of the economy in each case.
   a. Actual inflation is 5 percent, and expected inflation is 3 percent.
   b. Actual inflation is 3 percent, and expected inflation is 5 percent.
   c. Actual inflation is 5 percent, and expected inflation is 5 percent.
   d. Actual inflation is 3 percent, and expected inflation is 3 percent.

2. Illustrate the effects of the following developments on both the short-run and long-run Phillips curves. Give the economic reasoning underlying your answers.
   a. a rise in the natural rate of unemployment
   b. a decline in the price of imported oil
   c. a rise in government spending
   d. a decline in expected inflation

3. Suppose that a fall in consumer spending causes a recession.
   a. Illustrate the immediate change in the economy using both an aggregate-supply/aggregate-demand diagram and a Phillips-curve diagram. On both graphs, label the initial long-run equilibrium as point A and the resulting short-run equilibrium as point B. What happens to inflation and unemployment in the short run?
   b. Now suppose that over time expected inflation changes in the same direction that actual inflation changes. What happens to the position of the short-run Phillips curve? After the recession is over, does the economy face a better or worse set of inflation–unemployment combinations?

4. Suppose the economy is in a long-run equilibrium.
   a. Draw the economy's short-run and long-run Phillips curves.
   b. Suppose a wave of business pessimism reduces aggregate demand. Show the effect of this shock on your diagram from part (a). If the Fed undertakes expansionary monetary policy, can it return the economy to its original inflation rate and original unemployment rate?
   c. Now suppose the economy is back in long-run equilibrium and then the price of imported oil rises. Show the effect of this shock with a new diagram like that in part (a). If the Fed undertakes expansionary monetary policy, can it return the economy to its original inflation rate and original unemployment rate? If the Fed undertakes contractionary monetary policy, can it return the economy to its original inflation rate and original unemployment rate? Explain why this situation differs from that in part (b).

5. The inflation rate is 10 percent, and the central bank is considering slowing the rate of money growth to reduce inflation to 5 percent. Economist Milton believes that expectations of inflation change quickly in response to new policies, whereas economist James believes that expectations are very sluggish. Which economist is more likely to favor the proposed change in monetary policy? Why?

6. Suppose the Federal Reserve's policy is to maintain low and stable inflation by keeping unemployment at its natural rate. However, the Fed believes that the natural rate of unemployment is 4 percent when the actual natural rate is 5 percent. If the Fed based its policy decisions on its belief, what would happen to the economy? How might the Fed come to realize that its belief about the natural rate was mistaken?

7. Suppose the Federal Reserve announced that it would pursue contractionary monetary policy to reduce the inflation rate. Would the following conditions make the ensuing recession more or less severe? Explain.
   a. Wage contracts have short durations.
   b. There is little confidence in the Fed's determination to reduce inflation.
   c. Expectations of inflation adjust quickly to actual inflation.

8. As described in the chapter, the Federal Reserve in 2008 faced a decrease in aggregate demand caused by the housing and financial crises and a decrease in short-run aggregate supply caused by rising commodity prices.
   a. Starting from a long-run equilibrium, illustrate the effects of these two changes using both an aggregate-supply/aggregate-demand diagram and a Phillips-curve diagram. On both diagrams, label the initial long-run equilibrium as point A and the resulting short-run equilibrium as point B. For each of the following variables, state whether it rises or falls or whether the impact is ambiguous: output, unemployment, the price level, the inflation rate.
   b. Suppose the Fed responds quickly to these shocks and adjusts monetary policy to keep unemployment and output at their natural rates. What action would it take? On the same set of graphs from part (a), show the results. Label the new equilibrium as point C.
   c. Why might the Fed choose not to pursue the course of action described in part (b)?

Go to CengageBrain.com to purchase access to the proven, critical Study Guide to accompany this text, which features additional notes and context, practice tests, and much more.

Final Thoughts

Six Debates over Macroeconomic Policy

I t is hard to open up the newspaper without finding some politician or editorial writer advocating a change in economic policy. The president should raise taxes to reduce the budget deficit, or he should stop worrying about the budget deficit. The Federal Reserve should cut interest rates to stimulate a flagging economy, or it should avoid such moves in order not to risk higher inflation. Congress should reform the tax system to promote faster economic growth, or it should reform the tax system to achieve a more equal distribution of income. Such economic issues are central to the continuing political debate in the United States and other countries around the world.

Previous chapters have developed the tools that economists use to analyze the behavior of the economy as a whole and the impact of policies on the economy. This final chapter considers six classic questions about macroeconomic policy. Economists have long debated these questions, and they will likely continue to do so for years to come. The knowledge you have accumulated in this course provides the foundation upon which we can discuss these important, unsettled issues. It should help you choose a side in these debates or, at least, help you see why choosing a side is so difficult.

36-1 Should Monetary and Fiscal Policymakers Try to Stabilize the Economy?

In the preceding three chapters, we saw how changes in aggregate demand and aggregate supply can lead to short-run fluctuations in production and employment. We also saw how monetary and fiscal policy can shift aggregate demand and, thereby, influence these fluctuations. But even if policymakers *can* influence short-run economic fluctuations, does that mean they *should?* Our first debate concerns whether monetary and fiscal policymakers should use the tools at their disposal in an attempt to smooth the ups and downs of the business cycle.

36-1a Pro: Policymakers Should Try to Stabilize the Economy

Left on their own, economies tend to fluctuate. When households and firms become pessimistic, for instance, they cut back on spending, and this reduces the aggregate demand for goods and services. The fall in aggregate demand, in turn, reduces the production of goods and services. Firms lay off workers, and the unemployment rate rises. Real GDP and other measures of income fall. Rising unemployment and falling income help confirm the pessimism that initially generated the economic downturn.

Such a recession has no benefit for society—it represents a sheer waste of resources. Workers who lose their jobs because of declining aggregate demand would rather be working. Business owners whose factories are idle during a recession would rather be producing valuable goods and services and selling them at a profit.

There is no reason for society to suffer through the booms and busts of the business cycle. The development of macroeconomic theory has shown policymakers how to reduce the severity of economic fluctuations. By "leaning against the wind" of economic change, monetary and fiscal policy can stabilize aggregate demand and, thereby, production and employment. When aggregate demand is inadequate to ensure full employment, policymakers should boost government spending, cut taxes, and expand the money supply. When aggregate demand is excessive, risking higher inflation, policymakers should cut government spending, raise taxes, and reduce the money supply. Such policy actions put macroeconomic theory to its best use by leading to a more stable economy, which benefits everyone.

36-1b Con: Policymakers Should Not Try to Stabilize the Economy

Monetary and fiscal policy can be used to stabilize the economy in theory, but there are substantial obstacles to the use of such policies in practice.

One problem is that monetary and fiscal policy do not affect the economy immediately but instead work with a long lag. Monetary policy affects aggregate demand primarily by changing interest rates, which in turn affect spending, particularly residential and business investment. But many households and firms set their spending plans in advance. As a result, it takes time for changes in interest rates to alter the aggregate demand for goods and services. Many studies

indicate that changes in monetary policy have little effect on aggregate demand until about six months after the change is made.

Fiscal policy works with a lag because of the long political process that governs changes in spending and taxes. To make any change in fiscal policy, a bill must go through congressional committees, pass both the House and the Senate, and be signed by the president. It can take years to propose, pass, and implement a major change in fiscal policy.

Because of these long lags, policymakers who want to stabilize the economy need to look ahead to economic conditions that are likely to prevail when their actions will take effect. Unfortunately, economic forecasting is highly imprecise, in part because macroeconomics is such a primitive science and in part because the shocks that cause economic fluctuations are intrinsically unpredictable. Thus, when policymakers change monetary or fiscal policy, they must rely on educated guesses about future economic conditions.

Too often, policymakers trying to stabilize the economy end up having the opposite effect. Economic conditions can easily change between the time a policy action begins and the time it takes effect. Because of this, policymakers can inadvertently exacerbate rather than mitigate the magnitude of economic fluctuations. Some economists have claimed that many of the major economic fluctuations in history, including the Great Depression of the 1930s, can be traced to destabilizing policy actions.

One of the first rules taught to physicians is "do no harm." The human body has natural restorative powers. Confronted with a sick patient and an uncertain diagnosis, often a doctor should do nothing but leave the patient's body to its own devices. Intervening in the absence of reliable knowledge merely risks making matters worse.

The same can be said about treating an ailing economy. It might be desirable if policymakers could eliminate all economic fluctuations, but that is not a realistic goal given the limits of macroeconomic knowledge and the inherent unpredictability of world events. Economic policymakers should refrain from intervening often with monetary and fiscal policy and be content if they do no harm.

Quick Quiz   *Explain why monetary and fiscal policy work with a lag. Why do these lags matter in the choice between active and passive policy?*

IN THE NEWS
·············

How Long Will the Fed Keep Interest Rates at Zero?

In the aftermath of the financial crisis of 2008–2009, the Federal Reserve reduced its target for the federal funds rate to about zero, where it remained as this book was going to press in 2013. This article discusses the Fed's policy.

In Defense of the Fed's New Interest-Rate Policy

By Frederic S. Mishkin and Michael Woodford

At the most recent meeting of its Federal Open Market Committee, the Federal Reserve broke new ground by announcing the explicit criteria it would use to begin raising its target for the federal-funds rate. The FOMC said it will keep the rate near zero as long as the unemployment rate remains above 6.5%, and the inflation

rate one to two years ahead is projected to be no higher than 2.5%.

The Fed's increased clarity about its intentions is highly desirable. This is especially so now, when the current funds-rate target cannot be further lowered, yet aggregate demand remains insufficient. A commitment not to raise rates in the future as soon as might have been expected is an obvious way the FOMC can loosen current financial conditions. Yet the new approach has downsides that the Fed needs to address.

Providing policy criteria to the public is a significant improvement over the Fed's previous guidance to markets—in which the FOMC

stated that near-zero rates were "likely to be warranted at least through mid-2015." Pledging to keep rates unchanged for more than two years, regardless of what happens in the meantime, would be reckless—and of course was not what the central bank intended. But date-based guidance runs the risk that announcement of a distant date will be taken to indicate that the Fed has pessimistic information about the economy's future prospects. This gives households and firms a reason to sit on their cash rather than spend or invest it—which will hold the economy back.

Still, the Fed's new approach has invited confusion about its longer-run policy

36-2 Should the Government Fight Recessions with Spending Hikes Rather Than Tax Cuts?

When George W. Bush became president in 2001, the economy was slipping into a recession. He responded by cutting tax rates. When Barack Obama became president in 2009, the economy was again in recession, the worst in many decades. He responded with a stimulus package that offered some tax reductions but also included substantial increases in government spending. The contrast between these two policies illustrates a second classic question of macroeconomics: Which instrument of fiscal policy—government spending or taxes—is better for reducing the severity of economic downturns?

36-2a Pro: The Government Should Fight Recessions with Spending Hikes

John Maynard Keynes transformed economics when he wrote *The General Theory of Employment, Interest and Money* in the midst of the Great Depression of the 1930s, the worst economic downturn in U.S. history. Since then, economists have understood that the fundamental problem during recessions is inadequate aggregate demand. When firms are unable to sell a sufficient quantity of

targets. Many have read the FOMC statement as an important departure from the policy framework codified as recently as January 2012: The Fed is now taken to have a numerical target for unemployment alongside its inflation target, and the inflation target appears to have increased from 2% to 2.5%.

In fact, the Fed stated in its Jan. 25, 2012 policy statement that it would not be appropriate to specify a fixed goal for employment, because the maximum level of sustainable employment is difficult to estimate and is not something that can be controlled by the Federal Reserve.

This is a very important clarification. The central bank needs to reiterate that it does not have a "target" unemployment rate and is not determined to achieve a specific unemployment rate regardless of the amount of monetary stimulus required to reach it. That type of overreaching ended badly in the 1970s, with rising inflation and unemployment.

The Fed also needs to clarify that the threshold of 2.5% for the inflation rate in no way suggests that it is weakening its commitment to its long-run inflation target of 2%. It would be dangerous to weaken this commitment, as it would lead to a permanent ratcheting up of inflationary expectations and inflation.

Instead, the Fed's new approach is a temporary policy to keep interest rates low for longer, to make up for the inadequate nominal GDP growth that has occurred since 2008. Once the nominal GDP growth shortfall has been eliminated, it will be appropriate to again conduct policy much as was done before the crisis. That means ensuring a long-run inflation rate of 2% in terms of the PCE (personal consumption expenditure) deflator, and an average unemployment rate that is consistent with price stability.

It would have been better if the FOMC had explained its temporary policy by describing the size of the nominal growth shortfall that needed to be made up. A stated intention to "catch up" to a

particular nominal GDP path would have clarified that how long interest rates will remain low will depend on economic outcomes, while emphasizing the central bank's intention to return to a path consistent with its long-run inflation target.

It is too late to change the way that the FOMC has chosen to talk about the conditions that will determine the duration of the near-zero funds rate. Still, future Fed statements or speeches are needed to clarify the nature of the policy regime toward which the current transitional policy is expected to lead.

Doing so can help reduce the uncertainty about future financial conditions that may otherwise be created by the new communications policy.

Mr. Mishkin and Mr. Woodford are both professors of economics at Columbia University.

goods and services, they reduce production and employment. The key to ending recessions is to restore aggregate demand to a level consistent with full employment of the economy's labor force.

To be sure, monetary policy is the first line of defense against economic downturns. By increasing the money supply, the central bank reduces interest rates. Lower interest rates in turn reduce the cost of borrowing to finance investment projects, such as new factories and new housing. Increased spending on investment adds to aggregate demand and helps to restore normal levels of production and employment.

Fiscal policy, however, can provide an additional tool to combat recessions. When the government cuts taxes, it increases households' disposable income, which encourages them to increase spending on consumption. When the government buys goods and services, it adds directly to aggregate demand. Moreover, these fiscal actions can have multiplier effects: Higher aggregate demand leads to higher incomes, which in turn induces additional consumer spending and further increases in aggregate demand.

Fiscal policy is particularly useful when the tools of monetary policy lose their effectiveness. During the economic downturn of 2008 and 2009, for example, the Federal Reserve cut its target interest rate to almost zero. The Fed cannot reduce interest rates below zero, because people would hold onto their cash rather than lending it out at a negative interest rate. Thus, once interest rates are at zero, the Fed loses its most powerful tool for stimulating the economy. In this circumstance,

President Barack Obama delivers remarks at the groundbreaking of a road project funded by the American Recovery and Reinvestment Act, Friday, June 18, 2010, in Columbus, Ohio.

it is natural for the government to turn to fiscal policy—taxes and government spending—to prop up aggregate demand.

Traditional Keynesian analysis indicates that increases in government purchases are a more potent tool than decreases in taxes. When the government gives a dollar in tax cuts to a household, part of that dollar may be saved rather than spent. (That is especially true if households view the tax reduction as temporary rather than permanent.) The part of the dollar that is saved does not contribute to the aggregate demand for goods and services. By contrast, when the government spends a dollar buying a good or service, that dollar immediately and fully adds to aggregate demand.

In 2009, economists in the Obama administration used a conventional macroeconomic model to calculate the magnitude of these effects. According to their computer simulations, each dollar of tax cuts increases GDP by $0.99, whereas each dollar of government purchases increases GDP by $1.59. Thus, increases in government spending offer a bigger "bang for the buck" than decreases in taxes. For this reason, the policy response in 2009 featured fewer federal tax cuts and more increases in federal spending.

Policymakers focused on three kinds of spending. First, there was spending on "shovel-ready" projects. These were public works projects such as repairs to highways and bridges on which construction could begin immediately, putting the unemployed back to work. Second, there was federal aid to state and local governments. Because many of these governments are constitutionally required to run balanced budgets, falling tax revenues during recessions can make it necessary for them to lay off teachers, police, and other public workers; federal aid prevented that outcome or, at least, reduced its severity. Third, there were increased payments to the jobless through the unemployment insurance system. Because the unemployed are often financially stretched, they were thought to be likely to spend rather than save this extra income. Thus, these transfer payments were thought to contribute more to aggregate demand—and thereby production and employment—than tax cuts would. According to the macroeconomic model used by the Obama administration, the $800 billion stimulus package would create or save more than 3 million jobs by the end of the president's second year in office.

It is impossible to know for sure what effect the stimulus in fact had. Because we get only one run at history, we cannot observe the counterfactual—what would have happened without the stimulus package. One thing is clear: While the economic downturn of 2008–2009 was severe, it could have been worse. In the Great Depression of the 1930s, real GDP fell by 27 percent and unemployment reached 25 percent. In the recent recession, real GDP fell by only 4 percent and unemployment reached only 10 percent. As judged by either GDP or unemployment, the downturn of 2008–2009 did not approach the magnitude of the Great Depression.

36-2b Con: The Government Should Fight Recessions with Tax Cuts

There is a long tradition of using tax policy to stimulate a moribund economy. President Kennedy proposed a tax reduction as one of his major economic initiatives; it eventually passed under President Johnson in 1964. President Reagan also signed into law significant tax cuts when he became president in 1981. Both of these tax reductions were soon followed by robust economic growth.

Tax cuts have a powerful influence on both aggregate demand and aggregate supply. They increase aggregate demand by increasing households' disposable income, as emphasized in traditional Keynesian analysis. But they can also increase aggregate demand by altering incentives. For example, if the tax reductions take the form of an expanded investment tax credit, they can induce increased spending on investment goods. Because investment spending is the most volatile component of GDP over the business cycle, stimulating investment is a key to ending recessions. Policymakers can target investment specifically with well-designed tax policy.

At the same time that tax cuts increase aggregate demand, they can also increase aggregate supply. When the government reduces marginal tax rates, workers keep a higher fraction of any income they earn. As a result, the unemployed have a greater incentive to search for jobs, and the employed have a greater incentive to work longer hours. Increased aggregate supply, along with the increased aggregate demand, means that the production of goods and services can expand without putting upward pressure on the rate of inflation.

There are various problems with increasing government spending during recessions. First of all, consumers understand that higher government spending, together with the government borrowing needed to finance it, will likely lead to higher taxes in the future. The anticipation of those future taxes will induce consumers to cut back spending today. Moreover, like most taxes, those in the future will likely cause a variety of deadweight losses. As businesses look ahead to a more highly distorted future economy, they may reduce their expectations of future profits and reduce investment spending today. Because of these various effects, government-spending multipliers may be smaller than is conventionally believed.

It is also far from clear whether the government can spend money both wisely and quickly. Large government spending projects often require years of planning, as policymakers and voters weigh the costs and benefits of the many alternative courses of action. By contrast, when unemployment soars during recessions, the need for additional aggregate demand is immediate. If the government increases spending quickly, it may end up buying things of little public value. But if it tries to be careful and deliberate in planning its expenditures, it may fail to increase aggregate demand in a timely fashion.

Tax cuts have the advantage of decentralizing spending decisions, rather than relying on a centralized and highly imperfect political process. Households spend their disposable income on things they value. Firms spend their investment dollars on projects they expect to be profitable. By contrast, when the government tries to spend large sums of money fast, subject to various political pressures, it may end up building "bridges to nowhere." Ill-conceived public projects may employ some workers, but they create little lasting value. Moreover, they will leave future generations of taxpayers with significant additional debts. In the end, the short-run benefits of additional aggregate demand from increased government spending may fail to compensate for the long-run costs.

Quick Quiz *According to traditional Keynesian analysis, which has a larger impact on GDP—a dollar of tax cuts or a dollar of additional government spending? Why?*

36-3 Should Monetary Policy Be Made by Rule Rather Than by Discretion?

As we learned in the chapter on the monetary system, the Federal Open Market Committee (FOMC) sets monetary policy in the United States. The committee meets about every six weeks to evaluate the state of the economy. Based on this evaluation and forecasts of future economic conditions, it chooses whether to raise, lower, or leave unchanged the level of short-term interest rates. The Fed then adjusts the money supply to reach that interest-rate target, which will normally remain unchanged until the next meeting.

The FOMC operates with almost complete discretion over how to conduct monetary policy. The laws that created the Fed give the institution only vague recommendations about what goals it should pursue. A 1977 amendment to the 1913 Federal Reserve Act said the Fed "shall maintain long run growth of the monetary and credit aggregates commensurate with the economy's long run potential to increase production, so as to promote effectively the goals of maximum employment, stable prices, and moderate long-term interest rates." But the act does not specify how to weight these various goals, nor does it tell the Fed how to pursue whatever objective it might choose.

Some economists are critical of this institutional design. Our third debate over macroeconomic policy, therefore, focuses on whether the Fed should have its discretionary powers reduced and, instead, be committed to following a rule for how it conducts monetary policy.

36-3a Pro: Monetary Policy Should Be Made by Rule

Discretion in the conduct of monetary policy has two problems. The first is that it does not limit incompetence and abuse of power. When the government sends police into a community to maintain civic order, it gives them strict guidelines about how to carry out their job. Because police have great power, allowing them to exercise that power however they wanted would be dangerous. Yet when the government gives central bankers the authority to maintain economic order, it gives them few guidelines. Monetary policymakers are allowed undisciplined discretion.

One example of the abuse of power is that central bankers are sometimes tempted to use monetary policy to affect the outcome of elections. Suppose that the vote for the incumbent president is based on economic conditions at the time he is up for reelection. A central banker sympathetic to the incumbent might be tempted to pursue expansionary policies just before the election to stimulate production and employment, knowing that the resulting inflation will not show up until after the election. Thus, to the extent that central bankers ally themselves with politicians, discretionary policy can lead to economic fluctuations that reflect the electoral calendar. Economists call such fluctuations the *political business cycle*.

The second, subtler problem with discretionary monetary policy is that it might lead to more inflation than is desirable. Central bankers, knowing that there is no long-run trade-off between inflation and unemployment, often announce that their goal is zero inflation. Yet they rarely achieve price stability. Why? Perhaps it is because, once the public forms expectations of inflation, policymakers face a short-run trade-off between inflation and unemployment. They are tempted to renege on their announcement of price stability to achieve lower unemployment. This discrepancy between announcements (what policymakers *say* they are going to do) and actions (what they subsequently in fact do) is called the *time inconsistency of policy*. Because policymakers are so often time inconsistent, people are skeptical when central bankers announce their intentions to reduce the rate of inflation. As a result, people always expect more inflation than monetary policy-makers claim they are trying to achieve. Higher expectations of inflation, in turn, shift the short-run Phillips curve upward, making the short-run trade-off between inflation and unemployment less favorable than it otherwise might be.

One way to avoid these two problems with discretionary policy is to commit the central bank to a policy rule. For example, suppose that Congress passed a law requiring the Fed to increase the money supply by exactly 3 percent per year. (Why 3 percent? Because real GDP grows on average about 3 percent per year and because money demand grows with real GDP, 3 percent growth in the money supply is roughly the rate necessary to produce long-run price stability.) Such a law would eliminate incompetence and abuse of power on the part of the Fed, and it would make the political business cycle impossible. In addition, policy could no longer be time inconsistent. People would now believe the Fed's announcement of low inflation because the Fed would be legally required to pursue a low-inflation monetary policy. With low expected inflation, the economy would face a more favorable short-run trade-off between inflation and unemployment.

Other rules for monetary policy are also possible. A more active rule might allow some feedback from the state of the economy to changes in monetary policy. For example, a more active rule might require the Fed to increase monetary growth by 1 percentage point for every percentage point that unemployment rises above its natural rate. Regardless of the precise form of the rule, committing the Fed to some rule would yield advantages by limiting incompetence, abuse of power, and time inconsistency in the conduct of monetary policy.

36-3b Con: Monetary Policy Should Not Be Made by Rule

There may be pitfalls with discretionary monetary policy, but there is also an important advantage to it: flexibility. The Fed has to confront various circumstances, not all of which can be foreseen. In the 1930s, banks failed in record numbers. In the 1970s, the price of oil skyrocketed around the world. In October 1987, the stock market fell by 22 percent in a single day. From 2007 to 2009, house prices dropped, home foreclosures soared, and the financial system experienced significant problems. The Fed must decide how to respond to these shocks to the economy. A designer of a policy rule could not possibly consider all the contingencies and specify in advance the right policy response. It is better to appoint good people to conduct monetary policy and then give them the freedom to do the best they can.

Moreover, the alleged problems with discretion are largely hypothetical. The practical importance of the political business cycle, for instance, is far from clear. In some cases, just the opposite seems to occur. For example, President Jimmy Carter appointed Paul Volcker to head the Fed in 1979. Nonetheless, in October of that year, Volcker switched to a contractionary monetary policy to combat the high rate of inflation that he had inherited from his predecessor. The predictable result of Volcker's decision was a recession, and the predictable result of the recession was a decline in Carter's popularity. Rather than using monetary policy to help the president who had appointed him, Volcker took actions he thought were in the national interest, even though they helped to ensure Carter's defeat by Ronald Reagan in the November 1980 election.

The practical importance of time inconsistency is also far from clear. Although most people are skeptical of central-bank announcements, central bankers can achieve credibility over time by backing up their words with actions. In the 1990s and 2000s, the Fed achieved and maintained a low rate of inflation, despite the

FYI

Inflation Targeting

Over the past few decades, many central banks around the world have adopted a policy called *inflation targeting*. Sometimes this takes the form of a central bank announcing its intentions regarding the inflation rate over the next few years. At other times it takes the form of a national law that specifies an inflation goal for the central bank.

Inflation targeting is not a commitment to an ironclad rule. In all the countries that have adopted inflation targeting, central banks are left with a fair amount of discretion. Inflation targets are usually set as a range—an inflation rate of 1 to 3 percent, for example—rather than a particular number. Thus, the central bank can choose where in the range it wants to be. Moreover, the central bank is sometimes allowed to adjust its target for inflation, at least temporarily, if some event (such as a shock to world oil prices) pushes inflation outside the target range.

Although inflation targeting leaves the central bank with some discretion, the policy does constrain how that discretion is used. When a central bank is told simply to "do the right thing," it is hard to hold the central bank accountable, because people can argue forever about what is right. By contrast, when a central bank has an inflation target, the public can more easily judge whether the central bank is meeting its goals. Inflation targeting does not tie the hands of the central bank, but it does increase the transparency and accountability of monetary policy. In a sense, inflation targeting is a compromise in the debate over rules versus discretion.

Compared with other central banks around the world, the Federal Reserve was slow to adopt a policy of inflation targeting, although some commentators had long suggested that the Fed had an implicit inflation target of about 2 percent. In January 2012, the Federal Open Market Committee made the policy more explicit. Its press release read as follows:

The inflation rate over the longer run is primarily determined by monetary policy, and hence the Committee has the ability to specify a longer-run goal for inflation. The Committee judges that inflation at the rate of 2 percent, as measured by the annual change in the price index for personal consumption expenditures, is most consistent over the longer run with the Federal Reserve's statutory mandate. Communicating this inflation goal clearly to the public helps keep longer-term inflation expectations firmly anchored, thereby fostering price stability and moderate long-term interest rates and enhancing the Committee's ability to promote maximum employment in the face of significant economic disturbances. ◢

ever-present temptation to take advantage of the short-run trade-off between inflation and unemployment. This experience shows that low inflation does not require that the Fed be committed to a policy rule.

Any attempt to replace discretion with a rule must confront the difficult task of specifying a precise rule. Despite much research examining the costs and benefits of alternative rules, economists have not reached consensus about what a good rule would be. Until there is consensus, society has little choice but to give central bankers discretion to conduct monetary policy as they see fit.

Quick Quiz   *Give an example of a monetary policy rule. Why might your rule be better than discretionary policy? Why might it be worse?*

36-4 Should the Central Bank Aim for Zero Inflation?

One of the *Ten Principles of Economics* discussed in Chapter 1, and developed more fully in the chapter on money growth and inflation, is that prices rise when the government prints too much money. Another of the *Ten Principles of Economics* discussed in Chapter 1, and developed more fully in the preceding chapter, is that society faces a short-run trade-off between inflation and unemployment. Put together, these two principles raise a question for policymakers: How much inflation should the central bank be willing to tolerate? Our fourth debate is whether zero is the right target for the inflation rate.

36-4a Pro: The Central Bank Should Aim for Zero Inflation

Inflation confers no benefit on society, but it imposes several real costs. As we have discussed, economists have identified six costs of inflation:

- Shoeleather costs associated with reduced money holdings
- Menu costs associated with more frequent adjustment of prices
- Increased variability of relative prices
- Unintended changes in tax liabilities due to nonindexation of the tax code
- Confusion and inconvenience resulting from a changing unit of account
- Arbitrary redistributions of wealth associated with dollar-denominated debts

Some economists argue that these costs are small, at least for moderate rates of inflation, such as the 3 percent inflation experienced in the United States during the 1990s and 2000s. But other economists claim these costs can be substantial, even for moderate inflation. Moreover, there is no doubt that the public dislikes inflation. When inflation heats up, opinion polls identify inflation as one of the nation's leading problems.

The benefits of zero inflation have to be weighed against the costs of achieving it. Reducing inflation usually requires a period of high unemployment and low output, as illustrated by the short-run Phillips curve. But this disinflationary recession is only temporary. Once people come to understand that policymakers are aiming for zero inflation, expectations of inflation will fall and the short-run trade-off will improve. Because expectations adjust, there is no trade-off between inflation and unemployment in the long run.

Reducing inflation is, therefore, a policy with temporary costs and permanent benefits. Once the disinflationary recession is over, the benefits of zero inflation persist into the future. If policymakers are farsighted, they should be willing to incur the temporary costs for the permanent benefits. This was precisely the calculation made by Paul Volcker in the early 1980s, when he tightened monetary policy and reduced inflation from about 10 percent in 1980 to about 4 percent in 1983. Although in 1982 unemployment reached its highest level since the Great Depression, the economy eventually recovered from the recession, leaving a legacy of low inflation. Today, Volcker is considered a hero among central bankers.

Moreover, the costs of reducing inflation need not be as large as some economists claim. If the Fed announces a credible commitment to zero inflation, it can directly influence expectations of inflation. Such a change in expectations can improve the short-run trade-off between inflation and unemployment, allowing the economy to reach lower inflation at a reduced cost. The key to this strategy is credibility: People must believe that the Fed is actually going to carry through on its announced policy. Congress could help in this regard by passing legislation that makes price stability the Fed's primary goal. Such a law would decrease the cost of achieving zero inflation without reducing any of the resulting benefits.

One advantage of a zero-inflation target is that zero provides a more natural focal point for policymakers than any other number. Suppose, for instance, that the Fed were to announce that it would keep inflation at 3 percent—the rate experienced during much of the previous two decades. Would the Fed really stick to that 3 percent target? If events inadvertently pushed inflation up to 4 or 5 percent, why wouldn't it just raise the target? There is, after all, nothing special about the number 3. By contrast, zero is the only number for the inflation rate at which the Fed can claim that it has achieved price stability and fully eliminated the costs of inflation.

36-4b Con: The Central Bank Should Not Aim for Zero Inflation

Price stability may be desirable, but the benefits of zero inflation compared to moderate inflation are small, whereas the costs of reaching zero inflation are large. Estimates of the sacrifice ratio suggest that reducing inflation by 1 percentage point requires giving up about 5 percent of one year's output. Reducing inflation from, say, 4 percent to zero requires a loss of 20 percent of a year's output. People might dislike inflation of 4 percent, but it is not at all clear that they would (or should) be willing to pay 20 percent of a year's income to get rid of it.

The social costs of disinflation are even larger than this 20 percent figure suggests, for the lost income is not spread equitably over the population. When the economy goes into recession, all incomes do not fall proportionately. Instead, the fall in aggregate income is concentrated on those workers who lose their jobs. The vulnerable workers are often those with the least skills and experience. Hence, much of the cost of reducing inflation is borne by those who can least afford to pay it.

Economists can list several costs of inflation, but there is no professional consensus that these costs are substantial. The shoeleather costs, menu costs, and others that economists have identified do not seem great, at least for moderate rates of inflation. It is true that the public dislikes inflation, but the public may be misled into believing the inflation fallacy—the view that inflation erodes living standards. Economists understand that living standards depend on productivity, not monetary policy. Because inflation in nominal incomes goes hand in hand with inflation in prices, reducing inflation would not cause real incomes to rise more rapidly.

Moreover, policymakers can reduce many of the costs of inflation without actually reducing inflation. They can eliminate the problems associated with the nonindexed tax system by rewriting the tax laws to take account of the effects of inflation. They can also reduce the arbitrary redistributions of wealth between creditors and debtors caused by unexpected inflation by issuing indexed government bonds, as in fact the Clinton administration did in 1997. Such an act insulates holders of government debt from inflation. In addition, by setting an example, the policy might encourage private borrowers and lenders to write debt contracts indexed for inflation.

Reducing inflation might be desirable if it could be done at no cost, as some economists argue is possible. Yet this trick seems hard to carry out in practice. When economies reduce their rate of inflation, they almost always experience a period of high unemployment and low output. It is risky to believe that the central bank could achieve credibility so quickly as to make disinflation painless.

Indeed, a disinflationary recession can potentially leave permanent scars on the economy. Firms in all industries reduce their spending on new plants and equipment substantially during recessions, making investment the most volatile component of GDP. Even after the recession is over, the smaller stock of capital reduces productivity, incomes, and living standards below the levels they otherwise would have achieved. In addition, when workers become unemployed in recessions, they lose job skills, permanently reducing their value as workers.

A little bit of inflation may even be a good thing. Some economists believe that inflation "greases the wheels" of the labor market. Because workers resist cuts in nominal wages, a fall in real wages is more easily accomplished with a rising price level. Inflation thus makes it easier for real wages to adjust to changes in labor market conditions.

What Is the Optimal Inflation Rate?

In the aftermath of the financial crisis and recession of 2008–2009, economists started wondering whether higher inflation might be desirable.

Low-Inflation Doctrine Gets a Rethink, But Shift Is Unlikely

By Jon Hilsenrath

For the past quarter century, inflation has been a bogeyman that eats wealth and causes instability. But lately some smart people—including the chief economist at the International Monetary Fund and a senior Federal Reserve researcher—have been wondering aloud if a little more of it might actually be a good thing.

For several reasons, however, the idea isn't likely to gain traction any time soon.

The new argument for inflation goes like this: Low inflation and the low interest rates that accompany it leave central banks little room to maneuver when shocks hit. After Lehman Brothers collapsed in 2008, for example, the U.S. Federal Reserve quickly cut interest rates to near zero, but couldn't go any lower even though the economy needed a lot more stimulus.

Economists call this the "zero bound" problem. If inflation were a little higher to begin with, and thus interest rates were a little higher, the argument goes, the Fed would have had more room to cut interest rates and provide more juice to the economy.

Right now, the Fed and other big central banks have their sights set on inflation of around 2%. Economists had used a "Three Bears" approach to come up with this number—for a long time it seemed like it was not too hot and not too cold. But low and stable inflation could in theory mean something steady at a slightly higher rate.

IMF chief economist Olivier Blanchard, in a recent paper, said maybe the U.S. central bank's future inflation goal should be 4% instead. John Williams, head of the San Francisco Fed's research department, argued last year that higher targets might be needed to provide a cushion for future crises. . . .

There are other reasons some would welcome a little more inflation now. Governments in the U.S. and elsewhere, and many U.S. households, are sitting on mountains of debt. A little more inflation could in theory reduce the burden of servicing and paying that off, because while debt payments are often fixed, the revenue and income that households and governments generate to pay it off would rise with inflation.

But there are problems with the welcome-more-inflation argument.

The first is that it isn't yet clear that the "zero bound" on interest rates that Mr. Blanchard worries about is the economy's biggest problem. Thus addressing it might not be worth the costs that would be associated with higher inflation.

After the Fed pushed interest rates to near zero in December 2008, Chairman Ben Bernanke found alternatives to more interest-rate cuts: buying mortgage-backed securities and Treasury bonds and funneling credit to auto-loan, student-loan and credit-card markets. Those additional steps were no panacea, but they helped end the recession even if they didn't produce growth fast enough to bring unemployment down quickly. . . .

There is also a thornier problem. Suppose for a moment that Mr. Blanchard is right, and central banks around the world would be better prepared to fight future crises with a little higher inflation. Getting from 2% to 4% could be a very messy process. Investors, businesses and households might well conclude a one-time shift to a higher inflation target actually means less commitment to stable inflation. Expectations of higher inflation could become a self-fulfilling prophecy. Instead of getting 4% inflation, central banks could end up with 5%, or 6% or 7%.

A higher inflation goal "would have a fairly immediate and disruptive effect" on markets, said Bruce Kasman, chief economist at J.P. Morgan Chase.

Mr. Bernanke has acknowledged the allure of a higher inflation goal. In written answers to lawmakers in December, he said a higher inflation target could in theory make it possible for the Fed to push inflation-adjusted interest rates lower, stimulating borrowing and economic growth.

But the opposite could happen, too. The prospect of higher inflation could cause interest rates to shoot up and make the burden of future borrowing even heavier. This is a particular problem for countries, like the U.S., that issue a lot of short-term debt and for people with adjustable-rate mortgages.

Mr. Bernanke concluded he didn't want to mess with people's fragile expectations. He said switching to a higher target would risk causing "the public to lose confidence in the central bank's willingness to resist further upward shifts in inflation, and so undermine the effectiveness of monetary policy going forward."

The 2% inflation goal that is so popular with central bankers around the world might not have been the ideal target in retrospect. But it looks like everybody is tied to it, for better or worse, for the foreseeable future. ◢

In addition, inflation allows for the possibility of negative real interest rates. Nominal interest rates can never fall below zero, because lenders can always hold on to their money rather than lending it out at a negative return. If inflation is zero, real interest rates can also never be negative. However, if inflation is positive, then a cut in nominal interest rates below the inflation rate produces negative real interest rates. Sometimes the economy may need negative real interest rates to provide sufficient stimulus to aggregate demand—an option ruled out by zero inflation.

In light of all these arguments, why should policymakers put the economy through a costly and inequitable disinflationary recession to achieve zero inflation? Economist Alan Blinder, who was once vice chairman of the Fed, argued in his book *Hard Heads, Soft Hearts* that policymakers should not make this choice:

> The costs that attend the low and moderate inflation rates experienced in the United States and in other industrial countries appear to be quite modest—more like a bad cold than a cancer on society. . . . As rational individuals, we do not volunteer for a lobotomy to cure a head cold. Yet, as a collectivity, we routinely prescribe the economic equivalent of lobotomy (high unemployment) as a cure for the inflationary cold.

Blinder concludes that it is better to learn to live with moderate inflation.

Quick Quiz   *Explain the costs and benefits of reducing inflation to zero. Which are temporary and which are permanent?*

36-5 Should the Government Balance Its Budget?

A persistent macroeconomic debate concerns the government's finances. Whenever the government spends more than it collects in tax revenue, it covers this budget deficit by issuing government debt. In our study of financial markets, we saw how budget deficits affect saving, investment, and interest rates. But how big a problem are budget deficits? Our fifth debate concerns whether fiscal policymakers should make balancing the government's budget a high priority.

36-5a Pro: The Government Should Balance Its Budget

The U.S. federal government is far more indebted today than it was three decades ago. In 1980, the federal debt was $712 billion; in 2012, it was $11.3 trillion. If we divide today's debt by the size of the population, we learn that each person's share of the government debt is about $36,000.

The most direct effect of the government debt is to place a burden on future generations of taxpayers. When these debts and accumulated interest come due, future taxpayers will face a difficult choice. They can choose some combination of higher taxes and less government spending to make resources available to pay off the debt and accumulated interest. Or, instead, they can delay the day of reckoning and put the government into even deeper debt by borrowing once again to pay off the old debt and interest. In essence, when the government runs a budget deficit and issues government debt, it allows current taxpayers to pass the bill for some of their government spending on to future taxpayers. Inheriting such a large debt cannot help but lower the living standard of future generations.

In addition to this direct effect, budget deficits have various macroeconomic effects. Because budget deficits represent *negative* public saving, they lower national saving (the sum of private and public saving). Reduced national saving causes real interest rates to rise and investment to fall. Reduced investment leads over time to a smaller stock of capital. A lower capital stock reduces labor productivity, real wages, and the economy's production of goods and services. Thus, when the government increases its debt, future generations are born into an economy with lower incomes as well as higher taxes.

There are, nevertheless, situations in which running a budget deficit is justifiable. Throughout history, the most common cause of increased government debt has been war. When a military conflict raises government spending temporarily, it is reasonable to finance this extra spending by borrowing. Otherwise, taxes during wartime would have to rise precipitously. Such high tax rates would greatly distort the incentives faced by those who are taxed, leading to large deadweight losses. In addition, such high tax rates would be unfair to those generations of taxpayers who already have to make the sacrifice of fighting the war.

Similarly, it is reasonable to allow a budget deficit during a temporary downturn in economic activity. When the economy goes into a recession, tax revenue falls automatically because the income tax and the payroll tax are levied on measures of income. If the government tried to balance its budget during a recession, it would have to raise taxes or cut spending at a time of high unemployment. Such a policy would tend to depress aggregate demand at precisely the time it needed to be stimulated and, therefore, would tend to increase the magnitude of economic fluctuations.

Yet not all budget deficits can be justified as a result of war or recession. U.S. government debt as a percentage of GDP increased from 26 percent in 1980 to 50 percent in 1995. During this period, the United States experienced neither a major military conflict nor a major economic downturn. Yet the government consistently ran a sizable budget deficit, largely because the president and Congress found it easier to increase government spending than to increase taxes.

The budget deficits that the U.S. government has run in recent years can, perhaps, be rationalized by the wars in Iraq and Afghanistan and the effects of the recessions in 2001 and 2008–2009. But it is imperative that this deficit not signal a return to the unsustainable fiscal policy of an earlier era. As the economy recovers from the most recent recession and unemployment returns to its natural rate, the government should bring spending in line with tax revenue. Compared to the alternative of ongoing budget deficits, a balanced budget means greater national saving, investment, and economic growth. It means that future college graduates will enter a more prosperous economy.

"What?!? My share of the government debt is $36,000?"

36-5b Con: The Government Should Not Balance Its Budget

The problem of government debt is often exaggerated. Although the government debt does represent a tax burden on younger generations, it is not large compared to the average person's lifetime income. The debt of the U.S. federal government is about $36,000 per person. A person who works 40 years for $50,000 a year will earn $2 million over his lifetime. His share of the government debt represents less than 2 percent of his lifetime resources.

Moreover, it is misleading to view the effects of budget deficits in isolation. The budget deficit is just one piece of a large picture of how the government chooses to raise and spend money. In making these decisions over fiscal policy, policymakers affect different generations of taxpayers in many ways. The government's budget deficit or surplus should be considered together with these other policies.

For example, suppose the government reduces the budget deficit by cutting spending on public investments, such as education. Does this policy make younger generations better off? The government debt will be smaller when they enter the labor force, which means a smaller tax burden. Yet if they are less educated than they could be, their productivity and incomes will be lower. Many estimates of the return from schooling (the increase in a worker's wage that results from an additional year in school) find that it is quite large. Reducing the budget deficit rather than funding more education spending could, all things considered, make future generations worse off.

Single-minded concern about the budget deficit is also dangerous because it draws attention away from various other policies that redistribute income across generations. For example, in the 1960s and 1970s, the U.S. federal government raised Social Security benefits for the elderly. It financed this higher spending by increasing the payroll tax on the working-age population. This policy redistributed income away from younger generations toward older generations, even though it did not affect the government

IN THE NEWS

What Would an American Fiscal Crisis Look Like?

In recent years, the governments of several European nations have experienced fiscal crises as they have had to cope with ballooning government debt and dwindling investor confidence. Here is what such a crisis might look like in the United States.

It's 2026, and the Debt Is Due

By N. Gregory Mankiw

The following is a presidential address to the nation — to be delivered in March 2026.

My fellow Americans, I come to you today with a heavy heart. We have a crisis on our hands. It is one of our own making. And it is one that leaves us with no good choices.

For many years, our nation's government has lived beyond its means. We have promised ourselves both low taxes and a generous social safety net. But we have not faced the hard reality of budget arithmetic.

The seeds of this crisis were planted long ago, by previous generations. Our parents and grandparents had noble aims. They saw poverty among the elderly and created Social Security. They saw sickness and created Medicare and Medicaid. They saw Americans struggle to afford health insurance and

embraced health care reform with subsidies for middle-class families.

But this expansion in government did not come cheap. Government spending has taken up an increasing share of our national income.

Today, most of the large baby-boom generation is retired. They are no longer working and paying taxes, but they are eligible for the many government benefits we offer the elderly.

Our efforts to control health care costs have failed. We must now acknowledge that rising costs are driven largely by technological advances in saving lives. These advances are welcome, but they are expensive nonetheless.

If we had chosen to tax ourselves to pay for this spending, our current problems could have been avoided. But no one likes paying taxes. Taxes not only take money out of our pockets, but they also distort incentives and reduce economic growth. So, instead, we borrowed increasing amounts to pay for these programs.

Yet debt does not avoid hard choices. It only delays them. After last week's events in the bond market, it is clear that further delay is no longer possible. The day of reckoning is here.

This morning, the Treasury Department released a detailed report about the nature of the problem. To put it most simply, the bond market no longer trusts us.

For years, the United States government borrowed on good terms. Investors both at home and abroad were confident that we would honor our debts. They were sure that when the time came, we would do the right thing and bring spending and taxes into line.

But over the last several years, as the ratio of our debt to gross domestic product reached ever-higher levels, investors started getting nervous. They demanded higher interest rates to compensate for the perceived risk. Higher interest rates increased the cost of servicing our debt, adding to the upward pressure on spending. We found ourselves in debt. Thus, the budget deficit is only a small part of the larger issue of how government policy affects the welfare of different generations.

To some extent, forward-looking parents can reverse the adverse effects of government debt. Parents can offset the impact simply by saving and leaving a larger bequest. The bequest would enhance their children's ability to bear the burden of future taxes. Some economists claim that people do in fact behave this way. If this were true, higher private saving by parents would offset the public dissaving of budget deficits; as a result, deficits would not affect the economy. Most economists doubt that parents are so farsighted, but some people probably do act this way, and anyone could. Deficits give people the opportunity to consume at the expense of their children, but deficits do not require them to do so. If the government debt were actually a great problem facing future generations, some parents would help to solve it.

Critics of budget deficits sometimes assert that the government debt cannot continue to rise forever, but in fact, it can. Just as a bank evaluating a loan application

a vicious circle of rising budget deficits and falling investor confidence.

As economists often remind us, crises take longer to arrive than you think, but then they happen much faster than you could have imagined. Last week, when the Treasury tried to auction its most recent issue of government bonds, almost no one was buying. The private market will lend us no more. Our national credit card has been rejected.

So where do we go from here?

Yesterday, I returned from a meeting at the International Monetary Fund in its new headquarters in Beijing. I am pleased to report some good news. I have managed to secure from the I.M.F. a temporary line of credit to help us through this crisis.

This loan comes with some conditions. As your president, I have to be frank: I don't like them, and neither will you. But, under the circumstances, accepting these conditions is our only choice.

We have to cut Social Security immediately, especially for higher-income beneficiaries. Social Security will still keep the elderly out of poverty, but just barely.

We have to limit Medicare and Medicaid. These programs will still provide basic health care, but they will no longer cover many expensive treatments. Individuals will have to pay for these treatments on their own or, sadly, do without.

We have to cut health insurance subsidies to middle-income families. Health insurance will be less a right of citizenship and more a personal responsibility.

We have to eliminate inessential government functions, like subsidies for farming, ethanol production, public broadcasting, energy conservation and trade promotion.

We will raise taxes on all but the poorest Americans. We will do this primarily by broadening the tax base, eliminating deductions for mortgage interest and state and local taxes.

Employer-provided health insurance will hereafter be taxable compensation.

We will increase the gasoline tax by $2 a gallon. This will not only increase revenue, but will also address various social ills, from global climate change to local traffic congestion.

As I have said, these changes are repellant to me. When you elected me, I promised to preserve the social safety net. I assured you that the budget deficit could be fixed by eliminating waste, fraud and abuse, and by increasing taxes on only the richest Americans. But now we have little choice in the matter.

If only we had faced up to this problem a generation ago. The choices then would not have been easy, but they would have been less draconian than the sudden, nonnegotiable demands we now face. Americans would have come to rely less on government and more on themselves, and so would be better prepared today.

What I wouldn't give for a chance to go back and change the past. But what is done is done. Americans have faced hardship and adversity before, and we have triumphed. Working together, we can make the sacrifices it takes so our children and grandchildren will enjoy a more prosperous future.

Source: *New York Times*, March 27, 2011.

would compare a person's debts to his income, we should judge the burden of the government debt relative to the size of the nation's income. Population growth and technological progress cause the total income of the U.S. economy to grow over time. As a result, the nation's ability to pay the interest on the government debt grows over time as well. As long as the government debt grows more slowly than the nation's income, there is nothing to prevent the government debt from growing forever.

Some numbers can put this into perspective. The real output of the U.S. economy grows on average about 3 percent per year. If the inflation rate is 2 percent per year, then nominal income grows at a rate of 5 percent per year. The government debt, therefore, can rise by 5 percent per year without increasing the ratio of debt to income. In 2012, the federal government debt was $11.3 trillion; 5 percent of this figure is $565 billion. As long as the federal budget deficit is smaller than $565 billion, the policy is sustainable.

To be sure, very large budget deficits cannot persist forever. From 2009 to 2012, the federal budget deficit was over $1 trillion every year, but this astonishing number was driven by extraordinary circumstances: a major financial crisis, a deep economic downturn, and the policy responses to these events. No one suggests that a deficit of this magnitude can continue. But zero is the wrong target for fiscal policymakers. As long as the deficit is only moderate in size, there will never be a day of reckoning that forces government borrowing to end or the economy to collapse.

Quick Quiz   *Explain how reducing a government budget deficit makes future genera-tions better off. What fiscal policy might improve the lives of future generations more than reducing a government budget deficit?*

36-6 Should the Tax Laws Be Reformed to Encourage Saving?

A nation's standard of living depends on its ability to produce goods and services. This was one of the *Ten Principles of Economics* in Chapter 1. As we saw in the chapter on production and growth, a nation's productive capability, in turn, is determined largely by how much it saves and invests for the future. Our sixth debate is whether policy-makers should reform the tax laws to encourage greater saving and investment.

36-6a Pro: The Tax Laws Should Be Reformed to Encourage Saving

A nation's saving rate is a key determinant of its long-run economic prosperity. When the saving rate is higher, more resources are available for investment in new plant and equipment. A larger stock of plant and equipment, in turn, raises labor productivity, wages, and incomes. It is, therefore, no surprise that international data show a strong correlation between national saving rates and measures of economic well-being.

Another of the *Ten Principles of Economics* presented in Chapter 1 is that people respond to incentives. This lesson should apply to people's decisions about how much to save. If a nation's laws make saving attractive, people will save a higher frac-tion of their incomes, and this higher saving will lead to a more prosperous future.

Unfortunately, the U.S. tax system discourages saving by taxing the return to saving quite heavily. For example, consider a 25-year-old worker who saves $1,000 of his income to have a more comfortable retirement at the age of 70. If he buys a bond that pays an interest rate of 10 percent, the $1,000 will accumu-late at the end of 45 years to $72,900 in the absence of taxes on interest. But sup-pose he faces a marginal tax rate on interest income of 40 percent, which is typical for many workers once federal and state income taxes are added together. In this case, his after-tax interest rate is only 6 percent, and the $1,000 will accumulate at the end of 45 years to only $13,800. That is, accumulated over this long span of time, the tax rate on interest income reduces the benefit of saving $1,000 from $72,900 to $13,800—or by about 80 percent.

The tax code further discourages saving by taxing some forms of capital income twice. Suppose a person uses some of his saving to buy stock in a corporation. When the corporation earns a profit from its capital investments, it first pays tax on this profit in the form of the corporate income tax. If the corporation pays out the rest of the profit to the stockholder in the form of dividends, the stockholder pays tax on this income a second time in the form of the individual income tax. This double taxation substantially reduces the return to the stockholder, thereby reducing the incentive to save.

The tax laws again discourage saving if a person wants to leave his accumulated wealth to his children (or anyone else) rather than consuming it during his lifetime. Parents can bequeath some money to their children tax-free, but if the bequest becomes large, the estate tax rate can be as high as 40 percent. To a large extent, concern about national saving is motivated by a desire to ensure economic prosperity for future generations. It is odd, therefore, that the tax laws discourage the most direct way in which one generation can help the next.

In addition to the tax code, many other policies and institutions in our society reduce the incentive for households to save. Some government benefits, such as welfare and Medicaid, are means-tested; that is, the benefits are reduced for those who in the past have been prudent enough to save some of their income. Colleges and universities grant financial aid as a function of the wealth of the students and their parents. Such a policy is like a tax on wealth and, as such, discourages students and parents from saving.

There are various ways in which the tax code could provide an incentive to save, or at least reduce the disincentive that households now face. Already the tax laws give preferential treatment to some types of retirement saving. When a taxpayer puts income into an Individual Retirement Account (IRA), for instance, that income and the interest it earns are not taxed until the funds are withdrawn at retirement. The tax code gives a similar tax advantage to retirement accounts that go by other names, such as 401(k), 403(b), and profit-sharing plans. There are, however, limits to who is eligible to use these plans and, for those who are eligible, limits on the amount that can be put in them. Moreover, because there are penalties for withdrawal before retirement age, these retirement plans provide little incentive for other types of saving, such as saving to buy a house or pay for college. A small step to encourage greater saving would be to expand the ability of households to use such tax-advantaged savings accounts.

A more comprehensive approach would be to reconsider the entire basis by which the government collects revenue. The centerpiece of the U.S. tax system is the income tax. A dollar earned is taxed the same whether it is spent or saved. An alternative advocated by many economists is a consumption tax. Under a consumption tax, a household pays taxes only on the basis of what it spends. Income that is saved is exempt from taxation until the saving is later withdrawn and spent on consumption goods. In essence, a consumption tax automatically puts all saving into a tax-advantaged savings account, much like an IRA. A switch from income to consumption taxation would greatly increase the incentive to save.

36-6b Con: The Tax Laws Should Not Be Reformed to Encourage Saving

Increasing saving may be desirable, but it is not the only goal of tax policy. Policymakers also must be sure to distribute the tax burden fairly. The problem with proposals to increase the incentive to save is that they increase the tax burden on those who can least afford it.

It is undeniable that high-income households save a greater fraction of their income than low-income households. As a result, any tax change that favors people who save will also tend to favor people with high income. Policies such as tax-advantaged retirement accounts may seem appealing, but they lead to a less egalitarian society. By reducing the tax burden on the wealthy who can take advantage of these accounts, they force the government to raise the tax burden on the poor.

Moreover, tax policies designed to encourage saving may not be effective at achieving that goal. Economic theory does not give a clear prediction about whether a higher rate of return would increase saving. The outcome depends on the relative size of two conflicting forces, called the *substitution effect* and the *income effect*. On the one hand, a higher rate of return raises the benefit of saving: Each dollar saved today produces more consumption in the future. This substitution effect tends to increase saving. On the other hand, a higher rate of return lowers the need for saving: A household has to save less to achieve any target level of consumption in the future. This income effect tends to reduce saving. If the substitution and income effects approximately cancel each other, as some studies suggest, then saving will not change when lower taxation of capital income raises the rate of return.

There are ways to increase national saving other than by giving tax breaks to the rich. National saving is the sum of private and public saving. Instead of trying to alter the tax code to encourage greater private saving, policymakers can simply raise public saving by reducing the budget deficit, perhaps by raising taxes on the wealthy. This offers a direct way of raising national saving and increasing prosperity for future generations.

Indeed, once public saving is taken into account, tax provisions to encourage saving might backfire. Tax changes that reduce the taxation of capital income reduce government revenue and, thereby, lead to a larger budget deficit. To increase national saving, such a change in the tax code must stimulate private saving by more than the decline in public saving. If this is not the case, so-called saving incentives can potentially make matters worse.

Quick Quiz   *Give three examples of how our society discourages saving. What are the drawbacks of eliminating these disincentives?*

36-7 Conclusion

This chapter has considered six classic debates over macroeconomic policy. For each, it began with a controversial proposition and then offered the arguments pro and con. If you find it hard to choose a side in these debates, you may find some comfort in the fact that you are not alone. The study of economics does not always make it easy to choose among alternative policies. Indeed, by clarifying the inevitable trade-offs that policymakers face, it can make the choice more difficult.

Difficult choices, however, have no right to seem easy. When you hear politicians or commentators proposing something that sounds too good to be true, it probably is. If they sound like they are offering you a free lunch, you should look for the hidden price tag. Few if any policies come with benefits but no costs. By helping you see through the fog of rhetoric so common in political discourse, the study of economics should make you a better participant in our national debates.

Summary

- Advocates of active monetary and fiscal policy view the economy as inherently unstable and believe that policy can manage aggregate demand to offset the inherent instability. Critics of active monetary and fiscal policy emphasize that policy affects the economy with a lag and that our ability to forecast future economic conditions is poor. As a result, attempts to stabilize the economy can end up being destabilizing.

- Advocates of increased government spending to fight recessions argue that because tax cuts may be saved rather than spent, direct government spending does more to increase aggregate demand, which is key to promoting production and employment. Critics of spending hikes argue that tax cuts can expand both aggregate demand and aggregate supply and that hasty increases in government spending may lead to wasteful public projects.

- Advocates of rules for monetary policy argue that discretionary policy can suffer from incompetence, the abuse of power, and time inconsistency. Critics of rules for monetary policy argue that discretionary policy is more flexible in responding to changing economic circumstances.

- Advocates of a zero-inflation target emphasize that inflation has many costs and few if any benefits. Moreover, the cost of eliminating inflation—depressed output and employment—is only temporary. Even this cost can be reduced if the central bank announces a credible plan to reduce inflation, thereby directly lowering expectations of inflation. Critics of a zero-inflation target claim that moderate inflation imposes only small costs on society, whereas the recession necessary to reduce inflation is quite costly. The critics also point out several ways in which moderate inflation may be helpful to an economy.

- Advocates of a balanced government budget argue that budget deficits impose an unjustifiable burden on future generations by raising their taxes and lowering their incomes. Critics of a balanced government budget argue that the deficit is only one small piece of fiscal policy. Single-minded concern about the budget deficit can obscure the many ways in which policy, including various spending programs, affects different generations.

- Advocates of tax incentives for saving point out that our society discourages saving in many ways, such as by heavily taxing capital income and by reducing benefits for those who have accumulated wealth. They endorse reforming the tax laws to encourage saving, perhaps by switching from an income tax to a consumption tax. Critics of tax incentives for saving argue that many proposed changes to stimulate saving would primarily benefit the wealthy, who do not need a tax break. They also argue that such changes might have only a small effect on private saving. Raising public saving by decreasing the government's budget deficit would provide a more direct and equitable way to increase national saving.

Questions for Review

1. What causes the lags in the effect of monetary and fiscal policy on aggregate demand? What are the implications of these lags for the debate over active versus passive policy?

2. According to traditional Keynesian analysis, why does a tax cut have a smaller effect on GDP than a similarly sized increase in government spending? Why might the opposite be the case?

3. What might motivate a central banker to cause a political business cycle? What does the political business cycle imply for the debate over policy rules?

4. Explain how credibility might affect the cost of reducing inflation.

5. Why are some economists against a target of zero inflation?

6. Explain two ways in which a government budget deficit hurts a future worker.

7. What are two situations in which most economists view a budget deficit as justifiable?

8. Some economists say that the government can continue running a budget deficit forever. How is that possible?

9. Some income from capital is taxed twice. Explain.

10. What adverse effect might be caused by tax incentives to increase saving?

Quick Check Multiple Choice

1. Approximately how long does it take a change in monetary policy to influence aggregate demand?
   a. one month
   b. six months
   c. two years
   d. five years

2. According to traditional Keynesian analysis, which of the following will increase aggregate demand the most?
   a. $100 billion increase in taxation
   b. $100 billion decrease in taxation
   c. $100 billion increase in government spending
   d. $100 billion decrease in government spending

3. Advocates for setting monetary policy by rule rather than discretion often argue that
   a. central bankers with discretion are tempted to renege on their announced commitments to low inflation.
   b. central bankers following a rule will be more responsive to the needs of the political process.
   c. fiscal policy is a much better tool for economic stabilization than is monetary policy.
   d. it is sometimes useful to give the economy a burst of surprise inflation.

4. Which of the following is NOT an argument for maintaining a positive rate of inflation?
   a. It permits real interest rates to be negative.
   b. It allows real wages to fall without cuts in nominal wages.

   c. It increases the variability of relative prices.
   d. It would be costly to reduce inflation to zero.

5. Throughout U.S. history, what has been the most common cause of substantial increases in government debt?
   a. recessions
   b. wars
   c. financial crises
   d. tax cuts

6. Advocates of taxing consumption rather than income argue that
   a. a consumption tax is a better automatic stabilizer.
   b. taxing consumption does not cause any dead-weight losses.
   c. the rich consume a higher fraction of income than the poor.
   d. the current tax code discourages people from saving.

Problems and Applications

1. The chapter suggests that the economy, like the human body, has "natural restorative powers."
   a. Illustrate the short-run effect of a fall in aggregate demand using an aggregate-demand/aggregate-supply diagram. What happens to total output, income, and employment?
   b. If the government does not use stabilization policy, what happens to the economy over time? Illustrate this adjustment on your diagram. Does it generally occur in a matter of months or a matter of years?
   c. Do you think the "natural restorative powers" of the economy mean that policymakers should be passive in response to the business cycle?

2. Policymakers who want to stabilize the economy must decide how much to change the money supply, government spending, or taxes. Why is it difficult for policymakers to choose the appropriate strength of their actions?

3. The problem of time inconsistency applies to fiscal policy as well as to monetary policy. Suppose the government announced a reduction in taxes on income from capital investments, like new factories.
   a. If investors believed that capital taxes would remain low, how would the government's action affect the level of investment?
   b. After investors have responded to the announced tax reduction, does the government have an incentive to renege on its policy? Explain.
   c. Given your answer to part (b), would investors believe the government's announcement? What can the government do to increase the credibility of announced policy changes?
   d. Explain why this situation is similar to the time inconsistency problem faced by monetary policymakers.

4. Chapter 2 explains the difference between positive analysis and normative analysis. In the debate about whether the central bank should aim for zero inflation, which areas of disagreement involve positive statements and which involve normative judgments?

5. Why are the benefits of reducing inflation permanent and the costs temporary? Why are the costs of increasing inflation permanent and the benefits temporary? Use Phillips-curve diagrams in your answer.

6. Suppose the federal government cuts taxes and increases spending, raising the budget deficit to 12 percent of GDP. If nominal GDP is rising 5 percent per year, are such budget deficits sustainable forever? Explain. If budget deficits of this size are maintained for 20 years, what is likely to happen to your taxes and your children's taxes in the future? Can you personally do something today to offset this future effect?

7. Explain how each of the following policies redistributes income across generations. Is the redistribution from young to old or from old to young?
   a. an increase in the budget deficit
   b. more generous subsidies for education loans
   c. greater investments in highways and bridges
   d. an increase in Social Security benefits

8. What is the fundamental trade-off that society faces if it chooses to save more? How might the government increase national saving?

Go to CengageBrain.com to purchase access to the proven, critical Study Guide to accompany this text, which features additional notes and context, practice tests, and much more.

Glossary

A

ability-to-pay principle the idea that taxes should be levied on a person according to how well that person can shoulder the burden

absolute advantage the ability to produce a good using fewer inputs than another producer

accounting profit total revenue minus total explicit cost

adverse selection the tendency for the mix of unobserved attributes to become undesirable from the standpoint of an uninformed party

agent a person who is performing an act for another person, called the principal

aggregate-demand curve a curve that shows the quantity of goods and services that households, firms, the government, and customers abroad want to buy at each price level

aggregate-supply curve a curve that shows the quantity of goods and services that firms choose to produce and sell at each price level

appreciation an increase in the value of a currency as measured by the amount of foreign currency it can buy

Arrow's impossibility theorem a mathematical result showing that, under certain assumed conditions, there is no scheme for aggregating individual preferences into a valid set of social preferences

automatic stabilizers changes in fiscal policy that stimulate aggregate demand when the economy goes into a recession without policymakers having to take any deliberate action

average fixed cost fixed cost divided by the quantity of output

average revenue total revenue divided by the quantity sold

average tax rate total taxes paid divided by total income

average total cost total cost divided by the quantity of output

average variable cost variable cost divided by the quantity of output

B

balanced trade a situation in which exports equal imports

bank capital the resources a bank's owners have put into the institution

behavioral economics the subfield of economics that integrates the insights of psychology

benefits principle the idea that people should pay taxes based on the benefits they receive from government services

bond a certificate of indebtedness

budget constraint the limit on the consumption bundles that a consumer can afford

budget deficit a shortfall of tax revenue from government spending

budget surplus an excess of tax revenue over government spending

business cycle fluctuations in economic activity, such as employment and production

C

capital the equipment and structures used to produce goods and services

capital flight a large and sudden reduction in the demand for assets located in a country

capital requirement a government regulation specifying a minimum amount of bank capital

cartel a group of firms acting in unison

catch-up effect the property whereby countries that start off poor tend to grow more rapidly than countries that start off rich

central bank an institution designed to oversee the banking system and regulate the quantity of money in the economy

circular-flow diagram a visual model of the economy that shows how dollars flow through markets among households and firms

classical dichotomy the theoretical separation of nominal and real variables

closed economy an economy that does not interact with other economies in the world

club goods goods that are excludable but not rival in consumption

Coase theorem the proposition that if private parties can bargain without cost over the allocation of resources, they can solve the problem of externalities on their own

collective bargaining the process by which unions and firms agree on the terms of employment

collusion an agreement among firms in a market about quantities to produce or prices to charge

commodity money money that takes the form of a commodity with intrinsic value

common resources goods that are rival in consumption but not excludable

comparative advantage the ability to produce a good at a lower opportunity cost than another producer

compensating differential a difference in wages that arises to offset the nonmonetary characteristics of different jobs

competitive market a market with many buyers and sellers trading identical products so that each buyer and seller is a price taker

complements two goods for which an increase in the price of one leads to a decrease in the demand for the other

compounding the accumulation of a sum of money in, say, a bank account, where the interest earned remains in the account to earn additional interest in the future

Condorcet paradox the failure of majority rule to produce transitive preferences for society

constant returns to scale the property whereby long-run average total cost stays the same as the quantity of output changes

consumer price index (CPI) a measure of the overall cost of the goods and services bought by a typical consumer

consumer surplus the amount a buyer is willing to pay for a good minus the amount the buyer actually pays for it

consumption spending by households on goods and services, with the exception of purchases of new housing

corrective tax a tax designed to induce private decision makers to take account of the social costs that arise from a negative externality

cost the value of everything a seller must give up to produce a good

cost–benefit analysis a study that compares the costs and benefits to society of providing a public good

cross-price elasticity of demand a measure of how much the quantity demanded of one good responds to a change in the price of another good, computed as the percentage change in quantity demanded of the first good divided by the percentage change in price of the second good

crowding out a decrease in investment that results from government borrowing

crowding-out effect the offset in aggregate demand that results when expansionary fiscal policy raises the interest rate and thereby reduces investment spending

currency the paper bills and coins in the hands of the public

cyclical unemployment the deviation of unemployment from its natural rate

D

deadweight loss the fall in total surplus that results from a market distortion, such as a tax

demand curve a graph of the relationship between the price of a good and the quantity demanded

demand deposits balances in bank accounts that depositors can access on demand by writing a check

demand schedule a table that shows the relationship between the price of a good and the quantity demanded

depreciation a decrease in the value of a currency as measured by the amount of foreign currency it can buy

depression a severe recession

diminishing marginal product the property whereby the marginal product of an input declines as the quantity of the input increases

diminishing returns the property whereby the benefit from an extra unit of an input declines as the quantity of the input increases

discount rate the interest rate on the loans that the Fed makes to banks

discouraged workers individuals who would like to work but have given up looking for a job

discrimination the offering of different opportunities to similar individuals who differ only by race, ethnic group, sex, age, or other personal characteristics

diseconomies of scale the property whereby long-run average total cost rises as the quantity of output increases

diversification the reduction of risk achieved by replacing a single risk with a large number of smaller, unrelated risks

dominant strategy a strategy that is best for a player in a game regardless of the strategies chosen by the other players

E

economic profit total revenue minus total cost, including both explicit and implicit costs

economics the study of how society manages its scarce resources

economies of scale the property whereby long-run average total cost falls as the quantity of output increases

efficiency the property of society getting the most it can from its scarce resources

efficiency wages above-equilibrium wages paid by firms to increase worker productivity

efficient markets hypothesis the theory that asset prices reflect all publicly available information about the value of an asset

efficient scale the quantity of output that minimizes average total cost

elasticity a measure of the responsiveness of quantity demanded or quantity supplied to a change in one of its determinants

equality the property of distributing economic prosperity uniformly among the members of society

equilibrium a situation in which the market price has reached the level at which quantity supplied equals quantity demanded

equilibrium price the price that balances quantity supplied and quantity demanded

equilibrium quantity the quantity supplied and the quantity demanded at the equilibrium price

excludability the property of a good whereby a person can be prevented from using it

explicit costs input costs that require an outlay of money by the firm

exports goods produced domestically and sold abroad

externality the uncompensated impact of one person's actions on the well-being of a bystander

F

factors of production the inputs used to produce goods and services

federal funds rate the interest rate at which banks make overnight loans to one another

Federal Reserve (Fed) the central bank of the United States

fiat money money without intrinsic value that is used as money because of government decree

finance the field that studies how people make decisions regarding the allocation of resources over time and the handling of risk

financial intermediaries financial institutions through which savers can indirectly provide funds to borrowers

financial markets financial institutions through which savers can directly provide funds to borrowers

financial system the group of institutions in the economy that help to match one person's saving with another person's investment

firm-specific risk risk that affects only a single company

fiscal policy the setting of the level of government spending and taxation by government policymakers

Fisher effect the one-for-one adjustment of the nominal interest rate to the inflation rate

fixed costs costs that do not vary with the quantity of output produced

fractional-reserve banking a banking system in which banks hold only a fraction of deposits as reserves

free rider a person who receives the benefit of a good but avoids paying for it

frictional unemployment unemployment that results because it takes time for workers to search for the jobs that best suit their tastes and skills

fundamental analysis the study of a company's accounting statements and future prospects to determine its value

future value the amount of money in the future that an amount of money today will yield, given prevailing interest rates

G

game theory the study of how people behave in strategic situations

GDP deflator a measure of the price level calculated as the ratio of nominal GDP to real GDP times 100

Giffen good a good for which an increase in the price raises the quantity demanded

government purchases spending on goods and services by local, state, and federal governments

gross domestic product (GDP) the market value of all final goods and services produced within a country in a given period of time

H

horizontal equity the idea that taxpayers with similar abilities to pay taxes should pay the same amount

human capital the knowledge and skills that workers acquire through education, training, and experience

I

implicit costs input costs that do not require an outlay of money by the firm

imports goods produced abroad and sold domestically

incentive something that induces a person to act

income effect the change in consumption that results when a price change moves the consumer to a higher or lower indifference curve

income elasticity of demand a measure of how much the quantity demanded of a good responds to a change in consumers' income, computed as the percentage change in quantity demanded divided by the percentage change in income

indexation the automatic correction by law or contract of a dollar amount for the effects of inflation

indifference curve a curve that shows consumption bundles that give the consumer the same level of satisfaction

inferior good a good for which, other things being equal, an increase in income leads to a decrease in demand

inflation an increase in the overall level of prices in the economy

inflation rate the percentage change in the price index from the preceding period

inflation tax the revenue the government raises by creating money

informational efficiency the description of asset prices that rationally reflect all available information

in-kind transfers transfers to the poor given in the form of goods and services rather than cash

internalizing the externality altering incentives so that people take account of the external effects of their actions

investment spending on capital equipment, inventories, and structures, including household purchases of new housing

J

job search the process by which workers find appropriate jobs given their tastes and skills

L

labor force the total number of workers, including both the employed and the unemployed

labor-force participation rate the percentage of the adult population that is in the labor force

law of demand the claim that, other things being equal, the quantity demanded of a good falls when the price of the good rises

law of supply the claim that, other things being equal, the quantity supplied of a good rises when the price of the good rises

law of supply and demand the claim that the price of any good adjusts to bring the quantity supplied and the quantity demanded for that good into balance

leverage the use of borrowed money to supplement existing funds for purposes of investment

leverage ratio the ratio of assets to bank capital

liberalism the political philosophy according to which the government should choose policies deemed just, as evaluated by an impartial observer behind a "veil of ignorance"

libertarianism the political philosophy according to which the government should punish crimes and enforce voluntary agreements but not redistribute income

life cycle the regular pattern of income variation over a person's life

liquidity the ease with which an asset can be converted into the economy's medium of exchange

lump-sum tax a tax that is the same amount for every person

M

macroeconomics the study of economy-wide phenomena, including inflation, unemployment, and economic growth

marginal change a small incremental adjustment to a plan of action

marginal cost the increase in total cost that arises from an extra unit of production

marginal product the increase in output that arises from an additional unit of input

marginal product of labor the increase in the amount of output from an additional unit of labor

marginal rate of substitution the rate at which a consumer is willing to trade one good for another

marginal revenue the change in total revenue from an additional unit sold

marginal tax rate the amount that taxes increase from an additional dollar of income

market a group of buyers and sellers of a particular good or service

market economy an economy that allocates resources through the decentralized decisions of many firms and households as they interact in markets for goods and services

market failure a situation in which a market left on its own fails to allocate resources efficiently

market for loanable funds the market in which those who want to save supply funds and those who want to borrow to invest demand funds

market power the ability of a single economic actor (or small group of actors) to have a substantial influence on market prices

market risk risk that affects all companies in the stock market

maximin criterion the claim that the government should aim to maximize the well-being of the worst-off person in society

median voter theorem a mathematical result showing that if voters are choosing a point along a line and each voter wants the point closest to his most preferred point, then majority rule will pick the most preferred point of the median voter

medium of exchange an item that buyers give to sellers when they want to purchase goods and services

menu costs the costs of changing prices

microeconomics the study of how households and firms make decisions and how they interact in markets

model of aggregate demand and aggregate supply the model that most economists use to explain short-run fluctuations in economic activity around its long-run trend

monetary neutrality the proposition that changes in the money supply do not affect real variables

monetary policy the setting of the money supply by policymakers in the central bank

money the set of assets in an economy that people regularly use to buy goods and services from other people

money multiplier the amount of money the banking system generates with each dollar of reserves

money supply the quantity of money available in the economy

monopolistic competition a market structure in which many firms sell products that are similar but not identical

monopoly a firm that is the sole seller of a product without close substitutes

moral hazard the tendency of a person who is imperfectly monitored to engage in dishonest or otherwise undesirable behavior

multiplier effect the additional shifts in aggregate demand that result when expansionary fiscal policy increases income and thereby increases consumer spending

mutual fund an institution that sells shares to the public and uses the proceeds to buy a portfolio of stocks and bonds

N

Nash equilibrium a situation in which economic actors interacting with one another each choose their best strategy given the strategies that all the other actors have chosen

national saving the total income in the economy that remains after paying for consumption and government purchases

natural level of output the production of goods and services that an economy achieves in the long run when unemployment is at its normal rate

natural monopoly a monopoly that arises because a single firm can supply a good or service to an entire market at a smaller cost than could two or more firms

natural rate of unemployment the normal rate of unemployment around which the unemployment rate fluctuates

natural resources the inputs into the production of goods and services that are provided by nature, such as land, rivers, and mineral deposits

natural-rate hypothesis the claim that unemployment eventually returns to its normal, or natural, rate, regardless of the rate of inflation

negative income tax a tax system that collects revenue from high-income households and gives subsidies to low-income households

net capital outflow the purchase of foreign assets by domestic residents minus the purchase of domestic assets by foreigners

net exports spending on domestically produced goods by foreigners (exports) minus spending on foreign goods by domestic residents (imports)

nominal exchange rate the rate at which a person can trade the currency of one country for the currency of another

nominal GDP the production of goods and services valued at current prices

nominal interest rate the interest rate as usually reported without a correction for the effects of inflation

nominal variables variables measured in monetary units

normal good a good for which, other things being equal, an increase in income leads to an increase in demand

normative statements claims that attempt to prescribe how the world should be

O

oligopoly a market structure in which only a few sellers offer similar or identical products

open economy an economy that interacts freely with other economies around the world

open-market operations the purchase and sale of U.S. government bonds by the Fed

opportunity cost whatever must be given up to obtain some item

P

perfect complements two goods with right-angle indifference curves

perfect substitutes two goods with straight-line indifference curves

permanent income a person's normal income

Phillips curve a curve that shows the short-run trade-off between inflation and unemployment

physical capital the stock of equipment and structures that are used to produce goods and services

political economy the study of government using the analytic methods of economics

positive statements claims that attempt to describe the world as it is

poverty line an absolute level of income set by the federal government for each family size below which a family is deemed to be in poverty

poverty rate the percentage of the population whose family income falls below an absolute level called the poverty line

present value the amount of money today that would be needed, using prevailing interest rates, to produce a given future amount of money

price ceiling a legal maximum on the price at which a good can be sold

price discrimination the business practice of selling the same good at different prices to different customers

price elasticity of demand a measure of how much the quantity demanded of a good responds to a change in the price of that good, computed as the percentage change in quantity demanded divided by the percentage change in price

price elasticity of supply a measure of how much the quantity supplied of a good responds to a change in the price of that good, computed as the percentage change in quantity supplied divided by the percentage change in price

price floor a legal minimum on the price at which a good can be sold

principal a person for whom another person, called the agent, is performing some act

prisoners' dilemma a particular "game" between two captured prisoners that illustrates why cooperation is difficult to maintain even when it is mutually beneficial

private goods goods that are both excludable and rival in consumption

private saving the income that households have left after paying for taxes and consumption

producer price index a measure of the cost of a basket of goods and services bought by firms

producer surplus the amount a seller is paid for a good minus the seller's cost of providing it

production function the relationship between quantity of inputs used to make a good and the quantity of output of that good

production possibilities frontier a graph that shows the combinations of output that the economy can possibly produce given the available factors of production and the available production technology

productivity the quantity of goods and services produced from each unit of labor input

profit total revenue minus total cost

progressive tax a tax for which high-income taxpayers pay a larger fraction of their income than do low-income taxpayers

property rights the ability of an individual to own and exercise control over scarce resources

proportional tax a tax for which high-income and low-income taxpayers pay the same fraction of income

public goods goods that are neither excludable nor rival in consumption

public saving the tax revenue that the government has left after paying for its spending

purchasing-power parity a theory of exchange rates whereby a unit of any given currency should be able to buy the same quantity of goods in all countries

Q

quantity demanded the amount of a good that buyers are willing and able to purchase

quantity equation the equation M × V = P × Y, which relates the quantity of money, the velocity of money, and the dollar value of the economy's output of goods and services

quantity supplied the amount of a good that sellers are willing and able to sell

quantity theory of money a theory asserting that the quantity of money available determines the price level and that the growth rate in the quantity of money available determines the inflation rate

R

random walk the path of a variable whose changes are impossible to predict

rational expectations the theory that people optimally use all the information they have, including information about government policies, when forecasting the future

rational people people who systematically and purposefully do the best they can to achieve their objectives

real exchange rate the rate at which a person can trade the goods and services of one country for the goods and services of another

real GDP the production of goods and services valued at constant prices

real interest rate the interest rate corrected for the effects of inflation

real variables variables measured in physical units

recession a period of declining real incomes and rising unemployment

regressive tax a tax for which high-income taxpayers pay a smaller fraction of their income than do low-income taxpayers

reserve ratio the fraction of deposits that banks hold as reserves

reserve requirements regulations on the minimum amount of reserves that banks must hold against deposits

reserves deposits that banks have received but have not loaned out

risk aversion a dislike of uncertainty

rivalry in consumption the property of a good whereby one person's use diminishes other people's use

S

sacrifice ratio the number of percentage points of annual output lost in the process of reducing inflation by 1 percentage point

scarcity the limited nature of society's resources

screening an action taken by an uninformed party to induce an informed party to reveal information

shoe-leather cost the resources wasted when inflation encourages people to reduce their money holdings

shortage a situation in which quantity demanded is greater than quantity supplied

signaling an action taken by an informed party to reveal private information to an uninformed party

social insurance government policy aimed at protecting people against the risk of adverse events

stagflation a period of falling output and rising prices

stock a claim to partial ownership in a firm

store of value an item that people can use to transfer purchasing power from the present to the future

strike the organized withdrawal of labor from a firm by a union

structural unemployment unemployment that results because the number of jobs available in some labor markets is insufficient to provide a job for everyone who wants one

substitutes two goods for which an increase in the price of one leads to an increase in the demand for the other

substitution effect the change in consumption that results when a price change moves the consumer along a given indifference curve to a point with a new marginal rate of substitution

sunk cost a cost that has already been committed and cannot be recovered

supply curve a graph of the relationship between the price of a good and the quantity supplied

supply schedule a table that shows the relationship between the price of a good and the quantity supplied

supply shock an event that directly alters firms' costs and prices, shifting the economy's aggregate supply curve and thus the Phillips curve

surplus a situation in which quantity supplied is greater than quantity demanded

T

tariff tax on goods produced abroad and sold domestically

tax incidence the manner in which the burden of a tax is shared among participants in a market

technological knowledge society's understanding of the best ways to produce goods and services

theory of liquidity preference Keynes's theory that the interest rate adjusts to bring money supply and money demand into balance

total cost the market value of the inputs a firm uses in production

total revenue (for a firm) the amount a firm receives for the sale of its output

total revenue (in a market) the amount paid by buyers and received by sellers of a good, computed as the price of the good times the quantity sold

trade balance the value of a nation's exports minus the value of its imports; also called net exports

trade deficit an excess of imports over exports

trade policy a government policy that directly influences the quantity of goods and services that a country imports or exports

trade surplus an excess of exports over imports

Tragedy of the Commons a parable that illustrates why common resources are used more than is desirable from the standpoint of society as a whole

transaction costs the costs that parties incur in the process of agreeing to and following through on a bargain

U

unemployment insurance a government program that partially protects workers' incomes when they become unemployed

unemployment rate the percentage of the labor force that is unemployed

union a worker association that bargains with employers over wages, benefits, and working conditions

unit of account the yardstick people use to post prices and record debts

utilitarianism the political philosophy according to which the government should choose policies to maximize the total utility of everyone in society

utility a measure of happiness or satisfaction

V

value of the marginal product the marginal product of an input times the price of the output

variable costs costs that vary with the quantity of output produced

velocity of money the rate at which money changes hands

vertical equity the idea that taxpayers with a greater ability to pay taxes should pay larger amounts

W

welfare government programs that supplement the incomes of the needy

welfare economics the study of how the allocation of resources affects economic well-being

willingness to pay the maximum amount that a buyer will pay for a good

world price the price of a good that prevails in the world market for that good

Index

Page numbers in **boldface** refer to pages where key terms are defined.

A

Ability, wages and, 399–400
Ability-to-pay principle, **247**
Absolute advantage, **52**
Absolute value, 91
Accidents, associated with driving, 204
Account, unit of, **611**
Accountants, economists *vs.*, 262
Accounting, 554
Accounting profit, **262**
Acemoglu, Daron, 542–543
Active stabilization policy
  case against, 764
  case for, 761–763
Adjustment process, 638–639
Adverse selection, **464**, 574
Advertising, 338–343
  brand names, 342–343
  critique of, 339–340
  debate over, 339–340
  defense of, 340
  price of eyeglasses and, 340–341
  signaling theory of, 401
  as signal of quality, 341–342
Age, poverty correlated with, 418
Agent, **462**, 462–464
Aggregate demand, 707–708. *See also*
  Aggregate-demand curve; Model of aggregate demand and aggregate supply
  automatic stabilizers, 764–765
  changes in government purchases, 755
  changes in money supply, 751–752
  changes in taxes, 759–760
  crowding-out effect, 758–759
  economic fluctuations of, 707–714
  effects of shift in, 729–733
  fiscal policy and, 755–760
  formula for spending multiplier, 757
  Great Depression, 732–733
  monetary policy and, 746–755
  multiplier effect, 756
  Phillips curve, 771–773
  recession of 2008-2009, 733–736
  stabilization policy, 760–765
  theory of liquidity preference, 747–749
  World War II, 732–733
Aggregate-demand curve, **712**, 714–719. *See also* Aggregate demand; Model of aggregate demand and aggregate supply
  downward slope of, 714–717, 749–751
  exchange-rate effect, 716–717
  interest-rate effect, 715–716
  shifts in, 717–718
  wealth effect, 715
Aggregate supply, **712**, 712–714.
  See also Aggregate-supply curve; Model of aggregate demand and aggregate supply
  adverse shock to, 781
  economic fluctuations of, 707–714
  effects of shift in, 736–738
  fiscal policy and, 760
  oil and the economy, 738–740
  Phillips curve, 771–773
  stagflation, 737
  wage-price spiral, 737
Aggregate-supply curve, **713**, 719–728. *See also* Aggregate supply; Model of aggregate demand and aggregate supply
  menu costs, 725
  misperceptions theory, 726
  natural rate of output, 721
  shifts in, 721–722
  slopes upward in short run, 723–726
  sticky-price theory, 725
  sticky-wage theory, 724–725
  vertical in long run, 719
Airline industry, example of price discrimination, 317
Akerlof, George, 770
Algeria, OPEC as cartel, 356
Allin, Paul, 500
Alm, Richard, 420
American Airlines, 361
American Economic Review, 770, 773
American Indians, 338–339
American Recovery and Reinvestment Act, 799
"Analytics of Anti-Inflation Policy" (Samuelson & Solow), 770
Anarchy, State, and Utopia (Nozick), 423
Animals as common resources, 227
Annuity, 573
Antipoverty programs, 424–427
  benefits principle argument for, 247
  fighting poverty is public good, 220
  in-kind transfers, 426
  minimum-wage laws, 424–425
  negative income tax, 425–426
  welfare, 427
  work incentives and, 427
Antitrust laws
  Clayton Antitrust Act, 319, 360
  controversies over policy, 361–363
  increasing competition with, 319
  Microsoft case, 363–364
  oligopolies and, 361–363
  predatory pricing, 362–363
  resale price maintenance, 361–362
  restraint of trade, 360
  Sherman Antitrust Act, 319, 360
  tying, 363
Appreciation, **671**
Arbitrage, 315, 674
Argentina
  capital flight, 699
  economic growth of, 525
  GDP, 539
  inward-oriented policies of trade, 539
  underground economy in, 498–499
Arms races as prisoners' dilemma, 356–357
Arrow, Kenneth, 469
Arrow's impossibility theorem, **469**
Asset valuation, 576–580
Assumptions, 21–22, 710–711
Asymmetric information, 461, 462–467
  adverse selection, 464
  agents, 462–464
  gifts as signals, 465–466

hidden actions, 462–464
hidden characteristics, 464
lemons problem, 464
moral hazards, 462–464
principals, 462–464
public policy and, 467
screening to uncover private
information, 466
signaling to convey private
information, 465
AT&T, 319
Australia, underground economy in,
498–499
Austria, hyperinflation in, 642
Automatic stabilizers, 764–765
Automobile industry, safety
laws, 7–8
Autor, David, 597
Average cost, 6–7, 267–268
and marginal-cost curves, 269
pricing, deadweight losses
and, 320
Average fixed cost, **268**, 274
Average fixed cost (AFC) curve,
268, 270
Average revenue, **281**, 283, 304, 305
Average tax rate, **245**
Average total cost, **267**, 274
related to marginal cost and, 270
related to short- and long-run,
271–272
U-shaped, 269–270
Average total cost (ATC) curve, 268,
270, 283
Average variable cost, **268**, 274
Average variable cost (AVC) curve,
268, 270

B

Balance budget debate, 808–812
Balanced budget, 561
Balanced trade, **661**
Balance sheet, 618
Bangladesh
economic growth of, 525
GDP and quality of life in, 498
Bank capital, **620**, 620–622
Banks. *See also* Central bank; Euro-
pean Central Bank
bank capital, leverage, and fi-
nancial crisis of 2008-2009,
620–622

Fed lending to, 622–623
as financial intermediaries,
550–551
100-percent-reserve banking,
617–618
money creation with fractional-
reserve banking, 618–619
money multiplier, 619–620
money supply and, 617–622
runs, money supply and, 625
Bar graph, 37
Barro, Robert, 784, 789
Barter, 610
Bartlett, Bruce, 429
Base year, 492
Basket of goods and services, 506–507
Baum, L. Frank, 653
Bauman, Yoram, 208
A Beautiful Mind, (Nash), 351
Beauty premium, 400–401
Behavioral economics, **471**, 471–476
fairness and, 474–475
inconsistency and, 475
rationality and, 471–473
Benefits of beauty, 400–401
Benefits principle, **246**, 246–247
Benevolent social planner, 145
Benham, Lee, 340
Bentham, Jeremy, 421
Bernanke, Ben, 33, 615, 626–627,
700–701, 735, 788, 807
Bertrand, Marianne, 405
Biddle, Jeff, 400–401
Billion Prices Project, 511
Black Death, economics of, 389
Blacks
economics of discrimination,
403–408
poverty and, 418
Blanchard, Olivier, 734–735, 807
Blinder, Alan, 808
Bloomfield, Robert, 33
Bolivia
hyperinflation in, 648
underground economy in,
498–499
Bond, **548**, 549
Bond market, 548–549
Borda count, 469
Botswana, elephants as private
good, 227
Bowles, Erskine B., 250
Brain drain, 536
Brand-name product, 309
Brand names, economics of, 342–343

Braniff Airways, 361
Brazil
economic growth of, 525
GDP and quality of life in, 498
income inequality in, 416
Britain, purchasing-power parity, 678
Broken window fallacy, 14
Budget, 808–812
constraint, **436**, 436–437
Budget deficit, **238**, **555**
crowding out, 562
Federal government and, 238–240
fiscal challenge of, 238–240
life expectancy of elderly and rising
cost of healthcare, 238–240
market for loanable funds and,
561–563
in open economies, 692–694
Budget surplus, **238**, **555**
market for loanable funds and,
561–563
Bureau of Economic Analysis (BEA),
491, 662
definitions of investment and
GDP, 492–493
goal of, 493
Bureau of Labor Statistics (BLS),
586, 593
computing CPI, 506
Bush, George H. W., 429
Bush, George W., 788
appointed Bernanke, 615
government debt under, 564
reduced highest tax rate, 253
tax cuts under, 798
Business cycle, **15**, 708
Business-stealing externality, 337
Buyers
marginal, 137
number of, and shifts in
demand, 71
taxes on, affect market outcomes,
123–125
variables that influence, 71
willingness to pay, 136

C

Cameron, David, 500
Campbell, Doug, 498–499
Canada
economic growth of, 525
income inequality in, 416

NAFTA and, 187
tax burden in, 235
trade and distribution of
income, 184
Capital, **387**
aggregate-supply curve shifts
and, 721
bank, **620**, 620–622
cost of, 261–262
equilibrium in markets for,
387–388
factor of production, 386–389
human, 396–397, 404–405, 527,
530, 536
international flows of, 660–670
physical, **530**
Capital flight, **697**, 697–699
Capital flows from China, 699
Capital income, 388
Capital outflow, net, **664**, 664–665
equality of net exports and,
665–666
link between two markets, 689
in United States, 668–670
Capital requirement, **621**
Capital stock, population growth diluting of, 541–542
Capone, Al, 233
Carbon emissions, 200
Carbon tax, 208–209
Carnegie, Andrew, 453–454
Carney, John, 84
Cartel, **349**, 739. *See also* Organization
of Petroleum Exporting Countries
(OPEC)
markets with only few sellers,
349–350
public price fixing, 350
union as type of, 599–600
Carter, Jimmy, 634, 803
Catch-up effect, 533–535, **534**
Cause and effect, 43–45
Cavallo, Alberto, 511
Central bank, **615**. *See also* European
Central Bank; Federal Reserve
(Fed)
zero inflation debate, 804–808
Centrally planned economies, 10
Chamberlin, Edward, 342
Chance, wages and, 399–400
Charities, private solution to
externalities, 208–209
Chew, Victor, 148
Chile, unilateral approach to free
trade, 187

China
capital flows from, 699
economic growth of, 525
economic growth rate of, 524
GDP and quality of life in, 498
income inequality in, 416
trade and distribution of
income, 185
Chinese renminbi, 701
Choice. *See* Consumer choice;
Optimization
Christie, Chris, 84
Circular-flow diagram, **22**, 22–24, 485
Classical dichotomy, **639**, 639–640
Classical economics, assumptions of,
710–711
Clayton Antitrust Act, 319, 360
Clean Air Act, 207, 209
Clean air and water as common
resource, 226
Climate change, 208–209
Clinton, Bill
government debt and, 564
tax rates raised by, 252
welfare reform bill signed by, 427
Closed economy, 554, **660**
Club goods, **217**, 302
Coase, Ronald, 209
Coase theorem, **209**, 209–210
Collective bargaining, 598–601, **599**
College education, cost of, 398–399
College sports cartel, 365
Collusion, **349**
Combating inequality, reason,
428–429
Combs, Sean (Diddy), 9
Command-and-control policies, 202
Commodity money, **611**
Common resources, 214–215, **216**,
216–217, 223–227
animals as, 227
clean air and water, 226
congested roads, 226
elephants, 227
example of prisoners' dilemma,
357–358
importance of property
rights, 228
as natural monopoly, 302
oceans least regulated, 226
Tragedy of the Commons,
223–225
wildlife as, 226
Communism, collapse in Soviet
Union and Eastern Europe, 10–11

Comparative advantage, 52–58, **53**
absolute advantage, 52, 57
applications of, 55–58
opportunity cost and, 52–53
trade and, 53–54
world price and, 173
Compensating differentials, **396**
wage differences and, 404
Competition, 66–67
with differentiated products,
332–337
gender differences and,
408–409
imperfect, 330
international trade increases, 181
markets and, 66–67, 349–350
monopoly *vs.*, 303–304, 322
perfect, 330
Competitive firms
demand for labor, 374–380
long-run decision to exit or enter
a market, 288
long-run supply curve, 289
marginal-cost curve, 283–285
market supply with entry and
exit, 290–292
market supply with fixed number
of, 290
measuring profit in graph,
288–289
vs. monopoly, 303–304
profit maximization and,
282–289, 375
revenue of, 280–282
shift in demand in short run and
long run, 293
short-run decision to shut down,
285–286
short-run supply curve, 287
sunk costs and, 286–287
supply curve, marginal
cost as, 285
supply decision, 283–285
zero profit and, 292–293
Competitive market, 66, **280**, 280–282
characteristics of, 280
firms in, 279–280
long-run supply curve, 293–295
market supply with entry and
exit, 290–292
market supply with fixed number
of firms, 290
meaning of, 280
revenue of competitive firm,
280–282

shift in demand in short run and long run, 293
supply curve in, 289–295
zero profit and, 292–293
Complements, **70**
cross-price elasticity of demand, 98
perfect, **441**
Compounding, **570**
magic of, 572
rule of 70, 572
Concentration ratio, 330
Condorcet, Marquis de, 467
Condorcet paradox, **468**
Congestion
common resource and, 226
gas tax and, 204
traffic and toll roads, 226
Congestion pricing, 224–225
Congressional Budget Office, 29, 248, 589
Constant returns to scale, **273**, 531
Consumer choice
budget constraint, 436–437
consumer optimal choices, 442–443
deriving demand curve, 448–449
Giffen good, 449
income changes and, 444
income effect, 446–448
indifference curve, 438
inferior good, 444
interest rates and household saving, 454–456
marginal rate of substitution (MRS), 438, 443
normal good, 444
optimization, 442–449
perfect complements, 441
perfect substitutes, 441
preferences, 437–441
price changes and, 445–446
substitution effect, 446–448
theory of, 435–436, 449–456
wages affect labor supply, 450–453
Consumer price index (CPI), **506**, 506–513
Consumer surplus, 136–140, **137**
evaluating market equilibrium, 146–148
lower price raises, 138–139
market efficiency and, 144–150
measure, 139–140
price affects, 140

using demand curve to measure, 137–138, 139
willingness to pay, 136–137
Consumption, **489**
changes in, 717
as component of GDP, 489, 491
gap, 420
rivalry in, 216–217
tax, 243–244
trade expands set of opportunities, 51
Consumption-saving decision, 454
Cooper, Michael, 148
Cooperation
economics of, 353–360
prisoners' dilemma, 353–355
Coordinate system, 38–41
Coordination problems, 273
Copyright laws, 299–302
Core inflation, 511
Corporate income tax, 241, 250–251
Corporate management, 463
Corporation, 236
principal-agent problem, 463
Corrective taxes, **203**, 203–207
Correlation, positive and negative, 38–39
Costanza, George, 149
Cost-benefit analysis, **221**, 221–223
Cost curves
and their shapes, 268–270
typical, 270–271
Cost of living
allowance (COLA), 514
consumer price index, 506
measuring, 505–506, 509–512
Cost of reducing inflation, 782–789
costless disinflation, possibility of, 784–785
Greenspan era, 787–788
rational expectations, 784–785
recession of 2008–2009, 788–789
sacrifice ratio, 783–784
Volcker disinflation, 785–786
Cost(s), **141**, 260–262
average fixed, **268**, 274
average total, **267**, 271–272, 274, 290
average variable, **268**, 274
budget deficit and healthcare, 239
of capital, 261–262
economic profit *vs.* accounting profit, 262
economies of scale and, 180–182
explicit, **261**, 274
fixed, **266**, 266–267, 274

implicit, 261, 274
inconvenience, inflation and, 650–651
of inflation, 646–653
marginal. *See* Marginal cost
menu, **648**, 725
opportunity. *See* Opportunity cost
of possible sellers, 141
production and, 263–265
shoeleather, **647**, 647–648
in short run and long run, 271–273
social, 198–199, 313
sunk, 285, **286**, 286–287
of taxation, 155–156
total, **260**, 263, 274
transaction, **212**
variable, 266–267, **267**, 274
various measures of, 265–271
welfare, 310–313
Council of Economic Advisers, 29
Countries (OPEC)
application of supply, demand, and elasticity, 104–105
failure to keep price of oil high, 104–105
increase in price of crude oil, 114–115
Cowen, Tyler, 712–713
Cox, Michael, 420
CPI. *See* Consumer price index
Crandall, Robert, 361
Credit cards, money and, 614
Credit crunch, 622
Credit risk, bonds, 549
Cross-price elasticity of demand, **98**
Crowding out, **562**
Crowding-out effect, 758–759
Currency, **613**, 615
Current Population Survey, 586–587
Curves, 39–41
movements along, 40–41
shifts of, 40–41
slope of, 41–43
Customers, discrimination by, 406–407
Cyclical unemployment, 586, **589**

D

Dairy industry, 280–282
Date of maturity, bonds, 549
Deadweight loss, **159**, 160
changes in welfare, 159
debate, 162–163

determinants of, 160–163
elasticity and, 160–163
gains from trade and, 159–160
monopoly and, 311–313
tariffs and, 178
of taxation, 156–160, 234, 243
tax effects on market participants, 157–159
tax revenue and, 163–165
triangle, 312–313
Deaton, Angus, 501
DeBeers, 301
Debt finance, 549–550
Debt(s)
    dealing with, 808–812
    dollar-denominated, 805
    government, 561, 563–564, 806, 808–812
Default, bonds, 549
Deficits
    budget. *See* Budget deficit
    dealing with, 808–812
    trade, **661**, 668–670
    twin, 694
Deflation, 634, 652, **783**
    measuring a nation's income, 483–484
Defoe, Daniel, 527
Demand, 67–73. *See also* Aggregate demand; Model of aggregate demand and aggregate supply
    applications of, 101–107
    change in, 79, 81
    decrease in, 69
    disentangling supply and, 692
    elastic, 90, 92, 97–98
    elasticity of. *See* Demand elasticity
    equilibrium of supply and, 77–79
    excess, 78
    expectations and, 70–71
    income changes, 69–70
    increase in, 69, 80, 294
    individual, 68–69
    inelastic, 90, 92
    for labor, 374–380
    law of, 67, 79, 449
    market, 68–69
    market forces of supply and, 65
    number of buyers and, 71
    perfectly elastic, 94
    perfectly inelastic, 92
    price elasticity of, 93
    prices of related goods and, 70
    reducing smoking, 71–73

relationship between price and quantity demanded, 67–68
supply and, 77–83, 111–112, 375
tastes and, 70
Demand curve(s), 39–40, 67–68, **68**. *See also* Aggregate-demand curve
    demand schedule and, 138
    deriving, 448–449
    difference between competitive firm and monopoly, 303–304
    elasticity of linear, 97
    measuring consumer surplus with, 137–138, 139
    for monopoly, 304, 306
    price elasticity of demand and, 91, 93
    shifts in, 40–41, 69–73
    shifts in *vs.* movements along, 72
    slope of, 449
    variety of, 92–94
Demand deposits, **613**
Demand elasticity, 90–98
    cross-price elasticity of, 98
    income, 97–98
    price, 90–91
Demand schedule, **67**
    demand curve and, 68, 138
    for water, 348–349
Denhart, Christopher, 597
Dennie, Christian, 365
Department of Justice, antitrust laws, 319
Department of Labor, 506, 586, 599
Depreciation, 489, **671**
Derived demand, 374
Diamond, Jared, 542
Diamond, Peter, 166
Diminishing marginal product, **265**, **376**
Diminishing marginal utility, 421, 443
Diminishing returns, **533**, 533–535
Discount coupons, 317
Discounting, 318, 571
Discount rate, **623**
Discount window, 623
Discouraged workers, **591**
Discrimination, **403**
    by customers and governments, 406–407
    earnings and, 395–396
    economics of, 403–408
    by employers, 405–406
    in labor market, 405
    measuring labor-market discrimination, 403–405
    price, 314–318

profit motive and, 406
in sports, 407–408
Diseconomies of scale, 272–273, **273**
Disinflation, **783**
    costless, 786
    defined, 783
    rational expectations and possibility of costless, 784–785
    Volcker, 785–786
Disposable personal income, 489
Distribution
    of income in U.S., 415
    neoclassical theory of, 390
Diversification, **574**, 574–575
Dividend, 551
Dollar, exchange rate for, 700–701
Dominant strategy, **354**
Double coincidence of wants, 610
Dow Jones Industrial Average, 550
Downs, Anthony, 224
Drug interdiction, applications of supply, demand, and elasticity, 105–107
Duopoly, 348–349

E

Earned Income Tax Credit (EITC), 121, 426, 427
Easterlin, Richard, 500
Economica, 770
Economic fluctuations
    causes of, 728–740
    effects of shift in aggregate demand, 728–740
    effects of shift in aggregate supply, 736–738
    facts about, 710–714
    irregular and unpredictable, 708
    as output falls, unemployment rises, 711–712
    short-run, 712–714
Economic growth
    aggregate demand and aggregate supply to depict long-run, 722
    around world, 524–526
    diminishing returns and catch-up effect, 533–535
    education and, 536
    experiences, variety of, 525
    free trade and, 539
    health and nutrition, 536–537
    importance of long-run growth, 544
    investment from abroad, 535

natural resources as limit to, 532
population growth and, 540–544
production possibilities frontier and, 24–26
productivity and, 526–532
property rights and political stability, 537–539
public policy and, 532–544
research and development, 540
saving and investment, 533
Economic mobility, 420–421
Economic models, 22–26
Economic profit, **262**
Economic Report of the President, 29
Economics, **4**. *See also* Welfare economics
behavioral, **471**, 471–476
of Black Death, 389
of brand names, 342–343
of cooperation, 353–360
of discrimination, 403–408
of immigration, 384–385
within a marriage, 56–57
reasons for studying, 14
supply-side, and Laffer curve, 164–165
ten principles of, 4
of unions, 599–600
Economic variables, 513–517
Economic welfare
price discrimination and, 315
total surplus and, 145
Economies of scale, 272–273, **273**
as causes of monopoly, 302
lower costs through, 180–182
specialization and, 273
Economists
vs. accountants, 262
disagreement among, 30–31
as policy adviser, 27–30
propositions which most agree about, 32
as scientist, 20–27
thinking like, 19–20
and virtual realities, 33
in Washington, 28–29
Economy
centrally planned, 10
closed, 554, **660**
financial crisis, 734–735
increasing openness of U.S., 661–664
interest rates in U.S., 517
labor-force participation of men and women in U.S., 589–590

market, 10–11
money in U.S., 613–614, 615
oil and shifts in aggregate supply, 738–740
open, 554, **660**
parable for modern, 48–52
political, 462, **467**, 467–471
underground, 163, 498–499
unions, good or bad for, 600–601
U.S. deep economic downturn, 15
using policy to stabilize, 760–765, 796–798
Ecuador, OPEC as cartel, 356
Education
alternative view of, 401
cost of college, 5–6
economic growth and, 536
as positive externality, 199–200, 536
public policy and, 536
signaling theory of, 401
social optimum and, 200–201
state and local spending for, 241
type of human capital, 397
wages and, 397
Efficiency, **5**, **145**, 242–246
of equilibrium quantity, 147
government intervention and, 11–12
informational, **578**
lump-sum taxes, 245–246
marginal tax rates *vs.* average tax rates, 245
market. *See* Market efficiency
monopoly and, 311–313
production possibilities frontier and, 24
total surplus and, 145
trade-off between equity and, 252–253
Efficiency wages, **403**, **601**, 601–603
Efficiency-wage theories, 463
Efficient markets hypothesis, **577**, 577–578
Efficient scale, **270**, 291, 336
Effort, wages and, 399–400, 603
Einstein, Albert, 20
Elasticity, **90**, 166
along a linear demand curve, 96–97
applications of, 89–107
deadweight loss and, 160–163
of demand. *See* Demand elasticity

income elasticity of demand, 97–98
real world, 94
of supply, 98–101
tax incidence and, 126–128
Elephants, common resource, 227
Emmert, Mark, 365
Employers, discrimination by, 405–406
Employment. *See also* Jobs
moral hazard, 462–464
Employment gap, 398
"End of Four Big Inflations, The" (Sargent), 785
Entry/exit into market
firm's long-run decision to, 288
free, 331
long run market supply with, 290–292
monopoly, 300–303
Environmental Protection Agency (EPA), 203
Environmental regulations, 202
Equality, **5**, **146**
government intervention and, 12
of net exports and net capital outflow, 665–666
Equilibrium, **77**, 77–79
analyzing changes in, 79–83
for an oligopoly, 351–352
consumer and producer surplus in market, 146
decrease in supply affects, 81
increase in demand affects, 80
in labor market, 381–386
long-run, 332–335, 729
in markets for land and capital, 387–388
markets not in, 78
monetary, 635–636
in money market, 748, 749
Nash, 351
in open economy, 689–691
of supply and demand, 77–78
without international trade, 172–173
zero-profit, 292–293
Equilibrium interest rate, 749
Equilibrium price, **77**
Equilibrium quantity, **77**, 147
Equilibrium wages, 396–403
Equity
horizontal, 247, 249
tax, 249–251

taxes and, 246–251
trade-off between efficiency and, 252–253
vertical, **247**
Equity finance, 549–550
Essay on the Principle of Population as It Affects the Future Improvement of Society (Malthus), 540
Euro, 671
purchasing-power parity, 678
European Central Bank (ECB), 671
Evenett, Simon, 181
Eve Online, 33
Excess capacity, 335–336
Excess reserves, 618
Excess supply and demand, 77–78
Exchange-rate effect, 716–717, 746
Exchange rates, 670–678
Excise taxes, 237
Excludability, **216**, 216–217
Expectations
of free trade, 183
rational, 784–785
role of, 773–780
shift in Phillips curve, 773–782
shifts in demand curve, 70–71
shifts in supply curve, 76
Expected inflation, 776–778
short-run Phillips curve and, 778
Expenditures, nation's overall economy and, 484–486
Explicit costs, **261**, 274
Exports, **57**, **660**. *See also* International trade
gains and losses from exporting country, 174–175
net, **490**, 490–491, **660**
Externalities, **12**, 150, 195–**196**, 536
carbon tax, 208–209
Coase theorem, 209–210
command-and-control policies, 202
corrective taxes and subsidies, 203–205
of country living, 200
education as, 199
gas tax and, 204–205
internalizing, 199
market inefficiency and, 197–202
negative, 196, 198–199
positive, 196, 199–202
private solutions to, 208–211
public policies toward, 202–207
technology spillovers, 201–202
tradable pollution permits, 205–207
transaction costs, 211

F

Factors of production, 22–24, **374**, 527
competitive profit-maximizing firm, 375
demand for labor, 374–380
equilibrium in labor market, 381–386
land and capital, 386–389
linkages among, 388–389
markets for, 22–24, 373–390
production function and marginal product of labor, 375–376
shifting labor-demand curve, 378–380
supply of labor, 380–381
value of marginal product, 377–378
Fair Labor Standards Act of 1938, 117
Fairness, behavioral economics and, 474–475
Family tax liability, 236
Farming, applications of supply, demand, and elasticity, 102–104
Federal Deposit Insurance Corporation (FDIC), 625
Federal funds rate, **628**, 753–754
Federal government
budget deficit, 238–240
financial overview of, 234–241
receipts of, 235–237
spending, 237–240
Federal income tax rates (2013), 236
Federal Open Market Committee (FOMC), 616, 626–627, 745, 753–754, 761, 798–799, 802
Federal Reserve (Fed), 29, **615**
cost of reducing inflation, 782–783, 785, 787–789
exit strategy, 626–627
federal funds rate, 628
FOM, 616
Greenspan era, 787–788
lending to banks, 623
monetary policy and, 802–804
organization of, 615–616
Phillips curve during financial crisis, 788–789
problems in controlling money supply, 624–625
quantity of reserves, 622–623
rational expectations and disinflation, 784–785

reserve ratio, 623–624
role of interest-rate target in, 753–755
sacrifice ratio, 783–784
stock market and, 754–755
system, 615–617
tools of monetary control, 622–628
Volcker disinflation, 785–786
zero inflation debate, 805, 808
Federal tax burden, 248
Fiat money, **612**
FICA (Federal Insurance Contributions Act), 125
Final good, GDP includes value of, 487
Finance, 569–570, **570**
Financial aid, 317
Financial intermediaries, **550**, 550–552
banks, 550–552
mutual funds, 551–552
Financial resources, flow of, 664–665
Financial system, 547–548, **548**
Firms. *See also* Competitive firms
in circular-flow diagram, 22–24
marginal, 295
market supply with fixed number of, 290
as a natural monopoly, 302–303
profit-maximizing, 375
Firm-specific risk, 574–575, **575**
Fiscal challenge, 238–240
Fiscal cliff approaches, 167
Fiscal policy, **746**. *See also* Government spending
aggregate demand and, 755–760
aggregate supply and, 760
automatic stabilizers, 764–765
changes in government purchases, 755
changes in taxes, 759–760
crowding-out effect, 758–759
multiplier effect, 756
spending multiplier, formula for, 757
stabilization, 760–765, 796–798
Fisher, Irving, 645
Fisher effect, 644–646, **645**
Fixed costs, **266**, 266–267, 274
$5-a-day wage, 603
average, **268**, 274
Flypaper theory of tax incidence, 249–251
Fogel, Robert, 536–537

FOMC. *See* Federal Open Market Committee
Food aid, 538
Food Stamp program, 220, 426, 427
Food stamps, 596
Ford, Gerald, 14
Ford, Henry, 603
Ford Motor Company, 271–272
Foreclosures, 734–735
Foreign-currency exchange, 684–689
Foreign investment
    direct, 535, 664
    economic growth and, 535
    portfolio, 535, 664
Foundations of Economic Analysis (Samuelson), 476
Foundations of Neuroeconomic Analysis (Glimcher), 476
401(k), 813
403(b), 813
Fractional-reserve banking, **618**, 618–619
France
    tax burden in, 235
    tax rate and labor taxes, 166
Franklin, Ben, 233
Free rider, **218**
Free-silver debate, 652–653
Free To Be You and Me style, 56
Free trade, 171–188, 539
Frictional unemployment, **593**, 594
Friedman, Milton, 634, 637, 652, 773–780, 784
Full-employment output, 721
Full-reserve banking, 33
Fundamental analysis, **577**
Future value, **570**

G

G20 group of economies, 762
Gabon, OPEC as cartel, 356
Gains from trade
    comparative advantage, 52–58
    deadweight losses and, 159–160
    of exporting country, 174–175
    of importing country, 175–177
    production possibilities, 48–50
    specialization, 50–51
Gale, William, 429
Game theory, 347–359, **348**
Gasoline prices, incentive effects of, 8–9

Gasoline tax
    benefits principle and, 246–247
    as corrective tax, 203–205
    road congestion and, 204–205
Gates, Bill, 166, 167, 363–364
GDP. *See* Gross domestic product
GDP deflator, **494**, 494–495
    computing inflation rate, 495
    vs. consumer price index, 512–513
Gender. *See also* Women
    differences, 408–409
General Agreement on Tariffs and Trade (GATT), 187, 664
General Theory of Employment, Interest and Money, The (Keynes), 739, 747, 761, 798
Germany
    average income in, 523
    economic growth of, 525
    GDP and quality of life in, 498
    hyperinflation in, 642
    hyperinflation of early 1920s, 676
    income inequality in, 416
    inflation in, 14
    purchasing-power parity and, 673–678
    tax burden in, 235
    tax rate and labor taxes, 166
Giffen, Robert, 449
Giffen good, **449**, 450
Gifts as signals, 465–466
Gilbert, Daniel, 713
Glaeser, Edward L., 200–201
Glimcher, Paul, 476–477
Global Trade Alert, 181
Gold standard, 611
Goldstein, Jacob, 612
Gone with the Wind, 515
Good(s), 70
    club, **217**, 302
    complements, **70**
    CPI basket of, 506–510
    currently produced, GDP includes, 487
    different kinds of, 216–217
    excludability of, 216–217
    final, 487
    Giffen, **449**, 450
    inferior, **70**, 98, **444**, 445
    intermediate, 487
    international flows of, 660–670
    international trade increases variety of, 180
    marginal utility of, 443
    markets for, 22–24

    normal, **70**, 98, **444**
    private, **216**, 216–217
    public, 215–217, **216**, 218–223
    related, 70
    rivalry in consumption, 216–217
    substitutes, **70**
    tangible, 487
    types of, 217
Google, 300, 510–511
Google Price Index, 511
Goolsbee, Austan, 662–663
Government. *See also* Federal government
    balance budget debate, 808–812
    benefits of, 11–12
    budget deficits, 561–563, 692–694
    debate over spending hikes, 798–801
    discrimination by, 406–407
    regulation, 301
    revenue as percentage of GDP, 234
    tax revenue as percentage of GDP, 235
Government-created monopolies, 301–302
Government debt, 561
    crowding out, 562
    history of U.S., 563–564
Government policies
    price control and, 112–121
    supply, demand, and, 111–112
    taxes and, 121–128
Government purchases, **490**
    aggregate-demand curve shifts due to changes in, 718
    changes in, 755
    as component of GDP, 490, 491
Government spending. *See also* Fiscal policy
    three kinds of, 800
Graham, Carol, 500
Graphs, 37–45
    cause and effect, 43–45
    curves in, 39–41
    measuring profit in, 288–289
    of single variable, 37–38
    slope of, 41–43
    of two variables, 38–39
Great Britain
    caloric consumption and height of population, 536
    unilateral approach to free trade, 187

Great Depression, 797, 798, 800, 805
    bank runs during, 625
    shift in aggregate demand, 732–733
Great Moderation, 580
Great Recession, 398
Greenspan, Alan, 244, 579, 787–788
Greenspan era, 787–788
Greenstone, Michael, 398
Gross domestic product (GDP),
    483–484, **486**, 535
    beyond, 500–501
    components of, 488–491
    consumption, 489
    as economy's income and
        expenditure, 484–486
    exclusions from, 496–500
    GDP deflator, 494–495
    government purchases, 490
    government revenue as
        percentage of, 234
    government tax revenue as
        percentage of, 235
    investment, 489–490
    Lady Gaga's songs contribution
        to, 492–493
    measurement of, 486–488
    as measure of economic
        well-being, 496–500
    net exports, 490–491
    nominal. *See* Nominal GDP
    per capital, 491
    quality of life and, 398
    real growth in U.S. since 1900, 732
    underground economy and,
        498–499
Gross national product (GNP), 489, 535
Growth, production an, 523–524
Gucht, Karel De, 181
Guðmundsson, Eyjólfur, 33
"Guns and butter" tradeoff, 5

H

Hamermesh, Daniel, 4400–401
Hamilton Project, 398–399
Hard Heads, Soft Hearts (Blinder), 808
Health
    economic growth and, 536–537
    efficiency wages and, 601–602
    federal spending and, 237–238
Healthcare
    costs, budget deficit and, 239–240
    Obama's healthcare reform bill, 249
Health insurance, 573–574

Hilsenrath, Jon, 807
Hispanics, poverty and, 418
Holmes, Oliver Wendell, Jr., 155
Homo economics, 471
Homo sapiens, 472
Hong Kong, trade and distribution of
    income, 185
Hoover, Herbert, 505, 514
Horizontal equity, **247**, 249
Households
    in circular-flow diagram, 22–24
    decisions faced by, 3
    interest rates affect savings of,
        454–456
Housing
    in basket of goods of CPI, 508
    recession of 2008-2009 and,
        733–736
    rent control, 115–116
Huga, Katherine, 120
Human capital, 396–397, **397**, 527,
    530, 536
    economic growth and, 532–544
    education as, 397, 536
    health and nutrition as invest-
        ment in, 536–537
    per worker, 530
    role of, 404–405
Human-capital theory, 401
Human life, value of, 222–223
Human organs, market for, 148–150
Hume, David, 634, 639–640
Hungary, hyperinflation in, 642
Hyperinflation, 634
    in Bolivia, 648
    in Germany, 676
    money and prices during, 642
    nominal exchange rate during,
        676–677
    in Zimbabwe, 644

I

Imasogie, Osagie, 492
Immigration, 381
Imperfect competition, 330
Implicit costs, **261**, 274
Import quota, 31, 694
    compared to tariff, 179
    effects of, 695
Imports, **57**, **660**. *See also* International
    trade
    gains and losses of importing
        country, 175–177

Incentives, **7**, 7–9
    brand name quality, 342–343
    investment, 580
    savings, 558–560
    work, 427
Income
    capital, 388
    changes in affect consumer's
        choices, 444
    disposable personal, 489
    economic life cycle, 419
    effect, **446**, 446–448
    increase in, 444
    in-kind transfers as, 419
    measuring a nation's, 483–484
    national, 489
    nation's overall economy and,
        484–486
    other measures of, 489
    permanent, 419
    personal, 489
    political philosophy of redistrib-
        uting, 421–424
    shifts in demand and, 70
    transitory *vs.* permanent, 419
    U.S. distribution of, 414–416
Income effect, **446**, 446–448, **814**
    on labor supply, 453–454
Income elasticity of demand, **97**,
    97–98
Income inequality
    alternative measures of, 420
    around world, 416–417
    economic mobility, 420–421
    measurement of, 414–421
    poverty and, 413–414, 417
    in U.S., 414–416
Income redistribution, international
    differences in, 428–429
Income tax, 243
    corporate, 241, 250–251
    individual, 241
    negative, **425**, 425–426
Indexation, **514**, 514–515
Index funds, 552, 578–579
India
    average income in, 523
    economic growth of, 525
    GDP and quality of life in, 498
    income inequality in, 416
Indifference curve(s), **438**
    extreme examples of, 440–441
    four properties of, 439–440
    income effect, 446–448
    perfect complements, 411

834   INDEX

perfect substitutes, 411
preferences, 438–439
substitution effect, 446–448
Individual demand, 68–69
Individual income tax, 241
Individual retirement account
    (IRA), 813
Individual supply vs. market supply,
    74–75
Indonesia
    average income in, 523
    capital flight, 699
    economic growth of, 525
    GDP and quality of life in, 498
    OPEC as cartel, 356
    purchasing-power parity, 678
Industrial organization, 260
Industrial policy, 201–202
Inefficiency
    externalities and, 197–200
    of monopoly, 312–313
Inelastic demand, 90, 92
Inelastic supply, 98
Inequality
    alternative measures of, 420
    around world, 416–417
Infant-industry argument for trade
    restrictions, 185–186
Inferior good, **70**, **444**, 445
    income elasticity of demand
        and, 98
Inflation, **14**, 495, 506, 737
    arbitrary redistributions of
        wealth, 651–652
    brief look at adjustment process,
        638–639
    classical dichotomy and
        monetary neutrality, 639–640
    confusion and inconvenience,
        650–651
    core inflation, 511
    correcting economic variables for
        effect of, 513–517
    cost of reducing, 782–789
    costs of, 646–653
    effects of a monetary
        injection, 637
    effects of on box office
        receipts, 515
    expected, 776–778
    fall in purchasing power, 647
    Fisher effect, 644–646
    inflation-induced tax distortions,
        649–650
    inflation tax, 642–644

level of prices and value of
    money, 635
low-inflation doctrine, 807
measures of, 513
measuring a nation's income,
    483–484
menu costs, 648
money growth and, 633–634
money supply and, 15
money supply money demand,
    and monetary equilibrium,
    635–636
monitoring inflation in internet
    age, 510–511
online-based measures, 511
raises tax burden on saving, 650
relative-price variability and
    misallocation of resources,
    648–649
shoeleather costs, 647–648
short-run-trade-off between
    unemployment and, 15,
    773–792
six costs of, 805
special cost of unexpected,
    651–652
theory of, 634–646
velocity and quantity equation,
    640–642
zero, 804–808
Inflation fallacy, 647
Inflation-induced tax distortions,
    649–650
Inflation rate, 495, 506, **508**
    calculating of, 507
    high, 510–511
    nominal interest rate and, 646
    optimal, 807
Inflation targeting, 804
Inflation tax, 642–644, **643**
Information, asymmetry. See Asym-
    metric information
Informational efficiency, **578**
Information asymmetry, 462
In-kind transfers, **419**
    policies to reduce poverty, 426
    problems in measuring inequal-
        ity, 418–419
Input demand and output
    supply, 379
Input prices and supply, 75–76
An Inquiry into the Nature and Causes
    of the Wealth of Nations (Smith), 10,
    55, 273
Insolvency, 621

Insurance
    adverse selection, 464, 574
    health, 573–574
    market for, 573–574
    moral hazard, 464, 574
    social. See Social insurance taxes
    unemployment, **595**
Intangible services, GDP
    includes, 487
Intellectual property products,
    492–493
Interest-rate effect, 746
    aggregate-demand curve,
        715–716
Interest rate(s)
    affect household saving, 459–461,
        454–456
    equilibrium, 749
    federal funds rate, **628**, 753–754
    increase in, 455–456
    in long run and short run, 750
    nominal, 515–517, **516**, 645, 747
    real, 515–517, **516**, 645, 747
    subprime borrowers, 733–736
    supply and demand for loanable
        funds, 557–558
    targets in Fed policy, role of,
        753–755
    theory of liquidity preference,
        747–749
    in U.S. economy, 517
Intermediate good, 487
Internalizing the externality, **199**
International Monetary Fund,
    734–735
International trade, 171–188
    analysis of oligopoly and, 353
    benefits of, 180–182
    comparative advantage, 173
    determinants of, 172–173
    effects of tariffs, 177–179
    equilibrium without, 172–173
    gains and losses of exporting
        country, 174–175
    gains and losses of importing
        country, 175–177
    import quota compared to
        tariff, 179
    lessons for policy of, 179–180
    multilateral approach to free
        trade, 187
    outsourcing and, 184–185
    relative demand for skilled and
        unskilled labor and, 397–398
    restriction of, 179

of United States, 57–58
winners and losers from,
174–182
world price, 173
International transactions, prices for,
670–673
Internet
and inflation, 510–511
shopping through, 510–511
Intrinsic value, 611
Intuit, 319
Inventory, GDP and, 490
Investment, **489**, 489–490, 555–556,
563–564
accelerator, 756
aggregate-demand curve shifts
due to changes in, 717–718
as component of GDP, 489–490
demand for loanable funds and,
557–558
economic growth and, 533, 535
foreign, 535, 664
higher education as, 398–399
incentives, 560–561
in people, 397
price level and, aggregate-demand curve downward slope,
715–716
saving, and their relationship to
international flows, 666–667
tax credit, 560
U.S. trade deficit and, 668–670
Invisible hand, 10–12, 14, 148–149, 499
Inward-oriented policies, 539
IRA. *See* Individual retirement
account (IRA)
Iran, OPEC as cartel, 356
Iraq, OPEC as cartel, 356
Israel, shifts in labor supply and,
382–383
Italy, purchasing-power parity and,
673–678

J

Japan
average income in, 523
economic growth of, 525
GDP and quality of life in, 498
income inequality in, 416
inflation rate, 634
purchasing-power parity and,
674–676, 678
tax rate, 167

trade and distribution of
income, 184
underground economy in,
498–499
work hours, 167
Jensen, Robert, 450
Jobs
argument for trade restrictions,
182–183
characteristics of, 396–403
number, 593
Jobs, Steve, 167
Job search, **593**, 593–595
public policy and, 594–595
some frictional unemployment is
inevitable, 594
Jones, Charles, 500
Junk bonds, 549

K

Kahn, Mathew, 200
Kasman, Bruce, 807
Kennedy, John F., 417, 762–763
Kennedy, Robert, 496
Kenya, elephant poaching, 227
Kestenbaum, David, 612
Keynes, John Maynard, 29, 34, 477,
739, 747, 761–762, 798
Keynesians in White House, 762–763
Klenow, Peter, 500
Kobylarz, Thaddeus J., 492
Kremer, Michael, 552
Krugman, Paul, 184–185
Kumar, Sanat, 612–613
Kuwait, 356, 738–740

L

Labor
aggregate-supply curve shifts
and, 721
alternative measures of
underutilization, 591
demand for, 374–380
international trade and demand
for skilled and unskilled,
397–398
jobs argument for trade
restrictions, 182–183
marginal product of,
375–376, 379
supply of, 380–381

taxes on, 162–163
technology and demand for
skilled and unskilled, 397
Labor demand
minimum wage and, 119
shifts in, 383–384
Labor force, **587**
Labor-force participation rate, **587**
Labor market
adverse selection, 464
discrimination, measuring,
403–405
equilibrium in, 381–386
minimum wage effects on, 118
racial discrimination in, 405
Labor supply
income effects on, 453–454
shifts in, 381–383
wages and, 450–453
Labor tax, deadweight loss of, 162–163
Lady Gaga, songs contribution to
GDP, 492–493
Laffer, Arthur, 164–165, 208
Laffer curve, 164–165
Lahart, Justin, 538
Laissez faire, 147
Lamy, Pascal, 181
Land
equilibrium in markets for,
387–388
factor of production, 386–389
Landsburg, Steven E., 183
Law of demand, **67**, 449
Law of one price, 674
Law of supply, **73**
Law of supply and demand, **79**
Learning by doing, 57
Left-digit bias, 473–474
Lender of last resort, 616
Leverage, 620–622, **621**
Leverage ratio, **621**
Liberalism, **422**, 422–423
Libertarianism, **423**, 423–424
Libya, OPEC as cartel, 356
Life cycle, **419**
Lighthouses as public goods, 221
Lin, Jeremy, 662, 663
Lindert, Peter, 428
Lindsay, Alistair, 350
Liquidity, **611**
of asset, 749
of money, 749
theory of liquidity preference,
747–749
trap, 753

Loanable funds
> market for, 556–565, 684–686
> supply and demand for, 557–558, 684–689

Local government, 240–241
> receipts for, 240–241
> spendings for, 241

Logic of self-interest, 351

Long run
> aggregate-supply curve, 719–723, 731–734
> costs in, 271–273
> decision to exit or enter a market, 288
> disinflationary monetary policy in, 783
> equilibrium, 332–335, 729
> interest rates in, 750
> market supply, 290–292
> Phillips curve, 773–775
> rent control, 115–116
> shift in demand, 293
> supply curve, 293–295

Looney, Adam, 398

Losses. *See also* Deadweight loss
> of exporting country, 174–175
> of importing country, 175–177

Lowrey, Annie, 510

Lucas, Robert, 784, 789

Lump-sum tax, **245**, 245–246

Luxuries
> income elasticity of demand and, 98
> price elasticity of demand and, 90

Luxury tax, 128

M

Macroeconomics, **27**, **484**
> analyzing fluctuations of, 729
> quantities fluctuate together in, 710
> six debates over policy for, 795–816
> theory of open economy for, 683–684

Macroeconomic well-being, measuring, 500–501

Malawi, elephants as private good, 227

Mali, poor country, 528–529

Malmendier, Ulrike, 713

Malthus, Thomas Robert, 540–541

Mankiw, N. Gregory, 208, 250

Margin, 6

Marginal benefits, 6

Marginal buyer, 137

Marginal change, **6**

Marginal cost (MC), 6–7, 267–268, **268**, 274, 379
> markup over, monopolistic *vs.* perfect competition, 336
> pricing as regulatory system, 320
> pricing for natural monopoly, 320
> related to average total cost, 270
> related to price, 336
> rising, 268–269

Marginal cost (MC) curve, 268, 270, 283
> and average-cost curves, 269
> firm's supply decision and, 283–285

Marginal firm, 295

Marginal product, **264**
> demand for labor and value of, 377–378
> diminishing, 265, 376

Marginal product of labor (MPL), **376**, 379
> production function and, 375–376
> value of, 378

Marginal propensity to consume (MPC), 757
> defined, 757

Marginal rate of substitution (MRS), **438**, 443

Marginal revenue (MR), **282**, 283
> for competitive firm, 281
> curve for monopoly, 306
> monopoly, 304, 305

Marginal seller, 142

Marginal tax rate, 162, 236, **245**

Marginal utility
> diminishing, 421, 443
> of goods, 443

Market demand, 68–69

Market economy, **10**, 10–11

Market efficiency, 144–151

Market equilibrium, evaluating, 146–150

Market failure, **12**, 150–151, 321. *See also* Externalities
> insufficient variety as, 338–339

Market for loanable funds, **556**, 556–565, 684–686
> government budget deficits and surpluses, 561–563
> investment incentives, 560–561
> savings incentives, 558–560

supply and demand for loanable funds, 557–558

Market irrationality, 579

Market power, **12**, 150, 280, 301

Market risk, **575**

Market(s), **66**. *See also* Competitive market
> adverse selection and, 464
> bond, 548–549
> competition and, 66–67
> definition of, 90
> efficiency of, 135–136
> financial, **548**, 548–550
> firm's long-run decision to exit or enter, 288
> for foreign-currency exchange, 686–689
> free entry and exit of, 331
> for goods and services, 22–24
> for insurance, 573–574
> for land and capital, equilibrium in, 387–388
> with only few sellers, 348–349
> perfectly competitive, 66
> stock, 549–550
> tyranny of, 338–339

Market supply
> with entry and exit, long run, 290–292
> with fixed number of firms, short run, 290
> *vs.* individual supply, 74–75
> as sum of individual supplies, 74

Markup over marginal cost, 336

Maximin criterion, **422**

McGinty, Jo Craven, 148

McTeer, Robert D., Jr., 14

Median voter theorem, 469–471, **470**

Medicaid, 426, 427

Medicare, 125, 162, 167, 236–239

Medium of exchange, 551, **611**

Menu costs, **648**, 725

Mexico
> economic growth of, 525
> effect of capital flight on economy, 697
> GDP and quality of life in, 498
> income inequality in, 416
> living standards in, 13
> middle-income country, 528–529
> NAFTA and, 187
> purchasing-power parity, 678
> underground economy in, 498–499

Microeconomics, **27**, 461–462, **484**
Microsoft Corporation, 299–300, 319
   antitrust case against, 363–364
   Sherman Antitrust Act and, 319
Middle East, source of crude oil,
   738–740
Midpoint method, 91–92
Mill, John Stuart, 421
Miller, Nolan, 455
Minimum wage, 117–119
   advocates and opponents of, 119
   Fair Labor Standards Act of
     1938, 117
   labor market and, 118
   price floor, 117
   teenage labor market and,
     118–119
   who earns, 599
Minimum-wage laws, 424–425,
   596–598
   determinant of equilibrium
     wages, 402–403
   evaluating price controls,
     119–121
   policies to reduce poverty, 424
Misery index, 773
Misperceptions theory, aggregate-
   supply curve and, 726
Model of aggregate demand and
   aggregate supply, **712**, 712–714
   aggregate-demand curve,
     714–719
   aggregate-supply curve, 719–728
   origins of, 739
   Phillips curve, 771–773, 775
Monetary equilibrium, 635–636
Monetary neutrality, 639–640, **640**
   Fischer effect, 644–645
   revisited, 731
Monetary policy, **616**
   aggregate demand and, 746–755
   changes in money supply,
     751–752
   cost of reducing inflation, 783,
     785–786
   debate, policy made by rule or
     discretion, 802–804
   disinflation, 783
   effects of monetary injection,
     637–638
   expansionary, 753
   free-silver debate, 652–653
   inflation targeting, 804
   monetary injection, 752
   Phillips curve and, 773–775

role of interest-rate targets in Fed
   policy, 753–755
   stabilization policy arguments,
     760–763, 796–798
   theory of liquidity preference,
     747–749
   zero lower bound, 753
Monetary system, 609–610
   banks and the money supply,
     617–622
   Federal Reserve system, 615–617,
     622–628
   meaning of money, 610–615
Money, **610**
   commodity, 611
   creation with fractional-reserve
     banking, 618–619
   credit cards and, 614
   fiat, **612**
   functions of, 611
   future value, 570
   during hyperinflations, 642
   kinds of, 611–612
   measuring time value of, 570–572
   present value, 570–572
   quantity theory of, 634, **637**
   stock, 613
   in U.S. economy, 613–614
   value of, 635
   velocity of, 640–642
Money demand, 635–636
   theory of liquidity preference, 749
Money market
   equilibrium in, 748, 749
   and slope of the aggregate-
     demand curve, 751
Money multiplier, 619–620, **620**
Money stock, 613
Money supply, **616**, 635–636
   bank capital, leverage, and
     financial crisis of 2008-2009,
     620–622
   bank runs and, 625
   banks and, 612–622
   changes in, 751–752
   creation with fractional-reserve
     banking, 618–619
   discount rate, 623
   Fed's tools of monetary control,
     622–628
   Great Depression, 732–733
   inflation and, 15
   monetary neutrality, 640
   money multiplier, 619–620
   open-market operations, 622–623

problems in controlling, 624–625
   reserve requirements, 624
   theory of liquidity preference,
     747–748
Monopolistic competition,
   329–330, **330**
   advertising, 338–343
   characteristics of, 334–335
   competition with differentiated
     products, 332–337
   excess capacity, 335–336
   long-run equilibrium, 332–335
   markup over marginal cost, 336
   vs. perfect competition, 330–332,
     335–336, 344
   in short run, 332
   welfare of society and, 336–337
Monopoly, 67, 299–303, **300**
   antitrust laws, 319–321
   vs. competition, 303–304, 322
   competition *vs.*, 322
   deadweight loss and, 311–313
   drugs *vs.* generic drugs, 309–310
   economies of scale as, 302
   government-created, 301–302
   inefficiency of, 312–313
   markets with only few sellers,
     349–350
   natural, 217, 302–303
   perfect competition and,
     330–332, 344
   prevalence of, 322
   price discrimination, 314–318
   production and pricing decisions,
     303–310
   profit maximization, 306–308
   profit of, 308–309
   public ownership, 321
   public policy toward, 319–321
   regulation, 319–321
   resources, 300, 301
   revenue of, 304–306
   social cost, 313
   supply curve and, 308
   welfare cost of, 310–313
Monopsony, 386
Montero, Jenny, 121
Moral hazard, **462**, 462–464
   insurance, 464, 574
Morris, Eric A., 224
Mortgage-backed securities, 733
Mortgage defaults, 734
Movie industry, example of price
   discrimination, 317
Mullainathan, Sendhil, 405

Multiplier effect, **756**
    aggregate demand, 756
    formula for spending, 757
    other applications of, 758
Multiplier effects, 799
Municipal bonds, 549
Muskie, Edmund, 207
Mutual funds, **551**, 551–552
    as financial intermediaries,
      551–552
    index funds, 552
    portfolio, 551
Myth of the Great Depression,
    The (Potts), 713

N

Nader, Ralph, 8
Nagel, Stefan, 713
Namibia, elephants as private
    good, 227
NASDAQ (National Association of
    Securities Dealers Automated
    Quotation system), 550
Nash, John, 351
Nash equilibrium, **351**
National Collegiate Athletic Associa-
    tion (NCAA), 365
National defense
    important public goods, 219
    spending, 237
National Highway Traffic Safety
    Administration, 204
National income, 489
National income accounts, 554–556
National Institutes of Health, 220,
    237, 540
National Labor Relations Board
    (NLRB), 600
National saving, **555**, 809, 812–814
    economic well-being and, 812
    U.S. trade deficit and, 668–670
    ways to increase, 814
National Science Foundation,
    220, 540
National-security argument for trade
    restrictions, 184–185
Natural disasters, price and, 84–85
Natural monopoly, 217, **302**, 302–303
Natural-rate hypothesis, **778**
    natural experiment for, 778–779
Natural rate of output, **721**
Natural rate of unemployment, 586,
    588, **774**

monetary policy and, 775
natural-rate hypothesis, 778
Natural resources, 527, **530**
    aggregate-supply curve shifts
      and, 721
    limit to growth, 532
    population growth stretching of,
      540–541
Negative correlation, 39
Negative externality, 196, 198–199
Negative income tax, **425**, 425–426
Negative public saving, 809
Neoclassical theory of
    distribution, 390
Net capital outflow, **664**, 664–665
    equality of net exports and,
      665–666
    link between two markets, 689
    in United States, 668–670
Net exports, **490**, 490–491, **660**
    aggregate-demand curve shifts
      due to changes in, 718
    as component of GDP, 490–491
    exchange-rate effect, 716–717
    and net capital outflow, equality
      of, 665–666
    price level and, aggregate-
      demand curve downward
      slope, 716–717
    trade policy, 694–697
Net foreign investment, 664
Net national product (NNP), 489
Neuman, William, 120
Neuroeconomics revolution,
    476–477
Newell, Gabe, 33
Newton, Isaac, 20
New York Stock Exchange, 550
Nigeria
    average income in, 531
    GDP and quality of life in, 498
    income inequality in, 416
    living standards in, 13
    OPEC as cartel, 356
Nike, 338
Nocer, Joe, 365
Nominal exchange rates, **670**,
    670–672
    during hyperinflation, 676–677
Nominal GDP, **492**, 641
    numerical example of real *vs.*,
      492–494
    real GDP *vs.*, 491–496
    velocity and the quantity
      equation, 640

Nominal interest rate, 515–517, **516**, 747
    Fisher effect, 645
    inflation rate and, 646
    in U.S. economy, 517
Nominal variables, **639**
Normal good, **70**, **444**
    income change and, 444
    income elasticity of demand
      and, 98
Normative statements, **28**
North American Free Trade Agree-
    ment (NAFTA), 187, 664
Nozick, Robert, 423
Nunn, Nathan, 538
Nutrition, health and, 536–537

O

Obama, Barack, 15, 167, 181, 249, 250,
    253, 318, 428, 429, 662–663, 700,
    736, 788, 798–800
Observation, 20–21
Oceans, common resources, 226
Ohanian, Lee, 167
Ohanian, Lee E., 167
Oikonomos, 3
Oil industry, 738–740
Oligopoly, **330**, **347**
    analysis of, and international
      trade, 353
    cartels and, 349–350
    competition and, 349–350
    concentration ratio, 330
    duopoly example, 348
    economics of cooperation,
      353–360
    equilibrium for, 351–352
    game theory and, 355
    markets with only few sellers,
      348–353
    monopolies, 349–350
    OPEC as cartel, 356
    predatory pricing, 362–363
    prisoners' dilemma, 353–355
    public policy toward, 360–364
    public price fixing, 350
    resale price maintenance,
      361–362
    restraint of trade and antitrust
      laws, 360
    size affects market outcome,
      352–353
    tying, 363
Omitted variable, 43–44

OPEC. *See* Organization of Petroleum Exporting Countries
OPEC and world oil market, 356
   price ceilings and lines at gas pump, 114–115
Open economy, 554, **660**
   equality of net exports and net capital outflow, 665–666
   equilibrium in, 689–691
   Euro, 671
   flow of financial resources, 664–665
   flow of goods, 660–670
   government budget deficits, 692–694
   how policies and events affect, 692–700
   increasing openness of U.S. economy, 661–664
   international flows of goods and capital, 660–670
   market for foreign-currency exchange, 686–689
   market for loanable funds, 684–686
   nominal exchange rates, 670–672, 676–677
   political instability and capital flight, 697–699
   prices for international transactions, 670–673
   purchasing-power parity, 673–378
   real exchange rates, 672–673
   trade policy, 694–697
Open-market operation, 616, **622**, 622–623, 747–748, 753–754
Opportunity cost(s), **6**, **52**, 52–53, 260–261
   comparative advantage and, 52–53
   cost of capital as, 261–262
   economists *vs.* accountants, 262
   explicit and implicit costs, 261
   production possibilities frontier and, 24–26
Optimization
   consumer optimal choices, 442–443
   deriving demand curve, 448–449
   income changes and, 444
   income effect, 446–448
   price changes and, 445–446
   substitution effect, 446–448
   utility and, 443
Optimum, 198, 442

Ordered pair, 38
Organization for Economic Cooperation and Development (OECD), 428
Organization of Petroleum Exporting Countries (OPEC)
   nations in, 356
   oil and economy, 738–740
   and price of oil, 104–105
   shifts in Phillips curve, 780, 782
   supply shocks and, 780, 782
   world oil market and, 356
Organs (human), market for, 148–150
Origin, of graph, 38
Orrenius, Pia, 384–385
Orszag, Peter, 208
Oster, Emily, 56–57
Output, 750
   efficient level of, 311
   full-employment, 721
   levels of, 307
   natural rate of, **721**
   potential, 721
   unemployment rises as output falls, 711–712
Output effect, 305, 352
Output price, 378–379
Outsourcing, 183, 184–185
Outward-oriented policies, 539

P

Pakistan
   economic growth of, 525
   GDP and quality of life in, 498
Palestine, shifts in labor supply and, 382–383
Parker, Jonathan A., 712–713
Parking spots, 148–149
Patent, expiration of, 309–310
Patent protection, 201–202
Payroll tax, 236
   burden of, 125–126
Pell grants, 597
Peltzman, Sam, 8
Perception *vs.* reality, 31
Perfect competition
   monopolistic *vs.*, 335–336
   monopoly and, 330–332, 344
Perfect complements, **441**
Perfectly competitive markets, 66, 280
Perfectly elastic demand, 94
Perfectly elastic supply, 99
Perfectly inelastic demand, 92

Perfectly inelastic supply, 99
Perfect price discrimination, 315–316
Perfect substitutes, **441**
Permanent income, **419**
Perpetuity, bonds, 549
Personal income, 489
Peru, underground economy in, 498–499
Pharmaceutical drugs *vs.* generic drugs, 309–310
Phelps, Edmund, 773–780, 784
Phillips, A. W., 770
Phillips curve, **770**
   in 1960s, 779
   aggregate demand, aggregate supply, and, 771–773
   breakdown of, 780
   during financial crisis, 788–789
   long-run, 773–775
   natural-rate hypothesis, 778–779
   origins of, 770–771
   rational expectations, 784
   sacrifice ratio, 783–784
   shifts in, 773–782
   short-run, 777–778
   supply shocks and, 780–782
Physical capital, **530**
   per worker, 530
Pie chart, 37
Pigou, Arthur, 203
Pigovian taxes, 203
Pin factory, 273
Plumer, Brad, 33
Poland, hyperinflation in, 642
Political business cycle, 802–803
Political economy, 462, **467**, 467–471
   Arrow's impossibility theorem, 468–469
   Condorcet voting paradox, 467–468
   median voter theorem, 469–471
   politician's behavior, 471
Political instability, capital flight and, 697–699
Political stability, economic growth and, 537–539
Pollution
   clean air and water as common resource, 226
   corrective taxes and, 203–204
   Environmental Protection Agency (EPA), 203
   gas tax, 205
   as negative externality, 226

objections to economic analysis of, 207
regulation and, 203
social optimum and, 198
tradable pollution permits, 205–207
Population growth, economic growth and, 540–544
Porter, Eduardo, 428
Portfolio, mutual funds, 551
Positive correlation, 38
Positive externalities, 196, 199–202
technology spillovers, industrial policy, and patent protection, 201–202
Positive statements, **28**
Potts, David, 713
Poverty
correlated with age, race, and family composition, 418
fighting, as public good, 220
income inequality and, 413–414
in-kind transfers and, 419
policies to reduce, 424–427
Poverty line, **417**
Poverty rate, **417**, 417–418
Predatory pricing, 362–363
Preferences
consumer choice, 437–441
insufficient variety, 338–339
marginal rate of substitution, 433
representing with indifference curves, 438–439
utility and, 433
Prescott, Edward, 167
Present value, **570**, 570–572
Price ceiling, **112**
binding constraint, 112
lines at gas pump, 114–115
market outcomes and, 112–113
not binding, 112
rent control, 115–116
Price controls, food shortage and, 120–121
Price discrimination, **314**, 314–318
analytics of, 315–317
economic welfare and, 315
examples of, 317–318
in higher education, 318
moral of story, 315
parable about pricing, 314–315
rational strategy for a profit-maximizing monopolist, 315
willingness to pay and, 315
Price-earnings ratio, 551

Price effect, 305, 352
Price elasticity of demand, **90**, 90–91
computing, 91
determinants of, 90–91
elasticity and total revenue along a linear demand curve, 96–97
midpoint method, 91–92
total revenue and, 94–96
variety of demand curves, 92–94
Price elasticity of supply, **98**
computing, 99
determinants of, 98–99
variety of supply curves, 99–101
Price fixing, public, 350
Price floor, **112**
market outcomes and, 116–117
minimum wage as, 117–119
Price level, 750
consumption and, 715
exchange-rate effect, 716–717
investment and, 715–716
net exports and, 716–717
Price maker, 300
Price(s), 551. *See also* Consumer Price Index
advertising effect on, 340–341
allocation of resources and, 83
change in, 444–445
control on, 112–121
equilibrium, 77
higher price raises producer surplus, 143–144
during hyperinflations, 642
input prices and supply, 75–76
for international transactions, 670–673
law of one, 674
level of, 635
lower price raises consumer surplus, 138–139
marginal cost and, 336
market-clearing, 77
natural disasters and, 84–85
output, 378–379
purchase, of land or capital, 387
quantity demanded and, 67–68
quantity supplied and, 73
of related goods and demand, 70
relative, 437, 648–649
rental, of land or capital, 387
shortages and, 78
surplus and, 77–78
of trade, 54
when supply and demand shifts, 82

willingness to pay, 136–137
world, **173**
Price takers, 66, 174, 280, 300
Pricing
average-cost, 320
congestion, 224–225
marginal-cost, 320
predatory, 362–363
resale price maintenance, 361–362
tying, 363
value, 224–225
Principal, **462**, 462–464
bonds, 549
Principles of Political Economy and Taxation (Ricardo), 55
Prisoners' dilemma, **353**, 353–355
dominant strategy, 354
economics of cooperation, 353–355
examples of, 356–358
oligopoly as, 355
tit-for-tat strategy, 359
tournament, 359
welfare of society and, 358
Private goods, **216**, 216–217
Private saving, **555**
Producer price index, **509**
Producer surplus, **141**, 141–144
cost and willingness to sell, 141–142
evaluating market equilibrium, 146–148
higher price raises, 143–144
market efficiency and, 144–150
using supply curve to measure, 142–143
Product differentiation, 331
Production
cost of, 259–260, 263–265
within country, GDP measures value of, 487
factors of, 22–24, **374**, 527
growth and, 523–524
process, 301
resources, limited quantities of, 293–295
within specific interval of time, GDP measures value of, 487
Production function, **263**, 263–265, **376**, 377, 531
illustration, 534
marginal product of labor and, 375–376
total cost and, 263, 265

Production possibilities frontier, 49
 gains from trade, 48–50
Production possibilities frontier and,
 24, 24–26
Productivity, **13**, **527**
 determinants of, 526–532
 health and nutrition affects,
  536–537
 human capital per worker, 530
 importance of, 527
 living standards and, 527
 natural resources per worker, 530
 physical capital per workers, 530
 production function, 531
 relationship between living standards and, 13
 technological knowledge,
  530–531
 wages and, 384–386
Products
 advertising as signal of quality,
  341–342
 brand-name, 309
 competition with differentiated,
  332–337
Profit, **260**
 accounting, **262**
 as area between price and average total cost, 290
 economic, **262**
 measuring in graph for competitive firm, 288–289
 of monopoly, 308–309
Profit maximization, 282–283
 competitive firm's supply curve
  and, 282–289
 monopoly, 306–308
Progressive tax, **247**
Progressive tax code, 428–429
Property rights, **12**
 economic growth and, 537–539
 importance of, 228
 technology and, 202
Property taxes, 240–241
Proportional tax, **247**
Protection-as-a-bargaining-chip
 argument
 for trade restrictions, 186–187
Public choice, 467
Public good(s), 215–217, **216**,
 218–223, 540
 antipoverty programs, 220
 basic research, 219–220
 cost-benefit analysis, 221–223
 free-rider problem, 218

importance of property rights, 228
 lighthouses as, 221
 national defense, 219
 as natural monopoly, 302
 value of human life, 222–223
Public ownership, public policy toward monopolies, 321
Public policy, 12. *See also* Antitrust
 laws; Fiscal policy; Monetary
 policy
 asymmetric information and,
  466–467
 diminishing returns and catch-up
  effect, 533–535
 economic growth and, 532–544
 education and, 536
 free trade and, 539
 health and nutrition, 536–537
 investment from abroad, 535
 job search and, 594–595
 population growth and, 540–544
 property rights and political stability, 537–539
 research and development, 540
 saving and investment, 533
 toward externalities, 202–207
Public saving, **555**, 809–814
 budget deficit and, 814
 negative, 809
 saving incentives and, 814
Purchasing power, inflation and, 647
Purchasing-power parity,
 673–678, **674**
 basic logic of, 674
 hamburger standard, 677–678
 implications of, 674–676
 limitations of, 677
 as special case, 688
Putnam, Howard, 361

Q

Qatar, OPEC as cartel, 356
Qian, Nancy, 538
Quality
 advertising as signal of, 341–342
 brand names and, 342–343
 change in, and CPI, 511
 efficiency wages and, 602
 theory of efficiency wages and
  worker quality, 602
Quantity
 equilibrium, 77
 of reserves, Fed influences, 622–623

Quantity demanded, **67**
 change in, 80–81
 relationship between price and,
  67–68
Quantity discounts, 318
Quantity equation, 640–642, **641**
Quantity supplied, **73**
Quantity theory of money, 634, **637**
Quintiles, 248
Quotas, import, 31, 179

R

Race
 discrimination in labor
  market, 405
 discrimination in sports, 407–408
 median annual earnings by, 403
 poverty correlated with, 418
 segregated streetcars and, 406
Raffo, Andrea, 167
Randlett, Tom, 149
Random walk, **578**
 index funds and, 578–579
Rational expectations, **784**
 and possibility of costless
  disinflation, 784–785
Rationality, behavioral economics
 and, 471–473
Rational people, **6**
Rawls, John, 422–423
Reagan, Ronald, 30, 429, 634, 701,
 800, 803
 government debt and, 564
 tax cuts under, 165, 166, 252
Real exchange rates, **672**, 672–673
Real GDP, **492**
 vs. nominal GDP, 491–496
 numerical example of nominal
  vs., 492–494
 over recent history, 495–496
 of various countries, 498
Real interest rate, 515–517, **516**, 747
 Fisher effect, 644–645
 in U.S. economy, 517
Reality, perception *vs.*, 31
Real variables, **639**
Recession, 564, **707**, 708, 709, 710
 cultural and social effect of,
  712, 713
 government debate over spending hikes or tax cuts, 798–801
 real GDP and, 495
 Volcker's decision, 803

Recession (2008–2009), 733–736
    Phillips curve during and
        after, 788
*Reefer Madness: Sex, Drugs and Cheap
    Labor in the American Black Market*
    (Schlosser), 499
Regressive tax, **247**
Regulation
    of externalities, 202
    public policy toward monopolies,
        319–321
"Relationship between Unemploy-
    ment and the Rate of Change of
    Money Wages in the United
    Kingdom, 1861–1957"
    (Phillips), 770
Relative price
    budget constraints and,
        436–436
    consumer's choice and, 443
    variability and misallocation of
        resources, 648–649
Rent control, 31
    evaluating price controls, 120–121
    price ceiling, 115–116
    in short run and long run,
        115–116
Rent subsidies, 120–121
Resale price maintenance, 361–362,
    363–364
Research and development, economic
    growth and, 540
Reserve ratio, **618**, 623–624
Reserve requirements, 618, **624**
Reserves, **617**, 622–624
Resources
    common, 214–215, **216**, 216–217,
        223–227, 302
    flow of financial, 664–665
    limited quantities of production,
        293–295
    monopoly, 300, 301
    natural, 527, **530**, 721
    prices and allocation of, 83
    prisoners' dilemma, 357–358
    relative-price variability and
        misallocation of, 648–649
    scarcity of, 4
Retained earnings, 489
Revenue. *See also* Total revenue
    average, **281**
    of competitive firm, 280–282
    marginal, **282**
    of monopoly, 304–306
    tax, 157

Reverse causality, 44–45
Reyes, Nery, 120
Rhodes, Cecil, 301
Ricardo, David, 55
Right-to-work laws, 600
Rigobon, Roberto, 511
Risk
    firm-specific, **575**
    managing, 572–576
    market, **575**
    and return, trade-off between,
        575–576
Risk aversion, **572**, 572–573
Rivalry in consumption, **216**, 216–217
Road congestion, gasoline tax and, 204
Roback Jennifer, 406
Robe, Jonathan, 597
Robinson Crusoe, (Defoe), 527
Rockefeller, John D., 526
Rodriguez, Alex, 505
Rodríguez, Francisco, 121
Rogerson, Richard, 167
"Role of Monetary Policy, The"
    (Friedman), 773
Romer, Christina D., 700–701
Ruhm, Christopher J., 713
Rule of 70, 572
Rumsfeld, Donald, 734
Russia
    capital flight, 699
    GDP and quality of life in, 498
    income inequality in, 416
    inflation rate, 634
Ruth, Babe, 514

S

Sachs, Jeffrey, 542
Sacks, Daniel, 500
Sacrifice ratio, 783–784
Saez, Emmanuel, 166
Saldate, Edward, 149
Sales taxes, 240–241
Samsung, 300
Samuelson, Paul, 476, 770–771, 773,
    776–777, 779
Sargent, Thomas, 784–785
Sarkozy, Nicolas, 500
Satisficers, 472
Saudi Arabia, 356, 738–740
Saving(s), 547–548, **555**, 812–814
    defined, 556
    economic growth and, 533
    inflation raises tax burden on, 650

    interest rates affect household,
        454–456
    international flows, 666–667
    and investment in national in-
        come accounts, 554–556
    national, **555**, 668–670, 809,
        812–814
    negative public, 809
    private, **555**
    public, **555**, 809–814
    as supply for loanable funds,
        558–559
    tax law reform debate to
        encourage saving,
        812–814
Savings incentives, 558–560
Scarcity, **4**
Scarcity index, 121
Scatterplot, 38
Schlosser, Eric, 499
Schwarz, Andy, 365
Scientific judgments, differences
    among economists in, 30–31
Scientific method, 20–21
Screening, **466**
Seasonal adjustment, 488
Sectoral shifts, 594
Securitization, 733
Segregation, segregated streetcars
    and profit motive, 406
Sellers
    number of, and shifts in supply
        curve, 76
    taxes on, 123–123
    variables that influence, 76
Sensible tax, 208–209
Services
    CPI basket of, 506–509
    currently produced, GDP
        includes, 487
    intangible, 487
    markets for, 22–24
Shadow economy, 498–499
Shaw, George Bernard, 30, 528
Sherman Antitrust Act, 319, 360
Shi-Ling Hsu, 208
Shiller, Robert J., 476–477
Shoeleather costs, **647**, 647–648
Shortage, **78**
    lines at gas pump, 114–115
    price ceilings and, 113
Short run
    aggregate-supply curve slopes
        upward in, 722–726
    costs in, 271–273

disinflationary monetary policy in, 783
economic fluctuations, 721, 724–726, 709
increase in demand, 294
interest rates in, 750
market supply with fixed number of firms, 290
monopolistically competitive firm in, 332
monopolistic competitors in, 333
Phillips curve, 777–778
rent control, 115–116
shift in demand, 293
Shoup, Donald, 149
Shutdown, 285
competitive firm's short-run decision to, 285–286
near-empty restaurants and, 287
off-season miniature golf and, 287
Sichel, Daniel, 492
Siegel, Jeremy, 580
Sierra Club, 208
Signaling, 401, **465**
advertising, 401
to convey private information, 465
education, 401
gifts as, 465–466
Simon, Herbert, 472
Simpson, Alan K., 250
Singapore
economic growth rate of, 524
pursued outward-oriented policies, 539
trade and distribution of income, 185
Slope, 41–43
Smith, Adam, 10, 11, 14, 55, 148, 209, 273, 361, 499
Smith, Fred, 167
Smoking, reducing, 71–73
Social Choice and Individual Values (Arrow), 469
Social cost, 198
monopoly's profit, 313
Social insurance, **423**
Social insurance taxes, 236
Social Security, 125, 236, 248
budget deficit and, 238–240
federal spending and, 237
indexation of benefits under, 514–515
rise in government spending for, 238–239
tax, 162, 167

Social security disability payments, 597
Society
decisions faced by, 3–4
faces short-run trade-off between inflation and unemployment, 15
monopolistic competition and welfare of, 336–337
prisoners' dilemma and welfare of, 358
Solow, Robert, 770–771, 773, 776–777, 779
Soltas, Evan, 318
South Africa, income inequality in, 416
South Korea
caloric consumption and height of population, 537
capital flight, 699
economic growth rate of, 524
GDP to investment, 534
purchasing-power parity, 678
pursued outward-oriented policies, 539
trade and distribution of income, 185
unilateral approach to free trade, 187
Soviet Union
arms race and Cold War, 356–357
collapse of communism in, 10
Specialization
driving force of, 52–58
economies of scale and, 273
trade and, 50–51
Speculative bubble, 579
Spending and taxes, blur between, 250–251
Spending multiplier, formula for, 757
Sports, discrimination in, 407–408
Stabilization
automatic stabilizers, 764–765
debate, 796–798
policy arguments, 760–765
Stagflation, **737**, 780
Stagnation, 737
Standard of living
determinants of, 13
relationship between productivity and, 13
Standard & Poor's, 550
State government, 240–241
receipts for, 240–241
spendings for, 241

Statistical discrepancy, 488, 489
Steam, 33
Stevenson, Betsey, 500
Sticky-price theory, aggregate-supply curve and, 725
Sticky-wage theory, aggregate-supply curve and, 724–725
Stigler, George, 321
Stiglitz, Joseph E., 208
Stock, **549**
diversification of firm-specific risk, 574–575
efficient markets hypothesis, 577–578
fundamental analysis, 577
market irrationality, 579
random walks and index funds, 578–579
Stock index, 550
Stockman, David, 165
Stock market, 549–550
Federal Reserve and, 754–755
Store of value, 551, **611**
Strike, **403**, **599**
Structural unemployment, **593**
minimum-wage laws and, 596–598
Subprime borrowers, 733
Subsidies
market-based policy, 203–205
rent, 120–121
wage, 120–121
Substitutes, **70**
cross-price elasticity of demand, 98
perfect, **441**
price elasticity of demand, 90
Substitution
bias, 509
effect, **446**, 446–448
marginal rate of, **438**, 443
Substitution effect, **814**
Summers, Larry, 700
Sunk costs, 285, **286**, 286–287
Superstar phenomenon, 402
Supplemental Security Income (SSI), 425
Supply, 73–76. *See also* Aggregate supply; Money supply
applications of, 101–107
change in, 80–81
decrease in, 75, 81
elasticity of, 98–101
equilibrium of demand and, 77–79

excess, 77–78
increase in, 75, 102
individual, 74–75
inelastic, 98
input prices and, 75–76
of labor, 380–381
law of, **73**
market *vs.* individual, 74–75
number of sellers and, 76
perfectly elastic, 99
perfectly inelastic, 99
price elasticity of, 99, 100, 101
relationship between price and
    quantity supplied, 73–74
technology and, 76
Supply and demand, 77–83, 111–112
disentangling, 692
equilibrium of, 77
for foreign-currency exchange,
    684–689
law of, 79
for loanable funds, 684–689
market forces of, 65
shift in, 82
versatility of, 375
Supply curve(s), **74**
in competitive market, 289–295
monopoly and, 308
price elasticity of supply, 99–101
shifts in, 75–76
shifts in *vs.* movements along, 80
supply schedule and, 73–74, 142
using to measure producer sur-
    plus, 142–143
variety of, 99–101
Supply schedule, **74**
supply curve and, 73–74, 142
Supply shock(s), **780**
of the 1970s, 782
accommodating adverse, 781–782
adverse shock to aggregate sup-
    ply, 781
Phillips curve and, 780–782
role of, 780–782
Supply-side economics and Laffer
    curve, 165
Supply siders (economists), 760
Surplus, 77. *See also* Budget surplus;
    Consumer surplus; Total surplus;
    Trade surplus
    price floors and, 117
    producer. *See* Producer surplus
Sweden
    Laffer curve, 165
    purchasing-power parity, 678

tax burden in, 235
underground economy in,
    498–499
Switzerland, underground economy
    in, 498–499
Synergies, 319

T

Taiwan
    economic growth rate of, 524
    pursued outward-oriented
        policies, 539
    trade and distribution of
        income, 185
Tangible goods, GDP includes, 487
Tanzania, elephant poaching, 227
Tariff(s), 31, **177**, 694
    compared to import quotas, 179
    deadweight loss and, 178
    effects of in international trade,
        177–179
Tastes, shifts in the demand curve
    and, 70
Taxation, costs of, 155–156
Tax burden
    distribution of, 248–249
    divided, 127
    of U.S. compared to European
        companies, 235
Tax cuts
    under George W. Bush, 798
    under Kennedy, 762
    under Ronald Reagan, 252
    undex George H. W. Bush, 760
Tax debate, 166
Tax equity, 249–251
Taxes, 121–128, 242–246
    ability-to-pay principle, 247
    Barack Obama pledged to raise
        taxes, 253
    benefits principle and gasoline,
        246–247
    on buyers, market outcomes and,
        123–125
    carbon, 208–209
    changes in, 759–760
    consumption, 243–244
    corporate income, 241, 250–251
    corrective, **203**
    cuts under Reagan, 165
    deadweight loss of taxation,
        156–160, 163–165, 234, 243
    equity and, 246–251

excise, 237
expenditures, 250–251
gas, 204–205
high tax rates, 166
incidence, 122
income, 243
individual income, 241
inflation, 642–644
on labor, 162–163
Laffer curve and supply-side
    economics, 165–166
lump-sum tax, **245**, 245–246
luxury, 127
negative income, 425–426
payroll, 125–126
Pigovian, 203
progressive, **247**
property, 240–241
proportional, **247**
regressive, **247**
sales, 240–241
on sellers, market outcomes
    and, 122–123
social insurance, 236
value-added, 244
Tax expenditures, 250–251
Tax incidence, **122**, 249–251
    elasticity and, 126–128
    flypaper theory of, 249–251
Tax laws debate, 812–814
Tax rates
    average, **245**
    marginal, **245**
Tax revenue, 157, 163–166
Tax systems, 247
    administrative burden of,
        244–245
    design of, 233–234
Tax treatment, bonds, 549
Team Fortress 2, 33
Technological change, 379
Technological knowledge, 529, **530**,
    530–531
    changes in, 722
    specific, 219
Technological progress
    population growth promoting of,
        542–544
Technology
    demand for skilled and unskilled
        labor and, 397–399
    shifts in supply curve and, 76
    spillovers, 201–202
Teenage labor market, minimum
    wage and, 118–119

Temporary Assistance for Needy Families (TANF), 220, 425
Term, bonds, 549
Term auction facility, 623
Textile market, 172–187
Thailand
    capital flight, 699
    underground economy in, 498–499
Theory, 20–21
Theory of Justice (Rawls), 422
Theory of liquidity preference, 747–749
Time horizon, price elasticity of demand, 91
Time inconsistency of policy, 802–803
    practical importance of, 803–804
Time-series graph, 37, 38
Time value of money, measuring, 570–572
Tit-for-tat strategy, 359
Toll roads, 224–225
Total cost, **260**, 274
    average, **267**, 274
    production function and, 263–265
Total revenue, **94**, 95, **260**
    along a linear demand curve, 96–97
    for competitive firm, 281
    monopoly, 304, 305
    price elasticity of demand and, 94–96
Total surplus, 145, 147
Tradable pollution permits, 205–207
Trade. *See also* Free trade; Gains from trade; International trade
    agreements and World Trade Organization, 187
    benefits of, 10
    comparative advantage and, 53–54
    deadweight losses and gains from, 159–160
    equilibrium without international, 172–173
    interdependence and gains from, 47–48
    price of, 54
    restraint of, 360
    specialization and, 50–51
Trade balance, **660**
Trade barriers, 31
Trade deficit, **661**

measuring a nation's income, 484
of U.S., 668–670
Trade-offs, 4–5
    between equity and efficiency, 252–253
    between inflation and unemployment, 15
    policy decisions and, 28
    production possibilities frontier and, 24–26
    between risk and return, 575–576
Trade policy, **694**, 694–697
    import quota, 694
    tariff, 694
Trade restrictions
    arguments for, 182–187
    infant-industry argument for, 185–186
    jobs argument for, 183–184
    national-security argument, 184–185
    protection-as-a-bargaining-chip argument, 186–187
    tariffs, 31
    unfair-competition argument for, 186
Trade surplus, **660**
Traffic, congested roads as public goods or common resources, 226
Tragedy of the Commons, **223**, 223–225
Transaction costs, **211**
Transfer payments, 237, 248, 490
Transitivity, 468, 469
Transportation, 508
Truman, Harry, 28–29
Turnover, efficiency wages and, 602
Twin deficits, 694
Tying, 363–364
Tyranny of market, 338–339
Tyranny of the Market, The (Waldfogel), 338

U

Uganda, elephant poaching, 227
Ultimatum game, 474
Underground economy, 163, 498–499
Unemployment, 585–586
    benefits, 597
    cyclical, 586, **589**

efficiency wages and, 601–603
frictional, **593**
how long without work, 592
identifying, 586–593
job search and, 593–595
measuring a nation's income, 484
measuring of, 586–589
minimum-wage laws and, 596–598
natural rate of, 586, **588**, 774
rises as output falls, 711–712
short-run trade-off between inflation and, 15, 773–792
structural, **593**
wages of, 596–597
why some people always, 592–593
Unemployment insurance, **595**
Unemployment rate, **587**
    measures, 590–591
    since 1960, 588
Unfair-competition argument for trade restrictions, 186
Union, **402**, **608**
    collective bargaining and, 598–601
    determinant of equilibrium wages, 402–403
    economics of, 599–600
    good or bad for economy, 600–601
    type of cartel, 599–600
United Arab Emirates, OPEC as cartel, 356
United Kingdom
    advanced economy, 528
    economic growth of, 525
    income inequality in, 416
    tax burden in, 235
    underground economy in, 498–499
United States
    average income in, 523
    carbon tax, 208–209
    changing nature of exports, 662–663
    distribution of income in, 415
    economic growth of, 525
    financial institutions in, 548–553
    GDP and quality of life in, 498
    GDP to investment, 534
    government debt, history of, 563–564
    income inequality in, 414–416

inflation in, 14
inflation rate, 634
interest rates in, 517
international trade with, 57–58
living standards in, 13
money in, 613–614, 615
NAFTA and, 187
real GDP growth since 1900, 710
real GDP in, 495
tax burden compared to European countries, 235
tax rate, 166
trade and distribution of income, 184–185
trade deficit, 668–670
trade restrictions, 181
underground economy in, 498–499
various laws to manage use of fish and other wildlife, 226
Unit of account, **611**
Unsafe at Any Speed (Nader), 8
U.S. Department of Commerce, 491
U.S. exports, 662–663
U-shaped average total cost, 269–270
U.S. Justice Department, 360, 363–364
U.S. Supreme Court, antitrust laws, 319
Utilitarianism, **421**, 421–422
Utility, **421**, 443
    concept of, 573
    function, 573
Utility theory, 476–477

V

Value-added (VAT) tax, 244
Value of human life, cost-benefit analysis, 222–223
Value of marginal product, **377**, 377–378
Value pricing, 224–225
Values, differences among economists in, 31
Variable costs, 266–267, **267**, 274
    average, **268**, 274
Variables
    graphs of single, 37–38
    graphs of two, 38–39

nominal, **639**
omitted, 43–44
real, **639**
that influence buyers, 71
that influence sellers, 76
Variable tolling, 224–225
Varian, Hal, 408–409, 511
Varoufakis, Yanis, 33
Vedder, Richard, 596–597
Velocity of money, **640**, 640–642
Venezuela
    inflation rate, 634
    OPEC as cartel, 356
Vertical equity, **247**
Video games, economics of, 33
Vissing-Jorgenson, Annette, 712–713
Volcker, Paul A., 701, 782–783, 784, 785–786, 787
    decision led to recession, 803
    disinflation, 785–786
Voting systems, 468–469
    Arrow's impossibility theorem, 469
    Condorcet voting paradox, 467–468
    median voter theorem, 469–471

W

Wage-price spiral, 737
Wages
    $5-a-day, 603
    ability, effort, and chance, 399–400
    adverse selection and, 464
    beauty and, 400–401
    Black Death and, 389
    compensating differentials, 396
    determinants of equilibrium, 396–403
    education and, 397
    efficiency, 402–403, **601**, 601–603
    free trade and, 184–185
    human capital, 396–397
    immigration and, 384–385
    labor supply and, 450–453
    minimum, 117–119
    minimum-wage laws, unions, and efficiency wages, 402–403, 404–405
    productivity and, 384–386
    signaling, 401

sticky-wage theory, 724–725
superstar phenomenon, 402
theory of efficiency, 601–603
of unemployment, 596–597
Wage subsidies, 120–121
Wagner Act, 600
Waldfogel, Joel, 338–339
Wealth
    arbitrary redistributions of, 651–652
    effect, 715, 746
Wealth of Nations, The (Smith), 11, 361
Weil, David N., 846
Welfare, 237, 248, **425**, 427
    effects of free trade, 174
    effects of tariffs, 177–179
    policies to reduce poverty, 425
    tax affects, 158–159
Welfare cost of monopoly, 310–313
    deadweight loss, 311–313
Welfare economics, **135**, 136–151, 157–159, 197, 313
Wessel, David, 734–735
Whitehouse, Mark, 500
Why gold, 612–613
Willingness to pay, **136**, 136–137, 315
Willingness to sell, cost and, 141–142
Wolfers, Justin, 500–501
Women
    gender differences in competition, 408–409
    labor-force participation in U.S. economy of, 589–590
    labor force participation rates since 1950, 590
Wonderful Wizard of Oz, The (Baum), 652–653
Worker
    discouraged, **591**
    effort, 603
    health, 601–602
    human capital per, 530
    natural resources, 530
    physical capital per, 530
    quality, 602
    turnover, 602
Workfare, 427
Work incentives, antipoverty programs and, 427

World price, **173**
World Trade Organization (WTO),
    181, 187
        trade agreements and, 187
World War II, shift in aggregate
    demand, 732–733

X

X-coordinate, 38
Xi Jinping, 662

Y

Y-coordinate, 38

Z

Zero bound problem, 807
Zero economic profit, 334
Zero inflation, 804–808
Zero lower bound, 753

Zero profit
    competitive firms stay in
        business with, 292–293
    condition, 336
    equilibrium, 292–293
Zimbabwe
    economic growth rate of, 524
    hyperinflation in, 644
    inflation rate, 634
    underground economy in,
        498–499

Suggestions for Summer Reading

If you enjoyed the economics course that you just finished, you might like to read more about economic issues in the following books.

ABIJIT BANERJEE AND ESTHER DUFLO

Poor Economics

(New York: Public Affairs, 2011)

Two prominent development economists offer their proposal on how to fight global poverty.

YORAM BAUMAN AND GRADY KLEIN

The Cartoon Introduction to Economics

(New York: Hill and Wang, 2010)

Basic economic principles, with humor.

NARIMAN BEHRAVESH

Spin-Free Economics

(New York: McGraw-Hill, 2008)

A straightforward guide to major economic policy debates.

ALAN BLINDER

After the Music Stopped: The Financial Crisis, the Response, and the Work Ahead

(London: The Penguin Press HC, 2013)

A former vice chair of the Federal Reserve offers his take on what we have learned from the financial crisis that shook the world in 2008 and 2009.

WILLIAM BREIT AND BARRY T. HIRSCH

Lives of the Laureates

(Cambridge, MA: MIT Press, 2009)

Twenty-three winners of the Nobel Prize in Economics offer autobiographical essays about their life and work.

BRYAN CAPLAN

The Myth of the Rational Voter: Why Democracies Choose Bad Policies

(Princeton, NJ: Princeton University Press, 2008)

An economist asks why elected leaders often fail to follow the policies that economists recommend.

PAUL COLLIER

The Bottom Billion: Why the Poorest Countries Are Failing and What Can Be Done About It

(New York: Oxford University Press, 2007)

A former research director at the World Bank offers his insights into how to help the world's poor.

AVINASH DIXIT AND BARRY NALEBUFF

The Art of Strategy: A Game Theorist's Guide to Success in Business and Life

(New York: Norton, 2008)

This introduction to game theory discusses how all people—from corporate executives to criminals under arrest—should and do make strategic decisions.